CW01673265

HAYTON, McFARLANE AND MIT
ON EQUITY AND TRUSTS

HAYTON, McFARLANE AND MITCHELL ON EQUITY AND TRUSTS

FIFTEENTH EDITION

By

JESSICA HUDSON
Associate Professor of Law, University of New South Wales, Sydney

BEN McFARLANE
Professor of English Law, University of Oxford; Fellow of St John's College, Oxford

CHARLES MITCHELL
Professor of Law, University College London

SWEET & MAXWELL

THOMSON REUTERS

First Edition 1939 by J. A. Nathan
Second Edition 1951 by O.R. Marshall
Third Edition 1955 by O.R. Marshall
Fourth Edition 1961 by O.R. Marshall
Fifth Edition 1967 by O.R. Marshall
Sixth Edition 1975 by D.J. Hayton
Seventh Edition 1980 by D.J. Hayton
Eighth Edition 1986 by D.J. Hayton
Ninth Edition 1991 by D.J. Hayton
Tenth Edition 1996 by D.J. Hayton
Eleventh Edition 2001 by D.J. Hayton
Twelfth Edition 2005 by D.J. Hayton and C.C.J. Mitchell
Thirteenth Edition 2010 by C.C.J Mitchell
Fourteenth Edition 2015 by B. McFarlane and C.C.J. Mitchell

Published in 2022 by Thomson Reuters, trading as Sweet & Maxwell.
Thomson Reuters is registered in England & Wales, Company No.1679046.
Registered office and address for service: 5 Canada Square, Canary Wharf,
London E14 5AQ.

Typeset by Cheshire Typesetting Ltd, Cuddington, Cheshire.
Printed and bound by CPI Group (UK) Ltd Croydon, CR0 4YY

MIX
Paper | Supporting responsible forestry
FSC® C013604

For further information on our products and services, visit www.sweetandmaxwell.co.uk

A CIP catalogue record for this book is available from the British Library
ISBN (print): 9780414103795
ISBN (Proview): 9780414103825
ISBN (ebook): 9780414103818
ISBN (print and Proview): 9780414103801

ACKNOWLEDGMENTS

Grateful acknowledgement is made for permission to reproduce from the following works:

Extracts from cases originally published in full by the Incorporated Council for Law Reporting are reproduced with kind permission.

Extracts from cases originally published in All England Law Reports are reproduced by permission of RELX (UK) Limited, trading as LexisNexis.

Extracts from Journal of Equity cases are reproduced by permission of RELX (UK) Limited, trading as LexisNexis.

A. Burrows, "We Do This At Common Law But That In Equity" (2002) 22 O.J.L.S. 1 extracts used with permission of Oxford University Press Journals; permission conveyed through Copyright Clearance Center, Inc.

Ben McFarlane, "The Trust and its Civilian Analogues" in L. Smith (ed.), *The Worlds of the Trust* (Cambridge University Press, 2013), © B. McFarlane extracts reproduced with permission.

Ben McFarlane, "Form and Substance in Equity" in A. Robertson and J. Goudkamp (eds), *Form and Substance in the Law of Obligations* (Hart Publishing, 2019), extracts reproduced with permission of Bloomsbury Publishing.

Ben McFarlane, "Equity and the Justification of Private Rights" in Michael Crawford et al (eds), *Justifying Private Rights* (Hart Publishing, 2020), extracts reproduced with permission of Bloomsbury Publishing.

Charles Mitchell, "Commissioner of Stamp Duties (Queensland) v Livingston (1964)" in B. Sloan (ed.), *Landmark Cases in Succession Law* (Hart Publishing, 2019), extracts reproduced with permission of Bloomsbury Publishing.

Charles Mitchell, "Good Faith, Self-Denial and Mandatory Trustee Duties" (2018) 32 *Trust Law International* 92, extracts reproduced with the permission of Bloomsbury Professional, an imprint of Bloomsbury Publishing.

Charles Mitchell, "Johnson v Agnew (1979)" in C. Mitchell and P. Mitchell (eds), *Landmark Cases in the Law of Contract* (Hart Publishing, 2008), extracts reproduced with the permission of Bloomsbury Publishing.

Charles Mitchell and S. Watterson, "Remedies for Knowing Receipt" in C. Mitchell (ed.), *Constructive and Resulting Trusts* (Hart Publishing, 2010), extracts reproduced with permission of Bloomsbury Publishing.

Christian Daly and Charles Mitchell, "Paragon Finance plc v D.B. Thakerar & Co. (a firm) (1999)" in Charles Mitchell and Paul Mitchell (eds), *Landmark Cases in Equity* (Hart Publishing, 2012), extracts reproduced with permission of Bloomsbury Publishing.

Edelman, The Hon J, "Understanding Tracing Rules" *QUT Law Review*, [S.l.], v.16, n.2, pp.1–18, June 2016. ISSN 2201-7275. Available at: *https://lr.law.qut.edu.au/article/view/672*. Date accessed: 1

February 2021. doi: *https://doi.org/10.5204/qutlr.v16i2.672*. © Edelman, The Hon J extracts usage licensed under a Creative Commons Attribution Licence.

F.W. Maitland, Equity. *A Course of Lectures*, A.H. Chaytor and W.J. Whittaker (eds) (Cambridge: Cambridge University Press 2011), extracts reproduced with the permission of The Licensor through PLSclear.

Frame v Smith [1987] 2 S.C.R. 99; *Semelhago v Paramadevan* [1996] 2 S.C.R. 415 extracts reproduced with permission of the Supreme Court of Canada, 2022.

Henry Smith, "Equity as Meta-Law" (2021) 130 Yale L.J. 1050 extracts used with permission of Yale Law Journal Company Inc; permission conveyed through Copyright Clearance Center, Inc.

Jessica Hudson, "One Thicket in Fraud on a Power" (2019) 39 *Oxford Journal of Legal Studies* 577 © Jessica Hudson published by Oxford University Press extracts reprinted with permission.

Jessica Hudson, "Mere and Other Discretionary Objects in Australia" in Ying Khai Liew et al (eds), *Asia-Pacific Trusts Law*, Volume 1 (Hart Publishing, 2021), extracts reproduced with permission of Bloomsbury Publishing.

Jessica Hudson and Charles Mitchell, "Trustee Recoupment: A Power Analysis" (2021) 35 *Trust Law International* 3, extracts reproduced with the permission of Bloomsbury Professional, an imprint of Bloomsbury Publishing Plc.

Jonathan Garton, "*National Anti-Vivisection Society v Inland Revenue Commissioners* (1948)" in Charles Mitchell and Paul Mitchell (eds), *Landmark Cases in Equity* (Hart Publishing, 2012), extracts reproduced with permission of Bloomsbury Publishing.

Look Chan Ho, "Book Review" (2007) 21 *Trust Law International* 110, extracts reproduced with the permission of Bloomsbury Professional, an imprint of Bloomsbury Publishing Plc.

Lord Nicholls, "Trustees and Their Broader Community: Where Duty, Morality and Ethics Converge" (1995) 9 *Trust Law International* 71, extracts reproduced with the permission of Bloomsbury Professional, an imprint of Bloomsbury Publishing Plc.

N. Tiverios and B. McFarlane, "Controlling Private Punishment in Three Dimensions: Penalties and Forfeiture in England and Australia" in E. Bant et al (eds), *Punishment and Private Law* (Hart Publishing, 2021), extracts reproduced with permission of Bloomsbury Publishing.

P. Matthews, "*Burgess v Wheate* (1759)" in C. Mitchell and P. Mitchell (eds), *Landmark Cases in Equity* (2012), extracts reproduced with permission of Bloomsbury Publishing.

S. Douglas and B. McFarlane, "Sham Trusts" in H. Conway and R. Hickey (eds), *Modern Studies in Property Law*, Volume 9 (Hart Publishing, 2017), extracts reproduced with permission of Bloomsbury Publishing.

Steven Elliott and Charles Mitchell, "Remedies for Dishonest Assistance" (2004) 67 *Modern Law Review* 14, published by John Wiley & Sons, extracts reproduced with permission of Blackwell Publishing Ltd.

Ying Khai Liew, *Rationalising Constructive Trusts* (Hart Publishing, 2017) extracts reproduced with permission of Hart Publishing, an imprint of Bloomsbury Publishing Plc.

PREFACE

For this 15th edition, Jessica Hudson has joined Ben McFarlane and Charles Mitchell as a third co-author. Together we have given the text a new and much broader focus on the rules of equity of which the law of trusts forms part, signalled by a change in the title to "Equity and Trusts".

Since the last edition of this work, there has been something of a renaissance in judicial and academic thinking about the distinctiveness of equity as a body of legal rules and the important contributions which these make to enrich the operation of private law systems. In the context of the law of penalties and relief against forfeiture, for example, the Supreme Court in *Cavendish Square Holding BV v Makdessi* [2016] A.C. 1172 acknowledged that the jurisdictional classification of a rule as belonging to the common law or equity can affect its scope and effect and the remedies available to claimants. Similar judicial observations have been made regarding estoppels and rescission. Significant justifications for equity's continued role have been elaborated by legal theorists including Henry Smith, Matthew Harding and Irit Samet, and the courts have engaged with this scholarship as, for example, in *Akers v Samba Financial Group* [2017] A.C. 424 and *Serious Fraud Office v Litigation Capital Ltd* [2021] EWHC 1272 (Comm). Judicial theorising of important equitable concepts and rules has itself elucidated and clarified the law and prompted further academic work in response.

Inspired by these developments, we have re-orientated the scope and focus of the book to provide a more modern and sophisticated account of equity and its relationship with the common law. Traditional explanations of this relationship tend to say that the common law is sometimes unjust and that equity's role is to mitigate this problem. In our view, such accounts fail to explain the rich role that equity plays in correcting common law, in the specific sense of providing support for, or facilitating, the common law. The universality and generality of common law rules is a strength that equity supports, rather than a weakness or problem that equity corrects. The application of an equitable rule to a given case is not made necessary by the common law's failure. Rather, the point is that equity enables the common law to work as it should, by supplying clear and certain outcomes that are the fairest outcomes in the majority of cases, secure in the knowledge that equity will work as a "safety valve" to prevent common law rights being unfairly exploited.

The relationship between common law and equity is represented by the cover image we have chosen for this book. This shows tomato plants and marigolds deliberately planted together because the marigolds repel insect pests harmful to the tomato plants. In a similar way, lawmakers have developed the rules of common law and equity so that they work together and equity can prevent human pests from abusing the rules of common law. Of course, this comparison isn't exact—for one thing, tomato plants and marigolds can both get by on their own, while equity depends on the common law for its existence. But the picture captures the idea of a combination or system which is central to a proper understanding of equity.

This edition of the book contains three new opening chapters in Part I considering equity's contribution to the legal system as a form of secondary law, and discussion of select equitable doctrines showing this operation, such as promissory estoppel, fiduciary loyalty, relief against forfeiture, equitable assignment of legal choses in action, confidentiality, and the duty of due administration.

Parts II–VI on the creation and operation of express trusts, breach of trust, and the imposition of constructive and resulting trusts have been substantially re-written to take account of cases, legislation, and academic scholarship since the last edition. They also explain how all of these trusts illustrate the points made in Part I about the operation of equity as a secondary system of law. This point is also developed in Ben McFarlane's inaugural lecture at Oxford in March 2022. This can be viewed on the Oxford Law Faculty's YouTube site, entitled: "The Persistence of Equity: Lessons from the Trust".

The final Part VII on equitable remedies has also been re-written, again to take account of cases, legislation and academic scholarship since the last edition; to include consideration of the way that equity's remedies support its own doctrines, such as confidentiality and fiduciary loyalty; and discussion of the ways in which the equitable remedies of injunction, specific performance and declaration supplement the common law by providing remedies when for one reason or another the remedies available at common law are inadequate.

The text will support undergraduate and postgraduate courses on trusts, as well as courses with a broader scope that take in other equitable doctrines and remedies. As in previous editions, each chapter consists of text, cases and secondary materials and self-assessment questions to facilitate students' detailed engagement with and application of various topic areas. Our goal is to encourage students to think critically and at a higher conceptual level not only about trusts law but also about the nature and function of equitable rules and equity's overall contribution to the English legal system.

When writing this edition, we worked collectively to plan the book's core arguments and structure and we reviewed one another's work. Jessica Hudson took primary responsibility for Chapters 1–3 and 19–22, Ben McFarlane for Chapters 4–7, 12 and 16–17, and Charles Mitchell for Chapters 8–11, 13–15 and 18.

We thank our students at UNSW, Oxford and UCL, our academic colleagues and our friends in legal practice, whose energy, creativity and insights into equity and trusts are a continuing source of inspiration. We thank our copy-editor Kacey Mann for her hard work and high standards.

Jessica thanks Michael, Lachie and Elsie for their support and patience, and Alex Stefas for his fantastic research assistance.

Ben remains grateful as ever to Sarah, and to Iris and Mary.

Charles thanks Charlotte for her support. For their outstanding research assistance, he also thanks Abe Chauhan, Helena Ratcliff and Gianna Seglias.

Jessica Hudson
Ben McFarlane
Charles Mitchell
June 2022

CONTENTS

PART II CREATION OF EXPRESS TRUSTS

PART III OPERATION OF EXPRESS TRUSTS

TABLE OF CASES

References to paragraphs in **BOLD** indicate that the text is reproduced in part or in full

TABLE OF STATUTES

References to paragraphs in **BOLD** indicate that the text is reproduced in part or in full

TABLE OF STATUTORY INSTRUMENTS

References to paragraphs in **BOLD** indicate that the text is reproduced in part or in full

TABLE OF EU, INTERNATIONAL AND FOREIGN LEGISLATION

References to paragraphs in **BOLD** indicate that the text is reproduced in part or in full

PART I

INTRODUCTION

1

UNDERSTANDING EQUITY

1. What is Equity?

This book is about a defined body of legal rules and principles collectively referred to as equity, which forms part of the broader English legal system, and also forms part of other legal systems with a historical link to English law, such as Singapore, Hong Kong, Canada and Australia. It is helpful first to explain what we mean by equity. In this context, it refers not to a general concept of fairness or justice but rather, specifically, to the body of rules and principles, forming part of the current law, which have evolved from rules and principles applied and administered by the Court of Chancery. As noted by Williams JA in *Re Tyler*,[1] the distinction is between "equity which is capable of forensic enforcement in a suit or action" and "moral principle". 1-001

A. Equity and the Court of Chancery

The two senses of equity (as a general concept of fairness or justice; as a particular body of rules) are not mutually exclusive and there are overlaps and interconnections between them. The Court of Chancery grew out of the residuum of justice left in the King where his common law courts for some special reason brought about an unjust result, e.g. because they provided no remedy, or only an inadequate remedy.[2] The source of the injustice might, for example, have been the rigidity of the writ system, which meant that a deserving claim could not be formulated in such a way as to be accepted by a common law court; or strict evidential rules which meant that relevant facts could not be put before the court;[3] or the refusal of the common law courts to grant a remedy ordering the defendant to do something other than deliver up land or pay a sum of money. An aggrieved person would petition the King who would refer the complaint to his Chancellor as his right-hand man. The Chancellor, who was an ecclesiastic, with some knowledge of Roman law and canon law, first advised the King and his Council, but towards the end of the fifteenth century began making decrees on his own authority. He was concerned with affording relief in individual cases and made personal orders against parties who were imprisoned for contempt if they did not observe his decrees. Equity did not consist of rules and principles, but rather depended on the particular Chancellor's views of the merits 1-002

---

1 *Re Tyler* [1907] 1 KB 865 at 869.

2 For a short but illuminating account of the history and development of equity, see J. Hackney, *Understanding Equity and Trusts* (Fontana Press, 1987), Ch.1.

3 For fuller accounts see W.S. Holdsworth, *History of English Law*, Vol.1 (Methuen & Co., 1903), pp.395ff.; A. Kiralfy (ed.), *Potter's Historical Introduction to English Law*, 4th edn (Sweet & Maxwell, 1958), pp.152ff.; S.F.C. Milsom, *Historical Foundations of the Common Law*, 2nd edn (Oxford University Press, 1981), pp.82ff.; J.H. Baker, *Introduction to English Legal History*, 4th edn (Oxford University Press, 2002), Chs 6, 14, 15, 16. On the role of equity in overcoming common law limitations on procedure and evidence, see, e.g. M. Macnair, "Equity and Conscience" (2007) 27 O.J.L.S. 659.

of a particular case, and thus varied according to the Chancellor's conception of justice: or, as Selden remarked, according to the size of the Chancellor's foot.[4]

1-003 What begun as equity as the individual judge's perception of fairness, evolved into equity as a defined body of legal rules. This evolution was the product of various changes in the way that the Chancellor, and later the Court of Chancery decided cases, and in who decided them. The Chancellor and other judges appointed to the Court of Chancery changed from being mainly religiously trained ecclesiastics, such as Cardinal Wolsey (Chancellor from 1515–1529), to lawyers who were legally trained in civil law (in distinction to canon law), including in the doctrine of precedent, such as Sir Thomas More (1529–1533), who was a bencher of Lincoln's Inn and the first Chancellor since the fourteenth century to have been educated in the common law.[5] From 1660, cases were recorded more often and with more detail, including the arguments of counsel and the reasons upon which the judge based his decision. Those reasons initially were based on equity in the general sense, but with the accretion of recorded cases and influence of the doctrine of precedent, cases throughout the seventeenth century became increasingly to be decided on a judge's application of equity as a defined body of legal rules developed and applied by the Court of Chancery.

1-004 The development of the Court of Chancery, and the systematisation of its rules and principles, necessarily posed a problem for the administration of justice: in a single, non-federal legal unit such as England and Wales, how can it make sense to have two sets of courts where there is no clear divide between the jurisdiction of each? As Hackney has put it:[6]

> At the beginning of the nineteenth century, the court structure in England and Wales was in a mess. The population was subject to the jurisdiction of a dual system of superior courts. On the one side were the three 'common law' courts—the Common Pleas, the Queen's Bench and the Exchequer of Pleas – and on the other was the Court of Chancery . . . From any managerial viewpoint, this arrangement was ludicrous.

1-005 The Judicature Acts 1873–75 dealt with this procedural and managerial problem by allowing the procedural "fusion" which means that rules and principles of common law and equity are now administered in all courts concurrently.[7] Similar legislation has been enacted, at different times, in other common law jurisdictions.[8] The Judicature Act 1873 s.25 set out 10 cases in which the equitable and common law rules conflicted, stating that in each case the equitable rules were to prevail. In s.25(11), it then gave statutory force to the general rule that, in the case of conflict, a court should follow the equitable rules:

> Generally in all matters not hereinbefore particularly mentioned, in which there is any conflict or variance between the Rules of Equity and the Rules of Common Law with reference to the same matter, the Rules of Equity shall prevail.

1-006 The 1873 Act is no longer in force. The relevant legislation now is the Senior Courts Act 1981, s.49 of which states that:

> Every Court exercising jurisdiction in England or Wales in any civil cause or matter shall continue to administer law and equity on the basis that, wherever there is any conflict or variance between the rules of equity and the rules of common law with reference to the same matter, the rules of equity shall prevail.

---

4 F. Pollock (ed.), *Table Talk of John Selden* (Selden Society, 1927), p.43.
5 J.H. Baker, *Introduction to English Legal History*, 5th edn (Oxford University Press, 2019), p.115.
6 J. Hackney, *Understanding Equity and Trusts* (Fontana, 1987), Ch.1.
7 The governing legislation is now contained in the Senior Courts Act 1981.
8 New South Wales held out, retaining a dual court system, until 1972: see Law Reform (Law and Equity) Act 1972 (NSW).

B. Defining Equity

While we have thus distinguished equity as a body of legal rules from equity in the sense of some general principles of fairness, justice and equality, we have not yet articulated what these legal rules are, or a means for identifying them. This is not an easy task. The authors of *Meagher Gummow and Lehane's: Equity Doctrines & Remedies* point out this challenge in the following way:[9] **1-007**

> Equity can be described but not defined. It is the body of law developed by the Court of Chancery in England before 1873. Its justification was that it corrected, supplemented and amended the common law. It softened and modified many of the injustices in common law, and provided remedies where at law they were either inadequate or non-existent.

Certainly, it is not possible to identify equity by reference to a unifying subject, such as contract, or tort or land, for example. Equity also encompasses entire subject areas, such as the law of trusts, for example. Equity spans the public–private law divide, and includes procedural as well as substantive legal rules, and thus renders futile some of our more familiar means of demarking a subject area of law. **1-008**

Maitland, lecturing in the first decade of the twentieth century, defined equity as:[10] **1-009**

> . . . that body of rules administered by our English courts of justice which, were it not for the operation of the Judicature Acts, would be administered only by those courts which would be known as Courts of Equity. . . . This you may well say, is but a poor thing to call a definition. Equity is a certain portion of our existing substantive law, and yet in order that we may describe this portion and mark it off from other portions we have to make reference to courts that are no longer in existence. Still I fear that nothing better than this is possible. The only alternative would be to make a list of the equitable rules and say that Equity consists of those rules. This, I say, would be the only alternative, for if we were to inquire what it is that all these rules have in common and what it is that marks them off from all other rules administered by our courts, we should by way of answer find nothing but this, that these rules were until lately administered, and administered only, by our courts of equity.

As recognised by Maitland, there are some problems with understanding equity simply by reference to that body of legal rules administered by a court that no longer exists. A further problem is that equity is not static or fixed, and rules have evolved and developed since the Judicature Acts; some of which may be traced back to rules administered by a court of Equity prior to the reforms. An example is the doctrine of unconscionable bargains,[11] a means for a party to set aside, or resist the enforcement of, a contract, which evolved in its modern form after the Judicature Reforms, and a useful summary of which is given by Edelman J in the High Court of Australia in *Australian Securities and Investments Commission v Kobelt*:[12] **1-010**

> By the mid-twentieth century, the conscience of equity hardened so that mere "unfairness" or "unreasonableness" was not sufficient in any of the various categories. Claimants had to be subject to some "special" disadvantage – a disadvantage that must seriously affect their ability to make a judgment about their own interests. Moreover, there had to be a 'taking of advantage' of that special disadvantage. Although that

---

9 J.D. Heydon, M.J. Leeming and P.G. Turner, *Meagher, Gummow & Lehane's Equity: Doctrine & Remedies*, 5th edn (LexisNexis, 2014), para.1–005.

10 F.W. Maitland, *Equity – A Course of Lectures*, 2nd edn (Cambridge University Press, 1936), p.1.

11 See generally, *Multiservice Bookbinding Ltd v Marden* [1979] Ch. 84 at 110; *Boustany v Pigott* (1993) 69 P.&C.R. 298 at 303; *Credit Lyonnais Bank Nederland NV v Branch* [1997] 1 All E.R. 144 at 153; *Portman Building Society v Dusangh* [2000] 2 All E.R. (Comm) 221 at 229.

12 *Australian Securities and Investments Commission v Kobelt* [2019] HCA 18; 267 C.L.R. 1 at [282] [citations omitted].

taking of advantage did not, and does not, require that the victim suffer any "loss or detriment", it required much more than mere unreasonableness, being variously described in Australia as requiring "victimisation" or "exploitation". In England, in addition to these descriptions the courts also described equity as requiring conduct that is "morally reprehensible" or conduct that "shocks the conscience of the court". With some exceptions in application, these various epithets established a high bar for the vitiation of transactions in twentieth century equity on the ground of unconscionable conduct.

1–011 A definition of equity generated from a list of rules as administered by the Court of Chancery in 1873 would be underinclusive of those rules that have evolved and changed since then. More substantively, the historical description of equity provides us with little insight into the existence of any common themes or roles fulfilled by equity today, let alone why it is that we should continue to think about equity as a distinct body of rules.

1–012 Despite all this, judges and academics often look to the history of an equitable rule to understand it. History is relevant because it helps us to understand the nature of the problems that equity was developed to resolve, and thereby helps us to understand what equity does today, and why a particular role, at least initially, was performed by equity, rather than the common law or statute.

2. The Historical Development of Equity

A. Early Development

1–013 Equity was not developed in response to a mature and static legal system. Equity was developed within a novel common law system that was itself evolving concurrently with the gradual decline in feudalism after the Norman Conquest in 1066.[13] There are many accounts of the development of the common law and equity, and we are not aiming to give a comprehensive treatment here. The following discussion provides a high-level outline of some of the historical reasons why equity developed to perform certain roles within the English legal system.

1–014 As noted at para.1–002, the Court of Chancery grew out of the residuum of justice left in the King where the common law courts for some special reason brought about an unjust result; for example, because they provided no remedy, or an inadequate remedy. A plaintiff would petition the King, and later in the fourteenth century, the Chancellor, for a one-off form of relief based on the circumstances of the case. The Chancellor was the King's secretary of state, or "right-hand man" with much power. The Chancellor did much of the writing that had to be done in the King's name and could affix the Great Seal.

1–015 To commence a case in the common law courts, a plaintiff would purchase one of a closed list of writs from the Chancellor that allowed a plaintiff to commence an action for prescribed relief in the relevant court; provided the plaintiff could fit her case to the form of the writ.

1–016 The great range of human circumstances threw up situations that did not fit within the established list of writs. Sometimes, the Chancellor was moved to provide an ad hoc, one-off form of relief solely between the parties to the matter. Until the mid-thirteenth century, the Chancellor could do this by issuing a new form of writ for the plaintiff to take to the common law courts. However, the Chancellor's power to issue new writs was curtailed in the mid-thirteenth century, and the common law courts would quash the new forms of writ.[14] This meant that a deserving plaintiff would not be able to fit her case within a common law writ and would otherwise be left without any means of legal redress.

---

13 About which see generally: S.F.C. Milsom, *The Legal Framework of English Feudalism* (Cambridge University Press, 1972).

14 Provisions of Oxford 1258; Statute of Westminster II 1285. S.F.C. Milsom, *Historical Foundations of the Common Law*, 2nd edn (Oxford University Press, 1981), p.284.

In addition to the closed list of writs that only covered particular situations, a further limitation to the common law's ability to respond was the rules of procedure and evidence in application at the time. The ways in which questions were put to a jury, and the types of facts capable of being established by other modes of proof, such as trial by battle, meant that there were a range of facts that could not be established in a common law court, such as a plaintiff's or defendant's subjective state of mind. This further stifled the common law courts' ability to respond to a range of situations concerning a party's subjective state of mind or other facts that largely depended for their proof on oral testimony. **1–017**

John Baker, *Introduction to English Legal History*, 5th edn (Oxford University Press, 2019), pp.110–111, 346

In the King's Bench and Common Pleas [the fulfilment of the common law] was circumscribed by the writ system, the forms of pleading, the rules of evidence, the varying reliability of sheriffs, and the uncertainties of jury trial. The possibilities of technical failure were legion. And the growing strength of the substantive law could also work injustice, because the judges held that it was preferable to suffer hardship in individual cases than to make exceptions to clear rules. The stock example was that of a debtor who gave his creditor a sealed bond, but did not ensure that it was cancelled when he paid up. The law regarded the bond as incontrovertible evidence of the debt, and so payment was no defence against it. The debtor would suffer an obvious hardship of he was made to pay twice; but the mischief was a result of his own foolishness, and the law did not bend to protect fools. It was in the interests of certainty that deeds should prevail over mere words. Likewise, if a man made an oral contract where the common law required written evidence, he would find himself without remedy. Again if someone granted land to other on trust to carry out his wishes, he would find that at law his trusted grantees were absolute owners who could not be compelled to obey him. Now, it was not that the common law held that a debt was due twice, or that a promise or trust could be broken. Such propositions would have been dismissed as absurd. Those were merely the hard consequences of observing strict rules of evidence, rules which might well exclude the merits of a case from consideration by a court but which could not be relaxed generally without destroying certainty and condoning carelessness. For a creditor, promissee, or trustee to take unfair advantage of those strict rules was without question wrong; but it was a matter for their consciences rather than for the common law. **1–018**

Under the harsh logic of the common law it was "better to suffer a mischief to one man than an inconvenience to many, which would subvert the law. For if matter in writing could be so easily defeated and avoided by such a surmise, by naked breath, a matter in writing would be of no greater authority than a matter of fact".[15] **1–019**

The Chancellor, however, had another and different means to respond to these and other situations, which was to make a decree which bound only the parties to the suit and provided a one-off or ad hoc form of redress. The Chancellor's jurisdiction to award such decrees on his own authority was settled in the fifteenth century. To attain a decree, an aggrieved plaintiff would petition the Chancellor, who would respond by sending for the defendant to appear before the Chancellor, and to answer before the Chancellor about the plaintiff's complaints. The procedure was that the plaintiff would petition or send a "bill" to the Chancellor setting out their complaint, including the reason(s) why the Chancellor should intervene. These reasons varied, sometimes being that there was no remedy at law. In one petition, the plaintiff alleges that the defendants:[16] **1–020**

> . . . do continually threaten the said supplicant from day to day to kill him, so that he dare not approach his own country nor sue them at Common Law for fear of death: Wherefore may it please your most gracious lordship to grant your said supplicant writs directed to the [defendants] [commanding them] to come before you in your place on a certain pain . . . to answer concerning the said matters; considering, most

---

15 *Waberley v Cockerel* (1542) B. & M. 284 at 285.

16 "Petitions Addressed to Sir Michael De La Pole, 1383–1386", *Select Cases in Chancery* (1896) 10 SS 1, case 44, p.48.

> gracious lord, that the [defendant]s are so great in their country in kinsmen, alliances and friends, that the said supplicant cannot have right against them by any suit at Common Law; the which writs may it please you to grant the said supplicant for God and in way of charity.

1–021 Observe that the plaintiff alleges he is unable to pursue his case at common law because the notoriety and influence of the defendant is such that the plaintiff fears he will not have a fair trial. Observe also the plaintiff's prayer for the relief to be granted by the Chancellor "for God and in way of charity". The invocation of reasons such as "conscience", "God", "charity", "right" and "the law" were frequently used by plaintiffs in their petitions to the Chancellor and reflected the types of reasons upon which the Chancellor would act.

1–022 Another example is a petition to the Chancellor (undated) whereby the plaintiff sets out the facts of his complaint against the defendant and then concludes the petition by stating:[17]

> [and this] wrongfully and to the damage of the said supplicant of 100 marks, and to the great detriment of his poor estate if he be not aided by you, most gracious Lordship to consider this matter, and thereupon to ordain that the said suppliant may have restitution . . . and law and conscience demand, with the damages on this behalf: For God and in way of charity.

1–023 In another petition, the plaintiff, after setting out the facts of his complaint against the defendant, concludes with:[18]

> And so it is, most reverend [Lord], that the said suppliant cannot have any remedy in this behalf by the law of Holy Church, nor by the common law of the land: May it please your most gracious Lordship, in honour of God and on account of righteousness, to grant writs to cause the said Walter and Reginald [defendants] to come before you in the King's Chancery, which is the Court of Conscience, there to answer thereto as reason and conscience demand, otherwise the said suppliant is and will be without remedy, which God forfend.

1–024 If so moved, the Chancellor would issue a writ called a "subpoena" that would command the defendant to appear before the Chancellor and answer to the complaint. The defendant would have to swear an oath before the Chancellor and answer each allegation made by the plaintiff. The Chancellor's examination of the defendant was often referred to in the plaintiff's petition, as in for example:[19]

> May it please your most gracious Lordship to consider the premises, and that the said suppliant hath no remedy at common law, and to grant several writs under a certain pain directed to the said [defendants], [commanding them] to appear before you on a certain day, and to be examined on these matters, and on their examination to cause right to be done to the said suppliant, for God and in way of charity.

1–025 The Chancellor would make findings of fact, based on his interrogation of the defendant. This almost inquisitorial type of procedure was radically different to the procedure and modes of proof in the common law courts. The common law courts, by and large, did not have procedures and modes of proof capable of adducing facts as to a person's inner state of mind. The Chancellor, however, could make findings of fact based upon direct oral testimony of the parties, and other witnesses, and was not constrained to facts set out in a deed, written contract or other legal instrument, for example.[20]

---

17 "French Petitions of Various Dates", *Select Cases in Chancery* (1896) 10 SS 103, case 121, pp.118–119.
18 "French Petitions of Various Dates", *Select Cases in Chancery*, case 123, pp.120–121.
19 "French Petitions of Various Dates", *Select Cases in Chancery*, case 127, p.123.
20 M. Macnair, "Equity and Conscience" (2007) 27 O.J.L.S. 659.

Mike Macnair has explained that one of the meanings of "conscience" is "knowledge or belief of legally relevant facts which were not appropriately pleaded and proved"[21] going on to explain the "boundary between law and conscience" as being that between:[22] 1-026

> . . . facts [that] could not be proved at common law because of the structure of the system of pleadings and proofs, and in contrast . . . they could by their nature be proved by examining the defendant on oath with a view to extracting a confession.

The difference in procedural capabilities between common law courts and courts of Equity is significant for explaining why it is that certain matters could only be dealt with in Chancery, such as the oral declaration of a trust, or the subjective state of mind of a party. As a result, certain doctrines were necessarily equitable in origin, such as trusts, mistake, undue influence and other forms of equitable fraud. 1-027

Having ascertained the facts, the Chancellor would decide what type of relief, if any, was merited in the case and, if necessary, make orders compelling the defendant to take (in)action under the threat of imprisonment for contempt. 1-028

The whole process and means of compulsion is described in *Reynolde v Knott*:[23] 1-029

> . . . in the use of writs of *subpoena* . . . It is [Chancery's] business to examine the conscience, for when an act is good and always has been, their examination shall not make it bad, but their examination proves the act good and lawful in our law. And forasmuch as he cannot have remedy by our law, he sues there to have . . . judgment . . . to cause the defendant to make acquittance or release [of the debt]. And to execute this [judgment] the court can do nothing except order him to prison to be there until he is ready to do this; and thus this is all that the said court can do. And if the party would rather lie in prison than [to comply with the order to release the debt or cancel the bond] . . . the other (party) is without remedy, and this the Chancellor has no power to make the [debt] void.

Also referenced in the above passage is the limited effect of an order made by the Chancellor. The Chancellor's power was limited in that he could not change the law, or how it applied to determine the existence of the parties' legal relations. The Chancellor could only order the defendant in relation to how the defendant exercised or enforced the defendant's legal entitlement against the plaintiff. Further, and early on before Chancery was a court of record, orders were made in personam, binding only the parties to the case. The outcome of a case did not lay down a precedent that was legally binding in other cases. John Baker has explained:[24] 1-030

> By exercising this jurisdiction in conscience, the chancellor was not causing any of the 'inconvenience' which the law eschewed. In Chancery each case turned on its own facts, and the chancellor did not dispute or interfere with the general rules observed in courts of law. The decrees operated in personam; they were binding on the parties in the cause, but they were not judgements of record binding anyone else and they did not alter or contradict the law.

Despite the varied and ad hoc nature of the Chancery's activities, two loosely discernible patterns emerged over the fifteenth and sixteenth centuries as to the role of the Chancellor, and later of the court of Chancery. First, was to provide relief where the plaintiff had some right, or interest recognised 1-031

[21] Macnair, "Equity and Conscience", (2007) 27 O.J.L.S. 659, 674.
[22] Macnair, "Equity and Conscience", (2007) 27 O.J.L.S. 659, 676, see also 677–679.
[23] *Reynolde v Knott* (1459) 51 SS 147 at 152 (Prysot C.J.C.P.).
[24] Baker, *Introduction to English Legal History*, p.112 (citations omitted).

at law, but for some reason or another, the plaintiff was unable to obtain adequate relief owing to the limits of the remedy at law in the individual circumstances of the case. The common law courts were limited in the types of remedies they could award; largely to orders requiring a defendant to pay a sum of money to the plaintiff, orders for the delivery up of chattels, or possession of real property. The Chancellor, however, could make orders to direct a defendant to take action (or to not take action) on the threat of contempt of court. This meant that the Chancellor could make orders securing a wider range of remedial outcomes, including, but not limited to, the award of monetary awards, and orders for the reconveyance of title to land or other property.

1–032 The second role developed in response to a slightly different issue of where the common law either did not apply at all or would produce a result that was considered by the Chancellor to be wrong or unfair in the individual circumstances of the case. This might be because of the rigidity of the writ system, and/or because of the rules of procedure and evidence in application in the common law courts. As discussed above, the type of reasons upon which the Chancellor would decide whether or not the common law produced an "unfair" result, to begin with, was equity in the general sense of fairness, justice and equality; often expressed in terms of "conscience". Conscience is a term that has evolved in equity jurisprudence, having once been informed by the Chancellor's religious background and training, and later the legal training of the judges of the court of Chancery. Conscience is discussed further at paras 1–007 to 1–134.

1–033 History explains why equity developed to fulfil these two roles of complementing the common law and supplementing the common law. As will be discussed further below, these two roles help us to understand equity's functions today.

B. From Equity as General Principles to Equity as Positive Law

1–034 The history of equity is important not just for understanding how and why equity fulfils certain functions in our legal system today. History also helps us to understand the evolution of equity as general principles of fairness and morality, into equity as a defined body of legal rules, and in turn, the continuing and dynamic relationship between equity as a body of rules and general principles of morality and fairness.

1–035 In the Tudor period (1485–1603), Chancery was understood as a "court of conscience" in distinction from courts of common law that administered law conceived of as "rules applicable to given sets of facts".[25] This is because Chancery was not understood as administering a body of law, and was rather:[26]

> . . . just a myriad of single instances in which good conscience required more of people than the law demanded. . . . Nevertheless it prevailed over law, in that it could only function as a corrective to the common law if it had the last word. If, therefore, proceedings in other courts were brought unconscionably, the chancellor would enjoin the plaintiffs to surcease: this was called the 'common injunction'.

1–036 The relationship between equity and the common law came to a head with the *Earl of Oxford's Case*,[27] in which the Court of Chancery issued a common injunction to restrain a defendant from executing a judgment at law in ejectment. The Chancellor, Lord Ellesmere LC stated that:[28]

---

25 Baker, *Introduction to English Legal History*, 4th edn (2002) p.114.

26 Baker, *Introduction to English Legal History*, 4th edn (2002) p.114.

27 *Earl of Oxford's Case* (1615) 1 Ch. Rep. 1, examined by D. Ibbetson, "*The Earl of Oxford's Case* (1615)" in C. Mitchell & P. Mitchell (eds) *Landmark Cases in Equity* (Hart, 2013), Ch.1.

28 *Earl of Oxford's Case* (1615) 1 Ch. Rep. 1 at 5, 13.

> The Chancellor must give Account to none but only to the King and Parliament . . . The Chancellor sits in Chancery according to an absolute and uncontrollable Power, and is to judge according to that which is alleged and proved; but the Judges of Common Law are to judge according to a strict and ordinary (or limited) Power.

The common law courts, and Sir Edward Coke in particular, regarded Chancery as interfering with title to land[29] and also undermining the common law of contract by ordering a defendant to specifically perform a promise, thus taking away the defendant's choice "either to pay damages or to fulfil his promise".[30] **1-037**

The matter was resolved in 1616 by James I who issued a royal decree confirming the Chancellor's authority to entertain suits after judgments at law. Equity's prevalence over the law was later confirmed in the Judicature Act 1873.[31] **1-038**

During the periods of the Tudors and Stuarts and until the Judicature Reforms in 1873, equity evolved in that the types of reasons that were relied upon to determine the outcomes of cases developed from general principles of equity phrased in terms of what "conscience" demanded, to increasingly defined and generalisable rules derived from previous cases as applied to the next. There were multiple dynamics in this evolution, including the sheer volume of cases being heard by Chancery, the increased recording of Chancery cases, and legal training of the judges. Gradually, equity became an identifiable body of legal rules defining when some form of equitable relief was available, rather than some general principle(s) of fairness. John Baker has explained:[32] **1-039**

> After 1660 Chancery cases were regularly reported. . . . The effect of giving reasons for decisions, with a view to their being reported, was to complete the reduction of equity to a system of general principles. By 1676 a lord chancellor could repudiate the idea that equity had any dependence on his own inner conscience: "the conscience by which I am to proceed is merely *civilis et politica*, and tied to certain measures".[33] . . . Thus equity hardened into a kind of law. Trusts and mortgages were governed by rules as clear as any rules of common law. In matters of contract and tort, the Chancery normally followed the law. . . . It is true that equity remained, and still remains, more flexible than the common law, because it can take greater account of individual circumstances, for instance, remedies can be lost by delay, by intervention of third-party interests, or by a lack of probity on the part of the plaintiff. Guidelines at first seemed more helpful than rigid rules. . . . But the preoccupation of the court with matters of property, the high intellectual capacities of many chancellors and leaders of the Chancery Bar, and the superior quality of the later reports, all combined to render equity as certain and scientific as law. Precedents were as persuasive in equity as at law, and now even the Chancery would sooner suffer a hardship than a departure from known rules. . . .[34] "Nothing would inflict on me greater pain in quitting this place," said Lord Eldon LC in 1818, "than the recollection that I had done anything to justify the reproach that the equity of this court varies like the chancellor's foot."

The systematisation of equity brought with it a similar phenomenon to which equity first responded; there were various technicalities and complexities with equity procedure and doctrine, all of which were exacerbated with the growth in the caseload throughout the nineteenth century. Some of the problems with Chancery were famously skewered by Charles Dickens in *Bleak House,* a novel of 1851–1853 that centres upon a long running (fictional) case in the court of Chancery, *Jarndyce v* **1-040**

---

29 *Heath v Rydley* (1614) Cro. Jac. 335.
30 *Bromage v Genning* (1617) 1 Rolle. 368.
31 Judicature Act 1873 s.25(11).
32 Baker, *Introduction to English Legal History*, 4th edn (2002) p.119.
33 *Cooke v Fountain* (1676) 3 Swan. 585 at 660 (Lord Nottingham C).
34 *Galton v Hancock* (1743) 2 Atk. 427 at 439 (Lord Hardwicke C).

Jarndyce: a family dispute arising from a testator having written multiple inconsistent wills. Dickens is critical of the Court of Chancery, including in the following passages:[35]

> The raw afternoon is rawest, and the dense fog is densest, and the muddy streets are muddiest near that leaden-headed old obstruction, appropriate ornament for the threshold of a leaden-headed old corporation, Temple Bar. And hard by Temple Bar, in Lincoln's Inn Hall, at the very heart of the fog, sits the Lord High Chancellor in his High Court of Chancery. Never can there come fog too thick, never can there come mud and mire too deep, to assort with the groping and floundering condition which this High Court of Chancery, most pestilent of hoary sinners, holds this day in the sight of heaven and earth . . . some score of members of the High Court of Chancery bar ought to be – as here they are – mistily engaged in one of the ten thousand stages of an endless cause, tripping one another up on slippery precedents, groping knee-deep in technicalities, running their goat-hair and horse-hair warded heads against walls of words, and making a pretence of equity with serious faces . . . The lawyers have twisted it into such a state of bedevilment that the original merits of the case have long disappeared from the face of the earth. It's about a will and the trusts under a will – or it was once. It's about nothing but costs now. We are always appearing, and disappearing, and swearing, and interrogating, and filing, and cross-filing, and arguing, and sealing, and motioning, and referring, and reporting, and revolving about the Lord Chancellor and all his satellites, and equitably waltzing ourselves off to dusty death, about costs. That's the great question. All the rest, by some extraordinary means, has melted away.

1–041 These, and other problems with Chancery, ultimately led to multiple reforms of the English court system, including the fusion of the administration of common law and equity in the Judicature Reforms.[36] Whilst those reforms caused the disappearance of specific courts of Equity, the rules and principles of equity remained, and have continued to be developed. This raises the question of what role those rules and principles play in our current legal system.

3. The Modern Functions of Equity

A. Correction of the Common Law?

1–042 The history of equity tells us that it is a body of rules developed and applied by the Chancellor and later courts of Equity, in response to problems generated by the common law. It may thus seem that one of equity's roles is that identified by Aristotle as:[37]

> . . . a correction of the law where it is defective owing to its universality. In fact this is the reason why all things are not determined by law. That about some things it is impossible to lay down a law, so that a decree is needed. . . It is plain, then, what the equitable is, and that it is just and better than one kind of justice.

1–043 This idea of equity is also observed by Lord Ellesmere LC in *The Earl of Oxford's Case*:[38]

> The Cause why there is a Chancery is, for that Mens Actions are do divers and infinite, That it is impossible to make any general Law which may aptly meet with every particular Act, and not fail in some Circumstances. . . . The Office of the Chancellor is to correct Mens consciences for Frauds, Breach of Trusts, Wrongs and Oppressions, of what Nature soever they be, and to soften and mollify the Extremity of the Law. . .

---

35 C. Dickens, *Bleak House* (Penguin Classics, 2003).

36 Judicature Acts 1873–1875.

37 Aristotle, *Nicomachean Ethics* (W.D. Ross trans, Oxford University Press, 1908). The interconnections between equity and Equity are discussed in D. Klimchuk, "Aristotle and the Foundations of the Law of Equity" in D. Klimchuk, I. Samet and H. Smith (eds), *Philosophical Foundations of the Law of Equity* (Oxford University Press, 2020), Ch.2.

38 *Earl of Oxford's Case* (1615) Chan. Rep. 1, examined by Ibbetson, "*The Earl of Oxford's Case* (1615)".

Lord Ellesmere LC thus understood the body of rules we refer to as equity as responding to the problems that arise from some *ex ante* body of rules being too general to be able to deal with the full range of human interactions. Observe also that Lord Ellesmere LC describes the reasons for the Chancellor's intervention in terms other than equity as general principles of fairness. By 1615, the rules applied by the Court of Chancery to determine when relief would be awarded "to correct Mens consciences", were defined enough for Lord Ellesmere LC to refer to specific circumstances, such as a breach of trust, or fraud, for example. **1–044**

The body of legal rules we refer to as equity today thus developed from the application of equity in the sense of general moral principles. Both of these senses of equity have been described as "correcting" the common law in a manner that exemplifies the Aristotelian sense of equity, which has also been described as a "*correction* of the law where it is defective owing to its universality".[39] It is common for cases and commentaries to point to the common law's failings, injustices or problems and equity's role in correcting them. **1–045**

Whatever may have been the features of the common law requiring correction around 1400, the idea of equity applying to correct the common law should not be understood as meaning that there is some problem or deficiency with, or injustice caused by the common law today. As we will see through this chapter and book, equity's role is corrective in a very specific sense of providing support for, or facilitation of, the common law. The common law's universality or generality is a strength that equity supports, rather than a weakness or problem that equity corrects. The application of an equitable rule to a given case is not due to a problem or failing of the common law, but rather reflects the common law working precisely as it should. As we will explore in this chapter, equity's existence reflects the overall systemic advantages gained from having some secondary sub-system of rules that prevents the parties misusing the legal entitlements granted them by the *ex ante* sub-system of legal rules. Equity's supportive role is captured by Frederick Maitland who stated that "equity had come not to destroy the law but to fulfil it".[40] **1–046**

Building on Maitland's analysis, it will be argued here that today, equity can be understood to fulfil the following functions: **1–047**

(1) *complementing the common law* (sometimes referred to as equity's *concurrent or auxiliary jurisdiction*) by providing an equitable remedy in aid of a common law entitlement when a common law remedy is inadequate;

(2) *supplementing the common law* (sometimes referred to as equity's *exclusive jurisdiction*) by controlling A's exercise of A's legal entitlements, including by:
   (a) restraining A's exercise of an entitlement; and/or
   (b) generating a new duty of A, owed to B, that requires A to exercise (or not exercise) A's legal entitlement in some way.

B. Equity as a Complement to Common Law

Equity will not allow the claimant, B, to be without an adequate remedy, and an equitable remedy will be available to give effect to some common law entitlement where the remedy afforded at common **1–048**

[39] Aristotle, *Nicomachean Ethics*.
[40] F.W. Maitland, *Equity – A Course of Lectures*, 2nd edn (Cambridge University Press, 1936), p.17.

law is inadequate. We will see in Chapter 19, for example, that equitable remedies such as an order for specific performance and an injunction can compel performance of a common law duty.

1-049 Consider, for example, specific performance of a contract for the sale of title to land: a court order compelling the vendor to take action(s) as necessary to transfer title to land to the purchaser (assuming the purchaser likewise performs her side of the bargain). The overall effect of specific performance is that the parties are put in exactly the position they should be, according to the performance of their mutual obligations. This is very different to the outcome that might be reached by contractual damages, whereby the claimant will be paid a sum of money by the defendant that will aim to put her in the monetary equivalent of the position she expected to be in, had the defendant performed her obligation. Further, in some situations, the contractual remedy of damages would not even achieve this result; for example, where the property that is the subject of a contract for sale is unique, making the expectation measure of damages difficult to prove.

1-050 Another example is where an injunction is awarded to restrain a defendant from taking action that would result in a breach of the defendant's duty to the claimant. The duty might be contractual or tortious, for example. Damages are often found to be an inadequate remedy, and injunctions are awarded, for the torts of trespass to land and nuisance, reflecting the strong protection afforded by the law to a landowner's right to the quiet enjoyment of her property.[41]

1-051 Injunctions can be awarded to restrain other torts, too,[42] and breaches of contract, of which Sachs LJ observed in *Evans Marshall & Co Ltd v Bertola SA* that:[43]

> The courts have repeatedly recognised there can be claims under contracts in which, as here, it is unjust to confine a plaintiff to his damages for their breach. Great difficulty in estimating these damages is one factor that can be and has been taken into account. Another factor is the creation of certain areas of damage which cannot be taken into monetary account in a common law action for breach of contract. Loss of goodwill and trade reputation are examples. Generally, indeed, the grant of injunctions in contract cases stems from such factors.

1-052 Another type of equitable remedy sometimes awarded in aid of a common law right is a declaration.[44] This order declares the existence of the parties' legal entitlements and/or obligations and may also be awarded, either with an injunction, or alone.

1-053 Another important example of equity's complementing the common law is when an equitable remedy, such as an injunction, sometimes also coupled with a declaration, is awarded to effect judicial review of public power—equity's public law role is discussed further below.[45]

1-054 The way in which orders for specific performance or an injunction compel a defendant to take (in)action may take various forms; for example, empowering a person other than the defendant to

---

[41] See, e.g. *Hodgson v Duce* (1856) 2 Jur. N.S. 1014; *Eardley v Granville* (1876) 3 Ch. D. 826; *Litchfield-Speer v Queen Anne's Gate Syndicate (No.2) Ltd* [1919] 1 Ch. 407; *Anchor Brewhouse Developments Ltd v Berkley House (Docklands Developments) Ltd* (1987) 38 B.L.R. 82; *Harrow LBC v Donohue* [1995] 1 E.G.L.R. 257 (distinguishing acts of mere trespass—where damages might be substituted for an injunction—and dispossession, where a claimant is entitled as a matter of right to the protection of an injunction).

[42] As noted in J. Murphy, "Rethinking Injunctions in Tort Law" (2007) 27 O.J.L.S. 509, arguing that the law attaches just as much importance to the protection of non-property interests, and so should be just as willing to award injunctions to protect other interests besides proprietary interests, e.g. bodily integrity.

[43] [1973] 1 W.L.R. 349 at 380. See also *Manning v AIG Europe UK Ltd* [2004] EWHC 1760 (Ch); [2005] 1 B.C.L.C. 1 (breach of subordinated debt agreement); *Sheffield United Football Club Ltd v West Ham United Football Club Plc* [2008] EWHC 2855 (Comm); [2009] 1 Lloyd's Rep. 167 (breach of arbitration clause).

[44] See Chapter 19.

[45] See paras 1-135 to 1-148.

execute a conveyance which the latter has promised but refused to execute,[46] or, more generally, committing the defendant to prison on account of her contempt[47] (i.e. disobedience to the order of the court) until she complies with the court order and purges her contempt.

Orders for specific performance and injunction are thus also of a very different nature and significance from the defendant's perspective. They restrict the defendant's choices much more than the default position at common law which, in effect, allows the defendant to choose to perform her obligation or pay damages for breach. A defendant subject to an injunction or order for specific performance has no choice other than to obey the court order requiring her to take (in)action or be liable on contempt of court. **1-055**

It should not be surprising then that historically, and today, equitable remedies are not available as of right in response to common law rights. Even when a claimant establishes the existence of equitable jurisdiction on the basis of the inadequacy of a common law remedy, the award of equitable relief still depends on a range of discretionary factors. As will be discussed in later chapters,[48] these discretionary factors are carefully attuned to ensure fairness to both parties, including that the form of the order and surrounding circumstances are such that a defendant is not subject to an order she is unable to understand or perform, or that the court could not supervise. After all, as common law did not provide a remedy such as specific performance or an injunction, the common law rules on when the defendant comes under a duty to the claimant could allow such a duty to arise even if, given the content of the duty, such compulsion of the defendant would be inappropriate. It is therefore necessary for equity, in determining if such an order should be granted, to consider additional factors beyond those simply determining whether the defendant is under a duty to the claimant. **1-056**

In contrast, given the possibility of specific relief in equity, equitable rules defining when the defendant is under a duty to the claimant would already take account of at least some of the factors relevant to an order that the defendant must perform her duty. As Lionel Smith notes, for example, in relation to a trust:[49] **1-057**

> If the trustee has the trust property, he is not given the option of keeping it and paying compensation. In respect of trust property held by the trustee, a trust is always automatically specifically enforceable. There is no appeal to the discretion of the court, and no inquiry into whether damages would be adequate as a remedy. This is one of the things that is so foundational that people sometimes do not notice how interesting it is.

The trust provides an example of an important equitable intervention which cannot be seen as complementing or fulfilling the common law, and instead demonstrates a further role of equity, also identified by Maitland: that of supplementing the common law. **1-058**

---

46 Senior Courts Act 1981 s.39.

47 Sequestration of assets until compliance is also available against both individuals and corporations and is the only way of proceeding against corporations for contempt, although their directors may, of course, be imprisoned. Fines may also be imposed.

48 See Chapters 19 and 22.

49 See L. Smith, "Equity is Not a Single Thing" in D Klimchuk et al (eds) *Philosophical Foundations of the Law of Equity* (Oxford University Press, 2020), pp.144, 157.

C. Equity as a Supplement to Common Law

i. Equity's supplemental role

1-059 Today, there are a range of various equitable rules that, in one way or another, determine when the outcome that would otherwise be produced by the common law is unfair, such that the plaintiff has an entitlement to equitable relief; sometimes referred to as an "equity" for relief. This second function is different to the first outlined above of complementing a claimant's legal entitlements, as equity's rules and remedies are not aimed at producing the same outcome as mandated by the common law. Instead, equity provides for a different outcome than that provided by the common law.

1-060 This second function has sometimes been referred to in terms of equity's "correction", "modification" or "adjustment" of the common law. Care is needed, however, in understanding precisely what equity's effect is and why it applies. Equity does not correct or change the common law in the sense that the common law is defective or unfair in its general form. Equity does not change the existence or scope of the legal entitlements of the defendant (A), nor does equity change the existence and content of the common law rules themselves. Crucially, those common law rules, and A's legal entitlements arising under them, remain intact. Rather, equity alters the practical effect of those rules and entitlements in relation to the claimant (B), by intervening to control A's exercise of A's legal entitlements. It does so by changing the lawfulness of A's actions *as against B*. In other words, equity makes it unlawful, as against B, for A to exercise or not exercise a legal entitlement, where it would otherwise have been lawful for A to have done so, or not. In such a way, equity can in fact help to justify the existence of the general common law rules, by avoiding injustices to which those rules might otherwise give rise.

1-061 It is crucial to appreciate that equity is only a gloss on, or supplement to,[50] the common law. It has never shared the common law's aim of being a self-sufficient system that deals with all possible claims that might be made by a party. It would be a mistake to think, for example, that there is a common law of contract, and an opposing law of contract in equity; or that there is a common law of property, and an opposing law of property in equity. There is, rather, a set of common law rules and principles covering the whole domain of contract law, which is supplemented by equitable rules and principles which may, for example, regulate the ways and circumstances in which a party can assert the contractual rights she has acquired under those common law rules and principles. For example, in a case where a contract has been entered between A and B as a result of A's innocent misrepresentation to B, equity does not deny that the contract exists, but it limits the circumstances in which A can exercise her rights under the contract by giving B a power, in certain circumstances, to rescind the contract and thus unwind its effects.[51]

1-062 This supplemental nature of equity can be particularly important in understanding the trust, as Maitland explains:

Frederic Maitland, *Lectures on Equity*

Lecture II[52]

1-063 ...we ought to think of equity as supplementary law, a sort of appendix added on to our code, or a sort of gloss written round our code, an appendix, a gloss, which used to be administered by courts specially designed for that purpose, but which is now administered by the High Court of Justice as part of the code.

---

50 F.W. Maitland, *Equity – A Course of Lectures*, 2nd edn (Cambridge University Press, 1936), pp.18–19.

51 See further Chapter 20. Another example is provided by the equitable rules as to rectification: see Chapter 21.

52 The extract is from pp.18–19 of the 1909 edition A. Chaytor and W. Whittaker (eds) *Equity: Also The Forms of Action at Common Law* (Cambridge University Press, 1909).

The language which equity held to law, if we may personify the two, was not: "No, that is not so, you make a mistake, your rule is absurd, an obsolete one"; but "Yes, of course, that is so, but it is not the whole truth. You say that A is the owner of this land; no doubt that is so, but I must add that he is bound by one of those obligations which are known as trusts."

We ought not to think of common law and equity as of two rival systems. Equity was not a self-sufficient system, at every point it presupposed the existence of common law. Common law was a self-sufficient system. I mean this: that if the legislature has passed a short act saying "Equity is hereby abolished", we might have still got on fairly well; in some respects our law would have been barbarous, unjust and absurd, but still the great elementary rights, the right to immunity from violence, the right to one's good name, the rights of ownership and of possession would have been decently protected and contract would have been enforced. On the other hand had the legislature said, "Common Law is hereby abolished", this decree if obeyed would have meant anarchy. At every point equity presupposed the existence of common law. Take the case of the trust. It's of no use for Equity to say that A is the trustee of Blackacre for B, unless there be some court that can say that A is the owner of Blackacre. Equity without common law would have been a castle in the air, an impossibility. 1–064

Some more recent analyses of the role of equity, looking at both its function and its form, also build on this supplemental function of equity. In the extract below, Henry Smith argues that the distinctive feature of equity is that it operates as a secondary system of law, as meta-law, in that it presupposes the existence of, and responds to correct or mitigate problems caused by, the primary system of law. 1–065

Henry Smith, "Equity as Meta-Law"

(2021) 130 Yale L.J. 1050, 1054–1055

. . . a major theme of equity was, and is, to solve complex and uncertain problems by going to a new level of law. Equity is law about law, or meta-law. 1–066

What does it mean for equity to be meta-law? In the theory of language and in the theory of complex systems, orders are defined in terms of the domain of their operation. A meta-language takes a lower-order language as an input. Thus, when we talk about language, we need to use a meta-language. Likewise, a second-order component system acts on the output or the structure of the first-order system, but not vice versa. . . Similarly, some law regulates other law and needs to take it as an input. . . . meta-law in this sense is a theme of equity. 1–067

Going meta is usually done for functional reasons, and equity is no exception. Like other meta-systems, equity addresses a special class of problems--those of high complexity and uncertainty, which lack fore-seeability. By "complex," I do not mean complicated or having many parts. A system is complex when it is so interconnected that system behaviour is difficult to trace to individual elements. In complex systems such as brains, social networks, economies, and ecosystems--and the law--the action is in the connections, and not in the elements themselves. 1–068

Problems combining high complexity and uncertainty are those best suited for meta-law. Increased variance at one level can be better handled by going to a higher level through another system that acts on the first-order system from outside. . . . In law, complexity and its attendant uncertainty stem from at least three major phenomena. . . First, some problems involve many densely interacting elements and so are multiparty, multipolar, or, as is sometimes said, "polycentric." Multiple parties with conflicting customary rights and potential third-party effects would be a prime example. Second, conflicting presumptive rights that are each context-dependent lead to complexity and uncertainty, as in situations of good faith purchase or nuisances in which activities clash in a particular setting. And third, and quite characteristically for equity, deliberately caused or exploited uncertainty and complexity stem from the problem of opportunism, in which an actor takes unforeseen advantage of a rule that works under normal circumstances. The traditional heading for this phenomenon was "constructive fraud" and included much of unconscionability and violations of custom. 1–069

All of these types of problems—polycentricity, conflicting rights, and opportunism—are defined functionally. They are special because multiplex interactions lead to hard-to-foresee results. It is exactly here that law, in its normal aspirations of *ex ante* certainty, is at its weakest. As Aristotle put it, equity intervenes 1–070

> when law fails because of its generality. Courts have long cited this Aristotelian account, especially when it comes to the question of when equity will intervene. The question thus becomes: When does law fail and why would it fail because of its generality?

1-071 The account offered here allows us to fill in this picture: because regular law seeks generality and *ex ante* certainty, it cannot handle situations in which intense interactions can lead to unforeseen and undesired results. Equity is a second system that corrects these problems from without and thereby allows law to be more general and certain than it otherwise could be. Despite equity's reputation as a wild card, a combination of distinct law and equity can promote the law's ends—including rule-of-law values—better than could a more homogeneous legal system.

1-072 The account of equity that Article offers is functional, rather than jurisdictional or historical. While equity jurisdiction has left traces all over the law, and although equity is a major strand of the history of legal systems in the English-speaking world, the theory offered here focuses on a functional inquiry into what equity does. The jurisdiction and the history are relevant because they are the partly contingent vehicle through which a more basic function expresses itself. It is for that reason that we can speak of an "equitable" function rather than some anodyne "System II" of law that solves uncertain and complex problems with law's "System I".

1-073 This Article's reconstruction of equity goes against the grain in another way. Simply put, complexity is seen as the weakness of equity. And indeed equity's opponents have stressed its arbitrariness, epitomised by the "Chancellor's foot". I will argue that this view of equity gets things exactly backwards. Equity is part of law's response to the world's inevitable complexity. Explaining and justifying equity requires being clear on what functions it does and does not serve. The conventional view of equity is tenacious because it is plausible. Commentators are correct that not everything denominated "equitable" can receive a unified justification. And it is true that only by being justified functionally does equity deserve to survive. Putting these criticisms together, it would be hopeless to give a unified functional explanation of even a broad swath of such a seemingly variegated collection of legal odds and ends.

1-074 McFarlane and Stevens also employ this notion of equity as a secondary system in arguing that equitable rights have a characteristic form:[53]

> Our thesis is that much, although not all, of the law of Equity is distinguished by its *form*. Equitable rights concern rights in relation to other rights. It is, *in this sense*, a form of second-order, or meta law. This formal difference is a product of its historical origin, and an important part of its present function. A characteristically equitable right is one that has as its subject the right of another party. An example is the right of a beneficiary of a trust. Where T holds a legal freehold of land on trust for B, it is T's legal estate, not the land itself, that is the subject matter of the trust. B's right thus has T's right as its subject. In contrast, where O simply holds an unencumbered legal freehold of land, O's right does not have any other person's right at its subject.

ii. Controlling A's exercise of A's legal entitlements

1-075 A further division within equity's supplemental function can be made between: (a) restraining or preventing A's exercise of a legal entitlement against B, sometimes referred to as a proscriptive or disabling rule; and (b) generating a new duty–right relationship between A and B, as explained by McFarlane:[54]

> It would be no surprise if this function of controlling, in B's favour, the acquisition or enforcement of A's rights were to be particularly associated with equity. It accords both with the notion of equity as a supplementary, or secondary system, and with the ancient idea that equity can operate to correct problems

---

53 B. McFarlane and R. Stevens, "What's Special About Equity? Rights About Rights" in A.D. Klimchuk et al (eds), *Philosophical Foundations of the Law of Equity* (Oxford University Press, 2020), p.191.

54 B. McFarlane, "Form and Substance in Equity" in A. Robertson and J. Goudkamp (eds), *Form and Substance in the Law of Obligations* (Hart Publishing, 2019), Ch. 9.

> caused by the generality of primary rules.[55] Two warnings, should, however be noted. First, it is not argued here that rules controlling the acquisition or enforcement of rights are recognized only by equity; second, it is not argued that equity consists only of such rules. The key distinction made here is not between common law and equity as such, but rather between primary rules that define the parties' rights, and secondary rules that control, in favour of B specifically, A's acquisition or enforcement of rights. There is no reason, either historically or in the present law, why the common law cannot also recognize such secondary rules.[56] The ability of equity, historically, to recognize primary rules is a more difficult question, but it is clear that there are modern cases in which equity has gone beyond its traditional function of controlling the acquisition and enforcement of rights.[57] As a result it is not argued here that the function can explain *all* of modern equity. It is rather argued that it is at least important in understanding many areas in which equity as an impact on the law of obligations.

A distinction can be drawn between *primary rules* that define or generate the parties' legal entitlements, and *meta* or *secondary* rules that control the exercise of the legal entitlements generated by the primary system of rules. As McFarlane explains in the excerpt above, this division does not exactly map that between common law and equity. Many common law rules serve a primary function of defining the parties' legal entitlements, while some other common law rules have a meta-law or secondary function of controlling the exercise of those legal entitlements, such as the doctrine of waiver. As will be explained in more detail in Chapter 2, some equitable rules have this specific meta-law or secondary function of controlling, as against B, A's exercise of A's legal entitlement. **1–076**

An example of an equitable rule controlling A's exercise of a legal entitlement is provided by *Hughes v Metropolitan Rwy Co*.[58] The terms of B's lease gave A a power to terminate the lease if B failed to complete particular repairs within a six-month period. B had indeed failed to make those repairs, so A attempted to terminate the lease. However, during that period, A had entered into negotiations with B for the surrender of the lease, and had agreed to B's proposal to defer the repairs. This did not lead to a variation of the terms of the lease, but it did mean that A had led B reasonably to believe that A would not terminate the lease if B failed to complete the repairs within the six months, and B's decision not to undertake the repairs was likely to have been influenced by that belief. As a result, whilst A *did* have the contractual power to terminate the lease, equity could restrain A from exercising that power without first extending the time for completion, so that the six-month clock did not run during the parties' negotiations. As Lord Cairns LC put it in in his judgment:[59] **1–077**

> [t]he first principle upon which all Courts of Equity proceed [is that] . . . the person who might otherwise have enforced those rights will not be allowed to enforce them where it would be inequitable having regard to the dealings between the parties.

---

55 See D. Klimchuk, "Equity and the Rule of Law" in L. Austin and D. Klimchuk (eds), *Private Law and the Rule of Law* (Oxford University Press, 2014), discussing Aristotle's account in Aristotle, "Nicomachean Ethics" in J Barnes (ed.), *The Complete Works of Aristotle* (JO Urmson and WD Ross, trans), ii.1796 of the "equitable" as "a correction of law where it is defective owing to its universality".

56 . . . [C]ommon law rules of waiver are an example of rules that regulate in C's favour the enforcement of a right by D. A common law power to rescind a contract entered into as a result of duress or fraud is a further example, although its pedigree has been doubted: see W. Swadling, "Rescission, Property, and the Common Law" (2005) 121 L.Q.R. 123.

57 The development of breach of confidence to include misuse of private information and other breaches of privacy (such breaches often being referred to as 'torts': see, e.g. *TLU v Secretary of State for the Home Department* [2018] EWCA Civ 2217 at [15], [18] and [26] (Gross LJ)) provides one example: see further J. Goldberg and H. Smith, "Wrongful Fusion: Equity and Tort" in J. Goldberg, H. Smith and P. Turner (eds), *Equity and Law: Fusion and Fission* (Cambridge University Press, 2019), Ch.7.

58 (1877) 2 App. Cas. 439.

59 (1877) 2 App. Cas. 439 at 448.

iii. Generating a new legal entitlement for B against A

1–078 As will be discussed in Chapters 3 and 4, some equitable rules control A by imposing a duty–right relationship between A and B. Such rules, on first blush, might seem to be primary rules because they generate a right–duty relationship. However, on closer inspection, many of those rules are better understood as also having the meta-law or second order function, as the particular duty arises in order to control A's exercise of A's legal entitlement.[60] So, for example, the duties of administration applied to a trustee, who holds property for the benefit of others, generate new rights in the beneficiaries of the trust, but those duties relate to the specific rights which the trustee holds on trust.

1–079 Equity also generates new powers. For example, the law of express trusts allows a party who has a legal entitlement to set up a trust of that entitlement, thus giving her a power which does not exist at common law. As a result, equity not only restrains parties from exercising rights in an inappropriate way, but it can also positively increase parties' options, and thus increase their autonomy. We will examine the rules regulating the creation of express trusts in Chapters 4 to 9.

1–080 However, there are some cases, as we will see in Chapter 3, where equitable rules have developed so that they now impose a duty-right relationship which extends beyond simply controlling A's exercise of a legal entitlement.[61]

iv. Restraining equitable entitlements

1–081 Finally, it is important to appreciate that equity is not a one directional system. Even though equity is often understood in terms of being a supplement *to the common law*, it is a self-reflexive system. In other words, we have seen above that equity can control, in favour of B, A's legal entitlements: those legal entitlements include A's *equitable* rights and powers.[62] For example, it is possible for an equitable right to be held on trust. This may occur, for example, where T holds on trust for B, and B then declares a trust of B's equitable right in favour of B2. Indeed, such chains of trusts are important in practice, for example in the intermediated holding of securities.[63]

D. Equity Acting "In Personam"

1–082 An emphasis on equity's role as a secondary system can also be supported by the idea that equity acts specifically to control the lawfulness of A's conduct *as against B*. Equity thus controls A's exercise of a legal entitlement in relation to B, but does not deny the existence of that entitlement. For example, as noted above,[64] in a case where a contract has been entered between A and B as a result of A's innocent misrepresentation to B, equity does not deny that the contract exists, but it limits the circumstances in which A can exercise her rights under the contract by giving B a power, in certain circumstances, to rescind the contract and thus unwind its effects.[65] Further, as Maitland notes above,[66]

[60] B. McFarlane, "Form and Substance in Equity" in A. Robertson and J. Goudkamp (eds), *Form and Substance in the Law of Obligations* (Hart Publishing, 2019), Ch.9; B. McFarlane and R. Stevens, "What's Special About Equity? Rights Against Rights" in D. Klimchuk et al (eds), *The Philosophical Foundations of the Law of Equity* (Oxford University Press, 2020), Ch.9.
[61] See the discussion at paras 3–003 to 3–033 of proprietary estoppel and at paras 3–034 to 3–142 of breach of confidence.
[62] As noted by H. Smith, "Equity as Meta-Law" (2021) 130 Yale L.J. 1050, 1110, equity can thus have a "recursive" effect.
[63] See, e.g. B. McFarlane and R. Stevens, "Interests in Securities: Practical Problems and Conceptual Solutions" in L. Gullifer and J. Payne (eds), *Intermediated Securities: Legal Problems and Practical Issues* (Hart, 2010), Ch.2.
[64] See para.1–061.
[65] See further Chapter 20. Another example is provided by the equitable rules as to rectification: see Chapter 21.
[66] See para.1–063.

where A holds a freehold of land on trust for B, equity does not deny that A has significant rights and powers as a result of having that freehold; rather, it ensures that those significant legal entitlements are subject to control by B. Care must be taken, as it is easy to say, for example, that where A holds a right on trust for B, and the terms of the trust limit A's power to make a particular transfer of the trust property to C, then A has no power to make that transfer. That is not correct, however: simply by virtue of holding the right, A has the powers that go with such a right, which will generally include the power to transfer it. The transfer from A to C will therefore be valid, and C will acquire A's right. The point however is that the terms of the trust mean that A has no power *as against B* to make that transfer: this means that the transfer does not, by itself, extinguish B's right, and so it may still be possible for B to make a claim against C. We will consider such claims in Chapters 15 and 16.

This aspect of equity's operation can also be seen in Maitland's analysis:[67] **1–083**

> In fraud or breach of trust you obtain a judgment against me in a court of law; I complain to the Chancellor, and he after hearing what you have to say enjoins you not to put in force your judgment, says in effect that if you do put your judgment in force you will be sent to prison. Understand well that the Court of Chancery never asserted that it was superior to the courts of law; it never presumed to send to them such mandates as the Court of King's Bench habitually sent to the inferior courts, telling them that they must do this or must not do that or quashing their proceedings – the Chancellor's injunction was in theory a very different thing from mandamus, a prohibition, a certiorari or the like. It was addressed not to the judges, but to the party. You in breach of trust have obtained a judgment – the Chancellor does not say that this judgment was wrongly granted, he does not annul it, he tells you that for reasons personal to yourself it will be inequitable for you to enforce that judgment, and you are not to enforce it.

Note Maitland here is referring to the somewhat unusual case where equity's intervention occurs only after a common law judgment in A's favour: it would be more usual for B to invoke equity before the point where a judgment was obtained, and intervention after that point was particularly controversial, as shown by the disputes surrounding the *Earl of Oxford's Case*.[68] Nonetheless, the crucial point, applying generally, is that equity does not seek to deny A's legal entitlement, or thus to correct the rules giving rise to that entitlement; it instead protects B by controlling A's exercise of that entitlement as against B. **1–084**

One way to capture this aspect of equity's operation is to invoke the traditional idea that "equity acts in personam". Some care must be taken, however, in applying this maxim of equity as "no phrase has been more misused".[69] As a matter of history, the phrase refers only to a specific, narrow part of equity's operation: the enforcement of its orders. **1–085**

Ben McFarlane, "The Maxims of Equity" in John McGhee et al (eds), *Snell's Equity*, 34th edn (Sweet & Maxwell, 2020), para.5–018

> There was a procedural distinction in the means of execution available for common law judgments on the one hand and judgments of courts of equity on the other. In the former, there was the possibility of execution in rem: that is, against assets of the judgment debtor. Lacking local enforcement officers to effect such execution, equity had no similar mechanism and so judgments could be enforced only in personam: against the person of the debtor, through the threat of imprisonment if A did not comply with the judgment in B's favour. So, for example, if A refused to comply with an order of the Court of Chancery **1–086**

---

[67] The extract is from p.9 of the 1909 edition A. Chaytor and W. Whittaker (eds), *Equity: Also The Forms of Action at Common Law* (Cambridge University Press, 1909).

[68] (1615) 1 Rep. Ch. 1. See para.1–036.

[69] Holmes J. in *Tyler v Court of Registration* (1899) 175 Mass. 71, 76. See too W. Hohfeld, "Fundamental Legal Conceptions as Applied in Judicial Reasoning" (1917) Yale L.J. 710, 721.

that A should deliver up a document for cancellation, A might languish in prison, but in the meantime the document remained valid at law.[70]. . .

1–087 This point about the means of enforcement of judgments is now a matter of history. Since the Judicature Acts, the orders of the Chancery Division can be enforced by any of the legal writs of execution which may be applicable to the particular case. For example, an order for the payment of a sum of money can be enforced by a writ of fieri facias.[71]

1–088 As the discussion in *Snell* goes on to point out, the historical limit on the enforcement of *orders* of the Court of Chancery does not have a necessary connection to the nature of the *rights* that can arise in equity:[72]

For example, it is possible for B to have an in rem right (e.g. legal ownership of goods) protected by an in personam claim and remedy (an action in conversion against A and an order that A pay damages) which is in turn enforced by an in rem execution (property of A is sold off to meet the judgment debt owed by A to B).

1–089 That example of course concerns a legal rather than an equitable right, but it demonstrates that the method of enforcement does not control the nature of the underlying right. It should not therefore be thought that the maxim that "equity acts in personam", by itself, is inconsistent with equity generating proprietary, or in rem, rights in B. Certainly, as we will see throughout this book, not least when considering the trust, judges and legislation very commonly refer to "equitable property rights" or "equitable interests in property".

Swiss Bank Corp v Lloyds Bank Ltd

Chancery Division, [1979] Ch. 548 at 565–566

1–090 BROWNE-WILKINSON J. . . . Historically the courts of equity acted in personam. Whether equity was supplementing the common law by giving additional remedies or correcting the common law by imposing a different legal result, the courts of equity intervened by directing the defendant personally to do, or refrain from doing, a specific act. In deciding whether or not to intervene, the courts of equity required first, that the plaintiff should have some enforceable right and, secondly, that the conscience of the defendant was affected in some way so as to make the failure of the defendant to give effect to the plaintiff's rights contrary to justice.

1–091 The rights which the plaintiff asserted were normally either contractual rights or rights under a trust. In the realm of contracts equity supplemented the common law by ordering the party in default to perform the contract — instead of merely paying damages. In the realm of trusts equity ordered the legal owner of property, the trustee, specifically to carry out the trust which he had accepted. In matters involving property equity intervened by ordering that the defendant do deal with the property in question in a specific manner, whether the plaintiff's rights were founded in contract or trust.

1–092 But, although the basis of the equity jurisdiction was and still is founded on an order in personam, the courts of equity evolved the doctrine that, in the eyes of equity, that which ought to have been done is to be treated as having been done. Thus under a specifically enforceable contract for the sale of land, the purchaser is treated in equity as the owner of the property whether or not an order for specific performance has been made. Again, in the law of trusts the beneficiary is treated as immediately entitled to his interest in the trust property whether or not an order for the execution of the trust has been made against the trustee. In this way the plaintiff's rights, although founded upon the ability of the court to make an order in personam against the other contracting party or the trustee, become an interest in the property itself, an equitable interest. Once the position is reached that an order for specific performance could have been made against the legal owner if the matter had been brought before the court, thereafter the legal owner holds the property shorn of those rights in the property which the courts of equity would decree belong to another.

---

70 See (1459) Y.B. 37 Hen 6, Hil., pl.3, fo. 13 at 14 per Priscot C.J.

71 See RSC Ord.45 preserved by CPR Pt 50, Sch.1.

72 McFarlane, "The Maxims of Equity" in *Snell's Equity*, para.5–018.

These basic principles were not questioned on appeal, although the House of Lords upheld the Court of Appeal's decision reversing Browne-Wilkinson J's decision as to the parties' intention to create an equitable security interest.[73] A similar point is made by Lord Sumption in *Akers v Samba Financial Group,* where a beneficiary's interest under an express trust is described as having a "proprietary character" as "[a]n equitable interest possesses the essential hallmark of any right in rem, namely that it is good against third parties into whose hands the property or its traceable proceeds may have come . . .".[74] Note however that, in the same judgment, Lord Sumption also stated that:[75] **1–093**

> . . . equitable interests arise from equity's recognition that in some circumstances the conscience of the holder of the legal interest may be affected. When the asset is transferred to a third party, the question becomes whether the conscience of the transferee is affected.

It is clear therefore that Lord Sumption is using the term "in rem" in a specific, somewhat limited way. He is not suggesting that an equitable interest, like a legal property right, is prima facie binding on *all* third parties. Rather, the focus is on a particular set of third parties—those who acquire the trust property or its traceable proceeds—and in those cases the third party will be bound only if their conscience is affected, presumably by their acquiring knowledge of B's interest and the facts meaning the transfer was unauthorised, whilst still holding the trust property or its traceable proceeds. As we will discuss further in Chapter 12,[76] the "proprietary character" of an equitable interest, such as that of B, need not involve a *direct* entitlement of B to particular property. Rather, as Lionel Smith has argued, describing B as having "equitable property" or "equitable title" can be misleading:[77] **1–094**

> Equitable title suggests a direct relationship between a beneficiary and the trust property. This does not exist. All equitable proprietary rights require at least two people, in addition to the object of the right. I mean that the beneficiary's right itself cannot be understood as a direct relationship between the beneficiary and the trust property. The trustee has rights in the object; that is, rights in the trust property. The trust beneficiary's rights are rights in the rights the trustee holds in the object.

Smith's point is consistent with Lord Sumption's reference to the importance of "conscience" in determining if a third party receiving trust property can be subject to a claim of B. The point is that, just as B's initial acquisition of an interest under a trust depends on A's coming under a particular type of duty to B, so does B's possible claim against C (the third party receiving trust property from A) depend on B's showing that there are grounds for C's also now coming under a duty to B in relation to that property. We will explore such an "obligational" view of the nature of the trust further in Chapter 12. **1–095**

Certainly, it is dangerous to assume that particular consequences must follow simply because an equitable right can be described, in some senses, as "proprietary".[78] Rather, it seems such a label is applied *once* it has been determined that the right can have a particular effect, for example on a third party such as C, but that the label does not explain *why* that effect has been allowed to occur. This point is made in the following extract from a judgment considering the nature of a trustee's right of indemnity, which will be discussed at paras 12–028 to 12–029. **1–096**

---

73 *Swiss Bank Corp v Lloyds Bank Ltd* [1982] A.C. 584 (CA) 611 (HL).
74 *Akers v Samba Financial Group* [2017] UKSC 6; [2017] A.C. 424 at [80].
75 [2017] UKSC 6; [2017] A.C. 424 at [89].
76 See esp paras 12–015 to 12–018.
77 L. Smith, "Trust and Patrimony" (2008) 28 R.G.D. 379, 392.
78 See, e.g. B. McFarlane and S. Douglas, "Property, Analogy, and Variety" (2022) 42 O.J.L.S. 161, esp 177–182.

Carter Holt Harvey Woodproducts Australia Pty Ltd v Commonwealth

High Court of Australia, (2019) 268 C.L.R. 524 at [80]–[84]

1–097 BELL, GAGELER AND NETTLE JJ: Inasmuch as a court of equity will aid the beneficiaries in the enforcement of the terms of trust, the beneficiaries are described, especially in the revenue contexts, as having a beneficial interest in, or occasionally even beneficial ownership of, the trust assets. The beneficiaries' interest is not, however, to be conceived of as cut out of the trustee's legal estate but rather as engrafted onto it as a restriction on the manner in which the trustee may deal with trust assets. . . .

1–098 The trustee also has a right to be indemnified out of the trust assets in respect of liabilities properly incurred in the execution of the trust, which takes priority over the beneficiaries' claim on the trust assets. . . .

1–099 Possibly, the trustee's right of indemnity could be as well described as conferring a personal power. . . as a proprietary interest. But the choice of description should conform to, rather than dictate, the application of fundamental principles to "solving a concrete legal problem". The trustee's right to apply trust assets in satisfaction of trust liabilities is proprietary in that it may be exercised in priority to the beneficial interests of the beneficiaries. To describe it as constituting a beneficial interest in the trust assets, and so as property, thus acknowledges the characteristic blending of personal rights and obligations with proprietary interest which is the "genius" of the trust institution.

1–100 Consistently with the standard usage employed by judges and legislatures, we will refer in this book to "equitable property rights" and, indeed, some useful analogies can be drawn between such rights and legal property rights. It is however important to note at this early stage that there are some significant differences between such rights and legal property rights. Those differences are not based simply on the fact that, historically, equitable orders could only be enforced in personam; they may however be linked to equity's distinct secondary role, and its function in controlling legal entitlements, rather than denying them. Such an analysis has again been given by Maitland:[79]

Take the case of a trust. An examiner will sometimes be told that whereas the common law said that the trustee was the owner of the land, equity said that the *cestui que trust*[80] was the owner. Well here in all conscience there seems to be conflict enough. Think what this would mean were it really true. There are two courts of co-ordinate jurisdiction – one says that A is the owner, the other says that B is the owner of Blackacre. That means civil war and utter anarchy. Of course the statement is an extremely crude one, it is a misleading and a dangerous statement – how misleading, how dangerous, we shall see when we come to examine the nature of equitable estates. Equity did not say that the *cestui que trust* was the owner of the land, it said that the trustee was the owner of the land, but added that he was bound to hold the land for the benefit of the *cestui que trust*. There was no conflict here.

1–101 As was later pointed out by, for example, Hohfeld,[81] there is of course *some* conflict between common law and equity in Maitland's example. At common law, for example, A would be under no duty to B not to cut down ornamental trees on Blackacre; whereas, in equity, A is under such a duty to B.[82] Of course, if equity made no difference at all to the pre-existing common law position, it would have no purpose. The point though is that equity, in such a case, does not deny A's general rights to Blackacre (which are prima facie binding on the rest of the world); it rather recognises that, *as regards B*, A is under particular limits as to how those rights are exercised.[83]

79 The extract is from p.11 of the 1909 edition A. Chaytor and W. Whittaker (eds) *Equity: also The Forms of Action at Common Law* (Cambridge University Press, 1909).

80 This is an old-fashioned term for a beneficiary of a trust.

81 W. Hohfeld, "The Relations Between Equity and Law" (1913) 11 Mich. L.R. 537.

82 This example is used by Hohfeld: W. Hohfeld, "The Relations Between Equity and Law" (1913) 11 Mich. L.R. 537, 555.

83 For further discussion of the differing views of Maitland and Hohfeld, see B. McFarlane, "Avoiding Anarchy? Common Law v Equity and Maitland v Hohfeld" in P. Turner (ed.) *Equity and Law: Fusion and Fission* (Cambridge University Press, 2019), Ch.14.

E. Equitable Maxims

The idea that equity "acts in personam",[84] is an example of an equitable maxim. Further examples of such maxims recognised by the courts are:[85] "equity will not suffer a wrong to be without a remedy"; "equity follows the law"; "where there is equal equity, the law shall prevail"; "where the equities are equal, the first in time shall prevail"; "he who seeks equity must do equity"; "he who comes to equity must come with clean hands"; "delay defeats equities"; "equity is equality"; "equity looks to the intent rather than to the form"; "equity looks on done that which ought to be done"; "equity imputes an intention to fulfil an obligation"; and "equity will not assist a volunteer". **1–102**

The difference between a rule (whether defined by equitable or common law doctrine) and an equitable maxim was outlined by Mason CJ and McHugh J in the High Court of Australia decision in *Corin v Paton*:[86] **1–103**

> Of course it would be a mistake to set too much store by the maxim [equity would not assist a volunteer]. Like other maxims of equity, it is not a specific rule or principle of law. It is a summary statement of a broad theme which underlies equitable concepts and principles. Its precise scope if necessarily ill-defined and somewhat uncertain.

In *Pitt v Holt*,[87] Lord Walker referred, with tacit approval, to Mason CJ and McHugh J's judgment in *Corin v Paton*, to explain why a submission that relied upon the direct application of another equitable maxim, "equity does not act in vain" did not apply to determine the outcome in that case. Equitable maxims are expressed in such general terms as to make them meaningless in their application to a given set of facts; or the same set of facts might be relevant to more than one equitable maxim, the direct application of which would produce wholly inconsistent results. In *Yarnmouth v France*,[88] Lord Esher MR said:[89] **1–104**

> . . .I detest the attempt to fetter the law by maxims. They are almost invariably misleading: they are for the most part so large and general in their language that they always include something which really is not intended to be included in them.

In *Lissenden v C A V Bosch Ltd*,[90] Lord Wright referred to Lord Esher MR's statement set out above and went on to state:[91] **1–105**

> Indeed these general formulae are found in experience often to distract the court's minds from the actual exigencies of the case, and to induce the court to quote from them as offering a ready made solution.

So, whilst equitable maxims still have some limited relevance to the operation of equity,[92] they add little to our general understanding of equity, and there is equally little to be gained from a general **1–106**

---

84 See paras 1–082 to 1–101.
85 See McFarlane, "The Maxims of Equity" in *Snell's Equity*, Ch.5.
86 *Corin v Paton* (1990) 169 C.L.R. 540 at 557.
87 *Pitt v Holt* [2013] UKSC 26; [2013] 2 A.C. 108 at [136].
88 *Yarnmouth v France* (1887) 19 Q.B.D. 647.
89 *Yarnmouth v France* at 653.
90 *Lissenden v C A V Bosch Ltd* [1940] A.C. 412.
91 *Lissenden v C A V Bosch Ltd* at 435.
92 See, e.g. *HR Trustees Ltd v Wembley Plc* [2011] EWHC 2974 (Ch), where the maxim that "equity regards as done that which ought to be done" was relied on by Vos J to explain why the pension trustees' actions in exercising a power to amend the

discussion of them. We will not examine them further here but will consider their possible application in specific contexts in later chapters of the book.[93]

F. Equity and Conscience

i. General role of conscience

1–107 We noted above the role of the concept of conscience in the development of equity.[94] We have also seen examples of its use in the modern law, as seen in Lord Sumption's observation in *Akers v Samba Financial Group*,[95] that the ability of B, a beneficiary of a trust, to bring a claim against C, a third party receiving the trust property, depends on whether "the conscience of [C] is affected". We also note that, in *Australian Securities and Investments Commission v Kobelt*,[96] Edelman J, in discussing when equity may allow a party to set aside a transaction as unconscionable, referred to English courts as requiring conduct that is "morally reprehensible" or "shocks the conscience of the court". Similarly, when examining the circumstances in which a proprietary estoppel claim may succeed, and thus operate to generate, in equity, a new right of B, Lord Walker in *Cobbe v Yeoman's Row Management Ltd* stated that:[97] "If the other elements [of B's claim] appear to be present but the result does not shock the conscience of the court, the analysis needs to be looked at again."

1–108 Conscience, and unconscionability permeate equity. Historically, B only went to the Chancellor, and the Chancellor could only act, when there was either no relief available for B at law in aid of her common law rights, or B had no common law rights at all.[98] Some other moral framework and source of authority was needed to determine the dispute, which was found and expressed in terms of "conscience". As we have seen, "conscience" is still referred to in the cases. The High Court of Australia in *Kakavas v Crown Melbourne*[99] explained that "conscience" is "a metaphorical term, designating the common standard of civil right and expediency combined".[100] Conscience, or unconscionability, is expressed as an element of a claim, or as a reason why relief is or is not available. It is also a focus of some academic analysis of equity and its distinctive contribution to the legal system.[101] Equity's reliance on ideas such as conscience and unconscionability has also been criticised, on the basis that they are vague and open-ended concepts which lead to arbitrary and unpredictable decision-making that undermines the rule of law.[102]

---

terms of a pension scheme would be treated as effective, even though the trustees had not complied with formal requirements as to the exercise of that power.

93 See, e.g. paras 12–074, 17–070, 17–074, 22–036, 22–136 to 22–155.

94 See paras 1–010 to 1–033.

95 [2017] A.C. 424 at [89], set out at para.1–093.

96 *Australian Securities and Investments Commission v Kobelt* (2019) 267 C.L.R. 1 at [282], set out at para.1–010.

97 [2008] 1 W.L.R. 1752 at [92].

98 See paras 1–010 to 1–033.

99 *Kakavas v Crown Melbourne Ltd* (2013) 250 C.L.R. 392.

100 J. Pomeroy, *A Treatise on Equity Jurisprudence*, 5th edn (Bancroft & Whitney Co, 1941) Vol.1, p.74.

101 In addition to the excerpt next, see I. Samet, *Equity: Conscience Goes to Market* (Oxford University Press, 2018); P. Keane, "The 2009 WA Lee Lecture in Equity: The Conscience of Equity" (2010) 84 A.L.J 92; D. R. Klinck, "The Unexamined "Conscience" of Canadian Equity" (2001) 46 *McGill Law Journal* 571; J. Penner, "Equity, Justice and Conscience", in D. Klimchuk et al (eds), *Philosophical Foundations of the Law of Equity* (Oxford University Press, 2020), Ch.3.

102 See, e.g. P. Birks, "Equity in the Modern Law: An Exercise in Taxonomy" (1996) 26 U.W.A.L.R. 1, 16–17; P. Birks, "Equity, Conscience and Unjust Enrichment" (1999) 23 M.U.L.R. 1, 14–15; R. Havelock, "Conscience and Unconscionability in Modern Equity" (2015) J. Eq. 1, 23–28.

We will examine invocations of conscience in a number of specific contexts in this book and it is important to note that the term may be used in different ways, and be given different meanings, according to the particular context. It is nonetheless useful to make some general points here. **1–109**

First, it is wrong to think that equitable relief is available today on the basis of some idiosyncratic version of conscience, or unconscionability. B does not have a claim for equitable relief simply *because* the defendant has acted unconscionably or unfairly in the general senses of those terms.[103] This was made very clear, for example, by Lord Scott in *Cobbe v Yeoman's Row Management Ltd*, in rejecting B's proprietary estoppel claim:[104] "unconscionability of conduct may well lead to a remedy but, in my opinion, proprietary estoppel cannot be the route to it unless the ingredients for a proprietary estoppel are present." The point can be extended, of course, beyond proprietary estoppel to all other equitable doctrines: each has its own set of requirements which concertise what it means to act unconscionably, or inequitably, in *that specific context*. Criticisms of the use of conscience in judicial reasoning are therefore well-made if a judge simply labels a party's conduct as contrary to conscience, without explaining the particular reasons justifying equity's intervention.[105] **1–110**

Second, conscience is an idea that informs many equitable principles, and in different ways. It would be an error to assume that conscience, or unconscionability, has precisely the same content and meaning in each case and across each equitable rule, or even that it relates to the same person's conscience. There is a danger in thinking that a broad term such as conscience can be used to unify a set of doctrines or principles which are in fact distinct. **1–111**

These two points were both very well put by Lord Briggs, writing extra-judicially:[106] **1–112**

> . . . defining the underlying equitable principle too broadly, or at too high a level of abstraction, helps no-one, even if it may generate a comfortable glow of legal uniformity in the mind (or heart) of the writer and of the incautious reader. To say, as Lord Millett did, in the *Paragon* case, that:[107]
>
> > "a constructive trust arises *whenever* it would be unconscionable for the legal owner of the property to assert his own beneficial interest and deny the beneficial interest of another (emphasis added)"
>
> begs more questions than it answers. Lord Millett was using that compendious expression not by way of definition, still less for setting metes and bounds, but as the loose description of a cake which he then intended to cut into two very distinct slices. Unconscionable conduct may be a minimum condition, but never a sufficient condition, for the intervention of equity.

With those general points as to the role of conscience in mind, it is possible to outline some of the specific meanings that conscience can have when used in relation to equity. **1–113**

---

[103] The statutory regimes that deploy these concepts also have nuanced and particularised definitions for them, albeit sometimes wider than their equitable counterparts. See, e.g. in Australia, statutory standards of unconscionability in connection to the provision of financial services under the *Australian Securities and Investments Commission Act 2001* (Cth) s.12CB; see also contravention provisions for unconscionable conduct in relation to Australian consumer law under the *Competition and Consumer Act 2010* (Cth) Sch.2, ss.20–22.

[104] [2008] UKHL 55; [2008] 1 W.L.R. 1752 at [16].

[105] For an example of judicial reasoning criticised on this basis, see, e.g. *Pennington v Waine* [2002] EWCA Civ 227; [2002] 1 W.L.R. 2075, discussed at paras 5–105 to 5–125.

[106] Lord Briggs, "Equity in Business" (2019) 135 L.Q.R. 567, 583.

[107] *Paragon Finance Plc v DB Thakerar & Co* [1999] 1 All E.R. 400 at 409 (Millett LJ).

ii. A's conscience

1–114 Sometimes conscience expresses a focus on the defendant, who we are referring to here as A. In *Re Diplock*,[108] the Court of Appeal stated "[i]t is no doubt true that an equitable claim predicates that the conscience of the defendant must be affected." Conscience might refer to the subjective and inner state of mind of the defendant, or it might refer to the defendant's conduct, or a combination of both such that it would be "unconscionable" or "inequitable" for the defendant to act or not act in a particular way. Consider Lord Browne-Wilkinson's use of the idea of conscience in the summary of the "relevant principles of trust law":

Westdeutsche Landesbank Girozentrale v Islington LBC

House of Lords, [1996] A.C. 669 at 705–706

1–115 (i) Equity operates on the conscience of the owner of the legal interest. In the case of a trust, the conscience of the legal owner requires him to carry out the purposes for which the property was vested in him (express or implied trust) or which the law imposes on him by reason of his unconscionable conduct (constructive trust).

(ii) Since the equitable jurisdiction to enforce trusts depends upon the conscience of the holder of the legal interest being affected, he cannot be a trustee of the property if and so long as he is ignorant of the facts alleged to affect his conscience, i.e. until he is aware that he is intended to hold the property for the benefit of others in the case of an express or implied trust, or, in the case of a constructive trust, of the factors which are alleged to affect his conscience.

(iii) In order to establish a trust there must be identifiable trust property. The only apparent exception to this rule is a constructive trust imposed on a person who dishonestly assists in a breach of trust who may come under fiduciary duties even if he does not receive identifiable trust property.

(iv) Once a trust is established, as from the date of its establishment the beneficiary has, in equity, a proprietary interest in the trust property, which proprietary interest will be enforceable in equity against any subsequent holder of the property (whether the original property or substituted property into which it can be traced) other than a purchaser for value of the legal interest without notice.

1–116 These propositions are fundamental to the law of trusts and I would have thought uncontroversial. However, proposition (ii) may call for some expansion. There are cases where property has been put into the name of X without X's knowledge but in circumstances where no gift to X was intended. It has been held that such property is recoverable under a resulting trust. These cases are explicable on the ground that, by the time action was brought, X or his successors in title have become aware of the facts which gave rise to a resulting trust; his conscience was affected as from the time of such discovery and thereafter he held on a resulting trust under which the property was recovered from him. There is, so far as I am aware, no authority which decides that X was a trustee, and therefore accountable for his deeds, at any time before he was aware of the circumstances which gave rise to a resulting trust.

1–117 Those basic principles are inconsistent with the case being advanced by the bank. The latest time at which there was any possibility of identifying the "trust property" was the date on which the moneys in the mixed bank account of the local authority ceased to be traceable when the local authority's account went into overdraft in June 1987. At that date, the local authority had no knowledge of the invalidity of the contract but regarded the moneys as its own to spend as it thought fit. There was therefore never a time at which both (a) there was defined trust property and (b) the conscience of the local authority in relation to such defined trust property was affected. The basic requirements of a trust were never satisfied.

1–118 I turn then to consider the bank's arguments in detail. They were based primarily on principle rather than on authority. I will deal first with the bank's argument from principle and then turn to the main authorities relied upon by the bank.

---

[108] *Re Diplock* [1948] Ch. 465 at 488.

Lord Browne-Wilkinson went on to apply these principles to the facts of the case, finding that the "basic requirements of a trust were never satisfied" because there "was never a time at which [the supposed trustee had title to trust property and] the conscience of the [supposed trustee] . . . was affected". 1–119

The defendant's conscience is explicitly referenced in other equitable rules, such as proprietary and promissory estoppel.[109] An examination of the meaning and role of conscience across these rules[110] will show that the standard for assessment of the defendant's conscience varies across these doctrines according to defined sets of rules, so that unconscionability has a specific meaning in relation to proprietary and promissory estoppel, which is different to its meaning in the context of, for example, undue influence or unconscionable bargains. 1–120

Conscience as the defendant's knowledge, state of mind or fault, has been understood as demonstrating the close connection between equity as legal rules and equity in the general sense of moral or ethical standards. 1–121

Sinead Agnew, "The Meaning and Significance of Conscience in Private Law"

(2018) 77 C.L.J. 479, 481–482, 484

The contemporary definition of "conscience" includes the following descriptions: "(An) inward knowledge or consciousness", "a moral sense of right or wrong" and "the faculty or principle that leads to the approval of right thought or action and condemnation of wrong", "sense of guilt with regard to a thought or action". It also refers to "practice of or conformity with what is considered right". . . . therefore, our contemporary understanding of conscience refers to both the process of reasoning towards moral judgments and the standards by which we make them. It helps us to judge the moral quality of our past actions and to decide what we ought or ought not to do now or in the future. "Unconscionable" means "showing no regard for conscience"; not in accordance with what is right or reasonable . . . unreasonably excessive; egregious, blatant . . . having no conscience; not controlled by conscience; unscrupulous". This definition encompasses both a failure to act in accordance with what is morally right, and deliberate and flagrantly immoral behaviour. . . . 1–122

. . .Nevertheless, the language of conscience is helpful in describing the incidence of moral duties. There is support for the view that certain types of morally valuable behaviour, such as keeping our promises or returning something which does not belong to us, may be regarded as moral duties in the sense that they provide a reason to act with which we are "in some sense bound to confirm". It seems harsh to treat an individual as bound by a moral duty unless she has sufficient knowledge of the facts which require her to act in a specific way. The idea of conscience as applied knowledge helps us to understand this. If an individual's conscience is affected by knowledge, namely if she has knowledge of the relevant facts, she can reason morally as to what she ought to do, and it is not unreasonable to treat her as bound by a moral duty to do it. Conversely, if, due to the absence of factual knowledge, she is not capable of reasoning morally as to what she ought to do, she should not be treated as being subject to a binding moral duty. Therefore, it does not seem inappropriate to say that a moral duty may be experienced as a "demand of conscience". Beyond this, the language of conscience tells us little about moral duties: we do not expect it to help us identify the moral principles upon which a particular moral duty is grounded, nor to give detailed content to the duty or indicate how much knowledge is required to trigger it. 1–123

Similarly, the term "unconscionable" is apt to describe breaches of moral duty. On the basis that an individual has the requisite factual knowledge for the duty to arise in the first place, she may breach it in one of two ways. Her conscience may misfire because her moral understanding is defective, and it does not alert her to the correct moral course of action. There, her behaviour may be described as unconscionable in the very broadest sense of the word. She has failed to act in accordance with what is morally right. Alternatively, her conscience may work perfectly well, in the sense that she understands morally what the 1–124

---

[109] See paras In relation to promissory estoppel see paras 2–016 to 2–065. In relation to proprietary estoppel see paras 3–003 to 3–033.

[110] In relation to promissory estoppel see para.2–064. In relation to proprietary estoppel see para.3–032.

> correct course of action is, but she simply ignores or overrides the signals her conscience is sending her. In this instance, her behaviour is unconscionable in a narrower sense, as she has consciously and deliberately flouted moral standards. Although the term, "unconscionable" is wide enough to include both types of conduct, we tend to associate the adjective more closely with conscious and deliberate moral transgressions. . . .
>
> 1–125 Today, when the courts use the language of conscience in equity and (occasionally) at common law, they also appear to treat the idea of conscience as based on objective, rather than personal, standards, derived through the process of legal reasoning from "settled rules and decided cases". They have rejected any suggestion that the idea of unconscionability provides a basis for the court to create a general power to relieve a party from her legal obligations. Instead, what good conscience requires, and/or what is regarded as unconscionable, is informed by the principles and rationale of each doctrine. . . .
>
> 1–126 In English private law, the courts use the language of conscience and unconscionability in accordance with its ordinary meaning to describe the incidence of moral duties, and to indicate that a defendant is morally at fault.

1–127 Sinéad Agnew discusses how the courts use the ideas of conscience and unconscionability in relation to confidentiality, express trusts and knowing receipt. Agnew explains that conscience, at least in relation to these doctrines, conveys the idea that a defendant is only subject to a duty under one of these doctrines when she has the requisite knowledge of the relevant facts required for moral reasoning, going on to explain that:[111]

> . . . the language of conscience tells us that the courts regard the relevant equitable obligation as a moral duty, which will only arise if the defendant has the requisite factual knowledge. . . .
>
> The language of conscience plays a distinctive explanatory role in relation to equitable obligations. In the three examples [confidentiality, express trusts and knowing receipt], knowledge is an ingredient of the cause of action in the sense that it is a prerequisite to the recognition and enforcement of the relevant obligation. The courts do not need to use the language of conscience to tell us this, and thus it might appear to be superfluous at [the] doctrinal level. However, in fact the language of conscience tells us something about *why* factual knowledge is a doctrinal requirement, namely because, without it, the individual is not able to reason morally as to what she ought to do, and it is only when she can do this that equity will treat her as being subject to an enforceable equitable obligation. When the language of conscience is used in this way, equity is looking forwards: it asks if the defendant is capable of complying with a particular moral standard. If so, it will treat her as bound by a contiguous equitable duty, and require her to take positive action to comply with it.

1–128 Agnew also identifies limitations to the explanatory role of conscience, including that it operates at a high level of generality and does not identify specific values or principles why one or another equitable obligation should be enforced, nor the requisite degree of knowledge required before an obligation can be enforced.[112]

iii. B's conscience

1–129 "Conscience" is not confined to the state of a defendant's conduct or knowledge. The invocation of the conscience of equity requires "a scrutiny of the exact relations established between the parties' to determine 'the real justice of the case'."[113] The conduct of all suitors—claimant and defendant—will be

---

111 Agnew, "The Meaning and Significance of Conscience in Private Law" (2018) 77 C.L.J. 479, 486–487.

112 Agnew, "The Meaning and Significance of Conscience in Private Law" (2018) 77 C.L.J. 479, 488–490.

113 *Kakavas v Crown Melbourne Ltd* (2013) 250 C.L.R. 392 at [18], quoting *Jenyns v Public Curator* (1953) 90 C.L.R. 113 at 118–119.

judged according to a construct of values and standards referred to as "conscience."[114] The conscience of B, the party invoking equity, may therefore also be relevant.

Equity's scrutiny of B is evident in those equitable rules that operate upon B's subjective state of mind, such as undue influence, mistake or special disadvantage. All of these doctrines, in one way or another ask about B's inner state of mind, her motives and/or reasons for action and the external factors or forces impacting upon her. Other doctrines will also scrutinise B's conscience as assessed by reference to the objective manifestation of her intention, for example, where B is the settlor–beneficiary or settlor–trustee of an express trust. **1–130**

Equity's scrutiny of B is also seen when it comes to equitable discretionary factors relevant to awarding a remedy: we will consider these in Chapter 22. As exemplified by the equitable maxim that "He who comes to equity must come with clean hands",[115] it may be that B's own conduct can be a grounds for refusing equitable relief, particularly in a case where this will not prevent B having recourse to a different, common law remedy.[116] Henry Smith has argued, for example, that if one of the justifications of equitable intervention is to prevent A behaving opportunistically as regards B, it is also important for equity to have mechanisms to prevent *B* taking opportunistic advantage of the availability of an equitable remedy against A.[117] **1–131**

iv. The court's conscience

The conscience of the court can refer to the knowledge of the court,[118] and in particular to the types of facts that, prior to the Judicature Reform, could not be formally pleaded and proved by the parties in accordance with common law procedures.[119] The old common law courts were limited to certain modes of proof and this meant that some types of facts that could not be adduced and acted upon in common law courts.[120] The Chancellor, by contrast, was able to summon A to be examined and this allowed for a different range of facts and factual narratives to be within the knowledge of the court, and acted upon. This included, for example, the objective meaning of A's actions when those actions were an oral declaration of intention, rather than the execution of a legal instrument, or the inner (subjective) state of mind of A, or the effect of the A's conduct on B's state of mind. All these, and other facts, that could only be proven and taken into account by the Chancellor, were also encompassed by the label of "conscience". **1–132**

Given the changes in procedure today, according to which one court system administers common law and equity together with the same procedure, an idea of conscience that refers to facts that only the Chancellor could have known is less relevant. Nonetheless, it is still useful to bear this conception in mind, as it provides context to how the label of "conscience" is used in some cases. More importantly, it explains why certain equitable doctrines could only have developed as equitable doctrines, as they operate upon and respond to facts that could have only ever have been established in courts of equity. **1–133**

---

114 *Kakavas v Crown Melbourne Ltd* (2013) 250 C.L.R. 392 at [16] (the Court), referring to W. Gummow, *Change and Continuity: Statute, Equity, and Federalism* (Clarendon Press, 1999), pp.44–51.

115 See, e.g. *Royal Bank of Scotland Plc v Highland Financial Partners LP* [2013] EWCA Civ 328 at [158]–[172].

116 See paras 22–136ff and note N. McBride, "The Future of Clean Hands" in P. Davies et al (eds), *Defences in Equity* (Hart, 2018).

117 See, e.g. H. Smith, "Equitable Defences as Meta Law" in P. Davies et al (eds), *Defences in Equity* (Hart, 2018).

118 Macnair, "Equity and Conscience" (2007) 27 O.J.L.S. 659.

119 Macnair, "Equity and Conscience" (2007) 27 O.J.L.S. 659, 675–677.

120 See paras 1–026 to 1–030.

1–134 The conscience of the court has also been evoked in reference to a set of circumstances, as between A and B, which "shock the conscience of the court" and thus demand the intervention of equity.[121] In such cases, there is no overarching formulation as to when the conscience of the court will be thus shocked—the question is rather whether the specific requirements of the particular equitable doctrine in question (such as proprietary estoppel, or the jurisdiction to relieve against unconscionable transactions) has been met. Where, as in relation to proprietary estoppel, B seeks to use equity to generate a new claim against A, the reference to the conscience of the court can be used to permit A to point to particular facts (such as, for example, a relevant change of circumstances occurring after A made a promise to B) as providing A, in effect, with a defence to a prima facie claim of B.[122]

G. Equity and Public Law

1–135 Equity's relationship with, and impact upon, public law is just one instantiation of the broader story of equity's relationship with common law. The common law concerning the relationship between the state and individual citizen was subject to the same constraints—in terms of the writ system and rules of evidence and procedure—as the common law concerning the relationships between individuals. Public (common) law generated the same problems as the private (common) law, and so equity responded in the same ways: complementing the common law system by providing relief where the remedy at law was inadequate, and supplementing the common law when necessary, according to one or another of what came to be an increasingly systematised set of (equitable) rules.

1–136 The common law writ of mandamus, for example (one of the prerogative writs) was available to compel a public official to perform a duty, and was not available to prevent a public body from taking action that was not permitted by the relevant terms of the statute or regulation, but which the public body did not otherwise have a duty not to carry out. The Attorney-General, like any private individual, turned to the court of Chancery for equitable relief, in the form of injunctions or declarations, to vindicate the public interest in the proper exercise of public power.

1–137 Equity's role here was recognised "[l]ong before the development of modern public law"[123] and has been discussed by Sir Anthony Mason writing extra judicially:[124]

> Equitable doctrines and relief have extended beyond old boundaries into new territory where no Lord Chancellor's foot has previously left its imprint. In the field of public law, equitable relief in the form of the declaration and the injunction have played a critical part in shaping modern administrative law which, from its earliest days, has mirrored the way in which equity has regulated the exercise of fiduciary powers.

1–138 An early example of equitable relief being granted against public bodies at the suit of the Attorney-General was the application of equity's accounting procedures to monitor and control the trustees of municipal charities and local government bodies. Equity's accounting procedures will be discussed

---

121 See para.1–010.

122 For discussion of this point, see, e.g. B. McFarlane, *The Law of Proprietary Estoppel*, 2nd edn (Oxford University Press, 2021), paras 5–058ff.

123 *Bateman's Bay Local Aboriginal Land Council v Aboriginal Community Benefit Fund Pty Ltd* (1998) 194 C.L.R. 247 at [28]. See further *FAI Insurances Ltd v Winneke* (1982) 151 C.L.R. 342 at 350–351 (Gibbs CJ), 386–387 (Aickin J), 419–420 (Brennan J); *Ainsworth v Criminal Justice Commission* (1992) 175 C.L.R. 564 at 581–582; *Smethurst v Commissioner of the Australian Federal Police* [2020] H.C.A. 14 at [95] (Kiefel CJ, Bell and Keane JJ), [171]–[172] (Gordon J). See also: R. Pound, "Visitatorial Jurisdiction Over Corporations in Equity" (1936) 49 H.L.R. 369; M. Leeming, "Standing to Seek Injunctions Against Officers of the Commonwealth" (2006) 1 J. Eq. 3, 7.

124 Sir Anthony Mason, "The Place of Equity and Equitable Remedies in the Contemporary Common Law World" (1994) 110 L.Q.R. 238, 238.

in Chapter 13: what matters for now is that for several centuries, most welfare and municipal infrastructure spending in England was financed from charitable trusts.[125] As with any other charitable trust, the Attorney-General could seek equitable relief against the municipal corporation where that corporation was the trustee of the charitable trust.[126] Equity's role expanded by analogical extension and relief was awarded at the Attorney-General's suit to prevent the unauthorised use by municipal and other statutory bodies of funds, irrespective of whether the funds were held on trust or not.[127] By the end of the nineteenth century, it was relatively well settled that equitable relief would be available to the Attorney-General, whether acting on their own or at the relation of a private individual, to ensure that funds held by public bodies would be used and applied only in accordance with the applicable terms, whether those terms were sourced in charitable or statutory trusts, or other statutory and regulatory provisions.[128] From here, there was a further extension so that equitable remedies were available to control public bodies in the exercise of *statutory powers generally*, at the suit of the Attorney-General and sometimes, private individuals.[129] The basis for equitable relief was: "the public interest in the observance of statutory authorities, particular those with recourse to public revenues, of the limitations upon their activities which the legislature has imposed."[130]

Equity continued to control public power after the Judicature Reforms, and informed the development of administrative law principles and remedies for the judicial review of public power.[131] The role of the equitable remedies of injunction and declaration in judicial review of public power is now provided for in the Senior Courts Act 1981[132] which confers a power on the High Court to award a declaration or injunction where "it would be just and convenient" for the remedy to be awarded, having regard to the nature of the matters in respect of which relief by one of the prerogative writs might be granted. This statutory provision was a response to the Law Commission's recommendation for the declaration and injunction to be made available through a new method for judicial review. The Commission otherwise recommended that the "essential characteristics of these remedies remain",[133] including the discretionary nature of the remedies. **1–139**

125 About which see further J. Barratt, "Public Trusts" (2006) 69 M.L.R. 514; C. Mitchell "Charitable Endowment and Social Change: Cy-Près Orders and Schemes" (2020) 41 J.L.H. 29; S. Anderson, "Local Government" in W. Cornish et al, *Oxford History of the Laws of England* (Oxford University Press, 2010) Vol.XI, pp.431–437.

126 See, e.g. *Attorney-General v The Mayor of Norwich* (1837) 2 My. & Cr. 406; *The Attorney-General v Aspinall* (1837) 2 My. & Cr. 61; *Attorney-General v Corp of Lichfield* (1848) 11 Beav. 120.

127 Indeed, in some cases there was no need for analogy as one or more public powers were bestowed upon municipal corporations where the councillors were trustees of the corporate estate: *Attorney General v Belfast* Corp (1855) 4 Ir Ch. R. 119 at 160–161 (Lord Chancellor). See also *R. v Tower Hamlets LBC* [1988] A.C. 858 (HL) at 872 (Lord Bridge) referring to W. Wade, *Administrative Law*, 5th edn (Oxford University Press, 1982), pp.355–357.

128 *Attorney-General On the Relation Of The Byker Bridge Co v The Mayor, Alderman and Citizens of the City and County of Newcastle-Upon-Tyne and North-Eastern Railway Co* (1889) 23 Q.B.D. 492 at 497; affirmed on appeal *The Mayor, Aldermen and Citizens of the City and County of Newcastle-Upon-Tyne v Attorney-General On the Relation Of The Byker Bridge Co* [1892] A.C. 568; *The Attorney-General v The Guardians of the Poor of Southampton* (1849) 17 Sim 6; *Attorney-General v Andrews* (1850) 2 Mac. & G. 225.

129 Raising further issues as to standing, see, e.g. *Boyce v Paddington BC* [1903] 1 Ch. 109 at 114; *Bateman's Bay Local Aboriginal Land Council v Aboriginal Community Benefit Fund Pty Ltd* (1998) 194 C.L.R. 247 at 263–276.

130 *Bateman's Bay Local Aboriginal Land Council v Aboriginal Community Benefit Fund Pty Ltd* (1998) 194 C.L.R. 247 at 267 (Gaudron, Gummow and Kirby JJ). See also *Aukland Harbour Board v The King* [1924] A.C. 318 at 326–327 (Viscount Haldane).

131 See generally, Law Commission, *Remedies in Administrative Law*, (Law Com. No.73, 1976), Pt III.2–3. See also J. Beatson and M.H. Matthews, "Supreme Court Rules Reform of Administrative Law Remedies: The First Step" (1978) 41 M.L.R. 437.

132 Senior Courts Act 1981 s.31(2).

133 Law Com. WP No.40, *Remedies in Administrative Law* (1971) para.[43].

1–140 The inadequacies of the common law prerogative writs and need for the equitable injunction and declaration was explained in the following excerpt from *Ainsworth v Criminal Justice Commission*,[134] where a government body in Australia, the Criminal Justice Commission, issued a public report that made "highly critical" findings as to the conduct of the plaintiffs, and a recommendation that the plaintiffs not be permitted to participate in the gaming machine industry in the Australian state of Queensland. The Criminal Justice Commission failed to afford the plaintiffs procedural fairness, including by failing to allow the plaintiffs to address the evidence against them. Yet, the plaintiffs were unsuccessful in seeking relief based on the common law writs of mandamus and certiorari. Instead, an equitable remedy of a declaration provided a response.

Ainsworth v Criminal Justice Commission

High Court of Australia (1992) 175 C.L.R. 564 at 581–582

1–141 MASON C.J., DAWSON, TOOHEY and GAUDRON J.J.: . . . The claim for relief by way of mandamus is based on the view that the Commission is under a duty to investigate and report with respect to the appellants in relation to the introduction of poker machines into Queensland. That view is misconceived. The Commission is under no duty to investigate the appellants. . .

1–142 The Court should not make an order which constrains the Commission's freedom to decide that it will not pursue an investigation when the Court can make an order which will otherwise sufficiently protect the appellants. In saying that a declaration will otherwise sufficiently protect the appellants, we are mindful that this is not a case in which the appellants seek a writ of mandamus to compel the performance of a duty to do something which, if done, will or could result in the appellants obtaining a tangible benefit or entitlement such as a licence or franchise.

1–143 The function of certiorari is to quash the legal effect or the legal consequences of the decision or order under review. The report made and delivered by the Commission has, of itself, no legal effect and carries no legal consequences, whether direct or indirect. It is different when a report or recommendation operates as a precondition or as a bar to a course of action . . .

1–144 A report or a recommendation . . . [that has some legal effect] . . . may be quashed, that is to say its legal effect may be nullified by certiorari. But the Commission's report is not in that category. . . . There being no legal effect or consequence attaching to the report, certiorari does not lie to correct the failure of the Commission to comply with its duty to proceed in a way that was fair to the appellants.

1–145 It does not follow that, because mandamus and certiorari are inapplicable, the appellants must leave this Court without remedy. The law with respect to procedural fairness has developed in spite of the technical aspects of the prerogative writs. . . . Instead, the report has been made and delivered. . . And, although it had no legal effect or consequence, it had the practical effect of blackening the appellants' reputations. Prima facie, at least, these matters suggest that the appellants are entitled to declaratory relief . . .

1–146 . . . [the] power to grant declaratory relief . . . is a discretionary power [that] . . . is confined by the considerations which mark out the boundaries of judicial power. Hence, declaratory relief must be directed to the determination of legal controversies and not to answering abstract or hypothetical questions . . .

1–147 The present case involves no mere hypothetical question. At all stages there has been a controversy as to the Commission's duty of fairness. A report has been made and delivered . . . That report has already had practical consequences for the appellants' reputations. For all that is known, those consequences may extend well into the future. It is appropriate that a declaration be made in terms indicating that the appellants were denied natural justice. That may redress some of the harm done.

1–148 Equity's role is not limited to providing equitable relief where the common law remedy is inadequate. Equitable relief would also be available to supplement the substantive common law according to one or more equitable rules defining when equitable relief was available. For example, some of equity's controls on power, developed for example to control trustees, have informed a range of public law principles for judicial review of administrative or executive action; such as fraud on a power, good

[134] *Ainsworth v Criminal Justice Commission* (1992) 175 C.L.R. 564 at 581–582.

faith, adequacy of consideration and fiduciary loyalty.[135] Public law jurisprudence has relied upon equitable conceptions to express and rationalise the form of control on public power, an example of which is William Wade QC's explanation of the limitation upon the exercise of public power by reference to the trust:[136]

> . . . the notion of absolute or unfettered discretion is rejected. Statutory power conferred for public purposes is conferred as it were upon trust, not absolutely — that is to say, it can validly be used only in the right and proper way which Parliament when conferring it is presumed to have intended. . . the truth is that, in a system based on the rule of law, unfettered governmental discretion is a contradiction in terms.

4. The Fusion of Common Law and Equity?

Writing approximately 30 years after the Judicature Acts 1873–1875, Maitland predicted that "[t]he day will come when lawyers will cease to inquire whether a given rule be a rule of equity or a rule of common law: suffice that it is a well-established rule administered by the High Court of Justice."[137] Writing extra-judicially, a former Chief Justice of the High Court of Australia, French CJ, has colourfully stated, in response to Maitland's prediction:[138] **1–149**

> That day has come. Equity is part of a single body of law administered by most, if not all, Courts of the land albeit it retains its distinctive character and functions. Despite this and the passage of more than one hundred years there are still Jurassic Parks in which equity lawyers are cloned and roam in lush and ancient landscapes.

Certainly, the fusion of the administration of law and equity has removed one of the reasons for thinking about equity as a distinctive body of rules. Prior to the Judicature Reforms, it made sense to think about equity as a distinctive body of rules because in so doing we were able to identify and understand an entire court's jurisdiction and the legal rules according to which that court would award relief. As Maitland explained, the "bond which kept these various appendixes together. . . [is that]. . . [a]ll these matters were within the cognizance of Courts of equity and they were not within the cognizance of the courts of common law."[139] **1–150**

As a result of the procedural fusion, there is a long-standing and very contentious debate as to the extent to which rules and principles of common law on the one hand, and of equity on the other, are now, or should be, "fused". The debate is notable for the colour of the metaphors used and the strength of the language employed. To engage with this "fusion debate" it is necessary to separate out the questions of: (i) the current position, as determined by the Judicature Acts 1873–75 and later developments; and (ii) the approach that should be taken to the relationship between common law and equity. **1–151**

---

135 In relation to the influence or application of one or more equitable controls to determine the judicial review of administrative or executive action, see *Brownells Ltd v Irongmongers' Wages Board* (1950) 81 C.L.R. 108; R. French, "Public Law and Private Law: The Intersection" (Lecture, La Trobe University Law School, 30 October 2009) *https://cdn.hcourt.gov.au/assets/publications/speeches/current-justices/frenchcj/frenchcj30oct09.pdf*; P. Sales, "Use of Powers for Proper Purposes in Private Law" (2020) 136 L.Q.R. 384.

136 W. Wade, *Administrative Law*, 5th edn (Oxford University Press, 1982), pp.355–356 referred to with approval in *R. v Tower Hamlets LBC* at 872.

137 F.W. Maitland, *Equity – A Course of Lectures*, 2nd edn (Cambridge University Press, 1936), p.20.

138 Justice French, "The Equitable Gist in the Machinery of Administrative Justice" paper given at Recent Developments in Administrative Law hosted by the New South Wales Chapter of the Australian Institute of Administrative Law, 22 May 2003, accessed online at *http://www5.austlii.edu.au/au/journals/FedJSchol/2003/9.html*.

139 F.W. Maitland, *Equity – A Course of Lectures*, 2nd edn (Cambridge University Press, 1936), p.20.

A. The Descriptive Question: the Current Position

1–152 In *United Scientific Holdings Ltd v Burnley BC*, Lord Diplock stated that:[140]

> My Lords, if by 'rules of equity' is meant that body of substantive and adjectival law that, prior to 1875, was administered by the Court of Chancery but not by courts of common law, to speak of the rules of equity as being part of the law of England in 1977 is about as meaningful as to speak similarly of the Statute of Uses or of Quia Emptores. Historically all three have in their time played an important part in the development of the corpus juris into what it is today: but to perpetuate a dichotomy between rules of equity and rules of common law which it was a major purpose of the Supreme Court of Judicature Act 1873 to do away with, is, in my view, conducive to erroneous conclusions as to the ways in which the law of England has developed in the last hundred years. . . . Your Lordships have been referred to the vivid phrase traceable to the first edition of *Ashburner's Principles of Equity* where, in speaking in 1902 of the effect of the Supreme Court of Judicature Act, he says:[141] 'the two stream of jurisdiction [law and equity] though they run in the same channel, run side by side and do not mingle their waters.' My Lords, by 1977 this metaphor has in my view become both mischievous and deceptive. The innate conservatism of English lawyers may have made them slow to recognise that by the Supreme Court of Judicature Act 1873 the two systems of substantive and adjectival law formerly administered by the courts of law and Courts of Chancery (as well as those administered by courts of admiralty, probate and matrimonial causes) were fused. At the confluence of the Rhône and Saône, it may be possible for a short distance to discern the source from which each part of the combined stream came, but there comes a point at which this ceases to be possible. If Professor Ashburner's fluvial metaphor is to be retained at all, the waters of the confluent streams of law and equity have surely mingled now.

1–153 Lord Diplock's analysis was soon echoed by Lord Denning MR,[142] but in contemplating a substantive as well as a procedural fusion, it gives the Judicature Acts an impact far greater than they were seemingly intended to have,[143] and far greater than they were perceived to have had at the time. In *Salt v Cooper*, a case from 1880, for example, Jessel MR described the reform as "not any fusion, or anything of the kind; it was the vesting in one tribunal [of] the administration of Law and Equity in every cause, action or dispute which should come before that tribunal".[144]

1–154 Lord Diplock's analysis has, indeed, been powerfully criticised as involving a "fusion fallacy":[145] the fact that rules of common law and of equity can be applied by all courts does not mean that there is no longer any substantive difference between those rules, or that the distinction between common law and equity is no longer of significance. The position of B, a beneficiary of a trust, demonstrates this point. If T, the trustee, acts in breach of the terms of the trust and transfers the trust property to C, it may be possible for B to make a claim against C, based on B's initial right under

---

140 [1978] A.C. 904 at 924–925.

141 W. Ashburner, *Principles of Equity* (Butterworth & Co, 1902), p.23.

142 *Federal Commerce & Navigation Co Ltd v Molena Alpha Inc (The Nanfri)* [1978] 1 Q.B. 927 at 974 per Lord Denning MR: "Over 100 years have passed since the Judicature Act 1873. During that time the streams of common law and equity have flown together and combined so as to be indistinguishable the one from the other. We have no longer to ask ourselves: what would the courts of common law or the courts of equity have done before the Judicature Act? We have to ask ourselves: what should we do now do as to ensure fair dealing between the parties?"

143 See M. Leeming, "Equity, the Judicature Acts and Restitution" (2011) 5 J. Eq. 45, for a contextual account of the aims of the legislation.

144 (1880) 16 Ch.D. 544 at 549.

145 The term coined by the editors of *Equity: Doctrines and Remedies*. In, for example, the 3rd edn of that work (*Equity: Doctrines and Remedies*, R. Meagher et al (eds) (Butterworths Law, 1992), para.221), it was said that: "Those who commit the fusion fallacy announce or assume the creation by the Judicature system of a new body of law containing elements of law and equity but in character quite different from its components. The fallacy is committed explicitly, covertly, and on occasion with apparent inadvertence. But the state of mind of the culprit cannot lessen the evil of the offence." See now the 5th edn, J.D. Heydon et al (eds), (2014), paras 2.130–2.320.

the trust. B, in that sense, has an interest in the trust property. B's equitable interest, however, has a substantive effect that is quite different from the common law property right of a person, O, who simply owns property outright. If, for example, O's property is stolen and then sold by the thief to C, who buys in good faith and with no notice of O's initial property right, O will be able to assert that property right against C.[146] Where the property is goods, O's claim will arise in the tort of conversion. In contrast, if T, the trustee, sells the trust property in breach of the terms of the trust to C, who buys in good faith and with no notice of the trust in B's favour, B can bring no claim against C: in such a case, C is protected by a defence of bona fide purchase that is not available to him in reply to the claim by O.[147]

It is therefore clear that each of O's common law property right as outright owner, and B's equitable **1–155** interest under a trust, is subject to different substantive rules. This distinction between legal estates and interests on the one hand, and equitable interests on the other, is, for example, fundamental to the scheme of the Law of Property Act 1925,[148] and also to the scheme of the Land Registration Act 2002.[149] It is also necessary to make sense of the fact that the rules relating to the *acquisition* of an equitable interest differ from those applying to a legal property right. For example, a purchaser of land can acquire a legal estate in registered land only by registering as the holder of such a right; in contrast, such a purchaser can acquire an equitable interest as soon as the contract for the sale of the land is concluded.[150] If there were no substantive difference in the effect of the legal estate obtained on registration and this equitable interest, it would make no sense to permit the equitable interest to be acquired at that earlier stage, without registration.

As a result, and to continue with the maritime metaphors, Lord Diplock's view in the *United Scientific* **1–156** case may be taken as the high watermark of the substantive fusion approach: since then, the tide has turned and there now "seems to be little doubt that the Judicature Acts did not effect a substantive merger of law and equity".[151] The broader fusion debate continues, however, as to what approach *should* be taken to the relationship between common law and equity.

B. The Prescriptive Question: What Approach Should Be Taken?

In a very important contribution to the "fusion debate", Andrew Burrows (now Lord Burrows JSC) has **1–157** argued that a difference between two particular rules or principles cannot be justified *merely* by the fact that one of those rules or principles is part of common law, and the other part of equity. Rather, in such a case, care must be taken to ensure that there is a substantive justification for the different outcomes; if not, the law will be inconsistent and will fail in its aim of treating like cases alike.

---

146 See, e.g. *Farquarhson Bros and Co v King and Co* [1902] A.C. 325. Where the property consists of goods, O's claim against C will arise in the tort of conversion.

147 See, e.g. *MCC Proceeds Inc v Lehman Bros International (Europe)* [1998] 4 All E.R. 675.

148 See Law of Property Act 1925 s.1.

149 See, e.g. Land Registration Act 2002 Sch.3 para. 1 and para. 3, which allow *legal* leases and *legal* easements, in some circumstances, to count as overriding interests, but do not extend to equitable leases or equitable easements.

150 See paras 17–061ff.

151 J. Maxton, "Intermingling of Common Law and Equity" in M. Cope (ed.), *Equity: Issues and Trends* (Federation Press, 1995), p.25. See too Lord Evershed, "Reflections on the Fusion of Law and Equity after 75 Years" (1954) 70 L.Q.R. 326, 327.

Andrew Burrows, "We Do This At Common Law But That In Equity"

(2002) 22 O.J.L.S. 1, 4

1–158 [T]he fusion school of thought argues that the fusion of the administration of the courts brought about by the 1873–5 Acts, whilst not dictating the fusion of the substantive law, rendered this, for the first time, a realistic possibility. While there are areas where common law and equity can happily sit alongside one another, there are many examples of inconsistencies between them. It is important to remove the inconsistencies thereby producing a coherent or harmonized law. In developing the law it is legitimate for the courts to reason from common law to equity and vice versa. A harmonized rule or principle that has features of both common law and equity is at the very least acceptable and, depending on the rule or principle in question, may represent the best way for the law to develop.

1–159 [The fusion school of thought] is to be strongly preferred. There are numerous instances of inconsistencies between common law and equity; and to support fusion seems self-evident, resting, as it does, on not being slaves to history and on recognizing the importance of coherence in the law and of 'like cases being treated alike'.

1–160 Burrows then divides English private law into four categories. The first is where "the law has already reached the advanced position that common law and equity cannot be distinguished at all". Putting those relatively rare cases to one side, he then focusses on the remaining three categories:[152]

1–161 The first category is where common law and equity co-exist coherently and where the historical labels of common law and equity remain the best or, at least, useful terminology. I particularly have in mind here that greatest invention of equity, the trust. It is very hard—albeit not impossible as is shown by the approach in some other jurisdictions—to describe the trust without at some stage relying on, and referring to, the split between legal and equitable title. . .

1–162 The second category is where common law and equity co-exist coherently but, in contrast to the first category, there is nothing to be gained by adherence to those historical labels. If we are to taken fusion seriously, the labels common law and equity in the areas of law covered by this category should be abandoned at a stroke. . .

The third category is more complex. It comprises probably most of our civil law. In this category, in contrast to both of the first two categories, common law and equity do not co-exist coherently. If we are to take fusion seriously, what is needed is a change in the law, albeit often only a small change, so as to produce a principled product which may combine elements of law and equity.

1–164 The argument made by Burrows has not won universal acceptance.[153] It does however make a very important central point that any apparent differences between common law and equitable rules need to be carefully justified. For example, shortly after Burrows wrote, the Court of Appeal rejected the conventional view that there was a separate equitable doctrine of common mistake which could lead to the rescission of a contract, finding that such a doctrine would be inconsistent with the clear limits to the doctrine of common mistake as applied at common law.[154] More recently, the Supreme Court has considered whether there is any good reason to distinguish between the doctrines of actual undue influence and of duress: the mere fact that the former was developed in equity, and the latter

[152] Burrows, "We Do This At Common Law But That In Equity" (2002) 22 O.J.L.S. 1, 5–6.

[153] For different views, see, e.g. M. Leeming, "Equity, the Judicature Acts and Restitution" (2011) 5 J. Eq. 45; Samet, *Equity: Conscience Goes to Market* (2018), Ch.1.

[154] *Great Peace Shipping Ltd v Tsavliris Salvage (International) Ltd* [2002] EWCA Civ 1407; [2003] Q.B. 679, disapproving *Solle v Butcher* [1950] 1 K.B. 671. See too, e.g. *Halpern v Halpern (Nos 1 and 2)* [2007] EWCA Civ 291; [2008] Q.B. 195 at [70]–[77], where Carnwath LJ suggested that the "counter-restitution impossible" bar to rescission should operate in substantially the same way whether the claim rests on duress (at common law) or undue influence (in equity).

at common law does not, *in itself*, justify making the distinction.[155] Indeed, it was Lord Burrows himself who observed that in analysing past actual undue influence cases where equity intervened in response to influence exerted by a lawful threat, it would be "rational today to treat such cases as examples of duress" rather than of undue influence.[156]

Burrows' wider argument is significant when considering equitable remedies and, in fact, his analysis includes a detailed treatment of monetary remedies for civil wrongs, in which it is argued that such cases fall into the third category where "common law and equity do not co-exist coherently".[157] It may be the case, for example, that a remedy recognised in equity in fact closely resembles one available at common law, so that any differences in the rules applying to each remedy must be carefully examined. **1–165**

In relation to trusts, it is notable that even a committed fusionist such as Burrows regards the trust as falling into that first category of case, where common law and equity co-exist coherently, and it is helpful to continue to refer to particular rules by reference to their jurisdictional origin either in equity or at common law.[158] It may therefore be that the trust demonstrates how the somewhat illogical dual court system in place in England and Wales until the end of the nineteenth century in fact enriched English private law by producing some very useful concepts. As we will consider further in Chapter 12, however, it is not so clear that the "split between legal and equitable title" referred to by Burrows is the best way to characterise the trust, as that terminology suggests that the trust does in fact raise the problem of common law and equity giving different answers to the same fundamental question of "who has title to the property?".[159] **1–166**

C. Common Law and Equity: A Productive Paradox?

The argument has often been made that if one were creating a legal system from scratch, one would certainly not design a set of rules (common law), and then design a second set of rules (equity) which overlays the first set, making it necessary to have a third set of rules to determine whether the first or the second set governs cases where the two sets produce different outcomes.[160] It can nonetheless be claimed that this dual system allowed English law to produce a more nuanced, yet also more efficient, form of justice than might be achieved by a simpler, single set of rules. For example, Henry Smith has argued that equity continues to serve an important function by operating as "meta-law": in its role as a supplementary set of rules it can, for example, provide a "safety valve" to deal with cases where the application of common law rules lead to a clear injustice.[161] Equity can thus permit the common law to adopt rules of general application (which are thus clearer and easier to understand)[162] whilst ensuring that an individual party is not permitted to exploit the **1–167**

---

155 See *Pakistan International Airline Corp v Times Travel (UK) Ltd* [2021] UKSC 40, e.g. at [2], where Lord Hodge notes that: "the courts have developed the common law doctrine of duress to include lawful act duress by drawing on the rules of equity in relation to undue influence . . . morally reprehensible behaviour which in equity was judged to render the enforcement of a contract unconscionable in the context of undue influence has been treated by English common law as illegitimate pressure in the context of duress."

156 *Pakistan International Airline Corp v Times Travel (UK) Ltd* [2021] UKSC 40 at [90].

157 (2002) 22 O.J.L.S. 1, 9–12.

158 A. Burrows, "We Do This at Common Law But That in Equity" (2002) 22 O.J.L.S. 1, 5 (extracted at paras 1–158 to 1–162).

159 For discussion of this point see B. McFarlane, "The Persistence of Equity: Lessons from the Trust" (Inaugural Lecture, Oxford 2022): recording available at *https://www.youtube.com/watch?v=TNUQ96ik2tQ*.

160 See, e.g. S. Worthington, *Equity*, 2nd edn (Oxford University Press, 2006), Ch.2.

161 See paras 1–066 to 1–073 and also H. Smith, "Fusing the Equitable Function in Private Law" in K. Barker et al (eds) *Private Law in the Twenty-First Century* (Hart, 2017), Ch.9.

162 See too D. Klimchuk, "Equity and the Rule of Law" in L. Austin and D. Klimchuk (eds), *Private Law and the Rule of Law* (Oxford University Press, 2014), pp.251–255, drawing on Aristotle's observation that: "The nature of the equitable is a correction of law where it is defective owing to its universality."

generality of those rules to act in a way which would "shock the conscience of the court".[163] Smith explains that the dual layered system of the primary order law, and a secondary order or meta law, which is performed by equity, allows for each distinct sub-system to specialise in a given ideal; the primary system providing a set of general, simple and predictable rules, while the secondary system providing context sensitive and particular rules.[164] The secondary system of equity provides a safety net to deter the opportunism made possible by the universal application of relatively simple, stable and predictable rules.

1–168 Other scholars have also considered the unique contribution made by equity, including its role in preventing unconscionable reliance on legal rights.[165] Matthew Harding has argued that equity promotes the rule of law by contributing to the conditions under which law can be a normative guide for citizens' conduct.[166] Citizens are less likely to respect and take up the institutions of contract or property, for example, if the law allows for the unjust or unconscientious assertion of rights recognised by these areas of law. Equity's restraint of the unconscious assertion of legal rights prevents citizens from regarding law as a source of arbitrary force or evil open for manipulation by the unscrupulous and powerful. Irit Samet has similarly argued that equity helps to promote rule of law ideals, and also identifies its particular role as increasing the congruence between the practical effect of legal rules and the genuine moral standards which should guide behaviour, arguing that the concept of conscience is a "powerful tool" which equity can use to achieve this goal.[167]

1–169 It is therefore clear that the debate as to whether there are sufficient reasons to continue focussing on equity as a distinct set of rules and principles will continue. The approach taken in this book is that there are some general underlying functions which are characteristic of (although not unique to) equity and which continue to inform many, although not all, of the rules and principles that make up equity today. Equity does not apply because the common law as a whole is defective or unfair, or indeed because there is some problem with the rule that applies in an individual case. Equity is required because the common law is functioning precisely as it should in its provision of rules that define the parties' legal entitlements, such as property law or contract. Examples of this are rules for the creation or transfer of title to property and the creation of contracts, and which are expressed as generalised rules that largely focus upon the parties' objective manifestation of their intentions. Parties are less likely to be able to enter contracts or engage in property transfers if the rules providing for the creation of contracts or transfer of title to property are not relatively clear, stable, and predictable rules that apply on the basis of objectively ascertainable facts. Such rules, while necessary to the fulfilment of law's ends, are only possible because there is some other body of rules that responds to individualised and more subjective considerations. Such secondary rules can exist at common law,[168] but as a matter of history those rules developed chiefly in equity, which is no surprise given equity's

---

[163] That phrase is used to state a threshold for equitable intervention, through the doctrine of proprietary estoppel (see paras 2–003 to 2–033) by Lord Walker in *Cobbe v Yeoman's Row Management Ltd* [2008] UKHL 55; [2008] 1 W.L.R. 1752 at [92].

[164] See paras 1–066 to 1–073 and also Smith, "Fusing the Equitable Function" in K. Barker et al (eds) *Private Law in the Twenty-First Century* (Hart, 2017), Ch.9.

[165] Klimchuk, "Equity and the Rule of Law" in Austin and Klimchuk, *Private Law and the Rule of Law* (2014), Ch.11; M. Harding, "Equity and the Rule of Law" (2016) 132 L.Q.R. 278; P. Miller, "Equity as Supplemental Law" in D. Klimchuk, I. Samet and H. Smith (eds), *The Philosophical Foundations of the Law of Equity* (Oxford University Press, (2020), Ch.16; McFarlane and Stevens, "What's Special About Equity? Rights Against Rights" in Klimchuk, Samet and Smith (eds) *The Philosophical Foundations of the Law of Equity* (2020), Ch.9; Smith, "Equity is not a Single Thing" in Klimchuk, Samet and Smith (eds), *The Philosophical Foundations of the Law of Equity* (2020), Ch.7.

[166] Harding, "Equity and the Rule of Law" (2016) 132 L.Q.R. 278; M. Harding, "Equity and Institutions" in D. Klimchuk et al (eds), *Philosophical Foundations of the Law of Equity* (Oxford University Press, 2020), Ch.16.

[167] Samet, *Equity: Conscience Goes to Market* (2018), Ch.1.

[168] Rules as to waiver provide an example (as noted at para.1–076), and the common law also allows B to set aside a contract entered into through duress or fraud.

operation as gloss on, or supplement to, common law. In providing such rules, equity thus supports the common law by ensuring that the legal entitlements defined by the common law are not exploited or misused.

A significant part of equity's operation thus consists of controlling A's exercise of a legal entitlement as against B: we will consider such rules in Chapter 2. This does not mean, however, that equity's role is purely negative. In fulfilling its secondary function, it is also possible for equity to generate new entitlements in B that require A to act in a particular way and so place A under a duty to B. We will examine such cases in Chapter 3, and see there that they are consistent with the secondary or supplementary role of equity, as they function as a gloss on the lawfulness of A's exercise of some pre-existing entitlement. So, for example, the duties of administration owed by a trustee, A, to a beneficiary, B, generate new rights in B, but those duties aim to control A's exercise of A's rights and powers, and thus have a secondary aspect. We will also note in Chapter 3 that there are some, relatively rare, instances in which equity has gone further, and generates a new right in B which cannot reasonably be seen as secondary or supplemental in nature: this is the case, for example, with the development of the doctrine of breach of confidence to deal with invasions of privacy. In this case, equity operates in a primary way, recognising a duty on A which relates purely to A's conduct and not to any legal entitlement of A. **1–170**

One implication of this approach is that we can appreciate a much-less examined way in which meta-law or secondary rules enhance the overall legal system's commitment to the rule of law, which is by allowing the parties to use their legal entitlements for their own ends and on their terms. In other words, equity, sometimes, allows the parties to define the terms on which lawfulness of A's exercise of A's legal entitlement will be determined, and these rules confer on the parties a power to create relationships. Such powers, such as the power to create an express trust, or to make an equitable assignment, also continue to be a practically important means of promoting the autonomy of parties who hold rights.[169] **1–171**

Question

1. In *Dudley v Dudley* (1705) 24 E.R. 118 at 119 Lord Cowper stated: "Now equity is no part of the law, but a moral virtue, which qualifies, moderates, and reforms the rigour, hardness and edge of the law . . . [it] defends the law from crafty evasions, delusions, and new subtleties, invented and contrived to evade and delude the common law, whereby such as have undoubted right are made remediless." **Discuss.**

---

[169] See, e.g. S. Agnew and S. Douglas, "Self-Declarations of Trust" (2019) 135 L.Q.R. 67, 85–97; B. McFarlane, "Equity" in A. Gold et al (eds) *The Oxford Handbook of the New Private Law* (Oxford University Press, 2020), Ch.33; H. Dagan and I. Samet, "Express Trust: The Dark Horse of the Liberal Property Regime" in S. Degeling et al (eds) *Philosophical Foundations of the Law of Express Trusts* (Oxford University Press, forthcoming).

2

EQUITY'S RESTRAINING RULES

1. Introduction

A. Equity's Restraint of Powers and Rights

2-001 As we saw in Chapter 1, one of equity's characteristic functions is to restrain or control one party, A, in how she exercises or enforces a legal entitlement, such as a right or power, against B. Key to understanding these equitable rules is that they are concerned with A's exercise or enforcement of some other, pre-existing legal entitlement, which may itself arise and be defined by common law, statutory or equitable rules.

2-002 In understanding this function of equity, it is useful to distinguish between the different types of legal entitlement that A may have. One means of doing so is to look at the *source* of A's entitlement: common law, statute or equity. Another means is to look at the *type* of A's entitlement. In doing so, we can draw on the scheme developed by Wesley Hohfeld in distinguishing the different things that might be meant when we say that A has a right. For example, if A has a right that D pay £100 to A, then A's right against D correlates to a duty that D owes to A. In Hohfeld's scheme, a legal relation links two parties and one activity: in this case, the parties are A and D and the activity is D's payment of £100 to A. In that scheme, where the legal relation involves D's being under a duty to A, A has a *claim-right* against D. In our analysis here, we will generally limit the use of the word "right" to refer to such claim-rights.

2-003 There are however other cases in which the word 'right' is used to describe A's legal relations against D. For example, if we say that A has a right to rescind a contract entered into with D, then this does not mean that D is under any immediate duty to A. Rather, we mean that A has a *power* as against D: A can act in such a way as to change the legal relations between A and D. In such a case, it can be said that D has a liability to A: D's position can be changed by A's exercise of the power. So, in the Hohfeldian scheme, A's power correlates to a liability of D, whereas A's claim-right correlates to a duty of D.

2-004 When considering equity's restraining rules, the entitlements of A which are most commonly controlled are such claim-rights and powers. For example, consider a case where A holds a bank account on trust for B. Under A's contract with A's bank, A has various claim-rights against the bank, correlating to duties of the bank owed to A. The trust imposes certain duties on A, owed to B, in relation to those claim-rights. A's contract with the bank will also give A certain powers against the bank, and again the trust will impose certain duties on A, owed to B, in relation to those powers. In the absence of the trust, A would generally be free to exercise those rights and powers as A chooses; the intervention of equity now means that it would not be lawful, *as against B*, for A to exercise those rights and powers in particular ways.

2–005 In Chapter 1,[1] we also saw an example of equity intervening to control the exercise of a pure power, held by A against B. In *Hughes v Metropolitan Rwy Co*, it was held that A could be controlled, as against B, in its exercise of a power, arising under its contract with B, to terminate B's lease. As in the case of a trust, equity does not deny that A holds that legal entitlement; it rather restrains, in favour of B, a particular exercise of that entitlement.

2–006 Claim-rights and powers are not the only types of entitlement identified by Hohfeld. For example, A might say that she has a right, against D, to open up a competing shop near to D's shop. This does not involve a claim that D is under any duty to A. Rather, it means simply that A is *not* under a duty to D not to open the shop. Such an entitlement of A can be called a "privilege" or "liberty" against D and it describes a case where A is not under a duty to D in relation to a particular activity. One of the key points made by Hohfeld is that we can accept that A has a legal entitlement against D without also having to accept that D is under a duty to A—cases where A claims a liberty are very good examples of this. They also show the danger of the statement that A has a right to carry out an activity: this does not necessarily mean that D is under any duty to A not to interfere with that activity. So, there may be only one dessert left at a Law Faculty buffet. I have a right (in the sense of a liberty) against each of my colleagues to take that dessert, but if one of my colleagues takes it first, she commits no breach of duty against me.

2–007 A privilege or liberty thus arises where D has no claim-right against A. The fourth and final legal relation identified by Hohfeld arises where D has no power against A. It is described by Hohfeld as an "immunity" of A and correlates to a "disability" of D. If, for example, D is not A's agent and so has no power to enter into a contract with a third party on behalf of A, then A is immune from D's binding A to such a contract. Like a privilege or liberty, an immunity thus has a more negative quality than a claim-right or power, as it entails the absence of a particular type of legal relation between A and D.

2–008 Hohfeld's scheme is helpful to the extent that it provides a more accurate means of description and analysis of legal entitlements. In particular, it can help us to avoid various errors in legal analysis that occur if, for example, it is assumed that A's having a "right" in a general sense *necessarily* means that D is under a duty to A. For example, in *Glencore International AG v Commissioner of Taxation*,[2] the High Court of Australia considered B's application that the Australian Taxation Office should return copies of documents, containing legal advice given to B by A, which the Office had received following the "Paradise Papers" leaks. B's claim was based solely on the existence of legal professional privilege. One of the grounds on which the application was rejected that:[3]

> [B's] argument cannot be accepted. Fundamentally it rests upon an incorrect premise, namely that legal professional privilege is a legal right which is capable of being enforced, which is to say that it may found a cause of action. The privilege is only an immunity from the exercise of powers which would otherwise compel the disclosure of privileged communications . . . [B's case] seeks to transform the nature of the privilege from an immunity to an ill-defined cause of action which may be brought against anyone with respect to documents which may then be in the public domain.

2–009 It is, equally, important to be aware of the limits of Hohfeld's scheme. For example, it does not in itself provide reasons why a particular type of right should or should not exist. In the *Glencore* case cited above, for example, the mere fact that legal professional privilege operates as an immunity (meaning for example that a court does not have a power to order disclosure of particular documents)

---

1 See para.1–077.
2 [2019] HCA 26.
3 [2019] HCA 26 at [12]–[13].

does not mean that it cannot also support a linked, but independent claim-right. The point though is that justifications for such a claim-right would have to be provided: it is not enough for B to argue that the existence of the immunity *necessarily* means that other parties are also under a duty to B in relation to documents covered by the immunity. Nonetheless, it is necessary to have some awareness and understanding of the Hohfeldian scheme of legal relations, not least given its usage in a range of judicial and academic analyses of equity and trusts.

B. The Scope of this Chapter

This chapter outlines some examples of equity's restraining rules: promissory estoppel; relief against forfeiture and penalties; and fiduciary loyalty. It does not provide a complete account of those rules as its aim is rather to demonstrate some general points about the function of equity made in Chapter 1. We saw there that a characteristic function of equity, in supplementing the common law, is to control, in B's favour, A's exercise of legal entitlements. In each of the three cases examined in this chapter, that control consists of restraining A from exercising, as against B, such entitlements. **2–010**

It is not suggested here that these restraints are imposed for the same reasons. Rather, the point is that there is a common *form* to equity's intervention: the restraint of A's entitlement. This may occur via an injunction prohibiting A from taking action, or, in the event A has already exercised A's legal entitlement contrary to one or another equitable rule, one or more forms of other equitable relief may be available to require A (and sometimes third parties) to take action to reverse the consequences of A's action. The type of equitable relief that restrains A may thus take different forms depending on the circumstances of the case, and in particular, whether A has actually exercised the legal entitlement or not. What ties all the rules together is that the content of the rule, i.e. what it requires of A, is that A should not exercise A's legal entitlement in certain circumstances, or in other words, the rule is infringed if A exercises a legal entitlement when she should not have. **2–011**

Critically, equity's restraining rules exhibit the secondary or meta law function identified in Chapter 1 as they do not actually change the existence or scope of A's underlying legal entitlement. All they do is make it unlawful for A, as against B, to take action to exercise a legal entitlement in some way, and they define when equitable relief is available; either to prevent A from exercising her legal entitlement unlawfully, or to deal with the consequences of A having already exercised her legal entitlement. **2–012**

The chapter will also consider how equity's retraining rules achieve restraint through the generation of new equitable entitlements for B. This observation has implications for our understanding of equity's meta-law or secondary function, specifically that this function may itself generate rights in B. **2–013**

A further, general observation, is that the entitlements generated by equity's restraining rules can themselves be the object of equitable restraint. So, when thinking about equity, it is important to bear in mind that it is not just a restraint on common law legal entitlements. Equity is also a self-reflexive body of rules. **2–014**

Finally, there are other equitable rules not covered in this chapter, but which could be characterised as a form of restraint on the same basis that the rule makes it unlawful for A to take action to exercise a legal entitlement in some way, such as duties of administration, including those owed by an express trustee. Some of those rules will be examined in Chapter 4. **2–015**

2. Promissory Estoppel

A. A Restraint on A's Entitlements

2-016 A "traditional"[4] or "orthodox"[5] promissory estoppel allows B to prevent A from exercising some legal entitlement—for example, a right or power arising under a contract or some other legal relationship—contrary to a promise made by A to B.[6] If engaged, it restrains A from relying on that legal entitlement in a manner regarded by a court as unconscionable. The particular form of unconscionability which promissory estoppel is said to prevent is generally defined as A's exercising a legal entitlement against B when A, intending to induce some expectation of B, has made a promise to B, upon which B has reasonably relied in changing her position, so that B would suffer a detriment should A depart from A's promise.[7]

2-017 In *BP Exploration (Libya) v Hunt (No.2)*, for example, Goff J stated that promissory estoppel requires:[8]

> (1) a legal relationship between the parties; (2) a representation, express or implied, by one party that he will not enforce his strict rights against the other; and (3) reliance by the representee (whether by action or by omission to act) on the representation, which renders it inequitable, in all the circumstances, for the representor to enforce his strict rights, or at least to do so until the representee is restored to his former position.

2-018 The focus on the restraint of A's rights can be seen in the effect of a promissory estoppel, as explained by Goff J above, as well as in earlier authorities. For example, in *Hughes v Metropolitan Railway Co*, Lord Cairns LC stated:[9]

> [T]he person who otherwise might have enforced those rights will not be allowed to enforce them where it would be inequitable having regard to the dealings which have thus taken place between the parties.

2-019 In *Birmingham and District Land Company v London & North Western Railway Co*, Bowen LJ stated:[10]

> If persons who have contractual rights against others induce by their conduct those against whom they have such rights to believe that such rights will either not be enforced or will be kept in suspense or abeyance for some particular time, those persons will not be allowed by a Court of Equity to enforce the rights until such time has elapsed, without at all events placing the parties in the same position as they were before.

---

4 *Waltons Stores (Interstate) Ltd v Maher* (1988) 164 C.L.R. 387 at 400 (Mason CJ and Wilson J), 420 (Brennan J); *FJ & PN Curran Pty Ltd v Almond Investors Land Pty Ltd* [2019] VSCA 236 at [251] (the Court).

5 A phrase traced to *Bobko v The Commonwealth* unreported 22 April 1988 Supreme Court of Victoria, (Fullagar J), referred to in *Metropolitan Transit Authority v Waverley Transit Pty Ltd* [1991] 1 V.R. 181 at 205 (the Court).

6 *Waltons Stores (Interstate) Ltd v Maher* at 399–400 (Mason CJ and Wilson J), 426 (Brennan J); *Equitrust Ltd v Franks* [2009] NSWCA 128 at [70] (Handley AJA).

7 *Central London Property Trust Ltd v High Trees House Ltd* [1947] 1 K.B. 130 at 134 (Denning J); *Baird Textile Holdings Ltd v Marks and Spencer Plc* [2001] EWCA Civ 274 at [83]–[89] (Mance LJ); K. Handley, *Estoppel by Conduct and Election*, 2nd edn (Sweet & Maxwell, 2016) Ch.13.

8 [1979] 1 W.L.R. 783 at 810.

9 *Hughes v Metropolitan Railway Co* (1877) 2 App. Cas. 439 (HL) 448.

10 *Birmingham and District Land Co v London & North Western Railway Co* (1888) 40 Ch. D. 268 (CA) 286.

B. The Development of the Modern Doctrine

The following case is generally regarded as the basis of the modern doctrine of promissory estoppel. 2-020

Central London Properties Trust Ltd v High Trees House

[1947] K.B. 130 at 134–135

A let a block of flats situated in South London to B (a subsidiary company of A) for a term of 99 years from September 1937 at a rent of £2500 per year. By early 1940, given difficulties caused by the war, B had been able to sub-let only a small number of the flats A. A and B therefore agreed that the rent payable under the lease should be reduced to £1250, as from the beginning of the lease. B paid the reduced rent. By early 1945, all the flats were sub-let and in September 1945, A wrote to B to claim the full rent. In friendly proceedings, brought to establish the legal position, B argued first that the agreement to reduce the rent operated for the whole term of the lease, and second that A was only able to claim the full rent as from September 1945. 2-021

DENNING J.: . . . With regard to estoppel, the representation made in relation to reducing the rent, was not a representation of an existing fact. It was a representation, in effect, as to the future, namely, that payment of the rent would not be enforced at the full rate but only at the reduced rate. Such a representation would not give rise to an estoppel, because, as was said in *Jorden v Money*,[11] a representation as to the future must be embodied as a contract or be nothing. 2-022

But what is the position in view of developments in the law in recent years? The law has not been standing still since *Jorden v Money*. There has been a series of decisions over the last fifty years which, although they are said to be cases of estoppel are not really such. They are cases in which a promise was made which was intended to create legal relations and which, to the knowledge of the person making the promise, was going to be acted on by the person to whom it was made and which was in fact so acted on. In such cases the courts have said that the promise must be honoured . . . As I have said they are not cases of estoppel in the strict sense. They are really promises – promises intended to be binding, intended to be acted on, and in fact acted on . . . In each case the court held the promise to be binding on the party making it, even though under the old common law it might be difficult to find any consideration for it. The courts have not gone so far as to give a cause of action in damages for the breach of such a promise, but they have refused to allow the party making it to act inconsistently on it. It is in that sense, and that sense only, that such a promise gives rise to an estoppel. The decisions are a natural result of the fusion of law and equity: for the cases of *Hughes v Metropolitan Rwy Co*,[12] *Birmingham and District Land Co v London & North Western Rwy Co*[13] and *Salisbury (Marquess) v Gilmore*[14] afford a sufficient basis for saying that a party would not be allowed in equity to go back on such a promise. In my opinion, the time has now come for the validity of such a promise to be recognised. The logical consequences, no doubt, is that a promise to accept a smaller sum in discharge of a larger sum, if acted upon, is binding notwithstanding the absence of consideration: and if the fusion of law and equity leads to this result, so much the better. That aspect was not considered in *Foakes v Beer*. At this time of day however, when law and equity have been joined together for over seventy years, principles must be reconsidered in light of their combined effect. 2-023

Denning J went on to find that A's promise was that the rent should be reduced only as a "temporary expedient while the block of flats was not fully, or substantially fully let, owing to the conditions prevailing" and so it no longer applied by early 1945, when the flats were fully let. 2-024

---

11 [1951] 2 K.B. 215 at 219. See too *Baird Textiles Holdings Ltd v Marks & Spencer Plc* and *Greenhouse v Paysafe Financial Services Ltd* [2018] EWHC 3296 (Comm).

12 (1877) 2 App. Cas. 439 (HL).

13 (1999) 40 Ch. D. 268 (CA).

14 [1942] 2 K.B. 38.

2–025 In the following extract, Ben McFarlane suggests that is perhaps surprising that the *High Trees* case is seen as an application of promissory estoppel.

Ben McFarlane, "Understanding Equitable Estoppel: From Metaphors to Better Laws"

(2013) 66 *Current Legal Problems* 267, 281–282

2–026 The principle applying here [in the *High Trees* case] is that: (i) if B owes a duty to A; and (ii) B tenders, and A accepts, particular action (or inaction) by B as performance of that duty; then (iii) B's duty is discharged even if, in the absence of such acceptance from A, B's action (or inaction) would not have discharged that duty.

2–027 This principle, it is submitted, is the one recognized by Denning J in what has become the foundation of the modern law of promissory estoppel: his 'brilliant obiter dictum' in *Central London Property Trust v High Trees House Ltd*. The association of that judgment with the equitable doctrine of promissory estoppel is somewhat odd. First, as we have seen, Denning J made it very clear that his decision in that case did not depend on estoppel. Secondly, contrary to Denning J's analysis, the principle does not depend on A's having made a promise. Thirdly, and again contrary to Denning J's view, the principle does not appear to be peculiarly equitable.

2–028 As to the second point, it is submitted that the principle gives effect to A's actual consent in accepting the substitute performance, rather than to A's promise to accept such performance. The principle also differs from the promise-detriment principle as it is not focussed on the need to prevent B's suffering a detriment as a result of A's promise: in *High Trees* itself, B's action (paying a lower rent) was beneficial to B and B was not required to show that it would suffer any specific hardship if asked to pay the contractually due rent. As to the third point, the principle is also recognized at common law . . . the application of that common law doctrine, sometimes referred to as total waiver, is confirmed by section 11(2) of the Sale of Goods Act 1979 and was demonstrated by the decision of Gloster J in *The Bunga Saga Lima*.

2–029 In *High Trees* itself, it was for reasons of authority, rather than of principle, that Denning J invoked equity. The decision of the House of Lords in *Foakes v Beer* appears to establish that the general principle, operating where A accept substitute performance from B, cannot apply where B owes a debt to A and A accepts a lower sum in discharge of A's duty. As Lord Denning MR later noted, there are good reasons for thinking that such a restriction is unjustified in principle; the decision in *Foakes* itself can also be explained on a different basis. Nonetheless, no first instance judge, not even Denning J, would wish to have challenged the conventional understanding of *Foakes*. His Lordship, therefore, adopted one of his favourite tactics: the inconvenient rule was characterized as arising at common law; and an equitable exception was found. That equitable concept was said to be derived from decisions such as *Hughes v Metropolitan Rwy Co*. As will be seen, however, the principle applied in that case is quite different to one based on A's acceptance of a substitute performance and, indeed, has no application to cases such as *Foakes* or *High Trees*.

2–030 The classic case of estoppel, certainly, is one where A is prevented from denying the truth of a particular representation, made to B, on which B has relied in such a way that B would now suffer a detriment were A to go back on A's representation. This point is made well in the High Court of Australia case of *Waltons Stores (Interstate) Ltd v Maher*,[15] where Brennan J explains that the effect of an estoppel by representation is "not to create a right in one party against the other; it is to establish the state of affairs by reference to which the legal relationship between them is ascertained".[16] That principle cannot, however, be applied where A has instead made a promise as to A's future action, as there is then no statement of fact or law the truth of which A can be prevented from denying. The term "estoppel", as Denning J noted in the *High Trees* case, is an awkward one to apply to a principle that can give some legal effect to a promise of A. Certainly, the early cases, such as *Hughes v Metropolitan Railway* do

---

15 *Waltons Stores (Interstate) Ltd v Maher*.

16 *Waltons Stores (Interstate) Ltd v Maher* at 414 (Brennan J).

not themselves use the label "estoppel". The term "estoppel" has however stuck, in relation to promissory estoppel, as it captures the idea that A is precluded, or stopped, from acting in a particular way.

Indeed, if we take the formulation of promissory estoppel given by Goff J in *BP v Hunt*,[17] the label "equitable estoppel" also makes some sense, as the doctrine operates specifically to stop A from *exercising a legal entitlement, as against B, in a particular way*. This explains why, in *Thorner v Major*,[18] Lord Walker stated that promissory estoppel "must be based on an existing legal relationship (usually a contract, but not necessarily a contract relating to land)".[19] A's promise might be in relation to a legal entitlement, such as a right or a power, arising under a contract, or one which derives from some other source.[20] It is often said that the existence of a legal relationship is itself an independent element of promissory estoppel although we think the better view is that the need for A's promise to be in relation to some legal entitlement is an "inherent limit",[21] based on a conception of promissory estoppel as a restraint as to how A exercises a legal entitlement. **2-031**

The modern doctrine thus contrasts with the classic form of estoppel by representation: it does not prevent A *from pleading and proving facts* evidencing a particular state of affairs;[22] rather, promissory estoppel specifically prevents A from exercising a legal entitlement which A would otherwise be free to exercise against B. There is something of an irony here. In *High Trees* itself, Denning J did not formulate his principle in a way which is limited to promises that related to A's legal entitlements. Nor did he necessarily see the principle as purely equitable, rather regarding it as a principle arising from the "fusion of law and equity". Nonetheless, the orthodox modern doctrine of promissory estoppel, as encapsulated in Goff J's formulation, *is* consistent with equity's characteristic function of restraining A's exercise of legal entitlements. Indeed, it fits very well with the model set out in Chapter 1, as it does not, for example, deny that A has a particular right against B; it instead controls A's assertion of such a right. This explains, for example, why promissory estoppel can sometimes have a "suspensory" effect: it prevents A from asserting A's right against B to the extent necessary to avoid detriment to B, but as A's right remains, it can be asserted in the future when B has had the opportunity to avoid such detriment. **2-032**

Nonetheless, the somewhat dubious foundation of the *High Trees* case has led to some continued uncertainty in the law. First, the application of promissory estoppel to cases where B owes A a debt, and A promises to accept payment of a lower sum remains unclear, as the fundamental tension between the House of Lords' decision in *Foakes v Beer* and Denning J's approach in *High Trees* is yet to be resolved. Second, the role of detriment in promissory estoppel is not entirely settled—it is, of course, part of Goff J's formulation but, as McFarlane notes, it is difficult to find such detriment in a case where B simply relies on A's promise to do less than B is obliged to do under B's contract with A. **2-033**

C. A "Shield Not a Sword"

i. England: the orthodox position

Where B can establish a promissory estoppel, equitable relief is granted as necessary to prevent A from exercising A's legal entitlement against B. In some cases, as in *Hughes v Metropolitan Rwy Co*, it may be that B applies for an injunction to prevent such action by A: in that limited sense, promissory **2-034**

17 See para.2-017.
18 *Thorner v Major* [2009] UKHL 18, [2009] 1 W.L.R. 776.
19 *Thorner v Major* at [61].
20 McGhee (ed.), *Snell's Equity*, 34th edn (2020), para.12-026; *Waltons Stores (Interstate) Ltd v Maher*.
21 McGhee (ed.), *Snell's Equity*, 34th edn (2020), para.12-026.
22 See further J. Hudson, "The True Purpose of Estoppel by Representation" (2015) 32 J.C.L. 275; J. Hudson, "The Price of Coherence in Estoppels" (2017) 39 S.L.R. 1.

estoppel can ground a claim by B. Further, it is possible for B to use promissory estoppel to prevent A from asserting a defence to an independent claim of B, and so "while [B] cannot in terms found a cause of action on an estoppel, he may, as a result of being able to rely on an estoppel, succeed on a cause of action on which, without being able to rely on the estoppel, he would necessarily have failed."[23] It is therefore not strictly accurate to say that promissory estoppel can only operate as a defence.

2-035 However, the orthodox position, which still prevails in English law, is that a promissory estoppel cannot generate a new duty of A to B, and thus can only be used to protect B against an entitlement which A would otherwise be able to assert against B. This restriction on the orthodox scope of promissory estoppel has been expressed in different ways: that promissory estoppel is not a cause of action,[24] it is a defensive or negative equity,[25] or can only be a shield and not a sword.[26] The crucial point, however, is that the focus of the doctrine is on restraining A's exercise of a legal entitlement against B.

2-036 In *Combe v Combe*,[27] for example, in denying B's attempt to enforce A's promise to pay maintenance to B, Denning LJ stated that:[28]

> Much as I am inclined to favour the principle stated in the *High Trees* case, it is important that it should not be stretched too far, lest it should be endangered. That principle does not create new causes of action where none existed before. It only prevents a party from insisting upon its strict legal rights, when it would be unjust to allow him to enforce them, having regard to the dealings between the parties. . . . Seeing that the principle never stands alone as giving a cause of action in itself, it can never do away with the necessity of consideration when that is an essential part of the cause of action. The doctrine of consideration is too firmly fixed to be overthrown by a side-wind.

2-037 The reference to the doctrine of consideration can be seen as reflecting a desire that the equitable doctrine of promissory estoppel should not be permitted to undermine the requirements imposed at common law for an enforceable contract. We will consider this concern when considering the development of promissory estoppel in Australia, and when looking at proprietary estoppel in Chapter 4. Certainly, if promissory estoppel is limited, as it continues to be in England, to restraining A's exercise of a legal entitlement as against B, it is clearly not establishing general rules for the enforcement of agreements; rather than setting such primary rules, promissory estoppel remains as a secondary doctrine, thus fulfilling a characteristically equitable function.

ii. Australia: going beyond orthodoxy?

2-038 The orthodox limitation of promissory estoppel to being a restraint on A's exercise of a legal entitlement has come under pressure in the Australian case-law,[29] chiefly as a result of a complex, and contested, decision of the High Court of Australia.

---

23 *Amalgamated Investment and Property Co Ltd v Texas Commerce International Bank Ltd* [1982] Q.B. 84 (CA) 132 (Brandon LJ).

24 See, e.g. *Combe v Combe* [1951] 2 K.B. 215 at 219–220.

25 Handley, *Estoppel by Conduct and Election*, 2nd edn (2016), paras 13–029, 13–043.

26 All of which is set out in *Waltons Stores (Interstate) Ltd v Maher* (1988) 164 C.L.R. 387 at 399–402 (Mason CJ and Wilson J), referring to cases such as *Combe* at 220 (Denning LJ). See also D. Jackson "Estoppel as a Sword" (1965) 81 L.Q.R. 223; M. Barnes "Estoppels as Swords" [2011] L.M.C.L.W. 372; R. Halson "The Offensive Limits of Promissory Estoppel" [1999] L.M.C.L.Q. 256.

27 [1951] 2 K.B. 215.

28 [1951] 2 K.B. 215 at 219–220.

29 About this debate see generally: J.C. Campbell, "Waltons v Maher: History, Unconscientiousness and Remedy — The Minimum Equity" (2013) 7(3) J. Eq. 171; A. Robertson, "Three Models of Promissory Estoppel" (2013) 7(3) J. Eq. 226; J. Ward, "Sir Anthony Mason Oration" (Speech, Blue Mountains Law Society 2018 Succession Conference, 8 September 2018)

Waltons Stores (Interstate) Ltd v Maher

(1988) 164 C.L.R. 387 at 392, 397, 399–400, 406–408, 423–424, 425–426, 428–429, 447–448, 458

B, an owner of land, entered into negotiations with A, a retail company, to grant A a lease of the land, so that A could operate a business on the land. The planned arrangements involved B demolishing an existing building on the land and constructing a new one to A's specifications. Negotiations progressed and a draft lease was prepared, to which B suggested amendments. On 7 November, B's solicitor told A's solicitor that the agreement had to be concluded very soon if building work was to start as planned and that B did not wish to demolish part of the existing building until it was clear there were no problems with the planned lease. A's solicitors told B that B's suggested amendments were acceptable, and sent B fresh document including those amendments, along with a covering letter stating that they had not yet obtained A's approval to the amendments, but believed that "approval will be forthcoming. We will let you know tomorrow if any amendments are not agreed to." B signed the documents and returned them to A's solicitors and proceeded with the demolition work. Later in November, A had second thoughts about the lease and advised its solicitors to "go slow". In December, A became aware that B had started the demolition work. In January, B began construction of the new building. Neither A nor A's solicitors told B of any objections until January, at which point A's solicitors informed B that A would not proceed to exchange contracts. As a result of the lack of exchanged signed documents, there was no contractual agreement between the parties. However, the first instance judge, and the New South Wales Court of Appeal, found that A was estopped from denying the existence of a binding contract. **2–039**

MASON C.J. AND WILSON J.: The issue in this appeal is whether, in the light of the facts, [A] is estopped from denying the existence of a binding contract that it would take a lease of [B's] premises at Nowra and, if so, whether [B] can support the order made by the primary judge, affirmed by the New South Wales Court of Appeal, that [A] pay to [B] damages in lieu of specific performance of an agreement for a lease . . . **2–040**

. . . [On the evidence in the case] it would be difficult to sustain a finding that [B] actually believed that contracts had been exchanged or that a binding contract had come into existence. There was no evidence that [B] relied on [A's solicitors'] failure to notify amendments on 8 November as indicating that contracts had been exchanged. And, in any event, in the circumstances, such a belief, if it existed, could scarcely be described as a reasonably held belief in the absence of inquiry from, and confirmation by, [B's solicitors] . . . **2–041**

This brings us to the doctrine of promissory estoppel on which [B] relied in this Court to sustain the judgment in [B's] favour **2–042**

There has been for many years a reluctance to allow promissory estoppel to become the vehicle for positive enforcement of a representation by a party that he would do something in the future. Promissory estoppel, it has been said, is a defensive equity . . . **2–043**

. . . [B] asks us to drive promissory estoppel one step further by enforcing directly in the absence of a pre-existing relationship of any kind a non-contractual promise on which the representee has relied to his detriment. For the purposes of discussion, we shall assume that there was such a promise in the present case. The principal objection to the enforcement of such a promise is that it would outflank principles of the law of contract . . . **2–044**

[MASON C.J. and WILSON J. then considered some English and Australian decisions, including some applying proprietary estoppel[30]] One may therefore discern in the cases a common thread which links them together, namely, the principle that equity will come to the relief of a plaintiff who has acted to his detriment on the basis of a basic assumption in relation to which the other party to the transaction has 'played such a part in the adoption of the assumption' that it would be unfair or unjust if he were left free to ignore it'.[31] Equity comes to the relief of the plaintiff on the footing that it would be unconscionable conduct on the part of the other party to ignore the assumption . . .

The foregoing review of the doctrine of promissory estoppel indicates that the doctrine extends to the enforcement of voluntary promises on the footing that a departure from the basic assumptions underlying the transaction between the parties must be unconscionable. As failure to fulfil a promise does not of itself **2–045**

---

https://www.supremecourt.justice.nsw.gov.au/Documents/Publications/Speeches/2018%20Speeches/Ward_20180908.pdf; E. Bant and M. Bryan, "Fact, Future and Fiction: Risk and Reasonable Reliance in Estoppel" (2015) 35(3) O.J.L.S. 427.

30 See paras 3–003 to 3–033.

31 *Grundt v Great Boulder Mining Co* (1937) 59 C.L.R. 641 at 675 (Dixon J.).

amount to unconscionable conduct, mere reliance on an executory promise to do something, resulting in the promise changing his position or suffering detriment, does not bring promissory estoppel into play. Something more would be required . . .

2-046 . . . the crucial question remains: was [A] entitled to stand by in silence when it must have known that [B was] proceeding on the assumption that [B] had an agreement and that completion of the exchange was a formality? The mere exercise of its legal right not to exchange contracts could not be said to amount to unconscionable conduct on the part of [A]. But there were two other factors present in the situation which require to be taken into consideration. The first was the element of urgency that pervaded the negotiation of the terms of the proposed lease . . .

2-047 The second factor of importance is that [B] executed the counterpart deed and it was forwarded to [A's] solicitor on 11 November. The assumption on which [B] acted thereafter was that completion of the necessary exchange was a formality. The next their solicitor heard from [A] was a letter from its solicitors dated 19 January, informing him that [A] did not intend to proceed with the matter. It had known, at least since 10 December, that costly work was proceeding on the site.

2-048 It seems to us, in light of these considerations, that [A] was under an obligation to communicate with [B] within a reasonable time after receiving the counterpart deed and certainly when it learnt on 10 December that demolition was proceeding . . . [A's] inaction, in all the circumstances, constituted clear encouragement or inducement to [B] to continue to act on the basis of the assumption which [B] had made. It was unconscionable for it, knowing that [B was] exposing [B] to detriment by acting on the basis of a false assumption, to adopt a course of inaction which encouraged [B] in the course [B] had adopted. To express the point in the language of promissory estoppel [A] is estopped in all the circumstances from retreating from its implied promise to complete the contract.

2-049 BRENNAN J.: [Having considered some English and Australian decisions, including some applying proprietary estoppel][32]

2-050 The unconscionable conduct which it is the object of equity to prevent is the failure of a party, who has induced the adoption of the assumption or expectation and who knew or intended that it would be relied on, to fulfil the assumption or expectation or otherwise to avoid the detriment which that failure would occasion. The object of the equity is not to compel the party bound to fulfil the assumption or expectation; it is to avoid the detriment which, if the assumption or expectation goes unfulfilled, will be suffered by the party who has been induced to act or to abstain from acting thereon.

2-051 If this object is kept steadily in mind, the concern that a general application of the principle of equitable estoppel would make non-contractual promises enforceable as contractual promises can be allayed . . .

2-052 . . . there are differences between a contract and an equity created by estoppel. A contractual obligation is created by the agreement of the parties; an equity created by estoppel may be imposed irrespective of any agreement by the party bound. A contractual obligation must be supported by consideration; an equity crated by estoppel need not be supported by what is, strictly speaking, consideration. The measure of a contractual obligation depend on the terms of the contract and the circumstances to which it applies; the measure of an equity created by estoppel varies according to what is necessary to prevent detriment resulting from unconscionable conduct.

2-053 . . . there is a logical difficulty in limiting the principle [of equitable estoppel] so that it applies only to promises to suspend or extinguish existing rights. If a promise by A not to enforce an existing right against B is to confer an equitable right on B to compel fulfilment of the promise, why should B be denied the same protection in similar circumstances if the promise is intended to create a new legal right against A? There is no logical distinction to be drawn between a change in legal relationships effected by a promise which extinguishes a right and a change in legal relationships effected by a promise which creates one. Why should an equity of the kind to which *Combe v Combe* refers be regarded as a shield but not a sword?...

2-054 Moreover, unless the cases of proprietary estoppel are attributed to a different equity from that which explains the cases of promissory estoppel, the enforcement of promises to create new proprietary rights cannot be reconciled with a limitation on the enforcement of other promises. If it be unconscionable for an owner of property in certain circumstances to fail to fulfil a non-contractual promise that he will convey an interest in the property to another, is there any reason in principle why it is not unconscionable in similar circumstances for a person to fail to fulfil a non-contractual promise that he will confer a non-proprietary

[32] See paras 3-003 to 3-033.

legal right on another. It does not accord with principle to hold that equity, in seeking to avoid detriment occasioned by unconscionable conduct, can give relief in some cases but not in others . . .

In my opinion, to establish an equitable estoppel, it is necessary for a plaintiff to prove that (1) the plaintiff assumed that a particular legal relationship then existed between the plaintiff and the defendant or expected that a particular legal relationship would exist between them and, in the latter case, that the defendant would not be free to withdraw from the expected legal relationship; (2) the defendant has induced the plaintiff to adopt that assumption or expectation; (3) the plaintiff acts or abstains from acting in reliance on the assumption or expectation; (4) the defendant knew or intended him to do so; (5) the plaintiff's action or inaction will occasion detriment if the assumption or expectation is not fulfilled; and (6) the defendant has failed to act to avoid that detriment whether by fulfilling the assumption or expectation or otherwise . . . **2–055**

This is such a case . . . The retention of the counterpart deed [sent to A by B] and the absence of any demur as to the schedule of finishes or terms of the deed was tantamount to a promise by [A] that it would complete the exchange . . . **2–056**

DEANE J.: . . . [Summarised his analysis of promissory estoppel thus:] The unity, at law and in equity, of the general doctrine of estoppel by conduct was clearly established prior to the introduction of the Judicature Act system. The general proposition that the doctrine of estoppel by conduct did not extend to a representation or assumption of future fact was developed, in the context of the accepted unity of that doctrine, as applying indifferently both in equity and at law. There is no reason, in authority or in principle, for introducing into a fused system a dichotomy between equity and law in those cases where estoppel by conduct, under the nomenclature of promissory estoppel, is recognized as extending to at least some representations or assumptions about future fact. Nor, in a fused system where equitable and legal remedies are all generally available, is there any pragmatic reason why the application of the doctrine of estoppel by conduct to preclude departure, in some circumstances, from a representation or assumption of a future state of affairs should be seen as an exclusively equitable development. Finally, once it is recognized that the doctrine of estoppel is one of substantive law and equity, there is no reason why that doctrine cannot be applied as effectively in relation to a representation or assumption of a future state of affairs as to an existing state of affairs. **2–057**

[DEANE J., differing from MASON C.J. and WILSON J. on this point,[33] found on the facts that B had relied on the reasonable belief that there was already a contract between A and B, and the holdings below could be supported on that basis.] **2–058**

GAUDRON J.: Common law or evidentiary estoppel compels adherence to an assumption of fact by denying the person estopped the right to assert a contrary matter of fact. By so doing, it may operate to fashion a set of facts by reference to which is imposed a liability which otherwise does not exist . . . **2–059**

Equitable estoppel operates so as to compel adherence to an assumption as to rights. Sometimes that adherence can only be compelled by the recognition of an equitable entitlement to a positive right in the person claiming the benefit of the estoppel and the enforcement of correlative duties on the part of the person against whom the estoppel is successfully raised . . . Where equity compels adherence to an assumption in this manner, the resulting estoppel is generally referred to as "proprietary estoppel". On other occasions adherence to an assumption as to rights may be compelled by precluding the person estopped from asserting existing rights. It is in this manner that "promissory estoppel" has generally operated . . . **2–060**

[GAUDRON J., like DEANE J., found on the facts that B had relied on the reasonable belief that there was already a contract between A and B, as B believed that the exchange of contacts had occurred, and A was in part responsible for that belief of B by A's "imprudence in failing to inform [B] that exchange might not occur". A was therefore estopped from asserting any matter contrary to that assumption that exchange had occurred.] **2–061**

Waltons Stores is a controversial case as, in the analyses of Mason CJ and Wilson J, as well as those of Brennan and Deane JJ, it is accepted that the principles that underlie promissory estoppel can be used not merely to restrain A's exercise of an entitlement, but to generate a cause of action for B which can compel A to act in a particular way. Certainly, there are a large number of Australian decisions, **2–062**

---

33 At 439.

after *Waltons Stores*, in which a court has accepted that it is possible to respond to a successful promissory estoppel claim by ordering A to exercise a power in B's favour, or to otherwise compel A to act to protect B where B has relied to B's detriment on A's promise.[34] The legacy of the case is however contested in Australia,[35] not least because of the judges' disagreement as to the appropriate characterisation of the facts. According to Deane and Gaudron JJ, B had relied on a belief that there was *already* an enforceable contract between the parties, rather than on a belief that A *would* exercise its power to enter into such a contract with B, and so there was no strict need for B to invoke a promise-based principle. Moreover, as we will see in Chapter 4, it is accepted, even in English law, that *proprietary* estoppel can generate a cause of action for B which can compel A to act in a particular way, and the analyses of Mason CJ and Wilson J, as well as those of Brennan and Deane JJ, make use of proprietary estoppel cases to support an argument that equitable estoppel more generally (including promissory estoppel) can give rise to a cause of action. Whilst there are supporters of taking such a unified approach to equitable estoppel,[36] it could be argued that such an approach illegitimately blurs the boundary between proprietary and promissory estoppel and there is certainly some judicial caution, in Australia[37] as well as in England,[38] to unifying different doctrines in this way.[39]

2-063 The different analyses in *Waltons Stores* raise some important points about the functions of equity, and its relationship with common law. First, we can consider the function of promissory estoppel. As we have seen, Brennan J directly challenges the grounds for limiting the doctrine to "promises to suspend or extinguish existing rights", stating that "[t]here is no logical distinction to be drawn between a change in legal relationships effected by a promise which extinguishes a right and a change in legal relationships effected by a promise which creates one." This might seem to challenge the validity of our more general observation that equitable doctrines, characteristically, restrain the exercise of legal entitlements. Two points can be made, however, in response. First, there may well be good grounds for distinguishing rules which provide B with a defence to a right of A from rules which determine when duties arise: at common law, for example, waiver can provide B with a defence even if such consent, by itself, does not give rise to a new duty; similarly, B's contributory negligence can give A a partial defence, even if B does not owe a duty of care to A.[40] Second, even if promissory estoppel is allowed to generate a cause of action then, on the six point formulation given by Brennan J later in his judgment[41] it is still limited to cases where A's promise is to enter into a particular legal relationship with B. This goes beyond the "orthodox" scope of promissory estoppel, as applied in English law, and goes beyond the restraint of A's legal entitlements. Nonetheless, as suggested in the following extract, it is still consistent with the supplementary, or secondary nature of equity.

---

34 See, e.g. *E K Nominees Pty Ltd v Woolworths Ltd* [2006] NSWSC 1172 at [213], [281] (White J); *ACN 074 971 109 (as trustee for the Argot Unit Trust) v The National Mutual Life Association of Australasia Ltd* (2008) 21 V.R. 351 at [152]–[153], [167]–[172]. In *Cosmopolitan Hotel (Vic) Pty Ltd v Crown Melbourne Ltd* (2014) 45 V.R. 77, the promissory estoppel operated to bind A either to allow B to extend a lease or pay compensation to B. No equitable estoppel was found by the High Court on the facts: (2016) 260 C.L.R. 1.

35 See, e.g. *Saleh v Romanous* [2010] 79 N.S.W.L.R. 453 at [74], see also at [62], [73] (Handley AJA, Giles JA and Sackville AJA agreeing); *DHJPM Pty Ltd v Blackthorn Resources Ltd* [2011] 83 N.S.W.L.R. 728 at [93] (Handley AJA); *Hammond v JP Morgan Trust Australia* [2012] NSWCA 295 at [26] (Meagher JA, Basten JA and Bergin CJ in Eq agreeing).

36 See, e.g. E. Bant and M. Bryan, "Fact, Future and Fiction: Risk and Reasonable Reliance in Estoppel" (2015) 35(3) O.J.L.S. 427.

37 See, e.g. *Saleh v Romanous* and *Crown Melbourne Ltd v Cosmopolitan Hotel (Vic) Pty Ltd* (2016) 260 C.L.R. 1 where Keane J at [147] distinguishes between proprietary and promissory estoppel.

38 See, e.g. *Tinkler v HMRC* [2021] UKSC 39 at [28] (Lord Burrows).

39 See too B. McFarlane, "Understanding Equitable Estoppel: From Metaphors to Better Laws" (2013) 66 *Current Legal Problems* 267; J. Hudson, "The Price of Coherence in Estoppels" (2017) 39 S.L.R. 1.

40 See more generally R. Stevens, "Defenses" in A. Gold et al (eds) *The Oxford Handbook of the New Private Law* (OUP, 2020), Ch.32.

41 See para.2-055.

Ben McFarlane, "Equity and the Justification of Private Rights" in Michael Crawford et al (eds) *Justifying Private Rights* (Hart Publishing, 2020), pp.221, 239–240

It may nonetheless be possible, however, to justify Brennan J's focus on promises that relate to rights. It can be argued, for example, that the existence of certain legal powers, provided by private law (such as the power to transfer a right, or to enter a contract), whilst advantageous overall, carries certain risks: a party may abuse such a power by, for example, causing another to suffer a detriment through reasonable reliance on a promise that such a power will be exercised. A second-order rule can then control the risk inherent in the powers established by the primary legal rules, by offering some protection to the relying party. It can then be argued that the "shock" to the conscience of the court, justifying intervention, does not come merely from the fact that B has been left to suffer a detriment. After all, as the law does not usually protect B from economic loss, even where A has acted carelessly, it is difficult to sustain the argument that we all owe each other a duty not to cause one another loss thorough any form of induced reliance. Rather, the "shock" is more specific and comes from the risk of A's taking advantage of, or otherwise abusing, the existence of certain primary legal rules . . . The court's intervention is not about protecting B's pre-existing entitlement or enforcing A's pre-existing duty; it is rather concerned with mitigating a risk that comes from the existence of the power-conferring primary rules that form a key part of private law. **2–064**

Second, it should be noted that some Australian decisions have gone beyond the limit imposed by Brennan J and have allowed equitable estoppel to give rise to a cause of action even where A's promise to B is not that A will enter into a particular legal relationship with B.[42] At this point, it becomes harder to see the doctrine as fulfilling a characteristically equitable function. This does not necessarily mean, however, that equitable estoppel is undermining contract law in such cases. As noted in *Waltons Stores* by Mason CJ and Wilson J, as well as by Deane J, it is possible to distinguish equitable estoppel from contract law, even if both doctrines operate as means by which A can come under a duty to B as a result of a promise made by A to B. This can be done by focussing on the distinct aim of equitable estoppel as a means to prevent B's suffering a detriment, rather than as a doctrine which imposes a duty on A to perform A's agreement with B. As we will see in Chapter 4, this point is significant in English law, when considering the role of proprietary estoppel. It also shows that the distinction between equitable estoppel and contract law can be made without regarding the former as playing a characteristically equitable role of restraining the exercise of rights, or of responding to a potential abuse of the power to enter into legal relationships. This is important on Deane J's analysis in *Waltons Stores*, which, in the spirit of Denning J's judgment in the *High Trees* case, seeks to outline a set of principles which apply at common law as well as in equity. **2–065**

3. Fiduciary Loyalty

A. What is Fiduciary Loyalty?

i. The duty stated

A fiduciary must avoid being in a position where her personal interest may come into conflict with the principal's interest that the fiduciary is bound to protect,[43] and must avoid being in a position where **2–066**

[42] See, e.g. *W v G* (1996) 20 Fam. L.R. 49 and *Australian Crime Commission v Gray v National Crime Authority* [2003] NSWCA 318. For discussion see A. Robertson, "Three Models of Promissory Estoppel" (2013) 7 J. Eq. 226.

[43] *Bray v Ford* [1896] A.C. 44 at 51; *Boardman v Phipps* [1967] 2 A.C. 46 at 123; *Swain v Law Society* [1982] 1 W.L.R. 17 at 30–31; *FHR European Ventures LLP v Cedar Capital Partners LLC* [2014] UKSC 45; [2015] A.C. 250 at [5].

there may be a conflict between the interests of multiple principals.[44] A summary was given by the Supreme Court in *FHR European Ventures LLP v Mankarious*:[45]

> The following three principles are not in doubt, and they are taken from the classic summary of the law in the judgment of Millett LJ in *Bristol and West Building Society v Mothew*.[46] First, an agent owes a fiduciary duty to his principal because he is "someone who has undertaken to act for or on behalf of [his principal] in a particular matter in circumstances which give rise to a relationship of trust and confidence". Secondly, as a result, an agent "must not make a profit out of his trust" and "must not place himself in a position in which his duty and his interest may conflict" – and, as Lord Upjohn pointed out in *Phipps v Boardman*,[47] the former proposition is "part of the [latter] wider rule". Thirdly, "a fiduciary who acts for two principals with potentially conflicting interests without the informed consent of both is in breach of the obligation of undivided loyalty; he puts himself in a position where his duty to one principal *may* conflict with his duty to the other".

2-067 In this book, we use the label of "fiduciary duty" to mean a duty to avoid conflicts of interest that is owed by one who has undertaken to act for another and in whom trust and confidence have been reposed. We therefore use the label "fiduciary" to refer to a person who is subject to that duty. However, these labels have been used in different ways over time, and judges and academics do not always agree with how this label should be used.

Wood v Commercial First Business Ltd

Court of Appeal [2022] Ch. 123 at [36]–[37]

2-068 DAVID RICHARDS L.J. (with whom MALES and LAING L.JJ. agreed):. . . "Fiduciary relationship" is a protean term, capable of covering a wide range of different rights and obligations. It is worth quoting from the passage in *Finn: Fiduciary Obligations*...:

> "On the modern usage of 'fiduciary', Sealy concluded that it is not definitive of a single class of relationships to which fixed rules and principles apply. Rather, its use has generally been descriptive, providing a veil behind which individual rules and principles have been developed. This conclusion – an incontestable one – is the starting point of this work. In the following pages it will be suggested that it is meaningless to talk of fiduciary relationships as such. Once one looks to the rules and principles which actually have been evolved, it quickly becomes apparent that it is pointless to describe a person – or for that matter a power – as being fiduciary unless at the same time it is said for the purposes of which particular rules and principles that description is being used. These rules are everything. The description 'fiduciary', nothing. It has gone much the same way as did the general descriptive term 'trust' one hundred and fifty years ago."

2-069 The term "fiduciary relationship" is most commonly used with respect to well-established categories, such as trustee and beneficiary, director or manager and company, employer and employee, and principal and agent where the agent is authorised to act for and exercise powers of the principal. Subject to agreement to the contrary, those are relationships to which what might be called the full panoply of fiduciary obligations apply.

---

44 *Clark Boyce v Mouat* [1994] 1 A.C. 428 (PC); *Bristol & West Building Society v Mothew* [1998] Ch. 1 at 19; *FHR European Ventures LLP v Cedar Capital Partners LLC* [2014] UKSC 45; [2015] A.C. 250 at [5].

45 *FHR European Ventures LLP v Cedar Capital Partners LLC* [2014] UKSC 45; [2015] A.C. 250 at [5].

46 [1998] Ch. 1 at 18.

47 [1967] 2 A.C. 46 at 123.

ii. The duty distinguished from other duties

In the passage from *Bristol and West Building Society v Mothew*,[48] set out below, Millett LJ stresses the importance of distinguishing clearly between uniquely fiduciary duties and duties which trustees, other fiduciaries, and *non-fiduciaries* can owe, such as a duty of care and skill. In this case, the defendant solicitor acted for the purchasers of a house and for the claimant building society, which made the purchasers a loan towards the purchase of the house, on condition that the balance of the purchase price would be paid by the purchasers without further borrowing. The loan was to be secured by a mortgage over the house. The claimant instructed the defendant to report any proposal by the purchasers to create a second mortgage or otherwise borrow money to finance part of the purchase price. The solicitor knew they were arranging to create a second charge on the property to secure an existing debt, but failed to report this, due to an oversight. The claimant lent the money, the purchase was completed, the borrowers defaulted on their mortgage repayments, the claimant foreclosed, and the house was sold at a loss. The claimant sought to recover its loss on the transaction from the defendant. A simple claim for breach of contract, or negligence, was available but the courts had held that, in such a claim, a party cannot recover losses which are attributable to a general fall in the housing market. The claimant sought to argue that such limits on recovery did not apply to a claim for breach of fiduciary duty. The Court of Appeal found that, in any case, the defendant had committed no breach of fiduciary duty since his breach consisted simply of a failure to take due care and was unconnected to the fact that he was also acting for the purchasers. **2–070**

Bristol and West Building Society v Mothew

Court of Appeal [1998] Ch. 1 at 16, 18

MILLETT L.J.: Despite the warning given by Fletcher Moulton L.J. in *Re Coomber*,[49] this branch of the law has been bedevilled by unthinking resort to verbal formulae. It is therefore necessary to begin by defining one's terms. The expression "fiduciary duty" is properly confined to those duties which are peculiar to fiduciaries and the breach of which attracts legal consequences differing from those consequent upon the breach of other duties. Unless the expression is so limited it is lacking in practical utility. In this sense it is obvious that not every breach of duty by a fiduciary is a breach of fiduciary duty. I would endorse the observations of Southin J in *Girardet v Crease & Co*:[50] **2–071**

> "The word 'fiduciary' is flung around now as if it applied to all breaches of duty by solicitors, directors of companies and so forth. . . . That a lawyer can commit a breach of the special duty [of a fiduciary] . . . by entering into a contract with the client without full disclosure . . . and so forth is clear. But to say that simple carelessness in giving advice is such a breach is a perversion of words."

These remarks were approved by La Forest J in *LAC Minerals Ltd v International Corona Resources Ltd* where he said: "not every legal claim arising out of a relationship with fiduciary incidents will give rise to a claim for breach of fiduciary duty."[51] **2–072**

It is similarly inappropriate to apply the expression to the obligation of a trustee or other fiduciary to use proper skill and care in the discharge of his duties. If it is confined to cases where the fiduciary nature of the duty has special legal consequences, then the fact that the source of the duty is to be found in equity rather than the common law does not make it a fiduciary duty. The common law and equity each developed the duty of care, but they did so independently of each other and the standard of care required is not always the same. But they influenced each other, and today the substance of the resulting obligations is more significant than their particular historic origin. . . **2–073**

---

48 [1998] Ch. 1 at 16.
49 [1911] 1 Ch. 723 at 728.
50 (1987) 11 B.C.L.R. (2d) 361 at 362.
51 (1989) 61 D.L.R. (4th) 14 at 28.

2-074 This leaves those duties which are special to fiduciaries and which attract those remedies which are peculiar to the equitable jurisdiction and are primarily restitutionary or restorative rather than compensatory. A fiduciary is someone who has undertaken to act for or on behalf of another in a particular matter in circumstances which give rise to a relationship of trust and confidence. The distinguishing obligation of a fiduciary is the obligation of loyalty. The principal is entitled to the single-minded loyalty of his fiduciary. This core liability has several facets. A fiduciary must act in good faith; he must not make a profit out of his trust; he must not place himself in a position where his duty and his interest may conflict; he may not act for his own benefit or the benefit of a third person without the informed consent of his principal. This is not intended to be an exhaustive list, but it is sufficient to indicate the nature of fiduciary obligations. They are the defining characteristics of the fiduciary. As Dr. Finn pointed out in his classic work *Fiduciary Obligations*,[52] he is not subject to fiduciary obligations because he is a fiduciary; it is because he is subject to them that he is a fiduciary.

2-075 A similar approach to "fiduciary duty" is taken in the following extract.

Howard v Commissioner of Taxation

High Court of Australia (2014) 253 C.L.R. 83 at [56]–[57]

2-076 HAYNE and CRENNAN J.J.: . . . the appellant was bound not to obtain any unauthorised benefit from the relationship and not to be in a position of conflict. These obligations are peculiar to fiduciaries.[53] The obligations are[54] proscriptive, not prescriptive. They are not[55] quasi-tortious duties to act solely in the best interest of the principal. Nor are they obligations directed only to providing redress for loss or damage proceed to have been suffered by the person to whom the duties are owed.

2-077 Whether there are two distinct obligations, or they are properly to be seen[56] as "one 'fundamental rule' [which] embodies two themes", need not be explored. It is convenient, for the purposes of this case, to treat the obligations as if they are distinct, while recognising that both may, and often will, be engaged by the one set of facts.

2-078 In the following excerpt, Charles Mitchell makes the important distinction between fiduciary duties and the duties of, for example, a trustee to comply with the terms on which property is held.

Charles Mitchell, "Stewardship of Property and Liability to Account"

[2014] Conv. 215, 216–218

2-079 Lawyers often use the term "fiduciary duty" to describe a duty of undivided loyalty owed by a person who has assumed a position of trust and responsibility towards a principal: he must subordinate his personal interests to the interests of his principal and must not serve several principals with conflicting interests. Lawyers also use the term in a different sense, to describe any duty owed by a trustee or a person resembling a trustee. These meanings of the term "fiduciary duty" can overlap, as trustees and other stewards often owe a duty of undivided loyalty to their beneficiaries and principals. But the meanings are not identical, since trustees and other stewards also owe other duties.[57]

2-080 For example, they owe a duty of care. This differs from their duty of undivided loyalty, which is why Millett L.J. said in *Bristol & West Building Society v Mothew* that it would be "inappropriate to apply the expression ["fiduciary"] to the obligation of a trustee . . . to use proper skill and care in the discharge of his

52 P.D. Finn, *Fiduciary Obligations* (Law Book Co, 1977), p.2.

53 *Breen v Williams* (1996) 186 C.L.R. 71 at 113. See also R. Austin, "Moulding the Content of Fiduciary Duties", in A. J. Oakley (ed.), *Trends in Contemporary Trust Law* (Clarendon Press, 1996), pp.153, 156; Conaglen, *Fiduciary Loyalty: Protecting the Due Performance of Non-Fiduciary Duties*, pp.39–40.

54 *Breen v Williams* at 113 (Gaudron and McHugh JJ).

55 *Pilmer v Duke Group Ltd (In Liq)* (2001) 207 C.L.R. at 198.

56 *Chan v Zacharia* (1984) 154 C.L.R. 178 at 198.

57 Conaglen, *Fiduciary Loyalty: Protecting the Due Performance of Non-Fiduciary Duties*, Ch.3.

duties."[58] There would be no objection to describing a trustee's duty of care as a "fiduciary duty", if it were clear that this meant no more than "duty of care owed by a trustee". But in many cases, this is not clear, because the term might also mean "duty of undivided loyalty". So this usage is best avoided.

The same point can be made about the rule that a steward of property must comply with the terms of his authority. Express trustees are required to do this. Indeed, the High Court of Australia has said that "perhaps the most important duty of a trustee is to obey the terms of the trust".[59] Hence one could describe this limit on their powers as a "fiduciary duty of compliance with instructions", meaning no more than "a duty of compliance owed by a trustee". But, again, this language may create the false impression that the rules which prevent stewards from exceeding their authority coincide with the rules which require them to be loyal. So, again, this usage should be avoided. 2-081

Consider these dicta. In *HMRC v Holland* Lord Walker referred to "the fiduciary duty that a company director owes to his company not to make an unauthorised distribution of capital";[60] in *Pitt v Holt* Mummery L.J. said that if a "disposition [by a power-holder] is a misapplication of property outside the scope of the power . . . that will be a breach of fiduciary duty";[61] in *Sinclair Investments (UK) Ltd v Versailles Trade Finance Ltd* Lord Neuberger M.R. said that "a person entrusted with another person's money for a specific purpose has fiduciary duties to the other person in respect of the use to which those moneys are put";[62] and in *Ross River Ltd v Waveley Commercial Ltd* Lloyd L.J. said that "the essence of the fiduciary duty" owed by a director was that the company's "assets should have been kept intact, without being depleted by unauthorised payments".[63] 2-082

In all of these passages, their Lordships describe unauthorised disposals of property as breaches of "fiduciary duty". What they mean is that a person charged with administering and applying property for another person's benefit may not exceed the terms of his authority when dealing with the property, and that if he does this he will be required to restore the missing property in the same way that a trustee is required to reconstitute a trust fund depleted by unauthorised disposals. What their Lordships do not mean is that acting beyond one's powers is in itself necessarily a disloyal thing to do. 2-083

Of course, one can imagine cases where a steward of property might exceed his powers with a disloyal intention. If a trustee or director misappropriates the trust funds or the company's property for himself then he may simultaneously exceed his authority and improperly prioritise his personal interests over the interests of the beneficiaries or the company. But in this situation there are two problems with the transaction and not one. 2-084

Charles Mitchell, "Good Faith, Self-Denial and Mandatory Trustee Duties"

(2018) 32 T.L.I. 92, 92–95

. . . Unfortunately, however, the law in this area is in a serious terminological mess that reflects a deeper failure to think clearly about the law's different goals and the ways in which these should be achieved. 2-085

Significant problems have been caused by the loose way in which courts have used the term "fiduciary duties". This term has been applied to a duty of undivided loyalty (meaning a duty to prioritise a principal's interests over one's own interests and the interests of other people) and a duty to act in good faith,[64] a duty of confidence, a duty to act in accordance with terms of one's engagement or "to obey instructions"[65] (which in trusts law translates into a duty owed by trustees to comply with the terms of a trust deed[66]), a duty to act for a proper purpose (if that is different from acting within the terms of an engagement, which 2-086

58 [1998] Ch. 1 at 16.
59 *Youyang Pty Ltd v Minter Ellison Morris Fletcher* (2003) 212 C.L.R. 484 at [32].
60 [2011] Bus. L.R. 111 at [121].
61 [2012] Ch. 132 at [237].
62 [2012] Ch. 453 at [34].
63 [2013] EWCA Civ 910 at [118].
64 *Bristol & West Building Society v Mothew* [1998] Ch. 1 at 18.
65 *Crocs Europe BV v Anderson* [2013] 1 Lloyd's Rep 1 at [47].
66 *Youyang Pty Ltd v Minter Ellison Morris Fletcher* at [32].

may be doubted[67]), a duty to act with reasonable skill and care, and a duty to take all and only relevant matters into account when exercising discretionary powers.[68]

2-087 Describing all these duties as "fiduciary duties" has created uncertainty and confusion. In particular cases, it is not always clear which of these duties is being referred to when a court speaks of a defendant owing a "fiduciary duty". It is also unclear what point is being made when a single descriptor – "fiduciary" – is applied to all of the duties. Does this denote that they are all variants or aspects of a single duty? That seems unlikely, given their clear differences of content. But in that case, what common feature do they possess?

2-088 A possible answer is that they can all be imposed on someone who is in a fiduciary relationship with a principal, but this does not tell us anything very interesting about most of them, because most of them can also be imposed on other people. The exception is the loyalty duty, which is only imposed on people in fiduciary relationships. This view can be found in Matthew Conaglen's book, where he also argues – controversially – that the point of imposing the loyalty duty is to support the performance of the other duties.[69]

2-089 Another possible answer is that all the duties can be imposed on someone in a fiduciary relationship with a principal, and that when they are imposed on such a person their content may be more onerous, or at any rate differently focussed, than it would be if they were imposed on somebody else. So the reasonableness of her actions may be assessed against an elevated and/or more specifically purposed standard of care, the conscionability of her actions may be assessed against an elevated and/or more specifically purposed standard of good faith, and so on. That view has been taken by His Honour Dyson Heydon,[70] Joshua Getzler,[71] Lionel Smith,[72] and by Richard Nolan and Matthew Conaglen in an article which appeared after Conaglen's book.[73]

Loyalty

2-090 When the courts speak of a fiduciary owing a duty of "loyalty" or "undivided loyalty",[74] they have in mind both a duty of self-denial, meaning a duty to subordinate the fiduciary's personal interests to the interests of her principal, and also a duty to subordinate other people's interests to the principal's interests. These duties are manifested in the self-dealing and fair dealing rules which invalidate contracts for the sale of property between principals and their fiduciaries,[75] in rules which prohibit fiduciaries from making a profit

---

67 *Pitt v Holt* [2012] Ch. 132 at [96] (Lloyd LJ): "Cases of a fraud on the power are similar to [an appointment to someone who is not within the class of objects] . . . since the true intended beneficiary, who is not an object of the power, is someone other than the nominal appointee."

68 Duty to perform a trust in accordance with its terms: *Sinclair Investments (UK) Ltd v Versailles Trade Finance Ltd (in admin rec)* [2012] Ch. 453 at [34]. Duty to act for a proper purpose: *Bishopsgate Investment Management Ltd (in liq) v Maxwell (No.2)* [1994] 1 All. E.R. 261 at 265. Duty to take all and only relevant matters into account: *Pitt v Holt* [2013] 2 A.C. 108 at [73]. Duty of care: *Silven Properties Ltd v Royal Bank of Scotland Plc* [2004] 1 W.L.R. 997 at [29]. Duty of confidence: *Generics (UK) Ltd (trading as Mylan) v Yeda Research and Development Co Ltd* [2013] F.S.R. 13 at [79].

69 Conaglen, *Fiduciary Loyalty: Protecting the Due Performance of Non-Fiduciary Duties*, developing ideas in M. Conaglen, "The Nature and Function of Fiduciary Loyalty" (2005) 121 L.Q.R. 452; critiqued by R. Lee, "In Search of the Nature and Function of Fiduciary Loyalty: Some Observations on Conaglen's Analysis" (2007) 27 O.J.L.S. 327 (imposition of the loyalty duty protects a principal from harm caused by a fiduciary's self-serving behaviour; any support thereby given to the performance of other duties is an additional but not the only point of imposing the loyalty duty; performance of other duties by a fiduciary is insufficient to absolve them from liability for breach of the loyalty duty).

70 J.D. Heydon, "Modern Fiduciary Liability: The Sick Man of Equity?" (2014) 20 T. & T. 1006.

71 J. Getzler, "Am I My Beneficiary's Keeper? Fusion and Loss-Based Fiduciary Remedies" in S. Degeling and J. Edelman (eds), *Equity in Commercial Law* (Lawbook Co, 2005).

72 L. Smith, "Aspects of Loyalty" (Research Paper, 27 July 2017), *https://ssrn.com/abstract=3009894*.

73 R. Nolan and M. Conaglen, "Good Faith: What Does It Mean for Fiduciaries and What Does It Tell Us About Them?" in E. Bant and M. Harding (eds), *Exploring Private Law* (Cambridge University Press, 2010), especially pp.320–321, developing R.C. Nolan, "Controlling Fiduciary Power" (2009) C.L.J. 293, pp.312–313. This appears to mark a departure from the position taken in Conaglen's book, where he seems to say that the content of duties other than the duty of loyalty, is the same for fiduciaries and non-fiduciaries, but that the law increases the chances that the other duties will be performed by imposing the loyalty duty.

74 As in, e.g. *FHR European Ventures v Cedar Capital* at [5]; *AIB Group (UK) Plc v Mark Redler & Co Solicitors* [2014] UKSC 58, [2015] A.C. 1503 at [51].

75 *Fox v Mackreth* (1791) 2 Cox. Eq. Cas. 320, 30 E.R. 148; *Tito v Waddell (No.2)* [1977] Ch. 106 at 240–244; *Barnsley v Noble* [2014] EWHC 2657 (Ch) at [261] ff (not disturbed on appeal: [2017] Ch. 191).

out of their position in other ways,[76] and in rules which prohibit fiduciaries from serving two principals with conflicting interests.[77] All of these rules apply by default to parties who are in a fiduciary relationship with a principal, but they can all be disapplied by agreement provided that the principal is fully informed and has not been subjected to improper pressure.[78]

iii. Content of fiduciary loyalty

While there may be growing acceptance that the label of "fiduciary" should be used only in relation to those duties are that uniquely fiduciary, different views have been taken in the cases and commentaries as to what those duties are. It is uncontroversial that a fiduciary cannot lawfully act where there is a conflict between her personal interests and her principal's interests, and that she cannot lawfully act where there is a conflict between the interests of two different principals whom she serves. Whether fiduciary loyalty has a larger content is debated and jurisdictions have taken different views about which duties are uniquely fiduciary.[79] Some jurisdictions have a "thick" conception of fiduciary loyalty, which encompasses further duties or requirements such as a duty of care and duty of good faith.[80] This is in distinction to a "thin" conception of fiduciary loyalty, which is only comprised of the requirement to avoid a profit by reason or use of position; to avoid conflicts between a fiduciary's self-interest and duty; and, duties owed to multiple principals. An example of which is the excerpt from Hayne and Crennan JJ's judgment in the High Court of Australia case of *Howard v Commissioner of Taxation*, set out above.[81] Some arguments in favour of the "thin" conception are based on a process of exclusion explained by Millett LJ in *Mothew*, according to which fiduciary duties are "those duties which are peculiar to fiduciaries".[82] So, for example, Conaglen argues that the duty to act for a proper purpose cannot be a fiduciary duty because it is a duty owed by other non-fiduciary powerholders, whether or not they hold their powers in a fiduciary capacity—a conclusion with which we agree as we believe that this duty is best understood not as an aspect of the rules forbidding conflicts of interest, but as a rule ensuring a power-holder's compliance with the terms according to which a power is held. **2-091**

Conaglen also contends, rightly in our view, that the rule which forbids fiduciaries from making an unauthorised profit from their position is an extension of the "no conflicts" rule, and should not be understood as a separate rule underpinned by another principle.[83] Others think differently,[84] however, and this matters because it affects our understanding of the reasons why constructive trusts are imposed on the proceeds of a breach of fiduciary duty. This is a difficult issue and, as we discuss **2-092**

76 *Keech v Sandford* (1726) Sel Cas Temp King 61, 25 E.R. 223; *Boardman v Phipps; FHR European Ventures v Cedar Capital*.

77 *Moody v Cox* [1917] Ch. 271; *Bristol & West Building Society v Mothew; FHR European Ventures v Cedar Capital* at [5].

78 *Kelly v Cooper* [1993] A.C. 205; *Henderson v Merrett Syndicates Ltd* [1995] 2 A.C. 145 at 206.

79 Indeed, there is debate as to whether loyalty is a core fiduciary requirement at all, see S. Smith, "The Deed, Not the Motive: Fiduciary Law Without Loyalty" in P. Miller and A. Gold (eds), *Contract, Status and Fiduciary Law* (Oxford University Press, 2016), Ch.9.

80 See generally J. Getzler, "Rumford Market and the Genesis of Fiduciary Obligations" in A. Burrows and Lord Rodger of Earlsferry (eds), *Mapping the Law: Essays in Memory of Peter Birks* (Oxford University Press, 2006), pp.577–598; L. Smith, "Prescriptive Fiduciary Duties" (2018) 37 Q.U.L.J. 261; L. Smith, "Fiduciary Relationships: Ensuring the Loyal Exercise of Judgment on Behalf of Another" (2014) 130 L.Q.R. 608.

81 See paras 2-076 to 2-077. See also, *Breen v Williams* (1996) 186 C.L.R. 71 at 113 (Gaudron and McHugh JJ), 135–138 (Gummow J); Conaglen, *Fiduciary Loyalty: Protecting the Due Performance of Non-Fiduciary Duties* (2010).

82 Conaglen, *Fiduciary Loyalty: Protecting the Due Performance of Non-Fiduciary Duties* (2010), Ch.3.

83 See Conaglen, *Fiduciary Loyalty: Protecting the Due Performance of Non-Fiduciary Duties* (2010), see especially pp.33–40. For judicial statements of the same view, see *Boardman v Phipps* [1967] 2 A.C. 46 at 123; *FHR European Ventures v Cedar Capital* at [5].

84 See, e.g. L. Smith, "Fiduciary Relationships: Ensuring the Loyal Exercise of Judgement on Behalf of Another" (2014) 130 L.Q.R. 608, 625ff.

further in Chapter 17, it is complicated by the further question of whether the rule requiring fiduciaries to disgorge profits is a "duty-based" rule or a "disability-based" rule, and is an issue considered further below.

2–093 Another related debate is whether the rules that make up fiduciary loyalty, whatever they may be, are limited to proscriptive rules, or can be prescriptive too. This distinction has been introduced in Chapter 2 and is described by Lionel Smith as that between "proscriptive duties" "that stipulate what a person who owes these duties *must not* do" and "prescriptive duties" that require a duty holder to do something.[85] Jurisdictions that take the view that fiduciary loyalty is proscriptive, such as Australia,[86] tend to have a thinner conception of fiduciary loyalty as being comprised only of rules that constrain the fiduciary from taking action in circumstances where there is an actual or potential conflict, for example. This is in distinction to some cases[87] in England and Canada, for example, which have understood fiduciary loyalty as also encompassing prescriptive rules that require the fiduciary to act in some way. One example is *Children's Investment Fund Foundation (UK) v Attorney General*[88] where the Supreme Court held that a *member* of a charitable company held his power to vote on certain resolutions as a fiduciary and as such was required to vote in favour of the resolution on the basis it was in the best interests of the company. Another example is *Byers v Chen*[89] where the Board found that a de facto director had a "fiduciary duty" "to take all reasonable steps to intervene to prevent a payment being made from [the company's] account . . . for an improper purpose."[90] The Board went on to state that the director's "inaction amounted to a breach of her fiduciary duty to [the company]".[91] One consideration to bear in mind is that this case concerned a company director to which the Companies Act 2006[92] applied, the effect of which is to codify as a *fiduciary* the (prescriptive) duty to act in the best interests of the company.

iv. "No conflicts" rule strictly applied in practice

(1) Conflict between self-interest and duty

2–094 When it comes to applying the "no conflict" rule, it is important to identify the principal's interest with which the fiduciary's self-interest might conflict. Breach is not made out simply because the fiduciary's self-interest may conflict with any and all interests the principal might have at large. Lord Cranworth LC made this point in *Aberdeen Railway Co v Blaikie Bros*:[93]

> It is a rule of universal application, that no one having [fiduciary] duties to discharge, shall be allowed to enter into engagements in which he has, or can have, a personal interest conflicting, or which possibly may conflict, with the interests of those whom he is bound to protect. So strictly is this principle adhered to, that no question is allowed to be raised as to the fairness or unfairness of a contract so entered into.

---

85 Smith, "Prescriptive Fiduciary Duties" (2018) 37 Q.U.L.J. 1, 1.

86 *Breen v Williams* (1995) 186 C.L.R. 71 at 113 (Gaudron and McHugh JJ).

87 *Silven Properties Ltd v Royal Bank of Scotland Plc* [2003] EWCA Civ 1409 at [10], [29]; *Williams Lake Indian Band v Canada (Aboriginal Affairs and Northern Development)* 2018 S.C.C. 4 at [46], [55], [165], [176]. For a forceful argument in favour of the view that fiduciary duties are prescriptive rather than proscriptive, see Smith, "Prescriptive Fiduciary Duties" (2018) 37 Q.U.L.J. 261.

88 *Children's Investment Fund Foundation (UK) v Attorney General* [2020] UKSC 33, [2022] A.C. 155.

89 *Byers v Chen* [2021] UKPC 4, [2021] B.C.C. 462 at [92]–[93].

90 *Byers v Chen* [2021] UKPC 4, [2021] B.C.C. 462 at [93].

91 *Byers v Chen* [2021] UKPC 4, [2021] B.C.C. 462 at [93].

92 See Companies Act 2006 ss.172, 178; *Children's Investment Fund Foundation (UK) v Attorney General* [2020] UKSC 33, [2022] A.C. 155 at [42].

93 *Aberdeen Railway Co v Blaikie Bros* (1854) 1 Macq. 461 at 472.

The "no conflicts" rule only requires the fiduciary to avoid being in a position where her self-interest may conflict with the principal's interest in so far as the fiduciary is otherwise required or "bound" to protect or give effect to the principal's interest in some way. In other words, breach can be made out if there is an actual or *potential* conflict between the fiduciary's self-interest and her performance of some other duty owed to the principal. A solicitor may be in a position of conflict where her self-interest in a matter may undermine her performance of her duty to give advice to or represent her client, for example. **2–095**

Grimaldi v Chameleon Mining NL (No.2)

Full Court of the Federal Court of Australia (2012) 200 F.C.R. 296 at [179]–[180]

THE COURT: The concept of "duty" in the "conflict of duty and interest" formula of the first of these is convenient shorthand. It refers simply to the function, the responsibility, the fiduciary has assumed or undertaken to perform for, or on behalf of, his or her beneficiary. What that function or responsibility is, is a question of fact. It may be narrow and circumscribed, as is often the case with specific agencies; it may be broad and general, as is characteristically the case with the functions of company directors; its scope may have been antecedently defined or determined; it may have been ordained by past practice; it may be left to the fiduciary's discretion to determine; and it may evolve over time as is commonly the case with partnerships. Put shortly the actual function or responsibility assumed determines "[t]he subject matter over which the fiduciary obligations extend" for conflict of duty and interest and conflict of duty and duty purposes[94] . . . **2–096**

Having defined the scope of those duties [undertaken or assumed by the fiduciary] one must see whether he has committed some breach thereof by placing himself within the scope and ambit of those duties in a position where his duty and interest may possibly conflict. It is only at this stage that any question of accountability arises. **2–097**

One comment should be made about the term "interest" as used in the conflict formula. Put compendiously, the term signifies the presence of some personal concern of possible pecuniary value in a decision taken, or a transaction effected, within the scope of a fiduciary's duties. Importantly for present purposes, it may be a contingent or expectant one, as where a trustee uses a trust's shareholding in a company to vote himself onto the company's board from which position he will be likely to derive directors' fees[95] or where a dealing with an agent proceeds on the assumption that a success fee is to be paid if a transaction is effected.[96] **2–098**

The following two cases give examples of breach of the "no conflicts" rule, and the strict application of the rule. *Keech v Sandford*[97] and *Boardman v Phipps*,[98] reproduced below, both illustrate the firm line that has traditionally been taken by the courts against fiduciaries (including trustees): they have held that a fiduciary can be liable for breaching the "no conflicts" rule, although she has acted in good faith, despite her actions having left her principal better off than she would have been if the fiduciary had done nothing, and notwithstanding there was only a *potential* (rather than an actual) conflict between the fiduciary's interest and the interests of her principal.[99] **2–099**

94 *Birtchnell v Equity Trustees Executors & Agency Co Ltd* (1929) 42 C.L.R. 384 at 408.
95 *Dallow v Codd* [1946] Ch. 73 at 81.
96 *McCann v Switzerland Insurance Australia Ltd* (2000) 203 C.L.R. 579.
97 (1726) Sel. Cas. Temp. King 61.
98 [1967] 2 A.C. 46.
99 See also *Parker v McKenna* (1874) L.R. 10 Ch. App. 96; *Regal (Hastings) Ltd v Gulliver* [1967] 2 A.C. 134 at 134n., for discussion of which, see R. Nolan, "*Regal (Hastings) Ltd v Gulliver* (1942)" in C. Mitchell and P. Mitchell (eds), *Landmark Cases in Equity* (Hart Publishing, 2012).

Keech v Sandford

Lord Chancellor (1726) Sel. Cas. Temp. King 61

2–100 A person being possessed of a lease of the profits of a market devised his estate to a trustee in trust for his infant. Before the expiration of the term the trustee applied to the lessor for a renewal, for the benefit of the infant, which he refused, since the lease being only of the profits of a market, there could be no distress, and its enforcement must rest in covenant, by which the infant could not be bound. The infant sought to have the lease assigned to him, and for an account of the profits, on the principle that wherever a lease is renewed by a trustee or executor it shall be for the benefit of the cestui que use, which principle was agreed on the other side, though endeavoured to be differenced on account of the express proof of refusal to renew to the infant.

2–101 LORD KING L.C.: I must consider this as a trust for the infant, for I very well see, if a trustee, on the refusal to renew, might have a lease to himself, few trust estates would be renewed to cestui que use. Though I do not say there is fraud in this case, yet he should rather have let it run out than to have had the lease to himself. This may seem hard, that the trustee is the only person of all mankind who might not have the lease; but it is very proper that the rule should be strictly pursued, and not in the least relaxed; for it is very obvious what would be the consequences of letting trustees have the lease on refusal to renew to cestui que use.

2–102 So decreed, that the lease should be assigned to the infant, and that the trustee should be indemnified from any covenants comprised in the lease, and an account of the profits made since the renewal.

Boardman v Phipps

House of Lords [1967] 2 A.C. 46 at 100–104, 105–111, 115, 120, 125, 126–131, 133–134

2–103 The respondent, John Phipps, was one of the residuary legatees under the will of his father, who died in 1944. The residuary estate included 8,000 out of 30,000 issued shares in a private company, Lester & Harris Ltd. By his will the testator left an annuity to his widow and, subject to her interest, 5/18ths of his residuary estate to each of his three sons and 3/18ths to his only daughter. At the end of 1955 the trustees of the will were the testator's widow (who was senile and took no part in the affairs of the trust), his only daughter, Mrs Noble, and an accountant, Fox. The first appellant, Boardman, was at all material times solicitor to the trustees and also to the children of the testator (other than the respondent). The second appellant, Tom Phipps, was the younger brother of John and in the transactions which gave rise to the case he was associated with and represented by the first appellant, Boardman.

2–104 1956 Boardman and Fox decided that the recent accounts of Lester & Harris Ltd were unsatisfactory and with a view to improving the position the appellants attended the annual general meeting of the company in December 1956 with proxies obtained from two of the trustees, Mrs Noble and Fox. They were not satisfied with the answers given at the meeting regarding the state of the company's affairs. Shortly after this meeting the appellants decided with the knowledge of Mrs Noble and Fox to try to obtain control of Lester & Harris Ltd by themselves making an offer for all the outstanding shares in that company other than the 8,000 held by the trustees. The trustees had no power to invest in the shares of the company without the sanction of the court and Fox said in evidence that he would not have considered seeking such sanction. The appellants originally offered £2 5s per share, which they later increased to £3, but by April 1957 they had received acceptances only in respect of 2,925 shares and it was clear that as things then stood they would not go through with their offer. This ended the first phase in the negotiations which ultimately led to the acquisition by the appellants of virtually all the outstanding shares in Lester & Harris Ltd. During this phase the appellants attended the annual general meeting as proxies of the two trustees and obtained information from the company as to the prices at which shares had recently changed hands; but they made the offer to purchase on their own behalf.

2–105 The second phase lasted from April 1957 to August 1958. Throughout this period Boardman carried on negotiations with the chairman of Lester & Harris Ltd with a view to reaching agreement on the division of the assets of that company between the Harris family and the directors on the one hand and the Phipps family on the other. During this phase Boardman obtained valuable information as to the value of the company's assets and throughout he purported to act on behalf of the trustees. These negotiations proved abortive.

The third phase began in August 1958 with the suggestion by Boardman that he and Tom Phipps should acquire for themselves the outstanding shares in the company. The widow died in November 1958 and a conditional agreement for the sale of the shares was made on March 10, 1959. On May 26, 1959, the appellants gave notices making the agreements unconditional to buy 14,567 shares held by the chairman of the company and his associates at £4 10s per share. This, in addition to the earlier agreements to purchase 2,925 shares at £3 each and the purchase of a further 4,494 shares at £4 10s each, made the appellants holders of 21,986 shares. 2–106

Thereafter the business of the company was reorganised, part of its assets was sold off at considerable profit, and substantial sums of capital, amounting in the aggregate to £5 17s 6d per share, were returned to the shareholders, whose shares were still worth at least £2 each after the return of capital. The appellants acted honestly throughout. 2–107

The respondent, like the other members of the Phipps family, was asked by Boardman whether he objected to the acquisition of control of the company by the appellants for themselves; but Boardman did not give sufficient information as to the material facts to succeed in the defence of consent on the part of the respondent. At first the respondent expressed his satisfaction but later he became antagonistic and issued a writ claiming (i) that the appellants held 5/18ths of the above-mentioned 21,986 shares as constructive trustees for him (subject to a lien for their outlay on the purchase of the shares) and (ii) an account of the profits made by the appellants out of the said shares. 2–108

Wilberforce J. granted this relief,[100] his decision was affirmed by the Court of Appeal,[101] and their decision was affirmed in turn by a majority of the House of Lords (Lords Cohen, Hodson and Guest; Viscount Dilhorne and Lord Upjohn dissenting). 2–109

LORD COHEN: . . . As Wilberforce J. said,[102] the mere use of any knowledge or opportunity which comes to the trustee or agent in the course of his trusteeship or agency does not necessarily make him liable to account. In the present case had the company been a public company and had the appellants bought the shares on the market, they would not, I think have been accountable. The company, however, is a private company and not only the information but also the opportunity to purchase these shares came to them through the introduction which Mr Fox gave them to the board of the company and, in the second phase, when the discussions related to the proposed split up of the company's undertaking, it was solely on behalf of the trustees that Mr Boardman was purporting to negotiate with the board of the company. The question is this: when in the third phase the negotiations turned to the purchase of the shares at £4 10s a share, were the appellant debarred by their fiduciary position from purchasing on their own behalf the 21,986 shares in the company without the informed consent of the trustees and the beneficiaries? 2–110

Wilberforce J.[103] and, in the Court of Appeal,[104] both Lord Denning M.R. and Pearson L.J. based their decision in favour of the respondent on the decision of your Lordships' House in *Regal (Hastings) Ltd v Gulliver*.[105] I turn, therefore, to consider that case. Counsel for the respondent relied on a number of passages in the judgments of the learned Lords who heard the appeal, in particular on (i) a passage in the speech of Lord Russell of Killowen where he said:[106] 2–111

> "The rule of equity which insists on those, who by use of a fiduciary position make a profit, being liable to account for that profit, in no way depends on fraud, or absence of bona fides; or upon such questions or considerations as whether the profit would or should otherwise have gone to the plaintiff, or whether the profiteer was under a duty to obtain the source of the profit for the plaintiff, or whether he took a risk or acted as he did for the benefit of the plaintiff, or whether the plaintiff has in fact been damaged or benefited by his action. The liability arises from the mere fact of a profit having, in the stated circumstances, been made"

100 [1964] 1 W.L.R. 993.
101 [1965] Ch. 992 (Lord Denning M.R., Pearson and Russell LJJ).
102 *Phipps v Boardman* [1964] 1 W.L.R. 993 at 1011.
103 *Phipps v Boardman* at 1011.
104 [1965] Ch. 992.
105 [1942] 1 All E.R. 378.
106 *Regal (Hastings) Ltd v Gulliver* at 386.

(ii) a passage in the speech of Lord Wright where he says:[107]

"That question can be briefly stated to be whether an agent, a director, a trustee or other person in an analogous fiduciary position, when a demand is made upon him by the person to whom he stands in the fiduciary relationship to account for profits acquired by him by reason of his fiduciary position, and by reason of the opportunity and the knowledge, or either, resulting from it, is entitled to defeat the claim upon any ground save that he made profits with the knowledge and assent of the other person. The most usual and typical case of this nature is that of principal and agent. The rule in such cases is compendiously expressed to be that an agent must account for net profits secretly (that is, without the knowledge of his principal) acquired by him in the course of his agency. The authorities show how manifold and various are the applications of the rule. It does not depend on fraud or corruption."

2–112 These paragraphs undoubtedly help the respondent but they must be considered in relation to the facts of that case. In that case the profit arose through the application by four of the directors of Regal for shares in a subsidiary company which it had been the original intention of the board should be subscribed for by Regal. Regal had not the requisite money available but there was no question of it being ultra vires Regal to subscribe for the shares. In the circumstances Lord Russell of Killowen said:[108] "I have no hesitation in coming to the conclusion, upon the facts of this case, that these shares, when acquired by the directors, were acquired by reason, and only by reason, of the fact that they were directors of Regal, and in the course of their execution of that office." He went on to consider whether the four directors were in a fiduciary relationship to Regal and concluded that they were. Accordingly, they were held accountable. Counsel for the appellants argued that the present case is distinguishable. He puts his argument thus. The question one asks is whether the information could have been used by the principal for the purpose for which it was used by his agents. If the answer to that question is no, the information was not used in the course of their duty as agents. In the present case the information could never have been used by the trustees for the purpose of purchasing shares in the company; therefore purchase of shares was outside the scope of the appellants' agency and they are not accountable.

2–113 This is an attractive argument, but it does not seem to me to give due weight to the fact that the appellants obtained both the information which satisfied them that the purchase of the shares would be a good investment and the opportunity of acquiring them as a result of acting for certain purposes on behalf of the trustees. Information is, of course, not property in the strict sense of that word and, as I have already stated, it does not necessarily follow that, because an agent acquired information and opportunity while acting in a fiduciary capacity, he is accountable to his principals for any profit that comes his way as the result of the use he makes of that information and opportunity. His liability to account must depend on the facts of the case. In the present case much of the information came the appellants' way when Mr Boardman was acting on behalf of the trustees on the instructions of Mr Fox, and the opportunity of bidding for the shares came because he purported for all purposes except for making the bid to be acting on behalf of the owners of the 8,000 shares in the company. In these circumstances it seems to me that the principle of the Regal case applies and that the courts below came to the right conclusion.

2–114 That is enough to dispose of the case but I would add that an agent is, in my opinion, liable to account for profits which he makes out of the trust property if there is a possibility of conflict between his interest and his duty to his principal. Mr Boardman and Mr Tom Phipps were not general agents of the trustees, but they were their agents for certain limited purposes. The information which they had obtained and the opportunity to purchase the 21,986 shares afforded them by their relations with the directors of the company—an opportunity they got as the result of their introduction to the directors by Mr Fox—were not property in the strict sense but that information and that opportunity they owed to their representing themselves as agents for the holders of the 8,000 shares held by the trustees. In these circumstances they could not, I think, use that information and that opportunity to purchase the shares for themselves if there was any possibility that the trustees might wish to acquire them for the trust. Mr Boardman was the solicitor whom the trustees were in the habit of consulting if they wanted legal advice. Granted that he would not be bound to advise on any point unless he were consulted, he would still be the person they would consult if they wanted advice. He would clearly have advised them that they had no power to invest in shares of the company without the sanction of the court. In the first phase he would also have had to

---

107 *Regal (Hastings) Ltd v Gulliver* at 392.
108 *Regal (Hastings) Ltd v Gulliver* at 387.

advise on the evidence then available that the court would be unlikely to give such sanction: but the appellants learnt much more during the second phase. It may well be that even in third phase the answer of the court would have been the same but, in my opinion, Mr Boardman would not have been able to give unprejudiced advice if he had been consulted by the trustees and was at the same time negotiating for the purchase of the shares on behalf of himself and Mr Tom Phipps. In other words, there was, in my opinion, at the crucial date (March 1959) a possibility of a conflict between his interest and his duty.

In making these observations I have referred to the fact that Mr Boardman was the solicitor to the trust. Mr Tom Phipps was only a beneficiary and was not as such debarred from bidding for the shares, but no attempt was made in the courts below to differentiate between them. Had such an attempt been made it would very likely have failed, as Mr Tom Phipps left the negotiations largely to Mr Boardman, and it might well be held that, if Mr Boardman was disqualified from bidding, Mr Tom Phipps could not be in a better position. Be that as it may, counsel for the appellants rightly did not seek at this stage to distinguish between the two. He did, it is true, say that Mr Tom Phipps as a beneficiary would be entitled to any information that the trustees obtained. This may be so, but nonetheless I find myself unable to distinguish between the two appellants. They were, I think, in March 1959, in a fiduciary position vis-à-vis the trust. That fiduciary position was of such a nature that (as the trust fund was distributable) the appellants could not purchase the shares on their own behalf without the informed consent of the beneficiaries: it is now admitted that they did not obtain that consent. They are therefore, in my opinion, accountable to the respondent for his share of the net profits which they derived from the transaction. 2–115

I desire to repeat that the integrity of the appellants is not in doubt. They acted with complete honesty throughout, and the respondent is a fortunate man in that the rigour of equity enables him to participate in the profits which have accrued as the result of the action taken by the appellants in March 1959 in purchasing the shares at their own risk. As the last paragraph of his judgment clearly shows, the trial judge evidently shared this view. He directed an inquiry as to what sum was proper to be allowed to the appellants or either of them in respect of their or his work and skill in obtaining the said shares and the profits in respect thereof. The trial judge concluded by expressing the opinion that payment should be on a liberal scale. With that observation I respectfully agree. . . . 2–116

LORD HODSON: . . . The proposition of law involved in this case is that no person standing in a fiduciary position, when a demand is made on him by the person to whom he stands in the fiduciary relationship to account for profits acquired by him by reason of his fiduciary position and by reason of the opportunity and the knowledge, or either, resulting from it, is entitled to defeat the claim on any ground save that he made profits with the knowledge and assent of the other person . . . 2–117

. . . it is said on behalf of the appellants that information as such is not necessarily property and it is only trust property which is relevant. I agree, but it is nothing to the point to say that in these times corporate trustees, e.g. the Public Trustee and others, necessarily acquire a mass of information in their capacity of trustees for a particular trust and cannot be held liable to account if knowledge so acquired enables them to operate to their own advantage, or to that of other trusts. Each case must depend on its own facts, and I dissent from the view that information is of its nature something which is not properly to be described as property. We are aware that what is called 'know-how' in the commercial sense is property which may be very valuable as an asset. I agree with the learned judge[109] and with the Court of Appeal[110] that the confidential information acquired in this case, which was capable of being and was turned to account, can be properly regarded as the property of the trust. It was obtained by Mr Boardman by reason of the opportunity which he was given as solicitor acting for the trustees in the negotiations with the chairman of the company, as the correspondence demonstrates. The end result was that, out of the special position in which they were standing in the course of the negotiations, the appellants got the opportunity to make a profit and the knowledge that it was there to be made. . . . 2–118

Regal (Hastings) Ltd v Gulliver differs from this case mainly in that the directors took up shares and made a profit thereby, it having been originally intended that the company should buy these shares. Here there was no such intention on the part of the trustees. There is no indication that they either had the money or would have been ready to apply to the court for sanction enabling them to do so. On the contrary, Mr Fox, the active trustee and an accountant who concerned himself with the details of the trust property, was not prepared to agree to the trustees buying the shares and encouraged the appellants to 2–119

109 [1964] 1 W.L.R. 993 at 1008–1011.
110 [1965] Ch. 992.

make the purchase. This does not affect the position. As *Keech v Sandford* shows, the inability of the trust to purchase makes no difference to the liability of the appellants, if liability otherwise exists. The distinction on the facts as to intention to purchase shares between this case and *Regal (Hastings) Ltd v Gulliver* is not relevant. The company (Regal) had not the money to apply for the shares on which the profit was made. The directors took the opportunity which they had presented to them to buy the shares with their own money and were held accountable. Mr Fox's refusal as one of the trustees to take any part in the matter on behalf of the trust, so far as he was concerned, can make no difference. Nothing short of fully informed consent, which the learned judge found not to have been obtained, could enable the appellants in the position which they occupied, having taken the opportunity provided by that position, to make a profit for themselves. . .

2–120 The confidential information which the appellants obtained at a time when Mr Boardman was admittedly holding himself out as solicitor for the trustees was obtained by him as representing the trustees, the holders of 8,000 shares of Lester & Harris Ltd. As Russell L.J. put it:[111] "The substantial trust shareholding was an asset of which one aspect was its potential use as a means of acquiring knowledge of the company's affairs, or of negotiating allocations of the company's assets, or of inducing other shareholders to part with their shares." That aspect was part of the trust assets. Whether this aspect is properly to be regarded as part of the trust assets is, in my judgment, immaterial. The appellants obtained knowledge by reason of their fiduciary position, and they cannot escape liability by saying that they were acting for themselves and not as agents of the trustees. Whether or not the trust, or the beneficiaries in their stead, could have taken advantage of the information is immaterial, as the authorities clearly show. No doubt it was but a remote possibility that Mr Boardman would ever be asked by the trustees to advise on the desirability of an application to the court in order that the trustees might avail themselves of the information obtained. Nevertheless, whenever the possibility of conflict is present between personal interest and the fiduciary position the rule of equity must be applied. . . .

2–121 LORD GUEST: . . . I take the view that from first to last Mr Boardman was acting in a fiduciary capacity to the trustees. This fiduciary capacity arose in phase 1 and continued into phase 2, which glided into phase 3. In saying this I do not for one moment suggest that there was anything dishonest or underhand in what Mr Boardman did. He has obtained a clean certificate below and I do not wish to sully it; but the law has a strict regard for principle in ensuring that a person in a fiduciary capacity is not allowed to benefit from any transactions into which he has entered with trust property. If Mr Boardman was acting on behalf of the trust, then all the information that he obtained in phase 2 became trust property. The weapon which he used to obtain this information was the trust holding; and I see no reason why information and knowledge cannot be trust property. . . .

2–122 LORD UPJOHN (dissenting): On the evidence there was never any suggestion at any subsequent stage [after 1956] that Mr Fox or any other trustee would ever have contemplated any purchase of further shares. . . . In *Aberdeen Railway Co v Blaikie*[112] Lord Cranworth L.C. said, "and it is a rule of universal application that no-one having such duties to discharge shall be allowed to enter into engagements in which he has or can have a personal interest conflicting or which possibly may conflict with the interests of those whom he is bound to protect." The phrase 'possibly may conflict' requires consideration. In my view it means that the reasonable man would think that there was a real sensible possibility of conflict; not that you could imagine some situation arising which might, in some conceivable possibility in events not contemplated as real sensible possibilities by any reasonable person, result in a conflict. . . [*Regal (Hastings) Ltd v Gulliver* and *Keech v Sandford* bear no relation to this case].

2–123 This case, if I may emphasise it again, is one concerned not with trust property or with property of which the persons to whom the fiduciary duty was owed were contemplating a purchase but, in contrast to the facts in *Regal*, with property which was not trust property or property which was ever contemplated as the subject-matter of a possible purchase by the trust. . . .

2–124 . . . this question whether the appellants were accountable requires a closer analysis than it has received in the lower courts. This analysis requires detailed consideration:

---

[111] [1965] Ch. 992 at 1031.
[112] (1854) 1 Macq. 461 at 471.

(1) The facts and circumstances must be carefully examined to see whether in fact a purported agent and even a confidential agent is in a fiduciary relationship to his principal. It does not necessarily follow that he is in such a position.
(2) Once it is established that there is such a relationship, that relationship must be examined to see what duties are thereby imposed on the agent, to see what is the scope and ambit of the duties charged on him.
(3) Having defined the scope of those duties one must see whether he has committed some breach thereof by placing himself within the scope and ambit of those duties in a position where his duty and interest may possibly conflict. It is only at this stage that any question of accountability arises.
(4) Finally, having established accountability it only goes so far as to render the agent accountable for profits made within the scope and ambit of his duty.

Before applying these principles to the facts, however, I shall refer to the judgment of Russell L.J. which proceeded on a rather different basis. He said: **2–125**

> "The substantial trust shareholding was an asset of which one aspect was its potential use as a means of acquiring knowledge of the company's affairs, or of negotiating allocations of the company's assets, or of inducing other shareholders to part with their shares. That aspect was part of the trust assets."

My Lords, I regard that proposition as untenable.

In general, information is not property at all. It is normally open to all who have eyes to read and ears to hear. The true test is to determine in what circumstances the information has been acquired. If it has been acquired in such circumstances that it would be a breach of confidence to disclose it to another, then courts of equity will restrain the recipient from communicating it to another. In such cases such confidential information is often and for many years has been described as the property of the donor, the books of authority are full of such references; knowledge of secret processes, "know-how", confidential information as to the prospects of a company or of someone's intention or the expected results of some horse race based on stable or other confidential information. But in the end the real truth is that it is not property in any normal sense, but equity will restrain its transmission to another if in breach of some confidential relationship. **2–126**

With all respect to the views of Russell L.J., I protest at the idea that information acquired by trustees in the course of their duties as such is necessarily part of the assets of trust property which cannot be used by the trustees except for the benefit of the trust. Russell L.J. referred to the fact that two out of three of the trustees could have no authority to turn over this aspect of trust property to the appellants except for the benefit of the trust; this I do not understand, for if such information is trust property not all the trustees acting together could do it for they cannot give away trust property. **2–127**

We heard much argument on the impact of the fact that the testator's widow was at all material times incapable of acting in the trust owing to disability. Of course trustees must act all of them and unanimously in matters affecting trust affairs, but they never performed any relevant act on behalf of the trust at all; I quoted Mr Fox's answer earlier for this reason. At no time after going to the meeting in December 1956, did Mr Boardman or Tom rely on any express or implied authority or consent of the trustees in relation to trust property. They understood rightly that there was no question of the trustees acquiring any further trust property by purchasing further shares in the company, and it was only in the purchase of other shares that they were interested. **2–128**

There is, in my view, and I know of no authority to the contrary, no general rule that information learnt by a trustee during the course of his duties is property of the trust and cannot be used by him. If that were to be the rule it would put the Public Trustee and other corporate trustees out of business and make it difficult for private trustees to be trustees of more than one trust. This would be the greatest possible pity for corporate trustees and others may have much information which they may initially acquire in connection with some particular trust but without prejudice to that trust can make it readily available to other trusts to the great advantage of those other trusts. **2–129**

The real rule is, in my view, that knowledge learnt by a trustee in the course of his duties as such is not in the least property of the trust and in general may be used by him for his own benefit or for the benefit of other trusts unless it is confidential information which is given to him (i) in circumstances which, regardless of his position as a trustee, would make it a breach of confidence for him to communicate to anyone, for it has been given to him expressly or impliedly as confidential; or (ii) in a fiduciary capacity, and its use would place him in a position where his duty and his interest might possibly conflict. Let me give one or **2–130** two simple examples. A, as trustee of two settlements X and Y holding shares in the same small company, learns facts as trustee of X about the company which are encouraging. In the absence of special circumstances (such, for example, that X wants to buy more shares) I can see nothing whatever which would make it improper for him to tell his co-trustees of Y who feel inclined to sell that he has information that this would be a bad thing to do. Another example: A as trustee of X learns facts that make him and his co-trustees want to sell. Clearly he could not communicate this knowledge to his co-trustees of Y until at all events the holdings of X have been sold for there would be a plain conflict, reflected in the prices that might or might possibly be obtained.

2–131 My Lords, I do not think for one moment that Lord Brougham in *Hamilton v Wright*,[113] quoted in the speech of my noble and learned friend, Lord Guest, was saying anything to the contrary; one has to look and see whether the knowledge acquired was capable of being used for his own benefit to injure the trust (my italics). That test can have no application to the present. There was no possibility of the information being used to injure the trust. The knowledge obtained was used not in connection with trust property but to enhance the value of the trust property by the purchase of other property in which the trustees were not interested. . . .

2–132 As a result of the information the appellants acquired, admittedly by reason of the trust holding, they found it worthwhile to offer a good deal more for the shares than in phase 1 of chapter 2. I cannot see that in offering to purchase non-trust shares at a higher price they were in breach of any fiduciary relationship in using the information which they had acquired for this purpose. I cannot see that they have, from start to finish, in the circumstances of this case, placed themselves in a position where there was any possibility of a conflict between their duty and interest.

2–133 I have dealt with the problems that arise in this case at considerable length but it could, in my opinion, be dealt with quite shortly. In *Barnes v Addy*,[114] Lord Selborne L.C., said:

> "It is equally important to maintain the doctrine of trusts which is established in this court, and not to strain it by unreasonable construction beyond its due and proper limits. There would be no better mode of undermining the sound doctrines of equity than to make unreasonable and inequitable applications of them."

That, in my judgment, is applicable to this case.

2–134 The trustees were not willing to buy more shares in the company. The active trustees were very willing that the appellants should do so themselves for the benefit of their large minority holding. The trustees, so to speak, lent their name to the appellants in the course of prolonged and difficult negotiations and, of course, the appellants thereby learnt much which would have otherwise been denied to them. The negotiations were in the end brilliantly successful. How successful Tom was in his reorganisation of the company is apparent to all. They ought to be very grateful.

2–135 In the long run the appellants have bought for themselves with their own money shares which the trustees never contemplated buying and they did so in circumstances fully known and approved of by the trustees. To extend the doctrines of equity to make the appellants accountable in such circumstances is, in my judgment, to make unreasonable and inequitable applications of such doctrines.

2–136 *Boardman* possesses some difficult features that have been well explained by Michael Bryan in his study of the case.[115] One is that none of the courts which heard the case gave a convincing explanation of the reason why Boardman and Tom Phipps were fiduciaries for John Phipps. Boardman gave advice on various matters as a solicitor to the trustees and beneficiaries, but he was not on a permanent retainer; nor were he or Tom ever appointed as an agent either for the trustees or the beneficiaries with instructions to deal with the company management. Bryan concludes that the only basis on which they can have been fiduciaries is that they were "self-appointed agents", in Wilberforce J's term,[116] i.e.

---

113 (1842) 9 Cl. & Fin. 111.
114 (1874) 9 Ch. App. 244 at 251.
115 M. Bryan, "*Boardman v Phipps* (1967)" in C. Mitchell and P. Mitchell (eds), *Landmark Cases in Equity* (Hart Publishing, 2012).
116 [1964] 1 W.L.R. 993 at 1007.

intermeddlers in the trust affairs who took it on themselves to act as though they were agents for the beneficiaries and who were accordingly treated as though they had been regularly appointed.

Another difficult point is that John Phipps's statement of claim did not expressly allege a conflict of interest. The idea that Boardman had placed himself in a position where his personal interest prevented him from giving disinterested advice to the trustees appeared for the first time in Lord Denning MR's judgment in the Court of Appeal.[117] He reasoned that the articles of the company gave existing shareholders a right of pre-emption when another shareholder wished to sell his shares; hence when the directors were negotiating the sale of the company shares with Boardman and Tom Phipps, the trustees might have asked Boardman for advice as to whether they should exercise their pre-emption rights and if they had done so, there would then have been a conflict between his personal interests and his principal's interests. In the House of Lords the majority spoke in vague terms of a conflict of interest without identifying even this precisely what the conflict was. In this respect, *Boardman* can only be seen as a harsh decision, which most probably turned on a potential rather than an actual conflict of interest; furthermore this was a conflict that did not directly affect the claimant, who was not a trustee with pre-emption rights as a shareholder and was merely a beneficiary of the trust. **2–137**

(2) Conflict between duty and duty

In addition to avoiding a conflict between self-interest and duty, a fiduciary must also avoid being in a position where there is a potential for conflict between duties owed to multiple principals. This aspect of the "no conflict" rule applies with the same stringency: the fiduciary will be liable for actual and potential conflict, despite acting in good faith. **2–138**

In *Commonwealth Bank of Australia v Smith*, excerpted below, a bank provided financial advice to one of its customers such that a fiduciary relationship arose, and the bank breached its fiduciary obligation to avoid being in a position where it owed conflicting duties to multiple clients. This was because the bank, via its representative, Mr Dungan, advised one of its clients, the respondents, to purchase a hotel where the vendor was another of the bank's customers for whom the bank had been acting in trying to bring about a sale of the hotel. In the excerpt, the Full Court of the Federal Court of Australia (Davies, Sheppard and Gummow JJ) also consider the issues of when a fiduciary duty is owed, and the defence of informed consent, both of which are discussed further below. **2–139**

Commonwealth Bank of Australia v Smith

Full Court of the Federal Court of Australia (1992) 42 F.C.R. 390 at 391–393

THE COURT: It remains to deal with fiduciary relationship. It is not a novel proposition that where a bank gives to a customer advice upon financial affairs, then in addition to any contractual rights the customer may have (something which does not arise on this appeal) the relationship between the parties may be such as to found either or both a common law duty of care and a fiduciary duty. . . . **2–140**

A bank may be expected to act in its own interests in ensuring the security of its position as lender to its customer, but it may have created in the customer the expectation that nevertheless it will advise in the customer's interests as to the wisdom of a proposed investment. This may be the case where the customer may fairly take it that to a significant extent his interest is consistent with that of the bank in financing the customer for a prudent business venture. In such a way the bank may become a fiduciary and occupy the position of what Brennan J. has called "an investment adviser"[118]. . . **2–141**

The present case, like those just considered, is not one where one would properly describe the parties as acting in a commercial transaction at arm's length and each with the assistance of fully independent **2–142**

[117] [1965] Ch. 992 at 1020.

[118] *Daly v The Sydney Stock Exchange Limited* (1986) 160 C.L.R. 371 at 384–385.

professional advice. Such considerations would be of significance in tending to show the absence of a fiduciary relationship.[119] The starting points for consideration of the present problem are the findings that Mr Dungan assumed the role of introducing the parties and bringing them together, that he then acted as the respondents' financial adviser in the matter, and that they evinced complete faith in him. . . .

2–143 In our view, the primary judge was correct in concluding on the facts that the bank became the investment adviser of the respondents in the matter of the purchase of the Weeroona Hotel and that a fiduciary relationship arose. The question then was one of (i) identifying the relevant incidents of that relationship and duties arising from it, and (ii) determining whether there had been a breach of duty leading to loss for which there was an obligation upon the bank to compensate the respondents.

2–144 The crucial incident of the fiduciary relationship in this case arose from the conflicting interests between the two sets of customers of the bank. As Von Doussa J. put it, and we agree, Mr Dungan had become the representative of one customer of the bank, No Justice Pty Limited, that is to say, in substance, of two other customers, Messrs Gwynne and Hart, in helping to bring about the sale of their business to two other customers of the bank. Not only must the fiduciary avoid, without informed consent, placing himself in a position of conflict between duty and personal interest, but he must eschew conflicting engagements. The reason is that by reason of the multiple engagements, the fiduciary may be unable to discharge adequately the one without conflicting with his obligation in the other. Thus, it has been said, after ample citation of authority, that where an adviser in a sale is also the undisclosed adviser of the purchaser, an actual conflict of duties arises . . .

2–145 In such a case, it is not to the point that the fiduciary himself may not stand to profit from the transaction he brings about between the parties. The prohibition is not against the making of a profit (though many cases of breach of fiduciary duty involve the wrongful acquisition of a profit, rather than the infliction of a loss) but of the avoidance of conflict of duties, something described in forceful terms by Lord Cozens-Hardy M.R. in *Moody v Cox and Hatt*.[120] It is true that the evidence did not show that the bank was pressing Messrs Gwynne and Hart to sell, or that their company was having trouble in meeting its commitments. But, as we have indicated, it would not be necessary for such facts to exist in order for the fiduciary obligations that we have described to arise. Nor, of course, is it to the point that the appellants did not act with fraudulent intent.[121]

2–146 It frequently is said that the fiduciary will be absolved by the giving of fully informed consent to the existence of what otherwise would be a conflict. There is no precise formula which will determine in all cases if fully informed consent has been given; it is a question of fact in all the circumstances of each case.[122] The circumstances of the case may include (as they do here) the importance of obtaining independent and skilled advice from other parties.

2–147 In the present appeal, counsel for the appellants relied strongly on the disclosure which Mr Dungan made. At an early stage . . . Mr Dungan told [the respondents] of his relationship with the vendor and of the existence of a conflict. In counsel's submission, that was sufficient. The difficulty with that submission is that the matter did not stop there. Mr Dungan did not tell the respondents to go to someone else for advice. On the contrary, he persuaded them not to do so. He did his best to encourage them not to see either an accountant or a hotel broker. He did encourage them to go to the solicitor for the vendor, but with the unfortunate result that the solicitor was in a position of conflict. Had [the respondents] sought advice from that solicitor about the merits of the transaction, the solicitor would have been in an impossible position. This is because the acceptance of the double engagement would have placed the solicitor in a dilemma. As Lord Cozens-Hardy M.R. put it in *Moody v Cox*:[123]

> "He ought before putting himself in that position to inform the client of his conflicting duties, and either obtain from that client an agreement that he should not perform his full duties of disclosure or say – which would be much better – 'I cannot accept this business'"

---

119 *Hospital Products Limited v United States Surgical Corporation* (1984) 156 C.L.R. 41 at 70, 119, 146.

120 (1971) 2 Ch. 71 at 81–82.

121 *Nocton v Lord Ashburton* (1914) A.C. 932 at 957.

122 *In re Pauling's Settlement Trusts* (1962) 1 W.L.R. 86 at 108 (Wilberforce J), whose judgment on this issue was untouched by the Court of Appeal, (1964) Ch. 303. Turner LJ had spoken to the same effect in *Life Association of Scotland v Siddal* (1861) 3 De G.F. and J. 58 at 73, and also had there said that the question was whether the party had been fully informed of his rights "and of all the material facts and circumstances of the case".

123 *Moody v Cox* [1917] 2 Ch. 71 at 81.

. . . We agree with the following statement by the learned primary Judge:- **2–148**

"Even if Mr Dungan had disclosed to the applicants that he was acting for the vendor . . . and then giving particulars of the hotel business he would still have been placed in an impossible position when the applicants sought his advice on the merits of the transaction and enquired whether they should offer less than the vendor's asking price. He could give no answer on these matters without running into conflict with his duty to at least one side in the negotiations. In the circumstances of this case Mr Dungan ought never to have advised the applicants at all on the merits of the transaction ... He should have explained to them the need to get advice on the questions raised by them from someone who is independent. When Mr Smith asked if he should seek accounting advice, he should have been told to do so."

The failure of Mr Dungan to act in the manner indicated in that passage leads equity to afford its remedies for breach of duty, including that of compensation. **2–149**

v. Loyalty and exclusivity

It is often said that the essence of fiduciary duties is the notion of undivided loyalty.[124] However, for the reasons given by James Penner in the following excerpt, the rules requiring fiduciaries to act exclusively in the interests of their principals are not really concerned with loyalty, as that idea is commonly understood. Hence, it may be more apt to speak of fiduciaries owing a duty of "deliberative exclusivity",[125] meaning that when exercising their judgment on behalf of their principals, they are not required to identify subjectively with their principal's interests, but they are required to exclude their own, and any third party's interests from consideration. **2–150**

James Penner, "Distinguishing Fiduciary, Trust, and Accounting Relationships"

(2014) 8 J. Eq. 201, 206–208

. . . I do not agree that the concept of loyalty, or at least not any concept of loyalty which relates to the commonsense concept of loyalty, has anything really to do with understanding the fiduciary relationship.[126] In my view, the application of the rules governing fiduciaries, in particular the no-conflict rule (including the special applications of that rule, the self-dealing and fair-dealing rules, and the 'no-profit' rule), is not about ensuring loyalty. The rule addresses the fact that where an exercise of a power is taken in cases where the trustee's judgment is impaired, that exercise can be set aside. This idea of impairment follows from the recognition that, even with the best intentions in the world, where one is interested in a transaction one cannot even oneself be sure that one has made an unbiased decision; judgment in these circumstances is moreover compromised by the human propensity to rationalise a decision favouring oneself. That is it, and one needn't invoke any notion of loyalty to explain the law. There are also positive reasons to reject loyalty as an underlying organising value or virtue for the fiduciary relationship. To summarise them: **2–151**

(1) The notion of loyalty is both over- and under-inclusive. Many wrongs that are properly characterised as disloyal have nothing to do with fiduciary relationships.[127] A low-level employee who steals from his employer can certainly be characterized as disloyal, but there is no breach of any fiduciary **2–152**

---

[124] See, e.g. *Boardman v Phipps* [1967] 2 A.C. 46 at 123; *Grimaldi v Chameleon Mining NL (No.2)* (2012) 200 F.C.R. 296 at [174]; *FHR European Ventures LLP v Cedar Capital Partners LLC* [2015] A.C. 250 at [5]; *AIB Group (UK) Plc v Mark Redler & Co* [2014] 3 W.L.R. 1367 at [51].

[125] J.E. Penner, "Distinguishing Fiduciary, Trust, and Accounting Relationships" (2014) 8 J. Eq. 201, 206–208.

[126] J.E. Penner, "Is Loyalty a Virtue, and Even If It Is, Does It Really Help Explain Fiduciary Liability?" in A. Gold and P. Miller (eds), *Philosophical Foundations of Fiduciary Law* (Oxford University Press, 2014).

[127] At least on the discretionary model which both Smith and I endorse.

relationship here for there is none.[128] Conversely, fiduciaries who have been found liable under the rules do not necessarily act disloyally. In no way could the actions of Boardman in the leading U.K. case of *Boardman v Phipps* be said to have been "disloyal".[129]

2–153 (2) To act disloyally, which would be required for fiduciary liability on this view, is to reveal a state of mind, an animus against the principal; disloyalty is an offence requiring mens rea. As *Boardman* also tells us,[130] this is not required for fiduciary liability.

2–154 (3) To be loyal to someone is to give them "deliberative priority" in relation to others to whom one is not expected to be loyal. To be loyal to my friends requires me to take their interests more seriously than those of people who are not my friends. But to act loyally does not require one not to take one's own interests into account. To act loyally is not to act selflessly. A principal, by contrast, is entitled to the "deliberative exclusivity" of his fiduciary. The powers the fiduciary exercises are exercised in the interests of their principal, and no one else. This is most obviously the case with a trustee-fiduciary. They must exercise the trust discretions with only the trust beneficiaries in mind because it is beneficially their property, not his.

2–155 (4) Lastly, loyalty concerns a relationship in which the loyal person must emotionally identify with the object of her loyalty, such that she understands her life to go better when the life of the object of her loyalty goes better. Moreover, relations of loyalty give rise to the possibility of "epistemic bias"; the identification involved lends itself to forming favourable but false or at least dubious beliefs about the object of loyalty. . . While there is a weak sense in which fiduciaries should identify with their principals, generally thinking that their role in serving their principals is worthwhile, discharging the role of fiduciary does not require any sympathy or identification of this kind, in the sense that how the life of the fiduciary will go tracks in any really important way whether her principal flourishes. Being a fiduciary is just a job, after all. Once again, the case of the trustee-fiduciary makes this point particularly clearly. One of the main tasks of the family trustee-fiduciary is to stand back and take a clear-eyed view of the beneficiaries, untainted by personal "identification", drawing upon personal knowledge of the beneficiaries of course, but not being swayed by likes or dislikes . . . Indeed, in the case of family trusts, one of the whole purposes of placing powers in the hands of impartial trustees is to provide an antidote to the false beliefs which persons close to the beneficiaries might form based on their identification with them. . .

vi. Why are fiduciary duties imposed?

2–156 Penner's comments lead into the larger question of why fiduciary duties are imposed.[131] On one view of this question, fiduciary duties force fiduciaries to act altruistically, which is desirable because the inter-personal trust engendered by altruistic behaviour is a social good with an inherent moral value, because trust is critical to the individual flourishing of socially interdependent human beings, and because trust enables people to cooperate effectively towards the achievement of larger, socially desirable goals.[132] However, there are problems with this understanding of fiduciary duties. The idea of "trust" is only vaguely explained by those who place it at the centre of their analysis. Moreover, it is a purposive concept: we trust people to do things for us, and this creates the difficulty that if the things we trust them to do are bad rather than good, then trusting people to do them may itself be a bad rather than a good thing. Also, imposing fiduciary duties by law does not seem a good way to reinforce trust between the members of society: if people avoid conflicts of interest only because the

---

128 Or at least none in respect of a duty not to steal. In Australia, the employer–employee relationship has been described as a fiduciary one. . . . most recently in *Commonwealth Bank v Barker* (2014) 312 A.L.R. 356 at [16], [30]. With respect, it would seem correct to treat only those employees as fiduciaries who undertake an advisory or agent-like role vis-à-vis their employers.

129 [1967] 2 A.C. 46.

130 See also *Regal (Hastings) Ltd v Gulliver* [1967] 2 A.C. 134.

131 For an overview of the literature, see P.B. Miller, "Justifying Fiduciary Duties" (2013) 58 McGill L.J. 969.

132 See, e.g. T. Frankel, "Fiduciary Law" (1983) 71 California L.R. 795; R. Flannigan, "The Fiduciary Obligation" (1989) 9 O.J.L.S. 285; M. Harding, "Trust and Fiduciary Law" (2013) 33 O.J.L.S. 81.

law requires them to, how far can they be trusted? Further, as Remus Valsan[133] argues, the reason is not because humans are inclined to act self-interestedly and are too weak consciously to resist this urge while managing another person's interests, for although this may be true of some fiduciaries, it cannot account for the rule that liability arises even when a fiduciary's honesty and good intentions are un-impugned.

On another view, the point of fiduciary duties is to enable fiduciaries to make better decisions for their principals by requiring them to exercise disinterested judgment;[134] another, more elaborate, version of this argument holds that the point of fiduciary duties is to support the proper performance of other duties owed by fiduciaries by insulating them from temptation:[135] the idea here is that a fiduciary charged with taking decisions in her principal's interest will find it easier to do this carefully if she is not distracted by the prospect of personal advancement. Instrumental arguments of this sort do not treat conflicts of interest as morally problematic in themselves. Yet, the terms in which the courts speak of fiduciary breaches, and the stringency with which breaching fiduciaries are treated, suggest that they are perceived—by the courts at least—as morally wrongful. Furthermore, if the point of fiduciary duties is to reduce the risk of fiduciaries breaching their non-fiduciary duties, then why do their breaches of fiduciary duty attract more stringent treatment than their breaches of the non-fiduciary duties which it is supposedly the job of their fiduciary duties to support?[136] **2–157**

vii. From "disability" to "duty"

We have spoken of the "duty" owed by fiduciaries to act in their principals' interests. However, this "duty" was not originally conceived of as a primary duty, the breach of which could trigger a secondary duty to pay compensation or disgorge gains. The origins of fiduciary duties lie in equitable rules that were understood to operate differently, to disable fiduciaries from entering certain types of transaction.[137] The disability conception is underpinned by the idea that fiduciaries were legally "incapable" of entering into certain kinds of transactions, and meant that the rules governing fiduciary loyalty were understood as disabling or preventing a fiduciary from taking action, rather than rules that required performance of a duty, the breach of which triggered a secondary obligation to disgorge profits or pay compensation. In recent years, however, fiduciary duties have been partially reconceptualised by all of the Commonwealth courts, with the result that the law is now in an uneasy state of transition. This development is described by Charles Mitchell in the following passage. **2–158**

---

133 R. Valsan, "Fiduciary Duties, Conflict of Interest and Proper Exercise of Judgment" (2016) 62 McGill L.J. 1.

134 See, e.g. I. Samet, "Guarding the Fiduciary's Conscience—A Justification of a Stringent Profit-Stripping Rule" (2008) 28 O.J.L.S. 763; L. Smith, "Deterrence, Prophylaxis and Punishment in Fiduciary Obligations" (2013) 7 J. Eq. 87; L. Smith, "Fiduciary Relationships: Ensuring the Loyal Exercise of Judgment on Behalf of Another" (2014) 130 L.Q.R. 608; J.E. Penner, "Distinguishing Fiduciary, Trust, and Accounting Relationships" (2014) 8 J. Eq. 201; P.B. Miller, "The Fiduciary Relationship" in A. Gold and P. Miller (eds), *Philosophical Foundations of Fiduciary Law* (Oxford University Press, 2014).

135 The leading proponent of this argument is Matthew Conaglen, in his article "The Nature and Function of Fiduciary Loyalty" (2005) 121 L.Q.R. 121 and his book, *Fiduciary Loyalty: Protecting the Due Performance of Non-Fiduciary Duties*. See also P. Birks, "The Content of Fiduciary Obligation" (2000) 34 Israel L.R. 3.

136 R. Lee, "In Search of the Nature and Function of Fiduciary Loyalty: Some Observations on Conaglen's Analysis" (2007) 27 O.J.L.S. 327.

137 See further Michael et al, *Underhill and Hayton: Law of Trusts and Trustees*, 19th edn (LexisNexis, 2022), [29.10]–[29.13]. For an illuminating historical account, see J. Grower, *From Disability to Duty: From Constructive Fraud to Equitable Wrongs* (PhD thesis, UCL, 2021).

Charles Mitchell, "Equitable Compensation for Breach of Fiduciary Duty"

(2013) 66 C.L.P. 307, 313–316

2–159 In his famous judgment in *Earl of Chesterfield v Janssen*, delivered in 1751, Lord Hardwicke L.C. said that the Chancery court would "relieve against every species of fraud", including fraud

> "which may be presumed from the circumstances and condition of [two] parties contracting: and this goes farther than the rule of law; which is, that it must be proved, not presumed; but it is wisely established in this court to prevent taking surreptitious advantage of the weakness or necessity of another . . . ."[138]

2–160 Here is another source of modern fiduciary doctrine, and also of the modern doctrine of undue influence. These are now understood to be separate, though overlapping, doctrines,[139] but a century after Lord Hardwicke's judgment they were still hardly distinguishable in Joseph Story's great treatise on *Equity Jurisprudence*, where he wrote of "constructive frauds . . . which arise from some peculiar confidential, or fiduciary relation between the parties".[140] Story included relations between parents and children, attorneys and solicitors and clients, principals and agents, guardians and wards—and trustees and beneficiaries. Contracts of sale between such parties were prohibited, and in cases where "confidence [was] reposed, and one party [had] it in his power, in a secret manner, for his own advantage, to sacrifice those interests, which he [was] bound to protect", that party was not "permitted to hold any such advantage".[141]

2–161 Story did not think that this rule placed fiduciaries under a duty to refrain from disloyal behaviour, and his discussion of "trustee duties" makes no mention of the rule.[142] In this he was followed by other treatise writers of the nineteenth century, such as James Hill and Thomas Lewin. They saw things differently, writing that trustees and other fiduciaries were "incapable" of entering legally binding contracts with their principals, or that they could not do so because they were subject to an "equitable disability".[143] The same language appears in cases throughout the nineteenth and twentieth centuries.[144] It embodies a particular idea of the rules affecting fiduciaries' disloyal behaviour.[145] This is that fiduciary relationships are governed by a set of proscriptive rules that disable fiduciaries from acting in certain ways, rather than a set of prescriptive rules requiring them to perform certain duties, breaches of which trigger secondary obligations to disgorge profits or pay compensation. In modern times this idea of fiduciary disability has

---

138 (1751) 2 Ves. Sen. 125 at 155–156.

139 R.P. Meagher, J.D. Heydon and M.J. Leeming, *Meagher, Gummow and Lehane's Equity: Doctrines and Remedies*, 2nd edn (Butterworths LexisNexis, 2002), para.15–100; D. O'Sullivan, S. Elliott, and R. Zakrzewski, *The Law of Rescission* (Oxford University Press, 2008), paras 8.07–8.08; M. Conaglen, "Fiduciaries" in J. McGhee (ed.), *Snell's Equity*, 32nd edn (Sweet & Maxwell, 2010), pp.232–241. But note, R.A. Bigwood, *Exploitative Contracts* (Oxford University Press, 2003), Ch.8, especially pp.406–423, cautioning against the potentially misleading nature of such statements.

140 J. Story, *Commentaries on Equity Jurisprudence: As Administered in England and America* (1836), Vol.I 304.

141 J. Story, *Commentaries on Equity Jurisprudence: As Administered in England and America*, Vol.I 320.

142 J. Story, *Commentaries on Equity Jurisprudence: As Administered in England and America,* Vol.II 509 ff.

143 J. Story, *Commentaries on Equity Jurisprudence: As Administered in England and America*, Vol.II 506; J. Hill, *A Practical Treatise on the Law Relating to Trustees* (1845), pp.554–557; T. Lewin, *A Practical Treatise on the Law of Trusts* 3rd edn (1857), pp.460–473. Cf. A. Underhill, *A Practical and Concise Manual of the Law Relating to Private Trusts and Trustees*, 5th edn (Butterworth & Company, 1901), pp.243, 250; E. Vinter, *A Treatise on the History and Law of Fiduciary Relationship* (London: Stevens & Sons, 1932), Ch. 1; L. A. Sheridan, *Fraud in Equity: A Study in English and Irish Law* (Pitman, 1957), p.185; D. O'Sullivan, S. Elliott and R. Zakrzewski, *The Law of Rescission* (Oxford University Press, 2008), paras 8.09–8.10.

144 *Ex parte Bennett* (1805) 10 Ves. Jun. 381 at 385; *Downes v Grazebrook* (1817) 3 Mer. 200 at 200; *Carter v Palmer* (1842) 7 Cl. & F. 657 at 707; *Re Bloye's W.T.* (1849) 1 Mac. & G. 488 at 495; *Grand Junction Canal Co v Dimes* (1850) 2 H. & T. 92 at 100; *Franks v Bollans* (1868) L.R. 3 Ch. App. 717 at 718; *McPherson v Watt* (1877) 3 App. Cas. 254 at 266; *Re Canadian Oil Works Corp* (1875) L.R. 10 Ch. App. 593 at 601; *Clare v Joseph* [1907] 2 K.B. 369 at 378–9; *Bath v Standard Land Co Ltd* [1911] 1 Ch. 618 at 634; *Transvaal Lands Co v New Belgium (Transvaal) Land and Development Co* [1914] 2 Ch. 488 at 502; *Taylor v Davies* [1920] A.C. 636 at 647; *Furs Ltd v Tomkies* (1936) 54 C.L.R. 583 at 592; *Re Bulmer* [1937] Ch. 499 at 503; *Scott v Scott* (1963) 109 C.L.R. 649; *Regal (Hastings) Ltd v Gulliver* [1967] 2 A.C. 134 at 159; *Tito v Waddell (No.2)* [1977] Ch. 106 at 248; *Guinness Plc v Saunders* (1987) 3 B.C.C. 271 at 287; and [1990] 2 A.C. 663 at 669 (arguendo); *HR v JAPT* [1997] O.P.L.R. 123 at [29].

145 And also, of the doctrine of undue influence: *Henchman v East India Co* (1797) 8 Bro. P.C. 85; *Agnew v Länsförsäkringsbolagens AB* [2001] 1 A.C. 223 at 264.

been championed by Lord Millett, who has emphasised in extra-judicial writings that an order directing a fiduciary to account for unauthorised profits "is not a monetary award for wrongdoing",[146] but an order that gives effect to a rule that the fiduciary is legally incapable of keeping such gains for himself.

A different way of thinking about fiduciary duty emerged in the case law of the late twentieth century. . . . This envisages that a fiduciary owes a positive duty "not to promote his personal interest . . . in circumstances in which there is a conflict or a real or substantial possibility of a conflict between his personal interests and those of the persons whom he is bound to protect".[147] Breach of this duty is conceptualised as a civil wrong that triggers a secondary duty to account for unauthorised gains,[148] or to pay compensation for loss.[149] **2–162**

This new idea sits very uneasily alongside the old thinking. The courts have held that it does not matter which version of fiduciary obligation is correct for the purposes of the causation rules[150] and limitation rules[151] governing claims for unauthorised profits. Nor does this clearly affect the question whether the principal's claim to such profits is proprietary or merely personal. . . But it goes to the heart of the question whether a principal can have compensation for loss, and now that the courts have moved to the position that he can, the disability model has come under great pressure. As Conaglen has written, the authorities currently require us to think that the "remedies of rescission, accounts of profits and proprietary constructive trusts operate on the basis that the fiduciary was under a disability", but that "where a compensatory remedy is sought the claim. . . takes on the characteristics of a duty-based claim".[152] It is doubtful that this can be sustained. There is a strong likelihood that the number of compensatory claims will increase over the next few years, and that one effect of this will be that the disability model yields to the breach of duty model in the context of claims for unauthorised gains.[153] This in turn may have knock-on consequences for issues such as the proper classification of such claims for the purposes of the limitation rules, a topic that is anyway in need of a serious rethink. . . **2–163**

B. When is Fiduciary Loyalty Imposed?

i. Recognised status-based fiduciary relationships

As Joshua Getzler has explained,[154] the idea that fiduciary duties should be imposed on parties in certain types of relationship is sourced in late medieval and early modern legal rules that: constrained co-owners from dealing with the shared property without due consideration of one another's interests; prevented the exploitation of wards by their guardians; required bailees and agents to prioritise **2–164**

[146] Lord Millett, "Book Review" (2002) 2 O.U.C.L.J 291, 295. See too Lord Millett, "Bribes and Secret Commissions" [1993] *Restitution Law Review* 7, 20, endorsed in *A-G for Hong Kong v Reid* [1994] 1 A.C. 324 at 337; Lord Millett, "Proprietary Restitution" in S. Degeling and J. Edelman (eds), *Equity in Commercial Law* (2005) p.324; Lord Millett, "Bribes and Secret Commissions Again" (2012) 71 Cambridge Law Journal 583, 585 and 591–92.

[147] *Hospital Products Ltd v United States Surgical Corp* at 103.

[148] *New Zealand Netherlands Society "Oranje" Inc v Kuys* [1973] 1 W.L.R. 1126 at 1129; *Chan v Zacharia* (1984) 154 C.L.R. 178 at 189; *Maguire v Makaronis* (1997) 188 C.L.R. 449 at 468; *United Pan-Europe Communications NV v Deutsche Bank AG* [2000] 2 B.C.L.C. 461 at [44]; *Walsh v Deloitte & Touche Inc* [2002] 4 L.R.C. 454 at [13]; *Lindsley v Woodfull* [2004] 2 B.C.L.C. 131 at [28]–[30].

[149] Many Commonwealth cases have been decided in the past 20 years in which equitable compensation for breach of fiduciary duty has been awarded or its availability has been recognized in principle. English cases include *Swindle v Harrison* [1997] 4 All E.R. 705; *Nationwide Building Society v Balmer Radmore (a firm)* [1999] P.N.L.R. 606; *Longstaff v Birtles* [2002] 1 W.L.R. 470 at [35]–[37]; *DEG-Deutsche Investitions und Entwicklungsgesellschaft mbH v Koshy* [2004] 1 B.C.L.C. 131 at [142]–[147]; *Také Ltd v BSM Marketing Ltd* [2009] EWCA Civ 45; *Bank of Ireland v Jaffery* [2012] EWHC 1377 (Ch).

[150] *Murad v Al-Saraj* [2005] W.T.L.R. 1573 at [49].

[151] *DEG-Deutsche Investitions und Entwicklungsgesellschaft mbH v Koshy* at [104]–[109].

[152] Conaglen, "Fiduciaries", in *Snell's Equity*, 32nd edn (2010) pp.221–222.

[153] Another likely effect will be the increasing use of the term "damages" to describe compensatory awards for breach of fiduciary duty. This usage is already widespread and there is no sign of the courts "stamp[ing it] out", as advocated in Lord Millett, "Equity's Place in the Law of Commerce" (1998) 114 L.Q.R 214, 225.

[154] Getzler, "Rumford Market and the Genesis of Fiduciary Obligations" in *Mapping the Law: Essays in Memory of Peter Birks* (2006), pp.590–597.

their principals' interests when dealing with third parties on their principals' behalf; and, regulated the activities of office holders. The courts of Chancery drew on these bodies of doctrine when developing the rule that trustees owe fiduciary duties to their beneficiaries, a rule which has formed part of English trust law since at least the early eighteenth century.[155] During the nineteenth and twentieth centuries, the courts then drew on the example of the trustee–beneficiary relationship in turn to hold that fiduciary duties should also be owed by other parties in analogous relationships.[156]

2–165 Certain features of the trustee–beneficiary relationship have been thought particularly relevant to the question whether an analogy can be drawn between this relationship and others. Trustees assume office voluntarily and thereby acquire powers whose exercise affects the beneficiaries' property rights and legal relations with third parties. Beneficiaries have a reasonable expectation that the trustees will not abuse their powers and position in a way that detrimentally affects them. Other relationships possess similar features and have consequently been held to be fiduciary relationships as a matter of law. Examples are the relationships between the executor or administrator and the beneficiary of a deceased person's estate,[157] between a solicitor and a client,[158] between a principal and an agent,[159] between partners,[160] between a company promoter and the company,[161] and between a company director and the company.[162]

2–166 These fiduciary relationships are status-based: they arise as a matter of law as a result of the parties' being in a particular relationship, the existence of which itself may depend on the prior application of some other legal rules, such as those to determine the existence of the express trust, or relationship of agency, for example.

2–167 In comparison with the difficulty in identifying when fiduciary loyalty applies on the facts, the status-based approach may seem to be a relatively easy and an uncontroversial means of explaining when fiduciary loyalty applies. There can be some challenges with a status-based approach, and while they may not matter in all cases, they may present difficulties in others. One is that some status-based relationships depend on the prior application of another set of legal rules to determine the existence of the relationship and which are not always themselves clear or certain. For example, a trustee is typically fiduciary, although the label of "trustee" has different meanings for different purposes,[163] and it is not always clear whether or not someone is a trustee of a type that is typically fiduciary. Likewise, in relation to agents. "[C]onsiderable terminological confusion"[164] surrounds the meaning of "agent",

---

155 *Keech v Sandford* (1726) Sel. Cas. Ch. 61, though trustees were not regularly described as "fiduciaries" in this sense until the nineteenth century: eg, *Woodhouse v Meredith* (1820) 1 J. & W. 204 at 213 (arguendo); *Hoghton v Hoghton* (1852) 15 Beav. 278 at 287–288 (arguendo); *New Sombrero Phosphate Co v Erlanger* (1877) 5 Ch.D. 73 at 118; *Boswell v Coaks (No. 1)* (1886) 11 App. Cas. 232 at 245; *Bray v Ford* [1896] A.C. 44 at 51–52.

156 See, e.g. *Re West of England & South Wales District Bank, Ex p. Dale & Co* (1879) 11 Ch.D. 772 at 778 per Fry J: "a fiduciary relationship . . . is one in respect of which if a wrong arise, the same remedy exists against the wrong-doer on behalf of the principal as would exist against a trustee on behalf of the cestui que trust."

157 *Re Diplock* [1948] Ch. 465; *Commissioner of Stamp Duties (Queensland) v Livingston* [1965] A.C. 694 at 707.

158 *Nocton v Lord Ashburton* [1914] A.C. 932; *McMaster v Byrne* [1952] 1 All E.R. 1362; *Clark Boyce v Mouat* [1994] 1 A.C. 428; *Hilton v Barker Booth & Eastwood (a firm)* [2005] 1 W.L.R. 567. See too S. Degeling and M. Legg, "Fiduciary Obligations of Lawyers in Australian Class Actions: Conflicts between Duties" (2014) 37 U.N.S.W.L.J. 914.

159 *Lowther v Lowther* (1806) 13 Ves. 95 at [103]; *Parker v McKenna* (1874) 10 Ch. App. 96 at 124–125; *Boston Deep Sea Fishing Co v Ansell* (1888) 39 Ch. D. 389; *Hurstanger Ltd v Wilson* [2008] Bus. L.R. 216; *FHR European Ventures LLP v Cedar Capital Partners LLC* [2015] A.C. 250.

160 *Bentley v Craven* (1853) 18 Beav. 75; *Thompson's Trustee v Heaton* [1974] 1 All E.R. 1239; *John Taylors (a firm) v Masons* [2005] W.T.L.R. 1519.

161 *Lydney Iron Ore Co v Bird* (1886) 33 Ch. D. 85 at 94; *Gluckstein v Barnes* [1900] A.C. 240.

162 *Re West of England & South Wales District Bank, Ex p. Dale & Co* (1879) 11 Ch. D. 772; *Furs Ltd v Tomkies* (1936) 54 C.L.R. 583; *Regal (Hastings) Ltd v Gulliver* [1967] 2 A.C. 134; Companies Act 2006 s.175.

163 L. Sealy, "The Director as Trustee" [1967] C.L.J. 83.

164 *Scott v Davis* (2000) 204 C.L.R. 333 at [227].

for example. Lord Herschell in *Kennedy v De Trafford*[165] remarked that "[n]o word is more commonly and constantly abused than the word 'agent'."

Added to this is that the rules for determining when a certain relationship exists sometimes presuppose the existence of fiduciary status itself.[166] The existence of agency,[167] or an express trust,[168] for example, is sometimes conditioned upon the pre-existence of fiduciary status. In these instances, it is difficult to then rely upon the existence of agency or an express trust to explain fiduciary status. If someone is an agent or express trustee because they are fiduciary, that underlying agency or trustee status cannot in turn be the reason for fiduciary status. **2–168**

The limits to agency status for explaining the existence of fiduciary duties has been recognised in the following two cases. **2–169**

Prince Eze v Conway

Court of Appeal, [2019] EWCA Civ 88 at [38]–[39]

ASPLIN L.J. (with whom PETER JACKSON L.J. agreed): Whether the law of bribery is engaged is dependent upon the nature and extent of the fiduciary duties owed by the recipient of the benefit or promise of a benefit, if any, the nature of the transaction in question and the relevant circumstances. The enquiry is inevitably extremely fact sensitive. This was acknowledged by Lord Upjohn in *Boardman v Phipps*[169] [who stated] **2–170**

> "The facts and circumstances must be carefully examined to see whether in fact a purported agent and even a confidential agent is in a fiduciary relationship to his principal. It does not necessarily follow that he is in such a position. . ."

It is clear from the authorities that in order for the law of bribery and secret commissions to be engaged there must be a relationship of trust and confidence between the recipient of the benefit or the promise of a benefit and his principal (used in the loosest of senses) which puts the recipient in a real position of potential conflict between his interest and his duty. Not all agents will be in such a position and the relationship may arise where there is no agency at all. It is not helpful, therefore, to consider what might be considered to be the paradigm of any particular type of agent, whether an "introducing agent" or otherwise. It all depends on the nature of the individual's duties and which of those duties is engaged in the precise circumstances under consideration. Although the relationship of principal and agent is a fiduciary one, not every person described as an "agent" is the subject of fiduciary duties and a person described as an agent may owe fiduciaries duties in relation to some of his activities and not others. **2–171**

Caution was again urged by David Richards LJ (with whom Males and Laing LJJ agreed) in *Wood v Commercial First Business Ltd,* stating:[170] **2–172**

> While it was important not to be too prescriptive about what functions qualify a person as an agent with fiduciary duties and what functions do not, it was dangerous to equate the term agent with the status of a fiduciary . . . The breadth and uncertainty of the duties of agent to their principals makes the label "fiduciary" "extremely fact dependent".

---

165 *Kennedy v De Trafford* [1897] A.C. 180 at 188. See further R. Leow, "Understanding Agency as a Proxy Power" (2019) 78 C.L.J. 99.

166 See further, *Wood v Commercial First Business Ltd* [2021] EWCA Civ 471; [2022] Ch. 123 at [26] ff; M. Conaglen, "The Fiduciary Status of Agents" in P. Davies (ed.), *Intermediaries in Commercial Law* (Hart Publishing, 2022 forthcoming); J. Hudson, "Justifying Equity's Control of Power: Status and Beyond" in P. Miller and J. Oberdiek (eds), *Oxford Studies in Private Law Theory: Volume 1* (Oxford University Press, 2023 forthcoming).

167 See, e.g. P. Watts, *Bowstead and Reynolds on Agency*, 21st edn (Sweet & Maxwell, 2019), Art.1: "[a]gency is the fiduciary relationship which exists between two persons . . .".

168 Trusts Act 2019 (New Zealand) s.13, 'The characteristics of an express trust are . . . (a) it is a fiduciary relationship . . .'

169 [1967] 2 A.C. 47 at 127.

170 *Wood v Commercial First Business Ltd* [2021] EWCA Civ 471; [2022] Ch. 123.

2–173 As emphasised in the two cases, an agent's fiduciary status is not a fait accompli and depends on the terms undertaken by the agent. Agents can act self-interestedly, or otherwise in a position of conflict, if permitted by the terms of the agency agreement.[171] A similar comment can be made in relation to express trustees, who are typically fiduciaries, although can act self-interestedly where the trust terms provide. This is explained in *Space Investments Ltd v Canadian Imperial Bank of Commerce Trust Co (Bahamas) Ltd* by Lord Templeman, who stated, ". . . as a general rule, a trustee is not allowed to derive a benefit from trust property, that general rule may be altered by the express terms of the trust instrument."[172] Likewise, solicitors can act self-interestedly where the terms of the retainer allow.[173]

ii. Fact-based or "ad hoc" fiduciary relationships

2–174 There are additionally fact-based fiduciary relationships where fiduciary duties are imposed on an ad hoc basis, according to the factual circumstances of a case. To give some examples: an army sergeant owed a fiduciary duty to the Crown which he breached when he took bribes to escort smugglers' lorries through police checks with the aid of his military uniform;[174] a solicitor who took it on himself to negotiate on behalf of trustees and beneficiaries for the purchase of company shares owed them a fiduciary duty as a "self-appointed agent" which he breached when he bought some of the shares for himself;[175] a broker owed a fiduciary duty in adopting a role of intermediary and in representing to the client that the terms offered by a third party were "competitive";[176] and a financier owed a fiduciary duty to an applicant for a loan that he breached when the applicant supplied him with confidential information that he communicated to a third party who used it to conclude a deal to the profit of the third party and the financier.[177]

2–175 Various cases concerning joint ventures also show that although these are business arrangements—in which the parties are often contracting at arm's length who owe one another no fiduciary duties—situations can arise where one joint-venturer is reasonably entitled to expect that the other will act in their joint interest to the exclusion of her own several interests, with the result that a fiduciary duty is owed.[178] Other cases show that although the employment relationship is not generally a fiduciary relationship either, some employees can owe fiduciary duties to their employers while the employment relationship subsists.[179]

---

171 *Kelly v Cooper* [1993] A.C. 205 at 214; *New Zealand Netherlands Society "Oranje" Inc v Kuys* [1973] 1 W.L.R. 1126 at 1129–1130; *Wood v Commercial First Business Ltd* [2021] EWCA Civ 471; [2022] Ch. 123 at [26]; *Prince Eze v Conway* [2019] EWCA Civ 88 at [39]. This point is also made in R. Leow, "Understanding Agency as a Proxy Power" (2019) 78 C.L.J. 99; Conaglen, "The Fiduciary Status of Agents" in *Intermediaries in Commercial Law* (Hart Publishing, 2022 forthcoming).

172 *Space Investments Ltd v Canadian Imperial Bank of Commerce Trust Co (Bahamas) Ltd* [1986] 1 W.L.R. 1072 at 1075. See also *New Zealand Netherlands Society "Oranje" v Kuys* [1973] 1 W.L.R. 1126 at 1129–1130. An express trustee has various powers of recoupment that can be exercised self-interestedly and for the trustee's own benefit, as discussed in J. Hudson and C. Mitchell, "Trustee Recoupment: A Power Analysis" (2021) 35 T.L.I. 3. See also: C. Mitchell, "Good Faith, Self-Denial and Mandatory Trustee Duties" (2018) 32 T.L.I. 92.

173 *Beach Petroleum v Kennedy* (1999) 48 N.S.W.L.R. 1 at 188; *Canadian National Railway Co v McKercher LLP* [2013] SCC 39 at [37].

174 *Reading v Attorney General* [1949] 2 K.B. 232.

175 *Boardman v Phipps*, discussed at paras 2–103ff. Cf. *English v Dedham Vale Properties Ltd* [1978] 1 W.L.R. 93.

176 *Medsted Associates Ltd v Canaccord Genuity Wealth (International) Ltd* [2019] EWCA Civ 83 at [29]–[33].

177 *United Pan Europe Communications NV v Deutsche Bank AG* [2000] 2 B.C.L.C. 461.

178 *Lac Minerals Ltd v International Corona Resources Ltd* (1989) 61 D.L.R. (4th) 14; *Hospital Products Ltd v US Surgical Corp* (1984) 156 C.L.R. 41; *Noranda Australia Ltd v Lachlan Resources* (1988) 14 N.S.W.L.R. 1; *John v James* [1991] F.S.R. 397 at 433; *Elliott v Wheeldon* [1993] B.C.L.C. 53 at 57; *Murad v Al-Saraj* [2005] EWCA Civ 959; [2005] W.T.L.R. 1573; *Chirnside v Fay* [2007] 1 N.Z.L.R. 433; *Ross River Ltd v Waveley Commercial Ltd* [2013] EWCA Civ 910; [2014] 1 B.C.L.C. 545.

179 *University of Nottingham v Fishel* [2000] I.C.R. 1462; *Neary v Dean of Westminster* [1999] I.R.L.R. 288; *Generics (UK) Ltd v Yeda Research and Development Co Ltd* [2012] EWCA Civ 726; [2013] Bus. L.R. 777. See also A. Frazer, "The

There are other cases that have found that, in certain circumstances, an adviser may owe fiduciary obligations in giving advice. In *Commonwealth Bank of Australia v Smith*[180] a fiduciary relationship arose in relation to a bank's provision of financial advice to its customers. The Full Court of the Federal Court of Australia cited the following passage from Brennan J's decision in *Daly v Sydney Stock Exchange*:[181] **2–176**

> Whenever a stockbroker or other person who holds himself out as having expertise in advising on investments is approached for advice on investments and undertakes to give it, in giving that advice the adviser stands in a fiduciary relationship to the person whom he advises. The adviser cannot assume a position where his self-interest might conflict with the honest and impartial giving of advice.

Such decisions are all very context-specific and although the courts have often described the circumstances in which fiduciary duties are imposed, their comments do not amount—and are not usually meant to amount—to finely grained tests that can predictably discriminate between cases where duties are imposed and cases where they are not. For example,[182] in *Reading v Attorney General*, Asquith LJ said that a fiduciary relationship exists:[183] **2–177**

> (a) whenever the plaintiff entrusts to the defendant property. . . and relies on the defendant to deal with such property for the benefit of the plaintiff or for purposes authorized by him, and not otherwise. . . and (b) whenever the plaintiff entrusts to the defendant a job to be performed. . . and relies on the defendant to procure for the plaintiff the best terms available.

In *Attorney-General v Blake*, Lord Woolf MR said that:[184] **2–178**

> [The most important] category of fiduciary relationship. . . is the relationship of trust and confidence, which arises whenever one party undertakes to act in the interests of another or places himself in a position where he is obliged to act in the interests of another.

In *Arklow Investments Ltd v Maclean*, Henry J said that:[185] **2–179**

> The [fiduciary] concept captures a situation where one person is in a relationship with another which gives rise to a legitimate expectation, which equity will recognise, that the fiduciary will not utilise his or her position in such a way which is adverse to the interests of his principal.

In *Grimaldi v Chameleon Mining NL (No.2)*, Finn J said that "there is no generally agreed and unexceptionable definition of who is a fiduciary", but that the following description sufficed for the purposes of the case:[186] **2–180**

Employee's Contractual Duty of Fidelity" (2015) 131 L.Q.R. 53; R. Flannigan, "Employee Fiduciary Accountability" [2015] J.B.L. 189.

180 *Commonwealth Bank of Australia v Smith* (1991) 42 F.C.R. 390 at 391–392, see paras 2–140ff.

181 (1987) 160 C.L.R. 371 at 385, see also at 377 (Gibbs CJ); *Hodgkinson v Simms* [1994] 3 S.C.R. 37; *Aequitas v Aefc* [2001] NSWSC 14 at [307] (Austin J); *Australian Securities and Investments Commission v Citigroup Global Markets Australia Pty Ltd (ACN 113 114832) (No.4)* [2007] FCA 963 at [283].

182 See also *Hospital Products Ltd v US Surgical Corp* (1984) 156 C.L.R. 41 at 96–97; *Frame v Smith* [1987] 2 S.C.R. 99 at [136], adopted in *International Corona Resources Ltd v LAC Minerals Ltd* [1989] 2 S.C.R. 574; *Hodgkinson v Simms* [1994] 3 S.C.R. 377 at [29]–[37]; *Perez v Galambos* [2009] 3 S.C.R. 247 at [67]–[68].

183 [1949] 2 K.B. 232 at 236.

184 [1998] Ch. 439 at 454.

185 [2000] 1 W.L.R. 594 at 598.

186 (2012) 200 F.C.R. 296 at [177].

> . . . a person will be in a fiduciary relationship with another when and insofar as that person has undertaken to perform such a function for, or has assumed such a responsibility to, another as would thereby reasonably entitle that other to expect that he or she will act in that other's interest to the exclusion of his or her own or a third party's interest.

2–181 These are apt descriptions of fact-based, as well as status-based fiduciary relationships. But a legal test needs to explain the cases which fall outside its scope as well as those which fall within it, and on that measure these dicta do less well, since there are relationships which possess the features that are said to be relevant and which are not fiduciary under English law. An example is the doctor–patient relationship,[187] where there are power and an assumption of responsibility on one side; and, on the other side, vulnerability to abuse of that power and a reasonable expectation that the power will not be abused.

2–182 Again, it often happens that one commercial party has significant power to affect the financial interests of another commercial party, but the courts rarely find that such relationships are fiduciary, and will only do so when there is strong evidence that one has agreed to act in the interests of the other. Thus, in *JP Morgan Bank v Springwell Navigation Corp*, Gloster J held that:[188]

> . . . the mere fact that one party to a commercial relationship "trusts" the other does not predicate a fiduciary relationship. The word "trust", like the word "advice", has a variety of meanings. In a broad sense, trust is an important element in many commercial dealings. . . Springwell no doubt "trusted" Chase to conduct itself in a commercially appropriate manner. But I do not consider that Springwell had any legitimate expectation that, in its commercial dealings with Springwell, Chase would subordinate its interests to those of Springwell.

2–183 On the same theme, in *Frame v Smith*, Wilson J said that:[189]

> Because of the requirement of vulnerability of the beneficiary at the hands of the fiduciary, fiduciary obligations are seldom present in dealings of experienced businessmen of similar bargaining strength acting at arm's length. . . The law takes the position that such individuals are perfectly capable of agreeing as to the scope of discretion or power to be exercised, i.e., any "vulnerability" could have been prevented through the more prudent exercise of their bargaining power and the remedies for the wrongful exercise or abuse of that discretion or power. . . are adequate in such a case.

2–184 These comments reflect the courts' general attitude that they should not introduce uncertainty into commercial dealings by the "over-ready use of equitable concepts such as fiduciary obligations",[190] and that arm's length commercial parties should be entitled (and even encouraged) to act in their own self-interest, negotiate the best possible deal for themselves, and take whatever profit-making opportunities come their way. As Sales J said in *Vercoe v Rutland Fund Management Ltd*:[191]

---

[187] *Sidaway v Board of Governors of the Bethlem Royal Hospital* [1985] A.C. 871 at 884: "there is no comparison to be made between the relationship of doctor and patient with that of solicitor and client, trustee and cestui qui trust or the other relationships treated in equity as of a fiduciary character." The High Court of Australia takes the same view: *Breen v Williams* (1996) 186 C.L.R. 71; but the Supreme Court of Canada does not: *McInerny v Macdonald* [1992] 2 S.C.R. 138; cf. *Norberg v Wynrib* [1992] 2 S.C.R. 226 at 272.

[188] [2008] EWHC 1186 (Comm) at [574], followed in *Barclays Bank Plc v Svizera Holdings BV* [2014] EWHC 1020 (Comm) at [8] and *Bailey v Barclays Bank Plc* [2014] EWHC 2882 (QB) at [88].

[189] [1987] 2 S.C.R. 99 at 137–138, followed in *International Corona Resources Ltd v LAC Minerals Ltd* [1989] 2 S.C.R. 574 at [149].

[190] *Cobbe v Yeoman's Row Management Ltd* [2008] UKHL 55; [2008] 1 W.L.R. 1752 at [81] per Lord Walker.

[191] [2010] EWHC 424 (Ch) at [343].

> . . . a degree of self-seeking and ruthless behaviour [in commercial dealings] is expected and accepted. . . In a fiduciary relationship, by contrast, self-seeking behaviour is required to be reined in on the grounds that special obligations of trust have been assumed by the fiduciary to the other party.

The role and relevance of some of these indicators of a fiduciary relationship, such as vulnerability, were examined by the Law Commission[192] in a report on Fiduciary Duties of Investment Intermediaries. The Commission explained that some of the factors identified in some of the various case formulations, such as vulnerability, trust, discretion and confidence, for example, are "indicators of fiduciary status, rather than its defining feature",[193] echoing a similar point made by the Supreme Court of Canada in *Hodgkinson v Simms*, that "the concept of vulnerability is not the hallmark of [the] fiduciary relationship",[194] although it is an indicator that one may exist. **2–185**

Added to this is that the concepts of power, discretion and vulnerability are not at large, and it is not *any* sense of each that are indicators of a fiduciary relationship on the facts. The existence of a legal power, for example, is not in and of itself sufficient for a fiduciary relationship to arise. Examples of non-fiduciary power-holders include a mortgagee with a power of sale over the mortgagor's property, which the mortgagee holds on their own behalf and can exercise self-interestedly;[195] a third party donee of a power of appointment under an express trust may be permitted by the trust terms to exercise the power self-interestedly or otherwise in a position of conflict.[196] In all these, and other situations,[197] the power-holder does have a legal power to change another's legal status, who is vulnerable to the exercise of power, and yet fiduciary duties do not apply. **2–186**

One commercial party may have significant power to affect the interests of another, yet the courts will only find such relationships are fiduciary when there is strong evidence that one has agreed to act in the interests of the other.[198] As Leggatt LJ said at first instance in *Sheikh Al Nehayan v Kent*:[199] **2–187**

> At a basic level any contracting party is entitled to rely on the other party to perform its contractual obligations without having to monitor performance or even if... it is unable to monitor performance. The kind of trust and confidence characteristic of a fiduciary relationship is different. ... It is founded on the acceptance by one party of a role which requires exercising judgment and making discretionary decisions on behalf of another and constitutes trust and confidence in the loyalty of the decision-maker to put aside his or her own interests and act solely in the interests of the principal.

Nor does any type of vulnerability indicate a fiduciary relationship. It is only the vulnerability that arises from the particular circumstance in which the fiduciary holds a power or discretion over the principal. An example is where a fiduciary relationship arises in favour of a principal such as a large **2–188**

---

192 Law Commission, *Fiduciary Duties of Investment Intermediaries*, para.[3.24].
193 Law Commission, *Fiduciary Duties of Investment Intermediaries*, para.[3.22].
194 *Hodgkinson v Simms* [1994] 3 S.C.R. 377 at 405 (La Forest J).
195 *Downsview Nominees Ltd v First City Corp Ltd* [1993] A.C. 295 at 315; *Yorkshire Bank Plc v Hall* [1999] 1 W.L.R. 1713 at 1728; *Barns v Queensland National Bank Ltd* (1906) 3 C.L.R. 925 at 942–943.
196 As in *Gisborne v Gisborne* (1877) 2 App. Cas. 300, 305 at 309; *Cloutte v Storey* [1911] 1 Ch. 18 at 30–32; *Re Wills Trusts Deeds* [1964] Ch. 219; *Basel Trust Corp v Ghirlandina* [2008] J.L.R. 1; *IBM United Kingdom Holdings Ltd v Dalgleish* [2017] EWCA Civ 1212 at [46].
197 An express trustee has various powers of recoupment that can be exercised self-interestedly and for the trustee's own benefit, as discussed in J. Hudson and C. Mitchell, "Trustee Recoupment: A Power Analysis" (2021) 35 T.L.I. 3.
198 See, e.g. *International Corona Resources Ltd v LAC Minerals Ltd* [1989] 2 S.C.R. 574 at [149]; *Barclays Bank Plc v Svizera Holdings BV* [2014] EWHC 1020 (Comm); [2015] 1 All E.R. (Comm) 788 at [8]; *Bailey v Barclays Bank Plc* [2014] EWHC 2882 (QB) at [88].
199 [2018] EWHC 333 (Comm) at [165].

company or municipal council, who would not normally be considered as "vulnerable" in the general sense, and yet may be "vulnerable" in a sense tending towards a finding of fiduciary duties.[200]

2–189 The Law Commission,[201] after examining the different approaches to identifying a fiduciary relationship on the facts, came down to suggesting that the legitimate expectation approach was "a useful way to determine when fiduciary relationships arise", going on to express the "key test" for whether a fiduciary relationship arises as being "whether there is a legitimate expectation that one party will act in another's interest".[202]

2–190 As Sarah Worthington has pointed out, the Law Commission's "key test" "repeats the question rather than delivering the answer: *when* is there a legitimate expectation that one party will act in another's interest?"[203] An answer given by some cases and commentaries is similar to the idea expressed by Millett LJ in *Bristol & West Building Society v Mothew*, excerpted above[204] of "*an undertak[ing] to act for or on behalf of another* in a particular matter in circumstances that give rise to a relationship of trust and confidence".[205] In other words, a putative fiduciary undertaking to act for, or in the interests of another, is when that other, the principal, will have a reasonable or legitimate expectation sufficient to give rise to a fiduciary relationship.[206]

2–191 As with some of the other conceptual indicators, it is not any undertaking that renders a person a fiduciary, or engenders a legitimate expectation on the part of the putative principle. Each of the mortgagee and third party donee of a power of appointment under an express trust undertake to only exercise power in particular ways and not in others, and which would engender a legitimate expectation or a degree of trust as to how power is to be exercised (and not) on the other's part. Yet neither are fiduciaries.

2–192 A more promising line of inquiry may be to focus on the terms of the undertaking according to which a power or discretion is held, and to identify the terms that attract fiduciary loyalty and those that do not. This is the precise exercise undertaken in cases[207] confronted with a legal power that is held outside the traditional status-based relationships. For example, in *Re Wills Trusts Deeds*, Buckley J found that fiduciary loyalty applied to a power-holder ". . . because [the settlor] . . . reposes a confidence in [the power-holder] . . . to perform vicariously on his, the settlor's behalf."[208] Buckley J went on to state that the "distinguishing characteristic" attracting fiduciary loyalty is "the settlor's intention that the donee shall, in the exercise of the power, act on the settlor's behalf".[209] Similarly, in *Basel Trust Corp v Ghirlandina*, powers were subject to fiduciary loyalty when they are " . . . exercisable to promote the interests of the beneficiaries as a whole".[210]

---

200 See, e.g. *Wingecarribee Shire Council v Lehman Brothers Australia Ltd (in liq)* (2012) 301 A.L.R. 1; *ABN AMRO Bank NV v Bathurst Regional Council* (2014) 224 F.C.R. 1; *Australian Securities and Investments Commission v Citigroup Global Markets Australia Pty Ltd (No.4)* [2007] FCA 963; (2007) 160 F.C.R. 35.

201 Law Commission, *Fiduciary Duties of Investment Intermediaries*, para.[3.24].

202 Law Commission, *Fiduciary Duties of Investment Intermediaries*, para.[3.24].

203 S. Worthington, "Four Questions on Fiduciaries" (2016) 2 C.J.C.C.L. 723, 731.

204 See paras 2–071ff.

205 See, e.g. *FHR European Ventures LLP v Cedar Capital Partners LLC* [2014] UKSC 45; [2015] A.C. 250 at [5] (emphasis added); *Farrar v Miller* [2018] EWCA Civ 172 at [75]; *Sheikh Tahnoon v Kent* [2018] EWHC 333 (Comm) at [158]–[159].

206 Law Commission, *Fiduciary Duties of Investment Intermediaries*, para.[3.23], referring to J. Edelman, "When do Fiduciary Duties Arise?" (2010) 126 L.Q.R. 302; P. Finn, "The Fiduciary Principle" in T. Youdan (ed.), *Equity, Fiduciaries and Trusts* (Toronto: Carswell, 1989), p.46.

207 See *Lord Vesty's Executors v IRC* [1949] 1 All E.R. 1108 at 1115, 1132, also emphasised that on construction of the trust terms, the power was held on behalf of the beneficiaries; *Re Skeats' Settlement* (1889) 42 Ch. D. 522 at 527; *Basel Trust Corp v Ghirlandina* [2008] J.L.R. 1; *Weller v Ker* (1866) L.R. 1 Sc. & D. 11; *Re Wills Trusts Deeds* [1964] Ch. 219; *Mercanti v Mercanti* (2016) 50 W.A.R. 495 at [397]–[398], special leave to appeal refused in *Mercanti v Mercanti* [2017] HCASL 59.

208 *Re Wills Trusts Deeds* [1964] Ch. 219 at 228.

209 *Re Wills Trusts Deeds* [1964] Ch. 219 at 229.

210 *Basel Trust Corp v Ghirlandina* [2008] J.L.R. 1 at 34.

Terms requiring power to be held and exercised for and on behalf of another have been identified as "[t]he critical feature"[211] of the accepted status-based relationships as well. Company directors hold their powers on terms that require them to act for and on behalf of the company, and for this reason are subject to fiduciary loyalty.[212] An agent and express trustee are usually subject to terms requiring power to be held for and on behalf of the principal or beneficiary, and to this extent fiduciary loyalty applies. Fiduciary loyalty does not apply when the terms allow the agent or trustee to exercise power on her own behalf. **2–193**

The terms are a generic phrase to encompass the ways in which a power-holder should and should not exercise power, and will be derived from different sources across different contexts. The trust terms are discussed further in Chapter 10. In some contexts, the terms will be derived from the meanings attributed to the parties' actions, including their actions in entering a contract. This in turn helps to explain the significance attributed to the contract in some cases as reflecting the importance of the terms according to which a power is held, and which is an issue discussed further below. **2–194**

C. Scope of Fiduciary Duties

Once the court has decided that two parties are in a fiduciary relationship, "that relationship must be examined to see. . . what is the scope and ambit of the duties" that should be imposed on the fiduciary.[213] As Lord Browne-Wilkinson has observed, it is not the case that "all fiduciaries owe the same duties in all circumstances",[214] and as Lord Wilberforce has said, a person "may be in a fiduciary position quoad a part of his activities but not quoad other parts; each transaction, or group of transactions, must be looked at".[215] The courts must therefore determine "the subject matter over which the fiduciary obligations extend",[216] by asking what function or responsibility the fiduciary has assumed, and in Finn J's words:[217] **2–195**

> [this] may be narrow and circumscribed, as is often the case with specific agencies; it may be broad and general, as is characteristically the case with the functions of company directors; its scope may have been antecedently defined or determined; it may have been ordained by past practice; it may be left to the fiduciary's discretion to determine; and it may evolve over time as is commonly the case with partnerships.

And in *Birtchnell v Equity Trustees, Executors and Agency Co Ltd*, Dixon J explained:[218] **2–196**

> The subject matter over which the fiduciary obligations extend is determined by the character of the venture or undertaking for which the partnership exists, and this is to be ascertained, not merely from the express agreement of the parties, . . . but from the course of dealing actually pursued by the firm.

---

211 *Hospital Products Ltd v United States Surgical Corp* (1984) 156 C.L.R. 41 at 96–97 (Mason J).

212 Companies Act 2006 s.172(1).

213 *Boardman v Phipps* [1967] 2 A.C. 46 at 127 per Lord Upjohn. See too *University of Nottingham v Fishel* [2000] I.C.R. 1462 at 1490–1493; *Ross River Ltd v Waveley Commercial Ltd* [2013] EWCA Civ 910; [2014] 1 B.C.L.C. 545 at [12].

214 *Henderson v Merrett Syndicates Ltd* [1995] 2 A.C. 145 at 206. See too *Re Coomber* [1911] 1 Ch. 723 at 728–729.

215 *New Zealand Netherlands Society "Oranje" Inc v Kuys* [1973] 1 W.L.R. 1126 at [1130]. See too *United Pan-Europe Communications NV v Deutsche Bank AG* [2000] 2 B.C.L.C. 461 at [47]; *Saltri III Ltd v MD Mezzanine SA SICAR (t/a Mezzanine Facility Agent)* [2012] EWHC 3025 (Comm); [2013] 1 All E.R. (Comm) 661 at [123].

216 *Birtchnell v Equity Trustees* (1929) 42 C.L.R. 384 at 408 (Dixon J). See also *Chan v Zacharia* (1983) 154 C.L.R. 178 at 195; *Hospital Products Ltd v United States Surgical Corp* (1984) 156 C.L.R. 41 at 102; *Streeter v Western Areas Exploration Pty Ltd (No.2)* (2011) 278 A.L.R. 291 at [70].

217 *Grimaldi v Chameleon Mining NL (No.2)* (2012) 200 F.C.R. 296 at [179].

218 (1929) 42 C.L.R. 384 at 408.

2–197 This means that the scope of the fiduciary's duty will accommodate itself to the facts giving rise to it such that later certain conduct, such as conflict or profit is not a breach of fiduciary duty where it would otherwise have been.

2–198 An example is *Medsted Associates Ltd v Canaccord Genuity Wealth (International) Ltd*,[219] where some wealthy clients engaged the services of a broker as an introducing agent to facilitate the clients' investments in derivatives written by a financial institution via an intermediary. Longmore LJ (with whom Peter Jackson and Asplin LJJ agreed) found that the broker owed a fiduciary duty in acting on behalf of the clients in introducing them to an intermediary and representing the terms being offered to the clients as "competitive".[220] The issue was whether the broker was in breach of its fiduciary duty due to its receipt of a commission from a third party in connection with the broker's introduction of the clients to the intermediary. The Court of Appeal found there was no breach because the scope of the broker's fiduciary duty was limited by the fact that the clients knew from the outset that a commission would be paid to the broker.[221]

2–199 The scope of fiduciary duties can be of particular significance in the corporate context where directors or other corporate office-holders, who are typically fiduciary, may have other interests as a shareholder or hold other roles, such as being a director and/or shareholder of other (sometimes competitor) companies. In the following extract, Sarah Worthington argues that the courts should take a more nuanced approach to the scope of the fiduciary duty owed by directors under English law, as the current rules are operating unfairly in "corporate opportunity" cases.

Sarah Worthington, "Fiduciary Duties and Proprietary Remedies: Addressing the Failure of Equitable Formulae"

(2013) 72 C.L.J. 720, 746–747

2–200 [A] line of cases [has been] focused on determining whether an opportunity is a "corporate opportunity" (i.e. an opportunity which, given the specific ambit of the director's fiduciary duty, might legitimately be pursued for the benefit of the company),[222] or, similarly, a "partnership opportunity".[223] There is good reason to suppose that modern courts are drawing this line in the wrong place,[224] and that deeper thought about the precise import of the general rule against conflicts of duty and interest would see wider adoption of the approach taken in the partnership case of *Aas v Benham*.[225] It must surely be true that even fiduciaries have a private sphere of operation,[226] despite some assertions

---

[219] *Medsted Associates Ltd v Canaccord Genuity Wealth (International) Ltd* [2019] EWCA Civ 83 at [32] (Longmore LJ with whom Peter Jackson and Asplin LJJ agreed).

[220] *Medsted Associates Ltd v Canaccord Genuity Wealth (International) Ltd* [2019] EWCA Civ 83 at [32].

[221] *Medsted Associates Ltd v Canaccord Genuity Wealth (International) Ltd* [2019] EWCA Civ 83 at [34], [44].

[222] Earlier cases on the equitable rule vary in their approach, some taking a narrow view of which opportunities are caught: *Balston Ltd v Headline Filters Ltd* [1990] F.S.R. 385 at 412; *Industrial Development Consultants Ltd v Cooley* [1972] 1 W.L.R. 443; and, some a wider view: *Bhullar v Bhullar* [2003] EWCA Civ 424; *O'Donnell v Shanahan* [2009] EWCA Civ 751.

[223] *Aas v Benham* [1891] 2 Ch. 244.

[224] See the discussion in L. Sealy and S. Worthington, *Sealy & Worthington's Cases and Materials in Company Law*, 10th edn (Oxford University Press, 2013), pp.372ff. The explanation is perhaps simple: the courts' focus has been on establishing the existence of a fiduciary breach, rather than identifying its precise genesis.

[225] [1891] 2 Ch. 244.

[226] See Lindley LJ in *Aas v Benham* [1891] 2 Ch. 244 at 256, giving the example of a partner using his increased scientific knowledge, gleaned from working with the partnership, to publish a book on the subject, being a book which did not in any way compete with the partnership business: this profit would not be recoverable by the other partners.

to the contrary,[227] and that not every successful profit-making endeavour can be captured by the principal.[228]

For example, most modern companies have unrestricted objects. This cannot mean that directors have a duty to present to the company for its approval every personal investment they propose to make, or otherwise run the risk that the company will be able to claim the gain as a disloyal profit made in breach of the conflict rule on the basis that every opportunity is a potential corporate opportunity. Yet, taken at face value, that is just the proposition advanced in *Bhullar v Bhullar*,[229] where the court held that the director had one capacity only, and that was as a fiduciary. In that case, the directors had purchased on their own account a block of land adjacent to one already owned by the company. The court held that this had been acquired in breach of their fiduciary obligations, and was therefore held on constructive trust for the company. Since the company was in the business of buying property for investment, that conclusion might not seem unreasonable. On those bald facts, the acquisition was certainly one within the scope of the fiduciary endeavour. . . This would be true whether or not the company had the funds to make the investment, or would, if given the choice, have decided to do so. All those matters are for the principal to determine, not for the fiduciary to presume. But in this particular case the company was a family-owned company, and on the breakdown of the family relationship the other side of the family had insisted that no further property investments be made. That was taken by the court as going merely to the issue of the principal's choice, in the way just noted. But on another reading, the assertion goes instead to the issue of scope. If, as a result of the bar on future investment, the company is no longer a company interested in property investment (notwithstanding that its corporate capacity was not so limited), then the defendant fiduciaries' acquisition would not involve a conflict; indeed, it would not be disloyal in any way. The court, however, refused to accept that scope could be limited in this way. **2–201**

A more nuanced approach to the scope of a director's fiduciary duty was taken by the High Court of Australia in *Howard v Commissioner of Taxation*.[230] A company director received a sum of money in relation to his personal involvement in a joint venture investment in a golf course. An argument was made that the director held that sum on constructive trust for the company, on the basis the director's self-interest in the joint venture investment conflicted with the company's interests. This argument was rejected, and one of the main reasons for this was that the scope of the director's fiduciary duty to the company did not encompass the director's personal involvement in the joint venture investment. The joint venture did not compete with the company, and nor was the investment opportunity pursued by the joint venture one which the director was obliged to pursue for the company. **2–202**

Howard v Commissioner of Taxation

High Court of Australia, (2014) 253 C.L.R. 83 at [34]

FRENCH C.J. and KEANE J.: Despite their broad judicial formulations fiduciary duties are not infinitely extensible. That point was made in *Chan v Zacharia*[231] which concerned the content of the fiduciary duties of members of a partnership inter se. The limits of those duties were to be determined by the character of the venture for which the partnership existed, the express agreement of the parties and the course of dealings actually pursued by the firm.[232] The scope of the fiduciary duty generally in relation to conflicts of interest must accommodate itself to the particulars of the underlying relationship which give rise to the duty so that it is consistent with and conforms to the scope and limits of that relationship. It is to be **2–203**

---

227 *O'Donnell v Shanahan* [2009] EWCA Civ 751 at [69] (Rimer LJ), suggesting, in the context of directors as fiduciaries, that a director was always a director; he did not have "off-duty" time. Similarly, see *Bhullar v Bhullar* [2003] EWCA Civ 424 at [41]: a fiduciary has "one capacity and one capacity only".
228 Hence the suggestion here of a strict and limiting "scope" or "line of business" test.
229 [2003] EWCA Civ 424.
230 *Howard v Commissioner of Taxation* (2014) 253 C.L.R. 83.
231 (1984) 154 C.L.R. 178.
232 *Chan v Zacharia* (1984) 154 C.L.R. 178 at 196 (Deane J).

> "moulded according to the nature of the relationship and the facts of the case".[233] By way of example, company directors are frequently shareholders. The decisions they take as directors may therefore affect their personal interests. They do not breach their fiduciary obligations merely because in promoting the interests of the company they are also promoting their own.[234] On the other hand, a decision taken by directors to advantage themselves other than as members of the general body of shareholders would constitute an abuse of fiduciary powers.[235]

D. The Significance of Contract

2–204 We have seen already how the terms of the parties' arrangement can mean that those who are usually status-based fiduciaries may not owe fiduciary duties in respect of all or some of their powers,[236] and further, that the terms requiring a power or some other discretion to be exercised for or on behalf of another, will often be the essential or critical feature pointing towards to ascription of fiduciary duties.[237] As mentioned already, *the terms* is a generic label to refer to the ways in which a power may, and sometimes should, be exercised, and together define a sphere of permission for the lawful exercise of power. The terms can be derived from multiple sources, depending on the nature of the relationship in question. For some those relationships where the terms are the meanings attributed to the parties' volitional actions in manifesting their expressions of intention and consent, then any valid contract will provide evidence of the terms in this regard.

2–205 A contract may contain terms requiring power to be exercised for or on behalf of another, tending towards application of a fiduciary duty. The contract may instead contain terms indicating that power can be exercised self-interestedly, or may expressly state that one party is not acting in a fiduciary capacity,[238] tending against a finding of fiduciary duty, or a modification of the scope of such duty. On this topic, Mason J made the following comments in *Hospital Products Ltd v United States Surgical Corp:*[239]

> That contractual and fiduciary relationships may co-exist between the same parties has never been doubted. Indeed, the existence of a basic contractual relationship has in many situations provided a foundation for the erection of a fiduciary relationship. In these situations it is the contractual foundation which is all important because it is the contract that regulates the basic rights and liabilities of the parties. The fiduciary relationship, if it is to exist at all, must accommodate itself to the terms of the contract so that it is consistent with, and conforms to, them. The fiduciary relationship cannot be superimposed upon the contract in such a way as to alter the operation which the contract was intended to have according to its true construction.

2–206 Similarly, in *Henderson v Merrett Syndicates Ltd*, Lord Browne-Wilkinson said:[240]

> the extent and nature of the fiduciary duties owed in any particular case fall to be determined by reference to any underlying contractual relationship between the parties. Thus, in the case of an agent employed under a contract, the scope of his fiduciary duties is determined by the terms of the underlying contract. Although an agent is, in the absence of contractual provision, in breach of his fiduciary duties if he acts

---

233 *Hospital Products Ltd v United States Surgical Corp* (1984) 156 C.L.R. 41 at 102.
234 *Hirsche v Sims* [1894] A.C. 654, at 600–661.
235 *Harlowe's Nominees Pty Ltd v Woodside (Lakes Entrance) Oil Co NL* (1968) 121 C.L.R. 483 at 492–494.
236 See para.2–173.
237 See paras 2–192 to 2–194.
238 *Australian Securities and Investments Commission v Citigroup Global Markets Australia Pty Ltd (No.4)* [2007] FCA 963; (2007) 160 F.C.R. 35.
239 (1984) 156 C.L.R. 41 at 97.
240 [1995] 2 A.C. 145 at 206. See too *Hilton v Barker Booth & Eastwood* [2005] UKHL 8; [2005] 1 W.L.R. 567 at [30].

> for another who is in competition with his principal, if the contract under which he is acting authorises him so to do, the normal fiduciary duties are modified accordingly: see *Kelly v Cooper*.[241] The existence of a contract does not exclude the co-existence of concurrent fiduciary duties (indeed, the contract may well be their source); but the contract can and does modify the extent and nature of the general duty that would otherwise arise.

Kelly v Cooper was a Privy Council decision from Bermuda. The defendant estate agents were instructed by the claimant to sell his house on a commission basis. The claimant's neighbour also instructed the defendants to sell his house. A purchaser offered to buy the neighbour's house and his offer was accepted. The purchaser then offered to buy the claimant's house. The defendants failed to tell the claimant that the purchaser had agreed to buy the neighbour's house and as a result the claimant agreed to sell his house for a lower price than he could have negotiated if he had known that the purchaser planned to amalgamate the two properties. The court held that the defendant's failure to disclose the information did not entail a breach of fiduciary duty. The reason was that a term was implied into the contract between the claimant and the defendants that in the ordinary course of business, the defendants could act for many sellers and treat information that they obtained from each seller as confidential. Hence, the fiduciary duty they would otherwise have owed to the claimant, not to act for another principal with conflicting interests, was displaced by the parties' contract. Lord Browne-Wilkinson explained:[242] **2–207**

> First, agency is a contract made between principal and agent; second, like every other contract, the rights and duties of the principal and agent are dependent upon the terms of the contract between them, whether express or implied. It is not possible to say that all agents owe the same duties to their principals: it is always necessary to have regard to the express or implied terms of the contract.

It is important to remember that any contract is important only as showing the parties' intentions and consent for how the putative fiduciary is to hold and exercise her power or discretion. The contract it is not per se determinative and the question of whether or not a power or discretion is held for, or on behalf of, another will depend on the whole course of dealing between the parties, in so far as it is relevant to the parties' intentions and consent for how power should and should not be exercised. This means that where the parties' extra-contractual actions indicate their intentions for a power or discretion to be held by the putative fiduciary for an on behalf of the other party, a fiduciary relationship may arise prior to formation of, or outside of the parties' contractual relationship.[243] One implication is that parties who engage in pre-contractual dealings sufficient to give rise to a fiduciary relationship should be wary in their subsequent contractual or other attempts to exclude or modify fiduciary duties as this may itself result in a breach of any pre-existing fiduciary relationship. **2–208**

---

241 [1993] A.C. 205.

242 *Kelly v Cooper* [1993] A.C. 205 at 212–2–214.

243 See, e.g. *United Dominions Corp Ltd v Brian Pty Ltd* (1985) 157 C.L.R. 1 where the parties' dealing prior to entry into a partnership agreement were sufficient to constitute a fiduciary relationship: *Australian Securities and Investments Commission v Citigroup Global Markets Australia* at [325] where Jacobson J indicated that the parties' pre-contractual dealings "would have pointed strongly towards the existence of a fiduciary relationship in Citigroup's role as an adviser", although no fiduciary relationship was ultimately found as the pleaded case eschewed reliance upon the parties' pre-contractual dealings, see [306]. See further J. Campbell, "Fiduciary Relationships in a Commercial Context" (Sydney Law School Research Paper No. 14/26, 3 March 2014), *https://ssrn.com/abstract=2404202*.

E. Termination of Fiduciary Relationships

2–209 The courts do not recognise "the concept of a fiduciary obligation which continues notwithstanding the determination of the particular relationship which gives rise to it".[244] Fiduciary duties come to an end with the ending of the relationship which led to their imposition.[245] However, a fiduciary cannot escape liability for breach of fiduciary duty by resigning her post and then taking an opportunity for herself that previously came to her in her fiduciary capacity.[246] Also, a fiduciary's duty of confidentiality can extend beyond termination of the relationship giving rise to confidentiality.[247] Confidentiality is discussed in Chapter 3.

F. Defence of Informed Consent

2–210 A defence to liability for breach of fiduciary duty is informed consent, whether given before or after the facts of breach.[248] A principal cannot validly consent to a breach of duty unless she is sui juris and her consent must not have been procured by the fiduciary taking improper advantage of the parties' relationship.[249]

2–211 The principal's consent must furthermore be informed: the fiduciary must make "full and frank disclosure of all material facts".[250] In the High Court of Australia decision in *Maguire v Makaronis*, Brennan CJ, Gaudron, McHugh and Gummow JJ explained that:[251]

> What is required for a fully informed consent is a question of fact in all the circumstances of each case and there is no precise formula which will determine in all cases if fully informed consent has been given. ...

2–212 At minimum, this includes disclosure of the nature and extent of the breach of fiduciary duty.[252] For example, a fiduciary who receives a commission from a third party should disclose facts as to the third party's identity, the terms upon which the commission is paid, and how it is calculated.

2–213 The quality and means of disclosure expected of the fiduciary will be calibrated to circumstances and relevant experience of the principal, "[t]he sufficiency of disclosure can depend on the sophistication and intelligence of the persons to whom disclosure must be made".[253] The principal's actions must objectively show that she has turned her mind to the question of whether to consent to the fiduciary's breach.

---

244 *Attorney General v Blake* [1998] Ch. 439 at 453 per Lord Woolf MR, adding that: "Equity does not demand a duty of undivided loyalty from a former employee to his former employer".

245 *Walsh v Shanahan* [2013] EWCA Civ 411 at [34].

246 *Industrial Development Consultants Ltd v Cooley* [1972] 1 W.L.R. 443; *Canadian Aero Services Ltd v O'Malley* (1973) 40 D.L.R. (3d) 371; *Abbey Glen Pty Co v Stumborg* (1978) 85 D.L.R. (3d) 35; Contrast *Queensland Mines Ltd v Hudson* (1978) 18 A.L.R. 1; *Island Export Finance Ltd v Umunna* [1986] B.C.L.C. 460; *Framlington Group Plc v Anderson* [1995] 1 B.C.L.C. 475; *Foster Bryant Surveying Ltd v Bryant* [2007] Bus. L.R. 1565.

247 *Prince Jefri Bolkiah v KPMG* [1999] 2 A.C. 222 (HL) at 235; *Glencairn IP Holdings Ltd v Product Specialities Inc (t/a Final Touch)* [2020] EWCA Civ 609; [2021] Ch. 201 at [66].

248 *Regal (Hastings) Ltd v Gulliver* (1942) [1967] 2 A.C. at 134n., 150; *Bamford v Bamford* [1970] Ch. 212 at 238; *New Zealand Netherlands Society "Oranje" Inc v Kuys* [1973] 1 W.L.R. 1126 at 1132.

249 *Gibson v Jeyes* (1801) 6 Ves. 266; *Coles v Trecothick* (1804) 9 Ves. 234; *Morse v Royal* (1806) 12 Ves. 355; cf. *Fox v Mackreth* (1788) 2 Bro. C.C. 400.

250 *New Zealand Netherlands Society "Oranje" Inc v Kuys* [1973] 1 W.L.R. 1126 at 1132. See too *Dunne v English* (1874) L.R. 18 Eq. 524 at 533; *Boardman v Phipps* [1967] 2 A.C. 46 at 109; *Newgate Stud Co v Penfold* [2004] EWHC 2993 (Ch); [2008] 1 B.C.L.C. 46 at [227]; *Sharma v Sharma* [2013] EWCA Civ 1287; [2014] B.C.C. 73 at [43]; *FHR European Ventures LLP v Cedar Capital Partners LLC* [2014] UKSC 45; [2015] A.C. 250 at [5].

251 *Maguire v Makaronis* (1997) 188 C.L.R. 449 at 466.

252 *Wingecarribee Shire Council v Lehman Brothers Australia Ltd (in liq)* (2012) 301 A.L.R. 1 at [742].

253 *Farah Constructions Pty Ltd v Say-Dee Pty Ltd* (2007) 230 C.L.R. 89 at [107] (the Court).

It has been said that a fiduciary owes a positive duty to disclose conflicts of interest to her principal.[254] This may be correct to the extent that the duty of disclosure being referred to is some other non-fiduciary duty, such as the duties imposed by general law or statute on some financial advisers, or directors, to make certain disclosures. We otherwise take the view that a duty to disclose is not a fiduciary duty and a failure to disclose is thus not itself a breach of fiduciary duty. Disclosure and consent merely "provide a mechanism by which the fiduciary can avoid liability" if she wishes to act despite a conflict of interests.[255] As such, the burden of proving the elements of the defence lies on the fiduciary.[256] Equally, a fiduciary's failure to disclose and/or the absence of principal consent are not elements a plaintiff must show to make out a claim based on fiduciary duty, nor is an absence of informed consent itself sufficient to constitute a breach of fiduciary duty. **2–214**

This point was expressly addressed in *Maguire v Makaronis*, where Brennan CJ, Gaudron, McHugh and Gummow JJ stated that:[257] **2–215**

> . . . if the appellants were to escape the stigma of an adverse finding of breach of fiduciary duty, with consequent remedies, it was for them to show, by way of defence, informed consent by the respondents to the appellants acting. . . with divided loyalty. . . it should be noted that, contrary to what appeared to be suggested by the respondents in argument, there was no duty as such on the appellants to obtain an informed consent from the respondents. Rather, the existence of an informed consent would have gone to negate what otherwise was a breach of duty.

G. Consequences of Breach and Remedies in Outline

Fiduciary loyalty makes it unlawful for A to exercise a legal entitlement, where it would otherwise have been lawful for A to take such action. While it may be possible for B to get an injunction prohibiting A from taking action to exercise a legal entitlement (see further Chapter 19), fiduciary loyalty does not actually disable or limit A from exercising that entitlement. A can exercise her legal entitlement in breach of fiduciary duty. Breach triggers the availability of a range of equitable personal and proprietary remedies as necessary to address the consequences of the fiduciary's breach including; equitable monetary remedies against the fiduciary such as equitable compensation or an account of profits (discussed in Chapter 18); a constructive trust against the fiduciary or third party (discussed in Chapter 17); rescission against the fiduciary or a third party (see Chapter 20), as well as other forms of third party personal liability (discussed in Chapter 14). **2–216**

4. Relief Against Forfeiture (and Penalties)

A. A Doctrine and a Rule

Broadly speaking, the doctrine of relief against forfeiture allows a court to order equitable relief in favour of B, to restrain A from exercising a right or power to end an interest of B, in the specific circumstances where A's legal entitlement arises under a contract with B, and because of B's failure to act in **2–217**

---

254 *Item Software (UK) Ltd v Fassihi* [2004] EWCA Civ 1244; [2005] 2 B.C.L.C. 91 at [41]–[44] and [63]–[65]; cf. Companies Act 2006 s.177; *Medsted Associates Ltd v Canaccord Genuity Wealth (International) Ltd* [2019] EWCA Civ 83 at [44].

255 Conaglen, *Fiduciary Loyalty: Protecting the Due Performance of Non-Fiduciary Duties*, p.190. See too M. Harding, "Two Fiduciary Fallacies" (2007) 2 J. Eq. 1.

256 *Hurstanger Ltd v Wilson* [2007] EWCA Civ 299; [2007] 1 W.L.R. 2351 at [35]. The principal must have been made aware of the facts, but it is not necessary that he understood their legal characterisation, i.e. that they would constitute a breach of fiduciary duty: *Sharma v Sharma* [2013] EWCA Civ 1287; [2014] B.C.C. 73 at [47], approving *Knight v Frost* [1999] B.C.C. 819 at 828.

257 *Maguire v Makaronis* (1997) 188 C.L.R. 449 at 466. See also *Blackmagic Design Pty Ltd v Overliese* (2011) 191 F.C.R. 1 at [110].

a particular way. A classic example occurs where, under the terms of B's lease with A, A has a power to re-enter the property, and thus terminate B's lease, if B fails to pay rent. If, despite the failure to pay as required by the contract, B can make up for the deficit in rent (and pay any relevant interest and costs to A), then a court may, at B's request, grant an injunction restraining A from exercising her power to re-enter and terminate B's lease.

2–218 The doctrine of relief against forfeiture is closely associated with the rule against penalties. In English law, as stated by Lords Neuberger and Sumption in *Cavendish Square Holding BV v Makdessi*,[258] this rule prevents A from enforcing a term in A's contract with B if the term responds to B's breach of the contract and "imposes a detriment [on B] out of all proportion to any legitimate interest of [A] in the enforcement of the primary obligation."

2–219 The doctrine and the rule, in one way or another, thus deal with the phenomenon whereby A and B attempt to establish not only the terms of their primary legal relationship, but also what will happen if a particular event, such as B's failure to perform a term of the contract, does not occur. The courts have been careful to emphasise that neither the doctrine nor the rule can be used simply to relieve B from the consequences of what may in the event prove to be an onerous or possibly even a commercially imprudent bargain.[259] Rather, each has a specific, more limited focus. Nonetheless, each has attracted adverse comment as, where they apply, each of the doctrine and the rule undeniably prevents A from invoking the express terms of A's contract with B: each is thus a limit on the parties' freedom to contract.[260]

2–220 Both rules have equitable origins[261] such that it is necessary to understand one in order to understand the other, although their paths have digressed.[262] In *Cavendish Square Holdings BV v Makdessi*,[263] the Supreme Court affirmed that the *equitable* penalties rule is now subsumed into the *common law* rule on penalties. This means that, in English law, there is now only one rule against penalties, and its nature and effect is determined by what was the common law rule. It might therefore be said that the rule has no place in a textbook on equity. However, the position in other common law jurisdictions is not so clear.[264] Moreover, precisely because of this reclassification, the rule against penalties can tell us something important about why it matters whether a principle is seen as legal or equitable.

2–221 Relief against forfeiture can be seen as characteristically equitable. It does not deny the existence of A's legal entitlement against B, such as A's power to forfeit B's lease; rather it supplements the common law by controlling A's exercise of that entitlement as against B. This can be seen, for example, by the fact that, if B does not comply with the conditions for relief, A can assert A's underlying power. Similarly, where the rule against penalties is seen as equitable, it can operate not to deny A's contractual right to receive (for example) a large sum of money from B should B fail to perform

---

258 [2015] UKSC 67; [2016] A.C. 1172. The appeal was heard alongside *ParkingEye Ltd v Beavis*.

259 See, e.g. Lord Roskill in *Export Credit Guarantee Department v Universal Oil Products Co* [1983] 1 W.L.R. 399 at 403.

260 See, e.g. Lords Neuberger and Sumption in *Cavendish Square Holding BV v Makdessi* [2015] UKSC 67; [2016] A.C. 1172 at [33]: "The penalty rule is an interference with freedom of contract."

261 *Vauxhall Motors Ltd (Formerly General Motors UK Ltd) v Manchester Ship Canal Co Ltd* [2018] EWCA Civ 1100; [2019] Ch. 331 at [35] (Lewison LJ); upheld on appeal: *Manchester Ship Canal Co Ltd v Vauxhall Motors Ltd (Formerly General Motors UK Ltd)* [2019] UKSC 46; [2020] A.C. 1161.

262 *Vauxhall Motors Ltd (Formerly General Motors UK Ltd) v Manchester Ship Canal Co Ltd* [2018] EWCA Civ 1100; [2019] Ch. 331 at [37] (Lewison LJ).

263 [2015] UKSC 67; [2016] A.C. 1172.

264 For the position in Australia, for example, see *Andrews v Australia and New Zealand Banking Group Ltd* (2012) 247 C.L.R. 205, joint judgment of French CJ, Gummow, Crennan, Kiefel and Bell JJ at [39]. For a comprehensive account of the jurisdictional divergences see N. Tiverios, *Contractual Penalties in Australia and the United Kingdom: History, Theory and Practice*, Ch.3, and for an overview see N. Tiverios and B. McFarlane, "Controlling Private Punishment in Three Dimensions: Penalties and Forfeiture in England and Australia" in E. Bant et al (eds), *Punishment and Private Law* (Hart Publishing, 2021), p.351.

B's contractual duties to A, but rather to control A's enforcement of that right against B. This means, for example, that A could be allowed to enforce that right, but only to a certain extent and, perhaps, that circumstances arising after the time when A and B made their contract can be taken into account by the court in deciding how to control A's enforcement of the right. The common law form of the rule, in contrast, simply denies the offending term and that A has an enforceable right against B, by stating that, as a matter of legal policy, A and B simply do not have the power to create such a contractual right. On this view, as Lords Neuberger and Sumption put it in *Cavendish Square Holding BV v Makdessi*, a penalty clause is a "species of agreement which the common law considers to be by its nature contrary to the policy of the law".[265]

The characterisation of the rule against penalties as either equitable or legal is thus not a pure matter of history, but rather reflects a conceptual difference between two quite different techniques for dealing with a problematic right or power of A. Those two responses are described by Tiverios and McFarlane as follows:[266] **2-222**

> The first response consists of a court holding that the parties did not have the power to create the purported objectionable right. The most direct means of doing so is to say that the purported right is void: it was never brought into being or acquired by [A]. The second response consists instead of recognising that the right does exist, but limiting the extent to which it can be enforced or asserted.

B. Relief Against Forfeiture

The availability of equitable relief against forfeiture depends on whether: (i) the court's jurisdiction to grant relief is enlivened, and (ii) the court should exercise its discretion to control A in the circumstances. The part of the doctrine considered here[267] applies where the term A wishes to invoke has the purpose of securing to A the benefits of B's performance of a primary condition (such as e.g. B's payment of rent), and those benefits can still in substance be obtained by A (e.g. by B making a late payment, but with interest and costs to compensate A for the delay). There is then no good reason for A to insist on a forfeiture, with the detriment it would impose on B. As Lord Neuberger explained in *Cukurova Finance International Ltd v Alfa Telecom Turkey Ltd*:[268] **2-223**

> The commonest cases in which equity has power to intervene were identified by Lord Wilberforce[269] as mortgages, which give rise to the equity of redemption, and leases, which commonly contain re-entry clauses. The paradigm case for relief in such instances is where the primary object of the bargain is to secure a stated result which can be effectively attained when the matter comes before the court, and where the forfeiture provision is added by way of security for the production of that result.

i. Does the jurisdiction to relieve against forfeiture arise?

The scope of the court's jurisdiction to relieve against forfeiture is determined by whether (a) the legal entitlement that B is seeking to prevent A from exercising is one that secures B's performance of a **2-224**

---

[265] *Cavendish Square Holding BV v Makdessi* at [9].

[266] Tiverios and McFarlane, "Controlling Private Punishment in Three Dimensions: Penalties and Forfeiture in England and Australia" in E. Bant et al (eds), *Punishment and Private Law* (Hart Publishing, 2021), p.352.

[267] The doctrine can also apply where the forfeiture is affected by "fraud, accident, mistake or surprise" and where A's knowledge of those circumstances is such that it would be unconscionable for A to insist on the forfeiture: see, e.g. *Shiloh Spinners Ltd v Harding* [1973] A.C. 691 (HL) at 722.

[268] *Cukurova Finance International Ltd v Alfa Telecom Turkey Ltd* [2013] UKPC 2 at [90].

[269] *Shiloh Spinners Ltd v Harding* [1973] A.C. 691 (HL) at 722.

condition: usually, but not necessarily,[270] an obligation to pay a sum of money to A; and (b) A's legal entitlement allows A to forfeit or determine a propriety or possessory right of B.[271] In such a case, A's legal entitlement can be seen to operate simply as security for the performance of the primary condition, so that if that condition can be in substance performed by B, then A has no good reason to insist on the forfeiture.

2–225 This means that, if A's right or power is not in the nature of security for B's performance, then the jurisdiction for relief is not available.[272] The mere fact that A's right or power arises on a breach of a duty by B does not mean that A's legal entitlement functions as security in that sense; it may be, for example, that A's entitlement instead facilitates performance by A of her duty to B.[273]

2–226 Traditional cases include where A attempts to exercise a right of re-entry to forfeit B's right of possession under a lease, or to exercise a power of sale over mortgaged property, thus determining B's equity of redemption under a mortgage. The doctrine can though apply beyond land. In *Cukurova Finance International Ltd v Alfa Telecom Turkey Ltd,* for instance, the Privy Council applied it where A sought to retain shares that B had transferred to A as security for payment of a debt, and Lord Neuberger stated that:[274]

> there is no principled basis upon which the jurisdiction can be limited to real property. Nor is there any authority for such a distinction.

2–227 Relief is however limited to cases where B stands to lose a "proprietary or possessory right". This limit was confirmed by the Supreme Court in *The Manchester Ship Canal Co Ltd v Vauxhall Motors Ltd (Formerly General Motors UK).*[275] Under the licence agreement, Vauxhall had a right to discharge surface water and trade run-off into a canal via a spillway on MSCC's land. The licence was granted in "in perpetuity" and allowed MSCC to terminate the licence if Vauxhall's annual payment was in arrears after notice had been given. Vauxhall was in arrears and after notice was given, MSCC sought to terminate the licence and determine Vauxhall's right to drain water and trade run-off over MSCC's land. The Supreme Court held that Vauxhall's interest qualified as a possessory one, having regard to the duration of the licence and nature of control granted to Vauxhall, such that the jurisdiction was enlivened, and relief was granted.

2–228 In the Supreme Court in the *Manchester Ship Canal* case, A had argued that relief should not be available where B had a right in land which, whilst conferring possession, was not a recognised proprietary right. That argument was rejected on the basis that, as pointed out by Lord Briggs, "[there are] powerful reasons why, now that it is settled that equitable relief may apply to forfeiture of possessory rights in relation to a wide range of chattels and other personalty, it should also do so in relation to possessory rights over land." It had also been argued by B that, even if its licence did not give it possession, the doctrine should still be available, as it should be extended beyond "proprietary and possessory rights". On the facts, the Supreme Court did not have to decide on that submission, but it is clear that Lord Briggs (with whom Lord Carnwath, Lady Black and Lord Kitchin agreed) was against

---

[270] See, e.g. *Shiloh Spinners Ltd v Harding*, where it was confirmed that relief is in principle available where B's duty was to keep the premises leased to B in good repair.

[271] See, e.g. *Shiloh Spinners Ltd v Harding* [1973] A.C. 691 (HL) at 722.

[272] *Scandinavian Trading Tanker Co AB v Flota Petrolera Ecuatoriana ("The Scaptrade")* [1983] 2 A.C. 694; *Vauxhall Motors Ltd (Formerly General Motors UK Ltd) v Manchester Ship Canal Co Ltd* [2018] EWCA Civ 1100; [2019] Ch. 331 at [40].

[273] As in *Scandinavian Trading v Flota*.

[274] *Cukurova v Alfa* at [92].

[275] *Manchester Ship Canal Co Ltd v Vauxhall Motors Ltd (Formerly General Motors UK Ltd)* [2019] UKSC 46; [2020] A.C. 1161: see Lord Briggs at [49]–[51]. Lady Arden, in her concurring judgment, was however reluctant to impose such a limit based on the type of right held by the party seeking relief: see at [69] and [83]–[87].

such an extension, fearing it would cause uncertainty, particularly in commercial cases, and that it "would set at nought the careful development of the principled limitation of the jurisdiction to the forfeiture of proprietary or possessory rights, worked out over many years in a succession of broadly coherent authorities".[276]

Lady Arden, in contrast, preferred not to confine the scope of the jurisdiction by reference to the nature of B's interest. **2–229**

The Manchester Ship Canal Co Ltd v Vauxhall Motors Ltd (Formerly General Motors UK)

Supreme Court, [2020] A.C. 1161 at 1181–1183

The doctrine of relief from forfeiture is an equitable doctrine. I would approach it from the standpoint of equity rather than through the prism of property law. Equity is a body of principles which alleviates the strict application of rules of law in appropriate cases. In this case, the relevant rule of law is that the court will enforce the terms of the parties' agreement because there is no reason in law why it should not be enforced. Equity serves to finesse rules of law in deserving cases. It thus makes the system of law in England and Wales one which is more likely to produce a fair result than would be possible if equity did not exist. This must surely be one of the reasons why the law of England and Wales is held in high regard in the world. **2–230**

Some uncertainty is inevitable

Some element of uncertainty in the application of the doctrine of relief from forfeiture is inevitable. Equity in general operates by principles rather than by rules. That means that relief from forfeiture is not an automatic consequence if particular conditions are fulfilled but instead is given in appropriate cases. It is not a foregone conclusion that once the conditions for relief are shown relief will necessarily be granted and that inevitably means an element of uncertainty about its availability. **2–231**

Another element of inherent uncertainty arises from the fact that the doctrine of relief from forfeiture is a general doctrine and will apply to new circumstances, such as where the court has to deal with a particular form of property, or (as here) interest in or in relation to property, for the first time. The most obvious new circumstances are the creation of new forms of property or interest in property, such as shares in a registered company or aircraft. Thinking ahead, it may be applied in the future to forms of property which only exist in the cybersphere, or to rights which are treated as to all intents and purposes as rights to property.[277] I note that the view that the law of forfeiture may yet expand in this general area is supported by Professor Ben McFarlane in *Snell's Equity*,[278] cited by Lewison LJ in his judgment in this case.[279] **2–232**

It inevitably follows that there will be respects in which the equitable doctrine of relief from forfeiture will be "unfenced". So, while I agree with Lord Briggs JSC that there is a need for there to be certainty in this area of the law, especially in the commercial field, I would go further and conclude that certainty for the purposes of a general doctrine of equity differs from that which results from a hard-edged rule of law. As Sir Richard Arden MR explained in *Eaton v Lyon*:[280] "At Law a covenant must be strictly and literally performed: in Equity it must be really and substantially performed according to the true intent and meaning of the parties, so far as circumstances will admit . . ." **2–233**

Types of rights or types of cases?

As Lord Briggs JSC explains, equitable relief from forfeiture is a remedy of ancient origin. It is inevitably difficult, given the long history of equity, to say that the doctrine was ever finally constituted in a particular form. Rather it kept evolving as the social and economic life of the nation changed: the law of equity developed and keeps on developing. Questions such as this case raises as to whether particular forms of property interest are or are not within the reach of the doctrine would have no meaning in a society which did not discover the utility of them until later in its history. **2–234**

---

276 [2019] UKSC 46; [2020] A.C. 1161 at [50].

277 See, e.g. M. Solinas, "Bitcoiners in Wonderland: Lessons from the Cheshire Cat" [2019] L.M.C.L.Q. 433.

278 33rd edn (2015), para.13–023.

279 [2018] EWCA Civ 1100; [2019] Ch. 331 at [50]–[51].

280 (1798) 3 Ves. 689 at 692.

2–235 As time went on, the doctrine applied to both real and personal property and to intangible as well as tangible property, as need arose. I would prefer to express no view on the wider definition of an interest in property involved in the claimants' alternative argument since it does not need to be decided on this appeal and has not been fully argued. There is a degree of uncertainty in the concept of possessory rights in relation to land, and it may be that an extension to rights to use property may not involve any significant further degree of uncertainty.

The fundamental principle giving rise to relief from forfeiture

2–236 What then is the principle on which equity acts when it grants relief from forfeiture? The fundamental principle was, as Lord Briggs JSC has said, that equity intervenes to restrain forfeiture where (1) the right had been conferred to secure the performance of some other covenant and (2) although the covenantor had breached his covenant, he was now in a position to perform it and to pay any compensation that might be appropriate.[281]. . .

2–237 Moreover, this was a statement of general principle, not limited to any particular sort of property.

2–238 Given the ability of relief of forfeiture to prevent A from enforcing an agreed contractual term, it is perhaps no surprise that the majority in the *Manchester Ship Canal* case were not prepared to extend the scope of the doctrine beyond cases where B has a proprietary or possessory right. Nonetheless, as pointed out by Lady Arden, if the focus of the doctrine is on preventing A from using a right or power intended to function as security for a different purpose, then it is far from obvious why the nature of B's right should set a limit on the operation of the doctrine.

ii. Should relief be granted, and if so, on what terms?

2–239 Factors relevant to the court's consideration of whether to exercise its discretion[282] to award relief against forfeiture include:[283] (a) whether the result the parties intended to be secured by the forfeiture clause can effectively be attained by some other means than forfeiture of B's interest; (b) B's conduct and whether B's breach that is the trigger for the forfeiture clause was wilful, and the gravity of B's breach(es); and (c) the disparity of the value of B's interest as compared with the damage caused to A by B's breach.

2–240 It has been suggested that:[284]

. . . the central question is whether B can show that it would be unconscionable for A to insist on enforcing a clause designed as security for a primary stipulation. This depends on whether the clause would impose a burden on B, or give A a benefit,[285] that is excessive when compared to that which would arise through performance of the secured duty. It may be that the concept of A's "legitimate interest in performance", whilst it has emerged in the context of the rule against penalties, is potentially useful in determining the availability of relief against forfeiture. . . . Once it is decided to award relief against forfeiture, it will be necessary for the court to determine on what terms, if any, relief is to be granted to B. Usually, the terms of relief require B to put A, as closely as possible, in the position A would have been in had the secured condition been met by

281 See *Peachy v Duke of Somerset* (1721) Prec. Ch. 568.

282 The discretionary nature of this decision is confirmed in *Vauxhall Motors Ltd (Formerly General Motors UK Ltd) v Manchester Ship Canal Co Ltd* [2018] EWCA Civ 1100; [2019] Ch. 331 at [72].

283 See, e.g. *Shiloh Spinners Ltd v Harding* [1973] A.C. 691 (HL) at 722–724.

284 McGhee (ed.), *Snell's Equity*, 34th edn (2020), para.13–031.

285 In *Vauxhall Motors Ltd (Formerly General Motors UK Ltd) v Manchester Ship Canal Co Ltd* [2018] EWCA Civ 1100; [2019] Ch. 331 Lewison LJ stated at [75] that the first instance judge, in exercising the discretion to grant relief, had been entitled to take into account the "windfall" that would accrue to A if relief were refused.

B. This might mean it is necessary for B to pay an agreed sum, with interest and costs.[286] Conversely, where B is not ready and willing to perform the secured obligation, then relief will usually be denied.[287]

The effect of granting relief against forfeiture is to force A to accept something different to that which A agreed to; for example, a later payment by B. In granting relief, the court needs to find terms that prevent A taking advantage of the forfeiture clause to acquire a benefit substantially in excess of that which A would have acquired through B's performance, while at the same time ensuring A is not otherwise deprived of the substance of the benefit that would have arisen from B's performance. This is something on which judges may disagree, as was shown by the Board of the Privy Council's decision in *Cukurova Finance International Ltd v Alfa Telecom Turkey Ltd*,[288] where a majority awarded relief against forfeiture on terms that did not require B to pay interest on the late payment. This was on the basis that A had earlier refused B's offer of a repayment in full.[289] In dissent, Lord Neuberger[290] and Lord Sumption[291] disagreed, on the basis that relief should have been awarded on terms requiring B to pay interest, and thereby holding the parties more closely to their agreed terms. **2–241**

C. Penalties

The modern law of penalties evolved from instances where courts of equity would grant relief restraining A from enforcing a contractual right against B, where that right arose in consequence of B's failure to perform a condition. An example of a legal entitlement of A that could thus be constrained is one arising from a term requiring B to pay a sum of money, or transfer or forfeit some right in A's favour, in the event of B's breach of a pre-existing duty to A.[292] In such a case, the parties have agreed a remedy to be payable by B in event of B's breach of B's primary obligation, as an alternative to the remedial regime otherwise provided at law. *If* the term was penal relative to the primary obligation B has breached, then relief would usually be granted by restraining A from enforcing the penal term in full. **2–242**

The equitable pedigree of the rule:[293] **2–243**

is traceable to the preparedness of a court of equity to restrain the enforcement at common law of penal bonds i.e. bonds providing for the payment of a sum of money upon the non-payment of principal and interest due under another instrument. The common law courts adopted the doctrine and applied it to situations other than penal bonds.

As noted above,[294] the rule against penalties has since been clearly identified as a common law rule by the Supreme Court in *Cavendish Square Holding BV v Makdessi*.[295] In summary, a term will be **2–244**

---

286 *Shiloh Spinners v Harding* at 722 (Lord Wilberforce).

287 See, e.g. *Else (1982) Ltd v Parkland Holding* [1994] 1 B.C.L.C. 130 at 145 (Hoffmann LJ), although and exceptionally relief may be granted where B is unable or unwilling to remedy breach, see further McGhee (ed.), *Snell's Equity*, 34th edn (2020), para.13–032

288 [2013] UKPC 20.

289 *Cukurova v Alfa* at [47]–[48] (Lord Mance, with whom Lord Kerr and Lord Clarke agreed).

290 *Cukurova v Alfa* at [95]–[110].

291 *Cukurova v Alfa* at [179]–[187].

292 Tiverios, *Contractual Penalties*, Ch.2.

293 *Talal El Makdessi v Cavendish Square Holding BV* [2013] EWCA Civ 1539 at [44] (Christopher Clarke LJ); see also *Cavendish Square Holding BV v Makdessi* [2015] UKSC 67; [2016] A.C. 1172 at [4]–[5].

294 See para.2–220.

295 *Cavendish Square Holding BV v Makdessi* [2015] UKSC 67; [2016] A.C. 1172 at [6]–[18], and at [42] where it is stated that in the modern laws of both England and Scotland, "the penalty rule is an aspect of the law of contract".

a penalty if it: (a) attaches a secondary obligation, such as B's duty to pay a sum of money, or transfer property, or A's right to retain or forfeit B's property, to B's breach of a primary contractual obligation owed to A, and (b) if the term imposes a detriment on B that is "out of all proportion to any legitimate interest of" A in the enforcement of the primary obligation.[296] As a common law rule, the penalties rule renders the impugned clause void or entirely unenforceable. The common law penalties rule is thus a limit to the scope of the parties' power to determine the content of the secondary legal relations that arise in consequence of one party's breach of the primary legal relationship.

2-245 There are many important and difficult questions about the law of penalties. These include the concept of a *secondary* obligation[297] and the rules for construction of the parties' agreement. In relation to the question of whether a clause is penal, there are further questions around the concept of A's legitimate interest in performance,[298] when a penalty is "exorbitant or unconscionable",[299] and the time at which this assessment is made.[300]

2-246 Examination of these and other issues are beyond the scope of this Chapter, and this is even more so given that the penalties rule, today, is not an equitable rule. Nonetheless, in other common law jurisdictions, such as Australia, the penalties rule continues as an equitable rule that operates as a restraint on A's enforcement of a legal right arising under a contract.[301] We will therefore focus here on aspects of the rule where its characterisation as either equitable or legal may have an impact.

i. Scope of the rule

2-247 The scope of the rule in English law is limited in that it can only apply to clauses that create a secondary obligation consequent upon B's breach of some primary obligation that B owes to A.[302] A clause will not fall within the remit of the rule if B's obligation is not triggered by B's breach of a primary obligation, but rather by the failure of B to fulfil a condition which B was *not* under a duty to A to perform.[303] This leads to the somewhat odd point that B is given more protection (as B then has a chance of invoking the rule against penalties) where B is in breach of contract, rather than having merely failed to perform a non-obligatory condition.[304] This point is also inconsistent with the historical origin of the rule: it was applied to conditional bonds, and those bonds did not generally impose a duty on B to perform the condition they secured. It is also inconsistent with the scope of relief against forfeiture, which can apply even where the condition secured is not one which B had a duty to perform. This also

---

296 *Cavendish Square Holding BV v Makdessi* at [32].

297 *Cavendish Square Holding BV v Makdessi* [2015] UKSC 67; [2016] A.C. 1172 [74]–[83]; McGhee (ed)., *Snell's Equity*, 34th edn (2020), para.13-011.

298 See McGhee (ed.), *Snell's Equity*, 34th edn (2020), para.13-017; For a detailed discussion of the term, reflecting also on its use in other related areas of the law, see S. Rowan, "The 'Legitimate Interest in Performance' in the Law of Penalties" [2019] C.L.J. 148.

299 See McGhee (ed.), *Snell's Equity*, 34th edn (2020), para.13-019.

300 See McGhee (ed.), *Snell's Equity*, 34th edn (2020), para.13-020.

301 *Andrews v Australia and New Zealand Banking Group Ltd* (2012) 247 C.L.R. 205, joint judgment of French CJ, Gummow, Crennan, Kiefel and Bell JJ at [39]. For a comprehensive account of the jurisdictional divergences see Tiverios, *Contractual Penalties*, Ch.3.

302 See, e.g., *Cavendish Square Holding BV v Makdessi* [2015] UKSC 67; [2016] A.C. 1172 at [73].

303 See, e.g. *Euro London Appointments Ltd v Claessens International Ltd* [2006] EWCA Civ 385: B's failure to perform the condition of paying a sum of money within a certain period was not itself a breach of contract by B, and so the penalties rule could not apply. See too *Export Credits Guarantee Department v Universal Oil Products Co* [1983] 1 W.L.R. 399 (HL) at 402: if A's right arises when B breaches a duty owed to X, then again the penalties rule cannot apply.

304 The illogical nature of this position was pointed out by Lord Denning (who referred to it as an "absurd paradox") and Lord Devlin in *Bridge v Campbell Discount Co Ltd* [1962] A.C. 600 (HL) at 630 and 633.

means that, whilst courts are alert to the substance rather than mere form of any agreement,[305] the penalties rule can thus be easily avoided by the parties through careful drafting.

ii. When is a clause penal?

If a clause falls within the scope of the penalties rule, there is the second inquiry as to whether it is penal in nature, the test for which is explained in *Cavendish Square Holding BV v Talal El Makdessi*:[306] **2–248**

> The true test is whether the impugned provision is a secondary obligation which imposes a detriment on the contract-breaker out of all proportion to any legitimate interest of the innocent party in the enforcement of the primary obligation. The innocent party can have no proper interest in simply punishing the defaulter. His interest is in performance or in some appropriate alternative to performance. In the case of a straightforward damages clause, that interest will rarely extend beyond compensation for the breach, and we therefore expect that Lord Dunedin's four tests[307] would usually be perfectly adequate to determine its validity. But compensation is not necessarily the only legitimate interest that the innocent party may have in the performance of the defaulter's primary obligations.

Lord Hodge formulated the test as "whether the sum or remedy stipulated as a consequence of a breach of contract is exorbitant or unconscionable when regard is had to the innocent party's interest in the performance of the contract."[308] Lord Toulson endorsed that formulation, warning that "it is impossible to lay down abstract rules about what may or may not be 'extravagant or unconscionable'" and how the test applies will "depends on the particular facts and circumstances established in the individual case" and that "'exorbitant' and 'unconscionable' are strong words".[309] Lord Toulson also agreed with Lord Mance, who stated that " 'unconscionable' in this context means much the same as 'extravagant'".[310] **2–249**

These formulations of the rule are clearly influenced by, and consistent with, the test as developed by courts of equity, and have been largely adopted in Australia, where the rule against penalties is still regarded as a rule of equity. The equitable or common law characterisation of the rule does not seem to have an impact on the assessment of whether a clause is penal. **2–250**

iii. Effect

In English law, the effect of a clause being a penalty is that it is ineffective or void as a "species of agreement which the common law considers to be by its nature contrary to the policy of the law".[311] The terms will not create any legal entitlement in A's favour and impose no duty upon B. This does not mean the contract fails, and the clause will be severed from the valid terms.[312] As a result, A will be left to her remedy at law for B's breach of contract, if any. **2–251**

---

305 See eg the notion of a "disguised" penalty referred to (but not defined) in *Cavendish Square Holding BV v Makdessi* [2015] UKSC 67; [2016] A.C. 1172 at [77] and [258].

306 *Cavendish Square Holding BV v Makdessi* [2015] UKSC 67; [2016] A.C. 1172 at [32].

307 These are set out in *Dunlop Pneumatic Tyre Co Ltd v New Garage and Motor Co Ltd* [1915] A.C. 79 at 86–87 (Lord Dunedin).

308 *Cavendish Square Holding BV v Makdessi* [2015] UKSC 67; [2016] A.C. 1172 at [255].

309 *Cavendish Square Holding BV v Makdessi* [2015] UKSC 67; [2016] A.C. 1172 at [293].

310 *Cavendish Square Holding BV v Makdessi* [2015] UKSC 67; [2016] A.C. 1172 at [293].

311 *Cavendish Square Holding BV v Makdessi* [2015] UKSC 67; [2016] A.C. 1172 at [9].

312 The court has the power to sever the penal clause and enforce the remainder of the contract. See *The Angelic Star* [1988] 1 Lloyd's Rep. 122 at 126 per Ralph Gibson LJ: "The rule is, in my judgment, not designed to strike down any more of a lawful contract than is necessary to give effect to the Court's purpose of applying public policy; and, moreover, the rule should be applied so as to interfere as little as possible with the proper enforcement of a lawful contract according to its terms".

2–252 This absolute effect contrasts with the pro tanto effect of the penalties rule in equity. According to the equitable characterisation of the penalties rule,[313] it is a rule which, like the other equitable rules, restrains A's exercise of her (valid) legal entitlement *to the extent* enforcement would be out of all proportion to A's legitimate interest in B's performance. This is significant in cases where B has failed to perform a condition, but there has been no breach of contract by B: in such a case, of course, there is no remedy for breach of contract claim for A to fall back on.

2–253 This difference in effect is a significant implication flowing from the characterisation of the penalties rule as equitable or common law, and as discussed next, reflects the different types of justifications underpinning each formulation of the rule.

D. Assessing the Doctrine and the Rule: Equity or Common Law

2–254 A consideration of the doctrine against forfeiture and the rule against penalties highlights the continuing importance placed upon the characterisation of a rule as legal or equitable. As an equitable rule, the penalties doctrine restrains A's exercise of a secondary right that secures B's performance of a primary condition, preventing A from using that secondary right to gain some benefit substantially different to that which A would have received from B's performance.[314] This reflects the rationale that A should only be allowed to exercise a legal entitlement for the purpose for which it was conferred: in this case, to give A the benefits of B's performance of the primary condition. The doctrine against forfeiture can be seen to have precisely the same aim. Indeed, we will examine other equitable doctrines, such as fraud on a power, that have a similar concern of ensuring that a power is exercised for the purpose it was conferred.[315]

2–255 As a common law rule, in contrast, the doctrine of penalties relates to the types of remedies that the law will grant in response to a breach of contract, and "engages broader social and economic considerations, one of which is that the law will not generally make a remedy available to a party, the adverse impact of which on the defaulter significantly exceeds any legitimate interest of the innocent party".[316] Framed differently, the common law rule is a limit on the parties' ability to agree to a remedial regime applicable on breach: rather than limiting A's ability to enforce a right, it instead denies A the power to create such a right in the first place. One consequence of this analysis is that the rule can apply only where the contested clause operates on a breach of contract by B, rather than on B's failure to perform a condition; another is that it denies A any ability to enforce the penal clause, rather than controlling the extent to which the clause can be enforced by A.

2–256 The position now adopted in English law, which sees the doctrine of relief against forfeiture as equitable, and the rule against penalties as legal, may also make it more important to separate out the scope of operation of the doctrine and the rule. This, however, is no easy task.

---

313 See further McGhee (ed.), *Snell's Equity*, 34th edn (2020), para.13–023; Tiverios, *Contractual Penalties*, Ch.7.

314 See *Andrews v Australia and New Zealand Banking Group* at [10]–[11]. For discussion, see Tiverios, *Contractual Penalties*, Ch.3

315 See paras 11–030ff.

316 *Cavendish* at [29] (Lords Neuberger and Sumption) and [86]. See too Keane J. in *Paciocco Australia and New Zealand Banking Group* Ltd (2016) 258 C.L.R. 525 at [253]: "The real objection, as a matter of public policy, to a penalty clause which operates upon breach of contract is that it is no part of the law of contract to allow one party to punish the other for non-performance".

Cavendish Square Holdings BV v Makdessi

Supreme Court, [2016] A.C. 1172 at [17]

LORD NEUBERGER and LORD SUMPTION (with whom LORD CARNWATH agreed): . . . The relationship between penalty clauses and forfeiture clauses is not entirely easy. Given that they had the same origin in equity, but that the law on penalties was then developed through common law while the law on forfeitures was not, this is unsurprising. Some things appear to be clear. Where a proprietary interest or a "proprietary or possessory right" (such as a patent or a lease) is granted or transferred subject to revocation or determination on breach, the clause providing for determination or revocation is a forfeiture and cannot be a penalty, and, while it is enforceable, relief from forfeiture may be granted.[317] **2–257**

What is less clear is whether a provision is capable of being both a penalty clause and a forfeiture clause. It is inappropriate to consider that issue in any detail in this judgment, as we have heard very little argument on forfeitures—unsurprisingly because in neither appeal has it been alleged that any provision in issue is a forfeiture from which relief could be granted. But it is right to mention the possibility that, in some circumstances, a provision could, at least potentially, be a penalty clause as well as a forfeiture clause. We see the force of the arguments to that effect advanced by Lord Mance and Lord Hodge JJSC in their judgments.[318] **2–258**

It has been suggested that the relationship between the doctrine and the rule may be important in explaining why English law continues to confine the doctrine to cases where B loses a "proprietary or possessory right", and the rule to cases where the contested clause responds to a breach of contract by B. **2–259**

Nick Tiverios and Ben McFarlane, "Controlling Private Punishment in Three Dimensions: Penalties and Forfeiture in England and Australia"

in Elise Bant et al (eds), *Punishment and Private Law* (Hart Publishing, 2021), p.369

It is important to note that whilst most usually applied to secondary obligations of B to pay a sum of money to A, that rule [against penalties] can extend to other agreed sanctions triggered by a breach of contract, such as a duty of B to transfer a right to A,[319] or a power of A to retain a sum of money, or right, already transferred by B to A.[320] If the security-based strand of relief against forfeiture were not limited to the loss of possessory or proprietary rights, it could apply to limit A's ability to enforce a right in cases (such as where the right is not triggered by B's breach of contract) where, following the Supreme Court's decision in *Cavendish*, the courts have expressly decided not to intervene in the context of the rule against penalties. Put simply, any removal of the "proprietary or possessory right" threshold in the context of the doctrine of relief against forfeiture will blur the distinction between the scope of operation of the rule against penalties and the doctrine of relief against forfeiture, and undermine the unanimous view in *Cavendish* that the rule applies only to regulate agreed remedies payable on breach of contract. **2–260**

---

317 See *BICC Plc v Burndy Corp* [1985] Ch. 232 at 246–247, 252 (Dillon LJ) and *The Scaptrade* [1983] 2 A.C. 694 at 701–703 (Lord Diplock). But this does not mean that relief from forfeiture is unavailable in cases not involving land: see *Çukurova v Alfa* especially at 956–957, and the cases cited there.

318 See *Cavendish Square Holding BV v Makdessi* [2015] UKSC 67; [2016] A.C. 1172 at [160]–[161] (Lord Mance) and [230]–[238] (Lord Hodge)].

319 See, e.g. *Cavendish Square Holding BV v Makdessi* [2015] UKSC 67; [2016] A.C. 1172 at [84] (Lords Neuberger and Sumption), [157] (Lord Mance) and [230] (Lord Hodge).

320 See, e.g. *Signia Wealth Ltd v Vector Trustees Ltd* [2018] EWHC 1040 (Ch) at [653], where Marcus Smtih J. stated that: "it is clear that the penalty doctrine extends to deposits, forfeiture clauses and provisions that require a party in breach of contract to transfer property to the other party at less than its full value."

Questions

1. A sells B 1,000 widgets under a hire-purchase agreement according to which B hires 100 widgets from A for a period of one year, during which time B pays a monthly hire fee of $10, payable on the first day of each month. B has also agreed to insure the widgets during the one-year hire period. At the end of the one-year hire period B has an option to purchase the widgets from A for a price of $1,000 to A. B grants A security for B's payment of the monthly hire fee in the form of A's power to terminate the agreement and thereby forfeit B's lease of the widgets and B's option to purchase the widgets from A, exercisable if B is in breach of any of B's obligations under the hire-purchase agreement.
   (a) Three months into the hire period B has failed to insure the widgets. B is struggling financially, and insurance is expensive. B asks A whether insurance is necessary and A replies to B: "don't worry about taking out insurance for the widgets. The lawyers who drew up the hire-purchase agreement always insist the lessee pay for insurance but it all seems a bit much to me. I will not take any action against you for not insuring the widgets." B is grateful for A's accommodation and responds: "ok I will not insure the widgets." B misses a payment of the hire fee amount due on 1 March. On 10 March, A writes to B terminating the hire-purchase agreement and demanding B return the widgets and repay the outstanding hire fee. B replies indicating that B has paid the outstanding hire fee and is able to pay the next month's hire fee as well. A still wants to exercise A's power of termination because the price of widgets has increased significantly since the parties entered into the hire-purchase agreement and A can sell the widgets to C for $5,000. Can A do this?

(2) A is a social media and online marketing consultant, providing advice on online marketing strategies for clients, as well as introductions to social media influencers who provide marketing services on various online social media platforms.
   (a) B is a highly successful organic chef who produces high-quality organic snacks and meals that B sells to a range of customers online. B has an online marketing and data analytics bachelor's degree from a leading English university and can do the online marketing for B's business. B decides however to engage A to do all this for B, thereby allowing B to have more time to focus on new recipes and product design. A recommends that B engage the services of a social media influencer to market B's products. To that end A introduces B to X, a high-profile social media influencer who has a healthy lifestyle blog and millions of online followers. B adopts A's recommendations and enters into a marketing agreement with X according to which B pays a fee to X for X to market B's products online. Unbeknown to B, X pays A a fee under an agreement between A and X according to which A will market X's services in return for a fee payable by X upon X's entry into an online marketing agreement upon A's introduction.
   (b) A competitor of B, C, is also a highly successful organic chef who produces high-quality organic snacks and meals that C sells to a range of customers online. Unlike B, C has no online marketing or data analytics qualifications or experience and cannot event operate a computer. B engages A to design and manage C's online marketing for C's business as C does not have the time, let alone the capability to do this. A recommends that C engage Z to provide automated processing services to increase the online traffic on C's social media accounts, and thereby give the appearance to "real" online customers that C's products are very popular. C does not entirely understand A's recommendation and while very

impressed by A's expertise, C decides not to engage Z replying to A, "I do not like the idea of paying money for online robots to pretend to like my food!"

(c) Both B and C have signed consultancy agreements with A, which contain the following terms: "*By agreeing to engage my services, you acknowledge that I may receive fees and commissions from third parties.*"

Advise A.

3

GENERATIVE EQUITY

1. Introduction

This Chapter outlines a range of equitable rules that show how equity is generative of right–duty relationships that require A to take action to exercise A's legal entitlement in favour of B: proprietary estoppel; confidentiality; due administration; and equitable assignment. 3–001

As with the rules discussed in Chapter 3, the rules discussed here also exhibit a secondary or meta law function of controlling A's exercise of a legal entitlement. The rules however do more than merely restraining A in A's exercise, as against B of such an entitlement. Indeed, some of the rules in this Chapter show how equity can confer a power on the parties to generate such right–duty relationships, and to vary the content or terms of such relationships. Some equitable rules allow the parties to determine the existence and content of the meta law that governs how they exercise their pre-existing legal entitlements. It has often been noted that equitable doctrines, such as the trust, or the rules of equitable assignment, are very useful in practice in allowing parties to deal with their rights in commercially useful ways. It is important to see *how* equity achieves these effects, and we show here that the effects are consistent with equity's supplementary function of controlling, in favour of B, A's exercise of A's legal entitlements. 3–002

2. Proprietary Estoppel

A. The Effects of Proprietary Estoppel

In Chapter 2,[1] we considered the doctrine of promissory estoppel and saw that, in its orthodox formulation, as applied in English law, it operates to restrain A's exercise of a legal entitlement, and so cannot in itself impose a new duty on A to B. It has long been recognised, however, that proprietary estoppel operates differently. As Lord Denning MR put it in *Crabb v Arun DC*:[2] 3–003

> . . . there are estoppels and estoppels. Some do give rise to a cause of action. Some do not. In the species of estoppel called proprietary estoppel, it does give rise to a cause of action . . . The new rights and interests, so created by estoppel, in or over land, will be protected by the courts and in this way give rise to a cause of action.

In that case, it seems that the effect of B's successful proprietary estoppel claim was that A, an owner of land adjoining B's land, could be compelled by the court to grant B a right of way over A's 3–004

---

1 See paras 2–003 to 2–033.

2 (1976) Ch. 179 at 187.

land. A power held by A as owner of that land thus had to be exercised in B's favour. Similarly, in *Thorner v Major*,[3] the House of Lords confirmed that proprietary estoppel could be used by B to compel A's personal representatives to honour an assurance made by A to B that A's land would pass to B on A's death. This had a very significant practical effect: A had not left a valid will, and the intestacy rules would have led to B's acquiring nothing on A's death. B's proprietary estoppel claim, however, allowed him to acquire land with an estimated value of well over £2 million.

Thorner v Major

House of Lords, [2009] 1 W.L.R. 776 at [29], [60]–[61]

3-005 Peter Thorner [A] owned Steart Farm. David Thorner [B], whose father was a cousin of Peter, worked on Steart Farm, as well on his parents' farm for over 30 years. A did not pay B for the work on A's farm. A had no close family and B believed that, on A's death, B would inherit A's farm. In reliance on that belief, B continued to work for A and did not pursue other opportunities. A made no express promise to leave the farm to B, but B's belief developed over a period of 15 years and was reinforced by particular conduct of A. In fact, A did make a will leaving the farm to B. However, that will also included pecuniary legacies to people with whom A later fell out, and so A destroyed the will. A did not make a new will and so died intestate. Under the intestacy rules, the farm passed to other relatives of A, not to B. At first instance, B's proprietary estoppel claim succeeded and it was found that A's personal representatives had to convey title to the farm to B. The Court of Appeal reversed this result, finding that B had no proprietary estoppel claim as A had not made a sufficiently clear assurance that he would leave the farm to B.

3-006 The House of Lords restored the order of the first instance judge, essentially because it found there was no reason, on the facts, for the Court of Appeal to have reversed the finding that A had made a sufficiently clear assurance to B.

3-007 LORD WALKER: This appeal is concerned with proprietary estoppel . . . most scholars agree that the doctrine is based on three main elements, although they express them in slightly different terms: a representation or assurance made to the claimant; reliance on it by the claimant; and detriment to the claimant in consequence of his (reasonable) reliance . . .

3-008 . . . The evidence showed a continuing pattern of conduct by [A] for the remaining 15 years of his life and it would not be helpful to try to break that pattern into discrete elements (and then treat each as being, on its own, insignificant). To my mind the [first instance] judge did find that [A's] assurances, objectively assessed, were intended to be taken seriously and to be relied on. In the end it is a short point; I do not think that there was sufficient reason for the Court of Appeal to reverse the trial judge's finding and conclusion . . .

3-009 In my opinion, it is a necessary element of proprietary estoppel that the assurances given to [B] (expressly or impliedly, or, in standing-by cases, tacitly) should relate to identified property owned (or, perhaps, about to be owned) by the defendant. That is one of the main distinguishing features between the two varieties of equitable estoppel, that is promissory estoppel and proprietary estoppel. The former must be based on an existing legal *relationship* (usually a contract, but not necessarily a contract relating to land). The latter need not be based on an existing legal relationship, but it must relate to *identified property* (usually land) owned (or, perhaps, about to be owned) by the defendant. It is the relation to identified land of the defendant that has enabled proprietary estoppel to develop as a sword, and not merely a shield: see Lord Denning M.R. in *Crabb v Arun District Council*.

B. Three Strands

3-010 Whilst Lord Walker in *Thorner v Major* gave a general formulation of the "three main elements" of proprietary estoppel, there is also much scholarly opinion in favouring of separating out the doctrine into distinct strands:[4] at one general level, those strands do have common elemental themes, but at a

[3] [2009] UKHL 18; [2009] 1 W.L.R. 776 (HL).

[4] See, e.g. J. Mee, "Proprietary Estoppel, Promises and Mistaken Belief" in S. Bright (ed.), *Modern Studies in Property Law: Volume VI* (Hart Publishing, 2011), pp.175, 181–183 and J. Mee, "Thorner v Major (2009): Proprietary Estoppel and Inheritance" in B. Sloan (ed.), *Landmark Cases in Succession Law* (Hart Publishing, 2019); K. Low, "Nonfeasance in Equity"

greater level of detail, they have differing content and effects. Indeed, Lord Walker, in an earlier case, noted that "synthesis and unification, however desirable as objectives, have their dangers."[5]

For example, Lord Walker refers to the first element of proprietary estoppel as a "representation or assurance" but also later refers to "standing-by cases", where the relevant conduct of A consists of failing to intervene when B, to A's knowledge, acts with a mistaken belief as to B's rights in relation to particular land. It has therefore been argued that there are in fact three distinct strands of proprietary estoppel. The first, where A makes a representation as to B's existing rights, can be seen as simply an application of the standard rules of estoppel by representation, discussed in Chapter 2:[6] where B has relied on A's representation, and so would now suffer a detriment if A were allowed to deny it, A can be prevented from denying the truth of the representation.[7] The second, applying in a "standing-by case" is based on A's acquiescence in B's mistaken belief: it can be used to prevent A from asserting a right that is inconsistent with B's mistaken belief. As Lord Neuberger put it:[8] **3–011**

> The classic case of proprietary estoppel, standing by whilst one's neighbour builds on one's land believing it to be his property, can be characterised as acquiescence.

Unlike the representation-based strand, this type of proprietary estoppel is distinctively equitable. Certainly, where it operates to prevent A from asserting A's right against B, it can be seen as restraining A's exercise, as against B, of a legal entitlement. However, the courts have also used the principle as a means by which A can come under a duty to B, such as a duty to grant B a right,[9] for example to prevent B suffering a detriment as a result of B's reliance on the mistaken belief which A failed to correct. Even where the acquiescence principle thus generates a cause of action, it can still be seen as characteristically equitable, in a sense discussed in Chapter 2.[10] This is because, as Irit Samet has argued, the principle reflects a responsibility which A has as a result of A's holding of a right.[11] It can therefore be seen as secondary, or supplementary, as it mitigates a practical problem which can arise for B as a result of having a system of private rights: reliance on a mistaken belief as to the existence of such rights. **3–012**

The third strand of proprietary estoppel is the most practically important and was applied in *Thorner v Major*. It depends on an assurance or, synonymously, a promise made by A to B and thus, crucially, can apply not only where B acts in reliance on a belief that B currently has a right, but also where B acts in reliance on A's promise that B *will*, in the future, acquire a right. The principle therefore is not a true form of estoppel at all, as it does not operate simply to prevent A denying the truth of a particular matter of fact or law. As we have seen, it also does more than simply restrain A's enforcement of a legal entitlement against B, as it can generate a new duty of A to B. In some cases, as in *Thorner v Major*, A (or A's personal representatives) will be compelled to transfer A's land (and any linked property) to B; in others, as in *Crabb v Arun DC*, A will be compelled to grant B a property **3–013**

(2012) 128 L.Q.R. 63, 72–73; B. McFarlane, *The Law of Proprietary Estoppel*, 2nd edn (Oxford University Press, 2020), Ch.1.

5 *Cobbe v Yeomans Row Management Ltd* [2008] UKHL 55; [2008] 1 W.L.R. 1752 at [48].

6 See paras 2–030 to 2–032.

7 See, e.g. *Hopgood v Brown* [1955] 1 W.L.R. 213 CA.

8 *Fisher v Brooker* [2009] UKHL 41; [2009] 1 W.L.R. 1764 at [62].

9 See, e.g. *Duke of Beaufort v Patrick* (1853) 17 Beav. 60, 51 E.R. 954: the court held not only that A could not seek possession of A's land from B, but also that A should be compelled to convey part of that land to B, at an appropriate price.

10 See para.2–063.

11 I. Samet, "Proprietary Estoppel and Responsibility for Omissions" (2015) 78 M.L.R. 85.

right in A's land; in others, A (or A's personal representatives) will be made to pay a sum of money to B.[12]

3–014 If made out, the acquiescence-based and promise-based strands of proprietary estoppel both generate an entitlement to some form of equitable relief, usually referred to as an "equity for relief" or "estoppel equity".[13] These strands of proprietary estoppel are fundamentally different to estoppel by representation. They are not concerned with the state of affairs according to which the parties' legal relations should be determined, but with what those legal relations are. In other words, the acquiescence-based and promise-based strands of proprietary estoppel generate new legal relations between A and B. This distinction has been described by the Full Court of the Court of Appeal of Tasmania in the following terms:[14]

> Estoppel by representation as to existing fact, and estoppel by convention, are common law estoppels by conduct. They operate to preserve particular states of affairs between parties. On the other hand, equitable estoppels are themselves a source of rights and obligations that arise upon satisfaction of necessary elements, albeit subject to equitable discretion.[15]

3–015 We will focus here on the promise-based strand of proprietary estoppel. It has been suggested that the principle which underlies it consists of A's being under a liability to ensure that B suffers no detriment as a result of B's reasonable reliance on A's promise to B: in the next extract, this is referred to as the "promise-detriment" principle. Whereas the representation-based and acquiescence-based strands depend on principles which can apply more broadly, even where no land is involved, the promise-based strand is said, as in Lord Walker's analysis above, to apply only where A's promise to B relates to land (or possibly other property) of A. This gives rise to two related questions: first, why is the promise-based strand, unlike promissory estoppel, allowed to give rise to a new duty of A to B? Second, why is the promise-based strand limited to cases where A's promise relates to land (or possibly other property)? We will consider those questions in the next section.

C. Justifying the Effects of Proprietary Estoppel

3–016 It is also clear that the promise-based strand of proprietary estoppel goes beyond the orthodox scope of promissory estoppel: it does not simply restrain A, as against B, in the exercise of a legal entitlement. Nonetheless, its requirements, as set out by Lord Walker in the extract above, closely resemble those of promissory estoppel. Indeed, as we saw in Chapter 2 when considering the analyses of the judges in the High Court of Australia in *Walton Stores v Maher*,[16] it can even be argued that promissory and proprietary estoppel form part of a broader principle focussed on A's responsibility to ensure B does not suffer a detriment as a result of B's reasonable reliance on A. Why then is proprietary estoppel allowed to operate differently and to give rise to a cause of action?

3–017 As seen in the extract above from *Thorner v Major*, Lord Walker's explanation of this different effect is that the representation or assurance in a proprietary estoppel case related to specific property. As the following extract suggests, however, this does not seem to provide a convincing justification.

---

12 See, e.g. *Campbell v Griffin* [2001] EWCA Civ 990; [2001] W.T.L.R. 981 (where the duty to pay the sum was secured by an equitable charge on A's property); *Jennings v Rice* [2002] EWCA Civ 159; [2003] 1 P. & C.R. 8; and *Powell v Benney* [2007] EWCA Civ 1283; [2008] 1 P. & C.R. DG12 (where the duty was not so secured).

13 See, e.g. *Pascoe v Turner* [1979] 1 W.L.R. 431; *Thorner v Major*. The decision in *Dillwyn v Llewellyn* (1862) 4 De G.F. & J. 517 appears to have been based on an analogy with part performance of a contract but may perhaps today be seen as a proprietary estoppel case.

14 *Rae & Partners Pty v Shaw* [2020] TASFC 14 at [157].

15 See J. Hudson, "The Price of Coherence in Estoppels" (2017) 39 Syd L.R. 1, 3–8.

16 See paras 2–039ff.

Ben McFarlane and Sir Philip Sales, "Promises, Detriment, and Liability: Lessons from Proprietary Estoppel"

(2015) 131 L.Q.R. 610, 621–623

Does the fact that A's promise relates to specific property make any difference in considering the justification of the principle applied, in case such as *Thorner*, under the promise-based strand of proprietary estoppel? In giving an affirmative answer to that question, Lord Walker referred to Lord Denning M.R.'s judgment in *Crabb*. There, distinguishing between "estoppels and estoppels", Lord Denning said that only the proprietary form could give rise to a cause of action. In doing so, he referred in turn to his own judgment (shortly to be overturned on appeal to the House of Lords) in *Moorgate Mercantile Co Ltd v Twitchings*, to support the point that the effect of estoppel on a true owner of property may be that: 'his own title to the property, be it land or goods, has been held to be limited or extinguished, and new rights and interests have been created therein.' 3–018

Lord Walker's statement in *Thorner* can thus be traced back to Lord Denning M.R.'s analysis in *Moorgate Mercantile*. That earlier case cannot impose a limit on the promise-detriment principle as it concerned the application of the general doctrine of estoppel by representation, as applied to a representation by A as to the ownership of property. As such a representation is as to a matter of fact, or mixed fact and law, it can lead to A's being precluded from denying its truth. That preclusion may then assist B in establishing the ingredients of a claim against A. Even in that case, however, the estoppel itself does not generate a cause of action; rather it prevents A's denial of a matter crucial to B's establishing an independent claim against A. Further, Lord Denning relied on the statutory recognition, in what is now s 21(1) of the Sale of Goods Act 1979, that where a third party sells A's goods to B without A's consent or actual authority, A may by his conduct be 'precluded from denying the seller's authority to sell'. As has been judicially noted, however, that principle seems not to be based on a true estoppel, whereby A would simply be prevented, as against B, from denying the third party's authority; it is rather an example of the third party's having ostensible authority, so that B acquires a 'real title and not merely a metaphorical title by estoppel'. 3–019

As a result, it seems the line of authority invoked by Lord Walker in *Thorner* provides no support for the limitation on the promise-based principle stated in that case. It therefore seems that, whilst proprietary estoppel is often said to be a means of limiting the freedom of an owner of property, this may simply be a description of the context in which the promise-detriment principle is most often invoked, rather than a justification of its basis and hence a limit on its scope. It has been observed that there is no clear reason why the promise-detriment principle should be capable of applying only to promises relating to property held by A . . . 3–020

Certainly, an insistence on a promise in relation to property provides a fragile basis on which to limit the promise-detriment principle. Why should what is usually a person's most valuable asset (their home, their farm) be vulnerable to the operation of the principle, but not other parts of their fund of wealth? Indeed, as suggested by the additional formal requirements attaching to a contract for the sale or other disposition of an interest in land, it seems that it ought to be harder, rather than easier, to justify the application of the principle to promises relating to land. The crux of the matter, we suggest, is that the requirements of the promise-detriment principle, such as the need for a promise, the role of the extent of B's detriment in limiting any liability of A, and the residual role of unconscionability, provide for an appropriate fair balance between the interests of A and B, rendering unnecessary an arbitrary restriction to promises relating to land . . . 3–021

It may be that the current limit on the promise-detriment principle in English law cannot be conceptually justified but depends instead on a contingent factor: the absence of a case at the highest level exposing the injustice of that limit. In *Waltons Stores*,[17] the facts revealed the absurdity of a position in which the principle might assist a potential lessee, relying to his or her detriment on a promise that a lease would be granted, but not a potential lessor, similarly relying on a promise that a lease would be taken. The fact that the potential lessee's promise does not relate to any land, or about to be owned, by that promise should not be decisive in determining whether any liability can arise as a result of that promise. 3–022

---

[17] *Waltons Stores (Interstate Ltd) v Maher* (1988) 14 C.L.R. 387: see paras 2–039ff.

3–023 It is worth noting that the argument made by McFarlane and Sales in the extract above is not that English law should adopt a unified model of equitable estoppel, whereby each of promissory and proprietary estoppel can give rise to a cause of action in all cases; it is rather that a specific principle which lies behind at least part of the law of proprietary estoppel (and perhaps also part of the law of promissory estoppel) should not be limited to cases where A's promise to B related to land (or possibly other property) of A. As we noted in Chapter 2,[18] this need not mean that the principle would apply to *all* cases where B would suffer a detriment as a result of B's reasonable reliance on A's promise: it can be argued, for example, that the principle should be limited to cases where A's promise is to exercise a power to enter into a legal relationship with B. If so, the principle could still be seen to have a characteristically equitable, supplementary function, as it would mitigate a practical risk to B that arises from parties having the power to enter into such relationships. There would however still be a question, as there is even with the current promise-based strand of proprietary estoppel, of the relationship of the principle to the law of contract.

D. The Promise-Based Strand and Contract Law

3–024 The relationship of proprietary estoppel to contract law can be seen to raise a more general question about the interaction of common law and equity: to what extent does equity contradict, or undermine, common law rules? This can be seen by considering a sharp debate about the impact of the Court of Appeal's decision in *Crabb v Arun DC*.[19] Lord Denning MR acknowledged there that proprietary estoppel can operate as a cause of action; as a result, A, the defendant council, could be compelled to honour an apparent agreement to grant a right of way over its land to B, who owned a farm neighbouring the council's land. In a note on the case, Patrick Atiyah argued that, by thus enforcing an agreement because of B's reliance on it, rather than because of anything which met the orthodox definition of consideration, the Court of Appeal's decision revealed:[20]

> the extraordinary conceptual morass into which English contract law is falling, largely because of outmoded ideas about the purpose and nature of the doctrine of consideration.

3–025 Atiyah's argument was that equity, in the form of proprietary estoppel, was being used by the judges as an alibi:[21] as a way to do justice to B without having to reform the common law. The problem, in Atiyah's view, was that the "outmoded" doctrine of consideration was thus left in place, when the more transparent solution would be simply to confront that doctrine directly. This goes to a point discussed in Chapter 1:[22] if equity is seen as a means to *correct* the common law, this always raises the question of why the common law should not just be changed directly.

3–026 Peter Millett (later Lord Millett) had been B's counsel in *Crabb v Arun DC*. He responded to Atiyah's "interesting, if intemperate" note[23] by explaining why it had not been possible for B to make the argument that there was an enforceable contract between A and B. Not only had there been a lack of consideration, on the orthodox definition, as there had been no request by A for B to act in a particular way in exchange for A's promise or performance; further, the council officials with whom B had dealt had

---

[18] See paras 2–062 to 2–065.
[19] See para.3–003.
[20] (1976) 92 L.Q.R. 174.
[21] To adopt a term later used by Bernard Rudden in this context: "Equity as Alibi" S. Goldstein (ed.) *Equity and Contemporary Legal Developments* (Hebrew University of Jerusalem, 1992).
[22] See paras 1–042 to 1–047.
[23] (1976) 92 L.Q.R. 342.

no power to bind the council to a contract; the agreement reached had in any case not been intended to be legally binding, nor was it sufficiently certain to be contractually binding; and, as the agreement had only been made orally, it was prevented by statutory formality requirements from being enforceable.[24] A proprietary estoppel claim could succeed only because, even whilst it may in some cases have a similar *effect* to a contractual claim, it had a different basis and different requirements:[25]

> The apparent similarity of the results achieved . . . is . . . deceptive. The claims are different, require different facts to be proved, and have different consequences.

Millett's analysis is very persuasive. It would be an error to think that a proprietary estoppel claim is simply a form of contractual claim, in which detrimental reliance replaces consideration as a reason to make A's promise binding. First, as Millett noted, there are other differences in the requirements of the claims. This can be seen, for example, in the analysis of Hoffmann LJ (as he then was) in *Walton v Walton*.[26] The first instance judge had dismissed B's proprietary estoppel claim on the basis that A's promise to B had not been intended to create legal relations between the parties. Hoffmann LJ explained that, whilst that would be fatal to a contractual claim, it was not an obstacle to a proprietary estoppel claim. **3–027**

> *Walton v Walton*
>
> CA, 14 April 1994
>
> HOFFMANN LJ: Intention to create legal relations is a familiar concept in the law of contract. It means an intention to bring into existence an immediately binding contract; to make an offer which, when accepted, will constitute a contract, or to accept an offer with the intention of being bound. But in many cases of promises made in a family or social context, there is no intention to create an immediately binding contract. There are several reasons why the law is reluctant to assume that there was. One which is relevant in this case is that such promises are often subject to unspoken and ill-defined qualifications. Take for example the promise in this case. When it was first made, Mrs Walton did not know what the future might hold. Anything might happen which could make it quite inappropriate for the farm to go to the plaintiff. But a contract, subject to the narrow doctrine of frustration, must be performed come what may. This is why [the plaintiff's counsel] has always accepted that Mrs Walton's promise could not have been intended to become a contract. **3–028**
>
> But none of this reasoning applies to equitable estoppel, because it does not look forward into the future and guess what might happen. It looks backwards from the moment when the promise falls due to be performed and asks whether, in the circumstances which have actually happened, it would be unconscionable for the promise not to be kept. **3–029**

This does not mean, of course, that *any* promise is capable of giving rise to a proprietary estoppel claim. As confirmed in *Thorner v Major*, where *Walton v Walton* was relied on, A's promise must be one which B could reasonably understand as seriously intended as capable of being relied upon. The crucial point though is that the requirements of a proprietary estoppel claim differ from those of a contractual claim. This is linked to the second point which supports Millett's analysis: the *effect* of each claim is different. Where a contract is formed, A is under an immediate duty to B, and a remedy given to B will generally aim to ensure that B is put in the same position as B would have been had that duty been performed. In contrast, it is clear that, in responding to a successful promise-based **3–030**

---

24 (1976) 92 L.Q.R. 342, 346.

25 (1976) 92 L.Q.R. 342, 346.

26 CA, 14 April 1994. Whilst the decision was not included in any official reports, it has been influential, both in England and abroad: see e.g. *Thorner v Major*.

proprietary estoppel claim, a court will not always aim to protect B's expectation. As Lewison LJ stated in *Habberfield v Habberfield*:[27] "the expectation is not determinative of the relief to be granted". Rather, the court has a "wide judgmental discretion";[28] as Aldous LJ noted in *Jennings v Rice*, one of the many cases in which the remedy ordered had a lower value that B's expectation: "If the conscience of the court is involved, it would be odd that the amount of the award should be set rigidly at the sum expected by the claimant."[29]

3–031 There is currently some uncertainty, both in England and Australia, as to the principles a court should apply in determining its response to a successful promise-based proprietary estoppel claim.[30] Nonetheless, it is clear that, even though the claim is based on a promise, the court is not compelled to ensure B ends up in the same position as if the promise had been kept. As Millett noted, there is thus clear ground between the effects of proprietary estoppel and of a contract. This helps to explain why, for example, the strict formality requirements that apply to a *contract* for the sale or other disposition of an interest in land[31] have never been applied to a proprietary estoppel claim.[32]

3–032 It can therefore be argued that, whilst a proprietary estoppel claim may be a means to give some legal effect to A's promise to B, this does not mean that it undermines contract law as it does not provide an alternative means for a promise to impose an immediate duty on A arising as a result of A's promise to B. As explained by Hoffmann LJ in *Walton v Walton*, in a proprietary estoppel claim, a court instead looks at a later point, seeing whether it would at that point be unconscionable for A to go back on A's promise and leave B without a remedy. As noted in Chapter 1,[33] this shows one of the ways in which the idea of conscience may be relevant in equity: if, for example, circumstances change after the time of A's promise then, even if the change would not be significant enough to attract the contractual doctrine of frustration, a court can take that into account in deciding on whether B's proprietary estoppel claim succeeds and, if so, what order should be made against A.

3–033 Indeed, it could even be argued that the possibility of such a promise-based proprietary estoppel claim helps us to justify the stricter requirements applying to a contractual claim,[34] by providing a means of protection for parties who might otherwise suffer detriment, in practice, owing to the absence of a contract. For example, when recommending strict formality requirements for a valid contract for the sale or other disposition of an interest in land, the Law Commission expressly adverted to proprietary estoppel as a means to protect B when those rules might otherwise lead to injustice. Importantly, such an equitable claim does not change, or correct, those limits on a contractual claim; it leaves the limits intact, and rather supplements the common law by providing a different means of dealing with a practical injustice which might otherwise result from the operation of those rules.

---

27 [2019] EWCA Civ 890 at [71].

28 *Jennings v Rice* at at [24] (Robert Walker LJ). See too e.g. *Davies v Davies* [2016] EWCA Civ 463 at [39] (Lewison LJ).

29 *Jennings v Rice* at [21].

30 See, e.g. the competing views identified by Lewison LJ in *Davies v Davies* at [39]. It is possible that, in England, some clarity will be provided by the decision of the Supreme Court in *Guest v Guest* (on appeal from [2020] EWCA Civ 387). For discussion see e.g. A. Robertson, "The Reliance Basis of Proprietary Estoppel Remedies" (2008) 72 *Conveyancer and Property Lawyer* 295; J. Campbell, "Waltons v Maher: History, Unconscientiousness and Remedy – The Minimum Equity" (2013) 7 J. Eq. 171; Y. Liew, "The 'Prima Facie Expectation Relief' Approach in the Australian Law of Proprietary Estoppel" (2019) 39 O.J.L.S. 183.

31 In England, see Law of Property (Miscellaneous Provisions) Act 1989 s.2.

32 For discussion, see e.g. *Whittaker v Kinnear* [2011] EWHC 1479 (QB) at [28]–[30] and *Farrar v Miller* [2018] EWCA Civ 172 at [57]–[58], Lord Neuberger, "The Stuffing of Minerva's Owl? Taxonomy and Taxidermy in Equity" [2009] C.L.J. 537, p.546, B. McFarlane, "Proprietary Estoppel and Failed Contractual Negotiations" [2005] Conv. 501. Such analyses all show the difficulties with Lord Scott's contrary obiter comment in *Cobbe v Yeoman's Row Management Ltd* [2008] 1 W.L.R. 1752 at [29].

33 See paras 1–103 to 1–134.

34 See B. McFarlane, "Equity and the Justification of Private Rights" in M. Crawford et al (eds) *Justifying Private Rights* (Hart, 2020), Ch.11.

3. Confidentiality

A. Overview

The equitable doctrine of confidentiality generates a legal relationship between A and B, according to which A is under a duty to B not to use certain information, and B has a correlative right against A. B may be entitled to injunctive relief preventing A from using or communicating the information, or relief that requires A to take action as necessary to prevent the future use of the information, for example by returning or destroying documents. If A has breached the duty of confidence, B may be entitled to relief that addresses the consequences of A's misuse. This can include equitable compensation, account of profits, and sometimes a constructive trust. **3-034**

Confidentiality applies when the subject information has the necessary quality of confidentiality, and A knew, or had sufficient notice, that the information was confidential.[35] The doctrine:[36] **3-035**

> depends on the broad principle of equity that he who has received information in confidence shall not take unfair advantage of it. He must not make use of it to the prejudice of him who gave it without obtaining his consent.

A classic example[37] of the doctrine is *Prince Albert v Strange*.[38] An injunction was granted to prevent A from publishing a catalogue that described etchings made by Prince Albert and Queen Victoria. A had already submitted to an injunction against exhibiting or publishing the etchings and had agreed to part with the etchings themselves. The Prince had sent the etchings to a printer to be copied and A had surreptitiously obtained copies of the etchings and prepared a catalogue of them to advertise their exhibition to the public. In the extract below, justifying the injunction against the publication of the catalogue, Lord Cottenham indicates that confidentiality extends beyond the situations where B can show some proprietary right, such as ownership of a document, or where there is a pre-existing relationship of confidence between A and B, such as that between solicitor and client or doctor and patient. Lord Cottenham therefore makes clear that it is the confidential nature of the information itself that is the reason why A should not misuse the information. **3-036**

> *Prince Albert v Strange*
>
> Court of Queen's Bench, (1849) 1 Mac. & G. 25 at 41–47
>
> LORD COTTENHAM LC: . . . The importance which has been attached to this case arises entirely from the exalted station of the Plaintiff, and cannot be referred to any difficulty in the case itself; the precise facts may not have occurred before, but those facts so clearly fall within established principles, that the application of them is not attended with any difficulty. The right of the Plaintiff to an injunction restraining the Defendant from exhibiting, copying, or in any manner publishing or parting with, or disposing of any of the etchings in question, is perfectly clear from the facts of the case, and is not now disputed by the Defendant; and the only question I have to decide is whether, this right being so established and admitted, the Defendant is to be permitted to publish the catalogue in question, in which he announces his intention of exhibiting the etchings which he is so restrained from doing, and in which he announces to **3-037**

---

35 *Coco v Clark (Engineers) Ltd* [1969] R.P.C. 41 at [47], endorsed by the CA in *Murray v Yorkshire Fund Managers* [1998] 2 All E.R. 1015 at 1020; *Attorney General v Jonathan Cape* [1975] 3 All E.R. 484 at [494]; *Fraser v Thames Television Ltd* [1983] 2 All E.R. 101 at 116.

36 *Seager v Copydex Ltd* [1967] 1 W.L.R. 923 at 931.

37 Some specific works on confidentiality include: R. Toulson and C. Phipps, *Confidentiality*, 3rd edn (Sweet & Maxwell, 2012); T. Aplin et al (eds), *Gurry on Breach of Confidence*, 2nd edn (Oxford University Press, 2012); P. Stanley, *The Law of Confidentiality: A Restatement* (Hart, 2008). See also McGhee et. al (eds), *Snell's Equity*, 34th edn (2020), Ch.9.

38 *Prince Albert v Strange* (1849) 1 Mac. & G. 25.

> the public that every purchaser of the catalogue will be presented (by permission) with a facsimile of the autograph of either Her Majesty or of the Prince, engraved from the original, the selection being left to the purchaser. . . .
>
> 3–038 Upon the first question, therefore, that of property, I am clearly of opinion that the exclusive right and interest of the Plaintiff in the composition or work in question being established, and there being no right or interest whatever in the Defendant, the Plaintiff is entitled to the injunction of this Court to protect him against the invasion of such right and interest by the Defendant, which the publication of any catalogue would undoubtedly be; but this case by no means depends solely upon the question of property, for a breach of trust, confidence, or contract, would of itself entitle the Plaintiff to an injunction. The Plaintiff's affidavits state the private character of the work or composition, and negative any licence or authority for publication, the gifts of some of the etchings to private friends certainly not implying any such licence or authority, and state distinctly the belief of the Plaintiff, that the catalogue and the descriptive and other remarks therein contained, could not have been compiled or made, except by means of the possession of the several impressions of the said etchings surreptitiously and improperly obtained. . . .
>
> 3–039 The Plaintiff's affidavits state the private character of the work or composition, and negative any licence or authority for publication, the gifts of some of the etchings to private friends certainly not implying any such licence or authority, and state distinctly the belief of the Plaintiff, that the catalogue and the descriptive and other remarks therein contained, could not have been compiled or made, except by means of the possession of the several impressions of the said etchings surreptitiously and improperly obtained. To this case no answer is made, the Defendant saying only that he did not, at the time, believe that the etchings had been improperly obtained, but not suggesting any mode by which they could have been properly obtained, so as to entitle the possessor to use them for publication. . . .
>
> 3–040 . . . upon the evidence on behalf of the Plaintiff, and in the absence of any explanation on the part of the Defendant, I am bound to assume that the possession of the etchings by the Defendant or Judge has its foundation in a breach of trust, confidence, or contract,. . . and upon this ground also I think the Plaintiff's title to the injunction sought to be discharged, fully established. . . .
>
> 3–041 . . . The cases referred to. . . have no application to cases in which the court exercises an original and independent jurisdiction, not for the protection of a merely legal right, but to prevent what this court considers and treats as a wrong. . . arising from a. . . breach of. . . confidence, as in the present case. . . In the present case, where privacy is the right invaded, postponing the injunction would be equivalent to denying it altogether. The interposition of this court in these cases, does not depend upon any legal right, and to be effectual, it must be immediate. . .

3–042 The Prince also sought delivery up of all copies of the etchings. At trial, this part of the order was resisted. The Court of Appeal upheld the order made at trial, where Knight Bruce V-C stated:[39]

> It is. . . said, that neither the copies of the catalogue, nor the impressions that have been taken, can be delivered, or be directed to be delivered up, in as much as the defendant contends that he is entitled to the property in the materials on which they are printed. With regard to catalogues, no such question, I think, arises. They must be either cancelled or destroyed; and without destruction they can hardly be cancelled. With regard to the impressions, it might possibly be right to attend to the defendant's claim, had the impressions been upon a material of intrinsic value—upon a material not substantially worthless, except for the impressions which, by the wrongful act of the defendants, had been placed there. That case, however, does not arise. The material here is substantially worthless, except for that in which the defendant has no property. There can consequently be no reason why the effectual destruction of subject should not be directed by the court. . .

39 (1849) 2 De. G. & Sm. 652 at 716.

Confidentiality controls A's exercise or enjoyment of A's freedom (in Hohfeld's terms, a privilege or liberty)[40] to use the subject information. This point is made by Lewison LJ in *Racing Partnership Ltd v Done Bros (Cash Betting) Ltd*:[41] **3–043**

> The starting point, in my judgment, is freedom of speech. Unless there is a contrary obligation, a person is free to communicate what he sees or hears. In order to attract an obligation not to communicate information, the information must have the necessary quality of confidence about it.

In addition, there is an individual's right to freedom of expression in Art.10 of the ECHR.[42] The equitable doctrine of confidentiality controls how A exercises A's freedom or privilege to use and/or disseminate information. **3–044**

As such, the application of the doctrine requires the court to balance the competing interests served by A's legal entitlement, in this instance A's freedom to use or communicate information, and B's interest in confidentiality. It will not be the case that B's interest always prevails, and the doctrine of confidence will not be applied in such a way as to interfere unjustifiably with A's freedom of expression whether it be A's freedom to use or disseminate information, or A's right to communicate certain information as protected by Art.10 of the ECHR.[43] It is also the case that the strength of A's interest will vary in particular contexts: some types of communication are more valuable than others: as Lady Hale noted in *Campbell v MGN Ltd*:[44] **3–045**

> ... [there are] undoubtedly different types of speech, just as there are different types of private information, some of which are more deserving of protection in a democratic society than others. Top of the list is political speech. The free exchange of information and ideas on matters relevant to the organisation of the economic, social and political life of the country is crucial to any democracy. Without it, it can scarcely be called a democracy at all. This includes revealing information about public figures, especially those in elective office, which would otherwise be private but is relevant to their participation in public life. Intellectual and emotional speech and expression are also important in a democracy, not least because they enable the development of individuals' potential to play a full part in society and in our democratic life. Artistic speech and expression is important for similar reasons, in fostering both individual originality and creativity and the free-thinking and dynamic society we so much value. No doubt there are other kinds of speech and expression for which similar claims can be made.

Key to understanding confidentiality is that it is not concerned with how A acquires the information: it may have been communicated by B to A, or A may have acquired the information in other lawful or unlawful ways. As we will see below,[45] the tort of invasion of privacy which, at least to some extent, has evolved from the equitable doctrine of confidentiality, also controls the use of information when it is private, *as well as* the means by which such information is acquired. Confidentiality, on the other **3–046**

---

40 See para.2–007.

41 *Racing Partnership Ltd v Sports Information Services Ltd* [2020] EWCA Civ 1300 at [183] (with whom Phillips LJ agreed).

42 See, e.g. *Campbell v Mirror Group Newspapers Ltd* [2004] UKHL 22; [2004] 2 A.C. 457 at [29], per Lord Nicholls.

43 Art.10 Freedom of expression: 1. Everyone has the right to freedom of expression. This right shall include freedom to hold opinions and to receive and impart information and ideas without interference by public authority and regardless of frontiers. This Article shall not prevent States from requiring the licensing of broadcasting, television or cinema enterprises. 2. The exercise of these freedoms, since it carries with it duties and responsibilities, may be subject to such formalities, conditions, restrictions or penalties as are prescribed by law and are necessary in a democratic society, in the interests of national security, territorial integrity or public safety, for the prevention of disorder or crime, for the protection of health or morals, for the protection of the reputation or rights of others, for preventing the disclosure of information received in confidence, or for maintaining the authority and impartiality of the judiciary.

44 *Campbell v Mirror Group Newspapers Ltd* at [148].

45 See paras 3–114ff.

hand, controls only what A does with the information, irrespective of whether it has been obtained by A lawfully or not.

3–047 Confidentiality is significant for our understanding of equity for multiple reasons. First, it is an example of an equitable rule that applies to control A's exercise of a *liberty or privilege*, as distinct from A's power or claim-right. Second, as discussed further below,[46] it is an example of the courts' changing conception of equitable rules from being disability imposing rules to duty imposing rules: there is thus a parallel to the discussion in Chapter 2 of fiduciary duties.[47] Third, it shows the development of equitable doctrine according to changing social conditions, and its responsiveness to broader legal change(s), such as an individual's right to privacy under the ECHR.[48] Fourth, there is the interplay between equity's protection of confidentiality and the unresolved role of common law in protecting against invasions of privacy. Before discussing these issues further, we must first consider an outline of the scope and elements of confidentiality.

B. Elements

3–048 In *Coco v A.N. Clark (Engineers) Ltd*,[49] Megarry J outlined the elements necessary to B's action based on confidentiality:[50]

> First, the information itself . . . must 'have the necessary quality of confidence about it'. Secondly, that information must have been communicated in circumstances importing an obligation of confidence. Thirdly, there must have been an unauthorised use of the information to the detriment of the party communicating it.

3–049 As explained by Arnold LJ in *Racing Partnership Ltd v Sports Information Services Ltd*,[51] Megarry J's formulation "has repeatedly been cited with approval at the highest level".[52]

3–050 The first element is that the subject matter relates to information[53] that has the necessary quality of confidentiality. This first element had once been focussed on the quality of the information as assessed in light of the circumstances in which A acquired the information, such as a pre-existing relationship between A and B. The focus has changed to whether B has a reasonable expectation as to the confidentiality of the information.[54] This might be the case where information is available to one or more persons and not generally available to others, provided that the person (or group) who controls the information does not intend that it should become available to others.[55]

---

46 See paras 3–081 to 3–136.

47 See paras 2–158 to 2–163.

48 Art.8 Right to respect for your private and family life, home and correspondence: 1. Everyone has the right to respect for his private and family life, his home and his correspondence. 2. There shall be no interference by a public authority with the exercise of this right except such as is in accordance with the law and is necessary in a democratic society in the interests of national security, public safety or the economic well-being of the country, for the prevention of disorder or crime, for the protection of health or morals, or for the protection of the rights and freedoms of others.

49 *Coco v AN Clark (Engineers) Ltd* [1969] RPC 4.

50 *Coco v AN Clark (Engineers) Ltd* at 47.

51 *Racing Partnership v Sports Information Services Ltd* [2020] EWCA Civ 1300 at [44].

52 *Racing Partnership v Sports Information Services Ltd* [2020] EWCA Civ 1300 at [45], citing see Lord Griffiths in *Attorney General v Guardian Newspapers Ltd (No.2) ("Spycatcher")* [1990] 1 A.C. 109 at 268, Lord Nicholls of Birkenhead in *Campbell v MGN* at [13] and Lord Hoffmann in *Douglas v Hello! Ltd (No 3)* [2008] 1 A.C. 1 at [111].

53 *Campbell v Mirror Group Newspapers Ltd* [2004] UKHL 22; [2004] 2 A.C. 457 at [11]; dissenting in the result, although not on this issue.

54 *Campbell v Mirror Group Newspapers Ltd* at [21] (Lord Nicholls) at [85] (Lord Hope), and [96] and at [137] (Baroness Hale). See too, e.g. *HRH Prince of Wales v Associated Newspapers Ltd* [2006] EWCA Civ 1776; [2008] Ch. 57 at [34] (Lord Phillips).

55 *Prince of Wales v Associated Newspapers Ltd* [2008] Ch. 57 (CA) at [33]–[34] (the Court).

Satisfying this first element means that B must be able to identify clearly and precisely the information to which her expectation of confidentiality attaches.[56] This requirement is not concerned with whether the information is accurate or false, albeit this may relate to whether B's expectation of confidentiality is reasonable.[57] Further, confidence applies neither to useless information, nor to trivia.[58] **3–051**

Once information is generally available or accessible, B can no longer have a reasonable expectation of confidentiality.[59] However, information that is publicly available may nonetheless be *private* information; the dissemination or use of which can be restrained under the tort of invasion of privacy. This tort developed out of the equitable doctrine of confidence, but is now best understood as a separate or freestanding cause of action.[60] **3–052**

The second element is concerned with A's knowledge, actual or constructive, that the information is confidential. In *Coco v AN Clark (Engineers) Ltd*, Megarry J stated that:[61] **3–053**

> It seems to me that if the circumstances are such that any reasonable man standing in the shoes of the recipient of the information would realise that upon reasonable grounds the information was being given to him in confidence, then this would suffice to impose on him the equitable obligation of confidence.

However, the test for whether A did or should have realised the information was confidential has been expressed in different ways in a range of cases.[62] **3–054**

Attorney General v Guardian Newspapers Ltd (No.2) ("Spycatcher")

House of Lords, [1990] 1 A.C. 109 at 281–282

LORD GOFF: I start with the broad general principle (which I do not intend in any way to be definitive) that a duty of confidence arises when confidential information comes to the knowledge of a person (the confidant) in circumstances where he has notice, or is held to have agreed, that the information is confidential, with the effect that it would be just in all the circumstances that he should be precluded from disclosing the information to others. I have used the word "notice" advisedly, in order to avoid the (here unnecessary) question of the extent to which actual knowledge is necessary; though I of course understand knowledge to include circumstances where the confidant has deliberately closed his eyes to the obvious. The existence of this broad general principle reflects the fact that there is such a public interest in the maintenance of confidences, that the law will provide remedies for their protection. **3–055**

I realise that, in the vast majority of cases, in particular those concerned with trade secrets, the duty of confidence will arise from a transaction or relationship between the parties—often a contract, in which event the duty may arise by reason of either an express or an implied term of that contract. It is in such cases as these that the expressions "confider" and "confidant" are perhaps most aptly employed. But it is well settled that a duty of confidence may arise in equity independently of such cases; and I have expressed the circumstances in which the duty arises in broad terms, not merely to embrace those cases where a third party receives information from a person who is under a duty of confidence in respect of it, knowing that it has been disclosed by that person to him in breach of his duty of confidence, but also to include certain situations, beloved of law teachers—where an obviously confidential document is wafted by an electric fan out of a window into a crowded street, or where an obviously confidential document, such as a private diary, is dropped in a public place, and is then picked up by a passer-by. I also have in mind the situations **3–056**

---

56 *Amway Corp v Eurway International Ltd* [1974] R.P.C. 82 at 86–87; *Fraser v Thames Television Ltd* [1984] 1 Q.B. 44 at 63; *De Maudsley v Palumbo* [1996] F.S.R. 447.

57 *McKennitt v Ash* [2006] EWCA Civ 1714; [2007] 3 W.L.R. 194 at [80], (Buxton LJ); *BUQ v HRE* [2015] EWHC 1272 (QB) at [43] (Warby J).

58 *Attorney General v Guardian Newspapers (No.2)* [1990] 1 A.C. 109 at 281 (Lord Goff).

59 *Attorney General v Guardian Newspapers (No.2)* at 281 (Lord Goff).

60 See paras 3–114 to 3–124.

61 *Coco v AN Clark (Engineers) Ltd* at 48.

62 Some of which are summarised by Arnold J in *Primary Group (UK) Ltd v Royal Bank of Scotland* [2014] EWHC 1082 (Ch) at [210]–[235].

> where secrets of importance to national security come into the possession of members of the public—a point to which I shall refer in a moment. I have however deliberately avoided the fundamental question whether, contract apart, the duty lies simply "in the notion of an obligation of conscience arising from the circumstances in or through which the information was communicated or obtained". . . or whether confidential information may also be regarded as property. . .

3–057 After a review of many relevant authorities, Arnold LJ in *Primary Group (UK) Ltd v Royal Bank of Scotland*[63] concluded that the court must "consider the matter from the perspective of the reasonable person standing in the position of the recipient of the information"[64] suggesting that, in some circumstances, this element would be satisfied where a reasonable person would make further inquiries revealing the confidential nature of the information.[65]

3–058 One of the implications of the removal of the requirement for a pre-existing relationship of confidence is that the doctrine imposes a duty upon anyone who acquires the confidential information in the requisite circumstances, i.e. when they know or ought to know of its confidential nature. This means that the third party or stranger who chances on confidential information, for example, an unintended recipient of an email or letter, is subject to the same primary duty of confidentiality as a person to whom B confides confidential information, such as a solicitor or doctor.

3–059 A distinction is made however, between the primary liability of a recipient of confidential information, and a person, C, who assists in A's misuse of confidential information, but does not have or otherwise misuse the information herself. As Lord Neuberger stated in *Vestergaard Frandsen A/S v Bestnet Europe Ltd*:[66]

> [W]hile a recipient of confidential information may be said to be primarily liable in a case of its misuse, a person who assists her in the [breach] can be liable, in a secondary sense . . . as I see it, consistently with the approach of equity in this area, she would normally have to know that the recipient was abusing confidential information. Knowledge in this context would of course not be limited to her actual knowledge, and it would include what is sometimes called 'blind-eye knowledge'. The best analysis of what that involves is to be found in *Royal Brunei Airlines Sdn Bhd v Tan*.[67]

3–060 The third element of B's claim is that the actual or potential breach by A of A's duty of confidentiality, consisting of A's misuse of the information. The substance of B's right is to control A's use of the information,[68] and is not limited to controlling A's ownership or possession of physical documents or electronic material upon which information might be recorded. In *Brake v Guy*,[69] HHJ Paul Matthews explained:[70]

> The law is not here concerned with the ownership of pieces of paper on which information is recorded, but with rights to control the information itself. It would make no sense to say that, if the confidential clerk took away the employer's information in his head, he could reveal it to the authorities as evidence of wrongdoing, but if he had a poor memory and copied the relevant documents, or simply took them, intending to return them later, he could not.

---

63 *Primary Group (UK) Ltd v Royal Bank of Scotland.*
64 *Primary Group (UK) Ltd v Royal Bank of Scotland* at [237].
65 *Primary Group (UK) Ltd v Royal Bank of Scotland* at [240].
66 *Vestergaard Frandsen A/S v Bestnet Europe Ltd* [2013] UKSC 31; [2013] W.L.R. 1556 at [26].
67 *Royal Brunei Airlines Sdn Bhd v Tan* [1995] 2 A.C. 378 PC. For discussion of the *Tan* case, see paras 14–112 to 14–152.
68 *Racing Partnership v Sports Information* at [46].
69 *Brake v Guy* [2021] EWHC 670 (Ch).
70 *Brake v Guy* at [52].

While the existence of A's duty of confidentiality depends on A's knowledge (objectively assessed), breach does not depend on A's conscious misuse. A's subconscious use of confidential information may give rise to a claim of breach of confidence.[71] Use of information may amount to a breach where it is communicated or published, or where it is utilised by A in some other way such as in a production process. The duty of confidence is "not merely not to communicate the information to a third party" but is rather "not . . . to make any use of it or cause any use to be made of it by others".[72] **3-061**

Some cases have left open whether breach depends on A's use of information resulting in some detriment to B, as explained by Lord Goff in *Attorney-General v Guardian Newspapers (No.2)*:[73] **3-062**

> I would also, like Megarry J. in *Coco v. A. N. Clark (Engineers) Ltd*,[74] wish to keep open the question whether detriment to the plaintiff is an essential ingredient of an action for breach of confidence. Obviously, detriment or potential detriment to the plaintiff will nearly always form part of his case; but this may not always be necessary. Some possible cases where there need be no detriment are mentioned in the judgment of Megarry J. to which I have just referred[75] and in Gurry, *Breach of Confidence* . . . In the present case the point is immaterial, since it is established that in cases of Government secrets the Crown has to establish not only that the information is confidential, but also that publication would be to its "detriment" in the sense that the public interest requires that it should not be published. That the word "detriment" should be extended so far as to include such a case perhaps indicates that everything depends upon how wide a meaning can be given to the word "detriment" in this context.

Even if not a necessary condition to establish breach, detriment may be relevant to B's claim for relief, and, for example, to the extent of any monetary award, or whether an injunction should be awarded on the basis that the detriment is significant and/or could not otherwise be addressed by a money order.[76] **3-063**

Finally, it has been suggested that detriment is not a condition for breach and A's use, and even acquisition of the information, alone amounts to breach by A.[77] This, however, is based on the view that the doctrine of confidentiality extends to protect B's right to privacy and protects against an infringement of B's autonomy. As we will see below, later cases have since indicated that the law has developed to the point that the tort of privacy is now separate from the equitable doctrine of confidentiality and so has different and distinct requirements. **3-064**

C. Limiting Principles and "Defences"

In addition to the three elements or requirements identified by Megarry J, there are further requirements or limiting principles[78] that determine B's claim, including for example the public interest in disclosure. This is in addition to the range of other equitable defences and discretionary factors that might militate against relief being granted to B. **3-065**

---

71 As, for example, in *Seager v Copydex Ltd* [1967] 1 W.L.R. 923; *Paymaster (Jamaica) Ltd v Grace Kennedy Remittance Services Ltd* [2017] UKPC 40 at [38]–[41].

72 *Prince Jefri Bolkiah v KPMG* [1999] 2 A.C. 222 HL at 235, (Lord Millett).

73 *Spycatcher* at 281–282. See also, *Federal Bank of the Middle East Ltd v Hadkinson* [2000] 2 All E.R. 395 at 413, per Mummery LJ.

74 [1969] R.P.C. 41 at 48.

75 *Spycatcher* at 48.

76 See, e.g. *Sun Valley Foods Ltd v Vincent* [2000] F.S.R. 825 at 838, (Jonathan Parker J).

77 *Tchenguiz v Imerman* [2010] EWCA Civ 908; [2010] 2 F.L.R. 814 at [68], (Lord Neuberger MR).

78 *Peter Pan Manufacturing Co v Corsets Silhouette Ltd* [1964] 1 W.L.R. 96; *British Syphon Co v Homewood* [1956] 1 W.L.R. 1190; *Spycatcher*; *Attorney General v Blake* [1998] Ch. 439.

Imerman v Tchenguiz

Court of Appeal, [2011] Fam 116; [2010] EWCA Civ 908 at [74]–[75]

3–066 LORD NEUBERGER MR: A claim based on confidentiality is an equitable claim. Accordingly, the normal equitable rules apply. Thus, while one would normally expect a court to grant the types of relief we have been discussing, it would have a discretion whether to refuse some or all such relief on familiar equitable principles. Equally, the precise nature of the relief which would be granted must depend on all aspects of the particular case: equity fashions the appropriate relief to fit the rights of the parties, the facts of the case, and, at least sometimes, the wider merits. But, as we have noted, where the confidential information has been passed by the defendant to a third party, the claimant's rights will prevail as against the third party, unless he was a bona fide purchaser of the information without notice of its confidential nature.

3–067 In *Istil Group Inc v Zahoor*,[79] after a full and illuminating survey of the authorities, Lawrence Collins J held that, where a privileged document had been seen by an opposing party through fraud or mistake, the court has power to exercise its equitable confidentiality jurisdiction, and "should ordinarily intervene, unless the case is one where the injunction can properly be refused on the general principles affecting the grant of a discretionary remedy . . .", a view which he discussed in the ensuing paragraphs. On the facts of that case, he concluded that an injunction should be refused "on the ground [of] the public interest in the disclosure of wrongdoing and the proper administration of justice".[80]

3–068 In *Lachaux v Independent Print Ltd*,[81] Sir Michael Tugendhat explained that the "public interest in the emergence of the truth" is "commonly held to override what would otherwise be a duty of confidentiality".[82] This principle has been explained as being that "the true doctrine is that there is no confidence in an iniquity"[83] and is explained further by Lord Goff as the "third limiting principle" in the following excerpt.

Attorney General v Guardian Newspapers Ltd (No. 2) ("Spycatcher")

House of Lords, [1990] 1 A.C. 109 at 282–284

3–069 LORD GOFF: The third limiting principle is of far greater importance. It is that, although the basis of the law's protection of confidence is that there is a public interest that confidences should be preserved and protected by the law, nevertheless that public interest may be outweighed by some other countervailing public interest which favours disclosure. This limitation may apply, as the learned judge pointed out, to all types of confidential information. It is this limiting principle which may require a court to carry out a balancing operation, weighing the public interest in maintaining confidence against a countervailing public interest favouring disclosure.

3–070 Embraced within this limiting principle is, of course, the so called defence of iniquity. In origin, this principle was narrowly stated, on the basis that a man cannot be made "the confidant of a crime or a fraud".[84] But it is now clear that the principle extends to matters of which disclosure is required in the public interest.[85] It does not however follow that the public interest will in such cases require disclosure to the media, or to the public by the media. There are cases in which a more limited disclosure is all that is required.[86] A classic example of a case where limited disclosure is required is a case of alleged iniquity in the Security Service. Here there are a number of avenues for proper complaint. . . . Like my noble and learned friend, Lord Griffiths, I find it very difficult to envisage a case of this kind in which it will be in the public interest for allegations of such iniquity to be published in the media. In any event, a mere allegation of iniquity is not of itself sufficient to justify disclosure in the public interest. Such an allegation will only do so if, following

[79] [2003] EWHC 165 (Ch); [2003] 2 All E.R. 252 at [74].
[80] *Istil Group Inc v Zahoor* [2003] EWHC 165 (Ch); [2003] 2 All E.R. 252 at [115].
[81] *Lachaux v Independent Print Ltd* [2015] EWHC 3677 (QB).
[82] *Lachaux v Independent Print Ltd* at [42].
[83] *Gartside v Outram* (1857) 26 L.J. Ch. (NS) 113 at 114 (Sir William Page Wood VC).
[84] *Gartside v Outram* at 114.
[85] *Beloff v Pressdram Ltd* [1973] 1 All E.R. 241 at 260; *Lion Laboratories Ltd v Evans* [1985] Q.B. 526 at 550.
[86] *Francome v Mirror Group Newspapers Ltd* [1984] 1 W.L.R. 892.

> such investigations as are reasonably open to the recipient, and having regard to all the circumstances of the case, the allegation in question can reasonably be regarded as being a credible allegation from an apparently reliable source.
>
> In cases concerned with Government secrets, as appears from the judgments of two Chief Justices[87]—it is incumbent upon the Crown, in order to restrain disclosure of Government secrets, not only to show that the information is confidential, but also to show that it is in the public interest that it should not be published. The relevant passages in the above judgments are set out in the speech of my noble and learned friend, Lord Keith of Kinkel, and I need not repeat them. The reason for this additional requirement in cases concerned with Government secrets appears to be that, although in the case of private citizens there is a public interest that confidential information should as such be protected, in the case of Government secrets the mere fact of confidentiality does not alone support such a conclusion, because in a free society there is a continuing public interest that the workings of government should be open to scrutiny and criticism. From this it follows that, in such cases, there must be demonstrated some other public interest which requires that publication should be restrained. **3-071**
>
> Finally, I wish to observe that I can see no inconsistency between English law on this subject and article 10 of the European Convention on Human Rights. This is scarcely surprising, since we may pride ourselves on the fact that freedom of speech has existed in this country perhaps as long as, if not longer than, it has existed in any other country in the world. The only difference is that, whereas article 10 of the Convention, in accordance with its avowed purpose, proceeds to state a fundamental right and then to qualify it, we in this country (where everybody is free to do anything, subject only to the provisions of the law) proceed rather upon an assumption of freedom of speech, and turn to our law to discover the established exceptions to it. In any event I conceive it to be my duty, when I am free to do so, to interpret the law in accordance with the obligations of the Crown under this treaty. The exercise of the right to freedom of expression under article 10 may be subject to restrictions (as are prescribed by law and are necessary in a democratic society) in relation to certain prescribed matters, which include "the interests of national security" and "preventing the disclosure of information received in confidence." It is established in the jurisprudence of the European Court of Human Rights that the word "necessary" in this context implies the existence of a pressing social need, and that interference with freedom of expression should be no more than is proportionate to the legitimate aim pursued. I have no reason to believe that English law, as applied in the courts, leads to any different conclusion. **3-072**

The standard of disclosure or use of information in the public interest has been described in different ways in the cases, including that non-disclosure would be "destructive of the country or its people including matters medically dangerous to the public".[88] A broader formulation of public interest includes the discovery or prevention of the commission of a crime,[89] or the revelation of some other illegal or immoral dealing.[90] **3-073**

Lord Goff in the excerpt above also explains the overlap between the "iniquity defence" and A's freedom of expression under art.10 of the ECHR. As explained by Lord Goff, the doctrine of confidentiality will not be applied in a way that is disproportionate to A's right to freedom of expression enshrined by art.10 of the ECHR, and English courts have developed a clear procedure that is to be followed when balancing the interaction of B's right under confidentiality and art.10,[91] largely modelled on that applied when balancing B's claim for misuse of private information, embodied by art.8, against art.10.[92] **3-074**

---

87 *Attorney General v Jonathan Cape Ltd* [1976] Q.B. 752 at 770 (Lord Widgery C.J.); *Commonwealth of Australia v John Fairfax & Sons Ltd* 147 C.L.R. 39 at 51–53 (Mason J. as he then was).

88 *Beloff v Pressdram Ltd* [1973] 1 All E.R. 241 at 260, (Ungoed Thomas J).

89 *Tournier v National Provincial and Union Bank of England* [1924] 1 K.B. 461 CA at 480–481, 483–484, 486.

90 See further: *Heythrop Zoological Gardens Ltd (t/a Amazing Animals) v Captive Animals Protection Society* [2016] EWHC 1370 (Ch) at [27]–[29]; *Axon v Ministry of Defence* [2016] EWHC 787 (QB) at [104]; *Brevan Howard Asset Management v Reuters Ltd* [2017] EWHC 644 (QB) (affirmed on appeal: [2017] EWCA Civ 950) at [44].

91 *Campbell v Mirror Group Newspapers Ltd.* See too *Commissioner of Police of the Metropolis v Times Newspapers Ltd* [2011] EWHC 2705 (QB) at [73]–[93].

92 For this balancing between art.8 and art.10, see paras 3-075 to 3-080.

Court of Appeal [2008]

3–075 That procedure comprises a two-stage assessment, first, asking whether B has a reasonable expectation of confidentiality, and second, whether B's expectation is outweighed by countervailing interests; whether formulated under the iniquity defence, or an individual freedom of expression under art.10.

Prince of Wales v Associated Newspapers Ltd

Court of Appeal, [2008] Ch. 57 at [65]–[69]

3–076 LORD PHILLIPS C.J. (on behalf of the COURT): Whether a publication, or threatened publication, involves a breach of a relationship of confidence, an interference with privacy or both, it is necessary to consider whether these matters justify the interference with article 10 rights that will be involved if the publication is made the subject of a judicial sanction. A balance has to be struck. Where no breach of a confidential relationship is involved, that balance will be between article 8 and article 10 rights and will usually involve weighing the nature and consequences of the breach of privacy against the public interest, if any, in the disclosure of private information.

3–077 What is the position where the disclosure relates to "information received in confidence?" The authors of *The Law of Privacy and the Media*,[93] express the view that it would be surprising if this consideration was ignored. We agree. It is a factor that article 10(2) recognises is, of itself, capable of justifying restrictions on freedom of expression.

3–078 There is an important public interest in the observance of duties of confidence. Those who engage employees, or who enter into other relationships that carry with them a duty of confidence, ought to be able to be confident that they can disclose, without risk of wider publication, information that it is legitimate for them to wish to keep confidential. Before the Human Rights Act 1998 came into force the circumstances in which the public interest in publication overrode a duty of confidence were very limited. The issue was whether exceptional circumstances justified disregarding the confidentiality that would otherwise prevail. Today the test is different. It is whether a fetter of the right of freedom of expression is, in the particular circumstances, "necessary in a democratic society". It is a test of proportionality. But a significant element to be weighed in the balance is the importance in a democratic society of upholding duties of confidence that are created between individuals. It is not enough to justify publication that the information in question is a matter of public interest. To take an extreme example, the content of a budget speech is a matter of great public interest. But if a disloyal typist were to seek to sell a copy to a newspaper in advance of the delivery of the speech in Parliament, there can surely be no doubt that the newspaper would be in breach of duty if it purchased and published the speech.

3–079 For these reasons, the test to be applied when considering whether it is necessary to restrict freedom of expression in order to prevent disclosure of information received in confidence is not simply whether the information is a matter of public interest but whether, in all the circumstances, it is in the public interest that the duty of confidence should be breached. The court will need to consider whether, having regard to the nature of the information and all the relevant circumstances, it is legitimate for the owner of the information to seek to keep it confidential or whether it is in the public interest that the information should be made public.

3–080 In applying the test of proportionality, the nature of the relationship that gives rise to the duty of confidentiality may be important. Different views have been expressed as to whether the fact that there is an express contractual obligation of confidence affects the weight to be attached to the duty of confidentiality.

D. Scope—From Confidentiality to Privacy and Back

3–081 In the past few decades, the law's evolving protection of an individual's autonomy and dignity via recognition of the right to privacy and to control of the dissemination of information about one's private life has greatly impacted upon the scope of the equitable doctrine of confidence. Two stages of evolution occurred. First, the equitable doctrine of confidence was extended to control A's use of private information in *Campbell v Mirror Group Newspapers Ltd*.[94] Second, the tort of invasion of

---

93 Sir Michael Tugendhat and Iain Christie (eds), *The Law of Privacy and the Media*, Second Cumulative Supplement (Oxford University Press, 2006), para.6.111.

94 *Campbell v Mirror Group Newspapers Ltd*.

privacy was recognised, in cases such as *Vidal-Hall v Google Inc* and *Lloyd v Google LLC*, and the rule against misuse of private information now has an existence that is separate from the equitable rule from which it evolved. Further, the requirements and effect of the tort of invasion of privacy must now be distinguished from the requirements and effects of the equitable doctrine of confidence. We will consider these stages in turn.

i. Stage 1: The use of the equitable doctrine of confidence to protect against invasions of privacy

As is explained in the following except, it fell to the equitable doctrine of confidence to protect an individual's right to privacy as *Wainwright v Home Office*[95] had confirmed that English law did not recognise a tort of invasion of privacy. 3-082

Campbell v Mirror Group Newspapers Ltd

House of Lords, [2004] 2 A.C. 457 at [11]–[17], [43]–[52]

Breach of confidence: misuse of private information

LORD NICHOLLS: In this country, unlike the United States of America, there is no over-arching, all-embracing cause of action for "invasion of privacy".[96] But protection of various aspects of privacy is a fast developing area of the law, here and in some other common law jurisdictions. The recent decision of the Court of Appeal of New Zealand in *Hosking v Runting*[97] is an example of this. In this country development of the law has been spurred by enactment of the Human Rights Act 1998. 3-083

The present case concerns one aspect of invasion of privacy: wrongful disclosure of private information. The case involves the familiar competition between freedom of expression and respect for an individual's privacy. Both are vitally important rights. Neither has precedence over the other. The importance of freedom of expression has been stressed often and eloquently, the importance of privacy less so. But it, too, lies at the heart of liberty in a modern state. A proper degree of privacy is essential for the well-being and development of an individual. And restraints imposed on government to pry into the lives of the citizen go to the essence of a democratic state.[98] 3-084

The common law or, more precisely, courts of equity have long afforded protection to the wrongful use of private information by means of the cause of action which became known as breach of confidence. A breach of confidence was restrained as a form of unconscionable conduct, akin to a breach of trust. Today this nomenclature is misleading. The breach of confidence label harks back to the time when the cause of action was based on improper use of information disclosed by one person to another in confidence. To attract protection the information had to be of a confidential nature. But the gist of the cause of action was that information of this character had been disclosed by one person to another in circumstances "importing an obligation of confidence" even though no contract of non-disclosure existed.[99] The confidence referred to in the phrase "breach of confidence" was the confidence arising out of a confidential relationship. 3-085

This cause of action has now firmly shaken off the limiting constraint of the need for an initial confidential relationship. In doing so it has changed its nature. In this country this development was recognised clearly in the judgment of Lord Goff of Chieveley in *Attorney General v Guardian Newspapers Ltd (No 2)*. Now the law imposes a 'duty of confidence' whenever a person receives information he knows or ought to know is fairly and reasonably to be regarded as confidential. Even this formulation is awkward. The continuing use of the phrase 'duty of confidence' and the description of the information as "confidential" is not altogether comfortable. Information about an individual's private life would not, in ordinary usage, be 3-086

---

95 *Wainwright v Home Office* [2003] UKHL 53; [2004] 2 A.C. 406.
96 *Wainwright*.
97 [2004] NZCA 34.
98 *R. v Dyment* [1988] 2 S.C.R. 417 at 426.
99 See the classic exposition by Megarry J in *Coco v AN* at 47–48.

called "confidential". The more natural description today is that such information is private. The essence of the tort is better encapsulated now as misuse of private information.

3-087 In the case of individuals this tort, however labelled, affords respect for one aspect of an individual's privacy. That is the value underlying this cause of action. An individual's privacy can be invaded in ways not involving publication of information. Strip searches are an example. The extent to which the common law as developed thus far in this country protects other forms of invasion of privacy is not a matter arising in the present case. It does not arise because, although pleaded more widely, Miss Campbell's common law claim was throughout presented in court exclusively on the basis of breach of confidence, that is, the wrongful publication by the "Mirror" of private information.

3-088 The European Convention on Human Rights, and the Strasbourg jurisprudence, have undoubtedly had a significant influence in this area of the common law for some years. The provisions of article 8, concerning respect for private and family life, and article 10, concerning freedom of expression, and the interaction of these two articles, have prompted the courts of this country to identify more clearly the different factors involved in cases where one or other of these two interests is present. Where both are present the courts are increasingly explicit in evaluating the competing considerations involved. When identifying and evaluating these factors the courts, including your Lordships' House, have tested the common law against the values encapsulated in these two articles. The development of the common law has been in harmony with these articles of the Convention.[100]

3-089 The time has come to recognise that the values enshrined in articles 8 and 10 are now part of the cause of action for breach of confidence. As Lord Woolf CJ has said, the courts have been able to achieve this result by absorbing the rights protected by articles 8 and 10 into this cause of action.[101] Further, it should now be recognised that for this purpose these values are of general application. The values embodied in articles 8 and 10 are as much applicable in disputes between individuals or between an individual and a non-governmental body such as a newspaper as they are in disputes between individuals and a public authority. . . .

3-090 LORD HOFFMAN: This House decided in *Wainwright v Home Office* that there is no general tort of invasion of privacy. But the right to privacy is in a general sense one of the values, and sometimes the most important value, which underlies a number of more specific causes of action, both at common law and under various statutes. One of these is the equitable action for breach of confidence, which has long been recognised as capable of being used to protect privacy. Thus in the seminal case of *Prince Albert v Strange* the defendant was a publisher who had obtained copies of private etchings made by the Prince Consort of members of the royal family at home. The publisher had got them from an employee of a printer to whom the Prince had entrusted the plates. Knight Bruce V-C, in granting an injunction restraining the publication of a catalogue containing descriptions of etchings, said that it was:[102]

> "an intrusion—an unbecoming and unseemly intrusion . . . offensive to that inbred sense of propriety natural to every man—if intrusion, indeed, fitly describes a sordid spying into the privacy of domestic life—into the home (a word hitherto sacred among us) . . ."

3-091 But although the action for breach of confidence could be used to protect privacy in the sense of preserving the confidentiality of personal information, it was not founded on the notion that such information was in itself entitled to protection. Breach of confidence was an equitable remedy and equity traditionally fastens on the conscience of one party to enforce equitable duties which arise out of his relationship with the other. So the action did not depend upon the personal nature of the information or extent of publication but upon whether a confidential relationship existed between the person who imparted the information and the person who received it. Equity imposed an obligation of confidentiality upon the latter and (by a familiar process of extension) upon anyone who received the information with actual or constructive knowledge of the duty of confidence.

3-092 Thus the cause of action in *Prince Albert v Strange* was based upon the defendant's actual or constructive knowledge of the confidential relationship between the Prince Consort and the printer to whom he had entrusted the plates of his etchings. It was not essential that the information should concern the Prince's family life or be in any other way personal. Any confidential information would have done. Nor was

---

100 *Reynolds v Times Newspapers Ltd* [2001] 2 A.C. 127 at 203–204.
101 *A v B Plc* [2003] Q.B. 195 at 202.
102 *Prince Albert* at 698.

it essential that the defendant should have intended widespread publication. Communication to a single unauthorised person would have been enough. Many of the cases on breach of confidence are concerned with the communication of commercially valuable information to trade rivals and not with anything that could be described as a violation of privacy.

In recent years, however, there have been two developments of the law of confidence, typical of the capacity of the common law to adapt itself to the needs of contemporary life. One has been an acknowledgement of the artificiality of distinguishing between confidential information obtained through the violation of a confidential relationship and similar information obtained in some other way. The second has been the acceptance, under the influence of human rights instruments such as article 8 of the European Convention, of the privacy of personal information as something worthy of protection in its own right. 3–093

The first development is generally associated with the speech of Lord Goff of Chieveley in *Attorney General v Guardian Newspapers Ltd (No 2)*[103] where he gave, as illustrations of cases in which it would be illogical to insist upon violation of a confidential relationship, the "obviously confidential document . . . wafted by an electric fan out of a window into a crowded street" and the "private diary . . . dropped in a public place". He therefore formulated the principle as being that: 3–094

> "a duty of confidence arises when confidential information comes to the knowledge of a person . . . in circumstances where he has notice, or is held to have agreed, that the information is confidential, with the effect that it would be just in all the circumstances that he should be precluded from disclosing the information to others."

This statement of principle, which omits the requirement of a prior confidential relationship, was accepted as representing current English law by the European Court of Human Rights in *Earl Spencer v United Kingdom*[104] and was applied by the Court of Appeal in *A v B plc*.[105] It is now firmly established. 3–095

The second development has been rather more subtle. Until the Human Rights Act 1998 came into force, there was no equivalent in English domestic law of article 8 of the European Convention or the equivalent articles in other international human rights instruments which guarantee rights of privacy. So, the courts of the United Kingdom did not have to decide what such guarantees meant. Even now that the equivalent of article 8 has been enacted as part of English law, it is not directly concerned with the protection of privacy against private persons or corporations. It is, by virtue of section 6 of the 1998 Act, a guarantee of privacy only against public authorities. Although the Convention, as an international instrument, may impose upon the United Kingdom an obligation to take some steps (whether by statute or otherwise) to protect rights of privacy against invasion by private individuals, it does not follow that such an obligation would have any counterpart in domestic law. 3–096

What human rights law has done is to identify private information as something worth protecting as an aspect of human autonomy and dignity. And this recognition has raised inescapably the question of why it should be worth protecting against the state but not against a private person. There may of course be justifications for the publication of private information by private persons which would not be available to the state—I have particularly in mind the position of the media, to which I shall return in a moment—but I can see no logical ground for saying that a person should have less protection against a private individual than he would have against the state for the publication of personal information for which there is no justification. Nor, it appears, have any of the other judges who have considered the matter. 3–097

The result of these developments has been a shift in the centre of gravity of the action for breach of confidence when it is used as a remedy for the unjustified publication of personal information. It recognises that the incremental changes to which I have referred do not merely extend the duties arising traditionally from a relationship of trust and confidence to a wider range of people. As Sedley LJ observed in a perceptive passage in his judgment in *Douglas v Hello! Ltd*,[106] the new approach takes a different view of the underlying value which the law protects. Instead of the cause of action being based upon the duty of good faith applicable to confidential personal information and trade secrets alike, it focuses upon the protection of human autonomy and dignity—the right to control the dissemination of information about one's private life and the right to the esteem and respect of other people. 3–098

---

[103] At 281.
[104] (1998) 25 E.H.R.R. CD 105.
[105] [2003] Q.B. 195 at 207.
[106] [2001] Q.B. 967 at 1001.

3–099 These changes have implications for the future development of the law. They must influence the approach of the courts to the kind of information which is regarded as entitled to protection, the extent and form of publication which attracts a remedy and the circumstances in which publication can be justified.

Douglas v Hello! Ltd (No.3)

House of Lords, [2008] A.C. 1 at 47–48, 72

3–100 LORD HOFFMAN: . . . In recent years, English law has adapted the action for breach of confidence to provide a remedy for the unauthorised disclosure of personal information.[107] This development has been mediated by the analogy of the right to privacy conferred by article 8 of the European Convention on Human Rights and has required a balancing of that right against the right to freedom of expression conferred by article 10. But this appeal is not concerned with the protection of privacy.

3–101 LORD NICHOLLS: As the law has developed breach of confidence, or misuse of confidential information, now covers two distinct causes of action, protecting two different interests: privacy, and secret ("confidential") information. It is important to keep these two distinct. In some instances information may qualify for protection both on grounds of privacy and confidentiality. In other instances information may be in the public domain, and not qualify for protection as confidential, and yet qualify for protection on the grounds of privacy. Privacy can be invaded by further publication of information or photographs already disclosed to the public. Conversely, and obviously, a trade secret may be protected as confidential information even though no question of personal privacy is involved.

Imerman v Tchenguiz

Court of Appeal, [2011] Fam. 116, [2010] EWCA Civ 908 at [54]–[71]

3–102 LORD NEUBERGER M.R. (on behalf of the COURT): The law of confidence was developed by the Courts of Chancery over the 18th and 19th centuries. Typically, a claim for breach of confidence arose in the commercial context, and in circumstances where there was no question but that the defendant was entitled to have obtained the information concerned initially. Thus, in perhaps the most familiar and frequent category of case, involving trade secrets and the like, the claimant himself will have provided the defendant with the information, as, at the relevant time, the defendant will have been an employee or agent of the claimant. In such cases, the claimant cannot allege that the defendant is not entitled to have the information, let alone complain that he did anything legally wrong or morally culpable to obtain the information in the first place. What the claimant could do was to complain if the defendant made illicit copies of confidential papers or misused the information for his own, rather than his principal's, purposes.

3–103 The earliest cases on the topic pre-date even the days of Lord Eldon LC. However, the jurisprudence really starts with a number of his decisions and then continues throughout the 19th century. There are many reported cases but it is convenient to start with the celebrated case of *Prince Albert v Strange*, the facts of which are too well known to require repetition. . . .

3–104 It was only some 20 years ago that the law of confidence was authoritatively extended to apply to cases where the defendant had come by the information without the consent of the claimant. That extension, which had been discussed in academic articles, was established in the speech of Lord Goff of Chieveley in *Attorney General v Guardian Newspapers Ltd (No 2)*. He said, that confidence could be invoked "where an obviously confidential document is wafted by an electric fan out of a window . . . or . . . is dropped in a public place, and is then picked up by a passer-by".

3–105 The domestic law of confidence was extended again by the House of Lords in *Campbell v MGN Ltd*, effectively to incorporate the right to respect for private life in article 8 of the Convention, although its extension from the commercial sector to the private sector had already been presaged by decisions such as *Argyll v Argyll* and *Hellewell v Chief Constable of Derbyshire*.[108] In the latter case, Laws J suggested that the law recognised "a right of privacy, although the name accorded to the cause of action would be breach

[107] See *Campbell v Mirror*.
[108] [1995] 1 W.L.R. 804.

of confidence".[109] It goes a little further than nomenclature in that, in *Wainwright v Home Office*, the House of Lords held that there was no tort of invasion of privacy, even now that the Human Rights Act 1998 is in force. None the less, following its later decision in *Campbell*, there is now a tort of misuse of private information: as Lord Phillips of Worth Matravers MR put it in *Douglas v Hello! Ltd (No 3)* a claim based on misuse of private information has been "shoehorned" into the law of confidence.

As Lord Phillips MR's observation suggests, there are dangers in conflating the developing law of privacy under article 8 and the traditional law of confidence. However, the touchstone suggested by Lord Nicholls of Birkenhead and Lord Hope of Craighead in *Campbell*, namely whether the claimant had a "reasonable expectation of privacy" in respect of the information in issue, is, as it seems to us, a good test to apply when considering whether a claim for confidence is well founded. (It chimes well with the test suggested in classic commercial confidence cases by Megarry J in *Coco* namely whether the information had the "necessary quality of confidence" and had been "imparted in circumstances importing an obligation of confidence".) **3–106**

As stated in Stanley on *The Law of Confidentiality*:[110] **3–107**

> Cases asserting an 'old fashioned breach of confidence' may well be best addressed by considering established authority [whereas] cases raising issues of personal privacy which might engage article 8 . . . will require specific focus on the case law of the European Court of Human Rights.

However, given that the domestic law on confidentiality had already started to encompass privacy well before the 1998 Act came into force, and that, with the 1998 Act now in force, privacy is still classified as part of the confidentiality genus, the law should be developed and applied consistently and coherently in both privacy and 'old fashioned confidence' cases, even if they sometimes may have different features. Consistency and coherence are all the more important given the substantially increased focus on the right to privacy and confidentiality, and the corresponding legal developments in this area, over the past 20 years. **3–108**

If confidence applies to a defendant who adventitiously, but without authorisation, obtains information in respect of which he must have appreciated that the claimant had an expectation of privacy, it must, a fortiori, extend to a defendant who intentionally, and without authorisation, takes steps to obtain such information. It would seem to us to follow that intentionally obtaining such information, secretly and knowing that the claimant reasonably expects it to be private, is itself a breach of confidence. The notion that looking at documents which one knows to be confidential is itself capable of constituting an actionable wrong (albeit perhaps only in equity) is also consistent with the decision of the Strasbourg court that monitoring private telephone calls can infringe the article 8 rights of the caller . . . **3–109**

In our view, it would be a breach of confidence for a defendant, without the authority of the claimant, to examine, or to make, retain, or supply copies to a third party of, a document whose contents are, and were (or ought to have been) appreciated by the defendant to be, confidential to the claimant. It is of the essence of the claimant's right to confidentiality that he can choose whether, and, if so, to whom and in what circumstances and on what terms, to reveal the information which has the protection of the confidence. It seems to us, as a matter of principle, that, again in the absence of any defence on the particular facts, a claimant who establishes a right of confidence in certain information contained in a document should be able to restrain any threat by an unauthorised defendant to look at, copy, distribute any copies of, or to communicate, or utilise the contents of the document (or any copy), and also be able to enforce the return (or destruction) of any such document or copy. Without the court having the power to grant such relief, the information will, through the unauthorised act of the defendant, either lose its confidential character, or will at least be at risk of doing so. The claimant should not be at risk, through the unauthorised act of the defendant, of having the confidentiality of the information lost, or even potentially lost. **3–110**

In this connection, we were taken to the observation of Eady J in *White v Withers LLP*[111] that **3–111**

> the mere receipt of documents by the solicitors from their client, and their continued retention in connection with the matrimonial proceedings, simply cannot give rise to a cause of action.

---

109 [1995] 1 W.L.R. 804 at 807.

110 P. Stanley, *The Law of Confidentiality* (Hart Publishing, 2008), p.8.

111 [2009] 1 F.L.R. 383 at [8].

3–112 In our view, that observation (which may in any event have been limited to a cause of action in damages) should be taken as applying only to the receipt of documents by solicitors from their client; further, it should not be taken as suggesting that the claimant could not recover the documents from the solicitors.

3–113 The fact that the law of confidentiality was extended in *Campbell* for the purpose of giving effect to article 8 in English law, cannot, as we see it, mean that the law of confidentiality has somehow been circumscribed in other respects. The fact that misuse of private information has, as Eady J said in *White* "become recognised over the last few years as a wrong actionable in English law" does not mean that there has to be such misuse before a claim for breach of confidentiality can succeed, unless that was the position before the Human Rights Act 1998 came into force, which it was not.

ii. Stage 2: Recognition of a tort of invasion of privacy which is distinct from the equitable doctrine of confidence

3–114 Whilst the protection of privacy was thus developed via the equitable doctrine of confidence, English law now recognises the tort of invasion of privacy, which encompasses, among other things, the misuse of private information.[112] This means that, as was recognised by the Supreme Court in *PJS v News Group Newspapers Ltd* the action for misuse of private information has now been subsumed within the tort of invasion of privacy.[113]

Vidal-Hall v Google Inc (Information Commissioner intervening)

Court of Appeal, [2016] Q.B. 1003 at [17]–[51]

3–115 LORD DYSON MR and SHARP L.J.:

Whether misuse of private information is a tort for the purposes of paragraph 3.1(9) of Practice Direction 6B

The issue of classification or nomenclature has been the subject of some discussion in the cases, and amongst academics. So far as we are aware however—with the possible exception, on the defendant's case, of *Douglas v Hello! Ltd (No 3)*—this is the first case in which the "classification" question has made a difference. Put shortly, if a claim for misuse of information is not a tort for the purposes of service out of the jurisdiction, but is classified as a claim for breach of confidence, then on the authority of the *Kitechnology BV v Unicor GmbH Plastmaschinen*,[114] which is binding on us, the claimants will not be able to serve their claims for misuse of private information on the defendant.

3–116 Although the issue as framed in this appeal in one sense is a narrow one, it is none the less appropriate to look at it in the broader context. Fifteen years have passed since the coming into force of the Human Rights Act 1998 in October 2000, which incorporates into our domestic law the Convention for the Protection of Human Rights and Fundamental Freedoms. And it is a decade now since the seminal decision of the House of Lords in *Campbell v MGN Ltd*. The problem the courts have had to grapple with during this period has been how to afford appropriate protection to "privacy rights" under article 8 of the Convention, in the absence of a common law tort of invasion of privacy.

3–117 We were taken to a number of cases by Mr White to establish what is in fact an uncontroversial proposition—that the gap was bridged by developing and adapting the law of confidentiality to protect one aspect of invasion of privacy, the misuse of private information. This addressed the tension between the requirement to give appropriate effect to the right to respect for private and family life set out in article 8 of the Convention and the common law's perennial need (for the best of reasons, that of legal certainty) to appear not to be doing anything for the first time ...

---

112 *PJS v News Group Newspapers Ltd* [2016] UKSC 26; [2016] A.C. 1081.

113 *PJS v News Group Newspapers Ltd* at [57]–[62] (Lord Neuberger, with whom Baroness Hale, Lord Mance and Lord Reed agreed).

114 [1995] F.S.R. 765 (CA).

Thus, in *A v B plc*[115] Lord Woolf C.J., giving the judgment of the court, said that articles 8 and 10 of the Convention provided new parameters within which the courts would decide actions for breach of confidence, and that the court could act in a way that was compatible with Convention rights, as it was required to do under section 6 of the 1998 Act, by "absorbing the rights which articles 8 and 10 protect into the long-established action for breach of confidence". **3–118**

However, a number of things need to be said. First, there are problems with an analysis which fails to distinguish between a breach of confidentiality and an infringement of privacy rights protected by article 8, not least because the concepts of confidence and privacy are not the same and protect different interests. Secondly, as has been consistently emphasised by the courts, we are concerned with a developing area of the law. Although the process may have started as one of "absorption"[116] it is clear that, contrary to the submissions of the defendant, there are now two separate and distinct causes of action: an action for breach of confidence; and one for misuse of private information. Thirdly, it is also the case that the action for misuse of private information has been referred to as a tort by the courts. **3–119**

The speech of Lord Nicholls of Birkenhead in the *Campbell* has been highly influential in this process of development. In the Campbell case the claimant was the famous model, Naomi Campbell. The defendant newspaper published articles which disclosed her drug addiction, disclosed the fact that she was receiving therapy through a named self-help group, gave details of group meetings she attended and showed photographs of her in the street as she was leaving a group meeting. She sought damages against the newspaper for breach of confidentiality. The Court of Appeal allowed the newspaper's appeal, and Miss Campbell then succeeded in the House of Lords. Though the House was divided three to two (Lord Hope of Craighead, Baroness Hale of Richmond and Lord Carswell were in the majority, and Lord Nicholls and Lord Hoffmann were in the minority) the difference of opinion related to a narrow point arising on the facts of the case. But in the statements of general principle as to the way in which the law should strike the balance between the right to privacy and the right to freedom of expression, the House was unanimous . . . **3–120**

Mr White argues, vainly in our view, that Lord Nicholls did not say or mean that there were two causes of action. He also says that this latter passage was obiter. This is true. But it does not address the substance of the points made by Lord Nicholls which we think, with respect, are obviously correct. Actions for breach of confidence and actions for misuse of private information rest on different legal foundations. As Lord Nicholls said, they protect different interests: secret or confidential information on the one hand and privacy on the other. The focus of the actions therefore is also different. In the *Campbell*, Lord Hoffmann described the "shift in the centre of gravity" when the action for breach of confidence was used as a remedy for the unjustified publication of personal information. In those circumstances, he said, the focus was not on the duty of good faith applicable to confidential personal information and trade secrets alike, but the protection of human autonomy and dignity—the right to control the dissemination of information about one's private life and the right to the esteem and respect of other people. **3–121**

How then should the action for misuse of private information be characterised? Mr White says that in the cases where it has been referred to as a tort, classification or nomenclature was not in issue. This is true. None the less, in our view, these references cannot be dismissed as a mere loose use of language; they connote an acknowledgement, even if only implicitly, of the true nature of the cause of action. . . . **3–122**

. . . Against this background, we cannot find any satisfactory or principled answer to the question why misuse of private information should not be categorised as a tort for the purposes of service out of the jurisdiction. Misuse of private information is a civil wrong without any equitable characteristics. We do not need to attempt to define a tort here. But if one puts aside the circumstances of its "birth", there is nothing in the nature of the claim itself to suggest that the more natural classification of it as a tort is wrong. **3–123**

. . . we have concluded in agreement with the judge that misuse of private information should now be recognised as a tort for the purposes of service out the jurisdiction. This does not create a new cause of action. In our view, it simply gives the correct legal label to one that already exists. We are conscious of the fact that there may be broader implications from our conclusions, for example as to remedies, limitation and vicarious liability, but these were not the subject of submissions, and such points will need to be considered as and when they arise. **3–124**

---

115 [2003] Q.B. 195 at [4].

116 *A v B Plc* [2003] Q.B. 195 at [4] (Lord Woolf C.J.).

3–125 The equitable doctrine of confidentiality has now been treated as separate from the tort of invasion of privacy (including the misuse of private information).

Lloyd v Google LLC

Supreme Court, [2021] UKSC 50 at [97]–[99]

3–126 LORD LEGGATT (with whom LORD REED, LADY ARDEN, LORD SALES and LORD BURROWS agreed): The Court of Appeal in *Vidal-Hall* also held that the claims for damages for misuse of private information made by the claimants in that case were properly classified as claims in tort for the purpose of service out of the jurisdiction and had a real prospect of success. . . . the tort of misuse of private information evolved out of the equitable action for breach of confidence, influenced by the protection of the right to respect for private life guaranteed by article 8 of the Convention. The critical step in its emergence as a distinct basis for a claim was the identification of privacy of information as worthy of protection in its own right, irrespective of whether the information was imparted in circumstances which give rise to a duty of confidence . . . As Lord Hoffmann put it in *Campbell*:[117]

> "What human rights law has done is to identify private information as something worth protecting as an aspect of human autonomy and dignity."

3–127 The complaint in *Campbell* was about the publication of private information. Lord Nicholls of Birkenhead described the "essence of the tort", as "misuse of private information".[118] He also noted, however, that an individual's privacy can be invaded in ways not involving publication of information, and subsequent cases have held that intrusion on privacy, without any misuse of information, is actionable.[119] It is misuse of information, however, which is primarily relevant in this case, and I shall generally—as counsel did in argument—use the label for the tort of 'misuse of private information'.

3–128 To establish liability for misuse of private information (or other wrongful invasion of privacy), it is necessary to show that there was a reasonable expectation of privacy in the relevant matter. As the Court of Appeal (Sir Anthony Clarke MR, Laws and Thomas LJJ) explained in upholding a claim to restrain the publication of photographs taken in a public place of the child of the well-known author, JK Rowling, in *Murray v Express Newspapers plc*:[120]

> ". . . the question whether there is a reasonable expectation of privacy is a broad one, which takes account of all the circumstances of the case. They include the attributes of the claimant, the nature of the activity in which the claimant was engaged, the place at which it was happening, the nature and purpose of the intrusion, the absence of consent and whether it was known or could be inferred, the effect on the claimant and the circumstances in which and the purposes for which the information came into the hands of the publisher."

3–129 If this test is met, in cases where freedom of expression is involved the court must then undertake a "balancing exercise" to decide whether in all the circumstances the interests of the owner of the private information must yield to the right to freedom of expression conferred on the publisher by article 10 of the Convention . . .

3–130 Observe that an individual's right to privacy is afforded a greater scope of protection by the tort of invasion of privacy than by the equitable doctrine of confidence. The equitable doctrine controls only how A *uses* confidential information, and not the *means by which A obtains* that information. Further, the rules relate to different types of information and, while they may sometimes overlap, they have different criteria for assessment.

---

117 *Campbell v Mirror* at [50].
118 *Campbell v Mirror* at [14].
119 *Campbell v Mirror* at [15]. See *PJS v News Group Newspapers* at [58]–[60].
120 [2009] Ch. 481 at [36].

PJS v News Group Newspapers Ltd

[2016] A.C. 1081 at [25]–[26]

LORD MANCE (with whom LORD NEWUBERGER, BARONESS HALE and LORD REED agreed): 3–131

The distinction between rights of confidence and privacy rights

Mr Desmond Browne QC for the claimant submits the Court of Appeal also erred by too close an assimilation of a claim based on the tort of invasion of privacy with breach of confidence. Jackson L.J. recognised, correctly, that the former attracts greater protection than the latter. But he went on to suggest that, whether a claim for misuse of private information will survive when information is in the public domain "depends upon how widely known the relevant facts are". That suggests a quantitative test, measuring what has already been disclosed with what is yet undisclosed. That is a test which is not only appropriate but potentially decisive in the context of an application based on confidentiality, as witnessed famously by *Sunday Times v United Kingdom (No 2) ("Spycatcher No 2")*.[121] There, the loss of secrecy by 30 July 1987 was central to the European Court of Human Rights' conclusion that injunctions could after that date no longer be justified either as necessary to ensure a fair trial or to protect national security. The promotion of the efficiency and reputation of the Security Service constituted insufficient justification.

However, different considerations apply to the present privacy claim. First, as Mr Browne submits, 3–132
a quantitative approach overlooks the invasiveness and distress involved, even in repetition of private material. Second, open hard copy exposure, as well no doubt as further internet exposure, is likely to add significantly to the overall intrusiveness and distress involved. . . .

So while B's claim for misuse of private information may have evolved from the equitable doctrine of 3–133
confidentiality, recent English cases such as *Vidal-Hall v Google Inc* and *Lloyd v Google LLC* indicate that there are now separate rules dealing with confidential information and privacy. While they may overlap in the sense that they could apply to the same set of facts, the existence of two distinct rules reflects the different fundamental values they protect. Tanya Aplin[122] argues that the equitable doctrine of confidentiality should continue to have a separate existence from, and not be "eclipsed" by the tort of invasion of privacy:[123]

. . . breach of confidence and the tort of privacy serve different purposes. A breach of confidence action is largely (but not wholly) concerned with preserving and engendering respect for relationships of trust and confidence. In the context of personal information, there may be particular kinds of confidential relationship, such as doctor-patient, lawyer-client, or employer-employee that as a society we want to reinforce. A right of privacy, on the other hand, is concerned with protecting the dignity and autonomy of individuals and providing them with informational control critical to human development.[124] Allowing the two actions to co-exist may therefore help foster these distinct purposes.

In *Vidal-Hall v Google Inc*, the Court of Appeal acknowledged that the separation of a claim for 3–134
breach of privacy by misuse of private information from the equitable doctrine of confidentiality, and its classification as a tort may have "broader implications . . ." beyond private international law, including for remedies, limitation and vicarious liability.[125] In addition, there are implications for the

---

121 (1991) 14 E.H.R.R. 229 at [53]–[55].

122 T. Aplin, "The Relationship between Breach of Confidence and the Tort of Misuse of Private Information" (2007) 18 K.L.J. 329.

123 Aplin, "The Relationship between Breach of Confidence and the Tort of Misuse of Private Information"(2007) 18 K.L.J. 329, 335.

124 See *Hosking v Runting* [2005] 1 N.Z.L.R. 1 at 58 (Tipping J): "It is of the essence of the dignity and personal autonomy and wellbeing of all human beings that some aspects of their lives should be able to remain private if they so wish".

125 See, e.g. *Mosley v News Group Newspapers Ltd* [2008] EWHC 1777 (QB); [2008] E.M.L.R. 20 at [190], where Eady J, distinguished tort from "breach of confidence or any other equitable or restitutionary claim" in the context of a claim for

interrelationships between the now distinct claims regarding confidentiality and privacy and, and the "iniquity defence" and art.10 of the ECHR.[126]

3–135 A further implication relates to the scope of the equitable doctrine of confidence and whether the separation of the tort of invasion of privacy (encompassing misuse of private information) means that the equitable doctrine has contracted and no longer extends to information that is private, if not also confidential.

3–136 There are also implications for the form of the equitable doctrine of confidence. The recognition of the separation of the equitable doctrine of confidentiality and tort of privacy in cases like *Vidal-Hall v Google Inc* and *Lloyd v Google LLC* makes clear that the equitable doctrine of confidentiality is not itself a tort, and retains its existence as an equitable rule that controls how A uses confidential information in B's favour. As such, this removes some of the impetus for the remedial regime in response to confidentiality to be assimilated with that applying in response to torts, be it for invasion of privacy or other torts concerning trespass to the person, or more generally.

F. Implications for the Relationship Between Common Law and Equity

3–137 The development of the doctrine of confidence raises some important broader questions as to the relationship between common law and equity. First, in its scope and effects, the traditional doctrine is consistent with the characteristic role of equity, discussed in Chapter 1,[127] of allowing B to restrain A's exercise of legal entitlements. Indeed, cases often describe the doctrine of confidence as "restraining" or "preventing" A from using information. However, modern cases refer to the doctrine as imposing a duty on A not to misuse confidential information,[128] with B having a correlative right. The doctrine is thus seen as generating a claim-right of B against A, and the existence of a duty means that B is not limited to asking a court to restrain particular uses of information by A, but can also, for example, claim compensation for a misuse by A which has already occurred.

3–138 The duty characterisation better reflects the operation and effect of relief available in response to the doctrine. Indeed, even at the time of *Prince Albert v Strange*, it was clear that the doctrine of confidence could justify an order that A take specific action, such as destroying or delivering up catalogues containing confidential information. The duty-based analysis is also reflected in judicial references to the "the well-established equitable wrong of breach of confidence".[129]

3–139 The development of the doctrine from one which restrains A's exercise of a legal entitlement to one which also imposes a duty on A to B reflects the development seen in equity's approach to fiduciary relationships, as discussed in Chapter 2.[130] That development was also crucial in permitting the doctrine of confidence to be used as a means to develop what is now recognised as a free-standing tort of invasion of privacy.

3–140 It may thus seem that an equitable doctrine has taken on a characteristically common law role: defining the scope of tort liability.[131] Rather than performing a secondary or supplementary role by

---

exemplary damages. See also *Vestergaard Frandsen S/A v Bestnet Europe Ltd* at [26]. In *Marathon Asset Management LLP v Seddon* [2017] EWHC 300 (Comm); [2017] I.C.R. 791 at [132].

126 For a detailed discussion and examination, see *Brake v Guy*.

127 See paras 1–075 to 1–077.

128 See, e.g. *Spycatcher* at 281–282; *Campbell v Mirror Group Newspapers Ltd* at [44], [85] "duty of confidence"; *Lloyd v Google Inc at* [97] "duty of confidence".

129 See *Brake v Guy* at [3] (Matthews J.).

130 See paras 2–158 to 2–163.

131 For a helpful general discussion of the relationship between equity and tort, see J. Goldberg and H. Smith, "Wrongful Fusion: Equity and Tort" in J. Goldberg et al (eds) *Equity and Law: Fusion and Fission* (Cambridge University Press, 2019), p.309. They give the example, at pp.327–328, of the development in the United States of a now "well-established tort"

regulating A's exercise of legal entitlements, it has instead imposed a primary duty, the content of which is *not* related to any legal entitlement of A. The key point is thus not simply that the doctrine of confidence developed to recognise a duty of A owed to B; it is rather as to the content of that duty.

Certainly, we would agree that, when used as a means to protect B against invasions of privacy by A unrelated to any existing legal entitlement of A, the doctrine of confidence extended beyond the standard reach of equity. This is not in itself illegitimate, however: it is not surprising that, given the fused administration of common law and equity, some overlap in functions should occur. It is, nonetheless, significant that, after this extension occurred, the courts very soon began to recognise the distinct nature and requirements of, on the one hand, a new tort protecting privacy and, on the other, the standard equitable doctrine of confidence. That standard doctrine continues to control A by preventing A from taking action to exercise a legal entitlement; relevantly, a freedom or liberty to use information in some way, as well as by requiring A, in some cases, to take action to exercise that entitlement in B's favour. This secondary or meta-law effect is exemplified by those cases emphasising how the doctrine is an exception or limitation upon the starting position that A has a freedom or, in the case of an individual within the scope of art.10, a right, to communicate information. **3–141**

As such the doctrine of confidence, whilst it is duty-imposing, should still be understood as an example of equity's meta-law or secondary function in that it applies exceptionally to control A's freedom to use or communicate information as defined by the underlying primary system. Classifying confidentiality as a primary rule would conceal the incursion the rule makes upon A's freedom of expression, and is not representative of the significance the courts have placed upon the need to balance the competing interests between A's freedom of expression and B's right to confidentiality. **3–142**

4. Due Administration

A duty of due administration, at its most basic, is a requirement that A should exercise a set of legal entitlements in accordance with the terms on which they are held. This requirement is enforceable by another party, B, whose right to due administration is realised through one or more forms of equitable relief against A. Since duties of due administration relate to rights and powers held by A, they illustrate equity's characteristic function of empowering B to control A's exercise of legal entitlements which A could otherwise use as they chose. Duties of due administration are owed, for example, by express trustees, company directors and other corporate officers,[132] partners,[133] mortgagees,[134] and personal representatives when administering deceased estates.[135] **3–143**

We will examine the content and operation of the duty of due administration owed by express trustees in Chapters 10 and 11, and associated equitable remedies in Chapters 13, 14 and 15. The aim of the discussion in this Chapter is to give an overview of the different contexts in which a duty of due administration arises, and to highlight the generative nature of the equitable rules in this area, and their secondary or meta law function. **3–144**

---

of "misappropriation of likeness" which arose initially from the application of the equitable doctrine of confidence, as the courts moved from "second-order" to primary intervention.

132 See, e.g. *Re Duckwari Plc* [1999] Ch. 253 at 262; *Bairstow v Queens Moat Houses Plc* [2001] EWCA Civ 712; [2001] 2 B.C.L.C. 531 at 548; *Sinclair Investments (UK) Ltd v Versailles Trade Finance Ltd* [2011] EWCA Civ 347; [2012] Ch. 453 at [34].

133 *National Commercial Banking Corp of Australia Ltd v Batty* (1986) 160 C.L.R. 251 at 275 (Brennan J).

134 *Yorkshire Bank Plc v Hall* [1999] 1 W.L.R. 1713 at 1728; *Downsview Nominees Ltd v First City Corp Ltd* [1993] A.C. 295 at 315 (the Board); *Barns v Queensland National Bank Ltd* (1906) 3 C.L.R. 925 at 943 (the Court).

135 *Commissioner of Stamp Duties (Qld) v Livingston* [1965] A.C. 694 at 707, 717 (the Board); *Marshall (Inspector of Taxes) v Kerr* [1995] 1 A.C. 148 at 166.

A. When Does the Duty Arise?

3–145 Duties of due administration can arise in different ways. They may be created intentionally as is the case for express trusts, most agency relationships, deceased estates, and partnership. They may be imposed by law for reasons unrelated to the parties' intentions, as in a case of knowing receipt of trust property. They may also arise by force of statute, as in a case where a personal representative receives a deceased estate on an intestacy. The duty may also arise through a combination of these factors, as is the case for company directors and other corporate officers. Situations where duties of due administration arise can also be referred to as "custodial"[136] or "stewardship"[137] arrangements.

Charles Mitchell, "Stewardship of Property and Liability to Account"

[2014] Conv. 215, 215

3–146 It often happens that one person controls property that she must administer and apply for the benefit of another, to whom she must account for what she does with the property. Express trustees are the obvious example, but other relationships are also centred on the stewardship of property. "Stewardship" is not a legal term of art, and the word is used here in an everyday sense to describe the control and management of property for the benefit of another person.[138]

3–147 Stewards of property must usually exercise their powers to manage and disburse the property in certain ways: for example, they must handle the property with reasonable care; they must act in their principal's and not in their own interests; and they must comply with the terms of their authority.

3–148 An express trustee's duty of due administration has been described by Powell J in *Spellson v George*[139] as subjecting the trustee "to a personal obligation to hold, and to deal with, the trust property for the benefit of some identified, or identifiable, person or group of persons", and as a "fundamental proposition" and one of the "essential elements of a private trust, be it a discretionary trust or some other form of trust".[140] The duty of due administration correlates to a trust beneficiary's "right to have the trust property properly managed and to have the trustee account for his management".[141] These passages were referred to without disapproval by the Privy Council in *Schmidt v Rosewood Trust Ltd*.[142]

3–149 Partners have been said to owe to one another "the common duty of a trustee to apply the partnership property exclusively for the benefit of the partnership in accordance with the partnership deed."[143] A partner's equitable duty of due administration, and correlative rights, is mirrored in legislation[144] which itself "introduced no great change to the law".[145] The same duty of due administration is owed

---

136 See, e.g. *Agricultural Land Management v Jackson (No.2)* [2014] WASC 102; 48 W.A.R. 1 at [373]–[375] (Edelman J).

137 See, e.g. C. Mitchell, "Stewardship of Property and Liability to Account" (2014) 78 Conv. 215.

138 In medieval times, a steward managed the affairs of a household or estate. Modern judicial references to the "stewardship of assets", using the term in the loose sense employed in this article can be found in, e.g. *Bairstow v Queens Moat Houses Plc* at [53]; *Ultraframe (UK) Ltd v Fielding* [2006] F.S.R. 17 at [513]; *Relfo Ltd (In Liquidation) v Varsani* [2012] EWHC 2168 (Ch) at [21]; *Bieber v Teathers Ltd (In Liquidation)* [2013] 1 B.C.L.C. 248 at [59].

139 *Spellson v George* (1987) 11 N.S.W.L.R. 300.

140 *Spellson v George* at 313–316.

141 *Spellson v George* at 315.

142 *Schmidt v Rosewood Trust Ltd* [2003] UKPC 26; [2003] 2 A.C. 709 at [59]–[60].

143 *Commissioner of State Revenue v Rojoda Pty Ltd* (2020) 268 C.L.R. 281 at [32] (Bell, Keane, Nettle and Edelman JJ). See also *Crawshay v Collins* (1808) 15 Ves. Jun. 218 at 226; *Gardner v M'Cutcheon* (1842) 4 Beav. 534 at 542–543; *Clegg v Fishwick* (1849) 1 Mac. & G. 294 at 298–299.

144 Partnership Act 1890.

145 *Sandu v Gill* [2006] Ch. 456 (CA) at [25] (Neuberger L.J.), citing N. Lindley, *A Treatise on the Law of Partnership* (1860), para.1–06.

by personal representatives when administering a deceased person's estate, as discussed by Viscount Radcliffe in the next excerpt.

Stamp Duties Comr (Queensland) v Livingston

Privy Council, [1965] A.C. 694 at 707

When [A] died she had the interest of a residuary legatee in the testator's unadministered estate. The nature of that interest has been conclusively defined by decisions of long-established authority, and its definition no doubt depends upon the peculiar status which the law accorded to an executor for the purposes of carrying out his duties of administration. There were special rules which long prevailed about the devolution of freehold land and its liability for the debts of a deceased, but subject to the working of these rules whatever property came to the executor *virtute officii* came to him in full ownership, without distinction between legal and equitable interests. The whole property was his. He held it for the purpose of carrying out the functions and duties of administration, not for his own benefit; and these duties would be enforced upon him by the Court of Chancery, if application had to be made for that purpose by a creditor or beneficiary interested in the estate. Certainly, therefore, he was in a fiduciary position with regard to the assets that came to him in the right of his office, and for certain purposes and in some aspects he was treated by the court as a trustee. "An executor," said Kay J. in *In re Marsden*[146] "is personally liable in equity for all breaches of the ordinary trusts which in Courts of Equity are considered to arise from his office." He is a trustee "in this sense." 3–150

It may not be possible to state exhaustively what those trusts are at any one moment. Essentially, they are trusts to preserve the assets, to deal properly with them, and to apply them in a due course of administration for the benefit of those interested according to that course, creditors, the death duty authorities, legatees of various sorts, and the residuary beneficiaries. They might just as well have been termed "duties in respect of the assets" as trusts. 3–151

In a discussion of this decision Charles Mitchell has explained:[147] 3–152

At the heart of Viscount Radcliffe's analysis is the proposition that a personal representative owes a duty to the estate beneficiaries "to preserve the assets" of an unadministered estate, "to deal properly with them, and to apply them in a due course of administration".[148] This rule is an old one: there are cases stretching back for many years which say that proving a will connotes acceptance of the testator's instructions and that it follows from such acceptance that the executors can only exercise their powers in a manner authorised by the testator.[149] In this respect their duty is the same as that owed by trustees, who must comply with the terms of the trust deed and cannot validly exercise their powers in an unauthorised way.[150]

Cases and commentaries draw analogies and distinctions across the different situations to which this one fundamental relationship of due administration applies: express trustees are compared with directors;[151] partners[152] and executors, for example. While these different occurrences of the duty have strong similarities, however, there are also significant differences between them. For example, the label of "trustee" has been applied to executors to identify the fact that they are subject to a duty of due administration, but this usage can be confusing as there are important differences between the 3–153

---

146 (1884) 26 Ch.D. 783 at 789.

147 C. Mitchell, "Commissioner of Stamp Duties (Queensland) v Livingston (1964)" in B. Sloan (ed.) *Landmark Cases in Succession Law* (Hart Publishing, 2019), p.273.

148 *Stamp Duties Comr (Queensland) v Livingston* [1965] A.C. 694 at 707.

149 *Stiles v Guy* (1832) 4 Y. & C. Ex. 571 at 575: "The executors, by proving the will, took upon themselves, and accepted the trust, and were bound, therefore, to discharge the duties they voluntarily imposed upon themselves." See also *Mucklow v Fuller* (1821) Jac. 198; *Booth v Booth* (1838) 1 Beav. 125, 128.

150 *Youyang Pty Ltd v Minter Ellison Morris Fletcher* (2003) 212 C.L.R. 484 at [32].

151 See further L.S. Sealy, "The Director as Trustee" [1967] C.L.J. 83.

152 See, e.g. *Knox v Gye* (1872) L.R. 5 H.L. 656 at 675–679; *Commissioner of State Revenue v Rojoda Pty Ltd* at [27]–[35].

express trust and other types of legal structure. These include the way in which these relationships are created, who they can be enforced by, their terms, and the transmissibility of an entitlement to due administration, and any other entitlements created by the terms.[153]

3–154 There are further important differences between these and other stewardship arrangements where A's power or legal entitlement is devolved in different ways.[154] Sometimes A has title to specific property and has the power and other legal entitlements incidental to that title, such as when A is an express trustee or personal representative of a deceased estate. For other arrangements, A does not have title to specific property and rather has a power: an agent, for example, does not have title to the principal's property, but has a power to bind the principal; a director does not have title to the company's property, but has a power to deal with the company's title to property. At other times, power may be devolved in both ways, such as a partner who has title (and powers held as an incident of that title) over partnership property as well as a power to act as an agent for the other partners. It is particularly important to distinguish between these different types of powers: the mere fact that A holds rights on trust for B does not, for example, mean that A is B's agent.[155]

3–155 No matter how power is devolved, the special feature of all these stewardship arrangements is that A is not free to exercise power as she wishes and holds her power subject to a duty of due administration, which requires A's adherence to the terms according to which power (or other legal entitlement) is held. "Terms" is a generic descriptor of the instructions given to A about the ways in which she should and should not exercise her power or other legal entitlement. The terms matter because they are the mandate for the given stewardship arrangement, expressing the law's ends in recognising and giving effect to that arrangement. Those ends might differ according to context: the law may seek to give effect to the parties' choices or to achieve some other goal. We will see in the context of express trusts that the terms are derived from the parties' expressed intentions regarding the ways in which the trustee should and should not exercise her powers as titleholder with regard to the trust property.

3–156 Equity's rules affecting the creation and enforcement of relationships of due administration play an important role in preserving, if not enhancing, the conditions under which stewardship arrangements play out in property law. The existence and operation of express trusts, agency relationships, companies, and deceased estates, for example, all depend upon the law's creation of legal powers, as well as equity's further rules of due administration that ensure such powers are exercised in the ways they should be, and provide some response to an unauthorised execution. Due administration thus supports whatever the law's ends may be regarding particular legal relationships and institutions[156] and gives parties extra choices as to how rights and powers can be held, supporting their decisions, for example, to set up a trust or an agency relationship.[157]

---

153 Mitchell, "Commissioner of Stamp Duties (Queensland) v Livingston (1964)" in *Landmark Cases in Succession Law* (2019), pp.270–271.

154 *Gangat v Jassat* [2021] EWHC 2644 (Ch) at [118]–[119] (Eason Rajah QC): "where A has control of property belonging to B in circumstances where viewed objectively B is entitled to expect A to administer that property for the benefit of B, then equity enforces A's obligation of due administration by requiring A to account for his dealings with B's property. In many cases, the property will be vested in A, but that is not a requirement."

155 See A. Televantos "Trusteeship, Ostensible Authority, and Land Registration: The Category Error in *Wishart*" [2016] Conv. 81, arguing that this point was overlooked by the court in *Credit and Mercantil Plc v Kaymuu Ltd* [2015] EWCA Civ 655. See further B. McFarlane and A. Televantos, "Third Party Effects in Private Law" in P. Miller and J. Oberdiek (eds) *Oxford Studies in Private Law Theory: Vol 1* (Oxford University Press, 2020).

156 See further M. Harding, "Equity and Institutions" in D. Klimchuk et al (eds), *Philosophical Foundations of the Law of Equity* (Oxford University Press, 2020), Ch. 16.

157 *Schmidt v Rosewood Trust Ltd* at [59]–[60].

B. Content and Breach

A relationship of due administration is grounded in the "fundamental juristic principle" that "any form of authority may only be exercised for the purposes conferred, and in accordance with its terms".[158] **3–157** The content of every duty of due administration depends on the terms on which A holds A's powers. Sometimes these may *require* A to exercise a power, in which case the terms generate a duty-right relationship between A and B. Alternatively, the terms may *prohibit* the exercise of power in some situations. Duties of administration are thus like the other equitable controls considered in this Chapter: they not only restrain A by making it unlawful, as against B, to act in particular ways, but can also positively require A to act in other ways.

The question of whether A has complied with the terms on which her legal entitlements are held **3–158** depends on the immediate effect of A's exercise of power and A's subjective purpose (i.e. the effect A intends to achieve). It is sometimes said that A owes a duty to obey these terms, and sometimes said that A cannot validly commit a "fraud on a power". This is discussed further in Chapter 11.[159] The point for now is that A will have breached her duty of due administration if her (in)action results in an immediate effect that is not permitted by the terms, or if A's purpose, i.e. the effect A intends to achieve, is not permitted by the terms.

Another feature of A's duty of due administration is A's duty to account, which requires A to provide **3–159** certain information to B and take action as necessary to produce the subject property (or its value) in accordance with the history of A's dealings with the property that appears in the accounts, as corrected to allow only for authorised dealings.[160] This duty and its various facets are discussed in relation to the express trustee in Chapter 10, but is should be borne in mind that the principles discussed there are of general application to those who owe duties of due administration,[161] including agents, partners, company directors, receivers and managers, as well as mortgagees.

A may be subject to other duties in addition to a duty of due administration, such as a duty of care **3–160** or fiduciary loyalty. The existence and content of these and other duties will largely be a function of the terms. The importance of distinguishing between fiduciary loyalty and a duty of administration, as well as the way in which fiduciary loyalty accommodates itself to the terms, has been discussed above.[162] We will see in Chapter 10 how the terms of an express trust may exclude or modify the scope of a trustee's duty of care, duty to segregate, and duty of fiduciary loyalty.

---

158 For consideration of the role of such relationships in promoting parties' autonomy, see, e.g. McFarlane and Televantos, "Third Party Effects in Private Law" in *Oxford Studies in Private Law Theory: Vol 1* (2020); and H. Dagan and I. Samet, "Express Trust: The Dark Horse of the Liberal Property Regime" in S. Degeling et al (eds) *Philosophical Foundations of the Law of Express Trusts* (Oxford University Press, forthcoming).

159 See paras 11–030 to 11–077.

160 As to an express trustee's obligation to account, see para.10–059. In relation to other power-holders, such as company directors and agents, see, e.g. *Re Lands Allotment Co* [1894] 1 Ch. 616 at 638 (Kay LJ); *Re International Vending Machines Pty Ltd and Companies Act* [1962] N.S.W.R. 1408 at 1420; *O'Halloran v R T Thomas & Family Pty Ltd* (1998) 45 N.S.W.L.R. 262; *Agricultural Land Management v Jackson (No.2)* [2014] WASC 102; 48 W.A.R. 1 at [363] (Edelman J).

161 Executors: *Freeman v Fairlie* (1812) 3 Mer. 29 at 43; *Ottley v Gilby* (1845) 8 Beav. 602; *Wroe v Seed* (1863) 4 Giff. 425 at 428–429; *Re Bosworth* (1889) 58 L.J. Ch. 432. Administrators: Administration of Estates Act 1925 s.21. See also Administration of Estates Act 1925 s.25(b): estate beneficiaries can apply for an order that personal representatives supply them with information relating to administration of the estate. About which see further Mitchell, "Stewardship of Property and Liability to Account" (2014) 78 Conv. 215, Pt D.

162 See paras 2–197 to 2–207

C. A Right to Due Administration Distinguished from "Beneficial Ownership"

3–161 There is a difference between relationships of due administration requiring A's adherence to the terms on which she holds legal entitlements, and a smaller class of relationships where the terms on which A holds legal entitlements stipulate that B should have the beneficial enjoyment of these. Sometimes, the terms may require A to transfer her title to property to B, or otherwise deal with property in B's favour, and B is described as having a correlative right to benefit. B's right is then sometimes described as having an entitlement to the benefit of property, also known as "equitable/beneficial interest/ownership" or "an equitable proprietary right". If B has such an entitlement, then B may have further legal entitlements, such as a power to direct A to transfer title to B, or to deal with A's title in some way.[163]

3–162 Confusingly, the right to due administration is sometimes described in similar terms, i.e as an obligation requiring A to hold property for the benefit of B. However, B may have a right to due administration, i.e. a right to insist that A acts in accordance with instructions, in cases where B is not also entitled to beneficial enjoyment, and it follows that the two types of relationship are not identical. A clear example is provided by *Commissioner of Stamp Duties (Queensland) v Livingston*:[164] as noted above.[165] There Viscount Radcliffe held that B, as a party entitled on an intestacy, had a right to enforce A's duty of due administration, but because the estate was still being administered, and B could not tell what, if any, property B would receive once the debts of the deceased had been met, it could not also be said that B had beneficial ownership of any property. The importance of this distinction has been recognised in *Marshall v Kerr*, where Lord Browne-Wilkinson stated "...it is crucial to appreciate that the property settled by [the legatee] comprised, not the assets in the deceased's estate...but a separate chose in action, the right to due administration of his estate".[166] Furthermore, as we shall discuss next, an entitlement to beneficial enjoyment is not a necessary pre-requisite to someone having an entitlement to due administration.

D. Who Has a Right to Due Administration?

3–163 Across the different relationships of due administration, B is the person to whom the duty of due administration is owed and who can seek equitable relief as necessary to compel A's due administration, and relief against A, or a third party, in the event of A's maladministration, such as an unauthorised exercise of power. In the context of an express trust, B might be a beneficiary, an object of a discretionary power,[167] or in relation to charitable trusts, the Attorney-General,[168] Charity Commission for England and Wales[169] or any person interested in the trust.[170] Company directors owe their duties of due administration to the company; an agent owes her duty of due administration to her principal,

---

163 In the trusts context this is referred to as the "rule in *Saunders v Vautier*" and is discussed further in Chapter 12.

164 [1965] A.C. 694.

165 See para.3–150.

166 See further Mitchell, "Commissioner of Stamp Duties (Queensland) v Livingston (1964)" in *Landmark Cases in Succession Law* (2019), pp.270–271.

167 See, e.g.: *The Serious Fraud Office v Litigation Capital Ltd* [2021] EWHC 1272 at [203]–[205]; Mitchell, "Commissioner of Stamp Duties (Queensland) v Livingston (1964)" in *Landmark Cases in Succession Law* (2019); J. Hudson "Mere and Other Discretionary Objects in Australia" in Y.K. Liew and M. Harding (eds) *Asia-Pacific Trusts Law, Volume 1* (Hart Publishing, 2021), Ch.2.

168 *Wallis v Solicitor-General for New Zealand* [1903] A.C. 173 at 181–182.

169 Charities Act 2011 s.15(1)(2) and s.114. As to charitable trusts generally, see Chapter 9.

170 Charities Act 2011 s.115, discussed in H. Jing, "Enforcing Charitable Trusts: A Study on the English Necessary Interest Rule" (2022) 42 *Legal Studies* 228.

and for deceased estates, the personal representatives owe their duty of due administration to the estate beneficiaries and estate creditors.[171]

In some contexts, it is not always easy to identify who has a right to due administration, particularly where power is held over a potentially largely defined range of objects, or where the duty is not owed to an individual person interested in the exercise of power, such as for charitable trusts, or companies, for example. Equitable or beneficial ownership (also referred to as an "equitable proprietary interest") has sometimes been regarded as a pre-requisite to also having a right to due administration, particularly in the express trusts context, where we will see in later chapters[172] that some claims against a trustee and third parties have sometimes been confined to beneficiaries with an "equitable proprietary interest". Against this view, however, are instances where persons have a right to due administration yet have no "equitable proprietary interest", within the express trust context, and across other relationships of due administration. **3–164**

In the following extract, Charles Mitchell observes that the duties owed by trustees to perform the trust and account for their dealings with trust property are identical to the duties owed by personal representatives while administering a deceased person's estate to implement her wishes and account for their dealings. Further, these duties are owed to the estate creditors and to the legatees or next-of-kin, none of whom has any equitable proprietary interest in the assets being administered, legal ownership of which is vested in the administrators. This is the ratio of a Privy Council decision, *Commissioner of Stamp Duties (Queensland) v Livingston*,[173] where Viscount Radcliffe followed earlier House of Lords' decisions to the same effect. **3–165**

Charles Mitchell, "*Commissioner of Stamp Duties (Queensland) v Livingston* (1964): Rights of Estate Beneficiaries and Trust Beneficiaries Compared"

in Brian Sloan (ed.) *Landmark Cases in Succession Law* (Hart Publishing, 2019), pp.265–268, 273–274

Commissioner of Stamp Duties (Queensland) v Livingston[174] reaffirmed the proposition, established by earlier cases, that residuary legatees have no "beneficial interest" in the assets which make up a testator's estate during administration.[175] They can, however, prevent the executors from disposing of these assets in an unauthorised transaction and they can demand the return of such assets from third parties to whom they have been improperly transferred. Residuary legatees have these rights although nothing may remain in the estate for them once administration is complete because by then the assets have all been paid to the creditors. *Livingston* therefore establishes that duties can be imposed on an owner of property respecting her stewardship of the property, and that another person can be given corresponding rights against her, and rights against third parties with whom she has improperly dealt, although this other person has no right to beneficial enjoyment of the property and may never acquire one. This idea has been generalised within the law governing the administration of estates, which gives the same rights to general and specific legatees (where a testator has made general and specific legacies), next of kin (in cases of intestacy) and estate creditors (whether or not there is a will). . . . **3–166**

[The facts of *Livingston* were as follows.] Hugh Livingston died in 1948. By his will he left one-third of his residuary estate to his widow, Jocelyn Livingston. She remarried after his death and became Jocelyn **3–167**

---

171 *Commissioner of Stamp Duties (Queensland) v Livingston* at 707, 712–714; Mitchell, "Commissioner of Stamp Duties (Queensland) v Livingston (1964)" in *Landmark Cases in Succession Law* (2019).

172 See para.15–135.

173 [1965] A.C. 694.

174 [1965] A.C. 694.

175 HMRC considers that the question of when an administration period ends "is essentially one of fact and will depend on individual circumstances" but that it "may in some cases coincide with the date when the residue of the estate can be identified": HMRC, *Trusts, Settlements and Estates Manual* (28 March 2018 version).

Coulson. However, she died intestate in 1950, before the administration of Livingston's estate had been completed, and before any residue had been ascertained and any final balance payable or attributable to the residuary legatees had been determined. Livingston had been domiciled and resident in New South Wales at the time of his death and his will had been proved there. Coulson had also been domiciled and resident in New South Wales at the time of her death. However, Livingston's estate included property in Queensland, and the question was whether Queensland succession duty was payable by Coulson's executors in respect of her share of the Queensland property. The duty was payable under the relevant legislation only if Coulson had died possessed of a "beneficial interest" in the property, language which was understood by the court to signify an interest akin to the "beneficial interest" which a trust beneficiary has in the trust fund. The Privy Council held that Coulson had not had such an interest. She had only had a personal right against Livingston's executors which had been "capable of being invoked for any purpose connected with the proper administration of his estate".[176] It might have been said in a "loose and general way" that this right amounted to an "interest" in the assets which made up the unadministered estate, but not that this was a "beneficial interest" of the requisite kind.[177] So the duty was not payable.

3–168 The Privy Council's advice was given by Viscount Radcliffe. He found that a residuary legatee's interest in the testator's unadministered estate had been "conclusively defined by decisions of long-established authority"[178] [viz *Lord Sudeley v Attorney General*[179]and *Dr Barnardo's Homes National Inc Assoc v Special Commissioners of Income Tax*[180]].

3–169 . . . Viscount Radcliffe held on the strength of these authorities that property received by an executor by virtue of his office comes to him "in full ownership, without distinction between legal and equitable interests", but he holds this property "for the purpose of carrying out the functions and duties of administration, not for his own benefit"; hence he holds the property, subject to duties which can be enforced by a residuary legatee,

> "to preserve the assets, to deal properly with them, and to apply them in a due course of administration for the benefit of those interested according to that course, creditors, the death duty authorities, legatees of various sorts, and the residuary beneficiaries."[181]

3–170 It followed that residuary legatees have a corresponding (and "transmissible") set of personal rights against the executor.[182] However, what equity does not do is:[183]

> "to recognise or create for residuary legatees a beneficial interest in the assets in the executor's hands during the course of administration. Conceivably, this could have been done, in the sense that the assets, whatever they might be from time to time, could have been treated as a present, though fluctuating, trust fund held for the benefit of all those interested in the estate according to the measure of their respective interests. But it never was done."

3–171 Since the executor cannot take the estate for himself, and since neither the estate creditors nor any of the estate beneficiaries has an equitable beneficial interest in the estate assets during administration, it followed that nobody has such an interest in these assets. However, there was nothing wrong with this conclusion, for equity brings such interests into being only in situations where there is a need for them, and there was no need for them in *Livingston* because

---

176 *Commissioner of Stamp Duties (Queensland) v Livingston* at 717.

177 Ibid at 717, quoting *Lord Sudeley v Attorney General* [1897] A.C. 11 at 15 (Lord Herschell). Cf. *Gartside v IRC* [1968] A.C. 553 at 617 (Lord Wilberforce), accepting that the word "interest" is "capable of a very wide and general meaning", but emphasising that "the wide spectrum that it covers makes it all the more necessary, if precise conclusions are to be founded upon its use, to place it in a setting"; he also endorsed Viscount Radcliffe's dictum in *Commissioner of Stamp Duties (Queensland) v Livingston* at 719 that the word "has to do duty in several quite different legal contexts to express rights of very different characters and that to transfer a meaning from one context to another may breed confusion".

178 Ibid at 707.

179 [1897] A.C. 11.

180 [1921] 2 A.C. 1.

181 *Commissioner of Stamp Duties (Queensland) v Livingston* at 707.

182 Ibid at 710.

183 Ibid at 707–8.

"the court will control the executor in the use of his rights over assets that come to him in that capacity ... [by enforcing] remedies which do not involve the admission or recognition of equitable rights of property in those assets."[184]

... At the heart of Viscount Radcliffe's analysis is the proposition that a personal representative owes a duty to the estate beneficiaries "to preserve the assets" of an unadministered estate, "to deal properly with them, and to apply them in a due course of administration".[185] This rule is an old one: there are cases stretching back for many years which say that proving a will connotes acceptance of the testator's instructions and that it follows from such acceptance that the executors can only exercise their powers in a manner authorised by the testator.[186] In this respect their duty is the same as that owed by trustees, who must comply with the terms of the trust deed and cannot validly exercise their powers in an unauthorised way.[187] Since personal representatives and trustees are both the owners of property vested in them on the agreed basis that they will hold and apply it for the benefit of other people who are vulnerable to abuses of their power, it is no surprise to find that they are also generally required to avoid conflicts of interest and to prioritise the interests of the estate or trust beneficiaries over their own interests and those of other people.[188] Out of this requirement flows the further rule that they must disgorge any unauthorised profits which they make from their position.[189] **3–172**

For these duties to be meaningful, the persons to whom they are owed must be afforded a realistic opportunity to enforce them. This means that they must be told that their rights exist and they must be given access to the information which they need to determine whether any breach of duty is contemplated or has been committed. This is why trustees owe additional duties to take reasonable steps to inform the beneficiaries that they are beneficiaries, to keep an accurate record of their dealings with the trust property[190] and to supply the beneficiaries with information relating to the trust affairs when they are requested to do so.[191] These principles were restated in *Schmidt v Rosewood Trust Ltd*, where Lord Walker said that ownership of an "equitable proprietary right" in trust assets is "neither [a] sufficient nor [a] necessary" basis for requiring disclosure of trust documents.[192] The reason why persons interested in the proper administration of a trust are entitled to the information contained in the trust deeds and trust accounts is a different one, namely that this will enable them to monitor the trustees and prevent them from committing unauthorised actions. It followed, in Lord Walker's view, that there is "no reason to draw any bright dividing line either between [the interests of beneficiaries under fixed and discretionary trusts] ... or between the rights of an object of a discretionary trust and those of the object of a mere power (of a fiduciary character)".[193] **3–173**

In the same way, and for the same reason, personal representatives must keep accurate records and produce these for inspection by estate beneficiaries.[194] A statutory provision also entitles estate beneficiaries to apply for an order that the personal representatives should supply them with information relating to the administration of the estate.[195] **3–174**

---

184 Ibid at 712.

185 Ibid at 707.

186 *Stiles v Guy* at 575: "The executors, by proving the will, took upon themselves, and accepted the trust, and were bound, therefore, to discharge the duties they voluntarily imposed upon themselves." See also *Mucklow v Fuller* (1821) Jac. 198; *Booth v Booth* (1838) 1 Beav. 125 at 12.

187 *Youyang v Minter Ellison* at [32].

188 *Re Thomson* [1930] 1 Ch. 203. ...

189 *Vyse v Foster* (1874) L.R. 7 H.L. 318 at 329 (Lord Cairns LC): "a trustee or an executor who uses trust-money in trade must account for the profits which he makes by that use of it". See also *Piety v Stace* (1799) 4 Ves. Jun. 620 (executor); *Docker v Somes* (1834) 2 My. & K. 655.

190 *Pearse v Green* (1819) 1 J. & W. 135; *Springett v Dashwood* (1860) 2 Giff. 521.

191 For this principle in the context of testamentary trusts, see *Burrows v Walls* (1855) 5 De G.M. & G. 233; *Brittlebank v Goodwin* (1868) L.R. 5 Eq. 545 at 550. More generally, see also *Talbot v Marshfield* (1868) 3 Ch. App. 622; *Re Tillott* [1892] 1 Ch. 86. But note that the reasons for confidential discretionary decision making need not be disclosed, following *Re Londonderry's Settlement* [1965] Ch. 918.

192 [2003] 2 A.C. 709 at [54].

193 Ibid at [66].

194 Executors: *Freeman v Fairlie* (1812) 3 Mer. 29 at 43; *Ottley v Gilby* (1845) 8 Beav. 602; *Wroe v Seed* (1863) 4 Giff. 425 at 428–429; *Re Bosworth* (1889) 58 L.J. Ch. 432. Administrators: Administration of Estates Act 1925 s.21.

195 Administration of Estates Act 1925 s.25(b).

3–175 In the following extract, Jessica Hudson explains that objects of various discretionary powers of appointment, who do not have any "equitable proprietary interest" *do* have a right to due administration.

Jessica Hudson, "Mere and Other Discretionary Objects in Australia"

in Ying Khai Liew et al (eds) *Asia-Pacific Trusts Law*, Vol.1 (Hart Publishing, 2021), pp.23–24

3–176 To sum up, the objects from an open class of an exhaustive power and the mere object of a non-exhaustive power (with an open or closed class of objects) are thus in the same position in that they have neither a collective entitlement to the benefit of trust property, nor an individual entitlement. It is for this reason that these objects have significance for our understanding of Australia's approach to the conferral of the right to due administration, in particular, whether a right to due administration can accrue to objects who do not have, on either a collective or individual basis, an entitlement to the benefit of trust property.

3–177 The *right to due administration* is the central mechanism for control of the trustee in her exercise of power over trust property. This right is described in various ways, such as a "right to due administration"[196] and a "right to have the trust property properly managed and to have the trustee account for his management".[197] The "right to due administration" is a general and collective description of specific entitlements . . . that give substance to the trustee's essential duty to exercise her power over trust property in accordance with the trust terms,[198] and the requirements for power to be exercised properly and in good faith, whether those powers are held by a trustee or third-party donee. . . . This "right"[199] is the basis for equitable relief as necessary to ensure the due administration of a trust, which, depending on the circumstances, might include orders for access to trust information,[200] declaratory or specific relief consequent upon an unauthorised or improper exercise of power,[201] recovery of misapplied property from third parties,[202] and orders for an account against the trustee.[203]

3–178 Given the centrality of this right to the enforcement of a trust, the question of to whom this right accrues is important. . . .

3–179 The first category of cases[204] contain express judicial recognition that a right to due administration accrues to a mere object. An illustrative example is *Wright v Stevens*, where Hallen J found that an object of an exhaustive power to appoint new beneficiaries from an *open* class of objects defined as a "person . . . residing in or otherwise carrying on business in Dorrigo in New South Wales or surrounding area as defined by post code 2453" had "a chose in action which a court of equity will protect",[205] including to seek relief in relation to an unauthorised exercise of a power of appointment, or a trustee's unauthorised distribution of trust funds.

3–180 In *Randall v Lubrano*,[206] Holland J emphatically stated that "there is no doubt in my mind that [the objects of a mere power] . . . would be proper parties to seek relief in this Court"[207] in response to a trustee's misapplication of trust funds or other breach of trust. Again, in *Public Trustee v Smith*[208] White J found that a mere object "was entitled to enforce due administration of the trust",[209] despite not being

---

196 *Chief Commissioner of Stamp Duties (NSW) v Buckle* (1998) 192 C.L.R. 226 at 242.
197 *Spellson v George* at 315–316.
198 *Youyang v Minter* at [32].
199 "Right" refers to an equity for relief that is subject to equitable discretion . . .
200 *Spellson v George*.
201 *Karger v Paul* [1984] V.R. 161.
202 *Strang v Owens* (1925) 42 W.N. (NSW) 183.
203 *Youyang v Minter Ellison*.
204 In addition to the cases discussed next, see also: *Kennon v Spry* (2008) 238 C.L.R. 306 at [77] (French CJ), [125] (Gummow and Hayne JJ), cf [161] (Heydon J) . . .
205 *Wright v Stevens* [2018] NSWSC 548 at [56], [94], [235]–[246].
206 *Randall v Lubrano* (Supreme Court of New South Wales, Holland J, 31 October 1975), published as an annexure to *McDonald v Ellis* (2007) 72 N.S.W.L.R. 605.
207 *Randall v Lubrano* at 622.
208 *Public Trustee v Smith* [2008] NSWSC 397 at [14]–[30], [77].
209 *Public Trustee v Smith* at [107].

> "the beneficial owner of the trust property".[210] In *Australian Securities & Investments Commission v Carey (No 6)* French J (as the former Chief Justice of the High Court of Australia then was) stated ". . . there are some rights enjoyed, even by the beneficiaries of a non-exhaustive discretionary trust with an open class of beneficiaries . . . " including "a right to enforce the proper management of the trust by the trustee."[211]
>
> There are a further four categories of cases that recognise a mere object, or an object from an open class of an exhaustive power, has an entitlement: (a) to seek relief in relation to an unauthorised exercise of power; (b) to bring derivative proceedings to assert rights accruing to the trustee; (c) to access trust information; (d) to replacement of the trustee. . . . **3–181**

A similar point is made by Hui Jing in relation to charitable trusts, where the Attorney-General, Charity Commission or a person with a necessary interest in the charity can enforce the right to due administration of the charitable trust. Again, the right to due administration is enforceable by someone who does not have an "equitable proprietary interest". Further, Jing explains the rationale behind this rule:[212] **3–182**

> The central concern of a charitable trust lies in the establishment of mechanisms to hold a charity trustee accountable for its performance of duties, so as to the protect the public benefit flowing from the execution of the charitable purposes. In England, Parliament introduced the "necessary interest rule" through the passage of the Charities Act, allowing "any person interested in"[213] a charitable trust to bring charity proceedings against a defaulting trustee in its administration of charitable assets. . . . Practically, although it is recognised that the Attorney General "[represents] the Crown as *parens patriae* to enforce the execution of charitable trusts",[214] this "protector"[215] or "guardian"[216] mechanism has been extensively criticised due to its lack of resources (in terms of both personnel and funds) dedicated to supervising the administration of charitable trusts. . . . Since the reforms of the Charities Act 1960 (England and Wales), the function of the Attorney General has largely been replaced by the Charity Commission for England and Wales (Commission). However, the establishment of the Commission does not completely alleviate the concerns over the supervision and enforcement of charitable trusts, for not all charitable trusts are required to register with the Commission,[217] and more notably, it is questionable whether the Commission is capable of effectively performing its monitoring role . . . One might argue that, aside from the Attorney General and the Commission, settlors are interested in seeing charitable assets being properly used, and therefore they are ideal candidates to play an overseeing role. But this approach is also not free of problems, as too much reliance on settlors to supervise charitable trusts will contribute to the risk that they may use charitable trusts as a vehicle for illegal purposes, such as money laundering or tax evasion.

After reviewing the cases considering whether a person has a necessary interest to bring proceedings to enforce a charity trustee's duty of due administration, and comparing these with the cases considering the position of a discretionary object Jing makes the argument that:[218] **3–183**

> The way in which the courts have applied and construed this rule suggests the *same* conceptual basis for the recognition of an interested person's standing to sue under charitable trusts and that for discretionary objects. Irrespective of whether an express trust is for persons or for purposes, it is the concern of securing its due administration and execution that lies at the heart of the assessment of a person's eligibility to sue.

---

210 *Public Trustee v Smith* at [108], see also: [107], [139].

211 *Australian Securities and Investments Commission v Carey (No.6)* (2006) 153 F.C.R. 509 at [21] (French J).

212 Jing, "Enforcing Charitable Trusts", p.229. As Jing notes, the statutory rule was introduced in England in the Charitable Trusts Act 1853.

213 Charities Act 2011 s.115. . . .

214 *Wallis v Solicitor-General for New Zealand* at 181–182.

215 *Perpetual Trustees Victoria Limited v Barns & Another* [2012] VSCA 77 at [42].

216 *National Anti-Vivisection Society v Inland Revenue Commissioners* [1948] A.C. 31 at 63.

217 Charities Act 2011 s.30(2).

218 Jing, "Enforcing Charitable Trusts", pp.244–245 [emphasis in original].

3–184 As we will see in later chapters, the fact that a discretionary object without an "equitable proprietary interest" does have a right to due administration has important analytical implications for our understanding of the express trust relationship, the nature of a beneficiary's interest thereunder[219] and the justification(s) for various claims against the trustee and third parties, such as a claim to information against a trustee[220] and a proprietary claim to trust property against a third-party recipient.[221]

3–185 A right to due administration does not mean that the right-holder can seek relief requiring the transfer of property or payment of money to her directly. A right to due administration facilitates the transfer of property or money back into the fund or estate to be administered in accordance with the relevant set of terms. Hence orders for relief will require payment or transfer to the (perhaps replacement) trustee, executor or other administrator. Sometimes, however, a different form of relief might be granted, requiring payment of money or transfer of property direct to the claimant, such as a trust beneficiary. This difference is because the claimant, in addition to having a right to due administration, also has an entitlement to the benefit of property under the relevant set of terms. If the claimant, such as a trust beneficiary has an entitlement to the benefit of trust property and satisfies other conditions so that she has a power to call for the trust property from a third party,[222] then she may be able to seek relief that short circuits[223] the step of the return of that property to the trustee and instead requires the transfer of trust property directly to her.[224]

E. Operation and Effect

3–186 The terms and the duty of due administration are sometimes described as limitations on the scope of A's power,[225] or, in other words, as rules that disable or disempower A from acting otherwise than in accordance with the terms. In principle, it would be possible for a legal system to control a power-holder by disabling or disempowering in the event of maladministration. That is not, however, the path taken by English law and those jurisdictions in which a duty of due administration operates as a form of secondary or meta law.

3–187 A duty of due administration, and the terms that give content to it, do not actually limit the scope of or disable the underlying power.[226] Equity does not negate the legal outcomes produced by A satisfying whatever are the relevant rules providing for the exercise of A's power, or other legal entitlement. For example, even if acting beyond the terms of the agency, an agent can validly transfer the principal's title to specific property to a third party, if the agent complies with the relevant rules for assignment of the subject property.[227] The same point has been made in relation to express trust-

---

219 See Chapter 12.

220 See paras 10–063 to 10–078.

221 See para.15–135.

222 About which see further paras 12–064 to 12–073.

223 J. Hudson, "Equitable Ownership and Restitution of Misapplied Trust Property" (2017) 11 J. Eq. 245, 267.

224 As explained in *Akers v Samba Financial Group* [2017] UKSC 6; [2017] A.C. 424 at [46], [82].

225 See, e.g. *Pitt v Holt* [2011] EWCA Civ 197; [2012] Ch. 132 at [231] [emphasis added]; *Pitt v Holt* [2013] UKSC 26; [2013] 2 A.C. 108 at [93]; *British Airways Plc v Airways Pension Scheme Trustee Ltd* [2018] Pens. L.R. 19 at [44] (Patten LJ); R. Grantham, "The Powers of Company Directors and the Proper Purpose Doctrine" (1993–95) 5 K.C.L.J. 16, 32–4; R. Nolan, "Controlling Fiduciary Power" [2009] C.L.J. 293, 293–300.

226 See further J. Hudson, "One Thicket in Fraud on a Power" (2019) 39 O.J.L.S. 577; S. Agnew and B. McFarlane, "The Paradox of the Equitable Proprietary Claim" in S. Agnew et al (eds), *Modern Studies in Property Law*, 10th edn (Hart Publishing, 2019), Ch.17, referred to on this point in *The Serious Fraud Office v Litigation Capital Ltd* [2021] EWHC 1272 (Comm) at [276]–[277] (Foxton J).

227 As in: *Re David Payne & Co Ltd* [1904] 2 Ch. 608; *John v Dodwell* [1918] A.C. 563; *Reckitt v Barnett, Pembroke & Slater Ltd* [1928] 2 K.B. 244 at 268 (Russel LJ) affirmed on appeal in *Reckitt v Barnett, Pembroke and Slater Ltd* [1929] A.C. 176 at 183;

ees:[228] if A holds a right on trust for B, and, in breach of the terms of the trust, A then transfers that right to C, the transfer is valid, and C acquires the right. There is then a distinct question of whether the circumstances of C's acquisition are such that B can bring a claim against C.[229]

There are, however, some specific powers where the legal rules creating them condition an effective execution on the lawfulness of execution, such as a trustee or donee's power to vary the terms of an express trust.[230] These powers are limited in that they can *only* be effectively exercised lawfully. This is however a result of the legal rules defining the power, and not of equity's rules requiring due administration. We will discuss some of these powers in Chapter 11. **3–188**

Consistently with the arguments made about the function and operation of other equitable rules, a relationship of due administration is a "gloss" on the lawfulness of the exercise of A's power or other legal entitlement. Due administration makes it unlawful for A, as against B, to act (or not act) when it would otherwise would have been lawful for A to have done so. This relationship of due administration is realised through the award of various forms of equitable relief that aim to prevent the power-holder taking action(s) to exercise a power, such as injunctive relief (see Chapter 19), or relief to reverse the consequences of an unauthorised exercise of power, such as equitable money remedies available against the power-holder[231] and third-parties,[232] or various proprietary remedies against the power-holder and/or third parties.[233] All these remedies prevent or address the consequences of an unauthorised execution so that it is *as if* the power-holder were disabled from exercising power in an unauthorised manner. Equity's remedies are required precisely because a relationship of due administration is (just) a gloss on the lawfulness of execution and does *not* disempower or disable A from exercising her power in an unauthorised manner. **3–189**

The secondary or meta law function can be rationalised as allowing the legal system to pursue what are otherwise inconsistent commitments. These are, on the one hand, the need for legal powers to be defined by legal rules that are relatively predictable, stable and certain. These qualities secure legal powers as a form of freedom understood as a temporal horizon for action. They also ensure legal powers supply part of the necessary legal framework for a range of legal relationships and institutions, the diversity of which helps to promote the parties' autonomy,[234] and that such powers operate in a manner that preserves the conditions under which citizens are disposed to have faith in and be guided by law.[235] **3–190**

If however, A's power was actually limited by the terms such that an effective execution depended upon due administration, then the law's ends in conferring and creating powers under contract, or property, for example, would be undermined. This is because the content a duty of due administration might be defined by an infinitely diverse range of terms with high degrees of complexity that may not be understood by the parties subject to them. Further, A's adherence to the terms depends not just on **3–191**

Tobin v Broadbent (1947) 75 C.L.R. 378; *Great Investments Ltd v Warner* [2016] FCAFC 85; (2016) 243 F.C.R. 516. See further *Criterion Properties Plc v Stratford UK Properties LLC* [2004] UKHL 28 (HL) at [4].

228 *Rolled Steel Products (Holdings) Ltd v British Steel Corp* [1986] Ch. 246 at 303–304; *Wellington Capital Ltd v Australian Securities and Investments Commission* (2014) 254 C.L.R. 288 at [60].

229 See, e.g. *Akers* [2017] UKSC 6; [2017] A.C. 424 and the discussion at paras 12–008 to 12–019 and Chapter 15.

230 Such as a power to vary the terms of an express trust (see paras 10–079 to 10–083) and some agent's powers have been understood in this way too.

231 See Chapter 13.

232 See Chapter 14.

233 See Chapter 15.

234 See, e.g. McFarlane and Televantos, "Third Party Effects in Private Law" in *Oxford Studies in Private Law Theory: Vol 1* (2020); and Dagan and Samet, "Express Trust: The Dark Horse of the Liberal Property Regime" in *Philosophical Foundations of the Law of Express Trusts* (forthcoming).

235 See Harding, "Equity and Institutions" in *Philosophical Foundations of the Law of Equity* (2020).

the objective variables, such as the effect of execution and the meaning of the terms, it also depends on the power-holder's subjective belief that her purpose is proper. To deny all effect to A's exercise of a power in such cases would cause great uncertainty for third parties; instead, equity protects B not by invalidating the transaction between A and C, but by giving B relief against A and, in certain circumstances, against C.[236]

3–192 Equity thus operates as a gloss on A's authority, redefining the lawfulness, as against B, of an exercise of power or other legal entitlement. Equity then provides a range of remedial responses to address the consequences of an unauthorised execution. In the particular case that one or another remedy is awarded, equity's effect is as if the power-holder were disabled. This effect, however, is *in personam*, applying only as between the parties and has not come at the expense of re-writing the rules defining the underlying power itself: those rules remain intact and are supplemented by equity, not corrected by it.

5. Equitable Assignment of Legal Choses in Action

A. Introduction

3–193 Consider a case in which D, a debtor, is under a duty to pay £500 to A in one year's time. A is in need of money immediately and wishes to raise it by dealing with that right against D. One way to do so would be for A simply to transfer that right to B, asking for payment from B in return. B of course would pay less than £500, given that B would have to wait for payment from D, but A, if allowed to transfer the right to B, would at least receive something immediately. The difficulty for A is that common law does not give A such a power to transfer A's right against D: it is simply not possible for A, without D's consent, to re-direct D's duty so that is owed to B rather than to A. There are a number of explanations for common law's refusal to give A such a power. The most convincing is simply that the reason for which D came under the duty to A does not necessarily justify giving A the unilateral power to change D's duty so that it becomes instead a duty to B. For example, in the very common case where A's right against D arose because of a contract between A and D, D can point out that D agreed only to pay A, and to owe a duty to A.

3–194 In our example, where D is under a duty to pay £500 to A, A's right against D can be described as a "chose in action". This is to distinguish it from a "chose in possession". As stated by Channell J in *Torkington v Magee* a:[237] "'Chose in action' is a known legal expression used to describe all personal rights of property which can only be claimed or enforced by action, and not by taking physical possession." So, where A owns a car, or has a freehold of land, A has a chose in possession; but where D has a duty to pay £500 to A, A has a legal entitlement which cannot be enforced by taking possession. One reason to make the distinction between these different types of right is that, whilst the common law does generally allow the transfer of a chose in possession, such as ownership of a car, or a freehold of land, it does not generally permit the transfer of a chose in action, such as A's right to be paid £500 by D. In our example, A's right is a "legal" chose in action as A's right against D arises at common law.

3–195 What then can A do in our example? Fortunately for A, there is a concept of equitable assignment which can apply in our case. Equitable assignment is a broad term, and is used in a number of different contexts. For example, it can be applied to the type of case we will consider in Chapter 6, where

---

[236] See, e.g. *Akers* at [89] (Lord Sumption) and paras 12–008 to 12–019 and Chapter 15.

[237] [1902] 2 K.B. 427 (DC) at 430–431. Channell J's definition was not question in the successful appeal, [1903] 1 K.B. 644.

T holds on trust for B, and B wishes to deal with B's equitable interest under the trust by transferring that interest to B2. It can also be applied to a case we will consider in Chapter 5, where A holds a right which can be transferred to B (such as shares in a company), but the requirements for such a transfer have not been met, so that A remains entitled to the shares, and B then claims instead that an "equitable assignment" has occurred, with the result that A now holds the shares for the benefit of B. We will consider those types of equitable assignment in those later chapters. Our focus here is only on the form of equitable assignment which can assist A where A holds a common law right, such as a right to be paid £500 by D, which cannot be transferred at common law.

In our example, it has also been possible for A, since the coming into force of s.25(6) of the Judicature Act 1873, for A to make a statutory assignment to B of A's right to be paid £500 by D.[238] The power to make such a statutory assignment is now regulated in England by s.136 of the Law of Property Act 1925, and by similar provisions in other common law jurisdictions. As we will see below,[239] however, there are some situations in which statutory assignment of A's chose in action is not possible, but A can make an equitable assignment—so, for example, if A wishes to give B the benefit of part only of D's debt to A, equitable assignment is possible, but statutory assignment is not. Further, there are requirements for a valid statutory assignment, such as the use of writing, and the need to give written notice to D, which do not apply to an equitable assignment. Equitable assignment therefore remains a practically very important means of realising the value of A's rights. **3–196**

There are two key reasons for limiting our focus, in this Chapter, to this particular form of equitable assignment.[240] First, it provides a further example of equity's characteristic role of supplementing the common law by providing rules which regulate A's exercise of legal entitlements and, like the other equitable doctrines considered in this Chapter, it does not simply restrain A from exercising A's entitlement, it also operates to generate a duty of A to B in response to A's choice to do so. Second, this form of equitable assignment raises important broader questions about the relationship between common law and equity. In particular, if it is regarded as a means for A to *transfer* A's entitlement to B, so that A loses the entitlement and B gains it, it would seem to operate as a primary rather than a secondary rule. Moreover, it would involve a direct contradiction of the common law rule (that the right cannot be transferred): a correction of the common law, not a supplement to it. We agree, however, with commentators who have argued that the rules applying to this form of equitable assignment show clearly that, despite the potentially misleading language often used to describe equitable assignment, it does *not* in fact involve a transfer of A's right to B. Rather, it retains the characteristic equitable function of recognising that A has an entitlement, but then regulating, in favour of B, A's exercise of that entitlement. **3–197**

We recognise that the overall economic or practical effect of an equitable assignment is the same *as if* B steps into A's shoes and becomes the new holder of A's right against D. It is certainly true that, by allowing A to deal with A's right in this way, equity has provided a commercially valuable means for A to realise the value of A's legal entitlement. Equitable assignment is one of the main legal mechanisms for the provision of finance for a range of commercial, public and personal pursuits. **3–198**

---

238 There are also statutory provisions which allow for the transfer of specific types of choses in action, such as copyright (see Copyright, Designs and Patents Act 1988 s.90) and policies of life assurance (Policies of Assurance Act 1867).

239 See paras 3–240 to 3–249.

240 Note the term "equitable assignment" is used to cover a number of different situations, beyond the one considered here. So, for example, the application of the principle in *Re Rose* [1949] Ch. 78 (see paras 5–023 to 5–041) is sometimes said to involve an "equitable assignment" (see e.g. *Pennington v Waine* [2002] EWCA Civ 227; [2002] 1 W.L.R. 2075 at [51] and [116]), but it is distinct from the situation considered in this Chapter.

Ying Khai Liew, *Guest on the Law of Assignment*

3rd edn, (Sweet & Maxwell, 2021), para.1.04

3–199 In 1872, in his *Principles of Economical Philosophy*,[241] I.H. Macleod stated:

> "If we were asked – who made the discovery which has most deeply affected the fortunes of the human race? We think, after full consideration, we might safely answer – The man who first discover that a Debt is a Saleable Commodity."

3–200 In particular, assignment enables a business to sell to a bank or other financial institution debts due or growing due from its customers, though such debt are not presently payable, thus obtaining an immediate case payment in return for the transfer to the financier of its right to future payment from its customers. This in turn enables the business to allow its customers to purchase goods or services on credit, which it would be less disposed to do had it to wait for its money. But there are many other situations, for example, debt collection, the satisfaction or reduction of existing or future indebtedness, the creation of security for a loan, the sale of a business as a going concern, loan participation or the gift of intangible property to another family member, where assignment has an important role to play.

3–201 However, it is crucial to appreciate that equitable assignment does not take the form of a transfer of A's right to B and this can be seen in some important aspects of its operation. This means that whilst equitable assignment is often referred to by judges as a "transfer", we need to be careful and consider the precise operation of the rules. In particular, we need to consider not only the practical effect of this type of equitable assignment, but also *how* the effect is achieved.

3–202 Some care must also be taken in interpreting references to choses in action as "property". As we will discuss in Chapter 12, the term "property" is used in many different contexts, and may have different meanings depending on the context. If it is used to refer, in a general sense, to assets of value, then a chose in action, such as A's right to be paid £500 to B, certainly counts as property. A's ability to use the mechanism of equitable assignment to deal with that right and realise its value can also contribute to a description of A's right as "property". However, that cannot, by itself, mean that it is *therefore* possible for A to make a genuine transfer of that right to B. The danger lies in assuming either that, because A's right has value, it must be capable of being transferred, or that, because an equitable assignment is possible, A's right counts as property, and so must be capable of being transferred. It all depends on the nature of an equitable assignment: in our view, the possibility of such an assignment is not evidence that a chose in action can be transferred; it is rather a response to the fact that it *cannot* be.

B. Effect

i. Not a transfer

3–203 Edelman and Elliott have noted that: "The dominant modern conception of equitable assignment is that it involves rights against the debtor which are held by the assignor being transferred to the assignee." We will see that this transfer model is often reflected in the language used by judges when discussing equitable assignment. Nonetheless, as Edelman and Elliott go on to argue, there are some significant problems with this transfer model of equitable assignment.

---

[241] I.H. Macleod, *Principles of Economical Philosophy*, 2nd edn (1872), p.481. See also Zweigert and Kotz, *An Introduction to Comparative Law*, 3rd edn (Clarendon Press, 1998), p.448.

James Edelman and Steven Elliott, "Two Conceptions of Equitable Assignment"

(2015) 131 L.Q.R. 228, 230

As to the objection of principle [to the transfer model of equitable assignment], consider the common example of assignment of contractual rights such as debts. If one party is unilaterally to transfer rights owed to him by another then the other party to the contract will be placed under an obligation to a person to whom he has never undertaken to be bound. This point is powerfully made by Associate Professor Tham.[242] In the context of assignment of contractual rights the notion of the transfer of the contractual rights makes no conceptual sense. Suppose the debtor is an individual with a contractual debt to a bank creditor. If the bank assigns the debt to an assignee, what has been "transferred"? Can the assignee, a person about whom the debtor has no knowledge and with whom the debtor has no relationship, make any demands of the debtor? If so, on what basis can the assignee do this? The debtor has not agreed to incur a debt to the assignee, either expressly or impliedly . . . **3-204**

A second difficulty with the transfer conception of equitable assignment is how it is possible to make sense of it as a matter of history. Consider, for example, the equitable assignment of a legal right, a common law debt. Prior to the Judicature Act reforms, how could a court of Chancery have held that common law rights had been transferred from one party to another? How could the same court then have enforced the transferred common law right for the purposes of giving a common law remedy to the grantee of a common law right against the debtor? And if this was not historically possible, what has changed so that it would be possible today, post-Judicature Act reforms? **3-205**

The argument of Edelman and Elliott, that an equitable assignment does not involve a transfer of A's right to B, is supported by the very thorough analysis of Tham. It is also consistent with the effect of an equitable assignment: the key point being that, in contrast to a statutory assignment, an equitable assignment does not shift D's duty to A into a duty to B, so as to allow B a direct claim against D. Rather, D's duty remains owed to A, so if B wishes to enforce B's rights as an equitable assignee, B must ensure that A enforces A's right against D. If A refuses to enforce against D, there is no need for two separate sets of proceedings, as B can bring one set of proceedings, joining both A and D as defendants. We agree with the view of commentators such as Edelman and Elliott and Tham that this procedural device cannot obscure the substantive point that, in an equitable assignment, B is enforcing A's right against D, rather than enforcing B's own right directly against D. **3-206**

The critical point, in our view, is that if an equitable assignment were allowed to operate as a transfer, so that B acquires a direct right against D, this would mean a direct contradiction between the positions at common law and in equity. There is no reason why equity should not equally respect the reasons for which the common law denied A a power to transfer to B A's right to be paid £500 by D. Of course, statutory assignment of a chose in action is now possible, and its effect is either identical to, or very close to, that of a transfer, as B is allowed to bring a direct claim against D where a statutory assignment has occurred. However, the possibility of a statutory assignment does not change the nature of an equitable assignment, which existed before statutory assignment was introduced and, as we will see,[243] has different requirements as well as different effects. **3-207**

This view is supported, for example, by the analysis of Kerr LJ in *MH Smith v Mainwaring*.[244] That case involved insurer's subrogation: A, the insured party, had been a victim of a tort by D. B, the insurer, had paid out under A's policy, compensating A for damage caused by D. In such a case, B, as insurer has a right of subrogation and so can institute proceedings against D, in effect taking over **3-208**

---

[242] See especially C.H. Tham, "The Nature of Equitable Assignment and Anti-Assignment Clauses" in J. Neyers et al (eds) *Exploring Contract Law* (Hart Publishing, 2009), p.283.

[243] See paras 3-240 to 3-249.

[244] (1986) 2 Lloyd's Law Rep. 244.

A's right against D. However, A was a company which had since been dissolved, so it did not exist when B issued its claim. B argued that this did not matter. The Court of Appeal disagreed, finding that insurer's subrogation did not give B a direct right against D: rather, B had to claim through A, so A had to be joined to proceedings, and this could only occur if A was re-instated on the companies register, as the "right of action is vested in the assured [A]". Importantly for our purposes, Kerr LJ drew an analogy with equitable assignment:[245]

> It must be borne in mind that the right of subrogation which is acquired by insurers upon payment of a claim is no more than an equitable right against their assured [A] . . . the right of subrogation does not have the effect of transferring to the insurers any cause of action which the assured may have against the wrongdoer. Such transfer can only be effected by a legal assignment to the insurers . . . Alternatively, if the insurer encounters difficulty in persuading the assured to bring the action in respect of the claim for which he has indemnified him, or if he refuses to allow his name to be used, then he can join him in the action in order to compel him to do so, in the same way as the holder of an equitable assignment can bring an action against the debtor or wrongdoer by joining the assignor. If the assignor or, as in this case, the assured is no longer in existence, because the company has been dissolved, then unfortunately for the insurer none of those things can be done by him, since he himself has no cause of action against the wrongdoer . . . To contend, as counsel for the insurers [B] suggested, that the problem is only one of form and not substance, is as untenable in the present state of the law as it would be in relation to the different consequences of an equitable, as opposed to legal, assignment.

3–209 In *Roberts v Gill*,[246] the dispute similarly did not involve an equitable assignment, but rather when a claim could be amended to include a derivative action brought by a beneficiary of a will on behalf of the deceased estate. Again, however, equitable assignment was referred to, and Lord Collins stated that:[247] "the starting point is that if an equitable assignee sues a third party, the assignor must be joined as defendant" and also that: "[i]t is plain that, other than in the most exceptional circumstances . . . even in the case of an equitable assignment, the assignee cannot proceed to judgment without joining the assignor."

3–210 It is nonetheless true that, in *Roberts v Gill*, the transfer model of equitable assignment does have some effect in the reasoning of Lord Collins. The need to join A, the assignor, is seen as chiefly a procedural one, and so it is stated that in some cases B can validly commence proceedings against D without joining A, even if A does need to be joined before judgment is obtained against D.[248] This analysis can be criticised,[249] however, as it risks overlooking the characteristically equitable nature of an equitable assignment: it does not involve B acquiring A's legal right against D (and thus contradicting the common law prohibition on such transfers); it rather involves A's keeping that entitlement, but equity then controlling, in B's favour, how A exercises that entitlement. As will be seen in the next section, there is thus a close analogy between an equitable assignment and a trust.

ii. Similarity to a trust

3–211 In our example, where A has a right to be paid £500 by D, and wishes to realise the value of that right, one option is for A, in return for payment from B, to declare that A holds A's right against D on trust for

---

245 (1986) 2 Lloyd's Law Rep. 244 at 246–247.
246 [2011] 1 A.C. 240 (HL).
247 [2011] 1 A.C. 240 (HL) at [71].
248 [2011] 1 A.C. 240 (HL) at [67].
249 See, e.g. J. Edelman and S. Elliott, "Two Conceptions of Equitable Assignment" (2015) 131 L.Q.R. 228, 243–245; C.H. Tham, *Understanding the Law of Assignment* (Cambridge University Press, 2019), Ch.3.

B. It is possible, and indeed common, to have a trust of a chose in action. The fact that A's right cannot be transferred presents no difficulty as the trust does not involve a transfer: rather, A keeps the right and instead comes under duties to B (including a duty of due administration) in relation to that right. As A now holds the right for B's benefit, equity ensures that A's entitlements must be exercised for B's benefit. So, for example, if A refuses to enforce the right against D, B can compel A to do so, and B can do this in a single set of proceedings, joining both A and D as defendants. Further, B is protected if A goes into insolvency: as the chose in action against D is held on trust, it is not available to A's creditors. A trust of a chose in action is also relatively easy for A to create: there is no need for any writing or other formality, and the trust is valid even if neither A nor B has given any notice to D.

There are some very important similarities between an equitable assignment and a declaration of trust. This is true both as to the requirements for an equitable assignment and as to its effects. So, if an equitable assignment is made, B is protected in the event of A's insolvency, as A's chose in action is not available to A's creditors, only to B. As we saw at para.3–206, following an equitable assignment, B can also use a single set of proceedings to enforce A's right against D. Indeed, Edelman and Elliott, have argued that equitable assignment is best understood as the creation of a trust and that this was how equitable assignment was, until relatively recently, generally understood. 3–212

James Edelman and Steven Elliott, "Two Conceptions of Equitable Assignment"

(2015) 131 L.Q.R. 228, 229

The alternative conception of equitable assignment [i.e. the alternative to the transfer model of equitable assignment] is that an equitable assignment involves the creation of a trust. Unless statute effects a conveyance of the assigned rights, the rights never pass from assignor to assignee. The rights remain with the assignor and they are held for the benefit of the assignee. On this alternative conception, equitable assignment is not a transfer of rights but it is a creation of new rights or powers of the assignee in equity which encumber the existing rights held by the assignor . . . 3–213

This alternative conception of equitable assignment as involving a trust was espoused by Blackstone and Story.[250] 3–214

Chee Ho Tham has developed a model of equitable assignment of a legal chose if action as involving not only a trust of A's right against D, but also a limited but irrevocable agency relationship, in which B has the power to extinguish A's right against D by accepting performance directly from D. This "trust plus" conception helps to explain those cases in which, following an equitable assignment, D's payment of a debt directly to B gives D a good discharge. It also helps to make sense of cases in which the courts have found that, even where the contract between A and D prohibits an equitable assignment of A's right, it is still possible for A to set up a trust of A's right in favour of B: those cases are difficult to explain if an equitable assignment is identical to a trust. 3–215

It is also possible to regard B, an equitable assignee, as having a right which is very similar to the right of a beneficiary of a trust, without taking a view on whether the equitable assignment in fact creates a trust. In the following analysis, for example, it is said that an equitable assignee, like a beneficiary of a trust, has a right that relates to A's right, because A is under a duty to B that relates to a specific right held by A.[251] 3–216

---

[250] W. Blackstone, *Commentaries on the Laws of England* (1765), Book 2, Ch.30; J. Story, *Commentaries on Equity Jurisprudence* (Little, Brown, 1884), p.689, para.1040.

[251] See too B. McFarlane, *The Structure of Property Law* (Hart Publishing, 2008) pp.27–29.

Ben McFarlane and Robert Stevens, "The Nature of Equitable Property"

(2010) 4 *Journal of Equity* 1, 7

3–217 For example, if A has a personal right against Z, and makes an equitable assignment of that right in favour of B, B is not regarded as having an equitable property right. Nonetheless, B has acquired a right that is capable of binding C, a party who later acquires a right in relation to A's right against Z. For example, if A goes into bankruptcy, B's right, as an equitable assignee, will bind A's trustee in bankruptcy. This can be explained by analysis B's right as a right against A's right against Z. As there has been no statutory assignment, B has not acquired A's right.

3–218 Whilst there are thus slight differences in the models of equitable assignment proposed by Edelman and Elliott, and Tham, and McFarlane and Stevens, each is consistent with the characteristic role of equity in supplementing, rather than correcting, the common law. On each model, equitable assignment does not contradict the common law position that it is not possible for A to transfer to B A's right to be paid £500 by D; rather, equity controls A's exercise of that entitlement, and does so by imposing a duty on A that relates to A's exercise of that entitlement.

C. Requirements

i. Intention

3–219 The fundamental requirement of equitable assignment is that A (the assignor) must manifest her immediate intention to give B (the assignee) the benefit of A's right against D (the debtor, or obligor). For example, in *William Brandt's Sons & Co v Dunlop Rubber Co Ltd*,[252] A, the seller, told D, the buyer, to pay the price directly to A's bank, B. By mistake, D paid the price to A. B then sued A to recover the debt. A's instruction to D had not used the term "assignment" but it was nonetheless found that A's intention to give B the immediate benefit of the price was clear. Lord Macnaghten stated that:[253]

> ... the document does not, on the face of it, purport to be an assignment nor use the language of an assignment. An equitable assignment does not always take that form. It may be addressed to the debtor. It may be couched in the language of command. It may be a courteous request. It may assume the form of mere permission. The language is immaterial if the meaning is plain. All that is necessary is that the debtor should be given to understand that the debt has been made over by the creditor to some third person.

3–220 Of course, as it is to be expected given that the effect of an equitable assignment is to impose on A a duty which may have consequences for third parties, the intention cannot be a purely private one of A. There is a need for:[254]

> some outward expression by the assignor of his intention to make an immediate disposition of the subject matter of the assignment. It must be possible to identify some act on the assignor's part from which his intention then and there to divest himself – in favour of the assignee – of the right or interest to be assigned, on the terms which have been agreed, can be inferred.

---

252 [1905] A.C. 454 (HL).
253 [1905] A.C. 454 (HL) at 460.
254 *Finlan v Eyton Morris Winfield* [2007] EWHC 914 (Ch) at [33] (Blackburne J), cited with approval by Foxton J in *Serious Fraud Office v Litigation Capital Ltd* [2021] EWHC 1272 (Comm) at [262].

As we will see in Chapter 5,[255] these points as to equitable assignment apply equally to a self-declaration of a trust: it is not necessary for A to use particular words, but there must be a sufficient outwards expression of A's intention to come under a duty to use A's rights for the benefit of B. **3–221**

ii. Identification

For an equitable assignment to occur, it is also necessary for the particular rights of A in relation to which it operates to be clearly identified: "the subject-matter of the assignment should be so described as to be capable of being identified at the time of the alleged assignment.[256] This is to ensure that A, B, D, and any relevant third parties can be clear as to the extent of any duties imposed as a result of the equitable assignment. Again, as we will see in Chapter 5,[257] this requirement applies in the same way to a self-declaration of a trust. **3–222**

iii. A's right must be capable of being the subject matter of an equitable assignment

Before considering some clearly established limits on when equitable assignment is possible, we need first to consider a suggested limit which has not been adopted by English law. There is a view that, if the dealing contemplated by A can be carried out by means of a statutory assignment of A's chose in action,[258] then the form of equitable assignment considered in this Chapter is not possible: if A fails to meet the requirements for the statutory assignment, then equity can assist B only if the rule in *Re Rose* applies,[259] as A has done everything A needs to do to make the statutory assignment, or there is some other grounds for recognising that A holds the chose in action on trust for B. That view has found favour in Australia,[260] and could be supported by the argument that allowing the form of equitable assignment considered in this Chapter to continue to operate would undermine the requirements for statutory assignment. The view has not, however, been accepted in England, where it has instead been said that the introduction of statutory assignment was not intended to restrict the availability of that form of equitable assignment: as Lord Macnaghten put it in *William Brandt's Sons v Dunlop Rubber Co Ltd*:[261] "The statute does not forbid or destroy equitable assignments or impair their efficacy in the slightest degree." On this view, where statutory assignment is possible, A has an additional means of dealing with A's chose in action, but can still choose to deal with that right purely in equity.[262] **3–223**

The first clear limit to consider is that whilst a chose in action can generally be the subject matter of an equitable assignment, it is different from "a mere right of action", i.e. a remedy to enforce a chose in action, such as right to recover damages for breach of contract, or a legal right to recover damages arising out of an assault.[263] This distinction is explained in *Investors Compensation Scheme Ltd v West* **3–224**

---

255 See paras 5–012 to 5–022 and Chapter 7.

256 *Serious Fraud Office v Litigation Capital Ltd* at [260].

257 See paras paras 7–073 to 7–079.

258 The requirements of a statutory assignment are discussed at paras 3–240 to 3–249. For example, statutory assignment is available only where A seeks to give B the benefit of the whole of A's chose in action and so the argument discussed here does not apply if A wishes to give B only part of the benefit of such a right.

259 [1949] Ch. 78: see paras 5–023 to 5–041.

260 See, e.g. *Olsson v Dyson* (1969) 120 C.L.R. 365 and *Corin v Patton* (1990) 169 C.L.R. 540.

261 [1905] A.C. 454 at 461.

262 Support for the English position is provided by e.g. Tham, *Understanding the Law of Assignment* (2019), pp.434–436.

263 *Torkington v Mage* at 433.

Bromwich Building Society,[264] where a claim for rescission of a mortgage was held to not be a chose in action. Lord Hoffman explained:[265]

> a chose in action is property, something capable of being turned into money. *Snell's Equity*[266] defines choses in action as "all personal rights of property which can only be claimed or enforced by action, and not by taking physical possession." . . . what is assignable is the debt or other personal right of property. It is recoverable by action, but what is assigned is the chose, the thing, the debt or damages to which the assignor is entitled. The existence of a remedy or remedies is an essential condition for the existence of the chose in action but that does not mean that the remedies are property in themselves, capable of assignment separately from the chose. So, for example, there may be joint and several liability; a remedy for the recovery of a debt or damages may be available against more than one person. But this does not mean that there is more than one chose in action. The assignee either acquires the right to the money (or part of the money) or he does not. If he does, he necessarily acquires whatever remedies are available to recover the money or the part which has been assigned to him.

3–225 The distinction is important because it is not in general possible to assign a (bare) right of action. An exception exists where the assignee (B) has a genuine and substantial interest in the suit,[267] such as a restitutionary claim for money had and received under an unenforceable loan agreement.[268] An assignee will likely have such an interest when they have taken assignment of the chose itself, as:[269]

> the right to a remedy is an incident of the ownership of the chose. The remedy is not something that is capable of being sold or assigned separately from the right to which it relates. . . . A chose in action can be assigned but not a particular remedy by which that chose can be enforced.

3–226 Second, not all choses in action can be the subject matter of an equitable assignment. In some cases, the right is inherently unassignable as the identity of the person to whom the obligation is owed is an essential aspect of the cause of action.[270] For example, in *Peters v General Accident Fire & Life Assurance Corp Ltd*,[271] rights under a motor insurance policy were personal to the original policyholder and incapable of being assigned to a purchaser of the vehicle in respect of which the policy had been issued. The identity of the insured driver was material to the obligation undertaken by the insurer.

3–227 Further, where a right is created by contract, the parties may expressly or impliedly make the right one which cannot be the subject matter of an equitable assignment. This is the case even if, absent the contractual prohibition, the right is one which could be assigned in equity.

Linden Gardens Trust Ltd v Lenesta Sludge Disposals Ltd

House of Lords, [1994] 1 A.C. 85, 106–108

3–228 One issue raised in the dispute concerned the effect of a contractual prohibition on the assignment of the benefit of a contract between A, an owner of property, and D, who was undertaking building work on the property for A. A attempted to make an assignment to B, and B argued that the contractual prohibition on assignment was ineffective.

---

264 *Investors Compensation Scheme Ltd v West Bromwich Building Society* [1998] 1 W.L.R. 896 (HL).

265 *Investors Compensation Scheme Ltd v West Bromwich Building Society* at 915 (Lord Hoffman).

266 29th edn (Sweet & Maxwell, 1990), p.71.

267 *Ellis v Torrington* [1920] 1 K.B. 399 at 406; *Trendtex Trading Corp v Credit Suisse* [1982] A.C. 679 at 703.

268 As in *Equuscorp Ptd Ltd v Haxton* (2012) 246 C.L.R. 498.

269 *Re GP Aviation Group International Ltd* [2013] EWHC 1447 (Ch); [2014] 1 W.L.R. 166 at [28]. See too *Simpson v Norfolk and Norwich University Hospital NHS Trust* [2011] EWCA Civ 1149 at [13]–[15].

270 *Tolhurst v Associated Portland Cement Manufacturers Ltd* [1902] 2 K.B. 660 at 676–667.

271 *Peters v General Accident Fire & Life Assurance Corp Ltd* [1938] 2 All E.R. 267.

> LORD BROWNE-WILKINSON: "It was submitted that it is normally unlawful as being contrary to public policy to seek to render property inalienable. Since contractual rights are a species of property, it is said that a prohibition against assigning such rights is void as being illegal. This submission faces formidable difficulties both in authority and in principle . . . **3–229**
>
> . . . an attempted assignment of contractual rights in breach of a contractual prohibition is ineffective to transfer such contractual rights . . . If the law were otherwise, it would defeat the legitimate commercial reason for inserting the contractual prohibition, viz., to ensure that the original parties are not brought into direct contractual relations with third parties." **3–230**

As with many judicial discussions of assignment, Lord Browne-Wilkinson's language suggests that an equitable assignment involves a transfer, as it would entail "direct contractual relations" between the assignee, B, and the obligor, D. Nonetheless, even on the model of equitable assignment which we adopt, where A retains A's entitlement against D, but comes under an equitable duty to B in relation to that entitlement, there remain good reasons for protecting D from such effects where there is a non-assignment clause in the contract between A and D. For example, it may be that D has actual or potential claims against A which D would seek to set-off against the debt D owes to A; if, however, an equitable assignment is made to B, and notice of the assignment is given to D, D's ability to set off such claims is then limited.[272] It is worth noting that, even where A's chose in action cannot be assigned in equity, either because of its inherent nature or a contractual prohibition, the courts have recognised that A can create a trust of that chose in action in B's favour.[273] This has depended on the recognition that the declaration of a trust does not have exactly the same effects as an equitable assignment:[274] for example, it seems that the trust would not affect D's ability to set-off claims against A arising under a pre-existing contract with A, even if D later gains notice of the trust. **3–231**

Third, an immediate equitable assignment can be made only where A has an existing chose in action: A cannot immediately deal with a right that A does not yet have. This straightforward rule is sometimes expressed as being that A cannot assign "future property", or in terms of colourful metaphors, but it has a clear logical basis as explained by Windeyer J in the High Court of Australia decision in *Norman v Federal Commissioner of Taxation*:[275] **3–232**

> As it is impossible for anyone to own something that does not exist, it is impossible for anyone to make a present gift of such a thing to another person, however sure he may be that it will come into existence and will then be his to give. He can, of course, promise that when the thing is his he will make it over to the intended donee. But in the meantime he may change his mind and when the time comes refuse to carry out his promise, even though it were by deed. A court of law could not compel him to perform it. A court of equity would not. Courts of equity never had the objections to all agreements about future interests that, until the seventeenth century, were deeply rooted in the common law. Equity did not share the view that such agreements were void on the ground of maintenance. But things not yet in existence could only be the subject of agreement, not of present disposition. And, in relation to promises and agreements, equity has been faithful to its maxim that it does not come to the aid of volunteers. For equity a deed does not make good a want of consideration.

In applying this limit, a key distinction is between A's right to be paid a sum of money by D (or to some other act of performance by D) in the future, which *is* a presently existing chose in action capable **3–233**

---

272 See *Business Computers Ltd v Anglo-African Leasing Ltd* [1977] 1 W.L.R. 578 at 585 (Templeman J): once D has notice of the equitable assignment, "a debt which is neither accrued nor connected may not be set off even though it arises from a contract made before the assignment."

273 See *Don King Productions Inc v Warren* [2000] Ch. 291; *Barbados Trust Co v Bank of Zambia* [2007] EWCA Civ 148.

274 See *Don King Productions Inc v Warren* at 317–319 (Lightman J); *Barbados Trust Co v Bank of Zambia* [2007] EWCA Civ 148 at [43] (Waller LJ); [88] (Rix LJ) and [139] (Hooper LJ).

275 (1963) 109 C.L.R. 9 at 23–25.

of assignment; and the thing that A will receive as a result of D's performance, which is "future property" that cannot be assigned. One metaphor sees the presently existing chose in action as a tree, that in the future bears fruit (the thing received by A upon C's performance). This metaphor was used by Kitto J in the High Court of Australia decision of *Shepherd v Federal Commissioner of Taxation*,[276] which concerned the validity of a partial assignment to B of A's rights under a royalties agreement which obliged D to pay A a sum of money. The quantum of D's obligation was conditional upon how many products were sold by D utilising some technology developed by A. A question arose as to whether A's purported assignment would be ineffective as an attempted assignment of future property, which depended on whether A purported to assign "part of the right to the royalties or of the royalties themselves as after-acquired property".[277] The High Court of Australia[278] held that A had a presently existing right to payment by D, even though the quantum to be paid by D was not fixed from the point at which the right was created, and depended upon D's actions, Kitto J explained:[279]

> It is true also that what [A's] right under the licence agreement would yield in royalties in those years – indeed, whether it would yield any royalties at all in those years – no doubt depended upon contingencies partly within the control of [D]. It was for [D] to decide how many [products], if any, [D] would manufacture in accordance with [A's] inventions and try to sell. Market conditions would then determine how successful [D's] efforts to sell would be. But whatever [D] might do or desire to do, the existence of [A's] contractual right would be unaffected, though the quantum of its product might be. The tree, though not the fruit, existed at the date of the assignment as a proprietary right of [A] of which he was competent to dispose; and he assigned ninety per centum of the tree.

3–234 There can be some complicated questions as to whether and when A's chose in action exists, which will depend upon the application of the particular legal rules relevant to A's chose in action. The question of whether a right under a contract is presently existing or not will depend upon the meanings attributed to the parties' actions in manifesting their intentions, i.e. construction of the contractual terms. In *Shepherd v Federal Commissioner of Taxation*, Owen J dissented on the basis that A intended to assign the royalties as after acquired property, and which meant that on Owen J's findings, there was no assignment of "future property".[280]

3–235 In the context of company dividends, a shareholder's right to dividends does not exist as a presently existing chose in action; that is, as a debt owed by the company, until dividends are declared by the company. Prior to any such declaration by the company, the shareholder has only a mere hope or expectancy that dividends might be declared. Once declared, the shareholder then has a presently existing chose in action, i.e. a right to be paid a sum of money by the company in the future. At this point, the actual dividends, being the sum to be paid by the company, is "future property" and A cannot assign the dividends (as opposed to A's right to be paid dividends) until paid by the company.[281]

3–236 What A *can* do in relation to a chose in action before it exists, is to enter into an agreement with B to assign to B, A's chose in action *when* it exists at some point in the future. Such an agreement can be effective to impose an immediate duty on A, but *only* if B provides some value in return. In contrast, an immediate equitable assignment of an existing chose in action can be made even if B provides nothing in return.

---

[276] *Shepherd v Federal Commissioner of Taxation* (1965) 113 C.L.R. 385 at 396.
[277] *Shepherd v Federal Commissioner of Taxation* at 391 (Barwick CJ).
[278] *Shepherd v Federal Commissioner of Taxation* at 392–393 (Barwick CJ), 395–396 (Kitto J).
[279] *Shepherd v Federal Commissioner of Taxation* at 396.
[280] *Shepherd v Federal Commissioner of Taxation* at 399–400.
[281] As in *Norman v Federal Commissioner of Taxation* (1963) 109 C.L.R. 9.

Norman v Federal Commissioner of Taxation

High Court of Australia, (1963) 109 C.L.R. 9 at 25, 29–30

WINDEYER J.: If we turn from attempted gifts of future property to purported dispositions of it for value, the picture changes completely. The common law objection remains. But in equity a would-be present assignment of something to be acquired in the future is, when made for value, construed as an agreement to assign the thing when it is acquired. A court of equity will ensure that the would-be assignor performs this agreement, his conscience being bound by the consideration. The purported assignee thus gets an equitable interest in the property immediately the legal ownership of it is acquired by the assignor, assuming it to have been sufficiently described to be then identifiable. The prospective interest of the assignee is in the meantime protected by equity. These principles, which now govern assignments for value of property to be acquired in the future, have been developed and established by a line of well-known cases, of which *Holroyd v Marshall*;[282] *Collyer v Isaacs*;[283] *Tailby v Official Receiver*;[284] and *In re Lind; Industrials Finance Syndicate Ltd v Lind*[285] are the most important. "And so", to use Maitland's words, "lawyers easily slipped into the way of saying that inequity one could make an assignment of goods hereafter to be acquired though one could not do so at law. This was a compendious way of putting the matter and was not likely to deceive any equity lawyer"... **3–237**

An agreement to assign will be effective as an equitable assignment if it be for value; for then equity looks on that as done which ought to be done. But this does not mean that there cannot be in equity an actual assignment of a chose in action as distinct from an agreement to assign. I think there can, and that it can be by way of gift. In such a case equity enforces the assignment, not by compelling the assignor to do something, but by refusing to allow him to act in a way inconsistent with what he has done, that is by restraining him from derogating from his gift. His conscience becomes bound, not by value received, but because, as between him and the assignee, his gift was complete. **3–238**

It should be noted again that the application of equitable assignment to future rights of A corresponds exactly to the position in relation to trusts: it is not possible for A to self-declare a trust of a right that A does not yet hold; but, as we will see in Chapter 5,[286] if A makes a binding agreement, for which B provides value, that A will hold a right on trust when A acquires it, that agreement can give rise to a trust as soon as A later acquires the right. **3–239**

iii. Absence of further requirements; comparison with statutory assignment

Having set out the requirements for an equitable assignment of an existing chose in action held by A against D, it is worth noting some things which are *not* required. First, an equitable assignment of an existing chose in action can take place even if no value is provided by B. The requirement of value arises only where B instead seeks to show that A is under a duty to B in relation to a future right of A. **3–240**

Second, the equitable assignment is complete even before any notice of it is given to D. As Cotton LJ stated in *Gorringe v Irwell India Rubber and Gutta Percha Works*: "Though there is no notice to the debtor the title of the assignee is complete as against the assignor." In that case, this meant that, whilst no notice of the assignment had been given to D before A went into liquidation, the equitable assignment to B was still complete, and so A's liquidator was prevented from enforcing A's right against D for the benefit of A's creditors: the right had to be used for the benefit of B alone. **3–241**

Third, no formalities are required for a valid equitable assignment of a legal chose in action, such as D's debt to A. Fourth, an equitable assignment can be made of part only of a chose in action: there is no need for A to assign the whole chose in action to B. **3–242**

---

282 (1862) 10 H.L.C. 191.

283 (1881) 19 Ch.D 342.

284 (1888) 13 App. Cas. 523.

285 (1915) 2 Ch. 345.

286 See paras 5–076 to 5–086.

3-243 These four points all demonstrate the close link between the requirements of an equitable assignment and those of a self-declaration of trust. The final three points also show an important contrast between an equitable assignment of a legal chose in action and a statutory assignment of such a right. Such a statutory assignment does require formality—both writing signed by A and express written notice to D—and it cannot be used to make a partial assignment, as explained by Windeyer J in the High Court of Australia decision in *Norman v Federal Commissioner of Taxation*:[287]

> It has been held that the statutory method of assignment is not available for the assignment of parts of debts or choses in action . . . There were some earlier decisions to the contrary; but they must be taken to be overruled. The later decisions should, I consider, be followed by this Court. They are in accordance with general principle. The conclusion does not depend simply on a literal interpretation of the statutory language and of the phrase "absolute assignment". Before the statute an assignee was permitted to bring his action at law in the name of the assignor when he was seeking to recover a whole debt assigned to him. If a debt had been broken into parts this procedure was not appropriate. A creditor cannot recover a debt piecemeal in a court of law. Therefore, when part of a debt was assigned, proceedings to enforce the assignment had to be brought in a court of equity. And the assignee, not the assignor, would be the plaintiff in the suit. The assignor (the creditor) as legal owner, the debtor and any assignees of other parts of the debt were all necessary parties, so that all the obligations of the debtor and the rights of all persons interested in the fund might be established by the decree. This was the rule of the Chancery Court. It is still the law . . .

3-244 The crucial point is that, where a statutory assignment occurs, it is "effectual in law" to "pass and transfer" to B, from the date of the written notice to D, three things, as set out by s.136(1) of the Law of Property Act 1925:

> (a) the legal right to such debt or thing in action;
> (b) all legal and other remedies for the same; and
> (c) the power to give a good discharge for the same without the concurrence of the assignor [A].

3-245 There is room for debate as to whether s.136 thus effects a transfer of A's right against D, or just of particular powers that go with that right. In any case, however, a statutory assignment does bring D into direct legal relations with B. This is, in our view, its key difference with equitable assignment, and explains why the requirements of statutory assignment offer greater protection to D.

Ben McFarlane and Robert Stevens, "What's Special About Equity? Rights About Rights"

in Dennis Klimchuk et al (eds) *Philosophical Foundations of the Law of Equity* (Oxford University Press, 2020) 191, pp.207–208

3-246 There are at least five differences between equitable and statutory assignment. These differences appear arbitrary, until it is realized that despite sharing a name, the form of equitable assignment is quite different from that of a statutory assignment, and the different form justifies the substantive differences.[288]

3-247 First, a statutory assignment must be made in writing. Formal requirements such as these are common for the transfer of many types of right (eg title to land, equitable rights, intellectual property rights). The only types of right that can be transferred by agreement alone, without any formality or registration requirement, are rights to goods. Equitable assignment requires no formality because it involves no

[287] (1963) 109 C.L.R. 9 at 29–30.

[288] The substantive differences also show the danger of the view, expressed by Gloster LJ in *First Abu Dhabi Bank PJSC v BP Oil International Ltd* [2018] EWCA Civ 14 at [37], that "the equitable assignee is owner of the chose".

transfer. Second, statutory assignment requires that notice (in writing) be given to the debtor. A debtor must know to whom his obligation is owed so that he can perform with respect to the correct party. Again, equitable assignment does not require any notice to be given to the debtor, any more than does the declaration of a trust over a debt, because it involves no transfer of the obligation owed by the debtor.

Third, a statutory assignee can, indeed must, sue in his own name. The right is now vested in him, and so he is the proper party. In contrast, the requirement that an equitable assignee join the assignor, noted above, is not a procedural quirk, but reveals the structure of what has been done. Fourth, the statute requires that the assignment must be absolute. A partial transfer of a debt is not absolute, and cannot constitute a statutory assignment. If a debtor disputes a debt, it would prejudice him if a debt could be split up into the hands of multiple different creditors, each of whose claims he would then have to resist individually. Again, this may be contrasted with an equitable assignment. An equitable assignment involves the transfer of nothing. The debtor is not prejudiced by an assignee creating many different rights in third parties, and so partial "equitable" assignment of a debt, to as many parties as is desired, is unobjectionable. Finally, we cannot transfer what we do not have. A statutory assignment of future property is therefore not possible. By contrast, as an equitable assignment involves the imposition of a duty in relation to a right, a duty can arise immediately and bite in relation to a right when that right is later acquired. **3–248**

The analysis above is consistent with our view that an equitable assignment of a legal chose in action does not change the existence or scope of A's relationship with D, and D remains liable to A, not to B. The effect of the equitable assignment is rather that A is subject to an equitable duty in favour of B, so that B can control how A exercises A's entitlement against D. In other words, the equitable assignment affects a change to the lawfulness of A's actions, as against B, in exercising her chose in action against D; it does not affect the chose in action itself. This is consistent with equity's characteristic function of supplementing, rather than correcting or contradicting, the common law. **3–249**

Questions

(1) "Proprietary estoppel operates as a sword, whereas promissory estoppel operates as a shield." Discuss.

(2) "The doctrine of confidentiality is best regarded as a rule of tort rather than a rule of equity." Do you agree and why does it matter?

(3) "Equitable assignment of a legal chose in action is the same as the transfer of legal title to property, the only difference being that the property being assigned is equitable." Is this the best way of understanding equitable assignment? Why does it matter?

(4) Z owes A debt of £100 repayable on 30 June.

  (a) On 1 April, A says in a conversation to B, "I give you the £100 I will get from Z on 30 June".
  (b) On 2 April, A says in a conversation to D, "I assign to you the debt owed to me from Z, repayable on 30 June".
  (c) On 3 April, A says in a conversation to F, "I assign to you half the debt owed to me from Z, repayable on 30 June".
  (d) On 4 April, A signs a document titled "Assignment of debt to E", stating "I assign to E the debt owed to me by Z of £100, repayable on 30 June", gives the document to E along with Z's contact details.
  (e) On 5 April, E writes to Z directing Z to repay Z's debt to E directly and encloses a copy of the document titled "Assignment of debt to E".

Who can enforce the debt against Z and give good discharge to Z?

(5) One of equity's main functions is understood as being to control A from unconscientiously asserting A's legal entitlement(s). Does "unconscionability" import a wide-ranging judicial discretion to determine the parties' legal relations according to equity in the general sense of fairness?

4

INTRODUCTION TO TRUSTS

1. The Diversity of Trusts

A. Trusts Beyond English Law

Our focus on this book is on the English law of trusts. The English law of trusts, however, should not be confused with the law of trusts more generally. First, other common law jurisdictions may take different views on aspects of the operation of the trust, even if those aspects might be seen as a fundamental part of the English law of trusts. For example, the *Saunders v Vautier* principle,[1] discussed in detail in Chapter 12,[2] allows all of the beneficiaries of a trust, acting together, to call for the trust property to be transferred to them by the trustees: if that power is exercised by the beneficiaries, they then have the trust property itself, and the trust comes to an end. This principle may be seen to be a fundamental aspect of the rights of the beneficiaries, recognising their ultimate right to control of the trust property. It is not, however, part of the law of trusts in jurisdictions in the United States.[3] Similarly, as we will discuss in detail in Chapter 8, the "beneficiary principle" forms a key part of the English law of trusts, and prevents a settlor (S) establishing a trust for a non-charitable purpose,[4] rather than for the benefit of individuals. However, many offshore common law jurisdictions have legislated to reject, or make wide-ranging exceptions to, that principle,[5] and so accommodate within their law of trusts the situation where T holds property subject to a duty, enforced by a party appointed by S, to hold that property for a particular, non-charitable purpose. 4–001

Secondly, many civil law jurisdictions allow parties to set up legal structures that share some important features with the English trust. Such structures may fall within definitions of a trust that are intended to have a supra-jurisdictional application. For example, the Hague Convention on the Law Applicable to Trusts and on their Recognition[6] sets out general rules, agreed to by the jurisdictions that have ratified or acceded to the Convention,[7] as to when an arrangement governed by foreign 4–002

---

1 (1841) 4 Beav. 115.

2 See paras 12–064 to 12–073.

3 See para.12–069 and note the discussion by P. Matthews, "The Comparative Importance of the Rule in *Saunders v Vautier*" (2006) 122 L.Q.R. 266.

4 Trusts for exclusively charitable purposes are permitted under English law: see Chapter 9.

5 See, e.g. Bermuda Trusts (Special Provisions) Act 1989 ss.12A and 12B (extracted at paras 8–056 to 8–057). Other offshore jurisdictions permitting non-charitable purpose trusts include the Cayman Islands; the British Virgin Islands; Jersey; Guernsey; and the Isle of Man.

6 Signed on 1 July 1985, it came into force on 1 January 1992.

7 These jurisdictions include England (as part of the UK), Australia, Canada, Italy, the Netherlands and Switzerland. For the use to which the Convention has been put in Italy, in recognising trusts where the only non-Italian element is the foreign law chosen to govern the trust, see e.g. A. Braun, "The Trust Interno" in D. Hayton (ed.), *The International Trust*, 3rd edn (Jordan, 2011); M. Lupoi, "Trusts in Italy as a Living Comparative Law Laboratory" (2013) 19 *Trusts & Trustees* 302.

law must be recognised and enforced as a trust. The definition of a trust under the Convention is influenced by, but clearly different from, the English concept of the trust: it includes, for example, a trust for a non-charitable purpose. It is nonetheless useful to consider, as an attempt to produce a definition of the trust capable of applying across both common law and civil law jurisdictions.[8]

Hague Convention on the Law Applicable to Trusts and on their Recognition (1985) art.2

4–003 For the purposes of this Convention, the term "trust" refers to the legal relationships created—inter vivos or on death—by a person, the settlor, when assets have been placed under the control of a trustee for the benefit of a beneficiary or for a specified purpose.

A trust has the following characteristics—

(a) the assets constitute a separate fund and are not a part of the trustee's own estate;
(b) title to the trust assets stands in the name of the trustee or in the name of another person on behalf of the trustee;
(c) the trustee has the power and the duty, in respect of which he is accountable, to manage, employ or dispose of the assets in accordance with the terms of the trust and the special duties imposed upon him by law.

The reservation by the settlor of certain rights and powers, and the fact that the trustee may himself have rights as a beneficiary, are not necessarily inconsistent with the existence of a trust.

B. Diversity Within English Law

4–004 We have seen that English law has no monopoly on the trust concept. There is also diversity as to the nature of a trust even within English law. Certainly, judges and commentators have generally been reluctant to provide a comprehensive definition of the trust.[9] As David Hayton has stated:[10]

> It is universally acknowledged that, due to the inductive development of the trust, there is no true or conclusive definition of a trust that can enable one to determine whether or not certain legal relationships in particular circumstances give rise to a trust rather than some other legal concept. Instead, one can only look at certain core characteristics that reflect the rules that distinguish trusts from other legal concepts.

4–005 The difficulty of producing a neat definition of a trust should not be seen as a weakness in the trust concept, but rather as a product of its great practical utility and the diverse range of its applications. Indeed, it is worth noting the exact words used by Maitland when praising the trust:[11]

> If we were asked what is the greatest and most distinctive achievement performed by Englishmen in the field of jurisprudence I cannot think that we should have any better answer to give than this, namely, the development from century to century of the trust idea.

---

8 Note however that the definition adopted has been criticised as "shapeless" owing to its being divorced from the principles of any specific legal system: see, e.g. M. Lupoi, "The Shapeless Trust" (1995) T. & T. 15, 15: "Before the Hague Convention you would know a trust when you met one. That is no longer so."

9 Even when attempts have been made to provide a definition, they have generally been prefaced with a disclaimer: see, e.g. *Re Scott* [1948] S.A.S.R. 193 at 196: "No definition of a 'trust' seems to have been accepted as comprehensive and exact"; A. Scott and W. Fratcher, *The Law of Trusts*, 4th edn (Little, Brown and Company, 1989), para.2.3: "All that one can properly attempt to do is to give such a description of a legal concept that others will know in a general way what one is talking about."

10 D. Hayton, "'Trusts' in Private International Law" (2014) 366 *Recueil des Cours* 17, 17.

11 F. Maitland, *Selected Historical Essays* (Cambridge University Press, 1936), p.129.

Maitland's praise is thus not for the invention of the trust, but rather for its *development*. This development means that, even within English law itself, there is diversity over time as the trust concept has been adapted, often to suit the changing desires of parties wishing to set up a trust. The courts have also developed the law relating to when a trust can arise by operation of law, and this "flexibility of equity" was said, by Lady Arden in *Prickly Bay Waterside Ltd v British American Insurance Co Ltd*,[12] to make: **4–006**

> an important and beneficial contribution to the legal system of the jurisdiction in question because it enables equity to respond to the need for different sorts of transactions, and also because in that way it contributes to the development of society and to the growth of its economy.

Nonetheless, as long as these caveats are kept in mind, the following may provide a helpful working model of the trust. **4–007**

> *Underhill and Hayton: Law Relating to Trusts and Trustees*
>
> P. Matthews et al (eds), 22nd edn (Sweet and Maxwell, 2022), Article 1.1
>
> A trust is an equitable obligation binding a person (called a trustee) to deal with property (called trust property) that is owned and controlled by him as a discrete fund, segregated from his personal estate, to carry out particular purposes, or (more often) for the benefit of particular persons (called beneficiaries), of whom the trustee may himself be one, and any one of whom may enforce the obligation. Trusts are often created intentionally by legally valid declarations of trust by property owners, when they are called express trusts; but they can also be created by operation of law . . . **4–008**

i. The Modern Express Trust

As we noted in Chapter 1[13] and Chapter 3,[14] the ability to set up an express trust confers a valuable, autonomy-enhancing power[15] on a holder of property. The modern range of options provided by English law to a party setting up a trust (referred to as S, for settlor) can be seen by considering the discretionary trust.[16] A precedent used in the creation of such a trust is set out in Chapter 10.[17] The key feature of such a trust is that, rather than being instructed simply to hold the property for the benefit of specific, named beneficiaries, the trustees are given a choice either as to the extent of the benefit to be received by each beneficiary or, more usually, as to who amongst a class of possible beneficiaries will receive any of the trust property. Whilst such trusts are far from being a purely modern creation, their current popularity depends on the fact that, from the 1970s onwards, the courts have accepted that S can create a valid trust which confers powers on T to choose who, amongst a potentially very wide class of possible people, might benefit from distributions of the property held on trust. **4–009**

In such a modern trust S may, for example, transfer property to T[18] to hold on trust for a named charity, such as the Red Cross, but subject to a power held by T to distribute any or all of the trust **4–010**

---

12 [2022] UKPC 8 at [32].
13 See para.1–079.
14 See para.3–190.
15 See, e.g. B. McFarlane, "Equity" in A. Gold et al (eds), *The Oxford Handbook of the New Private Law* (Oxford University Press, 2020); S. Agnew and S. Douglas, "Self-Declarations of Trust" (2019) 135 L.Q.R. 67, 85–87; H. Dagan and I. Samet, "Express Trust: The Dark Horse of the Liberal Property Regime" in S. Degeling et al (eds), *Philosophical Foundations of the Law of Express Trusts* (Oxford University Press, forthcoming).
16 See further paras 7–124ff.
17 See paras 10–084ff.
18 In practice, there will often be more than one trustee, but we will refer to "T" in the singular for ease of exposition.

property to anyone other than certain named individuals. As we will see in Chapter 7,[19] it is possible for S to confer such a wide power on T. Usually, in such a case, S's intention is that T will, within the period permitted by the trust, distribute all the trust property, so that the Red Cross will, in the end, receive nothing. Hence the parties benefitting from the trust in practice will be those people chosen by T to receive distributions of the trust property in the exercise of T's discretionary powers. S can also retain some control over T's exercise of those powers: first, of course, in the choice of the particular trustees; second by making any exercise of the power by T subject to the consent of another party; and third, by providing T with a document, often referred to as a "letter of wishes" which sets out how S would like T to exercise the power of distribution.[20] Even if, as is likely, the letter does not form part of the terms of the trust,[21] so that T has no legal duty to comply with it, T has a duty to take the wishes of S into account when exercising the discretionary power.[22]

4-011 Such a modern trust clearly differs in important respects from the simple example introduced above, where S transfers property to T to hold for the benefit of B. Indeed, S may have no real intention to benefit the party fulfilling the role of beneficiary in the modern trust: the Red Cross in our example. As a result, the compatibility of such a trust with traditional rules of trusts law has been questioned.[23] Certainly, there is an important question, which we will consider at a number of points in this book, as to just how much flexibility equity can legitimately allow parties, if such parties want to gain all the advantages that flow from setting up a trust.

4-012 Whatever one's view as to the precise boundaries of the trust concept, the differences between the possible types of trust, caused by the development of the trust concept over time, mean that, in Hackney's words:[24]

> One of the greatest errors in creative thinking in trust law is to begin unguardedly, 'This is a trust therefore. . .' and to proceed to attribute to it the characteristics of the express private institutional trust. There are many different kinds of trust, the only common feature of which may be that they involve, or once involved, identifiable property and are subject to a legal regime originating solely in Equity. Perhaps it would better reflect the origin of the jurisdiction to say that there are many different kinds of trustee, ranging from the willing manager to the entrapped villain.

4-013 Two observations may be made to support Hackney's point in this passage. First, judges have suggested that, even when dealing simply with what Hackney calls the "express private institutional trust", where S transfers property to T to hold on trust for beneficiaries, different rules may have to

---

19 See paras 7–102ff, discussing *Re Hay's S.T.* [1982] 1 W.L.R. 202.

20 For analysis of the role of a letter of wishes, see, e.g. *Breakspear v Ackland* [2008] EWHC 220 (Ch); [2009] Ch. 32; D. Hayton, "English Fiduciary Standards and Trusts Law" (1999) 32 *Vanderbilt Journal of Transnational Law* 555, 573–577. And note the discussion at paras 10–077 to 10–078.

21 There are three main reasons why S would choose to express her intentions in a letter of wishes rather than through the terms of the trust. First, S's wishes may be of a general and somewhat vague nature and therefore lack the certainty required of a binding trust duty: see para.7–005ff. Second, if the wishes were to be made part of the trust, it might then seem that S is the true beneficiary of the trust, which would make the trust assets potentially available to creditors of S, or S's spouse in ancillary relief proceedings, and could also allow the value of those assets to be taken into account when S's tax liability is assessed. Third, whilst a court, on application by a beneficiary of a trust, or even by a party likely to receive a benefit through the exercise of a power by T, is likely to order disclosure to that party of a document setting out the terms of the trust, it is more likely to find that a letter of wishes was intended by S to be, and should remain, confidential (see *Breakspear v Ackland* [2008] EWHC 220 (Ch); [2009] Ch. 32 at [66]) and so S can thus express preferences in a wish letter without allowing, for example, other family members to discover those wishes.

22 See *Pitt v Holt* [2013] UKSC 26; [2013] 2 A.C. 108 at [66] per Lord Walker: "[S's] wishes are always a material consideration in the exercise of fiduciary discretions."

23 See, e.g. L. Smith, "Massively Discretionary Trusts" (2017) 70 C.L.P. 17; H. Dagan and I. Samet, "What is Wrong with Massively Discretionary Trusts", *Law Quarterly Review*, forthcoming.

24 J. Hackney, *Understanding Equity and Trusts* (Fontana, 1987), p.28.

be applied in different contexts. On this view, for example, a "traditional trust" which operates to "govern the ownership-management of property for a group of potential beneficiaries over a lengthy number of years"[25] may be distinguished from a "commercial trust" where "the trustee's duties are likely to be closely defined and may be of limited duration".[26] So, even if the basic equitable principles applicable, for example, to a breach of the duty of due administration by the trustee, extend to each of those cases, the different context of the trusteeship may have a bearing on the relief provided by the court in the event of such a breach. Moreover, whilst employers' pension schemes operate through the mechanism of a trust, it would be surprising if the rights of employees who are the beneficiaries of such a trust and have made contributions to the pension scheme were to be treated in exactly the same way as those of beneficiaries who have given no value in return for their rights under the trust and are simply recipients of the bounty of S.[27]

ii. Constructive and Resulting Trusts

The second observation on Hackney's point relates to his reference to the "many different kinds of trustee, ranging from the willing manager to the entrapped villain". The former may, for example, be a trust corporation, paid remuneration from the trust funds in return for exercising its investment and management skills in relation to those funds.[28] The trust in such a case is an *express trust*: it arises because S successfully exercised her power to set up a trust.[29] There are also other forms of trust. These non-express trusts arise for some reason other than S's successful exercise of a power to set up a trust. They are instead imposed by operation of law, and are generally split into two groups: *constructive trusts* and *resulting trusts*.[30] **4–014**

The exact dividing line between a constructive trust and a resulting trust is unclear,[31] but also relatively unimportant. The important divide is between express trusts on the one hand and constructive and resulting trusts on the other. This is because, whenever a trust is non-express and thus imposed by law, we need to examine carefully why the trust has arisen. Such trusts are imposed to protect a claimant (the beneficiary of the constructive or resulting trust) but it is also necessary to ask why that protection takes the form of a trust, rather than of, for example, a simple personal right for the claimant to be paid money by the defendant. This question is addressed in detail in Chapters 16 and 17. **4–015**

This does not mean, however, that constructive and resulting trusts can be neatly parcelled off from express trusts. On the contrary, we will encounter both resulting and constructive trusts during our **4–016**

---

25 *A.I.B. Group (UK) Plc v Mark Redler & Co Solicitors* [2014] UKSC 58; [2015] A.C. 1503 at [67], per Lord Toulson.

26 *A.I.B. Group (UK) Plc v Mark Redler & Co Solicitors* [2014] UKSC 58; [2015] A.C. 1503 at [70]. This case is discussed in detail at paras 13–058 to 13–085.

27 See, e.g. *Scully v Coley* [2009] UKPC 29 at [29].

28 As noted by Lord Walker in *Pitt v Holt* [2013] UKSC 26; [2013] 2 A.C. 108 at [66], offshore trusts are "usually run by corporate trustees whose officers and staff (especially if they change with any frequency) may know relatively little about the settlor, and even less about the settlor's family". S trusts such a trustee to be professional in carrying out its role; she does not trust it in the same way one might trust a friend.

29 Although as we will see at paras 4–026 to 4–028, the assent of the trustee(s) is required for the intended trust to be fully established, and it is also possible for beneficiaries to disclaim their interests under the trust.

30 Note that "statutory trusts" may comprise a further group of trusts imposed by law, where the trust is imposed by operation of statute: see, e.g. Administration of Estates Act 1925 s.33. The term "implied trusts" is often seen in legislative provisions which also apply to constructive and resulting trusts (see, e.g. Law of Property Act 1925 s.53(2): see para.6–027) but its meaning is unclear (it is often used to refer to both resulting and constructive trusts: see, e.g. *Cowcher v Cowcher* [1972] 1 W.L.R. 425 at 430) and such trusts are therefore of little independent significance.

31 See, e.g. *Ali v Dinc* [2020] EWHC 3055 (Ch) at [229], where Sarah Worthington QC (Hon) (sitting as a Deputy High Court Judge) notes that "there seems to be no compelling consistency in terminology" in relation to the constructive and resulting trust labels. See too paras 16–046 to 16–053 and 17–214 to 17–215.

examination, in Chapters 5–15, of express trusts. For example, if S transfers property to T intending that T hold it on a particular trust, but the trust fails as S has not properly exercised her power to set up an express trust, the basic position is that T will then hold that property on a resulting trust for S.[32] Similarly, if S has made a promise to B that, if and when she receives particular property, she will set up a trust of that property for B, and B has provided value for that promise, a constructive trust may arise as soon as S receives that property, providing B with protection even if S does not comply with the promise to set up an express trust.[33]

4–017 Moreover, where an express trust has been set up, a key feature of B's right under that trust is that it is capable of binding C, a third party who acquires the trust property as a result of an unauthorised transfer by T. In such a case, it has been said that the trust that binds C is a constructive trust.[34] So, even if B's right arises under an express trust, B may need to rely on a constructive trust to assert that right against C.

4–018 It has therefore been argued that understanding constructive and resulting trusts is crucial to understanding the practical operation of rules relating to express trusts, and, indeed, to understanding the conceptual foundations of the trust in English law.[35] At the very least, it is important not to overlook trusts imposed by law when attempting to make general statements about the English law of trusts.

4–019 For example, it is easy to regard the creation of a trust by a settlor as similar, for example, to the creation of a lease by a party with a freehold of land: in each case, a party holding property allocates the benefit of that property in particular ways. On such a model, it might then seem that a trust involves fragmentation of the property initially held outright by the settlor. Certainly, that view of the trust seems to have informed the doubts held in some civil law jurisdictions as to the acceptability of the trust, as such systems often have a clear antipathy to the fragmentation of property.[36] Moreover, on that model, trusts imposed by law may seem inherently dubious, as involving the courts exercising a power to redistribute the defendant's property:[37] after all, there is no concept, for example, of constructive leases. It is, however, possible to accept that a settlor can use a trust to allocate the benefit of property without also accepting that the initial right held by the settlor is thereby fragmented. If, for example, S transfers property to T to hold on trust for B, it is the underlying property right that is transferred and held on trust, and that right remains intact. It is not split up, but is rather encumbered by the terms of the trust, and the duties they impose on T.[38] As stated by Bell, Keane, Nettle and Edelman JJ in *Commissioner of State Revenue v Rojoda Pty Ltd*:[39] "it is fundamental that the creation of a trust involves the creation of new equitable obligations, which are 'annexed to the

---

32 See paras 16–059ff.

33 See paras 5–076 to 5–086 and 17–072 to 17–076.

34 See *Independent Trustee Services Ltd v GP Noble Trustees Ltd* [2013] Ch. 91 at [77]–[79] per Lloyd LJ: see further para.17–216. It has similarly been said that, where T uses the trust property in an unauthorised way and acquires a new asset, that asset will be held by T on constructive trust for B: *Re EVTR* [1987] B.C.L.C. 646 at 651 per Dillon LJ: see further paras 15–077 to 15–084.

35 See, e.g. S. Dix (trans.), M. Lupoi, *Trusts: A Comparative Study* (Cambridge University Press, 2000), Ch.2, arguing that constructive and resulting trusts are at "the heart of the trust"; B. McFarlane, "The Centrality of Constructive and Resulting Trusts" in C. Mitchell (ed.), *Constructive and Resulting Trusts* (Hart Publishing, 2010).

36 As discussed by P. Matthews, "The Compatibility of the Trust with the Civil Law Notion of Property" in L. Smith (ed.), *The Worlds of the Trust* (Cambridge University Press, 2013), pp.313–340.

37 There is certainly a general view in English law that the courts can redistribute property rights only if given a statutory power to do so: it is seen, for example, in the antipathy of the English courts to the "remedial constructive trust": see para.17–005.

38 This point is made by, e.g. P. Matthews, "The Compatibility of the Trust with the Civil Law Notion of Property" in *The Worlds of the Trust* (2013). See further paras 12–081 to 12–082.

39 [2020] HCA 7; [2020] 268 C.L.R. 281 at [44] (Bell, Keane, Nettle and Edelman JJ).

trust property'[40] or 'engrafted'[41] or 'impressed upon it'[42]." This is consistent with the supplementary nature of equity, as discussed in Chapter 1:[43] equity does not contradict the common law position that T holds the right, it rather imposes limits on how T may now use that right. The same occurs when a constructive or resulting trust is recognised: the court does not deny that the defendant has the particular right in question; it simply finds that, as a result of her conduct, the defendant came under a duty to hold that right for the benefit of the claimant.

2. The Parties to a Trust

With the warnings given above as to the diversity of trusts firmly in mind, it is possible to describe some of the basic features of the English trust, by examining the positions of the parties generally involved in the creation or operation of a trust. We will set out the basic roles played by each party and also consider the influence of each on the operation of a trust. **4–020**

A. The Settlor

i. Basic Role

It should first be noted that a trust can arise without a settlor: this is the case where a trust arises by operation of law.[44] An express trust does however require a settlor, as such a trust arises as a result of the settlor's successful exercise of a power to set up a trust. In Chapters 5 to 9 we will consider the rules that determine whether such a power has been successfully exercised. A settlor's power to set up a trust generally stems from the fact that the settlor (S) holds property outright. In such a case, S can then create a trust in one of two ways. The first entails a transfer to the trustee (T): S transfers the property to T, but subject to the terms of a trust in favour of the beneficiary (B).[45] The second method, recognised by the courts long after the first method,[46] consists of a self-declaration of trust: S becomes a trustee herself, retaining her right to the property, but declaring that she now holds that right on trust for B. In each case, then, S has created a situation where a party, the trustee, has legal entitlements, but is now subject to control, by equitable rules, as to how those entitlements may be exercised. It is also possible for a party to have the power to set up a trust of particular property even if she is not herself free to use that property for her own benefit. For example, there are many trusts in which the trustees are given, by the terms of the initial trust, a power to create new trusts over the trust property: if such a power is exercised, an express trust is created, even though the trustees exercising that power did not hold the property outright, but rather held it on the terms of the initial trust. **4–021**

---

40 *DKLR Holding Co (No.2) Ltd v Commissioner of Stamp Duties* [1980] 1 N.S.W.L.R. 510 at 519. See also Maitland, *Equity: also The Forms of Action at Common Law* (1929), pp.17–18; Maitland, *Equity: A Courts of Lectures*, 2nd edn (rev) (1936) p.17. *DKLR Holding Co (No.2) Ltd v Commissioner of Stamp Duties* (1982) 149 C.L.R. 431 at 474 per Brennan J and *Re Transphere Pty Ltd* (1986) 5 N.S.W.L.R. 309 at 311 per McLelland J.

41 *Re Transphere Pty Ltd* (1986) 5 N.S.W.L.R. 309 at 311.

42 *DKLR Holding Co (No.2) Ltd v Commissioner of Stamp Duties* (1982) 149 C.L.R. 431 at 474.

43 See paras 1–061 to 1–064.

44 See para.4–014.

45 See, e.g. the example discussed at para.4–010. As we discuss in Chapter 9, it is also possible for S to create a charitable trust by transferring property to T to hold for a particular charitable purpose, but for ease of exposition we will focus here on the creation of a private trust.

46 The validity of a gratuitous self-declaration of trust was not recognised until 1811: *Ex p. Pye* (1811) 18 Ves. Jun. 140.

4-022 S's power to set up a trust can be successfully exercised even if S does not invoke it by expressly stating that the arrangement she wishes to set up is a trust. As stated by Aikens LJ in *Williams v Central Bank of Nigeria*:[47]

> Put very generally, in English law an express trust is created when a person (the settlor) directs that certain identified property (the trust property) will be held either by him or others (as trustees) under a legal obligation which binds the trustees to deal with that property, which is owned by them as a separate fund, for the benefit of another (the beneficiary) who has an equitable proprietary interest in the trust property and its fruits from the moment that the trust is created.[48] Thus, if it is intended that a document is to create an express trust, it is sufficient that it demonstrates with reasonable certainty: (a) that there is an intent to create a trust; (b) that the trust property is intended to be kept separately from other property of the trustee; (c) the identity of the trust property; (d) the person(s) intended to be beneficiary(ies); and (e) the purpose of the trust and that it is administratively workable.[49]

ii. The Creation of the Trust

4-023 As argued in the following extract, care should be taken not to exaggerate the role of the settlor in the creation of an express trust.

Y.K. Liew and C. Mitchell, "The Creation of Express Trusts"

(2017) 11 Journal of Equity 133, 133–134

4-024 . . . it is only partly true to say, as Charles Rickett has said,[50] that the settlor's intention "brings the trust into being" and it is actively misleading to say, as he has also said, that the intention to which an express trust responds is a "unilateral one".[51] We agree with Rickett that settlors need not form an agreement with the beneficiaries and trustees, with the consensual meeting of minds that an agreement entails.[52] However, we consider that these parties must all consent to the creation of the trust, either by agreement or by independent action,[53] and since a settlor cannot create all the rights which typically vest in the beneficiaries of an express trust without the consent of the trustee and beneficiaries, the intentions which enliven these rights are not "unilateral" but "multilateral". We therefore prefer Rickett's own previous statement that the "intention to be established must be that of both the settlor and the trustee",[54] though we would add that the beneficiaries' consent in also required.

4-025 The need for the consent of the trustee is often hidden: it will necessarily be present, of course, where S declares that she holds on trust; and where S instead sets up a trust by means of transferring the trust property to T, S will generally have obtained the consent of T to act as

---

47 [2013] Q.B. 499 at [37]. The court was considering a procedural aspect of the substantive dispute eventually determined by the Supreme Court: [2014] A.C. 1189.

48 See *Underhill & Hayton: Law of Trusts and Trustees* (18th edn, 2010), paras 1.1 and 3.1. There are of course other ways of creating express trusts with which we are not concerned.

49 See *Underhill & Hayton: Law of Trusts and Trustees* (18th edn, 2010), para.7.1.

50 C. Rickett, "Instrumentalism in the Law of Truss: The Disturbing Case of the Constructive Trust Upon an Express Trust" (2016) 47 V.U.W.L.R. 463, 466.

51 ibid.

52 The distinction we make here between agreement and consent has also been made by Lionel Smith in work on fiduciary obligations: L. Smith, "Contract, Consent, and Fiduciary Relationships" in P. Miller and A. Gold (eds) *Contract, Status, and Fiduciary Law* (OUP, 2016).

53 C. Rickett, "The Classification of Trusts" (1999) 18 N.Z.U.L.R. 305, 310. See too P. Birks, *Unjust Enrichment* (2nd edn, OUP, 2005), p.28: "[express] trusts arise from declarations of trust accepted by the trustee."

54 C. Rickett, "Instrumentalism in the Law of Truss: The Disturbing Case of the Constructive Trust Upon an Express Trust" (2016) 47 V.U.W.L.R. 463, 466.

trustee.[55] Further, where S transfers property to T and S's objective intention is that T should hold on trust, then this will have some effect, even if T declines to act as trustee. This is captured in the idea that "a trust will not fail for want of a trustee". So, the trust is "sufficiently created" as to give B, the intended beneficiary, important protection: T of course cannot refuse the duties of trustee and keep the property for T's own benefit,[56] so B is able to bring a claim preventing T from doing so. Such a claim can also be brought against a third party receiving the property from T.[57] To that extent, despite T's lack of consent to act as trustee, the trust property is "ring-fenced" and B has "proprietary" protection. If T knows of the trust, but has not consented to act as trustee, then "a limited range of duties are imposed on [T] for as long as he has the [property], the point of which is to preserve the trust property and stop him from acting against the beneficiaries' interests".[58] A central aim of these rules is to hold things in place until a willing trustee is found, who will accept all the terms of the trust which S hopes to set up.

As the trust involves significant duties on T, such as the duty of due administration,[59] it is no surprise that T "cannot be compelled to accept the burdens of . . . trusteeship against his or her will."[60] Those full-blown trust duties can therefore only arise once T has consented. Once T has consented, the duties are of course binding and so cannot be unilaterally ended by T. **4–026**

A beneficiary of a trust, B, will acquire rights and powers (these can be referred to as B's "equitable interest") rather than duties and so, it seems, there is no requirement for B to consent before B's equitable interest arises.[61] However, as is the case with a gift, B may in fact prefer *not* to have such rights and powers and so B must have the option of disclaiming (i.e. refusing) the equitable interest which S intends to confer on B.[62] As stated by Lord Lindley in *Hardoon v Belilios*:[63] "No one can be made the beneficial owner of [property] against his will. Any attempt to make him so can be defeated by disclaimer." A disclaimer is not possible if B has already accepted B's interest under the trust:[64] in such a case, B can dispose of that equitable interest to a third party, or instead can give it up by releasing it.[65] As explained by HHJ Paul Matthews (sitting as a Judge of the High Court) in *Smith v Michelmores Trust Corp Ltd*:[66] "A release is a giving up of the interest which the beneficiary had,[67] whereas a disclaimer is the avoidance of the interest in the first place.[68]" **4–027**

---

55 Y.K. Liew and C. Mitchell, "The Creation of Express Trusts" (2017) 11 J. Eq. 133, 135. The analysis here at paras 4–025 to 4–027 is based on that of Liew and Mitchell.

56 See e.g. *Re Birchall* (1889) 40 Ch. D. 436.

57 The third party is not bound if she is a bona fide purchaser for value without notice of B's rights: see further para.15–164ff.

58 Y.K. Liew and C. Mitchell, "The Creation of Express Trusts" (2017) 11 J. Eq. 133, 137.

59 See paras 3–143 to 3–192 and 11–024 to 11–029.

60 *Scarpuzza v Scarpuzza* [2011] WASC 65 at [47].

61 See e.g. *Standing v Bowring* (1886) 31 Ch. D. 282 at 288 and 290; *re Stratton's Disclaimer* [1958] Ch. 42 (CA) at 54 (Jenkins LJ); *Commissioner of Taxation v Carter* [2022] HCA 10 at [33]–[48] (Edelman J). It can alternatively be said that B's assent is required, but is assumed if there is no evidence of a disclaimer: see e.g. *Smith v Michelmore Trust Corp Ltd* [2021] EWHC 1425 (Ch) at [71]; *Commissioner of Taxation v Carter* [2022] HCA 10 at [27]–[31] (Gageler, Gordon, Steward and Gleeson JJ).

62 See e.g. *Naas v Westminster Bank Ltd* [1940] A.C. 366.

63 [1901] A.C. 118 (PC) at 123.

64 See e.g. *Bence v Gilpin* (1868) L.R. 3 Exch. 76 at 81. The position has been changed by statute in some jurisdictions: see e.g. Trusts (Jersey) Law 1984 art.10A.

65 See e.g. *re Gulbenkian's Settlments* (No.2) [1970] Ch. 408 at 415, 418.

66 [2021] EWHC 1425 (Ch) at [69].

67 *Re Guinness's Settlement* [1966] 1 W.L.R. 1355.

68 *Re Paradise Motor Co Ltd* [1968] 1 W.L.R. 1125 at 1143.

4-028 A valid disclaimer will have retrospective effect,[69] and so B will be treated as if B's equitable interest never arose. This does not mean, however, that T is then free to use the property for T's own benefit, as that would clearly be inconsistent with the terms on which T acquired the property. As a result, T will then hold the property on trust for S (or, if S has died, S's estate):[70] this is an example of a resulting trust, a form of trust imposed by law.

iii. The Need for Trust Property

4-029 Care should also be taken with the requirement for trust property. The standard way of describing a trust is to refer to the "property" held by the trustee, and we will use that formulation throughout this book. However, as we saw in Chapter 1, a characteristic focus of equity is on the control of legal entitlements, and the entitlements held on trust need not count as "property" for all purposes. For example, it is clear that, where S has a personal right against X, such as the personal right against a bank constituted by S's bank account, S can set up a trust of that personal right. The trust need not relate to any physical thing. As once stated by Lord Shaw:[71]

> The scope of the trusts recognised in equity is unlimited. There can be a trust of a chattel or of a chose in action, or of a right or obligation[72] under an ordinary legal contract, just as much as a trust of land.

4-030 Indeed, in many trusts, the initial trust property consists simply of a bank account in the name of the trustees. As Briggs J noted in *Re Lehman Brothers (International) Europe*:[73]

> [N]o-one doubts the beneficial interest of clients in a solicitor's client account. Yet the subject matter of that fund consists entirely of the solicitor's purely personal rights as a customer of the client account bank or banks.

4-031 Further, it has also been accepted that S can set up a trust of a non-assignable personal right. In *Don King Productions Inc v Warren*,[74] for example, the Court of Appeal recognised that a trust could arise in relation to S's contractual rights under contracts for the promotion and management of boxers. Those contracts involved the conferral of personal services and many of them in any case contained a term preventing S from assigning the benefit of the contract.[75] The key point seems to be that if S declares that she holds such a right on trust for B, no transfer of that right occurs:[76] S retains the right, but comes under a duty to B to deal with that right for B's benefit.[77] The declaration of trust

---

69 *Jervis v Wolferstan* (1874) L.R. 18 Eq. 18. See too *Commissioner of Taxation v Carter* [2022] HCA 10 at [48], where Edelman J makes the important point that "when considering questions about the retrospective effects of a disclaimer, whether of rights at common law or in equity, it is always necessary to appreciate why the question is being asked."

70 See *Jervis v Wolferstan* (1874) L.R. 18 Eq. 18.

71 *Lord Strathcona Steamship Co Ltd v Dominion Coal Co Ltd* [1926] A.C. 108 at 124.

72 It is however difficult to see how an obligation can be held on trust: see para.4-059.

73 [2010] EWHC 2914 at [241]. The decision of Briggs J was affirmed on appeal: [2011] EWCA Civ 1544.

74 [2000] Ch. 291.

75 See too *Barbados Trust Co Ltd v Bank of Zambia* [2007] EWCA Civ 148; [2007] 2 All E.R. (Comm) 445.

76 See e.g. *Commissioner of State Revenue v Rojoda Pty Ltd* [2020] HCA 7; [2020] 268 C.L.R. 281 at [44] (Bell, Keane, Nettle and Edelman JJ).

77 It is important to note that, as we saw at paras 3-203 to 3-210, on one view, an equitable assignment of a legal chose in action does not involve a transfer of that chose in action. On that view, further differences between an equitable assignment and a declaration of trust must be identified, if it is to make sense, in a case where a party has a non-assignable chose in action, for the law to allow the latter but not the former: see para.3-215.

does not, therefore, allow B to bring any direct claim against the other party to S's contract and, to that extent, is not inconsistent with the purpose behind the non-assignment clause.

A legal entitlement (such as a bank account, or a non-assignable contractual right) can thus be the subject matter of a trust even if that legal entitlement, for many purposes, would not count as "property". If that point is borne in mind, referring to the "trust property" causes no harm.[78] However, it seems that the point is not infrequently overlooked.[79] For example, in each of *AA v Persons Unknown*[80] and *Ruscoe and Moore v Cryptopia Ltd*,[81] a court had to consider if particular digital assets, such as cryptocurrencies, were capable of being held on trust. To do so, each court relied on the approach adopted by Lord Wilberforce, in *National Provincial Bank v Ainsworth*,[82] when deciding if Mrs Ainsworth's "deserted wife's equity" counted as "property". However, in that case, the House of Lords was dealing with whether such a right counts as property in the specific sense of being capable of binding a third party who had acquired a right in the land after Mrs Ainsworth's right had arisen: this is clear both from the context of the case, and the requirements formulated by Lord Wilberforce.[83] Clearly, then, there is no need for a legal entitlement to pass that test before it can be held on trust: a bank account, for example, would not pass the *Ainsworth* test, as the customer's right binds only the bank, and not third parties; yet a bank account can clearly be held on trust. **4–032**

As a result, we agree with the suggestion that it is more accurate to think of the subject matter of the trust as a right, rather than as property.[84] After all, even in a case where the property held on trust is a physical thing, such as land, it is the trustees' estate in land (their rights and powers in relation to the land) that are held on trust, and not the land itself.[85] Certainly, it would be unfortunate if "the flexibility of equity" were limited by adopting an unduly narrow view of what legal entitlements can be held on trust, based on applying definitions of "property" developed in quite different contexts.[86] **4–033**

iv. Influence on the Operation of the Trust

The basic position in English law is that, after having set up a trust, S "drops out of the picture".[87] So, if S transfers property to T to hold on trust for B then, simply in her capacity as settlor, S has no rights against T, and no duties to B. If S wishes to have any such rights, S must reserve them expressly under the terms of the trust: for example, where the trust assets include shares in a family company, S might **4–034**

---

78 Although note care is also needed when considering the nature of a beneficiary's rights under a trust: see Chapter 12.

79 See e.g. B. McFarlane, "Trusts, Property, and Rights" in S. Degeling et al (eds) *Philosophical Foundations of The Law of Express Trusts* (Oxford University Press, forthcoming). See too B. McFarlane, "The Persistence of Equity: Lessons from the Trust" (Inaugural Lecture, Oxford, 2022): recording available at: *https://www.youtube.com/watch?v=TNUQ96ik2tQ*.

80 [2019] EWHC 3556 (Comm).

81 [2020] NZHC 728. See too *B2C2 Ltd v Quoine PTC Ltd* [2019] SGHC (I) 3 at [142] (reversed on appeal: [2020] SGCA (I) 2).

82 [1965] A.C. 1175 at 1248.

83 Two of the requirements are whether the right in question is "identifiable by third parties" and "capable in its nature of assumption by third parties": [1965] A.C. 1175 at 1248. See too K. Low, "Trusts of Cryptoassets" (2021) 43 Tru. L.I. 191, 194.

84 See, e.g. *Carter Holt Harvey Woodproducts Australia Pty Ltd v The Commonwealth* [2019] HCA 20 at [24] where it is said that the term "trust assets" is "simply shorthand for. . .the rights held on trust by the trustee". See too B. McFarlane and R. Stevens, "The Nature of Equitable Property" (2010) 4 J. Eq. 1; R. Chambers, *An Introduction to Property Law in Australia*, 4th edn (Thomson Reuters, 2018), 13.90. See further Chapter 12.

85 See, e.g. W. Swadling, "Property" in *English Private Law*, edited by A. Burrows, 3rd edn (Oxford University Press, 2013), paras 4.144 to 4–4.153.

86 See too S. Delacroix and N. Lawrence, "Bottom-up Data Trusts: Disturbing The 'One Size Fits All' Approach to Data Governance" (2019) 9 *International Data Privacy Law* 236, 245 noting that an objection to data trusts based on the idea that data is not capable of being property "betrays a misunderstanding" of the nature of a trust. For a very helpful analysis of the relevant rights that may be the subject matter of a trust in relation to certain types of data, see J. Lau, J. Penner, and B. Wong, "The Basic of Public and Private Data Trusts" [2020] Sing J. L. Studies 90.

87 See, e.g. D. Hayton, "'Trusts' in Private International Law" (2014) 366 *Recueil des Cours* 17, 20–21.

stipulate that T is not to sell those shares unless S has consented to such a sale. As noted above,[88] there are also means by which S may assert some practical influence in the operation of the trust, even without reserving any rights under the terms of the trust itself.

4–035 Matters are obviously different where S sets up a trust by means of a self-declaration of trust. In this case, S becomes the trustee and will have a very significant influence on the operation of the trust *in her capacity as trustee*.[89] Note, too, that it is possible for S to set up a trust, either by transfer or self-declaration, in which S is herself one of the beneficiaries of the trust:[90] in that case, S will acquire rights *in her capacity as a beneficiary*.[91]

4–036 The basic principle that S drops out of the picture is important for two reasons. First, it shows that, even in the case where the trust is set up by a transfer to T, rather than by a self-declaration by S, a trust is quite different from a contract between S and T.[92] If T and S sought to achieve a trust-like arrangement by contract, T's duties in relation to the trust property would give rise to rights enforceable by S, as the other contracting party.[93] In contrast, in English trusts law, the duties of T correlate (although not exclusively)[94] to rights held by B, the beneficiary of the trust. For the same reason, the relationship of S and T differs from the relationship of principal and agent: the principal may terminate such a relationship, thereby ending the actual authority of the agent to act on the principal's behalf, whereas, unless S expressly reserved such a power when setting up the trust, it is not possible for S to revoke a trust.[95]

4–037 Secondly, it will often be the case that S has decided to set up a trust precisely because S wishes to dispose immediately of her initial rights in the trust property. In the context of estate planning, for example, S may wish to make an immediate settlement of property, in the hope that S's death will occur more than seven years after that disposition, so that the property disposed of will not count towards the calculation of estate duties (such as inheritance tax) on S's death. The point is that the estate planning advantages of such a transaction depend on the fact that, by making the transfer into a trust, S no longer has rights to the trust property. Indeed, if S is regarded as having reserved a benefit to herself under the terms of the trust, the trust property is still treated as part of her estate on death, and so the estate planning advantages of the transaction are lost.

4–038 Similarly, part of S's motive in setting up a trust may be to place particular assets beyond the reach of her actual or potential creditors by disposing of her rights in those assets.[96] The trust can have this effect only because S is regarded as dropping out of the picture after having set up the trust. So if, for example, S retains rights under the trust, a court may order that creditors of S (or, for example, S's

---

88 See para.4–010.

89 See paras 4–045 to 4–062.

90 Note there can be no self-declaration of trust where S is the sole beneficiary, as such an arrangement is no different in substance from S's retaining her initial outright ownership of the trust property.

91 See paras 4–063 to 4–068.

92 See further P. Matthews et al (eds) *Underhill & Hayton: Law of Trusts and Trustees*, 20th edn (Sweet & Maxwell, 2022), 1.27–1.32.

93 Even in a case where the Contract (Rights of Third Parties) Act 1999 applies to give a third party the right to enforce a contract, the promisor retains rights under the contract and (subject to the conditions imposed by s.2 of the Act) the promisor and promisee may be able to vary or rescind the contract.

94 This is because, for example, a co-trustee or former trustee can also have a claim against T: see para.11–015.

95 See e.g. *North v Wilkinson* [2018] EWCA Civ 161; [2018] 4 W.L.R. 41 at [2], where David Richards LJ notes the "significant, and generally irreversible, consequences" of setting up a trust: see para.7–001.

96 Note that s.423 of the Insolvency Act 1986 (which deals with transactions defrauding creditors, whether those transactions take the form of a trust or not) can apply where S acts with a substantial purpose of putting assets beyond the reach of actual or future creditors, allowing a court to make an order restoring the property to S for the benefit of S's creditors. Note too that s.37 of the Matrimonial Causes Act 1973 gives the court a jurisdiction to set aside dispositions made with the intention of defeating a spouse's claim to ancillary relief.

spouse in ancillary relief proceedings) should be able to have access to those rights.[97] Such an order, indeed, can be made even if T merely has a power, rather than a duty, to make distributions of the trust property to S: in such a case, the making of the order amounts to a "judicious encouragement"[98] of T to exercise that power in favour of S.[99]

Where S acts, at least in part, for such reasons, it is worth asking why S would set up a trust in favour of B, rather than simply making an outright gift of the property to B. Consider, for example, a case in which S wishes to make a lifetime disposition, in the hope of limiting tax liability on her death, and has three grandchildren who are all at university. S could make an immediate gift of the property, perhaps dividing it equally between the grandchildren. There is, however, no flexibility in such a gift: it may turn out, for example, that, shortly after the gift is made, one of the grandchildren wins the lottery, whereas another is involved in an accident and requires expensive medical care. By setting up a discretionary trust, in which T has a power to choose when and how to make distributions of the trust property, S can both: (i) dispose of her property; and (ii) ensure that there is some flexibility as to how that property will be distributed between the grandchildren. A further advantage of a discretionary trust, as opposed to an outright gift, is that creditors of each grandchild will not generally have access to the trust fund, as each grandchild acquires a definite asset only if and when a distribution is made.[100] **4–039**

It might also be thought that the advantage to S of such a discretionary trust, as compared to an outright gift, is that the tax liability of each grandchild (at least prior to a distribution in his or her favour) will be limited. Certainly, it has been held that the interest of a beneficiary under a discretionary trust, as it is not a right to receive any specific distribution of property may lack "the necessary quality of definable extent which must exist before it can be taxed".[101] Parliament, however, does not simply sit back and allow assets to be put beyond the reach of taxation so easily. Indeed, the general rule[102] for any lifetime trust established after 22 March 2006 is that inheritance tax (IHT) is payable as an "entry charge" of 20% of the value of the property (to the extent that the value exceeds the tax-free IHT allowance),[103] a periodic charge to IHT of a maximum of 6% on the value of the assets every 10 years, and as an "exit charge" calculated as a proportion of the most recent periodic charge (if any).[104] Further, if the trust is a discretionary trust and the income received by the trustees from the trust property is not distributed to beneficiaries, the trustees are liable to pay income tax on that income at the trust rate, which at present matches the highest rate of income tax. **4–040**

---

97 See, e.g. *Tasarruf Mevduati Sigorta Fonu v Merrill Lynch Bank and Trust Co (Cayman) Ltd* [2011] UKPC 17; [2012] 1 W.L.R. 1721 (equitable execution could be ordered in relation to a power held by S to revoke a trust).

98 See *Thomas v Thomas* [1996] 2 F.C.R. 544. For discussion, see C. Mitchell, "Judicious Encouragement or Judicial Bullying?" [2017] Conv. 287.

99 See, e.g. *Whaley v Whaley* [2012] 1 F.L.R. 735 (if a discretionary trustee is likely to advance capital to a spouse in the foreseeable future, this can be taken into account in an order for ancillary relief).

100 Although, as noted at para.4–038, the spouse of one of the grandchildren, in ancillary relief proceedings, may claim that the likelihood of that grandchild receiving a distribution under the discretionary trust should be taken into account in assessing the relief.

101 *Gartside v Inland Revenue Commissioners* [1968] A.C. 553 at 617 per Lord Wilberforce. See too *Sainsbury v Inland Revenue Commissioners* [1970] Ch. 712.

102 There are exceptions for particular types of trust, such as trusts for the benefit of a bereaved minor or a disabled person: note that the failure to set up such a special trust, with its attendant tax advantages, was the initial cause of the difficulties in *Pitt v Holt* [2013] 2 A.C. 108.

103 That allowance is often referred to as the "nil rate band": in 2021/22 it is £325,000. A surviving spouse can take advantage of any of the allowance unused by the deceased spouse. There are also other allowances, exemptions and forms of relief which can avoid or reduce an IHT charge.

104 The exit charge is calculated on a similar basis if the exit occurs within 10 years of the settlement.

4-041 The basic point that S, on setting up a trust, drops out of the picture might be seen as a counter-balance to the fact that S, in choosing the terms of the trust, has a wide initial power to dictate the operation of the trust. It is certainly true that S's intentions, as objectively expressed in the terms of the trust,[105] are critical when defining the content of T's duties, and those duties in turn shape the rights of B. Nonetheless, it is possible to exaggerate S's influence. First, as we have noted,[106] the *Saunders v Vautier* principle[107] allows all of the beneficiaries of a trust, acting together, to call for the trust property to be transferred to them by the trustees, even if such a transfer is inconsistent with the terms of the trust. So, for example, if T holds on trust for B alone, and S has stipulated that B is to receive the trust capital (rather than just the income) only on reaching the age of 25, B, on reaching the age of 18 and thus becoming an adult, can terminate the trust and call for the transfer of the trust capital. One way to understand this principle is that, although T has an initial duty not to transfer the capital to B until B is 25, that duty is owed to B alone (as once the trust is up and running, S drops out of the picture) and so B, if an adult and of sound mind, is free to waive the duty.[108]

4-042 Second, consider a case in which S stipulates that T is to hold family shares on trust for B, and is not permitted to sell those shares without the consent of X. In breach of the terms of the trust, T sells the shares. In such a case, B has the power to "adopt the investment"[109] and treat it as trust property, so that T now holds the proceeds of sale of the shares on trust for B.[110] S clearly did not intend that such a situation could arise, but, again, as the duties imposed by the trust are owed to B and not to S, it is B who has the power to adopt the investment. In effect, then, the terms of the trusts have been informally varied. There is also a formal, statutory mechanism by which trusts can be varied:[111] its existence shows again that the terms of the trust as chosen by S are not necessarily definitive.

4-043 Further, whilst it is certainly the case, as we will see in Chapter 7, that the courts are generally keen, where possible, to give effect to the expressed, objective intention of S as to the terms of a trust, some limits are placed on S not only by the rights of B, but also by the general rules of the English law of trusts. For example, as we have already noted,[112] those general rules prohibit the creation of a private purpose trust, whereby T holds trust property not for the benefit of individuals but rather subject to a duty to apply it to a particular, non-charitable purpose.

4-044 One way of explaining such limits is to note that the interests of settlor, trustee, and beneficiary are not the only ones that must be considered when shaping the law of trusts. It can be argued, for example, that there is a general public interest in preventing property from being insulated from the claims of the creditors of *any* person, as would occur, for example, if a private purpose trust was permitted, and in preventing property from becoming effectively inalienable, as might occur in the absence of the rule against perpetuities.[113] The fact that some jurisdictions permit private purpose trusts, and have greatly extended, or even abolished, perpetuity periods[114] does not undermine this

105 See para.7-007.
106 See para.4-001.
107 (1841) 4 Beav. 115. See paras 12-064 to 12-073.
108 Note that it is not difficult for S to avoid the operation of the *Saunders v Vautier* power: S can, for example, set up a trust under which B's right to the trust capital is conditional on B's reaching the age of 25. See further para.12-068.
109 See *Wright v Morgan* [1926] A.C. 788 at 798, per Viscount Dunedin.
110 See further paras 15-010ff.
111 Under the Variation of Trusts Act 1958.
112 See paras 4-002 to 4-003. See further Chapter 8.
113 The rule against perpetuities has two aspects: first that the (very few, if any) permitted non-charitable purpose trusts cannot continue indefinitely (a rule against inalienability); second, the vesting of interests in individuals cannot be postponed for too long a period (a rule against remoteness of vesting): see Perpetuities and Accumulations Act 2009.
114 For a survey of the position in the US, see M. Schanzenbach and R. Sitkoff, "Perpetuities or Taxes? Explaining the Rise of the Perpetual Trust" (2006) 27 *Cardozo Law Review* 2465. For a wider international survey, see A. Hofri-Winogradow, "Trust Proliferation: A View From the Field" (2017) 31 *Trust Law International* 152.

point; it simply demonstrates that the public interest of one jurisdiction may differ from that of another.[115]

B. The Trustee

i. Holding the Trust Property

The trust property is vested in the trustee (T). As noted above,[116] that trust property need not consist of ownership of any physical thing, but may instead be a personal right against another party held by T, even a non-assignable personal right. As we noted in Chapter 1,[117] the trust property may also be an equitable interest held by T. This will be the case, for example, where nominees, acting for T, hold the trust property on trust for T. In such a case, the trust between T and B may be seen as a sub-trust, as the right held by T on trust for B is itself an equitable interest under a trust.[118] **4–045**

It might be thought that, at least where the trust property does not consist of an equitable interest, the creation of a trust involves S transferring legal title in the trust property to T, and equitable title in that property to B; or, in the case of a self-declaration, it involves S retaining legal title and giving equitable title to B. There are, however, at least two problems with such an analysis. First, the assumption it rests on, that S's initial property consists of both a legal and an equitable title, has been rejected by the House of Lords. In Lord Browne-Wilkinson's words in *Westdeutsche Landesbank Girozentrale v Islington LBC*:[119] **4–046**

> A person solely entitled to the full beneficial ownership of money or property, both at law and in equity, does not enjoy an equitable interest in that property. The legal title carries with it all rights. Unless and until there is a separation of legal and equitable estates, there is no separate equitable title. Therefore to talk about [S] "retaining" its equitable interest is meaningless. The only question is whether the circumstances under which the money was paid were such as, in equity, to impose a trust on [T]. If so, an equitable interest arose for the first time under that trust.

Secondly, as noted above,[120] the creation of a trust need not involve any fragmentation of the property initially held by S, and does not involve any transfer from S to B.[121] Rather, T acquires the very same property as held by S, but subject to a duty, owed to B, to comply with the terms of the trust. As James LJ put it in *Smith v Anderson*:[122] **4–047**

> A trustee is a man who is the owner of the property and deals with it as principal, as owner and as master, subject only to an equitable obligation to account to some persons to whom he stands in the relation of trustee.

---

115 Even within a single jurisdiction, there is a distinction between the policies given effect to, perhaps in the name of the public interest, in domestic law and those still more important policies that must be given effect to by the courts of that jurisdiction even when applying foreign law: see arts 15, 16 and 18 of the Hague Convention on the Law Applicable to Trusts and on their Recognition.

116 See paras 4–029 to 4–033.

117 See para.1–081.

118 See further paras 6–084ff.

119 [1996] A.C. 669 at 706.

120 See para.4–019.

121 See *Commissioner of State Revenue v Rojoda Pty Ltd* [2020] HCA 7; [2020] 268 C.L.R. 281 at [44] (Bell, Keane, Nettle and Edelman JJ).

122 (1880) 15 Ch.D. 247 at 275.

4-048 This analysis is consistent with the argument made in Chapter 1 as to the supplementary nature of equity, which does not contradict the common law position, but rather controls the exercise of common law rights.[123] It is also supported, for example, by the approach adopted in the old and factually complex case of *Burgess v Wheate*:[124] in the absence of any legislative provision dealing with the situation, if T holds property subject to a trust, and (perhaps because of the death of B and an absence of any party who can succeed to B's rights under the trust) there is no longer any person to whom T owes their "equitable obligation to account", then T is free to use the property for their own benefit. In the absence of anyone who can enforce the duty imposed by the trust, there is no reason for equity to intervene, and T is free to enjoy their ownership of the trust property. As Paul Matthews has observed:[125]

> The decision in *Burgess v Wheate* is like a salutary shock to the system. We are brought up to think that the last thing a trustee can do is to keep the property for himself. What that case shows is that, indeed, *as a last resort*, and only when there is no one else to affect his conscience, it really *is* the last thing he can do. The trustee is a true owner, and has the owner's rights, subject only to the effect on his conscience. If and when that effect runs out, he nevertheless remains the owner, untramelled by any equity. Of course the law has moved on since *Burgess v Wheate*, and the range of persons who may affect the conscience of the trustee is—quite rightly—larger than it was then. So the chances of a trustee finding himself able lawfully to enjoy the property by virtue of the disappearance of all those who might affect his conscience are correspondingly smaller. But the true principle is there, and in analysing the nature of the trust, and in explaining it to those from outside the common law tradition,[126] we ignore it at our peril.

4-049 The point that T has more than a mere legal title is also apparent when considering the impact of T's ownership of the trust property on third parties. If, for example, the trust property consists of a contractual right held by T against X, then T is free to enforce that right against X. Where appropriate, T may be awarded an equitable remedy, such as specific performance; T can otherwise receive damages in the usual measure from X. There is no suggestion that any discount should be made because T has "only" legal title to the trust property.[127] Similarly, if the trust property consists of ownership of tangible property, and X wrongfully interferes with that property, T can again get full damages against X, without any discount being made.[128] Indeed, the fact that T is treated, as against strangers such as X, as having a full entitlement to the trust property is actually an advantage to B, since the benefits acquired by T in asserting the right against X will also be held by T on trust for B.

ii. Responsibilities and Powers of the Trustee

4-050 Where T has accepted her role as trustee of an express trust, she is subject to three main types of duty. It is important to note that those duties are owed to the beneficiary B[129] and not to S, the settlor.[130]

---

[123] See paras 1-059 to 1-081.

[124] (1759) 1 Eden 177.

[125] P. Matthews, "*Burgess v Wheate* (1759)" in C. Mitchell and P. Mitchell (eds), *Landmark Cases in Equity* (Hart Publishing, 2012).

[126] This is a reference to the point discussed at para.4-019: the hostility of civil lawyers to the trust is sometimes based on the assumption, falsified by, e.g. *Burgess v Wheate*, that a trust necessarily involves a fragmentation of S's right into distinct legal and equitable titles.

[127] Indeed, it is T who is the appropriate party to bring any claim against X: see, e.g. *Vandepitte v Preferred Accident Insurance Corporation of New York* [1933] A.C. 70 at 79.

[128] See, e.g. *Leigh & Sillavan Ltd v Aliakmon Shipping Co Ltd* [1986] A.C. 785 at 812–813 and 819.

[129] Obviously a trust may have more than one beneficiary but for ease of exposition we will refer here to a singular "B".

[130] See para.4-034.

First, T has a duty of due administration, as discussed in Chapter 3;[131] secondly, T will usually owe fiduciary duties, as discussed in Chapter 2; thirdly, T will usually owe a duty to take reasonable care in exercising their powers under the trust when, for example, managing or investing the trust property.[132]

Where T is in breach of any of these duties, T may be personally liable to B, and we will examine such liability in Chapter 13. It is possible for the terms of the trust to exclude or limit such liability, but the existence of the trust depends on T's being under some enforceable duties to B. As Millett LJ stated in *Armitage v Nurse*:[133] **4–051**

> there is an irreducible core of obligations owed by the trustees to the beneficiaries and enforceable by them which is fundamental to the concept of a trust. If the beneficiaries have no rights enforceable against the trustees there are no trusts. But I do not accept [that] these core obligations include the duties of skill and care, prudence and diligence. The duty of the trustees to perform the trusts honestly and in good faith for the benefit of the beneficiaries is the minimum necessary to give substance to the trusts, but in my opinion it is sufficient.

Millett LJ's statement makes clear that, whilst T cannot be given the freedom to depart recklessly or dishonestly from the terms of the trust, the third of the three duties of T that we have identified, the duty of care, may be excluded by the express terms of a trust, and therefore cannot be seen as a fundamental part of what it means to be a trustee. Where it does apply, the duty is no different in its operation from the standard duty of care that arises, for example, when a defendant carries out a service for a claimant. The basic rules applicable to a claim by B in relation to a breach of a duty of care by T are therefore no different to those applying to a standard negligence claim arising in contract or tort.[134] **4–052**

We will examine the responsibilities of trustees in detail in Chapter 10. We also consider there the powers of trustees, and it is important to note that trustees do have powers which they can use for their own benefit. For example, where T has properly incurred expenses in the due administration of the trust, T is able to use the trust property to meet those expenses, and this claim takes priority over any claim of B.[135] Indeed, where B is a sole adult beneficiary with an absolute entitlement to the trust property,[136] B may be liable to pay any outstanding properly incurred expenses which remain even after T has used all of the trust property to meet those costs.[137] **4–053**

iii. Trusteeship as an Office

We have seen, when considering the role of S, the settlor of a trust, that a trust differs from a contract. This is underlined by the fact that trusteeship is conceived not merely as a set of duties that bind T (the party who, in an express trust, has initially agreed to act as trustee), but also as an office. For example, if T is not properly performing her duties as trustee, B can apply to court to have T replaced by a new trustee, in whom the trust property will then be vested. If T, a sole trustee, dies, then the trust **4–054**

131 See paras 3–143 to 3–192 and 11–024 to 11–029.
132 See now Trustee Act 2000 s.1.
133 [1998] Ch. 241 at 253.
134 See *Bristol & West Building Society v Mothew* [1998] Ch. 1 at 16–18; although note that a different approach is advocated by, e.g. J. Getzler, "Am I My Beneficiary's Keeper? Fusion and Loss-Based Fiduciary Remedies" in S. Degeling and J. Edelman (eds), *Equity in Commercial Law* (Law Book Co, 2005).
135 See paras 10–128 to 10–137 and 12–028 to 12–029.
136 Or where the beneficiaries between them are collectively entitled absolutely: see e.g. *Buchan v Ayre* [1915] 2 Ch. 474 at 477.
137 See *Hardoon v Belilios* [1901] A.C. 118.

continues, with T's personal representative becoming trustee and having the power to appoint a new trustee, in whom the trust property will again be vested.

4–055 Further evidence of the clear differences between the position of T and that of a party to a simple contract is provided by the powers of the courts to supervise the proper operation of a trust. As Lord Walker observed in *Schmidt v Rosewood Trust Ltd*:[138]

> It is fundamental to the law of trusts that the court has jurisdiction to supervise and if appropriate intervene in the administration of a trust, including a discretionary trust.

4–056 As we will see in Chapter 7,[139] even if S has set up a discretionary trust, and has thus given T the power to make decisions as to the distribution of the trust property, a court may still have a role to play in executing and enforcing the trust, not only by replacing T with new trustees if necessary but also, potentially, by agreeing to a scheme of distribution proposed by the beneficiaries of the trust, or even by devising its own scheme of distribution.[140]

4–057 In considering the duties of T, we saw that a trust necessarily involves a relationship between T and B. The notion of trusteeship as involving an office can be seen as involving the depersonalisation of that relationship.[141] As the trust can continue if T dies or is replaced, its existence does not depend on the precise identity of the trustee at any time; what matters is that the trust property is vested in someone. This point can also be seen in a fundamental aspect of the trust: the protection given to B in the event of T's insolvency. As long as the trust property is preserved, B is protected from the risk of T's insolvency, as any assets held on trust cannot be used to meet the claims of T's creditors.[142] This result flows, at least in part, from the fact that, as it would have been a breach of the terms of the trust for T to use the trust property to pay her own creditors, those creditors cannot benefit from the fact of T's insolvency.[143] It also shows that the personality, or creditworthiness, of T is not critical to the core duty of the trust: the duty of due administration.[144]

4–058 One way of explaining both the nature of trusteeship as an office, and the fact that T's creditors cannot have access to the trust assets, is to treat the trust as depending on T's simultaneous holding of two separate patrimonies. The concept of a patrimony is more familiar to civil lawyers, and this explanation of the trust is most prominent outside purely common law systems, as its attraction, in part, lies in its ability to explain some important features of the trust without relying on the divide between common law and equity.[145] Roughly speaking, a patrimony consists of the total assets and liabilities of any legal person. The general rule, in English law as in civilian systems, is that *all* of a defendant's assets are available to meet *any* of the defendant's liabilities. That is not true, however, if the defendant is a trustee: whilst T is fully entitled, as against parties other than B, to the trust property, those assets are not available to meet T's liabilities to T's creditors. One way to explain this result

---

138 [2003] UKPC 26; [2003] 2 A.C. 709 at [36].

139 See paras 7–124ff.

140 See *Re Baden's Deed Trusts (No.1)* [1971] A.C. 424 at 457 (extracted at paras 7–126ff).

141 See, e.g. B. McFarlane, "The Trust and its Civilian Analogues" in L. Smith (ed), *The Worlds of the Trust* (Cambridge University Press, 2013), pp.512, 522.

142 See, e.g. Insolvency Act 1986 s.283(3)(a): in the case of an individual becoming bankrupt, "property held by the bankrupt on trust for any other person" is excluded from the bankrupt's estate and so is not available to the trustee in bankruptcy to use to meet the claims of the bankrupt's creditors. For the justification of taking the same approach in relation to companies, where there is no such legislative provision, see e.g. *Carter Holt Harvey Woodproducts v Commonwealth of Australia* [2019] HCA 20 at [25]–[27] (Kiefel CJ, Keane and Edelman JJ) (extracted at paras 12–114 to 12–117).

143 See too paras 12–111 to 12–120.

144 See paras 3–143 to 3–192.

145 See, e.g. K. Reid, "Patrimony not Equity: The Trust in Scotland" (2000) 8 *European Review of Private Law* 427; G. Gretton, "Trusts Without Equity" (2000) 49 I.C.L.Q. 599.

is to see the trust as forming an exception to the general rule that each legal person has only one patrimony. On this view it can said that, a trustee, exceptionally, has two patrimonies:[146] their general patrimony and a special trust patrimony, which is not available to meet T's general liabilities. Or it could be said that the trust assets are outside T's patrimony, and form part of a separate, independent patrimony held by no-one.[147]

There are, however, difficulties with applying this patrimonial explanation of the trust in English law.[148] First, the civilian concept of a patrimony consists of both assets and liabilities, whereas the property held on trust by T consists only of assets: it is not possible for T to hold a liability on trust for B.[149] Second, consider a case in which the trust property includes land, and T, acting responsibly and consistently with the terms of the trust, enters into a contract with X under which X is to make repairs to a building on that land.[150] If T fails to pay X, and X makes a claim against T under the contract, X's position is essentially the same as any other creditor of T, and thus the same as if the contract had been to repair T's own home. It is very important to note that, whilst it is common to talk of "trust creditors" or "liabilities of the trust", as stated by Kiefel CJ, and Keane and Edelman JJ in *Carter Holt Harvey Woodproducts v Commonwealth of Australia*:[151] **4–059**

> the trust is not a separate entity and therefore does not have a separate solvency status from the trustee. A trustee is personally liable for debts incurred as trustee.

The trust is not a legal person,[152] and so is not an entity that can owe debts, have creditors, or own property: it is the *trustee* who does those things. Nor is the trustee, when making the contract with X, acting as an agent for B and thus imposing a liability on B. This means, first, that X has no direct access to the trust assets to satisfy X's claim and secondly, that *all* of T's non-trust assets are available to meet X's claim.[153] The general position, then, is that English law does not make a distinction between debts incurred by T in her capacity as trustee and any other debts of T.[154] As Lord Hodge put it in *Investec Trust (Guernsey) Ltd v Glenalla Properties Ltd*:[155] **4–060**

> A trust is not a legal person. Its assets are vested in trustees, who are the only entities capable of assuming legal rights and liabilities in relation to the trust. In particular, they are not agents for the beneficiaries, since their duty is to act independently . . . The legal personality of a trustee is unitary. Although a trustee has duties specific to his status as such, when it comes to the consequences English law does not distinguish between his personal and his fiduciary capacity. It follows that the trustee assumes those liabilities personally and without limit, thus engaging not only the trust assets but his personal estate.

---

146 This has been suggested as the basis of the Scottish trust: see, e.g. *Ted Jacob Engineering Group Inc v Robert Matthew Johnston-Marshall and Partners* [2014] CSIH 18 at [90] per Lord Drummond Young; Scottish Law Commission, *Report on Trust Law* (Scots Law Com. No.239, 2014) para.3.4, accepting the analyses of Reid and Gretton in the articles cited in the previous footnote.

147 That seems to be the basis, for example, of the "*patrimoine d'affectation*" model adopted for example in Quebec.

148 The discussion in this paragraph is based on the analysis of L. Smith, "Trust and Patrimony" (2008–09) 28 E.T. & P.J. 332.

149 The statement of Lord Shaw in *Lord Strathcona Steamship Co Ltd v Dominion Coal Co Ltd* [1926] A.C. 108 at 124 (set out at para.4–029) therefore seems over-broad, as it suggests that a liability may be held on trust.

150 This example is taken from L. Smith, "Trust and Patrimony" (2008–09) 28 E.T. & P.J. 332, 338.

151 [2019] HCA 20 at [24].

152 See further L. Smith, "Mistaking the Trust" (2011) H.K.L.J. 747.

153 See the principles set out in *Investec Trust (Guernsey) Ltd v Glenalla Properties Ltd* [2018] UKPC 7 at [59] (extracted at para.12–119).

154 Where the debt to X is properly incurred, T will have a right of indemnity against the trust fund (although only after discharging any liability T has for any other breach of trust), and X may be subrogated to that right of indemnity so as to have access to the trust property to meet T's debt: see, e.g. *Re Frith* [1902] 1 Ch. 342. See further para.12–120.

155 [2018] UKPC 7 at [59]. See too para.12–119.

iv. Influence on the Operation of the Trust

4-061 We have seen that, particularly in a modern discretionary trust, significant powers may be given to T to choose how to distribute the trust property;[156] it is also common for T to be given, for example, powers to set up new trusts that will bind all or part of the original trust property.[157] In such a case, T clearly has a significant influence on the operation of the trust and, whilst T's purported exercise of a power conferred by the trust may be subject to challenge if T does not take into account the expressed wishes of S,[158] there is no duty on T to comply with any such wishes which do not form part of the terms of the trust.

4-062 In general, when exercising powers under the trust, T must do their best to hold the balance fairly between different beneficiaries or classes of beneficiaries. If T exercises a power with the intention of achieving a result that is not permitted by the terms of the trust, or of favouring one group of beneficiaries over another without justification, then that exercise may be regarded as unauthorised, so that T has a duty to reconstitute the trust fund by replacing any property disposed of by the exercise of the power.[159] T may also play a paternalistic role in the operation of the trust. Even if all of the beneficiaries interested in a particular trust agree that T should exercise their powers under the trust in a particular way, T can refuse to do so if they consider that such an action would not be in the best objective interests of some of the beneficiaries.[160] In such a case, then, the beneficiaries cannot force T to act in a particular way. As we have seen,[161] however, the beneficiaries, acting together, could exercise their *Saunders v Vautier*[162] power to call for the trust property to be vested in them by T, thus terminating the trust.

C. The Beneficiary[163]

i. Basic Role

4-063 We have seen that, in English law, a trust without a beneficiary can exist only if it is a charitable trust.[164] It is not possible for S to set up a trust where T's duty is simply to apply the trust property for a non-charitable purpose. This principle of English law—it is not a part of the trusts law of many offshore jurisdictions, nor is it a requirement of the definition of a trust adopted by the Hague Convention on the Law Applicable to Trusts and on their Recognition[165]—is often referred to as "the beneficiary principle" and will be discussed in detail in Chapter 8. It shows that, outside the context of charitable trusts, the existence of a beneficiary is a necessary part of the English trust. Such a beneficiary is able to enforce the duties imposed on T: if there were no means of enforcing such duties,

---

156 See para.4-039.

157 For a case concerning a challenge to the exercise of such a power, see *Re Hay's S.T.* [1982] 1 W.L.R. 202 (extracted at paras 7-102ff).

158 See para.4-010.

159 See paras 11-030 to 11-077, discussing the "fraud on a power" rule.

160 *Re Brockbank* [1949] Ch. 206: subject to the beneficiaries' power to direct the trustees to retire and appoint other designated persons to become trustees in their place, under the Trusts of Land and Appointment of Trustees Act 1996 s.19.

161 See para.4-041.

162 *Saunders v Vautier* (1841) 4 Beav. 115.

163 Obviously a trust may have more than one beneficiary but for ease of exposition we will refer here to a singular "B" as beneficiary.

164 See para.4-002. Charitable trusts are discussed in Chapter 9.

165 See para.4-003.

there would be no restriction on T's use of the trust property which is, as we have seen,[166] fully vested in T.

Indeed, it could even be said that the need for a beneficiary is such that, in some cases, the law itself identifies a beneficiary. In Chapter 16,[167] we will examine the type of resulting trust that arises where S transfers property to T to hold subject to a particular trust, but, for some reason,[168] S does not successfully exercise her power to set up a trust, and so the intended express trust fails. In such a case, given S's clear intention that T should not be free to use the trust property for T's own benefit, and S's equally clear intention to establish a trust, the result is that T holds the intended trust property on trust for S.[169] **4–064**

The right acquired by B under a trust is often referred to as a "beneficial interest". The holding of such an interest gives B a great advantage as compared to, say, having a purely personal right to compel T to honour a promise, made to S, to use the trust property for B's benefit. First, B is protected in T's insolvency.[170] Second, if T transfers the trust property to C, and has no power under the terms of the trust to do so, it may be possible for B to make a claim against C, and to show that C has also come under a duty to B not to use that trust property for C's own benefit.[171] The possibility of making such a claim against C may be vital if T is insolvent and so cannot in practice perform her duty to dip into her own pocket and reconstitute the trust fund. Third, if T uses the trust property to acquire new property then, whether or not T had a power under the terms of the trust to do so, B can choose to impose a duty on T to hold that new property subject to the terms of the initial trust.[172] **4–065**

It is important to note that a beneficiary of a discretionary trust is also protected in each of these three ways. Even though such a party has no entitlement to any specific part of the trust property, as T owes a duty to B in relation to the trust property, B is protected in T's insolvency; and B may be able to ensure that C does not use the property for C's own benefit but instead transfers the property to a new T to hold on the terms of the original discretionary trust; and B can also, if acting with the consent of the other beneficiaries of the discretionary trust, impose a duty on T in relation to the new property acquired by T by the use of the initial trust property. It therefore seems that, whether the trust is discretionary or not, the three key advantages to B are based not on B's having a current entitlement to the full enjoyment or benefit of any specific property, but rather on B's holding a right that correlates to T's duty not to use particular property other than in compliance with the terms of the trust. Indeed, these three protections of B are also available to another party who benefits from a duty of due administration, but does not have "equitable ownership" of any property: that is, a party who stands to acquire property, as a legatee or as someone entitled in an intestacy, on the distribution of the estate of a deceased person.[173] **4–066**

These points are relevant to the long-standing and continuing controversy over the nature of B's interest under a trust: we will examine it in detail in Chapter 12. **4–067**

---

166 See paras 4–045 to 4–049.

167 See paras 16–059ff.

168 The reason may, for example, be a failure to identify the beneficiaries of the trust with sufficient certainty (see paras 7–090ff), or a failure to identify a complete set of beneficial entitlements, as occurs, for example, if S conveys to T to hold on trust for B for B's life, without specifying for whom T should hold on trust after B's death.

169 See, e.g. J. Mee "'Automatic' Resulting Trusts: Retention, Restitution or Reposing Trust?" in C. Mitchell (ed.), *Constructive and Resulting Trusts* (Hart Publishing, 2010).

170 See para.4–057.

171 See para.4–042: see further Chapter 15.

172 See further Chapter 15.

173 See, e.g. *Commissioner for Stamp Duties v Livingston* [1965] A.C. 694 at 714, where it was accepted that a residuary beneficiary under an unadministered estate can assert "the estate's right of property": the same must be true of a beneficiary of a discretionary trust. See paras 3–165ff and 12–031ff.

ii. Influence on the Operation of the Trust

4-068 It might be thought that where an express trust has been set up by S, B is merely a passive recipient of S's bounty, and so has little influence on the operation of the trust. We have seen, however, that this is not the case. First, in English law at least, the *Saunders v Vautier* principle[174] allows all of the beneficiaries of a trust, acting together, to call for the trust property to be transferred to them by the trustees, even if such a transfer would be inconsistent with the conditions that S sought to impose on particular beneficiaries' access to the trust property.[175] Second, even if T acts in a way which is inconsistent with the terms of the trust, B can adopt that transaction and thus compel T to hold any rights acquired as a result of T's action on the terms of the initial trust.[176] Third, and more generally, the duties imposed on T by the terms of the trust correlate to rights held by B, and so it is B who has the ultimate power to police the trust: even though a court may intervene to execute a trust,[177] it will only do so at B's invitation.

Questions

1. Which party has most influence in the operation of a trust: the settlor, the trustee, or the beneficiary?
2. Does the nature of equity as a supplementary body of rules help us to understand the nature of the trust?
3. "Any attempt to provide a general definition of the trust is doomed to failure." Do you agree?
4. "Significantly, a trust, unlike a corporation, has no legal personality." **Discuss**.

---

174 (1841) 4 Beav. 115. See paras 12-064 to 12-073.

175 Note too that a variation of the terms of the trust may be possible, where sought by B, under the Variation of Trusts Act 1958.

176 See para.4-042.

177 See paras 7-143 to 7-144.

PART II

CREATION OF EXPRESS TRUSTS

5

CONSTITUTION OF TRUSTS

1. Introduction

In this chapter and the four that follow, we consider various rules governing the creation of express trusts. In this chapter, our focus is on the situation where a settlor wishes to create an express trust by transferring property[1] to a trustee to hold on trust for a beneficiary. This is not the only means, however, by which a party may acquire a beneficial interest under a trust. Such a right will also arise if a settlor retains property, but declares that she holds that property on trust for the beneficiary. In addition, a party may instead acquire a beneficial interest not under an express trust, but under a trust imposed by law. It is important to keep those two possibilities in mind when considering cases where a settlor wishes to create an express trust by transferring property to a trustee to hold on trust for a beneficiary. If it turns out that the settlor has not successfully constituted the trust as intended, the planned beneficiary will still acquire a beneficial interest if she can show instead: (i) that the settlor in fact retained the property and declared a trust of it; or (ii) that a resulting or constructive trust of the property has arisen in her favour. **5–001**

In Chapter 6, we will examine the formality requirements that govern the means by which a party can acquire a beneficial interest under a trust. In Chapter 7, we will look at the rules which hold that three things must be certain before it can be said that a valid trust has been created: the settlor's intention to create the trust; the subject-matter of the trust; and the objects of the trust. In Chapter 8, we consider the principle that a valid trust must have a beneficiary. Consistently with this principle, trusts for private purposes are not generally valid under English law; exceptionally, however, trusts for charitable purposes are valid, and these are discussed in Chapter 9. **5–002**

2. Completely Constituted Trusts

A. Transferring Property to Trustees

In this chapter, our focus is on the situation where a settlor wishes to create an express trust by transferring property to a trustee to hold on trust for a beneficiary. This means of creating a trust can take effect (i.e. the trust can be "completely constituted") only if the property is indeed transferred to the trustee. So, if formality rules govern the transfer of such property, those formality rules must be satisfied. For example, if the subject matter of the trust is legal title to registered land, the conveyance to **5–003**

---

[1] Note that by "property" here we mean legal entitlements that may be held on trust (this includes a personal right, such as a bank account): in some other contexts, "property" has a more limited meaning: see paras 4–029 to 4–033.

the trustees must take the form of a deed,[2] and the transfer must be entered onto the Land Register.[3] Legal title to chattels must be transferred by delivery or by deed of gift. A bill of exchange must be transferred by endorsement[4] and a copyright by writing.[5] If the intended trust property is itself an equitable interest under another trust, then again the transfer must be in writing.[6]

5-004 In the case of testamentary trusts, the deceased's property is transferred to the settlor's executors, or the administrators of her estate, by virtue of her death.[7] Once those personal representatives have paid all the debts owed by the deceased, as well as relevant taxes and expenses of administering the estate, they are placed under equitable obligations[8] to transfer the relevant property according to the terms of the deceased's will, or, in the event of intestacy, according to the statutory rules as to distribution.[9] So, if the deceased made a valid will instructing that property should go to trustees to hold for a beneficiary, that trust will be constituted by means of a transfer to the trustees, as long as debts, taxes and expenses do not exhaust the relevant property. This testamentary trust will be completely constituted even if the named trustee disclaims (i.e. refuses to accept the property) or is unable to take the property because of incapacity or death.[10] In such a case, whoever succeeds to the legal title to the property will take it subject to the trust: once a trust is constituted, equity will not allow it to fail for want of a trustee.[11]

B. Self-Declaration of Trust

5-005 If a settlor wishes to create an express inter vivos trust,[12] it is also possible to do so by retaining property and declaring that she will hold that property as trustee upon certain trusts.[13] In such a case, of course, no transfer of the trust property is required. The three certainties must be present:[14] in particular, it must be clear that the settlor intended to hold the property subject to a duty to use it for the benefit of others, or for a charitable purpose. There is no need for a particular formula or phrase to be used and the settlor may indeed be unaware of the concept of a trust: the requirement, as we will see in Chapter 7,[15] is for some form of expression which in the circumstances shows that the settlor intended to hold the property subject to a binding duty.[16]

---

2 Law of Property Act 1925 s.52.
3 Land Registration Act 2002 ss.4 and 27.
4 Bills of Exchange Act 1882 s.31; Cheques Act 1957 ss.1, 2.
5 Copyright Designs and Patents Act 1988 s.90(3).
6 Law of Property Act 1925 s.53(1)(c): see 6-051ff.
7 Administration of Estates Act 1925 ss.1, 9, 25, and 32.
8 *Commissioner of Stamp Duties v Livingston* [1965] A.C. 694; *Marshall v Kerr* [1995] 1 A.C. 148.
9 See Administration of Estates Act 1925 s.46.
10 *Sonley v Clock Makers' Co* (1780) 1 Bro. C.C. 81; *Re Smirthwaite's Trusts* (1871) L.R. 11 Eq. 251.
11 *Re Armitage* [1972] Ch. 438 at 445 (where it is pointed out that very exceptionally the trust can fail if the personality of the named trustee is vital to the carrying out of the trust).
12 An inter vivos trust takes effect during the settlor's life and so is different from a testamentary trust.
13 For discussion see, e.g. S. Agnew and S. Douglas, "Self-Declarations of Trust" (2019) 135 L.Q.R. 67.
14 See Chapter 7.
15 See paras 7-005ff.
16 See, e.g. *Paul v Constance* [1977] 1 W.L.R. 527 (see paras 7-018 to 7-033). Note the resemblance, discussed at para.3-221, to the requirements for an equitable assignment of a legal chose in action.

C. The Basic Rule: An Unsuccessful Transfer to Trustees Is Not a Self-Declaration of Trust

We have seen so far that there are two different ways in which a settlor may create an express trust: (i) by transfer to trustees; (ii) by self-declaration. Each method results in the acquisition of a beneficial interest by the beneficiary; but there is a fundamental difference between them. In the former case, the settlor no longer holds the property, and the beneficiary's rights are against the transferees of the property; in the latter case, the settlor retains the property, and the beneficiaries' rights are against her. That crucial difference means that, if the settlor intends to create a trust by means of a transfer to trustees, but fails to make that transfer, those facts alone do *not* permit the intended beneficiary to claim that an express trust has arisen by means of a self-declaration of trust by the settlor. It is clear, after all, that the settlor had no such intention to hold property on trust for the beneficiary, as she rather intended to transfer the property to trustees to hold on trust. This very important principle is often known as the rule in *Milroy v Lord*. **5–006**

Milroy v Lord

Court of Appeal in Chancery (1862) 4 De G.F. & J. 264

Thomas Medley executed what was treated as a voluntary deed,[17] which purported to assign 50 shares in the Louisiana Bank to Samuel Lord upon trust for the benefit of the plaintiffs. The shares were transferable only by entry in the books of the bank; but no such transfer was ever made. At the relevant time Samuel Lord held a general power of attorney authorising him to transfer Thomas Medley's shares, and Thomas Medley, after the execution of the settlement, gave him a further power of attorney authorising him to receive the dividends on the bank shares. Thomas Medley lived for three years after the execution of the deed, during which period the dividends were received by Samuel Lord and remitted by him to the plaintiffs, sometimes directly and sometimes through Thomas Medley. There was thus a perfect gift of the dividends. Shortly after the execution of the deed, the settlor had delivered to Samuel Lord the certificates for the shares; and on the death of the settlor, Samuel Lord gave up the certificates to the settlor's executor. The shares stood in the settlor's name before and at the time of his death. At first instance Stuart V.C. held that a trust had been created for the claimant but this decision was reversed on an appeal by the executor. **5–007**

TURNER L.J. (with whom KNIGHT-BRUCE L.J. agreed): Under the circumstances of this case, it would be difficult not to feel a strong disposition to give effect to this settlement to the fullest extent, and certainly I have spared no pains to find the means of doing so, consistently with what I apprehend to be the law of the court; but, after full and anxious consideration, I find myself unable to do so. I take the law of this court to be well settled, that, in order to render a voluntary settlement valid and effectual, the settlor must have done everything which, according to the nature of the property comprised in the settlement, was necessary to be done in order to transfer the property and render the settlement binding upon him. He may, of course, do this by actually transferring the property to the persons for whom he intends to provide, and the provision will then be effectual, and it will be equally effectual if he transfers the property to a trustee for the purposes of the settlement, or declares that he himself holds it in trust for those purposes; and if the property be personal, the trust may, as I apprehend, be declared either in writing or by parol; but, in order to render the settlement binding, one or other of these modes must, as I understand the law of this court, be resorted to, for there is no equity in this court to perfect an imperfect gift. The cases, I think, go further to this extent: that if the settlement is intended to be effectuated by one of the modes to which I have referred, the court will not give effect to it by applying another of those modes. If it is intended to take effect by transfer, the court will not hold the intended transfer to operate as a declaration of trust, for then every imperfect instrument would be made effectual by being converted into a perfect trust. These are the principles by which, as I conceive, this case must be tried. **5–008**

---

[17] The deed (apparently executed in Louisiana) was expressed to be made in consideration of one dollar. In *Prest v Petrodel Resources Ltd* [2013] UKSC 34; [2013] 2 A.C. 415 at [49], a transfer for a nominal consideration of £1 was also treated as gratuitous for the purpose of applying presumptions as to resulting trusts: see para.16–022.

5-009 Applying, then, these principles to the case, there is not here any transfer either of the one class of shares or of the other to the objects of the settlement, and the question therefore must be whether a valid and effectual trust in favour of those objects was created in the defendant Samuel Lord or in the settlor himself as to all or any of these shares. Now it is plain that it was not the purpose of this settlement, or the intention of the settlor, to constitute himself a trustee of the bank shares. The intention was that the trust should be vested in the defendant Samuel Lord, and I think therefore that we should not be justified in holding that by the settlement, or by any parol declaration made by the settlor, he himself became a trustee of these shares for the purposes of the settlement. By doing so we should be converting the settlement or the parol declaration to a purpose wholly different from that which was intended to be effected by it and, as I have said, creating a perfect trust out of an imperfect transaction. . .

5-010 The more difficult question is whether the defendant Samuel Lord did not become a trustee of these shares. Upon this question I have felt considerable doubt; but in the result, I have come to the conclusion that no perfect trust was ever created in him. The shares, it is clear, were never legally vested in him; and the only ground on which he can be held to have become a trustee of them is that he held a power of attorney under which he might have transferred them into his own name; but he held that power of attorney as the agent of the settlor; and if he had been sued by the plaintiffs as trustee of the settlement for an account under the trust, and to compel him to transfer the shares into his own name as trustee, I think he might well have said: "These shares are not vested in me; I have no power over them except as the agent of the settlor, and without his express directions I cannot be justified in making the proposed transfer, in converting an intended into an actual settlement." A court of equity could not, I think, decree the agent of the settlor to make the transfer, unless it could decree the settlor himself to do so, and it is plain that no such decree could have been made against the settlor. In my opinion, therefore, this decree cannot be maintained as to the fifty Louisiana Bank shares. . .

5-011 In a case such as *Milroy v Lord*, it is only natural for a judge to feel "a strong disposition to give effect to this settlement to the fullest extent";[18] after all, the settlor did intend that the claimant would acquire a beneficial interest. The rule applied in that case must, however, be correct. Given that the settlor clearly intended to set up the trust by means of a transfer to a trustee, it would be inconsistent with that specific intention to find a self-declaration of trust by the settlor.

D. The Scope of the Basic Rule

i. Finding a Genuine Self-Declaration

5-012 The rule in *Milroy v Lord*, however, applies only if it is the case that the settlor intended to set up the trust by means of a transfer to trustees, and failed to make that transfer. The rule does not prevent a court from finding that, on the facts, the settlor instead intended to, and indeed did, make a self-declaration of trust. Of course, when interpreting the facts of a particular case, a court may be influenced by the "strong disposition" to give effect to the planned trust, and therefore find that the settlor intended a self-declaration rather than a transfer.[19]

T. Choithram International SA v Pagarani

Privy Council [2001] 1 W.L.R. 1

5-013 Pagarani (referred to in the Privy Councils' advice as TCP) was a wealthy businessman who was dying of cancer. A month before he died, he organised an elaborate ceremony at his London bedside to establish a philanthropic foundation in the form of a Jersey trust of which he was settlor and one of the trustees. He executed the trust deed in the presence of three (of the other six) trustees and of his accountant and

[18] (1862) 4 De G.F. & J. 264 at 274 (see para.5-008).

[19] See too *Paul v Constance* [1977] 1 W.L.R. 527, reproduced at paras 7-018ff.

the First Secretary of the Indian High Commission. They recollected him as orally making an immediate absolute gift of all his wealth in his shareholdings and credit balances with four British Virgin Island companies by stating that: "I give to the Foundation". However, English law does not recognise foundations as legal persons like companies, and legal title to the property was not vested in the other trustees before Pagarani died. On his death some of his children therefore sought to establish that the attempted gift was ineffective.

LORD BROWNE-WILKINSON: . . . Their Lordships then turn to the central and most important question: on the basis that TCP intended to make an immediate absolute gift "to the foundation" but had not vested the gifted property in all the trustees of the foundation, are the trusts of the foundation trust deed enforceable against the deposits and the shares or is this (as the judge and the Court of Appeal held) a case where there has been an imperfect gift which cannot be enforced against TCP's estate whatever TCP's intentions. **5–014**

The judge and the Court of Appeal understandably took the view that a perfect gift could only be made in one of two ways, viz (a) by a transfer of the gifted asset to the donee, accompanied by an intention in the donor to make a gift; or (b) by the donor declaring himself to be a trustee of the gifted property for the donee. In case (a), the donor has to have done everything necessary to be done which is within his own power to do in order to transfer the gifted asset to the donee. If the donor has not done so, the gift is incomplete since the donee has no equity to perfect an imperfect gift.[20] Moreover, the court will not give a benevolent construction so as to treat ineffective words of outright gift as taking effect as if the donor had declared himself a trustee for the donee.[21] So, it is said, in this case TCP used words of gift to the foundation (not words declaring himself a trustee): unless he transferred the shares and deposits so as to vest title in all the trustees, he had not done all that he could in order to effect the gift. It therefore fails. Further it is said that it is not possible to treat TCP's words of gift as a declaration of trust because they make no reference to trusts. Therefore the case does not fall within either of the possible methods by which a complete gift can be made and the gift fails. **5–015**

Though it is understandable that the courts below should have reached this conclusion since the case does not fall squarely within either of the methods normally stated as being the only possible ways of making a gift, their Lordships do not agree with that conclusion. The facts of this case are novel and raise a new point. It is necessary to make an analysis of the rules of equity as to complete gifts. Although equity will not aid a volunteer, it will not strive officiously to defeat a gift. This case falls between the two common form situations mentioned above. Although the words used by TCP are those normally appropriate to an outright gift—"I give to X"—in the present context there is no breach of the principle in *Milroy v Lord* if the words of TCP's gift (ie to the foundation) are given their only possible meaning in this context. The foundation has no legal existence apart from the trust declared by the foundation trust deed. Therefore the words "I give to the foundation" can only mean "I give to the trustees of the foundation trust deed to be held by them on the trusts of foundation trust deed". Although the words are apparently words of outright gift they are essentially words of gift on trust. **5–016**

But, it is said, TCP vested the properties not in *all* the trustees of the foundation but only in one, i.e. TCP. Since equity will not aid a volunteer, how can a court order be obtained vesting the gifted property in the whole body of trustees on the trusts of the foundation? Again, this represents an over-simplified view of the rules of equity. Until comparatively recently the great majority of trusts were voluntary settlements under which beneficiaries were volunteers having given no value. Yet beneficiaries under a trust, although volunteers, can enforce the trust against the trustees. Once a trust relationship is established between trustee and beneficiary, the fact that a beneficiary has given no value is irrelevant. It is for this reason that the type of perfected gift referred to in class (b) above is effective since the donor has constituted himself a trustee for the donee who can as a matter of trust law enforce that trust. **5–017**

What then is the position here where the trust property is vested in one of the body of trustees, viz. TCP? In their Lordship's view there should be no question. TCP has, in the most solemn circumstances, declared that he is giving (and later that he has given) property to a trust which he himself has established and of which he has appointed himself to be a trustee. All this occurs at one composite transaction taking place on 17 February. There can in principle be no distinction between the case where the donor declares himself **5–018**

---

20 *Milroy v Lord* (1862) 4 De G.F. & J. 264; *Richards v Delbridge* (1874) L.R. 18 Eq. 11; *Re Rose, Midland Bank Executor and Trustee Co Ltd v Rose* [1949] Ch. 78; *Rose v IRC* [1952] Ch. 499.

21 *Milroy v Lord* (1862) 4 De G.F. & J. 264.

> to be sole trustee for a donee or a purpose and the case where he declares himself to be one of the trustees for that donee or purpose. In both cases his conscience is affected and it would be unconscionable and contrary to the principles of equity to allow such a donor to resile from his gift. Say, in the present case, that TCP had survived and tried to change his mind by denying the gift. In their Lordship's view it is impossible to believe that he could validly deny that he was a trustee for the purposes of the foundation in the light of all the steps that he had taken to assert that position and to assert his trusteeship. In their Lordships' judgment in the absence of special factors where one out of a larger body of trustees has the trust property vested in him he is bound by the trust and must give effect to it by transferring the trust property into the name of all the trustees.[22]

5-019 As noted by Lord Browne-Wilkinson, the facts of the *Pagarani* case were somewhat unusual. It seems that Pagarani was regarded as having said, in effect: "As sole owner of the assets and as legal trustee of the Foundation I now hold my property on trust for the charitable purposes of the Foundation." The court was able to interpret his intention in this way because the case differed from *Milroy v Lord* in two important respects. First, it was not clear that the settlor intended to establish the trust by way of transfer as, although he had an intention to make a gift to the "Foundation", the Foundation had no legal personality in English law and so no transfer could be made to it.[23] Second, as the settlor was one of the trustees of the Foundation, it was possible to say that the settlor did in fact intend a self-declaration of trust, and the language of a gift to the "Foundation" in fact meant that the settlor intended to hold the property on the terms of the trust set out in the Foundation's trust deed. It was therefore possible to find, consistently with the rule in *Milroy v Lord*, that the settlor had intended, and succeeded, in constituting an express trust by means of a self-declaration.[24]

5-020 It is important to note that an intention to set up a trust by way of transfer does not preclude the possibility of the settlor *also* making a self-declaration of trust, to take effect immediately and to operate in the period pending the transfer. For example, as in *Re Ralli's Will Trusts*,[25] a settlor may both promise to transfer existing and future property to trustees to hold on trust *and* also declare that particular existing property held by the settlor is, pending transfer to the trustees, to be *immediately* subject to the planned trusts. In such a case, that declaration cannot create a trust over future property not currently in the hands of the settlor, but it will operate to bind the identified, existing property of the settlor, even if the promise to transfer the property to trustees is not honoured.[26]

5-021 It is also crucial to note that, in a case where a donor simply wants to make an absolute gift to a donee (so that no trust is intended), but fails to satisfy the requirements of a valid transfer, the intention to make an absolute gift does *not* suffice for the court to find a declaration of trust by the donor.[27]

---

22 As it happened, the relevant companies had altered their share registers after Pagarani's death so that legal title to the shares was actually vested in the remaining six trustees. Hence the Privy Council concluded that the administrators of Pagarani's intestate estate could not claim the shares or the deposit balances with the companies.

23 Compare the discussion at paras 8-036ff of gifts to unincorporated associations.

24 See, e.g. *Curtis v Pulbrook* [2011] 1 B.C.L.C. 638 at [43], where Briggs J regarded *Pagarani* as a case in which "by a benevolent construction an effective gift or implied declaration of trust may be teased out the words used". The suggestion in *Pennington v Waine* [2002] EWCA Civ 227; [2002] 1 W.L.R. 2075 at [59] that the trust in *Pagarani* was a constructive one therefore seems unnecessary: see further paras 5-104ff.

25 [1964] Ch. 288.

26 See *Re Ralli's W.T.* [1964] Ch. 288 (see paras 5-051 to 5-064). Buckley J held that Helen's existing reversionary interest under the will of her deceased father was bound by the declaration of trust, so that when it passed into possession, the rights thus acquired were held subject to the terms of the trust benefitting the children of Helen's sister.

27 See, e.g. *Richards v Delbridge* (1874) L.R. 18 Eq. 11. See too *Deslauriers v Guardian Asset Management Ltd* [2017] UKPC 34, stating at [41] that "[The donor's] intention to deal with the property so as to deprive himself of its beneficial ownership must be clearly evinced", and holding that no such intention was present on the facts of the case.

In a passage which has received judicial approval,[28] Maitland analysed this important principle by considering a case in which an intending donor attempts, but fails, to make a gift by transferring property to another:[29]

> It would be an imperfect gift, and being an imperfect gift the court will not regard it as a declaration of trust. I have made quite clear that I do not intend to make myself a trustee. I mean to give. The two intentions are very different—the giver means to get rid of his rights, the man who is intending to make himself a trustee intends to retain his rights but to come under an onerous obligation. The latter intention is far rarer than the former. Men often mean to give things to their kinsfolk, they do not often mean to constitute themselves trustees. An imperfect gift is no declaration of trust.

Sinéad Agnew and Simon Douglas have also emphasised the distinction between an absolute gift and a declaration of trust, whilst suggesting that it was not fully upheld by the court in the *Pagarani* case:[30] **5-022**

> The principal distinction between gifts and self-declarations of trust is that in the former the donor *transfers* rights to another, whereas in the latter the settlor *holds* rights for another. These transactions are completed in different ways. In the case of a gift, the donor's donative intention must be backed up with some act, such as a physical delivery or execution of a deed, that evinces the donor's intention irrevocably to transfer rights. In the case of a self-declaration of trust, because the settlor continues to hold their rights, something a little more subtle is required: the settlor must do some act, which the law can take cognizance of, which demonstrates that they are now holding those rights in a different capacity, i.e. an act that shows they are no longer held for himself, but for a beneficiary. The most obvious is the settlor's "declaring" of this intention. It is this declaration, as opposed to general donative intent seen in the context of a gift, that marks out self-declared trusts, albeit that, as *Choithram International SA v Pagarani* demonstrates, this distinction is not always adequately observed.

ii. Where the Settlor Has Done Everything in Her Power to Effect the Planned Transfer to Trustees

(1) The Rule in *Re Rose*

In *Milroy v Lord*, Turner LJ stated that:[31] **5-023**

> I take the law of this court to be well settled, that, in order to render a voluntary settlement valid and effectual, the settlor must have done everything which, according to the nature of the property comprised in the settlement, was necessary to be done in order to transfer the property and render the settlement binding upon him.

In a case where a transfer to trustees is planned, that statement can be interpreted in one of two ways: either: (i) the planned transfer must occur; or (ii) it also suffices if the settlor has done everything in her power to effect the transfer. **5-024**

The difference between those two interpretations was crucial in the following case, where the second interpretation of Turner LJ's statement was adopted. **5-025**

---

[28] See, e.g. *Pennington v Waine* [2002] EWCA Civ 227; [2002] 1 W.L.R. 2075 at [53].
[29] F.W. Maitland, *Equity – A Course of Lectures*, 2nd edn (Cambridge University Press, 1936), p.73.
[30] S. Agnew and S. Douglas, "Self-Declarations of Trust" (2019) 135 L.Q.R. 67, 72.
[31] (1862) 4 De G.F. & J. 264, 274.

Re Rose, Midland Bank Executor & Trustee Co Ltd v Rose

Chancery Division [1949] Ch. 78

5-026 The testator, Rose, had given a number of shares in his will to Hook, but the gift was subject to a qualification: "if such shares have not been transferred to him previously to my death". The question for the court was whether particular shares had already been transferred to Hook. Rose had intended to make an *inter vivos* transfer of certain shares to Hook and had executed a transfer document in the required form and handed it, with the share certificate, to Hook. By the time of Rose's death, however, Hook had not been registered as the new holder of the shares. As a result, it was clear that legal title to the shares remained in Rose at the time of his death. The residuary legatee under the will claimed the shares on the basis that: (i) Hook had no right in the shares at the time of Rose's death; but (ii) the testamentary gift to Hook was also ineffective, as the qualification applied, as the term "transfer", in that qualification, included Rose's execution of a transfer document. Jenkins J., however, accepted an argument made on Hook's behalf that, at his death, Rose held his legal title to the shares on trust for Hook.

5-027 JENKINS J.: It is argued on behalf of the residuary legatee that the testator's transfer of the 5,000 preference shares to Mr Hook, owing to the fact that the transfer was not registered in his lifetime, was at the time of the testator's death in the state of being an incomplete or inchoate gift. I was referred to the well known case of *Milroy v Lord*, and also to the recent case of *Re Fry*.[32] Those cases, as I understand them, turn on the fact that the deceased donor had not done all in his power, according to the nature of the property given, to vest the legal interest in the property in the donee. In such circumstances it is, of course, well settled that there is no equity to complete the imperfect gift. If any act remained to be done by the donor to complete the gift at the date of the donor's death the court will not compel his personal representatives to do that act and the gift remains incomplete and fails.

5-028 In *Milroy v Lord*, the imperfection was due to the fact that the wrong form of transfer was used for the purpose of transferring certain bank shares. The document was not the appropriate document to pass any interest in the property at all. . . In this case, as I understand it, the testator had done everything in his power to divest himself of the shares in question to Mr Hook. He had executed a transfer. It is not suggested that the transfer is not in accordance with the company's regulations. He had handed that transfer together with the certificates to Mr Hook. There was nothing else the testator could do. It is true that Mr Hook's legal title would not be perfected until the directors passed the transfer for registration, but that was not an act which the testator had to do, it was an act which depended on the discretion of the directors. Therefore it seems to me that the present case is not *in pari materia* with the two cases to which I have been referred. . .

5-029 What actually happened was that the transfer having been executed and the certificates handed over by the testator in his lifetime, Mr Hook's title under the transfer was in fact completed by registration after the testator's death. In my judgment, therefore, the position is that the shares had been transferred to Mr Hook previously to the testator's death within the meaning of clause 3(g) of the will, and his title under the transfer to him was perfected after the death by registration, and he takes the shares comprised in the transfer by the virtue of the transfer and not under the will.

5-030 The reasoning of Jenkins J was approved by the Court of Appeal in a different case, which also happened to involve a donor called Rose. In *Re Rose, Rose v IRC*,[33] it was again necessary to determine when a transfer had occurred. The question arose this time in relation to tax. Rose had transferred shares absolutely to his wife, and also to trustees on trust. The Crown claimed estate duty on the basis that the gifts had been completed only when the shares were registered in the names of the transferees. If, however, it could be shown that the gifts had been completed at an earlier point, that estate duty would not be payable. It was therefore argued that the gifts were, in the eyes of equity at least, complete when Rose completed the required transfer forms and handed them to the donees.

---

32 [1946] Ch. 312.

33 [1952] Ch. 499.

The Court of Appeal (the panel included Jenkins LJ) accepted that argument, adopting the "view of the limitations of *Milroy v Lord*" espoused by Jenkins J (as he then was) in the first *Re Rose* case.[34] Lord Evershed MR stated that:[35] **5–031**

> If a man executes a document transferring all his equitable interest, say, in shares, that document, operating, and intended to operate, as a transfer, will give rise to and take effect as a trust; for the assignor will then be a trustee of the legal estate in the shares for the person in whose favour he had made an assignment of his beneficial interest. And I do not think that the case of *Milroy v Lord* is an authority which compels the court to hold that in this case—where, in the terms of Turner L.J.'s judgment, the settlor did everything which, according to the nature of the property comprised in the settlement, was necessary to be done by him in order to transfer the property—the result necessarily negatives the conclusion that, pending registration, the settlor was a trustee of the legal interest for the transferee.

Jenkins LJ added his agreement:[36] **5–032**

> I agree with [Lord Evershed M.R.] that the case of *Milroy v Lord* by no means covers the question with which we have to deal in the present case. If the deceased had in truth transferred the whole of his interest in these shares so far as he could transfer the same, including such right as he could pass to his transferee to be placed on the register in respect of the shares, the question arises, what beneficial interest had he then left? The answer can only be, in my view, that he had no beneficial interest left whatever: his only remaining interest consisted in the fact that his name still stood on the register as holder of the shares; but having parted in fact with the whole of his beneficial interest, he could not, in my view, assert any beneficial title by virtue of his position of registered holder. In other words, in my view the effect of these transactions, having regard to the form and the operation of the transfers, the nature of the property transferred, and the necessity for registration in order to perfect the legal title, coupled with the discretionary power on the part of the directors to withhold registration, must be that, pending registration, the deceased was in the position of a trustee of the legal title in the shares for the transferees.

The analysis of Jenkins J and of the Court of Appeal in the two (otherwise unconnected) *Re Rose* cases thus makes it clear that the rule in *Milroy v Lord* is limited in this way: if a donor intends to make a transfer, and has done everything in her power to effect it, equity can regard the transfer as complete, with the consequence that the donee has an immediate beneficial interest and the donor holds on trust for the transferee. As Windeyer J put it in *Norman v Federal Commissioner of Taxation*:[37] **5–033**

> in equity there is a valid gift of property transferable at law if the donor, intending to make, then and there, a complete disposition and transfer to the donee, does all that on his part is necessary to give effect to his intention and arms the donee with the means of completing the gift according to the requirements of the law. . .

This analysis can apply not only where the donor plans to make an absolute gift, but also where a settlor intends to transfer property to trustees to hold on trust for B: in the latter case, it seems that the settlor then holds the property for B, on the terms of the intended trust.[38] **5–034**

---

[34] [1952] Ch. 499 at 511 per Lord Evershed MR.
[35] [1952] Ch. 499 at 510–511.
[36] [1952] Ch. 499 at 517–518. Morris LJ agreed with both Jenkins LJ and Lord Evershed MR.
[37] (1963) 109 C.L.R. 9 at 28–29.
[38] In *Re Rose, Rose v IRC* [1952] Ch. 499, for example, Rose intended two distinct transfers of shares: one to his wife absolutely, another to trustees to hold on trust, and the Court of Appeal regarded its analysis as applying in the same way to each of those intended transfers.

5-035 In *Mascall v Mascall*,[39] for example, the Court of Appeal applied the principle where a father had attempted to transfer legal title to registered land to his son. The father had executed the relevant transfer form and handed over the land certificate: "all that remained was for the son, in the ordinary way of conveyancing, to submit the transfer for stamping and then to ask the Land Registry to register his title".[40] At that stage, the transfer was regarded in equity as complete and so, although the father and son later fell out and the transfer form was returned by the Inland Revenue (to whom it had been sent for stamp duty purposes) to the father, it was no longer possible for the father to revoke the gift. Browne-Wilkinson LJ stated that:[41]

> The basic principle underlying all the cases is that equity will not come to the aid of a volunteer. Therefore, if a donee needs to get an order from a court of equity to complete his title, he will not get it. If, on the other hand, the donee has under his control everything necessary to constitute his title completely without any further assistance from the donor, the donee needs no assistance from equity and the gift is complete. It is on that principle, which is laid down in *Re Rose*, that in equity it is held that a gift is complete as soon as the settlor or donor has done everything that the donor has to do, that is to say, as soon as the donee has within his control all those things necessary to enable him, the donee, to complete his title.

5-036 As this statement shows, care must be taken when invoking the maxim that "equity will not assist a volunteer". There are many situations in which a claimant who has given no value can acquire rights in equity. The most obvious is where a settlor successfully exercises her power to set up a trust for the claimant, either by a transfer to trustees or by a self-declaration. Once a trust has been completely constituted, the courts will give effect to it and will enforce the rights of a beneficiary, regardless of whether the beneficiary has given any value in exchange for these rights.[42] As Lord Browne-Wilkinson subsequently noted in the *Choithram* case:[43] "Once a trust relationship is established between trustee and beneficiary, the fact that a beneficiary has given no value is irrelevant". The rule in *Re Rose* similarly depends on the idea that, as the donor has done what is necessary, in the eyes of equity at least, to complete the gift, the donee acquires an equitable interest, regardless of whether she has provided any value in exchange for it.

(2) Justifying the Rule in *Re Rose*

5-037 As noted above,[44] the approach taken in *Re Rose* depends on adopting the second of the two possible interpretations of a statement of Turner LJ in *Milroy v Lord*.[45] The first of those interpretations is equally consistent with the result in that earlier case and might be thought to provide a clearer fit with the logic of the reasoning: if a settlor intends to set up a trust by means of a transfer of property to a trustee, that express trust can take effect only if the property is in fact transferred. The complication introduced by *Re Rose* is that a transfer can be said to be effective *in equity*, even if the conditions for the transfer of the property at common law have not been met.

5-038 There are, however, two obvious objections to the analysis adopted in *Re Rose*. First, property is either transferred or it is not; if there are rules as to what is necessary for such a transfer (such as the need for registration in relation to shares or land), then why should equity bypass those rules and

---

39 (1985) 50 P. & C.R. 119.
40 (1985) 50 P. & C.R. 119 at 125 per Lawton LJ.
41 (1985) 50 P. & C.R. 119 at 126.
42 *Paul v Paul* (1882) 20 Ch.D. 742.
43 *T Choithram International SA v Pagarani* [2001] 1 W.L.R. 1 at 12.
44 See 5-025.
45 (1862) 4 De G.F. & J. 264.

directly contradict the common law by finding that a transfer has occurred? Moreover, if the common law rules are to be ignored, how can we then tell what is necessary in equity for a transfer to occur? In *Pennington v Waine*,[46] for example, a case that also concerned a planned gift of shares, Clarke LJ held that a transfer occurred in equity as soon as the donor executed the share transfer form, even if that form was not then given to the donee;[47] in contrast, Arden LJ (with whom Schiemann LJ agreed) stated that:[48] "the ratio of *Re Rose (Rose v IRC)* was as I read it that the gifts of shares in that case were completely constituted when the donor executed share transfers and delivered them to the transferees even though they were not registered in the register of members of the company until a later date."

The second objection to the analysis adopted in *Re Rose* is that it seems to depend on a particular transaction being effective to transfer the donor's equitable interest in property, but not her legal interest. It is clear, however, that if the donor simply owns property absolutely, it is misleading to think of her as having both a distinct legal interest and a distinct equitable interest. Equity has no reason to intervene where A simply holds a legal right to property, and, in the absence of grounds for equitable intervention, there can be no distinct equitable interest. In Lord Browne-Wilkinson's words in *Westdeutsche Landesbank Girozentrale v Islington LBC*:[49] **5–039**

> A person solely entitled to the full beneficial ownership of money or property, both at law and in equity, does not enjoy an equitable interest in that property. The legal title carries with it all rights. Unless and until there is a separation of legal and equitable estates, there is no separate equitable title.

A justification for the rule in *Re Rose* could meet those objections if it takes into account the supplementary nature of equity: in such cases, equity does not seek to contradict the common law, by finding that a transfer has occurred even though the donor in fact retains the property. Rather, equity recognises that the donor (A) has the property, but allows the donee (B) to control A's exercise of that legal entitlement: this is consistent with the characteristic function of equity discussed in Chapters 1 to 3. For example, in *Mascall v Mascall*,[50] Browne-Wilkinson LJ focussed on the point that if "the donee has under his control everything necessary to constitute his title completely without any further assistance from the donor, the donee needs no assistance from equity and the gift is complete".[51] The idea here may be that, if, as a result of the donor's actions, the donee obtains a power, through her own actions, to acquire the relevant property, then a trust arises. This view has some merit, but it is far from being fully worked out in the case-law, and gives rise to some difficult questions. For example, once the donee factually has the power to complete the transfer (e.g. by registration) does that mean that the trust continues even if the donee then loses that factual power (as occurred in *Mascall*, when the transferee lost possession of the transfer form)? If so, why does the fact that the donee at one point had the power to complete the transfer subject the donor to an ongoing duty? **5–040**

It could alternatively be said that where the donor has done everything necessary to complete the transaction, it would then be unconscionable for her to attempt to rescind the gift and a constructive trust of the property therefore arises to give effect to the donor's duty to make the transfer. The **5–041**

46 [2002] EWCA Civ 227; [2002] 1 W.L.R. 2075; paras 5–104 to 5–125.
47 [2002] 1 W.L.R. 2075 at [106] and [110]. See too Murray J in *Collins v Simonsen* [2019] EWHC 2214 (QB) at [58].
48 [2002] 1 W.L.R. 2075 at [65].
49 [1996] A.C. 669 at 706. The case is an important authority on resulting trusts, and so is examined in detail in Chapter 16: as to this specific point, see too para.4–046.
50 (1985) 50 P. & C.R. 119 at 126.
51 See too *Kaye v Zeital* [2010] EWCA Civ 159 at [42]–[43] where Rimer LJ stated that the principle applies only where A has done "all within his power to procure the transfer" to B, and that this requirement had not been met on the facts of the case, as B did not have access to the share certificate required to complete the transfer.

reasoning of Arden LJ (with whom Schiemann LJ agreed) in *Pennington v Waine*[52] seems to be consistent with that analysis. The difficulty, however, is in explaining precisely why the mere fact that the donor *tried* to make a gift then makes it unconscionable for the donor to change her mind and decide not to proceed.[53] After all, if the maxim that "equity will not assist a volunteer" means anything,[54] it means that no duty is imposed on a donor simply because she intended, and tried, to make a gift. In conclusion then, the effect of the rule in *Re Rose* is consistent with equity's characteristic secondary or supplementary function: it does not, despite some loose judicial language, involve equity pretending that a right of A has been transferred to B, but rather recognises that A is under a duty to B in relation to a right still held by A. The difficulty, however, is as to whether there is a good justification for that duty, which explains why A is no longer allowed to change her mind and use her retained right for her own benefit, rather than for the benefit of B.[55]

iii. Where the Planned Transfer Does not Occur, but the Property Ends Up in the Hands of the Intended Trustee by Other Means

(1) The Basic Rule: Only the Settlor (or Her Authorised Agent) Can Constitute a Trust

5-042 Consider a case in which the settlor, S, plans to set up a trust by transferring property to a trustee, T, to hold on trust for a beneficiary, B. It may even be that S has made a gratuitous promise to T that she will transfer a specific painting to T to hold on trust for B. S dies, however, without having made that planned transfer of the painting. Clearly the rule in *Milroy v Lord* means that B cannot claim that S held the painting on trust for B. If, however, S's title to the painting came into T's hands by some other means, should the courts then regard that trust as completely, even if coincidentally, constituted, so that B acquires the planned beneficial interest?

5-043 The basic answer is no: the settlor (or her duly authorised agent) must be responsible for the trust property becoming duly vested in the trustees.[56] That answer obtains even if, as in our example, S made a gratuitous promise to T to make the transfer: the point is that the gratuitous promise does not create a duty owed by S and that, in the absence of a transfer authorised by S, the planned trust has not been completely constituted.

Re Brooks' Settlement Trusts

Chancery Division [1939] Ch. 993

5-044 By the terms of a marriage settlement the income of the settled fund was directed to be paid to the wife during her life and the fund was to be held in trust for such of her issue as she might by deed or will appoint; in default of any appointment the fund was to be held in trust in equal shares for all her children who being sons should attain the age of twenty-one years or being daughters should attain that age or marry. In 1929 one of her children (AT) executed a voluntary settlement whereby he assigned to Lloyds Bank as trustees, "all the part or share, parts or shares and other interest whether vested or contingent to which the settlor is now or may hereafter become entitled whether in default of appointment, or under any appointment hereafter to be made or on failure of any such appointment of and in the trust property [under the marriage settlement]". By an appointment in pursuance of her power under the marriage settlement, AT's mother

52 [2002] 1 W.L.R. 2075 at [64]–[65].

53 See too Y.K. Liew, "Unconscionability and the Case Against Lumping: Three Case Studies" (2021) 27 T.&T. 181.

54 See para.1–102.

55 For consideration of possible justifications for *Re Rose*, see e.g. P. Luxton, "In Search of Perfection: the *Re Rose* Rule Rationale" [2012] Conv. 70 and YK Liew, *Rationalizing Constructive Trusts* (Hart Publishing, 2017) Ch.9.

56 *Re Brooks's ST* [1939] 1 Ch. 993; *Re Adlard* [1954] Ch. 29.

in 1939 appointed him a sum of £3,517 and released her life interest. Thereupon Lloyds Bank Ltd, who had by then become trustees of the marriage settlement as well as of AT's voluntary settlement, took out a summons asking whether they should pay AT the £3,517. Farwell J. held that AT was entitled to require payment of the sum appointed, and could not be compelled to permit the bank to retain the £3,517.

FARWELL J.: When one looks at the voluntary settlement, at first sight the answer would seem to be quite clearly that the trustees' duty was to retain the sum of £3,517 as part of the funds which the son had voluntarily settled, and the language of the voluntary settlement would seem to leave no doubt on that score, because the settlor assigned to the bank "all the part or share parts or shares and other interest whether vested or contingent to which the settlor is now or may hereafter become entitled whether in default of appointment or under any appointment hereafter to be made or on failure of any such appointment of and in the trust property which is now or may at any time hereafter become subject to the trusts of the wife's settlement." One would say, looking at the language of the settlement, that it would be difficult to find words more apt to embrace in the voluntary settlement all the interests which the son had then or might thereafter have under the marriage settlement and that accordingly the answer should be that it is the duty of the trustees to retain this as part of the voluntary settlement fund. But, when one considers the legal position in this matter, a different aspect seems to appear. If the matter could be tested simply as one of construction, the answer would appear to be in favour of the trustees of the voluntary settlement; but the question is not one of construction only, and I have to consider whether the attempt to assign that which the son has now become entitled to by virtue of the exercise of the power is enforceable against him. **5–045**

The legal position in the case of a special power of appointment is not in any doubt at all. Referring to *Farwell on Powers*,[57] I find this statement of principle, which will be found in exactly the same language in earlier editions of the book, and therefore is not in any way the creation of the editor: **5–046**

> "The exercise of a power of appointment divests (either wholly or partially according to the terms of the appointment) the estates limited in default of appointment and creates a new estate, and that, too, whether the property be real or personal."

The effect of this is that in the case of a special power the property is vested in the persons who take in default of appointment, subject, of course, to any prior life interest, but liable to be divested at any time by a valid exercise of the power, and the effect of such an exercise of the power is to defeat wholly or pro tanto the interests which up to then were vested in the persons entitled in default of appointment and to create new estates in those persons in whose favour the appointment had been made. That being so, it is, in my judgment, impossible to say that until an appointment has been made in favour of this son the son had any interest under his mother's settlement other than an interest as one of the people entitled in default of appointment; he had an interest in that; but that interest was liable to be divested, and, if an appointment was made in favour of the son, then to that extent the persons entitled in default were defeated and he was given an interest in the funds which he had never had before and which came into being for the first time when the power was exercised. No doubt it is quite true to say that the appointment has to be read in to the marriage settlement, but, in my judgment, that is not sufficient ground for saying that at the time when this voluntary settlement was made the son had any interest at all in the fund other than his vested interest in default of appointment; for the rest, he had nothing more than a mere expectancy, the hope that at some date his mother might think fit to exercise the power of appointment in his favour, but, until she did so choose, he had nothing other than his interest in default of appointment to which he could point and say: "That is a fund to which I shall become entitled in future or to which I am contingently entitled." Apart from this he was not contingently entitled at all; he had no interest whatever in the fund until the appointment had been executed. **5–047**

If that be the true view, as I believe it to be, the result must be that, whatever the language of the settlement may be, the settlor under the voluntary settlement was purporting to assign to the trustees something to which he might in certain circumstances become entitled in the future, but to which he was not then entitled in any sense at all, and if that be so, then it is plain on the authorities that the son cannot be compelled to hand over or to permit the trustees to retain this sum and that he is himself entitled to call upon them to pay it over to him. . . **5–048**

[57] 3rd edn (1916), p.310 [edited by Farwell J himself].

5–049 Notwithstanding the fact that the language of this voluntary settlement as a matter of construction is wide enough to comprise this interest, the principle of law which I have stated makes it impossible to enforce the settlement to that extent and prevents the settlor from being compelled by this Court to transfer or permit the trustees to retain this money as part of the funds subject thereto.

5–050 In *Re Brooks' Settlement Trusts*, then, AT had made a gratuitous promise to make a transfer of property he might receive under an existing marriage settlement, to Lloyds Bank to hold on trust. Lloyds Bank then became trustees of the marriage settlement, and, under its terms, were under a duty to pay a sum of money to AT. Lloyds Bank could not instead immediately hold that money on the terms of AT's promised voluntary settlement: that trust would only be completely constituted if AT, or his agent, authorised Lloyds Bank to hold on the terms of the voluntary settlement;[58] AT was under no duty to do so as his promise was gratuitous. The case thus makes very clear that a trust will not be completely constituted if, in the absence of the planned transfer by the settlor, the planned trust property happens to end up in the hands of the planned trustee. The law is not, however, as clear as it might be, owing to some further decisions that we will now consider.

(2) A Challenge to the Basic Rule: *Re Ralli's Will Trusts*

5–051 In *Re Ralli's Will Trusts*,[59] the approach taken by Buckley J in obiter dicta does not attempt to set up an exception to the basic rule, but seems rather to challenge its existence.

Re Ralli's Will Trusts

Chancery Division [1964] Ch. 288

5–052 In 1899, Helen Ralli became entitled, under a trust set up in her father's will, to one-half of her father's residuary estate subject to her mother's life interest. The mother died in 1961 so Helen's reversionary interest then fell into possession. In 1924, Helen in her marriage settlement had covenanted to assign to the trustees thereof as soon as circumstances would admit all her existing and after-acquired property upon certain trusts for her children which failed (Helen dying a childless widow) and ultimately upon trusts for the benefit of the children of Helen's sister, Irene, who were volunteers. A subsequent clause in the marriage settlement was held on its proper construction to declare that all property currently held by Helen and comprised within the terms of the covenant should be subject immediately to the trusts of the marriage settlement, pending assignment to the trustees. Helen died in 1956 without having assigned her reversionary interest acquired in 1899 under her father's will. The plaintiff (who was married to Helen's sister) was the sole surviving trustee of the 1924 marriage settlement. It so happened that in 1946 he had also become a trustee of the Helen's father's will trust and was now also the sole surviving trustee of that trust. He therefore claimed that Helen's reversionary interest under the father's will trusts was now held by him on the trusts of the marriage settlement (which benefitted his daughters). The defendants, Helen's personal representatives, disputed this, claimed that her estate was entitled to the reversionary interest, as Helen had made no transfer of it to the trustees of the marriage settlement.

5–053 BUCKLEY J. held that the vested reversionary interest, being existing property of Helen at the time she made what he construed as an independent declaration of trust pending assignment to the trustees of her marriage settlement, was held on the trusts of the marriage settlement.[60] He then continued:

5–054 If this view is right, this disposes of the case, but I think I should go on to state what would be my view, if I were mistaken in the view I have expressed. The investments representing the share of residue in question

---

[58] *Re Adlard* [1954] Ch. 29. Note that s.53(1)(c) of the Law of Property Act 1925 would apply in such a case to require AT's authority to be in signed: see *Grey v IRC* [1960] A.C. 1, discussed at paras 6–053ff. Any authority given to Lloyds Bank before its receipt of the property, if given gratuitously, and not otherwise irrevocable, could be revoked before receipt: *Re Bowden* [1936] Ch. 71, although cf. *Re Burton's Settlements* [1955] Ch. 82 at 104 per Upjohn J.

[59] [1964] Ch. 288.

[60] [See para.5–020.]

stand in the name of the plaintiff. This is because he is now the sole surviving trustee of the [father's] will. Therefore, say the defendants, he holds these investments primarily on the trusts of the will, that is to say, in trust for them as part of Helen's estate. The plaintiff is, however, also the sole surviving covenantee under clause 7 of the [marriage] settlement, as well as the sole surviving trustee of that settlement. This, however, affords him no answer, say the defendants, to their claim under the will unless the plaintiff, having transferred the property to them in pursuance of the trusts of the will, could compel them to return it in pursuance of their obligation under the covenant, and this, they say, he could not do. . . .

The plaintiff, on the other hand, contends that, as he already holds the investments, no question of his having to enforce the covenant arises. The fund having come without impropriety into his hands is now, he says, impressed in his hands with the trusts on which he ought to hold it under the settlement; and because of the covenant it does not lie in the mouth of the defendants to say that he should hold it in trust for Helen's estate. He relies on *Re Bowden*[61] in which case a lady by a voluntary settlement purported to assign to trustees inter alia such property as she should become entitled to under the will of her father, who was still alive, and authorised the trustees to receive the property and give receipts for it. In due course her father died and the property to which the lady became entitled under his will was transferred to the trustees of the settlement. Many years later the lady claimed that the property belonged to her absolutely. Bennett, J. [held] that she was not entitled to the property. . . **5–055**

Counsel for the defendants says that *Re Bowden* and *Re Adlard's Settlement Trust*[62] are distinguishable from the present case because in each of those cases the fund had reached the hands of the trustees of the relevant settlement and was held by them in that capacity, whereas in the present case the fund is, as he maintains, in the hands of the plaintiff in the capacity of trustee of the will and not in the capacity of trustee of the settlement. He says that *Re Burton's Settlements*,[63] the complicated facts of which I forbear to set out here, should be distinguished on the ground that, when the settlement there in question was made, the trustee of that settlement and the trustee of the settlement under which the settlor had expectations was the same, so that the settlor by her settlement gave directions to the trustee of the settlement under which she had expectations, who then already held the relevant fund. **5–056**

Counsel for the plaintiff says that the capacity in which the trustee has become possessed of the fund is irrelevant. Thus in *Strong v Bird*,[64] an imperfect gift was held to be completed by the donee obtaining probate of the donor's will of which he was executor, notwithstanding that the donor died intestate as to her residue and that the donee was not a person entitled as on her intestacy. Similarly in *Re James*,[65] a grant of administration to two administrators was held to perfect an imperfect gift by the intestate to one of them, who had no beneficial interest in the intestate's estate. **5–057**

In my judgment the circumstance that the plaintiff holds the fund because he was appointed a trustee of the will is irrelevant. He is at law the owner of the fund and the means by which he became so have no effect on the quality of his legal ownership. The question is: for whom, if any one, does he hold the fund in equity? In other words, who can successfully assert an equity against him disentitling him to stand on his legal right? It seems to me to be indisputable that Helen, if she were alive, could not do so, for she has solemnly covenanted under seal to assign the fund to the plaintiff and the defendants can stand in no better position. It is, of course, true that the object of the covenant was not that the plaintiff should retain the property for his own benefit, but that he should hold it on the trusts of the settlement. It is also true that, if it were necessary to enforce performance of the covenant, equity would not assist the beneficiaries under the settlement, because they are mere volunteers; and that for the same reason the plaintiff, as trustee of the settlement, would not be bound to enforce the covenant and would not be constrained by the court to do so, and indeed, it seems, might be constrained by the court not to do so. As matters stand, however, there is no occasion to invoke the assistance of equity to enforce the performance of the covenant. It is for the defendants to invoke the assistance of equity to make good their claim to the fund. To do so successfully they must show that the plaintiff cannot conscientiously withhold it from them. When they seek to do this, he can point to the covenant which, in my judgment, relieves him from any fiduciary obligation that he would otherwise owe to the defendants as Helen's representatives. In so doing the plaintiff is **5–058**

---

61 [1936] Ch. 71.
62 [1954] Ch. 29.
63 [1955] Ch. 82.
64 (1874) L.R. 18 Eq. 315.
65 [1935] Ch. 449.

> not seeking to enforce an equitable remedy against the defendants on behalf of persons who could not enforce such a remedy themselves: he is relying on the combined effect of his legal ownership of the fund and his legal right to enforce the covenant. That an action on the covenant might be statute-barred is irrelevant, for there is no occasion for such an action.
>
> **5-059** Had someone other than the plaintiff been the trustee of the will and held the fund, the result of this part of the case would, in my judgment, have been different; and it may seem strange that the rights of the parties should depend on the appointment of the plaintiff as a trustee of the will in 1946, which for present purposes may have been a quite fortuitous event. The result, however, in my judgment, flows—and flows, I think, quite rationally—from the consideration that the rules of equity derive from the tenderness of a court of equity for the consciences of the parties. There would have been nothing unconscientious in Helen or her personal representatives asserting her equitable interests under trusts of the will against a trustee who was not a covenantee under clause 7 of the [marriage] settlement, and it would have been unconscientious for such a trustee to disregard those interests. Having obtained a transfer of the fund, it would not have been unconscientious in Helen to refuse to honour her covenant, because the beneficiaries under her settlement were mere volunteers: nor seemingly would the court have regarded it as unconscientious in the plaintiff to have abstained from enforcing the covenant either specifically or in damages, for the reason, apparently, that he would have been under no obligation to obtain for the volunteers indirectly what they could not obtain directly. In such circumstances Helen or her personal representatives could have got and retained the fund. In the circumstances of the present case, on the other hand, it is not unconscientious in the plaintiff to withhold from Helen's estate the fund which Helen covenanted that he should receive: on the contrary, it would have been unconscientious in Helen to seek to deprive the plaintiff of that fund, and her personal representatives can be in no better position. The inadequacy of the volunteers' equity against Helen and her estate consequently is irrelevant, for that equity does not come into play; but they have a good equity as against the plaintiff, because it would be unconscientious in him to retain as against them any property which he holds in consequence of the provisions of the settlement.
>
> **5-060** For these reasons I am of opinion that in the events which have happened the plaintiff now holds the fund in question on the trusts of the marriage settlement, and I will so declare.

5-061 First, Buckley J's analysis of this point is that it is expressly stated to be obiter: the result in the case was determined by the fact that Helen had made an inter vivos self-declaration of trust that she would hold her current property (including her beneficial interest under the trusts of her father's will) on the trusts of the marriage settlement.[66]

5-062 Second, on the obiter analysis, everything turned on the coincidence that the plaintiff, Helen's brother-in-law, was both the trustee of Helen's father's will, under which Helen had a beneficial interest, *and* the trustee of Helen's marriage settlement, and thus the party to whom Helen, if she had kept her promise to do so, would have transferred property (including her interest under her father's will) on trust to be held for the benefit of the plaintiff's daughters. Buckley J. took the view that, whilst no-one could have sued Helen to force her to abide by her gratuitous promise to transfer property to the trustees of the marriage settlement, as property subject to that promise was now coincidentally in the hands of a trustee of that marriage settlement, Helen (and thus her personal representatives) could not now prevent the trustee from applying that property according to the terms of the marriage settlement trusts.

5-063 On the facts of *Re Ralli* itself, this no doubt suited the trustee, as the beneficiaries of the marriage settlement trusts were his daughters; but the general approach of Buckley J. could, in practice, cause grave difficulties for professional trustees who act as such in relation to a very large number of different trusts. It seems that, even if they received property to hold on the basis of one such trust, they may in fact hold it on the terms of another one of those trusts, if the beneficiary of the former trust made a promise (even a gratuitous one) to effect a transfer of it to the latter trust.

---

[66] See para.5-020.

Whatever its practical consequences might be, the obiter reasoning of Buckley J in *Re Ralli* appears to be a direct challenge to the reasoning in *Re Brook's Settlement Trusts*; but unfortunately it seems that the earlier decision was not cited to the court. Buckley J. did however rely on *Strong v Bird*,[67] and we will now consider that decision, though it seems at most to be an exception to the basic rule established in *Re Brook's*, rather than a rejection of that rule. **5-064**

(3) An Exception to the Basic Rule? *Strong v Bird*

In itself, the decision in *Strong v Bird*[68] is of quite limited effect, but later cases have used it as the basis for an exception to the general rule that, where a settlor plans to set up a trust by means of a transfer to trustees, the trust will be completely constituted only if the planned transfer is made by the settlor or her authorised agent. **5-065**

Consider a case in which a debtor (D) owes a creditor (C) £100. C dies and appoints D as her executor. What effect does this have on the debt? Generally, of course, it is the job of an executor to enforce outstanding debts owed to the deceased, but can we really say that C expected D, after C's death, to collect the debt that D himself owes to C? The common law certainly treated D's appointment[69] as executor as extinguishing or releasing his debt to C,[70] on the basis that C must have intended such a result.[71] As an administrator (who carries out the same essential role as an executor where the deceased dies intestate) is not specifically chosen by the deceased, the common law did not treat the appointment of the administrator as the release of any debt due to the deceased from the administrator.[72] In equity, however, the position was different: even if the debt had been formally extinguished D (whether C's executor or administrator) had to account for the debt to the estate, so that the £100 was available to pay off creditors of the estate or to be distributed among the beneficiaries.[73] **5-066**

In *Strong v Bird*, the Court of Chancery resolved this difference by ruling that the logic of the common law's approach should prevail, so that D did not have to account to the estate for the debt, as long as C had indeed manifested an intent to forgive the debt in his lifetime and this intent had continued until C's death. So, C's merely saying to D, "I forgive this debt" would not by itself release the debt, either at law or in equity;[74] but as Sir George Jessel MR ruled in *Strong v Bird*, things are different if: **5-067**

> [D] proves to the satisfaction of the court a continuing intention [of C] to give; and it appears to me that there being the continuing intention to give, and there being a legal act which transferred ownership or released the obligation—for it is the same thing—the transaction is perfected, and [D] does not want the aid of a court of Equity to carry it out, or make it complete, because it is complete already, and there is no equity against him to take the property away from him.

---

67 (1874) L.R. 18 Eq. 315.

68 (1874) L.R. 18 Eq. 315.

69 The appointment itself discharges the debt even if the executor dies before taking out probate: see, e.g. *Wankford v Wankford* (1704) 1 Salk. 299; *Re Applebee* [1891] 3 Ch. 422; *Jenkins v Jenkins* [1928] 2 K.B. 501.

70 See, e.g. *Re Bourne* [1906] 1 Ch. 697; *Bone v Stamp Duties Commissioner* (1974) 132 C.L.R. 38.

71 See, e.g. *Bone v Stamp Duties Commissioner* (1974) 132 C.L.R. 38 at 53 per Mason J.

72 *Wankford v Wankford* (1704) 1 Salk. 299; *Seagram v Knight* (1867) 2 Ch. App. 628; *Re Gonin* [1977] 2 All E.R. 720 at 734. Now see Administration of Estates Act 1925 s.21A added by Limitation Amendment Act 1980 s.10.

73 *Berry v Usher* (1805) 11 Ves. 87; *Jenkins v Jenkins* [1928] 2 K.B. 501.

74 *Strong v Bird* (1874) L.R. 18 Eq. 315 at 317–318 per Sir George Jessel MR: "It is what the law calls nudum pactum, a promise made without an actual consideration passing, and which consequently cannot be supported as a contract. It is not a release, because it is not under seal. Therefore the mere circumstance of saying 'I forgive you' will not do."

5-068 How then does *Strong v Bird* bear on the general rule that a trust by way of transfer to trustees is completely constituted only if the transfer is made by the settlor or her agent? First, it might be thought that the language of gifts and ownership seems strange when considering the release of a debt, but there is an obvious analogy between making a gift of £100 and releasing a debt of £100. The "gift" in *Strong v Bird* was considered complete as a result of C's having appointed D as executor with the intention of forgiving the debt. Second, however, it is important to note the limits of *Strong v Bird*: essentially, equity left the common law position undisturbed in a case where C appointed D as an executor and had an ongoing intention to release a debt. It certainly was not a case in which a donee invoked the assistance of equity in order to complete an imperfect gift, nor was it one in which an exception was recognised to the general rule that a trust by way of transfer to trustees is completely constituted only if the transfer is made by the settlor or her agent.

5-069 Later decisions, however, extended the impact of *Strong v Bird*. For example, in *Re Stewart*, Neville J said:[75]

> Where a testator has expressed the intention of making a gift of personal estate to one who upon his death becomes his executor, the intention continuing unchanged, the executor is entitled to hold the property for his own benefit. The reasoning is first that the vesting of the property in the executor at the testator's death completes the imperfect gift made in the lifetime and secondly that the intention of the testator to give the beneficial interest to the executor is sufficient to countervail the equity of beneficiaries under the will, the testator having vested the legal estate in the executor.

5-070 *Re Stewart* has been followed many times at first instance[76] and treated as good law by the Court of Appeal.[77] In *Re James*,[78] Farwell J extended *Re Stewart* to perfect an imperfect gift of real property made by a donor to his housekeeper who, on the donor's intestacy, had herself appointed by the court one of two administratrices of the deceased donor's estate, thereby obtaining legal title to the house. This extension has been doubted by Walton J in *Re Gonin*[79] and was rejected by the British Virgin Islands' Court of Appeal in *Re Pagarani*:[80] after all, it is the *choice* of the testator in appointing her debtor as her executor that extinguishes the debt at law, so that the fortuitous appointment by the court of an administrator who was a debtor of the intestate did not extinguish the debt. *Strong v Bird*, therefore, would have been differently decided if the defendant had been an administrator and not an executor.

5-071 It thus seems that "the rule in *Strong v Bird*" has now developed far beyond the principle in the case itself, and may now allow an imperfect immediate[81] gift of specific[82] existing[83] real or personal property[84] to be perfected if the intended donee is appointed the testator's executor or administrator, alone or with others, so long as the intention to make the gift continues unchanged till the testator's

---

75 [1908] 2 Ch. 251 at 254.

76 *Re Comberback* (1929) 73 Sol. Jo. 403; *Re James* [1935] Ch. 449; *Re Nelson* (1967) 91 Sol. Jo. 533: see also *Re Ralli's WT* [1964] Ch. 288; *Re Gonin* [1979] Ch. 16.

77 *Re Freeland* [1952] Ch. 110, counsel unreservedly accepting *Re Stewart*.

78 [1935] Ch. 449.

79 [1979] Ch. 16.

80 (1999) 2 O.F.L.R. 1. The issue was not considered by the Privy Council on the appeal from that decision: *T. Choithram International SA v Pagarani* [2001] 1 W.L.R. 1 (which is excerpted at paras 5-013 to 5-018).

81 *Re Innes* [1910] 1 Ch. 188; *Re Freeland* [1952] Ch. 110; *Re Gonin* [1979] Ch. 16; *Re Pink* [1912] 2 Ch. 528 at 536–539; *Simpson v Simpson* [1992] 1 F.L.R. 601. *Re Goff* (1914) 111 L.T. 34 is out of line since the donor only intended to forgive the debt if the donor predeceased the donee.

82 *Re Innes* [1910] 1 Ch. 188 at 193.

83 *Morton v Brighouse* [1927] 1 D.L.R. 1009.

84 *Re James* [1935] Ch. 449.

death.[85] Whilst the perfection of the gift thus prevents any claim to the property by those beneficially entitled to the deceased's estate, it probably does not, however, bar a claim to that property by creditors of the deceased, since the common law rule as to the release of a debt by appointment of the debtor as executor did not avail against creditors.[86]

It therefore seems that a limited exception, of doubtful pedigree, has been recognised to the general rule that a trust by way of transfer to trustees is completely constituted only if the transfer is made by the settlor or her agent. The exception applies where: (i) the settlor did not complete the planned transfer during her life; but (ii) the settlor appointed the planned trustee as an executor of her estate, or the planned trustee was appointed as an administrator of that estate;[87] and (iii) the settlor's intention to make the transfer on trust continued until her death, so that she had at that time "a present intention of giving".[88] **5–072**

E. Summary

We have now considered the basic rule in *Milroy v Lord*, the scope of that rule, and its application in practice. It is perhaps helpful to summarise the results. First, the basic rule states that, if a settlor intends to set up a trust by making a transfer to trustees to hold on trust for B, but fails to make the planned transfer, the settlor's intention to benefit B does not suffice to allow B to claim that the settlor instead declared a trust and so held the property on trust for B. This is because there is a clear distinction between: (i) intending to benefit B by transferring to trustees to hold on trust for B; and (ii) intending to benefit B by retaining property and declaring a trust of that property in favour of B.[89] Secondly, however, if it can be found that the settlor did in fact declare that she held the property on trust for B, that declaration will be given effect to and, it seems, in a case where it was clear that the settlor wished to benefit B, a court may adopt a "benevolent" interpretation of the facts in order to find such a declaration.[90] Thirdly, if, although the requirements for a valid transfer of legal title to the property were not met, the settlor nonetheless did everything in her power to make that transfer, the settlor will hold her legal title to the property subject to the planned trusts.[91] Fourthly, whilst the basic rule is that the planned transfer to trustees must be completed by the settlor or her agent,[92] an exception is permitted where the planned trustee receives the planned trust property as an executor or administrator on the death of the settlor, provided that the settlor had a continuing intention to set up the trust at the time of her death.[93] **5–073**

---

85 It seems that contrary expressions before death may be ignored if the intent to make the imperfect gift is confirmed in the will: *Re Stoneham* [1919] 1 Ch. 149 at 158. For cases on contrary intention see *Re Freeland* [1952] Ch. 110; *Re Eiser's WT* [1937] 1 All E.R. 244; *Re Wale* [1956] 1 W.L.R. 1346; *Morton v Brighouse* [1927] 1 D.L.R. 1009 (property imperfectly given to X subsequently specifically bequeathed to Y).

86 *Bone v Stamp Duties Commissioner* (1974) 132 C.L.R. 38.

87 Note that in *Carter v Hungerford* [1917] 1 Ch. 260 at 273, Astbury J suggested that the rule would also apply to protect an executor from the claims of those entitled under the settlor's will if the executor, mistakenly believing herself to be bound to do so, transferred property to the settlor's intended donees. This seems, however, to be an extension too far, as an executor, unlike a settlor, is subject to fiduciary duties and should not be able thus to defeat those entitled under the settlor's will purely in order to complete a transfer that the settlor died without completing.

88 *Re Innes* [1910] 1 Ch. 188 at 193, applied in, e.g. *Re Freeland* [1952] Ch. 110 at 116.

89 See *Milroy v Lord* (1862) 4 De G.F. & J. 264: see paras 5–006 to 5–011.

90 See, e.g. *T Choithram International SA v Pagarani* [2001] 1 W.L.R. 1: see paras 5–012 to 5–022.

91 *Re Rose, Rose v IRC* [1952] Ch. 499, approving *Re Rose, Midland Bank Executor & Trustee Co Ltd v Rose* [1949] Ch. 78.

92 *Re Brook's Settlement Trusts* [1939] Ch. 993: see paras 5–042 to 5–050; although note that the basic rule is challenged by *obiter* observations of Buckley J in *Re Ralli's Will Trusts* [1964] Ch. 288.

93 See *Re Stewart* [1908] 2 Ch. 251, giving a very expansive interpretation to the principle in *Strong v Bird* (1874) L.R. 18 Eq. 315: see paras 5–069 to 5–072.

3. Incompletely Constituted Trusts and Constructive Trusts

5–074 Consider a case in which the settlor plans to set up a trust in B's favour by making a transfer to trustees to hold on trust for B. If such a transfer is not made,[94] B cannot claim to have acquired a beneficial interest under such a trust. If, equally, the settlor made no self-declaration of a trust in favour of B, then it will be impossible for B to show that the settlor created an express trust in her favour: there is no completely constituted express trust. As previously noted,[95] however, it may still be possible for B to claim a beneficial interest if B can show that a non-express trust has arisen, i.e. a trust that was not created by the settlor's successful exercise of a power to create a trust, but was rather imposed by law. There are many different bases on which such a constructive trust might arise,[96] and we will examine such trusts in more detail in Chapter 17. We will consider here only the types of constructive trust that are most likely to be relevant in cases of an incompletely constituted express trust.[97]

A. The General Position: "Equity Will Not Assist a Volunteer"

5–075 The general position as to the possibility of B's claiming a right under a constructive trust is very clear: the mere fact that the settlor intended, and perhaps even attempted, to set up a trust for B does not, in itself, suffice to give rise to a constructive trust. It is often said that such a trust can be imposed on a party holding property only in response to the prospect of unconscionable conduct by that party, and there is nothing unconscionable in the settlor's conduct if she either repents of the intention to set up a trust for B, or dies having failed to constitute the planned trust. This general position can be explained by invoking the maxim that "equity will not assist a volunteer".[98] It is far from clear, however, that the maxim is helpful. As noted above,[99] caution must be exercised as, *if* an express trust has been completely constituted, B will acquire a beneficial interest under that trust even if she provided nothing in exchange for the settlor's exercise of the power to set up a trust. The maxim does however reflect the basic point that equity has no reason to intervene and impose a constructive trust where B has simply failed to receive a gift.

B. Special Circumstances: When a Constructive Trust May Arise

i. Promise by the Settlor for which B Provides Consideration

5–076 The general position considered in the preceding paragraph applies where A simply intended, and failed, to make a transfer to trustees to hold on trust for B. Things may be different, however, if A also made a *promise* to make such a transfer and thus to set up a trust for B. If B is regarded as having provided consideration for that promise, and A's promise relates to specific property which A holds at the time of the promise, or later acquires, then a constructive trust may be imposed on that property, either immediately or as soon as A acquires it.[100] This means, of course, that the property is then held

---

94 Either under the general rule regulating the transfer of such property, or under the apparently different equitable rules applied in, e.g. *Re Rose, Rose v IRC* [1952] Ch. 499: see paras 5–023 to 5–036.

95 See para.5–041.

96 For a general consideration of the diversity of such circumstances, see paras 17–006 to 17–010.

97 We will not consider resulting trusts here, as the circumstances in which a resulting trust may arise (considered in Ch.16) are very unlikely to assist B in our case where the settlor planned to set up an express trust.

98 See, e.g. *Re Plumptre's Marriage Settlement* [1910] 1 Ch. 609; *Re D'Angibau* (1880) 15 Ch.D. 228.

99 See para.5–036.

100 As noted at para.3–239, the same basic rules apply to an equitable assignment of future legal choses in action of A.

by A directly on trust for B, rather than (as planned) by trustees who received the property from A. The rule in *Milroy v Lord* is not, however, departed from as that rule simply means that an unsuccessful attempt to set up a trust by means of a transfer to trustees cannot be recharacterised as a successful self-declaration of trust. The rule does not, therefore, prevent a constructive trust arising in favour of B and binding property held by A.

Pullan v Koe

Chancery Division [1913] 1 Ch. 9

A marriage settlement of 1859 contained a covenant by the husband and wife to transfer the wife's after-acquired property of the value of £100 or upwards to the trustees of the marriage settlement. In 1879 the wife received £285 and paid it into her husband's banking account, on which she had power to draw. Shortly afterwards part of the money was invested in two bearer bonds which remained at the bank until the husband's death in 1909. The bonds then passed into the hands of his executors. The plaintiffs, trustees of the marriage settlement, claimed against the defendants, the husband's executors that, as soon as the wife received the £285, it was held by her on a trust enforceable in favour of all persons within the marriage consideration, as such persons were to be considered as having provided consideration for the promise, contained in the covenant, to transfer such property to the trustees of the settlement. As a result, it was claimed, the bearer bonds were also then held subject to such a trust, even though, because of the expiry of the statutory limitation period, it was no longer possible for the trustees to enforce the wife's covenant at common law. **5–077**

SWINFEN EADY J.: [The defendants] insisted that, although they still retained the bonds, they were under no liability to the plaintiffs. They put their case in this way—that the plaintiff trustees could not follow the bonds into their hands, that the only liability of the husband was upon his covenant, and the claim of the trustees was for damages only, and that as this claim accrued in 1879 it was long since barred by the Statutes of Limitation. . . . **5–078**

[The husband] received the bonds, purchased with his wife's money, with full notice of the trusts of the settlement, and knowing that the £285 and the bonds purchased with part of it were bound by the covenant. The trustees having traced the property into his hands are entitled to claim it from his executors. **5–079**

It was contended that the bonds never in fact became trust property, as both the wife and husband were only liable in damages for breach of covenant, and that the case was different from cases where property which has once admittedly become subject to the trusts of an instrument has been improperly dealt with, and is sought to be recovered. In my opinion as soon as the £285 was paid to the wife it became in equity bound by and subject to the trusts of the settlement. The trustees could have claimed that particular sum, could have obtained at once the appointment of a receiver of it, if they could have shown a case of jeopardy, and, if it had been invested and the investment could be traced, could have followed the money and claimed the investment. **5–080**

This point was dealt with by Jessel M.R. in *Smith v Lucas*,[101] where he said: **5–081**

> "What is the effect of such a covenant in equity? It has been said that the effect in equity of the covenant of the wife, as far as she is concerned, is that it does not affect her personally, but that it binds the property: that is to say, it binds the property under the doctrine of equity that that is to be considered as done which ought to be done. That is in the nature of specific performance of the contract no doubt. If therefore, this is a covenant to settle the future-acquired property of the wife, and nothing more is done by her, the covenant will bind the property."

Again in *Collyer v Isaacs*[102] Jessel M.R. said: **5–082**

> "A man can contract to assign property which is to come into existence in the future, and when it has come into existence, equity, treating as done that which ought to be done, fastens upon that property, and the contract to assign thus becomes a complete assignment. If a person contract for value, e.g. in this marriage settlement, to settle all such real estate as his father shall leave him by will, or purports

[101] (1881) 18 Ch.D. 531 at 543.
[102] (1882) 19 Ch.D. 342 at 351.

actually to convey by the deed all such real estate, the effect is the same. It is a contract for value which will bind the property if the father leaves any property to his son."

5-083 Again the trustees are entitled to come into a Court of Equity to enforce a contract to create a trust, contained in a marriage settlement, for the benefit of the wife and the issue of the marriage, all of whom are within the marriage consideration. The husband covenanted that he and his heirs, executors, and administrators should, as soon as circumstances would admit, convey, assign, and surrender to the trustees the real or personal property to which his wife should become beneficially entitled. The trustees are entitled to have that covenant specifically enforced by a Court of Equity. In *Re D'Angibau*[103] and in *Re Plumptre's Marriage Settlement*[104] it was held that the Court would not interfere in favour of volunteers, not within the marriage consideration, but here the plaintiffs are the contracting parties and the object of the proceeding is to benefit the wife and issue of the marriage.

5-084 The specific decision in *Pullan v Koe* thus depends in part on the special rules relating to marriage settlements: even though the promise made in the covenant of the husband and wife appears to be gratuitous, as it was made before and in consideration of marriage, it is regarded as having been made for value,[105] and that value is deemed to have been provided by the spouses, their children and remoter issue.[106] As a result, if the promise of the husband or wife relates to property later acquired by one of them, he or she is subject to an immediate duty to abide by the promise, and that duty can be enforced by the trustees of the marriage settlement, or by anyone who is deemed to have provided consideration for it.

5-085 The general principle underlying *Pullan v Koe* is, however, much broader: we will consider it in more detail in Chapter 17.[107] As can be seen from the statement of Jessel MR in *Collyer v Isaacs*,[108] for example, it can apply to *any* promise, made for value, to transfer property to trustees to hold on trust. Indeed, the underlying principle of equity is broader still, as it applies to a simple promise for value to transfer property absolutely (such as a contract to transfer land) and also to a promise for value to hold rights as security,[109] or to, for example, grant a lease[110] or easement[111] over the promisor's land. That principle is often said to depend on the maxim that "equity looks on as done that which ought to be done":[112] e.g. as the promisor in *Pullan v Koe* had promised to transfer the property on trusts, that transfer could be considered as completed, so that the planned beneficiaries under those trusts are regarded as having acquired an immediate beneficial interest.

5-086 The maxim that "equity looks on as done that which ought to be done", like most equitable maxims, is, however, somewhat unhelpful.[113] The point in *Pullan v Koe*, for example, was not that the wife was under a moral obligation to honour the promise in the covenant; it was rather that the wife could be

---

103 (1880) 15 Ch.D. 228 at 242.

104 [1910] 1 Ch. 609 at 616.

105 If, for example, a trust is created after marriage and contains a true recital that it was made in pursuance of an ante-nuptial promise to create the trust it will be treated as having been made for value: *Re Holland* [1902] 2 Ch. 360.

106 Such parties are "within the marriage consideration". Old cases allowing children of a former marriage or a possible later remarriage or illegitimate children to be within the scope of marriage consideration can now only be supported on the basis that such children's interests were so closely interwoven with the interests of the children of the marriage that the latter could only benefit on terms allowing the former to benefit: *Rennell v IRC* [1962] Ch. 329 at 341; *Re Cook's S.T.* [1965] Ch. 902 at 914.

107 See paras 17-072 to 17-076.

108 (1882) 19 Ch.D. 342 at 351 (see para.5-082).

109 The principle is therefore the basis of the modern law of secured lending: see, e.g. *Holroyd v Marshall* (1862) 10 H.L.C. 191 and *Tailby v Official Receiver* (1888) 13 App. Cas. 523.

110 See, e.g. *Walsh v Lonsdale* (1882) 21 Ch.D. 9.

111 See, e.g. *McManus v Cooke* (1887) 35 Ch.D. 681.

112 See, e.g. *Smith v Lucas* (1881) 18 Ch.D. 531 at 543 per Jessel MR (see para.5-081).

113 See para.17-049.

said to owe a *duty* to a party who could be regarded as the promisee, and as having provided consideration for the promise. As that duty related to specific property, and was a duty to use that property not for the wife's own benefit, but on the terms of the marriage settlement, the wife thus held the property on trust. The trust was a constructive one[114] as it did not depend on the wife's actually exercising her power to set up the promised trust; it rather arose immediately, as soon as she acquired the relevant property.

(1) The Principle and Future Property

Pullan v Koe demonstrates that, if a settlor makes a promise to set up a trust of property that she does not yet have ("after-acquired" or "future" property), a constructive trust of such property may arise when the settlor does acquire that property if, at that point, the settlor is under a duty, enforceable in equity, to honour the promise. The principle is therefore important when considering a settlor's attempts to deal with future property. It is of course impossible for a settlor, whatever her intentions may be, to set up an immediate trust of future property:[115] if the settlor does not have the property, then she cannot hold it on trust for B; nor can it can be transferred to trustees to hold on trust for B. **5–087**

Some care is needed, however, as future property must be distinguished from an existing right held by a settlor to obtain property in the future.[116] For example, we noted above[117] that in *Re Ralli's Will Trusts*, Helen Ralli was able to declare an immediate trust of her right, acquired under her father's will, to have the benefit of property on the death of her mother. Under such a remainder interest, a party has direct access to the benefit of the property only on the occurrence of a particular event; but the interest is itself an existing right with which the party can deal, for example by declaring a trust. In contrast, no such right exists if a party simply has the hope of inheriting property upon the death of a relative, or of receiving property under the exercise of a power of appointment, or of acquiring royalties arising on sales of a book. **5–088**

What happens then if A attempts to make an immediate gift to B of such future property? At law, an assignment of future property has no effect, as the donor has no right to transfer.[118] In equity, equally, there can be no transfer of any right by A to B; however, the principle underlying *Pullan v Koe* can apply *if* B gave valuable consideration: the failed attempt at an immediate assignment is then treated by equity as a *promise* to make such an assignment, with the effect that, if and when A acquires the property, she will hold it on constructive trust for B.[119] In a case where A instead attempts to transfer future property to trustees to hold on trust for B, and B provides consideration, it therefore seems that, if and when A acquires that property, A will hold it on trust for B. There is no contradiction of the rule in *Milroy v Lord*, as B's beneficial interest arises under a constructive trust, and does not depend on recharacterising the failed attempt to set up a trust by transfer as a self-declaration of trust. Similarly, if A attempts to make an immediate self-declaration of trust in favour of B in relation to future property, then, if B provided consideration, a constructive trust can again arise if and when A acquires that property. **5–089**

---

114 As acknowledged in, e.g. *Lysaght v Edwards* (1876) 2 Ch.D. 499 at 509–510 per Jessel MR.
115 See, e.g. *Re Ellenborough* [1903] 1 Ch. 697; *Williams v C.I.R.* [1965] N.Z.L.R. 395.
116 See *Re Earl of Midleton's WT* [1969] 1 Ch. 600 at 607. See too paras 3–232ff.
117 See para.5–020.
118 *Holroyd v Marshall* (1862) 10 H.L. Cas. 191 at 220; *Re Tilt* (1896) 74 L.T. 163.
119 See, e.g. *Re Lind* [1915] 2 Ch. 345 at 360. This principle is discussed further paras 17–072 to 17–076.

(2) Limits to the Principle: Covenants to Settle

5-090 The type of constructive trust recognised in *Pullan v Koe* depends on the settlor, S, being under a duty, enforceable in equity, to honour her promise to set up the trust in favour of the planned beneficiary, B. It does not arise, therefore, if the settlor's promise is gratuitous because a promise for which no consideration is provided is not regarded, in equity, as giving rise to an enforceable duty. This is the case even if the gratuitous promise was made in a deed[120] executed by the settlor and the planned trustee. The use of a deed means that the planned trustee has a right at common law to sue the settlor for failing to honour the promise,[121] but it does not lead to a constructive trust in favour of the planned beneficiaries, as the promise is still gratuitous and so does not give rise to a duty enforceable in equity: this is, therefore, a further context in which the maxim that "equity will not assist a volunteer" has some weight.

5-091 For example, consider a case in which S covenants (i.e. promises in a deed) to pay £10,000, and to transfer her unique fifth dynasty Ming vase, to B, a volunteer. The use of a deed means that B has a valid claim at law against S if S does not honour the promise. B cannot obtain specific performance of the promise to transfer the unique vase, as S's promise is gratuitous and so is not enforceable in equity. There is no reason, however, for equity to prevent B from enforcing his common law claim against S and recovering damages reflecting the value of the rights that S promised to transfer.[122]

5-092 What if S's promise, again gratuitous and again made in a deed, was instead made to T and was a promise to pay £10,000 to T and to transfer her unique fifth dynasty Ming vase to T, so that T would hold the cash and the vase on trust for B, a volunteer? Such a promise is often referred to as a "covenant to settle". In such a case, if S made the promise with the express or implied intent that T shall hold the benefit of the covenant on trust for B, then a completely constituted trust has been created in B's favour.[123] It is not a trust of the cash or the vase, but is rather a trust of T's right, at common law, to sue S. As we have seen,[124] once a trust has been completely constituted in B's favour, it is irrelevant that B is a volunteer who has given nothing in exchange: T is under a duty of due administration,[125] and this can be enforced by B. It is worth noting that such a "trust of the benefit of a covenant" can arise even if the covenant relates solely to "after-acquired" or "future" property: i.e. property that S does not hold at the time of the covenant. The point is that whilst S cannot, of course, hold property that she does not yet have on trust,[126] T has a right against S as soon as the covenant is made, and that existing chose in action may then be held by T on trust.[127] If such a trust is found, this means that,

---

120 Such a promise is often referred to as a covenant.

121 See, e.g. *Cannon v Hartley* [1949] Ch. 213. For the requirements of a deed, see Law of Property (Miscellaneous Provisions) Act 1989 s.1. Note too s.56 of the Law of Property Act 1925, which allows B to acquire a right under a deed made between S and another even if B is not a party to it, if certain conditions are met: see *Beswick v Beswick* [1968] A.C. 58 and *Amsprop Trading Ltd v Harris Distribution Ltd* [1997] 1 W.L.R. 1025.

122 See *Cannon v Hartley* [1949] Ch. 213 (assuming of course that the promise made in the deed was not vitiated by, e.g. fraud, undue influence or unconscionable conduct).

123 See *Fletcher v Fletcher* (1844) 4 Hare 67. See too *Cox v Barnard* (1850) 8 Hare 310 at [312] and [313]; *Milroy v Lord* (1862) 4 De G.F. & J. 264 at 278.

124 See paras 5-035 to 5-036.

125 See paras 3-143 to 3-192.

126 See para.5-087.

127 See, e.g. *Kwok Chi Leung Karl v Commissioner of Estate Duty* [1988] 1 W.L.R. 1035 at 1040 per Lord Oliver: "A chose in action is no less a chose in action because it is not immediately recoverable by action", applied in *Re Landau* [1997] 3 All E.R. 322 at 328.

even if T does not wish to sue S, B can force T to do so,[128] and any damages acquired by T by means of that common law claim against S will then be held by T on trust for B. In such a case, of course, B's claim does not depend on a constructive trust; it is rather based on the existence of an express trust of T's cause of action against S.

B can take advantage of this possibility, therefore, only if it can be shown that S intended to set up such a trust of T's right to sue S. The courts were, at one point, quite willing to infer such an intention, if only to give some means of redress to B in a case where S failed to honour the promise to transfer the property to T to hold on trust for B.[129] Since the middle of the twentieth century, however, it has instead been emphasised, quite justifiably, that such a trust of the benefit of a covenant can be found only if there was a genuine intention on the part of S and T to set up such a trust.[130] After all, S has made no promise directly to B, and the most likely interpretation of the parties' transaction is that S intended B to acquire a beneficial interest, but only in relation to the property referred to in the covenant, and only after a transfer of that property to T.[131] **5–093**

What is B's position then, if S has made a gratuitous promise in a deed to transfer property to T to hold on trust for B, and it cannot be shown that S intended T to hold the benefit of the right to enforce the covenant on trust for B? First, there is now the possibility that the Contract (Rights of Third Parties) Act 1999 may apply to give B a direct claim against S, even in the absence of a trust of the benefit of the covenant. The position is not, however, entirely clear;[132] and, in any case, such a claim does not involve any trust. If S does not perform the promise in the covenant, T does then have a right at common law to sue S and B might then claim that T holds such damages on trust for B, as the covenant was not intended to benefit T. The difficulty for B, however, is that S may well argue that substantial damages should not be paid: after all, the right to enforce the promise belongs to T, and T is unlikely to have suffered any loss as a result of S's failure to perform. In practice, it may be that S's promise was to transfer property into an existing settlement whereby T already holds some assets on trust for B. In such a case, T will have to consider whether their existing duties as trustee mean that T should sue S in an attempt to recover damages that can then be held on trust for B. T will of course wish to have access to the trust funds to meet any costs incurred in suing S, but, where T has asked for directions from the court in such a case, the courts have held that T cannot use the trust funds to claim common law damages from S.[133] In fact, this response is so well-established that there is now no need for a trustee in T's position to bother the court: T has a complete defence if B claims that T was in breach of trust by not suing S for damages.[134] It therefore seems that the courts have accepted that **5–094**

---

128 Procedurally, B's claim to force T to sue S, and T's claim against S, can be combined in one action by means of what is known as a *Vandepitte* procedure (named for *Vandepitte v Preferred Accident Insurance Corp of New York* [1933] A.C. 70). See too para.3–208.

129 See, e.g. *Fletcher v Fletcher* (1844) 4 Hare 67: the intention was not express but was inferred in rather special circumstances. Further examples of such inferences can be found: e.g. *Cox v Barnard* (1850) 8 Hare 310; *Watson v Parker* (1843) 6 Beav. 283; *Dowling v Dowling* [1917] V.L.R. 208.

130 See, e.g. *Re Kay's Settlement* [1939] Ch. 329; *Re Schebsman* [1944] Ch 83; *Re Cook's ST* [1965] Ch. 902.

131 See, e.g. *Re Plumptre's MS* [1910] 1 Ch. 609; *Re Pryce* [1917] 1 Ch. 234. That interpretation is perhaps further supported if the covenant relates only to "after-acquired" property of S: i.e. property which S does not hold at the time of the covenant. It may be going too far, however, to suggest (as W.A. Lee (1969) 85 L.Q.R. 313 does) that there can never be the trust of the benefit of such a covenant: for example, in *Davenport v Bishop* (1843) 2 Y. & C.C.C. 451, Knight Bruce VC indicated at 460 that such a trust can arise. See too *Lloyd's v Harper* (1880) 16 Ch.D. 290 and *Royal Exchange Assurance v Hope* [1928] Ch. 179.

132 For discussion of this point, which turns ultimately on whether a promise, enforceable because made in a deed, counts as a contract, see, e.g. R. Stevens, "The Contracts (Rights of Third Parties) Act 1999" (2004) 120 L.Q.R. 292 at 313–314. In *Prudential Assurance Co Ltd v Ayres* [2007] EWHC 775 (Ch); [2007] 3 All E.R. 946, the question as to the scope of the 1999 Act was not raised in relation to a supplemental deed.

133 See, e.g. *Re Pryce* [1917] 1 Ch. 234; *Re Kay's Settlement* [1939] Ch. 329; *Re Cook's Settlement Trusts* [1965] Ch. 902.

134 *Re Ralli's WT* [1964] Ch. 288 at 301–302.

B would derive no benefit from T's suing S.[135] This reflects the fact that, although made in a deed, S's promise to set up a trust is simply a promise to make a gift.

ii. Proprietary Estoppel

5–095 The doctrine of proprietary estoppel, which we considered in Chapter 3,[136] provides another means by which A's promise to make a gift to B, whether directly or by means of a trust in B's favour, may give rise to a constructive trust for B. The doctrine does not require B to have provided anything of value in exchange for S's promise. When applied to promises,[137] it has three principal requirements:[138] (i) A made a promise that B will acquire a right in relation to identified property and the promise is such as could be reasonably understood by B as seriously intended to be capable of being relied upon;[139] (ii) B reasonably relied on that promise by acting, or not acting, in a particular way;[140] and (iii) as a result of that reliance, B would now suffer a detriment if A were wholly free to renege on the promise.[141] Those three requirements are inter-related, and they are underpinned by the notion of unconscionability,[142] so that, if they appear to have been satisfied, but it would not "shock the conscience of the court" to refuse B's claim, then B's proprietary estoppel claim may still fail.[143]

5–096 If the doctrine of proprietary estoppel applies it may (but need not) result in the enforcement of A's promise.[144] If it is thus found that A is under a duty to perfect the promised gift to B, A will hold the relevant property subject to that duty, and a constructive trust thus arises in B's favour. The doctrine does not, however, necessarily lead to the enforcement of A's promise. Certainly, it will not be enforced if the value of A's promise is "out of all proportion" to the extent of the potential detriment B will suffer

---

135 T might of course argue that T should receive substantial damages on his own behalf as T has a right to the value of the promised performance by S, and that value is substantial even if B would be the principal beneficiary of S's performance. The success of such a claim would depend on the application of rules as to damages (compare, e.g. the case, postulated by Lord Goff in *Alfred McAlpine Construction Ltd v Panatown* [2001] 1 A.C. 518 at 547, where "a wealthy man who lives in a village decides to carry out at his own expense major repairs to, or renovation, or even construction of the village hall, and himself enters a contract with a builder to carry out the work to the existing building which belongs to another"). As T's claim is then for damages for himself, and not for B, then of course it is right that T should not have access to the trust funds to bring such a claim, and so, even were substantial damages available on this basis, this prospect does not undermine the reasoning in the cases cited at fn.133.

136 See paras 3–003 to 3–033.

137 The promise-based strand of proprietary estoppel is most relevant in the current context. It is also possible to identify an acquiescence-based strand and a representation-based strand of proprietary estoppel: see paras 3–011 to 3–012. The former can apply where the defendant has failed to take reasonable steps to correct the claimant's mistaken belief as to the claimant's current rights, even though the defendant knew of the claimant's belief and of the true position: see, e.g. *Willmott v Barber* (1880) 15 Ch. D. 96 at 105–106; *Fisher v Brooker* [2009] 1 W.L.R. 1764 at [62]. The latter can apply where one party has made a representation as to a matter of existing fact, or mixed fact and law, intending that the other party should rely on it, and the other party does so rely: see, e.g. *Hopgood v Brown* [1955] 1 W.L.R. 213.

138 *Thorner v Major* [2009] 1 W.L.R. 776 at [29] per Lord Walker.

139 See, e.g. *Thorner v Major* [2009] 1 W.L.R. 776 at [5], per Lord Hoffmann.

140 It is often said, following the analysis of Lord Denning MR in *Greasley v Cooke* [1980] 1 W.L.R. 1306, that there is a "presumption of reliance", but it is very difficult to see why the burden of proving an element of the claim should not, as usual, be on the claimant, and the validity of such a presumption has been doubted, both in relation to estoppel generally (see, e.g. *Steria Ltd v Hutchison* [2007] I.C.R. 445 at [129], per Neuberger LJ) and in relation specifically to proprietary estoppel (see *Sidhu v van Dyke* (2014) 251 C.L.R. 505).

141 See, e.g. *Gillett v Holt* [2001] Ch. 210 at 232.

142 See *Gillett v Holt* [2001] Ch. 210 at 225 per Robert Walker LJ: the elements of proprietary estoppel "cannot be treated as subdivided into three or four watertight compartments".

143 See *Cobbe v Yeoman's Row Management Ltd* [2008] 1 W.L.R. 1752 at [92] per Lord Walker. See para.3–032.

144 See, e.g. *Pascoe v Turner* [1979] 1 W.L.R. 431; *Thorner v Major* [2009] 1 W.L.R. 776. The decision in *Dillwyn v Llewellyn* (1862) 4 De G.F. & J. 517 appears to have been based on an analogy with part performance of a contract, but may perhaps today be seen as a proprietary estoppel case.

as a result of her reliance if A reneges on the promise.[145] In such a case A will be under a lesser duty, such as a duty to pay a sum of money to B:[146] in that case, no constructive trust arises, as A holds no property on trust for B.

In a case where A has made a promise to transfer specific, identifiable property to T to hold on trust for B, it therefore seems that, if B has reasonably relied on that promise and would as a result suffer a detriment were A to renege on the promise, the doctrine of proprietary estoppel may apply[147] and, depending on the extent of B's potential detriment, may lead to A's being under a duty to perform her promise, and thus to a constructive trust in B's favour.[148] In a case where A's promise was to transfer property into an existing settlement where T already holds on trust for B, and T has relied on the promise by, for example, incurring expenses on B's behalf in relation to the improvement or management of the property that T has promised to convey, it may be possible to regard such reliance as having been incurred on B's behalf and so as capable of supporting a proprietary estoppel claim by B. **5–097**

iii. Donatio Mortis Causa

The doctrine of *donatio mortis causa* may apply where A attempts to make a deathbed gift, but fails to transfer property as planned to the donee, B.[149] Where it applies, its effect is that A, at her death, holds the subject matter of the planned gift subject to a constructive trust for B, and so the trust thus binds A's personal representatives when they acquire the property on A's death.[150] There is no reason in principle why the doctrine could not apply in a case where the planned deathbed gift was intended to have effect by means of a transfer to T to hold on trust for B: A would then hold that property on constructive trust for B. **5–098**

As confirmed by Jackson LJ in *King v Dubrey*,[151] the doctrine will apply if three requirements are met: **5–099**

> (i) [A] contemplates his impending death. (ii) [A] makes a gift which will only take effect if and when his contemplated death occurs. Until then [A] has the right to revoke the gift. (iii) [A] delivers dominion over the subject matter of the gift to [B].

---

145 See, e.g. *Jennings v Rice* [2002] EWCA Civ 159; [2003] 1 P. & C.R. 8; note however that the Supreme Court's judgment in *Guest v Guest*, expected in late 2022, may clarify the law on this point.

146 See, e.g. *Jennings v Rice* [2002] EWCA Civ 159; [2003] 1 P. & C.R. 8; *Powell v Benney* [2007] EWCA Civ 1283. In *Campbell v Griffin* [2001] EWCA Civ 990; [2001] W.T.L.R. 981 and *McGuane v Welch* [2008] EWCA Civ 785; [2008] 2 P. & C.R. 24, the duty to pay a sum of money was secured by a charge on the land that had been promised to B.

147 It seems to be the case, in general, that a proprietary estoppel claim, like a contractual claim, depends on A having made a promise to B rather than to a third party (see B. McFarlane, *The Law of Proprietary Estoppel*, 2nd edn (Oxford University Press, 2014), paras 8–34 to 8–35); however, on the facts of our hypothetical, where the promise is made to T in relation to a planned trust for B's benefit, then it may well still be possible for B to show that it was reasonable in the circumstances for B to have regarded A's promise as one that was seriously intended as capable of being relied on *by B*.

148 Similarly, the doctrine may apply to assist B in a case where an attempted self-declaration of trust by A has failed or cannot be proved. In *McGuane v Welch* [2008] EWCA Civ 785; [2008] 2 P. & C.R. 24, for example, it was held that a document containing a self-declaration of trust in B's favour of a lease held by A could not be given in evidence, as the stamp duty on the declaration had not been paid, nor had any undertaking to pay that duty been given to the court by a solicitor (see per Mummery LJ at [27]). It was held however that B could still rely on the doctrine of proprietary estoppel. Given the circumstances in which B procured A's agreement to the parties' arrangement, and the limited detriment to B, it was held that A was not under a duty to give effect to that arrangement by holding the lease on trust for B, and instead was merely under a duty to compensate B for his expenditure incurred in reliance on the arrangement, such duty secured by a charge over A's lease: see, e.g. per Mummery LJ at [46].

149 The origins, as well as the name, of the doctrine, can be traced to Roman law, but the English doctrine differs in its requirements from that recognised in Roman law: *Sen v Headley* [1991] Ch. 425 at 432.

150 See, e.g. *Duffield v Elwes* (1827) 1 Bli. N.S. 497 at 543 per Lord Eldon: "this is a good *donatio mortis causa*, raising by operation of law a trust; a trust which being raised by operation of law is not within the Statute of Frauds". See too *Sen v Headley* [1991] Ch. 425 at 439 per Nourse LJ; *Keeling v Keeling* [2017] EWHC 1189 (Ch) at [59].

151 [2015] EWCA Civ 581; [2016] Ch. 221 at [50].

5–100 As to the first requirement, it is not enough that A is simply aware of ageing, or of the general inevitability of death: A must have in mind "impending death within the near future. Not the mere possibility that it may occur at some future date or even months away."[152] As to the second requirement, a condition to that effect need not be expressed and will normally be implied from the fact that the gift was made when A was ill.[153] To comply with the third requirement, A must give B[154] possession of the subject-matter of the gift, or the means or part of the means of getting at that subject-matter (e.g. by delivering car keys[155] or a key to a box containing essential indicia of title),[156] intending to part with dominion over the property to which the key relates.

5–101 Where the planned gift relates, for example, to a chose in action, the doctrine may apply where A has delivered a document which is necessary to prove title to the chose in action.[157] It is not necessary that the document should contain all the terms on which the subject-matter of the chose in action is held.[158] The doctrine can also apply where there has been delivery of title deeds to land,[159] or of a share certificate,[160] or of a cheque payable to A.[161] The mere delivery by A to B of a cheque drawn by A on A's own account does not allow the doctrine to apply, however, as the cheque is not a document giving B the right to any *specific* property held by A.[162]

5–102 In *King v Dubrey*, whilst noting that the concept of *donatio mortis causa* (DMC) was well-established in Roman law and later in English law, Jackson LJ also observed that:[163]

> the doctrine of DMC in the context of English law is an anomaly. It enables [A] to transfer property on his death without complying with any of the formalities of section 9 of the Wills Act or section 52 of the Law of Property Act. Thus the doctrine paves the way for all of the abuses which those statutes are intended to prevent . . . The doctrine obviously served a useful purpose in the social conditions prevailing under the later Roman Empire. But is serves little useful purpose today, save possibly as a means of validating deathbed gifts. Even then considerable caution is required. What [A] says to those who are ministering to him in the last hours of his/her life may be a less reliable expression of his/her wishes than a carefully drawn will . . . In my view therefore it is important to keep DMC within its proper bounds. The court should resist the temptation to extend the doctrine to an ever wider range of situations.

5–103 Indeed, on the facts of *King v Dubrey* itself, it was found that the first requirement of the doctrine had not been met, as A was not contemplating her imminent death at the time of her dealings with B.[164]

---

152 [2015] EWCA Civ 581; [2016] Ch. 221 at [90] (Patten LJ). See too at [55] and [68] (Jackson LJ).
153 See *Re Mustapha* (1891) 8 T.L.R. 160; *Re Lillingston* [1952] 2 All E.R. 184.
154 Where S's plan was to transfer T to hold on trust for B, delivery to T would presumably suffice.
155 *Woodard v Woodard* (1991) 21 Fam. Law 470 (not necessary to hand over the car's log book).
156 *Re Lillingston* [1952] 2 All E.R. 184; *Sen v Headley* [1991] Ch. 425.
157 *Moore v Darton* (1851) 4 De G. & Sm. 517; *Re Dillon* (1890) 44 Ch.D. 76; *Birch v Treasury Solicitor* [1951] Ch. 298.
158 *Birch v Treasury Solicitor* [1951] Ch. 298; disapproving dicta in *Re Weston* [1902] 1 Ch. 680 and *Delgoffe v Fader* [1939] Ch. 922.
159 *Sen v Headley* [1991] Ch. 425.
160 *Dufficy v Mollica* [1968] 3 N.S.W.L.R. 751 at 759.
161 *Re Mead* (1880) 15 Ch.D. 651.
162 *Re Beaumont* [1902] 1 Ch. 889; *Re Leaper* [1916] 1 Ch. 579.
163 [2015] EWCA Civ 581; [2016] Ch. 221 at [51]–[54].
164 See too *Davey v Bailey* [2021] EWHC 445 (Ch): the doctrine did not apply as the relevant statements of A were simply general testamentary wishes and not deathbed gifts; *Keeling v Keeling* [2017] EWHC 1189 (Ch) at [71] where it was said that "the facts come nowhere close to satisfying the requirements of this exceptional principle."

iv. Other Cases of Unconscionable Conduct?

We have considered a number of means by which a constructive trust may arise in B's favour where A planned, but failed, to make a gift of that property to B (either directly or by means of a trust where T was to hold the property on trust for B). At an abstract level, it might be said that the need to prevent unconscionable conduct by A underlies the recognition of such constructive trusts and, indeed, of any trust imposed by law. However, as noted in Chapter 1,[165] a broad and unparticularised notion of unconscionability, if not given effect to through specific principles, is a very uncertain guide when attempting to establish rights and duties. This does not mean that the law cannot develop: new, specific principles can emerge, identifying and responding to particular forms of unconscionable conduct. Such principles need to be invoked, however, only if none of the existing rules give rise to a constructive trust. It is useful to bear these points in mind when considering the following extract. **5–104**

Pennington v Waine

[2002] 1 W.L.R. 2075 (CA)

Ada owned 1,500 out of 2,000 shares in C Ltd. She told her nephew, Harold, who was company secretary, that she was going to give him 400 of those shares and wanted him to become a director. She then instructed Pennington, a partner in the firm of accountants which acted as the company auditors, to prepare a share transfer form. She executed the form and returned it to Pennington. He then put the form in the file relating to the company which he kept in his office. He subsequently told Harold of Ada's gift, saying that Harold need take no further action, and he asked Harold to sign the necessary form of consent to act as director now that he had qualifying shares. Harold signed the form and Ada as director countersigned it. Ada then made a will bequeathing 620 shares to Harold, assuming that after her death he would then have 1,020 of the 2,000 shares. A month later she died. The question was whether the 400 shares formed part of her estate or had instead been effectively given to Harold. **5–105**

ARDEN L.J. (with whom SCHIEMANN L.J. agreed): . . . The legal title to a share may today be conveyed by the execution and registration of an instrument of transfer (section 182(1) of the Companies Act 1985). However, the equitable interest in a share may pass under a contract of sale even if the contract is not completed by registration.[166] In addition, a share may also be the subject of a valid equitable assignment: see for example *Re Rose, Rose v IRC*. **5–106**

This appeal raises the question of what is necessary for the purposes of a valid equitable assignment of shares by way of gift. If the transaction had been for value, a contract to assign the share would have been sufficient: neither the execution nor the delivery of an instrument of transfer would have been required. However, where the transaction was purely voluntary, the principle that equity will not assist a volunteer must be applied and respected. This principle is to be found in *Milroy v Lord* and other cases. . . . Accordingly the gift must be perfected, or "completely constituted". **5–107**

. . .the principle that equity will not assist a volunteer at first sight looks like a hard-edged rule of law not permitting much argument or exception. Historically the emergence of the principle may have been due to the need for equity to follow the law rather than an intuitive development of equity. The principle against imperfectly constituted gifts led to harsh and seemingly paradoxical results. Before long, equity had tempered the wind to the shorn lamb (i.e. the donee). It did so on more than one occasion and in more than one way. **5–108**

First it was held that an incompletely constituted gift could be upheld if the gift had been completed to such an extent that the donee could enforce his right to the shares as against third parties without forcing the donor to take any further step. Accordingly, if a share transfer has been executed by the donor and duly presented to the company for registration, the donee would be entitled, if necessary, to apply to the court for an order for rectification of the share register under section 359 of the Companies Act 1985. Such an **5–109**

[165] See paras 1–110 to 1–113.

[166] *Hawks v McArthur* [1951] 1 All E.R. 22.

order would not, of course, be granted if for example the directors had a discretion to refuse to register the transfer and had timeously passed a valid resolution to decline to register the transfer.[167]

5-110 That exception was extended in *Re Rose, Rose v IRC* and other cases by holding that for this exception to apply it was not necessary that the donor should have done all that it was necessary to be done to complete the gift, short of registration of the transfer. On the contrary it was sufficient if the donor had done all that it was necessary for him or her to do. . . .

5-111 Secondly equity has tempered the wind (of the principle that equity will not assist a volunteer) to the shorn lamb (the donee) by utilising the constructive trust. This does not constitute a declaration of trust thus does not fall foul of the principle[168] that an imperfectly constituted gift is not saved by being treated as a declaration of trust. Thus, for example, in *T. Choithram International SA v Pagarani*,[169] the Privy Council held that the assets which the donor gave to the foundation of which he was one of the trustees were held upon trust to vest the same in all the trustees of the foundation on the terms of the trusts of the foundation. This particular trust obligation was not a term of the express trust constituting the foundation but a constructive trust adjunct to it.[170]. . .

5-112 Thirdly, equity has tempered the wind to the shorn lamb by applying a benevolent construction to words of gift . . . In [*T. Choithram International SA v Pagarani*][171] [t]he Privy Council held that the gift to the "Foundation" could only properly be construed as a gift to the purposes declared by the trust deed and administered by the trustees. [Arden L.J. then cited the paragraphs of Lord Browne-Wilkinson's advice extracted above[172]]. . .

5-113 Accordingly the principle that, where a gift is imperfectly constituted, the court will not hold it to operate as a declaration of trust, does not prevent the court from construing it to be a trust if that interpretation is permissible as a matter of construction, which may be a benevolent construction. The same must apply to words of gift. An equity to perfect a gift would not be invoked by giving a benevolent construction to words of gift or, it follows, words which the donor used to communicate or give effect to his gift.

5-114 The cases to which counsel have referred us do not reveal any, or any consistent single policy consideration behind the rule that the court will not perfect an imperfect gift. The objectives of the rule obviously include ensuring that donors do not by acting voluntarily act unwisely in a way that they may subsequently regret. This objective is furthered by permitting donors to change their minds at any time before it becomes completely constituted. This is a paternalistic objective, which can outweigh the respect to be given to the donor's original intention as gifts are often held by the courts to be incompletely constituted despite the clearest intention of the donor to make the gift. Another valid objective would be to safeguard the position of the donor: suppose, for instance, that (contrary to the fact) it had been discovered after Ada's death that her estate was insolvent, the court would be concerned to ensure that the gift did not defeat the rights of creditors. But, while this may well be a relevant consideration, for my own part I do not consider that this need concern the court to the exclusion of other considerations as in the event of insolvency there are other potent remedies available to creditors where insolvents have made gifts to defeat their claims.[173] There must also be, in the interests of legal certainty, a clearly ascertainable point in time at which it can be said that the gift was completed, and this point in time must be arrived at on a principled basis.

5-115 There are countervailing policy considerations which would militate in favour of holding a gift to be completely constituted. These would include effectuating, rather than frustrating, the clear and continuing intention of the donor, and preventing the donor from acting in a manner which is unconscionable. . . .

5-116 If one proceeds on the basis that a principle which animates the answer to the question whether an apparently incomplete gift is to be treated as completely constituted is that a donor will not be permitted to change his or her mind if it would be unconscionable, in the eyes of equity, vis à vis the donee to do so, what is the position here? There can be no comprehensive list of factors which makes it unconscionable for

---

167 See *Buckley on the Companies Acts*, 15th edn (LexisNexis UK, 2000) [359.277].

168 See *Milroy v Lord* (1862) 4 De G.F. & J. 264 and *Jones v Lock* (1865) 1 Ch. App. 25.

169 [2001] 1 W.L.R. 1. See paras 5-013 to 5-019.

170 [Note that this analysis of the specific duty to vest the property in all the trustees does not mean that the core trust in *Pagarani* must be regarded as constructive: as made clear by Arden LJ in her judgment (see, e.g. at [60]), and in her later judgment in *Shah v Shah* [2011] W.T.L.R. 519 at [14]–[20], that core trust in *Pagarani* depended on the finding that a valid self-declaration of trust had been made, and so the trust was thus express and not constructive.

171 [2001] 1 W.L.R. 1.

172 See paras 5-013 to 5-018.

173 See, e.g. ss.339 and 423 of the Insolvency Act 1986.

the donor to change his or her mind: it must depend on the court's evaluation of all the relevant considerations. What then are the relevant facts here? Ada made the gift of her own free will: there is no finding that she was not competent to do this. She not only told Harold about the gift and signed a form of transfer which she delivered to Mr Pennington for him to secure registration: her agent also told Harold that he need take no action. In addition Harold agreed to become a director of the company without limit of time, which he could not do without shares being transferred to him. If Ada had changed her mind on (say) 10 November 1998, in my judgment the court could properly have concluded that it was too late for her to do this as by that date Harold signed the form 288A, the last of the events identified above, to occur.

There is next the pure question of law: was it necessary for Ada deliver the form of transfer to Harold?. . . the ratio of *Re Rose, Rose v IRC* was as I read it that the gifts of shares in that case were completely constituted when the donor executed share transfers and delivered them to the transferees even though they were not registered in the register of members of the company until a later date. **5–117**

However, that conclusion as to the ratio in *Re Rose, Rose v IRC* does not mean that this appeal must be decided in the appellants' favour. Even if I am correct in my view that the Court of Appeal took the view in *Re Rose, Rose v IRC* that delivery of the share transfers was there required, it does not follow that delivery cannot in some circumstances be dispensed with. Here, there was a clear finding that Ada intended to make an immediate gift. Harold was informed of it. Moreover, I have already expressed the view that a stage was reached when it would have been unconscionable for Ada to recall the gift. It follows that it would also have been unconscionable for her personal representatives to refuse to hand over the share transfer to Harold after her death. In those circumstances, in my judgment, delivery of the share transfer before her death was unnecessary so far as perfection of the gift was concerned. **5–118**

It is not necessary to decide the case simply on that basis. After the share transfers were executed Mr Pennington wrote to Harold on Ada's instructions informing him of the gift and stating that there was no action that he needed to take. I would also decide this appeal in favour of the respondent on this further basis. If I am wrong in the view that delivery of the share transfers to the company or the donee is required and is not dispensed with by reason of the fact that it would be unconscionable for Ada's personal representatives to refuse to hand the transfers over to Harold, the words used by Mr Pennington should be construed as meaning that Ada and, through her, Mr Pennington became agents for Harold for the purpose of submitting the share transfer to the Company. This is an application of the principle of benevolent construction to give effect to Ada's clear wishes. Only in that way could the result "This requires no action on your part" and an effective gift be achieved. Harold did not question this assurance and must be taken to have proceeded to act on the basis that it would be honoured. **5–119**

[CLARKE L.J. gave a separate judgment holding that mere execution of the signed share transfer form on its own amounted to a valid equitable assignment,[174] but, if he were wrong on that, then he agreed with ARDEN L.J.'s reasons.] **5–120**

On one reading, *Pennington v Waine* opens the door to a beneficial interest arising in favour of B (presumably under a constructive trust) whenever "it would be unconscionable, in the eyes of equity, vis-à-vis [B]"[175] for A to change her mind and not proceed with a planned gift to B. There would then be no specific principle as to when B can thus claim a beneficial interest, as "[t]here can be no comprehensive list of factors which makes it unconscionable for the donor to change her mind. It must depend on the court's evaluation of all the relevant considerations."[176] As previously noted,[177] however, such an approach would leave the law in a very uncertain state, causing problems, for example, to third parties dealing with property which apparently belongs absolutely to A, but which might later turn out to have been impressed with a constructive trust arising because of A's earlier plan to make a gift of the property to B. **5–121**

174 For a criticism of this analysis, see para.5–038.
175 [2002] EWCA Civ 227; [2002] 1 W.L.R. 2075 at [64] (see para.5–116).
176 [2002] 1 W.L.R. 2075 at [64] (see para.5–116).
177 See para.1–112. See too the concerns expressed by J. Edelman, "Two Fundamental Questions for the Law of Trusts" (2013) 129 L.Q.R. 67, 79–81.

5–122 It is therefore not surprising that in *Curtis v Pulbrook*, Briggs J (as he then was, now Lord Briggs) gave the following analysis of the decision, which seeks to limit the scope for applying an undefined notion of unconscionability:[178]

> In *Pennington v Waine*, Arden L.J. (with whom Schiemann L.J. agreed) identified three routes by which, in the context of a defective voluntary transfer of shares, the court might avoid the rigorous application of the principle that equity will not compel the completion of an imperfect gift, in the absence of a valid declaration of trust. She described all three as methods whereby a court of equity might temper the wind to the shorn lamb. The first is where the donor has done everything necessary to enable the donee to enforce a beneficial claim without further assistance from the donor.[179] The second is where some detrimental reliance by the donee upon an apparent although ineffective gift may so bind the conscience of the donor to justify the imposition of a constructive trust.[180] The third is where by a benevolent construction an effective gift or implied declaration of trust may be teased out of the words used.[181] On its facts, *Pennington v Waine* appears to have been an example of sufficient detrimental reliance by the donee, who had agreed to become a director of the subject company upon an assumption that he had received an effective gift of qualifying shares in it.[182]

5–123 The analysis of Briggs J provides a useful limit to the impact of the decision in *Pennington v Waine*, in effect regarding it as an application of the doctrine of proprietary estoppel.[183] The difficulty with that reading on the facts may be that the extent of Harold's detriment, arising as a result of his act of becoming director, is likely to have been limited and so, if the doctrine of proprietary estoppel were applied, there would at least be a question of whether enforcing Ada's promise would be a disproportionate response. It should also be noted that the promise-based strand of proprietary estoppel is usually applied only where the promise relates, at least in part, to some land of the promisor.[184]

5–124 The focus on detrimental reliance has not been shared in all applications of *Pennington v Waine*. In *Khan v Mahmood*,[185] registered title to land was held jointly by A and B, with each having a 50% share in equity. After being charged with benefit fraud for failing to disclose his interest in the land, A signed a form purporting to transfer that registered title, for no consideration, to B alone, but that form was not submitted to the Land Registry, as A did not pay his solicitor the £60 required for the Land Registry fee.[186] The form was shown to B however and B paid £400 in stamp duty.[187] It was found that the parties' beneficial interests had been altered as a result, so that A and B held their registered title on trust for B alone. Marcus Smith J noted that *Pennington* had "relaxed somewhat the strict requirement that <u>everything</u> must be done which, according to the nature of the property, is necessary to be done to effect the transfer" and also emphasised that the "touchstone is one of *unconscionability*".[188] He also rejected the suggestion that such a trust could arise only in response to actual or potential detrimental reliance, stating that: "Unconscionability, as it seems to me, focuses more on the conduct

---

178 [2011] EWHC 167 (Ch) at [43].
179 See [2002] EWCA Civ 227; [2002] 1 W.L.R. 2075 at [55]–[56] and *Rose v IRC* [1952] Ch. 499.
180 See [2002] EWCA Civ 227; [2002] 1 W.L.R. 2075 at [59] (see para.5–111).
181 See [2002] 1 W.L.R. 2075 at [60]–[61] (see paras 5–112), based on *T Choithram International SA v Pagarani* [2001] 1 W.L.R. 1.
182 See [2002] EWCA Civ 227; [2002] 1 W.L.R. 2075 at [64]–[66] (see para.5–116).
183 In *Shah v Shah* [2010] EWCA Civ 1408; [2011] W.T.L.R. 519, the third of the three *Pennington v Waine* methods of "tempering the wind" was adopted: the donor of shares had sent a signed transfer form, but not the share certificate, to the donee, but had also stated that he held the shares on trust for the donee. The donee thus acquired a beneficial interest under a self-declaration of trust, which was sufficiently clear that no "benevolent construction" was needed: see per Arden LJ at [20].
184 See paras 3–017ff.
185 [2021] EWHC 597 (Ch).
186 As noted at [19], it is unlikely that the Land Registry would in any case have accepted a form signed by A alone purporting to deal with A and B's joint registered title.
187 [2021] EWHC 597 (Ch) at [43].
188 [2021] EWHC 597 (Ch) at [40]–[41] (emphasis in original).

of the donor, whereas reliance focuses more on the conduct of the donee in respect of the donor's gift."[189] In that case, nonetheless, there was more than a simple failure by A to complete a gift—for example, both A and B had asserted for some time afterwards that A had no interest in the relevant property and it was only when their relations later broke down that A claimed otherwise.

It is of course easy to understand why, in a case such as *Pennington v Waine*, a court may wish to reach a result which upholds the clear intentions of A: in that case, Ada had clearly wished to ensure that, on her death, Harold would have a majority shareholding in the company, and that outcome depended on Harold having acquired, during Ada's life, a beneficial interest in the 400 shares that she intended to transfer to him. Similarly in *Khan v Mahmood*, whilst there was no evidence of detrimental reliance by B, the parties had conducted themselves on the basis that A no longer had any interest in the land.[190] As Turner LJ noted in *Milroy v Lord*, it is only natural for a judge to feel "a strong disposition to give effect to [the donor's intentions] to the fullest extent".[191] As we will see in the next chapter, that same sentiment is often apparent in cases where a failure to comply with a formality rule threatens to frustrate A's clear intentions. However, the rules as to constitution of trusts, like formality rules, are there for a reason,[192] and, if they have not been satisfied, and neither a transfer to trustees nor a self-declaration of trust by A can be found on the facts, a constructive trust should be imposed only if there is a specific reason why A should hold A's rights subject to a duty to B. Certainly, the frustration of A's intentions caused by a failure successfully to exercise a power to give B a beneficial interest should not, in itself, provide sufficient grounds for the imposition of a constructive trust. 5–125

Questions

1. In *T Choithram International SA v Pagarani*, Lord Browne-Wilkinson said that: "Although equity will not assist a volunteer, it will not strive officiously to defeat a gift." Is it possible to reconcile those two aspects of equity's approach to the constitution of trusts?

2. Samit is registered freehold owner of land in Wales, the registered shareholder of 10,000 OK Ltd shares, a depositor of £12,000 with Bigg Bank, and is entitled to XYZ Ltd shares held for him by Eric, executor of his father's will.

   Samit executes a transfer form in Dawn's favour in relation to the registered land, and gives it to his solicitor, who then posts it to Dawn's solicitor. It arrives at Dawn's solicitor's office, but the office is in the process of moving to new premises, and the form is lost. Samit orally tells Frances he is holding his OK Ltd shares on trust for her, tells George he is holding his Bigg account on trust for him, and tells Eric to transfer the XYZ shares absolutely to Jennifer. Eric signs a duly completed share transfer form and encloses it with the relevant share certificate in an envelope which he gives to Jennifer, who accidentally throws it out with some old newspapers and empty envelopes.

---

189 [2021] EWHC 597 (Ch) at [44]. See too *Nosnehpetsj Ltd v Watersheds Capital Partners Ltd* [2020] EWHC 1938 (Ch) where it is stated at [41] that three factors supported the finding of unconscionability in *Pennington*: (i) A's intention to make an immediate gift; (ii) B had been informed of the gift; (iii) it would have been unconscionable to recall the gift. Whilst it is unclear how the third factor adds anything, note the lack of reference to detrimental reliance. For discussion of the specific factual context, which included A's having claimed tax relief on the basis of the supposed transfer to B, see A. Morris, "No Longer Waning: *Pennington* Revived?" (2021) 35 *Trust Law International* 50.

190 [2021] EWHC 597 (Ch) at [44].

191 (1862) 4 De G.F. & J. 264 at 274 (see para.5–008).

192 As noted, e.g. by Arden LJ in *Pennington v Waine* [2002] EWCA Civ 227; [2002] 1 W.L.R. 2075 at [62] (see para.5–114).

One month later a financial disaster strikes Samit, who now wishes to sell all the above property and use the proceeds of sale to meet his debts. Advise him. Would your answer be different in respect of the OK Ltd shares if he had made a further declaration of trust of 3,000 OK shares in favour of Keith?

3. Under Andy's father's will property is settled on trust for Wendy (Andy's mother) for life, remainder to Andy and Ben equally, but Wendy has an express power to appoint the capital between Andy and Ben as she sees fit. Andy, in a signed document, assigns "All my interest under my father's will trusts to Bigg Bank on trust for Steve for life, remainder to Theresa".

   Advise the bank if Wendy dies either: (i) without having made an appointment so that Andy receives £450,000 under his father's will trusts; or (ii) having appointed £500,000 to Andy a month before her death, so that Andy then also receives assets worth a further £200,000 under his father's will trusts.

   Would your advice differ if, instead, Andy had assigned to the Bank, inter alia "all such assets whatsoever as shall come into my possession on my mother's death under the terms of my father's will trusts"? Would any of your advice to the bank differ if unknown to Andy the bank happened to be trustee of his father's will trusts?

4. "When it comes to Chancery judges directing trustees not to sue on covenants that are not themselves the subject-matter of a trust, the judges cannot justify their directions simply on the negative basis that 'Equity will not assist a volunteer' because Equity is positively intervening to prevent trustees exercising their common law rights." **Discuss.**

5. Is the following approach to questions arising in connection with completely and incompletely constituted trusts a sound one?

   (a) Ask if a trust has been completely constituted by property having been transferred by S to trustees on trust for B. Note too the general rule that the transfer has to be effected by S or S's agent, and the exception to that rule resulting from the extension of the *Strong v Bird* decision. Note also that the rule in *Re Rose* may apply to allow a court to find B has acquired an interest under a constructive trust.

   (b) If a completely constituted trust by transfer cannot be found, ask if a trust has been completely constituted by a declaration of trust by S, of property currently held by S, in favour of B. Note that, in a case where it is clear that S intended a trust for B, a court may adopt a "benevolent construction" of the facts in order to find such a self-declaration. The mere fact, however, that S intended to set up a trust for B by means of a transfer to trustees cannot, in itself, justify a court in finding that S declared a trust.

   (c) If no completely constituted trust has arisen, either by transfer to trustees or by self-declaration, then consider if a constructive trust has arisen in B's favour. The mere fact that S intended to make a gift to B cannot suffice for such a trust to arise, but, in suitable circumstances, B may be able to invoke the doctrine of proprietary estoppel or of donatio mortis causa. If B has provided consideration for S's promise to make a gift, B may be able to rely on the principle applied in *Pullan v Koe*.

   (d) If no express trust or constructive trust has arisen in relation to the property initially held by S, but S made a promise in a deed (a covenant) to T to make a transfer to T to hold on trust for B, then ask if S intended that T should hold the benefit of T's common law right to sue on that covenant on trust for B. If so, B can then compel T to sue S and claim substantial damages which will be held by T on trust for B.

6

FORMAL REQUIREMENTS

1. Introduction

A. Formality Rules

The law provides that certain transactions, such as the creation or transfer of equitable interests, must take a particular form, e.g. they must be carried out in writing. Such rules, in general, may serve one or more of a number of purposes. For example, to ensure that a party with legal entitlements (e.g. an owner of property, or the holder of an equitable interest) seriously considers what she is doing before exercising her power to give away her entitlements, or to undertake duties to another in relation to those entitlements. Further, to ensure that documentary evidence exists that will make fraud more difficult and forestall problems that might otherwise arise in determining who is entitled to what, especially after many years have elapsed, when memories have faded and the main actors may even have died.[1] This chapter will consider the content and scope of the formality rules governing the creation and transfer of equitable interests under a trust, and the consequences of non-compliance with these rules.[2] **6–001**

We will focus on four formality rules. In relation to lifetime (i.e. inter vivos) dealings with property, we will consider: (i) the Law of Property (Miscellaneous Provisions) Act 1989 s.2; (ii) the Law of Property Act 1925 s.53(1)(b); and (iii) the Law of Property Act 1925 s.53(1)(c). The first of those is a general formality rule, not specific to trusts, that regulates contracts for the sale or other disposition of an interest in land. The second is specific to trusts, although it applies only in relation to land, as it regulates the means by which a party can prove a declaration of a trust of land. The third applies to the disposition of existing equitable interests, whether or not relating to land, and so is relevant, for example, when a beneficiary of trust seeks to assign her beneficial interest to another party. Additionally, in relation to testamentary dispositions, we will consider: (iv) the Wills Act 1837 s.9. This is a general formality rule, not specific to trusts, that regulates testamentary dispositions. **6–002**

It may first be useful to make four points. First, there is a distinction between formal requirements that apply specifically to the creation of a trust and those that apply generally to the transfer of, or other dealings with, a particular type of property. For example, as we saw in Chapter 5, if a settlor **6–003**

---

1 See L. Fuller, "Consideration and Form" (1941) 41 Columbia L.R. 799. See too P. Critchley, "Taking Formalities Seriously" in S. Bright and J. Dewar (eds), *Land Law: Themes and Perspectives* (Oxford University Press, 1998).

2 Note too that Law of Property Act 1925, s.53(1)(a) (see para.6–027) is relevant where a party attempts to create or dispose of an interest in land (this includes equitable interests, but does not apply to proving an interest arising under a declaration of trust, which is instead covered by s.53(1)(b) of the 1925 Act): see e.g. *Murray v Guinness* (Ch D, Lightman J, 29 April 1998) where s.53(1)(a) governed an attempt to create an immediate equitable charge in relation to land, whilst Law of Property (Miscellaneous Provisions) Act 1989 s.2 (see para. 6–013) governed a contractual undertaking to execute a legal mortgage.

wishes to transfer property to trustees to hold on trust, the general rule is that the intended trust will be constituted only if the transfer is made successfully. This may require compliance with formality rules, if such rules regulate the transfer of the type of property in question.[3] Such formality rules, however, apply whether or not a trust is intended.

6–004 Second, there are no formality rules that specifically govern the creation of a trust. If a settlor holds property other than land, and wishes to give another party a beneficial interest in that property, the settlor can do so simply by means of an *oral* declaration of trust. This is the case even if the beneficiary is a volunteer: a party who has provided no consideration and who simply benefits from the settlor's generosity. As Jeffrey Hackney has noted:[4]

> I can informally transfer to you my economic advantages in chattels of huge value by a few significantly chosen words, and once simply done that act cannot be revoked. No other device in the legal system approaches the massive power of these spoken words in Equity: "I declare myself trustee of this for you."[5]

6–005 Indeed, whilst the Law of Property Act s.53(1)(b) imposes a formality rule for the declaration of trusts in relation to land, that rule, as we will see,[6] regulates the means by which such trusts can be *proved*, not the means by which they can be created.

6–006 Third, it is generally true that formality rules, where they apply, regulate attempts by a party to exercise a legal power, such as the power to come under a particular duty to another, the power to make a transfer of particular property, or the power to dispose of property on death. As a result, such rules may be relevant when considering, for example, a party's attempt to make a particular type of contract,[7] or a beneficiary's attempt to exercise the power to assign her beneficial interest to another.[8] In contrast, if a party claims that a trust has arisen by operation of law, and thus by means of a constructive or resulting trust, it is unlikely that a formality rule will be relevant, as such trusts do not depend on any party having exercised a power to set up a trust. It is therefore important to note that, even if a particular formality rule prevents B from showing that A successfully exercised a power to give B a beneficial interest in property, this does not necessarily prevent B from showing that she acquired such an interest by means of a resulting or constructive trust.[9]

6–007 Fourth, in understanding the operation of formality rules, it is important to distinguish between lifetime and testamentary dispositions, as the Wills Act 1837 regulates the latter but not the former. We will now examine how that distinction is made.

B. Lifetime and Testamentary Dispositions Distinguished

6–008 A lifetime disposition is a disposition of property that takes effect during the lifetime of the person disposing of the property. A testamentary disposition is a disposition that takes effect after death,

---

3 See para.5–003.

4 J. Hackney, *Understanding Equity and Trusts* (Fontana Press, 1987), p.109.

5 Note too that the settlor does not have to use any specific words or formula to set up the trust. The question is rather whether an objective intention to declare a trust has been sufficiently manifested: see, e.g. *Paul v Constance* [1977] 1 W.L.R. 527.

6 At paras 6–027ff.

7 See the Law of Property (Miscellaneous Provisions) Act 1989 s.2.

8 See the Law of Property Act 1925 s.53(1)(c).

9 See, e.g. Law of Property (Miscellaneous) Provisions Act 1989 s.2(5), providing that "nothing in [s.2] affects the creation or operation of resulting, implied or constructive trusts"; and Law of Property Act 1925 s.53(2), providing that "[t]his section does not affect the creation or operation of resulting, implied or constructive trusts", thereby putting such trusts outside the reach of the s.53(1)(b) and s.53(1)(c) formality rules. Note too that s.53(1)(a) of the 1925 Act similarly allows an interest in land to be created or disposed of without writing, if this occurs "by operation of law".

and will be effective only if made in the form of a valid will. A will is "an instrument by which a person makes a disposition of his property to take effect after his decease and which is in its own nature ambulatory and revocable during his life".[10] The party making the will is the testator or testatrix.

There are various reasons why it might matter whether a disposition is testamentary in character. One is that a testamentary disposition can always be revoked during the lifetime of the testator,[11] but a disposition which is not testamentary may or may not be revocable, depending on its terms. Another reason is that a disposition will be void if it is testamentary and the disponor fails to comply with the formality rules contained in the Wills Act 1837. If the disposition is void, the benefit of the property will go not to the intended recipient, but rather to the estate of the testator, and this provides a reason for a party taking a share of that estate to try to persuade a court to characterise a particular disposition as testamentary. **6–009**

In *Chopra v Bindra*,[12] for example, the deceased had owned a house with his sister, and they had executed a deed stating that, whilst they each held a distinct beneficial interest in the house as tenants in common, on either of their deaths, the survivor would be entitled to the whole proceeds of sale of the house. The wife of the deceased, who was the sole beneficiary under his will, claimed, inter alia, that this provision in the deed was invalid, as it was a testamentary disposition that did not comply with the formality requirements imposed by the Wills Act 1837. The Court of Appeal rejected that argument, as the deed "disposed of the proceeds of the unsold house with immediate effect and was irrevocable" whereas "[i]t is the essence of a testamentary disposition that it is only intended to take effect after the testator's death and is revocable during the testator's lifetime".[13] **6–010**

This does not mean, however, that every document intended to operate on death and containing a power of revocation is necessarily testamentary in character. In *Baird v Baird*,[14] for example, the deceased was employed by a company that provided its employees with a pension scheme, the rules of which stated that a member could (revocably) nominate a beneficiary to receive a "death benefit" if the member died while he was in employment; if no valid nomination was made then the death benefit would go to his spouse. The deceased nominated his brother, married, and then died without altering his nomination. His brother claimed the death benefit, but his widow argued that the nomination constituted a testamentary disposition, and was void for non-compliance with statutory formality rules applying to wills. The Privy Council held that the nomination was not a testamentary disposition. Such a disposition can occur only in relation to property that belongs to a testator in his lifetime, and the deceased had not owned any of the death benefit, having merely had the contractual right to require the trustees to pay it to his nominee after his death.[15] **6–011**

---

10 *Baird v Baird* [1990] 2 A.C. 548 at 556, adopting T. Jarman, R. Jennings and J. Harper, *Jarman on Wills*, 8th edn (Sweet & Maxwell, 1951), p.26.

11 See, e.g. *Baird v Baird* [1990] 2 A.C. 548 at 557 per Lord Oliver: "an essential characteristic of a will is that, during the lifetime of the testator, it is a mere declaration of his present intention and may be freely revoked or altered."

12 [2009] EWCA Civ 203; [2009] 2 F.L.R. 786.

13 [2009] 2 F.L.R. 786 at [15] per Rimer LJ.

14 [1990] 2 A.C. 548.

15 [1990] 2 A.C. 548 at 557, applying *Re Danish Bacon Co Ltd Staff Pension Fund Trusts* [1971] 1 W.L.R. 248.

2. Lifetime Dispositions

A. Law of Property (Miscellaneous Provisions) Act 1989 s.2

6–012 As noted above,[16] this is a formality rule, not specific to trusts, that regulates contracts for the sale or other disposition of an interest in land.

Law of Property (Miscellaneous Provisions) Act 1989 s.2

6–013 (1) A contract for the sale or other disposition of an interest in land can only be made in writing and only by incorporating all the terms which the parties have expressly agreed in one document or, where contracts are exchanged, in each.

(2) The terms may be incorporated in a document either by being set out in it or by reference to some other document.

(3) The document incorporating the terms or, where contracts are exchanged, one of the documents incorporating them (but not necessarily the same one) must be signed by or on behalf of each party to the contract.

(4) Where a contract for the sale or other disposition of an interest in land satisfies the conditions of this section by reason only of the rectification of one or more documents in pursuance of an order of a court, the contract shall come into being, or be deemed to have come into being, at such time as may be specified in the order.

(5) This section does not apply in relation to—

(a) a contract to grant such a lease as is mentioned in section 54(2) of the Law of Property Act 1925 (short leases);
(b) a contract made in the course of a public auction; or
(c) a contract regulated under the Financial Services Act 1986;

and nothing in this section affects the creation or operation of resulting, implied or constructive trusts.

(6) In this section—

"disposition" has the same meaning as in the Law of Property Act 1925; "interest in land" means any estate, interest or charge in or over land or in or over the proceeds of sale of land.

(7) Nothing in this section shall apply in relation to contracts made before this section comes into force.

(8) Section 40 of the Law of Property Act 1925 (which is superseded by this section) shall cease to have effect.

i. The Scope of s.2

6–014 A contract to create a trust of any interest in land,[17] and a contract to dispose of an equitable interest in land, e.g. a life interest or a co-owner's equitable interest under a trust of land, is governed by the Law of Property (Miscellaneous Provisions) Act 1989 s.2.[18] The section provides that the contract

---

[16] See para.6–002.

[17] No formality rule applies to a contract to create a trust in relation to property other than land: see, e.g. *Chinn v Collins* [1981] A.C. 533 at 548; nor to a contract to transfer an existing beneficial interest in property other than land: see, e.g. *Neville v Wilson* [1997] Ch. 144, extracted at paras 6–110 to 6–121.

[18] The 1989 Act does not apply to the exercise of an option to purchase an interest in land (*Spiro v Glencrown Properties Ltd* [1991] Ch. 537) nor to a lock-out agreement not to consider any further offers if the purchaser exchanges contracts within two weeks (*Pitt v PHH Asset Management Ltd* [1994] 1 W.L.R. 327) nor to a collateral contract (*Record v Bell* [1991] 1 W.L.R. 853) nor to an agreement supplemental to a completed contract (*Tootal Clothing Ltd v Guinea Properties*

is void unless all the terms are in one document signed by both parties or in exchanged documents signed by each exchanger (or by a person acting on her behalf),[19] though it is possible to incorporate terms set out in another document by referring to that document. The s.2 formality rule is also important to the law of trusts because, as we will see in Chapter 17,[20] a trust may arise as a result of a contract for the sale of an interest in land, even before that contract has been performed by the conveyance of the interest itself. Such a trust, however, depends on there being a valid contract, and so cannot arise if the formality rule has not been satisfied.

ii. The Consequences of Non-Compliance

It is important to note that if s.2 is not complied with, there is no contract between the parties. Formerly, under both the Statute of Frauds 1677 s.4 and the Law of Property Act 1925 s.40, it was instead the case that an oral contract for the sale of an interest in land was valid, but unenforceable. The basic validity of the contract gave the courts the space to develop the equitable doctrine of part performance, under which specific performance of the contract could be ordered if some part of the contract had been performed and the claimant would therefore suffer some detriment if the contract were not enforced.[21] However, the nature and operation of the doctrine of part performance were unclear,[22] and one of the aims of the 1989 Act[23] was to avoid the complications of the doctrine by making clear that if the formality rule is not complied with, there is simply no contract between the parties. **6–015**

In the report which led to the enactment of the 1989 Act, the Law Commission, whilst emphasising the benefits of removing the doctrine of part performance from contracts, noted that there still might be situations where injustice could be caused if, in the absence of a contractual claim, a party were to have no recourse. It therefore noted that various non-contractual claims might be available to such a party: for example, a proprietary estoppel claim might be available if, as a result of reasonable reliance on the defendant's non-contractual promise, the claimant would now suffer a detriment if the defendant were wholly free to revoke that promise; and an unjust enrichment claim might arise if the claimant had transferred benefits to the defendant on the shared understanding that there was indeed a contract between the parties.[24] **6–016**

As noted in Chapter 3, it is indeed the case that, since the 1989 Act came into force, the courts have recognised that such non-contractual claims may arise in a case where s.2 has not been complied **6–017**

Management Ltd (1992) 64 P. & C.R. 452). However it does apply to variations: *McCausland v Duncan Lawrie Ltd* [1997] 1 W.L.R. 38. If the parties omit an agreed term (of the sale contract, rather than of some collateral agreement: *North Eastern Properties Ltd v Coleman* [2010] 1 W.L.R. 2715) then rectification can sometimes (but not always) be obtained so that the rectified document complies with the 1989 Act: *Wright v Robert Leonard (Developments) Ltd* [1994] E.G.C.S. 69; cf. *Oun v Ahmad* [2008] EWHC 545 (Ch). For discussion of rectification, see Chapter 21.

19 A signature for the purposes of the 1989 Act must be a personal signature: *Firstpost Homes Ltd v Johnson* [1995] 1 W.L.R. 1567. Note though that e.g. a typed name at the end of an email can constitute a signature if there is "authenticating intention": see e.g. *Neocleous v Rees* [2019] EWHC 2462 (Ch).

20 At paras 17–061 to 17–071.

21 *Steadman v Steadman* [1976] A.C. 536 as narrowly interpreted in *Re Gonin* [1979] Ch. 16.

22 For discussion of the doctrine see *Yaxley v Gotts* [2000] Ch. 162 at 171–172 per Robert Walker LJ, and for a helpful survey of the history and nature of the doctrine, see P. Matthews, "The Words Which Are Not There: A Partial History of the Constructive Trust" in C. Mitchell (ed.), *Constructive and Resulting Trusts* (Hart Publishing, 2010), pp.25–44.

23 See Law Commission, *The Transfer of Land: Formalities for Contracts of Sale etc. of Land* (HMSO, 1987), Law Com. No.164, HC Paper No.2 (Session 1987–88) para.5.4 and *Yaxley v Gotts* [2000] Ch. 162 at 188 per Beldam LJ: "Section 2 of the 1989 Act was primarily intended to overcome the complexities which had arisen from the doctrine of part-performance and from problems caused by the interpretation of section 40 of the Law of Property Act 1925." Beldam LJ had been Chair of the Law Commission at the time of its work on the issue.

24 Law Commission, *The Transfer of Land: Formalities for Contracts of Sale etc. of Land* (HMSO, 1987), Law Com. No.164, HC Paper No.2 (Session 1987–88) para.5.4.

with.[25] The difficulty for the claimant, of course, lies in showing that she has established all the requirements of a non-contractual claim.

6–018 In *Cobbe v Yeoman's Row Management Ltd*,[26] for example, the parties had made an oral agreement in principle that land would be sold to the claimant if planning permission were obtained and, in reliance on that agreement, and with the encouragement of the defendant vendor, the claimant had prepared the successful planning application. The judgment at first instance,[27] affirmed by the Court of Appeal,[28] was that the doctrine of proprietary estoppel applied and the defendant, who had refused to sell the land to the claimant, was ordered to pay the claimant a sum of around £2 million, equal to half of the increase in the value of the defendant's land resulting from the award of planning permission. The House of Lords, however, found that the ingredients of proprietary estoppel were absent: as Lord Neuberger later noted,[29] the parties' agreement in principle had left some important points outstanding, and it was therefore not possible for the claimant to show that he had reasonably relied on a promise which could be seen as one seriously intended by the defendant as capable of being relied upon. Nonetheless, the House of Lords held that a claim in unjust enrichment was made out,[30] as the claimant had performed valuable work for the defendant on the shared understanding that, if planning permission were obtained, that work would be rewarded. It was also held, however, that the extent of the claimant's award was not related to the increase in value of the defendant's land resulting from the claimant's work, but was limited instead to the usual market value of the services rendered by the claimant, plus other costs incurred: a sum estimated at around £150,000.[31]

6–019 The decision of the House of Lords in the *Cobbe* case thus demonstrates that a failure to comply with s.2 does not rule out all claims. In that case, however, Lord Scott made the following statement:[32]

> There is one further point regarding proprietary estoppel to which I should refer. Section 2 of the 1989 Act declares to be void any agreement for the acquisition of an interest in land that does not comply with the requisite formalities prescribed by the section. Subsection (5) expressly makes an exception for resulting, implied or constructive trusts. These may validly come into existence without compliance with the prescribed formalities. Proprietary estoppel does not have the benefit of this exception. The question arises, therefore, whether a complete agreement for the acquisition of an interest in land that does not comply with the s. 2 prescribed formalities, but would be specifically enforceable if it did, can become enforceable via the route of proprietary estoppel. It is not necessary in the present case to answer this question, for the second agreement was not a complete agreement and, for that reason, would not have been specifically enforceable so long as it remained incomplete. My present view, however, is that proprietary estoppel cannot be prayed in aid in order to render enforceable an agreement that statute has declared to be void. The proposition that an owner of land can be estopped from asserting that an agreement is void for want of compliance with the requirements of s. 2 is, in my opinion, unacceptable. The assertion is no more than the statute provides. Equity can surely not contradict the statute.

---

25 See para.3–026. For a proprietary estoppel claim, see, e.g. *Yaxley v Gotts* [2000] Ch. 162; *Kinane v Mackie-Conteh* [2005] EWCA Civ 45; [2005] W.T.L.R. 345; *Herbert v Doyle* [2010] EWCA Civ 1095; [2011] 1 E.G.L.R. 119; *Whittaker v Kinnear* [2011] EWHC 1479 (QB). For an unjust enrichment claim, see *Cobbe v Yeoman's Row Management Ltd* [2008] UKHL 55; [2008] 1 W.L.R. 1752.

26 [2008] UKHL 55; [2008] 1 W.L.R. 1752.

27 [2005] EWHC 266 (Ch); [2005] W.T.L.R. 625.

28 [2006] EWCA Civ 1139; [2006] 1 W.L.R. 2964.

29 *Thorner v Major* [2009] UKHL 18; [2009] 1 W.L.R. 776 at [93]: "there was total uncertainty as to the nature or terms of any benefit (property interest, contractual right, or money) and, if a property interest, as to the nature of that interest (freehold, leasehold or charge), to be accorded to Mr Cobbe." That is perhaps putting matters at their highest, but it was certainly true that the parties had not decided whether the land was to be conveyed to Mr Cobbe, or to a company to be set up by him, nor how security was to be provided for a planned overage provision in the vendor's favour.

30 [2008] UKHL 55; [2008] 1 W.L.R. 1752 at [40]–[44].

31 [2008] 1 W.L.R. 1752 at [44], although note the reluctance of Lord Mance at [96] to support any such estimate.

32 [2008] 1 W.L.R. 1752 at [29].

On the view adopted by Lord Scott, then, in a case where s.2 prevents a contractual claim, B cannot turn to proprietary estoppel—although, owing to the express provision in s.2(5), the claimant may be able to rely on principles very similar to those of proprietary estoppel in order to show that a constructive trust has arisen.[33] Lord Scott's obiter suggestion[34] has been subject to sustained judicial doubt[35] and, it is submitted, should be rejected. **6–020**

First, Lord Scott's view that s.2 renders an *agreement* void is incorrect: the section expressly regulates *contracts* and so it does not therefore rule out a non-contractual claim, even if that claim depends in part on A's having made an oral promise to B. **6–021**

Second, and contrary to Lord Scott's view of the doctrine, proprietary estoppel does not operate to prevent the defendant from denying the existence of a contract, or the grant of a right; rather, as we saw in Chapter 3, it provides a means by which an independent claim may be made.[36] Given the clear differences between a contractual claim and a proprietary estoppel claim,[37] it is difficult to see how recognising the latter claim is inconsistent with either the express wording or underlying policy of the s.2 formality requirement. **6–022**

Third,[38] Lord Scott's view leads to the strange position that, in a case where the parties have reached an agreement that would be contractually binding but for s.2, no proprietary estoppel claim can be made; whereas, in cases where it is clear that, even without s.2, there would be no contract between the parties, the courts have allowed proprietary estoppel claims without any consideration of the s.2 point.[39] **6–023**

Fourth, as there is no reported case in which a proprietary estoppel claim has failed simply on the basis of a failure to comply with formality rules, the effect of Lord Scott's view would be to force courts to rely on s.2(5) by finding that a constructive trust has arisen even if, on the facts of the case, it is clear that A does not in fact hold any property on trust for B.[40] **6–024**

Finally, it was suggested above[41] that formality rules regulate situations where a party attempts to exercise a power, and it seems reasonably clear that the doctrine of proprietary estoppel operates to impose a liability on A where necessary to prevent a specific form of unconscionable behaviour: as this form of liability is thus imposed by law it would be strange if it were regulated by a formality rule. **6–025**

It is therefore submitted that s.2 has no impact on a proprietary estoppel claim: if the requirements of such a claim are established, it should be permitted, whether or not a constructive trust can be **6–026**

---

33 The links, for example, between proprietary estoppel and the "common intention" constructive trust will be considered at paras 17–198 to 17–202.

34 It was not necessary for the decision in the case, as the proprietary estoppel claim failed in any case: see para.6–018.

35 See, e.g. *Whittaker v Kinnear* [2011] EWHC 1479 (QB) where Bean J stated at [30] that "notwithstanding Lord Scott's dicta in *Cobbe*, proprietary estoppel in a case involving the sale of land has survived the enactment of s.2 of the 1989 Act"; *Farrar v Miller* [2018] EWCA Civ 172 at [57] (Kitchin LJ): "There are in my view strong arguments for saying that s 2 of the 1989 Act is concerned only with the requirements of a valid contract for the sale or other disposition of land." See too *Sahota v Prior* [2019] EWHC 1418 at [26]–[29].

36 See paras 3–003 to 3–009.

37 See paras 3–027 to 3–033.

38 This point is noted by, e.g. B. McFarlane, "Proprietary Estoppel and Failed Contractual Negotiations" [2005] Conv. 501 and Lord Neuberger, "The Stuffing of Minerva's Owl? Taxonomy and Taxidermy in Equity" [2009] C.L.J. 537, 546.

39 See, e.g. *Crabb v Arun DC* [1976] Ch. 179.

40 Note that there is already evidence of this problem in the case-law: e.g. in *Yaxley v Gotts* [2000] Ch. 162, there was said to be a constructive trust, yet it does not appear that the defendant held any property on trust, as the court's order was that the defendant should grant the claimant the promised lease, or pay him its value.

41 See para.6–006.

found.[42] There is no need to resort to s.2(5), as the basic s.2 rule, which is limited to *contracts*, simply does not apply. As Lord Neuberger, writing extra-judicially, put it:[43]

> [Where proprietary estoppel is concerned] I suggest that s. 2 has nothing to do with the matter. . . the estoppel rests on the finding that it would be inequitable for the defendant to insist on his strict legal rights. So the fact that, if there was a contract, it would be void is irrelevant: indeed the very reason for mounting the proprietary estoppel claim is that there is no enforceable contract.

B. Law of Property Act 1925 s.53(1)(b)

Law of Property Act 1925 s.53

6–027 (1) Subject to the provisions hereinafter contained with respect to the creation of interests in land by parol:

(a) No interest in land can be created or disposed of except by writing signed by the person creating or conveying the same, or by his agent thereunto lawfully authorised in writing, or by will, or by operation of law;

(b) A declaration of trust respecting any land or any interest therein must be manifested and proved by some writing signed by some person who is able to declare such trust or by his will;

(c) A disposition of an equitable interest or trust subsisting at the time of the disposition, must be in writing signed by the person disposing of the same, or by his agent thereunto lawfully authorised in writing or by will.

(2) This section does not affect the creation or operation of resulting, implied or constructive trusts.

i. The Scope of s.53(1)(b)

6–028 The formality rule imposed by s.53(1)(b) applies only to a declaration of trust "respecting any land or any interest therein". It varies from the rules imposed by s.53(1)(a) and s.53(1)(c) as it does not regulate the creation of rights, but only the means by which such creation can be proved.[44] So, for example, if an oral trust of land is declared, but later written evidence of the trust signed by a party who is able to declare such a trust[45] comes into being, the beneficiary can prove that the trust existed *from the moment of its oral declaration*.[46]

6–029 As the effect of a failure to comply with s.53(1)(b) thus differs from that in relation to s.53(1)(a), a dividing line needs to be drawn between the two formality rules. It would seem that s.53(1)(a) must be interpreted as covering the creation of equitable interests in land *other than* equitable interests

---

42 Note that in *McGuane v Welch* [2008] EWCA Civ 785; [2008] 2 P. & C.R. 24 at [35], it was held that the particular nature of the parties' agreement "left no space for the insertion of a constructive trust", yet a proprietary estoppel claim, based on that oral agreement, was nonetheless allowed to arise.

43 Lord Neuberger, "The Stuffing of Minerva's Owl? Taxonomy and Taxidermy in Equity" [2009] C.L.J. 537, 546.

44 As noted by W. Swadling, "The Nature of the Trust in *Rochefoucauld v Boustead*" in C. Mitchell (ed.), *Constructive and Resulting Trusts* (Hart Publishing, 2010), p.108, s.53(1)(b) does not mean that the trust is unenforceable: rather, it simply regulates the means by which the trust can be proved.

45 Note that this later writing does not itself need to take the form of a declaration, as long as it provides evidence of the trust: see e.g. *Ong v Ping* [2017] EWCA Civ 2069.

46 See, e.g. *Gardner v Rowe* (1825) 2 S. & S. 346, affirmed (1828) 5 Russ. 258: the deed confirming the earlier oral declaration was executed only after the settlor went into insolvency, but it enabled proof of the declaration which was made before the insolvency, and the beneficial interest under the trust therefore bound the assignees in bankruptcy.

arising under a declaration of trust (e.g. restrictive covenants).[47] The fact that a slightly more lenient rule applies under s.53(1)(b) may perhaps be justified by the fact that, owing to the possibility of statutory overreaching,[48] and the fact that an equitable interest under a trust cannot be protected by the entry of a notice on the land register,[49] the existence of a beneficial interest under a trust of land causes fewer problems for third parties dealing with the land than the presence of a different type of equitable interest.

A settlor may create a trust of land either by declaring that she herself will henceforth hold the land on specified trusts, or by conveying the land to trustees and declaring specified trusts on which the trustees are to hold the land. In both cases, proof of the declaration of the trusts must be in writing specifying the beneficiaries, the trust property, and the nature of the trusts,[50] and the writing may be comprised in linked documents.[51] **6-030**

The signed writing must be "by some person who is able to declare such trust". So, for example, the sub-section would be satisfied if S conveyed Blackacre to T and at the same time declared signed written trusts for B. Again, if T1 and T2 held property on trust for A for life, remainder to B, but with power for the trustees to declare new trusts in favour of C or her issue, then the sub-section would be satisfied if T1 and T2 exercised this power in signed writing. In contrast to s.53(1)(a) or (c), there is no express reference in s.53(1)(b) to the possibility of an agent's signature, but this may simply be because a duly authorised agent, acting on behalf of a settlor, can be seen as "some person who is able to declare such trust". **6-031**

The signatory (or principal if signature by an agent is permitted) should be the person who, at the time of the signature, would be entitled to the enjoyment of the land if no declaration of trust had been made.[52] So, if S declares themselves trustee of land for B, the relevant person would be S; and if, subsequently, B declares that she holds her equitable interest on trust for C, the relevant person would be B.[53] However, if S conveys land to T and orally declares a trust for B, then subsequent written evidence of the trust signed by T satisfies s.53(1)(b).[54] If S instead conveys land or transfers other property to T to hold to S's order and on some later date S then tells T to hold on trust for B, this amounts to S's disposing of her subsisting equitable interest to B: a disposition that, as we will see below,[55] will be void under s.53(1)(c) unless in writing signed by S or her agent.[56] **6-032**

ii. The Consequences of Non-Compliance

If A either transfers land to B, or buys land in B's name, on an oral understanding with B that B will hold the land on trust for A, then case law assumes that, to satisfy s.53(1)(b), it is necessary for some **6-033**

---

47 In view of Law of Property Act 1925 s.52(1), s.53(1)(a) cannot be restricted to legal interests and in order to prevent s.53(1)(a) from making s.53(1)(b) otiose, para.(b) should be construed in line with the maxim *generalia specialibus non derogant* (i.e. general clauses cannot derogate from special clauses), so that declarations of trust of land fall outside the scope of s.53(1)(a): *Hagan v Waterhouse* (1991) 34 N.S.W.L.R. 308 at 385–386.

48 See Trusts of Land and Appointment of Trustees Act s.6 and Law of Property Act 1925 ss.2 and 27. See too para.10-031 and *City of London Building Society v Flegg* [1998] A.C. 54.

49 See Land Registration Act 2002 s.33.

50 *Smith v Matthews* (1861) 3 De G. F. & J. 139; *Morton v Tewart* (1842) 2 Y. & C. Ch. Cas. 67.

51 *Forster v Hale* (1798) 3 Ves. Jun. 696.

52 T. G. Youdan, "Formalities for Trusts of Land and the Doctrine in *Rochefoucauld v Boustead*" [1984] C.L.J. 306, 316–320.

53 *Tierney v Wood* (1854) 19 Beav. 330; *Kronheim v Johnson* (1877) 7 Ch.D. 60.

54 *Gardner v Rowe* (1828) 5 Russ. 258; *Smith v Matthews* (1861) 3 De G.F. & J. 139; *Mountain v Styak* [1922] N.Z.L.R. 131. If the oral trusts had been for A herself then she would have an equitable interest under a constructive trust which she could then sub-settle: *Tierney v Wood* (1854) 19 Beav. 330.

55 At paras 6-051ff.

56 *Grey v IRC* [1960] A.C. 1.

writing proving the trust to be signed by B.[57] What if B refuses to provide such writing, and instead attempts to keep the land for her own benefit? It would clearly be unconscionable for B, in such a case, to decide to keep the land for herself and to rely on the statute to prevent A proving any trust of the property: after all, the s.53(1)(b) formality rule derives from the Statute of Frauds,[58] which was enacted with the express purpose of *preventing* fraud. It is, fortunately, clear that, in such a case, A will be able to assert a beneficial interest against B. There is, however, a debate as to the best explanation for this undoubted position, and as to the nature of the trust that A can assert against B. There are two principal views.

6-034 On the first view, the trust asserted by A is an express one, arising as a result of the oral declaration of trust. A is allowed to prove that declaration by means other than signed writing, as it would be fraudulent in the circumstances for B to rely on s.53(1)(b), and a "statute cannot be used as an instrument of fraud".[59] On this view, of course, the crucial issue is to define what conduct counts as fraud sufficient to prevent a party relying on the formality rule.[60] On the second view, the trust asserted by A is a constructive one, which does not arise as a result of the oral declaration of trust, but is rather imposed on the facts[61] to prevent the particular form of unconscionable conduct that would consist of B receiving property on the basis of a promise to hold it on trust, and then holding that property free from the promised trust. On this view, of course, the crucial issue is to define the precise form of unconscionable conduct involved.[62] Before considering those views in more detail, it is useful to examine a key authority.

Rochefoucauld v Boustead

Court of Appeal [1897] 1 Ch. 196

6-035 In 1868, the plaintiff, the Comtesse de la Rochefoucauld, held an equity of redemption in coffee plantations in Ceylon (the Delmar Estates).[63] Legal title to the properties was held by the mortgagee, a Dutch company. The defendant, Mr Boustead, managed the plantations on behalf of the plaintiff. The Comtesse was unable to repay the mortgage debts and was concerned that the Dutch company would enforce its security by exercising its power to sell the land to a stranger. She therefore agreed with the defendant that, when the Dutch company auctioned off the estates, he would buy the titles to those estates at a price sufficient to cover the mortgage debt and expenses, and that he would hold those titles on trust for

---

57 See, e.g. *Re Duke of Marlborough* [1894] 2 Ch. 133; *Smith v Matthews* (1861) 3 De G.F. & J. 139; *Gardner v Rowe* (1828) 5 Russ. 258; *Mountain v Styak* [1922] N.Z.L.R. 131.

58 See Statute of Frauds 1677 s.7.

59 For academic support for that view, see, e.g. W Swadling, "The Nature of the Trust in *Rochefoucauld v Boustead*" in C. Mitchell (ed.), *Constructive and Resulting Trusts* (2010). For discussion of the principle that "equity will not allow a statute to be used as an instrument of fraud" see G. Allan, "Once a Fraud, Forever a Fraud: The Time Honoured Doctrine of Parol Agreement Trusts" (2014) 34 L.S. 419.

60 See further paras 6-048 to 6-050.

61 For academic support for that view, see, e.g. B. McFarlane, "Constructive Trusts Arising on Receipt of Property *Sub Conditione*" (2004) 120 L.Q.R. 667; N. Hopkins, "Conscience, Discretion and the Creation of Property Rights" (2006) 26 L.S. 475; S. Gardner, "Reliance-Based Constructive Trusts" in C. Mitchell (ed.), *Constructive and Resulting Trusts* (2010); Y.K. Liew "*Rochefoucauld v Boustead* (1897)" in C. Mitchell and P. Mitchell (eds), *Landmark Cases in Equity* (Hart Publishing, 2012).

62 Note that, whilst they agree that the trust is constructive and not express, there is no unanimity on this point between the commentators cited at fn.61. See further paras 17-085 to 17-086.

63 Note that *Rochefoucauld* itself involved land outside the English jurisdiction. The formality rule imposed by the Statute of Frauds 1677 s.7 was still considered relevant as it was said to affect the means of proof, in an English court, of the trust: see [1897] 1 Ch 196, 207, relying on *Leroux v Brown* (1852) 12 CB 80, which dealt with Statute of Frauds 1677 s. 4. It is not clear that a modern court would adopt the same view of s.53(1)(b): see L Collins et al (eds) *Dicey, Morris and Collins: The Conflict of Laws*, 15th edn (Sweet & Maxwell, 2013) at para.7-031.

her, subject to a lien for his expenditure.[64] In 1873, the defendant bought the titles from the mortgagee, with the conveyance saying nothing of the planned trust for the plaintiff. Without her knowledge, he then mortgaged the titles to the estates to secure his own borrowings. In 1894, the plaintiff sought a declaration that he had bought the titles as trustee for her, for an account of his dealings as trustee with the estates, and for payment of the amount found to be due. By then, the titles had already been sold, but the plaintiff alleged that the proceeds of sale were sufficient to repay the defendant all she owed him, and that a surplus remained, which he should pay her.

The defendant denied that he had bought the titles as trustee for the plaintiff, and said that in any case the alleged trusts could not be proved by any writing signed by him, and that the Statute of Frauds 1677 s.7 (the predecessor of s.53(1)(b) of the Law of Property Act 1925) precluded the admission of oral evidence to make good the plaintiff's allegation. Kekewich J. heard the plaintiff's oral testimony but did not admit it into evidence, on the ground that he was precluded from doing so by section 7. Hence he found that the plaintiff had not proved that the defendant had agreed to hold the titles on trust for her, and dismissed the claim. The Court of Appeal held that Kekewich J. had been wrong to use section 7 to keep out the claimant's evidence. Admitting that evidence, the court held that it proved the plaintiff's case. The defendant also sought to rely on the six-year limitation period in the Trustee Act 1888 s.8(1)(b), which governed claims for breach of trust against constructive trustees, but the court held that the trust was express, so that no limitation period applied. Hence the court granted the relief sought. 6–036

LINDLEY L.J. delivered the judgment of the court (which consisted of LORD HALSBURY L.C., LINDLEY and A.L. SMITH L.JJ.): The question raised by this appeal is whether the plaintiff is entitled to an account from the defendant of the proceeds of sale of certain coffee estates in Ceylon. The estates in question are known as the Delmar estates. They formerly belonged to the plaintiff; they were mortgaged first to Barings and then to a Dutch company, and on May 27, 1873, they were sold and conveyed to the defendant. In form the conveyance was to him absolutely, but the plaintiff insists that the estates were conveyed to the defendant as a trustee for the plaintiff, subject, however, to the repayment to the defendant of the amount which he paid for them and of the expenses which he has incurred in managing the estates. The estates were sold by the defendant or his mortgagees many years ago without the knowledge of the plaintiff, and she says that the proceeds of sale were more than sufficient to repay to the defendant all his advances, and that a considerable surplus remained which the defendant ought to have paid over to her. The defendant, in answer to this claim, says (1.) the estates were conveyed to him, not as a trustee for the plaintiff, but as beneficial owner; (2.) the trusts alleged by the plaintiff cannot be proved by any writing signed by the defendant, and the Statute of Frauds affords a defence to the action; (3.) the plaintiff's claim, even if proved, is barred (a) by the defendant's bankruptcy, (b) by the Statute of Limitations, (c) by the plaintiff's laches, an the equitable doctrines applicable to delay independently of the statute. 6–037

Kekewich J. decided against the plaintiff on the first ground—namely, that there was no trust in favour of the plaintiff. This view of the case rendered it unnecessary for him to consider the other defences. The plaintiff has appealed from this decision; and, as we have been unable to take the same view as the learned judge of the effect of the evidence, it will be necessary for us to deal with all the other defences relied upon by the defendant. 6–038

The circumstances under which the Delmar estates were conveyed to the defendant are to be gathered from the verbal testimony of the plaintiff, the defendant, and Mr Duff, and a mass of correspondence both before and after the conveyance. The correspondence after the conveyance is relied upon by the plaintiff as being inconsistent with the defendant's contention that he acquired the estates for himself beneficially, free from any trust in favour of the plaintiff. 6–039

[The Court then stated the leading facts in the history of the case, and examined the parties' correspondence, and summed up as follows:] We come, therefore, to the conclusion that the plaintiff has proved that the estates in question were conveyed to the defendant on May 27, 1873, upon trust for her, but subject to a charge in his favour in respect of all sums advanced by him in order to obtain the estates from the Dutch company in the first instance, and of all sums advanced by him in order to work them as coffee plantations after he had acquired them. 6–040

64 Y.K. Liew, "*Rochefoucauld v Boustead* (1897)" in C Mitchell & P Mitchell (eds) *Landmark Cases in Equity* (2012) suggests, drawing on the Law Times report of the case, (1897) 75 L.T. 502, 504–505, that this route was adopted as the Comtessse was concerned about possible claims to her interest in the plantations by her recently-divorced husband, and she wanted her husband to believe that she no longer had any rights in the plantations.

6-041 This conclusion renders it necessary to consider whether the Statute of Frauds affords a defence to the plaintiff's claim. The section relied upon is s.7, which has been judicially interpreted in *Forster v Hale*[65] and *Smith v Matthews*.[66] According to these authorities, it is necessary to prove by some writing or writings signed by the defendant, not only that the conveyance to him was subject to some trust, but also what that trust was. But it is not necessary that the trust should have been declared by such a writing in the first instance; it is sufficient if the trust can be proved by some writing signed by the defendant, and the date of the writing is immaterial. It is further established by a series of cases, the propriety of which cannot now be questioned, that the Statute of Frauds does not prevent the proof of a fraud; and that it is a fraud on the part of a person to whom land is conveyed as a trustee, and who knows it was so conveyed, to deny the trust and claim the land himself. Consequently, notwithstanding the statute, it is competent for a person claiming land conveyed to another to prove by parol evidence that it was so conveyed upon trust for the claimant, and that the grantee, knowing the facts, is denying the trust and relying upon the form of conveyance and the statute, in order to keep the land himself. . .

6-042 The defence, based on the Statute of Frauds, is met by the plaintiff in two ways. First, she says that the documents signed by the defendant prove the existence of the trust alleged; secondly, she says that if those documents do not prove what the trust is with sufficient fulness and precision, the case is one of fraud which lets in other evidence, and that with the aid of other evidence the plaintiff's case is established. In our opinion the plaintiff is correct in this contention. We are by no means satisfied that the letters signed by the defendant do not contain enough to satisfy the Statute of Frauds. Whether this is so or not, the other evidence is admissible in order to prevent the statute from being used in order to commit a fraud; and such other evidence proves the plaintiff's case completely. . .

6-043 Having come to the conclusion that the plaintiff has proved her case by evidence admissible by our law, it is necessary to consider the other defences raised. . .

6-044 The next defence is the Statute of Limitations. The trust which the plaintiff has established is clearly an express trust within the meaning of that expression as explained in *Soar v Ashwell*.[67] The trust is one which both plaintiff and defendant intended to create. This case is not one in which an equitable obligation arises although there may have been no intention to create a trust. The intention to create a trust existed from the first. The defendant is not able in this case to claim the benefit of s.8 of the Trustee Act, 1888, and the statute which is applicable is the Judicature Act 1873 s.25, subs. 2, which enacts as follows: "No claim of a cestui que trust against his trustee for any property held on an express trust, or in respect of any breach of such trust, shall be held to be barred by any Statute of Limitations." The Statutes of Limitations, therefore, afford no defence if the plaintiff's action is to be regarded as one brought by a cestui que trust against his trustee seeking for an account of trust property.

6-045 [The court also rejected the defence of laches, and concluded:] The appeal must be allowed and the judgment be reversed. It must be declared that the defendant purchased the Delmar estates as a trustee for the plaintiff, but subject to a charge for the amount paid to the Dutch company. An account must then be directed of the defendant's dealings and transactions with the Delmar estates. The account will be an account as between a trustee and his cestui que trust, not an account as between mortgagor and mortgagee, and there must be no account on the footing of wilful default. The defendant must be allowed all his advances and outlays, with colonial interest; but he ought only to be charged simple interest at 4 per cent on balances in his hands, unless it appears that he has made more. Minutes had better be prepared and signed, and, if necessary, they can be mentioned to the Court. The defendant must pay the costs of the action up to the hearing and the costs of the appeal.

6-046 It might therefore seem clear that the Court of Appeal adopted the first view: the Comtesse was permitted to prove the expressly declared trust without producing any signed writing, as it was necessary to stop Boustead using the formality rule as an instrument of fraud.[68] There are, however,

---

[65] (1798) 3 Ves. Jun. 696.

[66] (1861) 3 D.F. & J. 139.

[67] [1893] 2 Q.B. 390.

[68] That is certainly the argument made by W. Swadling, "The Nature of the Trust in *Rochefoucauld v Boustead*" in C. Mitchell (ed.), *Constructive and Resulting Trusts* (2010). See too A.B. Douglas, "Trusts, Formalities and the Doctrine in *Rochefoucauld v Boustead*" [2021] Conv. 128, arguing that B's fraud disabled B from invoking the formality rule to deny A's interest under the trust.

some difficulties with applying that view on the specific facts of *Rochefoucauld*.[69] Moreover, there are certainly later decisions in which the trust recognised in *Rochefoucauld* has been described as a constructive trust.[70] We need to know more about constructive trusts in order to understand the debate, and so we will examine these and other points for and against each of the two views in more detail in Chapter 17.[71] At this point, however, it is useful to ask why it might matter which of the two views is to be preferred.

There is no difference between the views when it comes to considering the possible application of a limitation period to A's claim against B. On the express trust view, as made clear in *Rochefoucauld*, no statutory limitation period applies; but even on the constructive trust view, as the case is one in which B agreed to hold on trust, it is again accepted that no statutory limitation period applies.[72] There are, however, two broader reasons for asking which of the two views is to be preferred. **6–047**

First, consider a case in which A transfers land to T subject to an oral agreement that T is to hold the land on trust for B. Such a "three-party" case can be contrasted with the "two-party" case in which A transfers land to T subject to an oral agreement that T is to hold on trust for A. In the three-party case, it seems clear, on either of the two views, that T should not be free to use the land for her own benefit. On the first view, however, it may be that T's potential fraud can be adequately addressed by finding that T holds the land on a trust for *A;*[73] or, to the same effect, that no risk of fraud arises, because if the oral trust for B cannot be proved, and, to that extent, fails, then a resulting trust arises for A.[74] On the second view, in contrast, it may be that the form of unconscionable conduct to which equity responds consists of T's reneging on the promise subject to which the property was acquired: in that case, T's promise must be enforced, and so a constructive trust is imposed in favour of *B*.[75] On the first view, of course, if a resulting trust arises for A, A will then have another chance to give B the beneficial interest in the land; but A may die before then, or may change her mind, and in such a case, the difference between the two views may be of critical importance to B.[76] **6–048**

Second, consider a case in which A transfers land to T subject to an oral agreement that T will allow A (or B) to make some limited use of the land, as a licensee. On the first view, there is of course no express trust, as no party has attempted to set up a trust, and so the principle applying in **6–049**

---

69 See Y.K. Liew, "*Rochefoucauld v Boustead* (1897)" in C. Mitchell and P. Mitchell (eds), *Landmark Cases in Equity* (2012), preferring the second, constructive trust view of the case.

70 See, e.g. *Paragon Finance v Thakerar* [1999] 1 All E.R. 400 at 409 per Millett LJ; *Gissing v Gissing* [1971] A.C. 886 at 905 per Lord Diplock; *Bannister v Bannister* [1948] 2 All E.R. 133.

71 At paras 17–077 to 17–093.

72 See, e.g. *Paragon Finance Plc v DB Thakerar & Co* [1999] 1 All E.R. 400 at 408–409. where Millett LJ distinguishes between different types of constructive trust when considering the relevant limitation rules. It is conceivable that a similar approach could be adopted when considering, for example, the application of conflicts of laws rules, so that a constructive trust arising in a case where the defendant had agreed to hold on trust would be treated in the same way as an express trust.

73 As argued by, e.g. J.D. Feltham, "Informal Trusts and Third Parties" [1987] Conv. 246. N. Hopkins, *The Informal Acquisition of Rights in Land* (Sweet & Maxwell, 2000), pp.37–38 argues that the prevailing position should be a trust for A, and that a trust for B should arise only in "exceptional circumstances where intervention in [B]'s favour is the only means of preventing fraud". This view was also adopted by HHJ Matthews in *Solomon v McCarthy* [2020] 1 WLUK 130 at [43].

74 See paras 16–059ff and compare, e.g. *Hodgson v Marks* [1971] Ch. 892.

75 As argued by, e.g. T. Youdan, "Formalities for Trusts of Land and the Doctrine in *Rochefoucauld v Boustead*" (1984) 43 C.L.J. 306 and "Informal Trusts and Third Parties: A Response" [1988] Conv. 267, as well as by, e.g. B. McFarlane, "Constructive Trusts Arising on Receipt of Property *Sub Conditione*" (2004) 120 L.Q.R. 667 and S. Gardner, "Reliance-Based Constructive Trusts" in C. Mitchell (ed.), *Constructive and Resulting Trusts* (2010). This view is supported by the analysis of Patten LJ in *de Bruyne v de Bruyne* [2010] EWCA Civ 519 at [51] referring to a principle giving rise to a constructive trust where the defendant's unconscionable conduct is "in the form of a denial or refusal to carry out the agreement to hold the property for the benefit of the third party which was the only basis upon which the property was transferred".

76 Taxation rules may also apply differently if B's right is acquired not as a result of the initial transaction, but as a result of a later gift by A. As noted at para.4–037, the timing of a gift may be crucial, for example, in determining its consequences for inheritance tax.

Rochefoucauld provides no assistance for A or B. On the second view, however, if a constructive trust can arise where it would be unconscionable for T to renege on a promise subject to which she acquired property, then there is a strong argument that T's promise should be enforced whether or not it is a promise to hold on trust.[77] Of course, in a case where T's promise is simply to allow A or B a licence, or other forms of personal right, no trust should arise;[78] but the principle may still be important in allowing a court to enforce T's promise even if it is not otherwise binding.[79]

6-050 It is, therefore, of some importance to know not only that A can assert a beneficial interest in a case such as *Rochefoucauld*, but also *why* A is permitted to do so. The debate between the express and constructive views of the case will be examined further in Chapter 17.[80]

C. Law of Property Act 1925 s.53(1)(c)

6-051

Law of Property Act 1925 s.53

(1) Subject to the provisions hereinafter contained with respect to the creation of interests in land by parol. . .

(c) A disposition of an equitable interest or trust subsisting at the time of the disposition, must be in writing signed by the person disposing of the same, or by his agent thereunto lawfully authorised in writing or by will.

(2) This section does not affect the creation or operation of resulting, implied or constructive trusts.

i. The Scope of s.53(1)(c): Three Key Cases

6-052 For the purposes of s.53(1)(c), an "equitable interest" comprises an interest in land or in other property.[81] The formality rule, therefore, may potentially be relevant whenever a beneficiary of a trust intends to deal with her beneficial interest. It provides that any transaction which amounts to a disposition must be in signed writing or it is void. In contrast to declarations of trusts of land under s.53(1)(b), then, written evidence of oral dealings with equitable interests, created after the event, will not rescue a disposition from the effects of non-compliance with s.53(1)(c). Equally, if an initial oral attempt at a disposition is followed by a later signed document that is itself capable of making a disposition, the document will take effect and the date of its execution will determine the date of the disposition.[82]

---

77 This argument can be used, for example, to explain the result in *Binions v Evans* [1972] Ch. 359 and the analysis of the relevant law adopted by the Court of Appeal in *Ashburn Anstalt v Arnold* [1989] Ch. 1; *Lloyd v Dugdale* [2001] EWCA Civ 1754; [2002] 2 P. & C.R. 13 and *Chaudhary v Yavuz* [2011] EWCA Civ 1314; [2013] Ch. 249. See further B. McFarlane, "Constructive Trusts Arising on Receipt of Property *Sub Conditione*" (2004) 120 L.Q.R. 667, 691–693.

78 Although note that in the cases cited at fn.77, the courts did continue to use the language of constructive trust. When applied to cases where T did not promise to hold on trust, however, this language is inappropriate, as noted by, e.g. W. Swadling, "Property" in A. Burrows (ed.), *English Private Law*, 3rd edn (Oxford University Press, 2013), para.4.126; S. Bright, "The Third Party's Conscience and Land Law" [2000] Conv. 398, 402.

79 If T's promise to A is contractually binding, then, even if it is made for B's benefit, B may acquire a right to enforce it under the Contract (Rights of Third Parties) Act 1999. But note that if T's oral promise is made as part of the contract of sale between A and T, then s.2 of the Law of Property (Miscellaneous Provisions) Act 1989 operates to ensure that it is not contractually binding, and so the 1999 Act cannot then assist B.

80 See paras 17–077 to 17–093.

81 Assumed in *Grey v IRC* [1960] A.C. 1; *Oughtred v IRC* [1960] A.C. 206; *Vandervell v IRC* [1967] 2 A.C. 291; and treated as well established in *Re Tyler's Fund Trusts* [1967] 1 W.L.R. 1269 at 1274. The context must oust Law of Property Act 1925 s.205(1) (ii), (x).

82 This may of course have consequences for taxation purposes, as in *Grey v IRC* [1960] A.C. 1. See B. Green, "*Grey, Oughtred* and *Vandervell*—A Contextual Reappraisal" (1984) 47 M.L.R. 385, 391–392.

The signed writing may comprise linked documents.[83] If the assignee of an equitable interest is themselves to hold the assigned equitable interest as a trustee, the writing need not contain the particulars of the trust: those details may be communicated orally,[84] although if the interest is in land then some subsequent written evidence will be necessary to satisfy s.53(1)(b).

The key question in establishing the scope of the s.53(1)(c) formality rule is as to the meaning **6–053**
of a "disposition". Its predecessor, the Statute of Frauds 1677 s.9, referred instead to "grants and assignments" of an equitable interest. Whilst a "disposition" undoubtedly includes "grants and assignments",[85] its meaning has been taken to be wider than this, and it includes other types of transaction, as can be seen from the decision of the House of Lords in *Grey v IRC*.

Grey v Inland Revenue Commissioners

House of Lords [1960] A.C. 1

On February 1, 1955, Hunter, as settlor, transferred 18,000 shares of £1 each to trustees (the appellants) as **6–054**
nominees for himself. The appellants were also the trustees of six other settlements, in favour of Hunter's children, which Hunter had previously created. On February 18, 1955, Hunter orally directed the trustees to divide the 18,000 shares into six parcels of 3,000 shares each and to appropriate the parcels to the trusts of the six settlements, one parcel to each settlement. On March 25, 1955, the trustees executed six deeds of declaration of trust (which Hunter also executed in order to testify to the oral direction previously given by him) declaring that since February 18, 1955, they had held each of the parcels of 3,000 shares on the trusts of the relevant settlement. The Commissioners of Inland Revenue assessed the deeds of declaration of trust to ad valorem stamp duty on the basis it was those deeds which had created the trusts of the shares, and they were therefore taxable as instruments transferring an interest in property. The appellants argued instead that the deeds had merely recorded and confirmed the earlier transfer, which had taken place as a result of Hunter's oral instructions, and so were not taxable.

The starting point and end point of the transaction can be explained by way of a diagram, with the arrow **6–055**
linking the trustees to the parties for whom they hold on trust:

Stage 1: Trustees (holding shares)	Stage 2: Trustees (holding the same shares)
↓	↓
Hunter	Beneficiaries of the settlements

The question was whether, in order to get from Stage 1 to Stage 2, signed writing in compliance with s.53(1) **6–056**
(c) was required. If so, the stamp duty was payable, as the written instrument made the transfer, it did not merely record it. A unanimous House of Lords, agreeing with a majority of the Court of Appeal, held that compliance with s.53(1)(c) was indeed required to get from Stage 1 to Stage 2, and thus agreed with the IRC that stamp duty was payable.

VISCOUNT SIMONDS (with whom LORD REID agreed, stated the facts, continued): These facts give **6–057**
rise to the plain question whether the oral directions given by Mr Hunter, which are recited in each of the instruments, were effective or were, having regard to section 53(1)(c) of the Law of Property Act, 1925, wholly ineffective. In the former event the instruments would not, and in the latter would, be chargeable with ad valorem duty. . .

Briefly, then, were the several oral directions given by Mr Hunter dispositions by him of the equitable **6–058**
interest in the shares held by the appellants as nominees for him?

If the word "disposition" is given its natural meaning, it cannot, I think, be denied that a direction given **6–059**
by Mr Hunter, whereby the beneficial interest in the shares theretofore vested in him became vested in another or others, is a disposition. But it is contended by the appellants that the word "disposition" is to

[83] *Re Danish Bacon Co Ltd Staff Pension Fund* [1971] 1 W.L.R. 248.
[84] *Re Tyler's Fund Trusts* [1967] 1 W.L.R. 1269.
[85] *Halley v Law Society* [2003] W.T.L.R. 845 at [69]ff.

be given a narrower meaning and (so far as relates to inter vivos transactions) be read as if it were synonymous with "grants and assignments" and that, given this meaning, it does not cover such a direction as was given in this case. As I am clearly of the opinion, which I understand to be shared by your Lordships, that there is no justification for giving the word "disposition" a narrower meaning than it ordinarily bears, it will be unnecessary to discuss the interesting problem that would otherwise arise. It was for this reason that your Lordships did not think it necessary to hear learned counsel for the appellants in reply on this part of the case.

6–060 My Lords, the argument for narrowing the meaning of "disposition" was that the Law of Property Act 1925, was a consolidating Act, that among the Acts which it consolidated was the Statute of Frauds 1677 s.9, that that section enacted that "all grants and assignments of any trust or confidence shall likewise be in writing, signed by the party granting or assigning the same, or by such last will or devise, or else shall likewise be utterly void and of none effect," and that therefore the word "disposition" in section 53(1)(c) of the Act of 1925 is to be given the same meaning as would be given to "grants and assignments" in section 9 of the Statute of Frauds.

6–061 My Lords, the principles applicable to the construction of a consolidating Act are not in doubt. The presumption is that such an Act is not intended to alter the law, but this prima facie view must yield to plain words to the contrary.[86] If the Law of Property Act 1925 was a typical consolidating Act, the question would be whether the alteration from "grants and assignments" to "disposition" changed the law by enlarging the area of void transactions—a question that might not be easy to answer. But the Act of 1925 cannot be thus regarded. . .

6–062 LORD RADCLIFFE (with whom LORD COHEN and LORD KEITH agreed): My Lords, if there is nothing more in this appeal than the short question whether the oral direction that Mr Hunter gave to his trustees on February 18, 1955, amounted in any ordinary sense of the words to a "disposition of an equitable interest or trust subsisting at the time of the disposition", I do not feel any doubt as to my answer. I think that it did. Whether we describe what happened in technical or in more general terms, the full equitable interest in the eighteen thousand shares concerned, which at that time was his, was (subject to any statutory invalidity) diverted by his direction from his ownership into the beneficial ownership of the various equitable owners, present and future, entitled under his six existing settlements. . .

6–063 In my opinion, it is a very nice question whether a parol declaration of trust of this kind was or was not within the mischief of section 9 of the Statute of Frauds. The point has never, I believe, been decided and perhaps it never will be. Certainly it was long established as law that while a declaration of trust respecting land or any interest therein required writing to be effective a declaration of trust respecting personalty did not. Moreover, there is warrant for saying that a direction to his trustee by the equitable owner of trust property prescribing new trusts of that property was a declaration of trust. But it does not necessarily follow from that that such a direction, if the effect of it was to determine completely or pro tanto the subsisting equitable interest of the maker of the direction, was not also a grant or assignment for the purposes of section 9 and therefore required writing for its validity. Something had to happen to that equitable interest in order to displace it in favour of the new interests created by the direction: and it would be at any rate logical to treat the direction as being an assignment of the subsisting interest to the new beneficiary or beneficiaries or, in other cases, a release or surrender of it to the trustee.

6–064 I do not think, however, that that question has to be answered for the purposes of this appeal. It can only be relevant if section 53(1) of the Law of Property Act 1925 is treated as a true consolidation of the three sections of the Statute of Frauds concerned and as governed, therefore, by the general principle, with which I am entirely in agreement, that a consolidating Act is not to be read as effecting changes in the existing law unless the words it employs are too clear in their effect to admit of any other construction. But, in my opinion, it is impossible to regard section 53 of the Law of Property Act 1925 as a consolidating enactment in this sense.

6–065 The approach of the House of Lords in *Grey v IRC* can be summarised simply: the term "disposition" in s.53(1)(c) is apt to cover a case where a party ensures that his trustees now hold on trust for others, rather than for himself, and there is no need to consider whether such an arrangement would have fallen within the scope of the Statute of Frauds 1677 s.9, as Parliament in 1925 did not intend simply to

[86] See *Gilbert v Gilbert* [1928] P. 1 at 8, per Scrutton LJ.

replicate the effect of that earlier provision. In *Grey*, there was a disposition of an equitable interest as, at Stage 1, Hunter had the beneficial interest in the shares, whereas, at Stage 2, the beneficial interest in the same shares was shared by the beneficiaries of the six settlements.

In *Vandervell v IRC*, the House of Lords had to consider a slightly different situation, which it distin- **6–066**
guished from that in *Grey v IRC*.

Vandervell v Inland Revenue Commissioners

House of Lords [1967] 2 A.C. 291

In 1958 Vandervell decided to make a gift to the Royal College of Surgeons to found a chair of pharma- **6–067**
cology, using 100,000 shares in a private company held by a bank on trust for him. The shares would be transferred to the RCS. The RCS would then be entitled to the dividends declared on the shares, which would suffice to set up the chair. Vandervell could of course have received the dividends himself, and then paid them over to the RCS, but he would then have been assessed to surtax on the dividends. The RCS, as a charity, would not have to pay such tax on the dividends. Once the dividends had been declared, however, Vandervell wanted the RCS to release the shares to a trustee company which acted as trustee of a settlement he had made in favour of his children. Hence it was arranged that the shares would be transferred to RCS subject to an option, vested in the trustee company, to purchase the shares for £5,000.

Vandervell orally directed the bank to transfer full ownership of the shares to RCS, and during the tax **6–068**
years 1958–59 and 1959–60 dividends on the shares, amounting to £162,500 and £87,500, respectively, were paid. In October, 1961, the trustee company then exercised its option and paid RCS £5,000 for the shares. Vandervell was then assessed to surtax on the dividends on the basis that the transaction amounted to a settlement of property of which he had not absolutely divested himself, so that the dividends fell to be treated for surtax purposes as his income and not that of any other person.

It is important to note that the IRC made two main arguments. First, it was said that Vandervell's oral **6–069**
direction to the bank to transfer full ownership of the shares to the RCS was an attempted disposition of his beneficial interest in the shares, and was void as it did not comply with s.53(1)(c). If that argument were accepted, Vandervell would retain the beneficial interest in the shares and be liable for the surtax. Second, even if the oral direction did not fall within s.53(1)(c) and so was valid, Vandervell nonetheless had a sufficient interest in the shares to be liable for the surtax because the option to purchase the shares, vested in the trustee company, was in fact held on a resulting trust for Vandervell.

In the House of Lords, the IRC succeeded on the *second* argument: we will consider this aspect of the **6–070**
law of resulting trusts in Chapter 16.[87] Here, we will consider only the first argument, and so the following extracts concern the s.53(1)(c) point only.

The relevant stages of the transaction can again be explained by way of a diagram, with the arrow **6–071**
linking the trustees to the parties for whom they hold on trust:

Stage 1: Trustees (holding shares) Stage 2: RCS

↓

Vandervell

There is no arrow at Stage 2 as the RCS did not hold the shares on trust, although the trustee company did **6–072**
of course have an option to buy the shares from the RCS. The question was whether, in order to get from Stage 1 to Stage 2, signed writing in compliance with s. 53(1)(c) was required. A unanimous House of Lords held that compliance with s. 53(1)(c) was *not* required to get from Stage 1 to Stage 2.

LORD UPJOHN:. . . the object of [s. 53(1)(c)], as was the object of the old Statute of Frauds, is to prevent **6–073**
hidden oral transactions in equitable interests in fraud of those truly entitled, and making it difficult, if not impossible, for the trustees to ascertain who are in truth the beneficiaries. When the beneficial owner, however, owns the whole beneficial estate and is in a position to give directions to his bare trustee with

[87] See para.16–061.

regard to the legal as well as the equitable estate there can be no possible ground for invoking the section where the beneficial owner wants to deal with the legal estate as well as the equitable estate.

6–074 I cannot agree with Diplock L.J. [in the Court of Appeal decision in the case] that prima facie a transfer of the legal estate carries with it the absolute beneficial interest in the property transferred; this plainly is not so, e.g. the transfer may be on a change of trustee; it is a matter of intention in each case. If, however, the intention of the beneficial owner in directing the trustee to transfer the legal estate to X is that X should be the beneficial owner, I can see no reason for any further document or further words in the document assigning the legal estate also expressly transferring the beneficial interest; the greater includes the less. X may be wise to secure some evidence that the beneficial owner intended him to take the beneficial interest in case his beneficial title is challenged at a later date but it certainly cannot, in my opinion, be a statutory requirement that to effect its passing there must be some writing under section 53(1)(c).

6–075 Counsel for the Crown admitted that where the legal and beneficial estate was vested in the legal owner and he desired to transfer the whole legal and beneficial estate to another he did not have to do more than transfer the legal estate and he did not have to comply with section 53(1)(c); and I can see no difference between that case and this.

6–076 As I have said, that section is, in my opinion, directed to cases where dealings with the equitable estate are divorced from the legal estate and I do not think any of their Lordships in *Grey v IRC*[88] and *Oughtred v IRC*[89] had in mind the case before your Lordships. To hold the contrary would make assignments unnecessarily complicated; if there had to be assignments in express terms of both legal and equitable interests that would make the section more productive of injustice than the supposed evils it was intended to prevent. . .

6–077 LORD WILBERFORCE: On November 14, 1958, [Vandervell's] solicitor received from the bank a blank transfer of the shares, executed by the bank, and the share certificate. So at this stage [Vandervell] was the absolute master of the shares and only needed to insert his name as transferee in the transfer and to register it to become the full legal owner. He was also the owner in equity. On November 19, 1958, the solicitor. . . on behalf of [Vandervell], who intended to make a gift, handed the transfer to the College, which in due course, sealed it and obtained registration of the shares in the College's name. The case should then be regarded as one in which [Vandervell] himself has, with the intention to make a gift, put the College in a position to become the legal owner of the shares, which the College in fact became. If [Vandervell] had died before the College had obtained registration, it is clear on the principle of *Re Rose*[90] that the gift would have been complete, on the basis that he had done everything in his power to transfer the legal interest, with an intention to give, to the College. No separate transfer, therefore, of the equitable interest ever came to or needed to be made and there is no room for the operation of the subsection. What the position would have been had there simply been an oral direction to the legal owner (viz. the bank) to transfer the shares to the College, followed by such a transfer, but without any document in writing signed by [Vandervell] as equitable owner, is not a matter which calls for consideration here. . .

6–078 It has been suggested that it is difficult to reconcile the decision in *Vandervell v IRC* with that in *Grey v IRC*.[91] Certainly, the argument rejected by the House of Lords in *Vandervell v IRC* was a fairly simple one: (i) *Grey v IRC* establishes that "disposition" is to be given its natural interpretation, and is not limited to "grants and assignments"; (ii) Vandervell initially had a beneficial interest in the shares (Stage 1 in the diagram above) and he wished to move to a situation where he no longer had that beneficial interest (Stage 2): as this involves his getting rid of (i.e. disposing) his beneficial interest, it must be a "disposition" of that interest.

6–079 As seen in the extract above, the House of Lords gave two reasons for rejecting that argument. First, there is Lord Wilberforce's use of *Re Rose*,[92] a case we considered in Chapter 5.[93] That analysis, however, is far from convincing: in *Re Rose*, the taxpayer, who started with legal title to the shares, did

---

88 [1960] A.C. 1.
89 [1960] A.C. 206.
90 *Re Rose, Midland Bank Executor & Trustee Co Ltd v Rose* [1949] Ch. 78.
91 See, e.g. B. Green, "*Grey, Oughtred* and *Vandervell*—A Contextual Appraisal" (1984) 47 M.L.R. 385.
92 [1949] Ch. 78.
93 See paras 5–023 to 5–041.

all he could to transfer them by executing a share transfer and delivering the transfer and the share certificate to the transferee. To say that Vandervell had done all he could to vest the shares in the RCS was to beg the s.53(1)(c) question of what a holder of a subsisting equitable interest must do to transfer that interest.

Second, there is Lord Upjohn's analysis. Importantly, it looks to the *purposes* of the s.53(1)(c) formality rule, stating that the object of the rule is "to prevent hidden oral transactions in equitable interests in fraud of those truly entitled, and making it difficult, if not impossible, for the trustees to ascertain who are in truth the beneficiaries".[94] It could be argued that a special formality rule for the disposition of equitable interests is required to give a beneficiary, for example, protection against risks that are specific to her position as a beneficiary, such as the risk of the trustee performing the trust in favour of the wrong person. Equally, a trustee should be concerned about that risk, as performing the trust in favour of the wrong person may lead to the trustee's being under a liability to the true beneficiary. **6-080**

The formality rule contained in s.53(1)(c) can, on Lord Upjohn's analysis, be seen as protecting both the beneficiary and the trustee against this risk. Consider a case in which a fraudster, X, goes to the trustee, T, falsely claims that B transferred her beneficial interest to X, and demands that T perform the trust in favour of X. The advantage of s.53(1)(c) is that T can insist on X's producing some writing signed by B before acceding to that demand. **6-081**

On this view, then, Lord Upjohn's analysis can be seen as stating that the purpose of s.53(1)(c) is to protect both B and T from a risk that is peculiar to their position as beneficiary and trustee: the risk that the trustee will perform the trusts in favour of the wrong person. On that analysis, there is no need for writing to get from Stage 1 to Stage 2 in *Vandervell*, as the relevant transaction *necessarily involves the trustee*. The transaction required legal title to the shares to vest in the RCS, and that was only possible with the co-operation of the trustee who, of course, held such title to the shares. The case can therefore be distinguished from *Grey* as the transaction in that earlier case was not of a type that necessarily involves the trustee.[95] **6-082**

The limited meaning given to the concept of "disposition" in *Vandervell* is also consistent with the approach of the Supreme Court in *Akers v Samba Financial Group*.[96] We will examine this case in more detail in later chapters,[97] but its resolution turned on whether T's transfer to C of shares which T held on trust for B was a "disposition" of B's property for the purposes of s.127 of the Insolvency Act 1986. Of course, given the different statutory context, there is no requirement for the term "disposition" to be given the same meaning in that provision as in s.53(1)(c). Nonetheless, it is significant that, even on the assumption that C would take the shares free from any claim of B, the Supreme Court found that there was no disposition of B's equitable interest, as T had rather transferred T's own right to the shares to C, and there was then a separate question of whether C was subject to any claim by B. It can equally be said that, in *Vandervell*, even though, in contrast to *Akers*, the transfer to the third party occurred with B's consent, the act of the trustee in transferring the subject matter of the trust itself to a third party was not a disposition of B's rights: it was simply a transfer of the rights held by T.[98] **6-083**

---

94 [1967] 2 A.C. 291 at 311 (extracted at para.6-070).

95 See too R. Nolan, "*Vandervell v IRC*: A Case of Overreaching" [2002] C.L.J. 169, 188: Nolan's analysis is different from any considered by the House of Lords, but is based on the idea that, as the trustees transferred legal title to the shares with the consent of Vandervell, "[t]he gift of the shares also overreached Vandervell's equitable interest in them. Consequently, the Royal College acquired the shares free of that interest". There is a link with Lord Upjohn's analysis, as overreaching requires a transfer by the trustees (which they have power to make: see para.10-031) and so the trustees are necessarily involved in the transaction.

96 [2017] UKSC 6; [2017] AC 424.

97 See e.g. paras 12-078 to 12-082 and 15-002.

98 See e.g. B. McFarlane and R. Stevens, "What's Special About Equity? Rights About Rights" in D. Klimchuk et al (eds) *Philosophical Foundatuions of the Law of Equity* (Oxford University Press, 2020), pp.191, 200-201.

6-084 Lord Upjohn's analysis is also helpful when considering the somewhat controversial question of whether s.53(1)(c) applies where B, the beneficiary of an existing trust, declares that she holds that beneficial interest on trust for another, thus creating a sub-trust. If the aim of the formality rule were simply to protect B from the risk of fraud, there is an argument that such a declaration should be regarded as a "disposition": that would certainly make life harder for X, a fraudster seeking to get the economic value of B's beneficial interest by falsely claiming that B declared a sub-trust in X's favour.[99] But why should B receive special protection against the risk of such fraud? After all, *anyone* holding a right (other than a right in land) is subject to the risk that X might falsely claim that an oral declaration of trust had been made in X's favour. Since there is no general formality rule regulating how such declarations of trust are to be made or proved, why should B, the holder of a purely equitable interest, receive special protection?

6-085 There is, therefore, a strong argument that s.53(1)(c) does not apply to a declaration of a sub-trust by a party, B, with an existing beneficial interest.[100] Certainly, Lord Upjohn's analysis of the purpose of the formality rule supports that view. No writing is required in such a case, as none is needed to protect either B, or the existing trustee T, from the risk that T might perform the trust in favour of the wrong person. Consider a case in which X, a fraudster, falsely claims that B declared a sub-trust in X's favour. Crucially, even if B had made such a declaration, it would not give X a direct claim against T and so would not mean that T had to perform the trusts in favour of X. The point is that, as such a declaration would merely create a sub-trust (so that T holds on trust for B who then holds on trust for X), it would not change the fact that T's duty is owed to B, and so T cannot be forced to perform the trusts in favour of X,[101] unless B asks T to do so.

6-086 It has instead been suggested that, at least in cases where the sub-trust declared by B in favour of X is purely "passive",[102] and so does not require the exercise of any powers by B, B should be treated as "dropping out of the picture", so that X would then have a direct claim against T.[103] If that were the case, then, applying Lord Upjohn's analysis, writing would be required for the declaration of such a passive sub-trust. The conclusion that B might thus drop out of the picture position is not, however, dictated by authority,[104] and it seems hard to defend in principle: the effect of declaring a trust, whether a sub-trust or not, is that the party declaring it continues to hold the trust property, but subject to duties to the beneficiary.[105] As noted in Chapter 1, the sub-trust is another example of

---

99 B. Green, "*Grey, Oughtred* and *Vandervell*—A Contextual Appraisal" (1984) 47 M.L.R. 385, 396–399 therefore argues that a declaration of a sub-trust should fall within the scope of s.53(1)(c). For a contrary view, see P. Matthews, "All About Bare Trusts—Part 2" [2005] P.C.B. 336, 336–340.

100 See, e.g. *Sheffield v Sheffield* [2013] EWHC 3927 (Ch) at [78]–[86].

101 In *Nelson v Greening & Sykes (Builders) Ltd* [2008] 1 E.G.L.R. 59 at [57], Lawrence Collins LJ noted that, in such a case, T may choose to deal directly with X, "as a matter of practicality", but also noted there that this does not mean that T holds directly for X.

102 It is certainly the case that s.53(1)(c) does not apply where B has powers to exercise under the sub-trust: see, e.g. *Onslow v Wallis* (1849) 1 Mac. & G. 506.

103 See, e.g. *Grey v IRC* [1958] Ch. 690 at 715 per Lord Evershed MR.

104 The conclusion is said to derive support from *Grainge v Wilberforce* (1889) 5 T.L.R. 436 and *Re Lashmar* [1891] 1 Ch. 258. The former case, however, simply decided that, in a claim for specific performance of a contract to convey land, an intermediate trustee under a settlement of that land did not need to be a party to the conveyance: that result can be explained on the basis that the planned conveyance would in any case overreach the interests of any intermediate beneficiaries. The latter case simply decided that a party with no beneficial interest in property, and with no duties to perform as trustee of that property, could not claim that property from the party holding legal title to it. So, as noted by Lawrence Collins LJ in *Nelson v Greening & Sykes (Builders) Ltd* [2008] 1 E.G.L.R. 59 at [57], the relevant cases "do not bind this court to hold that as a matter of law an intermediate trustee ceases to be a trustee". See too *Sheffield v Sheffield* [2014] W.T.L.R. 1039 at [82] where HHJ Pelling QC, analysing *Grainge v Wilberforce* and *Re Lashmar*, stated that "there is nothing in these authorities that is necessarily inconsistent with the conclusion of the Court of Appeal in *Nelson*".

105 See too C.H. Tham, "Exploding the Myth that Sub-Trustees 'Drop Out'" (2017) 31 *Trust Law International* 76.

equity, in its characteristic way, controlling legal entitlements, this time B's entitlements as beneficiary of the head trust. As observed by Lawrence Collins LJ (as he then was) in *Nelson v Greening & Sykes (Builders) Ltd*,[106] even if the *practical* effect of the sub-trust is that B becomes merely a conduit to pass on the economic benefits of the trust property to X, that does not mean that its *legal* effect is to dispose of B's beneficial interest. On the contrary, B's beneficial interest must continue to exist, as otherwise there would be no subject-matter to the sub-trust for X.[107]

As demonstrated by the decision of the Court of Appeal in the next instalment of the Vandervell saga, *Re Vandervell (No.2)*, there are further situations in which a dealing with a beneficial interest does not amount to a disposition, and so can be carried out orally. 6–087

Re Vandervell (No.2)

Court of Appeal [1974] Ch. 269

Recall that, on receiving full title to the shares, the RCS granted the Vandervell trustee company (VT) an option to buy those shares for £5,000. Remember too that, as we noted at para.6–068, the House of Lords in *Vandervell v IRC* decided that VT held that option on resulting trust for Vandervell. When, in October 1961, the possibility of such a trust became apparent to Vandervell, he orally instructed VT to exercise the option, using money held by VT on a trust benefitting Vandervell's children. VT did so. The intention of V and VT was that the shares would then be held on the same trust for Vandervell's children, and the dividends later declared on the shares were added to the fund held on the children's trusts. The revenue then suggested that, as s.53(1)(c) had not been complied with, Vandervell was still liable for surtax on the dividends declared after October 1961. In January 1965, to resolve any doubts as to the position from that point onwards, V executed a deed transferring any rights he had in the option, shares, or dividends to VT to hold on the trusts of the children's settlement. V died in 1967. Owing to their concern as to the possible surtax liability of Vandervell's estate for dividends declared between October 1961 and January 1965, his executors sought a declaration that Vandervell (and hence now his estate) had been entitled to all dividends on the shares during that period. The executors' argument was based on the contention that the attempted oral dealings with the shares in October 1961 did not dispose of Vandervell's beneficial interest. The argument was that, as he had the beneficial interest in the option, and the shares were acquired by the exercise of that option, any transfer of the beneficial interest in the shares to the children was a disposition of Vandervell's initial beneficial interest, and so s.53(1)(c) applied, with the effect that the disposition occurred only in January 1965, when signed writing was used. 6–088

The relevant stages of the transaction can again be explained by way of a diagram, with the arrow linking the trustees to the parties for whom they hold on trust: 6–089

Stage 1: VT (holding option)	Stage 2: VT (holding shares)
↓	↓
Vandervell	Vandervell's children

---

[106] [2008] 1 E.G.L.R. 59 at [57]: "saying (as Lord Evershed MR said) [in *Grey v IRC* [1958] Ch. 690 at 715] that the practical effect [of the sub-trust] would seem to amount to or be capable of amounting to the 'getting rid' of the trust of the equitable interest then subsisting, is not the same as saying that as a matter of law it does get rid of the intermediate trust. What he was saying was that in the case of a trust and sub-trust of personal property the trustees may decide that as a matter of practicality it is more convenient to deal directly with the beneficiary of the sub-trust."

[107] In *Re Lehman Brothers International (Europe) Ltd* [2010] EWHC 2914 (Ch) at [397] (affirmed [2012] 2 B.C.L.C. 151) Briggs J referred to the "structure of trusts and sub-trusts between the legal owner and ultimate beneficial owner in relation to intermediated securities" (see para.1–081) and noted that under such a structure, the depositary holding legal rights to the shares recognises one party (B) as its beneficiary and that party in turn recognises another (B2) as its beneficiary: the implication is that, even though holding on a sub-trust for B2, B does not simply drop out of the picture. See further B. McFarlane and R. Stevens, "Interests in Securities: Practical Problems and Conceptual Solutions" in L. Gullifer and J. Payne (eds), *Intermediated Securities* (2010), pp.46–48.

The trust at Stage 1 is the resulting trust found to exist in relation to the option in *Vandervell v IRC*.

6–090 At first instance, Megarry J. accepted the argument of the executors and held that, until January 1965, VT held the shares on trust for Vandervell, although, in its capacity as trustees for the children's settlement, VT had a lien for £5,000 in order to recover the money, taken from the children's settlement in order to exercise the option. The Court of Appeal, however, held that compliance with s.53(1)(c) was *not* required to get from Stage 1 to Stage 2. The judges were unanimous in their decision, but not as to their reasons.

6–091 LORD DENNING M.R.: . . .There is a complete fallacy in [the executors'] argument. A resulting trust for the settlor [such as the resulting trust of the option in favour of Vandervell] is born and dies without any writing at all. It comes into existence whenever there is a gap in the beneficial ownership. It ceases to exist whenever that gap is filled by someone becoming beneficially entitled. As soon as the gap is filled by the creation or declaration of a valid trust, the resulting trust comes to an end. In this case, before the option was exercised, there was a gap in the beneficial ownership. So there was a resulting trust for Mr. Vandervell. But, as soon as the option was exercised and the shares registered in the trustees' name, there was created a valid trust of the shares in favour of the children's settlement. Not being a trust of land, it could be created without any writing. . .

Estoppel

6–092 Even if [counsel for the executors] were right in saying that Mr Vandervell retained an equitable interest in the shares, after the exercise of the option, the question arises whether Mr Vandervell can in the circumstance be heard to assert that claim against his children. Just see what happened. He himself arranged for the option to be exercised. He himself agreed to the shares being transferred to the trustee company. He himself procured his products company to declare dividends on the shares and to pay them to the trustee company for the benefit of the children. Thenceforward the trustee company invested the money and treated it as part of the children's settlement. If he himself had lived, and not died, he could not have claimed it back. He could not be heard to say that he did not intend the children's trust to have it. Even a court of equity would not allow him to do anything so inequitable and unjust. Now that he has died, his executors are in no better position.

Conclusion

6–093 [Counsel for the executors] realized that the claim of the executors here had no merit whatsoever. He started off by reminding us that "hard cases make bad law". He repeated it time after time. He treated it as if it was an ultimate truth. But it is a maxim which is quite misleading. It should be deleted from our vocabulary. It comes to this: "Unjust decisions make good law": whereas they do nothing of the kind. Every unjust decision is a reproach to the law or to the judge who administers it. If the law should be in danger of doing injustice, then equity should be called into remedy it. Equity was introduced to mitigate the rigour of the law. But in the present case it has been prayed in aid to do injustice on a large scale—to defeat the intentions of a dead man—to deprive his children of the benefits he provided for them – and to expose his estate to the payment of tax of over £600,000. I am glad to find that we can overcome this most unjust result.

6–094 LAWTON L.J.: . . .On or about October 10, 1961, the trustee company acquired the shares with money taken by them from the children's settlement. In my judgment the inference from this course of conduct is that Mr. Vandervell intended that to happen which did happen and that when the directors of the trustee company used money from the children's settlement to pay for the shares he intended that company to hold the shares not for himself but for the trusts of the children's settlement. If the trustee company had used this money otherwise than for the benefit of the children they would have been in breach of trust, and as Mr. Vandervell knew what was happening and intended it to happen, he would have been guilty of aiding and abetting them.

6–095 The result in law is that after the transfer the trustee company held the shares for the benefit of the children's settlement as Mr. Vandervell had intended it should. This followed from the operation of the rule that if A uses B's money to buy property, in the absence of any evidence to show otherwise, A holds that property for the benefit of B. It follows that once the transfer of the shares had been registered the beneficial interest in them was held by the trustee company on the trusts of the children's settlement so that no declaration of trust was necessary.

6–096 STEPHENSON L.J.: I have had more doubt than Lord Denning M.R. and Lawton L.J. whether we can overturn the judgment of Megarry J. in what I have not found an easy case. . . Lord Denning M.R. and Lawton L.J. are able to hold that no such disposition [i.e. no written disposition complying with s. 53(1)(c)]

> is needed because (1) the option was held on such trusts as might thereafter be declared by the trustee company or Mr. Vandervell himself, and (2) the trustee company has declared that it holds the shares in the children's settlement. . . I should be more confident of the second if it had been pleaded or argued either here or below and we had had the benefit of Megarry J.'s views upon it. . . I see, as perhaps did counsel, difficulties in the way of a limited company declaring a trust by parole or conduct and without a resolution of the board of directors, and difficulties also in the way of finding any declaration of trust by Mr. Vandervell himself in October or November 1961, or any conduct then or later which would in law or equity estop him from denying that he made one.
>
> However, Lord Denning M.R. and Lawton L.J. are of opinion that these difficulties, if not imaginary, are not insuperable and that these shares went into the children's settlement in 1961 in accordance with the intention of Mr. Vandervell and the trustee company—a result with which I am happy to agree as it seems to me to be in accordance with the justice and the reality of the case. **6–097**

The decision of the Court of Appeal in *Re Vandervell (No.2)* is generally regarded as a difficult one to explain satisfactorily. Lord Denning MR's concern to do justice is understandable, but an inevitable consequence of formality rules is that they may seem to lead to unwelcome outcomes in specific cases; their justification lies instead in the benefits they provide in the vast majority of cases where the rule is complied with. There are certainly some problems with Lord Denning's reasoning as to resulting trusts: whilst it is true that such a trust can arise, and even be proved in relation to land, without any writing, it does not necessarily follow that no writing is required to dispose of an interest under such a trust. It is not obvious, for example, that the result in *Grey v IRC* would have been different if the initial trust of the shares for Hunter had arisen under a resulting trust. **6–098**

As to estoppel, we noted above[108] that proprietary estoppel may assist a claimant in a case where a formality rule prevents an agreement from having contractual effect, and may, in a suitable case, lead to the imposition of a trust. It may therefore be relevant where there has been a failure to comply with s.53(1)(c), but only if the requirements of the doctrine have been made out on the facts. The principal difficulty with using proprietary estoppel reasoning, or any other form of estoppel reasoning, to explain *Re Vandervell (No.2)*, is that there was no evidence of any action in reliance by the beneficiaries of the children's settlement, nor of any detriment they would suffer (other than the absence of a gift). **6–099**

Lawton LJ's reasoning is perhaps more convincing, as it focusses on the potentially important fact that the option held by the trustee company was exercised by using part of the funds held by those trustees for the children's settlement. As Lawton LJ noted, where A uses B's money to buy property, a trust may arise and, as it is imposed by law, such a trust can arise without any formality. Such a constructive or resulting trust,[109] like proprietary estoppel, may therefore be relevant where there has been a failure to comply with s.53(1)(c), but, again, only if the requirements of the doctrine have been made out on the facts. The difficulty in *Re Vandervell (No.2)* is that, whilst money held on trust for the children was used to acquire the shares, the sum paid was far lower than the market value of the shares, thanks to the terms of the option. The existence of the option, held on trust for Vandervell, was therefore just as crucial to the acquisition of the shares as the payment of the £5,000, held on trust for the children. However, it may still be possible to support Lawton LJ's analysis, if it is combined with Stephenson LJ's point that Vandervell intended the children to have the beneficial interest in the shares: it could perhaps be said that Vandervell had abandoned any intention to acquire an interest in the shares, leaving the trust for the children to take effect; or, similarly, that Vandervell's oral attempt to dispose of the beneficial interest in the shares, whilst incapable of effecting such a disposition in **6–100**

[108] At paras 6–020 to 6–026.

[109] There is some debate as to the classification of the trust arising in a case where B's money is used by A, without B's consent, to acquire property for A: see paras 17–210ff.

itself, can still be used to rebut any presumption of resulting trust that might otherwise have arisen when the shares were acquired through the exercise of the option.[110]

6–101 In considering *Re Vandervell (No.2)*, it is also useful to return to Lord Upjohn's analysis of the purposes of the s.53(1)(c) formality rule.[111] If we view the relevant transaction in the case as consisting of just two stages,[112] it can be said that, as was also the case in *Vandervell v IRC*, but not in *Grey v IRC*, the transaction was of such a type that the trustee was *necessarily involved* in it. After all, the option could not be exercised without action by the trustee company (VT). However a difficulty arises if we take a different view of the transaction and break it down into a further stage. If the transaction is thus broken down then there are two possibilities. Case (i) is that the option must first have been exercised, so that VT then held the shares on trust for Vandervell, and that beneficial interest in the shares was then transferred from Vandervell to the children. In that case, *Grey v IRC* must apply at the second stage, to the transfer of the beneficial interest in the shares from Vandervell to the children. Case (ii) is that the beneficial interest in the option was first transferred from Vandervell to the children, so that VT held the option on trust for the children, and only then was the option exercised for their benefit. In that case, *Grey v IRC* must apply at the first stage, to the transfer of the beneficial interest in the option from Vandervell to the children.

6–102 Nonetheless, even if it is accepted that the transaction has thus to be broken down into a further stage, it may just still be possible to explain the result in *Re Vandervell (No.2)*. One suggestion is that Vandervell did not simply transfer a beneficial interest to the children; rather, he surrendered or waived his beneficial interest (either in the option or in the shares), thereby creating a moment when the trustee company (VT) held the option or shares outright. At that point, VT could then orally declare a trust in favour of the children, as such a declaration certainly does not require writing. This suggestion depends on the view that a surrender of a beneficial interest to a trustee is outside the scope of s.53(1)(c): after all, as such a transaction, like the transfer of the shares in *Vandervell v IRC*, terminates a trust, it does not create any risk that the trustee will be confused as to the identity of the beneficiary.

ii. The Scope of s.53(1)(c): Summary

6–103 After this consideration of the three key decisions—*Grey v IRC*; *Vandervell v IRC*; and *Re Vandervell (No.2)*—it may be useful to summarise the scope of s.53(1)(c). First, it clearly applies to a simple transfer of a beneficial interest: such a transfer creates a risk that the trustees may be unaware of the identity of the new beneficiary and so falls within the mischief identified by Lord Upjohn in *Vandervell v IRC*. As a result, it also applies, as in *Grey v IRC*, to an instruction by the beneficiary to the trustees that they should now hold the trust property for a new beneficiary. It could be argued that, on the facts of *Grey*, there was no risk of the trustees' being confused, given that they received their instructions from Hunter. The problem, however, is that a transfer of a beneficial interest does not *necessarily* involve the trustees, and the usefulness of the s.53(1)(c) formality rule in limiting disputes would be undermined if an exception were permitted where it could be shown that the initial beneficiary had made an oral communication to the trustees.

6–104 Second, as shown by *Vandervell v IRC*, s.53(1)(c) does not apply where the trustees, at the request of those beneficially entitled, transfer the trust property outright to a third party. Such a transaction terminates the trust and necessarily involves the trustees, and so it falls outside the mischief identified by Lord Upjohn. Green has argued that this gives rise to the unwelcome possibility, in a case such as

---

110 See paras 16–025ff for consideration of the presumption of resulting trust.

111 Discussed at para.6–082.

112 As in the diagram at para.6–089.

Grey v IRC, that the initial beneficiary can direct the trustee to transfer the trust property to another trustee to hold on trust for new beneficiaries, and such a transaction, if carried through by the trustees, can occur without the need for compliance with s.53(1)(c).[113] That does indeed seem to be the effect of *Vandervell v IRC*,[114] but it is far from clear that the possibility is unwelcome: given that the trustees are necessarily involved in the transaction, the need for signed writing does not arise.

Third, it seems that a declaration of a sub-trust by a beneficiary does not fall within the scope of s.53(1)(c), as the beneficiary of the sub-trust has no direct claim against the head trustee so that, again, the need for signed writing does not arise, as the transaction does not change the identity of the party to whom the head trustee owes their duties under the trust. **6–105**

Fourth, it has also been held that s.53(1)(c) does not apply in a case where B disclaims an existing beneficial interest, thereby putting an end to that interest: "a disclaimer operates by way of avoidance and not by way of disposition."[115] Since a disclaimer ends the trust, we can certainly say that it causes no risk that the trustee might perform the trust in favour of the wrong person, and so it seems to lie outside the mischief identified by Lord Upjohn in *Vandervell v IRC*. **6–106**

As for the scope of s.53(1)(c), it is also worth noting that the formality rule applies only where B's interest is "subsisting at the time of the disposition". So, if an employee exercises her contractual right to nominate a person to receive moneys payable under a pension trust fund in the event of the employee's death in service, s.53(1)(c) does not apply, as the employee has simply exercised a power to direct what will occur in the future, and has not dealt with an existing beneficial interest.[116] **6–107**

Finally, s.53(1)(c) has been expressly disapplied in certain contexts where equitable interests are the subject of frequent financial trading, and the markets dependent on such trading would grind to a halt if signed writing were required for every disposition of such equitable interests. For example, a party with a stock portfolio including shares in a public company very rarely holds legal title to such shares: the shares are "dematerialised"[117] and the party instead holds a derivative equitable interest in the shares. Trading in such shares would be very inconvenient if every sale of such shares required signed writing.[118] So the Uncertificated Securities Regulations 2001[119] disapply s.53(1)(c). The sub-section has also been disapplied, for similar reasons, in relation to financial collateral arrangements,[120] and the scope of the exemption has been given a broad interpretation, so as to ensure the underlying aim of simplifying activities carried out under a financial collateral arrangement.[121] **6–108**

---

113 B. Green, "*Grey, Oughtred* and *Vandervell*—A Contextual Appraisal" (1984) 47 M.L.R. 385, 411.

114 On the overreaching analysis of the case adopted by Nolan, the effect of *Vandervell v IRC* in such a case would depend on whether the transaction was seen as having two stages (an overreaching transfer to the new trustees, followed by a declaration of trust, neither of which require writing) or just one (in which case *Grey v IRC* might apply): R. Nolan, "*Vandervell v IRC*: A Case of Overreaching" [2002] C.L.J. 169, 186–187.

115 *Re Paradise Motor Co Ltd* [1968] 1 W.L.R. 1125 at 1143 per Danckwerts LJ.

116 *Re Danish Bacon Co Ltd Staff Pension Fund* [1971] 1 W.L.R. 248; *Baird v Baird* [1990] 2 A.C. 548: see para.6–011. Similarly, if B takes out a policy on her life where rights to a money payment crystallise only on her death, B's nomination that on her death T is to receive the payment and hold it on trust for B2 does not require signed writing as it is not a disposition of a *subsisting* equitable interest.

117 See para.1–081.

118 See, e.g. Law Commission, "Intermediated Securities: Who Owns Your Shares?: A Scoping Paper" (2020) 7.41ff.

119 SI 2001/3755. See reg.38(5). Note however the regulations only apply to transfers within the CREST system and so the Law Commission (fn.118 at 7.59) have proposed extending the disapplication of s.53(1)(c).

120 Financial Collateral Arrangements (No.2) Regulations 2009 (SI 2009/2462), reg.4(2).

121 See *Mills v Sportsdirect.com Retail Ltd* [2010] 2 B.C.L.C. 143 at [70].

iii. The Effect of Non-Compliance

6–109 We have seen that a failure to comply with a particular formality rule, whilst it may prevent B from showing that A successfully exercised a power to give B a right, does not necessarily prevent B from showing that she acquired a very similar right by some other means. This is also true of s.53(1)(c). In particular, it is important to note that, whilst the section requires signed writing for a disposition of a beneficial interest, no such writing is required for a *contract* for the disposition of such an interest, at least if the interest itself is not an interest in land. As we will consider in more detail in Chapter 17,[122] a contract for the transfer of property may, in certain circumstances, give rise to a constructive trust of that property in favour of the planned transferee. A combination of those two points means that, even in the absence of a written transfer of B1's beneficial interest, B2 may acquire valuable equitable proprietary rights by showing that, as a result of B1's oral contractual promise to make such a transfer, B1 now holds that beneficial interest on constructive trust for B2. Some doubt was cast on this analysis by some of the members of the House of Lords in *Oughtred v IRC*,[123] but it was confirmed by the Court of Appeal in *Neville v Wilson*.

Neville v Wilson

Court of Appeal [1997] Ch. 144

6–110 Shareholders of a company (JEN) agreed to liquidate it informally and they also orally agreed to divide up between themselves that company's equitable interest in shares in a private company.

6–111 NOURSE L.J. (giving the judgment of the court to which ROSE and ALDOUS L.JJ also contributed):. . . The effect of the agreement, more closely analysed, was that each shareholder agreed to assign his interest in the other shares of JEN's equitable interest in exchange for the assignment by the other shareholders of their interests in his own aliquot share. Each individual agreement having been a disposition of a subsisting equitable interest not made in writing, there then arises the question whether it was rendered ineffectual by s.53 of the Law of Property Act 1925. . .

6–112 The simple view of the present case is that the effect of each individual agreement was to constitute the shareholder an implied or constructive trustee for the other shareholders, so that the requirement for writing contained in sub-s.(1)(c) of s.53 was dispensed with by sub-s.(2). That was the view taken by Upjohn J. at first instance and by Lord Radcliffe in the House of Lords in *Oughtred v IRC*. In order to see whether it is open to us to adopt it in this court, we must give careful consideration to those views and to the other speeches in the House of Lords.

6–113 In *Oughtred v IRC*[124] a mother and son were the tenant for life and absolute reversioner respectively under a settlement of shares in a private company. By an oral agreement made on 18 June 1956 they agreed that on 26 June the son would exchange his reversionary interest under the settlement for shares in the same company owned by the mother absolutely, to the intent that her life interest in the settled shares should be enlarged into an absolute interest. On 26 June the mother and the son released the trustees by a deed which recited, amongst other things, that the settled shares were "accordingly now held in trust for [the mother] absolutely", and that it was intended to transfer them to her. On the same day the trustees transferred the settled shares to the mother by deed, the consideration being expressed to be ten shillings. It was held by Lord Keith of Avonholm, Lord Denning and Lord Jenkins, (Lord Radcliffe and Lord Cohen dissenting), that the transfer was assessable to ad valorem stamp duty. The basis of decision adopted by the majority was that, even if the oral agreement was effective to pass the equitable interest in the settled shares to the mother, the transfer, as the instrument by which the transaction was completed, was none the less a conveyance on sale within s.54 of the Stamp Act 1891.

---

[122] See paras 17–061 to 17–071.

[123] [1960] A.C. 206.

[124] [1960] A.C. 206.

Upjohn J., having said that s.53(2) of the 1925 Act was a complete answer to the argument that s.53(1)(c) applied, continued:[125] 6–114

> "This was an oral agreement for value, and, accordingly, on the making thereof Peter the vendor became a constructive trustee of his equitable reversionary interest in the trust funds for the appellant. No writing to achieve that result was necessary, for an agreement of sale and purchase of an equitable interest in personalty (other than chattels real) may be made orally, and s.53 has no application to a trust arising by construction of law."

Lord Radcliffe, having expressed the view that the judgment of Upjohn J. was correct and agreeing with his reasons, said:[126] 6–115

> "The reasoning of the whole matter, as I see it, is as follows: On June 18, 1956, the son owned an equitable reversionary interest in the settled shares; by his oral agreement of that date he created in his mother an equitable interest in his reversion, since the subject-matter of the agreement was property of which specific performance would normally be decreed by the court. He thus became a trustee for her of that interest *sub modo*; having regard to sub-s.(2) of s.53 of the Law of Property Act, 1925, sub-s.(1) of that section did not operate to prevent that trusteeship arising by operation of law."

Lord Cohen, the other member of the minority, said:[127] 6–116

> "Before your Lordships, counsel for the Crown was prepared to agree that, on the making of the oral agreement, Peter became a constructive trustee of his equitable reversionary interest in the settled funds for the appellant, but he submitted that, none the less, s. 53(1)(c) applied and, accordingly, Peter could not assign that equitable interest to the appellant except by a disposition in writing. My Lords, with that I agree, but it does not follow that the transfer was a conveyance of that equitable interest on which ad valorem stamp duty was payable under the Stamp Act, 1891."

Having held that the transfer was not such a conveyance, he dissented on that ground.

Lord Denning said:[128] 6–117

> "I do not think it necessary to embark on a disquisition on constructive trusts; because I take the view that, even if the oral agreement of June 18, 1956, was effective to transfer Peter's reversionary interest to his mother, nevertheless, when that oral agreement was subsequently implemented by the transfer, then the transfer became liable to stamp duty. But I may say that I do not think the oral agreement was effective to transfer Peter's reversionary interest to his mother. I should have thought that the wording of s.53(1)(c) of the Law of Property Act 1925 clearly made a writing necessary to effect a transfer, and s.53(2) does not do away with that necessity."

The views of their Lordships as to the effect of s.53 can be summarised as follows. Lord Radcliffe, agreeing with Upjohn J., thought that sub-s.(2) applied. He gave reasons for that view. Lord Cohen and Lord Denning thought that it did not. Although neither of them gave reasons, they may be taken to have accepted the submissions of Mr. Wilberforce Q.C.[129] Lord Keith and Lord Jenkins expressed no view either way. We should add that when the case was in this court, Lord Evershed M.R., in delivering the judgment of himself, Morris and Ormerod L.JJ., said:[130] 6–118

> "In this court the case for the Crown has, we think, been somewhat differently presented, and in the end of all, the question under s.53 of the Law of Property Act [1925] does not, in our judgment, strictly call for a decision. We are not, however, with all respect to the learned judge, prepared to accept, as we understand it, his conclusion on the effect of s.53 of the Law of Property Act."

The basis of this court's decision was the same as that adopted by the majority of the House of Lords.

---

125 [1958] Ch. 383 at 390.
126 [1960] A.C. 206 at 227.
127 Ibid. at 230.
128 Ibid. at 233.
129 See [1960] A.C. 206 at 220–222.
130 [1958] Ch. 678 at 687.

6–119 We do not think that there is anything in the speeches in the House of Lords which prevents us from holding that the effect of each individual agreement was to constitute the shareholder an implied or constructive trustee for the other shareholders. In this respect we are of the opinion that the analysis of Lord Radcliffe, based on the proposition that a specifically enforceable agreement to assign an interest in property creates an equitable interest in the assignee, was unquestionably correct.[131] A greater difficulty is caused by Lord Denning's outright rejection of the application of s.53(2), with which Lord Cohen appears to have agreed.

6–120 So far as it is material to the present case, what sub-s.(2) says is that sub-s.(1)(c) does not affect the creation or operation of implied or constructive trusts. Just as in *Oughtred v IRC* the son's oral agreement created a constructive trust in favour of the mother, so here each shareholder's oral or implied agreement created an implied or constructive trust in favour of the other shareholders. Why then should sub-s.(2) not apply? No convincing reason was suggested in argument and none has occurred to us since. Moreover, to deny its application in this case would be to restrict the effect of general words when no restriction is called for, and to lay the ground for fine distinctions in the future. With all the respect which is due to those who have thought to the contrary, we hold that sub-s.(2) applies to an agreement such as we have in this case.

6–121 For these reasons, we have come to the conclusion that the agreement entered into by the shareholders of JEN in about April 1969 was not rendered ineffectual by s.53 of the 1925 Act.

6–122 The reasoning in *Neville v Wilson* has been criticised.[132] For example, Chadwick LJ later stated, in an obiter observation, that: "I am far from persuaded that s.53(2) of the Law of Property Act 1925 can have any application in a case where it is sought to avoid the effect of s.53(1)(c) by relying on an oral contract to make the disposition which s.53(1)(c) requires to be in writing."[133] Nonetheless, there is further judicial support for the reasoning,[134] and there is nothing illogical in having a formality requirement that applies to a disposition of an equitable interest, but not to a contract to make such a disposition. For example, if a party has full legal title to shares, the transfer of that title may require registration, but no formality rule applies to a contract to make such a transfer.

6–123 There is an important practical question as to whether the principle in *Neville v Wilson* is limited, as was assumed by the Court of Appeal in that case,[135] to *specifically enforceable* contracts for the disposition of an equitable interest.[136] This was not in issue in the case itself: the shares were in a private company, and so the contract was specifically enforceable, as damages are an inadequate remedy where the claimant cannot acquire equivalent property on the open market.[137] The conventional view is that a contract for the transfer of property must indeed be specifically enforceable if it is to give rise to a constructive trust, but we will examine challenges to that view in Chapter 17,[138] when considering that particular type of constructive trust.[139]

---

131 Cf. *London and South Western Rly Co v Gomm* (1882) 20 Ch.D. 562 at 581, per Jessel MR.

132 See, e.g. R. Nolan, "The Triumph of Technicality" [1996] C.L.J. 436; S. Worthington, *Equity*, 2nd edn (Oxford University Press, 2006), pp.236–234.

133 *United Bank of Kuwait Plc v Sahib* [1997] Ch. 107 at 129.

134 See, e.g. Upjohn J in *Oughtred v IRC* [1958] Ch. 383; Lord Radcliffe in *Oughtred v IRC* [1960] A.C. 206 at 227–228; Megarry J in *Re Holt's Settlement* [1969] 1 Ch. 100; and Goff and Shaw LJJ in *DHN Food Distributors Ltd v Tower Hamlets LBC* [1976] 1 W.L.R. 852 at 865, 867. See too Lord Cohen in *Oughtred v IRC* [1960] A.C. 206 at 230, stating that, at least when the purchase price has been paid, B can no longer claim, as against the purchaser, to be entitled to the benefit of the property.

135 [1997] Ch. 144 at 157 [extracted at para.6–119].

136 In *Chinn v Collins* [1981] A.C. 533, when considering non-specifically enforceable contractual dealings with an equitable interest in shares, Lord Wilberforce stated at 548 that: "Dealings related to the equitable interest in these [shares] required no formality. As soon as there was an agreement for their sale accompanied or followed by payment of the price, the equitable title passed at once to the purchaser and all that was needed to perfect his title was notice to the trustee or the nominee."

137 See paras 19–032ff.

138 See paras 17–068 to 17–071.

139 Note that in *Chinn v Collins* [1981] A.C. 533 at 548, Lord Wilberforce assumed at 548 that, even in the absence of specific enforceability, dealings in an equitable interest in shares required no formality: see fn.136.

3. Testamentary Dispositions: The Wills Act 1837

A. Introduction

As noted above,[140] the Wills Act 1837, which is not specific to trusts, prescribes special formalities for the validity of testamentary dispositions. **6–124**

Wills Act 1837 ss.9 and 15[141]

9. No will shall be valid unless— **6–125**

(a) it is in writing, and signed by the testator, or by some other person in his presence and by his direction; and
(b) it appears that the testator intended by his signature to give effect to the will; and
(c) the signature is made or acknowledged by the testator in the presence of two or more witnesses present at the same time;[142] and
(d) each witness either—
    (i) attests and signs the will; or
    (ii) acknowledges his signature, in the presence of the testator (but not necessarily in the presence of any other witness), but no form of attestation shall be necessary.

15. If any person shall attest the execution of any will to whom or to whose wife or husband any beneficial devise, legacy, estate, interest, gift, or appointment, of or affecting any real or personal estate (other than and except charges and directions for the payment of any debt or debts), shall be thereby given or made, such devise, legacy, estate, interest, gift, or appointment shall, so far only as concerns such person attesting the execution of such will, or the wife or husband of such person, or any person claiming under such person or wife or husband, be utterly null and void, and such person so attesting shall be admitted as a witness to prove the execution of such will, or to prove the validity or invalidity thereof, notwithstanding such devise, legacy, estate, interest, gift, or appointment mentioned in such will.[143] **6–126**

B. Scope

Under s.1 of the Wills Act 1837, the term "will" extends to any "testamentary disposition". The meaning of that term is therefore crucial to the scope of the Wills Act, as we have already discussed.[144] It follows that if a party intends to set up a trust that will take effect on her death, but not before then, the starting point[145] is that the power to set up such a trust must be exercised in writing, signed by that party, and attested by two witnesses, with s.15 providing that certain persons cannot act as valid witnesses. **6–127**

---

140 See para.6–002.

141 Section 9 supersedes the Statute of Frauds 1677 s.5, and was itself substituted by the Administration of Justice Act 1982 s.17.

142 [Note that the requirement for witnesses to be present was relaxed in relation to wills made between 31 January 2020 and 31 January 2022 in response to social distancing rules imposed during the COVID-19 pandemic: see Wills Act 1837 (Electronic Communications) (Amendment) (Coronavirus) Order 2020, amending the definition of "presence" in s.9(1)(c) and (d) to include "presence by means of videoconference or other visual transmission".]

143 Note that the Wills Act 1968 s.1 stipulates that: "For the purposes of section 15 of the Wills Act 1837 the attestation of a will by a person to whom to whose spouse there is given or made any such disposition as described in that section shall be disregarded if the will is duly executed without his attestation and without that of any other such person."

144 See paras 6–008 to 6–011.

145 Some express exceptions are made, e.g. under s.11 of the Wills Act 1837 for "any soldier being in actual military service, or any mariner or seaman at sea". See P. Critchley, "Privileged Wills and Testamentary Formalities: A Time to Die?" [1999] C.L.J. 49.

6–128 The probate doctrine of incorporation by reference may assist in satisfying these formal requirements. For example, if the will states that: "I devise Blackacre to X upon trusts which I have communicated to her by letter dated November 11, 2008", then, as the will refers to a written instrument, already existing at the date of the will, and in such terms that the written instrument can be ascertained, the doctrine of incorporation applies.[146] Consequently the incorporated letter will be admitted to public probate as part of the testator's will, and the trust as set out in the letter can take effect as a simple express trust, arising as a result of the testator's successful exercise of her power to set up such a trust.

C. The Effect of Non-Compliance: Secret Trusts and Mutual Wills

6–129 We have seen throughout this chapter that a failure to comply with a particular formality rule, whilst it may prevent B from showing that A successfully exercised a power to give B a particular right to property, does not necessarily prevent B from showing that she acquired a very similar right by some other means.

6–130 One such other means is the doctrine of secret trusts. The doctrine of fully secret trusts may assist B where, for example, a will states that "I leave Blackacre to X absolutely", but X had in fact agreed with the testator to hold Blackacre on trust for B. The doctrine of half secret trusts, which has slightly different requirements, may assist B where, for example, a will states that "I leave Blackacre to X on trust" and, before the will was made, X had agreed with the testator to hold Blackacre on trust for B. The point is that where a person has died, having been induced to leave property by will to X[147] on the oral understanding[148] that X will hold the property on trust for B, it would be unconscionable for X to decide to keep the property for her own benefit. As a result, equity recognises that, despite the absence of the requisite formalities, X holds the property thus received on trust for B.

6–131 There is, therefore, a clear link between secret trusts and cases where land is transferred subject to an oral understanding that is to be held on trust.[149] Indeed, the courts have often justified the doctrine of secret trusts on the basis that a statute cannot be used as an instrument of fraud:[150] the principle also relied on in *Rochefoucald v Boustead*[151] in relation to what is now s.53(1)(b) of the Law of Property Act 1925.[152] Again, as noted above,[153] the crucial question is as to what counts, in this context, as fraud?[154] Different answers are given to that question in cases of fully and of half secret trusts, and so we will consider the two separately before comparing them.

---

146 *In the Goods of Smart* [1902] P. 238; *Re Jones* [1942] Ch. 328, restricted by *Re Edwards WT* [1948] Ch. 440.

147 Or, indeed, to fail to make a will on the basis that X, the intestate successor, has agreed to hold the property thus received on trust for B.

148 A good practical precaution, if the deceased is concerned about the question of proof, is to have a document signed by X and put into the possession of B.

149 Note that the undertaking can take a variety of forms: the obligation of X may be, for example, to transfer the property to B, to hold on trust for B, to pass the property by will to B on X's death, or even to pass by will to B whatever property remains after X has had recourse to it in X's lifetime (as in *Ottaway v Norman* [1972] Ch. 698).

150 *Jones v Badley* (1868) 3 Ch. App. 362 at 364; *McCormick v Grogan* (1869) L.R. 4 H.L. 82 at 88–89; *Blackwell v Blackwell* [1929] A.C. 318 at 336–367.

151 [1897] 1 Ch. 196. See paras 6–035 to 6–050. The link between that doctrine and secret trusts is drawn, for example, by Patten LJ in *de Bruyne v de Bruyne* [2010] EWCA Civ 519 at [51].

152 *Jones v Badley* (1868) 3 Ch. App. 362 at 364; *McCormick v Grogan* (1869) L.R. 4 H.L. 82 at 88–89; *Blackwell v Blackwell* [1929] A.C. 318 at 336–367.

153 See paras 6–048 to 6–050.

154 Note too that, despite the references to fraud, it is not the case that the claimant, B, must necessarily meet the higher standard of proof applicable to allegations of deceit: the requirements of a secret trust need be proved only to the usual civil standard of the balance of probabilities: see *Re Snowden, deceased* [1979] Ch. 528 at 537 (disagreeing with *Ottaway v Norman* [1972] Ch. 698 at 712).

In considering secret trusts, it is important to realise that a will, when admitted to probate, is a public document. If a testator wishes to set up a particular trust on her death, but does not want others to know of that trust or its terms, she may try to take advantage of the doctrine of secret trusts. It is tempting to think that such trusts were necessary only in a bygone age when, for example, a husband did not want his wife to know that he had made provision in his will for his mistress or her children. Today, however, anyone who remarries may not want their new family to know that they have made testamentary provision for their children from previous marriages. **6–132**

The results of an empirical survey of private client practitioners carried out in 2001 suggest that secret trusts are still used, or at least considered, by modern day testators.[155] An unusual example is provided by *Re Freud, Deceased*,[156] where the court had to consider the interpretation of a clause in the will of Lucien Freud, the painter, which, on its face, gave his residuary estate (estimated to be worth, after tax, around £42 million) absolutely to two parties, his solicitor and one of his children, also acting as executrices of the will. A previous will had made the same bequest, but referred on its face to a trust, the terms of which were not set out in the will. The court accepted that "when considering the significance of this change of wording it is unrealistic to suggest that Lucien Freud did not have an appreciation of secret trusts." The evidence of his solicitor was that the bequest was made subject to a secret trust and the court noted that "the law recognises secret trusts, it is common place for solicitors to be appointed as trustees, and one reasonable explanation for a clause which confers a beneficial gift on a solicitor is that the testator intended to impose a fully secret trust."[157] In concluding that the terms of the will did not themselves impose any trust, the court effectively proceeded on the assumption that the solicitor's evidence was correct and that a secret trust was in place. **6–133**

We will also consider the doctrine of mutual wills. Consider a case in which two parties (H and W)[158] agree to make identical wills, so that, on the death of either party, their property will pass either to the survivor of the two, if there is one, or to B. The first party to die, H, abides by the agreement, and so his property passes under his will to the survivor, W. W then revokes her earlier will, and instead makes a new will, complying with all relevant formality requirements, leaving her property to Z. In such a case, B may have a claim to W's estate, even though W revoked the earlier will, and instead left her estate to Z. W's later will is admitted to probate, and the property vests in her personal representatives, but on trust to give effect to the terms of the agreement upon which the mutual wills were made, i.e. upon trust for B. There is a question as to whether or not the doctrine of mutual wills rests on the same underlying principle as the doctrine of secret trusts, and we will consider that question below.[159] **6–134**

D. Fully Secret Trusts

A fully secret trust is one where neither the existence of the trust nor its terms are disclosed by the will.[160] As noted by Brightman J in the following extract, there are three key requirements for such a trust to arise where the will, on its face, makes an absolute bequest to X: (i) the intention of the testator that X will hold property subject to a duty; (ii) communication of that intention to X; and (iii) acceptance of that duty by X, either expressly or by acquiescence. **6–135**

---

155 R. Meager, "Secret Trusts: Do They Have a Future?" [2003] Conv. 203.

156 [2014] EWHC 2577 (Ch); [2014] W.T.L.R. 1453.

157 [2014] EWHC 2577 (Ch); [2014] W.T.L.R. 1453 at [61] and [56]. Freud certainly did not lack access to legal advice: it is noted at [2] that he spoke to his solicitor, a partner in a reputable firm, "almost daily for about 20 years before he died".

158 The cases often involve a husband and a wife, but this is not, of course, a requirement of the doctrine.

159 At paras 6–209 to 6–211.

160 It can also arise in cases of intestacy: *Sellack v Harris* (1708) 2 Eq. Ca. Abr. 46.

Ottaway v Norman

Chancery Division [1972] Ch. 698

6–136 A testator, Harry Ottaway, by will devised his bungalow (with fixtures, fittings and furniture) to his housekeeper Miss Hodges in fee simple, and gave her a legacy of £1,500 and half the residue of his estate. It was alleged that Miss Hodges had orally agreed with the testator to leave the bungalow, etc., by her will to the claimants, who were the testator's son and daughter-in-law, Mr and Mrs William Ottaway. Further, it was alleged that she had orally agreed to leave them whatever money was left at her death. By her will Miss Hodges left all her property away from the claimants, who therefore brought an action against Miss Hodges' executor, Mr Norman, for a declaration that he held the appropriate parts of Miss Hodges' estate on trust for them. Brightman J. upheld the claim except in respect of the money.

6–137 BRIGHTMAN J.:. . . It will be convenient to call the person on whom such a trust is imposed the "primary donee" and the beneficiary under that trust the "secondary donee". The essential elements which must be proved are: (i) the intention of the testator to subject the primary donee to an obligation in favour of the secondary donee; (ii) communication of that intention to the primary donee; and (iii) the acceptance of that obligation by the primary donee either expressly or by acquiescence. It is immaterial whether these elements precede or succeed the will of the donor. I am informed that there is no recent reported case where the obligation imposed on the primary donee is an obligation to make a will in favour of the secondary donee as distinct from some form of inter vivos transfer. But it does not seem to me that that can really be a distinction which can validly be drawn on behalf of the defendant in the present case. The basis of the doctrine of a secret trust is the obligation imposed on the conscience of the primary donee and it does not seem to me that there is any materiality in the machinery by which the donor intends that that obligation shall be carried out. . .

6–138 I find as a fact that Harry Ottaway intended that Miss Hodges should be obliged to dispose of the bungalow in favour of the plaintiffs at her death, that he communicated that intention to Miss Hodges and that Miss Hodges accepted the obligation. I find the same facts in relation to the furniture, fixtures and fittings which passed to Miss Hodges under clause 4 of Harry Ottaway's will. I am not satisfied that any similar obligation was imposed and accepted as regards any contents of the bungalow which had not devolved on Miss Hodges under clause 4 of Harry Ottaway's will.

6–139 I turn to the question of money. In cross-examination William Ottaway said the trust extended to the house, furniture and money:

> "Everything my father left to Miss Hodges was to be in the trust. The trust comprised the lot. She could use the money as she liked. She had to leave my wife and me whatever money was left."

6–140 In cross-examination Mrs Ottaway said that her understanding was that Miss Hodges was bound to make a will giving her and her husband the bungalow, contents and any money she had left. "She could please herself about the money. She did not have to save it for us. She was free to spend it." It seems to me that two questions arise. First as a matter of fact what did the parties intend should be comprised in Miss Hodges's obligation? All money which Miss Hodges had at her death, including money which she had acquired before Harry's death and money she acquired after his death from all sources? Or, only money acquired under Harry's will? Secondly, if such an obligation existed would it as a matter of law create a valid trust? On the second question I am content to assume for present purposes but without so deciding that if property is given to the primary donee on the understanding that the primary donee will dispose by his will of such assets, if any, as he may have at his command at his death in favour of the secondary donee, a valid trust is created in favour of the secondary donee which is in suspense during the lifetime of the primary donee, but attaches to the estate of the primary donee at the moment of the latter's death. There would seem to be at least some support for this proposition in an Australian case to which I was referred: *Birmingham v Renfrew*.[161] I do not, however, find sufficient evidence that it was Harry Ottaway's intention that Miss Hodges should be compelled to leave all her money, from whatever source derived, to the plaintiffs. This would seem to preclude her giving even a small pecuniary legacy to any friend or relative. I do no think it is clear that Harry Ottaway intended to extract any such far-reaching undertaking from Miss Hodges or that she intended to accept such a wide obligation herself. Therefore the obligation, if any, is in my view to be confined to money derived under Harry Ottaway's will. If the obligation is confined to money

[161] (1937) 57 C.L.R. 666.

> derived under Harry Ottaway's will, the obligation is meaningless and unworkable unless it includes the requirement that she shall keep such money separate and distinct from her own money. I am certain that no such requirement was ever discussed or intended. If she had the right to mingle her own money with that derived from Harry, there would be no ascertainable property on which the trust could bite at her death.[162]
>
> There is another difficulty. Does money in this context include only cash or cash and investments, or all moveable property of any description? The evidence is quite inconclusive. In my judgment the plaintiff's claim succeeds in relation to the bungalow and in relation to the furniture, fixtures and fittings which devolved under clause 4 of Harry Ottaway's will subject, of course, to normal wastage and fair wear and tear, but not to any other assets. **6–141**

It is clear that nothing short of an express or implied acceptance by X will raise a trust.[163] Communication and acceptance must be of a definite legally binding obligation of X, not of a mere hope or confidence expressed by the testator.[164] In the case of a fully secret trust,[165] communication and acceptance[166] may be effected at any time during the life of the testator, whether before or after the execution of the will and communication may be made through an agent.[167] If X is told in the testator's lifetime that she is to hold the property on trust, but is not informed of the terms of the trust, X holds the property on a resulting trust for the testator's residuary legatee or devisee, or if there is no such person, or the property is residuary property, then for the testator's intestate successors.[168] Of course, if X is not told of the testator's intention to impose a trust at all, then no trust arises, as X does not act unconscionably by using the property for her own benefit. **6–142**

E. Half-Secret Trusts

A half-secret trust is one where the existence of the trust is disclosed by the will but the terms are not. It can be argued that such a case differs fundamentally from one in which a fully secret trust might arise. Where the existence of the trust is disclosed by the will, it is clear from the face of the will that X, the recipient of the bequest, is not free to use that property for her own benefit, and can only do so to the extent that she is permitted by the terms of the trust. So, if no half-secret trust can be established, X will hold the bequest on resulting trust for the testator's estate. It could then be argued that it should not be possible for B, the intended beneficiary, to avoid the formality requirements in the Wills Act 1837 and to establish a beneficial interest, as such a result is not necessary to prevent unconscionable conduct by X. As X will in any case hold the property on resulting trust, where is the risk of fraud?[169] **6–143**

---

[162] On this principle see *Henry v Hammond* [1913] 2 K.B. 515 at 521; endorsed in *Re Chelsea Cloisters Ltd* (1980) 41 P. & C.R. 98 at 101, and followed in *Azam v Iqbal* [2008] Bus. L.R. 168.

[163] *Wallgrave v Tebbs* (1855) 2 K. & J. 313.

[164] See *Att-Gen v Chamberlain* (1904) 90 L.T. 581; *Re Snowden (Deceased)* [1979] Ch. 528 at 534; *Kasperbauer v Griffith* [2000] W.T.L.R. 333 at 343.

[165] Compare the different position for a half-secret trust: see para.6–144.

[166] The full extent of the property to be covered by the obligation must be communicated and accepted so that where a secret trust for a £5,000 legacy has been communicated to and accepted by the trustee, and the legacy is increased by £5,000 in a further codicil but nothing is said to the trustee, the further £5,000 is not caught by the secret trust: *Re Colin Cooper, (Deceased)* [1939] Ch. 580 at 586. The further £5,000 is taken beneficially by the fully secret "trustee".

[167] *Moss v Cooper* (1861) 1 J. & H. 352. If the agent were unauthorised but the legatee did not approach the testator to clarify the matter, there is a question as to whether this amounts to acquiescence?

[168] *Re Boyes* (1884) 26 Ch. D. 531. In *Re Keen* [1937] Ch. 236, which concerned a half-secret trust, X had agreed to be bound by the terms unknown to X and contained in a letter handed to him by the testator in an envelope to be kept sealed until after the testator's death: the half-secret trust failed on other grounds: see para.6–149.

[169] This is the argument made, in relation to an inter vivos transfer of land from A to X where X orally agrees to hold on trust for B, by, for example, HHJ Matthews in *Solomon v McCarthy* [2020] 1 WLUK 130 at [43]: see paras 6–048 and 17–091 to 17–093.

6–144 In *Blackwell v Blackwell*,[170] however, the House of Lords considered and rejected that argument, concluding instead that there is a doctrine of half-secret trusts, which provides that they are governed by the same basic requirements as fully secret trusts (intention of the testator; communication to X; and acceptance by X). There is, however, at least one important difference between the two forms of secret trust:[171] in a fully secret trust, the communication and acceptance can occur at any point before the death of the testator; in relation to a half secret trust, it must occur before the will is made.[172] We will ask whether this difference is justified after considering the following extract from *Blackwell v Blackwell*.

Blackwell v Blackwell

House of Lords [1929] A.C. 318

6–145 A testator by a codicil bequeathed £12,000 to five persons upon trust to invest according to their discretion and "to apply the income. . . for the purposes indicated by me to them." Before the execution of the codicil the objects of the trust were communicated in outline to four of the legatees and in detail to the fifth, and the trust was accepted by all of them. The fifth legatee also made a memorandum of the testator's instructions, on the same day as (though a few hours after) the execution of the codicil. The plaintiffs (the residuary legatees) now claimed a declaration that no valid trust in favour of the objects so communicated had been created, on the ground principally that parol evidence was inadmissible to establish the purposes indicated by the testator. Eve J. and the Court of Appeal held that the evidence was admissible, and here proved a valid secret trust for the persons named by the testator in his instructions to the legatees. The plaintiffs' appeal to the House of Lords was unsuccessful.

6–146 VISCOUNT SUMNER (with whom LORD HAILSHAM L.C., LORD BUCKMASTER, LORD CARSON, and LORD WARRINGTON agreed):. . . In itself the doctrine of equity, by which parol evidence is admissible to prove what is called "fraud" in connection with secret trusts, and effect is given to such trusts when established, would not seem to conflict with any of the Acts under which from time to time the legislature has regulated the right of testamentary disposition. A court of conscience finds a man in the position of an absolute legal owner of a sum of money, which has been bequeathed to him under a valid will, and it declares that, on proof of certain facts relating to the motives and actions of the testator, it will not allow the legal owner to exercise his legal right to do what he will with his own. This seems to be a perfectly normal exercise of general equitable jurisdiction. The facts commonly, but not necessarily, involve some immoral and selfish conduct on the part of the legal owner. The necessary elements, on which the question turns, are intention, communication and acquiescence. The testator intends his absolute gift to be employed as he and not as the donee desires; he tells the proposed donee of this intention and, either by express promise or by the tacit promise, which is satisfied by acquiescence, the proposed donee encourages him to bequeath the money in the faith that his intentions will be carried out. For the prevention of fraud equity fastens on the conscience of the legatee a trust, a trust, that is, which otherwise would be inoperative; in other words it makes him do what the will in itself has nothing to do with; it lets him take what the will gives him and then makes him apply it as the court of conscience directs, and it does so in order to give effect to wishes of the testator which would not otherwise be effectual.

6–147 To this, two circumstances must be added to bring the present case to the test of the general doctrine, first, that the will states on its face that the legacy is given on trust but does not state what the trusts are, and further contains a residuary bequest, and, second, that the legatees are acting with perfect honesty,

---

170 [1929] A.C. 318.

171 It may be that, in *Re Freud, deceased* [2014] EWHC 2577 (Ch); [2014] W.T.L.R. 1453 (for which see para.6–133) the testator changed his will so as to establish a fully secret trust, rather than a half-secret trust, precisely in order to avoid any disputes about the timing of the communication and acceptance.

172 See, e.g. *Re Keen* [1937] Ch. 236; *Re Bateman's WT* [1970] 1 W.L.R. 1463. If a testator, having created a valid half-secret trust, subsequently tells the trustee not to hold for the old beneficiaries but to hold for new beneficiaries, then the trust for the new beneficiaries will fail (see, e.g. *Re Keen* [1937] Ch. 236). It is also possible that the revocation of the old trusts will fail on the basis that it was conditional on the creation of valid new trusts, although it should succeed if construed as unconditional (by analogy with, e.g. *Re Finnemore* [1992] 1 W.L.R. 793 on conditional revocation of wills), with the effect that the property will pass to the residuary legatee (or the statutory next-of-kin).

> seek no advantage to themselves, and only desire, if the court will permit them, to do what in other circumstances the court would have fastened it on their conscience to perform.
>
> Since the current of decisions down to *Re Fleetwood*[173] and *Re Huxtable*[174] has established that the principles of equity apply equally when these circumstances are present as in cases where they are not, the material question is whether and how the Wills Act affects this case. It seems to me that, apart from legislation, the application of the principle of equity which was made in *Fleetwood's case* and *Huxtable's case* was logical, and was justified by the same considerations as in the cases of fraud and absolute gifts. Why should equity forbid an honest trustee to give effect to his promise, made to a deceased testator, and compel him to pay another legatee, about whom it is quite certain that the testator did not mean to make him the object of his bounty? In both cases the testator's wishes are incompletely expressed in his will. Why should equity, over a mere matter of words, give effect to them in one case and frustrate them in the other? No doubt the words "in trust" prevent the legatee from taking beneficially, whether they have simply been declared in conversation or written in the will, but the fraud, when the trustee, so called in the will, is also the residuary legatee, is the same as when he is only declared a trustee by word of mouth accepted by him. I recoil from interfering with decisions of long standing, which reject this anomaly, unless constrained by statute. . . **6–148**
>
> The limits, beyond which the rules as to unspecified trusts must not be carried, have often been discussed. A testator cannot reserve to himself a power of making future unwitnessed dispositions by merely naming a trustee and leaving the purposes of the trust to be supplied afterwards, nor can a legatee give testamentary validity to an unexecuted codicil by accepting an indefinite trust, never communicated to him in the testator's lifetime: *Johnson v Ball*,[175] *Re Boyes*,[176] *Riordan v Banon*,[177] *Re Hetley*.[178] To hold otherwise would indeed be to enable the testator to "give the go-by" to the requirements of the Wills Act, because he did not choose to comply with them. It is communication of the purpose to the legatee, coupled with acquiescence or promise on his part, that removes the matter from the provision of the Wills Act and brings it within the law of trusts, as applied in this instance to trustees, who happen also to be legatees. . . **6–149**

Viscount Sumner's reasoning thus purports to justify treating fully secret and half-secret trusts differently when it comes to the timing of the required communication and acceptance. The argument goes that a testator cannot be permitted, through the medium of a valid will which imposes a trust but does not set out the beneficial interests of that trust, to reserve to herself a power to create the beneficial interests in an informal non-testamentary manner, so giving the go-by to the requirements of the Wills Act 1837.[179] It seems odd, however, that this scruple as to undermining the formality rules should appear at this point, as it is clear from fully secret trust cases[180] that the need to enforce the understanding subject to which X has acquired property can, in general, be given effect to without jeopardising the Wills Act.[181] Indeed, there are a number of other jurisdictions that have not accepted the special rule as to the timing of communication and acceptance of half-secret trusts.[182] **6–150**

---

173 (1880) 15 Ch.D. 594, where a testatrix by a codicil bequeathed to X all her personalty "to be applied as I have requested him to do." Before the execution of the codicil she had stated to X the trusts on which she intended the property to be held, and X made a memorandum of the details in her presence. Hall VC held that external evidence was admissible to prove the terms of the understanding between X and the testatrix.

174 [1902] 2 Ch. 793.

175 (1851) 5 De G. & Sm. 85.

176 (1884) 26 Ch.D. 531.

177 (1876) 10 I.R. Eq. 469.

178 [1902] 2 Ch. 866.

179 See too *Re Keen* [1937] Ch. 236 at 246, 248.

180 See, e.g. *McCormick v Grogan* (1869) L.R. 4 H.L. 82; *Ottaway v Norman* [1972] Ch. 698.

181 Note too that the case from which the special rule as to half-secret trusts is often said to derive, *Johnson v Ball* (1851) 5 De G. & Sm. 85, has been persuasively criticised: see W. Holdsworth, "Secret Trusts" (1937) 53 L.Q.R. 501.

182 e.g. Ireland: *Re Browne* [1944] Ir. R. 90; *Re Prendiville* (unreported, but noted [1992] Conv. 202 by J. Mee); New South Wales: *Ledgerwood v Perpetual Trustee Co Ltd* (1997) 41 N.S.W.L.R. 532; USA: American Law Institute, *Restatement (3rd) of Trusts* (American Law Institute, 2003), §18, comment (b).

6–151 It has been suggested that there is another means of defending the rule that the communication and acceptance of a half-secret trust must occur before the will is made. It involves seeing half-secret trusts as depending on the probate doctrine of incorporation by reference. It is certainly true that, as noted above,[183] that doctrine can apply only where the incorporated document exists at the time of the will referring to it. It is, however, hard to see why this should have any bearing on the operation of half-secret trusts. The essential point is that, whilst the doctrine of incorporation by reference operates within the scope of the formality requirements for testamentary dispositions, secret trusts are imposed precisely where those requirements have not been met: they operate independently of the Wills Act.[184] There are, further, some important differences between the doctrine of half-secret trusts and the probate doctrine of incorporation by reference:[185] in the former, for example, the terms of the trust, set out in the communication and acceptance, need not be in writing; and in the latter, for example, X does not need to be aware of the document incorporated.

6–152 The distinction between half-secret trusts and incorporation by reference also casts doubt on another supposed special requirement for half-secret trusts: that the communication of the trusts and the terms of the trust must not conflict with the wording of the will, for to allow otherwise would be to allow oral evidence to contradict the express words of the will.[186] Thus, leaving property to four persons "to be dealt with in accordance with my wishes which I have made known to them" is ineffective to create a half-secret trust unless the wishes were communicated to all four.[187] Furthermore, if property is left by will to X as trustee, evidence is not admissible to show that X was meant to have some part of that property beneficially.[188] In contrast, if the wording of the will gives property "to X absolutely" or "to X relying on her, but not by way of trust, to carry out my wishes . . ." then oral evidence is admissible to prove a fully-secret trust, contradicting the express words of the will, for to allow otherwise would be to allow the possibility of fraud.[189]

6–153 It is, again, difficult to see why the rules should differ as between fully secret and half secret trusts. There is, doubtless, an argument that there should be no doctrine of half-secret trusts, as the prospect of unconscionability or fraud is adequately dealt with by the resulting trust that would arise if there were no such doctrine.[190] Given, however, that the House of Lords rejected that argument in *Blackwell v Blackwell*,[191] holding that the principle behind fully secret trusts is applicable, there is no obvious reason why that principle should be applied differently.

---

183 At para.6–128.

184 See, e.g. *Blackwell v Blackwell* [1929] A.C. 318 at 335 (extracted at para.6–145); *Re Snowden, deceased* [1979] Ch. 528 at 535. However, as P. Critchley, "Instruments of Fraud, Testamentary Dispositions, and the Doctrine of Secret Trusts" (1999) 115 L.Q.R. 631 at 641 correctly states, "the mistake is to confuse 'outside the will' with 'outside the Wills Act'": a disposition by way of secret trust is a testamentary disposition, being revocable and ambulatory, so as to fall within the Wills Act. It is the harmful effect of the secret trustee's wrongful conduct that justifies equity's intervention.

185 In addition, if the doctrine of incorporation by reference is to apply, the will itself must refer to the document to be incorporated with sufficient precision to enable it to be identified: *Re Edwards' WT* [1948] Ch. 440; and a beneficiary of a half-secret trust who witnesses the will, unlike a beneficiary-witness named in an incorporated document, does not forfeit his or her beneficial interest: *Re Young* [1951] Ch. 344.

186 *Re Keen* [1937] Ch. 236.

187 *Re Spence* [1949] W.N. 237, following *Re Keen* [1937] Ch. 236.

188 See, e.g. *Re Rees* [1950] Ch. 204; *Re Tyler* [1967] 1 W.L.R. 1269.

189 *Re Spencer's Will* (1887) 57 L.T. 519; *Re Williams* [1933] 1 Ch. 244.

190 The argument is well made by, e.g. J. Hackney, *Understanding Equity & Trusts* (Sweet & Maxwell, 1987), p.103.

191 [1929] A.C. 318.

F. Fully and Half Secret Trusts: Applying the Concepts

Before looking at the basis and possible justification of secret trusts, it is useful to consider some specific points that have arisen in applying the relevant principles. **6–154**

i. Attestation of Will by Secret Beneficiary

Section 15 of the Wills Act 1837 sets out the general position that a party cannot take an interest under a will if her attestation of the will as a witness is vital to its validity.[192] In *Re Young*[193] there was a bequest by a testator to his wife with a direction that on her own death she should leave the property for the purposes which had been communicated to her (i.e. on a half-secret trust). Before execution of his will, a direction was given by him, and accepted by his wife, that she would leave a legacy of £2,000 to the testator's chauffeur. The chauffeur then witnessed the testator's will. Danckwerts J held that the chauffeur had not forfeited his legacy under the Wills Act 1837 s.15: **6–155**

> the whole theory of the formulation of a secret trust is that the Wills Act has nothing to do with the matter because the forms required by the Wills Act are entirely disregarded, since the persons do not take by virtue of the gift in the will, but by virtue of the secret trusts imposed upon the beneficiary who does in fact take under the will.

Even if this view of secret trusts is accepted, however, there is still a strong policy argument in favour of applying s.15, as its function is presumably to ensure attestation by an impartial witness with nothing to gain or lose by her testimony. Danckwerts J, however, took a narrow view of the rule, no doubt because of its potential to frustrate the intentions of the testator. **6–156**

ii. Beneficiary Predeceasing the Testator

If a testator leaves property to X on trust for B, and B predeceases the testator, the gift to B will lapse, just as an inter vivos trust for B fails if B is not alive when the trust is created.[194] As a result, no beneficial interest passes to B's estate. The same result should apply whether the trust in B's favour is set out expressly in the will, or is a secret trust. The point in each case is that B acquires no right until the death of the testator and so, if B dies before then, B has no right to pass on to her estate. **6–157**

In *Re Gardner (No.2)*,[195] however, Romer J held that in a secret trust case B's interest did *not* lapse when B died before the testator, as B obtained an interest as soon as the terms of the secret trust were communicated to and accepted by X.[196] This reasoning was based on the idea that the source of B's right was not the will itself, but rather the obligation accepted by X. Even if this is accepted, however, the problem is that B's right under the trust can arise only when the trust is constituted by X's receipt of the trust property.[197] After all, until that point, a testator could simply change her mind and make **6–158**

---

192 See para.6–126.

193 [1951] Ch. 344.

194 *Re Corbishley's Trusts* (1880) 14 Ch.D. 846; *Re Tilt* (1896) 74 L.T. 163: both concerned with personalty where a gift to B gave B an absolute interest. For realty a gift by will after 1837 to B gave an absolute interest whilst till 1925 a gift by deed to B gave B only a life interest in the absence of proper words of limitation.

195 [1923] 2 Ch. 230.

196 [1923] 2 Ch. 230 at 233.

197 See paras 5–003 to 5–004.

a different testamentary disposition, or, indeed, die insolvent and with no unencumbered property to pass to X. The authority of *Re Gardner (No.2)* is thus very weak indeed.

iii. Bequest to Two on a Promise by One

6–159 The orthodox position was laid down in *Re Stead* by Farwell J:[198]

> If A induced B either to make, or to leave unrevoked, a will leaving property to A and C as tenants in common, by expressly promising or tacitly consenting, that he and C will carry out the testator's wishes and C knows nothing of the matter until after the testator's death, A is bound, but C is not bound: *Tee v Ferris;*[199] the reason stated being, that to hold otherwise would be to enable one beneficiary to deprive the rest of their benefits by setting up a secret trust. If, however, the gift were to A and C as joint tenants, the authorities have established a distinction between those cases in which the will is made on the faith of an antecedent promise by A and those in which the will is left unrevoked on the faith of a subsequent promise. In the former case the trust binds both A and C: *Russell v Jackson;*[200] *Jones v Bradley,*[201] the reason stated being that no person can claim an interest under a fraud committed by another; in the latter case A and not C is bound: *Burney v Macdonald*[202] and *Moss v Cooper,*[203] the reason stated being that the gift is not tainted with any fraud in procuring the execution of the will. Personally, I am unable to see any difference between a gift made on the faith of an antecedent promise and a gift left unrevoked on the faith of a subsequent promise to carry out the testator's wishes; but apparently a distinction has been made by the various judges who have had to consider the question. I am bound, therefore, to decide in accordance with these authorities. . . .

6–160 The position in a case where A but not C accepted the secret trust is, therefore, that A's share is bound by the secret trusts, but C's share is not[204] *unless* it is the case that *both* (i) A and C take as joint tenants; and (ii) A's acceptance occurred before the will was made. In such a case, both A and C are bound, as the testator made the will on the basis of A's acceptance and if C were to take free from any trust, C would be profiting from A's fraud. As Perrins has suggested,[205] however, the timing of A's acceptance is not necessarily a reliable test as to whether the gift to C was induced by A's acceptance: it may be, for example, that the testator was induced not to amend an existing will by A's acceptance. It is interesting to note, however, that the current law distinguishes between the fraud or unconscionable conduct necessary in general for a secret trust to arise, and the heightened form of fraud that consists in accepting the secret trust *before* the will is made, finding that the latter can have an impact not only on the accepting party but also on an innocent party receiving property under the will jointly with that accepting party.

---

198 [1900] 1 Ch. 231 at 247. The principles here discussed apply only to fully secret trusts. In the case of half-secret trusts, if the will permits communication to be made to one only of several trustees, a communication made before or at the time of the execution of the will to one only of the trustees binds all of them, the trust being a joint office: *Blackwell v Blackwell* [1929] A.C. 318; *Re Spence* [1949] W.N. 237; *Ward v Duncombe* [1893] A.C. 369; *Re Gardom* [1914] 1 Ch. 662 at 673.

199 (1856) 2 K. & J. 357.

200 (1852) 10 Hare 204.

201 (1868) L.R. 3 Ch. 362.

202 (1845) 15 Sim. 6.

203 (1861) 1 J. & H. 352.

204 Where A and C take under the will as joint tenants, but A is bound and C is not, a severance of the joint tenancy is imposed.

205 B. Perrins, "Can You Keep Half a Secret?" (1972) 88 L.Q.R. 225, 228.

iv. Trustee Disclaiming after Testator's Death, or Predeceasing the Testator

Generally, a gift by will to X is said to lapse if X predeceases the testator.[206] However, if the gift is to X on trust for B and B survives the testator, X's predecease will not cause the gift to lapse, as equity will not allow a trust to fail for want of a trustee.[207] In *Re Maddock*, a case concerning a fully secret trust, Cozens-Hardy LJ suggested that "if the legatee renounces and disclaims, or dies in the lifetime of the testator, the persons claiming under the memorandum [i.e. the secret beneficiaries] can take nothing".[208] **6–161**

As to disclaimer after the testator's death,[209] if a person named as a half-secret trustee disclaimed the office then it would seem clear that the testator's personal representative would hold on the trusts for the secret beneficiaries. Notwithstanding the suggestion of Cozens-Hardy LJ, it is difficult, again, to argue for applying a different rule to a fully secret trust and, in *Blackwell v Blackwell*, Lord Buckmaster suggested that if a fully secret trustee disclaimed then "the court having once admitted the evidence of the trust, would interfere to prevent its defeat".[210] **6–162**

As to the predecease of X, however, it seems that Cozens-Hardy LJ's suggestion should apply, and to both fully and half-secret trusts. The point, again, is that the secret trust is constituted only when the trust property is acquired by a party who, as a result of the communication and acceptance of the testator's intention, is under a duty to the beneficiary. If X's pre-decease prevents X receiving the trust property, no such trust can arise. **6–163**

v. Secret Trusts of Interests in Land

As discussed above,[211] the Law of Property Act 1925 s.53(1)(b) requires a declaration of trust respecting any land or any interest therein to be proved in signed writing. Does this formality rule apply to secret trusts, so that the acceptance of the trust by X must be proved by writing signed by either the testator or X? It is of course prudent for a testator, even if no land is involved, to ensure that some such signed document exists, in order to make it easier for the beneficiaries to prove the terms and existence of a secret trust. The impact of the absence of such writing, where land is involved, depends on the broader question as to the basis of secret trusts, which we will now examine. It will be suggested as a result of that analysis that no signed writing is required for proof of a secret trust of land: this is either because the fraud that prevents X from relying on the Wills Act 1837 to deny the trust also prevents X from relying on s.53(1)(b), or because the secret trust is a constructive one, arising to prevent a particular form of unconscionable conduct by X, and so falls within s.53(2) of the Law of Property Act 1925. **6–164**

---

206 Exceptionally, if issue predecease a testator leaving issue of their own surviving the testator, the gift takes effect in favour of the surviving issue: Wills Act 1837 s.33. The persons benefiting from this exception will not be able to disregard the deceased legatee-trustee's undertaking: cf. *Huguenin v Baseley* (1807) 14 Ves. Jun. 273.

207 The testator's personal representative will step in as trustee. See, e.g. *Mallott v Wilson* [1903] 2 Ch. 494; *Re Armitage (Deceased)* [1972] Ch. 438.

208 [1902] 2 Ch. 220 at 231.

209 If X instead attempts to revoke his or her acceptance of the secret trust *before* the testator dies, the effect of the testator going ahead with the bequest to X may depend on whether or not X's revocation gave the testator sufficient time to consider whether to make, and then to make, any consequent change to the will.

210 [1929] A.C. 318 at 328.

211 See paras 6–027 to 6–032.

G. Justifying Secret Trusts

6–165 In the foregoing discussion, we noted[212] that judges have drawn a distinction between the transfer of property to X, which occurs as a result of the will, and the imposition of the secret trust on that property, which occurs outside the will, in response to X's conduct in agreeing to hold the property for the benefit of B.[213] In *Re Snowden*, for example, Megarry J stated that:[214]

> the whole basis of secret trusts . . . is that they operate outside the will, changing nothing that is written in it, and allowing it to operate according to its tenor, but then fastening a trust on the property in the hands of the recipient.

6–166 That analysis, whilst accurate, does not mean that secret trusts can be justified simply as express trusts,[215] arising outside the will[216] as a result of the testator's successful exercise of a power to set up a trust. As Patricia Critchley has persuasively argued, the important question is not whether a secret trust arises outside the will, but whether it arises outside the Wills Act.[217] The latter applies formality requirements to "testamentary dispositions" and the creation of an express trust arising only on the testator's death, whether or not contained in a will, is undoubtedly such a disposition. The fact that a secret trust arises outside the will is the phenomenon that we need to explain, not the explanation for the trust.

6–167 An alternative view, consistent with the analyses of the House of Lords in *McCormick v Grogan*[218] (as applied in *Ottaway v Norman*[219]) and in *Blackwell v Blackwell*,[220] is that secret trusts depend on the principle that equity will not allow a statute to be used as an instrument of fraud: X is not permitted to rely on the formality rules in the Wills Act 1837 if the result would be that X would be free to use property entirely for her own benefit, having agreed instead to hold that property on trust for B (or to hold it subject to some other condition). As noted above,[221] a similar analysis was applied by the Court of Appeal in *Rochefoucald v Boustead*,[222] when permitting a trust of land to be proved orally. On this view, secret trusts are essentially express trusts, arising as a result of the testator's successful exercise of her power to set up a trust.[223]

6–168 There is another view that can be taken, both of the type of trust recognised in *Rochefoucauld* and of secret trusts. On this view, the trusts are constructive trusts,[224] imposed to prevent the particular form

---

212 See, e.g. para.6–155.

213 See, e.g. *Re Young* [1951] Ch. 344; *Re Gardner (No.2)* [1923] 2 Ch. 230; *Blackwell v Blackwell* [1929] 2 A.C. 318 at 340, 342.

214 [1979] Ch. 528 at 535.

215 If secret trusts are express trusts arising outside the will, then s.53(1)(b) would apply to require signed writing for the proof of an express trust of land, as suggested by, e.g. A.J. Oakley, *Constructive Trusts*, 3rd edn (Sweet & Maxwell, 1992), pp.262ff.

216 This theory of secret trusts has sometimes been called the "dehors" theory, using the French word for "outside"; but as acerbically noted by J. Hackney, *Understanding Equity & Trusts* (1987), p.106: "Sloganising in French or Latin is plainly no substitute for analysis, and the notion lacks convincing explanation."

217 P. Critchley, "Instruments of Fraud, Testamentary Dispositions, and the Doctrine of Secret Trusts" (1999) 115 L.Q.R. 631, 636–641.

218 (1868) L.R. 4 H.L. 82 at 88–89.

219 [1972] Ch. 698; extracted at paras 6–136 to 6–141.

220 [1929] A.C. 318; extracted at paras 6–145 to 6–149.

221 See para.6–046.

222 [1897] 1 Ch. 196.

223 This does not mean, however that, on this view, a secret trust of land must be proved in writing: the same fraud that prevents reliance on the Wills Act 1837 also prevents reliance on s.53(1)(b) of the Law of Property Act 1925.

224 See, e.g. *Re Cleaver* [1981] 1 W.L.R. 939 at 947; *Re Basham* [1986] 1 W.L.R. 1498 at 1504; *Kasperbauer v Griffith* [2000] W.T.L.R. 333 at 342, per Peter Gibson LJ. This is also the view taken by Y.K. Liew, *Rationalising Constructive Trusts* (Hart Publishing, 2017) Ch.4.

of unconscionable conduct of X that consists of acquiring property as a result of a promise made in relation to that property, and then keeping the property whilst breaking the promise.[225] Constructive trusts are not expressly exempted from the Wills Act 1837 (which contains no equivalent to s.2(5) of the Law of Property (Miscellaneous Provisions) Act 1989 or s.53(2) of the Law of Property Act 1925),[226] but such trusts are imposed by law as a result of X's conduct and not as a result of the testator's successful exercise of a power to create a trust. As a result, the recognition of a constructive trust does not involve a "testamentary disposition".[227]

The differences between these two views will be discussed further in Chapter 17,[228] as part of our general examination of constructive trusts. Three points are worth making here. First, on either view, the key question concerns the sufficiency of X's conduct—either to raise the prospect of using a statute as an instrument of fraud,[229] or to raise the prospect of a particular form of unconscionable conduct. As to the fraud analysis, it should be noted that fraud in this context cannot be coterminous with the tort of deceit, as a secret trust can arise even if X, when agreeing to the trust, fully intends to give effect to it.[230] As to the unconscionability analysis, it should be noted that different views can be taken of the particular mischief targeted by the doctrine: is it, for example, the prospect of the testator suffering the detriment of having her intentions frustrated as a result of relying on X's promise;[231] or is it the prospect of X enjoying the benefit of property contrary to the terms of the promise subject to which X acquired that property?[232] **6–169**

Second, on the fraud analysis, there is a question as to the constitutional validity of the maxim that a statute cannot be used as an instrument of fraud:[233] it could be argued, for example, that it is for Parliament expressly to determine the scope of a formality rule, and that the courts should not read in exceptions. On the unconscionability analysis, the constructive trust arising lies outside the scope of the Wills Act 1837: it is imposed by law as a result of X's conduct, and therefore, as it does not **6–170**

---

225 See, e.g. *Gillett v Holt* [2001] Ch. 210 at 228 per Robert Walker LJ, referring in obiter dicta to secret trusts: "There must be an agreement between A [the testator] and B [the secret trustee] as to conferring a benefit on C [the secret beneficiary] because it is the agreement (and not C's moral claims) which would make it unconscionable for B to resile from his agreement." See too *de Bruyne v de Bruyne* [2010] EWCA Civ 519 at [51], per Patten LJ, referring to a principle giving rise to a constructive trust where the defendant's unconscionable conduct is "in the form of a denial or refusal to carry out the agreement to hold the property for the benefit of the third party which was the only basis upon which the property was transferred".

226 On this view of secret trusts, of course, there is no requirement for a secret trust of land to be proved in writing, as it is a constructive trust and so excepted from s.53(1)(b) of the Law of Property Act 1925 by s.53(2).

227 In the same way, see para.6–006, where it is noted that formality rules are generally limited to cases where it is claimed that a party has successfully exercised a power to give the claimant a right.

228 See paras 17–083 to 17–088.

229 For an analysis of the possible requirements of "fraud" in the context of secret trusts, see, e.g. P. Critchley, "Instruments of Fraud, Testamentary Dispositions, and the Doctrine of Secret Trusts" (1999) 115 L.Q.R. 631, 646–653. For the general question of what it might mean to say that a statute cannot be used as an instrument of fraud, see further paras 17–091 to 17–093.

230 Indeed, even if X maintains that intention throughout, a secret trust still arises, and is necessary in a half-secret trust case to rebut the claims of the testator's estate, as it might otherwise be argued that the property is held on resulting trust, and in a fully secret trust case to show that X, when later, e.g. giving the benefits of the property to B, is not making a gift (with, e.g. consequences under the Inheritance Tax Act 1984) but is instead performing the terms of the trust established on the testator's death.

231 As suggested by, e.g. S. Gardner, "Reliance-Based Constructive Trusts" in C. Mitchell (ed.), *Constructive and Resulting Trusts* (2010).

232 As suggested by, e.g. B. McFarlane, "Constructive Trusts Arising on Receipt of Property *Sub Conditione*" (2004) 120 L.Q.R. 667.

233 As noted by, e.g. P. Critchley, "Instruments of Fraud, Testamentary Dispositions, and the Doctrine of Secret Trusts" (1999) 115 L.Q.R. 631, 656–654.

arise as a result of the testator's power to deal with her property on death, it is not a "testamentary disposition".[234]

6–171 Third, doubts as to the validity of the doctrine of secret trusts may stem from the fact that it seems to give testators a simple means to avoid the general rule that there must be a public record of what happens to their property on death. Whether the fraud or the constructive trust argument is adopted, the facts triggering the secret trust—X's acceptance of the duty to hold property subject to conditions—are undoubtedly close to the facts involved in any express trust created by a transfer to a trustee.[235] However, this may contribute to a justification of secret trusts: if the power to create an express trust by transfer initially developed because equity considered that trustees should be bound by the conditions subject to which they received property, it is no surprise that equity should continue to intervene in such cases, even if a formality rule means that it cannot simply be said that the testator exercised a power to create a trust.[236]

H. Mutual Wills

i. Introduction

6–172 As we have said,[237] the doctrine of mutual wills can operate to impose a trust that gives effect to a testator's earlier promise to dispose of her property on death in a certain way, even if she attempted to renege on that promise, and left a valid will disposing of the property differently. As Mummery LJ said in *Fry v Densham–Smith*:[238]

> This illustrates the anomalous character of the doctrine of mutual wills: if and when it applies, absolute beneficial testamentary dispositions . . . do not take effect in accordance with their terms. The surviving party of a claimed mutual wills agreement is able to make further wills, but cannot, after the death of the first to die, effectively revoke dispositions already made in the mutual will. This irrevocable result can only be produced by an agreement made and acted on with that intention.

6–173 The key point therefore is that the survivor's promise was part of an agreement as to mutual testamentary dispositions made with a party who died earlier and who honoured that agreement. The doctrine of mutual wills thus shows "equity intervening to prevent unconscionable conduct",[239] and the precise form of unconscionable conduct targeted consists in breaching the terms of a binding agreement as to mutual testamentary dispositions, where the other party has acted on the basis of that agreement by disposing of her property in a particular way on death.

6–174 Before looking in more detail at the requirements, effect, and possible justifications of the doctrine, it is useful to consider the analysis of the Court of Appeal in the following extract.

---

[234] See para.6–006, where it is noted that formality rules are generally limited to cases where it is claimed that a party has successfully exercised a power to give the claimant a right.

[235] See W. Swadling, "The Nature of the Trust in *Rochefoucauld v Boustead*" in C. Mitchell (ed.), *Constructive and Resulting Trusts* (2010), p.107.

[236] See B. McFarlane, "The Centrality of Constructive and Resulting Trusts" in C. Mitchell (ed.), *Constructive and Resulting Trusts* (2010), pp.199–201. See too D. Wilde, "Secret Trusts: Dehors the Wills Act (Not the Will)" [2020] Conv. 163.

[237] See para. 6–134.

[238] [2010] EWCA Civ 1410; [2011] W.T.L.R. 387 at [30].

[239] *Gillett v Holt* [2001] Ch. 210 at 228 per Robert Walker LJ.

Re Walters

Court of Appeal [2009] Ch. 212

MUMMERY L.J. (with whom DYSON and MAURICE KAY L.JJ. agreed): Norris J. held that in 1998 Mr Harold Walters and his late wife, Freda ("the deceased") made a mutual wills contract pursuant to which they executed similar codicils amending their wills. The deceased died in 2006 leaving her will and codicil unrevoked. Mr Walters inherited her estate, but disputed the application of the mutual wills doctrine to him or to the deceased's estate in his hands. 6–175

The judge applied the principles summarised by Dixon J. in *Birmingham v Renfrew*:[240] 6–176

> "It has long been established that a contract between persons to make corresponding wills gives rise to equitable obligations when one acts on the faith of such an agreement and dies leaving his will unrevoked so that the other takes property under its dispositions. It operates to impose upon the survivor an obligation regarded as specifically enforceable. It is true that he cannot be compelled to make and leave unrevoked a testamentary document and if he dies leaving a last will containing provisions inconsistent with his agreement it is nevertheless valid as a testamentary act. But the doctrines of equity attach the obligation to the property. The effect is, I think, that the survivor becomes a constructive trustee and the terms of the trust are those of the will he undertook would be his last will."

This appeal is about (1) the sufficiency of the evidence for the finding of a mutual wills contract between Mr Walters and the deceased, and (2) the sufficiency in law of its terms. The litigation is regrettable. A family apparently united around the grandparents is now divided on the question whether they made a mutual wills contract. The decision on this appeal may not bring the dispute to an end. If the appeal fails, further issues may arise about the effect of the mutual wills on the ability of Mr Walters to deal with the assets derived from the deceased's estate. As recent cases have shown this equitable doctrine dating from the 18th century[241] continues to be a source of contention for the families of those who have invoked it. The likelihood is that in future even fewer people will opt for such an arrangement and even more will be warned against the risks involved. 6–177

In its *22nd Report on the Making and Revocation of Wills* the Law Reform Committee noted particular problems with the mutual wills doctrine. It recommended that the difficulties would "be better clarified by judicial development than by legislation".[242] The novel aspect of this case is that the survivor of the alleged contract is alive and gave evidence denying the alleged contract and disputing the application of the doctrine and its consequences. This feature was absent from all the authorities cited to the court. . .[243] 6–178

The Proceedings and the Judgment

On 16 March 2007 Andrew [a grandson of Mr and Mrs Walters who was also a solicitor and who drafted their wills] began these proceedings to have the deceased's 1988 will and the 1998 codicil proved in solemn form and for a declaration that the deceased's codicil takes effect as a valid and effective mutual will. . . 6–179

The judge considered the effect of the agreement made between Mr Walters and the deceased. He held that a valid mutual will was made. He rejected submissions on behalf of Mr Walters that the agreement was not intended to be a binding agreement and that it did not satisfy the requirements for mutual wills, because it did not record any express agreement not to revoke the wills so made . . . [The judge] did not regard the absence of any explicit mention of revocation as rendering "the mutual testamentary dispositions" incapable of enforcement as mutual wills, a reading which was reinforced by a consideration of the surrounding circumstances, in particular the covering letter of explanation. 6–180

As for the form of the relief to be granted on the mutual wills aspect of the case, the judge held that the declaration should be that the codicils executed by the deceased and Mr Walters on 18 May 1998 "take effect as valid and effective mutual wills *so as to bind the deceased's estate*."[244] He explained the 6–181

---

240 (1937) 57 C.L.R. 666 at 683.

241 Lord Camden L.C.'s judgment in *Dufour v Pereira* (1769) 1 Dick. 419.

242 Cmnd. 7902 (1980) p.26, 3.52.

243 *Re Oldham* [1925] Ch. 75; *Birmingham v Renfrew* (1937) 57 C.L.R. 666; *Re Cleaver, deceased* [1981] 1 W.L.R. 939; *Re Dale, deceased* [1994] Ch. 31; *Re Goodchild, deceased* [1996] 1 W.L.R. 694, affirmed [1997] 1 W.L.R. 1216; and *Birch v Curtis* [2002] EWHC 1158 (Ch); [2002] 2 F.L.R. 847.

244 [2007] EWHC 3060 (Ch) at [41].

italicised words by the fact that he had made no findings or holdings as to the scope of the agreement relating to mutual wills, which he regarded as a question of construction of the agreement embodied in clause 2 of the codicil. He confirmed that, as reflected in the form of declaration, the deceased's estate was bound by the agreement "when in due course it passes to Mr Walters or his executors". He added that he regarded the issue of Mr Walters's own estate as simply not before him. The declaration was made as to the deceased's estate, but nothing else.

Defendant's Submissions

6–182 On the first ground of appeal—the insufficiency of the terms of the contract—Mr Steinfeld submitted that it was vital to know all the terms of the contract for mutual wills. How else could the subject matter and terms of the constructive trust arising from it be determined? The judge had erred in failing to decide with sufficient particularity the scope and terms of the contract. The survivor was entitled to know exactly what he could or could not do with the assets that he acquired on the death of the deceased, or, indeed, with his own assets.

6–183 On the judge's findings it was unclear what property was affected by the supposed constructive trust and what Mr Walters was entitled to do with the deceased's property, which had been left to him absolutely under the 1988 will, and even what he was entitled to do with his own property during the rest of his life. There was a range of possibilities as to the scope of the contract which the judge had failed to determine. Was Mr Walters prevented from dealing with the deceased's estate at all in his lifetime? Or did the constructive trust only extend to the part of the deceased's estate left when he died? Did it extend to his estate at the date of the deceased's death? Or as at the date of his death? What was the position in relation to the Mill Hill house? What, if anything, could be done in relation to it?

6–184 The problem arising from lack of contractual certainty was, Mr Steinfeld submitted, well illustrated in two ways: first, by the form of the *quia timet* injunction originally sought in the claim form, but later abandoned because of the difficulty of formulating it; and secondly, and more immediately, by a very recent exchange between the parties about whether, if Mr Walters lost his appeal and was ordered to pay the costs, he would be entitled to use property coming to him absolutely from the deceased's estate to pay those costs. It was said on behalf of Andrew that Mr Walters would not be entitled to make that use of the deceased's property or make any other disposition of it inter vivos that would subvert the purpose for which the constructive trust was imposed to give effect to the contract.

6–185 It was also submitted by Mr Steinfeld that the terms of the declaration made by the judge were incorrect. The constructive trust did not affect the deceased's property in the hands of Mr Walters at all. The estate was expressly left to him absolutely. The trust would only bind his personal representatives as regards any property left by him on his death. The words "of the defendant" should be omitted from the declaration to make it clear that the constructive trust did not affect the assets of the deceased's estate in his hands. . .

Discussion and Conclusions

6–186 I turn to the legal submission that the contract found by the judge is not in law a valid and binding contract for mutual wills and that the judge was accordingly wrong in law to make the declaration in the form that he did, or at all.

6–187 In my judgment, Mr Steinfeld's submissions on insufficiency of the terms of the contract between Mr Walters and the deceased do not accurately reflect the fundamental principles of mutual wills.

6–188 It is a legally necessary condition of mutual wills that there is clear and satisfactory evidence of a contract between two testators. However, the argument resting on the alleged insufficiency or uncertainty of the terms of this contract is misconceived. The case for the existence of mutual wills does not involve making a contractual claim for specific performance or other relief. The claimant in a mutual wills case is not even a party to the contract and does not have to establish that he was.

6–189 The obligation on the surviving testator is equitable. It is in the nature of a trust of the property affected, so the constructive trust label is attached to it. The equitable obligation is imposed for the benefit of third parties, who were intended by the parties to benefit from it. It arises by operation of law on the death of the first testator to die so as to bind the conscience of the surviving testator in relation to the property affected.

6–190 It is a legally sufficient condition to establish what the judge described as "its irreducible core", which he analysed as a contract between two testators, T1 and T2:[245]

[245] [2007] EWHC 3060 (Ch) at [9].

> "that in return for T1 agreeing to make a will in form X and not to revoke it without notice to T2, then T2 will make a will in form Y and agree not to revoke it without notice to T1. If such facts are established then upon the death of T1 equity will impose upon T2 a form of constructive trust (shaped by the exact terms of the contract that T1 and T2 have made). The constructive trust is imposed because T1 has made a disposition of property on the faith of T2's promise to make a will in form Y, and with the object of preventing T1 from being defrauded."

In my judgment, that is an accurate and clear statement of the equitable principles. Mr Steinfeld accepted that. He agreed that Mr Walters would be bound by a constructive trust, but only if sufficient terms of the contract were established to raise one. **6–191**

The answer to the sufficiency point is, I think, summed up in a single sentence in *Snell's Equity*:[246] **6–192**

> "Mutual wills provide an instance of a trust arising by operation of law to give effect to an express intention of the two testators."

The intentions of Mr Walters and the deceased were sufficiently expressed in the contract to lay the foundations for the equitable obligations that bind the conscience of Mr Walters, as the survivor, in relation to the deceased's estate. The judge found all that he needed to find in order to hold that, contrary to the contentions of Mr Walters, mutual wills existed. Possible, and as yet unexplored, legal consequences of the application of the equitable principles do not negative the existence of the foundation contract or prevent a constructive trust from arising by operation of law on the death of the deceased. **6–193**

It had been accepted on behalf of Mr Walters in submissions to Norris J. that, if there was a valid contract for mutual wills, the doctrine operated by imposing a constructive trust on him as the survivor, because the deceased had performed her promise to leave her estate to him. In my judgment, the trust is immediately binding on him in relation to the deceased's property left to him on the basis of the contract. It is not postponed to take effect only after the death of Mr Walters when the property, or what may be left of it, comes into the hands of his personal representatives. **6–194**

Disputes about the actual operation of the trust in practice usually turn on construction of the contract in all the relevant circumstances. Of course, the disagreements can be resolved without litigation, if all the beneficiaries are agreed and have legal capacity to do so. If not, the disputes can be determined on an application to the court by Mr Walters in proceedings to which those interested are made parties. **6–195**

In this case the issues before the judge were the validity of the codicil and the existence of the mutual wills contract, both of which were unsuccessfully contested by Mr Walters. The judge determined those issues against him for sound reasons in an excellent judgment. He was not asked to rule on the possible legal consequences of the declaration for Mr Walters or for the beneficiaries arising on the death of the deceased. The judge prudently declined to be drawn into determining matters, such as the scope or extent of the constructive trust, which were neither raised in the pleadings nor in the submissions of the parties. As Bowen L.J. said in *Cooke v New River Co*,[247] the teaching of experience is that judgments should be given on points that the judge is bound to decide. Deciding more than is necessary could, "like the proverbial chickens of destiny", come home to roost sooner or later. Unnecessary opinions can be a source of future embarrassment, or even worse when, as here, no other points have been pleaded, investigated or argued. **6–196**

ii. The Requirements of the Doctrine

The doctrine does not apply simply because two parties make wills in almost identical terms. As Leggatt LJ stated in *Re Goodchild*:[248] **6–197**

> Two wills may be in the same form as each other. Each testator may leave his or her estate to the other with a view to the survivor leaving both estates to their heir. But there is no presumption that a present plan will be immutable in the future. A key feature of the concept of mutual wills is the irrevocability of the mutual intentions. Not only must they be binding when made, but the testators must have undertaken, and so

[246] 31st edn (2005), 22–31.
[247] (1888) 38 Ch.D. 56 at 71.
[248] [1997] 1 W.L.R. 1216 at 1225. See too *Birch v Curtis* [2002] EWHC 1158 (Ch); [2002] 2 F.L.R. 847 at [64]ff.

must be bound, not to change their intentions after the death of the first testator. The test must always be, suppose that during the lifetime of the surviving testator, the intended beneficiary did something which the survivor regarded as unpardonable, would he or she be free not to leave their combined estate to him? The answer must be that the survivor is so entitled unless the testators agreed otherwise when they executed their wills. Hence the need for a clear agreement.

6–198 The approach adopted in *Re Goodchild* is given effect to by Mummery LJ's statement in *Re Walters* that: "It is a legally necessary condition of mutual wills that there is clear and satisfactory evidence of a contract between two testators."[249] As a result, it must be shown that the parties' agreement to make specific dispositions of their property on death[250] was intended to be legally binding[251] and is sufficiently certain to be enforced.[252] The need for such a contract may be explained by the fact that the mutual wills doctrine extends beyond that of secret trusts, as it can apply not only to property received by the survivor under the will of the first testator, but to *any* property which the survivor promised to dispose of in a particular way in her will.[253] Secret trusts, in contrast, do not require a contractual agreement as such, as the principle applied there relates to *receipt* of property subject to a promise to hold that property subject to particular conditions. As the doctrine of mutual wills can have a wider effect, and relate to property acquired by the survivor independently of any promise made to the deceased (the first testator), a binding contract is required.

6–199 As Ying Khai Liew has observed, it is important to distinguish between cases where a promisor *acquires* property having made an undertaking to hold that property for another (as is the case with secret trusts) and cases where a promisor instead makes a promise in relation to property she already holds (as is the case with proprietary estoppel and, in some instances, mutual wills).[254] There are good reasons why equity may be quicker to enforce the promise in the first set of cases than in the second.[255] Certainly, it is significant that the doctrine of mutual wills can apply even if the agreement does not involve the survivor receiving any property under the will of the deceased,[256] and so can apply wholly to property already held by the survivor at the time of the agreement.

6–200 The doctrine of mutual wills can also apply even if the wills of the two parties do not mirror one another.[257] The parties are also free to set the terms of the agreement: it may be that the survivor is to receive a life interest in all or a specific part of property received from the first testator; it may be that the survivor is instead to have a life interest in all or a specific part of her own property as held at the date of death of the deceased.[258] Sometimes, it may appear that the survivor is to be absolute owner of all her property, subject only to a duty to bequeath to the agreed beneficiaries whatever she has left

---

[249] [2008] EWCA Civ 782; [2009] Ch. 212 at [36] (extracted at para.6–183). See too *Re Dale* [1994] Ch. 31 at 38 per Morritt J: there must be a "contract at law" and *Legg v Burton* [2017] EWHC 2088 (Ch); [2017] 4 W.L.R. 186 at [28]–[29].

[250] It is sometimes said that the agreement must be "not to revoke" the wills, but revocation may well be permissible, so long as a substitute will is made giving effect to the agreed dispositions.

[251] Hence it does not suffice if the parties make a non-contractual agreement trusting and confidently assuming that each will do as the other has asked: see, e.g. *Gray v Perpetual Trustee Ltd* [1928] A.C. 391; *Re Oldham* [1925] Ch. 75; *Re Goodchild* [1997] 1 W.L.R. 1216.

[252] *Re Walters* [2008] EWCA Civ 782; [2009] Ch. 212 at [36].

[253] See, e.g. *Re Dale* [1994] Ch. 31.

[254] See Y.K. Liew, "The Ambit of the Mutual Wills Doctrine" (2016) 132 L.Q.R. 664 and Y.K. Liew, "Explaining the Mutual Wills Doctrine" in B. Häcker and C. Mitchell (eds) *Current Issues in Succession Law* (Hart Publishing, 2016). See more generally, Y.K. Liew, *Rationalising Constructive Trusts* (Hart Publishing, 2017).

[255] See further paras 17–086 to 17–088.

[256] *Re Dale* [1994] Ch. 31.

[257] See, e.g. *Re Newey* [1994] 2 N.Z.L.R. 590.

[258] *Re Hagger* [1930] 2 Ch. 190.

at the time of death.[259] If the parties fail to make it clear which property is subject to the trust then this uncertainty may make it impossible for the survivor to know what dispositions she is entitled to make during her life, in which case an application to the court for directions may be required.[260]

Given that the doctrine of mutual wills requires a contractual agreement between the first and second testator, the question arises, whether s.2 of the Law of Property (Miscellaneous Provisions) Act 1989 has to be satisfied if the doctrine is to apply to any interest in land held by the survivor. In *Healey v Brown*,[261] the section was said to apply, with the effect that, whilst an interest in land acquired by the survivor under the will of the deceased was held on trust on the terms of the parties' oral agreement, an interest in land held independently by the survivor was not subject to any such trust, even though it was also covered by the oral agreement. This distinction reflects the different bases of the doctrines of secret trusts and of mutual wills. The preliminary question, however, is whether s.2 applies at all, and there are prior dicta inconsistent with the view taken on that point in *Healey*.[262] It can also be argued that, as Mummery LJ pointed out in *Re Walters*,[263] the doctrine of mutual wills is not concerned with enforcing a contract as such (after all, the beneficiary of the trust is not a party to the contract between the testators), but rather responds to the prospect of a specific form of unconscionable conduct. That unconscionable conduct consists of the survivor reneging on an agreement that is intended to be binding and on which the deceased is assumed to have relied when making her own testamentary dispositions. Indeed, it has been suggested that, where land is concerned, B could in any case recharacterise the claim as one depending on proprietary estoppel, rather than a mutual will as such, and then rely on the fact that, as discussed earlier in this Chapter,[264] the s.2 formality rule does not apply to proprietary estoppel claims.[265] As the law stands, however, if a mutual will deals with land, the parties' agreement should be put in signed writing, signed by both parties, and containing all the terms of the parties' contract. **6–201**

It seems that the principles underlying mutual wills extend to an agreement not to revoke existing wills, made prior to the agreement,[266] and also to an agreement made between two joint tenants, who agree not to sever their joint tenancy (thus ensuring that the survivor takes the whole interest by survivorship) and also that the survivor will then dispose of that interest in an agreed manner on her death.[267] **6–202**

iii. Effects of the Doctrine

Before the death of either party, the agreement is a purely contractual one made in consideration of the mutual promises of the two parties for the benefit of a third party.[268] If one of the parties attempts to revoke the agreement before either has died, that revocation, depending on the terms of the **6–203**

---

259 Such beneficiaries may well not have vested interests liable to be divested: the parties probably intend them to benefit only if alive on the survivor's death so that if they all predecease the second testator, his or her duty will cease.

260 As in *Edell v Sitzer* (2001) 4 I.T.E.L.R. 149, where the court declined to make an order as the parties had not made mutual wills. For further discussion, see P. Luxton, "*Walters v Olin*: Uncertainty of Subject Matter – An Insoluble Problem in Mutual Wills?" [2009] Conv. 498.

261 [2002] W.T.L.R. 849.

262 See, e.g. *Birmingham v Renfrew* (1957) 57 C.L.R. 666 at 690 per Dixon J; *Lewis v Cotton* [2001] W.T.L.R. 1117 at 1131.

263 [2009] Ch. 212 at [36] (extracted at para.6–188).

264 See paras 6–020ff.

265 See too *Legg v Burton* [2017] EWHC 2088 (Ch) at [27].

266 *Dufour v Pereira* (1769) 1 Dick. 419; *Re Fox* [1951] Ontario R. 378; *Edell v Sitzer* (2001) 4 I.T.E.L.R. 149 at [68].

267 *Re Newey* [1994] 2 N.Z.L.R. 590; *Manitoba University v Sandeman* (1998) 155 D.L.R. (4th) 40.

268 *Dufour v Pereira* (1769) 1 Dick. 419 at 421; *Birmingham v Renfrew* (1937) 57 C.L.R. 666; *Re Walters* [2008] EWCA Civ 782; [2009] Ch. 212.

parties' agreement, may be a breach of contract and so actionable by the other party.[269] If, however, the revoking party gives notice in sufficient time before the death of the other party, it would seem that the doctrine should not apply, even if the non-revoking party rejects the revocation and attempts to affirm the contract.[270] Whilst it is true as a matter of general contract law that an unaccepted repudiation is of no effect, this may simply reflect the suggestion made above,[271] that the doctrine of mutual wills is not concerned with enforcing a contract as such,[272] but rather with responding to a particular form of unconscionable conduct, and it is difficult to regard the conduct of the survivor as unconscionable if sufficient notice was given to the deceased who then failed to alter her will.

6–204 If there is no revocation of the agreement then, as confirmed in *Re Walters*,[273] on the death of the first party, an immediate trust arises in favour of B (the party to whom the second testator has promised to leave the property on her death).[274] As Lewison J stated in *Thomas and Agnes Carvel Foundation v Carvel*:[275]

> the trust does not arise under the will of the surviving testator. Nor does it arise under any previous will of the surviving testator. It arises out of the agreement between the two testators not to revoke their wills, and the trust arises when the first of the two dies without having revoked his will.

As was also confirmed in *Re Walters*,[276] the trust is a constructive one, imposed by law to prevent unconscionable conduct by the second testator.[277]

6–205 If, therefore, B dies after the first testator, but before the surviving testator, B has an existing interest at the time of her death, which does not lapse and instead forms part of B's estate.[278] B's interest is also unaffected if the surviving testator disclaims any benefits acquired under the will of the first testator.[279] It is the death of the first testator, who of course no longer has the opportunity to revoke her own will, which means that the agreement will necessarily be enforced in favour of B, even if the surviving testator revokes their will.

6–206 Whilst B has an existing interest from the time of the death of the first testator, the terms of the parties' agreement may be such that there is a form of "floating trust" which crystallises (i.e. takes final form) only on the death of the survivor.[280] The question can therefore arise as to what use of any relevant property the survivor may make during her life. If, for example, the parties' agreement was that all of the survivor's estate should be left to B, is it permissible for the survivor to make a large lifetime gift to charity, thereby reducing the size of her estate? As observed by Mummery LJ in *Re Walters*,[281] such questions "usually turn on the construction of the contract in all the relevant

---

[269] The breach is unlikely to give rise to substantial damages: *Lewis v Cotton* (2000) 3 I.T.E.L.R. 447 at [44]. B, the intended ultimate beneficiary, may have a claim under the Contract (Rights of Third Parties) Act 1999 if its requirements are met.

[270] As stated in *Lewis v Cotton* (2000) 3 I.T.E.L.R. 447 at [44].

[271] See para.6–201.

[272] See, e.g. *Re Walters* [2009] Ch. 212 at [36] per Mummery LJ (see para.6–188).

[273] [2009] Ch. 212 at [42] (see para.6–194).

[274] See too, e.g. *Birmingham v Renfrew* (1937) 57 C.L.R. 666; *Re Dale* [1994] Ch. 31.

[275] [2008] Ch. 395 at [27].

[276] [2009] Ch. 212 at [42] (see para.6–194).

[277] See, e.g. *Re Cleaver* [1981] 1 W.L.R. 939 at 947; *Re Basham* [1986] 1 W.L.R. 1498 at 1504; *Gillett v Holt* [2001] Ch. 210 at 228; *Birmingham v Renfrew* (1937) 57 C.L.R. 666 at 680.

[278] *Re Hagger* [1930] 2 Ch. 190.

[279] *Dufour v Pereira* (1769) 1 Dick. 419 at 421; *Stone v Hoskins* [1905] P. 194 at 197; *Re Hagger* [1930] 2 Ch. 190.

[280] See, e.g. *Re Goodchild* [1996] 1 W.L.R. 694 at 702 (affirmed [1997] 1 W.L.R. 1216), drawing on *Birmingham v Renfrew* (1937) 57 C.L.R. 666 at 689.

[281] [2009] Ch. 212 at [43]–[44] (see paras 6–195 to 6–196).

circumstances", and are far from intractable, with an application to court always available in the event of disagreement.

I. Justifying the Doctrine of Mutual Wills

In *Re Cleaver*, Nourse J said that cases on mutual wills are: **6–207**

> only one example of a wider category of cases, for example secret trusts, in which a court of equity will intervene to impose a constructive trust. . . The principle of all these cases is that a court of equity will not permit a person to whom property is transferred by way of gift, but on the faith of a clear understanding that it is to be dealt with in a partiuclar way for the benefit of a third person, to deal with that property inconsistently with that agreement or understanding. If he attempts to do so after having received the benefit of the gift equity will intervene by imposing a constructive trust on the property which is the subject matter of the agreement or understanding.

That analysis has been echoed in a number of other decisions.[282] It is certainly important to **6–208** note, when attempting to justify a trust arising under the doctrine of mutual wills, that the trust is constructive:[283] it does not arise in response to the deceased's successful exercise of a power to set up a trust, but is imposed by law to prevent a particular form of unconscionable conduct by the survivor. This is clear, for example, from the fact that, whilst the parties' agreement may simply be that B should acquire absolute title to property on the death of the survivor, the doctrine instead recognises that a trust arises in B's favour on the death of the first testator.

Besides Nourse J's analysis, there is also some academic support for the idea that the doctrine of **6–209** mutual wills has the same basis as that of secret trusts.[284] Care is needed, however. The doctrines seem to have different requirements, as well as a different scope. As noted above,[285] the requirement of a binding contract may explain why mutual wills, unlike secret trusts, can affect not only property acquired by the survivor under the will of the first testator, but also any other property that the survivor promised to bequeath in a particular way. Whereas the analysis of Nourse J assumes that mutual wills, like secret trusts, affect only property *transferred* to the defendant subject to an agreement, the mutual wills doctrine is in fact broader, and can affect property independently held by the defendant.[286]

The more limited scope of secret trusts means that, in considering that doctrine, it is possible to **6–210** suggest a justification which looks to the need to prevent the defendant from taking the benefit of property where that property was acquired subject to a promise to use it for the benefit of another person: it would be unconscionable for the defendant to keep the property and break the promise subject to which it was acquired. The mutual wills doctrine, however, can apply in the absence of any such receipt by the survivor, and so it seems that we cannot base a justification on the prospect of an unjust benefit to the survivor. Further, although a contract is required, basic contract law[287] cannot

---

282 See, e.g. *Re Basham* [1986] 1 W.L.R. 1498 at 1504; *Gillett v Holt* [2001] Ch. 210 at 228; *de Bruyne v de Bruyne* [2010] EWCA Civ 519 at [51].

283 In addition to the cases cited at fn.282, the characterisation of the trust as constructive has also been accepted in, e.g. *Charles v Fraser* [2010] EWHC 2154 (Ch); [2010] W.T.L.R. 1489 at [59] and *Shovelar v Lane* [2011] EWCA Civ 802; [2012] 1 W.L.R. 637 at [37].

284 See, e.g. S. Gardner, "Reliance-Based Constructive Trusts" in C. Mitchell (ed.), *Constructive and Resulting Trusts* (2010), p.75.

285 See para.6–198.

286 As apparent from *Re Dale* [1994] Ch. 31.

287 Those basic rules have now been supplemented by the Contract (Rights of Third Parties) Act 1999, but of course the doctrine long predated the Act and, in any case, there are differences between the operation of a contractual claim (or a claim under the 1999 Act) and the doctrine of mutual wills: see para.6–201.

provide the justification for mutual wills because, of course, the beneficiary of the trust is not the other contracting party (the first testator), but a third party to whom the survivor promised to leave the property.

6–211 It may therefore be necessary to look not only to the parties' agreement, but also to the reliance on it by the deceased, who honoured that agreement by making the agreed bequest.[288] That reliance is certainly required for the doctrine to operate. The question then is why equity responds to the prospect of the deceased suffering a detriment through such reliance by enforcing the survivor's promise in favour of the beneficiary, rather than, for example, by giving a remedy to the estate of the deceased. Certainly, as we saw in Chapter 3,[289] the doctrine of proprietary estoppel may be seen as concerned with avoiding the prospect of detriment arising through reliance, and it gives a claim to the party who has relied, and often limits the right arising by considering the extent of such detriment: there is no guarantee that the defendant's promise will be enforced. In the context of mutual wills, however, the definitive nature of the deceased's reliance means that she has irrevocably lost the opportunity to make a different testamentary disposition of her own estate and so the general principle suggested by Simon Gardner seems apposite:[290] the deceased has suffered a "loss of opportunity" and "if the law is to correct this loss, it must in fact require [the survivor] to hold the property in question on a constructive trust along the lines of his undertaking". The enforcement of the parties' agreement is also justified by the fact that, in contrast to proprietary estoppel, the doctrine of mutual wills requires a contract between the deceased and the survivor.[291] Once the contract and the deceased's reliance on it provides a justification for the survivor's being under a duty to honour the agreement, a trust necessarily arises, as the duty of the survivor relates to specific property held by the survivor, and involves a basic duty not to use that property for her own benefit.[292]

Questions

1. T1 and T2 hold shares on trust for X. What formalities are required in the following situations?
   (a) X assigns her equitable interest to Y;
   (b) X directs T1 and T2 to hold the shares on trust for Y;
   (c) X directs T1 and T2 to transfer the shares to T3 and T4 to hold on trust for Y;
   (d) X contracts with Y to transfer her equitable interest to him;
   (e) X declares herself a trustee of her interest for Y; and
   (f) X directs T1 and T2 that they henceforth have power to appoint the property to such of Y, Y's spouse and issue as they may see fit. A month later T1 and T2 declare that they therefore hold the property on trust for Y for life, remainder to his children equally.

---

[288] See e.g. Y.K. Liew, "The Ambit of the Mutual Wills Doctrine" (2016) 132 L.Q.R. 664 and Y.K. Liew, "Explaining the Mutual Wills Doctrine" in B. Häcker and C. Mitchell (eds), *Current Issues in Succession Law* (Hart Publishing, 2016), adopting a reliance-based analysis in order to explain those mutual wills cases which catch property held by the defendant prior to the making of the mutual wills.

[289] See paras 3–003 to 3–033.

[290] S. Gardner, "Reliance-Based Constructive Trusts" in C. Mitchell (ed.), *Constructive and Resulting Trusts* (2010), p.79. Gardner argues there that one general principle, concerned with enforcing detrimentally-relied on agreements, underpins a broad range of constructive trusts. It is however possible to accept the principle in the particular context of mutual wills, but not in relation to all the forms of constructive trust where Gardner suggests it applies. For the difficulties of applying this principle to certain cases of such trusts, see para.17–109.

[291] This suggests that, as noted by Robert Walker LJ in *Gillett v Holt* [2001] Ch. 210 at 228, it would be a mistake to go "too far in seeking a parallel between those principles [of mutual wills] and those of proprietary estoppel".

[292] See further B. McFarlane, "The Centrality of Constructive and Resulting Trusts" in C. Mitchell (ed.), *Constructive and Resulting Trusts* (2010).

2. Two years ago Brian transferred his cottage to Tom, orally telling Tom to hold it for Brian for life and then for Clarissa absolutely. He also transferred 10,000 ICI Plc shares, 8,000 Hanson Plc shares and 6,000 British Gas shares to his sister, Susan, orally telling her to hold them for himself or for such of their relatives as she might select. He soon told her to hold the ICI shares for Clarissa absolutely. Susan complied but said that she was now going to hold the Hanson shares for her cousin, Joy. Brian then told her to transfer the British Gas shares to Tom, who had already orally agreed to hold them on the same trusts as he held the cottage. Susan did so transfer the shares. A year ago Brian had a row with Clarissa and so told Tom: "Hold the cottage and the shares for me absolutely until I decide what to do about them." Last month he wrote a letter to Tom: "When I die I want you to transfer the cottage and the shares to Joy." A fortnight ago Brian died, having, by will, left everything to Eric.

   Advise Eric.

3. Is this a sound approach to gifts by will where secret trusts or mutual wills may be involved?
   (a) Consider if there appears to be: (i) incorporation by reference; (ii) a half-secret trust; (iii) a fully secret trust; or (iv) mutual wills.
   (b) If (i) ask whether the will refers to an ascertainable already existing document or attempts to incorporate a future document or an assortment of present and future documents.
   (c) If (ii) ask whether the terms of the obligation were communicated before or after the will and, if before, ask if they were communicated in accordance with the will, to a person who accepted them.
   (d) If (iii) ask whether there was an intention outside of the will to create a binding obligation, and whether the terms of the obligation were communicated in the testator's lifetime to a person who accepted the obligation.
   (e) If (iv) ask whether the parties accepted that the survivor would be legally obliged to carry out the arrangements.

4. In 2006 Alan made his will as follows: "Whatever I die possessed of I give to my wife Brenda." The will was witnessed by two of Alan's daughters, Diana and Edwina. Shortly afterwards, Alan asked Brenda if she would hold half the property she received under his will for their three daughters, Diana, Edwina and Freda equally. Brenda assented to this. In 2010 Freda ran away with a merchant seaman, Wayne. As a result Alan told Brenda to keep Freda's share for herself. A year ago Diana died, childless, and a week later Alan died after a long illness.

   How should his £150,000 estate be distributed? Would it make any difference if Brenda disclaimed all benefits due to pass to her under the will and relied, instead, upon her rights under the intestacy rules?

7

THE THREE CERTAINTIES

1. Introduction

An express trust can exist only if the trust property[1] is held by the trustee (i.e. the trust must be completely constituted),[2] any requisite formalities have been complied with,[3] and the "three certainties" are present: certainty of intention to create a trust; certainty of subject matter of the trust; and certainty of objects. As David Richards LJ stated in *North v Wilkinson*:[4] **7–001**

> The creation of a trust has significant, and generally irreversible, consequences. The settlor, by creating the trust, ceases to be entitled to the benefit of the property subject to the trust. If, as in the present case, he continues to hold the legal title to the property, he holds it, to the extent of the interest created by the trust, for the benefit of the beneficiaries of the trust and becomes subject to exacting fiduciary duties owed to the beneficiaries in relation to the trust property. The law therefore requires certainty on three crucial elements: the intended beneficiaries, the property to be subject to the trust and the intention of the settlor to create the trust. These elements must be established objectively by reference to the documents, words or conduct relied on as creating the trust. Statements as to the settlor's intention made subsequently are irrelevant. There is a parallel with the approach adopted to determine whether a contract has been made.

The three certainties are required to ensure that trustees hold specific property in respect of which they owe duties to beneficiaries which are capable of being enforced in practice by the courts. The existence of such duties is crucial to the existence of trusts. As Millett LJ stated in *Armitage v Nurse*:[5] **7–002**

> there is an irreducible core of obligations owed by the trustees to the beneficiaries and enforceable by them which is fundamental to the concept of a trust. If the beneficiaries have no rights enforceable against the trustees there are no trusts.

Certainty of subject matter and of objects are requirements of *all* trusts. If, for example, B claims that she has a beneficial interest under a constructive or resulting trust, then she needs to show that the defendant holds specific property subject to a duty to B. Certainty of intention, however, is a requirement only where a settlor exercises her power to set up a trust. Hence it does not apply to trusts imposed by law. In cases of the latter sort, the defendant still holds specific property subject to **7–003**

---

1 As discussed at paras 4–029 to 4–033, the "property" held on trust consists of the specific rights (in the sense of legal entitlements) held on trust.
2 See Chapter 5.
3 See Chapter 6.
4 [2018] EWCA Civ 161; [2018] 4 W.L.R. 41 at [2].
5 [1998] Ch. 241 at 253.

a duty to B, but that duty arises for some other reason, not because of the settlor's successful creation of an express trust.

7–004 There is a further difference between certainty of intention on the one hand and certainty of subject matter and of objects on the other. In the former case, we are concerned with the simple question of whether or not the settlor intended to create a trust. In relation to certainty of subject matter and of objects, however, we are not simply seeking a "Yes" or "No" answer when considering the acts of the settlor: we must ask, rather, what property was meant to be subject to the trust, and which people were meant to benefit (or not meant to benefit) from its performance? Whilst certainty of intention can be seen as relating to the preliminary question of whether the supposed trustee is under a duty *at all*, certainty of subject matter requires us to find specific property to which that duty relates, and certainty of objects requires us to be able to identify the content of that duty.

2. Certainty of Intention

7–005 An express trust can arise only if it can be shown that the settlor (S) intended to create a trust, either by transferring property to trustees to hold on trust,[6] or by declaring themselves to be the trustee of property that she owns.[7] Certainty of intention is required because the key event that gives rise to the trust is the settlor's exercise of a power to set up the trust. S can successfully self-declare a trust for B without B having any knowledge that S has exercised S's power to do so.[8]

7–006 As we saw in Chapter 4,[9] where a trust has been constituted by S having transferred property to T to hold on trust for B, T must consent to her role as trustee. If T, having received the property from S, refuses to act as trustee, or if S sets up a testamentary trust whereby T is to hold on trust for B, and T refuses to accept the property from S's personal representatives, then, if necessary,[10] a new trustee will be found,[11] and the property will be vested in that new trustee: "equity never allows a trust to fail for want of a trustee."[12] After receiving property from S, and before transferring it to the new trustee, S's chosen but reluctant T will not be free to use the property for their own benefit, and rather holds it on terms requiring them to transfer title to the new trustee: to that extent B can be said to have a beneficial interest without T necessarily having consented to act as trustee.[13] In the vast majority of cases, however, the trustees receive the property having previously agreed with the settlor that they will be trustees, and the beneficiaries know that they will be beneficiaries.

---

6 See paras 5–003 to 5–004.

7 See para.5–005.

8 See, e.g. *Fletcher v Fletcher* (1844) 4 Hare 67; *Re Lewis* [1904] 2 Ch. 656; *Rose v Rose* (1986) 7 N.S.W.L.R. 679 at 686; *Re Kayford* [1975] 1 W.L.R. 279. Indeed, there may be no beneficiaries for a period while income is being accumulated and the ultimate contingent beneficiary may not be born or otherwise ascertained for some time, especially for jurisdictions other than England where the accumulation period can be as long as the perpetuity period. Note however that it is possible for B to disclaim B's interest under the trust: see paras 4–027 to 4–028.

9 See paras 4–023 to 4–026.

10 Where B is the sole beneficiary and absolutely entitled under the trust, and is also adult and of sound mind, they will be able to exercise the *Saunders v Vautier* (1841) 4 Beav. 115 power to terminate the trust: see para.12–064ff) and so an order for the transfer of the property itself to B may well be appropriate.

11 Note that under Trustee Act 1925 s.36, S's personal representative will hold the property on trust for B, but with a power to appoint new trustees.

12 *Bisrat v Kebede* [2015] EWHC 840 (Ch) at [30]. See too, e.g. *Re Robinson* [1892] 1 Ch. 95 at 100: "If the gift is good in other respects the Court will take care that it shall not fail for want of a trustee." See too, e.g. *Mallott v Wilson* [1903] 2 Ch. 494; *Harris v Sharp* [2003] W.T.L.R. 1541; *Kynnersley v Wolverhampton City Council* [2008] W.T.L.R. 65.

13 *Fletcher v Fletcher* (1844) 4 Hare 67; *Childers v Childers* (1857) 1 De G. & J. 482.

A. The Test

S's intention to create a trust cannot, by itself, have that effect. Rather, an express trust arises where S has exercised her power to create a trust, and that requires not only intention, but also some external communication of that intention. It is important to note that, as in other parts of the law where rights can arise as a result on one party's exercise of a power to create such rights, S's intention must be judged objectively. 7–007

Byrnes v Kendle

High Court of Australia (2011) 243 C.L.R. 253

Kendle held legal title to a property but had signed an acknowledgment of trust in 1997 declaring that he held a half share of the interest in the property on trust for Byrnes, his estranged wife. It was now claimed that Kendle had committed breaches of his duties as trustee, by letting the house out to his son for five years for only a nominal rent. That claim was allowed by the High Court of Australia. One of the arguments made by Kendle in attempting to resist the claim was that he was not in fact a trustee as, although he had signed the acknowledgement of trust, he did not in fact have the required intention to create a trust of the property. That argument was rejected by all of the judges in the High Court decision. This extract reproduces the reasons for doing so given by Heydon and Crennan JJ., in a joint judgment. 7–008

HEYDON AND CRENNAN JJ.: In this court [Kendle] submitted that it was necesssary for [Byrnes] to establish a subjective intention by [Kendle] to create a trust. . . This submission is incorrect. The trial judge's estimate of [Kendle's] evidence about subjective intention, and the evidence itself, was irrelevant. The submission rests on a fundamental but very common misconception. . . 7–009

The authorities establish that in relation to trusts, as in relation to contracts, the search for "intention" is only a search for the intention as revealed in the words the parties, used, amplified by facts known to both parties. Thus in 1881 Sir George Jessel M.R. said:[14] 7–010

> "The settlement is one which I cannot help thinking was never intended by the framer of it to have the effect I am going to attribute to it; but, of course, as I very often say, one must consider the meaning of the words used, not what one may guess was the intention of the parties."

In 1934 Lord Wright said, speaking of a failed attempt to settle property on trust:[15] 7–011

> "the court, while it seeks to give effect to the intention of the parties, must give effect to that intention as expressed, that is, it must ascertain the meaning of the words actually used. There is often an ambiguity in the use of the word 'intention' in cases of this character. The word is constantly used as meaning motive, purpose, desire, as a state of mind, and not as meaning intention as expressed. The words actually used must no doubt be construed with reference to the facts known to the parties and in contemplation of which the parties must be deemed to have used them . . . But allowing for these and other rules of the same kind, the principle of the common law has been to adopt an objective standard of construction and to exclude general evidence of actual intention of the parties; the reason for this has been that otherwise all certainty would be taken from the words in which the parties have recorded their agreement or their dispositions of property."

Neither in England nor in Australia has the application of the principles for establishing and defining a trust been analysed with the sophistication devoted in England to their application in contract. However, in both English and Australia law the surrounding circumstances are material to the questions whether the words used created a trust and what its terms are. Accordingly, Conaglen was correct to say: 7–012

> "The court's focus when construing the terms of [a] bilateral arrangement [creating a trust] is on the objective meaning that those terms would convey to a reasonable person, just as it is when construing contractual arrangements."

---

14 *Smith v Lucas* (1881) 18 Ch. D. 531 at 542.
15 *Commissioners of Inland Revenue v Raphael* [1935] A.C. 96 at 142–143.

> The question is what the settlor or settlors did, not what they intended to do.
>
> 7–013 That truth tends to be obscured by constant repetition of the need to search for an "intention to create a trust". That search can be seen as concerning the first of the three "certainties" . . . But the "intention" referred to is an intention to be extracted from the words used, not a subjective intention which may have existed but which cannot be extracted from those words. This is as true of unilateral declarations of alleged trust as it is of bilateral covenants to create an alleged trust. It is as true of alleged trusts which are not wholly in writing as it is of alleged trusts which are wholly in writing. In relation to alleged trusts which are not wholly in writing, the need to draw inferences from circumstances in construing the terms of conversations may in practice widen the extent of the inquiry, but it does not alter its nature.
>
> 7–014 As with contracts, subjective intention is only relevant in relation to trusts when the transaction is open to some challenge or some application for modification[16] . . . But subjective intention is irrelevant both to the question of whether a trust exists and to the question of what its terms are.

B. Applying the Test in Practice

i. A General Donative Intention is Insufficient

7–015 No technical expressions or particular formulae are needed to create a trust: the circumstances must show however that the person holding the relevant property is intended to be subject to a legally binding *duty* to hold that property for others (or for herself and others). As Jessel MR said in *Richards v Delbridge*, when considering the rules applying to a self-declaration of trust:[17]

> It is true that [the settlor] need not use the words "I declare myself trustee", but he must do something which is equivalent to it, and use expressions which have that meaning; for, however anxious the Court may be to carry out a man's intention, it is not at liberty to construe words otherwise than according to their proper meaning . . . The cases in which the question has arisen are nearly all cases in which a man, by documents insufficient to pass a legal interest, has said "I give or grant certain property to B." . . . The true distinction appears to me to be plain, and beyond dispute: for a man to make himself a trustee there must be an expression of intention to become a trustee, whereas words of present gift show an intention to give property over to another, and not retain it in the donor's own hands for any purpose, fiduciary or otherwise.

7–016 As Jessel MR went on to note,[18] this approach accords with the principle in *Milroy v Lord*,[19] which was discussed in Chapter 5:[20] if S attempts to set up a trust for B by means of a transfer to trustees to hold for B, but that attempt fails, as the property remains with S, a court cannot then use S's undoubted general intention to benefit B as the basis on which to find a declaration of trust by S, as clearly S did *not* intend to hold the property herself on trust for B. If a declaration is to be found in such a case, there must be some additional evidence, such as some statement by S that justifies a court in finding that S exercised the power to bind the property in her own hands;[21] although where S clearly intended some form of gift to B, it has been suggested that it may be possible for a court, in some cases at least, to

---

16 [Three of the examples given of such a challenge or application were "an equitable challenge for mistake" (see para.7–071); an "allegation of 'sham'" (see paras 7–059ff); and a "claim for rectification" (see para.7–072).]

17 (1874) L.R. 18 Eq. 11 at 14, reaffirmed in *Clarence House Ltd v National Westminster Bank Plc* [2009] EWCA Civ 1311; [2010] 1 W.L.R. 1216 at [43] per Ward LJ. Note too the close analogy, discussed at paras 3–211 to 3–218 with the requirement of intention as applied to an equitable assignment of a legal chose in action.

18 (1874) L.R. 18 Eq. 11 at 15.

19 (1862) 4 De G.F. & J. 264.

20 See paras 5–006 to 5–011.

21 As was found to be the case in, e.g. *Re Ralli's W.T.* [1964] Ch. 288 and *T Choithram International SA v Pagarani* [2001] 1 W.L.R. 1: see paras 5–020 and 5–012 to 5–022.

look at the words used by S and, "by a benevolent construction . . . tease out" an implied declaration of trust.[22]

Besides the cases referred to by Jessel MR, where S has said "I give or grant certain property to B", there may also be cases, particularly in a domestic context, where legal title to property is vested in one party only (S), but there is some evidence that the property was treated, in practice, as held for the benefit of that party and another (B). Where the property involved is land, s.53(1)(b) of the Law of Property Act 1925 means that B can prove any such declaration of trust only by means of signed writing, and in the absence of such writing, B may then have to resort to a constructive or resulting trust in order to claim a beneficial interest.[23] In relation to property other than land, no such formality requirement applies. The question in such cases is simply whether any statement of S can be found which, when interpreted against the relevant facts (which include the nature of the parties' relationship), shows an objective intention that S should hold the property subject to a legal duty not to use it wholly for S's own benefit, but to use it for B's benefit too. The next extract provides an example of how that question may be resolved in practice. 7–017

Paul v Constance

Court of Appeal [1977] 1 W.L.R. 527

SCARMAN L.J. (with whom BRIDGE and CAIRNS L.J. agreed): Mr Dennis Albert Constance was a wage earner living in Cheltenham until he died on March 9, 1974. He was married to Bridget Frances Constance, the defendant in this action. But they parted in June 1965. In 1967 Mr Constance met Mrs Doreen Grace Paul, who is the plaintiff in this action. The two of them set up house together in December of that year, and they lived to all appearances as man and wife up to the date of Mr Constance's death. The house in which they lived was the property of the plaintiff. 7–018

In August 1969 Mr Constance was injured at his work. He claimed damages against his employers . . . his claim was disposed of by the payment to him of a sum of £950. This money he received by cheque early in 1973. He discussed with the plaintiff what to do with the money, and the evidence is clear that they decided it was to go into a bank account. The two of them went to see the manager of the St George's Square branch of Lloyds Bank in Cheltenham, and there they had a discussion about opening a bank account. According to the notes of evidence which the trial judge made, the two of them had a discussion with the bank manager. He explained to them the different sorts of accounts which they could open, and the decision was taken to open a deposit account. At that stage Mr Constance revealed that they were not married. It is perhaps of some significance in understanding this interview if one recalls the evidence that was given by a Mr Thomas, a fellow employee of Mr Constance's, who said that he knew that they were not married but most people did not. After Mr Constance had told the manager that they were not married the manager said: "Well, it will be in your name only then?" Mr Constance said: "Yes." Then Mr Constance asked the manager what was to happen if the plaintiff wanted to draw on the account, or if he wanted the plaintiff to draw on it, and the manager said that that could be done if she used a note with Mr Constance's signature on it authorising her to draw on the account. 7–019

The account that was opened on that day in February 1973 is at the very heart of this case. The account was maintained in Mr Constance's name from that date until the date of his death. Over the period between 1973 and his death, some 13 months later in 1974, further sums were paid into the account including, in particular, some sums which represented "bingo" winnings. It is clear from the evidence that Mr Constance and the plaintiff did play "bingo", and they played it really as a joint venture. They did have winnings from time to time, and at any rate three of such winnings—none of them very great—were 7–020

---

[22] *Curtis v Pulbrook* [2011] EWHC 167 (Ch); [2011] 1 B.C.L.C. 638 at [43], per Briggs J, applying *Pennington v Waine* [2002] EWCA Civ 227; [2002] 1 W.L.R. 2075. It is worth noting, however, that in *T Choithram International SA v Pagarani* [2001] 1 W.L.R. 1 at 11, per Lord Browne-Wilkinson, citing *Milroy v Lord* (1862) 4 De G.F. & J. 264, specifically said that "the court will not give a benevolent construction so as to treat ineffective words of outright gift as taking effect as if the donor had declared himself a trustee for the donee: see para.5–015.

[23] See paras 6–027 to 6–050.

paid into the account. It is clear from the plaintiff's evidence that they thought of those winnings as "their winnings": neither hers nor his alone, but theirs. Nevertheless, when the account was closed on the death of Mr Constance the ultimate balance, after the addition of interest, consisted largely of the initial sum of £950 representing Mr Constance's damages as a result of his injury at work. There was one withdrawal during this period, a sum of £150, and the evidence was that that money was divided between the two of them after part of it had been used for buying Christmas presents and some food.

7–021 The plaintiff began her action after the death of Mr Constance against his lawful wife, the defendant, who took out letters of administration for his estate since he died intestate. The plaintiff claims that the bank account in his name, to which I have referred, was held by him on trust for the benefit of himself and the plaintiff jointly. She claims that it was an express trust declared orally by him on numerous occasions. The defendant maintains that the whole fund contained in the account was the beneficial property of the deceased at the time of his death, and, as such, became part of his estate after death.

7–022 The matter came on for trial and on August 12 the Judge found in favour of the plaintiff. He found the existence of an express trust, a trust for the benefit of the plaintiff and the deceased jointly, and he ordered that the sum of £499.21 be paid to the plaintiff as representing one half share of the fund to which she was beneficially entitled.

7–023 The only point taken by the defendant on her appeal to this court goes to the question whether or not there was, in the circumstances of this case, an express declaration of trust.

7–024 Counsel for the defendant drew the attention of the court to the so-called three certainties that have to be established before the court can infer the creation of a trust. We are concerned only with one of the three certainties, and it is this:[24]

> "The words [that is the words of the declaration relied on] must be so used that on the whole they ought to be construed as imperative. [A little later on the learned author says:] No particular form of expression is necessary for the creation of a trust, if on the whole it can be gathered that a trust was intended. A trust may well be created, although there may be an absence of any expression in terms imposing confidence. A trust may thus be created without using the word 'trust' for what the court regards is the substance and effect of the words used."

7–025 Counsel for the defendant has taken the court through the detailed evidence and submits that one cannot find anywhere in the history of events a declaration of trust in the sense of finding the deceased man, Mr Constance, saying: "I am now disposing of my interest in this fund so that you, Mrs Paul, now have a beneficial interest in it." Of course, the words which I have just used are stilted lawyers' language, and counsel for the plaintiff was right to remind the court that we are dealing with simple people, unaware of the subtleties of equity, but understanding very well indeed their own domestic situation. It is right that one should consider the various things that were said and done by the plaintiff and Mr Constance during their time together against their own background and in their own circumstances.

7–026 Counsel for the defendant drew our attention to two cases [*Jones v Lock*[25] and *Richards v Delbridge*[26]], and he relies on them as showing that, though a man may say in clear and unmistakable terms that he intends to make a gift to some other person, for instance his child or some other member of his family, yet that does not necessarily disclose a declaration of trust; and, indeed, in the two cases to which we have been referred the court held that, though there was a plain intention to make a gift, it was not right to infer any intention to create a trust. . .

7–027 There is no suggestion of a gift by transfer in this case. The facts of those cases do not, therefore, very much help the submission of counsel for the defendant, but he was able to extract from them this principle: that there must be a clear declaration of trust, and that means there must be clear evidence from what is said or done of an intention to create a trust, or as counsel for the defendant put it, "an intention to dispose of a property or a fund so that somebody else to the exclusion of the disponent acquires the beneficial interest in it." He submitted that there was no such evidence.

7–028 When one looks to the detailed evidence to see whether it goes as far as that—and I think that the evidence does have to go as far as that—one finds that from the time that Mr Constance received his damages

---

24 *Snell's Equity*, 27th edn, p.111.
25 (1865) 1 Ch. App. 25.
26 (1874) L.R. 18 Eq. 11.

right up to his death he was saying, on occasions, that the money was as much the plaintiff's as his. When they discussed the damages, how to invest them or what to do with them, when they discussed the bank account, he would say to her: "The money is as much yours as mine." The judge, rightly treating the basic problem in the case as a question of fact, reached this conclusion. He said:

> "I have read through my notes, and I am quite satisfied that it was the intention of [the plaintiff] and Mr Constance to create a trust in which both of them were interested."

In this court the issue becomes: was there sufficient evidence to justify the judge reaching that conclusion of fact? In submitting that there was, counsel for the plaintiff draws attention first and foremost to the words used. When one bears in mind the unsophisticated character of Mr Constance and his relationship with the plaintiff during the last few years of his life, counsel for the plaintiff submits that the words that he did use on more than one occasion namely: "This money is as much yours as mine", convey clearly a present declaration that the existing fund was as much the plaintiff's as his own. The judge accepted that conclusion. I think he was well justified in doing so and, indeed, I think he was right to do so. There are, as counsel for the plaintiff reminded us, other features in the history of the relationship between the plaintiff and Mr Constance which support the interpretation of those words as an express declaration of trust. I have already described the interview with the bank manager when the account was opened. I have mentioned also the putting of the "bingo" winnings into the account, and the one withdrawal for the benefit of both of them. **7–029**

The question, therefore, is whether in all the circumstances the use of those words on numerous occasions as between Mr. Constance and the plaintiff constituted an express declaration of trust. The judge found that they did. For myself, I think he was right so to find. I therefore would dismiss the appeal. **7–030**

A question that went unaddressed by the court in *Paul v Constance* was as to the precise terms of the trust declared by Constance (S).[27] If the initial trust was such that S was holding on trust for himself and Paul (B) as joint tenants, and this beneficial joint tenancy was not severed before S's death then, on S's death, B would become solely entitled to the beneficial interest, and so could have claimed the full sum credited to the bank account. It seems to have instead been assumed that the initial trust involved S holding on trust for himself and B as beneficial tenants in common, each with an individual (but undivided) half share of the beneficial interest, so that on S's death, and in the absence of a will by S, his 50% share passed under the intestacy rules. **7–031**

The answer to this question as to the terms of the initial trust must also depend on S's objective intention, but of course, particularly where the parties are not alive to the technicalities, there is unlikely to be any clear intention on this point. **7–032**

To the extent that a default answer is necessary, it is probably right to say that, consistently with the result in *Paul v Constance*,[28] a tenancy in common should be preferred as it ensures that each party has an individual interest that can be passed on her death,[29] and so avoids the "gamble of the tontine".[30] **7–033**

---

27 Note that this question has also been overlooked, even by the House of Lords and Supreme Court, in relation to the common intention constructive trust of land: see, e.g. A. Briggs (2012) 128 L.Q.R. 183, commenting on *Jones v Kernott* [2011] UKSC 53; [2012] 1 A.C. 776 and *Stack v Dowden* [2007] UKHL 17; [2007] 2 A.C. 432.

28 Consistently too with the approach applied to common intention constructive trusts where, as discussed at paras 17–187 to 17–192, a tenancy in common seems to be assumed as the default position if one party is not intended to have a greater share than the other.

29 A joint tenancy carries with it the doctrine of survivorship which has been described as "odious in equity" (*R. v Williams* (1735) Bunb. 342 at 343) owing to its effect that the surviving joint tenant is wholly entitled.

30 That is, the point that a joint tenancy, if not severed, means that the survivor takes all, whereas those who die earlier take nothing.

ii. An Intention to Impose a Legally Binding Duty is Necessary

7–034 A trust arises only when the trustee holds property subject to a legally binding duty and so an express trust can arise only where S's objective, expressed intention was that such a duty should arise.[31] This point is important if S transfers property to T expressing confidence, a wish, or a hope that T will use the property for the benefit of B. Such transfers are most likely to occur in a testamentary context. Originally, the courts were only too ready to treat such words as creating a trust,[32] but the following extract is from a case which signalled a change in approach.

Lambe v Eames

Court of Appeal in Chancery (1870–71) L.R. 6 Ch. App. 597

7–035 John Lambe left his entire estate, including a freehold, to his widow "to be at her disposal in any way she may think best for the benefit of herself and family." When the widow died, she left the freehold on trust for one of her daughters, Elizabeth Eames, but subject to an annual payment for Henry Lambe, an illegitimate son of one of Lambe's sons. Elizabeth refused to make the annual payment to Henry, arguing that, by the terms of John's will, the widow had received the freehold subject to a trust for the benefit of herself and family, and that Henry, as an illegitimate child, did not qualify as "family". Henry argued instead that John's will had made an absolute gift of the freehold to his widow.

7–036 JAMES L.J.: If this will had to be construed irrespective of any authority, the construction would, in my opinion, not be open to any reasonable doubt . . . [The] question is whether [the words "to be at her disposal in any way she may think best for the benefit of herself and family"] create any trust affecting the property; and in hearing case after case cited, I could not help feeling that the officious kindness of the Court of Chancery in interposing trusts where in many cases the father of the family never meant to create trusts, must have been a very cruel kindness indeed. I am satsifed that the testator in this case would have been shocked to think that any person caling himself a next friend could file a bill in this Court, and, under pretence of benefitting the children, have taken the administration of the estate from his wife. I am satisfied that no such trust was intended, and that it would be a violation of the clearest and plainest wishes of the testator if we decided otherwise. . .

7–037 It is possible that in this case there may be some obligation on the widow to do something for the benefit of the children; but assuming that there is such an obligation, it cannot be extended to mean a trust for the widow for her life, and after her death for the children, in such shares as she may think fit to direct . . . [And] if there be any such obligation, I think it has been fairly discharged by the way in which she has made her will—giving part for the benefit of one member of the family, and part to a natural son, whom she might reasonably think it her duty to benefit.

7–038 The "very cruel kindness" consisted of the courts' former willingness, in interpreting a provision such as that in John Lambe's will, to find that the widow held the property subject to a trust for the benefit of herself and her children: this would secure a benefit to the children, but would equally hamper the widow's ability to deal with the property. The point made by James LJ is that a testator, particularly one such as John Lambe who made his will "in the prime of life, with a wife and young children", might well prefer his widow to have complete freedom to deal with the property, and so to be able to react to unforeseen events, trusting that she would discharge any moral duties to provide for other family members but not imposing any legal limits on her dealings.

---

[31] See e.g. *Hilton v Cosnier* [2018] EWHC 2728 (Ch) at [27]: a statement of S's current intention that his grandchildren should receive a particular property in the future was not sufficient to create an immediate trust with those grandchildren as beneficiaries with a future interest, as there was no intention of S's imposing an immediate duty on himself to the grandchildren. Similarly, in *Yusuf v Yusuf* [2019] EWHC 90 (Ch), it was stated at [111] that there was no declaration of trust where the relevant document "does not demonstrate an intention to create a trust at the time it was signed, but only an intention to sign some future document or documents".

[32] *Eade v Eade* (1820) 5 Madd. 118 at 121; *Palmer v Simmonds* (1854) 2 Drew. 221; *Gutty v Cregoe* (1857) 24 Beav. 185.

Since the 1870s, the courts have therefore drawn an important distinction between words which express a hope or desire that T *will* act in a certain way[33] and words which impose a duty that T *must* act in a certain way. The former, by themselves, do not give rise to a trust;[34] although of course the question is always whether, viewed in context, the true expressed, objective intention of S was to impose a duty on T.[35] For example, in *Re Adams and Kensington Vestry*,[36] a testamentary transfer from a husband to his widow "in full confidence that she will do what is right as to the disposal thereof between [S's] children" did not manifest an intention to impose a legally binding duty on T and so did not give rise to not trust.[37] **7–039**

In the specific context of a testamentary transfer to a spouse, the Administration of Justice Act 1982 s.22, states that: **7–040**

> Except where a contrary intent is shown, it shall be presumed that if a testator devises or bequeaths property to his spouse in terms which in themselves would give an absolute interest to the spouse but by the same instrument purports to give his issue an interest in the same property, the gift to the spouse is absolute notwithstanding the purported gift to the issue.

So, for example, if a testator leaves "all my property to my wife and after her death to our children", the wife will take the property absolutely and is under no obligation to hold it on trust for the children.[38] **7–041**

An intention that the party holding property (T) should be under *some* duty to B does not necessarily give rise to a trust; for a trust to arise, the duty must relate specifically to the trust property, and must be such that T has a duty not to use the property for her own benefit, unless and to the extent that T too is a beneficiary of the trust. In *North v Wilkinson*,[39] for example, the Court of Appeal noted that the first instance judge had erred by failing to consider if the agreement between the parties could be given effect to by "a conclusion other than a trust, in particular a personal obligation".[40] In that case, the practical difficulties involved in having a trust in favour of B of a percentage of A's business, where A was a sole trader,[41] were not insurmountable in theory, but, as "no thought at all had been given"[42] **7–042**

---

33 Such words are sometimes referred to as "precatory", with "precatory words" then being words that do not, by themselves, create a trust: see, e.g. *Re Brace* [1954] 1 W.L.R. 955 at 958; *Re Freud (Deceased)* [2014] EWHC 2577 (Ch); [2014] W.T.L.R. 1453 at [43], [46]. However, the term "precatory" is not very helpful, as some cases also refer to "precatory trusts": e.g. *Re Steele's WT* [1948] Ch. 603 at 607–608.

34 See, e.g. *Mussoorie Bank Ltd v Raynor* (1882) 7 App. Cas. 321 (no trust where S in S's will gives property to T "feeling confident that she will act justly to our children in dividing the same when no longer required by her").

35 By the Administration of Justice Act 1982 s.21, extrinsic evidence, including evidence of the testator's intention, may be admitted to assist in its interpretation: (a) in so far as any part of the will is meaningless; (b) in so far as the language used in any part of it is ambiguous on the face of it; and (c) in so far as evidence, other than evidence of the testator's intention, shows that the language used in any part of it is ambiguous in the light of the surrounding circumstances.

36 (1884) 27 Ch.D. 394.

37 See too, e.g. *Re Diggles* (1888) 39 Ch.D. 253 (no trust where the will states: "it is my desire that she allows A.G. an annuity of £25 during her life) "; *Re Johnson* [1939] 2 All E.R. 458 (no trust where the will states that "I request that C on her death leave her property to my four sisters").

38 The statutory presumption contained in s.22 can be displaced. See, e.g. *Harrison v Gibson* [2005] EWHC 2957 (Ch); [2006] 1 W.L.R. 1212: the testator had expressed a sufficiently clear intention that his widow had a life interest in the relevant property which was held on trust for the children in equal shares.

39 [2018] EWCA Civ 161.

40 [2018] EWCA Civ 161 at [38]. The primary focus of the parties' agreement had been on B's receiving a shareholding in a future company, and it was noted at [41]–[42] that the rights of a shareholder (contractual and some statutory right against the company) are quite different from those of a beneficiary of a trust.

41 For those difficulties, see [2018] EWCA Civ 161 at [44]–[46]: e.g. what is the position in relation to liabilities arising from the business: should the existence of such liabilities reduce B's share of the assets of the business?

42 [2018] EWCA Civ 161 at [44] and [46].

to such difficulties by the parties, it was regarded as unlikely that the parties had in fact intended to create a trust, rather than imposing a merely personal duty on A to B.[43] Note too that, even if it is intended to give B an equitable interest in A's property, this does not necessarily mean a trust arises: if, for example, A is to be free of any duty in relation to the property if A meets a debt owed to B, then the arrangement gives B a security interest (an equitable charge) rather than an interest under a trust.[44]

iii. The Relevance of Segregation of the Alleged Trust Property

7-043 In ascertaining whether S's expressed objective intention was to set up a trust of particular property, one relevant factor may be how that property was to be treated by the supposed trustee, T. If there is nothing to indicate that T (or, in the event of a claimed self-declaration, S) was to treat the property as separate from her own, that will be, at least, a strong indication that no trust was intended. After all, a key feature of a trust is that the trustee is not free to use the property entirely for her own benefit. As Channell J put it in *Henry v Hammond*:[45]

> It is clear that if the terms upon which the person receives the money are that he is bound to keep it separate, either in a bank or elsewhere, and to hand that money so kept as a separate fund to the person entitled to it, then he is a trustee of that money and must hand it over to the person who is his [beneficiary]. If on the other hand he is not bound to keep the money separate, but is entitled to mix it with his own money and deal with it as he pleases, and when called upon to hand over an equivalent sum of money, then, in my opinion, he is not a trustee of the money, but merely a debtor.

7-044 This point may be important in determining the nature of an agency relationship. For example, consider a case where an agent (A) collects money from customers on behalf of her principal (P). If the arrangement between A and P is that A is free to pay that money into her own bank account, but must settle up with P on a monthly basis by paying an equivalent sum over to P, then A simply owes a debt to P (i.e. A must pay P a particular sum of money) and does not hold the money received from customers on trust for P. The situation is thus similar to that of a bank receiving payment from a third party on behalf of a customer: the bank must credit the sum to the customer's account, thus increasing the debt it owes to the customer, but the bank does not hold the specific payment received on trust for the customer.[46] In contrast, if the arrangement between A and P is, for example, that A must pay the money into a separate bank account, then it may be possible to find an intention that A was to hold that money on trust for P. In that case, A's duty is not simply a personal obligation to pay a sum of money to P; rather A holds *specific* rights (the chose in action constituted by the bank account) on trust for P. The difference between those two cases will of course be crucial if, for example, A goes into insolvency:[47] if P can identify money held by A on trust for P, P can simply claim that money; whereas if

---

43 See too e.g. *Re Lester* [1942] Ch. 324 (a bequest of shares to A "subject to the payment" of certain annuities did not create a trust but rather imposed a personal duty on A).

44 See, e.g. *Re Oliver* (1890) 62 L.T. 533.

45 *Henry v Hammond* [1913] 2 K.B. 515 at 521, per Channell J. See too, e.g. *R. v Clowes (No.2)* [1994] 2 All E.R. 316 at 325; *Commissioners of Customs & Excise v Richmond Theatre Management Ltd* [1995] S.T.C. 257.

46 See, e.g. *First City Monument Bank Plc v Zumax Nigeria Ltd* [2019] EWCA Civ 294 at [81]–[84], Lewison LJ.

47 See, e.g. *Bailey v Angove's Pty Ltd* [2016] UKSC 47; [2016] 1 W.L.R. 3179 (see too para.17–220) and *Azam v Iqbal* [2007] EWHC 2025 (Admin); [2008] Bus. L.R. 168.

A is a collecting agent, P is simply an unsecured creditor who will have to settle for receiving a proportion of the total sum due from A.

The distinction between an agent who owes a debt to P and an agent who instead holds funds received on trust is also crucial when considering if a statutory limitation period applies to an action by P to recover sums due from A. P's claim against a collecting agent is purely contractual, and so is barred six years from the date of A's breach of contract.[48] In contrast, if a trust exists, P's claim is "to recover from the trustee trust property" and no statutory limitation period applies.[49] That difference was in issue in *Nelson v Rye*,[50] a decision discussed by Millett LJ in the following extract from *Paragon Finance plc v DB Thakerar & Co*:[51] **7-045**

> In *Nelson v Rye* the plaintiff was a solo musician who appointed the defendant his manager on terms that he would collect the fees and royalties which were due to him and pay his expenses and account to him annually for his net income after deducting his own commission. When the relationship came to an end the plaintiff claimed an account, and the question was whether the account should be limited to the six years before the issue of the writ or whether it should extend over the whole period of the relationship. . . **7-046**
>
> . . . [The] defendant's liability to account for more than six years before the issue of the writ in *Nelson v Rye* depended on whether he was, not merely a fiduciary (for every agent owes fiduciary duties to his principal), but a trustee, that is to say, on whether he owed fiduciary duties in relation to the money. **7-047**
>
> Whether he was in fact a trustee of the money may be open to doubt. Unless I have misunderstood the facts or they were very unusual it would appear that the defendant was entitled to pay receipts into his own account, mix them with his own money, use them for his own cash flow, deduct his own commission, and account for the balance to the plaintiff only at the end of the year. It is fundamental to the existence of a trust that the trustee is bound to keep the trust property separate from his own and apply it exclusively for the benefit of the beneficiary. Any right on the part of the defendant to mix the money which he received with his own and use it for his own cash flow would be inconsistent with the existence of a trust. So would a liability to account annually, for a trustee is obliged to account to his beneficiary and pay over the trust property on demand. . . **7-048**
>
> Unless the defendant was a trustee of the money which he received, however, the claim for an account was barred after six years. . . Accordingly, in so far as it decided that the defendant was liable to account without limit of time even if the money was not trust money, *Nelson v Rye* was wrongly decided. **7-049**

The basic point is that a trust requires T to be under a duty in relation to specific property: a duty just to pay B a sum of money, where that money can come from any source, does not count as a trust. There is, therefore, an overlap with the requirement of certainty of subject matter, and we will see below that the courts, particularly in modern commercial contexts, have been willing to find a trust even where T has a broad power to use and mix the trust funds.[52] It should therefore be emphasised that the overarching question is one as to S's expressed and objectively understood intention. The mere fact that T is permitted to mix funds does not, by itself, prevent the finding of a trust. **7-050**

For example, the mingling of funds received from S1 and S2 will not be fatal to the finding of a trust where T receives such funds to make investments for the parties which are to be held separately from T's own assets: an investment, such as a block of securities, can be held by T on trust for S1 and S2 in **7-051**

---

48 Limitation Act 1980 s.5. The contractual limitation applies even if the claim is an action for an account, as s.23 stipulates that: "An action for an account shall not be brought after the expiration of any time limit under this Act which is applicable to the claim which is the basis of the duty to account."

49 Limitation Act 1980 s.21(1)(b).

50 [1996] 1 W.L.R. 1378.

51 [1999] 1 All E.R. 400 at 415–416.

52 See paras 7-082 to 7-086.

their proportionate shares.[53] Similarly, where T adds funds of S1 and S2 to funds of T's own, and then makes investments to be held separately from T's own assets, those investments can be held on trust for S1, S2 and T in proportionate shares.[54] If T were then to sell such investments and, without authority from S1 and S2, to pay the proceeds into T's own bank account, S1 and S2 would each then have a right to trace into T's bank account and claim a proportionate share of that right:[55] once a trust has been established, unauthorised mingling by T does not, by itself, terminate the trust.[56]

iv. The Distinction between a Duty and a Power

7-052 In answering the key question of whether S had an expressed, objective intention to impose on T the required duty in relation to the trust property, it is useful to bear in mind the distinction between a duty and a power.[57] The distinction can be somewhat tricky to apply in practice. There may be cases in which T clearly is a trustee, holding property subject to specific duties, and B is clearly a beneficiary of that trust, but T also has authority to use the trust property so as to benefit C. The question then is whether T has merely been given a *power* to act so as to benefit C, or whether instead the terms of the settlement impose a *duty* on T to act in that way: only in the latter case does C, as well as B, acquire a beneficial interest under the trust; only in the latter case will the court be required to execute the trust if T fails to act for C's benefit. As we will see below,[58] the distinction between a power and a duty is also crucial in determining which particular test is to be applied in determining if the parties benefitting from the exercise of the power or duty have been defined with sufficient certainty.

7-053 The conceptual distinction between a power and a duty is clear, although it is complicated slightly by the fact that S may have intended T to hold a power in a fiduciary capacity, so that T, whilst not bound to exercise the power in a particular way, does have particular duties *in relation to* the power, such as a duty to consider seriously and fairly whether to exercise it. The existence of such duties distinguishes a fiduciary power from a bare power: a bare power exists where T has no duty to consider seriously and fairly whether to exercise the power.

7-054 In practice, however, in the context of a specific settlement, there may be only a very fine line between interpreting a term that potentially benefits C as giving T a fiduciary power or as instead imposing a trust under which C, as well as B, has a beneficial interest. For example, consider the following two cases: (i) T holds funds on trust for B, but with a power to make distributions of interest to C, X, Y or Z; and (ii) T holds funds on a discretionary trust for B and C, but with a power to distribute a certain proportion of those funds to X, Y or Z. It may not always be simple in practice to determine which of those two interpretations best accords with S's expressed, objective intentions: as Lord Wilberforce put it in *Re Baden's Deed Trusts (No.1)*: "A layman and, I suspect, also a logician, would find it hard to understand what difference there is."[59]

7-055 There are of course further possibilities. For example, if S makes a testamentary disposition to trustees on trust to B for life, S may combine that with a bare power for B to appoint the capital among such of S and B's children as B may see fit. If, then, B dies and that power has not been exercised, the capital will be held on a resulting trust for S's estate, as S has not directed any other parties for

---

53 *R. v Clowes (No.2)* [1994] 2 All E.R. 316; *Re Goldcorp Exchange* Ltd [1995] 1 A.C. 74.
54 *Re Lewis's of Leicester Ltd* [1995] 1 B.C.L.C. 428.
55 See, e.g. *Foskett v McKeown* [2001] 1 A.C. 102.
56 For discussion of the rules of tracing, and of the limits of the ability of a beneficiary to assert a claim in relation to assets acquired through an unauthorised use of trust assets, see paras 15-023ff.
57 See e.g. paras 4-009 to 4-010.
58 See paras 7-124ff.
59 [1971] A.C. 424 at 448 (also known as *McPhail v Doulton*; extracted at paras 7-126 to 7-142).

whose benefit the trustees should hold the property if the power is not exercised.[60] A different result obtains, of course, if S instead intended that, in default of B exercising the power to appoint among the children, the property should then be held for the children in equal shares: in that case there is a fixed trust for all of the children, but the beneficial interest of each child is subject to B's exercising the power to appoint the property wholly to the other children.[61]

There may be a very fine line between cases in which the court is, and is not, willing to infer that S intended such a fixed trust in the event of B's not fully exercising the power to appoint.[62] One relevant factor will be the width of the class: whilst a trust for equal division between the objects of an unexercised power of appointment may be a practical solution if the objects are all members of a narrow class (e.g. S's children), such a trust would be very unlikely to reflect S's intention if the class were very broad (e.g. all S's employees, ex-employees and their relatives and dependants). As Lord Wilberforce noted in *Re Baden (No.1)* in considering that very class:[63] **7–056**

> Equal division is surely the last thing the settlor ever intended: equal division among all may, probably would, produce a result beneficial to none. Why suppose that the court would lend itself to a whimsical execution?. . . Equal division may be sensible and has been decreed, in cases of family trusts, for a limited class, here there is life in the maxim "equality is equity", but the cases provide numerous examples where this has not been so. . .

In relation to a broad class of objects, it is of course possible for S to set up a discretionary trust, so that T does have to distribute the trust property, but there is no duty to divide it equally amongst members of the class. The difference between a discretionary trust and a power of appointment is that, in the former, T has a *duty* to distribute. There is therefore an extremely fine line between the cases where: (i) T holds on a discretionary trust for X, Y and Z, but subject to the possible exercise of a power of appointment by T in favour of C; and (ii) T has a power to appoint to X, Y and Z, and T is to hold on trust for C if the power of appointment is not exercised. **7–057**

Further, in our example where S makes a testamentary disposition to trustees on trust to B for life, with a bare power for B to appoint the capital among such of S and B's children as B may see fit, it would also be possible for S to provide expressly that, if B does not exercise that power of **7–058**

[60] See, e.g. *Re Weekes's Settlement* [1897] 1 Ch. 289: a bequest to B, S's husband, was made with a "power to dispose of all such property by will amongst our children in accordance with the power granted to him as regards the other property which I have under my marriage settlements" with no express gift over in default of B's exercise of that power. Romer J refused to infer that S intended that, should B fail to exercise the power, the property should be divided equally between the children, stating at 292: "The authorities do not show, in my opinion, that there is a hard and fast rule that a gift to A for life with a power to A to appoint among a class and nothing more must, if there is no gift over in the will, be held a gift by implication to the class in default of the power being exercised." See too *Re Combe* [1925] 1 Ch. 210; *Re Poulton's WT* [1987] 1 All E.R. 1068.

[61] See, e.g. *Wilson v Duguid* (1883) 24 Ch.D. 244, where, in contrast to *Re Weekes's Settlement* [1897] 1 Ch. 289, it was found on the facts that an inference could be made that S had intended a gift to the children equally if B did not exercise the power of appointment. Similarly, each child has an immediate beneficial interest, but one which is liable to be divested by B's exercise of the power, if there is a bequest "to W for life, remainder to our children equally, but so that W may instead appoint the capital between our children in such shares as she may see fit": see, e.g. *Re Llewellyn's Settlement* [1921] 2 Ch. 281; *Re Arnold* [1947] Ch. 131.

[62] It is of course also possible for S, for example, to stipulate that, in default of the exercise of the power of appointment, the trustees will hold on a discretionary trust, with the children as objects of that trust: see para.7–058.

[63] [1971] A.C. 424 at 451 (also known as *McPhail v Doulton*). See further paras 7–144 to 7–145. Lord Wilberforce's comments were made when considering how a court would execute a discretionary trust for such a class, but his point is clearly relevant to the question of establishing the likely intentions of S in relation to such a class.

appointment, the trustees will then hold on discretionary trust for the children. It is however very difficult for a court to *infer* such an intention to create a discretionary trust in default. Consequently the basic choice, if no express provision is made for the case where B does not exercise the power of appointment, is between a resulting trust for S's estate[64] and a trust for equal division amongst S the children.[65] The court will have to decide which of those possibilities best reflects S's expressed, objective intention.

C. Shams

i. The Doctrine

7-059 As emphasised by Heydon and Crennan JJ in the passage from *Byrnes v Kendle* set out above,[66] the court's focus when determining if S has exercised her power to set up a trust is on S's expressed, objective intention. As Lord Wright had noted in *Commissioners of Inland Revenue v Raphael*,[67] one of the cases relied on in *Byrnes*:[68] "It must be remembered at the outset that the court, while it seeks to give effect to the intention of the parties, must give effect to that as expressed, that is, it must ascertain the meaning of the words actually used." In *Byrnes*, however, an "allegation of sham" was recognised as one of the situations in which subjective intention may be relevant, as "the transaction is open to some challenge".[69]

7-060 In *Midland Bank Plc v Wyatt*,[70] for example, Mr and Mrs Wyatt, beneficial owners of their family home, signed a trust deed which stated that Mr Wyatt now held his beneficial share on trust for Mrs Wyatt and his two daughters. Mr Wyatt relied on this deed when the bank attempted to enforce a charging order against his interest in the home: he argued that his debts could not be enforced against that property, as he held it on trust for his wife and daughter. In the usual case, the signed deed would of course be conclusive evidence that S had indeed exercised his power to set up a trust.[71] It was held by the judge, however, that "the trust deed was executed by [Mr Wyatt], not to be acted upon but to be put in the safe for a rainy day" and the judge stated that: "I do not believe Mr Wyatt had any intention when he executed the trust deed of endowing his children with the interest, which at that time was his only real asset."[72] The finding then was that Mr Wyatt had intended only to rely on the trust deed if it was necessary to protect his interest in the home from execution by a creditor; despite signing the deed, he had not in fact exercised his power to set up a trust. The deed was intended by

---

64 As was found in, e.g. *Re Weekes's Settlement* [1897] 1 Ch. 289.
65 As was found in, e.g. *Wilson v Duguid* (1883) 24 Ch.D. 244.
66 (2011) 243 C.L.R. 253 at [42], [50]–[62] (extracted at paras 7-008 to 7-014).
67 [1935] A.C. 96 at 142.
68 (2011) 243 C.L.R. 253 at [106] (extracted at para.7-011).
69 (2011) 243 C.L.R. 253 at [63]. Note that s.423 of the Insolvency Act 1986 (which deals with transactions defrauding creditors, whether those transactions take the form of a trust or not) can apply where S acts with a substantial purpose of putting assets beyond the reach of actual or future creditors, allowing a court to make an order restoring the property to S for the benefit of S's creditors. That provision may of course apply even if there was no sham, and a trust was set up by S. Similarly, s.37 of the Matrimonial Causes Act 1973 gives the court a jurisdiction to set aside dispositions made with the intention of defeating a spouse's claim to ancillary relief.
70 [1995] 1 F.L.R. 697.
71 See, e.g. *National Westminster Bank Plc v Jones* [2001] 1 B.C.L.C. 98 at [59] per Neuberger J: "there is a very strong presumption that parties intend to be bound by the provisions of agreements into which they enter, and, even more, intend the agreements they enter into to take effect."
72 [1995] 1 F.L.R. 696 at 707.

Mr Wyatt to mislead and Mrs Wyatt had been "recklessly indifferent"[73] to the possibility of its being used to mislead third parties such as Mr Wyatt's actual or future creditors. As a result, his interest in the home was subject to no trust, and so the bank could proceed to enforce their charging order over that interest. Whilst the term "sham trust" is sometimes used in reference to a case such as *Midland Bank Plc v Wyatt*, as Birss J pointed out in *JSC Mezhdunarodniy Promyshlenniy Bank v Pugachev*:[74] "Despite the frequent references to a 'sham trust', there is not really any such thing. What may or may not be a sham are the acts or documents which purport to set up the trust."

The sham doctrine may also apply to a document signed by S apparently setting up a trust by way of a transfer to T. In *Rahman v Chase Bank (CI) Trust Co Ltd*,[75] for example, Rahman purported to set up a trust, governed by Jersey law, where any capital remaining in the trust fund on an appointed day was to be divided between certain of his relatives. Until that point, both the trustees and Rahman had various powers in relation to the trust property, including a power to make appointments to Rahman. The court, looking at what had happened in practice after the date of the document, found that, to the extent that it suggested that Rahman had set up a trust for the benefit of others, the document was a sham: in fact, the trustees held the property as nominees for Rahman, who therefore had the beneficial interest in the trust property. The judge held that "the trustee was never made the master of the assets. [Rahman] intended to and in fact retained control of the capital and income of the trust fund throughout this lifetime".[76] The terms of the document could therefore be disregarded:[77] the trustee in fact held the property on a bare trust for Rahman. **7–061**

It is important to note that, even if S has retained some significant practical control over the exercise of powers by T, this may be perfectly consistent with the finding that S intended to create a trust for the benefit of others, rather than a trust solely for S's own benefit:[78] after all, one of the main attractions of a trust (as opposed to an outright gift) is that it may be used by settlors as a means of benefitting other people whilst also keeping some control over the use of the trust property. However, in a case where S has transferred the property to T,[79] there comes a point where the extent of the duties owed by T to S mean that S has to be regarded as a beneficiary of the trust.[80] Such cases do not necessarily involve shams as such; it may be that S genuinely but mistakenly believed, perhaps as a result of poor **7–062**

---

[73] It was stated in *Midland Bank v Wyatt* [1997] 1 B.C.L.C. 242 at 245 that "a sham transaction will remain a sham transaction even if one of the parties to it merely went along with the 'shammer' not either knowing or caring about what he or she was signing." This was interpreted in *A v A* [2007] EWHC 99 (Fam) at [52] as demonstrating that "reckless indifference" by one party can suffice to show a common intention: see *JSC Mezhdunarodniy Promyshlenniy Bank v Pugachev* [2017] EWHC 2426 (Ch) at [150].

[74] [2017] EWHC 2426 (Ch) at [145].

[75] [1991] J.L.R. 103.

[76] [1991] J.L.R. 103 at 112.

[77] Note that there are cases, and *Rahman* may well have been one, where, even if the document is treated at face value, and the sham doctrine is not applied, it can still be said that the rights and powers given to S by the document are so extensive that S in fact has a beneficial interest in the trust property. Certain offshore jurisdictions, however, not wanting to deter potential settlors, have legislated to ensure that the reservation of certain types of rights and powers will not lead to a finding that S has a beneficial interest in the property, e.g. the Bermuda Trusts (Special Provisions) Act 1989 s.2 (as amended by the Trusts (Special Provisions) Amendment Act 2014).

[78] Similarly, the mere fact that T in practice acquiesced in S's wishes without considering the terms of the trust does not render the document setting up the trust a sham, as it may be that T is simply acting in breach of the trust genuinely set up in that document: see *A v A* [2007] EWHC 99 (Fam); [2007] 2 F.L.R. 467 at [42].

[79] Similarly, in a case where S attempts a self-declaration of trust: if the powers held by S are such that it cannot be said that S is under a duty not to use the trust property for S's own benefit then either there is no trust, or S is a beneficiary of the trust.

[80] Some off-shore jurisdictions have sought to minimise the risk to settlors of a court making such a finding by legislative provisions stating that the reservation by S of certain powers "shall not affect the validity of the trust nor delay the trust taking effect": see e.g. Trusts (Jersey) Law 1984 s.9A and fn.77.

legal advice, that the legal structure created was one in which S was not a beneficiary of a trust.[81] As a result, the term "illusory trust" has been used to refer to such cases.[82] There is no necessity to use such a label, however, as no distinct doctrine is being applied: the court is simply undertaking its usual task of establishing S's objective intentions as to what rights and duties have been created,[83] and then seeing if those rights and duties give rise to a trust and, if so, on what terms. We therefore agree with some recent judicial observations that the term "illusory trust" is unhelpful.[84]

7–063 Whether as a result of the finding of a sham or otherwise, the finding that an apparent trust on which S is holding property does not exist, or that an apparent trust for third parties is in fact a trust for S, can have very significant consequences for S. As can be seen from *Midland Bank v Wyatt*, it means that property which, according to the terms of the document, is held by S for others is in fact at S's free disposition and so is available to meet the claims of S's creditors. Similarly, in a case such as *Rahman*, the finding of a sham means that T holds the property on a bare trust for S: such an interest is again available to S's creditors and must be taken into account when assessing S's tax liability. As well as insulating assets from general creditors or trying to limit a tax bill, S may have wished to put assets beyond the reach of any claims by a spouse, or by a relative who would be entitled on S's death under a particular jurisdiction's "forced heirship" rules.

7–064 The onus of proving that a document which appears to create a proper trust is actually a sham is on the person making the allegation.[85] Whilst it is rarely invoked, the sham doctrine is generally relied upon *against* S, by a party such as one of S's creditors.[86] Certainly, it is not open to a purported settlor to deny the objective effect of her own acts by relying on her secret dishonest intention to produce a different outcome.[87] In *Official Assignee v Wilson*[88] the New Zealand Court of Appeal concluded from this that S's trustee in bankruptcy was also precluded from alleging the existence of a sham, as he could be in no better position than the "settlor" herself. However, it seems strongly arguable that, as the trustee in bankruptcy acts on behalf of S's creditors, his ability to have a transaction declared a sham should not be compromised by any deception practised by S; although, of course, the interests of any innocent third parties who have relied on the apparent trust must be taken into account.[89]

---

81 See *JSC Mezhdunarodniy Promyshlenniy Bank v Pugachev* [2017] EWHC 2426 (Ch) at [168], per Birss J: such a conclusion "is not the same thing as a finding of sham. The analysis is all concerned with what the effect of the deed truly is. It is not concerned with the subjective intentions of the parties to create a pretence to mislead."

82 Similarly, the mere fact that T in practice acquiesced in S's wishes without considering the terms of the trust does not render the document setting up the trust a sham: see fn.78.

83 The Privy Council's decision in *Webb v Webb* [2020] UKPC 22, for example, can be understood on this basis: see S. Agnew [2021] C.L.J. 18.

84 See e.g. *Clayton v Clayton (No.1)* [2016] NZSC 29; [2016] 1 N.Z.L.R. 551 at [123]; *JSC Mezhdunarodniy Promyshlenniy Bank v Pugachev* [2017] EWHC 2426 (Ch) at [169]. Contrast *Law Society v Dua* [2020] EWHC 3528 (Ch) at [143].

85 *A v A* [2007] EWHC 99 (Fam); [2007] 2 F.L.R. 467 at [69]; *National Westminster Bank Plc v Jones* [2001] 1 B.C.L.C. 98 at [68]. It is a serious allegation involving dishonesty, and "the more serious the allegation the less likely it is that the event occurred and, hence, the stronger should be the evidence before the court concludes that the allegation is established on the balance of probability": *Re H (Minors)* [1996] A.C. 563 at 586.

86 See too, e.g. *Hitch v Stone* [2001] S.T.C. 214. Note too that, even if there is no sham and S did set up such a trust, such creditors may then attempt to rely on the "claw-back" provisions of the Insolvency Act 1986, as discussed at fn 69.

87 See, e.g. *Shalson v Russo* [2005] Ch. 281 at [190]. In *Commissioner of Stamp Duties v Jolliffe* (1920) 28 C.L.R. 178, the High Court of Australia allowed S to rely on his own sham as against a taxing authority, but the dissent of Isaacs J has since been preferred: see, e.g. *Byrnes v Kendle* (2011) 243 C.L.R. 253.

88 [2008] 3 N.Z.L.R. 45.

89 See, e.g. *Re Yates (A Bankrupt)* [2004] EWHC 3448 (Ch); [2005] B.P.I.R. 476 at [219]–[220]; *National Westminster Bank Plc v Jones* [2001] 1 B.C.L.C. 98 at [60].

ii. Defining a Sham

The notion of a sham is not, of course, specific to the law of trusts. In *Snook v London and West Riding Investments Ltd*, Diplock LJ, albeit reluctantly,[90] suggested the following definition of the concept:[91] **7–065**

> it means acts done or documents executed by the parties to the "sham" which are intended by them to give to third parties or to the court the appearance of creating between the parties legal rights and obligations different from the actual legal rights and obligations (if any) which the parties intended to create. . .for acts or documents to be a "sham", with whatever legal consequences follow from this, all the parties thereto must have a common intention that the acts or documents are not to create the legal rights and obligations which they give the appearance of creating. No unexpressed intentions of a "shammer" affect the rights of a party whom he deceived.

It is therefore clear that a degree of dishonesty is involved in a sham.[92] Whose intention is relevant when considering if a document apparently setting up a trust is a sham? In *Re Esteem Settlement*, the Royal Court of Jersey held that, where the apparent trust was set up by S's transfer of property to T to hold on trust,[93] **7–066**

> in order to find a sham, the court must find that both the settlor and the trustee had the intention that the true position should be otherwise than as set out in the trust deed which they both executed.

That reasoning was also adopted by Rimer J in *Shalson v Russo*:[94] **7–067**

> When a settlor creates a settlement he purports to divest himself of assets in favour of the trustee, and the trustee accepts them on the basis of the trusts of the settlement. The settlor may have an unspoken intention that the assets are in fact to be treated as his own and that the trustee will accede to his every request on demand. But unless that intention is from the outset shared by the trustee (or later becomes so shared), I fail to see how the settlement can be regarded as a sham. Once the assets are vested in the trustee, they will be held on the declared trusts, and he is entitled to regard them as so held and to ignore any demands from the settlor as to how to deal with them. I cannot understand on what basis a third party could claim, merely by reference to the unilateral intentions of the settlor, that the settlement was a sham and that the assets in fact remained the settlor's property. One might as well say that an apparently outright gift made by a donor can subsequently be held to be a sham on the basis of some unspoken intention of the donor not to part with the property in it. But if the donee accepted the gift on the footing that it was a genuine gift, the donor's undeclared intentions cannot turn an ostensibly valid disposition of his property into no disposition at all. To set that sort of case up the donee must also be shown to be a party to the alleged sham. In my judgment, in the case of a settlement executed by a settlor and a trustee, it is insufficient in considering whether or not it is a sham to look merely at the intentions of the settlor. It is essential also to look at those of the trustee.

---

90 The statement set out here was prefaced by Diplock LJ's comment that: "it is, I think, necessary to consider what, if any, legal concept is involved in the use of this popular and pejorative word": [1967] 2 Q.B. 786 at 802.

91 [1967] 2 Q.B. 786 at 802. The reference to documents cannot mean that either all of a document is sham, or none of it: see *Hitch v Stone* [2001] EWCA Civ 63; [2001] S.T.C. 214. Rather, each apparent creation of rights within a document must be seen as a relevant "act", and will only be valid if accompanied by the necessary intention that those rights should genuinely be created.

92 See, e.g. *National Westminster Bank Plc v Jones* [2001] 1 B.C.L.C. 98 at [46], [59], endorsed in *A v A* [2007] EWHC 99 (Fam); [2007] 2 F.L.R. 467 at [53].

93 [2003] J.L.R. 188 at [54].

94 [2003] EWHC 1637 (Ch); [2005] Ch. 281 at [190].

7-068 In *A v A*, Munby J similarly stated that:[95]

> [there should be no finding of sham where] the trust property has been vested in someone who accepts that he holds the property as trustee on the trusts of a document which he believes to be a genuine instrument. He has no intention that the arrangement should be a sham . . . What is required is a common *intention* [of S and T], but reckless indifference will be taken to constitute the necessary intention.[96]

7-069 There may seem to be a discrepancy between this requirement of common intention and the point made above,[97] that a settlor setting up an express trust is exercising her own power to do so, and can therefore act unilaterally.[98] There are two plausible ways of resolving this tension. First, the sham doctrine can be seen as essentially evidential:[99] the court is asking when, in considering the intention of the settlor, it is possible to look beyond a signed document seemingly setting out that intention and to take account of factors such as the subsequent conduct of the relevant parties. Where that document has been executed by two parties, it seems that it can be disregarded only when both of those parties are, to some degree at least, involved in the deception. However, if a case were to involve a deed executed unilaterally and purporting to declare a trust of S's property, it is difficult to see how the intention of anyone other than S could be relevant.[100] Once the document is disregarded, the court can establish S's true intention. At that point, having made a decision as to the relevant evidence, and having undertaken an assessment of that evidence, the court can apply the standard test for the existence of an express trust.[101]

7-070 The second means of resolving the tension is to argue that there is no special sham doctrine as such, and that the cases can in fact be best seen as involving the application of the standard objective approach to evaluating S's intention. Douglas and McFarlane[102] have argued, for example, that the common intention requirement for a sham reflects the fact that S's intention is to be judged objectively, so that, once that common shamming intention is present, it is clear that, judged from the perspective of the reasonable person to whom S is communicating S's intention, the required intention to set up a trust is absent, as that party knows that the written document is not intended to be decisive.[103] On that view:[104]

---

95 [2007] EWHC 99 (Fam); [2007] 2 F.L.R. 467 at [46], [52].

96 Munby J. considered *Midland Bank v Wyatt* to be a case in which that test was satisfied, as Mrs Wyatt could be seen as having gone along with the sham "neither knowing or caring what [she was] signing": [2007] EWHC 99 (Fam); [2007] 2 F.L.R. 467 at [52], approving the analysis in *Re Esteem Settlement* [2003] J.L.R. 188 at [58].

97 See para.7-005.

98 This point is explored by J. Palmer [2008] N.Z.L.J. 319, although note the reply to Palmer's analysis by M. Conaglen, "Trusts and Intention" in E. Simpson and M. Stewart (eds), *Sham Transactions* (Oxford University Press, 2013), 7.36-7.66 and see too paras 4-023 to 4-026.

99 This seems to be the effect of the analysis in M. Conaglen, "Sham Trusts" [2008] CL.J. 176 and M. Conaglen, "Trusts and Intention" in *Sham Transactions* (2013).

100 See, e.g. *Painter v Hutchison* [2007] EWHC 758 (Ch); [2008] B.P.I.R. 170 at [111]-[112]. At [115], Lewison J offered one way of explaining this point: "where there is a simple unilateral declaration of trust, the settlor and the trustee are one and the same person. So even if it is necessary to consider the intention of both the settlor and the trustee, in practice that amounts to the same thing as considering the intention of the settlor alone."

101 This the argument of B. McFarlane and E. Simpson, "Tackling Avoidance" in J. Getzler (ed.), *Rationalizing Property, Equity and Trusts: Essays in Honour of Edward Burn* (Oxford University Press, 2003).

102 S. Douglas and B. McFarlane, "Sham Trusts" in H. Conway and R. Hickey (eds) *Modern Studies in Property Law*, Vol.9 (Hart Publishing, 2017), p.237.

103 So, in *JSC Mezhdunarodniy Promyshlenniy Bank v Pugachev* [2017] EWHC 2426 (Ch), it was found at [424] that: "at all material times [S] regarded all the assets in these trusts as belonging to him and intended to retain ultimate control" and at [434] that this would have been obvious to someone in the position of the director of T, the trustee company. So, if, properly interpreted, the trust documents did not fulfil that objective intention, they would have been, in that sense, sham documents: see [437].

104 S. Douglas and B. McFarlane, "Sham Trusts" in *Modern Studies in Property Law*, Vol.9 (2017), pp.237, 249.

just because a court is looking behind the written declaration of trust does not mean that it is adopting a subjective approach . . . the objective approach employed in trusts law requires the court to ask what the settlor's words meant *to a reasonable person in the position of the addressee*. Such a person in sham cases (usually the trustee, but sometimes a beneficiary) is privy not just to the "declaration of trust", but also to other communications which inform the trustee of the settlor's desire to keep hold of his assets. To ask what a reasonable person in the position of the trustee would have understood the settlor to mean, therefore, naturally forces the court to "look behind" the declaration of trust as the trustee was privy to other communications.

D. Mistakes

We have seen that S's intention to set up a trust has to be judged objectively, but that, on one view at least, S's subjective intention to deceive will be relevant when considering if a document apparently setting up a trust can be disregarded as a sham. S's inward thought processes may also be relevant where S did express a genuine intention to set up a trust, but her decision to exercise her power to set up a trust was vitiated by a mistake. In these circumstances the court may allow them to rescind the settlement, provided that her decision to create the trust was caused by her mistake, and she made a mistake sufficiently serious to render the trust voidable.[105] When deciding whether to allow rescission, the court will also take into account matters such as the interests of third parties. This is all examined in more detail in Chapter 20. **7–071**

It is also possible for there to be a mistake in the documents setting up the trusts, if those documents do not accurately record S's intention. In such a case, a court may order rectification of the documents, with retrospective effect, so that they accord with the relevant intention. We will consider rectification in Chapter 21. Where S signs a trust document, the usual position of course is that, consistent with S's intention, the trust document will be regarded as the exclusive source of the terms of the trust. If, however, S is mistaken as to the content of the document when signing it, this subjective flaw can justify a court in ignoring S's intention that the document be the sole source of the terms of the trust,[106] so that the court can instead look beyond the document to establish the trust terms of the trust. This still allows room for those true terms to be established by the standard objective test,[107] rather than through S's subjective intention alone.[108] **7–072**

3. Certainty of Subject-Matter

A. The Nature of the Test

A trust can exist only if a trustee (T) is under a duty in relation to specific property held by T: "the creation of a valid trust requires the existence at that time of some assets to which the trust would apply".[109] To establish a valid express trust the settlor (S) must therefore make it certain what property **7–073**

---

105 *Pitt v Holt* [2013] UKSC 26; [2013] 2 A.C. 108.

106 See e.g. S. Douglas, "Misuse of Rectification in the Law of Trusts" (2018) 134 L.Q.R. 138.

107 The contrary suggestions in *Day v Day* [2013] EWCA Civ 280; [2014] Ch. 114 (see e.g. Etherton C at 122) that S's subjective intention can also control the content of the trust terms on rectification are difficult to support: see S. Douglas, "Misuse of Rectification in the Law of Trusts" (2018) 134 L.Q.R. 138.

108 See e.g. B. McFarlane and S. Douglas, "Sham Trusts" in *Modern Studies in Property Law*, Vol.9 (2017), p.237 and S. Douglas, "Misuse of Rectification in the Law of Trusts" (2018) 134 L.Q.R. 138, applying to trusts the approach taken to relation to rectification of contracts by R. Stevens, "Objectivity, Mistake and the Parol Evidence Rule" in E. Peel and A. Burrows (eds) *Contract Terms* (Oxford University Press, 2007).

109 *North v Wilkinson* [2018] EWCA Civ 161 at [14] (David Richards LJ).

is to be held on trust.[110] For example, in *Boyce v Boyce*,[111] S bequeathed two houses to T on trust to convey whichever house Maria should choose to Maria and to convey the other to Charlotte. Maria died before S and so could not make a selection. It was held that the trust in favour of Charlotte was void for uncertainty of subject matter.

7–074 The need to identify the specific property to which B's right relates is certainly not unique to trusts: it is present in any case where B claims a legal or equitable property right. For example, no matter what the intention of the parties may have been, no property can pass in a sale of goods unless the specific goods have been identified, either by the terms of the parties' contract or by later ascertainment and appropriation.[112] As noted by Lord Mustill in *Re Goldcorp Exchange Ltd*,[113] this need for identification (as well as intention) is not some "arid legal technicality" but rather depends on "the very nature of things".[114] In that case, for example, the vendor had promised to sell a particular quantity of gold bullion to each customer, but the promise did not relate to any *specific* bullion, and so, even if a customer paid in advance, she could acquire no legal title. Seeking protection from the consequences of the vendor's insolvency, such customers instead claimed that a trust had arisen. This claim, as far as it related to any particular bullion,[115] failed for exactly the same reason: the subject-matter of the supposed equitable property right could not be identified.

B. Applying the Test

7–075 The test does not require the subject matter of a gift or trust to be identified before the time when the gift or trust takes effect. In a will, therefore, S can validly make a disposition of "the residue of my estate" as the property comprised in that residue will be clear by the time when the gift or trust takes effect, as the executors will have met any debts and taxes due from the estate and have distributed any specific legacies. Similarly, of course, a gift or trust in relation to "half of the residue of my estate" would be valid; a disposition of "the bulk of my residuary estate" would however be too uncertain,[116] unless clear guidance could be found as to a particular meaning of the term "bulk" intended by S. Similarly, if S directs, in her will, that property is to go to her spouse, and "such part of it as may not be required by [the spouse]" shall, on the spouse's death, be held on trust for their children, the attempt to set up an immediate trust for the children fails, as there is no certainty as to its subject matter, and so the spouse takes absolutely.[117] In *re Last*, however, S directed that all her property should go to her brother and "at his death anything, that is left, that came from me to go to my late husband's grandchildren". As the brother died without a will or anyone entitled on his intestacy, such remaining property would otherwise have gone to the Crown as bona vacantia, so Karminski J strained

---

110 *Palmer v Simmonds* (1854) 2 Drew. 221 at 227 ("the bulk of my residuary estate" cannot satisfy the certainty requirement though "my residuary estate" can); *Re London Wine Co (Shippers) Ltd* [1986] P.C.C. 121 (settlor cannot declare itself trustee of unascertained 20 out of 80 bottles of Château Lafite 1970 in its cellar though it could declare it held its holding of 80 bottles on trust as for three-quarters for itself and one-quarter for X).

111 (1849) 16 Sim. 476.

112 Sale of Goods Act 1979 s.16.

113 [1995] 1 A.C. 74 at 90.

114 This is in turn a reference to C. Blackburn, *The Effect of the Contract of Sale* (William Benning and Co, 1845), p.123.

115 The customers also attempted to claim that the pre-payment of the price was held on a trust imposed by law. No such trust could arise, however, as the contract had not imposed any limit on the use the vendors could make of the money: the claimed trust of the money therefore failed for the same reason as the trust claimed in *Westdeutsche Landesbank Girozentrale v Islington LBC* [1996] A.C. 669: see para.16–026.

116 *Palmer v Simmonds* (1854) 2 Drew 221.

117 See e.g. *Mussoorie Bank v Raynor* (1882) 7 App. Cas. 321 at 331; *re Dunstan* [1918] 2 Ch. 304. See too Administration of Justice Act 1982 s.22 (extracted at para.7–040).

to interpret the will in such a way as to allow the gift to the grandchildren to succeed. He achieved this result by finding that, on a construction of the will as a whole, the brother had only a life interest in the property, with the grandchildren entitled in equal shares on his death.[118]

Where S makes a lifetime transfer of property to T to hold on trust for B, the identity of the trust property will necessarily be certain by virtue of the transfer. However, identifiability problems can arise in cases where S purports to declare herself trustee of some of her property without clearly identifying that property. For example, if S purports to declare herself trustee for B of 20 of her 80 gold bars, then (just as would be the case if a contract for sale was made on those terms) B acquires no interest until 20 bars have been ascertained and appropriated to the transaction with B.[119] **7-076**

The position is different, however, if S declares a trust under which B has a 25% share of S's interest in the 80 gold bars. In such a case, the subject-matter of B's equitable property right *is* identified: it is all of the 80 gold bars. B's interest allows her a share in the benefit of S's single right to the identified 80 bars. For the same reason, property can pass immediately in a contract for the sale of a 25% share in S's right to the 80 bars. **7-077**

In *Hunter v Moss*,[120] the question was whether a trust could arise as a result of a declaration that S held 50 of his 950 shares in a particular private company on trust for B. The Court of Appeal affirmed the view of the first instance judge that there was sufficient certainty of subject-matter and so a trust arose. Dillon LJ stated that:[121] **7-078**

> Just as a person can give, by will, a specified number of his shares of a certain class in a certain company, so equally, in my judgment, he can declare himself a trustee of 50 of his ordinary shares in [a company] and that is effective to give a beneficial proprietary interest to the beneficiary under the trust.

This particular reasoning can be criticised. If S has made a will, then on her death, S's rights in all her assets are transferred to her executor, who is then obliged to implement S's wishes subject to the payment of debts, expenses and taxes. At no point does the executor have the free enjoyment of the property for herself. In contrast, where S purports to declare an inter vivos trust of property of which she is currently the full beneficial owner, it could be said that her attempt to constitute a trust of some of this property should be complete only when she has taken the further step of identifying the specific property to be held on trust. It could be argued that, until then, S has simply made an imperfect gift. **7-079**

It may nonetheless be possible to support the approach in *Hunter v Moss* on different grounds. The principle in the case was usefully summarised by Briggs J in *Re Lehman Brothers International (Europe)*,[122] who then went on to discuss the nature of the trust recognised in that case: **7-080**

> A trust of part of a fungible mass without the appropriation of any specific part of it for the beneficiary does not fail for uncertainty of subject matter, provided that the mass itself is sufficiently identified and provided also that the beneficiary's proportionate share of it is not itself uncertain . . . *Hunter v Moss* has not been without its academic and judicial critics, but its conclusion that there is no objection on the grounds of

---

118 [1958] P. 137. Note "bona vacantia" roughly translates as "ownerless goods": see para.16–068ff.

119 *Re London Wine Co Shippers Ltd* [1986] P.C.C. 121; *Re Stapylton Fletcher Ltd* [1995] 1 All E.R. 192; *Re Goldcorp Exchange* [1995] 1 A.C. 74. Some of the practical problems in the sale of goods context have now been remedied by Sale of Goods (Amendment) Act 1995.

120 [1994] 1 W.L.R. 452; criticised by D.J. Hayton (1994) 110 L.Q.R. 335; followed in an undefended case as applicable to intangibles but not tangibles: *Re Harvard Securities Ltd* [1997] 2 B.C.L.C. 369.

121 [1994] 1 W.L.R. 452 at 459.

122 [2010] EWHC 2914 (Ch) at [225]. The decision of Briggs J was affirmed by the Court of Appeal: [2011] EWCA Civ 1544; [2012] 2 B.C.L.C. 151.

uncertainty to a trust of part of a shareholding of a trustee has been generally followed, in this country,[123] in Hong Kong,[124] and in Australia.[125] . . . The difficulty with applying the Court of Appeal's judgment in *Hunter v Moss* to any case not on almost identical facts lies in the absence of any clearly expressed rationale as to how such a trust works in practice. There has not been unanimity among those courts which have followed *Hunter v Moss*, nor among the many academics who have commented on it, as to the correct approach. The analysis which I have found the most persuasive is that such a trust works by creating a beneficial co-ownership share in the identified fund, rather than in the conceptually much more difficult notion of seeking to identify a particular part of that fund which the beneficiary owns outright.[126]

7–081 On this view, the key point in *Hunter v Moss* is that S was dealing with shares and not, for example, with gold. A share, by definition, is simply a proportionate part of a total set of entitlements, held by the complete body of shareholders, in relation to a company.[127] So if S has 950 shares of the same type, S does not have 950 separate rights; rather, S has one right (essentially a contractual right against the company) and the content of that right is determined by the number of shares. An analogy can be drawn with a bank account: the customer has just one right, but the extent of the credit determines the content of that right. This means that a declaration of trust of 50 of S's 950 shares can therefore be interpreted as a declaration of trust under which B becomes beneficially entitled to a 1/19th share of S's chose in action against the company constituted by all of the 950 shares: it is thus the same as a declaration of trust of a 25% share of 80 gold bars.[128] In contrast, if S instead declares a trust of 20 of her 80 gold bars, that *cannot*, by itself, be interpreted as a declaration of trust of a 25% share of S's right to the whole 80 bars, as each gold bar is a specific thing, and has a specific existence independent of any broader right.

7–082 There is certainly some evidence that, following *Hunter v Moss*, the courts have been readier to find that the requirement for certainty of subject-matter has been met. In *Re Lehman Brothers International (Europe)*,[129] for example, it was reasonably clear that the parties had intended to create a system where T, acting as a hub for buying and selling shares and other securities for all Lehman affiliate companies in Europe, would acquire rights from third parties on behalf of the affiliates, and would then hold those rights on trust for the affiliates. On the collapse of Lehman Brothers, different companies within the group had different creditors, and some of those creditors disputed whether the parties' arrangements had indeed created a trust, instead arguing that T in fact held unencumbered title to the securities.

7–083 This argument was based on the fact that the parties had agreed that, although T held the securities for and on account of the affiliates, T was also free to deal with those securities for its own benefit (for example by lending them, or by transferring them to third parties in order to satisfy its own contracts with such third parties) provided that, when the affiliate accounts were settled at the end of each day, T was able to provide the correct number and type of securities to each affiliate. It

---

123 *Re Harvard Securities Ltd (in liq.)* [1997] 2 B.C.L.C. 369.

124 *Re CA Pacific Finance Ltd* [2000] 1 B.C.L.C. 494.

125 [2006] NSWSC 1379 [after a very thorough analysis of the authorities and of academic views].

126 [Reference was made here to R. Goode, "Are Intangible Assets Fungibles?" [2003] L.M.C.L.Q. 309 and the judgment of Campbell J in *White v Shortall* [2006] NSWSC 1379 at [212].]

127 See R. Goode "Are Intangible Assets Fungibles?" [2003] L.M.C.L.Q. 309, although note the contrary argument (in relation to private companies such as that in *Hunter v Moss*) made by G. Morton in S. Worthington (ed.), *Commercial Law and Commercial Practice* (Hart Publishing, 2003), pp.296–302.

128 Note that where S is dealing with shares in a public company, it is almost certain (see paras 1–081 and 6–108) that S has only an equitable interest, as the shares are held through intermediaries, and S's equitable interest is very likely to be a proportionate one in a bigger pool of such shares held by an intermediary higher up the chain: in such a case, any declaration of trust of S's shares is necessarily a dealing in relation to co-ownership of a bigger pool of such shares.

129 [2010] EWHC 2914 (Ch) at [225]. The decision of Briggs J was affirmed by the Court of Appeal: [2012] 2 B.C.L.C. 151.

was therefore argued that the apparent trust lacked certainty of subject-matter, as T's ultimate duty related purely to the number and type of securities and so did not relate to any specific property held by T, as that duty could be satisfied by using securities acquired from elsewhere, not the securities initially acquired on behalf of a particular affiliate.

Briggs J, whilst noting that the facts of the case were much more complicated than those in *Hunter v Moss*,[130] held that the certainty of subject matter requirement had nonetheless been satisfied. The point was that if, for example, T at one point acquired 100 ordinary ICI shares on behalf of an individual affiliate company (B), the subject matter of the trust would then be T's total holding of such shares, as well as any rights of T arising as a result of its future dealings with such shares (such as rights against third parties to whom T might lend the shares or sell the shares). It was argued that problems could arise if there was, at any point, a shortfall, so that the current rights held by T did not suffice to meet its duties to the affiliates; but Briggs J found that, as all the parties had consented to the arrangement, and thus to the possibility of a shortfall, it could be implied that they had consented to "bear the consequences of the shortfall equally".[131] **7–084**

Moreover, whilst there might be points in time when T had disposed of shares without gaining any rights against third parties as a result, and so (consistently with the terms of the agreement) would have to reconstitute the fund by acquiring such shares, "a trust does not fail for want of certainty merely because its subject matter is to consist of after-acquired property":[132] even though at a particular point its subject matter might be uncertain, the trust can be valid if "the terms of the trust are sufficient to identify its subject matter in the future."[133] On this point, it is worth noting that the arrangement between the parties was not gratuitous: T had a binding contractual duty to reconstitute the fund by acquiring the necessary shares. It may therefore be possible to draw on the principle applied in cases such as *Pullan v Koe*,[134] and to find that a trust therefore arose immediately on T's acquisition of such shares.[135] Nonetheless, a difficulty remains: if, as in *Lehman Brothers*, T is permitted to deal with the relevant property for T's own benefit, subject only to a duty to reconstitute the fund from *any* source, then can it be said that T has more than a merely personal duty, given that there is a point in time when T's duty does not relate to any *specific* rights held by T?[136] **7–085**

The broader issue in *Lehman Brothers*, which has arisen in a number of contexts, is the extent to which commercial parties can secure the advantages that come from establishing a trust, whilst at the same time giving the supposed trustee a wide power to deal with the trust property, or giving parties other than the supposed beneficiaries significant powers in relation to the decisions made by the trustees.[137] Briggs J's approach to this broader question is evident from his statement that:[138] **7–086**

> The law does not lightly allow contracting parties' purposes and intentions to be defeated by supposed uncertainty, and there is in my judgment no reason why the law should do so any more readily than normal merely because the issue is as to the validity of an intended trust. On the contrary, the law commonly recognises the creation of a trust as a necessary consequence of an intention that parties should share property

---

[130] [2010] EWHC 2914 (Ch) at [239].
[131] [2010] EWHC 2914 (Ch) at [244].
[132] [2010] EWHC 2914 (Ch) at [235].
[133] [2010] EWHC 2914 (Ch) at [225].
[134] [1913] 1 Ch. 9. See paras 5–076ff and 17–073ff.
[135] But note, strictly speaking, this trust is a constructive one.
[136] For discussion of this problem, see R. Stevens, "Floating Trusts" in P. Davies and J. Penner (eds) *Equity, Trusts and Commerce* (Hart Publishing, 2017).
[137] See too *Citibank NA v MBIA Assurance SA* [2007] EWCA Civ 11; [2007] 1 All E.R. (Comm) 475.
[138] [2010] EWHC 2914 (Ch) at [245].

> beneficially, in circumstances where the parties themselves have given no thought at all to the terms of the consequential trust, if indeed they even recognised its existence. In all such cases the law fills the consequential gaps by implication, and by importation of generally applicable principles.

7–087 It is useful to compare the decisions in *Lehman Brothers* and in *North v Wilkinson*.[139] In the latter case, the Court of Appeal considered a claim that A, a sole trader, had created a trust in B's favour of 5% of A's business assets. Drawing on *Hunter v Moss* and *Lehman Brothers*, David Richards LJ found that "such a trust would not lack certainty of subject matter" as it would attach to "5% of such fluctuating credit balance as from time to time existed during the currency of the trust". However, the trust claimed in *North v Wilkinson*, as noted earlier in this chapter,[140] would raise serious practical issues, to which the parties had not addressed their minds. As a result, it was held that, whilst such a trust was possible in theory, it could not be said in practice that the parties had intended to create it, given that they had not dealt with the obvious practical difficulties that would arise from a trust. In *Lehman Brothers*, in contrast, where the very well-advised parties clearly had intended a trust, the court was willing to give effect to that intention.

7–088 Indeed, as shown by Briggs J's drawing of an analogy with common intention constructive trusts of the family home,[141] this judicial desire to give effect, where possible, to an intention to establish a trust can be seen beyond the commercial sphere. *Hunter v Moss* itself provides an example of the court's willingness to take a practical, rather than an overly-technical, approach when applying the test for certainty of subject-matter. Rimer QC, deciding the case at first instance, stated that:[142]

> the question of whether in any particular case there is such certainty depends, or ought to depend, not on the application of any immutable principle based on the requirements of a need for segregation or appropriation, but rather on whether, immediately after the purported declaration of trust, the court could, if asked, make an order for the execution of the purported trust. In any particular case it could and will only do so if, inter alia, the subject matter of the trust is identified with sufficient certainty.

7–089 In *Re Golay's Will Trusts*,[143] for example, a gift in a will directing that B should receive "a reasonable income" was upheld as valid, as the testator was regarded as having "given a sufficient indication of his intention to provide an effective determinant of what he intends so that the court in applying that determinant can give effect to the testator's intention". This was because the term was interpreted as requiring an objective assessment of reasonableness, such as courts are accustomed to making, which did not depend on the testator's subjective or personal view. As we will now see, this emphasis on whether the terms of the supposed gift or trust are clear enough to enable the court to ensure that those terms have been complied with is also evident when considering the third of the three certainties.

---

139 [2018] EWCA Civ 161.

140 See para.7–042.

141 See para. 7–086. Briggs J went on to note ([2010] EWHC 2914 (Ch) at [245]) that, in the "protracted and difficult debate" as to the common intention constructive trust of the family home (as to which, see paras 17–121ff), it has never been suggested that the parties' failure to specify the extent of B's beneficial interest causes the trust to fail for uncertainty.

142 *Hunter v Moss* [1993] 1 W.L.R. 934 at 945 (affirmed on appeal: [1994] 1 W.L.R. 452).

143 [1965] 1 W.L.R. 969 at 971.

4. Certainty of Objects

A. The Nature of the Tests

The third of the three certainties, which can be referred to as requiring "certainty of objects", is, again, based on an underlying principle that is not unique to the law of trusts. A trust necessarily involves T holding property subject to a duty; a contract, for example, also involves a contracting party (call her D) being under a duty to another. Such a duty can exist only where it is possible for a court to enforce it. This means two things. First, a court must be able to *police* the duty: it must be able to tell if particular action by T (or D) is or is not a breach of the duty. Second, a court must be able to *enforce* the duty: in the event of T (or D)'s failure to perform the duty, the court must be able to make an order that gives effect to the content of the duty. A valid trust, like a valid contract, must therefore provide a court with sufficient information to police and enforce the supposed duty imposed on T or on D. **7–090**

There may also be relationships which a court must police, but need not enforce. This is the case where T has a *power* to act in a certain way, but no duty to act. For example, S may transfer property to T to hold on trust for B, but with a power for T to appoint up to one half of the property to "any of [S's] old friends". T has no duty to make any such appointment, and so a court will never be called upon to enforce the power. The court does need to ensure, however, that any purported exercise of the power by T is authorised. This means that if T chooses, for example, to exercise the power in favour of X, and B challenges the exercise of that power, the court needs to be able to tell if X is, or is not, an "old friend" of S. If the term "old friend" is so uncertain that a court will simply be unable to make such an assessment, then the power cannot be policed, and so it will be invalid. **7–091**

It is therefore clear that when a court deals with questions of certainty of objects, we first need to ask what limits S intended to impose on T, in order to see what information is required for a court to police and (if necessary) enforce such limits. We must first, therefore, consider the different possibilities. We will start with arrangements with the least demanding certainty of objects requirements, and move up to those with the most demanding. **7–092**

B. Identifying the Test to be Applied

i. Gifts Subject to a Condition Precedent

In *Re Barlow's Will Trusts*,[144] a testatrix (S) instructed her executor "to allow any member of my family and any friends of mine who may wish to do so to purchase" particular paintings in her estate at a low valuation. The term "friend" seems like a clear example of an uncertain term: how could a court tell in practice if X is or is not within that class? However, Browne-Wilkinson J held the disposition to be valid. His reasoning turned on the fact that the testatrix had effectively made a series of individual gifts to persons answering the description of her blood relations or friends, since the effect of the disposition was to confer on such persons a series of options to purchase at a low price. This was important as, if the disposition was invalidated, this would result in the loss of property to any person who clearly was, on any view, a member of S's family or friend of S. This suggested that as long as S had just one **7–093**

144 [1979] 1 W.L.R. 278.

friend (on anyone's definition of that word), invaliding the instruction to S's executor as regards friends would, in effect, deprive that person of a clear entitlement.

7-094 Certainly, there was no need to have a complete list of all family members and friends, as all that was required was for the executors to be able to say of any individual coming forward whether or not she had proved that she was a relation or friend. The risk of the executors allowing someone not truly entitled to buy a painting (e.g. X, who was not in fact a friend of S) could therefore be dealt with by other means, e.g. by presuming that, if X cannot show that she is clearly within the class of "member of my family" or "friends", then X is not within that class and no gift need be made to them.[145] Such an approach may create some practical difficulties for the executors, who may have awkward decisions to make, but that disadvantage, it seems, is the price of ensuring that the vested entitlements of any clear friends are upheld.

7-095 In *Re Barlow's Will Trusts*, Browne-Wilkinson J relied on *Re Allen*,[146] where the Court of Appeal had upheld a bequest "to the eldest of the sons of [S] who shall be a member of the Church of England and an adherent to the doctrine of that Church". By upholding this gift, the court gave the eldest son the chance to establish that he met the condition imposed on the gift. It was not necessary for the executors to be able to tell of a hypothetical X whether or not X met the condition: they simply had to consider, in turn according to age, each of the sons of S. As Lord Evershed MR observed in *Re Allen*,[147] a gift to "B if he is a tall man" should not be invalidated, as B, if he is 6ft 6ins, should not be deprived of the gift.

7-096 Certainly, if there are a small number of ascertainable possible recipients of the gift, it seems reasonable that each should be given the chance to show that she comes within the "core" meaning of the qualifying condition, even if that term is conceptually uncertain, in the sense that a clear meaning, enabling marginal cases to be decided, cannot be found.[148]

ii. Non-Fiduciary Powers

7-097 It is possible for a settlor S to give a party who is not a trustee a power in relation to trust property. For example, S could give property to trustees to hold on trust for B, whilst also giving P, S's sister, a power to order the trustees to advance up to half of the trust fund to any of S's friends. In such a case, there is a question as to whether S intended P to be under any duties in relation to the exercise of that power—such as, for example, a duty to consider periodically whether or not to exercise that power. Such duties are generally assumed to arise where S gives a power to a trustee, T, because T, as a trustee, has fiduciary duties.[149] If, instead, S gives a power to someone such as P who is not expected to have similar responsibilities, then there is no such presumption.[150]

7-098 Where P has no such duties, P may be called a holder of a "non-fiduciary power" or "bare power". In such a case, the court's only concern in policing the exercise of the power is to ensure that P does not

---

145 That was the approach taken to relatives by Megaw and Sachs LJJ in *Re Baden's Deed Trusts (No.2)* [1973] Ch. 9: see paras 7-155 to 7-171.

146 [1953] Ch. 810.

147 [1953] Ch. 810 at 817.

148 See, e.g. L. McKay, "Re Barlow and the Certainty of Objects Rule" [1980] Conv. 263 at 277; C.T. Emery, "The Most Hallowed Principle: Certainty of Beneficiaries of Trusts and Powers of Appointment" (1982) 98 L.Q.R. 551 at 564.

149 See paras 2-066 to 2-216 for a discussion of fiduciary duties.

150 Indeed, if the power given to P is one which P can also exercise for her own benefit, then it will be difficult to see it as a fiduciary power, as the ability to act in one's own self-interest is inconsistent with the basic nature of fiduciary duties: see paras 2-094 to 2-137.

exercise the power in favour of someone who is outside the class specified by S. This means that the court needs to be able to tell of any given person whether or not that person is inside the class: should P exercise the power in favour of X, and B then challenges that disposition, the court will then be able to tell if the exercise of the power was authorised. This test is often called the "given postulant" test or the "is or is not" test. It is of great importance in practice, as it also applies in the much more common case where a power is given to a trustee.

It seems that a power to make dispositions in favour of any "friend" of S will not pass this "is or is not" test, as the term is not sufficiently certain to enable a court to decide, in a marginal case, if X is nor is not in the class. This may be unfortunate for C, a party who was, on any view of the concept of friendship, a friend of S. It is important to note, however, that the invalidity of the power does not deprive C of any vested entitlement, but only of the possibility that P would have exercised the power in C's favour. This explains why the more relaxed test applied to conditional gifts[151] does not apply to powers. In *Re Gulbenkian's Settlement Trusts*,[152] the House of Lords therefore rejected the view of Lord Denning MR in the Court of Appeal that, in the case of a power,[153] it was only necessary to show that any one person is clearly within the class. Lord Upjohn stated that:[154] **7–099**

> with respect to mere powers, while the court cannot compel the trustees to exercise their powers, yet those entitled to the fund in default must clearly be entitled to restrain the trustees from exercising it save among those within the power. So the trustees, or the court, must be able to say with certainty who is within and who is without the power.

iii. Fiduciary Powers

Consider a case in which a settlor S gives property to a trustee T to hold on trust for a beneficiary B, whilst also giving T a power to advance up to half of the trust fund to any of S's friends. As in the case of a non-fiduciary power, the court will have to police the power by ensuring that it is not exercised in favour of anyone outside that class, and so the "is or is not" test will be applied. In this case, however, T's power is a fiduciary one because she holds it in her capacity as trustee. This means that T will be under further duties: the question is whether the existence of such duties means that a higher standard of certainty is required than in the case of a non-fiduciary power. Those questions were considered by Megarry VC in the following extract, which draws an explicit link between the nature of the duties that S seeks to impose and the certainty required of S's settlement. **7–100**

At various points in the extract Megarry VC refers to a "mere power" vested in trustees, by which he means a fiduciary power that the trustees need not exercise. Megarry VC uses this term to differentiate the power from a power that the trustees owe a duty to exercise in some way. Confusingly, the latter type of power is sometimes called a "trust power",[155] but, as it gives rise to a discretionary trust, we will examine it separately below.[156] **7–101**

---

[151] See paras 7–093 to 7–096.
[152] [1970] A.C. 508.
[153] The case itself concerned fiduciary powers, but the reasoning also applies to non-fiduciary powers.
[154] [1970] A.C. 508 at 525.
[155] As in, e.g. *Re Baden (No.1)* [1971] A.C. 424 (extracted at paras 7–126 to 7–142).
[156] See paras 7–124ff.

Re Hay's Settlement Trusts

Chancery Division [1982] 1 W.L.R. 202

7–102 By clause 4 of Lady Hay's settlement made in 1958, trustees held the trust fund

> "on trust for such persons or purposes for such interests and with such gifts over and (if for persons) with such provisions for their respective maintenance or advancement at the discretion of the Trustees or of any other persons as the Trustees shall by any deed or deeds revocable or irrevocable (but if revocable not after the expiration of 21 years from the date hereof) executed within 21 years from the date hereof appoint . . . and in default of such appointment in trust for the nieces and nephews of the Settlor now living in equal shares."

7–103 A proviso precluded any appointment being made to the settlor, any husband of her, and any trustee or past trustee. For the first five years income was to be accumulated and then the income was to be held on discretionary trusts for the nieces and nephews or charities until the clause 4 power of appointment was exercised or ceased to be exercisable (by expiry of the 21 years). In 1969 a deed of appointment was executed, clause 1 conferring a power of appointment on the trustees (exercisable till expiry of the 21-year period in the 1958 settlement) to hold "the trust fund and the income thereof on trust for such persons and such persons as shall be appointed." Clause 2 directed that the undisposed-of income (until full exercise of the clause 1 power) be held on discretionary trusts for the benefit of any persons whatsoever (the settlor, any husband of her, any existing or former trustee excepted) or for any charity. The questions arose: (i) whether or not the very wide power of appointment in the 1958 settlement was valid; and (ii) if it was valid then whether its purported exercise by the trustees in 1969 was void in creating a very wide discretionary trust that was either an impermissible delegation by the trustees of their power under the 1958 settlement, or was in itself void as th planned discretionary trust was administratively unworkable? The first question is our focus here, and it was decided in favour of validity; on the second question, however, it was decided that the very wide discretionary trust involved an impermissible delegation by the trustees of their powers under the 1958 settlement.

7–104 MEGARRY V.-C.: . . . The starting point must be to consider whether the power created by the first limb of clause 4 of the settlement is valid. . . . The essential point is whether a power for trustees to appoint to anyone in the world except a handful of specified persons is valid. Such a power will be perfectly valid if given to a person who is not in a fiduciary position: the difficulty arises when it is given to trustees, for they are under certain fiduciary duties in relation to the power, and to a limited degree they are subject to the control of the courts. . .

7–105 In *Re Manisty's Settlement*[157] a settlement gave trustees a discretionary power to apply the trust fund for the benefit of a small class of the settlor's near relations, save that any member of a smaller "excepted class" was to be excluded from the class of beneficiaries. The trustees were also given power at their absolute discretion to declare that any person, corporation or charity (except a member of the excepted class or a trustee) should be included in the class of beneficiaries. Templeman J. held that this power to extend the class of beneficiaries was valid. . .

7–106 I propose to approach the matter by stages. First, it is plain that if a power of appointment is given to a person who is not in a fiduciary position, there is nothing in the width of the power which invalidates it per se. The power may be a special power with a large class of persons as objects; the power may be what is called a "hybrid" power, or an "intermediate" power, authorising appointment to anyone save a specified number or class of persons; or the power may be a general power. Whichever it is, there is nothing in the number of persons to whom an appointment may be made which will invalidate it. The difficulty comes when the power is given to trustees as such, in that the number of objects may interact with the fiduciary duties of the trustees and their control by the court. The argument of counsel for the defendants carried him to the extent of asserting that no valid intermediate or general power could be vested in trustees.

7–107 That brings me to the second point, namely, the extent of the fiduciary obligations of trustees who have a mere power vested in them, and how far the court exercises control over them in relation to that power. In the case of a trust, of course, the trustee is bound to execute it, and if he does not, the court will see to its execution. A mere power is very different. Normally the trustee is not bound to exercise it, and the court will not compel him to do so. That, however, does not mean that he can simply fold his hands and ignore

[157] [1974] Ch. 17.

it, for normally he must from time to time consider whether or not to exercise the power, and the court may direct him to do this.

When he does exercise the power, he must, of course (as in the case of all trusts and powers) confine himself to what is authorised, and not go beyond it. But that is not the only restriction. Whereas a person who is not in a fiduciary position is free to exercise the power in any way that he wishes, unhampered by any fiduciary duties, a trustee to whom, as such, a power is given is bound by the duties of his office in exercising that power to do so in a responsible manner according to its purpose. It is not enough for him to refrain from acting capriciously; he must do more. He must "make such a survey of the range of objects or possible beneficiaries" as will enable him to carry out his fiduciary duty. He must find out "the permissible area of selection and then consider responsibly, in individual cases, whether a contemplated beneficiary was within the power and whether, in relation to the possible claimants, a particular grant was appropriate"[158] . . . 7–108

That brings me to the third point. How is the duty of making a responsible survey and selection to be carried out in the absence of any complete list of objects? This question was considered by the Court of Appeal in *Re Baden (No.2)*. That case was concerned with what, after some divergences of judicial opinion, was held to be a discretionary trust and not a mere power; but plainly the requirements for a mere power cannot be more stringent than those for a discretionary trust. The duty, I think, may be expressed along the following lines. The trustee must not simply proceed to exercise the power in favour of such of the objects as happen to be at hand or claim his attention. He must first consider what persons or classes of persons are objects of the power within the definition in the settlement or will. In doing this, there is no need to compile a complete list of the objects, or even to make an accurate assessment of the number of them: what is needed is an appreciation of the width of the field, and thus whether a selection is to be made merely from a dozen or, instead, from thousands or millions. . . . Only when the trustee has applied his mind to "the size of the problem" should he then consider in individual cases whether, in relation to other possible claimants, a particular grant is appropriate. In doing this, no doubt he should not prefer the undeserving to the deserving; but he is not required to make an exact calculation whether, as between deserving claimants, A is more deserving than B.[159] 7–109

If I am right in these views, the duties of a trustee which are specific to a mere power seem to be threefold. Apart from the obvious duty of obeying the trust instrument, and in particular of making no appointment that is not authorised by it, the trustee must, first, consider periodically whether or not he should exercise the power; second, consider the range of objects of the power; and third, consider the appropriateness of individual appointments. I do not assert that this list is exhaustive; but as the authorities stand it seems to me to include the essentials, so far as relevant to the case before me. 7–110

On this footing, the question is thus whether there is something in the nature of an intermediate power which conflicts with these duties in such a way as to invalidate the power if it is vested in a trustee. . .I do not see how mere numbers can inhibit the trustees from considering whether or not to exercise the power, as distinct from deciding in whose favour to exercise it. 7–111

The second ground of [claimed invalidity] seems to be that the power is so wide that it would be impossible for the trustees to consider in any sensible manner how to exercise it, and also impossible for the court to say whether or not they were properly exercising it. With respect, I do not see how that follows. If I have correctly stated the extent of the duties of trustees in whom a mere power is vested, I do not see what there is to prevent the trustees from performing these duties. [In *Re Baden (No.2)*,[160] the Court of Appeal explained] how the trustees should make a survey and consider individual appointments in cases where no complete list of objects could be compiled. I also have in mind that the settlor in the present case is still alive, though I do not rest my decision on that. 7–112

From what I have said it will be seen that I cannot see any ground on which the power in question can be said to be void. Certainly it is not void for linguistic or semantic uncertainty; there is no room for doubt in the definition of those who are or are not objects of the power. Nor can I see that the power is administratively unworkable. The words of Lord Wilberforce in *Re Baden (No.1)*[161] are directed to discretionary 7–113

[158] *Re Baden (No.1)* [1971] A.C. 424 at 449 and 457, per Lord Wilberforce.
[159] See *Re Gestetner, deceased* [1953] Ch. 672 at 688, approved in *Re Baden (No.1)* [1971] A.C. 424 at 453.
[160] [1973] Ch. 9.
[161] [1971] A.C. 424 at 457.

trusts, not powers. Nor do I think that the power is void as being capricious. In *Re Manisty's Settlement*[162] Templeman J. appears to be suggesting that a power to benefit "residents in Greater London" is void as being capricious "because the terms of the power negative any sensible intention on the part of the settlor". In saying that, I do not think that the judge had in mind a case in which the settlor was, for instance, a former chairman of the Greater London Council, as subsequent words of his on that page indicate. In any case, as he pointed out earlier, this consideration does not apply to intermediate powers, where no class which could be regarded as capricious has been laid down. Nor do I see how the power in the present case could be invalidated as being too vague, a possible ground of invalidity considered in *Re Manisty's Settlement*.[163] Of course, if there is some real vice in a power, and there are real problems of administration or execution, the court may have to hold the power invalid: but I think that the court should be slow to do this. Dispositions ought if possible to be upheld, and the court ought not to be astute to find grounds on which a power can be invalidated. Naturally, if it is shown that a power offends against some rule of law or equity, then it will be held to be void: but a power should not be held void on a peradventure. In my judgment, the power conferred by clause 4 of the settlement is valid.

7–114 [Megarry VC then accepted the argument that "clause 2 of the deed of appointment is void as being an excessive execution of the power" as it involved an impermissible delegation of that power by the trustees of the 1958 settlement to the trustees of the 1969 discretionary trust]. . .

7–115 That, I think, suffices to dispose of the case. I have not dealt with the submission which counsel for the defendants put in the forefront of his argument. This was that even if the power had been wide enough to authorise the creation of the discretionary trust, that trust was nevertheless as bad as being a trust in favour of "so hopelessly wide" a definition of beneficiaries "as not to form anything like a class so that the trust is administratively unworkable".[164] I do not propose to go into the authorities on this point. I consider that the duties of trustees under a discretionary trust are more stringent than those of trustees under a power of appointment,[165] and as at present advised I think that I would, if necessary, hold that an intermediate trust such as that in the present case is void as being administratively unworkable. In my view there is a difference between a power and a trust in this respect. The essence of that difference, I think, is that beneficiaries under a trust have rights of enforcement which mere objects of a power lack.

7–116 [He then held that the nieces and nephews living at the date of the settlement had become entitled to the trust fund on the expiration of 21 years from the date of the settlement by virtue of the gift over in default of any valid appointment within the 21 years.]

7–117 The analysis of Megarry VC is very helpful as it makes clear the link between the certainty of objects test and the nature of the duties owed by the holder of a power. Like the holder of a non-fiduciary power, the holder of a fiduciary power should not exercise the power in favour of someone outside the permitted class, and so the "is or is not" certainty test must be met.[166] In addition, however, the holder of a fiduciary power also has, at least,[167] the three duties identified by Megarry VC:[168] (i) to consider periodically whether or not he should exercise the power; (ii) to consider the range of objects of the power; and (iii) to consider the appropriateness of individual appointments.

7–118 As held by Megarry VC,[169] the width of the class does not in itself prevent T from fulfilling those duties. It is important that T can carry them out without having a complete list of all potential objects. In *Re Baden (No.2)*,[170] for example, Megaw LJ stated that (even in relation to a discretionary trust),

---

162 [1974] Ch. 17 at 27.

163 [1974] Ch. 17 at 24.

164 *Re Baden (No.1)* [1971] A.C. 424 at 457, per Lord Wilberforce.

165 See *Re Baden (No.1)* [1971] A.C. 424 at 457.

166 This may be the point that Templeman J had in mind in *Re Manisty's Settlement Trusts* [1974] Ch. 17 at 24 when stating that a power may be invalid if "too vague".

167 Note Megarry VC's statement that "I do not assert that this list is exhaustive": [1982] 1 W.L.R. 202 at 210 (extracted at para.7–110). See paras 2–091 to 2–093 for a discussion of the content of fiduciary duties.

168 [1982] 1 W.L.R. 202 at 210 (extracted at para.7–110).

169 Preferring the analysis of Templeman J in *Re Manisty's Settlement Trusts* [1974] Ch. 17 to the obiter views of Buckley LJ in *Blausten v IRC* [1972] Ch. 256.

170 [1973] Ch. 9 at 24.

there is no need for T to ascertain all of the possible objects: as long as a substantial number of objects can clearly be identified, T can proceed to consider how to exercise the power to select particular objects as recipients of part of the fund.

It could instead be argued, in the words of Lord Upjohn in *Re Gulbenkian's Settlement Trusts*,[171] that: **7–119**

> The trustees have a duty to select the donees of the donor's bounty from among the class designated by the donor; he has not entrusted them with any power to select the donees merely from known claimants who are within the class, for that is constituting a narrower class and the donor has given them no power to do this.

The practical difficulty, however, is that if a complete list of all potential objects were required, the flexibility available to S by conferring a power on trustees would be severely reduced. The most significant way of departing from S's intentions, of course, is to find that a power is invalid with the effect that those entitled in default of the exercise of the power take absolutely, without any chance for the power to be exercised. It is therefore reasonable for a court to presume that, in order for the power to be valid, S would be content with T, when considering the exercise of the power, to have an "appreciation of the width of the field",[172] rather than a duty to survey the whole field. This coincides with the point that we noted above in relation to certainty of subject matter:[173] the courts are prepared to take a practical view of certainty requirements in order to uphold, if possible, the intended arrangement. As Megarry VC phrased it:[174] **7–120**

> Dispositions ought if possible to be upheld, and the court ought not to be astute to find grounds on which a power can be invalidated.

Megarry VC did however consider whether the terms of the power were such as to make it "void as being capricious". In *Re Manisty's Settlement Trusts*,[175] Templeman J's view was that this ground of invalidity would arise if "the terms of the power negative any sensible intention on the part of the settlor." The point seems to be that, in discharging the three duties identified by Megarry VC, T needs to bear in mind the (expressed, objective) intention of the settlor: it will clearly be a key factor, for example, in considering the appropriateness of a particular possible distribution. If, however, the terms of the trust provide T with no evidence as to that intention, and there is no other evidence that T could draw on in considering what might be a sensible approach to the exercise of the power, then the power will be invalid. It would seem that this need for a "sensible intention on the part of the settlor" is not a requirement for a non-fiduciary power, as the holder of such a power is free in any case simply to refuse to consider whether to exercise it. **7–121**

It therefore seems that the need for the power to be non-capricious (i.e. for there to be evidence of a sensible intention on the part of the settlor, either from the terms of the power or from other circumstances) is a further requirement for the validity of a fiduciary power which does not apply to a non-fiduciary power. It should be emphasised, however, that this additional hurdle is extremely unlikely to cause any practical problems for S. After all, in practice, people do not tend to use settlements (especially ones drawn up with professional advice) as a means to act irrationally or mysteriously. Indeed, it is worth noting that the power in question in *Re Manisty's Settlement* was itself **7–122**

---

171 [1970] A.C. 508 at 524.
172 *Re Hay's Settlement Trusts* [1982] 1 W.L.R. 202 at 210 (extracted at para.7–109).
173 See para.7–089.
174 *Re Hay's Settlement Trusts* [1982] 1 W.L.R. 202 at 212 (extracted at para.7–113).
175 [1974] Ch. 17 at 27.

upheld, and the example given by Templeman J of a capricious power (a power to benefit "residents in Greater London") was queried by Megarry VC in *Re Hay's Settlement Trusts*,[176] on the basis that a sensible intention of the settlor might be evident if "the settlor was, for instance, a former chairman of the Greater London Council". Megarry VC also limited the potential reach of the non-capricious requirement by stating that it cannot apply where the power is an intermediate one (i.e. exercisable in favour of anyone in the world, bar those specifically excepted) as in such a case, "no class which could be regarded as capricious has been laid down".

7–123 Megarry VC also considered, and rejected, the argument that a fiduciary power will be invalid if it is "administratively unworkable", stating that this requirement applied only to discretionary trusts.[177] We will now consider the rules applying in the latter type of case.

iv. Discretionary Trusts

7–124 The distinction between a fiduciary power and a discretionary trust consists in the fact that the latter involves a duty on a trustee (T) to exercise the power in some way, and hence make some distribution of the trust property.[178] When holding property on a discretionary trust, T can be prevented from exercising her power in favour of a party outside the permitted class of objects and, as a fiduciary, she also has the duties outlined above.[179] The "is or is not" test and the non-capricious requirement must therefore apply to discretionary trusts as they do to a fiduciary power. The question is whether the addition of the duty to make some distribution should lead to further certainty requirements that apply to a discretionary trust but not to a fiduciary power.

7–125 This critical question was considered by the House of Lords in *Re Baden's Deed Trusts (No.1)*, which is also known as *McPhail v Doulton*.[180] It had been previously held by the Court of Appeal that a discretionary trust can be valid only if a complete list can be drawn up of all the objects of the trust, i.e. of all possible recipients of the trust property.[181] The majority of the House of Lords rejected that view and instead found that discretionary trusts should, with some small differences,[182] be subject to the same certainty test as applied by the House of Lords to fiduciary powers in *Re Gulbenkian's Settlement Trusts*:[183] the "is or is not" test. It should be noted that Lord Wilberforce in the following extract refers to a discretionary trust as a "trust power"[184] to distinguish it from what in *Re Hay's Settlement Trusts* Megarry VC called a "mere power" held in a fiduciary capacity.[185]

Re Baden's Deed Trusts (No.1), McPhail v Doulton

House of Lords [1971] A.C. 424

7–126 The facts and the issues appear clearly in the following speech of LORD WILBERFORCE with which LORD REID and VISCOUNT DILHORNE concurred, although dissenting speeches were delivered by LORD HODSON and LORD GUEST.

---

176 [1982] 1 W.L.R. 202 at 212 (extracted at para.7–113).
177 [1982] 1 W.L.R. 202 at 213 (extracted at para.7–115).
178 A discretionary trust need not be exhaustive however: the duty need not be to distribute all of the trust fund. For discussion see, e.g. Y. Grbich, "*Baden*: Awakening the Conceptually Moribund Trust" (1974) 37 M.L.R. 643, 643.
179 See para.7–117.
180 [1971] A.C. 424.
181 *IRC v Broadway Cottage Trusts* [1955] Ch. 20.
182 See further paras 7–146 to 7–149.
183 [1970] A.C. 508.
184 See too, e.g. *Re Baden (No.1)* [1971] A.C. 424 (extracted at paras 7–126 to 7–142).
185 See para.7–101.

LORD WILBERFORCE: My Lords, this appeal is concerned with the validity of a trust deed dated July 17, 1941, by which Mr. Bertram Baden established a fund for the benefit, broadly, of the staff of the respondent company Matthew Hall & Co Ltd. 7–127

The critical clauses are as follows: 7–128

"9. (a) The Trustees shall apply the net income of the Fund in making at their absolute discretion grants to or for benefit of any of the officers and employees or ex-officers or ex-employees of the Company or any relatives or dependants of any such persons in such amounts at such times and on such conditions (if any) as they think fit and any such grant may at their discretion be made by payment to the beneficiary or to any institution or person to be applied for his or her benefit and in the latter case the Trustees shall be under no obligation to see to the application of the money.

"(b) The Trustees shall not be bound to exhaust the income of any year or other period in making such grants as aforesaid and any income not so applied shall be dealt with as provided by clause 6(a) hereof enabling moneys to be placed with any Bank or to be invested.

"(c) The Trustees may realise any investments representing accumulations of income and apply the proceeds as though the same were income of the Fund and may also (but only with the consent of all the Trustees) at any time prior to the liquidation of the Fund realise any other part of the capital of the Fund which in the opinion of the Trustees it is desirable to realise in order to provide benefits for which the current income of the Fund is insufficient.

"10. All benefits being at the absolute discretion of the Trustees, no person shall have any right title or interest in the Fund otherwise than pursuant to the exercise of such discretion, and nothing herein contained shall prejudice the right of the Company to determine the employment of any officer or employee."

Clause 11 defines a perpetuity period within which the trusts are, in any event, to come to an end and clause 12 provides for the termination of the fund. On this event the trustees are directed to apply the fund in their discretion in one or more of certain specified ways of which one is in making grants as if they were grants under clause 9(a) . . . 7–129

In this House, the appellants contended that the provisions of clause 9(a) constitute a trust and not a power. If that is held to be the correct result both sides agree that the case must return to the Chancery Division for consideration, on this footing, whether this trust is valid. But here comes a complication. In the present state of authority, the decision as to validity would turn on the question whether a complete list (or on another view a list complete for practical purposes) can be drawn up of all possible beneficiaries. This follows from the Court of Appeal's decision in *Inland Revenue Comrs v Broadway Cottages Trust*[186] as applied in later cases by which, unless this House decides otherwise, the Court of Chancery would be bound. The respondents invite your Lordships to review this decision and challenge its correctness. So the second issue which arises, if clause 9(a) amounts to a trust, is whether the existing test for its validity is right in law and if not, what the test ought to be. 7–130

Before dealing with these two questions some general observations, or reflections, may be permissible. It is striking how narrow and in a sense artificial is the distinction, in cases such as the present, between trusts or as the particular type of trust is called, trust powers, and powers. It is only necessary to read the learned judgments in the Court of Appeal[187] to see that what to one mind may appear as a power of distribution coupled with a trust to dispose of the undistributed surplus, by accumulation or otherwise, may to another appear as a trust for distribution coupled with a power to withhold a portion and accumulate or otherwise dispose of it. A layman and, I suspect, also a logician, would find it hard to understand what difference there is. 7–131

It does not seem satisfactory that the entire validity of a disposition should depend on such delicate shading. And if one considers how in practice reasonable and competent trustees would act, and ought to act, in the two cases, surely a matter very relevant to the question of validity, the distinction appears even less significant. To say that there is no obligation to exercise a mere power and that no court will intervene to compel it, whereas a trust is mandatory and its execution must be compelled, may be legally correct enough, but the proposition does not contain an exhaustive comparison of the duties of persons who are 7–132

186 [1955] Ch. 20.
187 [1969] 2 Ch. 388.

trustees in the two cases. A trustee of an employees' benefit fund, whether given a power or a trust power, is still a trustee and he would surely consider in either case that he has a fiduciary duty; he is most likely to have been selected as a suitable person to administer it from his knowledge and experience, and would consider he has a responsibility to do so according to its purpose. It would be a complete misdescription of his position to say that, if what he has is a power unaccompanied by an imperative trust to distribute, he cannot be controlled by the court if he exercised it capriciously, or outside the field permitted by the trust.[188] Any trustee would surely make it his duty to know what is the permissible area of selection and then consider responsibly, in individual cases, whether a contemplated beneficiary was within the power and whether, in relation to other possible claimants, a particular grant was appropriate.

7–133 Correspondingly a trustee with a duty to distribute, particularly among a potentially very large class, would surely never require the preparation of a complete list of names, which anyhow would tell him little that he needs to know. He would examine the field, by class and category; might indeed make diligent and careful enquiries, depending on how much money he had to give away and the means at his disposal, as to the composition and needs of particular categories and of individuals within them; decide on certain priorities or proportions, and then select individuals according to their needs or qualifications. If he acts in this manner, can it really be said that he is not carrying out the trust?

7–134 Differences there certainly are between trusts (trust powers) and powers, but as regards validity should they be so great as that in one case complete, or practically complete ascertainment is needed, but not in the other? Such distinction as there is would seem to lie in the extent of the survey which the trustee is required to carry out; if he has to distribute the whole of a fund's income, he must necessarily make a wider and more systematic survey than if his duty is expressed in terms of a power to make grants. But just as, in the case of a power, it is possible to underestimate the fiduciary obligation of the trustee to whom it is given, so, in the case of a trust (trust power), the danger lies in overstating what the trustee requires to know or to enquire into before he can properly execute his trust. The difference may be one of degree rather than of principle; in the well-known words of Sir George Farwell[189] trusts and powers are often blended, and the mixture may vary in its ingredients.

7–135 I now consider whether the provisions of clause 9(a) constitute a trust or a power. Naturally read, the intention of the deed seems to me clear: clause 9(a), whose language is mandatory ("shall"), creates, together with a power of selection, a trust for distribution of the income, the strictness of which is qualified by clause 9(b) which allows the income of any one year to be held up and (under clause 6(a)) either placed, for the time, with a bank, or, if thought fit, invested. Whether there is, in any technical sense, an accumulation seems to me in the present context a jejune enquiry; what is relevant is that clause 9(c) marks the difference between "accumulations" of income and the capital of the fund: the former can be distributed by a majority of the trustees, the latter cannot. As to clause 10, I do not find in it any decisive indication. If anything it seems to point in favour of a trust, but both this and other points of detail are insignificant in the face of the clearly expressed scheme of clause 9. I therefore declare that the provisions of clause 9(a) constitute a trust and remit the case to the Chancery Division for determination whether on this basis clause 9 is (subject to the effects of section 164 of the Law of Property Act 1925) valid or void for uncertainty.

7–136 This makes it necessary to consider whether, in so doing, the court should proceed on the basis that the relevant test is that laid down in the *Broadway Cottages* case[190] or some other test. That decision gave the authority of the Court of Appeal to the distinction between cases where trustees are given a power of selection and those where they are bound by a trust for selection. In the former case the position, as decided by this House, is that the power is valid if it can be said with certainty whether any given individual is or is not a member of the class and does not fail simply because it is impossible to ascertain every member of the class. (The *Gulbenkian* case.[191]) But in the latter case it is said to be necessary, for the trust to be valid, that the whole range of objects (I use the language of the Court of Appeal) should be ascertained or capable of ascertainment.

7–137 The respondents invited your Lordships to assimilate the validity test for trusts to that which applies to powers. Alternatively, they contended that in any event the test laid down in the *Broadway Cottages* case was too rigid, and that a trust should be upheld if there is sufficient practical certainty in its definition for

188 cf. G. Farwell, *Farwell on Powers*, 3rd edn (Stevens & Son, 1916), p.524.
189 G. Farwell, *Farwell on Powers*, 3rd edn (1916), p.10.
190 [1955] Ch. 20.
191 [1970] A.C. 508.

it to be carried out, if necessary with the administrative assistance of the court, according to the expressed intention of the settlor. I would agree with this, but this does not dispense from examination of the wider argument. The basis for the *Broadway Cottages* case principle is stated to be that a trust cannot be valid unless, if need be, it can be executed by the court, and that the court can only execute it by ordering an equal distribution in which every beneficiary shares. So it is necessary to examine the authority and reason for this supposed rule as to the execution of trusts by the court.

Assuming, as I am prepared to do for present purposes, that the test of validity is whether the trust can be executed by the court, it does not follow that execution is impossible unless there can be equal division. As a matter of reason, to hold that a principle of equal division applies to trusts such as the present is certainly paradoxical. Equal division is surely the last thing the settlor ever intended; equal division among all may, probably would, produce a result beneficial to none. Why suppose that the court would lend itself to a whimsical execution? And as regards authority, I do not find that the nature of the trust, and of the court's powers over trusts, calls for any such rigid rule. Equal division may be sensible and has been decreed, in cases of family trusts for a limited class, here there is life in the maxim "equality is equity," but the cases provide numerous examples where this has not been so, and a different type of execution has been ordered, appropriate to the circumstances. . . . **7–138**

So I come to *Inland Revenue Comrs v Broadway Cottage Trusts*.[192] This was certainly a case of trust, and it proceeded on the basis of an admission, in the words of the judgment, "that the class of 'beneficiaries' is incapable of ascertainment." In addition to the discretionary trust of income, there was a trust of capital for all the beneficiaries living or existing at the terminal date. This necessarily involved equal division and it seems to have been accepted that it was void for uncertainty since there cannot be equal division among a class unless all the members of the class are known. . . **7–139**

. . . I think we are free to review the *Broadway Cottages* case. The conclusion which I would reach, implicit in the previous discussion, is that the wide distinction between the validity test for powers and that for trust powers, is unfortunate and wrong, that the rule recently fastened on the courts by the *Broadway Cottages* case ought to be discarded, and that the test for the validity of trust powers ought to be similar to that accepted by this House in *Re Gulbenkian's Settlement Trusts* for powers, namely that the trust is valid if it can be said with certainty that any given individual is or is not a member of the class. **7–140**

Assimilation of the validity test does not involve the complete assimilation of trust powers with powers. As to powers, I agree with my noble and learned friend Lord Upjohn in *Re Gulbenkian's Settlement* that although the trustees may, and normally will, be under a fiduciary duty to consider whether or in what way they should exercise their power, the court will not normally compel its exercise. It will intervene if the trustees exceed their powers, and possibly if they are proved to have exercised it capriciously. But in the case of a trust power, if the trustees do not exercise it, the court will; I respectfully adopt as to this the statement in Lord Upjohn's opinion.[193] I would venture to amplify this by saying that the court, if called on to execute the trust power, will do so in the manner best calculated to give effect to the settlor's or testator's intentions. It may do so by appointing new trustees, or authorising or directing representative persons of the classes of beneficiaries to prepare a scheme of distribution, or even, should the proper basis for distribution appear, by itself directing the trustees so to distribute. The books give many instances where this has been done and I see no reason in principle why they should not do so in the modern field of discretionary trusts.[194] Then, as to the trustees' duty of enquiry or ascertainment, in each case the trustees ought to make such a survey of the range of objects or possible beneficiaries as will enable them to carry out their fiduciary duty.[195] A wider and more comprehensive range of enquiry is called for in the case of trust powers than in the case of powers. **7–141**

Two final points: first, as to the question of certainty, I desire to emphasise the distinction clearly made and explained by Lord Upjohn,[196] between linguistic or semantic uncertainty which, if unresolved by the court, renders the gift void, and the difficulty of ascertaining the existence or whereabouts of members of the class, a matter with which the court can appropriately deal on an application for directions. There may be a third case where the meaning of the words used is clear but the definition of beneficiaries is so **7–142**

---

192 [1955] Ch. 20.

193 [1970] A.C. 508 at 525.

194 See *Brunsden v Woolredge* (1765) Amb. 507; *Supple v Lowson* (1773) Amb. 729; *Liley v Hey* (1842) 1 Hare 580; and *Lewin on Trusts* (16th edn, 1964), p.630.

195 cf. *Liley v Hey* (1842) 1 Hare 580.

196 [1970] A.C. 508 at 524.

hopelessly wide as not to form "anything like a class" so that the trust is administratively unworkable or in Lord Eldon L.C.'s words one that cannot be executed.[197] I hesitate to give examples for they may prejudice future cases, but perhaps "all the residents of Greater London" will serve. I do not think that a discretionary trust for "relatives" even of a living person falls within this category . . .

7–143 [The appeal was therefore allowed. It was declared that the provisions of clause 9(a) constituted a trust. The case was remitted for determination whether, on the basis of the test set out by the majority of the House of Lords, clause 9 was valid or void for uncertainty. On this remittal, Brightman J. held that the trust was valid, and this was confirmed by the Court of Appeal in *Re Baden's Deed Trusts (No.2)*.[198]]

7–144 We noted above[199] that the certainty of objects test is based on the need for the court to police limits and enforce duties. The important point about a discretionary trust, as opposed to a fiduciary power, is that the trustee has a duty to make at least some distribution, and the court may need to enforce that duty. It is therefore vital to know what form such enforcement might take. If the only option for the court is to order the trustee to divide the relevant property equally between all those within the class then, as Lord Wilberforce noted, it is necessary to have a complete list of all such objects.[200] That seems to have been the assumption behind the Court of Appeal's view, in *IRC v Broadway Cottage Trusts*,[201] that a discretionary trust is valid only if a complete list of objects can be drawn up.

7–145 Lord Wilberforce's rejection of that view depends on the (surely correct) point that a court is not so limited when it comes to enforcing a discretionary trust. Indeed, in a case such as *Re Baden (No.1)*, where the settlor has nominated a very wide class of objects, such equal division, which would perhaps see each party acquiring only a very small sum of money, is "surely the last thing the settlor ever intended; equal division among all may, probably would, produce a result beneficial to none".[202] As other means of enforcement are available,[203] the potential need to enforce the trustee's duty to make some distribution does not require a complete list of objects to be drawn up.

7–146 As Lord Wilberforce also noted, given the difficulties in some cases of distinguishing between a fiduciary power and a discretionary trust, it is also sensible to align the certainty tests applying in each case.[204] Indeed, it has since been held, by the Privy Council in *Schmidt v Rosewood Trust Ltd*,[205] that even if a party is only an object of a fiduciary power, rather than of a discretionary trust, that party "may also be entitled to protection from a court of equity, although the circumstances in which he may seek protection, and the nature of the protection he may expect to obtain, will depend on the court's discretion".[206] It therefore seems that, in exceptional cases at least, it may be possible for a court to step in and execute a fiduciary power.[207]

7–147 This does not mean, however, that the certainty tests to be applied to a fiduciary power and to a discretionary trust are necessarily identical. First, as to policing T's duties, Lord Wilberforce suggested, in relation to T's duty to survey the range of objects of the power, that: "A wider and more comprehensive range of enquiry is called for in the case of trust powers [ie a discretionary trust] than in the

---

197 *Morice v Bishop of Durham* (1805) 10 Ves. 521 at 527 (see paras 8–002 to 8–007).
198 [1973] Ch. 9 (extracted at para.7–155ff).
199 See para.7–090.
200 [1971] A.C. 424 at 450 (extracted at paras 7–137 to 7–138).
201 [1955] Ch. 20.
202 [1971] A.C. 424 at 451 (extracted at para.7–138).
203 [1971] A.C. 424 at 451 (extracted at para.7–138).
204 [1971] A.C. 424 at 448–449 (extracted at paras 7–134 to 7–142).
205 [2003] 2 A.C. 709.
206 [2003] 2 A.C. 709 at [51], per Lord Walker.
207 See *Mettoy Pension Trustees Ltd v Evans* [1991] 2 All E.R. 513 at 549, approved in *Schmidt v Rosewood Trust Ltd* [2003] UKPC 26; [2003] 2 A.C. 709 at [42], [51].

case of powers."[208] Secondly, as to enforcing T's duties, Lord Wilberforce suggested that there may be cases in which:

> the meaning of the words used is clear but the definition of beneficiaries is so hopelessly wide as not to form 'anything like a class' so that the trust is administratively unworkable or in Lord Eldon L.C.'s words one that cannot be executed.[209]

The first of Lord Wilberforce's points is hard to understand and seems to have had no practical effect: in later cases, such as *Re Hay's*, no distinction has been made between fiduciary powers and discretionary trusts in considering the nature of a fiduciary's duty to survey the range of objects. Even if the need for the discretionary trustee to make some exercise of the power justifies a somewhat higher duty in this respect, it is very difficult to translate it into a tangibly different certainty test. **7–148**

The second of Lord Wilberforce's points, in contrast, has had an impact, and there are cases in which discretionary trusts have failed on the grounds of administrative unworkability. The example hesitantly given by Lord Wilberforce was of a class of "all the residents of Greater London".[210] In *R. v District Auditor, Ex p. West Yorkshire MCC*,[211] an attempt to set up a discretionary trust "for the benefit of any or all or some of the inhabitants of the County of West Yorkshire" failed on the basis of administrative unworkability.[212] It has been assumed that the requirement of administrative workability applies only to discretionary trusts, and not to powers, even if fiduciary.[213] **7–149**

The requirement of administratively workability does therefore seem to be a distinction between discretionary trusts and fiduciary powers. It is not of great practical importance, even in the rare case where a trust or power in relation to such a class is set up. This is because fiduciary powers are subject to the non-capricious requirement,[214] and this may well also apply where the apparent arrangement would be administratively unworkable. The distinction does appear to be defensible as a matter of principle, if it is related to the fact that the discretionary trustee, unlike a fiduciary power-holder, has a duty to make some distribution, and the court may need to enforce that duty. It may then be possible to say that there are some decisions as to distribution that a fiduciary power-holder may validly make but which a court would not wish to undertake, as the role of the courts as even-handed purveyors of justice means that they should not also be involved in broad polycentric disputes as to, for example, how a large sum of money should be spent amongst the 2.5 million inhabitants of West Yorkshire.[215] **7–150**

v. Fixed Trusts

If a settlor (S) transfers property to a trustee (T) to hold on trust for various beneficiaries, each of whom is to receive a fixed share of the benefit of the property, then of course the identity of each beneficiary must be certain. This requirement causes no practical problems as S will naturally have identified the **7–151**

---

208 [1971] A.C. 424 at 457 (extracted at para.7–140).
209 [1971] A.C. 424 at 457 (extracted at para.7–141).
210 [1971] A.C. 424 at 457 (extracted at para.7–141).
211 (1986) R.V.R. 24.
212 See too *Re Harding (Deceased)* [2007] EWHC 3 (Ch); [2008] Ch. 235 at [15]: it is "common ground that a private trust for such a large class as the black community in four London Boroughs would be so large as to make a private trust unworkable, and hence void".
213 See, e.g. *Re Hay's Settlement Trusts* [1982] 1 W.L.R. 202 at 212 (extracted at para.7–115).
214 See para.7–121.
215 For example, whilst it might be permissible for T, as a private individual, to choose to spend the money on sports facilities for local residents, a court might not want to have to take a view as to whether the money should be spent on that purpose or instead on schools, or hospitals, or public transport, etc.

beneficiaries: if one or more of the beneficiaries cannot be found, this will not invalidate the trust and jeopardise the rights of the ascertainable beneficiaries, as the trustees can simply pay the shares of the missing beneficiaries into court, or otherwise ask the court for directions.[216]

7–152 A difficulty may arise, however, if the trust calls for equal division amongst members of a certain class, and the number within that class cannot be established, as that uncertainty means that the extent of any individual's beneficial interest cannot be established. In such a case, then, the "complete list" test, which no longer applies to discretionary trusts, must apply.

vi. Gifts Subject to a Condition Subsequent

7–153 We started this discussion by considering gifts subject to a condition precedent, such as where S transfers property to T to hold on trust for B *if* B meets a certain condition. A condition subsequent is imposed where, instead, B acquires her right but that right is forfeited if the condition occurs. We saw that the certainty test applied in the case of a condition precedent is very easy to satisfy, as, if there is a situation in which one person might clearly qualify for the gift, then that person should not lose their entitlement by means of the gift's being seen as invalid. The same concern, of protecting B's entitlement, leads to a very strict certainty test's being applied in the case of a gift subject to a condition subsequent. The condition must be described in such a way that the court can see from the outset precisely and distinctly upon the happening of what event the interest is to be forfeited.[217] The circumstances involving forfeiture must be clearly known in advance so that B knows precisely where she stands. The condition will also be invalid if it is repugnant to the essential alienability of the interest given[218] or if it is void on the grounds of public policy.[219]

C. Applying the Relevant Test

i. Applying the "Is or Is Not" Test

7–154 We have seen that the "is or is not" test, which states that a power or discretionary trust will be invalid if it is not possible to tell of any given person whether that person is or is not in the permitted class, is crucial in determining the validity of powers (both non-fiduciary and fiduciary) and discretionary trusts. Having determined by a majority that the test should apply to the discretionary trust that S attempted to set up in *Re Baden's Deed Trusts (No.1)*, the House of Lords remitted the case to the High Court so the test could be applied.

---

216 See too Trustee Act 1925 s.27, which gives trustees and personal representatives who have advertised properly and waited for beneficiaries to come forward immunity from liability if funds are then distributed only amongst ascertainable beneficiaries. Note too that, by means of a *Benjamin* order (named for *Re Benjamin* [1902] 1 Ch. 723), a court may allow a trustee or executor to distribute even if not all of the beneficiaries have been ascertained. See, e.g. *Re Green's W.T.* [1985] 3 All E.R. 455. The purpose in each case is to protect the trustees or executor from liability for the distribution; the beneficial interests of any unascertained beneficiaries do continue unless and until, for example, the relevant property is acquired by a bona fide purchaser for value without notice.

217 *Clavering v Ellison* (1859) 7 H.L. Cas. 707; *Blathwayt v Lord Cawley* [1976] A.C. 397 at 429. This is consistent with equity's general sensitivity to the effects of forfeiture, as discussed in paras 2–217 to 2–260.

218 *Re Scientific Investment Pension Plan Trusts* [1999] Ch. 53 at 59.

219 See, e.g. *Church Property Trustees of Newcastle Diocese v Ebbeck* (1960) 104 C.L.R. 394: a condition that B must "profess Protestant faith" was void for public policy as it was designed by the testator to encourage his three sons to divorce their Catholic wives. A condition designed to restrain marriage altogether will also be void as contrary to public policy: see, e.g. *Lloyd v Lloyd* (1852) 2 Sim. N.S. 255. See too J.-S. Beaudry and A. Nair, "Property, Equality and the Freedom to Discriminate: The Case of the Discriminatory Gift' in S. Farran. et al (eds) *Modern Studies in Property Law: vol 11* (Hart Publishing, 2021).

The critical clause in the trust deed (cl.9(a)) provided for grants "to or for the benefit of any of the officers and employees or ex-officers or ex-employees of [the defined company] or to any relatives or dependants of any such persons".[220] Brightman J decided at first instance that this class did pass the "is or is not" test, although in reaching that conclusion he held that the trustees and a court could assume that anyone who could not show that she was in the class was in fact outside the class. The Court of Appeal confirmed that result but each of the three judges provided different reasons for his decision. **7–155**

Re Baden's Deed Trusts (No.2)

Court of Appeal [1973] Ch. 9

SACHS L.J.: It is first to be noted that the deed must be looked at through the eyes of a businessman seeking to advance the welfare of the employees of his firm and those so connected with the employees that a benevolent employer would wish to help them. He would not necessarily be looking at the words he uses with the same eyes as those of a man making a will. Accordingly, whether a court is considering the concept implicit in relevant words, or whether it is exercising the function of a court of construction, it should adopt that same practical and common-sense approach which was enjoined by Upjohn J. in *Re Sayer*[221] and by Lord Wilberforce in *Re Baden (No.1)*,[222] and which would be used by an employer setting up such a fund. **7–156**

The next point as regards approach that requires consideration is the contention, strongly pressed by Mr Vinelott [counsel for S's executors, arguing that the trust was invalid], that the court must always be able to say whether any given postulant is not within the relevant class as well as being able to say whether he is within it. In construing the words already cited from the speech of Lord Wilberforce in *Re Baden (No.1)*,[223] (as well as those of Lord Reid and Lord Upjohn in *Re Gulbenkian's Settlement Trusts*)[224], it is essential to bear in mind the difference between conceptual uncertainty and evidential difficulties. That distinction is explicitly referred to by Lord Wilberforce in *Re Baden (No.1)*,[225] when he said: **7–157**

> ". . . as to the question of certainty. I desire to emphasise the distinction clearly made and explained by Lord Upjohn[226] between linguistic or semantic uncertainty which, if unresolved by the court, renders the gift void, and the difficulty of ascertaining the existence or whereabouts of members of the class, a matter with which the court can appropriately deal on an application for directions."

As Mr. Vinelott himself rightly observed, "the court is never defeated by evidential uncertainty," and it is in my judgment clear that it is conceptual certainty to which reference was made when the "is or is not a member of the class" test was enunciated. (Conceptual uncertainty was in the course of argument conveniently exemplified, rightly or wrongly matters not, by the phrase "someone under a moral obligation" and contrasted with the certainty of the words "first cousins.") Once the class of persons to be benefited is conceptually certain it then becomes a question of fact to be determined on evidence whether any postulant has on inquiry been proved to be within it: if he is not so proved, then he is not in it. That position remains the same whether the class to be benefited happens to be small (such as "first cousins") or large (such as "members of the X Trade Union" or "those who have served in the Royal Navy"). The suggestion that such trusts could be invalid because it might be impossible to prove of a given individual that he was *not* in the relevant class is wholly fallacious—and only Mr. Vinelott's persuasiveness has prevented me from saying that the contention is almost unarguable. **7–158**

It was suggested that some difficulty arises from the passage in the speech of Lord Wilberforce in *Re Baden (No. 1)*,[227] where he referred to the need of trustees "to make such a survey of the range of objects or **7–159**

---

220 See [1973] Ch 9 at 12.
221 [1957] Ch. 423 at 436.
222 [1971] A.C. 424 at 452.
223 [1971] A.C. 424 at 450: "can it be said with certainty that any given individual is or is not a member of the class?".
224 [1970] A.C. 508 at 518, 521 and 525.
225 [1971] A.C. 424 at 457.
226 *Re Gulbenkian's Settlement Trusts* [1970] A.C. 508 at 524.
227 [1971] A.C. 424 at 457.

possible beneficiaries as will enable them to carry out their fiduciary duty." The word "range," however, in that context has an inbuilt and obvious element of considerable elasticity, and thus provides for an almost infinitely variable range of vision suitable to the particular trust to be considered. In modern trusts of the category now under consideration it may be sufficient to know whether the range of potential postulants runs into respectively dozens, hundreds, thousands, tens of thousands or even hundreds of thousands. I cannot imagine that the above-quoted passage was intended to cast doubt, for instance, on the validity of wide-ranging discretionary trusts such as those of the Army Benevolent Fund. When looked at in the context of the rest of the speech this particular passage does not seem to me to cause any difficulty. In my judgment it refers to something quite different, to a need to provide a list of individuals or to provide a closely accurate enumeration of the numbers in the class: it relates to that width of the field from which beneficiaries may be drawn and which the trustees should have in mind so that they can adapt to it their methods of discretionary selection. Assessing in a business-like way "the size of the problem" is what the trustees are called on to do. . .

7-160 In agreement with the practical approach of Brightman J.,[228] I consider that the trustees, or if necessary the court, are quite capable of coming to a conclusion in any given case as to whether or not a particular candidate could properly be described as a dependant—a word that, as the judge said, "conjures up a sufficiently distinct picture." I agree, too, that any one wholly or partly dependent on the means of another is a "dependant." There is thus no conceptual uncertainty inherent in that word and the executors' contentions as to the effect of its use fail.

7-161 As regards "relatives" Brightman J., after stating, "It is not in dispute that a person is a relative of an . . . employee . . ., if both trace legal descent from a common ancestor:" a little later said: "In practice, the use of the expression 'relatives' cannot cause the slightest difficulty."[229] With that view I agree for the reasons he gave when he correctly set out the evidential position.

7-162 MEGAW L.J.: If this trust were to be held void for uncertainty because of the inclusion of the "dependants" in clause 9 (a), I think that few trusts would stand. I do not find any greater uncertainty in it than is inherent in, or can by ingenuity be conjured up in relation to, any ordinary, well understood word. . .

7-163 Then it is said that the deed is invalid because of the inclusion of the word "relatives." Brightman J.,[230] approached that question on the basis that: "It is not in dispute that a person is a relative of an officer or employee or ex-officer or ex-employee, if both trace legal descent from a common ancestor." He held that the executors' argument on this issue also failed. I agree, for the reasons given by the judge.

7-164 [The test set out by Lord Wilberforce in *Re Baden (No.1)*[231]] is this:

> ". . . the power is valid if it can be said with certainty whether any given individual is or is not a member of the class and does not fail simply because it is impossible to ascertain every member of the class."

7-165 The executors' argument concentrates on the words "or is not" in the first of the two limbs of the sentence quoted above: "if it can be said with certainty whether any given individual is *or is not* a member of the class." It is said that those words have been used deliberately, and have only one possible meaning; and that, however startling or drastic or unsatisfactory the result may be—and Mr. Vinelott does not shrink from saying that the consequence is drastic—this court is bound to give effect to the words used in the House of Lords' definition of the test. It would be quite impracticable for the trustees to ascertain in many cases whether a particular person was *not* a relative of an employee. The most that could be said is: "There is no proof that he is a relative." But there would still be no "certainty" that such a person was not a relative. Hence, so it is said, the test laid down by the House of Lords is not satisfied, and the trust is void. For it cannot be said with certainty, in relation to any individual, that he is not a relative.

7-166 I do not think it was contemplated that the words "or is not" would produce that result. It would, as I see it, involve an inconsistency with the latter part of the same sentence: "does not fail simply because it is impossible to ascertain every member of the class." The executors' contention, in substance and reality, is that it does fail "simply because it is impossible to ascertain every member of the class.". . .

7-167 In my judgment, much too great emphasis is placed in the executors' argument on the words "or is not." To my mind, the test is satisfied if, as regards at least a substantial number of objects, it can be said with

---

[228] [1972] Ch. 607 at 625.
[229] [1972] Ch. 607 at 625.
[230] [1972] Ch. 607 at 625.
[231] [1971] A.C. 424 at 450 and 454.

certainty that they fall within the trust; even though, as regards a substantial number of other persons, if they ever for some fanciful reason fell to be considered, the answer would have to be, not "they are outside the trust," but "it is not proven whether they are in or out." What is a "substantial number" may well be a question of common sense and of degree in relation to the particular trust: particularly where, as here, it would be fantasy, to use a mild word, to suggest that any practical difficulty would arise in the fair, proper and sensible administration of this trust in respect of relatives and dependants.

STAMP L.J.: There are, however, in my judgment serious difficulties in the way of a rejection of Mr. Vinelott's submission. . . **7–168**

The first difficulty, as I see it, is that the rejection of Mr. Vinelott's submission involves holding that the trust is good if there are individuals—or even one—of whom you can say with certainty that he is a member of the class. That was the test adopted by and the decision of the Court of Appeal in *Re Gulbenkian's Settlement Trusts*[232] where what was under consideration was a power of distribution among a class conferred upon trustees as distinct from a trust for distribution: but when the case came before the House of Lords that test was decisively rejected and the more stringent test upon which Mr. Vinelott insists was adopted. Clearly Lord Wilberforce in expressing the view that the test of validity of a discretionary trust ought to be similar to that accepted by the House of Lords in the *re Gulbenkian's Settlement Trusts*[233] did not take the view that it was sufficient that you could find individuals who were clearly members of the class; for he himself remarked, towards the end of his speech as to the trustees' duty of inquiring or ascertaining, that in each case the trustees ought to make such a survey of the range of objects or possible beneficiaries as will enable them to carry out their fiduciary duty. It is not enough that trustees should do nothing but distribute the fund among those objects of the trust who happen to be at hand or present themselves. . . **7–169**

If the matter rested there, it would in my judgment follow that, treating the word "relatives" as meaning descendants from a common ancestor, a trust for distribution such as is here in question would not be valid. Any "survey of the range of the objects or possible beneficiaries" would certainly be incomplete, and I am able to discern no principle upon which such a survey could be conducted or where it should start or finish. The most you could do, so far as regards relatives, would be to find individuals who are clearly members of the class—the test which was accepted in the Court of Appeal, but rejected in the House of Lords, in *Re Gulbenkian's Settlement Trusts*.[234] **7–170**

The matter does not, however, rest there. . .[Stamp L.J. then referred to *Harding v Glyn*,[235] in which a court executed a discretionary trust for relations by distributing to the testator's next of kin in equal shares]. . . Does it then make any difference that here the discretionary trust for relations was a reference not to the relations of a deceased person but of one who was living? I think not. The next of kin of a living person are as readily ascertainable at any given time as the next of kin of one who is dead. A trust for the next of kin of a person, without more, was not a trust for the next of kin according to the statutes which would regulate the distribution of the personal property of a deceased person had he died intestate, but a trust for his nearest blood relations.[236] To execute a discretionary trust for the relations or relatives of a living person by distribution among his nearest blood relations appears to me a satisfactory method of so doing; and, if it were necessary to give a construction to the word "relatives" in relating to a living person in an inter vivos settlement, to construe it as a reference to his nearest blood relations would be far more likely to give effect to the intention than a construction which embraced all who were descended from one of his ancestors. . .nothing could be more improbable than that [S] should have intended the trustees to be at liberty to make grants to a relative of an employee of whose very existence that employee might be ignorant. "Nearest blood relations or dependants" makes more sense. . . **7–171**

The only other challenge to the validity of the trust is directed against the use of the word "dependants" which it is said introduces a linguistic or semantic uncertainty. That in the context the word connotes financial dependence I do not doubt, and although in a given case there may be a doubt whether there be a sufficient degree of dependence to satisfy the qualification of being a "dependant," that is a question which can be determined by the court and does not introduce linguistic uncertainty. **7–172**

---

232 [1968] Ch. 126.
233 [1970] A.C. 508.
234 [1970] A.C. 508.
235 (1739) 1 Atk. 469.
236 *Re Gray's Settlement* [1896] 2 Ch. 802.

7–173 Stamp LJ's approach can be seen as more faithful to the specific language used by Lord Wilberforce in *Re Baden (No.1)*: it must be possible to tell of any given person whether she is *or is not* in the class. In other words, in considering if a given postulant, X, is a relative or dependant, it must be possible to put X in either in the "Yes" box or the "No" box. A discretionary trust would therefore be void if X had to go into a "Don't know" box. On that approach, the trust was valid (in a world before DNA testing) only because Stamp LJ was prepared to treat relatives as meaning "next-of-kin" or "nearest blood relations" in which case any postulant would fall within the "Yes" box or the "No" box.

7–174 The approach of Sachs and Megaw LJJ (as well as that of Brightman J at first instance)[237] could be seen as more faithful to the underlying policy of Lord Wilberforce's speech in *Re Baden (No.1)*, which was to develop the law so as to give S the flexibility to set up a discretionary trust with a potentially very wide class of objects. It is also consistent with the pragmatic, rather than overly-technical, approach to certainty tests that we have seen at a number of points in this chapter.[238] A key part of their approach is the assumption that if it cannot be shown that X is in the class, X must be treated as being out of the class. This may introduce an element of artificiality, but it enables a court to police the trustees, who know that they are at risk if exercising a power in favour of a party who has not demonstrated that she is within the permitted class.

7–175 Once such an assumption is adopted, however, the question arises of whether anything in fact remains of the certainty test: might any class, even "friends" be valid on the basis that anyone not clearly in the class must be treated as outside it? The practical problem in such a case might be that so few people would clearly qualify that T would not be able to exercise a genuine choice when deciding how to exercise the power. Megaw LJ sought to deal with this by imposing a requirement that there must be a "substantial" core of objects who are clearly within the class. This raises again the point raised by Lord Upjohn in *Re Gulbenkian's Settlement Trusts*:[239] the consequence is that the class is narrowed from that which S stated; but at least the trust is validated.

7–176 Sachs LJ, in contrast, sought to give some content to the certainty test by adopting the distinction between conceptual and evidential uncertainty.[240] This provides another means of invalidating a discretionary trust for "friends": the term in itself is inherently uncertain, as no stable definition can be provided. In practical terms, though, it is difficult to see why this matters: if it could be shown that sufficient people were clearly within the class (as the uncertain term nonetheless has a core meaning) then, given the assumption that anyone who cannot show she is in the class is outside it, the duties of the trustees could, it seems, be discharged in practice.

7–177 It might be thought that, given the differing approaches adopted in *Re Baden (No.2)*, the law is in an unsatisfactory state. It is certainly not the case, however, that the courts have subsequently had to deal with problems arising from the application of the "is or is not" test to powers and discretionary trusts, nor that the use of such wide powers and trusts has diminished. It seems rather that, with the confirmation in *Re Baden (No.2)* that key terms such as "relative" and "dependant" are sufficiently certain, well-advised settlors have felt no need to investigate the boundaries of the certainty test through the sort of idiosyncratic terms that are beloved of examiners but extremely rare in practice.

---

237 [1972] Ch. 607 at 626.

238 See paras 7–089 and 7–120.

239 [1970] A.C. 508 at 524 (extracted at para.7–119).

240 For further discussion of this distinction, see C. Emery, "The Most Hallowed Principle—Certainty of Beneficiaries of Trusts and of Powers of Appointment" (1982) 98 L.Q.R. 551.

ii. Resolving Apparent Uncertainty

It is possible for a settlor (S) to attempt to avoid certainty problems by identifying a party who can resolve a dispute as to whether X is or is not in the permitted class, or has or has not met a particular condition. It is clear that such a party's decisions may assist in relation to evidential uncertainty although, following *Re Baden (No.2)*,[241] such uncertainty is in any case unlikely to invalidate the planned arrangement. The more important question is as to the impact of such a party's decision on potential conceptual uncertainty caused by the inherent vagueness of the terms used to define a class. **7–178**

In *Re Tuck's Settlement Trusts*,[242] for example, S's settlement provided for payment of an income to B "if and when and so long as he shall be of the Jewish faith and be married to an approved wife". An approved wife was defined as "a wife of Jewish blood by one or both of her parents and who has been brought up in and has never departed from and at the date of the marriage continues to worship according to the Jewish faith". It was also provided that as to such facts, in the case of dispute or doubt, the decision of the Chief Rabbi in London of either the Sephardim or Ashkenazim communities "shall be conclusive". It was held by the Court of Appeal that these terms were conditions precedent and, given the lenient test applied in such cases,[243] they were certain enough even without the reference to the Chief Rabbi. **7–179**

In an obiter discussion, Lord Denning MR rejected the argument of counsel that the appointment of a party to resolve doubt could not save a settlement from conceptual (as opposed to evidential) uncertainty, stating instead that:[244] **7–180**

> I see no reason why a testator or settlor should not provide that any dispute or doubt should be resolved by his executors or trustees, or even by a third person . . . [If] the appointed person is ready and willing to resolve the doubt or difficulty, I see no reason why he should not do so. So long as he does not misconduct himself or come to a decision which is wholly unreasonable, I think his decision should stand. After all, that was plainly the intention of the testator or settlor.

Lord Denning's analysis can be contrasted with that of Jenkins J in *Re Coxen*:[245] **7–181**

> If the testator had insufficiently defined the state of affairs on which the trustees were to form their opinion he would not have saved the condition from invalidity on the ground of uncertainty merely by making their opinion the criterion, although the declaration by the trustees of this or that opinion would be an event about which in itself there could be no uncertainty.

This view was followed in *Re Jones*[246] and in *Re Wright's Will Trusts*[247] where a gift of property to trustees "to use the same at their absolute discretion for such people and institutions as they think have helped me or my late husband" failed for uncertainty. The point is that S had not intended the trustees to be able to appoint to anyone at all: a condition is attached and the trustees need some means of making sense of that condition. **7–182**

It may be that Lord Denning's approach can be reconciled to this by finding that, if a party is appointed by S to resolve doubts, this does not mean that the arrangement will necessarily be certain. **7–183**

---

241 [1973] Ch. 9: see paras 7–155 to 7–171.
242 [1978] Ch. 49.
243 See paras 7–093 to 7–096.
244 [1978] Ch. 49 at 61–62.
245 [1948] Ch. 747 at 761–762.
246 [1953] Ch. 125: "if at any time B shall in the uncontrolled opinion of the trustee have social or other relationship with C."
247 [1981] L.S. Gaz. 841. Also see *Tatham v Huxtable* (1950) 81 C.L.R. 639 at 653.

After all, the court[248] must have some means of reviewing any decision by the appointed party: in *Dundee General Hospital Board v Walker*,[249] a case heavily relied on by Lord Denning in *Re Tuck*,[250] Lord Reid pointed out (in a case where such a power had been given to trustees), that their decision could be challenged:

> if it can be shown that the trustees considered the wrong question, or that, although they purported to consider the right question, they did not really apply their minds to it or perversely shut their eyes to the facts, or that they did not act honestly or in good faith.

7–184 It must similarly be the case that the decision by the party appointed to resolve doubts can be challenged if it is so unreasonable that no reasonable person could have made it. In order to consider such challenges, it seems, the court will need *some* information as to the criteria to be used by the appointed party when making the decision, and so, whilst a decision by that party may assist in resolving some doubts, it would be a mistake to think that the underlying definition of the class can be wholly uncertain.

Questions

1. A testator who died a month ago by her will made the following bequests:
   (a) £10,000 to Ahmed and at his death the remaining part of what is left that he does not want for his own use to be divided equally between Xerxes and Yorick;
   (b) £50,000 to my trustees Tom and Tim to distribute among such of the inhabitants of Cambridge as they shall in their unfettered discretion think fit;
   (c) £100,000 to my said trustees to distribute among Brian, Charlene, David, Ellen, Oswald, Peter, Quentin and Raheem and such of my other business associates and old friends as they shall see fit;
   (d) residue to my son Simon trusting that he will see to it that my old friends shall have the contents of my wine cellar; and in case of any doubts he shall have power to designate who are my business associates and old friends.

   Consider the validity of these bequests, the testator having lived in Cambridge all her life.

2. Are the certainty tests applicable to fiduciary powers identical to those applying to discretionary trusts? Should they be?

3. Simon Settlor, who was 4ft 11ins tall, has just died. In his home-made will, he directed his executors:
   (a) to pay £2,000 to each of my small relatives;
   (b) to distribute £8,000 as they see fit among such persons as they consider to be friends of mine; and
   (c) to hold my residuary estate on trust to pay the income therefrom to my four daughters equally in their respective lifetimes but if a daughter marries a supporter of Fulham

[248] The jurisdiction of the court cannot be ousted: *Re Raven* [1915] 1 Ch. 673: *Re Wynn's WT* [1952] Ch. 271.
[249] [1952] 1 All E.R. 896.
[250] [1978] Ch. 49 at 61.

Football Club the share of such daughter shall accrue to the other daughters, as shall also be the case on the death of a daughter, but on the death of my last surviving daughter they shall distribute the capital within one year among such persons connected with me who have been benefited by me in my lifetime as they shall see fit.

Advise on the validity of the above bequests.

8

THE BENEFICIARY PRINCIPLE

1. Overview

According to many English cases, a trust cannot exist unless there is a person at whose behest the court can order the trustees to perform the trust and, further, this must be a person with an equitable beneficial interest in the trust property. This rule is known as the "beneficiary principle". One consequence of the principle is that trusts for abstract purposes are generally void, although an exception is made for trusts with charitable purposes and some less important exceptions are made for certain private purpose trusts. After describing the beneficiary principle as it has been stated in the leading cases, we discuss whether English law would do better to recognise an "enforcer principle" which would require only that trustees' duties are enforceable by *someone* and would not require that this person must have a beneficial interest in the trust property. This would not mean taking a large step, since English trusts law already holds that various parties have rights of due administration against trustees although they are not entitled to beneficial enjoyment of the trust property. This has already been discussed in Chapter 3.[1] **8–001**

2. Definition of the Beneficiary Principle

A trust exists only if the trustee holds certain property subject to a duty that is capable of enforcement and a court will not uphold any alleged trust that cannot be supervised and sanctioned by the court at the behest of someone in whose favour performance of the trust can be decreed. This rule was stated by Sir William Grant MR in *Morice v Bishop of Durham* who said that:[2] **8–002**

> There can be no trust, over the exercise of which this Court will not assume a control; for an uncontrollable power of disposition would be ownership, and not a trust.

In *Morice* the judges also held that the law does not generally permit trusts for abstract purposes because there is no person at whose behest an order for execution of a purpose trust can be made, although an exception is made for charitable purpose trusts. The rule that non-charitable purpose trusts are generally void was restated in *Leahy v Attorney General for New South Wales* where Viscount Simonds said that:[3] **8–003**

---

1 See paras 3–143 to 3–192.

2 (1804) 9 Ves. Jun. 399 at 405. For a discussion of the case in its historical context, see J. Getzler, "*Morice v Bishop of Durham* (1805)" in C. Mitchell and P. Mitchell (eds), *Landmark Cases in Equity* (Hart Publishing, 2012). See too *Morice v Bishop of Durham* (1805) 10 Ves. Jun. 521 at 539; *Re Astor's ST* [1952] Ch. 534 at 549.

3 [1959] A.C. 457 at 479.

> A gift can be made to persons (including a corporation) but it cannot be made to a purpose or to an object: so, also, a trust may be created for the benefit of persons as cestuis que trust but not for a purpose or object unless the purpose or object be charitable. For a purpose or object cannot sue, but, if it be charitable, the Attorney-General can sue to enforce it.

8–004 *Re Shaw*[4] was to like effect: in his will, the playwright George Bernard Shaw directed that funds should be held on trust for the purpose of undertaking research into the possibility of a 40-letter alphabet. This purpose was held not to be charitable and it followed that Shaw had attempted to create a private purpose trust which was not permissible. In Uthwatt J's words this was because:[5]

> one cannot have a trust, other than a charitable trust, for the benefit, not of individuals, but of objects. The reason has been often stated, that the court cannot control the trust. ... An object cannot complain to the court, which therefore cannot control the trust, and, therefore, will not allow it to continue.

8–005 It is now often said that *Morice* is the source of a rule known as the "beneficiary principle" which holds that trusts must generally "have ascertained or ascertainable beneficiaries".[6] In *Re Horley Town Football Club*, for example, Lawrence Collins J took *Morice* to stand for the following propositions:[7]

> The general rule is that a gift on trust must have a cestui que trust and must be for the benefit of individuals, unless charitable. It must have a definite object, and there must be someone in whose favour the court can enforce it. In general, in order to be valid, a non-charitable trust must have an ascertainable beneficiary in whose favour performance of the trust may be decreed. ... Consequently, trusts for purposes or objects are invalid, for a purpose or object cannot sue, but trusts for charitable purposes are valid because they are enforceable by the Attorney-General.

8–006 Looking at this passage, however, one can see that it contains two different ideas. One is that a trust is valid only if there is a person to whom the trustees owe duties and at whose behest the court can order the trustees to perform these duties. The other is that this person must usually have a beneficial interest in the trust property (an exception being made for charitable trusts). The first of these ideas was stated in *Morice* but not the second and it follows that *Morice* itself is not actually an authority for the "beneficiary principle", as stated by Lawrence Collins J, although this hardly matters now given that many other cases say the same thing.

8–007 However, there is a more important point that is worth bringing out here, namely that the second idea does not *necessarily* follow from the first. It may be that as matter of English legal history the two ideas became tangled up together so that courts came to define the trust as a legal relationship that involves beneficiaries with rights with respect to property which correspond with duties owed by trustees (and by extension from them, duties owed by third parties).[8] But even if this is how the trust developed historically, it does not follow that there is an insuperable conceptual obstacle to creating a trust under which the duty of the trustee is owed to a party who will not personally benefit from

---

4 [1957] 1 W.L.R. 729.

5 [1957] 1 W.L.R. 729 at 744–745, citing *Bowman v Secular Society* [1917] A.C. 406 at 441 and *Re Astor's ST* [1952] Ch. 534.

6 *Re Endacott* [1960] Ch. 232 at 246. Cf *Re Wood* [1949] Ch. 498 at 501; *Armitage v Nurse* [1998] Ch. 241 at 253; *Re St Andrew's (Cheam) Lawn Tennis Club Trust* [2012] EWHC 1040 (Ch); [2012] 1 W.L.R. 3487 at [45]; *Re Merchant Navy Ratings Pension Fund* [2015] EWHC 448 (Ch); [2015] P.L.R. 239 at [214] and [241].

7 [2006] EWHC 2386 (Ch); [2006] W.T.L.R. 1817 at [89], where he also cited *Leahy v Attorney-General of New South Wales* [1959] A.C. 457 at 478 and *Re Denley's Trust Deed* [1969] 1 Ch. 373.

8 As argued in P. Matthews "From Obligation to Property, and Back Again" in D.J. Hayton (ed.), *Extending the Boundaries of Trusts and Similar Ring-Fenced Funds* (Kluwer Law International, 2002).

performance of that duty.[9] And if such an arrangement were accepted as valid in English law, there would not be a "beneficiary principle", but a wider "enforcer principle", the key distinction between them being that an "enforcer" need not be a person who personally benefits from performance of the trust.

3. Exceptions to the Beneficiary Principle?

A. "Anomalous" Testamentary Private Purpose Trusts

According to the Court of Appeal in *Re Endacott*,[10] there are some anomalous cases, not to be extended, where testamentary trusts infringing the beneficiary principle have been held valid as concessions to human sentiment.[11] These are: **8–008**

- trusts for the maintenance of particular animals;[12]
- trusts for the erection or maintenance of graves and sepulchral monuments;[13]
- trusts for the saying of masses in private;[14] and
- trusts for the promotion and furtherance of fox-hunting.[15]

These trusts are sometimes referred to as "trusts of imperfect obligation": there is no one who can apply to the court to enforce the trust and so the trustees effectively owe no duty to carry out the specified purpose. The concession made by the courts is that the testamentary disposition is not regarded as invalid, and so the property is not held on an immediate resulting trust for the deceased's estate. The recipients of the property instead have a *power* to carry out the specified purpose. If they do not exercise that power, the property can be claimed by the party otherwise entitled (i.e. who would have had the benefit of the resulting trust had the disposition failed immediately).[16] As a result, the purported testamentary purpose trust is not validated as such; it is rather recharacterised as a trust for the benefit of the party otherwise entitled, where the trustees have a power to spend the fund on the specified purpose. It may therefore be questioned whether these cases do in fact constitute exceptions to the beneficiary principle, given that the "trustees" were not under a duty to apply the property to the specified purpose; they were merely given a power to do so. This suggests that the true concession made in the cases consisted in the courts having created limited exceptions to the rule that they do not treat words purporting to create a trust as in fact creating a power.[17] **8–009**

---

9 As argued in D.J. Hayton, "Developing the Obligation Characteristic of the Trust" (2001) 117 L.Q.R. 96.

10 [1960] Ch. 232 (residuary gift to a parish council "for the purpose of providing some useful memorial to" the testator held void for uncertainty and for infringing the beneficiary principle).

11 Note that such trusts would also infringe an "enforcer principle", in the absence of provisions appointing any party as an enforcer.

12 *Pettingall v Pettingall* (1842) 11 L.J. Ch. 176; *Re Dean* (1889) 41 Ch.D. 552. Such trusts are not charitable as they are confined to specific animals; many trusts for animals generally are charitable: *Re Wedgwood* [1915] 1 Ch. 113; and see para.9–267.

13 *Re Hooper* [1932] Ch. 38; *Mussett v Bingle* [1876] W.N. 170; *Pirbright v Salwey* [1896] W.N. 86; *Trimmer v Danby* (1856) 25 L.J. Ch. 424.

14 *Bourne v Keane* [1919] A.C. 815 at 874–875. The saying of public masses would be a charitable purpose.

15 *Re Thompson* [1934] Ch. 342, but the default beneficiary, a charity, only objected pro forma.

16 See, e.g. *Re Thompson* [1934] Ch. 342 at 344, where Clauson J ordered that the fund should be paid to the recipient on his undertaking to apply the money for the specific purpose, with the residuary legatee to have a power to apply for the funds if not spent on that purpose.

17 See, e.g. *IRC v Broadway Cottage Trust* [1955] Ch. 20 at 36; *Re Shaw* [1957] 1 W.L.R. 729 at 746.

8-010 It is also possible to query how anomalous these trusts are.[18] Regarding the maintenance of specific animals, such animals are regarded in law as chattels that belong to specific individuals who will benefit from the animals' upkeep, and so an analogy might be drawn between these cases and other cases, discussed below,[19] in which an apparent purpose trust has been characterised as a trust for the benefit of individuals who will personally gain from the performance of the purpose. The maintenance of private graves may be possible in any case under the Parish Councils and Burial Authorities (Miscellaneous Provisions) Act 1970 s.1, and if the relevant construction is part of the fabric of a church then the trust will be charitable and valid on that ground.[20] Gifts for the saying of masses in private are very close to gifts for the saying of masses in public, which are charitable, and it is only the dubious rule in *Re Hetherington*[21] that divides the two, by holding that the saying of prayers can only be for the public benefit (and thus legally charitable) if persons other than the priest can hear them being said and are thereby benefited by this edifying example.[22] Trusts for the promotion of fox-hunting may be truly anomalous, but the form of fox-hunting involved in the relevant case was made illegal by the Hunting Act 2004.

B. Apparent Purpose Trusts Benefitting Particular People

i. Absolute Gift with a Motive

8-011 It may be possible to characterise an apparent purpose trust as, in fact, an absolute gift to a specific person or persons, with the supposed purpose in fact constituting the donor's motive for the gift. In such a case, the gift will be valid, and cannot be challenged by, for example, a residuary legatee, but the recipient will take absolutely and will be under no duty to apply the money only for the specified purpose. In *Re Andrew's Trust*,[23] for example, a fund was subscribed solely for the education of the seven children of a deceased clergyman and not for the exclusive use of one child or for equal division among them but as necessary. After the formal education of the children had been completed, Kekewich J held that the children were entitled to the balance equally. He construed "education" in the broadest sense as an ongoing process that did not come to an end with the conclusion of formal education, and he treated the reference to education as expressing merely the motive of the gift, holding that:[24]

> If a gross sum be given, or if the whole income of property be given, and a special purpose be assigned for the gift this court [rebuttably] regards the gift as absolute and the purpose merely as the motive of the gift, and therefore holds that the gift takes effect as to the whole sum or the whole income as the case may be.

8-012 This approach was taken in *Re Osoba*,[25] where the court held that a bequest to the testator's widow upon trust "for her maintenance and for the training of my daughter Abiola up to university grade and for the maintenance of my aged mother" was a trust for the three women absolutely as joint tenants, with the reference to maintenance and training bearing solely on the testator's motive for the gift. As the widow and the mother had died by that point, the daughter was absolutely entitled as the sole

---

18 As argued in P. Matthews, "The New Trust: Obligations Without Rights?" in A.J. Oakley (ed.), *Trends in Contemporary Trust Law* (Oxford University Press, 1997).

19 At paras 8-011 to 8-013.

20 *Hoare v Osborne* (1866) L.R. 1 Eq. 585. See too para.9-206.

21 [1990] Ch. 1.

22 See para.9-207 for discussion.

23 [1905] 2 Ch. 48.

24 [1905] 2 Ch. 48 at 52-53, citing Page-Wood V.C. in *Re Sanderson's Trust* (1857) 3 K. & J. 497 at 503.

25 [1979] 2 All E.R. 393.

surviving joint tenant. Likewise, in *Re Bowes*[26] a trust to spend £5,000 on planting trees for shelter on the Wemmergill Estate was held to be a trust for the estate owners absolutely with the motive of having trees planted. The trust was therefore valid, but as the owners were absolutely entitled they could choose to spend the money as they wished.

It is clear that these cases, again, do not constitute an exception to the beneficiary principle. In each, there was a clear beneficiary or beneficiaries and there was no duty on the trustees to spend the fund solely for the specified purpose.[27] The difficulty in the cases is a factual rather than a legal one: is it right to say that, on the facts of the case, the donor intended the recipient to be free to spend the money as she wished, with the apparent purpose being only a motive for such a gift? It may be that the courts have strained to apply that interpretation, where the alternative has been that the donor's intended purpose trust will fail, and the recipient will receive nothing (unless she happens also to be the person entitled should a resulting trust arise). **8–013**

A more likely candidate as an exception to the beneficiary rule is *Re Abbott*.[28] A fund had been subscribed for the maintenance and support of two deaf and mute women. Stirling J held, not solely as a matter of construction of the documents by which the subscriptions had been sought, but as an inference from all the facts, that the surplus left after both women had died was held on resulting trust for the subscribers. His view, therefore, was that the subscribers had not intended the funds to be held on trust absolutely for the benefit of the women, with the reference to maintenance and support providing only a motive, but had rather intended the funds to be used for their benefit only whilst at least one survived. It may then be argued that, before the death of the survivor, the funds were held subject to a purpose trust, before resulting back to the donors on that death. The result is, however, also consistent with the analysis suggested above for the anomalous testamentary purpose trusts:[29] the attempted purpose trust failed immediately, and so the funds were held on resulting trust for the donors from that point, but the trustees had a power to spend the money on the specified purpose, such power ending only when the purpose could no longer be achieved. **8–014**

ii. *Re Denley*-Type Trusts

Re Denley's Trust Deed

Chancery Division [1969] 1 Ch. 373

In 1936 land was conveyed by a company to trustees so that, until the expiration of 21 years from the death of the last survivor of certain specified persons, the land should under clause 2(c) of a trust deed "be maintained and used as and for the purpose of a recreation or sports ground primarily for the benefit of the employees of the company and secondarily for the benefit of such other person or persons (if any) as the trustees may allow to use the same." The main question was dealt with as follows: **8–015**

GOFF J: It was decided in *Re Astor's Settlement Trusts*,[30] that a trust for a number of non-charitable purposes was not merely unenforceable but void on two grounds; first that they were not trusts for the benefit of individuals, which I refer to as "the beneficiary principle", and, secondly, for uncertainty. **8–016**

Counsel for the first defendant has argued that the trust in clause 2(c) in the present case is either a trust for the benefit of individuals, in which case he argues that they are an unascertainable class and therefore the trust is void for uncertainty; or it is a purpose trust, that is a trust for providing recreation, **8–017**

---

26 [1896] 1 Ch. 507.

27 Note too that it is possible to make an absolute gift to a recipient, with the value of the gift to be set by the money spent by that person on a specific purpose: *Re Sanderson's Trust* (1857) 3 K. & J. 497.

28 [1900] 2 Ch. 326.

29 See para.8–009.

30 [1952] Ch. 534.

which he submits is void on the beneficiary principle; or alternatively it is something of a hybrid having the vices of both kinds.

8-018 I think that there may be a purpose or object trust, the carrying out of which would benefit an individual or individuals, where that benefit is so indirect or intangible or which is otherwise so framed as not to give those persons any locus standi to apply to the court to enforce the trust, in which case the beneficiary principle would, as it seems to me, apply to invalidate the trust, quite apart from any question of uncertainty or perpetuity. Such cases can be considered if and when they arise. The present is not, in my judgment, of that character, and it will be seen that clause 2(d) of the trust deed expressly states that, subject to any rules and regulations made by the trustees, the employees of the company shall be entitled to the use and enjoyment of the land.

8-019 Apart from this possible exception, in my judgment the beneficiary principle of *Re Astor*,[31] which was approved in *Re Endacott (decd.)*,[32] see particularly by Harman L.J.,[33] is confined to purpose or object trusts which are abstract or impersonal. The objection is not that the trust is for a purpose or object per se, but that there is no beneficiary or cestui que trust. The rule is so expressed in *Lewin on Trusts*,[34] and, in my judgment, with the possible exception which I have mentioned, rightly so. In *Re Wood*[35] Harman J. said:

> "There has been an interesting argument on the question of perpetuity, but it seems to me, with all respect to that argument, that there is an earlier obstacle which is fatal to the validity of this bequest, namely, that a gift on trust must have a cestui que trust, and there being here no cestui que trust the gift must fail."

8-020 Again, in *Leahy v Att.-Gen. of New South Wales*[36] Viscount Simonds, delivering the judgment of the Privy Council, said:

> "A gift can be made to persons (including a corporation) but it cannot be made to a purpose or to an object: so, also [and these are the important words] a trust may be created for the benefit of persons as cestuis que trust but not for a purpose or object unless the purpose or object be charitable. For a purpose or object cannot sue, but, if it be charitable, the Attorney-General can sue to enforce it."

8-021 Where, then, the trust, though expressed as a purpose, is directly or indirectly for the benefit of an individual or individuals, it seems to me that it is in general outside the mischief of the beneficiary principle.

8-022 I am fortified in this conclusion by the dicta of Lord Evershed M.R. and Harman L.J. in *Re Harpur's Will Trusts, Haller v Att.-Gen.*[37]

8-023 Some further support for my conclusion is, I think, to be found in *Re Aberconway's Settlement Trusts*[38] where it was assumed that a trust for the upkeep and development of certain gardens which were part of a settled estate was valid.

8-024 I also derive assistance from what was said by North J. in *Re Bowes*.[39] That was a bequest of a sum of money on trust to expend the same in planting trees for shelter on certain settled estates. It happened that there was a father and a son of full age, tenant for life in possession and tenant in tail in remainder respectively; so that, subject to the son disentailing, they were together absolutely entitled, and the actual decision was that they could claim the money, but North J. said[40]:

> "If it were necessary to uphold it, the trees can be planted upon the whole of it until the fund is exhausted. Therefore, there is nothing illegal in the gift itself . . .";

and:[41]

---

31 [1952] Ch. 534.
32 [1960] Ch. 232.
33 [1960] Ch. 232 at 250.
34 16th edn, p.17.
35 [1949] Ch. 498 at 501.
36 [1959] A.C. 457 at 478.
37 [1962] Ch. 78 at 91, 96.
38 [1953] Ch. 647.
39 [1896] 1 Ch. 507.
40 [1896] 1 Ch. 507 at 510.
41 [1896] 1 Ch. 507 at 511.

> "I think there clearly is a valid trust to lay out money for the benefit of the persons entitled to the estate."

> The trust in the present case is limited in point of time so as to avoid any infringement of the rule against perpetuities and, for the reasons which I have given, it does not offend against the beneficiary principle; and unless, therefore, it be void for uncertainty, it is a valid trust. **8–025**

> There is, however, one other aspect of uncertainty which has caused me some concern; that is, whether this is in its nature a trust which the court can control, for, as Lord Eldon L.C. said in *Morice v Bishop of Durham*:[42] **8–026**

> "As it is a maxim that the execution of a trust shall be under the control of the court, it must be of such a nature that it can be under that control; so that the administration of it can be reviewed by the court; or, if the trustee dies, the court itself can execute the trust: a trust, therefore, which, in case of maladministration could be reformed; and a due administration directed; and then, unless the subject and the objects can be ascertained upon principles familiar in other cases, it must be decided that the court can neither reform maladministration nor direct a due administration."

> In my judgment, however, it would not be right to hold the trust void on this ground. The court can, as it seems to me, execute the trust both negatively by restraining any improper disposition or use of the land, and positively by ordering the trustees to allow the employees and such other persons (if any) as they may admit to use the land for the purpose of a recreation or sports ground. Any difficulty there might be in practice in the beneficial enjoyment of the land by those entitled to use it is, I think, really beside the point. The same kind of problem is equally capable of arising in the case of a trust to permit a number of persons—for example, all the unmarried children of a testator or settlor—to use or occupy a house or to have the use of certain chattels; yet no one would suggest, I fancy, that such a trust would be void. **8–027**

> In my judgment, therefore, the provisions of clause 2(c) are valid. **8–028**

Goff J reasoned that the attainment of the trust purposes would enure to the benefit of individuals who could be identified with sufficient certainty to make it a plausible reading of the trust deed that the settlor intended that those individuals should have standing to enforce the trust in their favour.[43] In effect, the trust was construed as being primarily for the benefit of particular people (the employees), with the specified way in which they were to be benefited being a secondary consideration. **8–029**

A *Re Denley*-type trust typically involves a relatively large, fluctuating class of beneficiaries and therefore varies, in its factual context, from the trusts which have previously been discussed. If, however, the class of parties benefitting from performance of the purpose is too widely drawn, the *Re Denley* analysis cannot apply, as it is then difficult to argue that the trust has any ascertainable beneficiaries.[44] It is, therefore, far from clear whether the *Re Denley*-type trust constitutes an exception to the beneficiary principle which was expressly invoked in Goff J's judgment.[45] Certainly, it is clear that the duties of the trustees can be enforced by parties who benefit from the performance of those duties and who can thus be seen as beneficiaries rather than as enforcers. **8–030**

Differing views have been expressed as to whether it is possible, in theory, for the beneficiaries of a *Re Denley*-type trust, acting together, to combine to terminate the trust and call for a transfer to **8–031**

---

42 (1805) 10 Ves. 522 at 539.

43 See too *Re Saxone Shoe Co's Trust Deed* [1962] 1 W.L.R. 934 (which would now be valid under the *McPhail v Doulton* [1971] A.C. 424 test for discretionary trusts); *Wicks v Firth* [1983] A.C. 214; *Grender v Dresden* [2009] EWHC 214 (Ch); [2009] W.T.L.R. 379 at [18]; *Re Merchant Navy Ratings Pension Fund* [2015] EWHC 448 (Ch); [2015] P.L.R. 239 at [241]. Persons named in a trust deed and benefiting directly or indirectly (e.g. as employees) but not intended to have a right to enforce the trust have no locus standi to apply to the court: *Shaw v Lawless* (1838) 5 Cl. & Fin. 129 at 153; *Gandy v Gandy* (1885) 30 Ch.D. 57 at 69–70.

44 See *Re Lipinski's Will Trusts* [1976] Ch. 235 at 248, discussed at para.8-053.

45 [1969] 1 Ch. 373 at 382–383. In *Grender v Dresden* [2009] W.T.L.R. 379 at [18], Norris J described the trust arising there as "a trust for a definable class of persons of the type recognized in *Re Denley*".

them of the trust property, thus exercising the *Saunders v Vautier* power.[46] The answer depends on which of two competing views of the *Re Denley*-type trust is taken. On the first, the beneficiaries do have the power, if acting together, to terminate the trust. The existence of the power may be merely theoretical, given the practical difficulties in gaining unanimity amongst the large, fluctuating class of beneficiaries, but the same can be said of a discretionary trust with a large class of actual or potential objects. On this view, the *Re Denley*-type trust is a standard trust for persons.[47] On the second view, the beneficiaries only have the power to ensure that the terms of the trust are complied with, and have no power to terminate the trust,[48] a reading of the case which suggests that it may implement an "enforcer principle" rather than a "beneficiary principle".

C. Quistclose Trusts

8–032 "*Quistclose* trusts" are named for *Barclays Bank Ltd v Quistclose Investments Ltd,*[49] a decision which was later reinterpreted in *Twinsectra Ltd v Yardley.*[50] In *Quistclose,* a company lent money to a second company for the purpose of paying a dividend to the shareholders of the second company. The second company became insolvent before the dividend was paid and the House of Lords held that the second company held the money for the first company on a resulting trust which arose on the failure of a primary express trust to pay the dividend. This was difficult to reconcile with the beneficiary principle which suggests that if the primary trust was a trust for a private purpose then it should have been void from the outset. Hence the *Quistclose* case was once thought to constitute a further exception to the beneficiary principle. Following *Twinsectra*, however, this is no longer the case. Lord Millett held there that in situations typified by *Quistclose*, where L lends money to B on the basis that it will not form part of B's general assets and will be used for a specified purpose, there are not two trusts—an express purpose trust, the failure of which triggers the imposition of a resulting trust—but only one: an express trust of the money that immediately arises in L's favour which is defeasible by the exercise of a power vested in B to apply the money for the specified purpose. This is discussed further in Chapter 16.[51]

D. Gifts for the Purposes of Unincorporated Associations

i. Unincorporated Associations

8–033 A group of people may decide to pool funds and use them to pursue a common purpose without forming a company with separate legal personality through which to carry out their plans. In such cases the associates have no legal personality as a group which is separate from their legal personality as individuals. As a result, they usually cannot hold legal rights nor can they be made subject to legal duties as a group; nor can they own property or enter into contracts as a group.[52] So far as

46 (1841) 4 Beav. 115: see paras 12–064 to 12–073.
47 This view was taken of a *Re Denley*-type trust in *Re Grant's WT* [1980] 1 W.L.R. 360.
48 The treatment of *Re Denley* in *Re Lipinski's Will Trusts* [1976] Ch. 235 at 247–249 is consistent with this second view.
49 [1970] A.C. 567.
50 [2002] 2 A.C. 164.
51 See paras 16–117 to 16–156 and 16–198 to 16–201.
52 Trade unions are often unincorporated associations but by the statutory magic of the Trade Union and Labour Relations Consolidation Act 1992 they can nevertheless make contracts and sue or be sued in their own names. Further, judgments can be enforced against them as if they were bodies corporate, and property may be vested in trustees on trust "for the union".

outsiders are concerned, an association is therefore legally identical with the individual members at any given time.

8–034 So far as the members' relationship with one another is concerned, this is typically governed by rules by which they agree to be bound when they become members, as noted by Beatson LJ in *Evangelou v McNicol*:[53]

> [An] unincorporated association ... has no separate legal personality from that of its individual members and as a matter of law is not a legal entity distinct from them, ... [like] a company or an industrial and provident society.
>
> The nature of the relationship between an unincorporated association and its individual members is governed by the law of contract:
>
> (a) The contract is found in the rules to which each member adheres when he or she joins the association.[54]
>
> (b) A person who joins an unincorporated association thus does so on the basis that he or she will be bound by its constitution and rules, if accessible, whether or not he or she has seen them and irrespective of whether he or she is actually aware of particular provisions.[55]
>
> (c) The constitution and rules of an unincorporated association can only be altered in accordance with the constitution and rules themselves.[56]
>
> Because the nature of the relationship between an unincorporated association and its individual members is governed by the law of contract the proper approach to the interpretation of the constitution and rules is governed by the legal principles as to the interpretation of contracts, and is a matter of law for the court ...

ii. Holding of Property by Unincorporated Associations

8–035 Whilst an unincorporated association cannot itself hold property, trustees or other people nominated under its constitution may hold property on a bare trust for the members. The existence of such a trust ensures that the property is insulated from the general creditors of those holding it. Such a trust does not, of course, constitute an exception to the beneficiary principle, because the beneficiaries of the trust are the members of the association. The particular rights of the beneficiaries will depend on the body's constitution and the express or implied contractual arrangements between the members.[57] As trustees, those holding the property may enter into contracts, thereby putting the property at risk vis-à-vis the claims of creditors, and may even be authorised to declare trusts binding the body's property.

iii. Gifts to Unincorporated Associations

8–036 Consider a simple case where A wishes to make a gift of £500 to her local tennis club, which is an unincorporated association and which is not devoted to exclusively charitable purposes. It may be that A's intention is for the money, like a subscription paid by a member, simply to become part of the general funds of the club, held by the trustees on trust for the current members, and to be spent as soon as convenient on general expenses. However, A may intend that the fund be held as a separate endowment, so that income but not capital is spent, managed separately from the body's general assets. The difficulty then is in giving effect to this fairly simple intention. The beneficiary principle

---

53 [2016] EWCA Civ 817 at [18]–[20].

54 See *Choudhry v Treisman* [2003] EWHC 1203 (Ch) at [38], per Stanley Burnton J.

55 *John v Rees* [1970] 1 Ch. 345 at 388; *Raggett v Musgrave* (1827) 2 C. & P. 556 at 557.

56 *Dawkins v Antrobus* (1881) 17 Ch.D. 615 at 621; *Harington v Sendall* [1903] 1 Ch. 921 at 926; and *Re Tobacco Trade Benevolent Society* [1958] 3 All E.R. 353 at 355.

57 *Re Bucks Constabulary Fund Friendly Society (No.2)* [1979] 1 W.L.R. 936.

means that the money cannot be held on a non-charitable purpose trust and if it is found that the only possible interpretation of the facts is that A intended to set up such a trust, the gift will fail and there will be a resulting trust to A or A's estate.[58]

(1) Lifetime Gifts: The Mandate Analysis

8–037 In *Conservative Central Office v Burrell*,[59] Brightman LJ suggested that where A contributes funds to an unincorporated association, for example by advancing them to its treasurer, she may choose to keep ownership of that property but give the treasurer a mandate to add the money to the general funds of the association and spend it accordingly. Once that has been done the mandate becomes irrevocable, but until then she has the right to restrain or have made good a misapplication of the fund. This construction is consistent with the beneficiary principle, as ownership of the property remains with the donor, and it also gives the donor some degree of control over the use of the property. It should also be noted that it is consistent with the power analysis that we have already seen applied to other situations,[60] as the basic model is that the recipient has a power but not a duty to apply funds to a particular purpose.

(2) Testamentary Gifts

8–038 The mandate analysis works well where A makes a lifetime transfer, but it cannot apply to a testamentary transfer as "no agency could be set up at the moment of death between a testator and his chosen agent".[61] Hence the analysis does not assist in the fairly common case where A wishes to leave funds in her will to a club. As has been judicially noted, however, "It would astonish a layman to be told there was a difficulty in his giving a legacy to an unincorporated non-charitable society which he had, or could have, supported without trouble during his lifetime".[62] In *Neville Estates Ltd v Madden*,[63] Cross J set out three possible interpretations of a testamentary gift to an unincorporated association: the first is an absolute gift to the current members as joint tenants;[64] the second is an absolute gift to the members where those members will hold the property subject to the terms of the contract between them as members to be bound by the rules of the association;[65] the third is a gift in trust to be applied for the purposes of the body.[66]

(a) Absolute gift to current members

8–039 It is of course possible that A might wish to make an absolute gift to the current members of the club.[67] In such a case, each member can claim her proportionate share and, as a simple gift to individuals

---

58 As in e.g. *Re St Andrew's (Cheam) Lawn Tennis Club Trust* [2012] EWHC 1040 (Ch); [2012] 1 W.L.R. 3487, in relation to land given to the club.

59 [1982] 1 W.L.R. 522 at 529–530.

60 See para.8–009.

61 As accepted by Brightman LJ in *Conservative Central Office v Burrell* [1982] 1 W.L.R. 522 at 530. See too *Re Wilson* [1908] 1 Ch. 839.

62 *Re Recher's Will Trusts* [1972] Ch. 526 at 536.

63 [1962] Ch. 526 at 540.

64 Considered at paras 8–039 to 8–041.

65 Considered at paras 8–042 to 8–051.

66 Considered at paras 8–052 to 8–053.

67 In *Neville Estates Ltd v Madden* [1962] Ch. 832, Cross J noted that a gift to existing members as joint tenants is one possible interpretation of a gift to an unincorporated body, but that interpretation can be applied only if consistent with A's actual intention.

has been made, there is no trust in play and no question of any breach of the beneficiary principle. The interpretation used in a case such as *Re Andrew's Trust*[68] can thus be applied, with any reference to the purposes of the club merely providing the motive for A's decision to make an absolute gift, rather than a binding restraint on the members' rights to the funds. An interesting question arises if there is a contract between the donees as members of the association (e.g. the constitution of the club by which they all agree with one another to be bound) which requires gifts to members as members to be treated as an accretion to the body's fund to be dealt with according to the body's rules.[69] In such a case, it seems that the donor's property will have to be so treated:[70] presumably, proportionate shares of the property are initially acquired but are then held by the members subject to a constructive trust, arising as a result of the members' contractual duties to each other.

If A's gift can thus be interpreted as an absolute gift to existing members of the club, it will be valid, and there is no question of a resulting trust arising. Indeed, in *Leahy v Attorney General of New South Wales*,[71] Viscount Simonds stated that, if nothing else is known about A's intentions, a simple gift to an unincorporated association without more is a gift to the members of the club at the date of the gift. As in the *Leahy* case itself, however, this presumption is easily displaced. In the usual case, it is clear that the gift is intended not as an absolute one to the individuals who happen to make up the club's membership at the time the gift takes effect, under which any of those individuals would immediately be free to take a proportionate part of the property. The gift is rather to the members *as members*. **8–040**

However, there is also a difficulty in saying that the money is to be held for the benefit of current *and future* members. In that case A's intention to benefit future members would require the capital to be kept intact and held on trust for only the income to be used, so that the capital would remain available for the benefit of future members, and this may infringe the rules against perpetuities.[72] On the other hand, if the gift were construed as a gift to the association on trust for carrying out purposes, with the gift being an endowment fund to be used for those purposes only, it would be an invalid attempt to set up a non-charitable purpose trust. **8–041**

(b) The "contract-holding"[73] analysis: an absolute gift of legal title to the current members, taking effect as an accretion to the body's funds which is to be dealt with (under a bare trust) according to the rules of the body by which the members are all contractually bound

It would be unfortunate if the law could not accommodate such a simple desire as the wish to give money to a club and in fact a way has been found to analyse the effect of a donation to an unincorporated association that avoids the foregoing problems. This analysis depends on finding a contractual link between all the members, as a result of which they are bound by the rules of the association, acquisition of property by which can then be explained as in the following extract. **8–042**

---

68 [1905] 2 Ch. 48: see para.8–011.

69 Like property caught by a donee's covenant to settle after-acquired property: *Pullan v Koe* [1913] 1 Ch. 9.

70 *Leahy v Attorney General for New South Wales* [1959] A.C. 457 at 478 per Viscount Simonds: "If it is a gift to individuals, each of them is entitled to his distributive share (unless he has previously bound himself by the rules of the society that it should be devoted to some other purpose)."

71 [1959] A.C. 457 at 477.

72 Discussion of this problem is omitted for reasons of space.

73 The term "contract-holding" is used as a shorthand for this analysis by e.g. Lawrence Collins J in *Re Horley Town Football Club* [2006] EWHC 2386 (Ch); [2006] W.T.L.R. 1817 at [43]–[46], [114].

Re Recher's Will Trusts

Chancery Division [1972] Ch. 526

8–043 By will dated May 23, 1957, a testator gave a share of her residue to what the judge interpreted as "the London and Provincial Anti-Vivisection Society" which had ceased to exist on January 1, 1957. The testator died in 1962. Consideration was first given to the question whether the gift would have been valid if the unincorporated society had existed at the time of her death.

8–044 BRIGHTMAN J.: Having reached the conclusion that the gift in question is not a gift to the members of the London and Provincial Society at the date of death, as joint tenants or tenants in common so as to entitle a member as of right to a distributive share, nor an attempted gift to present and future members beneficially, and is not a gift in trust for the purpose of the society, I must now consider how otherwise, if at all, it is capable of taking effect.

8–045 As I have already mentioned, the rules of the London and Provincial Society do not purport to create any trusts except insofar as the honorary trustees are not beneficial owners of the assets of the society, but are trustees on trust to deal with such assets according to the directions of the committee.

8–046 A trust for non-charitable purposes, as distinct from a trust for individuals, is clearly void because there is no beneficiary. It does not, however, follow that persons cannot band themselves together as an association or society, pay subscriptions and validly devote their funds in pursuit of some lawful non-charitable purpose. An obvious example is a members' social club. But it is not essential that the members should only intend to secure direct personal advantages to themselves. The association may be one in which personal advantages to the members are combined with the pursuit of some outside purpose. Or the association may be one which offers no personal benefit at all to the members, the funds of the association being applied exclusively to the pursuit of some outside purpose. Such an association of persons is bound, I would think, to have some sort of constitution; i.e. the rights and liabilities of the members of the association will inevitably depend on some form of contract inter se, usually evidenced by a set of rules. In the present case it appears to me clear that the life members, the ordinary members and the associate members of the London Provincial Society were bound together by a contract inter se. Any such member was entitled to the rights and subject to the liabilities defined by the rules. If the committee acted contrary to the rules, an individual member would be entitled to take proceedings in the courts to compel observance of the rules or to recover damages for any loss he had suffered as a result of the breach of contract. As and when a member paid his subscription to the association, he would be subjecting his money to the disposition and expenditure thereof laid down by the rules. That is to say, the member would be bound to permit, and entitled to require, the honorary trustees and other members of the society to deal with that subscription in accordance with the lawful directions of the committee. Those directions would include the expenditure of that subscription, as part of the general funds of the association, in furthering the objects of the association. The resultant situation, on analysis, is that the London and Provincial Society represented an organisation of individuals bound together by a contract under which their subscriptions became, as it were, mandated towards a certain type of expenditure as adumbrated in rule 1. Just as the two parties to a bipartite bargain can vary or terminate their contract by mutual assent, so it must follow that the life members, ordinary members and associate members of the London and Provincial Society could, at any moment of time, by unanimous agreement (or by majority vote if the rules so prescribe), vary or terminate their multipartite contract. There would be no limit to the type of variation or termination to which all might agree. There is no private trust or trust for charitable purposes or other trust to hinder the process. It follows that if all members agreed, they could decide to wind up the London and Provincial Society and divide the net assets among themselves beneficially. No one would have any locus standi to stop them so doing. The contract is the same as any other contract and concerns only those who are parties to it, that is to say, the members of the society.

8–047 The funds of such an association may, of course, be derived not only from the subscriptions of the contracting parties but also from donations from non-contracting parties and legacies from persons who have died. In the case of a donation which is not accompanied by any words which purport to impose a trust, it seems to me that the gift takes effect in favour of the existing members of the association as an accretion to the funds which are the subject-matter of the contract which such members have made inter se, and falls to be dealt with in precisely the same way as the funds which the members themselves have subscribed. So, in the case of a legacy. In the absence of words which purport to impose a trust, the legacy is a gift to the members beneficially, not as joint tenants or as tenants in common so as to entitle each

> member to an immediate distributive share, but as an accretion to the funds which are the subject-matter of the contract which the members have made inter se.
>
> In my judgment the legacy in the present case to the London and Provincial Society ought to be construed as a legacy of that type, that is to say, a legacy to the members beneficially as an accretion to the funds subject to the contract which they had made inter se. Of course, the testatrix did not intend the members of the society to divide their bounty between themselves, and doubtless she was ignorant of that remote but theoretical possibility. Her knowledge or absence of knowledge of the true legal analysis of the gift is irrelevant. The legacy is accordingly in my view valid, subject only to the effect of the events of January 1, 1957. **8–048**

The analysis in *Re Recher's Will Trusts*, sometimes referred to as the "second of Cross J's categories",[74] is very important as it provides the standard way of understanding the effect of a gift to an unincorporated association in the usual case where it is possible to find an express or implied contract between the members.[75] It is important to note that the analysis can apply even where the purposes of the body are "outward-looking" and so the donor's expectation is that the members will not in fact use the funds for their own benefit.[76] The point is that even if the donor's aim is to achieve that purpose, the legal means of fulfilling the aim is to "make a gift to an association formed for the pursuit of that purpose in the expectation that the subject matter of the gift will be so used, without imposing or attempting to impose any trust or obligation on the members, or the trustees, or the committee of the association".[77] **8–049**

Note that the analysis does not constitute an exception to the beneficiary principle: Brightman J makes clear in *Re Recher's Will Trusts* that in the standard case, where the gift does not include "any words which purport to impose a trust" the gift is made "to the members beneficially, not as joint tenants or tenants in common so as to entitle each member to an immediate distributive share, but as an accretion to the funds which are the subject matter of the contract which the members have made inter se". As Brightman J acknowledges, this does mean that the members at any point may decide to vary their contract and so "could decide to wind up the [club] and divide the net assets among themselves beneficially". The point here is the same as that examined above,[78] in relation to gifts subject to a motive: whilst it may be the case that the members thus choosing to wind up the club and take the money would be contrary to the donor's likely intention, this solution does at least permit the gift to be valid, and so avoids the resulting trust for the donor (or, in the case of a testamentary gift, to the donor's estate) that would arise if the gift were interpreted instead as an attempt to set up a non-charitable purpose trust. **8–050**

It is clear that the analysis in *Re Recher's Will Trusts* is the courts' preferred means of validating a gift to an unincorporated association, and that they will use it even if this requires a somewhat flexible interpretation of the facts of the case.[79] There are, nonetheless, some situations in which the **8–051**

---

[74] See, e.g. *Hanchett-Stamford v Attorney General* [2008] EWHC 330 (Ch); [2009] Ch. 173 at [29], referring to Cross J's analysis in *Neville Estates Ltd v Madden* [1962] Ch. 526 at 540.

[75] As noted by Lewison J in *Hanchett-Stamford v Attorney General* [2008] EWHC 330 (Ch); [2009] Ch. 173 at [29].

[76] See *Re Recher's WT* [1972] Ch. 526 at 542, doubting the approach adopted by the High Court of Australia in *Bacon v Pianta* (1966) 114 C.L.R. 634, where a gift to the Communist Party of Australia for "its sole use and benefit" was interpreted as an invalid attempt to set up a purpose trust.

[77] As noted by Vinelott J in *Re Grant's WT* [1980] 1 W.L.R. 360 at 367.

[78] At para.8–013.

[79] In *Re Horley Town Football Club* [2006] EWHC 2386 (Ch); [2006] W.T.L.R. 1817, for example, land was conveyed by a deed (referred to in the judgment as "the Deed") on trust "for the primary purpose of securing a permanent ground for The Horley Town Football Club", but Lawrence Collins J (at [114]) was nonetheless "satisfied that the Deed should be construed as a gift to the Club, as a 'contract-holding' gift to the Club and its members for the time being within category (2) in *Neville Estates v Madden*".

contract-holding analysis cannot be applied. First, it cannot apply if, on the facts, it is impossible to find any express or implied contract that binds all the members of the body.[80] Second, it cannot apply if, on the facts, it is not within the power of the members of the body, acting together, to agree to end any restrictions on the use of the body's property and to divide that property amongst themselves.[81] This is because, in the absence of such a power, it is impossible to find that a gift to the members, albeit subject to the members' contract, has been made.[82]

(c) Trust for the purposes of the association

8–052 Even if the members of the unincorporated body are bound by a contract, and have full potential control of the property, it may be that the terms of A's bequest make it clear that she intended the property to be held on trust for a particular purpose. In *Re Recher's Will Trusts*, for example, in applying the contract-holding analysis, Brightman J emphasised that it applied "[i]n the case of a donation which is not accompanied by any words which purport to impose a trust".[83]

8–053 Care must be taken, however. The fact that A's gift is expressed as a gift for a purpose does not necessarily mean that A will be viewed as having intended to set up a trust, and so it does not preclude the application of the contract-holding analysis.[84] Just as in the cases such as *Re Bowes*,[85] that were discussed earlier,[86] the reference to the purpose can be seen as a motive for the gift to the members subject to their contract, not as evidence of an intention to impose an absolute restriction of the use of the property. Further, just as in cases such as *Re Thompson*,[87] a court may well be keen to find that no trust was intended, in order to ensure that the gift can be validated under the contract-holding approach.[88] For example, in *Re Lipinski's Will Trusts*,[89] the testator's gift was made "for the Hull Judeans (Maccabi) Association in memory of my late wife, to be used solely in the work of constructing the new buildings for the association and/or improvements to the said buildings". Oliver J stated that:[90]

> Where the donee association is itself the beneficiary of the prescribed purpose, there seems to me to be the strongest argument in common sense for saying that the gift should be construed as an absolute one within the second category[91]—the more so where, if the purpose is carried out, the members can by appropriate action vest the resulting property in themselves, for here the trustees and the beneficiaries are the same persons.

---

80 See, e.g. *Conservative Central Office v Burrell* [1982] 1 W.L.R. 522.

81 See, e.g. *Re Grant's WT* [1980] 1 W.L.R. 360; *Re St Andrew's (Cheam) Lawn Tennis Club Trust* [2012] EWHC 1040 (Ch); [2012] 1 W.L.R. 3487.

82 See *Re Grant's WT* [1980] 1 W.L.R. 360 at 368 per Vinelott J: "It must, as I see it, be a necessary characteristic of any gift within the second category that the members of the association can by an appropriate majority, if the rules so provide, or acting unanimously if they do not, alter the rules so as to provide that the funds, or part of them, should be applied for some new purpose, or even distributed amongst the members for their own benefit."

83 [1972] Ch. 526 at 539.

84 See *Re Grant's WT* [1980] 1 W.L.R. 360 at 367 referring to *Re Turkington* [1937] 4 All E.R. 501 and *Re Lipinski's WT* [1976] Ch. 235.

85 [1896] 1 Ch. 507.

86 See paras 8–011 to 8–013.

87 [1934] Ch. 342. See para.8–015.

88 See, e.g. *Re Horley Town Football Club* [2006] EWHC 2386 (Ch); [2006] W.T.L.R. 1817.

89 [1976] Ch. 235.

90 [1976] Ch. 235 at 246.

91 i.e. the contract-holding analysis set out at para.8–042, which is the second of the three categories identified by Cross J in *Neville Estates Ltd v Madden* [1962] Ch. 832 at 849.

Oliver J also relied on cases where a purpose stated by the donor was seen as a motive for a gift, not as a binding restriction on the recipient's use of the property.[92]

4. An Enforcer Principle?

It seems difficult to argue against the proposition that there must be *someone* at whose behest a court can enforce a trust; if not, the apparent duty of the trustee to conform to the terms of the trust is a mere illusion. The question, however, is whether that person must be a beneficiary with an equitable proprietary interest in the trust property. On one view, noted above,[93] the decision in *Re Denley's Trust Deed* has already relaxed that requirement, by allowing the party enforcing the trust to be one of a defined group of individuals who directly benefits from the performance of a defined non-charitable purpose.[94] A more radical departure would entail the English courts permitting the "enforcer" of a trust, i.e. the person with a right to hold the trustees to account, to be someone with no beneficial interest and who does not benefit directly from the performance of the trust. **8–054**

Many offshore jurisdictions have embraced this enforcer model. They can be seen as having responded to a gap in the trusts "market" by enacting legislation validating non-charitable purpose trusts so long as the trust instrument appoints an enforcer (who could be the settlor or an independent or related third party) with provision for further enforcers after the enforcer's death or retirement. An example is provided by the following provisions of Bermuda law.[95] **8–055**

Bermuda Trusts (Special Provisions) Act 1989 ss.12A and 12B

12A. Purpose Trusts **8–056**

(1) A trust may be created for a non-charitable purpose or purposes provided that the conditions set out in subsection (2) are satisfied; and in this Part such a trust is referred to as a "purpose trust".
(2) The conditions are that the purpose or purposes are—
   (a) sufficiently certain to allow the trust to be carried out,
   (b) lawful, and
   (c) not contrary to public policy.
(3) A purpose trust may only be created in writing.
(4) The rule of law (known as the rule against excessive duration or the rule against perpetual trusts) which limits the time during which the capital of a trust may remain unexpendable to the perpetuity period under the rule against perpetuities shall not apply to a purpose trust.
(5) The rule against perpetuities (also known as the rule against remoteness of vesting) as modified by the Perpetuties and Accumulations Act 1989 shall apply to a purpose trust.

---

92 [1976] Ch. 235 at 249, relying on *Re Bowes* [1896] 1 Ch. 507.
93 At para.8–031.
94 As noted at para.8–031, however, that is not the only possible interpretation of the decision in *Re Denley's Trust Deed*.
95 The Bermudan legislation was the first jurisdiction to permit non-charitable purpose trusts. Other offshore jurisdictions have followed suit, some would say in a "race to the bottom". The original Bermudan legislation, unlike the current version set out above, required an enforcer to be expressly appointed. Much of the current legislation on purpose trusts, e.g. that of Guernsey and the Bahamas, has been influenced by the Special Trusts (Alternative Regime) Law 1997 (Cayman Islands), now contained in that jurisdiction's Trusts Law (2011 Revision), Part VIII. For discussion of this trusts regime, see, e.g. A. Duckworth, "STAR Trusts" (2013) 19 T. & T. 215.

8–057 **12B. Enforcement and Variation of Purpose Trust by the Court**

(1) The Supreme Court may make such order as it considers expedient for the enforcement of a purpose trust on the application of any of the following persons—

(a) any person appointed by or under the trust for the purposes of this subsection;
(b) the settlor, unless the trust instrument provides otherwise;
(c) a trustee of the trust;
(d) any other person whom the court considers has sufficient interest in the enforcement of the trust;

and where the Attorney-General satisfies the court that there is no such person who is able and willing to make an application under this subsection, the Attorney-General may make an application for enforcement of the trust.

(2) On an application in relation to a purpose trust by any of the following persons—

(a) any person appointed by or under the trust for the purposes of this subsection;
(b) the settlor, unless the trust instrument provides otherwise;
(c) a trustee of the trust,

the court may if it thinks fit approve a scheme to vary any of the purposes of the trust, or to enlarge or otherwise vary any of the powers of the trustees of the trust.

(3) Where any costs are incurred in connection with any application under this section, the Supreme Court may make such order as it considers just as to payment of those costs (including payment out of the property of the trust).

8–058 A clear aim of such legislation is to make the relevant jurisdiction appealing to settlors. This is achieved not only by permitting non-charitable purpose trusts but also, for example, by permitting settlors to reserve wide rights and powers to themselves without imperilling the validity of the trust or creating a risk that the trust documents will be regarded as a sham.[96] Of course, settlors are not attracted to such jurisdictions because the purpose trust regime allows them to make donations to their local tennis club. The attraction of such trusts is, rather, that they allow property to be insulated both from the creditors of the trustees and of the settlor and also, more importantly,[97] from the creditors of any other party (as no party has a beneficial entitlement to the property). This means, first, that such a trust may appeal to wealthy individuals who wish to place wealth offshore, where it will receive a more favourable tax treatment, and who can benefit from dispositions made by the trustees in exercise of the wide powers conferred on them, or on a party such as an enforcer. It also means, secondly, that a private purpose trust can be used in various financing arrangements, e.g. by enabling the parties to vest ownership of company shares in trustees who hold them for a limited private purpose such as "to hold shares in XYZ Ltd",[98] without any beneficial interests arising. Offshore jurisdictions are keen to cater for such needs as they derive benefits not only from the establishment of such trusts, for example by requiring that only licensed companies can act as trustees, but also from related financial services, the providers of which are taxed within the jurisdiction.[99]

---

96 See, e.g. Bermuda Trusts (Special Provisions) Amendment Act 2014, building on s.2(3) of the 1989 Act.

97 There may of course be cases where a court has a statutory power to make orders against a creditor (e.g. a divorcing spouse in ancillary relief proceedings) that relate not only to the property of that spouse, but also to property he or she is likely to receive in the future through the exercise of a power: see, e.g. *Whaley v Whaley* [2011] EWCA Civ 617; [2012] 1 F.L.R. 735.

98 It may, for example, hold those shares simply for the purpose of holding a controlling interest in a private company: see, e.g. Virgin Islands Special Trusts Act 2003.

99 As noted by e.g. D. Waters, "The Trust: Continual Evolution of a Centuries-Old Idea" [2007] J.T.C.P. 207, there is thus keen competition between such jurisdictions to appeal to potential settlors.

Should English law replace the beneficiary principle with an enforcer principle? Two linked sets of issues must be considered: policy matters and the conceptual nature of the trust in English law. As for policy, there may be a desire to "compete" with other trusts jurisdictions by catering for settlors who wish to set up non-charitable purpose trusts.[100] On the other hand, there may be a concern that such trusts can be used as a means to shield assets by ensuring that they remain free from the claims of *any* creditors. The beneficiary principle does at least ensure that trust assets, whilst protected from creditors of the trustees, will be available at some point to the creditors of those who eventually receive the trust assets. **8–059**

As for the conceptual nature of the trust, two basic views can be contrasted. The question is as to which of those views is regarded as best reflecting the *English* law of trusts.[101] We will examine these views in more detail in Chapter 12. On the first view, the essence of the trust lies in the holding of property subject to an equitable duty relating to the use of that property.[102] The question then is as to the nature of that duty: is there any reason why it must be owed to a party who benefits directly from its performance? There may be practical reasons for arguing that the answer is yes, and for doubting whether an enforcer will have sufficient incentive properly to supervise the trustees of a non-charitable purpose trust.[103] There may also be the conceptual concern that, in private law generally, duties tend to be owed to those who benefit from their performance, and an enforcer principle instead applies a more "public law" approach, under which the trustees' duties are seen not as correlative to a right of another, but rather as a burden of their office, or as a limit on their powers.[104] Nonetheless, if one views the trust in English law as consisting of the holding of property subject to a duty, the replacement of the beneficiary principle with an enforcer principle would not require a rethinking of the fundamental basis of the trust.[105] **8–060**

On the second view, the essence of the trust lies in the equitable proprietary rights of the beneficiaries, such rights being proprietary in the sense of giving the beneficiaries the ultimate right to control the use of the trust property, even if that right is residual and may, for its realisation, require the termination of the trust by the exercise of a *Saunders v Vautier* power.[106] On this view, replacing the beneficiary principle with an enforcer principle would indeed involve a fundamental shift in the conceptual nature of the English law of trusts.[107] **8–061**

---

[100] For example, the Scottish Law Commission, *Report on Trust Law*, paras 14.2–14.10 argues for legislation affirming the non-charitable purpose trust in Scottish law, and at para.1.3 the report says that it is "essential that Scottish trust law should be, and should be perceived as being, suitable for use in contemporary financial and economic conditions".

[101] It is undoubtedly true of some other trusts jurisdictions that a proprietary view of the trust is *not* adopted. For a general consideration of different views of the basis of the trust adopted in different jurisdictions, see, e.g. D. Clarry, "Fiduciary Ownership and Trusts in a Comparative Perspective" (2014) 63 I.C.L.Q. 901.

[102] See, e.g. D.J. Hayton, "Developing the Obligation Characteristic of the Trust" (2001) 117 L.Q.R. 96.

[103] The question arises whether the enforcer owes a duty to enforce the trust, and if so, to whom that duty is owed. It is interesting to note that under s.106(2) of the Cayman Islands Trust Law (2011 Revision), in relation to a pure purpose trust, the trust assets are to be regarded, as against the trustee and the enforcer as property "belonging to others" and if a trustee or enforcer has an intention "to defeat the trust" this shall be "regarded accordingly as an intention to deprive others of property" thereby potentially exposing the enforcer (or trustee) to criminal charges for theft.

[104] For an illuminating discussion of the different possible conceptions of "duty" in relation to the law of trusts, see J. Harris, "Trust, Power and Duty" (1971) 87 L.Q.R. 31.

[105] On this view, even though there is no party with a beneficial interest in the property under the trust, it could be said that there is no resulting trust for the settlor, as, in general, if the settlor has "expressly, or by necessary implication, abandoned any beneficial interest in the trust property, there is in my view no resulting trust" (*Westdeutsche Landesbank v Islington LBC* [1966] A.C. 669 at 708, per Lord Browne-Wilkinson) and that is true in a case where the settlor sets up a non-charitable purpose trust with an enforcer. That is certainly the case under, for example, a Cayman Islands STAR trust set up for a purpose: A. Duckworth, "STAR Trusts" (2013) 19 T. & T. 215, 218.

[106] This view seems to underpin the analysis of Vinelott J in *Re Grant's WT* [1980] 1 W.L.R. 360. For academic support for this view, see P. Matthews, "The Comparative Importance of the Rule in *Saunders v Vautier*" (2006) 122 L.Q.R. 266, 273–74.

[107] e.g. A. Duckworth, "STAR Trusts" (2013) 19 T. & T. 215, 215 describes that regime as one in which "the trust is freed at last from the idea that the trust is a matter of equitable ownership, a relationship between title-holder (trustee) and equitable

8-062 Against the second view is the fact that English law has already accepted the idea that property owners charged with administering the property in a particular way can owe duties of due administration to people who have no right to beneficial enjoyment of the property. As noted in Chapter 3,[108] examples of this are the objects of mere powers of appointment vested in the trustees (or other power-holders) under the terms of an express private trust; the Attorney General, Charity Commission and "persons interested" in charitable trusts under the Charities Act 2011 s.115; and estate beneficiaries and estate creditors during the administration of a deceased person's estate. Recognition of a general "enforcer principle" in English trusts law would not therefore represent a major step. This point is pursued further in Chapters 10 and 11 where the point is made that rights to due administration, including rights to seek information and hold trustees to account, are vested not only in the beneficiaries of express fixed trusts, but also in the beneficiaries of discretionary trusts and the objects of mere powers of appointment, and also in the trustees themselves.[109]

Questions

1. By his will Tony left:

   "£1,000,000 to my executor and trustee Eric to use the income to further the purposes of the UK Socialist Party so far as the law allows, such trust to be enforceable by the Leader from time to time of such Party";

   "£50,000 to the Treasurer of the Salford University Law Society to deal with it as the Society wishes";

   "£50,000 to the Treasurer of the Manchester Literary and Philosophical Society on trust to apply the income for the benefit of its members"; and

   "the proceeds of sale of my residuary estate to the Treasurer of the Manchester Mavericks Darts Club to apply half the income for the purposes of the Club and half the income for providing educational assistance to the children of Club members."

   Statute prevents the members of the Literary and Philosophical Society from winding up the Society and dividing its assets between themselves, while this is possible in the case of the Darts Club only if membership falls below five, although the rules can be changed by a 90% majority vote.

   Advise on the validity of the above bequests.

2. To what extent, if at all, does a *Re Denley*-type trust depart from traditional rules of trusts law?

3. Do you have any anxieties over a legal structure where a £20 million portfolio of shares, land and paintings is owned by a company, all of whose shares are held by a private trust company holding the shares on trust for the purpose of developing the value of the shares, and where the shares in the trust company are held by individuals on trust for the purpose of running the business of the trust company as trustee of only one trust?

---

owners (beneficiaries)". It is therefore inconsistent with the view that "if there are no equitable owners, there can be no trust—other than a resulting trust for the settlor".

108 See paras 3-143 to 3-192.

109 See paras 10-059 to 10-076 and 11-013 to 11-023.

9

CHARITABLE TRUSTS

1. Legal Forms Used by Charities

The Charities Act 2011 s.1(1) defines a charity as "an institution which (a) is established for charitable purposes only, and (b) falls to be subject to the control of the High Court in the exercise of its jurisdiction with respect to charities". The question whether purposes are legally charitable is the main subject of this chapter. **9–001**

Section 9(3) provides that "institution" means "an institution whether incorporated or not, and includes a trust or undertaking." Hence, while charities often have the form of a charitable trust,[1] i.e. a trust with legally charitable purposes, a charity might have some other form, e.g. that of an unincorporated association,[2] a chartered corporation,[3] a friendly society,[4] an industrial and provident society,[5] a company limited by guarantee (which differs from a company limited by shares, the form used by businesses which distribute profits as dividends to their shareholders),[6] or a Charitable Incorporated Organisation (CIO).[7] **9–002**

All of these bodies typically have written provisions detailing their purposes and the rules governing their administration. Confusingly, these provisions count as "trusts" for the purposes of the charities legislation whether or not they take effect by way of trust,[8] and their officers are referred to **9–003**

---

1 The Charity Commission has published a model trust deed for a charitable trust at *https://www.gov.uk/government/uploads/system/uploads/attachment_data/file/269509/gd2text.pdf*.

2 The Charity Commission has published a model constitution for a charitable unincorporated association at *https://www.gov.uk/government/uploads/system/uploads/attachment_data/file/278200/gd3text.pdf*.

3 There are only a few of these, and they are all very well-established charities with large funds, e.g. the older universities, the Church Commissioners, and the British Museum.

4 Friendly societies are incorporated mutual assurance associations which provide social or financial benefits, e.g. life assurance, funeral benefits. They are charitable only if their purpose is the relief of poverty.

5 A form generally used by housing associations. An industrial and provident society is a corporate body with members whose purpose is to carry on industry or conduct business, either as a co-operative (in which case it will not be charitable) or for the benefit of the community (in which case it will be charitable).

6 The Charity Commission has published model articles of association of a charitable company limited by guarantee at *https://www.gov.uk/government/uploads/system/uploads/attachment_data/file/269508/gd1textc.pdf*.

7 A legal form first introduced in 2010 which enables charities to acquire the benefits of incorporation without attracting the disadvantage of dual regulation by Companies House and the Charity Commission. There are two types: "foundation CIOs" whose only voting members are the charity trustees and which resemble an incorporated charitable trust, run by a small group of people (the charity trustees) who make all the key decisions; and "association" CIOs with a wider membership, including voting members other than the charity trustees. Model constitutions have been published by the Charity Commission at *https://www.gov.uk/government/uploads/system/uploads/attachment_data/file/390171/FoundationModelConstitution.pdf* and *https://www.gov.uk/government/uploads/system/uploads/attachment_data/file/390170/AssociationModelConstitution.pdf*.

8 Charities Act 2011 s.353. On occasion the loose usage of the term "trust" in this context has created problems of statutory interpretation when the question has arisen whether particular charitable bodies count as "trusts" for the purposes of other

as "trustees" in the legislation and in the Charity Commission literature, whether or not they are the trustees of a charitable trust.[9]

2. The Advantages of Charitable Status

9–004 Whatever form they take, charities enjoy various fiscal and legal advantages over institutions created for non-charitable reasons, reflecting the fact that charitable purposes enure to the public good.

A. Tax Advantages

9–005 Charities do not pay income or corporation tax on their property income and investment income which is applicable to charitable purposes only and is in fact applied solely for those purposes.[10] Nor do they pay capital gains tax in respect of gains made on disposals by them, provided that the gain is applied solely to charitable purposes.[11] Charities can obtain 80% relief as of right in respect of non-domestic rates for premises wholly or mainly used for charitable purposes and some discretionary relief in respect of the rest.[12] Charities are also exempt from stamp duty.[13] However they only have a few reliefs from value added tax in prescribed circumstances, e.g. relating to medical supplies, fuel for lifeboats, etc.[14]

9–006 Charities are exempt from tax on their trading income if the profits are used solely for charitable purposes, and either the trade is exercised in the course of the carrying out of a primary purpose of the charity, or the work in connection with the trade is mainly carried out by beneficiaries of the charity, or the charity can bring itself within a small scale trading exemption because its annual turnover falls below £5,000.[15] Charities can also avoid paying tax on trading that is not within these exemptions, by incorporating subsidiary trading companies and causing them to donate all their profits to the charities, with the result that their taxable profits are effectively kept at zero.[16]

9–007 No inheritance tax is payable on gifts to charities,[17] nor does a charge to capital gains tax arise on disposals of property to charities.[18] Individuals who make gifts of shares, securities and real property to charities are given relief from income tax by deducting a corresponding amount when calculating their net income for the tax year in which the gift is made.[19] Charities can also recover basic rate tax in respect of any gifts made to them under the gift aid scheme.[20]

---

legislation: *Hope Community Church, Wymondham v Phelan* [2020] EWHC 1240 (Ch); [2021] Ch. 51, and earlier authorities discussed there.

9 Charities Act 2011 s.177.

10 Income Tax Act 2007 ss.531, 532; Corporation Tax Act 2010 Pt 11.

11 Taxation of Chargeable Gains Act 1992 s.256.

12 Local Government Finance Act 1988 ss.43(5) and (6), 47 and 64(10).

13 Finance Act 1982 s.129.

14 Value Added Tax Act 1994 Sch.8, Groups 4, 5, 6, 8, 12 and 15 and Sch.9, Groups 6, 7, 10, 12 and 13. See HMRC, *VAT for Charities*, https://www.gov.uk/vat-*charities*.

15 Income Tax Act 2007 ss.524–526; Corporation Tax Act 2010 ss.478, 479.

16 A company donating its taxable profits to charity can get a tax deduction equal to the amount of the profits, so that no corporation tax is payable. In the hands of the charity the donation is taxable as income but is exempt from tax if it is applied for charitable purposes: Income Tax Act 2007 s.522; Corporation Tax Act 2010 s.473(1). See Charity Commission, *CC 35: Trustees, Trading and Tax: How Charities May Lawfully Trade* (2016), *https://assets.publishing.service.gov.uk/government/uploads/system/uploads/attachment_data/file/869136/CC35_PDF_v2.pdf*.

17 Inheritance Tax Act 1984 s.23.

18 Taxation of Chargeable Gains Act 1992 s.257.

19 Income Tax Act 2007 ss.431ff.

20 Income Tax Act 2007 ss.413ff.

In 2018, there were about 168,000 registered charities in England and Wales, with a total annual income of about £77 billion.[21] For the many small charities which have little or no income and no property, exemption from tax liabilities makes no difference as they incur no liability to tax in any case. For larger charities, tax exemptions can make a significant difference, and the overall cost to the Treasury of tax reliefs for charities and their donors was £5.7 billion in the tax year 2020/21.[22] **9–008**

B. Trust Law Advantages

As discussed in Chapter 8, trusts for abstract purposes are not generally permitted under English law, because there is no one at whose behest a court can order execution of the trust. However, a major exception is made for charitable trusts, the Attorney General having standing to take action against defaulting trustees where necessary.[23] It is also the Attorney General's responsibility to represent charities in disputes over the construction or validity of wills and of trust deeds where there is a charitable interest at stake, to intervene where necessary in disputes over the use or sale of charitable property, to direct schemes for the administration of charities where necessary, and to direct charitable bequests in cases where a charity has not been identified or no longer exists.[24] Note, also, that the few private (i.e. non-charitable) purpose trusts which are permitted are subject to perpetuity rules which do not apply to charitable trusts. **9–009**

In the case of a charitable trust, the requirement of certainty of objects is satisfied if the settlor has manifested a sufficiently clear general charitable intention to enable a *cy-près* scheme to be formulated for giving effect to her intention as nearly as possible.[25] Thus a charitable trust "for world-wide charitable purposes" or "for the poor" is valid, although a private discretionary trust for everyone in the UK would be void for uncertainty of objects. The *cy-près* doctrine is not discussed in this book. Briefly summarised, it is a doctrine which holds that where a charitable trust is impossible or impracticable from the outset there may be a resulting trust in favour of the settlor or their estate, just as there is where a private trust is initially ineffective or later fails;[26] however, if the settlor had a general charitable intention, the property will be applied *cy-près* under a scheme by the court or the Charity Commission, meaning that it will be applied to another charitable purpose which resembles the intended purpose as nearly as possible (the term "*cy-près*" deriving from the French "*aussi près que possible*").[27] **9–010**

Two other differences between charitable purpose trusts and private trusts for persons can be noted. Charity trustees can act by a majority instead of unanimously, as is required of private trustees **9–011**

---

21 Charity Commission, *Recent Charity Register Statistics* (September 2018), *https://www.gov.uk/government/statistics/charity-register-statistics/recent-charity-register-statistics-charity-commission*.

22 *Commentary for UK Charity Tax Relief Statistics: April 2012 to April 2021* (November 2021), *https://www.gov.uk/government/statistics/uk-charity-tax-relief-statistics-commentary/uk-charity-tax-statistics-commentary-april-1990-to-april-2020*.

23 The Charity Commission can also take action against charity trustees, as can other trustees and "any person interested in the charity" under the Charities Act 2011 s.115; for discussion, see Hui Jing, "Enforcing Charitable Trusts: A Study on the English Necessary Interest Rule" (2022) 42 L.S. 228.

24 On the Attorney General's role in disputes as to whether a trust is charitable, see *Brent LBC v Johnson* [2020] EWHC 933 (Ch).

25 *Morice v Bishop of Durham* (1804) 9 Ves. Jun. 399 at 405; *Re Harding, deceased* [2007] EWHC 3 (Ch); [2008] Ch. 235 at [21]–[22].

26 See paras 16–059 to 16–068.

27 For the history of the doctrine at common law, see G. Jones, *History of the Law of Charity* (Cambridge University Press, 1969) pp.72ff; C. Mitchell, "Charitable Endowment and Social Change: *Cy-Près* Orders and Schemes, 1837–1901" (2020) 41 J.L.H. 29. There have been several statutory restatements: Charities Act 1960 s.13; Charities Act 1993 s.13; Charities Act 2011 ss.62 and 63A (the latter section inserted by Charities Act 2022 s.6).

unless they are the trustees of a pensions trust,[28] or the trust deed authorises majority decisions;[29] and the six-year limitation period in the Limitation Act 1980 s.21(3) applies to an action against trustees by the beneficiary of a private trust for persons,[30] but not to an action by the Attorney General to enforce a charitable trust.[31]

C. Policing and Advice

9–012 Concerns over the negligent and corrupt mismanagement of charitable funds led to the appointment of Charity Commissioners in the 1850s.[32] They were public officials charged with the investigation and regulation of charities. Legislation subsequently expanded their duties and strengthened their powers,[33] and gave the Charity Commission legal status as a corporate body.[34]

9–013 In theory, the Charity Commission is an independent regulator, a non-ministerial government department accountable to Parliament for its efficiency but not for the way in which it pursues its objectives.[35] In practice, it has come under pressure to pursue political objectives, particularly in recent times,[36] e.g. from those who believe that the voluntary sector should be more heavily regulated,[37] from those who consider that the rules against political campaigning by charities should not be strictly enforced,[38] and from those who wish charities to broaden access to their facilities and services on pain of losing their charitable status.[39]

9–014 Most, though not all, charities are required by statute to register with the Charity Commission,[40] which has the power to decide whether or not bodies are legally charitable and can refuse to register those which are not. Registered charities with a gross annual income exceeding £250,000 must submit annual accounts and returns to the Commission,[41] which must ensure that these have been prepared accurately and honestly. All charities are also selectively targeted by HM Revenue and Customs to ensure that their accounts are in proper order, and that they are eligible for the tax exemptions which they claim.

9–015 The Charity Commission has wide powers to institute inquiries into the administration of charities, to require that people furnish them with information relevant to these inquiries, and to obtain

---

28 Pensions Act 1995 s.32.

29 *Re Whiteley* [1910] 1 Ch. 600 at 608.

30 See paras 13–181 to 13–183.

31 *Attorney General v Cocke* [1988] Ch. 414; though the six-year limitation period may apply to an action to enforce a charitable trust for the benefit of a defined class, even if the Attorney General is the claimant: *President and Scholars of the College of St Mary Magdalen, Oxford v Attorney General* (1857) 6 H.L. Cas. 189.

32 Charitable Trusts Acts 1853, 1855 and 1860. See R. Tompson, *The Charity Commission and the Age of Reform* (Routledge, 1979).

33 Charities Acts 1960, 1992, 1993, 2006 and 2011.

34 See now Charities Act 2011 s.13.

35 Charities Act 2011 s.13(4). For the Commission's objectives, functions, duties and incidental powers, see Charities Act 2011 ss.14–17 and 20.

36 D. Morris, "The Charity Commission for England and Wales: A Fine Example or Another Fine Mess" (2016) 91 Chi.-Kent L.R. 965.

37 See, e.g. Select Committee on Public Accounts, *28th Report: Charity Commission—Regulation and Support of Charities* (TSO, 1998), HC Paper No.408 (Session 1997–98), discussed in C. Mitchell, "Reviewing the Register" in C. Mitchell and S. Moody (eds), *Foundations of Charity* (Hart Publishing, 2000), pp.188–190.

38 e.g. Cabinet Office Strategy Unit, *Private Action, Public Benefit* (Cabinet Office, September 2002), pp.45–46, critiqued in S. Brodie, "The Charity Commission—Politicised and Politicising" (2010) 30 *Economic Affairs* 9; and see paras 9–106 to 9–130.

39 e.g. House of Lords and House of Commons Joint Committee on the Draft Charities Bill, *The Draft Charities Bill* (TSO, 2004), HL 167 and HC 660, pp.19–33; and see paras 9–049 to 9–105.

40 Charities Act 2011 Pt 4.

41 Charities Act 2011 Pt 8.

information relating to charities from the police and other public bodies.[42] Where misconduct or mismanagement in a charity's administration is discovered, the Commission can suspend or remove any of the charity's officers and appoint new ones as it thinks necessary.[43] It also has powers, corresponding to and concurrent with those possessed by the Attorney General, to go to the courts for the enforcement of obligations owed by charity trustees and others.[44] Appeals can be made from decisions, directions, and orders by the Commission to the First-tier Tribunal (General Regulatory Chamber), appeals from which can be made in turn to the Upper Tribunal (Tax and Chancery Chamber) and from there to the High Court.

As well as investigating possible misconduct and abuse of charitable funds with a view to taking remedial action, the Commission also provides charities with guidance and information in publications that can be accessed on its website. It is empowered to give advice to charity trustees to make the administration of their charity more effective,[45] and a trustee acting on such advice is deemed to have acted in accordance with the terms of the trust, provided no court decision has been obtained on the matter and the trustee has not withheld material facts when seeking the Commission's directions.[46] The Commission can also make schemes and orders to modernise the purposes and administration of charities, and give the trustees additional powers.[47] **9–016**

Between 2007/08 and 2015/16 the Commission's operating budget was reduced from £32.6 million to £20.2 million. By 2019/20 this had risen again to £29.3 million, but earlier staffing cuts had not been fully made up and the focus of the Commission's activities is narrower than it used to be, with a greater emphasis being laid on policing the sector. Previously the Commission often gave one-to-one advice to charity trustees on such matters as how to simplify their administration, alter their trusts, amend their governing documents, transfer property, and appoint new trustees.[48] Now it provides generic guidance through its website and gives one-to-one advice only in a limited range of circumstances.[49] The Commission has argued that this promotes self-reliance by trustees and creates space for the pro bono provision of advice by volunteers,[50] but the danger remains that it "will result in under-confident trustees . . . and that an unregulated market of advice providers will be created to the detriment of public trust and confidence".[51] **9–017**

3. Determining Charitable Status

A. Decision-Making Bodies

It will be seen from the foregoing discussion that institutions with charitable status enjoy advantages which cost the state money, in the form of foregone tax revenues and the costs of charity regulation. This suggests that decisions on legal entitlement to charitable status should be taken by a body with a democratic mandate, charged with undertaking a cost–benefit analysis of purposes to determine whether they merit the advantages flowing from charitable status. However, while Parliament has **9–018**

---

42 Charities Act 2011 Pt 5.
43 Charities Act 2011 ss.76–83, enhanced by the Charities (Protection and Social Investment) Act 2016.
44 Charities Act 2011 s.114.
45 Charities Act 2011 s.110.
46 Charities Act 2011 s.110(2).
47 Charities Act 2011 s.69.
48 Charity Commission, *Report for 1996*, paras 123–125.
49 Charity Commission, *Risk Framework: Application of the Charity Commission's Risk Framework* (January 2012), p.17.
50 S. Younger, "The Charity Commission's Strategy" [2013] P.C.B. 84.
51 A. Dunn, "Regulatory Shifts: Developing Sector Participation in Regulation for Charities in England and Wales" (2014) 34 L.S. 660, 665.

occasionally legislated to provide that a purpose is legally charitable,[52] decisions on charitable status are not generally taken by Parliament or indeed any other democratically accountable body, and are instead taken by unelected bodies, whose basic approach is to decide the question as though it were a "pure" question of law divorced from fiscal considerations.

9–019 The courts are sometimes asked to decide whether testamentary purpose trusts are charitable; HM Revenue and Customs must often decide whether an institution is a "charity" for the purposes of determining its entitlement to tax reliefs; local government rating departments must decide whether institutions are entitled to rates relief; and most significantly, the Charity Commission must decide applications by bodies to be included on the Register of Charities which it owes a statutory duty to maintain. The effect of registration by the Charity Commission is that for all purposes other than rectification of the Register, a body is conclusively presumed to be or to have been a charity at any time when it is or was registered.[53] If it refuses to register a body as a charity, an appeal can be made to the First-tier Tribunal (General Regulatory Chamber), from there to the Upper Tribunal (Tax and Chancery Chamber) and from there to the High Court.

B. Methodology

i. Analogising with Existing Charitable Purposes

9–020 When deciding whether the purposes of a trust or organisation are charitable, the courts and Charity Commission first ask whether such purposes have previously been held to be legally charitable. If not, then they ask whether an analogy can be drawn between the purposes under review and purposes which have previously been held to be legally charitable. For example, in *Scottish Burial Reform & Cremation Society Ltd v Glasgow Corp*,[54] the House of Lords held that the operation of crematoria was charitable by analogy with the provision of burial grounds, which itself had been held charitable by analogy with the upkeep of churchyards, which itself had been held charitable by analogy with the repair of churches. By these steps successive courts started with a religious charitable purpose and ended with a secular charitable purpose focused on public health.

9–021 The same process of analogising from one purpose to another is employed by the Charity Commission when deciding whether to register as charities institutions whose purposes have not previously been recognised as charitable.[55] It is also recognised by the Charities Act 2011 s.3(1)(m)(ii) which provides that purposes are charitable if they "may reasonably be regarded as analogous to, or within the spirit of" the purposes identified in s.3(1) as being charitable; s.3(1)(m)(iii) further states that purposes are charitable if they "may reasonably be regarded as analogous to, or within the spirit of" purposes held to be charitable under s.3(1)(m)(ii).

9–022 This approach to determining charitable status has been criticised as a formalistic charade that disguises value judgments made by decision-makers as to the desirability of using public money

---

52 e.g. Recreational Charities Act 1958 (reenacted as Charities Act 2011 s.5); Charities Act 2006 s.2 (reenacted as the Charities Act 2011 s.3), which was meant to codify the pre-existing law on charitable status, but which was amended to deem certain purposes to be charitable which had not previously been charitable. See para.9–041.

53 Charities Act 2011 s.37. The courts are bound by this provision when considering the validity of a gift to a body which has attained or subsequently attains registration: *Re Murawski's WT* [1971] 1 W.L.R. 707. It also binds rating authorities: *Wynn v Skegness UDC* [1967] 1 W.L.R. 52. But tax relief may be refused to registered charities which spend their money on non-charitable purposes: *IRC v Educational Grants Assoc Ltd* [1967] Ch. 123.

54 [1968] A.C. 138.

55 As discussed in Charity Commission, "RR1a: Recognising New Charitable Purposes" (October 2001), *https://www.gov.uk/government/uploads/system/uploads/attachment_data/file/358849/rr1atext.pdf*.

to underwrite the pursuit of particular purposes. A vivid example of this artificiality is the Canadian Federal Court of Appeal's decision in *Vancouver Regional FreeNet Association v MNR*,[56] that the provision of free public access to the "information super-highway", including the internet, is a charitable purpose by way of analogy to the charitable purpose of repairing roads and bridges. Reasoning of this kind brings the law into disrepute.

A further peculiarity of the law is that to a large extent the precedential value of decisions on charitable status is not altered by the fact that the consequences of charitable status have changed over time.[57] Several well-known cases extending charitable status to particular purposes were decided during the currency of the Mortmain and Charitable Uses Act 1736, which invalidated certain gifts of land to charitable purposes. Examples are *Trustees of the British Museum v White*[58] and *Thornton v Howe*.[59] When they were decided, the expansive view taken in these cases of (respectively) education and religion worked to the disadvantage of bodies with such purposes to whom gifts of land were made, as it meant that the gifts were rendered void.[60] However it now works to the advantage of voluntary bodies with such purposes which seek charitable status. **9–023**

ii. Changing Social and Economic Circumstances

When deciding whether purposes are legally charitable neither the courts nor the Charity Commission purport to consider whether one purpose is a better use of public money than another, nor do they attempt to align their findings on charitable status with current government policy, and they have declined to hold that a purpose is necessarily charitable merely by reason of the fact that Parliament has provided for it to be undertaken.[61] Since the 1990s, however, the Commission has laid more stress on the question whether changes in social and economic circumstances have made it more (or less) desirable for particular purposes to be pursued,[62] and it has departed from previous court decisions on this ground, a practice which it considers justified because the courts have done the same thing.[63] **9–024**

---

56 [1996] 3 F.C.R. 880.

57 Although to some extent changing social and economic circumstances are now taken into account when assessing the import of previous case law: see para.9–024.

58 (1826) 2 Sim. & St. 594.

59 (1862) 31 Beav. 14.

60 G. Jones, *History of the Law of Charity 1532–1827* (Cambridge University Press, 1969) Ch.7; P. Ridge, "Legal Neutrality, Public Benefit and Religious Charitable Purposes: Making Sense of *Thornton v Howe*" (2010) 31 J.L.H. 177, esp. at 191–195.

61 *General Nursing Council for England and Wales v St Marylebone Corp* [1959] A.C. 540 (nurses' self-regulatory body was authorised by Parliament but was not a charity because the nurses took a private benefit from its activities); followed in *Helena Partnerships Ltd v HMRC* [2012] EWCA Civ 569; [2012] 4 All E.R. 111 at [67]–[71] (provision of social housing by housing association was not charitable because the members took a private benefit). Cf. *Latimer v IRC* [2004] UKPC 13; [2004] 1 W.L.R. 1466 at [37]: the Government's "money is applicable and is applied for numerous non-charitable purposes. It is true that these are public purposes rather than private purposes; . . . but not all public purposes are charitable purposes."

62 But cf. the Commission's refusal to register Good News for Israel: Charity Commission, *Application for Registration of Good News for Israel* (5 February 2004), *https://www.gov.uk/government/uploads/system/uploads/attachment_data/file/324278/gnfidecision.pdf* (establishment of the state of Israel did not justify departing from *Keren Kayemeth Le Jisroel Ltd v IRC* [1931] 2 K.B. 465 to hold that the settlement of Jewish people in the Holy Land could be accepted as furthering a religious purpose when previously it could not).

63 e.g. *National Anti-Vivisection Soc v IRC* [1948] A.C. 31, departing from *Re Foveaux* [1895] 2 Ch. 501 to hold that anti-vivisection was not a charitable purpose. See too *IRC v McMullen* [1981] A.C. 1 at 15, per Lord Hailsham LC: "both the legal conception of charity, and within it the educated man's ideas about education, are not static, but moving and changing . . . with changes in ideas about social values." These dicta mark a departure from the Victorian judges' view that once a purpose had been held legally charitable, it would always be legally charitable, whatever contemporary social opinion might be about the usefulness of the purpose: *Philpott v St George's Hospital* (1859) 27 Beav. 107 at 111–112; *Re Foveaux* [1895] 2 Ch. 501 at 505.

Examples are its 1993 finding that rifle clubs were no longer charitable[64] and its 2001 finding that the General Medical Council was a charity.[65]

9–025 To the extent that such decisions reveal something of the decision-makers' policy calculations about public resource allocation, they bring some transparency to the decision-making process. But the question remains whether it is desirable for the Commission and the courts to formulate policy in this area at all? In *Dingle v Turner*, Lord Cross held that "in answering the question whether any given trust is a charitable trust the courts . . . cannot avoid having regard to the fiscal privileges accorded to charities",[66] but three other law lords in the case disassociated themselves from these remarks, considering that questions of public resource allocation are unsuited for judicial determination.[67] However, ignoring the issue does not make it go away: like it or not, the courts and the Charity Commission have effectively been left to decide such questions because successive governments have not wished to take responsibility for doing so.

4. Legally Charitable Purposes

9–026 The Charities Act 2011 s.2 provides that a purpose is legally charitable if it is one of the purposes listed in s.3 and it satisfies the public benefit requirement in s.4. The legislation therefore follows the case law in distinguishing between the question of whether a purpose is inherently beneficial and the question of whether it will enure to the benefit of the whole public, or a substantial part of it, rather than to the private advantage of a group of individuals. The latter question emerged as a distinct issue in the Victorian period when the courts first developed a "public benefit" rule as a means of denying charitable status to trusts for purposes which had previously been held legally charitable.[68] However, it was not until the twentieth century that the courts systematically distinguished inherently beneficial purposes and legally charitable purposes, "the former being merely one (albeit necessary) element of the latter together with the requirement that the purpose be carried on for the benefit of a sufficient section of the community".[69]

9–027 Jonathan Garton has suggested that each question can itself be sub-divided. The first question encompasses these questions: (a) whether a broadly described set of purposes are inherently beneficial in the abstract; and (b) whether a particular purpose identified in a trust deed or body's governing documents falls within a set of purposes that have been identified as inherently beneficial. Hence, for example, if a trust deed provided that the trust funds should be applied to the provision of advice on debt management, one would need to ask: (a) whether the relief and prevention of poverty are inherently beneficial purposes; and (b) whether the provision of debt management advice can be characterised as falling within the scope of relieving and preventing poverty. The second question

---

64 (1993) 1 Ch. Com. Dec. 4, departing from *Re Stephens* (1892) 8 T.L.R. 792.

65 Departing from *GMC v IRC* [1928] All E.R. 252; published online at: Charity Commission, *Decision of The Charity Commissioners for England and Wales Made on 2nd April 2001 Application For Registration as a Charity by the General Medical Council* (2 April 2001), *https://www.gov.uk/government/uploads/system/uploads/attachment_data/file/324270/GMC.pdf*.

66 [1972] A.C. 601 at 624.

67 [1972] A.C. 601 at 614.

68 *Cocks v Manners* (1871) L.R. 12 Eq. 574 at 585; *Yeap Cheah Neo v Ong Cheng Neo* (1875) L.R. 6 P.C. 381 at 396; *Re White* [1893] 2 Ch. 41 at 53. Discussion in P. Ridge, "Legal Neutrality, Public Benefit and Religious Charitable Purposes: Making Sense of *Thornton v Howe*" (2010) 31 J.L.H. 177, 199–202; M. Mills, "The Development of the Public Benefit Requirement for Charitable Trusts in the Nineteenth Century" (2016) 37 J.L.H. 269.

69 J. Garton, *Public Benefit in Charity Law: Principles and Practice* (Oxford University Press, 2013), para.1–22, identifying *Oppenheim v Tobacco Securities Trust Co Ltd* [1951] A.C. 297 as the case in which this step was decisively taken. The distinction was not clearly drawn in *Verge v Somerville* [1924] A.C. 496, although the case turned on the question whether a trust was legally charitable if it benefited those who were not poor.

divides into: (c) what constitutes a sufficient section of the public to justify treating a purpose as legally charitable; and (d) when does the pursuit of a purpose lead to more than an incidental benefit to a private class so that charitable status should be denied?[70]

Unfortunately, the courts have not distinguished these connected but conceptually different issues as clearly as they might have done. They have used the same language of "public benefit" when discussing them all, a practice which has caused confusion and misunderstandings. Some steps towards clarification were taken in the *Independent Schools Council* case, however, where the difference between the two main questions was explained in the following passage. **9–028**

R. (on the application of the Independent Schools Council) v Charity Commission for England and Wales

Upper Tribunal (Tax and Chancery) [2012] Ch. 214 at [44]

WARREN J. (CHAMBER PRESIDENT), UPPER TRIBUNAL JUDGES McKENNA AND OVEY: It is possible . . . to discern from the cases two related aspects of public benefit. The first aspect is that the nature of the purpose itself must be such as to be a benefit to the community: this is public benefit in the first sense. In that sense, the advancement of education, referred to in the Preamble under the guise of "schools of learning, free schools and scholars in universities", has the necessary element of benefit to the community . . . The second aspect is that those who may benefit from the carrying out of the purpose must be sufficiently numerous, and identified in such manner as, to constitute what is described in the authorities as "a section of the public": this is public benefit in the second sense. The decision in *Oppenheim's case*[71] illustrates these two aspects, which we will refer to as public benefit in "the first sense" and "the second sense". The advancement of education, as such, was of a nature which was beneficial to the community (and so of public benefit in the first sense); but the practical restriction of the benefits to children of employees of certain employers was in effect to render the trust a private trust, because it was not for the benefit of a sufficient section of the public. It was therefore not charitable. **9–029**

Conversely, as the Upper Tribunal also noted, "a trust to train pickpockets would not be charitable" even if the training were offered to everyone in the country, as in this case the anti-social nature of the trust's educational purpose would mean that it was not for the public benefit in the first sense, and so could never be legally charitable.[72] **9–030**

In the following overview of the law governing legally charitable purposes we shall first consider the purposes identified by the Charities Act 2011 s.3 as being inherently beneficial ("for the public benefit" in the first sense identified in the *Independent Schools Council* case) and then discuss the requirement in the Charities Act 2011 s.4 that legally charitable purposes must additionally be for the benefit of a significant section of the community ("for the public benefit" in the second sense identified in the case). **9–031**

A. Inherently Beneficial Purposes

The modern law of charity can be traced back to the Statute of Charitable Uses 1601. This statute appointed Poor Law Commissioners to investigate misappropriations of charity property. The preamble to the statute contained a list of objects which were understood to be legally charitable at that time, and which the courts later came to use as a reference point for the determination of cases, with **9–032**

[70] Garton, *Public Benefit in Charity Law: Principles and Practice* (2013), para.2–15.

[71] *Oppenheim v Tobacco Securities Trust Co Ltd* [1951] A.C. 297.

[72] *R. (on the application of Independent Schools Council) v Charity Commission for England and Wales* [2011] UKUT 421 (TCC); [2012] Ch. 214 at [48]. See too *Re Pinion* [1965] Ch. 85 at 105.

the result that, in addition to the objects listed in the preamble, other objects analogous to them or within the spirit and intendment of the preamble also came to be regarded as legally charitable.

Preamble to the Statute of Charitable Uses 1601

9–033 Whereas lands, chattels, money have been given by sundry well disposed persons: some for the relief of aged, impotent and poor people; the maintenance of sick and maimed soldiers and mariners, schools of learning, free schools, and scholars in universities; the repair of bridges, ports, havens, causeways, churches, sea banks and highways; the education and preferment of orphans; the relief, stock, or maintenance for houses of correction; the marriage of poor maids; the supportation aid and help of young tradesmen, handicraftsmen and persons decayed; the relief or redemption of prisoners or captives; the aid or ease of any poor inhabitants concerning payment of fifteens, setting out of soldiers and other taxes; which lands, chattels and money have not been employed according to the charitable intent of the givers by reason of frauds, breaches of trust and negligence. . .

9–034 In *Morice v Bishop of Durham*, the Preamble was identified by Sir William Grant MR and by Lord Eldon LC as the starting point for any judicial examination of the question whether the purposes of a trust were legally charitable.[73] They also stressed that popular notions of charity were beside the point when answering this question. According to Grant MR, the word charity:[74]

> in its widest sense denotes all the good affections, men ought to bear towards each other; in its most restricted and common sense, relief of the poor. In neither of these senses is it employed in this Court. Here its signification is derived chiefly from the Statute of Elizabeth. Those purposes are considered charitable, which that Statute enumerates, or which by analogies are deemed within its spirit and intendment; and to some such purpose every bequest to charity generally shall be applied.

9–035 Lord Eldon agreed, and approved a classification of legally charitable objects proposed by counsel that was founded on the Preamble. In Lord Eldon's words:[75]

> There are four objects, within one of which all charity, to be administered in this Court, must fall: 1st, relief of the indigent; in various ways: money: provisions: education: medical assistance: &c.; 2dly, the advancement of learning: 3dly, the advancement of religion; and, 4thly, which is the most difficult, the advancement of objects of general public utility.

9–036 This four-part classification of legally charitable objects was influential. It was taken up by Lord Macnaghten in *Special Commissioners for the Purposes of Income Tax v Pemsel*, where he said that:[76]

> "Charity" in its legal sense comprises four principal divisions: trusts for the relief of poverty; trusts for the advancement of education; trusts for the advancement of religion; and trusts for other purposes beneficial to the community, not falling under any of the preceding heads.

9–037 The four "*Pemsel* heads of charity", as they were known thereafter, then formed the starting-point for the courts and the Charity Commission throughout the twentieth century, until the enactment of the Charities Act 2006 s.2. Intended as a codifying measure, this section set out a list of 13 charitable purposes, retaining the first three *Pemsel* heads, and sub-dividing the fourth into ten new heads,

---

73 The facts and arguments in the case, and the judges' decisions, are well explained in J. Getzler, "*Morice v Bishop of Durham* (1805)" in C. Mitchell and P. Mitchell (eds), *Landmark Cases in Equity* (Hart Publishing, 2010).

74 (1804) 9 Ves. Jun. 399 at 405.

75 (1805) 10 Ves. Jun. 522 at 532.

76 [1891] A.C. 531 at 583.

including a residual category of purposes which swept in all the existing charitable purposes which did not fall under any of the other heads, and which allowed for the recognition of new charitable purposes by the analogising process familiar from the case law.

The Charities Act 2006 s.2 was reenacted as the Charities Act 2011 s.3, which is reproduced here along with s.5, which has replaced the Recreational Charities Act 1958, legislation which deemed the provision of recreational facilities to be a charitable purpose and thereby reversed the effect of *IRC v Baddeley*,[77] in which the House of Lords had held that the promotion of social well-being was not a charitable purpose falling within the fourth *Pemsel* head, and had thereby threatened the status of village halls which had generally been assumed to been charitable prior to the court's decision.[78] **9–038**

Charities Act 2011 ss.3 and 5

3 Descriptions of purposes

(1) A purpose falls within this subsection if it falls within any of the following descriptions of purposes – **9–039**

(a) the prevention or relief of poverty;
(b) the advancement of education;
(c) the advancement of religion;
(d) the advancement of health or the saving of lives;
(e) the advancement of citizenship or community development;
(f) the advancement of the arts, culture, heritage or science;
(g) the advancement of amateur sport;
(h) the advancement of human rights, conflict resolution or reconciliation or the promotion of religious or racial harmony or equality and diversity;
(i) the advancement of environmental protection or improvement;
(j) the relief of those in need because of youth, age, ill-health, disability, financial hardship or other disadvantage;
(k) the advancement of animal welfare;
(l) the promotion of the efficiency of the armed forces of the Crown or of the efficiency of the police, fire and rescue services or ambulance services;
(m) any other purposes—

(i) that are not within paragraphs (a) to (l) but are recognised as charitable purposes by virtue of section 5 (recreational and similar trusts, etc.) or under the old law,
(ii) that may reasonably be regarded as analogous to, or within the spirit of, any purposes falling within any of paragraphs (a) to (l) or sub-paragraph (i), or
(iii) that may reasonably be regarded as analogous to, or within the spirit of, any purposes which have been recognised, under the law relating to charities in England and Wales, as falling within sub-paragraph (ii) or this sub-paragraph.

(2) In subsection (1)—

(a) in paragraph (c), "religion" includes—

(i) a religion which involves belief in more than one god, and
(ii) a religion which does not involve belief in a god,

(b) in paragraph (d), "the advancement of health" includes the prevention or relief of sickness, disease or human suffering,
(c) paragraph (e) includes—

(i) rural or urban regeneration, and

[77] [1955] A.C. 572.
[78] Discussion at paras 9–270 to 9–271.

(ii) the promotion of civic responsibility, volunteering, the voluntary sector or the effectiveness or efficiency of charities,

(d) in paragraph (g), "sport" means sports or games which promote health by involving physical or mental skill or exertion,
(e) paragraph (j) includes relief given by the provision of accommodation or care to the persons mentioned in that paragraph, and
(f) in paragraph (l), "fire and rescue services" means services provided by fire and rescue authorities under Part 2 of the Fire and Rescue Services Act 2004.

(3) Where any of the terms used in any of paragraphs (a) to (l) of subsection (1), or in subsection (2), has a particular meaning under the law relating to charities in England and Wales, the term is to be taken as having the same meaning where it appears in that provision.
(4) In subsection (1)(m)(i), "the old law" means the law relating to charities in England and Wales as in force immediately before 1 April 2008.

5 Recreational and similar trusts, etc.

9–040 (1) It is charitable (and is to be treated as always having been charitable) to provide, or assist in the provision of, facilities for—
(a) recreation, or
(b) other leisure-time occupation,
if the facilities are provided in the interests of social welfare.
(2) The requirement that the facilities are provided in the interests of social welfare cannot be satisfied if the basic conditions are not met.
(3) The basic conditions are –

(a) that the facilities are provided with the object of improving the conditions of life for the persons for whom the facilities are primarily intended, and
(b) that –

(i) those persons have need of the facilities because of their youth, age, infirmity or disability, poverty, or social and economic circumstances, or
(ii) the facilities are to be available to members of the public at large or to male, or to female, members of the public at large.

(4) Subsection (1) applies in particular to—
(a) the provision of facilities at village halls, community centres and women's institutes, and
(b) the provision and maintenance of grounds and buildings to be used for purposes of recreation or leisure-time occupation,
and extends to the provision of facilities for those purposes by the organising of any activity.
But this is subject to the requirement that the facilities are provided in the interests of social welfare.

(5) Nothing in this section is to be treated as derogating from the public benefit requirement.

9–041 According to s.3(3), the terms in which the statutory heads of charity are expressed in s.3, such as "the advancement of religion", must be read in line with their meanings at common law. This is consistent with the Government's stated intention when putting the Charities Bill 2005 before Parliament, to codify the existing common law rules. In some respects, however, the statute went further than that, and changed the law, partly as a result of changes to the wording of the bill as it went through Parliament. Section 3(1)(a) recognises the prevention of poverty as a stand-alone charitable purpose, the first *Pemsel* head having previously been confined to the relief of poverty; s.3(2)(a)(ii) defines "religion" to include "a religion which does not involve belief in a god", a departure from cases which defined religion to mean belief in a god; and s.3(2)(d) defines "sport" to include "sports or games which promote health by involving . . . mental skill or exertion", the law previously having held that sporting purposes were charitable only to the extent that they involved physical effort and skill.

Some of the categories in s.3(1) overlap, so that some purposes might fit within two or more of the descriptions of purposes listed there. Examples are trusts for the relief of those suffering from financial hardship, which could fall within s.3(1)(a) and (j); trusts for the promotion of the arts, which could fall within s.3(1)(b) and (f); and trusts for the advancement of health and care of the sick, which could fall within s.3(1)(d), (g), (j) and (l). Since the Government's purpose was to state the law simply and clearly, this is unfortunate. **9–042**

B. Benefit to a Significant Section of the Community

i. Common Law Development

As noted above,[79] the rule first emerged in the nineteenth century that a valid charitable trust must provide an identifiable and demonstrable benefit for the community at large, or at least a significant section of it, as opposed to a private class of individuals. It is clear that a trust need not benefit every person in the country to be charitable. However, it is very far from clear whether there is a requirement that the number of people who could potentially benefit from the fulfilment of a purpose must be of any particular size, and if so whether this should be defined as "more than negligible" or in some other way, and whether the size of the trust fund should affect the number of people who should potentially be able to benefit from its application.[80] **9–043**

The courts have also attempted, but struggled, to articulate a clear test to distinguish between charitable trusts which benefit a group of people qua members of the public and private trusts which benefit a group of people qua private individuals. **9–044**

The House of Lords in *Oppenheim v Tobacco Securities Trust Co Ltd*[81] used the personal nexus test put forward in *Re Compton*:[82] they held that except in "poverty" cases no class of beneficiaries can constitute a section of the public if the distinguishing quality which links them together is a relationship to a particular person, e.g. through a common ancestor or a common employer. Thus a trust for the education of the children of employees of British American Tobacco Co Ltd or any of its subsidiary or allied companies was not a valid charitable trust. This was despite the fact that there were over 110,000 current employees. If the trust in *Oppenheim* had been for the education of the children of those employed or formerly employed in the tobacco industry, it would have been valid, as it would if the provision of education had been confined to children of those engaged in the tobacco industry in a particular place. **9–045**

The weaknesses of the personal nexus test are revealed in the dissenting speech of Lord MacDermott in *Oppenheim*, with whose approach the House of Lords were in obiter agreement in *Dingle v Turner*.[83] In the latter case, Lord Cross said that whether or not the potential beneficiaries of a trust can fairly be said to constitute a section of the public is a question of degree in all the circumstances of a case, and that much must depend on the purposes of the relevant trust. If that is correct, it means that whether **9–046**

---

79 See para.9–026.

80 Consider *Oppenheim v Tobacco Securities Trust Co Ltd* [1951] A.C. 297 at 306 and *Re Duffy (deceased)* [2013] EWHC 2395 (Ch), criticised in M. Synge, "Charitable Status: Not a Negligible Matter" (2016) 132 L.Q.R. 303. See too J. Jaconelli, "Adjudicating on Charitable Status—A Reconsideration of the Elements" [2013] Conv. 96, 96–97.

81 [1951] A.C. 297.

82 [1945] Ch. 123.

83 [1972] A.C. 601.

a purpose is inherently socially beneficial and whether the fulfilment of the purpose will enure to a significant section of society are connected issues, and that it is possible for the court to hold, e.g. that a trust for the relief of poverty is charitable although it enures to the benefit of many fewer people than would be required for a trust for the advancement of education to be charitable.[84]

9-047 Owing to the conflicting views expressed in the Lords in *Oppenheim* and *Dingle*, the lower courts and the Charity Commission have faced a dilemma in cases that compel a choice between the two views. The narrow personal nexus approach, although conducive to certainty, also leads to artificial manipulation of the legal forms so as to obtain fiscal advantages, e.g. in the case of a trust for the education of children of inhabitants of Bourneville, which might be invalidated under the broad approach as being in substance a trust benefiting employees of Cadbury Schweppes Plc. The broad approach, though less predictable in outcome, at least concerns itself with the substance of the matter and is not unduly preoccupied with form.

9-048 Note also that an institution's purposes cannot be for the public benefit if they do more harm than good, i.e. if the detriment resulting from their pursuit is greater than the benefit which they bring. This was established in *National Anti-Vivisection Society v IRC*,[85] where the House of Lords held that the appellant society's purpose of campaigning for the abolition of vivisection was not charitable because the harm that would result if the society's goals were achieved would outweigh the good.

ii. Statutory Developments and Their Aftermath

9-049 In 2006 the Government sought to alter the law in this area by enacting ss.3 and 4 of the Charities Act 2006. The Government believed that there was a common law presumption that the purposes of relieving poverty, advancing education, and advancing religion were "for the public benefit" in the second sense described in the *ISC* case.[86] Section 3(2) of the 2006 Act was enacted with the intention of abrogating this supposed rule. At the same time s.4 placed the Charity Commission under a new duty to issue guidance "to promote awareness and understanding" of the public benefit requirement, to which charity trustees would henceforth be required to "have regard" when exercising relevant powers and duties.

9-050 The Government stated that these measures were intended to simplify the law and to strengthen the Commission's ability as sector regulator to clarify and publicise the legal rules governing charitable status. The Government also had a political objective, however, which it did not make explicit when describing its aims in enacting the legislation: it wished to empower the Commission to revisit the charitable status of fee-charging charities, and particularly fee-charging schools and hospitals, whose purposes enured only to the benefit of a few well-off people, and for that reason, in the Government's view, should not have charitable status.

9-051 Sections 3 and 4 were later reenacted without any substantive change to their wording as ss.4 and 17 of the Charities Act 2011 (a consolidating statute). These are reproduced below, along with the Charities Act 2011 s.14, which lists the Commission's (rather nebulous) institutional objectives, and which was also copied across from the 2006 Act.

---

84 See also *Attorney General v Charity Commission for England and Wales* [2012] UKUT 420 (TCC); [2012] W.T.L.R. 977 at [64], where the Upper Tribunal (Tax and Chancery Chamber) came to exactly this conclusion.

85 [1948] A.C. 31. See too *R. (on the application of Independent Schools Council) v Charity Commission for England and Wales* [2011] UKUT 421 (TCC); [2012] Ch. 214 at [106].

86 See para.9-029. For the Government's understanding of the law, see, e.g. *Hansard*, HC Vol.448, cols 50–51 (26 June 2006), A. Milburn MP.

Charities Act 2011 ss.4, 14 and 17

4 The public benefit requirement

(1) In this Act "the public benefit requirement" means the requirement in section 2(1)(b) that a purpose falling within section 3(1) must be for the public benefit if it is to be a charitable purpose. 9–052
(2) In determining whether the public benefit requirement is satisfied in relation to any purpose falling within section 3(1), it is not to be presumed that a purpose of a particular description is for the public benefit.
(3) In this Chapter any reference to the public benefit is a reference to the public benefit as that term is understood for the purposes of the law relating to charities in England and Wales.
(4) Subsection (3) is subject to subsection (2).

14 The Commission's objectives 9–053

The Commission has the following objectives—

1 The public confidence objective
The public confidence objective is to increase public trust and confidence in charities.

2 The public benefit objective
The public benefit objective is to promote awareness and understanding of the operation of the public benefit requirement.

3 The compliance objective
The compliance objective is to promote compliance by charity trustees with their legal obligations in exercising control and management of the administration of their charities.

4 The charitable resources objective
The charitable resources objective is to promote the effective use of charitable resources.

5 The accountability objective
The accountability objective is to enhance the accountability of charities to donors, beneficiaries and the general public.

17 Guidance as to operation of public benefit requirement

(1) The Commission must issue guidance in pursuance of its public benefit objective (see paragraph 2 of section 14). 9–054
(2) The Commission may from time to time revise any guidance issued under this section.
(3) The Commission must carry out such public and other consultation as it considers appropriate –
  (a) before issuing any guidance under this section, or
  (b) (unless it considers that it is unnecessary to do so) before revising any guidance under this section.
(4) The Commission must publish any guidance issued or revised under this section in such manner as it considers appropriate.
(5) The charity trustees of a charity must have regard to any such guidance when exercising any powers or duties to which the guidance is relevant.

The Government's objectives in enacting these sections were not achieved. There are several reasons for this. One is that the Charities Act 2006 s.3(2) was premised on a mistaken view of the common law. There was no common law rule that the first three *Pemsel* purposes should be presumed to be "for the public benefit" in the second sense. The view that such a rule existed depended on a misreading of Lord Wright's dictum in *National Anti-Vivisection Society v IRC* that:[87] 9–055

[87] [1948] A.C. 31 at 42.

> The test of benefit to the community goes through the whole of Lord Macnaghten's classification [in the *Pemsel* case], though, as regards the first three heads, it may be prima facie assumed unless the contrary appears.

9-056 However, as the Upper Tribunal later noted in the *Independent Schools Council* case,[88] Lord Wright was speaking in this passage of "public benefit" in the first rather than the second sense.

9-057 Lord Wright's point was that purposes falling within the first three *Pemsel* heads can be assumed to be inherently beneficial, but that the contrary may appear if they are framed in an anti-social way (e.g. running a school for pickpockets, relieving poverty by killing the homeless). And as the Upper Tribunal also noted, even this was not to say that there is a "presumption" that the first three *Pemsel* heads are "for the public benefit" in the first sense, for in each case the court:[89]:

> will form its own view on the evidence before it whether the trust is for the public benefit and will do so, not by way of assumption, but by way of decision. It will no doubt take account of other decided cases; and it will take judicial notice of facts where appropriate. This is far from a 'presumption' in the usual sense.

9-058 Since Lord Wright did not say that purposes falling within the first three *Pemsel* heads are presumed to deliver benefits to a wide section of society, s.3(2) cannot have abolished a presumption that such purposes are "for the public benefit" in the second sense: no such presumption has ever existed. And if instead the sub-section abolished a presumption that such purposes are "for the public benefit" in the first sense, then this can have made "little, if any, difference" to the law,[90] because this was a "presumption" only in a very attenuated sense.

9-059 Problems were also caused by the measures taken by the Charity Commission in pursuit of its duty under the Charities Act 2006 s.4 to promote awareness and understanding of the public benefit requirement.[91] These can be partly attributed to the Commission's ambiguous status as a regulator with de facto law-making powers. Critics have contended that as an independent regulator the Commission is empowered only to apply the law defining public benefit as it is laid down by the courts and legislature, and that it has no authority to make or develop the law.[92] However, that is to ignore the reality that when deciding applications by voluntary bodies for registration the Commission has often made new law by analogising between old and new charitable purposes and departing from previous court decisions in light of changing social and economic circumstances.[93] Asking whether the Charities Act 2006 s.4 gave the Commission a new law-making power in relation to public benefit therefore misses the point that it already had such a power, although it is unfortunate that the government did not clarify this issue in the 2006 legislation, given the contentious nature of the policy directed against fee-charging charities that it expected the Commission to apply.

9-060 Following enactment of the 2006 Act, the Commission undertook a consultation process, and then published a generic guidance document[94] and supplementary documents on issues specific to various

---

88 *R. (on the application of Independent Schools Council) v Charity Commission for England and Wales* [2011] UKUT 421 (TCC); [2012] Ch. 214 at [63]. See too P. Luxton, "A Three-Part Invention: Public Benefit Under the Charity Commission" (2009) 11 C.L. & P.R. 19, 23.

89 [2011] UKUT 421 (TCC); [2012] Ch. 214 at [68]. See too *Attorney General v Charity Commission* [2012] W.T.L.R. 977 at [39].

90 [2011] UKUT 421 (TCC); [2012] Ch. 214 at [88].

91 A. Dunn, "Using the Wrong Policy Tools: Education, Charity, and Public Benefit" (2012) 39 J.L.S. 491.

92 P. Luxton, *Making Law: Parliament v The Charity Commission* (2009); C. Decker and M. Harding, "Three Challenges in Charity Regulation: The Case of England and Wales" in M. Harding et al (eds), *Not-for-Profit Law: Theoretical and Comparative Perspectives* (Cambridge University Press, 2014).

93 See paras 9-020 to 9-025.

94 Charity Commission, *Charities and Public Benefit* (January 2008).

charitable purposes[95] and on fee charging.[96] These documents set out certain principles for which there was little clear authority in the pre-existing case law. Most notably, the Commission asserted that "where benefit is to a section of the public, the opportunity to benefit must not be unreasonably restricted . . . by ability to pay any fees charged" (principle 2b) and also that "people in poverty must not be excluded from the opportunity to benefit" (principle 2c). Part of the Commission's fee-charging document is reproduced below, to illustrate its approach.

Charity Commission, *Public Benefit and Fee-Charging* (December 2008)

C. Fee-charging as a public benefit issue

. . . Fee-charging is likely to be a public benefit issue where: 9–061

the service or facility that is charged for forms a significant part of the charity's aims, or the way it carries out those aims; and/or
the fees that are charged for that service or facility are high.

A significant part of the charity's aims: where a charity's sole or main aim, or way it carries out its aims, is to provide a service or facility for which it charges, the level of fees it charges is significant when assessing whether the organisation is carrying out those aims for the public benefit. This is because it has a bearing on who has the opportunity to benefit from that service or facility and, in particular, the extent to which the charity can show that its aims meet public benefit principles 2b and 2c. 9–062

Where the service or facility that is charged for is an insignificant aspect of what the charity does, or is just one of many ways in which the charity carries out its aims, many of which are not charged for, then fee-charging is generally less of a public benefit issue. . . . 9–063

Charities charging low fees: where a charity charges low fees that most people can afford, then the fee-charging is unlikely to give rise to public benefit difficulties. In most cases it will not be necessary for those charities to demonstrate any further opportunities to benefit since the low fees do not prevent people from having the opportunity to benefit from the charity's services or facilities. . . . 9–064

Charities charging high fees: where a charity charges high fees that many people could not afford, the trustees must ensure that: 9–065

the benefits are not unreasonably restricted by a person's ability to pay; and that
people in poverty are not excluded from the opportunity to benefit.

The charity trustees must therefore demonstrate that there is sufficient opportunity for people who cannot afford those fees to benefit in a material way that is related to the charity's aims. . . .

Opportunities to benefit: there must be sufficient *opportunity* to benefit for people who cannot afford to pay the fees charged for the services or facilities provided by the charity. It does not mean that people who cannot afford the fees must actually benefit. What is important is that they must not be excluded from the opportunity to benefit, whether or not they actually choose to do so. However, the opportunity to benefit should be genuine and meaningful. If the opportunity to benefit that is provided is not genuine, or is meaningless or trivial, then it would count for very little in a public benefit assessment. 9–066

. . . Some fee-charging charity trustees might wish to argue that there are wider or remote benefits to the public at large that arise from carrying out their charity's aims and that these benefits should be regarded as opportunities to benefit for people who cannot afford the fees. 9–067

For example, this might include wider or remote benefits such as: 9–068

the general relief of public expenditure from a charity doing something that the state would otherwise have to provide, such as relieving the exchequer of the cost of educating children at state schools or treating patients at NHS hospitals; or

---

[95] Charity Commission, *The Prevention or Relief of Poverty for the Public Benefit* (December 2008); *The Advancement of Religion for the Public Benefit* (December 2008); *The Advancement of Education for the Public Benefit* (December 2008 version).

[96] *Public Benefit and Fee-Charging* (December 2008).

benefits to the nation from educating students who go on to become, for example, successful entrepreneurs or scientists; or

other sorts of wider or remote benefits to the public that might be claimed by any charity carrying out a charitable aim, such as encouraging charitable giving or volunteering.

9-069 In cases where such public benefits are clear and related to the charity's aims, they might be relevant when considering the public benefit of a fee-charging charity in relation to public benefit principle 1a. . . . However, we do not consider that they are opportunities to benefit in a "material way" for people who cannot afford the fees. For that reason we do not consider they are relevant when considering the extent to which a charity meets public benefit principles 2b and 2c. . . .

9-070 Fee-charging charities must ensure that there are sufficient opportunities to benefit for people who cannot afford the fees. There are many different ways of doing this.

9-071 This might be by:

offering free or subsidised access: enabling people who cannot afford the fees to access the service or facility by offering it at a reduced rate or for no fee, or via schemes or arrangements which offer financial assistance to help meet the cost of the fees;

providing other significant opportunities to benefit: providing other significant opportunities to benefit that do not involve free or subsidised access to the service or facility that is charged for.

9-072 *Trustees' discretion*: it is for the charity's trustees to decide what sorts of opportunities to benefit they wish, and are able, to provide for people who cannot afford the fees, taking into consideration what is appropriate in their charity's circumstances. However, what is provided must be sufficient to satisfy principles 2b and 2c.

9-073 **Satisfying Principles 2b and 2c:**

where a charity provides a sufficient amount of free or subsidised access (in the context of the charity's circumstances) to people who cannot afford the fees, this will satisfy principles 2b and 2c;

where a charity provides a combination of free or subsidised access and other significant opportunities to benefit, we can take into account the totality of the opportunities to benefit it provides;

where a charity provides other significant opportunities to benefit, but offers no free or subsidised access, the trustees must be able to demonstrate in what other ways the opportunities to benefit that the charity provides clearly satisfy principles 2b and 2c.

We will look at each case on its own merits and in the context of the individual charity's circumstances.

9-074 *Totality of benefits*: in assessing whether a charity provides sufficient opportunity to benefit for people who cannot afford the fees, we will consider the totality of the opportunities to benefit that the charity provides. . . .

9-075 *Percentage of free or subsidised access*: there is no "one-size-fits-all" amount, or percentage, of free or subsidised access that fee-charging charities must offer.

9-076 We cannot specify how many concessionary tickets a theatre should offer, or suggest a percentage of bursaries that all independent schools should offer, or say how many free beds should be available at a hospital.

9-077 It is primarily for the trustees of the charity to decide for themselves the extent to which they offer free or subsidised access, and how much to offer to how many people, provided they can show that people who cannot afford the fees have sufficient opportunity to benefit in a material way that is related to the charity's aims.

9-078 We have to consider what is reasonable and appropriate in each particular charity's circumstances. Offering free or subsidised access costs money and so can clearly impact on the financial situation of a charity. What is appropriate and sufficient will vary from charity to charity, depending upon, amongst other things: its charitable aims; the level of the fees charged; any relevant local needs or factors; and the resources available to the charity.

9-079 It is unusual for a charity that charges high fees to offer no free or subsidised access. Typically, most such charities offer concessions on fees, or assistance with fees, and might also provide other significant opportunities to benefit alongside offering some free or subsidised access. . . .

9-080 *Measures aimed at people who cannot afford the fees*: measures that are designed specifically, and exclusively, to assist people who cannot afford the fees are likely to provide greater opportunity to benefit than other measures.

For example, in the context of charitable independent schools, it means that bursaries (which are usually specifically aimed at assisting children from poorer families) are likely to provide a greater opportunity to benefit to people who cannot afford the fees than would be the case with scholarships (which are usually open to anyone to apply for and which are awarded solely on academic merit). 9-081

Bursaries usually still require the applicant to show academic merit (e.g. to meet entrance requirements) but should guarantee that children, whose parents or guardians are unable to pay the fees, are given sufficient opportunity to benefit. . . . 9-082

Providing other significant opportunities to benefit that meet local needs: it is possible that, in looking to ensure that the public benefit requirement is met, trustees will seek opportunities to work with other service and facility providers. We do not want charities, as a result of the public benefit requirement, to provide opportunities to benefit that are not desired or valued. Charity trustees should have regard to whether the way in which they propose providing other significant opportunities to benefit are relevant and desired. 9-083

If trustees decide to explore providing other significant opportunities to benefit to meet local needs, we recommend that they engage with their partners and local communities. This is so that they can properly and sufficiently discuss and evaluate local needs when deciding what sort of services, facilities or collaboration to provide. Trustees might want to use peer review or other forms of quality assessment to assist them. 9-084

Examples of other significant opportunities to benefit that are not wanted or required, because they do not meet the needs of the intended beneficiaries, might include: 9-085

> a charitable hospital that argues that it offered the local NHS hospital the use of a consultant specialising in children's illnesses but the NHS hospital refused the offer. Where the local NHS hospital caters only for elderly patients, or if it already has sufficient medical staff, the opportunity offered by the charity would have no effect in showing that it provides other significant opportunities to benefit. In this case, the charitable hospital might provide more significant opportunities to benefit if it consults the local NHS hospital about what it could offer that would be of more assistance to the NHS hospital and to benefit people locally;
>
> a charitable independent school that offers to provide teaching staff to the local state school for certain subjects but the subject areas offered are not required by the local state school. In this case, it would be more beneficial for the trustees of the independent school to consult other education providers locally about how to achieve the maximum impact from sharing resources. It could then target the charity's assistance to state schools and other educational establishments most in need of help in ways that are likely to make most difference to their students.

Following the publication of its public benefit guidance, the Commission undertook "public benefit assessments" of certain fee-paying schools and invoked principles 2b and 2c to justify its stance that such bodies could be assured of charitable status only if they created means-tested bursaries and made access to their facilities available to the public at large.[97] This policy was said to apply not only to new schools seeking to be registered as charities for the first time but also to existing schools which could lose their charitable status if they failed to comply with the public benefit requirement. 9-086

In 2012, proceedings for judicial review were brought against the Commission by a body representing around 1,000 charitable fee-charging schools. In *R. (on the application of Independent Schools Council) v Charity Commission for England and Wales*,[98] the applicant sought an order to quash principles 2b and 2c as founded on errors of law. The Upper Tribunal held among other things that an organisation is not charitable if it excludes the poor and that fee-charging charities owe a duty to provide benefits to members of the public who cannot afford their fees.[99] But it also held that it is for the trustees to decide, and not for the Charity Commission to proscribe, the nature and extent of 9-087

---

97 Charity Commission, *Highfield Priory School Ltd: Public Benefit Assessment Report* (July 2009).

98 [2011] UKUT 421 (TCC); [2012] Ch. 214.

99 [2011] UKUT 421 (TCC); [2012] Ch. 214 at [178]

such benefits provided that these exceed a de minimis level.[100] Moreover, if the trustees of an existing charity do not ensure that it delivers benefits to a sufficiently broad section of the public then it follows not that the charity should lose its charitable status, but that the trustees are in breach of their duty to apply the body's resources to its charitable purposes.[101] Hence the statement relating to fees in principle 2b was incorrect and although principle 2c was correctly stated, its significance was incorrectly explained in the guidance. The Upper Tribunal therefore ordered that these parts of the guidance should be quashed unless they were withdrawn by the Commission. In the event this was done and the guidance was rewritten.

9-088 Both sides claimed a victory. The applicant pointed to the Upper Tribunal's repudiation of the Commission's over-proscriptive approach, its affirmation of trustee autonomy and its findings about the results of non-compliance with the public benefit requirement. The Commission said it had been vindicated by the Upper Tribunal's finding that a trust is not charitable if it excludes the poor. It is doubtful, however, that this proposition is correct as a matter of law. The Upper Tribunal itself conceded that although they believed it to be "right as a matter of principle", "there is no case which decides [the] point",[102] and as Mary Synge demonstrates in the following extract, there are in fact many cases which hold, on the contrary, that some purposes can be for the public benefit in the second sense although they do not benefit the poor.

M. Synge, "Poverty: An Essential Element in Charity after All?"

[2011] C.L.J. 649 at 651–656

9-089 Whether or not poverty, and the needs of the poor, must be addressed in all cases of charity has proved to be a contentious aspect of charity law. On the one hand, there have been clear authoritative statements to the effect that poverty does not always need to be considered. Most notably, perhaps, in a Privy Council decision in 1924,[103] Lord Wrenbury made it clear that poverty is not "a necessary element" in charities under the fourth head[104] and, similarly, that education and religion "do not require any qualification of poverty to be introduced to give them validity."[105] On the other hand, the relevance of poverty has been argued on occasion, principally in relation to charities dealing with the aged or infirm and where fees are charged for the charity's services.

9-090 To say that poverty is not an essential element of charity is to say, first, that the relief of poverty does not need to be one of the purposes of the organisation and, secondly, that there is no requirement in charity law for the poor to be given the opportunity to benefit from an organisation's charitable purposes. It may well not accord with popular notions of charity, but that is because "charity" has a distinct legal meaning that is "clear and distinct, peculiar to the law" and "not depending upon or coterminous with the popular or vulgar use of the word".[106] The technical nature of the legal definition of charity was not changed by the Act.

9-091 The beneficiaries of a charity's purposes might comprise all poor, all rich, or a combination of poor and rich. For our purposes, "rich" means "not poor" and "poor" means "not rich". The two terms are thus

---

100 [2011] UKUT 421 (TCC); [2012] Ch. 214 at [215]–[220]. For an empirical study of private schools' practices in this regard, see R.J. Wilde et al, "Private Schools and the Provision of 'Public Benefit'" (2016) 45 *Journal of Social Policy* 305.

101 [2011] UKUT 421 (TCC); [2012] Ch. 214 at [191]–[195]. But note the possibility discussed at [194] that an institution might cease "to be able ever to carry out its objects in a manner which would be for the public benefit" so that its original character is "blotted out": in this case, "there may arise an obligation for its trustees to apply for a *cy-près* scheme".

102 [2011] UKUT 421 (TCC); [2012] Ch. 214 at [178].

103 *Verge v Somerville* [1924] A.C. 496.

104 At 499–500, referring to the four heads of charity (relief of poverty, education, religion and other purposes beneficial to the community) outlined in *Commissioners for Special Purposes of the Income Tax v Pemsel* [1891] A.C. 531 at 583.

105 Ibid. at 503. See too *Re Compton* [1945] Ch. 123 at 139.

106 *Pemsel's case* [1891] A.C. 531 at 581, per Lord Macnaghten.

mutually exclusive and require no further definition.[107] Whilst accepting the principle that a class need not be confined to the poor and that the rich may also benefit, the Commission maintains that, where all the beneficiaries may be rich, the poor must also be given material opportunities to benefit.

A class comprising only the rich might arise in the following ways: 9–092

- By an indifference to whether those who actually benefit are rich or poor
- By declaring that purposes are aimed at the rich or with a proviso or qualification that the poor shall not benefit (an "express exclusion on the terms")
- By describing a class of beneficiaries in such a way that only the rich could possibly fall within it (an "implied exclusion on the terms")
- By declaring purposes which can only benefit the rich because high fees are charged (an "implied exclusion in practice")

Except where purposes are clearly aimed at relieving poverty, very often there is no intention that a potential beneficiary's wealth should be taken into account in considering his eligibility to receive the benefits of the charitable purposes[108] and this lack of concern on the part of the donor is reflected in the courts' attitudes. It seems unlikely that an express exclusion on the terms would arise in practice and even less likely, if it did, that charitable status would be advocated or defended with any vigour.[109] An implied exclusion on the terms is more likely to arise and, indeed, has arisen in some cases[110] and, of course, an implied exclusion in practice is commonplace where fees are charged. 9–093

1. The relief of poverty

Clearly poverty is an essential element under the first head of charity. In the case of membership organisations, which are potentially non-charitable because of their non-public character, charitable status will only exist if the purpose, or one of the dominant purposes, is to relieve poverty.[111] Thus in *Re Hobourn Aero Components Limited's Air Raid Distress Fund*,[112] the Court of Appeal held that a fund which was primarily for contributing employees who had suffered from air raids did not constitute a charitable trust, principally on the ground that it was of a private and not public nature.[113] Had there been a requirement of poverty in those eligible for assistance, the trust would have been charitable, whereas the relief of distress from air raids (which would be capable of being charitable in a public context) would not render a private arrangement charitable.[114] 9–094

2. Advancement of education

In *Attorney-General v The Earl of Lonsdale*,[115] the Vice-Chancellor, Sir John Leach, dismissed outright an argument by counsel that a free school for the education of gentlemen's sons could not be charitable. He conceded that such an object would not be charitable "in popular language" but then stated that "in the view of the statute of Elizabeth, all schools for learning are so to be considered".[116] Nearly a century later, Lord Cozens Hardy M.R. refused to accept that a trust for the advancement of education could not be charitable unless there was an element of poverty: "There is no foundation for it in authority nor is there any foundation for it in reason."[117] 9–095

---

107 Thus avoiding the inevitably tortuous problems of scope and definition which the Commission fails to resolve: since the law does not rule out rich beneficiaries, there is no need to address any other class on the sliding scale between the wealthy and the impoverished.

108 For example, the services offered by a charitable lifeboat organisation are available to all distressed seamen, without regard to their means.

109 Some judicial dicta (below) which suggest that charitable status would be denied if the poor were excluded appear to be limited to such an express exclusion (it is submitted that this covers any exclusion of persons less rich than those included [so that, again, there is no need to consider various degrees of wealth]).

110 e.g. a school for the sons of gentlemen: *Attorney General v Earl of Lonsdale* (1827) 1 Simons 105.

111 *Spiller v Maude* 1864. S. 22n.; *Re Lacy* [1899] 2 Ch. 149.

112 [1946] Ch. 194.

113 Ibid. at p.203.

114 Ibid. at p.210; nor will restricting a non-charitable purpose to a particular locality: *Williams' Trustees v. IRC* [1947] A.C. 447 at 456.

115 57 E.R. 518 (in 1827).

116 Ibid. at p.520 (referring to the Charitable Uses Act 1601).

117 *R v Special Commissioners of Income Tax, ex parte University College of North Wales* (1909) 78 L.J.K.B. 576, 578.

9-096 Many fee-paying schools were founded for the education of the poor.[118] Fee-paying boarders were initially few in number, or introduced at a later date, but, typically, became the sole or main category of pupils. This evolution in educational provision led to many repeated calls for independent schools to be closed, or for fiscal privileges and/or charitable status to be removed,[119] but it did not hinder the unswerving attitude of the judiciary in attributing charitable status to them in the nineteenth and twentieth centuries.[120]

9-097 Provided purposes are actually seen as tending to advance education,[121] they have been held to be charitable without any consideration of the presence or absence of poverty.[122] A failure to attract charitable status, on the other hand, has not been due to the absence of poverty but other reasons, most notably lack of public character where education has been intended for relatives or employees.[123]

3. Advancement of religion

9-098 The relevance of poverty was central to *Pemsel's* case,[124] where the House of Lords held that the purposes of "advancing the missionary establishments among heathen nations of the Protestant Episcopal Church"[125] were charitable and entitled to income tax allowances. Three of their Lordships dismissed the "restricted"[126] view that charity implies the relief of poverty and that the testator must be found to have had an intention to provide such relief. They found the purposes to be charitable, notwithstanding that there was no intention to discriminate between rich and poor heathens.

9-099 As with education, the presence or absence of poverty has not been a determining factor in purposes for the advancement of religion.[127]

4. Cases falling under the fourth head

9-100 After identifying the fourth head of charity in *Pemsel's* case, Lord Macnaghten added that trusts within that category "are not the less charitable in the eye of the law, because incidentally they benefit the rich as well as the poor, as indeed, every charity that deserves the name must do either directly or indirectly".[128] Of course, in itself, this tells us only that the beneficiaries of a charitable trust are not required to be exclusively poor and not that poverty is an irrelevant consideration. Whilst it is authority for the proposition that the rich may benefit incidentally, it is not authority for saying that the rich cannot benefit in ways that are not merely incidental.[129] To suggest that it requires at least some poor to benefit, regardless of purpose and charges, would be to ignore the historical and factual context of the case.

9-101 Later dicta address more explicitly the relevance of poverty in charities under the fourth head. In *IRC v Baddeley*,[130] trusts were declared to be non-charitable because the purposes were not recognised by law as exclusively charitable. Lord Reid was clearly of the opinion that, had the purposes been exclusively within the fourth head, "the element of poverty is not necessary to make them valid charitable purposes".[131] In *Re Resch*,[132] Lord Wilberforce referred to Lord Wrenbury having "held generally that poverty is not a necessary qualification in trusts beneficial to the community".

---

118 Including Eton and Winchester.

119 See, for example, I. Williams, *The Alms Trade* (London 1989).

120 *Brighton College v Marriott* [1926] A.C. 192; *Abbey Malvern* [1951] Ch. 728.

121 The courts have interpreted "education" widely but not without limitation: *Re Pinion* [1965] Ch. 85; *Re Shaw* [1957] 1 W.L.R. 729.

122 e.g. *Re Gott* [1944] Ch. 193; *Re Koeppler Will Trusts* [1986] Ch. 423; *Smith v Kerr* [1902] 1 Ch. 774; *IRC v McMullen* [1981] A.C. 1.

123 *Re Compton* [1945] Ch. 123; *Oppenheim v. Tobacco Securities Trust Co. Ltd.* [1951] A.C. 297 at 306; *IRC v Educational Grants Association* [1967] Ch. 993.

124 [1891] A.C. 531.

125 Ibid. at p.532.

126 Ibid. at p.571, per Lord Herschell.

127 e.g. *Re Manser* [1905] 1 Ch. 68; *Re Hood* [1931] 1 Ch. 240; *Farley v Westminster Bank* [1939] A.C. 430; *Cocks v. Manners* (1871) L.R. 12 Eq. 574.

128 [1891] A.C. 531 at 583.

129 Recognised by Lord Wrenbury in *Verge v Somerville* [1924] A.C. 496 at 503.

130 [1955] A.C. 572.

131 Ibid. at 604.

132 [1969] 1 A.C. 514 at 542.

Again, numerous purposes have been found to be charitable under this head without any consideration of poverty[133] and charitable status has been denied on a number of grounds but not the absence of poverty.[134] **9–102**

5. Relief of the aged or infirm

The significance of poverty has been especially prominent where the purposes are concerned with the aged or infirm.[135] In these cases are to be found some of the most notable suggestions of a judicial reluctance[136] to accord charitable status to purposes that do not include an element of poverty. In the mid-twentieth century, academics debated whether a trust for the relief of "aged peers" or "impotent millionaires" would be charitable. Megarry noted the evolving cases of the time and identified the nub of the problem as it seeming "to accord ill with the spirit of the Statute to open the doors of charity to those who are wealthy and well able to provide for themselves, merely because they are aged".[137] Brunyate,[138] however, considered the example of a rich blind man and distinguished between gifts of money on the one hand and curing blindness or providing braille services on the other.[139] Taking a bolder approach than some, he noted: "to regard a rich man who is blind or maimed as in no sense a proper object of charity would surely be taking a very worldly view of human suffering".[140] The cases which addressed this issue over the following two decades[141] reflected this view and to relieve the needs of aged or impotent persons came to be regarded as charitable without any need for poverty, just as other prima facie charitable purposes had not been disqualified through an absence of poverty. **9–103**

After a period of reticence, where judges appeared to be reassured to find evidence which suggested that the testator had intended to benefit aged people who were also poor[142] or indigent,[143] a new confidence emerged in *Re Robinson*,[144] where Vaisey J. held, without hesitation, that a gift to people aged over 65 was charitable without any need for poverty. The requirement for some relief of a need attributable to age, however, was favoured as an approach and emphasised in *Joseph Rowntree Memorial Trust v Attorney General*.[145] Peter Gibson J. in that case considered a number of schemes for the provision of special housing for the elderly and found that the relief of that need was prima facie charitable without any qualification of poverty. Basing his decision on logic as well as judicial authority, he expressed his conclusion with utmost clarity: "It would be as absurd to require that the aged must be impotent or poor as it would be to require the impotent to be aged or poor, or the poor to be aged or impotent."[146] **9–104**

The question of whether poverty is essential in gifts for the relief of the infirm was to the fore in *Re Lewis*.[147] Roxburgh J., in construing gifts of £100 to blind boys and girls, boldly decided to "grasp the nettle" and decide whether or not the absence of "any element of poverty whatsoever" was fatal to finding that the gifts were charitable.[148] He was also happy to endorse the disjunctive interpretation (and its necessary consequences) adopted by Danckwerts J. and Vaisey J.[149] Like Peter Gibson J,[150] Roxburgh J. pointed **9–105**

---

133 e.g. *Re Good* [1905] 2 Ch. 60; *Scottish Burial and Cremation Society Ltd v Glasgow Corporation* [1968] A.C. 138.

134 e.g. *National Anti-Vivisection Society v IRC* [1948] A.C. 31; *IRC v City of Glasgow Police Athletic Association* [1953] A.C. 380 (likewise the "animal cases" contain no consideration of poverty: *Re Wedgwood* [1915] 1 Ch. 113; *Re Grove-Grady* [1929] 1 Ch. 557).

135 Perhaps because the preamble to the 1601 Act includes the relief of the "aged, impotent and poor people", without indicating whether a conjunctive or disjunctive interpretation was intended.

136 Or "great disinclination": *Re Lewis (Deceased)* [1955] Ch. 104 at 107.

137 (1951) 67 L.Q.R. 164.

138 (1945) 61 L.Q.R. 268; see too *Attorney General v Duke of Northumberland* (1877–78) L.R. 7 Ch. D. 745, 749.

139 Echoed by Peter Gibson J. in *Joseph Rowntree Memorial Trust Housing Association Ltd v Attorney-General* [1983] Ch. 159, 171.

140 61 L.Q.R. at p. 272. See too P.S. Atiyah, "Public Benefit in Charities" (1958) 21 M.L.R. 138, at p.140.

141 Briefly, but helpfully, reviewed in the *Joseph Rowntree* case, at pp. 172–173.

142 *Re Lucas* [1922] 2 Ch. 52.

143 *Re Glyn's Will Trusts* [1950] 2 All E.R. 1150n.

144 [1951] Ch. 198. See too *Re Neal* (1966) 110 S.J. 549; *Re Bradbury* [1950] W.N. 558.

145 [1983] Ch. 159. This emphasis on need is also discernible in *Re Resch*.

146 [1983] Ch. 159 at 171. See too *McGovern v Attorney General* [1982] Ch. 321 at 333 where the principle was reiterated without question.

147 [1955] Ch. 104.

148 Ibid. at p. 107.

149 In *Re Glyn's Will Trust* and *Re Robinson*.

150 In the *Joseph Rowntree* case.

to the illogical nature of the counter-argument that would mean that a trust for poor people would not be charitable unless they were also aged or infirm.

C. Political Purposes

9–106 In the context of charity law, "political purposes" have been defined by the courts to include attempts to change the law by legislation or oppose proposed changes to the law and attempts to influence local or national government home or foreign policy.[151] In *National Anti-Vivisection Society v IRC*, excerpted below, the House of Lords held that trusts for political purposes cannot be charitable because the courts have no means of judging whether a proposed change in the law would or would not be for the public benefit,[152] and because the law cannot stultify itself by holding that it is for the public benefit that the law itself should be changed.[153] These reasons are found to be inadequate by Jonathan Garton in a critique of the decision that is also excerpted below.

National Anti-Vivisection Society v IRC

House of Lords [1948] A.C. 31

9–107 The question was whether the appellant society was a body established for charitable purposes only, within the meaning of the Income Tax Act 1918, s.37, and accordingly entitled to exemption from income tax on the income it derived from its investments. The Special Commissioners for the Purposes of Income Tax held that the society was so entitled, but this decision was reversed by McNaghten J.,[154] whose judgment was upheld by the Court of Appeal.[155] The society appealed unsuccessfully.

9–108 LORD WRIGHT: . . . The claim of the appellant society . . . must fail . . . because its object is to secure legislation to give legal effect to it. It is, in my opinion, a political purpose within the meaning of Lord Parker's pronouncement in *Bowman v. Secular Society Ltd.*[156] Lord Parker was discussing in a different connexion the same question of the true criterion for deciding if charitable gifts are for the benefit of the public in the legal sense; he was there referring to the objects enumerated in the memorandum of association of the Secular Society Ltd. He said:

> "Now, if your Lordships will refer for a moment to the society's memorandum of association you will find that none of its objects, except, possibly, the first, are charitable. The abolition of religious tests, the disestablishment of the church, the secularization of education the alteration of the law touching religion or marriage, or the observation of the Sabbath, are purely political objects. Equity has always refused to recognize such objects as charitable. It is true that a gift to an association formed for their attainment may, if the association be unincorporated, be upheld as an absolute gift to its members, or, if the association be incorporated, as an absolute gift to the corporate body; but a trust for the attainment of political objects has always been held invalid, not because it is illegal, for everyone is at liberty to advocate or promote by any lawful means a change in the law, but because the court has no means of judging whether a proposed change in the law will or will not be for the public benefit, and therefore cannot say that a gift to secure the change is a charitable gift."

9–109 While I was preparing this part of my opinion my noble and learned friend Lord Simonds was kind enough to draw to my attention the passage which, in due course, your Lordships will hear quoted by him from a

---

151 See *Baldry v Feintuck* [1972] 1 W.L.R. 552; *Webb v O'Doherty* (1991) 3 Admin. L.R. 731; *Re Koeppler's WT* [1984] Ch. 243. In *Southwood v Attorney General* [2000] W.T.L.R. 1199 the Court of Appeal held that a trust to educate the public to accept that peace is best secured by demilitarisation and disarmament was political and non-charitable.

152 See also *Bowman v Secular Society* [1917] A.C. 406 at 442, per Lord Parker.

153 See also *Bonar Law Memorial Trust v IRC* (1933) 49 T.L.R. 220 (Conservative); *Re Ogden* [1933] Ch. 678 (Liberal); *Re Hopkinson* [1949] W.N. 29 (Socialist); *Re Strakosch* [1949] Ch. 529 (appeasing racial feeling); *Re Bushnell* [1975] 1 W.L.R. 1596 (furthering socialised medicine in a socialist state).

154 [1945] 2 All E.R. 529.

155 [1946] K.B. 185.

156 [1917] A. C. 406 at 442.

work of authority, *Tyssen on Charitable Bequests* . . . It is, I think, a very important contribution to this question. It appears to me to go to explain and justify Lord Parker's opinion. I refer especially to Tyssen's words: "the law could not stultify itself by holding that it was for the public benefit that the law itself should be changed" and again: "each court . . . must decide on the principle that the law is right as it stands." I am reminded of the words of a great common law judge who warned the courts against usurping the functions of the legislature. I do not regard the statements of Lord Parker and Tyssen as inconsistent but as complementary. In my opinion, the respondents' objection under this head is well founded. . .

LORD SIMONDS: . . . The first and shorter point is whether a main purpose of the society is of such a political character that the court cannot regard it as charitable. To this point little attention was directed in the courts below . . . As will appear in the course of this opinion, it is worthy of more serious debate. 9–110

My Lords, on the first point the learned Master of the Rolls cites in his judgment[157] a passage from the speech of Lord Parker in *Bowman v Secular Society Ltd*:[158] 9–111

> "A trust for the attainment of political objects has always been held invalid, not because it is illegal . . . but because the court has no means of judging whether a proposed change in the law will or will not be for the public benefit."

Lord Parker is here considering the possibility of a valid charitable trust and nothing else and when he says "has always been held invalid" he means "has always been held not to be a valid charitable trust." The learned Master of the Rolls found this authoritative statement upon a branch of the law, with which no one was more familiar than Lord Parker, to be inapplicable to the present case for two reasons, first, because he felt difficulty in apvplying the words to "a change in the law which is in common parlance a 'non-political' question", and secondly, because he thought they could not in any case apply, when the desired legislation is "merely ancillary to the attainment of what is *ex hypothesi* a good charitable object."

My Lords, if I may deal with this second reason first, I cannot agree that in this case an alteration in the law is merely ancillary to the attainment of a good charitable object. In a sense no doubt, since legislation is not an end in itself, every law may be regarded as ancillary to the object which its provisions are intended to achieve. But that is not the sense in which it is said that a society has a political object. Here the finding of the commissioners is itself conclusive. "We are satisfied," they say, "that the main object of the society is the total abolition of vivisection . . . and (for that purpose) the repeal of the Cruelty to Animals Act, 1876, and the substitution of a new enactment prohibiting vivisection altogether." This is a finding that the main purpose of the society is the compulsory abolition of vivisection by Act of Parliament. What else can it mean? and how else can it be supposed that vivisection is to be abolished? Abolition and suppression are words that connote some form of compulsion. It can only be by Act of Parliament that that element can be supplied . . . Coming to the conclusion that it is a main object, if not the main object, of the society, to obtain an alteration of the law, I ask whether that can be a charitable object, even if its purposes might otherwise be regarded as charitable. 9–112

My Lords, I see no reason for supposing that Lord Parker in the cited passage used the expression "political objects" in any narrow sense or was confining it to objects of acute political controversy. On the contrary he was, I think, propounding familiar doctrine, nowhere better stated than in a text-book, which has long been regarded as of high authority but appears not to have been cited for this purpose to the courts below (as it certainly was not to your Lordships), *Tyssen on Charitable Bequests*. The passage is worth repeating at length:[159] 9–113

> "It is a common practice for a number of individuals amongst us to form an association for the purpose of promoting some change in the law, and it is worth our while to consider the effect of a gift to such an association. It is clear that such an association is not of a charitable nature. However desirable the change may really be, the law could not stultify itself by holding that it was for the public benefit that the law itself should be changed. Each court in deciding on the validity of a gift must decide on the principle that the law is right as it stands. On the other hand, such a gift could not be held void for illegality."

157 [1946] K. B. 185 at 207.
158 [1917] A. C. 406 at 442.
159 (1st edn, 1898) at p.176.

9–114 Lord Parker uses slightly different language but means the same thing, when he says that the court has no means of judging whether a proposed change in the law will or will not be for the public benefit. It is not for the court to judge and the court has no means of judging. The same question may be looked at from a slightly different angle. One of the tests, and a crucial test, whether a trust is charitable, lies in the competence of the court to control and reform it. I would remind your Lordships that it is the King as *parens patriæ* who is the guardian of charity and that it is the right and duty of his Attorney-General to intervene and inform the court, if the trustees of a charitable trust fall short of their duty. So too it is his duty to assist the court, if need be, in the formulation of a scheme for the execution of a charitable trust. But, my Lords, is it for a moment to be supposed that it is the function of the Attorney-General on behalf of the Crown to intervene and demand that a trust shall be established and administered by the court, the object of which is to alter the law in a manner highly prejudicial, as he and His Majesty's Government may think, to the welfare of the state? This very case would serve as an example, if upon the footing that it was a charitable trust it became the duty of the Attorney-General on account of its maladministration to intervene. There is undoubtedly a paucity of judicial authority on this point . . . But in truth the reason of the thing appears to me so clear that I neither expect nor require much authority. I conclude upon this part of the case that a main object of the society is political and for that reason the society is not established for charitable purposes only.

J. Garton, "*National Anti-Vivisection Society v Inland Revenue Commissioners* (1948)"

in C. Mitchell and P. Mitchell (eds), *Landmark Cases in Equity* (Hart Publishing, 2012), pp.542–550

9–115 . . . Given that the House was not bound by precedent to recognise any rule to the effect that an otherwise valid charitable trust – i.e. one that had an exclusively charitable purpose and demonstrable public benefit – would fail if it had a political purpose, we might expect that their Lordships would have offered convincing justifications for the rule. The majority gave three reasons for their decision:

a) the court's inability to judge the public benefit of a change in law;
b) the inappropriateness of the court's usurping the legislature; and
c) the problem of requiring the Attorney-General to enforce a political trust.

Each is fallacious.

9–116 Our main concern must lie with the dictum of Lord Parker in *Bowman*, which was cited with approval by each of the majority judges in the *National Anti-Vivisection Society* case[160] and was clearly instrumental in their Lordships' reaching the conclusion that they did:[161]

> "[A] trust for the attainment of political objects has always been held invalid, not because it is illegal, for everyone is at liberty to advocate or promote by any lawful means a change in the law, but because the court has no means of judging whether a proposed change in the law will or will not be for the public benefit, and therefore cannot say that a gift to secure the change is a charitable gift."

Public benefit in this context refers to the common law requirement that for a purpose to be charitable, it must not only fall within the spirit and intendment of the list of charitable purposes contained in the Preamble to the Statute of Charitable Uses 1601 but must, conceptually,[162] be one which benefits the public. To the extent that an inability to determine public benefit is the stumbling block preventing a charitable purpose that is also political from being valid, we may say a number of things.

---

160 At 61 (Lord Simonds, with whom Viscount Simon concurred), 50 (Lord Wright) and 77 (Lord Normand).
161 *Bowman v Secular Society* [1917] A.C. 406 at 442.
162 It is another matter whether in practice a charity pursues its conceptually beneficial purpose in such a way as to meet the further requirement, confusingly also referred to as public benefit, that if access to its benefits is in any way restricted then an "appreciably important" section of the public must still be able to enjoy them: *Verge v Somerville* [1924] A.C. 496 at 499 (Lord Wrenbury).

The traditional criticism levelled is that the court ought to be perfectly able to judge whether a change in the law would be for the public benefit, for this is what it is to be a judge in the common law tradition. The position was summed up neatly by Leslie Sheridan 40 years ago:[163] **9–117**

> "Granted that a judge must decide cases on the basis of the law as it stands, he does not have to approve the eternal correctness of all our law . . . Nothing could be more stultifying of the legal system than the judges always sticking to precedent, never breaking new ground, taking no notice of changing social conditions, applying a rule in 1972 solely because there is a precedent of 1372."

The reality is that of course the court has on more than one occasion shown that it is capable of judging whether a change in the law would be for the public benefit, and two examples from both ends of the spectrum should suffice by way of illustration:[164] in the *National Anti-Vivisection Society* case itself . . . the change in the law sought out by the Society was found on the evidence to be "greatly to the public disadvantage";[165] whilst Slade J. in *McGovern v Attorney-General* would later describe Amnesty International's three main objects—securing the release of prisoners of conscience, opposing the detention without trial of prisoners of conscience and political prisoners, and opposing the death penalty, torture and inhumane treatment of all prisoners—as "philanthropic purposes of an excellent character",[166] despite the fact that they necessitated changes to the laws or the government policies in jurisdictions where relevant abuses occurred. **9–118**

However, an important aspect of Lord Parker's dictum has hitherto been overlooked. When read in the light of the House's comments in the *National Anti-Vivisection Society* case, that the court must weigh the benefits and detriments of a purpose in the balance when considering whether it is for the public benefit, the only logical conclusion is that the court is capable of judging on the evidence whether a purpose is charitable if pursued outside the political arena, but incapable of judging whether the same purpose is charitable if pursued through political action. This means we may conceive of a situation where the court can say that a society established for a particular purpose tends towards the public benefit (and is therefore charitable) because it seeks to effect that purpose through non-political means, but it is unable to say one way or the other whether another society established for the same purpose tends towards the public benefit (and is therefore not charitable) because it seeks to effect that purpose politically. If the purpose is the same in both cases, and if the end result is the same if either society is successful, then why does the public benefit, or rather the court's ability to judge the public benefit, disappear? **9–119**

If we assume no other variables then the only logical conclusion is that there must be something about the political process itself that has the potential to introduce a detriment capable of outweighing the public benefit otherwise inherent in a given purpose—*potential* here being key, as we know that there is nothing in the political process that *necessarily* outweighs the public benefit of an otherwise charitable purpose, for this would mean that a political purpose is not, on balance, for the public benefit, and Lord Parker's dictum is clear: the court cannot say either way whether a political purpose is for the public benefit. **9–120**

This is difficult, not least because Lord Simonds[167] and Lord Wright[168] both make it clear in their speeches that it is not the process but the end result—the change in the law—that is the problem. . . **9–121**

Lord Wright suggests that a second justification for the prohibition is that if the court were to recognise political purposes as charitable then this would usurp the functions of the legislature.[169] The idea is not pursued in any detail, and it is clear that approving as charitable an organisation with political objects would not in reality involve the court stepping on the shoes of Parliament. There are several reasons for this. **9–122**

---

163 L.A. Sheridan, "Charity versus Politics" (1973) 2 Anglo-American Law Review 4757. See too L.A. Sheridan, "The Political Muddle – A Charitable View" (1977) 19 Malaya Law Review 42, 65; C.E.F. Rickett, "Charity and Politics" (1982) 10 New Zealand University Law Review 169, 172.

164 See also F. Gladstone, *Charity, Law and Social Justice* (1982) 100–01, who wonders, in the context of a community association's campaign to procure the construction of a pedestrian crossing, "how many old-age pensioners would need to be knocked down before a court could judge that [the] crossing would be for the public benefit".

165 At 65 (Lord Simonds).

166 *McGovern v Attorney-General* [1982] Ch. 321 at 329.

167 At 62.

168 At 50.

169 At 50.

9–123 First, the decision whether to grant an organisation with political objects charitable status is, in itself, unlikely to be determinative of whether the organisation in fact goes on to pursue those objects. Unless structured around a testamentary purpose trust, which would fail if denied charitable status,[170] its trustees would still be free to carry on its political objects, though there may be resource implications in failing to obtain charitable status.

9–124 Secondly, even if a charity were to campaign for a change in the law as a result of a decision of the court, it would not follow that Parliament must respond by effecting that change, as Francis Gladstone observes:[171]

> "Apart from anything else, granting charitable status to such trusts is not at all the same thing as actually granting the reforms they seek. There is no guarantee that they will be successful; and if they are, it will be because they have convinced public opinion and Parliament of the need for reform, not because the judiciary has usurped the prerogative of Parliament."

9–125 Thirdly, it is fallacious to suggest that by granting charitable status to an institution campaigning for a change in the law, the court itself is advocating that change: in the spirit of Voltaire, the court could permit a charity to pursue a purpose in a manner of which it does not necessarily approve, so long as the purpose is otherwise charitable and there is public benefit. Furthermore, just as we have argued why two charities with the same broad purpose might seek to achieve it through different means and with different effects in the interests of the diversity of organised civil society, so too might two charities legitimately take different positions on the desirability or otherwise of a proposed change in the law; allowing one to pursue its object by campaigning for the change would not prevent the court from allowing the other to pursue the same object by campaigning against it.[172] Neither charity would be able to claim the "approval" of the court.

9–126 Additional support is lent to this argument if we contrast the court's attitude towards political trusts following the *National Anti-Vivisection Society* case with its long-standing attitude towards religious trusts, where it has no problem recognising the validity of trusts without approving or disapproving of any particular set of religious beliefs[173]. . .

9–127 The final argument against political purposes in the *National Anti-Vivisection Society* case, hitherto largely overlooked, is that if a political trust were to be upheld as charitable and its trustees defaulted or acted in breach of trust, this might place the Attorney-General, who has jurisdiction at common law to enforce charitable trusts, in a difficult position . . . Such a situation, the argument goes, would clearly give rise to a conflict of interest, and there would be strong incentive for the Attorney-General either to refuse to exercise his discretion to intervene[174] or to mount an ineffectual action for the sake of form. In other cases, where the object of the charitable trust was to advocate maintaining the status quo, the Attorney-General would presumably happily pull out all the stops to hold the trustees to account. The same line of reasoning could be applied today with regard to enforcement by the Charity Commission . . . This argument has been largely ignored by critics of the prohibition, but it can be easily dismissed: it overlooks the simple fact that charities are already free to pursue their purposes in ways that might conceivably bring them into conflict with the views of the government of the day—the activities that a charity carries out do not require State approval and, save where they reveal something about the true nature of the institution's purposes, . . . do not come under meaningful scrutiny. So whilst it is true that the Attorney-General and the Charity Commission might have an incentive to enforce certain political purposes over others, so too do they have a similar incentive with other charitable purposes under the current law.

---

170 Although an *inter vivos* purpose trust would also fail, the settlor would of course be in a position to select an alternative vehicle, such as a company or a society, to carry out the desired objects.

171 Gladstone at p.102.

172 See Rickett at p.171.

173 *O'Hanlon v Logue* [1906] 1 I.R. 247 at 259 (Lord Walker L.C.). See also *Gilmour v Coats* [1949] A.C. 426 at 457 (Lord Reid): '[S]ince diversity of religious beliefs arose and became lawful the law has shown no preference in this matter to any church and other religious body. Where a belief is accepted by some and rejected by others the law can neither accept nor reject, it must remain neutral'.

174 Note *Central Bayside General Practice Association Ltd v Commissioner of State Revenue* (2006) 228 C.L.R. 168 at [179], where by implication Callinan J. contemplates a similar situation, given that he argues that there would be no such conflict where a charity's objects are in line with those of the State.

The rule that political purposes are not charitable has been followed by the English courts and the Charity Commission[175] and by the courts of other Commonwealth jurisdictions. It remains the law in Canada.[176] However, it was repudiated by the High Court of Australia in *Aid/Watch Inc v Federal Commissioner of Taxation*,[177] where the court held that "the encouragement of public debate" on matters falling within an existing charitable head is a charitable purpose in its own right because it contributes to the culture of free political expression on which a representative system of government depends.[178] This decision was affirmed by federal legislation.[179] The rule denying chartable status to political purposes was also rejected by the New Zealand Supreme Court in *Re Greenpeace of New Zealand Inc*,[180] although the court did not whole-heartedly accept the *Aid/Watch* finding that the promotion of political debate is a charitable purpose in itself,[181] and held that courts must assess whether the achievement of a political purpose will enure to the public good.[182] **9–128**

Of the two approaches, *Aid/Watch* is preferable to *Greenpeace*, since it rightly recognises the promotion of public debate as a social good in itself and obviates the need for courts to become embroiled in contentious arguments about the merits or demerits of particular changes to the legal status quo.[183] We must therefore hope that the English courts and Charity Commission will move English law in the same direction, something which would be consistent with the emphasis that the Commission now places in its guidance document on the benefits flowing from the advocacy and campaigning work done by charities.[184] This is currently permissible to the extent that it is done not as an end in itself but as an ancillary means towards the achievement of a purpose that is itself charitable.[185] So, for example, Shelter, a charity which aims to relieve the homeless, can legitimately press for changes in the Government's housing policy. **9–129**

The recognition of political campaigning as a charitable purpose in itself has also been brought closer by the Charities Act 2011 s.3(1)(h), which states the advancement of human rights to be a charitable purpose.[186] The import of this sub-section was considered by the First-tier Tribunal (Charity) in 2013, in the course of deciding that the purposes of the Human Dignity Trust were not political, although these entailed campaigning for foreign states to amend their domestic laws to align them with international human rights norms, and bringing litigation against foreign states with this goal in mind.[187] The Tribunal reasoned that these norms were embodied in treaties to which the relevant **9–130**

---

175 e.g. *McGovern v Attorney General* [1982] Ch. 321; *The Margaret Thatcher Foundation* [1991] Ch. Comm. Rep. 39; *Southwood v Attorney General* [2000] W.T.L.R. 1199; *Hanchett-Stamford v Attorney General* [2008] EWHC 330 (Ch); [2009] Ch. 173.

176 *Vancouver Society of Immigrant and Visible Minority Women v M.N.R.* [1999] 1 S.C.R. 10.

177 (2010) 241 C.L.R. 539.

178 (2010) 241 C.L.R. 539 at [44]–[47].

179 Charities Act 2013 (Cth) s.12(1)(l); but note s.11(b): the purpose of promoting or opposing a political party or a candidate for political office is not charitable in itself.

180 (2014) 17 I.T.E.L.R. 296.

181 Their comments about this at [62] and [103] are ambiguous.

182 At [72]–[76].

183 M. Harding, "An Antipodean View of Political Purposes and Charity Law" (2015) 131 L.Q.R. 181 at 183; S. Barker, "Advocacy by Charities: What Is the Question?" (2020) 6 C.J.C.C.L. 1.

184 Charity Commission, *CC 9: Speaking Out—Guidance on Campaigning and Political Activities by Charities* (March 2008), *https://www.gov.uk/government/uploads/system/uploads/attachment_data/file/300222/cc9text.pdf*. The Commission has not always taken such a positive view of political activities by charities and in the past has sharply criticised bodies such as Oxfam and War on Want for overstepping the line.

185 *McGovern v Attorney General* [1982] Ch. 321 at 351; Charity Commission, *Decision to Register English PEN as a Charity*, 21 July 2008, reported at [2008] W.T.L.R. 1799..

186 For a case study of the decision taken by War on Want to rewrite its objectives so as to bring itself within s.3(1)(h), see H. Miller, "A Change in Charity Law for England and Wales: Examining War on Want's Foremost Adoption of the New Human Rights Charitable Purpose" (2012) 16 I.J.H.R. 1003.

187 *Human Dignity Trust v Charity Commission*, First-tier Tribunal (Charity), 9 July 2014, *http://charity.decisions.tribunals.gov.uk/documents/decisions/human-dignity-trust-v-charity-commission-judgment.pdf*.

states were signatories and were guaranteed by the states' constitutions. Hence litigation aimed at upholding the constitutional rights of the citizens of these states did not seek to change the states' laws but to enforce and uphold rights guaranteed by their constitutions. Technically this must have been correct, but the finding that bodies such as the Human Dignity Trust are legally charitable makes it harder to deny the same status to bodies who use the same means to accomplish similar ends, particularly if the *Aid/Watch* argument is accepted, that campaigning is a social good regardless of the outcomes which it produces.

D. Discriminatory Purposes

9–131 The Equality Act 2010 prohibits direct or indirect discrimination in relation to the "protected characteristics" of age, disability, gender reassignment, marriage and civil partnership, pregnancy and maternity, race, religion or belief, sex, and sexual orientation. However, the Equality Act 2010 s.193(2), reproduced below, permits charities to restrict benefits to a class of people defined by reference to a "protected characteristic" if this is either a "proportionate means of achieving a legitimate aim" or is "for the purpose of preventing or compensating for a disadvantage" connected to that characteristic.

9–132 This was considered in *Catholic Care (Diocese of Leeds) v Charity Commission for England and Wales*,[188] which concerned a charitable Catholic adoption agency that wished to amend its objects so as to limit its provision of adoption services to prospective foster parents who were heterosexuals. The agency argued that its proposed discrimination was proportionate to the achievement of a legitimate aim, namely "the prospect of increasing the number of children (particularly 'hard to place' children) placed with adoptive families". It argued that if it did not discriminate against same sex couples, it would lose funding from its Catholic supporters and be forced to close. This would mean that fewer children would be adopted, and the harm to them would exceed the harm suffered by same sex couples who could not adopt through the agency. Sitting in the Upper Tribunal, Sales J accepted that the agency's aim was a legitimate aim for the purposes of the Act. However, he did not accept that the evidence bore out the agency's case that the number of children placed in adoptive care would be increased by its continued work, as there was a surplus of potential adopters available through other adoption agencies. Hence it could not prove the "weighty and convincing reasons" required to justify its proposed discrimination against homosexuals.[189]

9–133 The Equality Act 2010 s.193(3) permits charities to treat people with disabilities more favourably than others when providing them with employment, so that, e.g. the Royal National Institute for the Blind can prefer employing visually impaired persons. Section 193(4) forbids charities to restrict the provision of benefits to a class defined by colour, and any trust that purports to do so will be read as though the reference to colour was absent. Thus a trust for "the black community of Hackney, Haringey, Islington and Tower Hamlets" was upheld as a valid charitable trust, but only on the basis

---

[188] [2012] UKUT 395 (TCC); [2013] 1 W.L.R. 2105, discussed in D. Morris, "Charities and the Modern Equality Framework—Heading for a Collision?" (2012) 65 C.L.P. 295. See also M. Harding, "Charitable Trusts and Discrimination: Two Themes" (2016) 2 C.J.C.C.L. 227; A. Parachin, "Why and When Discrimination Is Discordant with Charitable Status: The Problem with 'Public Policy', the Possibility of a Better Solution" (2020) 6 C.J.C.C.L. 305.

[189] [2012] UKUT 395 (TCC); [2013] 1 W.L.R. 2105 at [55] per Sales J. See also *R. (on the application of Cornerstone (North East) Adoption and Fostering Services Ltd) v Chief Inspector of Education, Children's Services and Skills (Ofsted)* [2021] EWCA Civ 1390; [2021] I.R.L.R. 993 (where a similar conclusion was drawn regarding a similarly discriminatory policy operated by an evangelical Christian fostering agency). But cf. *R. (on the application of Z) v Hackney LBC* [2020] UKSC 40; [2020] 1 W.L.R. 4327 (where a charitable housing association pursued a discriminatory policy of prioritising the housing needs of members of the Orthodox Jewish community, but where this policy was held to be a proportionate means of pursuing a legitimate aim).

that the word "black" was deleted.[190] Section 193(5) permits charities to discriminate in favour of, although not against, people defined by reference to their religious beliefs. Section 193(7) permits charities to benefit persons of one sex only.

Equality Act 2010 s.193

(1) A person does not contravene this Act only by restricting the provision of benefits to persons who share a protected characteristic if— 9–134

(a) the person acts in pursuance of a charitable instrument, and
(b) the provision of the benefits is within subsection (2).

(2) The provision of benefits is within this subsection if it is—

(a) a proportionate means of achieving a legitimate aim, or
(b) for the purpose of preventing or compensating for a disadvantage linked to the protected characteristic.

(3) It is not a contravention of this Act for—

(a) a person who provides supported employment to treat persons who have the same disability or a disability of a prescribed description more favourably than those who do not have that disability or a disability of such a description in providing such employment;
(b) a Minister of the Crown to agree to arrangements for the provision of supported employment which will, or may, have that effect.

(4) If a charitable instrument enables the provision of benefits to persons of a class defined by reference to colour, it has effect for all purposes as if it enabled the provision of such benefits—

(a) to persons of the class which results if the reference to colour is ignored, or
(b) if the original class is defined by reference only to colour, to persons generally.

(5) It is not a contravention of this Act for a charity to require members, or persons wishing to become members, to make a statement which asserts or implies membership or acceptance of a religion or belief; and for this purpose restricting the access by members to a benefit, facility or service to those who make such a statement is to be treated as imposing such a requirement.
(6) Subsection (5) applies only if—

(a) the charity, or an organisation of which it is part, first imposed such a requirement before 18 May 2005, and
(b) the charity or organisation has not ceased since that date to impose such a requirement.

(7) It is not a contravention of section 29 for a person, in relation to an activity which is carried on for the purpose of promoting or supporting a charity, to restrict participation in the activity to persons of one sex. . .

E. Purposes Must Be Exclusively Charitable

i. The Basic Rule

If, consistently with a trust's terms, trust property may be applied for purposes which are not charitable, it is not a charitable trust even though, consistently with the trust's terms, the property may be applied exclusively for purposes which are charitable. Hence these trusts are not exclusively charitable 9–135

190 *Re Harding (Deceased)* [2007] EWHC 3 (Ch); [2008] Ch. 235, applying the statutory precursor to s.193(4), the Race Relations Act 1976 s.34(1).

and so are void: "for worthy causes", for "charitable or benevolent purposes",[191] for purposes "connected with the education and welfare of children"[192] or "for the public good".[193] The same principle was applied in *Uturn UK CIC v Charity Commission*,[194] where the First-tier Tribunal affirmed the Commission's decision that it was not a charitable purpose to promote "street associations" where there was no guarantee that the associations would undertake exclusively charitable activities and would not deliver private benefits to individuals.

ii. Exceptions

9–136 Notwithstanding the basic rule, a benignant construction can sometimes save a charitable trust as in *Guild v IRC*[195] where the trust deed required funds to be used for a sports centre in North Berwick qualifying as a valid recreational charity under the Recreational Charities Act 1958 "or some similar purpose in connection with sport", and where the House of Lords held such "similar purpose" must likewise be a charitable purpose. Again, in *Armenian Patriarch of Jerusalem v Sorsino*,[196] a trust for the "education and advancement in life of Armenian children" was construed conjunctively and so for the charitable purpose of education.

9–137 If the purpose of a trust is charitable but it undertakes non-charitable activities which are incidental to the effective promotion of its purpose, then it is established for charitable purposes only.[197] However, if a trust has a non-charitable object as one of its purposes then it is not established for exclusively charitable purposes. In Slade J's words:[198]

> The distinction is between (a) those non-charitable activities authorised by the trust instrument which are merely incidental or subsidiary to a charitable purpose and (b) those non-charitable activities so authorised which themselves form part of the trust purpose. In the latter but not the former case the reference to non-charitable activities will deprive the trust of its charitable status.

9–138 Where a trustee is directed to apportion between charitable and non-charitable objects the trust is always good as to the charitable objects. The trust will be valid *in toto* if the non-charitable objects are certain and valid,[199] and, in the absence of apportionment by the trustee, the court will divide the fund equally between both classes of objects in accordance with the maxim that "equality is equity".[200] If the non-charitable objects are uncertain, then the trust will be good as to the charitable objects only, provided they are sufficiently well defined to reveal a general charitable intention.[201]

---

191 *Chichester Diocesan Fund v Simpson* [1944] A.C. 341; *Latimer v Inland Revenue Commissioner* [2004] UKPC 13; [2004] 1 W.L.R. 1466 at [32].

192 *Attorney General of the Bahamas v Royal Trust Co* [1986] 1 W.L.R. 1001 (welfare purposes not restricted to educational welfare purposes so as to qualify as charitable).

193 *Attorney General of Cayman Islands v Wahr-Hansen* [2001] 1 A.C. 75.

194 27 February 2012, *http://charity.decisions.tribunals.gov.uk/documents/decisions/Uturn_UK_Decision.pdf*. See too *Crocels Community Media Group v Charity Commission*, First-Tier Tribunal (Charity), 18 July 2016, *http://charity.decisions.tribunals.gov.uk/documents/decisions/crocels-v-charity-commission-decision-18july16.pdf*; Charity Commission, *Decision on the Application for Registration of the Countryside Alliance*, 23 March 2017, *https://assets.publishing.service.gov.uk/government/uploads/system/uploads/attachment_data/file/602740/Countryside_Alliance_Decision_Final.pdf*.

195 [1992] 2 A.C. 310.

196 (2002) 5 I.T.E.L.R. 125.

197 *Royal College of Surgeons of England v National Provincial Bank Ltd* [1952] A.C. 631; *Re Coxen* [1948] Ch. 747; *London Hospital Medical College v IRC* [1976] 1 W.L.R. 613.

198 *McGovern v Attorney General* [1982] Ch. 321 at 341.

199 *Re Douglas* (1887) 35 Ch. D. 472.

200 *Salusbury v Denton* (1857) 3 K. & J. 529.

201 *Re Clarke* [1923] 2 Ch. 407.

5. The Heads of Charity

The following discussion proceeds in accordance with the classificatory scheme of the Charities Act 2011 ss.3(1) and 5, which have been reproduced above.[202] **9–139**

A. Section 3(1)(a): "The Prevention or Relief of Poverty"

i. Inherently Beneficial Purposes

Section 3(1)(a) has its origins in that part of the preamble to the Statute of Charitable Uses 1601 which speaks of "the relief of aged, impotent and poor people". At common law, these words had to be read disjunctively so that a trust was charitable if the beneficiaries were either elderly, or ill, or poor.[203] Under the Charities Act 2011, the relief of those in need by reason of age and ill-health has been separated from relief of the poor and appears in s.3(1)(j). **9–140**

The "relief" of poverty and the "prevention" of poverty exist along a continuum of measures that can be taken for the benefit of the needy, and many charities aim to do both. But there is a difference between them, in that prevention entails addressing the causes, while relief entails addressing the consequences of poverty, and this is recognised by the wording of s.3(1)(a) which treats each as a stand-alone purpose. The prevention of poverty might be undertaken, for example, by charities that provide money management and debt counselling advice. **9–141**

"Poverty" is a relative term and the expression "poor people" is not necessarily confined to the destitute poor: it includes persons who have to "go short" in the ordinary acceptation of that term, due regard being had to their station in life and so forth.[204] The "working classes" do not ipso facto constitute a section of the poor,[205] but in *Re Niyazi's WT*[206] a gift of residue worth about £15,000 for "the construction of or as a contribution towards the construction of a working men's hostel" in Famagusta was held charitable. The size of the gift, the housing shortage in Famagusta, and the term "working men's hostel" provided a sufficient connotation of poverty to make the gift charitable. The Charity Commission now advises that:[207] **9–142**

> For a charity carrying out its aims in England and Wales, 'people in poverty' might typically mean households living on less than 60% of median income who go short in some unacceptable way. This includes those people who, despite working, might still fall into this category and people may qualify for assistance from a poverty charity whether or not they are eligible for state benefits.

---

202 See paras 9–039 and 9–040.

203 Age: *Re Robinson* [1951] Ch. 198; *Re Glyn's WT* [1950] 2 All E.R. 1150n.; *Re Bradbury* [1950] 2 All E.R. 1150n.; *Rowntree Memorial Trust Housing Association v Attorney General* [1983] Ch. 159; impotence: *Re Elliott* (1910) 102 L.T. 528; *Re Hillier* [1944] 1 All E.R. 480; *Re Lewis* [1955] Ch. 104.

204 *Re Segelman* [1996] Ch. 171; *Re Coulthurst* [1951] Ch. 661 at 666; *Re Young* [1953] 3 All E.R. 689: Charity Commission, *Decision to Register the AITC Foundation* (19 February 2004).

205 *Re Sanders' WT* [1954] Ch. 265 ("dwellings for the working classes and their families resident in the area of Pembroke Dock or within a radius of 5 miles therefrom" held not charitable).

206 [1978] 3 All E.R. 785.

207 Charity Commission, *The Prevention or Relief of Poverty for the Public Benefit* (December 2008 version), Pt C1.

ii. Provision of Benefit to the Community

9–143 Trusts for the relief of poverty (but not for the relief of elderly[208] or ill persons[209]) form an exception to the principle that the people benefiting from a charitable trust must not be a private class of individuals defined by reference to a personal nexus with a particular person. The exception covers both the poor relations of a named individual[210] and the poor employees of a particular employer and their families.[211] However, there must be a primary intent to relieve poverty, albeit among a particular class of person. If the primary intent is to benefit particular persons (e.g. A, B, C and their children for their relief in needy circumstances) the trust is a private one and not charitable.[212]

9–144 These principles are derived from *Dingle v Turner*,[213] parts of which are reproduced below. Following the enactment of the Charities Act 2006 s.3, which has been discussed above,[214] doubts were raised as to the continued validity of these rules. In particular, the Charity Commission doubted whether it remained a charitable purpose to provide financial assistance to a settlor's poor relations. The Attorney General therefore made a non-adversarial reference to determine whether the 2006 Act had altered the common law rules on this point, and in *Attorney General v Charity Commission for England and Wales*,[215] which is also excerpted below, the Upper Tribunal (Tax and Chancery Chamber) held that it had not.

Dingle v Turner

House of Lords [1972] A.C. 601

9–145 VISCOUNT DILHORNE: My Lords, I agree with Lord Cross that this appeal should be dismissed and with the reasons he gives for the conclusion.

9–146 With Lord MacDermott, I too do not wish to extend my concurrence to what my noble and learned friend Lord Cross has said with regard to the fiscal privileges of a legal charity. Those privileges may be altered from time to time by Parliament and I doubt whether their existence should be a determining factor in deciding whether a gift or trust is charitable.

9–147 LORD MACDERMOTT: My Lords, the conclusion I have reached on the facts of this case is that the gift in question constitutes a public trust for the relief of poverty which is charitable in law. I would therefore dismiss the appeal.

9–148 I do not find it necessary to state my reasons for this conclusion in detail. In the first place, the views which I have expressed at some length in relation to an educational trust in *Oppenheim v Tobacco Securities Trust Co Ltd*[216] seem to me to apply to this appeal and to mean that it fails. And, secondly, I have had the advantage of reading the opinion prepared by my noble and learned friend, Lord Cross of Chelsea, and find myself in agreement with his conclusion for the reasons he has given. But I would prefer not to extend my concurrence to what my noble and learned friend goes on to say respecting the fiscal privileges of a legal charity. This subject may be material on the question whether what is alleged to be a charity is sufficiently altruistic in nature to qualify as such, but beyond that, and without wishing to express any final view on the

---

208 *Re Dunlop* [1984] N.I. 408 (trust to found a home for old Presbyterian persons held to be for sufficient section of public to be charitable under fourth head of charity).

209 *Re Resch's WT* [1969] 1 A.C. 514.

210 *Re Scarisbrick* [1951] Ch. 622.

211 *Dingle v Turner* [1972] A.C. 601. See, too, *Cawdron v Merchant Taylors' School* [2009] EWHC 1722 (Ch); [2010] P.T.S.R. 507 at [29]–[34] (trust to benefit sons of the school's old boys killed or disabled in the First World War).

212 *Re Scarisbrick* [1951] Ch. 662; *Re Cohen* [1973] 1 W.L.R. 415; *Re Segelman* [1995] 3 All E.R. 676 at 686–692 (26 persons in the class which would increase with the birth of further members).

213 [1972] A.C. 601.

214 See paras 9–049 to 9–105.

215 [2012] UKUT 420 (TCC); [2012] W.T.L.R. 977.

216 [1951] A.C. 297.

matter, I doubt if these consequential privileges have much relevance to the primary question whether a given trust or purpose should be held charitable in law.

LORD HODSON: My Lords, I agree with my noble and learned friend, Lord Cross of Chelsea, that this appeal should be dismissed and with his reasons for that conclusion. With this reservation: that I share the doubts expressed by my noble and learned friends, Lord MacDermott and Viscount Dilhorne, as to the relevance of fiscal considerations in deciding whether a gift or trust is charitable. 9–149

LORD SIMON OF GLAISDALE: My Lords, I have had the advantage of reading the opinion of my noble and learned friend, Lord Cross of Chelsea, with which I agree. 9–150

LORD CROSS OF CHELSEA: My Lords, . . . Clause 8(e) was in the following terms: 9–151

> "(e) To invest the sum of ten thousand pounds in any of the investments for the time being authorised by law for the investment of trust funds in the names of three persons (hereinafter referred to as 'the Pension Fund Trustees') to be nominated for the purpose by the persons who at the time at which my Executors assent to this bequest are directors of E. Dingle & Company Limited and the Pension Fund Trustees shall hold the said sum and the investments for the time being representing the same (hereinafter referred to as 'the Pensions Fund') upon trust to apply the income thereof in paying pensions to poor employees of E. Dingle & Company Limited or of any other company to which upon any reconstruction or amalgamation the goodwill and the assets of E. Dingle & Company Limited may be transferred who are of the age of Sixty years at least or who being of the age of Forty five years at least are incapacitated from earning their living by reason of some physical or mental infirmity provided always that if at any time the Pension Fund Trustees shall for any reason be unable to apply the income of the Pension Fund in paying such pensions to such employees as aforesaid the Pension Fund Trustees shall hold the Pensions Fund and the income thereof upon trust for the aged poor in the Parish of St. Andrew, Plymouth."

Finally by clause 8(g) the testator directed his trustees to hold the ultimate residue of his estate on the trusts set out in clause 8(e).

The testator died on January 10, 1950. His widow died on October 8, 1966, having previously released her testamentary power of appointment over her husband's shares in E. Dingle & Co Ltd, which accordingly fell into the residuary estate. When these proceedings started in July 1970, the value of the fund held on the trusts declared by clause 8(e) was about £320,000 producing a gross income of about £17,800 per annum. 9–152

E. Dingle and Co Ltd was incorporated as a private company on January 20, 1935. Its capital was owned by the testator and one John Russell Baker and it carried on the business of a departmental store. At the time of the testator's death the company employed over 600 persons and there was a substantial number of ex-employees. On October 23, 1950, the company became a public company. Since the testator's death its business has expanded and when these proceedings started it had 705 full-time and 189 part-time employees and was paying pensions to 89 ex-employees. 9–153

The trustees took out an originating summons asking the court to determine whether the trust declared by clause 8(e) were valid and if so to determine various subsidiary questions of construction—as, for example, whether part-time employees or employees of subsidiary companies were eligible to receive benefits under the trust. To this summons they made defendants (1) representatives of the various classes of employees or ex-employees, (2) those who would be interested on an intestacy if the trusts failed, and (3) Her Majesty's Attorney-General. It has been common ground throughout that the trust at the end of clause 8(e) for the aged poor in the Parish of St Andrew Plymouth is dependent on the preceding trust for poor employees of the company so that although it will catch any surplus income which the trustees do not apply for the benefit of poor employees it can have no application if the preceding trust is itself void. 9–154

The contentions of the appellant and the respondents may be stated broadly as follows. The appellant says that in the *Oppenheim* case this House decided that in principle a trust ought not to be regarded as charitable if the benefits under it are confined either to the descendants of a named individual or individuals or the employees of a given individual or company and that although the "poor relations" cases may have to be left standing as an anomalous exception to the general rule because their validity has been recognised for so long, the exception ought not to be extended to "poor employees" trusts which had not been recognised for long before their status as charitable trusts began to be called in question. The respondents, on the other hand, say, first, that the rule laid down in the *Oppenheim* case with regard to educational trusts ought not to be regarded as a rule applicable in principle to all kinds of charitable trust 9–155 and, secondly, that in any case it is impossible to draw any logical distinction between "poor relations" trusts and "poor employees" trusts, and, that as the former cannot be held invalid today after having been recognised as valid for so long, the latter must be regarded as valid also.

9–156 By a curious coincidence within a few months of the decision of this House in the *Oppenheim* case the cases on gifts to "poor relations" had to be considered by the Court of Appeal in *Re Scarisbrick*.[217] Most of the cases on this subject were decided in the eighteenth or early nineteenth centuries and are very inadequately reported but two things at least were clear. First, that it never occurred to the judges who decided them that in the field of "poverty" a trust could not be a charitable trust if the class of beneficiaries was defined by reference to descent from a common ancestor. Secondly, that the courts did not treat a gift or trust as necessarily charitable because the objects of it had to be poor in order to qualify, for in some of the cases the trust was treated as a private trust and not a charity. The problem in *Re Scarisbrick* was to determine on what basis the distinction was drawn. The Court of Appeal held that in this field the distinction between a public or charitable trust and a private trust depended on whether as a matter of construction the gift was for the relief of poverty amongst a particular description of poor people or was merely a gift to particular poor persons. The fact that the gift took the form of a perpetual trust would no doubt indicate that the intention of the donor could not have been to confer private benefits on particular people whose possible necessities he had in mind; but the fact that the capital of the gift was to be distributed at once did not necessarily show that the gift was a private trust. . .

9–157 [His Lordship then reviewed the earlier cases leading up to *Gibson v South American Stores* and continued:] The facts in *Gibson v South American Stores (Gath & Chaves) Ltd*[218]—the case followed by Megarry J. in this case—were that a company had vested in trustees a fund derived solely from its profits to be applied at the discretion of the directors in granting gratuities, pensions or allowances to persons—

> "who . . . are or shall be necessitous and deserving and who for the time being are or have been in the company's employ . . . and the wives widows husbands widowers children parents and other dependants of any person who for the time being is or would if living have been himself or herself a member of the class of beneficiaries."

9–158 The Court of Appeal held that this trust was a valid charitable trust but it did so without expressing a view of its own on the question of principle involved, because the case of *Re Laidlaw*[219] which was unearthed in the course of the hearing showed that the Court of Appeal had already accepted the decision in *Re Gosling*[220] as correct.

9–159 In *Oppenheim v Tobacco Securities Trust Co Ltd*[221] this House had to consider the principle laid down by the Court of Appeal in *Re Compton*.[222] There the trustees of a fund worth over £125,000 were directed to apply its income and also if they thought fit all or any part of the capital—

> "in providing for or assisting in providing for the education of children of employees or former employees of British-American Tobacco Co, Ltd . . . or any of its subsidiary or allied companies . . .".

9–160 There were over 110,000 such employees. The majority of your Lordships—namely Lord Simonds (in whose judgment Lord Oaksey concurred), Lord Normand and Lord Morton of Henryton—in holding that the trust was not a valid charitable trust gave unqualified approval to the Compton principle. They held, that is to say, that although the "poverty" cases might afford an anomalous exception to the rule, it was otherwise a general rule applicable to all charitable trusts that no class of beneficiaries can constitute a "section of the public" for the purpose of the law of charity if the distinguishing quality which links them together is relationship to a particular individual either through common descent or common employment. My noble and learned friend, Lord MacDermott, on the other hand, in his dissenting speech, while not challenging the correctness of the decisions in *Re Compton* or in the *Hobourn Aero* case[223] said that

217 [1951] Ch. 622.
218 [1950] Ch. 177.
219 (January 11, 1935) unreported, the decision (and not the reasoning) only being available.
220 (1900) 48 W.R. 300.
221 [1951] A.C. 297.
222 [1945] Ch. 123.
223 [1946] Ch. 194.

he could not regard the principle stated by Lord Greene M.R. as a criterion of general applicability and conclusiveness. He said[224]:

> ". . . I see much difficulty in dividing the qualities or attributes which may serve to bind human beings into classes into two mutually exclusive groups, the one involving individual status and purely personal, the other disregarding such status and quite impersonal. As a task this seems to me no less baffling and elusive than the problem to which it is directed, namely, the determination of what is and what is not a section of the public for the purposes of this branch of the law."

He thought that the question whether any given trust was a public or a private trust was a question of degree to be decided in the light of the facts of the particular case and that viewed in that light the trust in the *Oppenheim* case was a valid charitable trust . . .

The *Oppenheim* case was a case of an educational trust and although the majority evidently agreed with the view expressed by the Court of Appeal in the *Hobourn Aero* case,[225] that the *Compton* rule was of universal application outside the field of poverty, it would no doubt be open to this House without overruling *Oppenheim* to hold that the scope of the rule was more limited. If ever I should be called on to pronounce on this question—which does not arise in this appeal—I would as at present advised be inclined to draw a distinction between the practical merits of the *Compton* rule and the reasoning by which Lord Greene M.R. sought to justify it. That reasoning—based on the distinction between personal and impersonal relationships—has never seemed to me very satisfactory and I have always—if I may say so—felt the force of the criticism to which my noble and learned friend Lord MacDermott subjected it in his dissenting speech in the *Oppenheim* case.[226] For my part I would prefer to approach the problem on far broader lines. The phrase "a section of the public" is in truth a phrase which may mean different things to different people. In the law of charity judges have sought to elucidate its meaning by contrasting it with another phrase "a fluctuating body of private individuals". But I get little help from the supposed contrast for as I see it one and the same aggregate of persons may well be describable both as a section of the public and as a fluctuating body of private individuals. The ratepayers in the Royal Borough of Kensington and Chelsea, for example, certainly constitute a section of the public; but would it be a misuse of language to describe them as a "fluctuating body of private individuals"? After all, every part of the public is composed of individuals and being susceptible of increase or decrease is fluctuating. So at the end of the day one is left where one started with the bare contrast between "public" and "private". No doubt some classes are more naturally describable as sections of the public than as private classes while other classes are more naturally describable as private classes than as sections of the public. The blind, for example, can naturally be described as a section of the public; but what they have in common—their blindness—does not join them together in such a way that they could be called a private class. On the other hand, the descendants of Mr Gladstone might more reasonably be described as a "private class" than as a section of the public, and in the field of common employment the same might well be said of the employees in some fairly small firm. But if one turns to large companies employing many thousands of men and women most of whom are quite unknown to one another and to the directors the answer is by no means so clear. One might say that in such a case the distinction between a section of the public and a private class is not applicable at all or even that the employees in such concerns as ICI or GEC are just as much "sections of the public" as the residents in some geographical area. In truth the question whether or not the potential beneficiaries of a trust can fairly be said to constitute a section of the public is a question of degree and cannot be by itself decisive of the question whether the trust is a charity. Much must depend on the purpose of the trust. It may well be that, on the one hand, a trust to promote some purpose, prima facie charitable, will constitute a charity even though the class of potential beneficiaries might fairly be called a private class and that, on the other hand, a trust to promote another purpose, also prima facie charitable, will not constitute a charity even though the class of potential beneficiaries might seem to some people fairly describable as a section of the public. 9–161

In answering the question whether any given trust is a charitable trust the courts—as I see it—cannot avoid having regard to the fiscal privileges accorded to charities. As counsel for the Attorney-General remarked in the course of the argument the law of charity is bedevilled by the fact that charitable trusts 9–162

224 [1951] A.C. 297 at 317.
225 [1946] Ch. 194.
226 [1951] A.C. 297. See also G. Cross, as Lord Cross then was, (1956) 72 L.Q.R. 187.

enjoy two quite different sorts of privilege. On the one hand, they enjoy immunity from the rules against perpetuity and uncertainty and although individual potential beneficiaries cannot sue to enforce them the public interest arising under them is protected by the Attorney-General. If this was all there would be no reason for the courts not to look favourably on the claim of any "purpose" trust to be considered as a charity if it seemed calculated to confer some real benefit on those intended to benefit by it whoever they might be and if it would fail if not held to be a charity. But that is not all. Charities automatically enjoy fiscal privileges which with the increased burden of taxation have become more and more important and in deciding that such and such a trust is a charitable trust the court is endowing it with a substantial annual subsidy at the expense of the taxpayer. Indeed, claims of trusts to rank as charities are just as often challenged by the Revenue as by those who would take the fund if the trust was invalid. It is, of course, unfortunate that the recognition of any trust as a valid charitable trust should automatically attract fiscal privileges, for the question whether a trust to further some purpose is so little likely to benefit the public that it ought to be declared invalid and the question whether it is likely to confer such great benefits on the public that it should enjoy fiscal immunity are really two quite different questions. The logical solution would be to separate them and to say—as the Radcliffe Commission proposed—that only some charities should enjoy fiscal privileges. But as things, are, validity and fiscal immunity march hand in hand and the decisions in the *Compton*[227] and *Oppenheim*[228] cases were pretty obviously influenced by the consideration that if such trusts as were there in question were held valid they would enjoy an undeserved fiscal immunity. To establish a trust for the education of the children of employees in a company in which you are interested is no doubt a meritorious act; but however numerous the employees may be the purpose which you are seeking to achieve is not a public purpose.[229] It is a company purpose and there is no reason why your fellow taxpayers should contribute to a scheme which by providing "fringe benefits" for your employees will benefit the company by making their conditions of employment more attractive. The temptation to enlist the assistance of the law of charity in private endeavours of this sort is considerable—witness the recent case of the Metal Box scholarships—*Inland Revenue Comrs v Educational Grants Association Ltd*[230]—and the courts must do what they can to discourage such attempts. In the field of poverty the danger is not so great as in the field of education—for while people are keenly alive to the need to give their children a good education and to the expense of doing so, they are generally optimistic enough not to entertain serious fears of falling on evil days much before they fall on them. Consequently the existence of company "benevolent funds", the income of which is free of tax does not constitute a very attractive "fringe benefit". This is a practical justification—although not, of course, the historical explanation—for the special treatment accorded to poverty trusts in charity law. For the same sort of reason a trust to promote some religion among the employees of a company might perhaps safely be held to be charitable provided that it was clear that the benefits were to be purely spiritual. On the other hand, many "purpose" trusts falling under Lord Macnaghten's fourth head if confined to a class of employees would clearly be open to the same sort of objection as educational trusts. As I see it, it is on these broad lines rather than for the reasons actually given by Lord Greene M.R. that the *Compton* rule can best be justified.

9–163 My Lords, I would dismiss this appeal.

9–164 *Appeal dismissed.*

Attorney General v Charity Commission

Upper Tribunal (Tax and Chancery Chamber) [2012] W.T.L.R. 977

9–165 WARREN J. (CHAMBER PRESIDENT) AND UPPER TRIBUNAL JUDGE MCKENNA: These proceedings concern a Notice of Reference . . . made by Her Majesty's Attorney General on 27 January 2011, by which he sought the Tribunal's determination of a number of issues relating to charities for the relief of poverty, in which the potential beneficiaries are connected by a family relationship to the founder, common employment or former employment, or their membership of an unincorporated organisation . . .

---

227 [1945] Ch. 123.
228 [1951] A.C. 297.
229 For a critical view of this approach see T.G. Watkin [1978] Conv. 277.
230 [1967] Ch. 993.

The Pre 2006 Act Position

The concept of public benefit prior to the 2006 Act was considered at [42]ff of the decision in *I.S.C.* [i.e. *R. (on the application of Independent Schools Council) v Charity Commission for England and Wales*[231]] . . . which explains . . . how it is possible to discern from the cases two related aspects of public benefit. The first aspect is that the nature of the purpose itself must be such as to be a benefit to the community: this was referred to as public benefit in the first sense . . . The second aspect is that those who may benefit from the carrying out of the purpose must be sufficiently numerous, and identified in such manner, as to constitute what is described in the authorities as "a section of the public": this is public benefit in the second sense. 9–166

. . . In our view, the purposes of the institutions with which we are concerned insofar as they relate to the relief of poverty . . . which were all charitable institutions prior to the 2006 Act, are all purposes which are for the public benefit in the first sense. The relief of poverty is, we consider, ordinarily to be seen a purpose of a nature which is for the public benefit just as ordinary education is of a nature which is for the public benefit. It is a purpose which is expressly mentioned in the Preamble and thus of a nature which is charitable. But just as there may be educational purposes which are not charitable because they are not for the public benefit in the first sense—the school for pickpockets again: see [48b] of the decision in *ISC* – it is possible that there could be a trust for the relief of poverty which is not for the public benefit in the first sense either. Indeed, in his speech in *National Anti- Vivisection Society v IRC*,[232] Lord Simonds gave practical examples of such a possibility and observed:[233] 9–167

> "If today a testator made a bequest for the relief of the poor and required that it should be carried out in one way only and the court was satisfied by evidence that that way was injurious to the community, I should say that it was not a charitable gift, though three hundred years ago the court might upon different evidence or in the absence of any evidence have come to a different conclusion."

. . . In the light of the discussion at [45] to [71] of *ISC* we do not think that the abolition of the presumption of public benefit in section 3(2) of the 2006 Act has had any impact on whether a trust for the relief of poverty is charitable or not. There is no presumption that a trust for the relief of poverty is for the public benefit, any more than there is a presumption that education is for the public benefit. In either case, the Court or Tribunal will form its own view on the evidence before it whether the trust is for the public benefit and it will do so, not by way of assumption, but by way of decision. It will no doubt take account of other decided cases; and it will take judicial notice of facts where appropriate. But as the Tribunal said at [68] of the decision in *ISC*, this is far from a "presumption" in the usual sense. 9–168

[The judges reviewed *Gibson v South American Stores (Gath & Chaves) Ltd*,[234] *Oppenheim v Tobacco Securities Trust Co Ltd*,[235] *Re Scarisbrick*,[236] and *Dingle v Turner*,[237] and drew these conclusions]: (a) First, to state the obvious, there is nothing in the [foregoing cases] which raises the slightest doubt that what we have referred to as public benefit in the first sense is a necessary requirement for a purpose to qualify as a charitable purpose. (b) Secondly, there is nothing in [the foregoing cases] which leads to the conclusion that what we have referred to as public benefit in the first sense has nothing to do with the public benefit requirement, but is (only) a separate and distinct requirement which has to be satisfied if a purpose is to be charitable. 9–169

Accordingly, it is an element of the "public benefit" as that term is understood for the purposes of charity law that the nature of the purpose has to be one which is capable of being of benefit to the community. Before the 2006 Act, the purposes of a trust, in order to be charitable, had to fall within, or within the spirit of, the Preamble. After the 2006 Act, the purposes of the trust must fall within section 2(2). But in each case, there is (or was) a requirement that the purpose is (or was) also one which is of its nature capable of being for the benefit of the community. Thus, a school for pickpockets fails the test even though 9–170

---

231 [2012] Ch. 214; see para.9–029.
232 [1948] A.C. 31 at 60.
233 Ibid. at 69–70.
234 [1949] Ch. 572; [1950] Ch. 177.
235 [1951] A.C. 297.
236 [1951] Ch. 622.
237 [1972] A.C. 601.

it is educational; and there may be a trust for the relief of poverty which is to be carried out in such a way that it fails the test too.

The Post-2006 Act Position

9–171 We now turn back to . . . [the position following the 2006 Act]. For an institution to be a charity, its purposes have to be "for the public benefit" and reference to the "public benefit" is a reference to the public benefit as that term is understood for the purposes of the law relating to charities in England and Wales. Mr Dibble submits that each limb of the public benefit test must be satisfied in relation to an institution if it is to be charitable. Accordingly, even if the purpose of a trust for the relief of poverty is for the public benefit in the first sense, it is not, if restricted to a narrow class, for the public benefit in the second sense and is therefore not charitable.

9–172 We reject that submission. It is clear, we consider, that whether or not an institution satisfies the public benefit requirement must be assessed by reference to the criteria which are relevant to its purposes. For instance, as is clear from the cases, what is or is not a sufficient section of the public to satisfy the second aspect of public benefit varies depending on the nature of the charity: a sufficient section of the public in relation to an educational institution may not be sufficient in relation to a religious institution and vice versa. Accordingly, it does not make sense to address in abstract the public benefit requirement under the 2006 Act. Rather, it has to be asked what that requirement is in relation to the particular institution under consideration. In the case of a trust for the relief of poverty which had a narrow class of direct beneficiary, the trust was nonetheless charitable under the law prior to the 2006 Act even though the class was not wide enough to establish public benefit in the second sense as applied to poverty trusts. In order that a trust for the relief of poverty with a narrow class of beneficiary should be charitable, the public benefit requirement as applied to such a trust required only that public benefit in the first sense be established. The 2006 Act has not, in our judgment, changed that. The "public benefit" as that term was understood for the purposes of the law of charity required, in the context of a trust for the relief of poverty, only that public benefit in the first sense should be shown. Of course, a trust for the relief of poverty might be one which is also for the public benefit in the second sense because the class of potential beneficiary is, on any view, a sufficient section of the community. But it does not follow from that consideration that every trust for the relief of poverty must be for the public benefit in the second sense. . .

B. Section 3(1)(b): "The Advancement of Education"

i. Inherently Beneficial Purposes

9–173 This group of charitable trusts has its origins in those parts of the preamble to the Statute of Charitable Uses 1601 which speak of "the maintenance of schools of learning, free schools and scholars in universities" and "the education and preferment of orphans". Providing students with a school or university education remains the purpose that most obviously falls within s.3(1)(b), but the advancement of education takes in a wider range of purposes than this. In *IRC v McMullen*,[238] the House of Lords held that it is charitable to provide sports facilities for children and young people at school and university because physical education and development are an integral part of the education of the young. At the time when the case was decided, the promotion of sport was not in itself a charitable object, but the law in this area has moved on, and s.3(1)(g) now recognises the advancement of amateur sport as a beneficial purpose.[239]

9–174 Various cases show that education also includes the encouragement of the arts and graces of life, including *Re Shaw's Will Trusts*[240] ("the teaching, promotion and encouragement in Ireland of self-control, elocution, oratory, deportment, the arts of personal contact, of social intercourse, and

---

238 [1981] A.C. 1.

239 For discussion see paras 9–259 to 9–260.

240 [1952] Ch. 163.

the other arts of public, private, professional and business life"); *Royal Choral Society v IRC*[241] (choral singing in London); *Re Levien*[242] (organ music); *Re Delius*[243] (the music of the composer Delius); *Re Dupree's Deed Trusts*[244] (encouragement of chess-playing among young people in Portsmouth); and *Re South Place Ethical Society*[245] (the study and dissemination of ethical principles and the cultivation of a rational religious sentiment). Some of these purposes would now appear to fall within other sub-sections, most notably s.3(1)(f), which recognises as a charitable purpose "the advancement of the arts, culture, heritage or science".

The Charity Commission has upheld as charitable Public Concern at Work (concerned with promoting business ethics and advising and protecting employees faced with ethical dilemmas at work)[246] and Full Fact (concerned with ensuring that factual inaccuracies in public statements are corrected by making correction requests and promoting general improvements to information made available to the public).[247] In the latter decision, the Commission accepted that:[248] **9–175**

> the structured provision of information which is factually accurate may be capable of being educational, where is it provided in furtherance of a genuinely educational purpose, to advance the knowledge or abilities of the recipients in a meaningful way and . . . is not promoting particular opinions or propaganda.

However, the Commission will pay particular attention to the quality of instruction offered by organisations which claim to be training their users outside formal educational establishments, and will decline to register them if it considers their activities to amount to nothing more the unstructured imparting of information.[249] **9–176**

The decision of Harman J in *Re Shaw*[250] (denying charitable status where George Bernard Shaw had bequeathed funds for pursuing inquiries into a new 40-letter alphabet) appeared to render doubtful the validity of trusts for the advancement of research, at any rate where no element of teaching was involved; but *Re Hopkins' Will Trusts* removes most of the doubts. There Wilberforce J held that:[251] **9–177**

> the word "education", as used by Harman J., must be used in a wide sense, certainly extending beyond teaching, and that the requirement is that, in order to be charitable, research must either be of educational value to the researcher or must be so directed as to lead to something which will pass into the store of educational material or so as to improve the sum of communicable knowledge in an area which education may cover . . . research of a private character, for the benefit only of the members of a society, would not normally be educational or otherwise charitable but I do not think that the research in the present case [into the works of Francis Bacon and whether he might have been the author of plays ascribed to Shakespeare]

---

241 [1943] 2 All E.R. 101; contrast *Associated Artists Ltd v IRC* [1956] 1 W.L.R. 752 (production of artistic dramatic works).
242 [1955] 1 W.L.R. 964.
243 [1957] Ch. 299.
244 [1945] Ch. 16.
245 [1980] 1 W.L.R. 1565.
246 [1994] 2 Ch. Comm Decisions 5.
247 Charity Commission, "Decision to Register Full Fact" (17 September 2014), *https://www.gov.uk/government/uploads/system/uploads/attachment_data/file/372962/Full_Fact_Decision.pdf*. The Commission had previously rejected Full Fact's application to register in 2009 under the head of "advancement of citizenship and civic responsibility" (see now s.3(1)(e) and (2)(c)(ii)), but accepted that its purposes were educational following a statement to that effect by the First-tier Tribunal, "*Full Fact v Charity Commission*" (26 July 2011), *http://www.charity.tribunals.gov.uk/Documents/FullFactdecision_26Jul11.pdf*.
248 ibid., at [23].
249 Charity Commission, *Decision on the Millennium College UK Ltd's Application for Registration as a Charity* (27 April 2004); *Decision on Living in Radiance's Application for Registration as a Charity* (24 August 2005).
250 [1957] 1 W.L.R. 729.
251 [1965] Ch. 669 at 680–681.

> can be said to be of private character, for it is inherently inevitable and manifestly intended that the result of any discovery should be published to the world.

9–178 In *McGovern v Attorney General*, Slade J summarised the governing principles as follows:[252]

> (1) A trust for research will ordinarily qualify as a charitable trust if, but only if (a) the subject matter of the proposed research is a useful subject of study; and (b) it is contemplated that knowledge acquired as a result of the research will be disseminated to others; and (c) the trust is for the benefit of the public, or a sufficiently important section of the public. (2) In the absence of a contrary context, however, the court will be readily inclined to construe a trust for research as importing subsequent dissemination of the results thereof. (3) Furthermore, if a trust for research is to constitute a valid trust for the advancement of education, it is not necessary either (a) that a teacher/pupil relationship should be in contemplation, or (b) that the persons to benefit from the knowledge to be acquired should be persons who are already in the course of receiving "education" in the conventional sense.

9–179 The rule that trusts for research purposes are charitable only if it is contemplated that the research will be published was revisited by the Charity Commission in its guidance document on *Public Benefit and the Advancement of Education*, where it stated that:[253]

> This does not mean that research has to be presented in a way that is understandable by everyone. It might only be capable of being understood by people who are experts in the field. What is important is that it is published and made publicly available so that everyone who is capable of understanding it has access to it, and its benefits or usefulness are widely available to everyone.

9–180 The idea expressed in *McGovern* that educational purposes are charitable only if capable of achieving "useful" outcomes recurs in decisions about teaching, research and the display of objects in museums, etc. These dicta suggest that courts and the Charity Commission are applying a "merits test" that is potentially problematic if it leads them to make subjective and ill-informed value judgments,[254] and even if their decisions are founded on expert evidence,[255] they must allow for legitimate differences of opinion between experts.

9–181 Trusts to disseminate political opinions are not charitable where this amounts to propaganda rather than education.[256] The rule that political purposes are not charitable has been discussed above.[257]

ii. Provision of Benefit to the Community

9–182 Trusts supporting the educational activities of schools are charitable, even if the schools are fee-charging institutions, provided that they do not make profits, or if they do, that these are used solely

---

252 [1982] Ch. 321 at 352.

253 (December 2008 version) para.E2.

254 G.E. Dal Pont, "Charitable Un-Educational Objects" (2020) 6 C.J.C.C.L. 191.

255 As in *Re Pinion (Deceased)* [1965] Ch. 85 where Wilberforce J and the CA relied on expert evidence to hold that a bequest of works of art to found a museum was not charitable because the works in question were a "mass of junk" (per Harman LJ at 107).

256 *Bonar Law Memorial Trust v IRC* (1933) 49 T.L.R. 220; *Re Hopkinson* [1949] 1 All E.R. 346; *Southwood v Attorney General* [2000] W.T.L.R. 1199; cf. *Re McDougall* [1957] 1 W.L.R. 81 (study of methods of government is a charitable object). For the same reason, a trust to persuade people to accept particular religious beliefs is not a charitable trust for an educational purpose: Charity Commission, *Decision on the Gnostic Centre's Application for Registration as a Charity* (16 December 2009), paras 12–18.

257 See paras 9–106 to 9–130.

for the charitable purposes of the institution.[258] In *R. (on the application of Independent Schools Council) v Charity Commission for England and Wales*,[259] the Upper Tribunal held that the trustees of fee-charging schools must make provision for the community as a whole that goes beyond a "de minimis or token level", but that it is for the trustees to decide what that should be "in all the circumstance of the particular school under consideration".[260] This case has already been discussed.[261]

In *Oppenheim v Tobacco Securities Trust Co Ltd*,[262] reproduced below, the House of Lords held that a trust for the education of beneficiaries who are ascertained by reference to some personal tie (e.g. of blood or contract), such as the relations of a particular individual, the members of a particular family, the employees of a particular firm or the members of a particular trade union, lacks the necessary element of public benefit and is not charitable. In contrast, a trust to educate the residents of a town[263] or the children of members of a particular profession[264] will be valid. **9–183**

Oppenheim v Tobacco Securities Trust Co Ltd

House of Lords [1951] A.C. 297

Investments were held by the respondents, Tobacco Securities Trust Co Ltd, on trust to apply the income in providing for "the education of children of employees or former employees of British-American Tobacco Co Ltd . . . or any of its subsidiary or allied companies without any limit of time being specified". The High Court and Court of Appeal held the trust void for perpetuity because it was not charitable on the ground that it lacked public benefit. **9–184**

LORD SIMONDS (with whom LORD NORMAND, LORD OAKSEY and LORD MORTON agreed): In the case of trusts for educational purposes the condition of the public benefit must be satisfied. The difficulty lies in determining what is sufficient to satisfy the test, and there is little to help your Lordships to solve it. **9–185**

If I may begin at the bottom of the scale, a trust established by a father for the education of his son is not a charity. The public element, as I will call it, is not supplied by the fact that from that son's education all may benefit. At the other end of the scale the establishment of a college or university is beyond doubt a charity. "Schools of learning and free schools, and scholars of universities" are the very words of the preamble to the [Charitable Uses Act 1601]. So also the endowment of a college, university or school by the creation of scholarships or bursaries is a charity, and nonetheless because competition may be limited to a particular class of persons. It is on this ground, as Lord Greene M.R. pointed out in *Re Compton*,[265] that the so-called "founder's kin" cases can be rested. The difficulty arises where the trust is not for the benefit of any institution either then existing or by the terms of the trust to be brought into existence, but for the benefit of a class of persons at large. Then the question is whether that class of persons can be regarded as such a "section of the community" as to satisfy the test of public benefit. These words "section of the community" have no special sanctity, but they conveniently indicate (1) that the possible (I emphasise the word "possible") beneficiaries must not be numerically negligible, and (2) that the quality which distinguishes them from other members of the community, so that they form by themselves a section of it, must be a quality which does not depend on their relationship to a particular individual. It is for this reason that a trust for the education of members of a family or, as in *Re Compton*, of a number of families cannot be regarded as charitable. A group of persons may be numerous, but, if the nexus between them is their personal relationship to a single *propositus* or to several *propositi*, they are neither the community nor a section of the community for charitable purposes. **9–186**

---

258 *Abbey Malvern Wells Ltd v Ministry of Local Government* [1951] Ch. 728; *Oppenheim v Tobacco Securities Trust Co Ltd* [1951] A.C. 297 at 306; *Customs & Excise Commissioners v Bell Concord Education Trust* [1990] 1 Q.B. 1040.

259 [2011] UKUT 421 (TCC); [2012] Ch. 214 at [69].

260 [2011] UKUT 421 (TCC); [2012] Ch. 214 at [215].

261 See paras 9–059 to 9–088.

262 [1951] A.C. 297.

263 *Re Tree* [1945] Ch. 325: a restriction to Methodists or members of the Church of England would seem valid.

264 *Hall v Derby Sanitary Authority* (1885) 16 Q.B.D. 163 approved in *Oppenheim v Tobacco Securities Trust Co* [1951] A.C. 297.

265 [1945] Ch. 123.

9–187 I come, then, to the present case where the class of beneficiaries is numerous, but the difficulty arises in regard to their common and distinguishing quality. That quality is being children of employees of one or other of a group of companies. I can make no distinction between children of employees and the employees themselves. In both cases the common quality is found in employment by particular employers. The latter of the two cases, by which the Court of Appeal held itself to be bound, the *Hobourn* case, is a direct authority for saying that such a common quality does not constitute its possessors a section of the public for charitable purposes. In the former case, *Re Compton*, Lord Greene M.R. had by way of illustration placed members of a family and employees of a particular employer on the same footing, finding neither in common kinship nor in common employment the sort of nexus which is sufficient. My Lords, I am so fully in agreement with what was said by Lord Greene in both cases, and by my noble and learned friend, then Morton L.J., in the *Hobourn* case, that I am in danger of repeating without improving upon their words. It appears to me that it would be an extension [of the legal definition of charity], for which there is no justification in principle or authority, to regard common employment as a quality which constitutes those employed a section of the community. It must not, I think, be forgotten that charitable institutions enjoy rare and increasing privileges, and that the claim to come within that privileged class should be clearly established. With the single exception of *Re Rayner*,[266] which I must regard as of doubtful authority, no case has been brought to the notice of the House in which such a claim as this has been made, where there is no element of poverty in the beneficiaries, but just this and no more, that they are the children of those in a common employment.

9–188 Learned counsel for the appellant sought to fortify his case by pointing to the anomalies that would ensue from the rejection of his argument. For, he said, admittedly those who follow a profession or calling—clergymen, lawyers, colliers, tobacco-workers and so on—are a section of the public; how strange then it would be if, as in the case of railwaymen, those who follow a particular calling are all employed by one employer. Would a trust for the education of railwaymen be charitable,[267] but a trust for the education of men employed on the railways by the Transport Board not be charitable? And what of service of the Crown, whether in the civil service or the armed forces? Is there a difference between soldiers and soldiers of the King? My Lords, I am not impressed by this sort of argument and will consider on its merits if the occasion should arise, the case where the description of the occupation and the employment is in effect the same, where in a word, if you know what a man does, you know who employs him to do it. It is to me a far more cogent argument, as it was to my noble and learned friend in the *Hobourn* case, that, if a section of the public is constituted by the personal relation of employment, it is impossible to say that it is not constituted by a thousand as by 100,000 employees, and if by a thousand, then by a hundred, and, if by a hundred, then by ten. I do not mean merely that there is a difficulty in drawing the line, though that, too, is significant. I have it also in mind that, though the actual number of employees at any one moment might be small, it might increase to any extent, just as, being large, it might decrease to any extent. If the number of employees is the test of validity, must the court take into account potential increase or decrease, and, if so, as at what date? . . .

9–189 LORD MACDERMOTT (dissenting): The question is whether it is of a public nature, whether, in the words of Lord Wrenbury in *Verge v Somerville*,[268] "it is for the benefit of the community or of an appreciably important class of the community." The relevant class here is that from which those to be educated are to be selected. The appellant contends that this class is public in character; the respondent bank (as personal representative of the last surviving settlor) denies this and says that the class is no more than a group of private individuals.

9–190 Until comparatively recently the usual way of approaching an issue of this sort, at any rate where educational trusts were concerned, was, I believe, to regard the facts of each case and to treat the matter very much as one of degree. No definition of what constituted a sufficient section of the public for the purpose was applied, for none existed; and the process seems to have been one of reaching a conclusion on a general survey of the circumstances and considerations regarded as relevant rather than of making a single, conclusive test. The investigation left the course of the dividing line between what was and what was not a section of the community unexplored, and was concluded when it had gone far enough to

---

266 (1920) 89 L.J. Ch. 369.

267 As to this see *Hall v Derby Sanitary Authority* (1885) 16 Q.B.D. 163.

268 [1924] A.C. 496 at 499.

establish to the satisfaction of the court whether or not the trust was public; and the decision as to that was, I think, very often reached by determining whether or not the trust was private.

If it is still permissible to conduct the present inquiry on these broad if imprecise lines, I would hold with the appellant. The numerical strength of the class is considerable on any showing. The employees concerned number over 110,000, and it may reasonably be assumed that the children, who constitute the class in question, are no fewer. The large size of the class is not, of course, decisive but in my view it cannot be left out of account when the problem is approached in this way. Then it must be observed that the propositi are not limited to those presently employed. They include former employees (not reckoned in the figure I have given) and are, therefore, a more stable category than would otherwise be the case. And, further, the employees concerned are not limited to those in the service of the "British American Tobacco Co Ltd or any of its subsidiary or allied companies"—itself a description of great width—but include the employees, in the event of the British American Tobacco Co Ltd being reconstructed or merged on amalgamation, of the reconstructed or amalgamated company or any of its subsidiary companies. No doubt the settlors here had a special interest in the welfare of the class they described, but, apart from the fact that this may serve to explain the particular form of their bounty, I do not think it material to the question in hand. What is material, as I regard the matter, is that they have chosen to benefit a class which is, in fact, substantial in point of size and importance and have done so in a manner which, to my mind, manifests an intention to advance the interests of the class described as a class rather than as a collection or succession of particular individuals . . . 9–191

The respondent bank, however, contends that the inquiry should be of quite a different character to that which I have been discussing. It advances as the sole criterion a narrower test derived from the decisions of the Court of Appeal in *Compton*,[269] and in *Hobourn*.[270] The basis and nature of this test appear from the passage in the judgment of the court in *Compton*,[271] where Lord Greene M.R., says: 9–192

> "In the case of many charitable gifts it is possible to identify the individuals who are to benefit, or who at any given moment constitute the class from which the beneficiaries are to be selected. This circumstance does not, however, deprive the gift of its public character. Thus, if there is a gift to relieve the poor inhabitants of a parish the class to benefit is readily ascertainable. But they do not enjoy the benefit, when they receive it, by virtue of their character as individuals but by virtue of their membership of the specified class. In such a case the common quality which unites the potential beneficiaries into a class is essentially an impersonal one. It is definable by reference to what each has in common with the others, and that is something into which their status as individuals does not enter. Persons claiming to belong to the class do so not because they are A.B., C.D. and E.F., but because they are poor inhabitants of the parish. If, in asserting their claim, it were necessary for them to establish the fact that they were the individuals A.B., C.D. and E.F., I cannot help thinking that on principle the gift ought not to be held to be a charitable gift, since the introduction into their qualification of a purely personal element would deprive the gift of its necessary public character. It seems to me that the same principle ought to apply when the claimants, in order to establish their status, have to assert and prove, not that they themselves are A.B., C.D., and E.F., but that they stand in some specified relationship to the individuals A.B., C.D., and E.F., such as that of children or employees. In that case, too, a purely personal element enters into and is an essential part of the qualification, which is defined by reference to something, i.e., personal relationship to individuals or an individual which is in its essence non-public."

The test thus propounded focuses upon the common quality which unites those within the class concerned and asks whether that quality is essentially impersonal or essentially personal. If the former, the class will rank as a section of the public and the trust will have the element common to and necessary for all legal charities; but, if the latter, the trust will be private and not charitable. It is suggested in the passage just quoted, and made clear beyond doubt in *Hobourn*,[272] that in the opinion of the Court of Appeal employment by a designated employer must be regarded for this purpose as a personal and not as an impersonal bond of union. In this connection and as illustrating the discriminating character of what I may call "the 9–193

[269] [1945] Ch. 123.
[270] [1946] Ch. 194.
[271] [1945] Ch. 123 at 129–130.
[272] [1946] Ch. 194.

Compton[273] test" reference should be made to that part of the judgment of the learned Master of the Rolls in *Hobourn*,[274] in which he speaks of the decision in *Hall v Derby Borough Urban Sanitary Authority*.[275] The passage runs thus:

> "That related to a trust for railway servants. It is said that if a trust for railway servants can be a good charity, so too a trust for railway servants in the employment of a particular railway company is a good charity. That is not so. The reason, I think, is that in the one case the trust is for railway servants in general and in the other case it is for employees of a particular company, a fact which limits the potential beneficiaries to a class ascertained on a purely personal basis."

9–194 My Lords, I do not quarrel with the result arrived at in the *Compton* and *Hobourn* cases, and I do not doubt that the *Compton* test may often prove of value and lead to a correct determination. But, with the great respect due to those who have formulated this test, I find myself unable to regard it as a criterion of general applicability and conclusiveness. In the first place I see much difficulty in dividing the qualities or attributes, which may serve to bind human beings into classes, into two mutually exclusive groups, the one involving individual status and purely personal, the other disregarding such status and quite impersonal. As a task this seems to me no less baffling and elusive than the problem to which it is directed, namely, the determination of what is and what is not a section of the public for the purposes of this branch of the law. After all, what is more personal than poverty or blindness or ignorance? Yet none would deny that a gift for the education of the children of the poor or blind was charitable; and I doubt if there is any less certainty about the charitable nature of a gift for, say, the education of children who satisfy a specified examining body that they need and would benefit by a course of special instruction designed to remedy their educational defects.

9–195 But can any really fundamental distinction, as respects the personal or impersonal nature of the common link, be drawn between those employed, for example, by a particular university and those whom the same university has put in a certain category as the result of individual examination and assessment? Again, if the bond between these employed by a particular railway is purely personal, why should the bond between those who are employed as railway men be so essentially different? Is a distinction to be drawn in this respect between those who are employed in a particular industry before it is nationalised and those who are employed therein after that process has been completed and one employer has taken the place of many? Are miners in the service of the National Coal Board now in one category and miners at a particular pit or of a particular district in another? Is the relationship between those in the service of the Crown to be distinguished from that obtaining between those in the service of some other employer? Or, if not, are the children of, say, soldiers or civil servants to be regarded as not constituting a sufficient section of the public to make a trust for their education charitable?

9–196 It was conceded in the course of the argument that, had the present trust been framed so as to provide for the education of the children of those engaged in the tobacco industry in a named county or town, it would have been a good charitable disposition, and that even though the class to be benefited would have been appreciably smaller and no more important than is the class here. That concession follows from what the Court of Appeal has said. But if it is sound and a personal or impersonal relationship remains the universal criterion I think it shows, no less than the queries I have just raised in indicating some of the difficulties of the problem, that the *Compton* test is a very arbitrary and artificial rule. This leads me to the second difficulty that I have regarding it. If I understand it aright it necessarily makes the quantum of public benefit a consideration of little moment; the size of the class becomes immaterial and the need of its members and the public advantage of having that need met appear alike to be irrelevant. To my mind these are considerations of some account in the sphere of educational trusts for, as already indicated, I think the educational value and scope of the work actually to be done must have a bearing on the question of public benefit.

9–197 Finally, it seems to me that, far from settling the state of the law on this particular subject, the *Compton* test is more likely to create confusion and doubt in the case of many trusts and institutions of a character whose legal standing as charities has never been in question. Take, for instance, a trust for the provision of university education for boys coming from a particular school. The common quality binding the members

[273] [1945] Ch. 123.
[274] [1946] Ch. 194 at 206.
[275] (1885) 16 Q.B.D. 163.

of that class seems to reside in the fact that their parents or guardians all contracted for their schooling with the same establishment or body. That the school in such a case may itself be a charitable foundation seems altogether beside the point and quite insufficient to hold the *Compton* test at bay if it is well founded in law.

I therefore return to what I think was the process followed before the decision in *Compton's case*, and, for the reasons already given, I would hold the present trust charitable and allow the appeal. I have only to add that I recognise the imperfections and uncertainties of that process. They are as evident as the difficulties of finding something better. But I venture to doubt if it is in the power of the courts to resolve those difficulties satisfactorily as matters stand. It is a long cry to the age of Elizabeth and I think what is needed is a fresh start from a new statute. **9–198**

Appeal dismissed. **9–199**

C. Section 3(1)(c): "The Advancement of Religion"

i. Inherently Beneficial Purposes

This category has its origin in the preamble to the 1601 Statute which spoke of "the repair of churches". **9–200** The courts soon held that the equity of the Statute extended to trusts advancing the religious purposes of the Church of England, and for a time these were the only religious purposes that were legally charitable. Trusts for the advancement of other religions were illegal and void,[276] and in cases where the settlor's words were held to manifest a general charitable intention, the property was liable to be redirected into Anglican purposes by application of the *cy-près* doctrine.[277] These rules came to be moderated with the advent of greater religious toleration. Trusts for Protestant Nonconformist purposes were made legally charitable by the Toleration Act 1688, subject to the proviso that nothing in them should assist persons denying the Trinity; this proviso was removed by the Unitarian Relief Act 1813. Trusts to advance Judaism were made legally charitable by the Jewish Relief Act 1846. The Catholic Relief Act 1791 abolished penalties for public adherence to Catholicism, but trusts for the furtherance of Catholicism remained void because they were illegal per se.[278] The Roman Catholic Charities Act 1832 then validated gifts for many Catholic purposes, including schools and churches, but gifts for the saying of requiem masses remained invalid as they were still deemed to be for a "superstitious use".[279] The hardship of this was abated by the Roman Catholic Charities Act 1860 s.1, by which the courts were empowered to apply funds settled for a "superstitious" use to other Catholic purposes at their discretion.

---

276 e.g. *Mitford v Reynolds* (1842) 1 Phillips 185 at 193, where Lord Lyndhurst LC held that a trust to build a Hindu temple in Dakka would not be charitable because "an application of the fund for the purpose of encouraging idolatry could [not] be for the benefit of the native inhabitants".

277 As in *Da Costa v Da Pas* (1754) Amb. 228, where the prerogative *cy-près* power was exercised to apply a void legacy to found a Jewish yeshiva (religious school) to pay for a Christian preacher at the Foundling Hospital.

278 *Cary v Abbot* (1802) 7 Ves. Jun. 490.

279 *West v Shuttleworth* (1835) 2 My. & K. 684; *Heath v Chapman* (1854) 2 Drew. 423; but cf. *Re Michel's Trust* (1860) 28 Beav. 39 at 42–43.

9–201 During the twentieth century the purposes of a wide range of theistic religions were recognised as legally charitable, including the Plymouth Brethren,[280] Sikh,[281] Islamic,[282] Hindu[283] and Spiritualist[284] religions. The Unification Church (the "Moonies") has been accorded charitable status,[285] and so has the Druid Network, a group with animistic beliefs in Nature.[286]

9–202 Rejecting the claim of an ethical society to be a charity for the advancement of religion, Dillon J said:[287]

> Religion is concerned with man's relations with God, and ethics are concerned with man's relations with man. The two are not the same, all are not made the same by sincere inquiry into the question: what is God? If reason leads people not to accept Christianity or any known religion, but they do believe in the excellence of qualities, such as truth, beauty and love, or believe in the platonic concept of the ideal, their beliefs may seem to them to be the equivalent of a religion, but viewed objectively they are not religion. . . . It seems to me that two of the essential attributes of religion are faith and worship: faith in a god and worship of that god. The Oxford English Dictionary gives as one of the definitions of religion: "A particular system of faith and worship." Then: "Recognition on the part of man of some higher unseen power as having control of his destiny, and as being entitled to obedience, reverence and worship."

9–203 On this definition, however, Buddhism is not a religion since it is a "realised" rather than a "revealed" religion: its adherents do not revere the Buddha as a "god", and believe that they should follow a spiritual path that he laid out which can ultimately lead to spiritual awakening. Dillon J failed to resolve this in his judgment, and though the Charity Commissioners later registered various Buddhist trusts as charitable, they were criticised for acting inconsistently with Dillon J's approach. The issue is now settled by the Charities Act 2011 s.3(2)(a)(ii), which says that for the purposes of s.3(1) religion includes "a religion which does not involve belief in a god".

9–204 The Charity Commission has refused to register the Church of Scientology,[288] finding that although Scientologists believe in a supreme being, this belief does not find expression in conduct indicative of reverence or veneration. This is hard to reconcile with the Supreme Court's decision in *R. (on the application of Hodkin) v Registrar General of Births, Deaths and Marriages*[289] that a chapel of the Church of Scientology was a "place of meeting for religious worship" for the purposes of the Places of Worship Registration Act 1855 s.2. Lord Toulson drew support for this conclusion from the wording of the Charities Act 2011 s.3(2)(a), which was not in point, but which he thought was an "indication that the understanding of religion in today's society is broad".

9–205 The Commission's approach to determining whether purposes are for "the advancement of religion" is set out in its decision on the application for registration by the Temple of the Jedi Order, reproduced

---

280 *Holmes v Attorney General The Times*, 12 February 1981; Charity Commission, "Decision on Preston Down Trust's Application for Registration" (3 January 2014), *https://www.gov.uk/government/uploads/system/uploads/attachment_data/file/336112/preston_down_trust_full_decision.pdf.*

281 cf. *Khaira v Shergill* [2014] UKSC 33; [2014] 3 W.L.R. 1.

282 cf. *Liverpool Muslim Society v Revenue and Customs Commissioners* [2014] UKFTT 1080 (TC); [2015] S.T.I. 142.

283 cf. *Varsani v Jesani* [1999] Ch. 219.

284 Charity Commission, *Decision on the Application for Registration of the Sacred Hands Spiritual Centre* (5 September 2003).

285 [1982] Charity Commissioners *Annual Report*, paras 36–38. The Attorney General dropped his action to deprive them of charitable status: *Hansard*, HC Vol.126, col.977 (3 February 1988).

286 Charity Commission, "Decision to Register the Druid Network as a Charity" (21 September 2010), *https://www.gov.uk/government/uploads/system/uploads/attachment_data/file/324236/druiddec.pdf.*

287 *Re South Place Ethical Society* [1980] 1 W.L.R. 1565 at 1571. The society was charitable under the second and fourth heads of charity. Lord Denning defined religion in a similar way in *R. v Registrar General, Ex p. Segerdal* [1970] 2 Q.B. 697 at 707.

288 Decision of 17 November 1999; criticised in P.W. Edge and J.M. Loughey, "Religious Charities and the Juridification of the Charity Commission" (2001) 21 L.S. 36.

289 [2013] UKSC 77; [2014] A.C. 610. Note also that the Church of Scientology has achieved recognition as a religious charity in other jurisdictions, e.g. Australia: *Church of the New Faith v Commissioner of Pay-roll Tax* (1983) 154 C.L.R. 120.

below. Among other things, the Commission states that "religion in charity law is characterised ... by a certain level of cogency, seriousness, cohesion and importance", consistently with Lord Nicholls's dictum in *R. (on the application of Williamson) v Secretary of State for Education and Employment* (which concerned the freedom to manifest religious beliefs under art.9(1) of the ECHR) that "religious belief" must be "coherent in the sense of being intelligible and capable of being understood."[290] However, his Lordship also emphasised that:

> too much should not be demanded in this regard. Typically, religion involves belief in the supernatural. It is not always susceptible to lucid exposition or, still less, rational justification. The language used is often the language of allegory, symbol and metaphor. Depending on the subject matter, individuals cannot always be expected to express themselves with cogency or precision. Nor are an individual's beliefs fixed and static. The beliefs of every individual are prone to change over his lifetime.

It is, moreover, a recurring theme of the caselaw that "the courts do not take it upon themselves to pass value judgments on different religions or on different sects within religions"[291] and are reluctant to adjudicate disputes about the correct interpretation of religious doctrine when these are agitated by members of religious groups.[292]

Trusts for adding to or repairing the fabric of a church[293] or for the upkeep of a churchyard[294] are charitable but not for the erection or upkeep of a particular tomb in a churchyard.[295] If a gift is made to an ecclesiastic in her official name and by virtue of her office then if no purposes are expressed in the gift the gift is for charitable religious purposes inherent in the office.[296] However, if the purposes are expressed in terms not confining them to exclusively charitable purposes then the charitable character of the trustee will not make the gift charitable.[297] **9–206**

ii. Provision of Benefit to the Community

In *Gilmour v Coats*,[298] reproduced below, the House of Lords held that a trust for a contemplative order of nuns who did not leave their cloisters nor allow the public into them was not charitable. The court does not have to accept as proved whatever a particular religion believes, and the benefits of the nuns' edifying example and their intercessory prayers were too vague and incapable of being proved to be **9–207**

---

290 [2005] UKHL 15; [2005] 2 A.C. 246 at [23]. See too *Afariogun v Charity Commission*, First-tier Tribunal (General Regulatory Chamber), 22 October 2021; P. Ridge, "Not-for-Profit Law and Freedom of Religion" in M. Harding (ed.) *Research Handbook on Not-For-Profit Law* (Edward Elgar, 2018); P. Ridge, "When is the Advancement of Religion Not a Charitable Purpose?" (2020) 6 C.J.C.C.L. 360.

291 *Buckley v Barlow* [2016] EWHC 3017 (Ch) at [33]. And note the judge's refusal at [37] to be influenced by the argument that the sect under consideration "crossed a line between eccentricity and downright blasphemy". See too *Gilmour v Coats* [1949] A.C. 426 at 455.

292 e.g. *Varsani v Jesani* [1999] Ch. 219 at 238; *Halal Meat Sellers Committee Ltd v HMC (UK) Ltd* [2020] EWHC 2190 (Comm) at [52]. Further see R. Meakin, "Taking the Queen's Shilling: The Implications for Religious Freedom for Religions Being Registered as Charities" (2017) 178 *Law & Justice* 57.

293 *Hoare v Osborne* (1866) L.R. 1 Eq. 585; *Re Raine* [1956] Ch. 417.

294 *Re Vaughan* (1866) 33 Ch. D. 187 at 192; *Re Douglas* [1905] 1 Ch. 279.

295 *Lloyd v Lloyd* (1852) 2 Sim. (N.S.) 225; *Re Hooper* [1932] 1 Ch. 38; see Parish Councils and Burial Authorities (Miscellaneous Provisions) Act 1970 s.1 (a burial or local authority may contract to maintain a grave or memorial for not exceeding 99 years).

296 *Re Rumball* [1956] Ch. 105.

297 *Re Simson* [1946] Ch. 299 (gift to vicar "for his work in the parish" charitable); *Farley v Westminster Bank* [1939] A.C. 430 (gift to vicar "for parish work" not charitable) applying *Dunn v Byrne* [1912] A.C. 407.

298 [1949] A.C. 426.

of tangible benefit for the public. Similarly, in *Re Hetherington*[299] it was held that a trust for Masses for the repose of particular souls was charitable only by implicitly restricting it to Masses that had to be held in public.

9–208 It cannot be said, however, that the courts and the Charity Commission have taken a consistent line towards religious bodies which conduct their religious services in private. The foregoing cases can be contrasted with *Neville Estates Ltd v Madden* where Cross J upheld as charitable a trust for the members from time to time of the Catford Jewish Synagogue although access to its services was restricted, because he felt "entitled to assume that some benefit accrues to the public from the attendance at places of worship of persons who live in this world and mix with their fellow citizens".[300] The Charity Commission has also registered as charitable both the Society of the Precious Blood[301] and the Preston Down Trust.[302] The first of these was an enclosed contemplative society of Anglican nuns, whose activities within their walls included holding services open to the public, providing religious and secular education of the public and relieving suffering, sickness, poverty and distress through their counselling service. The second is a trust for the advancement of the purposes of the Plymouth Brethren Christian Church, a body whose beliefs centre on the doctrine of separation from evil and whose practices include not only holding services for members only but also imposing physical separation between members and non-members in their daily lives, even if they are members of the same family.

Gilmour v Coats

House of Lords [1949] A.C. 426

9–209 The income of a trust fund was to be applied to the purposes of a Carmelite convent, if those purposes were charitable. The convent was comprised of an association of strictly cloistered and purely contemplative nuns who were concerned with prayers and meditation, and who did not engage in any activities for the benefit of people outside the convent. In the view of the Roman Catholic Church, however, their prayers and meditation caused the intervention of God for the benefit of members of the public, and their life inside the convent provided an example of self-denial and concentration on religious matters which was beneficial to the public. At first instance and in the Court of Appeal it was held that the trust was not a charitable one, and the House of Lords dismissed an appeal from this conclusion.

9–210 LORD SIMONDS (with whom LORD DU PARCQ, LORD NORMAND, LORD MORTON, and LORD REID agreed): I need not go back beyond the case of *Cocks v Manners*,[303] which was decided nearly eighty years ago by Wickens V.C. In that case the testatrix left her residuary estate between a number of religious institutions, one of them being the Dominican convent at Carisbrooke, a community not differing in any material respect from the community of nuns now under consideration. The learned judge used these words,[304] which I venture to repeat, though they have already been cited in the courts below:

> "On the Act [the statute of Elizabeth] unaffected by authority I should certainly hold that the gift to the Dominican convent is neither within the letter nor the spirit of it; and no decision has been referred to which compels me to adopt a different conclusion. A voluntary association of women for the purpose

---

299 [1990] Ch. 1 criticised by C. Rickett [1990] Conv. 34; further see *Nolan v Downes* (1917) 23 C.L.R. 546 and *Carrigan v Redwood* (1910) 30 N.Z.L.R. 244.

300 [1962] Ch. 832 at 853. Clearly, the benefited class was small, and in *Dingle v Turner* [1972] A.C. 601 at 625 Lord Cross said, "A trust to promote some religion among the employees of a company might perhaps be held to be charitable, provided it was clear that the benefits were to be purely spiritual." *Re Warre's WT* [1953] 1 W.L.R. 725 (retreat house not charitable) is of dubious authority.

301 Charity Commission, *Annual Report* (1989), paras 56–62; Decisions, Vol.3, p.11.

302 Charity Commission, "Decision on Preston Down Trust's Application for Registration" (3 January 2014), *https://www.gov.uk/government/uploads/system/uploads/attachment_data/file/336112/preston_down_trust_full_decision.pdf*. This was a controversial decision, not least because the Commission had reached the opposite conclusion only two years' previously.

303 (1871) L.R. 12 Eq. 574.

304 ibid. at 585.

of working out their own salvation by religious exercises and self-denial seems to me to have none of the requisites of a charitable institution, whether the word 'charitable' is used in its popular sense or in its legal sense. It is said, in some of the cases, that religious purposes are charitable, but that can only be true as to religious services tending directly or indirectly towards the instruction or the edification of the public; an annuity to an individual, so long as he spent his time in retirement and constant devotion, would not be charitable, nor would a gift to ten persons, so long as they lived together in retirement and performed acts of devotion, be charitable. Therefore the gift to the Dominican convent is not, in my opinion, a gift on a charitable trust."

Apart from what I have called the final argument, which I will deal with later, the contention of the appellant rests, not on any change in the lives of the members of such a community as this, nor, from a wider aspect, on the emergence of any new conception of the public good, but solely on the fact that for the first time certain evidence of the value of such lives to a wider public together with new arguments based on that evidence has been presented to the court. Never before, it was urged, has the benefit to be derived from intercessory prayer and from edification been brought to the attention of the court; if it had been, the decision in *Cocks v Manners* would, at least should, have been otherwise. 9–211

My Lords, I would speak with all respect and reverence of those who spend their lives in cloistered piety, and in this House of Lords spiritual and temporal, which daily commences its proceedings with intercessory prayers, how can I deny that the Divine Being may in His Wisdom think fit to answer them? But, my Lords, whether I affirm or deny, whether I believe or disbelieve, what has that to do with the proof which the court demands that a particular purpose satisfies the test of benefit to the community? Here is something which is manifestly not susceptible of proof. But, then it is said, this is a matter not of proof but of belief, for the value of intercessory prayer is a tenet of the Catholic faith, therefore, and in such a prayer there is benefit to the community. But it is just at this "therefore" that I must pause. It is, no doubt, true that the advancement of religion is, generally speaking, one of the heads of charity, but it does not follow from this that the court must accept as proved whatever a particular church believes. The faithful must embrace their faith believing where they cannot prove: the court can act only on proof. A gift to two or ten or a hundred cloistered nuns in the belief that their prayers will benefit the world at large does not from that belief alone derive validity any more than does the belief of any other donor for any other purpose. The importance of this case leads me to state my opinion in my own words but, having read again the judgment of the learned Master of the Rolls, I will add that I am in full agreement with what he says on this part of the case. 9–212

I turn to the second of the alleged elements of public benefit, edification by example, and I think that this argument can be dealt with very shortly. It is, in my opinion, sufficient to say that this is something too vague and intangible to satisfy the prescribed test. The test of public benefit has, I think, been developed in the last two centuries. Today it is beyond doubt that that element must be present. No court would be rash enough to attempt to define precisely or exhaustively what its content must be. But it would assume a burden which it could not discharge if now for the first time it admitted into the category of public benefit something so indirect, remote, imponderable and, I would add, controversial as the benefit which may be derived by others from the example of pious lives. 9–213

I must now refer to certain cases on which the appellant relied. They consist of a number of cases in the Irish courts and *Re Caus*,[305] a decision of Luxmoore J. A consideration of the Irish cases shows that it has there been decided that a bequest for the saying of masses, whether in public or in private, is a good charitable bequest: see, e.g., *Att.-Gen. v Hall*[306] and *O'Hanlon v Logue*.[307] And in *Re Caus* Luxmoore J. came to the same conclusion. I would expressly reserve my opinion on the question whether these decisions should be sustained in this House. So important a matter should not be decided except on a direct consideration of it. It is possible that, particularly in regard to the celebration of masses in public, good reason may be found for supporting a gift for such an object as both a legal and a charitable purpose. But it follows from what I have said in the earlier part of this opinion that I am unable to accept the view, which at least in the Irish cases is clearly expressed, that in intercessory prayer and edification that public benefit which is the condition of legal charity is to be found. Of the decision of Luxmoore J. in *Re Caus*, I would only say that his ratio decidendi is expressly stated to be,[308] "first, that it (i.e., a gift for the saying of masses) enables a 9–214

[305] [1934] Ch. 162.
[306] [1897] 2 I.R. 426.
[307] [1906] 1 I.R. 247.
[308] [1934] Ch. 162 at 170.

ritual act to be performed which is recognised by a large proportion of Christian people to be the central act of their religion, and, secondly, that it assists in the endowment of priests whose duty it is to perform the ritual act." The decision, therefore, does not assist the appellant's argument in the present case and I make no further comments on it.[309]

9–215 It remains, finally, to deal with the argument that the element of public benefit is supplied by the fact that qualification for admission to membership of the community is not limited to any group of persons but is open to any woman in the wide world who has the necessary vocation. Thus, it is said, just as the endowment of a scholarship open to public competition is a charity, so also a gift to enable any woman (or, presumably, any man) to enter a fuller religious life is a charity. To this argument, which, it must be admitted, has a speciously logical appearance, the first answer is that which I have indicated earlier in this opinion. There is no novelty in the idea that a community of nuns must, if it is to continue, from time to time obtain fresh recruits from the outside world. That is why a perpetuity is involved in a gift for the benefit of such a community, and it is not to be supposed that, to mention only three masters of this branch of the law, Wickens V.C., Lord Lindley or Lord Macnaghten failed to appreciate the point. Yet, by direct decision or by way of emphatic example, a community such as this is by them regarded as the very type of religious institution which is not charitable. I know of no consideration applicable to this case which would justify this House in unsettling a rule of law which has been established so long and by such high authority. But that is not the only, nor, indeed, the most cogent reason why I cannot accede to the appellant's argument. It is a trite saying that the law is life, not logic. But it is, I think, conspicuously true of the law of charity that it has been built up, not logically, but empirically. It would not, therefore, be surprising to find that, while in every category of legal charity some element of public benefit must be present, the court had not adopted the same measure in regard to different categories, but had accepted one standard in regard to those gifts which are alleged to be for the advancement of religion, and it may be yet another in regard to the relief of poverty. To argue by a method of syllogism or analogy from the category of education to that of religion ignores the historical process of the law. Nor would there be lack of justification for the divergence of treatment which is here assumed. For there is a legislative and political background peculiar to so-called religious trusts, which has, I think, influenced the development of the law in this matter.[310]

9–216 *Appeal dismissed.*

Charity Commission, *Decision on Application for Registration of the Temple of the Jedi Order*, 16 December 2016

Background

9–217 *The Temple of the Jedi Order ("TOTJO") applied to constitute* as a Charitable Incorporated Organisation ("CIO") and be entered onto the register of charities on 7 March 2016.

Decision

9–218 The Commission's decision made under section 208 of the Charities Act 2011 is to refuse the application to constitute and register TOTJO as a charity because it is not satisfied that the proposed CIO would be a charity at the time it would be registered. The Commission is not satisfied that TOTJO is established for exclusively charitable purposes for the advancement of religion and/or the promotion of moral and ethical improvement for the benefit of the public. The detailed reasoning is set out below.

---

[309] See *Re Hetherington* [1990] Ch. 1 on *Re Caus*.

[310] The Nathan Committee on Charitable Trusts rejected the suggestion of the representatives of the Roman Catholic Church that trusts for the advancement of religion should be defined to include "the advancement of religion by those means which that religion believes and teaches are means by which it does advance it": (1952) Cmnd. 8710, paras 129–130.

The issue for consideration

The issue to be determined is whether TOTJO would be established for exclusively charitable purposes for public benefit as defined by section 1 of the Charities Act 2011("the 2011 Act"). That is to say: 9–219

a. Do the purposes of the TOTJO fall within the descriptions of purposes in section 3 of the 2011 Act?
b. Are the purposes for the public benefit?

What are the purposes of the Society?

The purposes of the proposed CIO are: 9–220

> To advance the religion of Jediism, for the public benefit worldwide, in accordance with the Jedi Doctrine.[311]
> To advance such charitable purposes (according to the law of England and Wales) as the Trustees see fit from time to time.

... The definition of Jediism is "...a religion based on the observance of the Force, the ubiquitous and metaphysical power that a Jedi (a follower of Jediism) believes to be the underlying, fundamental nature of the universe." 9–221

Do the purposes fall within the descriptions of purposes in section 3 of the Charities Act 2011?

THE ADVANCEMENT OF RELIGION—section 3 (1)

The advancement of religion is a description of purposes in section 3 (1) of the 2011 Act. Religion is partially defined in section 3 (2) to include (i) a religion which involves belief in more than one god, and (ii) a religion which does not involve belief in a god. 9–222

The Commission, like the court, is not concerned with the truth or otherwise of the beliefs in question but will not recognise as a religion everything that chooses to call itself a religion.[312] The courts have held that "to give [a] purpose the name of "religious" or "education" is not to conclude the matter".[313] 9–223

The definition and characteristics of religion for the purposes of charity law are distilled from charity law and the partial statutory definition introduced by the Charities Act 2006. Recently, the Supreme Court has considered the meaning of "religious worship" for registered places of worship[314] in the case of *Hodkin*.[315] As the Commission's published guidance[316] pre-dates the *Hodkin* decision, it has considered the extent to which that decision, which did not relate to a matter of charity law, might influence how it assesses whether a particular purpose is charitable as being for the advancement of religion. 9–224

Lord Toulson, who gave the leading judgment in *Hodkin*, reviewed the relevant case law, including case law on the question from other jurisdictions.[317] At paragraph 57 he states that: 9–225

> "For the purposes of PWRA, I would describe religion in summary as a spiritual or non- secular belief system, held by a group of adherents, which claims to explain mankind's place in the universe and relationship with the infinite, and to teach its adherents how they are to live their lives in conformity with the spiritual understanding associated with the belief system. By spiritual or non-secular I mean a belief system which goes beyond that which can be perceived by the senses or ascertained by the application of science. I prefer not to use the word "supernatural" to express this element, because it is a loaded word which can carry a variety of connotations. Such a belief system may or may not involve belief in a supreme being, but it does involve a belief that there is more to be understood about

---

311 [Details appear in an Appendix.]
312 *Re Coats' Trusts, Coats v Gilmour* [1948] Ch. 340 (CA) 346–347.
313 *National Anti-Vivisection Society v I.R.C.* [1948] A.C. 31.
314 Section 2 of the Places of Worship Registration Act 1855.
315 *R (on the application of Hodkin) v Registrar General of Births, Deaths and Marriages* [2013] UKSC 77.
316 *The Advancement of Religion for the Public Benefit and Analysis of the law underpinning The Advancement of Religion for the Public Benefit, https://www.gov.uk/government/uploads/system/uploads/attachment_data/file/358531/advancement-of-religion-for-the-public-benefit.pdf*
317 He cites the judgments of Wilson and Deane JJ in *Church of the New Faith v Comr of Pay-Roll Tax (Victoria)* (1983) 154 CLR as helpful on the question.

mankind's nature and relationship to the universe than can be gained from the senses or from science. I emphasise that this is intended to be a description and not a definitive formula."

9–226 As regards the meaning of "religious worship", Lord Toulson interprets it as being:

> ". . . wide enough to include religious services, whether or not the form of service falls within the narrower definition adopted in *Segerdal*. This broader interpretation accords with standard dictionary definitions. The *Chambers Dictionary*, 12th ed (2011) defines the noun "worship" as including both "adoration paid to a deity, etc." and "religious service", and it defines "worship" as an intransitive verb as "to perform acts of adoration; to take part in religious service". Similarly, the *Concise Oxford English Dictionary*, 12th ed (2011), defines "worship" as including both "the feeling and expression of reverence and adoration of a deity" and "religious rites and ceremonies". The broader interpretation accords with the purpose of the statute in permitting members of a religious congregation, who have a meeting place where they perform their religious rites, to carry out religious ceremonies of marriage there. Their authorisation to do so should not depend on fine theological or liturgical niceties as to how precisely they see and express their relationship with the infinite (referred to by Scientologists as "God" in their creed and universal prayer). Those matters, which have been gone into in close detail in the evidence in this case, are more fitting for theologians than for the Registrar General or the courts."

9–227 The court in *Hodkin* has taken a broad view of what it means to be a religion and the requirements of religious worship, recognising the inherent difficulties of attempting to attach a narrowly circumscribed meaning to the word, including "the different context in which the issue may arise, the variety of world religions, developments of new religions and religious practices, and developments in the common understanding of the concept of religion due to cultural changes".[318] Lord Toulson emphasised this was not a definitive formula but intended to be a description.

9–228 From the statute and these cases, the Commission draws the principles that religion in charity law is characterised by belief in one or more gods or spiritual or non-secular principles or things, and a relationship between the adherents of the religion and the gods, principles or things which is expressed by worship, reverence and adoration, veneration intercession or by some other religious rite or service. In addition, that it must be capable of providing moral and ethical value or edification to the public[319] and characterised by a certain level of cogency, seriousness, cohesion and importance.[320]

9–229 The Commission has considered TOTJO against this framework and concluded that Jediism does not meet the characteristics of a religion for the purposes of charity law for the reasons set out below.

Belief in one or more gods or spiritual or non-secular principles or things

9–230 Jediism is based on the observance of the Force, described as "the ubiquitous and metaphysical power that a Jedi (a follower of Jediism) believes to be the underlying, fundamental nature of the universe". Jediism does not involve belief in a god but the statutory definition of religion includes religions which do not involve belief in a god. It is recognised that some religions for example Buddhism and Jainism do not believe in a god. The Commission considered whether Jediism is characterised by belief in a spiritual or non-secular principles or things.

9–231 The Jedi Doctrine states that Jedi believe "In the Force, and in the inherent worth of all life within it." The Teachings state "Jedi are in touch with the Force. We are open to spiritual awareness and keep our minds in tune with the beauty of the world"; and "Jedi believe in eternal life through the Force. We do not become obsessed in mourning those who pass. We may grieve at their passing but we are content, knowing that they will forever be a part of the Force and so always a part of us."

9–232 *The definition of Jediism also states "The Jedi religion is an inspiration and a way of life for many people throughout the world who take on the mantle of Jedi". TOTJO acknowledges that "there is some scope for followers to simply view Jediism as a philosophy or way of life . . . Some* Jedi prefer to avoid the word religion to describe their theological beliefs, ethical framework and way of life. We do not insist that members use the word religion . . . ."

---

318 Per Lord Toulson para 34.

319 *Cocks v Manners* (1871) L.R. 12 Eq. 585; *Gilmour v Coats* [1949] A.C. 426 at 444.

320 *Campbell and Cosaus v UK* (1982) 4 E.H.R.R. 293 at 304; *JP v South London and Maudsley NHS Foundation Trust* [2012] UKUT 486 (AAC); [2013] M.H.L.R. 148.

Based on the proposed governing document, the evidence received in support of the application and the content of the website of TOTJO, the Commission is not satisfied that the observance of the Force within Jediism is characterised by a belief in one or more gods or spiritual or non-secular principles or things which is an essential requirement for a religion in charity law. Despite being open to spiritual awareness, there is scope for Jediism and the Jedi Doctrine to be advanced and followed as a secular belief system. Jediism therefore lacks the necessary spiritual or non-secular element. The Commission noted that in *Hodkin* Lord Toulson did distinguish and exclude secular belief systems from the description of religion. 9-233

Relationship with the gods, principles or things which is expressed by worship, reverence and adoration, veneration, intercession or by some other religious rite or service

The Commission noted that TOTJO is an entirely web based organisation and the Jedi are predominantly, if not exclusively, an online community. The information available on TOTJO's website and provided in support of the application, to include the content of the sermons and transcripts of the Live Services which are based upon the Jedi Doctrine and recite the Creed (adopted from the Prayer of St. Francis of Assisi) were considered. The Commission also noted that TOTJO promotes meditation as a means of connecting with the Force. 9-234

Although these publications borrow from the prayers and texts of world religions, in the context of TOTJO the Commission is not satisfied that the "Live Services" on the website, the published sermons and the promotion of meditation evidence a relationship between the adherents of the religion and the gods, principles or things which is expressed by worship, reverence and adoration, veneration intercession or by some other religious rite or service. In particular, it is significant that Jediism may be adopted as a lifestyle choice as opposed to a religion and the website states that TOTJO provides "an online space for anyone to explore non-denominational spirituality." 9-235

Cogency, cohesion, seriousness and importance in the form of the belief system

It is clear that the law does not concern itself with the truth of a religion but based on principles distilled from case law, the Commission considers that a religion/belief system should be characterised by a certain level of cogency, seriousness, cohesion and importance. This requirement was discussed in *Campbell and Cosaus v UK*[321] in relation to a claim in the context of Article 2 of Protocol 1 of the European Convention on Human Rights which considered the requirement of the State to respect the right of parents to ensure their child's education and teaching is in conformity with their own religious and philosophical convictions. The European Court of Human Rights held that 'belief' in this context extends beyond just mere opinions or deeply held feelings: there must be a holding of spiritual or philosophical convictions which have an identifiable formal content. One may expect it to concern something relating to an important aspect of human life and it would require "a certain level of cogency, seriousness, cohesion and importance"[322] This approach has been applied by the Upper Tribunal in *JP v South London and Maudsley NHS Foundation Trust*.[323] 9-236

The definition of Jediism in Appendix A to the CIO Constitution states that it sources its terminology in the books, films and video games comprising the Star Wars. It uses the mythology of Star Wars and draws on many faiths, including, but not limited to: Taoism, Buddhism, Hinduism, Christianity, Sufism, Judaism, and Paganism. It also draws on a number of secular philosophical teachings including the existential phenomenology of Heidegger, Kierkegaard and Buber. 9-237

There is no worldwide authority or structure for Jediism. It is open to different interpretations and there are a spectrum of groups that classify themselves as Jedi. It appears that Jedi are an amorphous and diverse group with a framework that allows individuals to pursue Jediism in different ways and not as a religion but as a secular belief system. TOTJO has set out Jediism as it is understood and promoted by it. 9-238

The Jedi Doctrine promoted by TOTJO borrows heavily from other world religions and philosophical teachings but the Commission does not consider that the aggregate amounts to a sufficiently cogent and distinct religion. 9-239

---

321 (1982) 4 E.H.R.R. 293 at 304.

322 *Campbell and Cosaus v United Kingdom* (1982) 4 E.H.R.R. 1.

323 [2012] UKUT 486 (AAC); [2013] M.H.L.R. 148.

9–240 TOTJO confirm that Jediism may be adopted alongside any other religion, and that many interpretations of Jediism are possible. Also that TOTJO is open to different perspectives, self-realisation and individuals paths. It is inclusive and different viewpoints are accepted.

9–241 The TOTJO website confirms the diverse and differing nature of Jediism:

> "There are many Jedi communities across the internet with a great variety of beliefs, customs and policies. As a community we will do our best to address your concerns and take on board your views, but no one site may offer you exactly what you are looking for. If you'd feel more comfortable elsewhere maybe one of the other Jedi communities would correspond more to your needs."

9–242 The Commission noted the following analysis of Jediism presented by TOTJO in support of its application: "Jedi Religion, or Jediism, continues to be an incredibly decentralized system of belief. While various groups have sprung up to teach it to others, there remains a large amount of variance between individual Jedi and multiple Jedi organizations. Jedi teachings are generally considered suggestions and guides rather than rules, so the difference of teachings between groups is not necessarily viewed as improper or incorrect."[324]

9–243 The Commission also noted the decision of the Board of the New Zealand Charity Commission[325] declining registration of The Jedi Society Incorporated on the basis that "Jediism is not sufficiently structured, cogent or serious to advance religion; nor to advance moral or spiritual improvement in a charitable manner". On the basis of the evidence the Board considered that "the belief system is merely a collection of interconnected ideas based on the Star Wars universe, rather than structured cogent and serious religion."

9–244 The Commission considers that there is insufficient evidence that Jediism and the Jedi Doctrine as promoted by TOTJO is a sufficiently structured, organised or integrated system of belief to constitute a religion. There is insufficient evidence of an objective understanding of Jediism as opposed to a self-defining system which may be pursued outside the confines of a religion and in a secular manner. It comprises a loose framework of ideas with some common ground which individuals may interpret as they see fit. In particular, it is not obligatory to interpret and follow the Jedi Doctrine as a religion.

9–245 There is scope for individuals, consistent with Jediism and the Jedi Doctrine promoted by TOTJO, to pursue a spiritual path, a philosophy or way of life outside of the scope of a religion, as that term is defined in charity law. Any cogency and cohesion that is present is eroded by the individual's ability to develop themselves within a loose framework and follow an individual experiential philosophy or way of life as a secular belief system.

Doctrines and practice of benefit to the public—capable of providing moral and ethical value or edification to the public

9–246 The belief system to be a religion for the purposes of charity law must be capable of providing moral and ethical value or edification to the public. The court in *Cocks v Manners* stated "It is said, in some of the cases that religious purposes are charitable, but that can only be true as to religious services tending directly or indirectly towards the instruction or the edification of the public".[326] This statement was approved by Lord Simonds in *Gilmour v Coats*.[327]

9–247 Jediism as promoted by TOTJO draws on many moral and ethical frameworks from other religions and philosophies. The Commission accepts that moral and ethical frameworks rooted in other religions and philosophies may be capable of providing moral and ethical value or edification to the public. In addition, the Commission accepts that such moral and ethical frameworks, in the context of other religions, may to some extent be open to interpretation by individual followers. However, the Commission considered that the general lack of structure to support a coherent religious belief system and latitude for individual acceptance or rejection and interpretation of the Jedi Doctrine affects the capability of TOTJO to promote doctrines and practice of benefit to the public which provide moral and ethical value or edification to the public.

9–248 The Commission noted there is some evidence that Jediism upholds particular values which might be capable of having a positive and beneficial impact on the public. However, the morals and ethics are not formally set out and are open to individuals to accept, reject and interpret. Given the lack of formality

[324] *http://altreligion.about.com/od/alternativereligionsaz/a/jedi_religion.htm.*

[325] Dated 14 September 2015.

[326] (1871) L.R. 12 Eq. 585.

[327] [1949] A.C. 426 at 444.

around the expression and promotion of values and behaviours coupled with the ability of individuals to interpret and develop their own guidelines, the Commission is not satisfied that there is sufficient evidence to conclude that TOTJO promotes doctrines and practice of benefit to the public.

It is not evident that TOTJO reaches out into the community so as to have a positive impact. The Jedi Doctrine and services are accessible to the general public but the supporting information confirms that the pastoral care is focused on the provision of a support service for TOTJO's members who are in need to help them seek solutions themselves. This suggests an inward focus on its members rather than an outward focus on the general public. **9-249**

Summary of purpose—the advancement of religion

The Commission concluded that there is insufficient evidence that the characteristics of a religion in charity law are met for the reasons set out above. The Commission then considered whether the purposes might further another charitable purpose, the promotion of moral and ethical improvement for the benefit of the public, as an alternative to the advancement of religion. **9-250**

[The Commission went on to ask whether the purposes of TOTJO fell within the Charities Act 2011, s.3(1)(m), as being for the promotion of moral or ethical improvement, and concluded that they did not.] **9-251**

D. Section 3(1)(d): "The Advancement of Health or the Saving of Lives"

The Charities Act 2011 s.3(2)(b) states that for the purposes of s.3(1)(d) "the advancement of health" includes "the prevention or relief of sickness, disease or human suffering". This encompasses measures to ease the suffering, or to assist the recovery, of people who are sick, convalescent, disabled or infirm;[328] and a person may relevantly be "sick" if she suffers from a mental disorder or an addiction.[329] **9-252**

Section 3(1)(d) takes in the provision of medical and nursing services, whether in the community,[330] or in hospitals, hospices, care homes, rest homes, etc.[331] It also includes the promotion of health by the provision of other services, items and facilities for patients,[332] the welfare of health professionals,[333] the education and training of health professionals,[334] and the organisation and regulation of their activities.[335] The pursuit of medical research also falls within the scope of s.3(1)(d),[336] as does the education of the public with regard to health and safety matters.[337] However these last few purposes **9-253**

[328] *Re Lewis* [1955] Ch. 104 (blind); *Motability* [1977] Ch. Com. Rep. paras [51]–[56] (physically disabled); *Sarah Mary Collard Fund for the Provision of Guide Dogs* [1983] Ch. Com. Rep. paras [57]–[58].

[329] *Needham v Bowers* (1888) 21 Q.B.D. 436 ("institution for the reception of insane persons"); *Cawse v Committee of the Nottingham Lunatic Hospital* [1891] 1 Q.B. 585 ("lunatic hospital").

[330] *IRC v Peebleshire Nursing Assoc* 1927 S.C. 215; *Re Webster* [1912] 1 Ch. 106 (midwives).

[331] *Biscoe v Jackson* (1887) 35 Ch. D. 460; *Re Weir Hospital* [1910] 2 Ch. 124; *Re Welsh Hospital (Netley) Fund* [1921] 1 Ch. 655; *Kytherian Association of Queensland v Sklavos* (1958) 101 C.L.R. 56; *Re Smith (Deceased)* [1962] 1 W.L.R. 763; *Re Resch's WT* [1969] 1 A.C. 514.

[332] *Attorney General v Belgrave Hospital* [1910] 1 Ch. 73; *Re Adams* [1968] Ch. 80; Charity Commission, *Annual Report for 1966*, p.32. By extension a gift to provide accommodation for relations coming to visit patients is also charitable: *Re Dean's WT* [1950] 1 All E.R. 882.

[333] *Armagh County Infirmary Committee v Commissioner for Valuation for NI* [1940] N.I. 1 (house for visiting surgeon); *Re White's WT* [1951] 1 All E.R. 528 (rest home for nurses). See too *Re Pettit* [1988] 2 N.Z.L.R. 513 (relief of doctors' widows).

[334] *Re Lysaght* [1966] 1 Ch. 191 (medical studentships); *London Hospital Medical College v IRC* [1976] 1 W.L.R. 613 (student union at medical school).

[335] Including the promulgation and enforcement of professional standards: Charity Commission, *Decision on the Application for Registration as a Charity by the General Medical Council* (2 April 2001).

[336] *Taylor v Taylor* (1910) 10 C.L.R. 218; *Re Osmund* [1944] Ch. 206; *National Trust Co v Canadian Diabetes Assoc* (1993) 109 D.L.R. (4th) 232.

[337] *Re Hood* [1931] 1 Ch. 240 (temperance); *McGregor v Commissioner of Stamp Duties* [1942] N.Z.L.R. 164 (obstetrics and maternal welfare); *The League of Highway Safety and Safe Drivers Ltd* [1965] Ch. Com. Rep. 27 (road safety); *The Royal Association for Disability and Rehabilitation* [1977] Ch. Com. Rep. [57] (causes of disablement and the ways in which these may be reduced or eliminated); *Auckland Medical Aid Trust v CIR* [1979] 1 N.Z.L.R. 382 (human reproduction).

also fall within s.3(1)(b), and the saving of lives by rescue services, which falls under s.3(1)(d),[338] also falls under s.3(1)(l).

9–254 Controversy over complementary and alternative medical therapies such as homeopathy has led the Charity Commission to tighten up its guidance about the evidence it is willing to accept as proof of their efficacy. It will now accept evidence such as "peer reviewed research in recognised medical journals or acceptance by the Department of Health or other government health regulatory or health provision body", but it regards "testimonials from individuals who claim to have been cured or otherwise benefitted [to be] of minimal, if any, evidential weight."[339] The Commission also regards authorities which hold the promotion of faith healing to be a legally charitable purpose[340] to be justifiable only on the basis that this is a religious purpose as "the analysis applied in these cases would not be sufficient to establish that a health benefit has been demonstrated."[341] However, in cases where "claimed benefit is limited to, for example, the comfort and support of patients, then it may be possible to demonstrate benefit based on evidence of patient experience."[342] It also seems likely that the Commission would agree with the Scottish charity regulator that a different approach is justified where "an organisation intends to advance health by conducting or funding research into new treatments, since such activities are by their nature novel and experimental."[343]

9–255 In *Re Resch's WT*, Lord Wilberforce stated that a hospital may not be a charitable body if "the benefits it provides are not for the public, or a sufficiently large class of the public to satisfy the necessary tests of public character". However, he also considered that a private hospital which "provides only for persons of means who are capable of paying the substantial fees required as a condition of admission" does not necessarily fall foul of this rule, because "to provide, in response to public need, medical treatment otherwise inaccessible but in its nature expensive, without any profit motive, might well be charitable" albeit that "to limit admission to a nursing home to the rich would not be so".[344]

9–256 This case was distinguished by the Charity Commission when refusing to register Odstock Private Care Ltd.[345] The applicant company was formed, by means of a loan from an NHS foundation trust, to promote the undertaking of private patient work at the trust's district hospital. It did this by entering agreements with patients and insurance companies for the provision of private care, and then contracting with the trust to provide staffed facilities to enable this work to be carried out by clinicians. The company argued that its overall aim was to provide low-cost treatment to patients, using facilities which were available to the public at large and ploughing any surpluses back into additional NHS facilities at the hospital. However, the Commission took the view that the scheme was not available to the public at large, but only to those who could pay the fees, and so people living in poverty would not have access to its services. As the company did not provide financial assistance to patients on

---

338 *Thomas v Howell* (1874) L.R. 18 Eq. 198 (lifeboat); *Re Wokingham Fire Brigade Trusts* [1951] Ch. 373 (fire brigade).

339 Ibid.

340 *Re Kerin*, *The Times*, 24 May 1966; *Re Le Cren Clarke* [1996] 1 All E.R. 715.

341 Charity Commission, *The Use and Promotion of Complementary and Alternative Medicine: Making Decisions about Charitable Status: The Legal Framework* (December 2018) at 2, *https://assets.publishing.service.gov.uk/government/uploads/system/uploads/attachment_data/file/763304/CAM_Legal_framework.pdf*.

342 Charity Commission, *The Use and Promotion of Complementary and Alternative Medicine: Making Decisions about Charitable Status: The Legal Framework* (December 2018), at 3.

343 OSCR, *Meeting the Charity Test: Guidance* (20 August 2015), *https://www.oscr.org.uk/guidance-and-forms/meeting-the-charity-test-guidance/d-the-advancement-of-health/*.

344 [1969] 1 A.C. 514 at 540–541.

345 25 September 2007.

low incomes, they would need to fall back on insurance, but the cost of such insurance had not been shown to be affordable by all members of the community.[346]

E. Section 3(1)(e): "The Advancement of Citizenship or Community Development"

This head takes in a broad group of charitable purposes which are directed towards support for community and social infrastructure and whose focus is on the community rather than the individual. These include the promotion of urban and rural regeneration,[347] the promotion of community capacity building,[348] and the promotion of the voluntary sector.[349] **9–257**

F. Section 3(1)(f): "The Advancement of the Arts, Culture, Heritage, or Science"

Charities concerned with the advancement of art and culture, such as museums[350] and art galleries,[351] must satisfy a criterion of educational or artistic merit.[352] The advancement of "heritage" takes in the preservation and conservation of historic land and buildings,[353] as well as the preservation of historical traditions by folk clubs, country dancing societies, eisteddfods, etc. The advancement of science includes scientific research projects and charities connected with learned societies and institutions, e.g. the Royal College of Surgeons[354] and the Royal Geographical Society.[355] **9–258**

G. Section 3(1)(g): "The Advancement of Amateur Sport"

For many years, the promotion of sport was legally charitable only when it was ancillary to the pursuit of a charitable purpose[356] and it was not a charitable object in itself.[357] In 2003 the law was changed by the Charity Commission's decision to recognise as charitable "the promotion of community participation in healthy recreation by providing facilities for playing particular sports".[358] In this context, "facilities" meant not just land, building, and equipment, but also the organising of sporting activity **9–259**

---

346 For further discussion of private hospitals, see D. Morris, "Fee-Paying Hospitals and Charitable Status: A New Dawn or Lost Opportunities?" (2007) 18 K.L.J. 455; and cf. *Nuffield Health v Merton LBC* [2021] EWCA Civ 826; [2022] Ch. 1.

347 Charity Commission, *RR 2: Promotion of Rural and Urban Regeneration* (March 1999 version). cf. *Re Tenant* [1996] 2 N.Z.L.R. 633 (provision of creamery).

348 Charity Commission, *RR 5: The Promotion of Community Capacity Building* (November 2000 version).

349 Charity Commission, *RR 13: Promotion of the Voluntary Sector for the Benefit of the Public* (September 2004 version). See too Charity Commission, *Decision on the Application for Registration of the Charity Bank Ltd* (17 April 2002); Charity Commission, *Decision on the Application for Registration of Guidestar UK* (7 March 2003); Charity Commission, *RR 14: Promoting the Efficiency and Effectiveness of Charities and the Effective Use of Charitable Resources for the Benefit of the Public* (September 2004 version).

350 *Trustees of the British Museum v White* (1826) 2 Sim. & St. 594; *Re Holburne* (1885) 53 L.T. 212.

351 *Abbott v Fraser* (1874) L.R. 6 P.C. 96.

352 Charity Commission, *RR 10: Museums and Art Galleries* (August 2002 version), paras 6–12 and Annex A. See too *Re Pinion* [1965] Ch. 85.

353 *Re Verrall* [1916] 1 Ch. 100 (National Trust); *Re Cranstoun* [1932] 1 Ch. 537 (Elizabethan cottages); *Settle & Carlisle Railway Trust* [1990] Ch. Com. Rep. 23–26 (railway line). See too Charity Commission, *RR 9: Preservation and Conservation* (February 2001 version).

354 *Royal College of Surgeons of England v National Provincial Bank Ltd* [1952] A.C. 631.

355 *Beaumont v Oliviera* (1869) L.R. 4 Ch. 309.

356 School sports: *Re Mariette* [1915] 2 Ch. 284; *IRC v McMullen* [1981] A.C. 1. University and medical school sports: *London Hospital Medical College v IRC* [1976] 2 All E.R. 113. See too *Attorney General v Ross* [1985] 3 All E.R. 334. Army sports: *Re Gray* [1925] Ch. 362 (but doubted in *IRC v City of Glasgow Police Athletic Assoc* [1953] A.C. 380 at 391 and 401).

357 *Re Nottage* [1885] 2 Ch. 649 (yacht racing); *Re Clifford* (1911) 106 L.T. 14 (angling); *Re Patten* [1929] 2 Ch. 276 (cricket); *Re Birchfield Harriers* [1989] Ch. Com. Rep. paras 48–52 (athletics).

358 Charity Commission, *RR 11: Charitable Status and Sport* (April 2003 version).

such as that undertaken by community amateur sports clubs (CASCs). A CASC could therefore be a charity provided that: (1) the sport in question was capable of improving physical health and fitness; and (2) the club had an open membership, i.e. access to the club's facilities was available to anyone wishing to take advantage of them.[359] Some limits on club membership were tolerated, e.g. limited facilities and health of applicants,[360] but others not, e.g. tests of skill for admission and membership subscriptions which were unaffordable for most of the community served by the club.[361]

9–260 The law was then changed again by the Charities Act 2006. The Government's intention was simply to codify the pre-existing law, but an amendment was agreed to the statute as it passed through Parliament, with the result that s.3(2)(d) now provides that for the purposes of s.3(1)(g) "'sport' means sports or games which promote health by involving physical or mental skill or exertion". Hence it can now be a charitable purpose to undertake sport and games involving mental as well as physical skill or exertion—provided that these activities "promote health". In a guidance document published in 2003, the Charity Commission stated that the following sports did not appear to meet this criterion: angling; ballooning; billiards, pool and snooker; crossbow shooting; rifle and pistol shooting; flying; gliding; motor sports; and parachuting.[362] It seems likely that the Commission will take a similar line when construing the Charities Act 2011 s.3(2)(d). This is borne out by its 2015 decision not to register the Cambridgeshire Target Shooting Association as a charity, because although the evidence supported the contention that target shooting involves "physical and mental skill or exertion" it did not support the contention that target shooting "promotes health".[363] This may be contrasted with its 2011 decision to register the Hitchin Bridge Club after accepting evidence that "playing bridge among seniors . . . lower[s] the risk of developing Alzheimer's disease and other dementia by as much as 75%".[364]

H. Section 3(1)(h): "The Advancement of Human Rights, Conflict Resolution or Reconciliation or the Promotion of Religious or Racial Harmony or Equality and Diversity"

9–261 The promotion of human rights can be accomplished in various ways including monitoring human rights abuses, obtaining redress for the victims of such abuses, and campaigning in favour of the recognition of human rights, to the extent that political activity of this kind is ancillary to the charity's main purposes.[365] The advancement of conflict resolution or reconciliation includes the resolution of international conflicts, the promotion of international co-operation,[366] and relieving the suffering and distress arising through conflict on a national and international scale. It also includes mediation

---

359 *RR11* at para.7.

360 *RR11* at paras 16–17.

361 *RR11* at paras 18–19.

362 Charity Commission, *RR11: Charitable Status and Sport* (April 2003 version), para.11.

363 Charity Commission, *Decision on Application for Registration by Cambridgeshire Target Shooting Association*, 2 February 2015, paras 21–31.

364 Charity Commission, *Decision on Application for Registration by Hitchin Bridge Club*, 1 March 2011, para.19.

365 See further Charity Commission, *RR 12: The Promotion of Human Rights* (January 2005 version). For discussion of political activities, see paras 9–106 to 9–130. And for a survey of charities working in this field, see Charity Commission, *RS 16: Charities Working in the Field of Human Rights* (December 2007 version).

366 cf. *Re Koeppler's WT* [1986] Ch. 423 (trust to fund conferences to promote co-operation in Europe charitable as for the advancement of education).

and conciliation services,[367] and the promotion of restorative justice, where all the parties affected by a particular criminal offence come together to resolve collectively how to deal with its aftermath.[368]

The appeasement of racial feelings between Dutch- and English-speaking South Africans was held not to be a charitable purpose in *Re Strakosch*,[369] essentially because the court considered it to be a political purpose. Social attitudes subsequently underwent a considerable shift, however, and the enactment of the Race Relations Act 1968 indicated that Parliament considered the promotion of harmonious race relations to be for the public benefit. For this reason, the Charity Commissioners departed from *Re Strakosch* in 1983, when they stated that "promoting race relations, endeavouring to eliminate discrimination on grounds of race, and encouraging equality of opportunity" are charitable purposes.[370] **9–262**

Human rights organisations often have a political slant, and so the question frequently arises whether they fall foul of the rule that political purposes cannot be charitable. This has been discussed above.[371] **9–263**

I. Section 3(1)(i): "The Advancement of Environmental Protection or Improvement"

This head includes[372] the conservation of particular species of flora and fauna, of particular geographical areas,[373] and of the environment more generally,[374] along with the promotion of sustainable development and bio-diversity and the promotion of recycling and renewable energy resources.[375] Charities for the conservation of species or of particular land must produce independent expert evidence that the species or land in question are worthy of conservation.[376] **9–264**

In *Re Grove-Grady*,[377] the Court of Appeal struck down a trust to establish a sanctuary for wild birds and animals from which the public would be excluded, because the court could perceive no benefit to mankind in leaving the animals to their own devices in this way. However, ideas about environmental protection and the survival of endangered species have moved on. The Charity Commission's current approach to wildlife sanctuaries is to presume that they are not for the public benefit unless the public is given physical access to the site, but to take a flexible approach to the level of access needed, acknowledging that access "needs to be consistent with the aims of the charity so that visitors should not be allowed access at the expense of deterioration of a fragile . . . environment".[378] If an organisation can make out a case for limiting or excluding public access, it may still be able to satisfy the public benefit requirement, e.g. by allowing access to parts of the site, publishing books and videos about its activities, etc.[379] **9–265**

---

367 *Mediation in Divorce (Richmond-upon-Thames); The National Family Conciliation Council* [1983] Ch. Com. Rep. paras 28–34.
368 Charity Commission, *Decision on Application for Registration by Restorative Justice Consortium Ltd* (15 January 2003).
369 [1949] Ch. 529.
370 [1983] Ch. Com. Rep. paras 15–20. See too *Community Security Trust* (1995) 4 Decisions of the Charity Commissioners 8. The promotion of gender equality is also a charitable purpose: *Halpin v Seear* Ch. D. 27 February 1976; *Women's Service Trust* [1977] Ch. Com. Rep. paras 34–36.
371 See paras 9–106 to 9–130.
372 For a survey of charities working in this field, see Charity Commission, *Going Green: Charities and Environmental Responsibility* (December 2008 version), Pt 5.
373 *The Upper Teesdale Defence Fund* [1969] Ch. Comm. Rep. paras 23–24 (fund for preservation of flora and fauna of Upper Teesdale).
374 Charity Commission, *Decision on the Application for Registration of Environment Foundation* (24 January 2003).
375 Charity Commission, *Decision on the Application for Registration of Recycling in Ottery* (April 2002).
376 Charity Commission, *RR 9: Preservation and Conservation* (February 2001 version), paras A10–A15.
377 [1929] 1 Ch. 557.
378 Charity Commission, *RR 9: Preservation and Conservation* (February 2001 version), para.A19.
379 *RR9* para.A20. cf. *Attorney General. for New South Wales v Sawtell* [1978] 2 N.S.W.L.R. 200.

J. Section 3(1)(j): "The Relief of Those in Need by Reason of Youth, Age, Ill-health, Disability, Financial Hardship or other Disadvantage"

9–266 As previously noted,[380] "the relief of aged, impotent and poor people" was specified as charitable in the Preamble to the Statute of Charitable Uses 1601, but because these words are to be construed disjunctively,[381] the relief of those in need by reason of age,[382] and the relief of those in need by reason of ill-health or disability, are stand-alone charitable purposes—although they belong more obviously under s.3(1)(d). The Preamble also mentions "the education and preferment of orphans", and by analogy with this purpose, the promotion of the welfare of children generally is also a charitable purpose.[383]

K. Section 3(1)(k): "The Advancement of Animal Welfare"

9–267 Trusts for the protection or welfare of animals have been held charitable provided that they benefit, or promote the moral improvement of, the community.[384] Note, however, that in *National Anti-Vivisection Society v IRC*,[385] the House of Lords held among other things that anti-vivisection is not a charitable purpose because the practical benefits to mankind of retaining vivisection outweighed the moral benefits of abolishing it.

L. Section 3(1)(l): "The Promotion of the Efficiency of the Armed Forces of the Crown, or of the Efficiency of the Police, Fire and Rescue Services or Ambulance Services"

9–268 This sub-section was introduced by amendment as the Charities Bill 2005 went through Parliament primarily in order to safeguard the charitable status of the 15,000-odd service funds whose purposes are (broadly speaking) to support *esprit de corps* in the armed services.[386] Typically these include funds for increasing the physical fitness of service members through the provision of sporting facilities, equipment, and sporting competitions; funds to support messes (NCOs and Officers) and institutes (other ranks), including the provision of silver plate, etc.; benevolent funds for serving members, ex-serving members, widows/widowers of serving or ex-serving members, and dependents of serving or ex-serving members who are in need, etc.

M. Section 3(1)(m): Other Purposes

9–269 Section 3(1)(m)(i) deems other purposes to be charitable which do not fall under any other head, but which either fall within s.5 or were recognised as charitable in the case law predating the the Charities

---

[380] See para.9–140.

[381] *Re Robinson* [1951] Ch. 198; *Joseph Rowntree Memorial Trust Housing Assoc Ltd v Attorney General* [1983] Ch. 159.

[382] *Re Dunlop* [1984] N.I. 408 (home for elderly Presbyterians); *Joseph Rowntree Memorial Trust Housing Assoc Ltd v Attorney General* [1983] Ch. 159 (sheltered accommodation for the elderly). The Charities Act 2006 s.2(3)(e) specifies that "relief" of those in need under this head includes the provision of accommodation or care.

[383] *D v NSPCC* [1978] A.C. 171 at 228. See too *Re Sahal's WT* [1958] 1 W.L.R. 1243 (gift of house as children's home); Charity Commission, *Decision on the Application for Registration of the Internet Content Rating Association* (12 September 2002) (protection of children and young people from harm arising from contact with unsuitable material on the internet).

[384] *Re Wedgwood* [1915] 1 Ch. 113 (promotion of humane methods of slaughtering livestock); *Re Moss* [1949] 1 All E.R. 495 (welfare of cats and kittens); *Re Green's WT* [1985] 3 All E.R. 455 (rescue, maintenance, and benefit of cruelly treated animals).

[385] [1948] A.C. 31. See paras 9–107 to 9–127.

[386] *Hansard*, HL Vol.673, cols 131ff (28 June 2005).

Act 2006. Purposes falling into the latter category include: the payment of rates and taxes;[387] the discharge or reduction of the National Debt;[388] the provision of public works and public amenities;[389] the promotion of agriculture,[390] and of industry and commerce,[391] provided that the public benefit outweighs any private benefits derived by those involved;[392] the relief of unemployment;[393] the promotion of moral or spiritual welfare;[394] the relief of refugees;[395] and the relief of victims of accidents and disasters.[396]

N. Section 5: "The Provision of Facilities for Recreation or Other Leisure-time Occupation"

Section 5 concerns the provision of facilities for recreation or other leisure-time occupation. At common law, trusts of land for public use as a recreation ground had long been charitable,[397] but doubts about the provision of recreational facilities were created by the decision in *IRC v Baddeley*.[398] This concerned a trust to promote the moral, social and physical well-being of Methodists resident in West Ham and Leyton by the provision of facilities for moral, social and physical training and recreation. The court held that this was not a charitable trust, first, because the intended beneficiaries did not comprise a sufficient section of the community for the trust to merit charitable status, and, secondly, because the promotion of social well-being was not a charitable purpose. This decision prompted fears that village halls and similar institutions which had previously been considered legally charitable might not be charitable after all, and so the Recreational Charities Act 1958 was enacted to remove any doubt on this point. **9–270**

---

387 Dating back to the Preamble which refers to the "aid or ease of any poor inhabitants concerning payment of fifteens, setting out of soldiers and other taxes." See, e.g. *Nightingale v Goulburn* (1848) 2 Ph. 594.

388 *Attorney General v Zedra Fiduciary Services (UK) Ltd* [2020] EWHC 2988 (Ch); [2020] W.T.L.R. 1287; further proceedings [2022] EWHC 102 (Ch); [2022] W.T.L.R. 557.

389 *Attorney General v Heelis* (1824) 2 Sim. & St. 67 (town lighting, paving, drains and sewers); *Attorney General v Shrewsbury Corp* (1843) 6 Beav. 220 (repair and improvement of town's bridges, towers and walls); *Scottish Burial Reform and Cremation Soc v Glasgow Corp* [1968] A.C. 138 (crematorium); *Oxford Ice-Skating Assoc Ltd* [1984] Ch. Com. Rep. paras 19–25 (ice-rink). Because the provision of amenities and services of this kind is nowadays frequently undertaken by public authorities, many trusts for their provision have been made the subject of schemes under the Charities Act 1993 s.13. See further *Charities for the Maintenance of Highways, Bridges, and Similar Works* [1968] Ch. Com. Rep. paras 66–72.

390 *IRC v Yorkshire Agricultural Soc* [1928] 1 K.B. 611.

391 *IRC v White* (1980) 55 T.C. 61 (improvement of standards of craftsmanship); *Business in the Community* [1987] Ch. Com. Rep. paras 16–19. Note that the regulation of a trade is not a charitable purpose: *Wine Standards Board of the Vintners' Company* [1978] Ch. Com. Rep. paras 95–98.

392 *IRC v Oldham Training and Enterprise Council* [1996] S.T.C. 1218.

393 *Oldham TEC* at 1234; Charity Commission, *RR 3: Charities for the Relief of Unemployment* (March 1999 version).

394 *Re South Place Ethical Society* [1980] 1 W.L.R. 1565; *Public Concern at Work* (1994) 2 Decisions of the Charity Commissioners 5 (assistance to employees faced with moral and ethical issues of whistle-blowing). But cf. Charity Commission, *Decision on the Gnostic Centre's Application for Registration as a Charity* (16 December 2009), paras 50–57: furtherance of the applicant body's non-religious philosophical beliefs was not charitable because it had no demonstrable impact on the community.

395 *Re Morison* (1967) 117 N.L.J. 757.

396 *Re Hartley Colliery Accident Relief Fund* (1908) 102 L.T. 165n.; *Re North Devon and Somerset Relief Fund Trusts* [1953] 1 W.L.R. 1260. Disaster funds are entitled to charitable status only if the help is given to those in need: Charity Commission, *CC 40: Disaster Appeals* (January 2002 version).

397 *Re Hadden* [1932] 1 Ch. 133 (park); *Re Morgan* [1955] 1 W.L.R. 738 (recreation ground); *Brisbane CC v Attorney General for Queensland* [1979] A.C. 411 (park); *Bath and North Eastern Somerset Council v Attorney General* (2002) 5 I.T.E.L.R. 274 (recreation ground).

398 [1955] A.C. 572. See too *Londonderry Presbyterian Church House Trustees v IRC* [1946] N.I. 178; *Williams Trustees v IRC* [1947] A.C. 447.

9–271 The 1958 Act was replaced by the Charities Act 2011 s.5, which provides that it is a charitable purpose to provide facilities in the interests of social welfare, and that two criteria must both be satisfied before this can be said. The first is constant: the object of providing the facilities must be to improve the intended beneficiaries' conditions of life; but the second may be satisfied in alternative ways—by showing either that the beneficiaries have need of the facilities by reason of the factors enumerated in s.5(3)(b)(i), or that the facilities are available to members of the public at large, or to either male or to female members of the public at large (see s.5(3)(b)(ii)).[399] Bodies which might typically be expected to fall within the scope of these provisions include village halls, community centres and women's institutes.

Questions

1. "Because of the tax exemptions enjoyed by registered charities, decisions on charitable status entail decisions on resource allocation by the State. So they should be taken by a democratically elected body, with reference to Government policy on public resource allocation." **Discuss.**
2. "The courts and the Charity Commission have yet to produce a compelling reason why trusts of a political nature must fail. So long as it is otherwise exclusively charitable, and the appropriate public benefit test is satisfied, a trust for a political purpose should be upheld." **Discuss.**
3. "The Charity Commission cannot make new law, and can only state and apply existing law, when deciding whether to register voluntary bodies as charities, when issuing guidance to charities on the public benefit requirement, and when assessing registered charities to determine whether their activities are for the public benefit." **Discuss.**
4. Sam Smith is a rich industrialist who owns a majority shareholding in a large private company, Taurus Ltd. The company employs approximately one thousand people manufacturing widgets at an industrial plant in Manchester. Sam dies, leaving a valid will under which his residuary estate goes to his son Ben, and in which he also makes gifts, each of £500,000, to trustees to invest and apply the income therefrom to each of the following purposes:

   (a) to relieve poverty in Manchester, provided that past and present employees of Taurus Ltd and their relatives and dependents shall have priority over others when the money is applied;
   (b) to bring the residents of Manchester to a better understanding of the desirability of unilateral nuclear disarmament in the UK;
   (c) to arrange the legal adoption of children in Manchester by heterosexual couples who will bring them up in the Roman Catholic faith; and
   (d) to venerate the memory of Elvis Presley, who is not a deity, but a better appreciation of whose music will help us all to find our 'inner centres' and live in better harmony with one another.

   Advise Ben as to the validity of these bequests.

---

[399] Considered in *Gibbons v Smith* [2020] EWHC 1727 (Ch); [2020] W.T.L.R. 947 at [47]–[49] (railwaymen's sports and welfare club not charitable because membership by invitation only).

PART III

OPERATION OF EXPRESS TRUSTS

10

RESPONSIBILITIES AND POWERS OF TRUSTEES

1. Introduction

The creation of an express trust brings a new set of legal relationships into existence. Trustees acquire ownership of property (if they were not already the owners because they were the settlors of the relevant trust) and therefore have all the legal rights and powers that are incidental with ownership, e.g. to assign the property to other people. They may also acquire further powers within the trust structure, e.g. to appoint new trustees or to vary the terms of the trust. As discussed in Chapter 11, the exercise of all these powers is governed by rules which are typically enforceable by trustees against one another, and/or by the Attorney General, in the case of charitable trusts, and/or by the beneficiaries and probably also the objects of mere powers of appointment, in the case of trusts for persons. In this chapter we discuss the appointment, retirement and removal of trustees, their rights to remuneration and indemnification, the tasks which the trustees of many settlements must typically carry out and the powers they are given to do this. **10–001**

2. Appointment, Retirement and Removal of Trustees

A. Appointment

By definition, a trust is a legal form that entails ownership of property being vested in one or more trustees who are authorised—and indeed required—to use the property in particular ways chosen by the settlor. It follows that a trust cannot exist unless there is at least one trustee in whom ownership of trust property vests, and it is usual for more than one trustee to be appointed to ensure that they can monitor one another's conduct and to avoid the complications that might arise on the death of a sole trustee (where the sole trustee is a human being, although it is possible to appoint a corporation as trustee which is another way to avoid such problems). **10–002**

When a settlor creates a trust in her lifetime, she would normally appoint the first set of trustees herself, e.g. by appointing herself and others as trustees by a clause of the trust deed. After the trust has been created, the settlor has no right to appoint further trustees simply because she was the settlor, although she can give herself (or another person) such a power in the trust deed.[1] In the case of a testamentary trust, the settlor can do no more than appoint the first trustees, since the trust will not come into existence until after her death, but again she can give a power to appoint new trustees **10–003**

[1] For an example of such a clause see para.10–089.

on another person by a clause of the trust deed. Otherwise, new trustees may be appointable by the existing trustees under powers conferred by the Trustee Act 1925 s.36, or by beneficiaries under powers conferred by the Trusts of Land and Appointment of Trustees Act 1996 s.19, or by the court under powers conferred by the Trustee Act 1925 s.41.

10–004 The Trustee Act 1925 s.36 gives a power to appoint new trustees to the following persons in this order: (i) the person(s) nominated in the trust instrument (s.36(1)(a)); (ii) if there is no such person, or no such person able or willing to act, the surviving and continuing trustees (s.36(1)(b)); or (iii) if there is no surviving or continuing trustee, the personal representatives of the last or only surviving trustee (s.36(1)(b)). Where current trustees have a power to appoint new trustees, they must take the interests of all the beneficiaries into account when exercising this power, but they are entitled to exercise their independent judgment. Before 1996, therefore, even if all the beneficiaries were of full capacity and between them absolutely entitled, they could not force the trustees to use their s.36 power to appoint the beneficiaries' own nominee, and if the beneficiaries were dissatisfied with the trustees' choice of new trustees, all they could do was bring the settlement to an end under the rule in *Saunders v Vautier*[2] and create a new trust of which, as settlors, they could appoint whoever they chose. However, this could produce significant fiscal disadvantages and to help beneficiaries in this position, s.19 of the 1996 Act was enacted.

Trusts of Land and Appointment of Trustees Act 1996 s.19

19. Appointment and retirement of trustee at instance of beneficiaries

10–005 (1) This section applies in the case of a trust where—

(a) there is no person nominated for the purpose of appointing new trustees by the instrument, if any, creating the trust, and
(b) the beneficiaries under the trust are of full age and capacity and (taken together) are absolutely entitled to the property subject to the trust.

(2) The beneficiaries may give a direction or directions of either or both of the following descriptions—

(a) a written direction to a trustee or trustees to retire from the trust, and
(b) a written direction to the trustees or trustee for the time being (or, if there are none, to the personal representative of the last person who was a trustee) to appoint by writing to be a trustee or trustees the person or persons specified in the direction.

(3) Where—

(a) a trustee has been given a direction under subsection (2)(a),
(b) reasonable arrangements have been made for the protection of any rights of his in connection with the trust,
(c) after he has retired there will be either a trust corporation or at least two persons to act as trustees to perform the trust, and
(d) either another person is to be appointed to be a new trustee on his retirement (whether in compliance with a direction under subsection (2)(b) or otherwise) or the continuing trustees by deed consent to his retirement, he shall make a deed declaring his retirement and shall be deemed to have retired and be discharged from the trust.

(4) Where a trustee retires under subsection (3) he and the continuing trustees (together with any new trustee) shall (subject to any arrangements for the protection of his rights) do anything necessary to vest the trust property in the continuing trustees (or the continuing and new trustees). ...

---

2 See paras 12–064 to 12–073.

It is usual for a person who intends to create a trust to secure the consent of her intended trustees in advance. But settlors do not always do this, and even when they do, circumstances may change. The question may then arise, as to what should happen, e.g. if a testator creates a trust in her will and appoints trustees who are unwilling or unable to act? The answer in broad terms is that the trust will not fail for want of a trustee,[3] unless its operation was conditional on a particular trustee undertaking the trust,[4] but that some other trustee will have to be found, if necessary a court appointee, because a person "cannot be compelled to accept the burdens of ... trusteeship against his or her will",[5] and an intended trustee "may choose whether he will accept the trust, or not".[6] It follows that a settlor's intentions are not enough in themselves to create a trust because trustee consent is also required,[7] as indeed is beneficiary consent.[8] **10–006**

B. Retirement

When a trustee retires and a new trustee is appointed to fill the vacancy,[9] the retirement and new appointment are usually effected under s.36 of the Trustee Act 1925; where a new trustee is not appointed to fill the vacancy, the retirement is usually effected under s.39. Independently of statute, a trustee may retire under a power of retirement contained in the trust deed,[10] or by the consent of all the beneficiaries, provided that they are all of full capacity,[11] or by authority of the court, to which the trustee can apply to be discharged. **10–007**

Where one trustee is replaced with another it is essential that this is done properly as problems may ensue if it is not, e.g. the "old trustees" may remain liable to account for the trust property and the new "trustees" may only become trustees *de son tort*,[12] so that they are also liable to account for the trust property but at the same time their purported dealings with the trust property may be invalid, with possible consequences for the tax treatment of the settlement.[13] To avoid such problems, and to protect themselves from possible liability for actions of their successors or predecessors, outgoing and incoming trustees should therefore execute a deed of retirement and appointment (known as a "DORA"). This must also be done where trustees are compelled to retire and new trustees are appointed by beneficiaries under s.19 of the Trusts of Land and Appointment of Trustees Act 1996, as required by s.19(3). **10–008**

C. Removal

If the conditions in s.36 of the Trustee Act 1925 for replacing a trustee cannot be satisfied, removal will require an express power in the trust deed or an application to the court. The court's equitable **10–009**

3 *Re Willis* [1921] 1 Ch. 44; *Re Armitage* [1972] Ch. 438.
4 *Re Lysaght* [1966] Ch. 191.
5 *Scarpuzza v Scarpuzza* (2011) 4 A.S.T.L.R. 244 at [47].
6 *Robinson v Pett* (1734) 3 P. Wms 249 at 251.
7 As discussed in Y.K. Liew and C. Mitchell, "The Creation of Express Trusts" (2017) 11 J.Eq. 133.
8 *Naas v Westminster Bank Ltd* [1940] A.C. 366 at 396; *Smith v Michelmores Trust Corp Ltd* [2021] EWHC 1425 (Ch); [2021] W.T.L.R. 1051 at [64]–[72]; *Carroll v Toronto-Dominion Bank* (2021) 63 E.T.R. (4th) 1 at [27]; *Commissioner of Taxation v Carter* [2022] HCA 10 at [30], but compare [38]–[48].
9 If no one else can be found the Public Trustee will usually be willing to act.
10 *Lord Camoys v Best* (1854) 19 Beav. 414.
11 *Wilkinson v Parry* (1828) 4 Russ. 272 at 476.
12 See paras 14–013 to 14–016.
13 e.g. *Jasmine Trustees Ltd v Wells & Hind (a firm)* [2007] EWHC 38 (Ch); [2008] Ch. 194.

jurisdiction to remove trustees is independent of statute, as illustrated by *Letterstedt v Broers*,[14] reproduced below, which makes it clear that dishonest misconduct and want of capacity will both lead the court to remove a trustee.[15] Extreme incompetence may also lead a court to make such an order, as may a trustee being in a position of conflict (even without proof of loss).[16] But a breakdown of personal relations between trustee and beneficiary may not be enough to justify removal, for the reason stated by Sales J in *National Westminster Bank Plc v Lucas*:[17]

> There are many contexts in which trustees or those in equivalent positions, such as personal representatives of a deceased person, have to make judgments which involve striking a balance between different competing interests and which may thus adversely affect some persons claiming under the trust or in respect of the estate of the deceased. It is to be expected that in such cases there will often be an element of friction between the trustee or personal representative and those disappointed by their decisions. This is not in itself a good ground to remove the trustee or personal representative from their office.

10–010 Even so, where personal hostility between trustee and beneficiary have made proper administration of the trust impossible, this is a factor that the court can take into account when deciding whether to remove the trustee.[18]

Letterstedt v Broers

Privy Council (1884) 9 App. Cas. 371

10–011 The Board of Executors of Cape Town were the sole surviving executors and trustees of a will under which the appellant was a beneficiary. The appellant alleged misconduct in the administration of the trust, and claimed that the Board were unfit to be entrusted with the management of the estate and should be removed in favour of a new appointment. The Supreme Court of the Cape of Good Hope had refused the application to remove the Board. The beneficiary appealed successfully.

10–012 LORD BLACKBURN: . . . [The] whole case has been argued here, and, as far as their Lordships can perceive, in the court below, as depending on the principles which should guide an English court of equity when called upon to remove old trustees and substitute new ones. It is not disputed that there is a jurisdiction "in cases requiring such a remedy", as is said in Story's *Equity Jurisprudence*, s.1287, but there is very little to be found to guide us in saying what are the cases requiring such a remedy; so little that their Lordships are compelled to have recourse to general principles.

10–013 Story says, section 1289: "But in cases of positive misconduct, courts of equity have no difficulty in interposing to remove trustees who have abused their trust; it is not indeed every mistake or neglect of duty, or inaccuracy of conduct of trustees, which will induce courts of equity to adopt such a course. But the acts or omissions must be such as to endanger the trust property or to show a want of honesty, or a want of proper capacity to execute the duties, or a want of reasonable fidelity."

10–014 It seems to their Lordships that the jurisdiction which a court of equity has no difficulty in exercising under the circumstances indicated by Story is merely ancillary to its principal duty, to see that the trusts are properly executed. This duty is constantly being performed by the substitution of new trustees in the place of original trustees for a variety of reasons in non-contentious cases. And therefore, though it should appear that the charges of misconduct were either not made out, or were greatly exaggerated, so that the trustee was justified in resisting them, and the court might consider that in awarding costs, yet if satisfied that the continuance of the trustee would prevent the trusts being properly executed, the trustee might be

---

14 (1884) 9 App. Cas. 371.

15 See too *Thomas & Agnes Carvel Foundation v Carvel* [2007] EWHC 1314 (Ch); [2008] Ch. 395 at [51]; *Jones v Firkin-Flood* [2008] EWHC 2417 (Ch) at [283]ff.

16 *Long v Rodman* [2019] EWHC 753 (Ch) at [20]; *Manton v Manton* [2021] EWHC 125 (Ch); [2021] W.T.L.R. 245 at [17]–[18].

17 [2014] EWHC 653 (Ch); [2014] W.T.L.R. 637 at [83], affirmed [2014] EWCA Civ 1632; [2015] W.T.L.R. 635.

18 *Re EA Scott (1991 Chldren's Settlement No.1)* [2012] EWHC 2397 (Ch); [2012] W.T.L.R. 1439; *Brudenell-Bruce v Moore* [2014] EWHC 3679 (Ch); [2015] W.T.L.R. 373.

> removed. It must always be borne in mind that trustees exist for the benefit of those to whom the creator of the trust has given the trust estate.
>
> The reason why there is so little to be found in the books on this subject is probably that suggested by Mr Davey in his argument. As soon as all questions of character are as far settled as the nature of the case admits, if it appears clear that the continuance of the trustee would be detrimental to the execution of the trusts, even if for no other reason than that human infirmity would prevent those beneficially interested, or those who act for them, from working in harmony with the trustee, and if there is no reason to the contrary from the intentions of the framer of the trust to give this trustee a benefit or otherwise, the trustee is always advised by his own counsel to resign, and does so. If, without any reasonable ground, he refused to do so, it seems to their Lordships that the court might think it proper to remove him; but cases involving the necessity of deciding this, if they ever arise, do so without getting reported. It is to be lamented that the case was not considered in this light by the parties in the court below, for, as far as their Lordships can see, the Board would have little or no profit from continuing to be trustees, and as such coming into continual conflict with the appellant and her legal advisers, and would probably have been glad to resign, and get out of an onerous and disagreeable position. But the case was not so treated. 10–015
>
> In exercising so delicate a jurisdiction as that of removing trustees, their Lords do not venture to lay down any general rule beyond the very broad principle above enunciated, that their main guide must be the welfare of the beneficiaries. Probably it is not possible to lay down any more definite rule in a matter so essentially dependent on details often of great nicety. . . . 10–016
>
> It is quite true that friction or hostility between trustees and the immediate possessor of the trust estate is not of itself a reason for the removal of the trustees. But where the hostility is grounded on the mode in which the trust has been administered, where it has been caused wholly or partially by substantial over-charges against the trust estate, it is certainly not to be disregarded. 10–017
>
> Looking, therefore, at the whole circumstances of this very peculiar case, the complete change of position, the unfortunate hostility that has arisen, and the difficult and delicate duties that may yet have to be performed, their Lordships can come to no other conclusion than that it is necessary, for the welfare of the beneficiaries, that the Board should no longer be trustees. 10–018
>
> Probably if it had been put in this way below they would have consented. But for the benefit of the trust they should cease to be trustees, whether they consent or not . . . 10–019

3. Remuneration and Indemnification of Trustees

A. Remuneration

The basic rule is that trustees must administer the trust gratuitously for otherwise "the trust estate might be loaded and made of little value".[19] However the position has been much liberalised and modernised by the Trustee Act 2000. The main cases in which the trustee is now entitled to remuneration are as follows. 10–020

First, the court has an inherent jurisdiction to authorise a trustee to receive remuneration and it may also increase any remuneration authorised by the trust deed. The court must be satisfied that the trustee's services have been or will be of exceptional benefit to the estate.[20] Second, if the settlement authorises the trustee to charge for her services then she can do so.[21] Charging clauses used to be construed strictly, with the onus on the trustee to show that the charge she proposed to make was covered by the terms of the settlement. Thus, where a solicitor-trustee was authorised to make "professional charges", and even where the words "for her time and trouble" were added, she 10–021

---

19 *Robinson v Pett* (1734) 3 P. Wms. 249 at 251.

20 *Marshall v Holloway* (1820) 2 Swans. 432; *Docker v Somes* (1834) 2 My. & K. 655; *Re Freeman* (1887) 37 Ch.D. 148; *Re Macadam* [1946] Ch. 73; *Re Masters* [1953] 1 W.L.R. 51; *Re Worthington (Deceased)* [1954] 1 W.L.R. 526; *Re Duke of Norfolk's Settlement Trusts* [1982] Ch. 61; *Foster v Spencer* [1996] 2 All E.R. 672; *Brudenell-Bruce v Moore* [2014] EWHC 3679 (Ch); [2015] W.T.L.R. 373; *Re Portman Estate* [2015] EWHC 536 (Ch); [2015] W.T.L.R. 871.

21 For an example of such a clause see para.10–099.

could not charge for time and trouble expended other than in her position as solicitor.[22] However, the Trustee Act 2000 s.28(2) now treats a trustee entitled under the trust instrument to charge for services as being entitled to receive payment "in respect of services even if they are services which are capable of being provided by a lay trustee", so long as the trustee is "a trust corporation or is acting in a professional capacity".[23] Third, by s.29 of the Trustee Act 2000 a trustee which is a trust corporation is entitled to "reasonable remuneration",[24] while a human trustee who acts in a professional capacity and is not a sole trustee, is also entitled to reasonable remuneration if each other trustee has agreed in writing that she may be remunerated for services,[25] including services capable of being provided by a lay trustee.[26]

B. Indemnification

10–022 Although people are often willing to act as trustees without charge, e.g. because they are relations or friends of the settlor, few people would become trustees if they could not recoup themselves out of the trust funds for liabilities incurred while managing the trust affairs—something which they routinely incur as the trust has no legal personality and dealings with third parties can only be accomplished through the trustees acting personally.[27] Trust deeds often empower trustees to use trust property either to pay third parties directly or to indemnify trustees for costs and liabilities they have paid for out of their own resources.[28] This is also provided for by the Trustee Act 2000 s.31. This section reflects the established position that trustees only have a power to pay "proper costs incident to the execution of the trust".[29] However, trustees cannot claim for a liability that has been improperly incurred. Nor are trustees allowed to reimburse themselves out of the trust fund if they are themselves indebted to the trust, e.g. because they have incurred a compensatory liability for breach of trust, the reason being that a trustee's power to recoup depends on the state of accounts between them and the beneficiaries and it is limited to the balance, if any, in the trustee's favour.[30] Trustee powers of recoupment are discussed further below.[31]

4. Trustees' Administrative and Distributive Responsibilities

10–023 The trustees of many settlements, including family trusts and pension trusts, have two roles to perform: an administrative role, concerned with safeguarding and enhancing the trust fund, and a distributive role, concerned with distributing trust property to beneficiaries and/or objects of mere powers of appointment. To perform these roles trustees typically need to carry out various tasks: ascertainment of the trust terms; reduction of the trust property into possession; preservation of the trust property; investment of the trust property; distribution of the trust property; keeping of trust accounts; notification of beneficiaries and other interested parties; and provision of trust information to such parties.

---

22 *Re Chapple* (1884) 27 Ch.D. 584; *Re Orwell's Will Trusts* [1982] 1 W.L.R. 1337.
23 Trustee Act 2000 s.31(1).
24 As defined in s.29(3).
25 Trustee Act 2000 s.29(2).
26 Trustee Act 2000 s.29(4).
27 *Investec Trust (Guernsey) Ltd v Glenalla Properties Ltd* [2018] UKPC 7; [2019] A.C. 271 at [59].
28 For an example of such a clause see para.10–093 (clause 1.13).
29 *Holding & Management Ltd v Property Holding & Investment Trust Plc* [1989] 1 W.L.R. 1313 at 1324. See too *Re Grimthorpe* [1958] Ch. 615 at 623.
30 *Ex parte Edmonds* (1862) 4 De G.F. & J. 488 at 498; *Re Johnson* (1880) 15 Ch.D. 548; *Re British Power Traction & Lighting Co Ltd* [1910] 2 Ch. 470.
31 See paras 10–128 to 10–137.

A. Ascertainment of the Trust Terms

An essential first step when accepting office as a trustee is to familiarise oneself with the trust terms.[32] Trustees cannot carry out the settlor's wishes unless they know what the settlor wants them to do and how the settlor wants them to do it: which property is to be held on trust, for the benefit of which people or for what purposes, to be preserved, invested and distributed by the exercise of what powers and in accordance with what permissions. How much trouble trustees should take to familiarise themselves with these matters depends on the situation, however. As Newey J said in *Re Prudential Staff Pension Scheme*:[33] **10–024**

> It is doubtless incumbent on a trustee to familiarise himself, in general terms, with his powers. However, there can be no absolute rule that a trustee must be aware of every possibility inherent in his powers. ... If it is desirable that a trustee should be able to act in a particular way, and the trustee appreciates that his powers could potentially allow him to do so, it may well be his duty to clarify the extent of his powers .... If, at the other end of the spectrum, the trustee neither knows, nor ought reasonably to know, of any uncertainty of practical importance, he can be under no obligation to obtain advice on the precise scope of his powers; in fact, spending money on an unnecessary exercise of that kind might itself be in breach of duty.

Naturally, trustees may be able to discuss what the settlor expects of them prior to the trust's creation (and of course a settlor and trustee may be one and the same person). Afterwards the trustees may also be able to ask the settlor what she wants them to do in particular situations, and they may legitimately take her wishes into account even if these differ from her wishes at the time when the trust was first created[34] —although they must not surrender their discretions[35] and they need to avoid falling foul of the sham doctrine.[36] When courts speak of trustees owing a general duty "to obey the terms of the trust",[37] they commonly have two other sources of information in mind, however: namely, the clauses in the trust deed which specify the details of the settlement and rules of law which add further details unless these are excluded or varied by the settlor. **10–025**

In other words, many of the trust terms are typically laid out in the trust instrument but some are not. There are some terms which *must be* expressly stated or there will not be a trust, owing to rules which require certain matters to be stated with certainty, e.g. the identity of the trust property and object(s).[38] Other terms, however, may be supplied by the operation of statutory or equitable rules that require or permit trustees to do certain things. Examples are statutory rules which describe the scope of the trustees' investment powers and statutory rules which allow them to use trust property to pay trust expenses: whenever an express trust is created these powers vest in the trustees by default.[39] **10–026**

---

[32] *Harvey v Oliver* (1887) 57 L.T. 239 at 241; *Hallows v Lloyd* (1888) 39 Ch.D. 688 at 691; *Nestle v National Westminster Bank Plc* [1993] 1 W.L.R. 1260 at 1265; *Jones v Firkin-Flood* [2008] EWHC 2417 (Ch) at [240]. See too New Zealand Trusts Act 2019 s.23. Cf. Charity Commission, *CC3 Guidance: The Essential Trustee: What You Need to Know, What You Need to Do* (2018) para.4.1.

[33] [2011] EWHC 960 (Ch); [2011] P.L.R. 239 at [235].

[34] *Hartigan Nominees Pty Ltd v Rydge* (1992) 29 N.S.W.L.R. 405 at 431. *Abacus Trust Co (Isle of Man) Ltd v Barr* [2003] EWHC 114 (Ch); [2003] Ch. 409 at [23]–[25]; *Re Esteem Settlement* [2004] W.T.L.R. 1 at [166]; *Charman v Charman* [2005] EWCA Civ 1606; [2006] 1 W.L.R. 1053 at [12]; *Kain v Public Trust* [2021] NZCA 685 at [113]–[148].

[35] *Turner v Turner* [1984] Ch. 100.

[36] For discussion of which see paras 7–059 to 7–070.

[37] *Youyang Pty Ltd v Minter Ellison Moris Fletcher* (2003) 212 C.L.R. 484 at [32]. See too *Space Investments Investments Ltd v Canadian Imperial Bank of Commerce Trust Co (Bahamas) Ltd* [1986] 1 W.L.R. 1072 at 1075; New Zealand Trusts Act 2019 s.24.

[38] See Chapter 7.

[39] Trustee Act 2000 s.3 (trustee may invest trust property) and s.31 (trustee's indemnity for expenses).

B. Reduction of the Trust Property into Possession

10–027 On taking up her appointment, a trustee should "get the trust property in, protect it, and vindicate the rights attaching to it",[40] ensuring that all of it is under her control and that of the other trustees.[41] There was formerly a rule that title to the trust property therefore had to be vested in the joint names of all the trustees,[42] but it can now suffice for title to be vested in the name of a duly authorised nominee or custodian.[43] Where trust property includes choses in action, such as debts, trustees should be active in calling these in and they may incur personal liability if they unreasonably delay in doing this.[44] A person appointed as a new trustee of an existing trust must also investigate any suspicious circumstances suggesting that a breach of trust may have occurred, so that action can be taken to recover any missing funds if necessary.[45]

C. Preservation of the Trust Property

10–028 A trustee is expected to "preserve the assets of the trust except in so far as the terms of the trust permit [her] to do otherwise".[46] At any given moment, she must therefore be able to prove that she is still the owner of the trust property, unless she can show that she has disposed of it in an authorised way, e.g. by proving that she has distributed the property to a beneficiary.[47] "Preservation" of the trust property thus includes retaining ownership of the property unless this has been transferred to other people in an authorised transaction.

10–029 According to Peter Gibson LJ in *Duggan v Governor of HM Prison, Full Sutton*, "a trustee would normally have to keep trust monies separate not only from his own monies but also from other monies which the trustee holds for other beneficiaries."[48] However, *Duggan* appears to be the only English authority for the proposition that trustees are *required* to segregate trust property from their own property.[49] It is true that when an owner transfers property to another with an instruction to segregate this may be treated as evidence of the transferor's intention to create a trust.[50] It is also true that there

---

40 *CGU Insurance Ltd v One Tel Ltd (in liq.)* (2010) 242 C.L.R. 174 at [36], reaffirmed in *Fischer v Nemeske Pty Ltd* (2016) 257 C.L.R. 615 at [111].

41 *Wyman v Paterson* [1900] A.C. 271 at 288.

42 *Wyman v Paterson* [1900] A.C. 271 at 289. See also *Lewis v Nobbs* (1878) 8 Ch.D. 591; *Hallows v Lloyd* (1888) 39 Ch.D. 686 at 691; *Field v Field* [1894] 1 Ch. 425 at 429.

43 Trustee Act 2000 ss.16–23.

44 *Re Stevens* [1898] 1 Ch. 162 at 171; *Partridge v Equity Trustees Executors and Agency Co Ltd* (1947) 75 C.L.R. 149.

45 *Re Strahan* (1856) 8 De G.M. & G. 291; *Re Forest of Dean Coal Co* (1878) 10 Ch.D. 250; *Young v Murphy* [1996] 1 V.R. 279.

46 *AIB Group (UK) Plc v Mark Redler & Co Solicitors* [2014] UKSC 58; [2015] A.C. 1503 at [51]. See too *Low v Bouverie* [1891] 3 Ch. 82 at 99; *Alsop Wilkinson v Neary* [1996] 1 W.L.R. 1220 at 1223; *ED&F Man Capital Markets Ltd v Come Harvest Holdings Ltd* [2022] EWHC 229 (Comm) at [615].

47 Further see paras 13–009 to 13–017.

48 [2004] EWCA Civ 78; [2004] 1 W.L.R. 1010 at [42]. See also Chadwick LJ's statement to the same effect at [37]; and *Associated Alloys Pty Ltd v ACN 001 452 106 Pty Ltd (In Liq.)* (2000) 202 C.L.R. 588 at [34].

49 Solicitors who act as trustees are usually required to segregate the trust property from their own property not because they are trustees but because they must comply with the Accounts Rules issued by the Solicitors Regulation Authority; these are published online at *https://www.sra.org.uk/solicitors/standards-regulations/accounts-rules/*. These require solicitors to keep client money separate from the firm's own money (rule 4), to pay client money only into a client account (rule 2, but with a few exceptions), and to maintain any client account with a bank in England and Wales (rule 3). There is no rule that there must be a separate client account for each client. Nor is there any provision authorising a single account for all clients. In practice solicitors nonetheless have a single client account for all client monies, although sometimes they open a separate account temporarily for a specific large deposit from a particular client.

50 See e.g. *Henry v Hammond* [1913] 2 K.B. 515 at 521; *Customs & Excise Commissioners v Richmond Theatre Management Ltd* [1995] S.T.C. 257; and discussion at paras 7–043 to 7–051. See also *Prickly Bay Waterside Ltd v British American Insurance Co Ltd* [2022] UKPC 8 at [42], and discussion at paras 16–143 to 16–155.

are often good practical reasons for trustees to keep trust property separate from their own property. But there is no particular reason to place them under a *duty* to do this, breach of which triggers a compensatory liability, given that in cases where there has been mixing followed by a disposal that causes a loss the trustees are likely to incur liability for non-compliance with other rules in any case. This was the reason given by HHJ Matthews for doubting the soundness of *Duggan* in *Batt v Boswell*:[51]

> There can be no doubt that mixing trust and personal money, or trust and other trust money, increases the risks both of an unauthorised investment and of a misapplication of trust money, both of which are certainly breaches of trust. But mixing is not of itself either an unauthorised investment or a misapplication, because the mixed fund may be in the form of an authorised investment, and the trust funds remain intact, and continue to be available for distribution to those entitled. So, despite what [was said by the Court of Appeal in *Duggan*], it is not clear to me why a mere mixing should *itself* be a breach of trust.

The "preservation" of trust property can also include taking steps to stop it from deteriorating so that e.g. where the property is land trustees may have to spend trust money on repairs.[52] It may also be appropriate in some cases for trustees to insure it.[53] In the case of company shares, where the trustees hold a majority stake in a private company so that they are entitled to oversee the directors and take steps to replace them if their performance is unsatisfactory, the trustees may have to keep themselves informed about the company's affairs, liaise with the directors and take action against them if necessary.[54] This is discussed further in Chapter 13.[55] **10–030**

D. Investment of the Trust Property

According to Heydon and Crennan JJ in *Byrnes v Kendle*:[56] **10–031**

> Even if there is no direction in the trust instrument that the trust property be invested, it is the duty of the trustee to invest the trust property subject to the limits permitted by the legislation in force under the proper law of the trust and subject to any limits stated in the trust document.[57] If there are no limits of that kind, a trustee who receives a trust asset, like an executor of a deceased estate, must "lay it out for the benefit of the estate."[58] That is, it is the duty of a trustee to obtain income from the trust property if it is capable of yielding an income. If the property is money, it should be invested at interest or used to purchase income-yielding assets like shares. If the property consists of business assets, it should be employed in a business. If the property is lettable land, it should be let for rent.[59] And if the intended means of gaining an income turn out to be unsatisfactory, those means must be abandoned and others found.

---

51 [2022] EWHC 649 (Ch) at [120]. See also his review of the English case law cited to him on the point in [90]–[123]. And cf. *McLaughlin Estate v McLaughlin* (2001) 43 E.T.R. (2d) 65 at [31]: "while it is clearly prudent that a trustee segregate trust funds and this practice is to be encouraged, there is no absolute legal duty requiring that trustees segregate all trust funds in all circumstances." But cf. Jersey and Guernsey trust law, which both expressly provide for segregation: Trusts (Jersey) Law 1984 art.21(6); Trusts (Guernsey) Law 2007 s.27.

52 Trustees of a trust of land have statutory powers to repair the property under the Trusts of Land and Appointment of Trustees Act 1996 s.6(1), although s.8(1) provides that these can be excluded by a term of the trust instrument.

53 An express power to do which may be included in the trust instrument, and a statutory power to do which can be found in the Trustee Act 1925 s.19.

54 *Bartlett v Barclays Bank Trust Co Ltd* [1980] Ch. 515. Trustees who negligently fail to take such steps may incur a compensatory liability in the event of loss, but this may be excluded by a so-called "anti-*Bartlett*" clause in the trust instrument as in e.g. *Zhang Hong Li v DBS Bank (Hong Kong) Ltd* (2019) 22 H.K.C.F.A.R. 392.

55 See paras 13–097 to 13–110.

56 (2011) 243 C.L.R. 253 at [119].

57 *Stafford v Fiddon* (1857) 23 Beav. 386; *Adamson v Reid* (1880) 6 V.L.R. (E.) 164 at 167; *Gilroy v Stephens* (1882) 51 L.J. Ch. 834; *Re Jones* (1883) 49 L.T. 91; *Wharton v Masterman* [1895] AC 186 at 197.

58 *Rocke v Hart* (1805) 11 Ves. Jun. 58 at 60.

59 *Earl of Egmont v Smith* (1877) 6 Ch. D. 469 at 476; *Re Byrne* (1902) 19 W.N. (N.S.W.) 141.

10-031A A trustee wishing to implement an investment strategy by selling trust property or using trust money to buy new property must be able to assign ownership of the relevant trust asset to the buyer or seller free of the beneficiaries' equitable interest. This is accomplished by the doctrine of overreaching, by operation of which the beneficiaries' interest in trust property is extinguished when the trustee assigns ownership of the property to a third party in a transaction permitted by the trust terms.[60] This doctrine applies where trustees distribute trust property to authorised beneficiaries as well as where they exchange it for other property for reasons of investment.[61] In cases of the latter kind, the new property acquired by the trustees is thereafter held by the trustees as part of the trust fund for the beneficiaries,[62] an outcome that is often expressly stipulated in trust instruments.[63]

10-032 Trustees must familiarise themselves with their powers of investment so that they know whether particular types of investment are authorised by the trust instrument, or by the court,[64] or in default by the Trustee Act 2000. A properly drafted trust instrument will contain extensive powers of investment so that there is no need to apply to the court for wider powers, or otherwise to rely on the Trustee Act 2000. Trustees should review the portfolio of trust investments regularly,[65] and if lacking investment knowledge they should take professional advice and consider this before acting on it.[66] These principles now find statutory expression in ss.4 and 5 of the Trustee Act 2000, but notice that trustees might legitimately decide against diversification of a trust portfolio if they have been instructed by the settlor to retain particular assets within the trust fund.[67]

Trustee Act 2000 ss.4 and 5

4. Standard investment criteria

10-033 (1) In exercising any power of investment, whether arising under this Part or otherwise, a trustee must have regard to the standard investment criteria.

(2) A trustee must from time to time review the investments of the trust and consider whether, having regard to the standard investment criteria, they should be varied.

(3) The standard investment criteria, in relation to a trust, are—

(a) the suitability to the trust of investments of the same kind as any particular investment proposed to be made or retained and of that particular investment as an investment of that kind, and

---

60 The general doctrine of overreaching does not apply where trustees assign ownership of trust property to recipients in transactions that are not permitted by the trust terms or are entered for an improper purpose: *Independent Trustee Services Ltd v GP Noble Trustees Ltd* [2012] EWCA Civ 195; [2013] Ch. 91 at [106], reproduced at para.12–082; cf. C. Harpum, "Overreaching, Trustees' Powers and the Reform of the 1925 Legislation" [1990] C.L.J. 277, endorsed in *State Bank of India v Sood* [1997] Ch. 276 at 281; G. Ferris and G. Battersby, "The General Principles of Overreaching and the Reforms of 1925" (2002) 118 L.Q.R. 270, 270–272. See also paras 11–027, 11–073 to 11–077, 15–128, 15–140 and 15–149. Special rules apply in relation to trusts of land, for which see ss.2 and 27 of the Law of Property Act 1925, also discussed in the foregoing articles and more recently considered in e.g. *Baker v Craggs* [2018] EWCA Civ 1126; [2018] Ch. 617, noted by A. Televantos, "Overreaching and Trusts of Land" [2019] C.L.J. 516.

61 As noted in *Ali v Dinc* [2020] EWHC 3055 (Ch); [2021] 2 p. & C.R. 19 at [318]. See too paras 6–029 and 6–082.

62 *Byers v Saudi National Bank* [2022] EWCA Civ 43; [2022] 4 W.L.R. 22 at [25], approving *Lewin on Trusts*, 20th edn (2020), para.44–014.

63 See para.15–128. Clause 1.5.2 of the specimen trust deed reproduced below at para.10.085 expresses the same idea in a truncated form.

64 The court's powers are in the Trustee Act 1925 s.57, and the Variation of Trusts Act 1958.

65 *Nestlé v National Westminster Bank Plc* [1994] 1 All E.R. 118.

66 *Cowan v Scargill* [1985] Ch. 279; *Jones v AMP Perpetual Trustee Co NZ Ltd* [1994] 1 N.Z.L.R. 690. Pension trustees are required to seek advice by the Pensions Act 1995 s.36, for breach of which duty the defendant trustees were held liable in *Adams v Bridge* [2009] Pens. L.R. 153.

67 *Gregson v HAE Trustees Ltd* [2008] EWHC 1006 (Ch); [2009] 1 All E.R. (Comm.) 457 at [70]–[92].

(b) the need for diversification of investments of the trust, in so far as is appropriate to the circumstances of the trust.

5. Advice

(1) Before exercising any power of investment, whether arising under this Part or otherwise, a trustee must (unless the exception applies) obtain and consider proper advice about the way in which, having regard to the standard investment criteria, the power should be exercised. **10–034**

(2) When reviewing the investments of the trust, a trustee must (unless the exception applies) obtain and consider proper advice about whether, having regard to the standard investment criteria, the investments should be varied.

(3) The exception is that a trustee need not obtain such advice if he reasonably concludes that in all the circumstances it is unnecessary or inappropriate to do so.

(4) Proper advice is the advice of a person who is reasonably believed by the trustee to be qualified to give it by his ability in and practical experience of financial and other matters relating to the proposed investment.

Trustees acting within their investment powers are entitled to be judged by the standards of modern portfolio theory, which emphasises the risk level of the entire portfolio rather than the risk attaching to each investment in isolation.[68] This requires portfolio securities to have a low co-variance with each other, where a high co-variance means that the values of two assets are likely to move in the same direction, and a low co-variance means that they are likely to move in opposite directions. Having different types of investment within the trust portfolio is not enough in itself: e.g. land and government bonds are different types of investment, but movements in interest rates affect both in the same way. This is touched on by Lord Nicholls in the next excerpt. **10–035**

Lord Nicholls, "Trustees and Their Broader Community: Where Duty, Morality and Ethics Converge"

(1995) 9 Tru. L.I. 71 at 73–74

. . . It is not enough that a trustee should act honestly. Promotion of the trust purpose requires a trustee to be prudent and exercise the degree of care he would in conducting his own affairs but mindful, when making investment decisions, that he is dealing with another's property. The classic formulation of this standard of conduct was enunciated by Lindley L.J. in *Re Whiteley*.[69] The duty of a trustee is not to take such care only as a prudent man would take if he had only himself to consider; the duty is rather to take such care as an ordinary prudent man would take if he were minded to make an investment for the benefit of other people for whom he felt morally bound to provide. . . . This "ordinary prudent person conducting another's affairs" is the equitable counterpart of the reasonable man who is so ubiquitous in the common law. . . . A comment is needed here on the ordinary prudent person. His standards are the minimum standards expected of trustees. If the trustee is a person professing particular expertise in the management of trusts, and he has been appointed for that reason, his conduct will be judged by the standards he professes. A professional person, a trust corporation, held out as an expert, will be expected to display the degree of skill and care and diligence such an expert would have. **10–036**

Investment policy is aimed at producing a portfolio of investments which is balanced overall and suited to the needs of the particular trust. Different investments are accompanied by different degrees of risk, which are reflected in the expected rate of return. A large fund with a widely diversified portfolio of securities might justifiably include modest holdings of high risk securities which would be imprudent and out of place in a smaller fund. In such a case it would be inappropriate to isolate one particular investment **10–037**

68 On modern portfolio theory, see J. Langbein, "The Uniform Prudent Investor Act and the Future of Trust Investing" (1996) 81 Iowa L.R. 641; I.N. Legair, "Modern Portfolio Theory: A Primer" (2000) 14 Tru L.I. 75.

69 (1886) 33 Ch.D. 347 at 355.

out of a vast portfolio and enquire whether that can be justified as a trust investment. Such a 'line by line' approach is misplaced. The inquiry, rather, should be to look at a particular investment and enquire whether that is justified as a holding in the context of the overall portfolio. Traditional warnings against the need for trustees to avoid speculative or hazardous investments are not to be read as inhibiting trustees from maintaining portfolios of investments which contain a prudent and sensible mixture of low risk and higher risk securities. They are not to be so read, because they were not directed at a portfolio which is a balanced exercise in risk management.

10-038 Unless otherwise directed, the trustees of private trusts for persons must make investment decisions which are in the beneficiaries' best financial interests. If the trustees have strong moral objections, e.g. to the arms trade or the tobacco industry, but investment in companies which pursue such activities is likely to produce a better financial return than other investments, then the trustees must make such investments, though they can avoid this if they can identify other investments that are likely to perform equally well. This is the ratio of *Cowan v Scargill*.[70] Analogous but more elaborate rules govern the extent to which charity trustees can and should pursue an ethical investment policy that accords with the charitable purposes of the trust.[71]

Cowan v Scargill

Chancery Division [1985] Ch. 270

10-039 Under a mineworkers' pension scheme set up by the National Coal Board, a committee of management was formed of ten trustees (five appointed by the Board and five by the National Union of Mineworkers) to control and administer funds provided by members' contributions to the scheme and by contributions by the Board of approximately the same amount. The funds totalled some £3,000 million, with some £200 million available for investment each year. The committee had wide powers of investment which they used with the assistance of an advisory panel of experts. An investment plan was submitted by a sub-committee for approval, but the five union trustees on the committee of management objected to investments in oil, investments overseas, and the acquisition of land overseas. The five Board trustees sought the court's directions as to whether the union trustees were in breach of duty in holding up the adoption of the investment plan. Megarry V.-C. held that they were, because their objections could not be justified on broad economic grounds, and were only remotely in the interests of the beneficiaries, for whom there would be no advantage in excluding investments overseas or investments in competition with the coal industry.

10-040 MEGARRY V.-C.: . . . I turn to the law. The starting point is the duty of trustees to exercise their powers in the best interests of the present and future beneficiaries of the trust, holding the scales impartially between different classes of beneficiaries. This duty of the trustees towards their beneficiaries is paramount. They must, of course, obey the law; but subject to that, they must put the interests of their beneficiaries first. When the purpose of the trust is to provide financial benefits for the beneficiaries, as is usually the case, the best interests of the beneficiaries are normally their best financial interests. In the case of a power of investment, as in the present case, the power must be exercised so as to yield the best return for the beneficiaries, judged in relation to the risks of the investments in question; and the prospects of the yield of income and capital appreciation both have to be considered in judging the return from the investment.

10-041 The legal memorandum that the union obtained from their solicitors is generally in accord with these views. In considering the possibility of investment for "socially beneficial reasons which may result in lower returns to the fund", the memorandum states that "the trustees' only concern is to ensure that the return is

---

70 See also *Buttle v Saunders* [1950] 2 All E.R. 193.

71 *Butler-Sloss v Charity Commission for England and Wales* [2022] EWHC 974 (Ch); [2022] 3 W.L.R. 182, considering *Harries v Church Commissioners for England* [1992] 1 W.L.R. 1241. In 2014, the Charity Commission published general guidance on charity investments, which was updated in 2016 after the coming into force of the Charities (Protection and Social Investment) Act 2016: *Charities and Investment Matters: A Guide for Trustees (CC14)*; online at: *https://assets.publishing.service.gov.uk/government/uploads/system/uploads/attachment_data/file/857987/CC14_new.pdf*. Parts of this guidance will have to be amended in light of Green J's statement of legal principles in the *Butler-Sloss* case.

the maximum possible consistent with security"; and then it refers to the need for diversification. However, it continues by saying:

> "Trustees cannot be criticised for failing to make a particular investment for social or political reasons, such as in South African stock for example, but may be held liable for investing in assets which yield a poor return or for disinvesting in stock at inappropriate times for non-financial criteria."

This last sentence must be considered in the light of subsequent passages in the memorandum which indicate that the sale of South African securities by trustees might be justified on the ground of doubts about political stability in South Africa and the long-term financial soundness of its economy, whereas trustees could not properly support motions at a company meeting dealing with pay levels in South Africa, work accidents, pollution control, employment conditions for minorities, military contracting and consumer protection. The assertion that trustees could not be criticised for failing to make a particular investment for social or political reasons is one that I would not accept in its full width. If the investment in fact made is equally beneficial to the beneficiaries, then criticism would be difficult to sustain in practice, whatever the position in theory. But if the investment in fact made is less beneficial, then both in theory and in practice the trustees would normally be open to criticism. 10-042

This leads me to the second point, which is a corollary of the first. In considering what investments to make trustees must put on one side their own personal interests and views. Trustees may have strongly held social or political views. They may be firmly opposed to any investment in South Africa or other countries, or they may object to any form of investment in companies concerned with alcohol, tobacco, armaments or many other things. In the conduct of their own affairs, of course, they are free to abstain from making any such investments. Yet under a trust, if investments of this type would be more beneficial to the beneficiaries than other investments, the trustees must not refrain from making the investments by reason of the views that they hold. 10-043

Trustees may even have to act dishonourably (though not illegally) if the interests of their beneficiaries require it. Thus where trustees for sale had struck a bargain for the sale of trust property but had not bound themselves by a legally enforceable contract, they were held to be under a duty to consider and explore a better offer that they received, and not to carry through the bargain to which they felt in honour bound.[72] In other words, the duty of trustees to their beneficiaries may include a duty to "gazump", however honourable the trustees. As Wynn-Parry J. said trustees "have an overriding duty to obtain the best price which they can for their beneficiaries".[73] . . . 10-044

Powers must be exercised fairly and honestly for the purposes for which they are given and not so as to accomplish any ulterior purpose, whether for the benefit of the trustees or otherwise.[74] 10-045

Third, by way of a caveat I should say that I am not asserting that the benefit of the beneficiaries which a trustee must make his paramount concern inevitably and solely means their financial benefit, even if the only object of the trust is to provide financial benefits. Thus if the only actual or potential beneficiaries of a trust are all adults with very strict views on moral and social matters, condemning all forms of alcohol, tobacco and popular entertainment, as well as armaments, I can well understand that it might not be for the "benefit" of such beneficiaries to know that they are obtaining rather larger financial returns under the trust by reason of investments in those activities than they would have received if the trustees had invested the trust funds in other investments. The beneficiaries might well consider that it was far better to receive less than to receive more money from what they consider to be evil and tainted sources. "Benefit" is a word with a very wide meaning, and there are circumstances in which arrangements which work to the financial disadvantage of a beneficiary may yet be for his benefit.[75] But I would emphasise that such cases are likely to be very rare, and in any case I think that under a trust for the provision of financial benefits the burden would rest, and rest heavy, on him who asserts that it is for the benefit of the beneficiaries as a whole to receive less by reason of the exclusion of some of the possibly more profitable forms of investment. Plainly the present case is not one of this rare type of case. Subject to such matters, under 10-046

---

72 *Buttle v Saunders* [1950] 2 All E.R. 193.

73 *Buttle* at 195.

74 See *Duke of Portland v Topham* (1864) 11 H.L. Cas. 32, a case on a power of appointment that must apply a fortiori to a power given to trustees as such.

75 See, for example, *Re Towler's Settlement Trusts* [1964] Ch. 158; *Re CL* [1969] 1 Ch. 587.

a trust for the provision of financial benefits, the paramount duty of the trustees is to provide the greatest financial benefits for the present and future beneficiaries.

10-047 Fourth, the standard required of a trustee in exercising his powers of investment is that he must

> "take such care as an ordinary prudent man would take if he were minded to make an investment for the benefit of other people for whom he felt morally bound to provide".[76]

That duty includes the duty to seek advice on matters which the trustee does not understand, such as the making of investments, and on receiving that advice to act with the same degree of prudence. This requirement is not discharged merely by showing that the trustee has acted in good faith and with sincerity. Honesty and sincerity are not the same as prudence and reasonableness. Some of the most sincere people are the most unreasonable; and Mr Scargill told me that he had met quite a few of them. Accordingly, although a trustee who takes advice on investments is not bound to accept and act on that advice, he is not entitled to reject it merely because he sincerely disagrees with it, unless in addition to being sincere he is acting as an ordinary prudent man would act.

10-048 Fifth, trustees have a duty to consider the need for diversification of investments . . . The degree of diversification that is practicable and desirable for a large fund may plainly be impracticable or undesirable (or both) in the case of a small fund.

10-049 In the case before me, it is not in issue that there ought to be diversification of the investments held by the fund. The contention of the defendants, put very shortly, is that there can be a sufficient degree of diversification without any investment overseas or in oil, and that in any case there is no need to increase the level of overseas investments beyond the existing level. Other pension funds got on well enough without overseas investments, it was said, and in particular the N.U.M.'s own scheme had, in 1982, produced better results than the scheme here in question. . .

10-050 I shall not pursue this matter. Even if other funds in one particular year, or in many years, had done better than the scheme which is before me, that does not begin to show that it is beneficial to this scheme to be shorn of the ability to invest overseas. . .

10-051 Sixth, there is the question whether the principles that I have been stating apply, with or without modification, to trusts of pension funds. Mr. Stamler asserted that they applied without modification, and that it made no difference that some of the funds came from the members of the pension scheme, or that the funds were often of a very substantial size. Mr. Scargill did not in terms assert the contrary. He merely said that this was one of the questions to be decided, and that pension funds may be subject to different rules. I was somewhat unsuccessful in my attempts to find out from him why this was so, and what the differences were. What it came down to, I think, was that the rules for trusts had been laid down for private and family trusts and wills a long time ago; that pension funds were very large and affected large numbers of people; that in the present case the well-being of all within the coal industry was affected; . . .

10-052 I can see no reason for holding that different principles apply to pension fund trusts from those which apply to other trusts. Of course, there are many provisions in pension schemes which are not to be found in private trusts, and to these the general law of trusts will be subordinated. But subject to that, I think that the trusts of pension funds are subject to the same rules as other trusts. The large size of pension funds emphasises the need for diversification, rather than lessening it, and the fact that much of the fund has been contributed by members of the scheme seems to me to make it even more important that the trustees should exercise their powers in the best interests of the beneficiaries. In a private trust, most, if not all, of the beneficiaries are the recipients of the bounty of the settlor, whereas under the trusts of a pension fund many (though not all) of the beneficiaries are those who, as members, contributed to the funds so that in due time they would receive pensions. It is thus all the more important that the interests of the beneficiaries should be paramount, so that they may receive the benefits which in part they have paid for. I can see no justification for holding that the benefits to them should run the risk of being lessened because the trustees were pursuing an investment policy intended to assist the industry that the pensioners have left, or their union. . .

10-053 I reach the unhesitating conclusion that the trusts of pension funds are in general governed by the ordinary law of trusts, subject to any contrary provision in the rules or other provisions which govern the trust. In particular, the trustees of a pension fund are subject to the overriding duty to do the best that they

[76] See *Re Whiteley* (1886) 33 Ch.D. 347 at 355, per Lindley L.J. and see also at 350, 358; *Learoyd v Whiteley* (1887) 12 App. Cas. 727.

> can for the beneficiaries, the duty that in the United States is known as "the duty of undivided loyalty to the beneficiaries".[77]
>
> In considering that duty, it must be remembered that very many of the beneficiaries will not in any way be directly affected by the prosperity of the mining industry or the union. Miners who have retired, and the widows and children of deceased miners, will continue to receive their benefits from the fund even if the mining industry shrinks: for the scheme is fully funded, and the fund does not depend on further contributions to it being made . . . I cannot regard any policy designed to ensure the general prosperity of coal mining as being a policy which is directed to obtaining the best possible results for the beneficiaries, most of whom are no longer engaged in the industry, and some of whom never were. The connection is far too remote and insubstantial. Further, the assets of even so large a pension fund as this are nowhere near the size at which there could be expected to be any perceptible impact from the adoption of the policies for which Mr Scargill contends. . . **10–054**

Note, finally, that under some trusts different classes of beneficiary have different financial interests, all of which the trustees must take into account when making their investment decisions. For example, where there is a trust which confers a life interest on X and a remainder interest on Y, the trustees might conceivably attempt to optimise X's financial interest by investing for maximum income yield or to optimise Y's financial interest by investing for maximum capital growth. As a general rule, neither strategy would be permissible and the trustees would be expected "to administer the trust fund impartially or fairly, having regard to the different interests of beneficiaries."[78] Exceptionally, though, it seems that a trustee could validly prioritise the income needs of a penurious life tenant who was close to the settlor (e.g. the settlor's widow) over the interest of a remainderman who was a wealthy remoter relative or stranger, so as to tilt the balance in favour of the life tenant even if this could lead to the real value of the capital being eroded.[79] **10–055**

The latter finding might be explained on the basis that, in Chadwick LJ's words:[80] **10–056**

> Properly understood, the so-called duty to act impartially [as between different classes of beneficiary or other objects of a power] is no more than the ordinary duty which the law imposes on a person who is entrusted with the exercise of a discretionary power: that he exercises the power for the purpose for which it is given, giving proper consideration to the matters which are relevant and excluding from consideration matters which are irrelevant. If trustees do that, they cannot be criticised if they reach a decision which appears to prefer the claims of one interest over others. The preference will be the result of a proper exercise of the discretionary power.

E. Distribution of the Trust Property

The trustees of every private trust for persons must ultimately distribute the trust property to parties identified by the settlor as objects, but the circumstances in which they should do this can vary widely according to the choices made by the settlor. When to distribute, to whom, and in what amounts are all matters which might be tightly prescribed or left to the trustees' discretion. The less discretion trustees have, the less they have to think about when implementing the settlor's wishes. **10–057**

In a simple case where trustees are told only that they should hold property until the settlor instructs them to return it or transfer it to a named third party, they need only ensure that they obey **10–058**

---

77 *Blankenship v Boyle* 329 F. Supp. 1089 (1971) at 1095.

78 *Nestle v National Westminster Bank* [1994] 1 All E.R. 118 at 136. See too *Re Mulligan* [1998] 1 N.Z.L.R. 481. And cf *Stuart v Stuart* (1841) 3 Beav. 430; *Raby v Ridehalgh* (1855) 7 De G.M. & G. 104.

79 Ibid at 137.

80 *Edge v Pensions Ombudsman* [2000] Ch. 602 at 627. This case was not itself concerned with the exercise of investment powers in a way that benefited one class of beneficiaries more than other, but with the exercise of powers to amend the terms of a pension fund in a way that benefited one class of members more than another.

instructions when these arrive.[81] However, trustees may be given more complex tasks. Consider, for example, the position of trustees with a discretion exercisable as between the members of a wide class of objects. According to Lord Wilberforce in *Re Baden's Deed Trusts (No.1)* such a trustee would:[82]

> make it his duty to know what is the permissible area of selection and then consider responsibly, in individual cases, whether a contemplated beneficiary was within the power and whether, in relation to other possible claimants, a particular grant was appropriate. ... [The trustee] would examine the field, by class and category; might indeed make diligent and careful inquiries, depending on how much money he had to give away and the means at his disposal, as to the composition and needs of particular categories and of individuals within them; decide upon certain priorities or proportions, and then select individuals according to their needs or qualifications.

F. Keeping of Trust Accounts

10–059 Trustees should keep track of what they do with the trust property, keep accounts and produce these on demand, along with supporting documentation.[83] Trustees "who indefensibly fail to produce accounts may be ordered to pay not only the costs of proceedings to obtain the accounts but also the costs of taking the account which is ordered".[84] Every beneficiary "is entitled to see the trust accounts, whether his interest is in possession or not".[85] The point of this is not only that good book-keeping is essential for sound management, but also to empower entitled parties to monitor and enforce the trustees' performance of the trust, and trustees may therefore have to account not only to beneficiaries with a current vested interest, but also to beneficiaries with a future interest,[86] including people who are only the likely objects of a discretionary power which may never be exercised in their favour.[87] This is discussed further below.[88]

G. Notification of Beneficiaries and Other Interested Parties

10–060 For the same underlying reason (i.e. to ensure accountability of trustees to the people for whose benefit the trust was created), sui juris beneficiaries are entitled to be told that they are beneficiaries, and trustees should notify them this fact if the settlor has not told them already.[89] However, trustees

---

81 Examples of such trusts which are discussed elsewhere in this book include the trust on which the Royal College of Surgeons held the shares for Vandervell in *Vandervell v IRC* [1967] 2 A.C. 291 (see paras 6–066 to 6–083) and the trust on which Mark Redler & Co held the purchase money in its client account for AIB in *AIB Group (UK) Plc v Mark Redler & Co Solicitors* [2014] UKSC 58; [2015] A.C. 1503 (see paras 13–058 to 13–085).

82 [1971] A.C. 424 at 449.

83 *White v Lady Lincoln* (1803) 8 Ves. Jun. 363; *Pearse v Green* (1819) 1 Jac. & W. 135 at 140; *Eglin v Sanderson* (1862) 3 Giff. 434 at 440; *Re Cowin* (1886) 33 Ch.D. 179; *Re Rabaiotti's 1989 Settlement* [2000] W.T.L.R. 953; *Schmidt v Rosewood Trust Ltd* [2003] UKPC 26; [2003] 2 A.C. 709; *Byrnes v Kendle* (2011) 243 C.L.R. 253 at [42]; *Re EA Scott (1991 Children's Settlement No.1)* [2012] EWHC 2397 (Ch); [2012] W.T.L.R. 1439; *Hancock v Rinehart* (2015) 106 A.C.S.R. 207 at [339].

84 *Mason v Coleman* [2007] EWHC 3149 (Ch) at [93]. See too *Kemp v Burn* (1863) 4 Giff. 348; *Jefferys v Marshall* (1870) 23 L.T. 548; *Re Skinner* [1904] 1 Ch. 289; *Re Den Haag Trust* (1997/98) 1 O.F.L.R. 495.

85 *Armitage v Nurse* [1998] Ch. 241 at 261.

86 Including contingent interests: *Re Tillott* [1892] 1 Ch. 86; *Attorney General of Ontario v Stavro* (1995) 119 D.L.R. (4th) 750.

87 *Chaine-Nickson v Bank of Ireland* [1976] I.R. 393; *Spellson v George* (1987) 11 N.S.W.L.R. 300 at 315–316; *Hartigan Nominees Pty Ltd v Rydge* (1992) 29 N.S.W.L.R. 405; *Re Rabbaiotti's 1989 Settlement* [2000] W.T.L.R. 953; *Schmidt v Rosewood Trust Ltd* [2003] UKPC 26; [2003] 2 A.C. 709.

88 See paras 10–063 to 10–076.

89 *Brittlebank v Goodwin* (1868) L.R. 5 Eq. 541 at 550; *Hawkesley v May* [1956] 1 Q.B. 304; *Foreman v Kingstone* [2005] W.T.L.R. 823 at [85]. The beneficiary also has the right to be told the name and address of the trustee to whom a request can be made for a discretionary distribution: *Re Murphy's Settlement* [1999] 1 W.L.R. 282, where the judge treated the claimant as a primary object of a power of appointment in a discretionary trust.

need only take such steps to identify and communicate with beneficiaries as are reasonable in all the circumstances.

Where the objects of a power of appointment consist of more than one category of person, the court may consider that only some of these people were intended by the settlor ever to receive a distribution and, therefore, that the trustees need only tell these people that they are objects and need not tell the others.[90] Suppose, for example, that a settlor declares a discretionary trust for her descendants, her other relatives known to her trustees, and employees and ex-employees of X Co Ltd (which she founded). Depending on the situation, a court might decide that the latter two classes should be treated as peripheral. However, much must depend on the facts, and as David Fox has noted:[91] **10–061**

> Where the interests of different beneficiaries were opposed to each other (as where they were the respective objects of a special power and a gift over), then the due accountability of the donee of the power might require some of each group to be notified of their status. To leave all the powers of enforcement in, say, the beneficiary of a gift over might not be sufficient to ensure the donee was effectively accountable in respect of his distinctive duties to the objects of the power.

H. Provision of Trust Information

In *Re Londonderry's Settlement*,[92] the Court of Appeal drew a distinction between trust accounts and other "trust documents" which a beneficiary is entitled to see, and material which need not be made available for inspection, for example correspondence between the trustees, or between the trustees and beneficiaries, and the agenda for trustees' meetings. Further, while "trust documents" included minutes of trustees' meetings and other documents disclosing the content of the trustees' deliberations about the exercise of their discretions, these were exempt from the beneficiaries' right to inspect trust documents. Otherwise, the right of trustees not to give reasons for the exercise of their discretionary distributive functions would be undermined.[93] The court was attracted by the argument that the beneficiaries are equitable owners of trust documents created by the expenditure of trust money, suggesting that they should be able to see them all.[94] However, this analysis made it hard to explain why any trust documents should ever be treated as confidential, although the court thought that in some situations there are good reasons why they should be so treated. **10–062**

A further problem with the "proprietary" analysis is that it suggests that disclosure of trust documents should only be made in favour of a beneficiary with an "equitable proprietary interest" in trust property, although there can be other situations where this is an appropriate thing to do. Some of these other situations have already been discussed in Chapter 3, where we saw that it is not necessary for a person to show that they have an "equitable proprietary interest" before they can be entitled to enforce a right to due administration.[95] The shift from a proprietary analysis to an analysis which focuses on a right to due administration can also be seen in the express trust context in relation to a discretionary object's access to trust information. Thus, in *Schmidt v Rosewood Trust Ltd*,[96] where Lord Walker held that the court's jurisdiction to order disclosure forms part of its inherent jurisdiction to supervise the administration of trusts. Hence the court has a discretion to order disclosure to anyone **10–063**

---

90 *Re Manisty's Settlements* [1974] Ch. 17 at 25.

91 D. Fox, "Non-Excludable Trustee Duties" (2011) 17 T.&T. 17, 21.

92 [1965] Ch. 818.

93 *Re Beloved Wilkes' Charity* (1851) 3 Mac. & G. 440; *Wilson v Law Debenture Trust Corp* [1995] 2 All E.R. 337.

94 See too *O'Rourke v Derbishire* [1920] A.C. 581 at 626, per Lord Wrenbury: "The beneficiary is entitled to see all trust documents because they are trust documents and because he is a beneficiary. They are in a sense his own."

95 See paras 3–143 to 3–192.

96 [2003] UKPC 26; [2003] 2 A.C. 709.

with a sufficient interest in the due administration of a trust to make her a suitable person to monitor the trustees and (implicitly, though he did not spell this out) to sue them for breach of trust.

Schmidt v Rosewood Trust Ltd

Privy Council [2003] 2 A.C. 709 at [43]–[67]

10-064 The petitioner sought disclosure of documents relating to two settlements of which his late father had been a settlor. The petitioner was not himself a beneficiary of either settlement nor was he even the object of a mere power of appointment vested in the trustees. However, he was the administrator of his father's estate and his father (along with other people) was the object of a mere power of appointment vested in the trustees of one of the settlements. Further, the trustees of the second settlement had a mere power of appointment which could be exercised in favour of a class of objects and, also had a power to amend the trust terms by adding further people to this class of objects, if they belonged to a (widely defined) class of objects of the amendment power – and the petitioner belonged to this second class of objects. Hence the petitioner was a person who could be added to the class of objects of the mere power of appointment under the second settlement and if this were done, he would then become a person in whose favour this power of appointment could be exercised. Given the petitioner's personal relationship with the settlor, and other evidence of the settlor's intentions, there were good reasons to believe that the settlor would have wished the trustees to do this. The Privy Council concluded that the petitioner was therefore a person in whose favour it was appropriate to make the disclosure orders sought, rejecting the argument that this should not be done because the petitioner had no equitable "proprietary" interest in the property held by the trustees of the two settlements.

LORD WALKER (giving the advice of the Privy Council): . . .

Disclosure to Discretionary Beneficiaries: A Proprietary Basis?

10-065 Much of the debate before the Board addressed the question whether a beneficiary's right or claim to disclosure of trust documents should be regarded as a proprietary right. Mr Brownbill [counsel for the trustees resisting disclosure] argued that it should be classified in that way, and from that starting point he argued that no object of a mere power could have any right or claim to disclosure, because he had no proprietary interest in the trust property. Mr. Brownbill submitted that this point has been conclusively settled by the decision of the House of Lords in *O'Rourke v Darbishire*.[97] It is therefore useful to go straight to that case to see what it did decide.

10-066 The facts of the case were unusual. Sir Joseph Whitworth, a man of considerable wealth, had died in 1887. In 1884 he had made a will appointing three executors and leaving his residuary estate to charity. By a codicil made in 1885 he altered his will to leave his ultimate residue to his executors for their own benefit, with a precatory expression of his wishes that it should be used for charitable purposes. Two further codicils executed in 1886 extended the scope of the first codicil's gift to the executors. Sir Joseph's intestate successors would have been Mrs Uniacke (as to realty) and Mrs Uniacke and Mrs McGowan (as to personalty). Mrs McGowan threatened to challenge the will and codicils, but in 1889 there was a compromise between all interested parties. Then in 1916, after Mrs Uniacke, Mrs McGowan and the executors had all died, Mrs Uniacke's administrator (Mr O'Rourke) sought to challenge both the will and codicils and the compromise, alleging fraud by Mr Darbishire (who was one of the executors and had been Sir Joseph's solicitor). Mr O'Rourke sought to obtain disclosure of documents containing legal advice given to Sir Joseph during his lifetime, and to his executors after his death.

10-067 The House of Lords dismissed Mr O'Rourke's appeal, primarily because he had not made out even a prima facie case that the will and codicils were invalid, or that the communications had been promoting fraud. Viscount Finlay[98] referred to Mr O'Rourke's reliance on a "proprietary right" and Lord Sumner[99] referred to "what has been called the 'proprietary' ground". Lord Parmoor said:[100]

97 [1920] A.C. 581.
98 Ibid at 603.
99 Ibid at 617.
100 Ibid at 619–20.

"A cestui que trust, in an action against his trustees, is generally entitled to the production for inspection of all documents relating to the affairs of the trust. It is not material for the present purpose whether this right is to be regarded as a paramount proprietary right in the cestui que trust, or as a right to be enforced under the law of discovery, since in both cases an essential preliminary is either the admission, or the establishment, of the status on which the right is based."

It is on what was said by Lord Wrenbury that Mr Brownbill most relied. Lord Wrenbury said:[101] **10-068**

"If the plaintiff is right in saying that he is a beneficiary and if the documents are documents belonging to the executors as executors, he has a right to access to the documents which he desires to inspect upon what has been called in the judgments in this case a proprietary right. The beneficiary is entitled to see all trust documents because they are trust documents and because he is a beneficiary. They are in this sense his own. Action or no action, he is entitled to access to them. This has nothing to do with discovery. The right to discovery is a right to see someone else's documents. The proprietary right is a right to access to documents which are your own."

On the facts of the case, what Lord Wrenbury said was very apposite. If Mr O'Rourke was right in his claim, the executors had had no proper legal or equitable title to Sir Joseph's estate. The grant of probate to them should have been revoked and Mr O'Rourke (together with the representatives of Mrs McGowan) would have been entitled to the whole of the estate, including any documents which formed part of it.

[Lord Walker considered three earlier cases, *Clarke v Earl of Ormonde*,[102] *Re Cowin*[103] and *Re Tillott*,[104] **10-069** then continued:] ... In *Re Londonderry's Settlement*[105] the Court of Appeal had to consider one of the most important limitations on the right to disclosure of trust documents, that is the need to protect confidentiality in communications between trustees as to the exercise of their dispositive discretions, and in communications made to the trustees by other beneficiaries. That issue can alternatively be seen as an inquiry whether such confidential communications are indeed trust documents. The judgments of the three members of the court (Harman, Danckwerts and Salmon LJJ) are not easy to reconcile. All three referred to *O'Rourke v Darbishire* but Harman and Danckwerts LJJ found that Lord Wrenbury's general observations gave little assistance on the issue which concerned them. Only Salmon LJ expressly adopted the proprietary basis of the principle.[106]

Lord Wrenbury's observations in *O'Rourke v Darbishire* have also been cited in several Australian cases, **10-070** and they were referred to by Lord Lowry in *A T & T Istel Ltd v Tully*.[107] The Board does not find it surprising that Lord Wrenbury's observations have been so often cited, since they are a vivid expression of the basic distinction between the right of a beneficiary arising under the law of trusts (which most would regard as part of the law of property) and the right of a litigant to disclosure of his opponent's documents (which is part of the law of procedure and evidence). But the Board cannot regard it as a reasoned or binding decision that a beneficiary's right or claim to disclosure of trust documents or information must always have the proprietary basis of a transmissible interest in trust property. That was not an issue in *O'Rourke v Darbishire*.

Their Lordships consider that the more principled and correct approach is to regard the right to seek **10-071** disclosure of trust documents as one aspect of the court's inherent jurisdiction to supervise, and if necessary to intervene in, the administration of trusts. The right to seek the court's intervention does not depend on entitlement to a fixed and transmissible beneficial interest. The object of a discretion (including a mere power) may also be entitled to protection from a court of equity, although the circumstances in which he may seek protection, and the nature of the protection he may expect to obtain, will depend on the court's discretion.[108] Mr Brownbill's submission to the contrary effect tends to prove too much, since he would

---

101 Ibid at 626–7.
102 (1821) Jacob 108.
103 (1886) 33 Ch.D. 179.
104 [1892] 1 Ch. 86.
105 [1965] Ch. 918.
106 Ibid at 937.
107 [1993] A.C. 45 at 65.
108 See Lord Wilberforce in *Gartside v I.R.C.* [1968] A.C. 553 at 617–8 and in *McPhail v Doulton* [1971] A.C. 424 at 456–7; Templeman J in *Re Manisty's Settlement* [1974] Ch. 17 at 27–8; and Warner J in *Mettoy Pension Trustees Ltd v Evans* [1990] 1 W.L.R. 1587 at 1617–8.

regard the object of a discretionary trust as having a proprietary interest even though it is not transmissible (except in the special case of collective action taken unanimously by all the members of a closed class).

10-072 Their Lordships are therefore in general agreement with the approach adopted in the judgments of Kirby P and Sheller JA in the Court of Appeal of New South Wales in *Hartigan Nominees Pty Ltd v Rydge*.[109] That was a case concerned with disclosure of a memorandum of wishes addressed to the trustees by Sir Norman Rydge (who was in substance, but not nominally, the settlor). Kirby P said:[110]

> "I do not consider that it is imperative to determine whether that document is a 'trust document' (as I think it is) or whether the respondent, as a beneficiary, has a proprietary interest in it (as I am also inclined to think he does). Much of the law on the subject of access to documents has conventionally been expressed in terms of the 'proprietary interest' in the document of the party seeking access to it. Thus, it has been held that a cestui que trust has a 'proprietary right' to seek all documents relating to the trust.[111] This approach is unsatisfactory. Access should not be limited to documents in which a proprietary right may be established. Such rights may be sufficient; but they are not necessary to a right of access which the courts will enforce to uphold the cestui que trust's entitlement to a reasonable assurance of the manifest integrity of the administration of the trust by the trustees. I agree with Professor H A J Ford's comment,[112] that the equation of rights of inspection of trust documents with the beneficiaries' equitable rights of property in the trust assets 'gives rise to far more problems than it solves':
>
> > '... The legal title and rights to possession are in the trustees: all the beneficiary has are equitable rights against the trustees. ... The beneficiary's rights to inspect trust documents are founded therefore not upon any equitable proprietary right which he or she may have in respect of those documents but upon the trustee's fiduciary duty to keep the beneficiary informed and to render accounts. It is the extent of that duty that is in issue. The equation of the right to inspect trust documents with the beneficiary's equitable proprietary rights gives rise to unnecessary and undesirable consequences. It results in the drawing of virtually incomprehensible distinctions between documents which are trust documents and those which are not; it casts doubts upon the rights of beneficiaries who cannot claim to have an equitable proprietary interest in the trust assets, such as the beneficiaries of discretionary trusts; and it may give trustees too great a degree of protection in the case of documents, artificially classified as not being trust documents, and beneficiaries too great a right to inspect the activities of trustees in the case of documents which are, equally artificially, classified as trust documents.'"

10-073 Mahoney JA favoured the proprietary basis but recognised that it extended to information of a non-documentary kind.[113] Sheller JA considered that inquiry as to an applicant's proprietary interest was "if not a false, an unhelpful trail".[114] All three members of the court expressed reservations about the reasoning and conclusions in *Re Londonderry's Settlement*.

10-074 It will be observed that Kirby P said that for an applicant to have a proprietary right might be sufficient, but was not necessary. In the Board's view it is neither sufficient nor necessary. Since *In re Cowin* well over a century ago the court has made clear that there may be circumstances (especially of confidentiality) in which even a vested and transmissible beneficial interest is not a sufficient basis for requiring disclosure of trust documents; and *Re Londonderry's Settlement* and more recent cases have begun to work out in some detail the way in which the court should exercise its discretion in such cases. There are three such areas in which the court may have to form a discretionary judgment: whether a discretionary object (or some other beneficiary with only a remote or wholly defeasible interest) should be granted relief at all; what classes of documents should be disclosed, either completely or in a redacted form; and what safeguards should be imposed (whether by undertakings to the court, arrangements for professional inspection, or otherwise) to limit the use which may be made of documents or information disclosed under the order of the court.

---

109 (1992) 29 N.S.W.L.R. 405.

110 Ibid at 421–2.

111 See *O'Rourke v Darbishire* at 601, 603.

112 In his book (with Mr W A Lee) *Principles of the Law of Trusts*, 2nd ed (1990) Sydney, Law Book Co, at 425.

113 (1992) 29 N.S.W.L.R. 405 at 435.

114 Ibid at 444.

... [Lord Walker discussed some other cases,[115] before concluding as follows:] Their Lordships have already indicated their view that a beneficiary's right to seek disclosure of trust documents, although sometimes not inappropriately described as a proprietary right, is best approached as one aspect of the court's inherent jurisdiction to supervise (and where appropriate intervene in) the administration of trusts. There is therefore in their Lordships' view no reason to draw any bright dividing-line either between transmissible and non-transmissible (that is, discretionary) interests, or between the rights of an object of a discretionary trust and those of the object of a mere power (of a fiduciary character). The differences in this context between trusts and powers are (as Lord Wilberforce demonstrated in *McPhail v Doulton*[116]) a good deal less significant than the similarities. The tide of Commonwealth authority, although not entirely uniform, appears to be flowing in that direction. **10–075**

However the recent cases also confirm (as had been stated as long ago as *Re Cowin* in 1886) that no beneficiary (and least of all a discretionary object) has any entitlement as of right to disclosure of anything which can plausibly be described as a trust document. Especially when there are issues as to personal or commercial confidentiality, the court may have to balance the competing interests of different beneficiaries, the trustees themselves, and third parties. Disclosure may have to be limited and safeguards may have to be put in place. Evaluation of the claims of a beneficiary (and especially of a discretionary object) may be an important part of the balancing exercise which the court has to perform on the materials placed before it. In many cases the court may have no difficulty in concluding that an applicant with no more than a theoretical possibility of benefit ought not to be granted any relief. **10–076**

Difficult issues can also arise where a settlor provides the trustees with a letter of wishes to guide them in their exercise of discretionary powers (e.g. to appoint property to the beneficiaries of a discretionary trust). Such letters have special significance after the settlor's death, because while alive the settlor may in any event be consulted by the trustees before exercising their discretionary distributive functions.[117] Such letters are brought into existence for the purposes of the operation of the trust, and they must be handed on from a retiring trustee to the new trustee, some regard needing to be had to them before a discretionary decision is taken on any matter to which they refer, even if the trustees exercising their independent discretion then decide to ignore a particular wish.[118] Thus, a letter of wishes is a trust document that is legally significant, although not so significant as the trust deed itself unless, exceptionally, the settlor intends the letter to be legally binding so as to override the trust deed to the extent necessary to give effect to what was laid down in the letter.[119] **10–077**

Nevertheless, in *Breakspear v Ackland*,[120] Briggs J held that letters of wishes are generally subject to the principle that the exercise by trustees of their dispositive discretions should be regarded, from start to finish, as an essentially confidential process. A document brought into existence for the sole or predominant purpose of being used in such a process is itself properly to be regarded as confidential, so that the trustees ordinarily need not disclose it to beneficiaries merely because they ask to see it, unless, in the trustees' view, disclosure is in the interests of the sound administration of the trust, and the exercise of their discretions. **10–078**

---

115 *Chaine-Nickson v Bank of Ireland* [1976] I.R. 393; *Spellson v George* (1987) 11 N.S.W.L.R. 300; *A-G of Ontario v Stavro* (1994) 119 D.L.R. (4th) 750; *Re Murphy's Settlement* [1999] 1 W.L.R. 282.

116 [1971] A.C. 424.

117 See cases cited in fn.34.

118 *Bank of Nova Scotia Trust Co (Bahamas) Ltd v Ricart de Barletta* (1985) 1 *Butterworths Offshore Cases & Materials* 5, discussed by H. Thompson in (1994) 3 Jo. Int. T. & Corp. p.35. Further see D.J. Hayton (1999) 32 Vanderbilt Jo. of Transnat. Law 555, 573–576; N. Sanders and C. Yates, "Letters of Wishes and Their Ongoing Importance in a Trustee's Decision-making" (2022) 28 T. & T. 386.

119 *Chase Manhattan Equities Ltd v Goodman* [1991] B.C.L.C. 897 at 923.

120 [2009] Ch. 32. Cf. *Re Rabbaiotti's 1989 Settlement* [2000] W.T.L.R. 953; *Hartigan Nominees Pty Ltd v Rydge* (1992) 29 N.S.W.L.R 405.

5. Powers of Trustees

A. Trustees' Powers as Owners of Trust Property Distinguished from Other Powers

10-079 It is axiomatic that trustees are always the owners of real or personal property rights,[121] and ownership brings with it powers in relation to the relevant property. These include a power to assign ownership to others and a power to allocate enjoyment of the property to oneself or others. It follows that when settlors vest the ownership of rights in trustees (possibly including the settlors themselves) they vest them with powers in their capacity as owners, essentially because this is what "ownership" means. These powers can be distinguished from other powers which trustees may also be given, which do not fall out of their ownership of trust property, examples being powers to vary the trust terms and powers to appoint new trustees.

10-080 There are various reasons why this distinction matters. One, discussed in Chapter 11,[122] is that various rules govern the exercise of trustee powers and the effect of non-compliance with these rules can vary according to the type of power which has been exercised as well as with the rule which the trustees have not followed. Noticing that some, though not all, trustee powers are consequential on their ownership of trust property also enables us to understand how equity's recognition of the trust redefines a trustee's authority to exercise their powers as owner of the trust property, and it enables us to see that many of the so-called "powers" conferred on trustees in trust instruments are really just permissions to use their powers as owners in particular ways.

10-081 It is sometimes said that a trust is "annexed to", "impressed upon" or "engrafted onto" the trustees' ownership of trust property.[123] At a general level, such statements express the idea that trustees own property and therefore have "all the powers [and other legal entitlements] incidental to ownership"[124] but may not use these in whatever way they please and must use them in accordance with the instructions given by the settlor.[125] However, trusts do not redefine or limit the powers which trustees are given by the general law in their capacity as owners. For example, the fact that a trustee holds a freehold estate in land on trust does not affect her power to assign ownership of the estate: if they comply with the rules governing assignment of the estate then the assignment will be valid at common law even if it is contrary to the trust terms.[126] However, the trustee's failure to comply with the trust terms will have consequences in equity: the trustee cannot rely on the transfer to obtain a discharge from her duty to account for the trust property and in addition the assignee of the estate may incur a liability to the beneficiaries, depending on whether or not she is a bona fide purchaser for value without notice of the beneficiaries' equitable interest in the estate. It follows that the trustee is in a different position from other owners. They are free to exercise their

---

121 See e.g. *Smith v Anderson* (1880) 15 Ch.D. 247 at 275: "A trustee is a man who is the owner of the property and deals with it as principal as owner and as master, subject only to an equitable obligation to account to some persons to whom he stands in the relation of trustee and who are his cestuis que trust."

122 See paras 11-001 to 11-011.

123 e.g. *DKLR Holding Co (No.2) Pty Ltd v Commissioner of Stamp Duties* [1980] 1 N.S.W.L.R. 510 at 519; *First City Monument Bank Plc v Zumax Nigeria Ltd* [2019] EWCA Civ 294; [2019] W.T.L.R. 511 at [16]; *Commissioner of State Revenue v Rojoda Pty Ltd* (2020) 268 C.L.R. 281 at [44].

124 *Carter Holt Harvey Woodproducts Australia Pty Ltd v Commonwealth* (2019) 268 C.L.R. 524 at [82]. See too *DKLR Holding Co (No.2) Pty Ltd v Commissioner of Stamp Duties* [1980] 1 N.S.W.L.R. 510 at 518–520.

125 Cf. *Harries v Church Commissioners* [1992] 1 W.L.R. 1241 at 1246, reaffirmed in *Bhamani v Sattar* [2021] EWCA Civ 243 at [40].

126 *Rolled Steel Products (Holdings) Ltd v British Steel Corp* [1986] Ch. 246 at 303 *Akers v Samba Financial Group* [2017] UKSC 6; [2017] A.C. 424 at [51].

powers in whatever way they choose. The trustee is not and the overall effect of the trust is thus that her authority as owner is redefined, although the powers and legal entitlements that constitute her ownership are not.

An associated point is that the sphere of permission within which trustees may validly exercise their powers as owners is typically defined by clauses in trust instruments. Most obviously, this is the effect of clauses which describe the objects of the trust: the trustees are authorised to distribute trust property to the objects alone and they are not authorised to distribute the property to anyone else. Perhaps less obviously, this is also the effect produced by clauses which state that trustees have "powers" to do certain things with the trust property which they are already empowered to do by dint of the fact that they are the owners. To illustrate this point, we reproduce a discretionary trust precedent below. Consider e.g. paras 1.1 and 1.13 of the Schedule. These confer "additional powers" on the trustees to "make any kind of investment that they could make if they were absolutely entitled to the Trust Fund" and to "indemnify any Person for any liability relating to the Trust". As owners of the trust property, the trustees already have a power to pay trust money to the vendors of property which they wish to acquire for investment purposes or to people to whom they have incurred a liability while pursuing the trust affairs. The point of the clauses is to affirm that the trustees are authorised to use their power to assign the trust property for these purposes. **10–082**

In this regard, the clauses can be distinguished from clauses which confer a power on trustees (or third parties) which they would not otherwise have because the power does not derive from ownership of the trust property. An example is the power of appointment contained in clause 3.1, which enables the trustees to vary the terms of the trust. **10–083**

Discretionary Trust Precedent from J. Kessler, *Drafting Trusts and Will Trusts*, 14th edn (Sweet & Maxwell, 2019)

This Trust is made [date] between: **10–084**

1 [Name of settlor] of [address] ("the Settlor") of the one part and

2 2.1 [Name of first trustee] of [address] and
2.2 [Name of second trustee] of [address]

("the Original Trustees") of the other part.

Whereas:

1 The Settlor has [two] children:

1.1 [Adam Smith] ("[Adam]") who was born on [date] and
1.2 [Mary Smith] ("[Mary]") who was born on [date].

2 This Trust shall be known as the [Name-of-settlor Trust 2017].

Now this deed witnesses as follows:

1 Definitions

In this Trust: **10–085**

1.1 **"The Beneficiaries"** means:

1.1.1 The descendants of the Settlor.
1.1.2 The Spouses of the descendants of the Settlor.
1.1.3 The Surviving Spouses of the descendants of the Settlor.
1.1.4 The Surviving Spouse of the Settlor.

1.1.5 Any Person or class of Persons added to the class of Beneficiaries by the Trustees by deed with the consent in writing of:

1.1.5.1 the Settlor or
1.1.5.2 two Beneficiaries (if the Settlor has died or has no capacity to consent).

1.2 **"Spouse"** includes a civil partner within the meaning of section 1 Civil Partnership Act 2004 and a person is a "**Surviving Spouse**" whether or not they have remarried or entered into another civil partnership.
1.3 **"Person"** includes a person anywhere in the world and includes a Trustee.
1.4 **"The Trustees"** means the Original Trustees or the trustees of this Trust for the time being.
1.5 **"The Trust Fund"** means:

1.5.1 property transferred to the Trustees to hold on the terms of this Trust; and
1.5.2 all property from time to time representing the above.

1.6 **"The Trust Period"** means the period of 125 years beginning with the date of this Trust.
1.7 **"Trust Property"** means any part of the Trust Fund.

2 Trust Income

10–086 During the Trust Period and subject to the Overriding Powers below:

2.1 The Trustees may accumulate the whole or part of the income of the Trust Fund. That income shall be added to the Trust Fund.
2.2 The Trustees shall pay or apply the remainder of the income to or for the benefit of any Beneficiaries, as the Trustees think fit.

3 Overriding Powers

10–087 The Trustees shall have the following powers ("Overriding Powers"):

3.1 *Power of appointment*

3.1.1 The Trustees may appoint that they shall hold any Trust Property for the benefit of any Beneficiaries, on such terms as the Trustees think fit.
3.1.2 An appointment may create any provisions and in particular:

3.1.2.1 discretionary trusts;
3.1.2.2 dispositive or administrative powers; exercisable by any Person.

3.1.3 An appointment shall be made by deed and may be revocable or irrevocable.

3.2 *Transfer of Trust Property to another trust*

3.2.1 The Trustees may by deed declare that they hold any Trust Property on trust to transfer it to trustees of another trust, wherever established, to hold on the terms of that trust, freed and released from the terms of this Trust.
3.2.2 The Trustees shall only exercise this power if:

3.2.2.1 every Person who may benefit is (or would if living be) a Beneficiary; or
3.2.2.2 with the consent in writing of

(a) the Settlor, or
(b) two Beneficiaries (after the death of the Settlor).

3.3 *Power of advancement*
The Trustees may pay or apply any Trust Property for the advancement or benefit of any Beneficiary.
3.4 The Overriding Powers shall be exercisable only:

3.4.1 during the Trust Period; and
3.4.2 at a time when there are at least two Trustees, or the Trustee is a company carrying on a business which consists of or includes the management of trusts.

4 Default Clause

Subject to that, the Trust Fund shall be held on trust for [Adam and Mary in equal shares - or specify default trusts as appropriate] absolutely. 10–088

5 Appointment of Trustees

The power of appointing trustees is exercisable by the Settlor during [his] life and by will. 10–089

6 Further Provisions

The provisions set out in the schedule below shall have effect. 10–090
[For a shorter form, say instead:
"The standard provisions and all of the special provisions of the Society of Trust and Estate Practitioners (2nd Edition) shall apply."
And omit the schedule.]

7 Exclusion of Settlor and Spouse

Notwithstanding anything else in this Trust, no power conferred by this Trust shall be exercisable, and no provision shall operate so as to allow Trust Property or its income to become payable to or applicable for the benefit of the Settlor or the Spouse of the Settlor in any circumstances whatsoever. 10–091

8 Irrevocability

This Trust is irrevocable. 10–092
In witness, [etc.]

THE SCHEDULE: FURTHER PROVISIONS

1 Additional powers

The Trustees have the following additional powers: 10–093

1.1 *Investment*

1.1.1 The Trustees may make any kind of investment that they could make if they were absolutely entitled to the Trust Fund. In particular the Trustees may invest in land in any part of the world and unsecured loans.
1.1.2 The Trustees may invest in speculative or hazardous investments but this power may only be exercised at the time when there are at least two Trustees, or the Trustee is a company carrying on a business which consists of or includes the management of trusts.

1.2 *Joint property*

The Trustees may acquire property jointly with any Person and may blend Trust Property with other property.

1.3 *General power of management and disposition*

The Trustees may effect any transaction relating to the management or disposition of Trust Property as if they were absolutely entitled to it.

1.4 *Improvement*

The Trustees may develop or improve Trust Property in any way. Capital expenses need not be repaid out of income under section 84(2) of the Settled Land Act 1925, if the Trustees think fit.

1.5 *Income and capital*

1.5.1 The Trustees may acquire:

1.5.1.1 wasting assets and
1.5.1.2 assets which yield little or no income for investment or any other purpose.

1.5.2 The Trustees are under no duty to procure distributions from a company in which they are interested.

1.5.3 The Trustees may pay taxes and other expenses out of capital or income whether or not they would otherwise be so payable.

1.5.4 Generally, the Trustees are under no duty to hold a balance between conflicting interests of Beneficiaries.

1.5.5 Income may be set aside and invested to answer any liabilities which in the opinion of the Trustees ought to be borne out of income or to meet depreciation of the capital value of any Trust Property. In particular, income may be applied for a leasehold sinking fund policy.

1.6 *Application of trust capital as income*

The Trustees may apply Trust Property as if it were income arising in the current year. In particular, the Trustees may pay such income to an Income Beneficiary as his income, for the purpose of augmenting his income.

"**Income Beneficiary**" here means a Person to whom income of the Property is payable (as of right or at the discretion of the Trustees).

1.7 *Use of trust property*

1.7.1 The Trustees may acquire any interest in property anywhere in the world for occupation or use by an Income Beneficiary.

1.7.2 The Trustees may permit an Income Beneficiary to occupy or enjoy the use of Trust Property on such terms as they think fit.

1.7.3 The Trustees may lend trust money to an Income Beneficiary. The loan may be interest free and unsecured, or on such terms as the Trustees think fit. The Trustees may charge Trust Property as security for any debts or obligations of an Income Beneficiary.

1.7.4 "**Income Beneficiary**" here means a Person to whom income of the Property is payable (as of right or at the discretion of the Trustees).

1.7.5 This paragraph does not restrict any right of Beneficiaries to occupy land under the Trusts of Land and Appointment of Trustees Act 1996.

1.8 *Trade*

The Trustees may carry on a trade, in any part of the world, alone or in partnership.

1.9 *Borrowing*

The Trustees may borrow money for investment or any other purpose. Money borrowed shall be treated as Trust Property.

1.10 *Delegation*

A Trustee or the Trustees jointly (or other Person in a fiduciary position) may authorise any Person to exercise all or any functions on such terms as to remuneration and other matters as they think fit. A Trustee (or other Person in a fiduciary capacity) shall not be responsible for the default of that Person (even if the delegation was not strictly necessary or convenient) provided he took reasonable care in his selection and supervision. None of the restrictions on delegation in sections 12 to 15 Trustee Act 2000 shall apply.

1.11 *Nominees and custodians*

1.11.1 The Trustees may appoint a Person to act as their nominee in relation to such of the assets of the trust as they may determine. They may take such steps as are necessary to secure that those assets are vested in the nominee.

1.11.2 The Trustees may appoint a Person to act as custodian in relation to such of the assets of the trust as they may determine. The Trustees may give the custodian custody of the assets and any documents or records concerning the assets. The Trustees are not obliged to appoint a custodian of securities payable to bearer.

1.11.3 The Trustees may appoint a Person to act as nominee or custodian on such terms as to remuneration and other matters as they may think fit.

1.12 *Place of administration*

The Trustees may carry on the administration of this Trust anywhere they think fit.

1.13 *Indemnities*

The Trustees may indemnify any Person for any liability relating to the Trust.

1.14 *Security*

The Trustees may mortgage or charge Trust Property as security for any liability incurred by them as Trustees (and may grant a floating charge so far as the law allows).

1.15 *Supervision of company*

The Trustees are under no duty to enquire into the conduct of a company in which they are interested, unless they have knowledge of circumstances which call for inquiry.

1.16 *Appropriation*

The Trustees may appropriate Trust Property to any Person or class of Persons in or towards the satisfaction of their interest in the Trust Fund.

1.17 *Receipt by charities*

Where Trust Property is to be paid or transferred to a charity or non-charitable association or company, the receipt of the treasurer or appropriate officer of the organisation shall be a complete discharge to the Trustees.

1.18 *Release of powers*

The Trustees (or other Person in a fiduciary position) may by deed release wholly or in part any of their rights or functions and (if applicable) so as to bind their successors.

1.19 *Ancillary powers*

The Trustees may do anything which is incidental or conducive to the exercise of their functions.

1.20 *Power to pay insurance premiums out of income*

The Trustees may pay premiums of any insurance policy out of income.

1.21 *Waiver of income*

The Trustees may waive the payment of income before it becomes due.

MINORS

1.22 Where the Trustees may apply income for the benefit of a minor, they may do so by paying the income to the minor's parent or guardian on behalf of the minor, or to the minor if the minor has attained the age of 16. The Trustees are under no duty to inquire into the use of the income unless they have knowledge of circumstances which call for inquiry. **10–094**

1.23 Where the Trustees may apply income for the benefit of a minor, they may do so by resolving that they hold that income on trust for the minor absolutely and:

1.23.1 The Trustees may apply that income for the benefit of the minor during his minority.
1.23.2 The Trustees shall transfer the residue of that income to the minor on attaining the age of 18.
1.23.3 For investment and other administrative purposes that income shall be treated as Trust Property.

MENTALLY HANDICAPPED BENEFICIARY

Where income or capital is payable to a Beneficiary who does not have the mental capacity to appoint an attorney under a lasting power of attorney which related to the property and affairs of the Beneficiary, the Trustees **10–095** may (subject to the directions of the Court or a deputy appointed under the Mental Capacity Act whose powers include receiving such income or capital) apply that income or capital for the benefit of the Beneficiary.

DISCLAIMER

10-096 A Person may disclaim his interest in this Trust wholly or in part.

CONFLICTS OF INTEREST

10-097 1.24 In this paragraph:

1.24.1 **"Fiduciary"** means a Person subject to fiduciary duties under the Trust.
1.24.2 "An Independent Trustee", in relation to a Person, means a Trustee who is not:

1.24.2.1 a brother, sister, ancestor, descendant or dependent of the Person;
1.24.2.2 a spouse or Civil Partner of paragraph .1.2.1 above, or a spouse or Civil Partner of the Person;
1.24.2.3 a company controlled by one or more of any of the above.

1.25 Subject to subparagraph 3 below a Fiduciary may:

1.25.1 enter into a transaction with the Trustees, or
1.25.2 be interested in an arrangement in which the Trustees are or might have been interested, or
1.25.3 act (or not act) in any other circumstances;

even though his fiduciary duty under the Trust conflicts with other duties or with his personal interest.

1.26 Subparagraph .2 above only has effect if:

1.26.1 the Fiduciary first discloses to the Trustees the nature and extent of any material interest conflicting with his fiduciary duties, and
1.26.2 there is in relation to the Fiduciary an Independent Trustee in respect of whom there is no conflict of interest, and he considers that the transaction arrangement or action is not contrary to the general interest of the Trust.

1.27 The powers of the Trustees may be used to benefit a Trustee (to the same extent as if he were not a Trustee) provided that there is in relation to that Trustee an Independent Trustee in respect of whom there is no conflict of interest.

ABSOLUTE DISCRETION CLAUSE

10-098 1.28 The powers of the Trustees may be exercised:

1.28.1 at their absolute discretion; and
1.28.2 from time to time as occasion requires.

1.29 The Trustees are not under any duty to consult with any Beneficiaries or to give effect to the wishes of any Beneficiaries.

TRUSTEE REMUNERATION

10-099 1.30 A Trustee acting in a professional capacity is entitled to receive reasonable remuneration out of the Trust Fund for any services that the Trustee provides to or on behalf of this Trust.
1.31 For this purpose, a Trustee acts in a professional capacity if the Trustee acts in the course of a profession or business which consists of or includes the provision of services in connection with:

1.31.1 the management or administration of trusts generally or a particular kind of trust, or
1.31.2 any particular aspect of the management or administration of trusts generally or a particular kind of trust.

1.32 The Trustees may make arrangements to remunerate themselves for work done for a company connected with the Trust Fund.

COMMISSIONS AND BANK CHARGES

1.33 A Person may retain any reasonable commission or profit in respect of any transaction relating to this Trust even though that commission or profit was procured by an exercise of fiduciary powers (by that Person or some other Person) provided that: 10–100

1.33.1 The Person would in the normal course of business receive and retain the commission or profit on such transaction.
1.33.2 The receipt of the commission or profit shall be disclosed to the Trustees.

1.34 A bank may make loans to the Trustees and generally provide banking services upon its usual terms and shall not be liable to account for any profit so made even though the receipt of such profit was procured by an exercise of fiduciary powers (by the bank or some other Person).

LIABILITY OF TRUSTEES

1.35 The duty of reasonable care (set out in s.1, Trustee Act 2000) applies to all the functions of the Trustees. 10–101
1.36 A Trustee shall not be liable for a loss to the Trust Fund unless that loss was caused by his own fraud or negligence.
1.37 A Trustee shall not be liable for acting in accordance with the advice of Counsel, of at least ten years' standing, with respect to the Trust. The Trustees may in particular conduct legal proceedings in accordance with such advice without obtaining a Court Order. A Trustee may recover from the Trust Fund any expenses where he has acted in accordance with such advice.
1.38 The above sub-paragraph does not apply:

1.38.1 if the Trustee knows or has reasonable cause to suspect that the advice was given in ignorance of material facts;
1.38.2 if proceedings are pending to obtain the decision of the court on the matter;
1.38.3 in relation to a Trustee who has a personal interest in the subject matter of the advice; or
1.38.4 in relation to a Trustee who has committed a breach of trust relating to the subject matter of the advice.

1.39 The Trustees may distribute Trust Property or income in accordance with this Trust but without having ascertained that there is no Person who is or may be entitled to any interest therein by virtue of a relationship unknown to the Trustees. The Trustees shall not be liable to such a Person unless they have notice of his claim at the time of the distribution.
1.40 This paragraph does not prejudice any right of any Person to follow property or income into the hands of any Person, other than a purchaser, who may have received it.

APPOINTMENT AND RETIREMENT OF TRUSTEES

1.41 A Person may be appointed Trustee of the Trust even though he has no connection with the United Kingdom. 10–102
1.42 A Trustee may be discharged even though there is neither a trust corporation nor two Persons to act as trustees provided that there remains at least one trustee.

CHANGE OF GOVERNING LAW

The Trustees may during the Trust Period by deed with the consent of the Settlor during his life or of two Beneficiaries after his death declare that from the date of such declaration: 10–103

1.43 The law of any Qualifying Jurisdiction governs the validity of this Trust, and its construction, effects and administration, or any severable aspect of this Trust; and
1.44 The courts of any Qualifying Jurisdiction have exclusive jurisdiction in any proceedings involving rights or obligations under this Trust.
In this paragraph a "Qualifying Jurisdiction" is one which recognises trusts (as defined in the Hague Convention on the Law Applicable to Trusts and on their Recognition).

B. Some Trustee Powers

10–104 In this section we discuss some—though by no means all—of the powers which are commonly conferred on the trustees of family trusts and/or pension trusts, either by the terms of a trust instrument or by the trusts legislation: powers of appointment; powers of accumulation and maintenance; powers of advancement; powers of recoupment; powers of delegation; and powers of amendment.

(i) Powers of Appointment

10–105 Powers of appointment are powers to create beneficial interests in property in favour of identified objects. A power of appointment is described as a "general power" if the power holder can appoint an interest in property to anyone in the world including themselves. It is a "special power" if they can appoint to any member of a particular class of people, e.g. any issue of the settlor or any spouse or civil partner of such issue. It is a "hybrid" or "intermediate power" if it can be exercised in favour of anyone apart from a small, excepted class, e.g. the settlor, her spouse, and past and present trustees.[127]

10–106 A trust instrument may confer a power of appointment in relation to the trust property on the trustees (as in clause 3.1 of the trust precedent reproduced above) or on someone else. The effect of this is to empower the trustees (or other power holder) to decide, on behalf of the settlor, which of the objects of the power shall take the trust property and in what proportions. In Lord Romer's words, it is "as though the settlor had left a blank in the settlement which [the power-holder] fills up for him if and when the power is exercised."[128]

10–107 Where powers of appointment are conferred on people such as trustees or executors by reason of the fact that they hold a fiduciary office they are "fiduciary powers". Fiduciary power holders may not exercise their powers in a self-interested way where there is a conflict between their own interests and those of the people for whom they are fiduciaries (the beneficiaries in the case of a trust). Where powers of appointment are conferred on people in a personal capacity, and not because the settlor intends that the power should be exercised for the benefit of other people, they are "personal powers". Personal power holders are not caught by the "no conflicts" rule and can exercise their powers in a self-serving way if they so wish.

10–108 A trustee who has a power of appointment may or may not owe a duty to exercise the power, depending on the settlor's intentions. As previously noted in Chapter 7,[129] confusing terminology has been used to describe powers of appointment which are accompanied by a duty and powers which are not: powers of the first kind give rise to a discretionary trust, but are sometimes called "trust powers"; powers of the latter kind are called "mere powers". For example, if a trustee, T, is required to exercise a power to appoint the income generated by trust property as T sees fit to X's descendants, there is a discretionary trust or "trust power" of the income, as opposed to a mere power of appointment. T must distribute all of the income to one or more beneficiaries, although T may decide whether a particular beneficiary receives a lot or a little or nothing.[130]

10–109 To give another example, if T holds property on trust for A for life, then for B absolutely, but subject to the exercise of a mere power vested in T to appoint income or capital to X's descendants, T must distribute income to A during A's lifetime and capital to B after A's death, unless T chooses to exercise

---

[127] *Schmidt v Rosewood Trust Ltd* [2003] UKPC 26; [2003] 2 A.C. 709 at [35].
[128] *Muir v Muir* [1943] A.C. 468 at 483.
[129] See para.7–125.
[130] *McPhail v Doulton* [1971] A.C. 424 at 457; *Pitt v Holt* [2013] UKSC 26; [2013] 2 A.C. 108 at [63].

her power to appoint to X's descendants. At first sight it may seem that there is a fixed trust for A and B, but the effect of making their interests defeasible by T's exercise of the power of appointment in favour of X's descendants is to turn the trust for A and B into a discretionary trust, because T has a discretion to appoint some or all of the property to X's descendants and thereby reduce or extinguish A's and B's interests.

Powers of appointment are usually exercised by deed. A specimen deed of appointment is reproduced here by way of illustration. Note that the effect of this deed is not to transfer legal ownership of trust property to the nominated beneficiary but to create a fixed trust in her favour, although of course once they have been made the sole beneficiary of a fixed trust of the specified property they may be able to require the trustees to transfer legal title to them by virtue of the rule in *Saunders v Vautier*,[131] something that they may or may not wish to do, depending on fiscal and other considerations. **10–110**

Specimen Deed of Appointment out of a Discretionary Trust Supplemental to Will or Settlement from *Encyclopedia of Forms and Precedents*, 5th edn (2022 release)

In exercise of the power of appointment conferred by clause [number] of the [Will OR Settlement] and of any other powers, if any, enabling them, the Trustees [irrevocably OR subject to clause [number—provision for revocation]] appoint the property set out in [the Schedule] as and from the date of this deed to be held on the following trusts: **10–111**

1 as to the property set out in [Part 1 of the Schedule], on trust as to both capital and income for [adult beneficiary] absolutely; [and] **10–112**
2 as to the property set out in [Part 2 of the Schedule] on trust as to both capital and income for [minor beneficiary] but contingently on [minor beneficiary] attaining the age of [18 OR 21] years[; and] **10–113**
3 [[set out trusts (if any) in favour of other beneficiaries identifying the property to be held on those trusts],] provided that: **10–114**
4 if any person named in clause[s] [number(s) of subclause(s) containing contingent interests] above dies before attaining a vested interest but leaving a child or children living at their death, such child or children shall take absolutely, and if more than one in equal shares, so much of the trust property and the income of it as that person would have taken had they attained a vested interest; and **10–115**
5 if at any time the trusts declared by clause 2 [and clause 3], read in conjunction with clause 4 fail, then from the date of failure the property which was the subject of those trusts and the income from it shall be held on trust [set out alternative trusts for a living adult beneficiary]. **10–116**

(ii) Powers of Accumulation and Maintenance

A common device used by settlors who wish to provide for their infant children is to create a trust under which the children's interests are not immediately vested and the trustees are empowered to accumulate trust income until the children reach a specified age (e.g. 21 or 25) but are also empowered to spend trust income on the children's maintenance in the meantime. Settlements of this kind are called "accumulation and maintenance trusts" ("A&M trusts"). They are governed by a particular tax regime which differs from the regime which governs "interest in possession trusts", under which at least one beneficiary has an immediate right to be paid the trust income, but the details of these regimes lie beyond the scope of this work. **10–117**

A settlor may confer powers of accumulation and maintenance on the trustees by a clause of the trust deed, as illustrated by clause 2.1 and 2.2 of the foregoing trust precedent. Where a settlor made **10–118**

[131] As to which see paras 12–064 to 12–073.

no provision for such powers, trustees previously had to ask the court to grant permission to accumulate income or use trust property for maintenance under its supervisory jurisdiction, which might be granted according to circumstances, although these had to be exceptional before the expenditure of capital rather than income would be allowed. The position is now governed by the Trustee Act 1925 s.31, which gives the trustees default statutory powers, which may be ousted by a clause in a trust instrument to contrary effect. The general law governing trustee decision-making applies to exercises of the s.31 power: trustees must consciously decide whether to exercise the power in good faith after due consideration of all and only relevant circumstances.[132]

10–119 The length of the period during which trustees can be empowered to accumulate income is subject to statutory restrictions, although these have been liberalised in modern times. The legislation dates back to the Accumulations Act 1800 (the "Thellusson Act") which was enacted to prevent trusts such as that settled by Peter Thellusson, under which the trust income could be accumulated for the whole perpetuity period of the settlement.[133] Subsequent legislation meant that until 2009, where it was sought to give trustees a power to accumulate, it was crucial to restrict the accumulation to one of the six periods allowed by ss.164–166 of the Law of Property Act 1925 and s.13 of the Perpetuities and Accumulations Act 1964. However, the rule against excessive accumulation was abolished for most purposes by the Perpetuities and Accumulations Act 2009 s.13, which repeals the relevant sections of the 1925 and 1964 statutes. The effect is to give settlors considerable freedom to accumulate income within settlements, although the rule against perpetuities effectively limits the lifetime of a trust and so provides an upper limit on any accumulation.

(iii) Powers of Advancement

10–120 Where trustees have been empowered to accumulate income for the long-term benefit of minor beneficiaries, and there is an expectation that they will keep the trust capital intact until the beneficiaries reach a specified age, the settlor may nevertheless think it desirable to provide for unexpected occurrences by giving the trustees a power of advancement as well, i.e. a power to pay or apply trust capital for the advancement of the beneficiaries, as in clause 3.3 in the trust precedent reproduced above. Even in the absence of such a clause trustees have a default statutory power of advancement by virtue of the Trustee Act 1925 s.32.

10–121 Exercise of a power of advancement is accomplished in a similar way to the exercise of a power of appointment, as described above, although these powers differ insofar as the exercise of a power of appointment varies the trust terms and brings into existence an interest in the trust property that would otherwise never have existed (and might have an effect of defeating other interests in default), but the exercise of a power of advancement results in an object acquiring an interest in the property that they would have acquired later on in any case, assuming satisfaction of the relevant contingency.

10–122 When exercising a power of advancement trustees must be careful, for a mistake may mean that both capital and income disappear for good, as in *Re Pauling's Settlement Trusts*.[134] The father of the beneficiaries persuaded the trustees to fritter away much of the trust capital in ways that enabled the mother's overdraft to be paid off, a house to be bought for the parents absolutely and an overly high standard of living to be maintained for the family. The lesson is that requests for advancement of capital by young adults who are unemancipated from their parents' influence must be treated with

---

[132] *Wilson v Turner* (1883) 22 Ch. D. 521.

[133] See *Thellusson v Woodford* (1799) 4 Ves. 227, for a full account of which, see P. Polden, *Peter Thellusson's Will of 1797 and Its Consequences on Chancery Law* (Edwin Mellen Press, 2002).

[134] [1964] Ch. 303.

caution and that when moneys are requested for particular purposes they should be applied to those purposes by the trustees themselves if experience suggests that they will otherwise be spent by the parents on something else.

Further points are made about the exercise of powers of advancement in the next extract. 10–123

Kain v Hutton

New Zealand Supreme Court [2008] 3 N.Z.L.R. 589 at [56]–[59]

TIPPING J: ... Importantly, a power of advancement may be exercised only if there is some "good reason" to exercise it at the time and in the manner proposed.[135] That good reason must of course be of benefit to the person the subject of the advancement. But in spite of the width of the concept of benefit, *Pauling's* case shows that it is insufficient simply to make an advancement on the basis that any receipt of money or other property ahead of the date of vesting in possession must be of benefit to the recipient. The concept of benefit is wide but not wholly unrestricted. 10–124

For example, proposed advancements close to the date of vesting in possession should be viewed cautiously. Trustees must make sure that there really is a good reason to advance the date.[136] Similarly, advancements when the trustees are or should be aware that the beneficiary may be going to use the money or other property unwisely should also be viewed with caution, unless the advancement is by means of a protective trust.[137] 10–125

Need, as such, is not the touchstone but if there is a total absence of material or moral need the interests of those who take in default should be preferred to those of the proposed advancee. The position, in short, is that trustees may exercise their discretionary power to make an advancement only if they have formed the considered view that there is good reason to do so and it truly will be of benefit to the advanced beneficiary to exercise the power in the manner contemplated.[138] 10–126

In this respect powers of advancement are different from powers of appointment.[139] A person exercising a power of appointment is exercising a discretionary power to select who should take from a group of potential beneficiaries. That is a materially different task from that required of someone exercising a power of advancement. There, the essential question is whether a distribution should be made ahead of the time at which the beneficiary would otherwise receive possession of property in which they already have an interest. 10–127

(iv) Powers of Recoupment

The terms of private trusts for persons typically entitle beneficiaries to distributions out of trust property, but in some situations, a reduction may need to be made to the amounts paid so that the property can be used for other purposes. The process by which this is done is termed "recoupment". For example, where a trust fund is depleted because a beneficiary has been overpaid, the trustees can "recoup" the loss by using trust funds for this purpose that would otherwise have been distributed to the beneficiary at a later date; and where a trustee has paid trust expenses out of her own resources, she can "recoup" the cost of this by treating trust funds as her own so that the amount of property held on trust is reduced. 10–128

It is often said that trustees have a "right" to recoupment and that that this is secured by an equitable "lien" over the trust property. However, recoupment is possible in cases where the trustees have no legal right against anyone, e.g. a trustee can recoup against an overpaid beneficiary even if the 10–129

---

[135] See *Re Paulings Settlement Trusts* [1964] Ch. 303 at 333, per Willmer L.J.

[136] See *Lewin on Trusts*, 18th edn (Sweet & Maxwell, 2008), para.32–18 and *Pilkington v IRC* [1964] A.C. 612 at 640–641.

[137] See G. Thomas and A. Hudson, *The Law of Trusts* (Oxford University Press, 2004), para.14–31.

[138] See Thomas and Hudson, *The Law of Trusts* (2004), para.14–30 citing *Phillips v Phillips* (1853) Kay 40; *Re Kershaw's Trusts* (1840) L.R. 6 Eq. 322 and *Re Moxon's Will Trusts* [1958] 1 W.L.R. 165.

[139] Unless of course the express terms of the power circumscribe its exercise by reference to benefit in which case that will be an additional criterion as well as the standard requirement that the appointee be an object of the power.

beneficiary owes no legal obligation to repay the amount of the overpayment.[140] In such cases it is also difficult to understand what it means to say that the trustee has an equitable "lien", given that these are generally understood to be interests in property which secure the performance of a legal obligation. Given that trustees are the owners of the trust property, it is also hard to understand what it means to say that they have a "lien" over this property which they can enforce against themselves as owners.[141] A better analysis is therefore that trustees have a "power" to recoup in some situations, meaning that in some situations they have permission to use the trust property in particular ways; and in other situations they have a power to vary the trust terms.

10–130 The situations in which this is typically permissible are summarised in the following passage from an article by Jessica Hudson and Charles Mitchell, where they argue that trustees' powers of recoupment divide into two types. Where trust funds are depleted because something goes wrong in the administration of the trust, and a beneficiary is implicated in this problem, it is cured by the trustee's exercise of a power to vary the terms of that beneficiary's entitlement to the benefit of trust property. Where trustees pay trust expenses out of their own funds, they are permitted to reimburse themselves by treating trust property as forming part of their personal estate rather than part of the trust fund; they are allowed to do this because trust business requires them to enter legal relations with third parties in the absence of any other means of dealing with them and yet fairness demands that trustees should not have to pay such liabilities out of their own pockets.

J. Hudson and C. Mitchell, "Trustee Recoupment: A Power Analysis"

(2021) 35 Tru. L.I. 3, pp.4–7

Recoupment in an express private trust

Situations where recoupment is possible

10–131 There are five situations in which recoupment is typically carried out. First, where a trustee pays a beneficiary money to which she is not entitled under the trust terms, future payments to the beneficiary can be reduced by the amount of the overpayment.[142] Secondly, where a breach of trust is committed by a trustee who is also a beneficiary, future payments made to her in her capacity as beneficiary can be reduced to make good the loss sustained by the trust fund.[143] Thirdly, where a trustee commits a breach of trust at the instigation of a beneficiary they are jointly and severally liable for the loss; if the trustee is compelled to pay more than her fair share of their common liability, property that would have been distributed to the beneficiary can be used to reimburse the trustee.[144] Fourthly, where a beneficiary defaults on a duty she owes to contribute to the trust fund, payments to her out of the fund can be reduced by the amount of her

140 See e.g. *Re Musgrave* [1916] 2 Ch. 417 at 424–426; *Re Robertson* [1953] V.L.R. 685 at 689. See also *Test Claimants in the FII Group Litigation v HMRC* [2020] UKSC 47; [2022] A.C. 1 at [115]: recoupment itself is "not a claim at all"; *Burgess v BIC UK Ltd* [2018] EWHC 785 (Ch); [2018] Pens. L.R. 13 at [172]; *CMG Pension Trustees Ltd v CGI IT UK Ltd* [2022] EWHC 2130 (Ch) at [151].

141 Dicta stating that trustees have a lien in a "special sense" merely confirm that they do not have a lien: e.g. *Chief Commissioner of Stamp Duties (NSW) v Buckle* (1998) 192 C.L.R. 226 at [50]; *Carter Holt Harvey Woodproducts Australia Pty Ltd v Commonwealth* (2019) 268 C.L.R. 524 at [83].

142 *Fuller v Knight* (1843) 6 Beav. 205 at 210–211; *Dibbs v Goren* (1849) 11 Beav. 483 at 484; *Harris v Harris (No.2)* (1861) 29 Beav. 110; ... *Re Oppenheim* [1917] 1 Ch. 274 at 281–282; *MacPhillamy v Fox* (1932) 32 S.R. (N.S.W.) 427 at 431–3; *Re Robertson* [1953] V.L.R. 685 at 689, *Burgess v BIC UK Ltd* [2018] P.L.R. 13 at [162].

143 *Jacubs v Rylance* (1874) L.R. 17 Eq. 341 at 342; *Re Brown* (1886) 32 Ch.D. 597 at 603; ... *Re Dacre* [1916] 1 Ch. 344 at 347–8; ... *RWG Management Ltd v Commissioner for Corporate Affairs* [1985] V.R. 385 at 397.

144 *Lincoln v Wright* (1841) 4 Beav. 427 at 432; ... *Chillingworth v Chambers* [1896] 1 Ch. 685; *Fletcher v Collis* [1905] 2 Ch. 24; ... *Re Pauling's S.T. (No.2)* [1963] Ch. 576 at 583–4. The court also has a power to order recoupment from a beneficiary who instigates or requests a breach of trust in writing under the Trustee Act 1925, s.62.

liability.[145] Fifthly, where a trustee pays a third party to discharge a debt incurred by the trustee in carrying out trust business, she can reimburse herself out of the trust property.[146]

Two types of recoupment

Detailed rules govern the question of when recoupment is possible in each of these situations. We shall not discuss these because we have a broader aim, which is to advance a general theory of how recoupment works in every situation. As a first step, however, we must make some observations about the differences and similarities between the five situations and introduce a fundamental distinction between recoupment against a particular beneficiary (situations 1–4) and recoupment for expenses (situation 5). 10–132

Recoupment against a particular beneficiary

In situations 1–4, recoupment occurs against a particular beneficiary in the sense that it involves a change being made to that beneficiary's entitlement to the benefit of trust property. This entitlement is sometimes described as 'beneficial ownership' or 'equitable ownership'[147] because the trustees owe duties to exercise their powers over the trust property to put the beneficiary 'into a position where directly, or indirectly, or for all practical purposes, [she] ... enjoys or exercises the rights which the law has vested in the trustee'.[148] The trustees might do this, for example, by paying her money or granting her possession of the property ... 10–133

When a trustee recoups against a beneficiary her entitlement is adjusted by treating her as if she has received a distribution in advance of the date when it would otherwise have fallen due. Consider a very simple example of situation 1. A beneficiary is entitled to an annual income of £20, but in 2018 the trustees pay her £30 by mistake. They recoup by treating her as having received an advance payment of £10 which was not due until 2019 and the advance is then equalised by paying her £10 less in 2019. As a result, the overall value of the beneficiary's receipts remains the same – over 2018 and 2019 she receives £40 – but a change is made to the timing of her receipts as a way of correcting the overpayment. 10–134

In situations 2–4, recoupment operates in a similar way. The beneficiary is treated as though sums to which she would have become entitled were paid ahead of time to the extent that she must restore the trust fund (in situation 2), reimburse the breaching trustee (in situation 3), or pay money into the trust fund (in situation 4).[149] A corresponding reduction is made to the beneficiary's future entitlements to equalise the early advance. In situation 1, the beneficiary's liability to recoupment arises because she has received an unauthorised payment and the effect of recoupment is to authorise her early receipt of funds with retrospective effect. In situations 2–4, the beneficiary's liability to recoupment does not depend on the receipt of trust funds, but on the beneficiary having committed a breach of trust in her capacity as trustee, or on her having failed to reimburse a trustee who was liable for a breach that she instigated, or on her having failed to perform a duty to pay money into the trust fund. In all of these situations, recoupment authorises the use of trust funds to discharge the beneficiary's various obligations, but the mechanism by which this is achieved is the same as the mechanism used in situation 1: a change is made to the time when trust funds are used to confer a benefit on the beneficiary. 10–135

---

145 Older cases concern arrangements that have fallen into desuetude, such as marriage and other family settlements, as in e.g. *Priddy v Rose* (1817) 3 Mer. 86; *Smith v Smith* (1835) 1 Y. & C. Ex. 338; *Burridge v Row* (1842) 1 Y. & C. Ex. 183 at 193; *Re Weston* [1900] 2 Ch. 164. However, modern arrangements can also generate problems that fall into this category, e.g. where the "issue price" for a beneficiary's entitlements under an investment trust is payable in instalments and the beneficiary defaults on a payment.

146 *Worrall v Harford* (1802) 8 Ves. Jun. 4 at 8; *Re Blundell* (1888) 40 Ch. D. 370 at 376; *Stott v Milne* (1884) 25 Ch. D. 710 at 714–715; *Armitage v Nurse* [1998] Ch. 241 at 262; ... *Investec Trust (Guernsey) Ltd v Glenalla Properties Ltd* [2019] A.C. 271 at [59]; *Carter Holt Harvey Woodproducts Australia Pty Ltd v Commonwealth* (2019) 368 A.L.R. 390 at [29]–[33], [80]–[84]. See too Trustee Act 2000, s 31(1)(a).

147 For example, *Glenn v Federal Commissioner of Land Tax* (1915) 20 C.L.R. 490 at 498, 501–504. However, for the reasons identified later in this article, the accuracy of proprietary metaphors is to be doubted.

148 *DKLR Holding Co. (No.2) Pty Ltd v Commissioner of Stamp Duties* [1980] 1 N.S.W.L.R. 510 at 518–520.

149 [Footnotes omitted.]

Recoupment for expenses

10–136 A trustee has an indemnity for expenses properly incurred in the due administration of a trust.[150] The trustee is entitled to be indemnified both for payments she has made, and against liabilities she has incurred, to third parties. There are thus two limbs to the trustee's 'right of indemnity', as it is frequently called. One allows the trustee to use trust funds to discharge liabilities owed to third parties directly; this is described as the trustee's 'right of exoneration'. The other allows the trustee to reimburse herself out of trust funds for expenses she has already paid with her own money; this is the trustee's 'right of reimbursement' or 'recoupment'.[151] The exoneration limb and recoupment limb are different methods of achieving the same end, which is to ensure that a trustee is not left out of pocket through undertaking the proper administration of the trust. For example, it would be unfair to the trustee if she had to bear the burden of paying taxes or other expenses for which she is personally liable in her capacity as owner of the trust property,[152] or of paying litigation costs which she incurs while acting as trustee.[153] While exoneration and recoupment are directed towards the same end, however, they work differently. Exoneration allows a trustee to use trust property to pay a third party directly, while recoupment presupposes that the trustee has already paid the third party with her own money and allows the trustee to treat trust property as her own, free of her duties as trustee, to the extent required to make good her loss. ...

10–137 Recoupment in situation 5 differs from recoupment in situations 1–4. It is not targeted on a particular beneficiary's entitlement to trust property, albeit that it may affect the position of some or all of the beneficiaries by reducing the total amount available for distribution.[154] Indeed, if the trustee's expenses are larger than the trust fund, the beneficiaries' collective entitlements will be 'completely overwhelm[ed]';[155] but the effect of recoupment will always vary according to the size of the expense relative to the size of the trust fund and it may also vary according to rules governing the apportionment of expenses between income and capital interests ...

(v) Powers of Delegation

10–138 Where there is more than one trustee, as is usually the case, each trustee is personally responsible for administration of the trust and so should personally consider each act that needs to be done: if things turn out badly, it is no defence for a trustee to say that she was a "sleeping trustee" blindly relying on her co-trustees.[156] Nor can trustees collectively delegate their duties to another person, unless this is authorised by the trust deed or the Trustee Act 2000, which gives them broad powers to delegate their administrative, but not their distributive, functions.[157] Trustees of private trusts for persons must act unanimously unless the trust terms or court direct otherwise,[158] though the trustees of charitable trusts and pension trusts may act by a majority.[159]

---

150 There are many formulations of the circumstances in which the indemnity is available: see e.g. *Re Beddoe* [1893] 1 Ch. 547; *Re Grimthorpe* [1958] Ch. 615 at 623; *Chief Commissioner of Stamp Duties (NSW) v Buckle* (1998) 192 C.L.R. 226 at [47]; ... S. Donald, "The 'Proper' Approach to a Trustee's Right to Indemnity out of Trust Assets" (2014) 8 J. Eq. 283.

151 e.g. *Vacuum Oil Co Pty Ltd v Wiltshire* (1945) 72 C.L.R. 319 at 336–7; *Lemery Holdings Pty Ltd v Reliance Financial Services Pty Ltd* [2008] NSWSC 1344 at [47].

152 *Reid v Deane* [1906] V.L.R. 138; Re Reid [1943] S.A.S.R. 254; *Byrnes v Kendle* (2011) 243 C.L.R. 253 at [83], [143].

153 See generally *Easton v Landor* (1892) 62 L.J. Ch. 164 at 165; *Re Beddoe* [1893] 1 Ch. 547; ... *Price v Saundry* [2020] W.T.L.R. 233 at [29]–[31]; Rule 46.3 of the Civil Procedure Rules.

154 *Kemtron Industries Pty Ltd v Commissioner of Stamp Duties* [1984] 1 Qd. R. 576 at 587; *Chief Commissioner of Stamp Duties (NSW) v Buckle* (1998) 192 C.L.R. 226 at [48].

155 As in *Lane v Deputy Commissioner of Taxation* (2017) 253 F.C.R. 46 at [58].

156 *Munch v Cockerell* (1840) 5 Myl. & Cr. 178; *Bahin v Hughes* (1886) 31 Ch.D. 390; *Re Turner* [1897] 1 Ch. 536; *Head v Gould* [1898] 2 Ch. 250. There is no automatic vicarious liability for a co-trustee's breaches of trust, but a trustee will be liable for her own breach of trust if she fails to act jointly with the others and take reasonable steps to monitor her conduct: see, e.g. *Re Lucking's WT* [1968] 1 W.L.R. 866.

157 Trustee Act 2000 Pt IV.

158 *Luke v South Kensington Hotel Ltd* (1879) 11 Ch.D. 121; *Re Butlin's ST* [1976] Ch. 251 (rectification to allow majority decisions).

159 *Re Whiteley* [1910] 1 Ch. 600 at 608 (charitable trusts); Pensions Act 1995 s.32 (pension trusts).

The law's attitude towards the delegation of trustee responsibilities has shifted with the passing of time. The classical rule of equity was *delegatus non potest delegare* ("a delegate is not able to delegate"), reflected in Langdale MR's comment in *Turner v Corney*[160] that: 10–139

> trustees who take on themselves the management of property for the benefit of others have no right to shift their duty on other persons; and if they employ an agent, they remain subject to the responsibility towards their cestuis que trust, for whom they have undertaken the duty.

Accordingly, a trustee could not individually delegate her responsibilities to another trustee; nor could trustees collectively put the trust property into the hands of an agent. If they did this, and the agent dealt with the property to good effect, the beneficiaries could ratify the trustees' acts; but if the agent absconded with the property or negligently lost it, then the beneficiaries could hold the trustees liable to account for its value because the transfer to the agent was an unauthorised transaction. 10–140

By the 1880s, the courts had become concerned that this rule operated too harshly against trustees who needed to be able to delegate their investment functions to professionals with expertise in investing in an increasingly sophisticated financial marketplace. Hence in *Speight v Gaunt*[161] the Court of Appeal, affirmed by the House of Lords, held that trustees had an implied authority to delegate their managerial responsibilities to an agent if, in the circumstances, delegation was either reasonably necessary or in the ordinary course of affairs. If these conditions were satisfied, then the trustees would owe no continuing duty to account for property transferred to the agent. However, the trustees still had to be prudent in their selection and supervision, and could not employ an agent to do an act outside the scope of the agent's normal business.[162] Hence trustees could still be made liable for loss arising through an agent's default if they failed to exercise reasonable care in selecting and supervising the agent.[163] 10–141

The Trustee Act 1925 enlarged trustees' collective powers to delegate implementation of their decisions to an agent because s.23(1) enabled them to delegate whether or not there was any reasonable need for this, and lazy trustees could therefore delegate matters which they could have seen to themselves. However, they could not generally delegate the exercise of their discretion to decide what should be done. The collective powers of trustees to delegate their functions was later extended again by the Trustee Act 2000 ss.11 to 27.[164] 10–142

(vi) Powers of Amendment

Settlors may wish to empower trustees, or others, to amend the terms of their trusts for various reasons. One is that they wish to create a settlement with maximum flexibility, and possibly also to conceal the identity of the parties to whom they intend that beneficial enjoyment of the trust property should ultimately go. A device that is often used in offshore jurisdictions to achieve these goals is to create a discretionary trust for the benefit of a class of beneficiaries defined to include a named charitable body (which is in truth only a placeholder) and anyone added later by the exercise of a power of 10–143

---

160 (1841) 5 Beav. 515 at 517. See too *Chambers v Minchin* (1802) 7 Ves. Jun. 186; *Wood v Wightman* (1872) L.R. 13 Eq. 434.

161 (1883) 22 Ch.D. 727, affirmed (1883) 9 App. Cas. 1; discussed in C. Stebbings, *The Private Trustee in Victorian England* (Cambridge University Press, 2001), Ch.5, esp. pp.151–155.

162 *Fry v Tapson* (1884) 28 Ch.D. 268.

163 *Matthews v Brise* (1845) 10 Jur. (O.S.) 105.

164 An individual trustee may delegate her own functions, including distributive functions, under the Trustee Delegation Act 1999.

addition vested in the trustees.[165] Trusts of this kind are sometimes known as "Red Cross" trusts (after the charity that is often the only named beneficiary at the start) or as "black hole" trusts (because beneficial enjoyment of the property disappears into a "black hole"). Settlements of this kind were in issue in *Schmidt v Rosewood Trust Ltd*, discussed above.[166] Whether such drafting practices can be relied on to produce their intended effects is a disputed question.[167]

10–144 Another reason why settlors give trustees (or others) powers of amendment is that they cannot foresee the future and they want the relevant power holders to be able to change the trust terms in response to new circumstances which cannot be anticipated at the time when the trust is created. This is the main reason why powers of amendment are often vested in trustees and/or employers under occupational pension schemes. They are generally essential for the effective functioning of schemes, as David Pollard has written, because:[168] (1) schemes often last for a long time; (2) the pensions legislation and tax position of schemes is constantly changing; (3) pensions legislation often imposes new mandatory rules on trustees without overriding the existing terms of schemes or supplying employers or trustees with amendment powers; (4) the needs of employers and members in relation to retirement provision often change; and (5) discrimination laws have become directly applicable to pension schemes and this has created a need for amendments to the rules of many schemes. Given all this, as Arden LJ once said, it would be "crying for the moon" to expect the terms of a scheme to cover every eventuality,[169] and a better approach is to give employers and/or trustees) a broad power of amendment.

10–145 Examples of powers to amend the terms of occupational pension schemes include powers to increase the members' retirement age, to close the scheme to new members, to change or terminate the members' future accrual of benefits, to increase or remove the employers' liability to make contributions, to introduce, increase or remove the members' liability to make contributions, to convert a defined benefit scheme into a defined contribution scheme, and to replace the trustee.

Questions

1. "In *Cowan v Scargill*, Megarry V.-C. was too quick to dismiss the notion that trustees should sometimes take account of beneficiaries' interests that are not purely financial." **Discuss**.
2. "Clauses in trust deeds often purport to confer 'powers' on trustees, but sometimes the effect of these is not to give them powers but to give them permission to use their powers as owners of the trust property in particular ways." **Discuss**.
3. "It is often said that trustees have a 'lien' to secure their 'right' to take an indemnity out of the trust fund for costs they have personally incurred when carrying trust business. However, such statements are conceptually problematic." **Discuss**.

---

165 Compare clause 1.1.5 of the trust precedent reproduced above, which can be found at para.10–085.
166 [2003] 2 A.C. 709; see paras 10–063 to 10–076.
167 See paras 4–010 to 4–011.
168 D. Pollard, 'A "Two Steps" Tango: Amending Amendment Powers' (2015) 29 Tru.L.I. 16, 17–18.
169 *Stevens v Bell* [2002] P.L.R. 247 at [28].

11

RULES GOVERNING THE EXERCISE OF TRUSTEE POWERS

1. Introduction

A. Constraints on the Exercise of Trustee Powers

(i) General Rules of Property Law

As discussed in Chapter 10, trustees have powers which they use to perform their administrative role, which involves preserving, managing and investing the trust property, and their distributive role, which entails distributing property to authorised beneficiaries or applying it to authorised purposes. These powers may be vested in the trustees by reason of the fact that they own the trust property, an example being a power to assign the property to other parties, or they may be powers given to the trustees in addition to their powers as owners, an example being a power to amend the trust terms. When exercising powers of the first sort trustees may need to attend to general rules of property law governing transfers, e.g. if they wish to assign ownership of trust property they may have to comply with formality rules which affect all assignments of such property and which are not specific to trustees. We do not discuss rules of this kind in this chapter.[1] **11–001**

(ii) Oversight and Veto of Another Party

The exercise of trustee powers may also have been made subject to the oversight and veto of another party who has been empowered either to prevent the trustees from doing things she disapproves of, or to tell them what to do, e.g. when investing the trust fund.[2] Employers are commonly given powers to veto exercises of power by trustees under pension schemes, and the consent of the settlor or the beneficiaries may be needed for the trustees of certain family trusts to exercise powers of sale and investment or a power of appointment.[3] A person other than the trustees (who might or might not be **11–002**

---

1 But note that we outline the formality rules governing all assignments of property in Chapter 6 because settlors may have to comply with these in cases where they want to constitute a trust by transferring property to their intended trustees.

2 For a general discussion, distinguishing third party powers of consent, veto, direction and action, see R.C. Nolan, "Trustees and Third Party Powers" in R.C. Nolan et al (eds), *Trusts and Wealth Management in the Twenty First Century* (Cambridge University Press, 2018).

3 See e.g. G. Thomas, *Thomas on Powers*, 2nd edn (Oxford University Press, 2012) paras 7.107–7.128. Legislation also provides in some cases that the consent of beneficiaries is needed before trustees can exercise a statutory power, e.g. the Trustee Act 1925 s.32(1)(c) requires the trustees to obtain the life tenant's consent to the exercise of their statutory power of advancement.

the settlor[4]) might also be given such powers and described in the trust deed as the "protector" of the settlement. This is often done in offshore trusts,[5] less often in English trusts.[6] The word "protector" is not a legal term of art and is only an expression used by some drafters to describe a person who has powers to oversee and control the trustees.[7]

11-003 The settlor may or may not grant such powers intending that they be used to benefit the beneficiaries. In the former case, they are "fiduciary powers";[8] in the latter case they are "personal powers". A settlor might spell this out by stating e.g. that a power conferred on a protector "shall be absolute and shall not be a fiduciary power", or this might be implied, as e.g. where a settlor has appointed a person as protector who is also one of the beneficiaries. Fiduciary powers to tell trustees what to do and/or veto their decision-making may not be exercised in the power-holder's personal interests if these differ from the beneficiaries' interests,[9] but personal powers can be exercised in a self-interested way even in cases of conflict.[10] In either case, the power holder may not exceed the terms of her powers.[11] Where a person upon whose consent the valid exercise of a trustee power is predicated cannot give her consent it may be that the power can never be exercised; but although the courts have no general power to dispense with consents required by a trust deed or statute,[12] they may do so where this is permitted by statute,[13] or even in exceptional cases when acting under their inherent jurisdiction—as a court might do, e.g. where the person whose consent is needed cannot give it owing to a disability.[14] The decision whether to exercise a power of veto may also be taken by a court in the place of a fiduciary power-holder who is prevented from exercising the power by an inescapable conflict of interest.[15]

---

4 In which case the settlor is said to have "reserved" powers to herself under the trust. This is a popular device among settlors who wish to keep control of the trust property, particularly in offshore jurisdictions where this does not trigger the same fiscal disadvantages that might ensue in the UK. However, it creates a risk that their settlements may be struck down under the sham doctrine, for which see paras 7-059 to 7-070. For general discussion, see T.H. Tey, "Settlor's Reserved Powers" (2009) 23 Tru. L.I. 183; P.G. O'Hagan, "The Reluctant Settlor – Property, Powers and Pretences" (2011) 17 T. & T. 905; L. Ho, "'Breaking Bad': Settlors' Reserved Powers" in R.C. Nolan et al (eds) *Trusts and Modern Wealth Management in the Twenty First Century* (Cambridge University Press, 2018); D. Goodman and P. Hirsch, "To Reserve or not to Reserve? That Is the Question – Part I" (2019) 25 T. & T. 1025; D. Goodman and L. Johnson, "To Reserve or not to Reserve? What Can Possibly Go Wrong – Part II" (2020) 26 T. & T. 692.

5 R. Ham et al "Protectors" in D. Hayton (ed.) *The International Trust*, 3rd edn (LexisNexis Butterworths, 2011); A. Holden, *Trust Protectors* (Jordans, 2011); A. Duckworth "Protectors: Law and Practice" (2013) 19 T. & T. 98; M. Hubbard, *Protectors of Trusts* (Oxford University Press, 2013); P. Panico, *International Trust Laws*, 2nd edn (Oxford University Press, 2017), Ch.10.

6 Although the idea has a long history in English law. It made its first appearance in the Fines and Recoveries Act 1833; protectors have also been charged with protecting mentally incapable beneficiaries for many years: e.g. *Re Garrod* (1885) 31 Ch.D. 164; *Re Shortridge* [1895] 1 Ch. 278.

7 *JSC Mezhdunarodniy Bank v Pugachev* [2017] EWHC 2426 (Ch); (2017) 20 I.T.E.L.R. 905 at [180].

8 As in e.g. *IRC v Schroder* [1983] S.T.C. 480; *Re Osiris Trustees* (2000) 2 I.T.E.L.R. 404; *Re Circle Trust* [2007] W.T.L.R. 631; *Re Bird Charitable Trust and Bird Purpose Trust* [2008] W.T.L.R. 1505; *Blenkinsop v Herbert* (2017) 51 W.A.R. 264.

9 *JSC Mezhdunarodniy Bank v Pugachev* [2017] EWHC 2426 (Ch); (2017) 20 I.T.E.L.R. 905 at [180].

10 *Re Skeats' Settlement* (1889) 42 Ch.D. 522; *Lord Vestey's Executors v IRC* [1949] 1 All E.R. 1108; *JSC Mezhdunarodniy Bank v Pugachev* [2017] EWHC 2426 (Ch); (2017) 20 I.T.E.L.R. 905 at [186] and [203].

11 *Re Wright* [1920] 1 Ch. 108 at 118; *C v C (Ancillary Relief: Trust Fund)* [2009] EWHC 1491 (Fam); [2010] 1 F.L.R. 337 at [15].

12 *Re Forster's Settlement* [1942] Ch. 199.

13 e.g. Trusts of Land and Appointment of Trustees Act 1996 s.14, considered in *Bagum v Hafiz* [2015] EWCA Civ 801; [2016] Ch. 241.

14 *Re Cardross's Settlement* (1878) 7 Ch.D. 728; *Re Cooper* (1884) 27 Ch.D. 565; *Saipem SpA v Rafidain Bank* [1994] C.L.C. 253, further proceedings [2007] EWHC 3119 (Ch).

15 *Scully v Coley* [2009] UKPC 29 at [47]–[49], noting *Mettoy Pension Trustees Ltd v Evans* [1990] 1 W.L.R. 1587.

(iii) Rules of Trust Law

Whether or not the exercise of trustee powers is premised on another party's consent, there are also rules governing the exercise of trustee powers which affect every trust, although some of these can be disapplied by settlors, as we discuss in part 7 below. In the rest of this chapter, we consider the following rules: 11-004

- trustees may not act in a way that is contrary to the trust terms (the "excessive execution" rule);
- trustees may not exercise powers for an improper purpose (the "fraud on a power" rule);
- trustees may not take irrelevant considerations into account or overlook relevant considerations when deciding whether and if so how to exercise powers (the "adequate deliberation" rule);
- trustees may not exercise powers in bad faith (the "good faith" rule); and
- trustees must exercise powers with reasonable skill and care.

Another important rule governing the exercise of trustee powers is the "no conflicts" rule, which applies to all fiduciaries, including trustees, and which holds that they may not prioritise their own interests, or the interests of other people, over the beneficiaries' interests, unless the settlor has authorised them to do this. This rule is discussed in Chapter 3.[16] 11-005

Historically, most of these rules are sourced in decisions of the Chancery courts where the issue was whether a purported exercise of power was effective to create or vary or extinguish legal rights and duties.[17] (This is true, in fact, of all the rules apart from the rule that trustees should act with a reasonable degree of skill and care.) For example, it was held that beneficiaries' interests in trust property were not overreached if trustees purported to distribute trust property to a person other than a beneficiary, that a purported distribution of trust property to a beneficiary could be rescinded if the trustees and beneficiary had previously agreed that the beneficiary would transfer the property to someone who was not a beneficiary, and that a sale of trust property to a trustee could be rescinded. 11-006

In such cases, the courts did not say that the trustees had "breached a duty" not to do the things which they had done. Instead, the courts granted equitable relief to undo the legal effects intended by the trustees because they had failed to comply with the relevant rules, and the courts made different orders depending on the facts, e.g. holding that although ownership of property had been transferred to a recipient, the beneficiaries' equitable interest had not been overreached, or that the beneficiaries' equitable interest had been overreached but the transfer of legal title to the property could be rescinded. 11-007

In modern times, the rules have come to be expressed in the language of trustee "duties":[18] trustees are said to owe a "duty of due administration", a "duty to act for a proper purpose", a "duty to take all and only relevant considerations into account", a "duty of good faith", a "duty of skill and care" and a "fiduciary duty". This terminology can be convenient, but it creates a danger of misinterpretation. If everyone knows e.g. that a failure to comply with the "fraud on a power rule" and a 11-008

---

16 See paras 2–066 to 2–163.

17 This continues to be the question before the court in many cases where challenges are made to purported exercises of powers: see Warren J's observations in *IBM United Kingdom Holdings Ltd v Dalgleish* [2015] EWHC 389 (Ch); [2015] Pens. L.R. 99 at [55].

18 A parallel development has been the statutory statement of company directors' "duties" which appears in the Companies Act 2006 Part 10 Ch.2, which includes the s.171 "duty to act within powers", the s.172 "duty to promote the success of the company" and the s.175 "duty to avoid conflicts of interest".

failure to perform a "duty to act for a proper purpose" are one and the same thing, it may not matter which term is used to explain why a transfer of title to trust property can be rescinded if the trustees have acted for an improper purpose. However, a problem is created if the change of language leads the courts to make unwarranted assumptions about the remedies available for "breaches of duty" as opposed to "non-compliance with rules". This might occur if the language suggests by way of analogy with the "duty language" used at common law in breach of contract and tort cases that every breach of trustee "duty" must similarly result in liability to pay compensation for loss quantified by reference to similar rules to those developed at common law. This point is developed in Chapter 13, which concerns the compensatory liability of trustees where trust property is transferred to unauthorised recipients.[19] It is also touched on in Chapter 18 where compensatory liability for breach of fiduciary duty is discussed.[20]

11–009 In this chapter, the five rules listed above, and corresponding "duties" owed by trustees, are discussed in parts 2–6. In part 7 the question is considered whether any of these can be excluded by settlors and the point is made that some can, but others cannot because they are so fundamental to the idea of a trust that it cannot be said that a trust exists if they do not form part of the relationships between the trust parties.

11–010 The focus of all this discussion is on the content of the relevant rules; the results of non-compliance are discussed in later chapters contained in Part V, on "Breach of Trust", a term that is often used in a compendious way to describe every failure to comply with the rules described below.

11–011 Note, however, that breaches of trust do not always produce the same results and that these can differ according to circumstances: a non-compliant exercise of a power by trustees may be a nullity (e.g. where they purport to vary the trust terms but exceed the scope of the power); or it may be valid at common law but not in equity (e.g. where trustees purport to distribute trust property to a person who is not a beneficiary, so that she acquires legal ownership but the beneficiaries' equitable interest in the property subsists); and/or it may expose the trustees to personal compensatory liability (e.g. where they use trust money to purchase property in a transaction that is unauthorised and/or negligent).

11–012 Note, also, that various parties may have standing to enforce the trust law rules governing the exercise of trustee powers, depending on the circumstances. This is discussed in the next section, by way of preliminary to discussion of the rules themselves.

B. Who Can Enforce the Trust Law Rules?

11–013 It is uncontroversial that the beneficiaries of fixed trusts have standing to enforce the rules of trust law discussed in this chapter and to seek a variety of orders against trustees and third parties. Less straightforward is the question whether the same is true of other trust parties.

11–014 We can start by putting settlors to one side. It is well established that a settlor has no standing to bring a claim founded on a breach of trust merely by dint of the fact that she was the settlor.[21] She may, however, have standing to sue in some other capacity, e.g. if she has made herself a beneficiary or a trustee or has given herself powers of oversight and veto of the sort which have been described above.[22]

---

19 See paras 13–009 to 13–089.

20 See paras 18–007 to 18–025.

21 *Re Astor's Settlement Trusts* [1952] Ch. 534 at 542; *Re Murphy's Settlements* [1999] 1 W.L.R. 282 at 295.

22 See paras 11–002 to 11–003.

Proceedings for breach of trust can be brought by a trustee against a co-trustee or a former trustee,[23] and it is no answer to such a claim that the claimant trustee themselves participated in the breach,[24] because trustees owe a positive duty to rectify breaches of duty by other trustees of which they are, or reasonably should be, aware, and failure to do this will itself constitute a breach of trust.[25] The authorities establishing these propositions were reviewed by an Australian judge, Brooking J, in *Young v Murphy*. **11–015**

Young v Murphy [1996] 1 V.R. 279 at 281–285

Victoria Court of Appeal

... The standing of a trustee to take proceedings to have a breach of trust redressed against a trustee or former trustee or a stranger who has become liable to redress a breach of trust is well recognised. Not only may a trustee take such proceedings, but he runs the risk of himself committing a breach of trust if he fails to do so.[26] His obligation to take the proceedings (unless they would be futile) is part of his duty to get in the trust estate, which includes rights of action against co-trustees or former trustees and strangers for breach of trust. This is clear as a matter of both principle and authority. Moreover, since the trustee will take the proceedings for breach of trust for the benefit of the beneficiaries, he can sue even if he was a party to the breach of trust or some other breach of trust. The principle is shortly stated in *Snell's Equity*,[27] where it is said of a new trustee: **11–016**

> "If ... he discovers that breaches of trust have been committed, he must obtain satisfaction for them from the old trustee, just in the same way as an original trustee must get in any part of the trust estate which is outstanding: and the only excuse for not doing so is that it would be useless to take proceedings against the old trustees."

... The right and duty of a successor trustee to sue his predecessor for breach of trust is in *Re Lane's Will*[28] correctly founded on his duty to obtain all the property that belongs to the trust and for that purpose to get in from the preceding trustees or their representatives whatever the successor trustee finds to be necessary to reimburse the trust estate for losses sustained through breach of trust. Similarly in *Wentworth v Tompson*[29] the Full Court of New South Wales, in rejecting the suggestion that a trustee could not sue his co-trustees for breach of trust where he had been himself a party to that breach, observed that it was the duty of each trustee to recover the trust fund, for the benefit of the objects of it. In the same way, *Scott on Trusts*,[30] in asserting the right of a trustee who in breach of trust transfers property to a person who has notice of the trust or pays no value to sue the transferee notwithstanding his own breach of trust, rests that view on the circumstance that the trustee is suing for the benefit of the trust estate. Likewise it is said in *Scott*,[31] that a co-trustee is not debarred by his own misconduct from maintaining a suit to redress a breach of trust committed by a trustee, since the purpose of the suit is to maintain the interests of the beneficiaries.[32] ... **11–017**

---

23 *Young v Murphy* [1996] 1 V.R. 279 at 281; *Dalriada Trustees Ltd v Woodward* [2012] EWHC 21626 (Ch); [2012] W.T.L.R. 1489 at [37].

24 *Young* [1996] 1 V.R. 279 at 283.

25 *Walker v Symonds* (1818) 3 Swans. 1 at 71–72; *Re Forest of Dean Coal Mining Co* (1878) 10 Ch. D. 450 at 451.

26 *Scott on Trusts*, s.177, s.223 and s.223.3; Bogert, *Law of Trusts and Trustees*, s.592; Bogert, *Handbook of the Law of Trusts*, s.97; *Re Brogden* (1888) 38 Ch.D. 546.

27 29th ed., pp.286–7, correctly citing *Re Forest of Dean Coal Mining Co* (1878) 10 Ch.D. 450.

28 (1916) 97 Atl. 587.

29 (1859) 2 Legge 1238 at 1241.

30 4th ed., s.294.2.

31 Ibid at s.200.2.

32 [For this proposition the judge also cited: *Franco v Franco* (1796) 3 Ves. Jun. 76; *May v Selby* (1842) 1 Y.&C. (C.C.) 235; *Price v Blakemore* (1843) 6 Beav. 507; *Hughes v Key* (1855) 20 Beav. 395; *Baynard v Woolley* (1855) 20 Beav. 583 (where Sir John Romilly MR said that the books were full of cases in which trustees who had been guilty of breaches of trust had called on their co-trustees to replace funds); *Butler v Butler* (1872) 7 Ch.D. 116 at 120–121, per Baggallay LJ and at 1231, per Thesiger LJ; *Coverlid v Joel* (1879) 1 Q.B. 138 at 140.]

11–018 In general, if the trustee takes proceedings to have a breach of trust redressed, he need not make the beneficiaries parties. For in general the trustee sufficiently represents their interests for the purposes of proceedings to have a breach of trust redressed. As was said by Porter, MR in *Carson v Sloane*,[33] "If one of the cestuis que trust could follow this fund, why cannot the trustee who represents them all?" The right of the trustee in general to sue for breach of trust without making the beneficiaries parties is well established.[34]

11–019 But, while the trustee in general sufficiently represents the beneficiaries' interests for the purposes of proceedings to redress a breach of trust, they should be made parties if their interests may not be properly represented by the trustee. If it can be said that for any reason the trustee should not be regarded as a party who will properly represent the interests of all beneficiaries, then he should not be regarded as able to sue without joining any beneficiary. Cases of suggested fraud or collusion or a hidden interest of the trustee may be put to one side. The proceedings which the trustee brings may be such as to raise, or be capable of raising, questions between one beneficiary and another or questions between the beneficiaries and himself. In such a case the trustee does not sufficiently represent the interests of the beneficiaries for the purposes of the proceedings. Accordingly, if in the proceedings the trustee seeks the execution or administration of the trust in addition to seeking to have the breach of trust redressed, the beneficiaries will or may be necessary parties, since their interests inter se or their rights against the trustee may have to be determined. This is not so if in the proceedings the trustee seeks only to get in the trust fund, or seeks in addition only any account necessary for that purpose. On the other hand, in proceedings for the execution or administration of the trust the interests of the beneficiaries may conflict among themselves and there may in addition be a conflict of interest between the trustee and the beneficiaries with regard to the accounting by the trustee required for the purposes of the general distribution of the trust estate which is asked for in the proceedings. So a distinction is drawn between proceedings which seek merely to get back the trust fund and proceedings for the execution or administration of the trust. The former can be maintained by the trustee without joining the beneficiaries; the latter are or may be incapable of being so maintained.[35]

11–020 Proceedings to have a breach of trust redressed may also be taken "by a beneficiary against a trustee or a former trustee or the estate of a former trustee".[36] As discussed in Chapter 3,[37] this includes the beneficiary of a discretionary trust, although her interest is a mere expectancy, meaning that her right to beneficial enjoyment is contingent on the exercise of a discretionary dispositive power in her favour.[38] This proposition was confirmed in *Lewis v Tamplin* where the judge added that:[39]

---

33 (1884) 13 L.R. Ir. 139 at 147.

34 See, for example, *Greenwood v Wakeford* (1839) 1 Beav. 576; *Robinson v Evans* (1843) 7 Jur. 738; *Price v Blakemore* (1843) 6 Beav. 507; *Bridget v Hames* (1844) 1 Coll. 72; *Horsley v Fawcett* (1847) 11 Beav. 565; *Noble v Meymott* (1851) 14 Beav. 471; *Wentworth v Tompson* (1859) 2 Legge 1238; ... *Re Cross* (1882) 20 Ch.D. 109.

35 [The judge cited various authorities for these propositions, including: *Franco v Franco* (1796) 3 Ves. Jun. 76; *Horsley v Fawcett* (1847) 11 Beav. 565; *Chancellor v Morecraft* (1847) 11 Beav. 262; *Groom v Booth* (1853) 1 Drew. 548; the note to the report of *Devaynes v Robinson* (1857) 24 Beav. 86; *Re Jordan* (1904) 1 Ch. 260 at 263; and *Equity Trustees etc Co v Fenwick* (1905) V.L.R. 154 at 164.]

36 *Young v Murphy* [1996] 1 V.R. 279 at 281. See too *Re Cross* (1881) 20 Ch.D. 109; *Space Investments Ltd v Canadian Imperial Bank of Commerce Trust Co (Bahamas) Ltd* [1986] 1 W.L.R. 1072 at 1074; *Shimshon v MLC Nominees Pty Ltd* [2021] VSCA 363 at [13].

37 See paras 3–175 to 3–181.

38 *Gartside v IRC* [1968] A.C. 553 at 617. See too *Spellson v George* (1987) 11 N.S.W.L.R. 300 at 316, considered in *Schmidt v Rosewood Trust Ltd* [2003] UKPC 26; [2003] 2 A.C. 709 at [59]–[60]; *Armitage v Nurse* [1998] Ch. 241 at 261; *Johns v Johns* [2004] 3 N.Z.L.R. 202 at [34]; *Whaley v Whaley* [2011] EWCA Civ 617; [2012] 1 F.L.R. 735 at [112].

39 [2018] EWHC 777 (Ch); [2018] W.T.L.R. 215 at [39]. See also *Serious Fraud Office v Litigation Capital Ltd* [2021] EWHC 1272 (Comm) at [203]–[205] where Foxton J found that the object of a discretionary power of appointment "had the right to require the trustee . . . to administer the assets in accordance with the terms of the Settlement, and to seek relief in the event that the trustee dealt with any assets in breach of trust, including against any third party recipients of that property."

> A beneficiary or object may have rights in relation to the trust fund which are good, not only against the trustees, but also against third parties, which thus may properly be called property rights, without necessarily having a vested interest in possession or in remainder in a particular income stream or capital asset. If the trustee of a discretionary trust in breach of trust gave away a trust asset to a third party, no-one can doubt that even a discretionary object of the trust in whose favour an appointment could still be made would have standing to sue the third party for the return of the asset to the trust fund.

Prior to *Schmidt v Rosewood Trust Ltd*,[40] a contrast was drawn between the beneficiary of a discretionary trust and the object of a mere power of appointment: it was considered that the former was in a stronger position than the latter and that the former, but not the latter, could invoke the jurisdiction of the court to supervise and, if necessary, intervene in the administration of a trust with a view to obtaining trust information and bringing proceedings against the trustees if they were found to have committed a breach of trust. However, the Privy Council held in *Schmidt* that this was incorrect and that there is no clear distinction in this respect between the objects of trust powers (also known as the beneficiaries of a discretionary trust) and the objects of mere powers of appointment. According to Lord Walker, both can obtain orders requiring trustees to give them trust information in some situations—and there is no point in a court making such an order unless the person in whose favour it is made can bring proceedings in the event that she uncovers evidence of unauthorised dealings, something which the objects of a mere power of appointment are permitted to do in some other jurisdictions.[41] **11–021**

It may be that some objects of a mere power of appointment have a more realistic chance than others of being considered prime candidates for the exercise of a discretion in their favour and it may be that a court would consider them for that reason to be more suitable people than other objects to have rights to information and standing to sue in cases of breach.[42] As Neuberger J once said, the onerous burdens on trustees should not be unnecessarily increased by the courts making orders:[43] **11–022**

> which would be likely to result in trustees of discretionary private trusts being badgered with claims by many beneficiaries [scil: or objects of mere powers] for consideration to be given to their claims for trust moneys, or for accounts as to how trust moneys have been spent.

A consideration pulling in the other direction, however, is that the accountability of trustees is the heart of the trust concept, that settlors who create trusts necessarily intend that the trustees should be accountable to *someone*, and that in some cases it could defeat this intention if the courts denied that enforcement rights might be vested in people with no immediate (nor even any) right to enjoyment of trust property. This suggests that enforcement rights can appropriately be given to a person with no more than the hope of future enjoyment, and even, as we have already discussed in Chapter 3, that a settlor can give such rights to a person who has no prospect of beneficial enjoyment at all.[44] Indeed, the law already permits this, since it holds that charitable trusts are legally valid, that charitable trustees are generally subject to the rules described in this chapter, and that these rules are enforceable by the Attorney General, acting in the public interest. **11–023**

---

40 [2003] UKPC 26; [2003] 2 A.C. 709; discussed at paras 10–063 to 10–076.

41 Australian cases are identified and discussed in J. Hudson. "Mere and Other Discretionary Objects in Australia" in Y.K. Liew and M. Harding (eds), *Asia-Pacific Trusts Law, Volume 1: Theory and Practice in Context* (Hart Publishing, 2021), pp.24–27. See also *Lemos v Coutts (Cayman) Ltd* (2005–06) 8 I.T.E.L.R. 153 (Cayman Islands); *Freeman v Ansbacher (Trustees) Jersey Ltd* [2009] J.L.R. 1; [2010] W.T.L.R. 569 (Jersey).

42 As observed in R. Nolan, "Invoking the Administrative Jurisdiction: The Enforcement of Modern Trust Structures" in P.S. Davies and J. Penner (eds), *Equity, Trusts, and Commerce* (Hart Publishing, 2017) at pp.167–168.

43 *Re Murphy's Settlement* [1999] 1 W.L.R. 282 at 293.

44 See paras 3–163 to 3–185.

2. The "Excessive Execution" Rule and the Duty of Due Administration

11–024 The purported exercise of a power is ineffective if the power does not exist. So, for example, there are many cases concerning pension schemes where the exercise of a power of amendment (or some other power) has been declared ineffective because the trustees (and/or employers) were never given the relevant power.[45] For essentially the same reason, pensions cases also hold that a purported exercise of power is ineffective where its exercise is subject to conditions that are not satisfied.[46] The questions whether a trustee has a power, and whether her exercise of a power is subject to conditions, may be determined by legal rules which themselves generate the relevant power. So, for example, the questions whether a trustee has powers, as owner of trust property, to transfer, assign or deal with the property, and if so whether the exercise of these powers depends on conditions being satisfied, are governed by relevant rules of property law and legal rules about assignment of choses in action. When a trustee fails to comply with the relevant power-generating rules, her actions will be ineffective to produce the legal outcome which she sought to produce, e.g. a transfer of title to a third party, and in such cases it is sometimes said that the reason for this is that the trustee's purported exercise of power was "in excess of the power" or an "excessive execution".[47]

11–025 Confusingly, however, the language of "excessive execution" has also been used to describe another rule which holds that an exercise of power by a trustee or other power holder must cohere with the trust terms. This separate rule is also referred to as imposing a "duty of due administration", as discussed in Chapter 3, where the point is made that it applies across express trusts, deceased estates, partnerships, and other relationships.[48] The rule requiring a trustee's due administration stipulates that a trustee cannot secure a legal effect through an exercise of power, such as a third party's receipt of title, unless this is permitted by the trust terms. The point is to ensure that power holders carry out the intentions of the settlors who gave them their powers and, when it is conceived in this way, it is obvious why the rule applies to trustees, since it is a recurring theme of trusts law that trustees are made the owners of trust property, and thereby acquire rights and powers respecting the property, in order to carry out the settlor's intentions.

11–026 Typically, settlors intend that trust property should be preserved and managed, either for beneficiaries to whom the property will be distributed, or to further legally permissible abstract purposes, and these plans are usually reflected in the terms of trusts which specify the circumstances in which the trustees are and are not permitted to exercise their powers. This is the reason why the courts have said that a trustee's "paramount obligation" is "recovering, securing and duly applying the trust fund",[49] that she must get in the trust property when required to do so,[50] that if she or another trustee misapplies the property she must bring proceedings to recover it or otherwise obtain relief on the

---

45 *Schmidt v Air Products Canada Ltd* [1994] 2 S.C.R. 611; *Air Jamaica Ltd v Charlton* [1999] 1 W.L.R. 1399 at 1411; *UC Rusal Alumina Jamaica Ltd v Miller* [2014] UKPC 39; [2015] Pens. L.R. 15 at [46]; *British Airways Plc v Airways Pension Scheme Trustee Ltd* [2018] EWCA Civ 1533; [2018] Pens. L.R. 19 at [102].

46 *BESTrustees v Stuart* [2001] Pens. L.R. 283; *HR Trustees Ltd v Wembley Plc* [2011] EWHC 2974 (Ch); *Briggs v Gleeds (Head Office) (a firm)* [2014] EWHC 1178 (Ch); [2015] Ch. 212 at [2]–[7]; *BIC UK Ltd v Burgess* [2019] EWCA Civ 806; [2019] P.L.R. 17 at [23].

47 Language used in e.g. *Kater v Roget* (1840) 4 Y. & C. 18 at 18–19; *Re Burton's Settlements* [1955] Ch. 82 at 89–90; *Pitt v Holt* [2013] UKSC 26; [2013] 2 A.C. 108 at [60] and [80]; *IBM United Kingdom Holdings Ltd v Dalgleish* [2017] EWCA Civ 1212; [2018] I.C.R. 1681 at [173]–[175]; *Board of the Pension Protection Fund v Dalriada Trustees Ltd* [2020] EWHC 2960 (Ch); [2021] I.C.R 479 at [194].

48 See paras 3–163 to 3–185.

49 *Re Brogden* (1888) 38 Ch.D. 546 at 571.

50 *Maitland v Bateman* (1843) 13 L.J. Ch. 273; *M'Donnel v White* (1865) 9 H.L. Cas. 570 at 585; *Wyman v Paterson* [1900] A.C. 271.

beneficiaries' behalf,[51] and that she must "properly . . . preserve the trust fund", and "pay the income and the corpus to those who are entitled to them respectively".[52]

In *Youyang Pty Ltd v Minter Ellison Morris Fletcher* the High Court of Australia averred that "perhaps the most important duty of a trustee is to obey the terms of the trust".[53] Similarly, in *AIB Group (UK) Plc v Mark Redler & Co Solicitors* Lord Toulson said that a trustee owes "a duty to preserve the assets of the trust except in so far as the terms of the trust permit [her] to do otherwise",[54] and that "the basic right of a beneficiary is to have the trust duly administered in accordance with the provisions of the trust instrument, if any, and the general law."[55] This is why the beneficiaries' equitable interests in trust property are not overreached in cases where trustees purport to distribute trust property by transferring ownership to someone who is not a beneficiary,[56] or treat trust property as their own as a means of recouping themselves for the cost of paying liabilities which were not "properly incurred" in the course of trust business.[57] **11–027**

The courts can also give effect to the beneficiaries' rights to due administration in other ways, such as by making a declaration setting out the nature and extent of a beneficiary's interest,[58] or of a trustee's duties and powers;[59] by directing the trustee to exercise an obligatory discretionary power of appointment;[60] by directing the trustee to transfer trust assets to an absolutely entitled beneficiary;[61] or by issuing a prohibitory injunction, restraining the trustee from acting inconsistently with the terms of the trust.[62] Further, a trustee who is unsure whether a proposed course of action lies within her **11–028**

---

51 *Re Forest of Dean Coal Mining Co* (1879) 10 Ch.D. 450 at 453–454; *Young v Murphy* [1996] 1 V.R. 279, esp. at 281–282; *Evans v European Bank Ltd* (2004) 7 I.T.E.L.R. 19 at [116].

52 *Low v Bouverie* [1891] 3 Ch. 82 at 99.

53 (2003) 212 C.L.R. 484 at [32].

54 [2014] UKSC 58; [2015] A.C. 1503 at [51].

55 [2014] UKSC 58; [2015] A.C. 1503 at [64]. See also *Sneddon v Lord Advocate* [1954] A.C. 257 at 283; *Spellson v George* (1987) 11 N.S.W.L.R. 300 at 315–316; *Target Holdings Ltd v Redferns (a firm)* [1996] A.C. 421 at 434; *Chief Commissioner of Stamp Duties (NSW) v Buckle* (1998) 192 C.L.R. 226 at 242; *Burke v Hudson's Bay Co* [2010] 2 S.C.R. 273 at [87]; *Whaley v Whaley* [2011] EWCA Civ 617; [2012] 1 F.L.R. 735 at [112]; *Akers v Samba Financial Group* [2017] UKSC 6; [2017] A.C. 424 at [82].

56 *Harvey v Stacey* (1852) 22 L.J. Ch. 23; *Re Kerr's Trusts* (1877) 4 Ch. D. 600 at 604; *Clark v Revenue and Customs Commissioners* [2020] EWCA Civ 204; [2020] 1 W.L.R. 3354 at [45]. The same principle applies to expenditure by charity trustees: Charity Commission, *The Prevention or Relief of Poverty for the Public Benefit* (Charity Commission, December 2008), para.G1: "a breach of trust can arise where trustees act outside their duties or powers, including using their charity's property and other resources for something that falls outside the charity's aims."

57 *Re Beddoe* [1893] 1 Ch. 547 at 559; *Alsop Wilkinson v Neary* [1996] 1 W.L.R. 1220 at 1224; *Chief Commissioner of Stamp Duties (NSW) v Buckle* (1998) 192 C.L.R. 226 at [47]; *Carter Holt Harvey Woodproducts Australia Pty Ltd v Commonwealth* (2019) 268 C.L.R. 524 at [40] ("authorised liabilities incurred in the course of the business of the trust").

58 *Smith v Acton* (1858) 26 Beav. 210. The courts now have an unfettered discretion to make binding declarations under CPR r.40.20, but will not normally entertain theoretical questions with no practical application: *Padden v Arbuthnot Pensions and Investments Ltd* [2004] EWCA Civ 582 at [24], [31]. The proper form of a declaration of equitable interest under r.40.20 is discussed in *Powell v Wiltshire* [2004] EWCA Civ 534; [2005] Q.B. 117 at [39]–[45]. The Trusts of Land and Appointment of Trustees Act 1996 s.14(2)(b) enables a person with an interest in property subject to a trust of land to a declaration of the nature or extent of her interest, as in, e.g. *Oxley v Hiscock* [2004] EWCA Civ 546; [2005] Fam. 211 and *Vinaver v Milton Ashbury Ltd* [2006] EWCA Civ 363; [2006] W.T.L.R. 1675.

59 *Cowan v Scargill* [1985] Ch. 270; *University of London v Prag* [2014] EWHC 3564 (Ch).

60 *Re Locker's Settlement Trusts* [1977] 1 W.L.R. 1323.

61 *Re Knox's Trusts* [1895] 2 Ch. 483; *Re Sandeman's Will Trust* [1937] 1 All E.R. 368. See too the Trustee Act 1925 ss.44(vi) and 51(1)(d).

62 *Fox v Fox* (1870) L.R. 11 Eq. 142 (improper distribution of assets); *Buttle v Saunders* [1950] 2 All E.R. 193 (sale of assets at an undervalue); *Walbrook Trustees (Jersey) Ltd v Fattal* [2009] EWHC 1446 (Ch); [2010] 1 All E.R. (Comm) 526 (interim injunction restraining disposal of property by trustees before trial). It is no bar to the issue of an injunction restraining the unauthorised disposal of trust assets that the trustees have entered a binding contract with a third party: *Fouche v Superannuation Fund Board* (1952) 88 C.L.R. 609; and see too *Ord v Noel* (1820) 5 Madd. 438; *Dance v Goldingham* (1873) 8 Ch. App. 902.

powers may seek prior authorisation from the court,[63] which should act cautiously in such a case, and be mindful that such an order will "deprive the beneficiaries of any opportunity of alleging that [the trustee's action] constitutes a breach of trust and seeking compensation for any loss which may flow from that wrong".[64]

11–029 The courts' use of a single term—"excessive execution"—to describe two separate rules is confusing. As explained above, this language is sometimes used to describe a rule which renders an exercise of power ineffective for non-compliance with power generating rules such as the rules of property law, but is sometimes used to describe a rule which stipulates that a trustee can only use her powers in a manner which is permitted by the trust terms. This may create the false impression that there is only one rule of "excessive execution". However, the two rules described here are distinct, as is shown by cases concerning an unauthorised exercise of the trustee's power to transfer title to trust property to a third party where there is an effective exercise of the trustee's power according to the power generating rules providing for the transfer of the subject property, but the trustee's exercise of power is unauthorised because it is contrary to the trust terms. In such cases, provided the trustee complies with the legal rules governing transfer of the property, the transfer will be valid at common law even if it is contrary to the trust terms,[65] but the trustee's failure to comply with the trust terms may lead to the conclusion that the transfer was ineffective for the purposes of various equitable doctrines.[66]

3. The "Fraud on a Power" Rule and the Duty to Act for a Proper Purpose

11–030 The doctrine of "fraud on a power"[67] provides that a power holder may not exercise a power to produce a result that is inconsistent with the purposes of the person who conferred the power. The language of "fraud" is misleading in this context as it is possible for a power holder to commit a fraud on the power although she acts with good intentions. In *Vatcher v Paull* Lord Parker said that:[68]

> The term [fraud] in connection with frauds on a power does not necessarily denote any conduct on the part of the appointor amounting to fraud in the common law meaning of the term or any conduct which could properly be termed dishonest or immoral. It merely means that the power has been exercised for a purpose, or with an intention, beyond the scope of or not justified by the instrument creating the power.

11–031 A trustee would fall foul of the doctrine if she purported to exercise a power in a way that produced an outcome that was permissible on its face, but with the bad faith intention of achieving a larger purpose that was impermissible. For example, it could constitute a fraud on a power for trustees to appoint property to a beneficiary who had previously agreed to apply the property for the benefit of a person who was not an object, as in *Wong v Burt*,[69] excerpted below. Or again, as Lord Parker noted

---

[63] By proceedings pursuant to C.P.R. Pt 64. Further see L. Ho and R.C. Nolan, "The Performance Interest in the Law of Trusts" (2020) 136 L.Q.R. 402, 405–407.

[64] *Richard v Mackay*, Ch.D. 4 March 1987, reported [2008] W.T.L.R. 1667 at 1671, per Millett J. See too *X v A* [2005] EWHC 2706 (Ch); [2006] 1 W.L.R. 741 at [30]; *Tamlin v Edgar* [2011] EWHC 3949 (Ch) at [25]; *Cotton v Earl of Cardigan* [2014] EWCA Civ 1312; [2015] W.T.L.R. 39.

[65] *Rolled Steel Products (Holdings) Ltd v British Steel Corp* [1986] Ch. 246 at 303; *Akers v Samba Financial Group* [2017] UKSC 6; [2017] A.C. 424 at [51].

[66] See para.10–081.

[67] See P. Matthews, "The Doctrine of Fraud on a Power, Parts 1 and 2" [2007] P.C.B. 131 and 191.

[68] [1915] A.C. 372 at 378. See too *Duke of Portland v Topham* (1864) 11 H.L. Cas. 32 at 54.

[69] [2005] 1 N.Z.L.R. 91. See too *Lane v Page* (1755) Amb. 233; *Re Turner's Settled Estates* (1884) 28 Ch.D. 205; *Re Greaves* [1954] Ch. 434. But cf. *Netherton v Netherton* [2000] W.T.L.R. 1171, followed in *Re X Trust* (2003) 5 I.T.E.L.R. 119; *Kain v Hutton* [2008] 3 N.Z.L.R. 589.

in *Vatcher*,[70] it would be a fraud on a power for a father to exercise a power of appointment in favour of his child, although such an appointment was prima facie valid,[71] if he did this when the child was ill and intending to take the child's estate for himself on the child's death—and in such a case, the appointment would be a fraud on the power even if the child recovered.[72]

Wong v Burt

New Zealand Court of Appeal [2005] 1 N.Z.L.R. 91

HAMMOND J.: The essential facts relating to this issue can be shortly stated. 11–032

Clause 5 of William Wong's will, in summary, provided as follows: 11–033

- The residuary estate was to be held in trust with the net annual income payable to Estelle Wong until her death.
- After the death of Estelle Wong, the net annual income was to be payable in equal shares to those of Phillipa and Wong Liu Sheung who were still alive. It is of singular importance to this case that there was no substitutionary provision in favour of grandchildren, if one of those daughters predeceased Estelle; in that event, all the income was to be paid to the other surviving daughter.
- After the death of the last surviving child, the estate is to be distributed among the children, or grandchildren, or great grandchildren of Phillipa. The exclusion of Wong Liu Sheung's children appears to have been quite deliberate, as a result of a family falling out.

Clause 6 of the will conferred upon the trustees a discretion to pay to Estelle, out of the capital of the estate: 11–034

> ". . . such sum or sums as they in their absolute discretion may think fit if they shall consider it necessary, desirable or expedient so to do by reason of the state of my wife's health or her desire to travel or to acquire a home or by reason of a fall in the purchasing power of money or for any other reasons whatsoever whether similar or dissimilar to the foregoing."

When Phillipa Wong died in 1995 Mrs Estelle Wong became concerned as to the position of Mei-Ling and Matthew. She viewed the inability of these two children to take their mother's share of the estate income, in the event of their mother's death, as inappropriate, and unfair. 11–035

To overcome this disability, in 1996 the trustees distributed $250,000 of the capital of the William Wong estate to Estelle. Estelle then lent this sum of $250,000 to the Phillipa Estelle Wong Trust (PEW Trust). The beneficiaries of PEW are Mei-Ling and Matthew. 11–036

In effecting this payment of $250,000, the trustees relied on their powers under clause 6 of the will. The debt was then periodically forgiven over a period of years, and by this will. 11–037

The Claim in the High Court

Wong Liu Sheung bought proceedings in the High Court claiming that, in so proceeding, the trustees: 11–038

- had acted ultra vires the terms of the trust;
- breached their duty to exercise their discretion for a proper purpose; and
- breached their duty to act impartially and even handedly towards all classes of beneficiaries.

The Judgment in the High Court

Ronald Young J. dismissed this claim, in its entirety, in a judgment delivered on 6 May 2003. . . . 11–039

The Grounds of Appeal

Ms Peters argued that the exercise of the discretion by the trustees in the impugned respect was for an improper purpose. This submission rested essentially on two propositions. First, that the sole purpose of the exercise of the discretion was to "remedy" a perceived inequality that had arisen under clause 5 of the 11–040

[70] *Vatcher v Paull* [1915] A.C. 372 at 379–380.
[71] See too *Henty v Wrey* (1882) 21 Ch.D. 232.
[72] See too *Lord Hinchbrooke v Seymour* (1789) 1 Bro. C.C. 395.

will (the appellants really say as a device to circumvent the plain meaning of clause 5). Second, that the distribution made was to benefit a person who was not an object of the clause 6 discretion (i.e. not Estelle).

11–041 As to remedies, Ms Peters submitted that the $250,000 can be traced to the PEW Trust, and as such, the trustees of that trust hold the funds as constructive trustees for the William Wong estate.

11–042 Alternatively, the appellants submit that the trustees are personally liable. The essential issue both under clause 13 of the will (the exoneration provision) and s.73 is whether the trustees acted dishonestly. The appellants submit that the trustees' actions, particularly when they were specifically warned that the will prohibited the course of conduct proposed, amounted (at least) to "recklessness". . . .

The Law

11–043 The notion of a fraud on a power itself rests on the fundamental juristic principle that any form of authority may only be exercised for the purposes conferred, and in accordance with its terms. This principle is one of general application.

11–044 The particular expression, a "fraud on a power", applies to both a power and a discretion. The word "fraud" here denotes an improper motive, in the sense that a power given for one purpose is improperly used for another purpose.

11–045 Over the years a number of attempts have been made to categorise the circumstances in which a fraud on a power will arise. For instance, Hanbury and Martin, *Modern Equity*[73] divides the cases into three categories. The first arises where the appointment is made as a result of a prior agreement or bargain with the appointee as to what he or she will do with the proceeds. Secondly, there are those cases where the power is exercised improperly so as to benefit the appointor. The third category are those cases in which an appointment is drafted so that the intent appears to benefit objects of the power, but the real intent is to benefit non-objects.

11–046 These distinctions are useful for analytic and descriptive purposes, but it is necessary to recall that the sine qua non which makes the exercise of a discretion or power "improper" is the improper intention of the person exercising it. The central principle is that if the power is exercised with the intention of benefiting some non-object of the discretionary power, whether that person is the person exercising it, or anybody else for that matter, the exercise is void. If, on the other hand, there is no such improper intention, even although the exercise does in fact benefit a non-object, it is valid.[74]

11–047 In the case of a discretionary power to be exercised in favour of one of its objects, but in the "hope" that the recipient will benefit a non-object, the validity of such an exercise will depend upon whether the recipient had legal and moral freedom of action.[75]

11–048 The case law in this area is difficult, not so much for the underlying principles, which seem plain enough, but in their application to often quite complex estates, or interrelated transactions. Assume, for instance, a case in which a discretionary power is exercisable in favour of an adult male (X) who states that, if it is in fact exercised in his favour, he will give part of the relevant fund to his parents, Y and Z, who are not objects of the discretionary power. If the true intention of the appointment is to benefit the parents, the exercise is invalid. If that is not the case, but X is under some distinct pressure to benefit Y and Z, the exercise would also be invalid.[76] On the other hand, if X has genuine freedom of action and wishes to give Y and Z a benefit, then it appears that the exercise of the power would be good.[77]

11–049 As to the effect of a finding of a fraud on a power, it has long been held that where a power is successfully impugned, its exercise is totally invalid,[78] unless the improper element in the appointment can be severed from the remainder of that appointment.[79]

This Case

11–050 It is necessary at this point to add some further facts. On the evidence, Mrs Estelle Wong was devastated by the death from cancer of her daughter Phillipa, in August of 1995. Phillipa was then only 43 years old, and

---

73 16th edn, 2001, p.188.
74 See *Vatcher v Paull* [1915] A.C. 372 at 378, per Lord Parker.
75 *Birley v Birley* (1858) 25 Beav. 299.
76 *Re Dick* [1953] Ch. 343.
77 *Re Marsden's Trusts* (1859) 4 Drew. 594; and see Parker and Mellows, *The Modern Law of Trusts* (8th edn, Oakley), p.222.
78 *Re Cohen* [1911] 1 Ch. 37.
79 *Topham v Duke of Portland* (1858) 1 De G.J. & S. 517.

Matthew and Mei-Ling were teenagers. Estelle was very close to Phillipa. Although Phillipa's family were in Australia, Estelle spoke regularly to Phillipa, and she would frequently go to Australia to visit her daughter.

On one occasion, after she had returned from Australia, Estelle expressed concern to Mr Burt (who is now a retired chartered accountant and had a long association with the Wong family) "about the effect of Bill Wong's will". Estelle suddenly came to appreciate that, under the will, Phillipa's share of the income would not pass to her children. **11–051**

It was in those circumstances that advice was sought from Chapman Tripp on this issue. It seems that it was Mr Burt who calculated various figures, and "concluded that $250,000 would partly redress the situation and should be loaned to the PEW Trust, and successively forgiven". As Mr Burt put it, "the purpose of the loan and forgiveness programme was to restore the expected benefit that Mei-Ling and Matthew would have received on their mother's death had they been entitled under Bill's will to her life interest in the PW Estate Trust. . . . **11–052**

In their opinion (which was disclosed to the Court) Chapman Tripp advised that clause 5 must be read in "its plain words". The solicitors said, "In other words there is no statutory remedy to allow Phillipa's two children to receive the income that she would have received". The solicitors then detailed three options which, as they saw it, were "available to remedy this matter". One was to resort to the discretionary power available to the trustees under clause 6 of the will, which "[Estelle] could then invest in [her] own name". Estelle could then amend her will to provide for that sum to be left equally to Mei-Ling and Matthew. Secondly, the capital sum received from the estate could be loaned to the PEW Trust and then, on Estelle's death, the assets of that trust automatically vest in Mei-Ling and Matthew. A third option was identified as being an interest-free loan from the husband's estate, but repayable on Janice's death. **11–053**

Although some disadvantages in each of these alternatives were identified, it was at no point suggested by the solicitors that the potential difficulties relating to a fraud on a power might have to be addressed in relation to the first option. **11–054**

The evidence in the case in this respect is well documented and quite clear. In summary, on Phillipa's premature death, Mrs Estelle Wong became concerned that there was no gift-over provision as to income for Phillipa's children. A member of Chapman Tripp recorded in a file note: "this is of great concern to Mrs Wong and although she accepts that her late husband may never have anticipated their daughter predeceasing Mrs Wong she is adamant that it would have been his intention for Phillipa's share of the income to pass to her children". Thus it was that a scheme was settled by Mrs Wong, with the trustees, and after taking legal advice, which had the overt and pre-determined idea that the trustees would utilise clause 6 of the will to avoid the effect of clause 5 of the will, in the circumstances which had arisen. This exercise was not undertaken as a distinct, or separate advance to Mrs Wong or in the "hope" that Estelle Wong would benefit a non-object. The exercise was already constrained by a pre-considered course of action which also avoided Mrs Estelle Wong having to resort to any assets under her control or direction to assist her grandchildren. **11–055**

In our view, this deliberate, and pre-conceived, device amounted to a fraud on the power. If Mrs Estelle Wong had simply been advanced the money out of the estate and had then exercised genuine freedom of action to benefit the children (as for instance by setting up a trust for them), that would not have been unlawful. But what was knowingly erected was a deliberate scheme to subvert the terms of the will. What was overlooked was that the property was vested in those entitled in default of the exercise of the power, subject to its being divested by a proper exercise of the power in clause 6, and the steps in fact taken gave rise to a fraud on those entitled in default. **11–056**

Held: to the extent that the $250,000 could not be recovered by tracing into the PEW Trust, the trustees were personally accountable and were not protected by an exemption clause which provided that they should "not liable for any loss not attributable to dishonesty". **11–057**

Whether the "fraud on a power" rule differs from the "excessive execution" rule is a question to which the English courts have given inconsistent answers. One reason may be that the term "excessive execution" has been used to describe two different rules, as discussed above.[80] In *Vatcher v Paull* Lord Parker held that the "fraud on a power" doctrine concerns the exercise of a power "beyond the **11–058**

[80] See paras 11–024 to 11–025 and 11–029.

scope of or not justified by the instrument creating the power,"[81] which makes it look like the second version of the "excessive execution" rule, which invalidates an exercise of power by trustees which is not authorised by the trust terms. More recently, however, Lord Sumption held otherwise, in a passage of his judgment in a case concerning company directors, *Eclairs Group Ltd v JKX Oil & Gas Plc*, where he also spoke of the duty owed by directors to exercise their powers for a proper purpose as "substantially corresponding" to the doctrine of "fraud on a power".

Eclairs Group Ltd v JKX Oil & Gas Plc

Supreme Court [2015] Bus. L.R. 1395 at [14]–[15]

11–059 **LORD SUMPTION:**

The proper purpose rule

Part 10, Chapter 2 of the Companies Act 2006 codified for the first time the general duties of directors. The proper purpose rule is stated in section 171(b) of the 2006 Act, which provides that a director of a company must "only exercise powers for the purposes for which they are conferred". The rule thus stated substantially corresponds to the equitable rule which had for many years been applied to the exercise of discretionary powers by trustees. "It is a principle in this court", Wigram V-C had observed in *Balls v Strutt*,[82] "that a trustee shall not be permitted to use the powers which the trust may confer upon him at law, except for the legitimate purposes of the trust". Like other general duties laid down in the Companies Act 2006, this one was declared to be "based on certain common law rules and equitable principles as they apply in relation to directors and have effect in place of those rules and principles as regards the duties owed to a company by a director": section 170(3). Section 170(4) accordingly provides that the general duties are to be "interpreted and applied in the same way as common law rules or equitable principles, and regard shall be had to the corresponding rules and equitable principles in interpreting and applying the general duties".

11–060 The proper purpose rule has its origin in the equitable doctrine which is known, rather inappropriately, as the doctrine of "fraud on a power". For a number of purposes, the early Court of Chancery attached the consequences of fraud to acts which were honest and unexceptionable at common law but unconscionable according to equitable principles. In particular, it set aside dispositions under powers conferred by trust deeds if, although within the language conferring the power, they were outside the purpose for which it was conferred. So far as the reported cases show the doctrine dates back to *Lane v Page*[83] and *Aleyn v Belchier*,[84] but it was clearly already familiar to equity lawyers by the time that those cases were decided. In *Aleyn's case*, Lord Northington could say in the emphatic way of 18th century judges that "no point was better established". In *Duke of Portland v Topham*[85] Lord Westbury LC stated the rule in these terms:

> "that the donee, the appointor under the power, shall, at the time of the exercise of that power, and for any purpose for which it is used, act with good faith and sincerity, and with an entire and single view to the real purpose and object of the power, and not for the purpose of accomplishing or carrying into effect any bye or sinister object (I mean sinister in the sense of its being beyond the purpose and intent of the power) which he may desire to effect in the exercise of the power."

The principle has nothing to do with fraud. As Lord Parker of Waddington observed in delivering the advice of the Privy Council in *Vatcher v Paull*[86] it

> "does not necessarily denote any conduct on the part of the appointor amounting to fraud in the common law meaning of the term or any conduct which could be properly termed dishonest or

---

81 *Vatcher v Paull* [1915] A.C. 372 at 378. See too *Topham v Duke of Portland* (1869–70) L.R. 5 Ch. App. 40 at 59; G. Farwell, C.J.W. Farwell and F.K. Archer, *A Concise Treatise on Powers*, 3rd edn (Stevens & Sons, 1916), 458: "the essential notion is disposition beyond the scope of the power, not breach of trust by the donee."

82 (1841) 1 Hare 146.

83 (1754) Amb. 233.

84 (1758) 1 Eden 132.

85 (1864) 11 HL Cas 32 at 54.

86 [1915] A.C. 372 at 378,

> immoral. It merely means that the power has been exercised for a purpose, or with an intention, beyond the scope of or not justified by the instrument creating the power."

The important point for present purposes is that the proper purpose rule is not concerned with excess of power by doing an act which is beyond the scope of the instrument creating it as a matter of construction or implication. It is concerned with abuse of power, by doing acts which are within its scope but done for an improper reason. It follows that the test is necessarily subjective. "Where the question is one of abuse of powers," said Viscount Finlay in *Hindle v John Cotton Ltd*,[87] "the state of mind of those who acted, and the motive on which they acted, are all important".

While it is true that a power-holder's subjective reasons for exercising a power are important, however, there is no escaping from the fact that it is always a relevant question whether these reasons coincided with the purposes for which the power was given. In extra-judicial writing, Lord Sales therefore demurred from Lord Sumption's insistence in *Eclairs* that interpretation of a company's articles formed no part of the process by which it was determined whether the directors had exercised their powers for a proper purpose. In Lord Sales's view, while the doctrine of fraud on a power:[88] **11–061**

> was originally conceived, as so many equitable doctrines were, as something laid over the top of rights defined in law or a legal instrument, and imposing distinct norms of conduct from outside ... there is a strong case for saying that the doctrine should be taken to be more directly informed by what the parties have stipulated in their contract, or in a trust instrument or a will, as the case may be.

In the trusts context, this means that it is frequently necessary to construe the trust deed and other relevant trust documents to identify the settlor's reasons for conferring particular powers when deciding whether these have been exercised for a proper purpose[89]—and this is true whether or not the doctrine of fraud on a power is distinct from the excessive execution rule. It may not always be necessary, however, to identify exactly what it was that the power holder sought to achieve, as explained in the following extract. **11–062**

Hancock v Rinehart

New South Wales Supreme Court (2015) 106 A.C.S.R. 207 at [60]–[61].

BRERETON J.: In determining whether a power has been exercised for an extraneous or ulterior purpose, the Court determines first, as a matter of law, for what purpose or purposes the power may properly be exercised and secondly, as a matter of fact, whether the purpose for which the power was in fact exercised was within the category of permissible purposes.[90] In ascertaining the purpose for which the power was in fact exercised, the Court is concerned with the state of mind of the trustee and is informed by the surrounding circumstances, as was explained by the Privy Council in *Howard Smith Ltd v Ampol Ltd*:[91] **11–063**

> "Where the question is one of abuse of powers, the state of mind of those who acted, and the motive on which they acted, are all important, and you may go into the question of what their intention was, collecting from the surrounding circumstances all the materials which genuinely throw light upon that question of the state of mind of the directors so as to show whether they were honestly acting in

---

[87] (1919) 56 Sc. L.R. 625 at 630.

[88] P. Sales, "Use of Powers for Proper Purposes in Private Law" (2020) 136 L.Q.R. 384 at 387. See also his general discussion of the fraud on a power doctrine at 388–391.

[89] *Bank of New Zealand v Bank of New Zealand Officers Provident Association Management Board* [2003] O.P.L.R. 281 at [21]; *British Airways Plc v Airways Pension Scheme Trustee Ltd* [2018] EWCA Civ 1533; [2018] Pens. L.R. 19; *Airways Pension Scheme Trustee Ltd v Fielder* [2019] EWHC 29 (Ch); [2019] 4 W.L.R. 9.

[90] *Chameleon Mining NL v Murchison Metals Ltd* [2010] FCA 1129 at [112].

[91] [1974] A.C. 821 at 835, citing *Hindle v John Cotton Ltd* (1919) 56 Sc. L.R. 625 at 630–631 (Viscount Finlay).

discharge of their powers in the interests of the company or were acting from some bye-motive, possibly of personal advantage, or for any other reason."

11-064 In that respect, the burden of proof is born by those who allege a fraud on the power.[92] However, the crucial question is simply whether the power (or discretion) was exercised bona fide for a proper purpose, and an answer that it was not does not depend in every case on proof of what the extraneous purpose was, so long as it can be established that the power was not exercised bona fide for the purpose for which it was conferred. In other words, it may be discernible that the power (or discretion) could not have been exercised bona fide for a proper purpose, without proving for what collateral purpose it was in fact exercised.

11-065 Turning to the effects of the fraud on a power rules, Jessica Hudson has argued that these can vary with the particular type of power that has been exercised, so that it can mean different things in different cases to say that the exercise of a power for an improper purpose is "ineffective" because the trustee is "disabled" from exercising the power. In the following extract, she illustrates this point with various examples.

J. Hudson, "One Thicket in Fraud on a Power"

(2019) 39 O.J.L.S. 577, 583–588

3. Fraud on a Power—Express Trusts

A. Fraud on a Power Renders the Exercise of Some Equitable Powers Ineffective

11-066 The full potential of fraud on a power as a disability/immunity relation can be seen in the context of powers created under an express trust to vary, create or extinguish the equitable interest under that trust. It is necessary to explain the mechanics and operation of these powers to explain why fraud on a power does define the scope of such powers. Critically, these powers are only effective in creating, extinguishing or varying an equitable interest(s) to the extent that a court would order the person who holds title to the subject property, such as a trustee, to act in accordance with the exercise of power. As the analysis below will demonstrate, a court would not exercise its discretion to order a title holder to act in accordance with a fraudulent exercise of power. Thus, the effect of fraud on a power is that the purported exercise of power is ineffective. In this instance, the doctrine does limit the scope of power, and in this sense imposes an actual disability on the part of the donee of power that corelates to an object's immunity from a fraudulent exercise of power.

11-067 Take, for example, a power of appointment, which is a power granted to a person (the donee) to affect the equitable interests under a trust. An effective exercise might, for example, create a new equitable interest in favour of the appointee and this interest is interposed in priority to a beneficiary's pre-existing interest.[93] The subordination of the pre-existing equitable interest to the appointee's new equitable interest is also an example of overreaching.[94] There are other powers which overreach the equitable interest, and this process is discussed further below in section 3B in connection with the trustee's power of sale. Exercise of a power of appointment has no direct operation on the trustee title, which does not pass by the execution of a power of appointment,[95] although the trustee's title might pass simultaneously when a trustee exercises her power to transfer title concurrently with a power of appointment. Exercise of a power of appointment operates as a "mandate . . . to the trustees as to the mode of dealing with the legal title".[96] Once exercised, it is a direction to the trustee, who must deal with the trustee's title to trust property accordingly, for example by transferring legal title to the appointee.

---

92 *Askham v Barker* (1853) 17 Beav. 37 at 44 (Romilly MR); see also *NSW Medical Defence Union v Crawford* (1993) 31 N.S.W.L.R. 469 at 485–486 (Kirby P).

93 G. Farwell, *A Concise Treatise on Powers* (3rd edn, Stevens & Sons 1916) 1.

94 See further C. Harpum, "Overreaching, Trustees' Powers and the Reform of the 1925 Legislation" (1990) 49 C.L.J. 277, 282.

95 Farwell (fn.93) 3. See also T. Youdan, "Powers of Appointment" (2008) 27 Estates, Trusts & Pensions Journal 266.

96 *Cloutte v Storey* [1911] 1 Ch. 18 at 30.

If necessary, a court might order a trustee to act in accordance with the exercise of a power of appointment and, for example, require the trustee to transfer the trustee's title to the subject property to the appointee.[97] To the extent that a court would so compel a trustee, the exercise of a power of appointment is effective in creating a new equitable interest in favour of the appointee and extinguishing the beneficiary's pre-existing equitable interest. The appointee's equitable interest is to seek the court's assistance in compelling the trustee to act, and she only has an equitable interest to the extent a court would compel a trustee to act. **11–068**

Fraud on a power disables the exercise of a power of appointment as a court would not compel a trustee to act in accordance with a fraudulent exercise of a power of appointment. Indeed, to do so might render a trustee personally liable.[98] Understood in this way, the effect of fraud on a power is that any purported exercise of power is ineffective in creating a new equitable interest or extinguishing the existing equitable interest. Finally, any assignee of the appointee, even if for value, would have no equitable interest in relation to the trust property, because specific performance of the agreement between the assignee and appointee is not possible. The appointee does not have any equitable interest the subject of the agreement.[99] **11–069**

These arguments are drawn from the operation and effect of fraud on a power in the cases.[100] For example, in each of *Chadderton v Simpson*,[101] *Pryor v Pryor*,[102] *Re Crawshay*[103] and *Duke of Portland v Topham*,[104] the donee's fraudulent purpose meant there had been no effective exercise of the power of appointment nor extinction of the equitable interest under the trust. The fraudulent purpose "destroy[ed] the efficacy of the exercise of the power".[105] In each case, the beneficiary was able to rely on her pre-existing interest, whether that be to assert the beneficiary's proprietary claim to seek recovery of property[106] or to assert priority of equitable title in defence against another's proprietary claim.[107] **11–070**

Another way to test this understanding of the cases is to ask whether it is possible for a beneficiary to ratify or confirm a fraudulent exercise of a power to vary the equitable interests under an express trust. If ratification or confirmation were possible, this might tend to the view that prima facie a fraudulent exercise of power is effective, but susceptible to being set aside. However, this is not the case. Ratification or confirmation is not possible in relation to a fraudulent exercise of a power of appointment.[108] True, the same practical outcome as ratification might be achieved if all the beneficiaries entitled and the donee of the power execute a deed assigning the equitable interest(s) to the appointee and releasing the power respectively.[109] But the inability to ratify a fraudulent exercise of such a power is because there is nothing to confirm or ratify. **11–071**

The disabling effect of fraud on a power can also be observed in relation to other powers to vary the equitable interests under an express trust. In *Australian Super Pty Ltd v Woodward*, an improper exercise of **11–072**

---

97 *Cloutte* (fn.96).

98 Where the donee has a fraudulent purpose, the trustee's (and any co-trustee's) personal liability, generally speaking, turns on the trustee's knowledge, and liability between co-trustees is several; see e.g. *Mackechnie v Marjoribanks* (1870) 39 L.J. Ch. 604; *Re Deane* (1889) 42 Ch.D. 918; L. Tucker at al, *Lewin on Trusts* (19th edn, Sweet & Maxwell 2015) [29–316]. The requisite level of knowledge has been described in various terms, e.g. where the trustee "[has] . . . good reason to doubt the validity of the appointment" in *Harrison v Randall* (1852) 9 Hare 397 at 407 … .

99 As the case was in *Cloutte* (fn.96).

100 In addition to the cases discussed in the following text, see also *Lane v Page* (1754) Amb. 233 at 234–5; *Dick v Dick* [1953] Ch. 343; *Wellesley v Earl of Mornington* (1855) 2 K. & J. 143; *Farmer v Martin* (1828) 2 Sim. 502; *Redman v Permanent Trustee Company of New South Wales Ltd* (1916) 22 C.L.R. 84.

101 [1952] Ch 412.

102 (1864) 2 De G.J. & S. 205.

103 [1947] Ch. 356 affd [1948] Ch. 123.

104 (1864) 11 H.L. Cas. 32.

105 *Pryor v Pryor* [1952] Ch. 412 at 417.

106 For recognition of this claim, see e.g *Foskett v McKeown* [2001] 1 A.C. 102 at 127 (Lord Millett); *Akers v Samba Financial Group* [2017] A.C. 424 at [82]–[83] (Lord Sumption).

107 See also *Daubeny v Cockburn* (1816) 1 Mer. 626; *Re Marsden's Trust* (1859) 4 Drew. 594; *Cloutte v Storey* [1911] 1 Ch. 18.

108 *Daubeny* (fn.107) 806; *Cloutte* (fn.96) 32 … .

109 See e.g. *Preston v Preston* (1869) 21 L.T. 346.

a power to amend the trust terms[110] "w[as] . . . not . . . cognisable by a court of equity".[111] Fraud on a power likewise disables a power to appoint a trustee, protector or guardian.[112] This effect applies regardless of whether the power is exercised by a trustee or donee—although, where a power to vary the equitable interest(s) is exercised in conjunction with a trustee's power held incident of title to trust property, the analysis is more complicated, as discussed next, in section 3B.

B. Fraud on a Power as Applied to the Exercise of a Trustee's Powers Incident of Title to Trust Property

11–073 This section considers the effect of fraud on a power on the trustee's exercise of power to deal with her title to trust property and compares the effect of the doctrine on the power to overreach[113] and extinguish or vary the beneficiary's equitable interest[114] under the trust. These powers might be exercised concurrently to facilitate a single transaction, such as the sale or investment of trust property, or appointment of trust property to an object. As the analysis will show, fraud on a power has a different effect in relation to these different powers. In summary, and drawing on the analysis presented in section 3A, it will be seen that fraud on a power disables the power to overreach. However, it does not actually disable the trustee's power to deal with her title to trust property ...

11–074 This variation is a function of the trustee holding powers by virtue of multiple sources, such that the scopes of trustee's powers are affected by fraud on a power in two different ways. First, fraud on a power does not define or limit the scope of the trustee's power to deal with her title to the trust property, and thus does not actually disable the trustee from exercising this power. A trustee's power to deal with trust property is an incident of the trustee's title, the scope of which is determined by the relevant principles of equity, law and statute that determine the assignability of that title. If the trust property is land, then the scope of the trustee's power will be a function of the law of real property.[115] If the trust property is a chose in action, such as a debt, then the scope of the trustee's power is a function of the principles of the law of assignment, contained in equity or statute.[116] Likewise in relation to the trustee's power to deal with her title to an equitable chose in action, the scope of which is defined by the principles of equitable assignment[117] or a relevant statute.[118] The title holder's purpose is irrelevant to these regimes ... [and] the equitable pedigree of fraud on a power further explains why it cannot define the scope of the trustee's power to deal with her legal title at law, or her statutory powers to assign legal or equitable title. The trustee's power held incident of title will not be disabled by fraud on a power.

11–075 However, the exercise of this power may be susceptible to equitable relief that gives effect to an in-principle disability on the basis that fraud on a power has disabled the exercise of the separate and distinct power to overreach the beneficiary's interest under a trust. This is the second way in which fraud on a power may affect the trustee's exercise of powers. It is critical to understanding the overall effect the doctrine may

---

110 Likewise in *British Airways plc v Airways Pension Scheme Trustee Ltd* [2018] EWCA Civ 1533 at [110], [126]–[127]; *Re Courage Group's Pension Schemes* [1987] 1 W.L.R. 495 at 511–12; *Mercanti v Mercanti* (2016) 50 W.A.R. 495 at [98], [264]; special leave was refused in *Mercanti v Mercanti* [2017] HCASL 59.

111 [2009] FCAFC 168 [38] (the Court).

112 *Austec Wagga Wagga Pty Ltd v Rarebreed Wagga Pty Ltd* [2012] NSWSC 343 at [71].

113 A valid exercise of this power will: (i) extinguish the beneficiary's equitable interest in relation to the original trust property, and precludes any equitable proprietary claim against that property; (ii) create a new equitable interest in a third party or, if coupled with exercise of a power to transfer legal title, confer an absolute title in the third party; and (iii) if the trustee receives property in exchange, the equitable title under the trust will be annexed to the trustee's title to the new substitute property. See further *Independent Trustee Services v GP Noble Trustees Ltd* [2013] Ch. 91 at [76]–[77], [101]–[106]; *Akers v Samba Financial Group* [2017] A.C. 424 at [52]; D. Fox, "Overreaching" in P. Birks and A. Pretto (eds), *Breach of Trust* (Hart Publishing 2002); R. Nolan, "Administration of Funds in Equity" in P. Turner (ed), *Equity and Administration* (CUP 2016) 74–85. ...

114 [Footnote omitted.]

115 See e.g. Land Registration Act 2002.

116 See e.g. Law of Property Act 1925 ss. 53(1)(c) and 136; *William Brandt's Sons & Co v Dunlop Rubber Co Ltd* [1905] A.C. 454 at 462; *Corin v Patton* (1990) 169 C.L.R. 525, 556–59; D. Fox, "Assignment of Choses in Action" in J. McGhee (ed), *Snell's Equity* (33rd edn, Sweet & Maxwell 2015) ch.3; Y Liew, *Guest on the Law of Assignment* (3rd edn, Sweet & Maxwell 2018).

117 *William Brandt's* (fn.116) 462; McGhee (fn.116) ch.3; Law of Property Act 1925 s.53(1)(c). ...

118 Law of Property Act 1925) s.136; *King v Victoria Insurance Co Ltd* [1896] A.C. 250 at 254, 256; *FCT v Everett* (1979) 143 C.L.R. 440 at 447.

have of imposing an in-principle disability on the trustee's power to deal with her (legal or equitable) title to trust property.

Like the other powers to vary or extinguish the equitable interest under an express trust considered in section 3A above, the scope of the power to overreach, whether reposed in the trustee or a donee, is defined by fraud on a power. An exercise of this power is effective only to the extent a court would recognise its exercise. An improper purpose is a reason for a court to refuse to recognise a purported exercise of the power to overreach, and thus disables the exercise of this power. The immediate significance is that the beneficiary's equitable interest is unaffected and can be relied upon to seek relief to set aside an exercise of the trustee's power to deal with title to trust property. The overall effect is that this latter power is subject to an in-principle disability given the availability of equitable relief in response to the beneficiary's proprietary claim. 11–076

This pattern is borne out in cases[119] such as *Wong v Burt*,[120] where trustees transferred title to trust property to third parties (X) for improper purposes. Fraud on a power did not actually disable the exercise of the trustee's power to transfer title to X. X did receive title to the subject property. Fraud on a power did, however, disable the power to overreach, and the beneficiaries were able to rely on the pre-existing equitable interest to seek recovery of the property from X.[121] 11–077

4. The "Adequate Deliberation" Rule and the Duty to Consider All and Only Relevant Matters

This is often referred to as "the rule in *Re Hastings-Bass*",[122] although that case did not actually apply the rule in the form which it now takes, after a series of cases starting with *Mettoy Pension Trustees Ltd v Evans*[123] and culminating in *Pitt v Holt*.[124] For this reason, as Lord Walker said in *Pitt*, "the label 'the rule in *Hastings-Bass*' is a misnomer";[125] but he also said that it "is by now so familiar that it is best to continue to use it". 11–078

Re Hastings-Bass (Deceased)[126] concerned a tax avoidance scheme that went wrong. Hastings-Bass had a life interest under a settlement. Under applicable inheritance tax legislation, estate duty of 75% was payable on any property in which he had a life interest at the time of his death. To avoid this, the trustees used their power under the Trustee Act 1925 s.32 to advance property out of the settlement into a second settlement created by Hastings-Bass's sister, on trust for Hastings-Bass's son for life, with remainder interests to the son's children. This would have worked but for the House of Lords' later decision in a case about perpetuities, *Pilkington v IRC*.[127] The effect of this decision was that all of the interests in the sub-settlement of the fund in *Hastings-Bass*, other than the son's life interest, were void for perpetuity. Following Hastings-Bass's death, the Revenue argued that there had been no valid exercise of the trustees' power of advancement, because their purported exercise of the power had produced a result different from the one they had intended. Hence the sub-settlement had been a nullity, Hastings-Bass's life interest in the fund had continued until his death, and estate duty was payable. 11–079

The Court of Appeal held as a matter of law that where a trustee has acted in good faith the court should not hold his action to be ineffective:[128] 11–080

---

119 See also *Hillsdown Holdings Plc v Pensions Ombudsman* [1997] 1 All E.R. 862 at [139]; *Roadchef (Employee Benefits Trustees Limited) v Ingram Hill* [2014] EWHC 109 at [122], [126]–[131].

120 [2004] NZCA 174.

121 Ibid at [43] and [59].

122 See generally M. Ashdown, *Trustee Decision Making: The Rule in Re Hastings-Bass* (Oxford University Press, 2015).

123 [1990] 1 W.L.R. 1587.

124 [2013] UKSC 26; [2013] 2 A.C. 108.

125 [2013] UKSC 26; [2013] 2 A.C. 108 at [1].

126 [1975] Ch. 25.

127 [1964] A.C. 612 at 639.

128 [1975] Ch. 25 at 41.

> notwithstanding that it does not have the full effect which he intended, unless (1) what he has achieved is unauthorised by the power conferred on him or (2) it is clear that he would not have acted as he did (a) had he not taken into account considerations which he should not have taken into account or (b) had he not failed to take into account considerations which he ought to have taken into account.

11–081 The Revenue argued that the trustees would not have appointed property into the sub-settlement if they had known that the remainder interests would be void for perpetuity, that the case therefore fell within the scope of (2)(b) above, and hence that it was open to court to hold that the sub-settlement had been ineffective, producing the result that the tax was payable. However, the Court of Appeal held that even if the trustees had known this, they would still have advanced the capital in order to benefit Hastings-Bass's son for his life as this would itself have achieved the tax saving which the trustees had sought to achieve. Hence the appointment had been valid to the extent that it had benefited the son, Hastings-Bass had had no interest at the time of his death because he had disposed of it to his son, and the tax was not payable.

11–082 The Court of Appeal's statement of the circumstances in which the courts will treat the exercise of powers by trustees as ineffective was framed in a negative way—"the courts will not interfere unless"—but their formulation of principle was taken out of context and put into a positive form in *Mettoy Pension Trustees v Evans* where Warner J said that:[129]

> where a trustee acts under a discretion given to him by the terms of the trust, the court *will interfere* with his action if it is clear that he would not have acted as he did had he not failed to take into account considerations which he ought to have taken into account.

11–083 This positive formulation of the rule (or some variant of it) was then successfully invoked by trustees in a series of cases to escape the unforeseen tax consequences of transactions they had entered, in some cases following negligent advice given by their tax advisors.[130] By winning a declaration that such transactions should be set aside, the trustees were able to avoid paying the tax, obviating the need for them to sue their advisors for negligence, and for their advisors to claim on their insurance policies. For more than a decade HMRC made no attempt to intervene in these cases and so the trustees' arguments were unopposed, since there was no one else whose interest lay in opposing rescission of the relevant transactions (which suited the beneficiaries as much as the trustees and the others). However, it came to be felt in many quarters that (in Lord Neuberger's phrase) it was inappropriate for "Doctor Equity [to] administer a magical morning-after pill to trustees suffering from post-transaction remorse",[131] given that no other taxpayer could set transactions aside following the discovery that she could have arranged her affairs in a more tax-efficient way. In two conjoined appeals, *Pitt v Holt* and *Futter v Futter*,[132] the Supreme Court then took corrective action.

---

129 [1990] 1 W.L.R. 1587 at 1621 (emphasis added).

130 e.g. *Abacus Trust Co (Isle of Man) Ltd v NSPCC* [2001] S.T.C. 1344; *Green v Cobham* [2002] S.T.C. 820; *Burrell v Burrell* [2005] EWHC 245 (Ch); [2005] S.T.C. 569; *Sieff v Fox* [2005] EWHC 1312 (Ch); [2005] 1 W.L.R. 3811; *Jiggens v Low* [2010] EWHC 1566 (Ch); [2010] S.T.C. 1899.

131 Lord Neuberger, "Aspects of the Law of Mistake: *Re Hastings-Bass*" (2009) 15 T. & T. 189, 192. See also *Breadner v Granville- Grossman* [2001] Ch. 523 at [61]; *Futter v Futter* [2010] EWHC 449 (Ch); [2010] S.T.C. 982 at [1].

132 [2013] UKSC 26; [2013] 2 A.C. 108.

Pitt v Holt; Futter v Futter

Supreme Court [2013] 2 A.C. 108

These were conjoined appeals from two cases where the rule in *Hastings-Bass* had been successfully invoked at first instance. In *Pitt v Holt*, Pitt was injured in a road accident and received compensation. His wife was appointed as a receiver on his behalf under the Mental Health Act 1983, and the decisions she took in this capacity were subject to the same rules as decisions taken by a trustee. She decided, on advice, to put the money into a settlement that was worded in such a way that a significant inheritance tax charge would be triggered on Pitt's death. This result could easily have been avoided if the trust instrument had been worded in a slightly different way. 11–084

Futter concerned an offshore trust which held stockpiled gains. On advice, losses were triggered within the settlement with a view to setting these off against the gains when they were distributed to the beneficiary onshore. However, the trustees' advisors who had recommended this course of action had overlooked the Taxation of Chargeable Gains Act 1994, s 2(4), which prevented offsetting in this way. Hence a significant tax charge was incurred when the distributions were made. 11–085

In both cases,[133] the judges at first instance held that the rule in *Hastings-Bass* applied and that the relevant transactions would be rescinded with the result that no tax was payable. HMRC appealed, and the Court of Appeal held in both cases that the claims for relief based on the rule in *Hastings-Bass* should fail.[134] Lloyd L.J. held that the *Hastings-Bass* rule applies only where the trustees have breached a duty to consider all and only relevant considerations when exercising their discretion, and that trustees do not breach this duty in cases where they act on advice given by professional advisers who have been selected with reasonable care. 11–086

The Court of Appeal's decision on this point was upheld by the Supreme Court, but in *Pitt* the court also held that Mrs Pitt could rescind the settlement on the ground of mistake; rescission for mistake was not pleaded in *Futter*. The following excerpt is concerned only with the application of the rule in *Hastings-Bass* to both cases. 11–087

LORD WALKER (with whom LORD NEUBERGER, BARONESS HALE, LORD MANCE, LORD CLARKE, LORD SUMPTION and LORD CARNWATH agreed):

Introduction

These appeals raise important and difficult issues in the field of equity and trust law. Both appeals raise issues about the so-called rule in *Hastings-Bass*. One appeal (*Pitt v Holt*) also raises issues as to the court's jurisdiction to set aside a voluntary disposition on the ground of mistake. It is now generally recognised that the label "the rule in *Hastings-Bass*" is a misnomer. The decision of the Court of Appeal in *Re Hastings-Bass, decd*[135] can be seen, on analysis, to be concerned with a different category of the techniques by which trust law controls the exercise of fiduciary powers. That decision is concerned with the scope of the power itself, rather than with the nature of the decision-making process which led to its being exercised in a particular way.[136] The rule would be more aptly called "the rule in *Mettoy*", from the decision of Warner J. in *Mettoy Pension Trustees Ltd v Evans*.[137] But the misnomer is by now so familiar that it is best to continue to use it, inapposite though it is. 11–088

As *Mettoy's* case illustrates, the rule is concerned with trustees who make decisions without having given proper consideration to relevant matters which they ought to have taken into consideration. It has also been applied to other fiduciaries (in *Pitt v Holt* Mrs Pitt was acting as a receiver appointed by the Court of Protection). *Mettoy's* case was concerned with the rules of an occupational pension scheme, as are some other cases on the rule. But since the turn of the century there have been several cases concerned with family trusts, and in particular with tax-planning arrangements involving trusts, where the arrangements have for one reason or another proved unexpectedly disadvantageous, and the court has been asked to restore the status quo ante under the *Hastings-Bass* rule. . . 11–089

133 *Pitt v Holt* [2010] 1 W.L.R. 1199; *Futter v Futter* [2010] S.T.C. 982.
134 [2012] Ch. 132.
135 [1975] Ch. 25.
136 See R.C. Nolan, "Controlling Fiduciary Power" [2009] C.L.J. 293, especially pp. 294–295, 306–309.
137 [1990] 1 W.L.R. 1587.

11–090 [Lord Walker reviewed the case-law, and explained the facts and first instance decisions in the cases at issue, before turning to the decision of the Court of Appeal:] I have already indicated my general agreement with Lloyd L.J.'s judgment on the *Hastings-Bass* issue [with which Longmore and Mummery LJJ agreed] . . . In the core of his judgment Lloyd L.J. correctly spelled out the very important distinction between an error by trustees in going beyond the scope of a power (for which I shall use the traditional term "excessive execution") and an error in failing to give proper consideration to relevant matters in making a decision which is within the scope of the relevant power (which I shall term "inadequate deliberation"). *Hastings-Bass* and *Mettoy* were, as he rightly observed, cases in quite different categories. The former was a case of excessive execution and the latter might have been, but in the end was not, a case of inadequate deliberation. . .

11–091 Lloyd L.J. then addressed the difficult question of how a fraudulent appointment (that is, an appointment ostensibly within the scope of a power, but made for an improper purpose) is to be fitted into the classification. The exercise of an equitable power may be fraudulent in this sense whether or not the person exercising it is a fiduciary. A well-known example of trustees exercising a power for an improper purpose is provided by *Re Pauling's S.T.*,[138] in which a power ostensibly exercisable for the benefit of young adult beneficiaries was used to distribute trust capital to be frittered away on their improvident parents' living expenses.

11–092 There is Court of Appeal authority that a fraudulent appointment is void rather than voidable: *Cloutte v Storey*.[139] In that case the appointee under an improper appointment had charged his equitable interest as security for a loan (and in doing so made two false statutory declarations as to the genuineness of the appointment). It was held that the lender had no security, even though it had no notice of the equitable fraud. It is an authority which has bedevilled discussion of the true nature of the *Hastings-Bass* rule. Lightman J. in *Abacus Trust Co (Isle of Man) v Barr*[140] found the judgment of Farwell L.J. problematic and Lloyd L.J. shared his reservations.[141] So do I. It is hard to know what to make of Farwell L.J.'s observations:[142]

> "If an appointment is void at law, no title at law can be founded on it; but this is not so in equity: the mere fact that the appointment is void does not prevent a Court of Equity from having regard to it: eg, an appointment under a limited power to a stranger is void, but equity may cause effect to be given to it by means of the doctrine of election."

11–093 The decision in *Cloutte v Storey* may have to be revisited one day. For present purposes it is sufficient to note that a fraudulent appointment (that is, one shown to have been made for a positively improper purpose) may need a separate pigeon-hole somewhere between the categories of excessive execution and inadequate deliberation.

11–094 Lloyd L.J. considered the duties of trustees in exercising their discretion, and in particular the relevance of tax considerations.[143] He referred to some well-known authorities including *Re Baden's Deed Trusts*.[144] That case was directly concerned with the correct test for certainty of objects of a discretionary trust (or trust power) but the speech of Lord Wilberforce contains[145] a general discussion of fiduciary discretions which has been very influential in the development of the law. This includes a passage[146] as to the court's intervention if trustees fail to exercise a trust power (that is, a discretion which it is their duty to exercise in some way). After referring to Lord Upjohn's opinion Lord Wilberforce said:

> "I would venture to amplify this by saying that the court, if called upon to execute the trust power, will do so in the manner best calculated to give effect to the settlor's or testator's intentions. It may do so by appointing new trustees, or by authorising or directing representative persons of the classes of beneficiaries to prepare a scheme of distribution, or even, should the proper basis of distribution appear by itself directing the trustees so to distribute."

---

138 [1964] Ch. 303.
139 [1911] 1 Ch. 18.
140 [2003] Ch. 409 at [31].
141 [2012] Ch. 132 at [98].
142 [1911] 1 Ch. 18 at 31.
143 At [102]–[118].
144 [1971] A.C. 424.
145 At 448–457.
146 At 456–457.

Lloyd L.J. did not refer to that particular passage, but Warner J. had done so in *Mettoy's* case,[147] since in that case a decision as to the exercise of the power to augment benefits would have to be taken by someone. The passage serves as a reminder that where trustees have been in breach of duty by exercising a discretion with inadequate deliberation, setting aside their decision may not be the only course open to the court. 11-095

. . . Lloyd L.J.[148] reaffirmed the view that he had expressed in *Sieff v Fox* that "fiscal consequences may be relevant considerations which the trustees ought to take into account".[149] I agree. In the private client world trusts are mostly established by and for wealthy families for whom taxes (whether on capital, capital gains or income) are a constant preoccupation. It might be said, especially by those who still regard family trusts as potentially beneficial to society as a whole, that the greater danger is not of trustees thinking too little about tax, but of tax and tax avoidance driving out consideration of other relevant matters. 11-096

That is particularly true of offshore trusts. They are usually run by corporate trustees whose officers and staff (especially if they change with any frequency) may know relatively little about the settlor, and even less about the settlor's family. The settlor's wishes are always a material consideration in the exercise of fiduciary discretions. But if they were to displace all independent judgment on the part of the trustees themselves (or in the case of a corporate trustee, by its responsible officers and staff) the decision-making process would be open to serious question. . . 11-097

It is a striking feature of the development of the *Hastings-Bass* rule that it has led to trustees asserting and relying on their own failings, or those of their advisers, in seeking the assistance of the court . . . There may be cases in which there is for practical purposes no other suitable person to bring the matter before the court, but I agree with Lloyd L.J.'s observation[150] that in general it would be inappropriate for trustees to take the initiative in commencing proceedings of this nature. They should not regard them as uncontroversial proceedings in which they can confidently expect to recover their costs out of the trust fund. 11-098

Lloyd L.J. stated the correct principle, as he saw it [as follows]:[151] 11-099

> "It seems to me that the principled and correct approach to these cases is, first, that the trustees' act is not void, but that it may be voidable. It will be voidable if, and only if, it can be shown to have been done in breach of fiduciary duty on the part of the trustees. If it is voidable, then it may be capable of being set aside at the suit of a beneficiary, but this would be subject to equitable defences and to the court's discretion. The trustees' duty to take relevant matters into account is a fiduciary duty, so an act done as a result of a breach of that duty is voidable. Fiscal considerations will often be among the relevant matters which ought to be taken into account. However, if the trustees seek advice (in general or in specific terms) from apparently competent advisers as to the implications of the course they are taking, and follow the advice so obtained, then, in the absence of any other basis for a challenge, I would hold that the trustees are not in breach of their fiduciary duty for failure to have regard to relevant matters if the failure occurs because it turns out that the advice given to them was materially wrong. Accordingly, in such a case I would not regard the trustees' act, done in reliance on that advice, as being vitiated by the error and therefore voidable."

The requirement for breach of duty

. . . [Mr Robert Ham QC's] submissions centred on whether the court's jurisdiction under the *Hastings-Bass* rule is exercisable only if there is a breach of fiduciary duty on the part of the trustees (or other relevant fiduciary). He argued that this is a novel requirement which leads to arbitrary and unfair distinctions, especially in cases where incorrect advice on tax has been given by professional advisers who may or may not themselves be trustees. Mr Ham also had subsidiary but important arguments about the attribution to trustees of fault on the part of their advisers, and about the identification of relevant considerations for the purposes of the rule. 11-100

Mr Ham contended that the supposed need for establishing a breach of fiduciary duty, before the *Hastings-Bass* rule can come into play, was a novel requirement introduced in 2003 by Lightman J. in his judgment in *Barr's* case.[152] . . . In my view Lightman J. was right to hold that for the rule to apply the 11-101

[147] [1990] 1 W.L.R. 1587 at 1617–1618.
[148] [2012] Ch. 132 at [115].
[149] [2005] 1 W.L.R. 3811 at [86].
[150] At [130]
[151] At [127].
[152] [2003] Ch. 409 at [16]–[20].

inadequate deliberation on the part of the trustees must be sufficiently serious as to amount to a breach of fiduciary duty. Breach of duty is essential (in the full sense of that word) because it is only a breach of duty on the part of the trustees that entitles the court to intervene . . . It is not enough to show that the trustees' deliberations have fallen short of the highest possible standards, or that the court would, on a surrender of discretion by the trustees, have acted in a different way. Apart from exceptional circumstances (such as an impasse reached by honest and reasonable trustees) only breach of fiduciary duty justifies judicial intervention.

11–102 . . . Mr Ham's fallback position was that if a breach of duty was an essential requirement, there could be a breach without fault on the part of any individual trustee being established . . . It is undoubtedly correct that trustees may be liable for breach of trust even though they have acted in accordance with skilled professional advice. Such advice cannot protect trustees from potential liability for a loss to the trust fund resulting from a decision that is, judged objectively, beyond the trustees' powers and detrimental to the trust (though professional advice may lead to their obtaining relief under section 61 of the Trustee Act 1925). An example mentioned in argument is *Dunn v Flood*,[153] in which trustees had sold by auction 73 plots of freehold land at Reading, subject to special conditions which the court held to be severely depreciatory (as Fry L.J. put it,[154] "eminently calculated to frighten away purchasers"). The Court of Appeal, upholding North J., refused to force a doubtful title on a reluctant purchaser. The fact that the trustees had consulted respectable solicitors was no excuse. It was not a reasonable exercise of discretion.[155] But the trustee's breach of duty was not in the manner of their decision-making (as to which we know nothing other than that they consulted respectable solicitors) but the loss to the trust property that their unreasonable decision appeared to have caused.

11–103 Further examples are provided by the decision of the Court of Appeal in *Perrins v Bellamy*[156] and that of the Privy Council, on appeal from the Supreme Court of Victoria, in *National Trustees Co of Australasia Ltd v General Finance Co of Australasia Ltd*.[157] These cases, discussed by Lloyd L.J. [in] his judgment,[158] were both examples of action taken by trustees on professional advice which was unequivocally incorrect: one a sale of leaseholds when the trustees had no power of sale; the other a distribution (resulting from "some extraordinary slip" by solicitors of high standing) of a deceased beneficiary's vested share to persons who were not entitled to it under the intestacy law of Victoria in force at the beneficiary's death. As Lloyd L.J. observed, the issue in these cases:

> "is altogether different, as it seems to me, from the question whether, if trustees take advice properly, and act on that advice in a matter which is within their powers, the fact that the advice has misled them as to the true position in a relevant respect means that they acted in breach of fiduciary duty."

11–104 I respectfully agree. Trustees may be liable, even if they have obtained apparently competent professional advice, if they act outside the scope of their powers (excessive execution), or contrary to the general law (for example, in the Australian case, the law regulating entitlement on intestacy). That can be seen as a form of strict liability in that it is imposed regardless of personal fault. Trustees may also be in breach of duty in failing to give proper consideration to the exercise of their discretionary powers, and a failure to take professional advice may amount to, or contribute to, a flawed decision-making process. But it would be contrary to principle and authority to impose a form of strict liability on trustees who conscientiously obtain and follow, in making a decision which is within the scope of their powers, apparently competent professional advice which turns out to be wrong.

11–105 Such a result cannot be achieved by the route of attributing any fault on the part of professional advisers to the trustees as their supposed principals. Solicitors can and do act as agents in some clearly defined functions, usually of a ministerial nature, such as the receipt and transmission of clients' funds, and the giving and taking of undertakings on behalf of clients. But they do not and may not act as agents in the exercise of fiduciary discretions . . .

---

153 (1885) 28 Ch. D. 586.
154 Ibid. at 594.
155 Ibid. at 592 per Baggallay and Bowen L.JJ. and at 593–4 per Fry L.J.
156 [1899] 1 Ch 797.
157 [1905] A.C. 373.
158 At [124].

. . . In *Futter v Futter* Mr Cutbill, a partner in a London firm of solicitors, was involved both as a trustee and as a solicitor advising the trustees. The facts as to his involvement were found at first instance by Norris J.[159] It so happened, as already mentioned, that the judgment of Mr Engelhart Q.C. in *Pitt v Holt* was given on 18 January 2010, the first day of the hearing in *Futter v Futter*. In *Pitt v Holt* it had been common ground[160] that there was no need to identify a breach of duty by the trustees. It is not clear from Norris J.'s judgment whether the same incorrect concession was made and accepted before him. But Norris J. seems to have accepted *Sieff v Fox* as the leading authority from which to obtain guidance, and *Barr's* case received only a passing mention . . . in his judgment. Norris J. did not therefore make any clear finding about breach of fiduciary duty. He simply recorded and accepted Mr Cutbill's written evidence, which included the statement that "[Mr Futter] and I failed to pay any regard to the provisions of section 2(4) [TCGA] at the time, and therefore failed to consider the full tax implications". 11–106

The Court of Appeal was therefore in as good a position as Norris J. to make a finding about breach of duty on the part of the trustees. This court has before it all the written evidence and exhibits that were before the judge, and in the absence of concurrent findings below it is also in a position to make findings, if necessary, on that issue. I will return to it below when dealing with the disposal of the *Futter* appeal. 11–107

Finally, on this part of the case, there is the submission that the trustees' duty to take account of relevant considerations is to be interpreted as a duty to act on advice only if it is correct—in effect, a duty to come to the right conclusion in every case. I have left this submission until the end because it is to my mind truly a last-ditch argument. It involves taking the principle of strict liability for ultra vires acts . . . out of context and applying it in a different area, so as to require trustees to show infallibility of judgment. Such a requirement is quite unrealistic. It would tip the balance much too far in making beneficiaries a special favoured class, at the expense of both legal certainty and fairness. It is contrary to the well-known saying of Lord Truro L.C. in *Re Beloved Wilkes's Charity*[161] 11–108

> "that in such cases as I have mentioned it is to the discretion of the trustees that the execution of the trust is confided, that discretion being exercised with an entire absence of indirect motive, with honesty of intention, and with a fair consideration of the subject. The duty of supervision on the part of this court will thus be confined to the question of the honesty, integrity, and fairness with which the deliberation has been conducted, and will not be extended to the accuracy of the conclusion arrived at, except in particular cases."

The trustees' duty does not extend to being right ("the accuracy of the conclusion arrived at") on every occasion. . .

As a first footnote on the topic of fault, I would mention that in his judgment,[162] Lloyd L.J. observed that a claim by beneficiaries against trustees may often be precluded by an exoneration clause in the trust instrument. Mr Philip Jones Q.C. (for the Revenue) disputed this, pointing out that even if a trustee is exonerated from liability to pay equitable compensation, he is still liable to injunctive relief to prevent a threatened breach of trust, and personal and proprietary remedies may be available against persons who receive assets distributed in breach of trust. Moreover an exoneration clause does not protect a trustee against removal from office by order of the court. The Futter No. 3 and No. 5 settlements contain exoneration clauses in conventional terms, stating that "in the professed execution of the trusts and powers hereof no trustee shall be liable for a breach of trust arising from a mistake or omission made by him in good faith". I would not treat that clause as ousting the application of the *Hastings-Bass* rule, if it were otherwise applicable. 11–109

As a second footnote, there was some discussion in the course of argument as to the significance, in situations of this sort, of a possible claim for damages against professional advisers for financial loss caused by incorrect advice (or incorrect implementation of instructions). Mr Nugee referred to *Walker v Geo H Medlicott & Son*,[163] in which a strong Court of Appeal dismissed on two grounds a claim for damages for professional negligence in preparing a will. The second ground was that the aggrieved claimant's proper course was to mitigate his damage by seeking rectification of the will. That decision may 11–110

159 [2010] S.T.C. 982.
160 [2010] 1 W.L.R. 1199 at [22].
161 (1851) 3 Mac. & G. 440 at 448.
162 At [128].
163 [1999] 1 W.L.R. 727.

reflect the court's view of the particular facts of the case, and the feeling that if the drafting of the will had gone wrong other beneficiaries under it should not obtain adventitious benefits. In principle the possibility that trustees may have a claim for damages should have no effect on the operation of the *Hastings-Bass* rule. In practice it will be rare for trustees to have so strong a claim that they can be confident of obtaining a full indemnity for their beneficiaries' loss and their own costs. In the *Pitt* case this court was told that the claim against Frenkel Topping has been settled. Had it gone to trial the claim, even if successful in establishing duty and breach, might have faced difficulties over causation, since Mrs Pitt executed the SNT under the authority of an order of the Court of Protection, which had considered its terms. That court's apparent lack of awareness of the importance of section 89 of the Inheritance Tax Act 1984 is one of the most remarkable features of the whole sorry story. . .

Void or voidable?

11–111 Counsel on both sides readily admitted that they had hesitated over this point, but in the end they were all in agreement that Lloyd L.J. was right in holding that[164]

> "if an exercise by trustees of a discretionary power is within the terms of the power, but the trustees have in some way breached their duties in respect of that exercise, then (unless it is a case of a fraud on the power) the trustees' act is not void but it may be voidable at the instance of a beneficiary who is adversely affected."

11–112 In my judgment that is plainly right, and in the absence of further argument on the point it is unnecessary to add much to it. The issue has been clouded, in the past, by the difficult case *Cloutte v Storey*,[165] a case on appointments that are fraudulent in the equitable sense, that is made for a positively improper purpose. Here we are concerned not with equitable fraud, nor with dispositions which exceed the scope of the power, or infringe the general law (such as the rule against perpetuity). We are in an area in which the court has an equitable jurisdiction of a discretionary nature, although the discretion is not at large, but must be exercised in accordance with well-settled principles. . .

Disposal of the Hastings-Bass issues

11–113 In *Futter v Futter* the essential issue was whether the trustees of the No. 3 and No. 5 settlements, in deciding to take the steps which they took in March and April 2008, failed in their duty to take relevant considerations into account. Capital gains tax was a relevant consideration. Indeed, it is fairly plain that it was the paramount consideration, and the trustees thought about it a great deal. But the tax advice which they received and acted on was wrong, because an amendment to section 2(4) of TCGA had been overlooked. As Lloyd L.J. put it succinctly: "They did not overlook the need to think about CGT. They were given advice on the right point. The problem was that the advice was wrong."[166]

11–114 The only complication was that Mr Cutbill (the solicitor-trustee) was a member of both teams: the solicitors giving the erroneous advice, and the trustees receiving and acting on it. I agree with the Court of Appeal that it would be artificial to distinguish between the two trustees, who acted together in making and effectuating their decisions. I would if necessary go further and hold that the documentary evidence indicates that most if not all of the technical tax advice given by his firm came not from Mr Cutbill but from the assistant solicitor who was working with him, from January 2008, in a review of a number of different Futter family settlements. Until 27 March 2008 it was supposed, wrongly, that the No. 3 settlement's stockpiled gains were relatively small, and the fact that they amounted to about £188,000 led to a last-minute change of plan. On 28 March 2008 there was a telephone conversation between the assistant solicitor and Mr Bunce, Mr Futter's accountant, at which, without reference to Mr Cutbill, she definitely confirmed that Mr Futter's personal losses could be set off against the section 87 gains. Mr Cutbill seems to have been, very properly, reluctant to put the blame on a junior member of his firm, and of course his firm must take legal responsibility for any actionable mistake by any of its fee-earners. But the documents in exhibit "CDC 1" to Mr Cutbill's witness statement tend to confirm that he should not, as a trustee of the No. 3 and No. 5 settlements, be treated as having been personally in breach of fiduciary duty.

164 At [99].
165 [1911] 1 Ch. 18.
166 At [138].

In *Pitt v Holt* the position was even clearer. As her husband's receiver under the Mental Health Act 1983 Mrs Pitt was in a fiduciary position but there is no suggestion that she had any professional qualifications. She devoted herself, alternating with a carer, to looking after her disabled husband. As anyone in that position would, she took professional advice from solicitors and specialist consultants. After hearing from her legal advisers and the Official Solicitor the Court of Protection made an order on 1 September 1994 authorising (not directing) her to execute the SNT and she acted on that authority on 1 November 1994 . . . She had taken supposedly expert advice and followed it. There is no reason to hold that she personally failed in the exercise of her fiduciary duty. Unfortunately the advice was unsound. **11–115**

I would therefore dismiss the appeal in *Futter v Futter*, and the appeal in *Pitt v Holt* so far as it turns on the *Hastings-Bass* rule. **11–116**

Some points should be made about this decision. First, Lord Walker followed Lloyd LJ in characterising *Re Hastings-Bass* itself as a case of "excessive execution" rather than as a case of "inadequate deliberation". Their reason was that the Court of Appeal had decided the case "on the ground that the advancement, so far as not struck down by the rule against perpetuities, must stand unless it could not, in that attenuated form, reasonably be regarded as beneficial to the advancee".[167] This meant that Buckley LJ had stated the ratio of *Hastings-Bass* too broadly in his judgment,[168] and so there had never been a real foundation for *Mettoy* and the cases which had followed in its wake. **11–117**

Second, Lord Walker and Lloyd LJ both considered that the so-called "rule in *Hastings-Bass*", as it had evolved following *Mettoy*, was enabling trustees and their beneficiaries to escape the consequences of botched tax avoidance schemes too easily. The device they adopted to limit the scope of the rule, drawing on Lightman J's decision in *Abacus Trust Co (Isle of Man) Ltd v Barr*,[169] was to hold that the rule applies only when the trustees' failure to exercise their powers properly amounts to a breach of their duty to consider all and only relevant matters, and that trustees do not breach this duty where, in Lloyd LJ's words, they "seek advice (in general or in specific terms) from apparently competent advisers as to the implications of the course they are taking, and follow the advice so obtained".[170] The effect of this finding is that the rule in *Hastings-Bass* can no longer be invoked in many cases that would formerly have fallen within its scope, because the trustees have taken advice from apparently competent advisers. If the advice was negligent, the trustees can sue their advisers for tort or breach of contract.[171] Otherwise there is no remedy. **11–118**

In the Court of Appeal, Lloyd LJ said that "the trustees' duty to take relevant matters into account is a fiduciary duty",[172] meaning that it is a duty which they owe in their capacity as trustees. This explained why the court intervenes when they breach the duty, in the exercise of its supervisory jurisdiction over trust affairs. Given that he agreed with Lloyd LJ's reasoning, this must also have been what Lord Walker meant when he said that "the inadequate deliberation on the part of the trustees must be sufficiently serious as to amount to a breach of fiduciary duty."[173] We must therefore hope that in future cases his words are not taken out of context and misinterpreted to mean that the trustees must have breached some other duty, e.g. their duty to exercise their judgment in the exclusive interest of their principals[174] (suggesting incorrectly that the rule in *Hastings-Bass* applies only where **11–119**

167 [2013] UKSC 26; [2013] 2 A.C. 108 at [24], affirming [2011] EWCA Civ 197; [2012] Ch. 132.
168 In the passage quoted at para.11–080.
169 [2003] EWHC 114 (Ch); [2003] Ch. 409. In *Sieff v Fox* [2005] 1 W.L.R. 3811, Lloyd LJ had previously declined to follow Lightman J on this point, but in *Pitt v Holt* he changed his mind.
170 [2011] EWCA Civ 197; [2012] Ch. 132 at [127].
171 As to which, see T. Rosen Peacocke, "Liability of Professionals Retained by Settlors and Trustees following *Pitt v Holt/Futter v Futter*" (2011) 27 P.N. 200.
172 [2011] EWCA Civ 197; [2012] Ch. 132 at [127].
173 [2013] UKSC 26; [2013] 2 A.C. 108 at [73].
174 For which, see paras 2–066 to 2–163.

there has been a conflict of interest), or their duty of care (suggesting incorrectly that the exercise of discretionary dispositive powers can be impugned for having been made carelessly).[175]

11–120 Third, Lloyd LJ envisaged that a broad spectrum of matters might be relevant to the exercise of a discretionary power, but did not wish to be prescriptive as to what these might be as the circumstances of cases are various. He identified tax matters, the settlor's wishes and the beneficiaries' wishes, circumstances and needs.[176] Other cases have identified other matters material to the exercise of particular powers, e.g. the fact that beneficiaries of a discretionary trust are also the beneficiaries of a second trust.[177] It is worth emphasising, however, that the trustees are not required:[178]

> to go on endlessly in pursuit of perfect information in order to make a perfect decision. The reality of finite resources and the trustee's responsibility to preserve the fund for the benefit of all beneficiaries according to the terms of the deed means that there must be a limit.

11–121 Fourth, in a passage of his judgment that was endorsed by Lord Walker, Lloyd LJ said that "one practical consequence" of his reconceptualisation of the rule in *Hastings-Bass* as turning on a breach of duty would be that:[179]

> if in future it is desired to challenge an exercise by trustees of a discretionary power on this basis, it will be necessary for one or more beneficiaries to grasp the nettle of alleging and proving a breach of fiduciary duty on the part of the trustees. Only rarely would it be appropriate for the trustees to take the initiative in the proceedings. . .

11–122 It might be thought that trustees who have not acted fraudulently, and who are protected by an exemption clause from compensatory liability,[180] would have no financial reason to fear bringing proceedings with a view to establishing their own breach of duty (though reputational considerations might deter them from doing so). One might also have thought that if trustees were to bring such litigation this would be consistent with cases which hold that they not only have the power to sue one another for their breaches of duty but also have a duty to do so.[181] However, while the Trustee Act 2000 s.31 entitles trustees to recover expenses incurred in the course of trust business out of the trust fund, they are not usually entitled to be indemnified for their costs where they are successfully sued for breach of duty.[182] Could the trustees ask for a *Beddoe* order,[183] i.e. permission to bring proceedings on the basis of a pre-emptive indemnity out of the estate for their costs? Lord Walker seems to have ruled this out, stating that trustees "should not . . . confidently expect" to get one.[184]

---

175 This is Richard Wilson's understanding of the duty in [2014] P.C.B. 20, 22. We agree that a trustee might owe a duty to take care when gathering information prior to taking her decision – and indeed when communicating her decision to an agent after it has been made (cf. *Abacus Trust Co (Isle of Man) v Barr* [2003] EWHC 114 (Ch); [2003] Ch. 409)—but not that the making of a discretionary choice is itself an action that can be tested against a standard of care. See M. Ashdown, *Trustee Decision Making: The Rule in Re Hastings-Bass* (2015), paras 4.08ff.

176 [2011] EWCA Civ 197; [2012] Ch. 132 at [114]–[118].

177 *Goodrich v AB* [2022] EWHC 81 (Ch); [2022] W.T.L.R. 525 at [120]. See too *Edge v Pensions Ombudsman* [2000] Ch. 602 at 626–627, listing matters that could be relevant to pension trustees deciding whether to exercise a power to increase benefits.

178 *Alcoa of Australia Retirement Plan Pty Ltd v Frost* [2012] VSCA 238 at [60].

179 [2011] EWCA Civ 197; [2012] Ch. 132 at [130].

180 As to which see paras 11–145 to 11–147 and 13–159 to 13–166.

181 *Walker v Symonds* (1818) 3 Swans. 1 at 71–72; *Butler v Butler* (1877) 7 Ch. D. 116; *Carson v Sloane* (1884) 13 L.R. Ir. 139 at 147; *Young v Murphy* [1996] 1 V.R. 279.

182 See para.10–022.

183 Named for *Re Beddoe* [1893] 1 Ch. 547.

184 [2013] UKSC 26; [2013] 2 A.C. 108 at [69].

Fifth, if the absolutely entitled legal owner of property decides to do something with her property that triggers adverse tax consequences, she may well be unable to go back on this decision afterwards and say that it does not count. Why should beneficiaries be entitled to more favourable treatment when their trustees do the same thing? The answer given by trust lawyers is that the beneficiaries are vulnerable to flawed exercises of power by trustees, but arguably that is a problem for them that is internal to the trust relationship into which the settlor has put them, and it should be dealt with by giving them an action against the trustees. *Pitt* makes it harder for trustees and beneficiaries to use the rule in *Hastings-Bass*, but it remains controversial that they should be allowed to use it under any circumstances, given that other taxpayers are not so privileged.[185] **11–123**

Sixth, the claimants in *Pitt* and *Futter* did not only base their claims on the rule in *Hastings-Bass*: they also argued that their transactions should be set aside on the ground of mistake, and in this regard their claims were successful. Since then, trustees and other property owners whose disposals of property have triggered unexpected tax liabilities have tended to rely on mistake rather the rule in *Hastings-Bass* as the primary route to having these disposals rescinded, calculating that the requirements for such claims are easier to satisfy.[186] Policy issues of the kind noted in the previous paragraph apply to mistake claims by trustees as well.[187] **11–124**

5. Good Faith

If a trustee decides not to bother using any of her powers to benefit a beneficiary for capricious reasons, the court will intervene to remove the trustee or direct a payment that no trustee could refuse to make unless being spiteful or malicious. This is the ratio of *Klug v Klug*,[188] where legacy duty had to be paid by a beneficiary whose income was insufficient to pay the instalments. One of the trustees (the beneficiary's mother) declined to exercise a power of advancement in her favour to enable her to pay the duty and so she applied to the court. Neville J said:[189] **11–125**

> When the summons was previously before me, I decided that the trustees could in the exercise of their discretion under the powers of advancement, if they thought fit, advance out of capital a sum sufficient to pay this legacy duty. The public trustee thinks that their discretion should be so exercised, but his co-trustee, the mother, declines to join him in so doing, not because she has considered whether or not it would be for her daughter's welfare, that the advance should be made, but because her daughter has married without her consent, and her letters show, in my opinion, that she has not exercised her discretion at all. . . . In such circumstances, it is the duty of the court to interfere and to direct a sum to be raised out of capital sufficient to pay off . . . the legacy duty.

---

185 M. Bhandari, "Undoing Transactions for Tax Purposes: The *Hastings-Bass* Principle" in S. Elliott et al (eds), *Restitution of Overpaid Tax* (Hart Publishing, 2013).

186 C. Mitchell, "Rescission of Voluntary Settlements and Dispositions of Trust Property on the Ground of Mistake" [2017] P.C.B. 41; J Lee, "Tax, Equity and Artificiality" (2017) 31 Tru. L.I. 219; R. Lee, "Correcting Mistakes in Trust Planning: A Comparative post-*Pitt* Analysis" [2018] Conv. 45. Rectification of documents rather than rescission is sometimes the remedy sought: S. Douglas, "Misuse of Rectification in the Law of Trusts" (2018) 134 L.Q.R. 138; P.S. Davies and S Douglas, "Tax Mistakes post-*Pitt v Holt*" (2018) 32 Tru. L.I. 3.

187 A. Hofri-Winogradow and G. Weiss, "Trust Parties' Uniquely Easy Access to Rescission: Analysis, Critique and Reform" (2019) 82 M.L.R. 777.

188 [1918] 2 Ch. 67. See too Re *Lofthouse* (1885) 29 Ch.D. 921 (where trustees had refused to pay maintenance to a beneficiary under a discretionary power and Bacon VC ordered £400 p.a. to be paid; on appeal his order was discharged without more ado since the trustees were agreeable to pay £250 p.a.). There was an interventionist attitude in some 19th century cases concerning powers to benefit a beneficiary, especially if the beneficiary was a ward of court: *Re Hodges* (1878) 7 Ch.D. 754; *Re Roper's Trusts* (1879) 11 Ch.D. 271.

189 *Klug* [1918] 2 Ch. 67 at 71.

11–126 The capricious exercise (or non-exercise) of a discretionary power by trustees was also considered by Templeman J in *Re Manisty's Settlement*.

Re Manisty's Settlement

Chancery Division [1974] Ch. 17 at [25]–[27]

11–127 TEMPLEMAN J.: The court cannot insist on any particular consideration being given by the trustees to the exercise of the power. If a settlor creates a power exercisable in favour of his issue, his relations and the employees of his company, the trustees may in practice for many years hold regular meetings, study the terms of the power and the other provisions of the settlement, examine the accounts and either decide not to exercise the power or to exercise it only in favour, for example, of the children of the settlor. During that period the existence of the power may not be disclosed to any relation or employee and the trustees may not seek or receive any information concerning the circumstances of any relation or employee. In my judgment it cannot be said that the trustees in those circumstances have committed a breach of trust and that they ought to have advertised the power or looked beyond the persons who are most likely to be the objects of the bounty of the settlor. The trustees are, of course, at liberty to make further inquiries, but cannot be compelled to do so at the behest of any beneficiary. The court cannot judge the adequacy of the consideration given by the trustees to the exercise of the power, and it cannot insist on the trustees applying a particular principle or any principle in reaching a decision.

11–128 If a person within the ambit of the power is aware of its existence he can require the trustees to consider exercising the power and in particular to consider a request on his part for the power to be exercised in his favour. The trustees must consider this request, and if they decline to do so or can be proved to have omitted to do so, then the aggrieved person may apply to the court which may remove the trustees and appoint others in their place. This . . . is the only right and only remedy of any object of the power. . .

11–129 The court may also be persuaded to intervene if the trustees act "capriciously", that is to say, act for reasons which I apprehend could be said to be irrational, perverse or irrelevant to any sensible expectation of the settlor; for example, if they chose a beneficiary by height or complexion or by the irrelevant fact that he was a resident of Greater London . . . [Reasonable] trustees will endeavour, no doubt, to give effect to the intention of the settlor in making the settlement and will derive that intention not from the terms of the power necessarily or exclusively, but from all the terms of the settlement, the surrounding circumstances and their individual knowledge acquired or inherited . . . [They] have an absolute discretion and cannot be obliged to take any form of action, save to consider the exercise of the power and a request from a person who is within the ambit of the power.

11–130 Although the expression "good faith" is often used as a synonym for honesty, it is also used in a more technical sense to capture the ideas expressed in the foregoing passages, that a power holder must act in a candid, rational, and fair-minded way, and refrain from sharp practice and behaviour that is secretive, perverse, or misleading. For example, in *Hayes v Willoughby* Lord Sumption spoke of a rule that decision-making must be done in "good faith" as importing:[190]

> a requirement that there should be some logical connection between the evidence and the ostensible reasons for the decision, and . . . an absence of arbitrariness, of capriciousness or of reasoning so outrageous in its defiance of logic as to be perverse.

11–131 Equitable duties of good faith in this sense are imposed in a wide variety of circumstances and this makes it hard to pin down their content, as the requirements of good faith can vary from one situation to another. However, a theme running through the cases is that a power-holder must make a sincere and serious commitment to the purposes for which her powers have been given and this may require her to pay proper regard to the interests of those whose position will be affected by the exercise of

[190] [2013] UKSC 17; [2013] 1 W.L.R. 935 at [14]. See too *UC Rusal Alumina Jamaica Ltd v Miller* [2014] UKPC 39; [2015] P.L.R. 15 at [51].

these powers, even if she is not required to prioritise their interests over her own interests and those of other people. In other words, a power-holder may owe a duty of good faith whether or not she also owes a fiduciary duty, these two duties being distinct, as discussed in the following excerpt, where Charles Mitchell uses the term "duty of self-denial" as a synonym for fiduciary duty.

C. Mitchell, "Good Faith, Self-Denial and Mandatory Trustee Duties"

(2018) 32 Tru. L.I. 92, pp.96–98

Good Faith and Self-Denial

A good way to test the proposition that equitable duties of good faith and self-denial are distinct is to see whether there are cases where a defendant has been permitted to act in a self-serving way but is nevertheless bound by a duty of good faith. It turns out that there are many. **11–132**

One group of cases concerns the powers of sale vested in mortgagees, which they are entitled to use for their own benefit but which they are forbidden to use in ways that unfairly prejudice the mortgagors' position. As stated by the editors of *Fisher & Lightwood*:[191] **11–133**

> "while the mortgagee may look to his own interest, he must nevertheless pay some regard to the interests of the mortgagor. Thus, the mortgagee owes a general duty in equity to the mortgagor . . . to act in good faith and to use his powers for proper purposes. Insofar as consistent with the mortgagor's right to put his own interests first, the mortgagee must act fairly towards the mortgagor. Where their interests conflict, he is not entitled to act in a manner which unfairly prejudices or wilfully and recklessly sacrifices the interests of the mortgagor."

A second group of cases concerns powers affecting the management and distribution of trust property which are vested in the donee of a power who is permitted to exercise the power in a self-interested way, but who must give proper consideration to the beneficiaries' interests when deciding what to do, and must take decisions rationally and openly. Such powers are sometimes given by settlors to trust protectors (who may indeed be the settlors themselves),[192] and they are often given to employers under occupational pension schemes.[193] **11–134**

A third group of cases concern powers vested in the trustees of trusts for multiple beneficiaries including the trustees themselves: as James Penner has written, "such a trustee may be required, in exercising his judgment to distribute property, at least to consider the interests of all the objects, not just his own interests as one of the objects, and to do so in good faith."[194] ... [Consider, for instance,] *Re Mulligan (deceased)*,[195] where a settlor's widow was the life tenant of his estate, and also trustee (with a firm of solicitors); the remainderman was the settlor's nephew. The widow insisted on the adoption of an investment **11–135**

---

191 W. Clark et al (eds), *Fisher & Lightwood's Law of Mortgage* 12th edn (2006) [30.22], approved *Haydon-Baillie v Bank Julius Baer & Co Ltd* [2007] EWHC 1609 (Ch) at [185]. See too *Knight v Marjoribanks* (1849) 2 Mac. & G. 10 at 13–14; *Warner v Jacob* (1882) 20 Ch.D. 220 at 224; *Farrar v Farrars Ltd* (1888) 40 Ch.D. 395 at 398 and 410–411; *Kennedy v De Trafford* [1897] A.C. 180 at 185; *Cuckmere Brick Co Ltd v Mutual Finance Ltd* [1971] Ch. 949 at 965–6; *China and South Sea Bank Ltd v Tan* [1990] 1 A.C. 536 at 545; *Downsview Nominees Ltd v First City Corp Ltd* [1993] A.C. 295 at 317; *Yorkshire Bank plc v Hall* [1999] 1 All E.R. 879 at 895; *Medforth v Blake* [2000] Ch. 86 at 98, 102 and 103. Discussion in K.C.F. Loi, "Mortgagees Exercising Power of Sale: Nonfeasance, Privilege, Trusteeship and Duty of Care" [2010] J.B.L. 576.

192 *Re Z Trust* [1997] C.I.L.R. 248 (Cayman Islands); *Re Internine and Intertraders Trusts* (2005) [2010] W.T.L.R. 443 (Jersey); *Scaffidi v Montevento Holdings Pty Ltd* [2011] WASCA 146 [151]-[152] (Western Aus); *Blenkinsop v Herbert* [2017] WASCA 87 (Western Aus). Earlier days: *Duke of Portland v Lady Topham* (1864) 11 H.L. Cas. 32 at 54. Protectors can also be given powers which they are forbidden to exercise in a self-serving way: *Centre Trustees (CI) Ltd v Pabst* (2009) 12 I.T.E.L.R. 720 (Jersey); *JSC Mezhdunarodniy Promyshlenniy Bank v Pugachev* [2017] EWHC 2426 (Ch) at [186] and [203].

193 *Re Courage Group's Pension Schemes* [1987] 1 W.L.R. 495 at 514; *Imperial Group Pension Trust Ltd v Imperial Tobacco Ltd* [1991] 1 W.L.R. 589; *National Grid Co plc v Mayes* [1997] P.L.R. 157 at [85]-[92] (not contested on appeal); *IBM United Kingdom Holdings Ltd v Dalgleish* [2018] P.L.R. 1. Discussion in M. Thomas and B. Dowrick, "The Heart of the Matter – Re-thinking Good Faith in Occupational Pension Schemes" [2007] Conv. 495; D. Pollard, *The Law of Pension Trusts* (2013) Ch. 11.

194 J.E. Penner, "Distinguishing Fiduciary, Trust, and Accounting Relationships" (2014) 8 J. Eq. 201, p. 221

195 [1998] 1 N.Z.L.R. 481.

policy which maximised income at the expense of capital growth, a breach of trust not because she owed a duty of self-denial to subordinate her personal interest to the nephew's interest by adopting the opposite policy (she did not), but because she and the solicitor trustees both acted in bad faith when they failed to hold an even hand between her interest and the nephew's interest.

11–136 A fourth group of cases holds that where the rules of a partnership invest a majority of partners with powers, these may not be used against the minority unfairly, for example, to expel a partner without allowing her to advance her own case and giving this fair consideration,[196] or to arrange a meeting at which a partner is 'bounced' into resigning: in Neuberger J's words, "Bullying, seeking to trap and intentionally taking by surprise with a view to shock . . . must, in my view, amount to a breach of good faith."[197]

11–137 Similar rules have been exported from partnership law into company law and have been applied in a fifth group of cases, which concern small and closely-held companies that resemble "quasi-partnerships". These cases prohibit the unconscionable use of powers vested in the majority shareholders by the articles of association,[198] conduct which may lead either to orders for a just and equitable winding up of the company under the Insolvency Act 1986, s.122(1)(g) or to buy-out orders on the ground of unfair prejudice under the Companies Act 2006, s.994. In connection with the former provision, Lord Wilberforce said in *Ebrahimi v Westbourne Galleries Ltd* that it enables the court:[199]

> "to subject the exercise of legal rights to equitable considerations . . . of a personal character arising between one individual and another, which may make it unjust, or inequitable, to insist on legal rights, or to exercise them in a particular way."

11–138 In connection with the latter, Lord Hoffmann said in *O'Neill v Phillips* that:[200]

> "One of the traditional roles of equity, as a separate jurisdiction, was to restrain the exercise of strict legal rights in certain relationships in which it considered that this would be contrary to good faith. . . . [So there are] cases in which equitable considerations make it unfair for those conducting the affairs of the company to rely upon their strict legal powers . . . [for example, because they have used the rules in a way] which equity would regard as contrary to good faith."

11–139 In all of these cases, the courts have required defendants to engage in a fair, rational and transparent decision-making process when exercising discretionary powers, and it has been no answer to a complaint that a defendant has failed to do this that she could have arrived at the same conclusion – even the same self-serving conclusion – after following a better process than the one which she undertook. So a central point established by these cases is that although defendants might conceivably breach an equitable duty of good faith because they are actuated by self-interest, it does not follow that equitable duties of good faith and self-denial are one and the same duty. Good faith is a different concept from self-denial, just as it is a different concept from honesty, and a defendant can fail to act in good faith although she is honest and although she has no personal interest in the outcome produced by her bad faith conduct ...

6. Skill and Care

11–140 When performing her administrative role, a trustee is generally required to display no higher degree of diligence than people of ordinary prudence would exercise in the management of their own private affairs.[201] In the investment sphere, however, the trustee's duty is:

---

196 *Const v Harris* (1824) Turn. & R. 496 at 525; *Blisset v Daniel* (1853) 10 Hare 493; *Wood v Woad* (1874) L.R. 9 Ex. 190.

197 *Mullins v Laughton* [2003] Ch. 250 at [100].

198 Note also that shareholder agreements providing for the expulsion of shareholders are enforceable only if they are exercised in good faith and not used "for unworthy purposes": *Re LCM Wealth Management Ltd* [2013] EWHC 3957 (Ch) at [45]–[55].

199 [1973] A.C. 360 at 379.

200 [1999] 1 W.L.R. 1092 at 1098–9; applied in e.g. *Re Via Servis Ltd* [2014] EWHC 3069 (Ch). ...

201 *Learoyd v Whiteley* (1887) 12 A.C. 727 at 733, per Lord Watson.

> not to take such care only as a prudent man would take if he had only himself to consider; the duty rather is to take such care as an ordinary prudent man would take if he were minded to make an investment for the benefit of other people for whom he felt morally bound to provide.[202]

Moreover, with the advent of professional paid trustees and trust companies it has become established that a higher degree of care is expected of them, so that they are judged according to the standards of care which they profess,[203] although they should presumably be afforded the margin available to those called on to exercise their professional judgment in like circumstances.[204] **11–141**

In 2000, the equitable duty of care owed by trustees was replaced by a statutory duty of care which now applies to all trustee activities relating to investments, using agents, nominees and custodians, compounding liabilities, insuring, valuing, and auditing. The statutory duty does not substantially differ from the equitable duty, but s.1 of the Trustee Act 2000 states very clearly what approach should be taken by the courts when assessing whether a trustee has acted to a reasonably careful standard. **11–142**

Trustee Act 2000 s.1

The duty of care

(1) Whenever the duty under this subsection applies to a trustee, he must exercise such care and skill as is reasonable in the circumstances, having regard in particular— **11–143**

(a) to any special knowledge or experience that he has or holds himself out as having, and
(b) if he acts as trustee in the course of a business or profession, to any special knowledge or experience that it is reasonable to expect of a person acting in the course of that kind of business or profession.

Note that s.1(1)(a) involves a subjective element relating to any extra knowledge or experience of the trustee personally, while s.1(1)(b) objectively relates to persons engaged in the trustee's business or profession generally. In (b) there is a distinction between a trustee who carries on trust business in the course of practising generally as a solicitor or accountant, and a trustee who specialises in trust work in the course of the specific business of being a trustee: the latter will normally be governed by a higher standard. Note, too, that the statutory duty of care laid down in s.1 may be excluded by an express term of the trust instrument.[205] **11–144**

7. Mandatory and Default Rules

Can a settlor who wishes to make life easier for her trustees exclude the application of the foregoing rules to her settlement? The leading English case on this topic is *Armitage v Nurse*,[206] the facts of which are given elsewhere.[207] In brief, the case concerned the validity of a clause in a trust deed which **11–145**

---

202 *Re Whiteley* (1886) 33 Ch.D. 347 at 355, per Lindley LJ, endorsed in *Cowan v Scargill* [1985] Ch. 270 at 289; *Nestlé v National Westminster Bank Plc* [1994] 1 All E.R. 118 at 126, 140.

203 *Bartlett v Barclays Bank Trust Co* [1980] 1 All E.R. 139 at 152. See too Lord Nicholls, "Trustees and Their Broader Community: Where Duty, Morality and Ethics Converge" (1995) 9 Tru. L.I. 71, 73.

204 Cf. *Rubenstein v HSBC Bank Plc* [2012] EWCA Civ 1184; [2013] P.N.L.R. 9 at [89], accepting the principle that professionals are entitled to such a margin, although the defendant could not take advantage of this on the facts.

205 Trustee Act 2000 Sch.1 para.7. For general discussion of exemption clauses, see paras 13–159 to 13–166.

206 [1998] Ch. 241.

207 See para.13–161.

exempted the trustees from compensatory liability for loss to the trust fund unless caused by the trustees' "own actual fraud". Millett LJ held that this was a valid clause on which the defendant trustees could rely because the claimant beneficiary had not alleged that loss sustained by the trust fund had resulted from dishonest conduct by the trustees. According to the judge, the governing principles which produced this conclusion were: first, that if "beneficiaries have no rights enforceable against the trustees there are no trusts";[208] but, second, that a distinction can be drawn between rights that beneficiaries *must have*, and rights that they *may have but need not have*, there being "an irreducible core of obligations owed by the trustees to the beneficiaries and enforceable by them which is fundamental to the concept of a trust";[209] and, third, that "the minimum necessary to give substance to the trusts" was "the duty of the trustees to perform the trusts honestly and in good faith for the benefit of the beneficiaries".[210] The clause did not relieve the trustees from this duty since it did not shield them from liability for loss caused by dishonest conduct. Hence it was a valid clause and the trustees could rely on it.

11–146 Millett LJ clearly thought that the answer to the question posed above is no: at least some of the rules considered in this chapter cannot be disapplied by settlors, and the reason for this is that a trust is definitionally a relationship existing between trustees and beneficiaries with respect to property governed by an "irreducible core" set of rules—meaning that certain rules must govern the exercise of trustee powers, or to put the point in "duty language", that certain duties must be owed by the trustees before one can say that a trust exists at all. Extracting these principles from Millett LJ's judgment is not entirely easy, however, because the point at issue in *Armitage* was not whether a settlor can create a trust to which certain core rules do not apply, but whether a settlor can exempt the trustees from personal liability for loss caused by their non-compliance with these rules.

11–147 These two questions are connected, since a trustee would not need to be shielded from compensatory liability for non-compliance with a rule if the rule did not apply to them in the first place. It is important, though, to understand that they are separate questions, and that it would be possible for the law to say that some rules are mandatory, meaning that a settlor cannot validly create a trust to which they do not apply, but at the same time permit settlors to shield trustees from personal liability for non-compliance. And in fact, this is exactly what English law does, since it holds that some of the rules discussed in this chapter are so essential to the idea of a trust that one cannot say that a trust exists at all if property is transferred to a person described as a "trustee" to whom the rules do not apply. At the same time, however, the law permits settlors to shield honest trustees from personal liability for breach of mandatory rules. This might appear paradoxical, but only if one makes the incorrect assumption that the only point of the rules is to expose trustees to personal liability for breaching them—and it is far from clear that non-compliance with all the rules discussed in this chapter does produce this effect, and whether or not it does, most of the rules can produce other effects, too, since non-compliance may result in e.g. beneficiaries being able to assert an equitable interest in trust property which has been transferred to a third party in an unauthorised transaction or to win a court order that amendments to the trust terms are ineffective because they were made for an improper purpose.

11–148 The idea that certain rules must govern the exercise of trustee powers, or that certain "duties" must be owed by the trustees, was derived by Millett LJ from the scholarship of David Hayton.[211] It has since

---

[208] [1998] Ch. 241 at 253.
[209] [1998] Ch. 241 at 253.
[210] [1998] Ch. 241 at 253–254.
[211] D.J. Hayton "The Irreducible Core Content of Trusteeship" in A.J. Oakley (ed) *Trends in Contemporary Trust Law* (Oxford University Press: 1996).

gained widespread judicial acceptance,[212] albeit that there is not yet a judicial consensus as to which duties must be owed and which need not be. The same idea can also be found in the New Zealand Trusts Act 2019, a codifying measure which draws an identical distinction between "mandatory" and "default" trustee duties. The relevant sections are reproduced below and it is illuminating for English lawyers to consider which duties the New Zealand legislature has assigned to each category.

New Zealand Trusts Act 2019, Part 3(1): Duties of Trustee

21. Guiding principle in performing duties
In performing the mandatory duties set out in sections 23 to 27 and (except to the extent modified or excluded by the terms of the trust) the default duties set out in sections 29 to 38, a trustee must have regard to the context and objectives of the trust. **11–149**

Mandatory duties

22. Mandatory duties
The duties set out in sections 23 to 27 are mandatory duties that— **11–150**

(a) must be performed by the trustee; and
(b) may not be modified or excluded by the terms of the trust.

23. Duty to know terms of trust
A trustee must know the terms of the trust. **11–151**

24. Duty to act in accordance with terms of trust
A trustee must act in accordance with the terms of the trust. **11–152**

25. Duty to act honestly and in good faith
A trustee must act honestly and in good faith. **11–153**

26. Duty to act for benefit of beneficiaries or to further permitted purpose of trust
A trustee must hold or deal with trust property and otherwise act— **11–154**

(a) for the benefit of the beneficiaries, in accordance with the terms of the trust:
(b) in the case of a trust for a permitted purpose, to further the permitted purpose of the trust, in accordance with the terms of the trust.

27. Duty to exercise powers for proper purpose
A trustee must exercise the trustee's powers for a proper purpose. **11–155**

Default duties

28. Default duties
The duties set out in sections 29 to 38 are default duties that must be performed by the trustee unless modified or excluded in accordance with section 5(4) and (5). **11–156**

29. General duty of care
When administering a trust (other than when exercising a discretion to distribute trust property), a trustee must exercise the care and skill that is reasonable in the circumstances, having regard, in particular,— **11–157**

(a) to any special knowledge or experience that the trustee has or that the trustee holds out as having; and

[212] e.g. *Citibank NA v MBIA Assurance SA* [2007] EWCA Civ 11; [2007] 1 All E.R. (Comm.) 475 at [58] and [82]; *Spread Trustee Co Ltd v Hutcheson* [2011] UKPC 13; [2012] 2 A.C. 194 at [60]; *Children's Investment Fund Foundation (UK) v Attorney General* [2020] UKSC 33; [2022] A.C. 155 at [82]–[84]; *Webb v Webb* [2020] UKPC 22; [2021] 1 F.L.R. 448 at [89]. See too *Scaffidi v Montevento Holdings Pty Ltd* [2011] WASCA 146 at [149]; *Crossman v Sheahan* (2016) 115 A.C.S.R. 130 at [307]–[308]; *Clayton v Clayton (No.1)* [2016] 1 N.Z.L.R. 551 at [124]; *Zhang Hong Li v DBS Bank (Hong Kong) Ltd* (2019) 22 H.K.C.F.A.R. 392 at [65].

(b) if the person acts as a trustee in the course of a business or profession, to any special knowledge or experience that it is reasonable to expect of a person acting in the course of that kind of business or profession.

30. Duty to invest prudently

11–158 When exercising any power to invest trust property, a trustee must exercise the care and skill that a prudent person of business would exercise in managing the affairs of others, having regard, in particular,—

(a) to any special knowledge or experience that the trustee has or that the trustee holds out as having; and
(b) if the person acts as a trustee in the course of a business or profession, to any special knowledge or experience that it is reasonable to expect of a person acting in the course of that kind of business or profession.

31. Duty not to exercise power for own benefit

11–159 A trustee must not exercise a power of a trustee directly or indirectly for the trustee's own benefit.

32. Duty to consider exercise of power

11–160 A trustee must consider actively and regularly whether the trustee should be exercising 1 or more of the trustee's powers.

33. Duty not to bind or commit trustees to future exercise of discretion

11–161 A trustee must not bind or commit trustees to a future exercise or non-exercise of a discretion.

34. Duty to avoid conflict of interest

11–162 A trustee must avoid a conflict between the interests of the trustee and the interests of the beneficiaries.

35. Duty of impartiality

11–163 (1) A trustee must act impartially in relation to the beneficiaries, and must not be unfairly partial to one beneficiary or group of beneficiaries to the detriment of the others.
(2) This section does not require a trustee to treat all beneficiaries equally (but all beneficiaries must be treated in accordance with the terms of the trust).

36. Duty not to profit

11–164 A trustee must not make a profit from the trusteeship of a trust.

37. Duty to act for no reward

11–165 A trustee must not take any reward for acting as a trustee, but this does not affect the right of a trustee to be reimbursed for the trustee's legitimate expenses and disbursements in acting as a trustee ...

38. Duty to act unanimously

11–166 If there is more than 1 trustee, the trustees must act unanimously. ...

11–167 This statutory statement of trustee duties implemented the recommendations of the New Zealand Law Commission, which approached the question whether duties should be regarded as "mandatory" or "default" by starting with the principle that a trust cannot exist unless the trustees are accountable for what they do with the trust property to beneficiaries or other parties with enforcement rights, and then ask what duties are needed to give content to this idea.[213] The same approach has been taken by legal scholars who have taken up the idea that trustee duties should be placed into these two categories, although they have variously arrived at different (but overlapping) lists of duties which they consider to be mandatory.[214]

---

[213] New Zealand Law Commission, *Review of the Law of Trusts: A Trusts Act for New Zealand* (Report No. 130, 2013), Ch.5.

[214] D.J. Hayton, "The Irreducible Core Content of Trusteeship" in A.J. Oakley (ed.) *Trends in Contemporary Trust Law* (1996); J. Penner, "Exemptions" in P. Birks and A. Pretto (eds) *Breach of Trust* (Hart Publishing, 2002) pp.250–252; J.H. Langbein, "Mandatory Rules in the Law of Trusts" (2004) 98 North Western University L.R. 1105, 1121–1126; A.S. Butler and D.J. Flinn "What is the Least that We Can Expect of a Trustee? Exclusion of Trustee Duties and Exemption of Trustee Liability" [2010] N.Z.L.R. 459; D. Fox "Non-excludable Trustee Duties" (2011) 17 T. & T. 17; L. Ho, "Trusts: The Essentials" in L. Smith (ed),

Note that a trustee's fiduciary duty does not appear on the statutory list of mandatory duties, various aspects of this duty appearing instead as default duties: a duty not to exercise powers for the trustees' own benefit; a duty to avoid conflicts of interest; a duty not to profit; and a duty to act for no reward. The decision to treat all these duties as default rather than mandatory duties is in line with the common law position that settlors are free to create trusts under which trustees are authorised to exercise their powers in ways that subordinate the interests of particular beneficiaries to those of other people, i.e. to disapply the "no conflicts" rule that would otherwise apply to the trustees as fiduciaries,[215] provided that they act in good faith, meaning in a way that is true to the settlors' intentions. In practice this is frequently done, an example being discretionary trusts under which the trustees belong to the class of beneficiaries and are empowered to distribute property to some beneficiaries (possibly including themselves) and not the others.[216] The effect of all this is that trustees can find themselves in situations where they must attend to the interests of different beneficiaries who have conflicting interests, and in such cases they are said to owe a duty of "even-handedness and impartiality".[217] **11–168**

Questions

1. What are the connections between the rules on certainty of objects affecting the validity of discretionary trusts and powers of appointment and the rules governing the exercise of powers of appointment by trustees and donees of powers?
2. "The law took a seriously wrong turn when the courts began to let trustees use the rule in *Re Hastings-Bass* to avoid dispositions of trust property with unforeseen tax consequences. In *Pitt v Holt*, the Supreme Court put the law back on the right course." **Discuss.**
3. Five years ago, Sam transferred assets worth £5 million to Vic and Waldo, to hold on trust for Sam himself for his life, and thereafter to hold on a discretionary trust for Sam's children, Rachel and Tom, and their issue. The trust instrument also gives the trustees a power to appoint property out of the trust fund to Eve, Sam's wife.

   At the time of settling the trust, Sam wrote a letter of wishes to the trustees in which he stated: (i) that he would make generous provision to Eve in his will and that after his death the trustees should only exercise their power of appointment in her favour if she found herself in serious financial need; (ii) that he did not want his children to become dependent on the trust and that he wanted them to make their own way in the world; and (iii) that particular care should be taken in relation to Tom as he was a feckless young man with no ambition beyond spending other people's money.

   Three years ago, Sam died. Since then, Vic and Waldo have made regular distributions out of trust income to Rachel, but paid nothing to Tom. Tom has now complained about this, has demanded that they justify their "unfair" attitude towards distributing the trust property, and

---

The Worlds of the Trust (Cambridge University Press, 2013) pp.13–15; D. Clarry, "The Irreducible Core of a Guernsey Trust'" [2014] Jersey & Guernsey L.R. (online); C. Mitchell, "Good Faith, Self-Denial and Mandatory Trustee Duties" (2018) 32 Tru. L.I. 92.

215 As noted in New Zealand Law Commission *Review of the Law of Trusts: A Trusts Act for New Zealand* (Report No.130, 2013) p.109.

216 See e.g. *Jones v Firkin-Flood* [2008] EWHC 2417 (Ch) at [265]; *Whaley v Whaley* [2011] EWCA Civ 617; [2012] 1 F.L.R. 735 at [51].

217 See paras 10–055 to 10–056; and see too New Zealand Trust Act 2019 s.35, quoted at para.11–163.

has said that unless they pay him a sizeable annual income henceforth he will have them replaced as trustees.

Last year Eve remarried. Her new husband, Jeremy, is a highly successful businessman. He has suggested to her, and she has now suggested to Vic and Waldo, that the trustees should appoint £2 million out of the trust fund to Eve which she could then give to Jeremy to invest in his business.

Advise Vic and Waldo.

12

RIGHTS OF BENEFICIARIES AND THE NATURE OF A TRUST

1. Introduction

12-001 We noted in Chapter 4 that there is a debate about the true nature of the rights of B, a beneficiary of a trust.[1] In this long-running controversy, the key disagreement is as to the nature of a trust itself. On one view, which we will refer to here as the "proprietary view", the creation of a trust gives B a property right, arising in equity, in the trust property. A number of important rules and principles of trusts law, including some of those we have examined in Chapters 9, 11 and 12, and many of those we will examine in Chapters 15 and 16, are then explained as recognising and giving effect to B's equitable property right in the trust property. On another view, which we will refer to here as the "obligational view", the creation of a trust imposes particular duties on T, and the rights acquired by B are defined by the content of those duties. On this view, a different explanation needs to be found for those rules and principles of trusts law that might otherwise be seen as based on the proprietary nature of B's rights.[2]

12-002 It would be a mistake to say that, in analysing the nature of a trust, only two views are possible: whilst each of the proprietary and obligational views can be taken as marking one end of a spectrum, that spectrum is broad enough to include a large number of different views. It is nonetheless necessary, in coming to any conclusion as to the analysis of the rights of beneficiaries, and the nature of a trust, to consider and evaluate each of the proprietary view and the obligational view. It is also important to be aware of this debate when considering the impact of trusts on third parties, which is a matter we will consider in, for example, Chapters 14 and 15.

12-003 Throughout this book, we have seen a number of very important features of B's rights under a trust that differentiate B's position from that of a party with a purely personal right. We can, for example, compare B's position, where T holds property on trust for B, with that of a creditor, where a debtor has a simple duty to pay the creditor £100. First, B is protected in the event of T's insolvency; the creditor is not protected in the event of the debtor's insolvency. Second, if T makes an unauthorised transfer of the trust property to a third party, and that third party cannot establish a defence such as that of bona fide purchase for value,[3] B will be able to make a claim against that third party; if the debtor were to make a gift of £100 to a third party, rather than paying that £100 to the creditor, the creditor has no claim against that third party. Third, if T acquires new assets through an authorised or unauthorised

1 See para.4-067.
2 Of course, in many cases, an express trust will involve two or more trustees, and two or more beneficiaries. For ease of exposition, however, we will refer in this chapter to T and to B.
3 See paras 15-164ff.

use of the trust property, B can claim that those new assets are held subject to the terms of the initial trust in B's favour;[4] if the debtor takes £100 and, rather than giving it to the creditor, instead uses it to gamble and turns it into £1,000, the creditor has no claim to that £1,000.

12-004 It is therefore indisputable that there is a difference between the nature of B's rights, arising under a trust, and the right of the creditor, in the case of a pure debt. B, like the creditor, benefits from the existence of an obligation: T is under a duty to B, and the debtor is under a duty to the creditor. The crucial difference is that T's duty to B relates to specific property (the subject matter of the trust); the debtor's duty to the creditor does not. That explains the first and second of the three key differences between B's position and the position of the creditor that were noted in the preceding paragraph; on the view of the House of Lords in *Foskett v McKeown* it also explains the third.[5] For this reason, the difference between B's position and the creditor's position is consistently described by the courts[6] and the legislature[7] in the same way as it has been consistently described in this book: as turning on the fact that B has an equitable or beneficial interest in the trust property or, synonymously, an equitable or beneficial property right; or, in relation to some trusts at least, equitable or beneficial ownership of the trust property.[8]

12-005 It might therefore seem that the debate between the proprietary view and the obligational view of the trust is over before we have even begun. Yet the obligational view has attracted many eminent supporters over the centuries,[9] and lies behind a number of more recent analyses of the nature of the trust.[10] It is vital to note that proponents of an obligational view do not claim that the right of B under a trust is no different to the right of the creditor to be paid a debt of £100; nor do they seek to deny any of the three fundamental features of a right under a trust noted above. The debate is not as to what the basic rules and principles of the law of trusts should be; it is rather as to the best way to explain those rules and principles. On an obligational view, focussing on the particular nature of T's duties to B is the key to explaining why B's rights differ from those of the creditor, and to understanding the nature of the trust; on a proprietary view, the door is instead opened by focussing on B's direct link to the trust property.

12-006 It should not be thought that this debate is either illusory or unimportant. There is some substantial common ground between commentators currently engaged in the debate; but the differences in their positions, and between the proprietary view and the obligational view, are nonetheless real. Nor should it be thought that, because the debate interests academics, it is of only academic interest. It is true that, just as those favouring an obligational view do not deny the fundamental point that B has a right that is protected in T's insolvency and which may bind certain third parties, those adopting a proprietary view equally do not claim that B's right is identical in its effect to the full title enjoyed by O, a party who simply owns property outright. It is accepted on all sides, for example, that B will have no claim against C if C is a bona fide purchaser for value of the trust property without notice of the trust.[11]

---

4 See paras 15–143.

5 [2001] 1 A.C. 102. As noted at paras 15–133 to 15–137, however, that analysis can be questioned.

6 See, e.g. *Westdeutsche Landesbank Girozentrale v Islington LBC* [1996] A.C. 669 at 705; *Foskett v McKeown* [2001] 1 A.C. 102 at 110); *Independent Trustee Services Ltd v GP Noble Trustees Ltd* [2012] EWCA Civ 195; [2013] Ch. 91 at [77]; *Akers v Samba Financial Group* [2017] UKSC 6; [2017] A.C. 424 at [82].

7 See, e.g. Law of Property Act 1925, s.53(1)(c): see para.6–051.

8 See, e.g. *Shell UK Ltd v Total UK Ltd* [2011] Q.B. 86 (extracted at paras 12–093 to 12–104), referring to the case where B has rights under a fixed trust, rather than under a discretionary trust.

9 See paras 12–037 to 12–043.

10 See, e.g. L. Smith, "Unravelling Proprietary Restitution" (2004) 40 Can. Bus. L.J. 317; B. McFarlane & R. Stevens, "The Nature of Equitable Property" (2010) 4 J. Eq. 1; T. Cutts, "The Nature of 'Equitable Property': a Functional Analysis" (2012) 6 J. Eq. 44; J. Edelman, "Two Fundamental Questions for the Law of Trusts" (2013) 129 L.Q.R. 66.

11 See para.15–164.

In contrast, if O's property is stolen and then sold by the thief to C, who buys in good faith and with no notice of O's initial property right, O will be able to assert that property right against C.[12]

It is nonetheless clear that the accepted, key features of the trust cannot, by themselves, provide the answers to every practical question that may arise as to the operation of B's rights. As we will see later in this chapter,[13] there are a number of practical points which will be determined differently according to whether a court expressly or impliedly favours the proprietary view or the obligational view. **12–007**

2. The Debate

A. The Proprietary View

The proprietary view has long-standing and current academic support,[14] as it provides a straightforward explanation for two of the three key features of the trust discussed above.[15] It is also consistent with, and derives support from, the language often used by the courts. For example, in a careful analysis of the nature of B's rights against C, an innocent donee to whom T makes an unauthorised disposition of trust property, Lloyd LJ in *Independent Trustee Services Ltd v GP Noble Trustees Ltd*[16] explained that: **12–008**

> in the case of an innocent volunteer recipient of money which is the product of a breach of trust, the legal title is in the recipient but equitable title remains in the beneficiaries of the relevant trust throughout.

In *Foskett v McKeown*,[17] when analysing the third of the three features discussed above, Lord Browne-Wilkinson invoked the "hard-nosed property rights" of B in explaining why B could bring a claim in relation to the traceable proceeds of trust property against innocent donees who had received, and retained, such proceeds. **12–009**

One of the key features of B's rights under a trust is that B may be able to assert a claim against C, a third party who acquires the trust property as a result of an unauthorised transfer by T, as will be examined in Chapter 15. On the proprietary view, this can be explained by seeing B as having an equitable interest in the trust property, rather than only a right correlating to T's duty to B: a key feature of property rights, as opposed to personal rights, is that they are capable of binding third parties. As Richard Nolan has explained,[18] however, it is clear that B's position against C is not entirely the same as B's initial position against T. For example, under the terms of an initial express trust, T may have agreed to particular positive duties to manage and invest the trust property. C, merely by acquiring the trust property, will not be under those same positive duties to B; C's basic duty will instead simply be to restore the trust assets,[19] by giving them up either to a new trustee or (where B is the sole and **12–010**

---

[12] See, e.g. *Farquarhson Bros and Co v King and Co* [1902] A.C. 325. Where the property consists of goods, O's claim against C will arise in the tort of conversion.

[13] See paras 12–057 and 12–082.

[14] In addition to the articles referred to elsewhere in this Chapter, see e.g. A.W. Scott, 'The Nature of the Rights of the 'Cestui Que Trust" (1917) 17 Col. L. Rev. 269; P. Jaffey, "Explaining the Trust" (2015) 131 L.Q.R. 377; H. Dagan and I. Samet, "Express Trust: The Dark Horse of the Liberal Property Regime" in S. Degeling et al (eds) *Philosophical Foundations of the Law of Express Trusts* (Oxford University Press, forthcoming).

[15] See para.12–003.

[16] [2012] EWCA Civ 195; [2013] Ch. 91 at [77]–[80].

[17] [2001] 1 A.C. 102 at 109.

[18] R. Nolan, "Equitable Property" (2006) 122 L.Q.R. 232.

[19] See e.g. *Akers v Samba Financial Group* [2017] UKSC 6; [2017] A.C. 424 at [46] and [88].

absolutely entitled beneficiary) to B. As Nolan explains in the following extract, even on the proprietary view, it is therefore necessary to distinguish the core, negative duty of T—the duty not to use the trust property for T's own benefit, unless specifically authorised to do so by the terms of the trust—from the additional positive duties that T may have agreed to assume under the terms of the initial trust. It is important to note that the proprietary view does not entail the clearly incorrect proposition that *all* the rights of B under a trust are proprietary, and that none of those rights are based simply on the content of duties owed by T to B.[20]

Richard Nolan, "Equitable Property"

(2006) 122 L.Q.R. 232, 233, 261–262, 255–256

12–011 . . . In short, a beneficiary's core proprietary rights under a trust consist in the beneficiary's primary, negative right to exclude non-beneficiaries from the enjoyment of trust assets. Infringement of this primary right will generate secondary rights by which a beneficiary may also prevent (or at least restrict) access to assets by non-beneficiaries.[21] By contrast, a beneficiary's positive claims to access benefits from trust assets, which will exist in conjunction with his negative, exclusionary rights, may or may not themselves be regarded as proprietary by reason of their utility rather than their enforceability. . ..

12–012 The constant, negative, exclusionary aspect of an equitable property right under a trust may be conjoined with one of many possible fractions of positive benefit which a settlor can instruct trustees to carve out of the trust assets and deflect to a beneficiary: fixed interests or discretionary interests; interests in possession or remainder and so on. Whether the resulting bundle of rights itself satisfies and particular definition (usually statutory) of "property" or "proprietary interest" will depend on the definition used, which will necessarily vary, depending in turn on the purpose for which the definition is established. . .

12–013 Any positive claims to take benefit from assets by virtue of a trust are not the concern of third parties, unless they have for reasons beyond mere receipt of assets made themselves amenable to such claims. It is in this way, by limiting the extent of the claims which can be made against third parties, by limiting the proprietary claims founded on an equitable interest under a trust, that the Chancery courts have reconciled the perceived need to restrict the number of proprietary claims which may affect third parties with the huge flexibility that the law of trusts affords to intending settlers who want to apportion and allocate the various benefits from assets amongst several different people.

12–014 For the purposes of his analysis, Nolan adopts a particular meaning of "proprietary":[22]

an asset is termed "property" or "proprietary" when the component parts of that interest include a primary right to exclude any one of a very large and indefinite class of people from access to some enjoyment of the asset, whether or not those people have in fact consented to such exclusion, and secondary claims to vindicate that primary right.

---

20 See e.g. *Akers v Samba Financial Group* [2017] UKSC 6; [2017] A.C. 424 at [82], where Lord Sumption distinguishes between the personal right of B against T "to have the trust administered according to its terms" and B's proprietary right, enforceable against (particular) third parties. See further paras 12–078ff.

21 For the distinction between "primary rights" (those rights which arise from facts or events, rather than from an infringement of some other right) and "secondary rights" (those rights which arise from infringement of some other right), see J Austin, *Lectures on Jurisprudence* (1885) Lecture XLV, esp at pp 762 et seq. The distinction, as used here, is essentially between the extra-curial behaviour legitimated by a property right and its judicial vindication following infringement. It is not about the difference between property rights and restitutionary rights, as to which see P Birks, *Introduction to the Law of Restitution* (1985) at pp.50–52.

22 R. Nolan, "Equitable Property" (2006) 122 L.Q.R. 232, 235.

Certainly, whilst general debates as to the nature of property do of course continue, there is a significant body of support[23] for the idea that a proprietary right necessarily involves a "right to exclude" or, more precisely, that it imposes a prima facie duty of non-interference on the rest of the world. In this chapter, therefore, we will adopt that notion of property when defining and evaluating the proprietary view of the trust. **12–015**

It is important to bear in mind, however, that, whilst we have thus adopted a stable meaning of what it means for a right to be proprietary, other analyses may have adopted, expressly or impliedly, a different meaning. First, a term such as "property" may mean different things in different contexts.[24] In *Akers v Samba Financial Group*,[25] for example, the Supreme Court had to consider s.127 of the Insolvency Act 1986, which applies to render a disposition of a company's property void[26] if that disposition is made after winding up proceedings have commenced in relation to that company. The question was whether the provision could apply to a case in which the company (B) was a beneficiary of a trust: it was assumed that T had, in breach of trust, transferred shares held on trust for B to C, a third party against whom B would not be able to bring a claim to the shares. There was an initial question as to whether a beneficial interest under a trust could be regarded as "property". However, as Lord Sumption explained: **12–016**

> Section 436 of the Insolvency Act 1986 defines 'property' as including: 'money, goods, things in action, land and every description of property wherever situated and also obligations and every description of interest, whether present or future or vested or contingent, arising out of, or incidental to, property.' These are exceptionally wide words. It is plain that an equitable proprietary interest in property under a trust and a personal right to have the trusts of that property administered according to their terms are both 'property' for the purposes of the Act, including section 127.

The fact that the s.436 definition of "property" expressly includes "obligations" within its scope thus means that the characterisation of a beneficiary's interest as "property" for the purposes of s.127 of the Insolvency Act is compatible with each of the proprietary and obligational views of the trust. **12–017**

Second, the term "property" is often applied, not least by economists, to any valuable asset; it is sometimes also used to refer to any asset the value of which can be realised by trading, for example by means of transferring the asset to another person.[27] Neither of those usages of the term is relevant to the debate we are considering here, between the proprietary and obligational views of the trust.[28] This is because it is perfectly consistent with the obligational view to accept that B's right under a trust **12–018**

---

23 See, e.g. K. Gray, "Property in Thin Air" [1991] C.L.J. 252; T. Merrill "Property and the Right to Exclude" (1998) 77 Nebraska L.R. 730; S. Douglas & B. McFarlane, "Defining Property Rights" in J. Penner & H. Smith (eds) *Philosophical Foundations of Property Law* (Oxford University Press, 2013).

24 For discussion see e.g. B. McFarlane and S. Douglas, "Property, Analogy, and Variety" (2022) 42 O.J.L.S. 161.

25 [2017] UKSC 6; [2017] A.C. 424.

26 Such a disposition is prima facie void but the court has a discretion to uphold it nevertheless as s.127 states that: "In a winding up by the court, any disposition of the company's property, and any transfer of shares, or alteration in the status of the company's members, made after the commencement of the winding up is, unless the court otherwise orders, void. . . ."

27 See, e.g. *OBG Ltd v Allan* [2007] UKHL 21; [2008] 1 A.C. 1 at [309] per Lady Hale (dissenting). Lady Hale's argument there was that, because a chose in action is "property" in the sense of being an asset, separate to its holder, which can be transferred, it should be protected by means of a strict duty of non-interference prima facie binding on the rest of the world. It is submitted, however, that the view of the majority in that case is to be preferred, as the question of transferability differs from that of exclusion. There are, for example, some rights which do impose a strict general duty of non-interference but which cannot be effectively transferred (e.g. a non-assignable lease).

28 That is not to say, of course, that such meanings of property are never relevant. For example, the term "property" as used in the Insolvency Act 1986 is given a broad meaning by s.436 of that Act (see, e.g. *Bristol Airport Plc v Powdrill* [1990] Ch. 744) as its aim is to vest the realisable assets of the insolvent party in, e.g. the trustee in bankruptcy who can then realise the value in those assets to meet the debts of the insolvent party.

is valuable, and that its value can be realised by trading.[29] After all, a simple contractual right of a creditor to be paid £100 by a debtor can have both of those features.

12-019 Third, it is possible for a particular analysis to adopt a still different approach to defining "property". For example, in part of Lord Sumption's judgment in *Akers v Samba Financial Group* cited below,[30] it is the ability of an equitable interest to bind *particular* third parties—those who acquire the trust property or its traceable proceeds—which is said to show the proprietary nature of that interest. This definition of "property" is more limited than the one we are using in this chapter, as it does not involve *all* third parties being under a prima facie duty to B of non-interference with the trust property. The possible significance of this distinction will be explored further below.[31]

B. The Diversity of Trusts

i. Different Types of Trusts

12-020 As we saw in Chapter 4,[32] there is a great diversity to the law of trusts, both across jurisdictions and within English law, and so care must be taken in making general statements that purport to apply to all forms of trust. A good example is provided by the difference between a fixed trust and a discretionary trust.[33] In *Baker v Archer-Shee*,[34] for example, B was the life tenant under a trust of shares, i.e. T held shares subject to a duty to use those shares for the benefit of B during B's life, and then to use the shares for the benefit of others on B's death. T thus had a duty to pay dividends declared on the shares to B, although T was allowed to deduct expenses before making those payments. The shares, and T, were based in New York. To apply legislation determining B's tax liability,[35] it was necessary to ask if B could be regarded as owning the dividends as soon as they were paid to T, so that the dividends were chargeable to income tax immediately, whether or not the dividends were later remitted to B in the UK. A majority of the House of Lords held that, by virtue of her rights under the trust, B could be regarded, in effect, as the real owner of income produced by the trust property as soon as that income was produced, and could be assessed for income tax accordingly. Lord Wrenbury stated that B was "entitled in equity specifically during her life to the dividends upon the stocks".[36] The decision, albeit given in the particular context of applying specific tax legislation, thus provides support for the proprietary view.

12-021 In *Gartside v IRC*,[37] by way of contrast, the House of Lords considered the application of tax legislation in a case where B was the beneficiary of a discretionary trust rather than a fixed trust. The question under that legislation (which governed estate duty rather than income tax) was whether B, before receiving any distribution from T under the discretionary trust, had an "interest in possession" or even an "interest" in the trust property.[38] The House of Lords, allowing B's appeal from the decision of the

---

29 See paras 6-051ff for discussion of the methods by which B can realise the value of a right under a trust. It is of course possible for S, when setting up a trust, to ensure that B cannot transfer B's right; even in such a case, however, it may still be possible for B to realise the value of her right by declaring, in exchange for payment from C, a sub-trust in C's favour (compare, e.g. *Don King v Warren* [2000] Ch. 291 and see para.4-031).

30 See para.12-078.

31 See paras 12-079 to 12-082.

32 See paras 4-001 to 4-019.

33 See paras 4-009 to 4-011.

34 [1927] A.C. 844.

35 Income Tax Act 1918 Sch.D, Case 4.

36 [1927] A.C. 844 at 866.

37 [1968] A.C. 553.

38 Finance Act 1940 s.43.

Court of Appeal, held that, as the trust was a discretionary trust, B's right did not count as such an interest. Lord Wilberforce explained this in the following words.[39]

> No doubt in a certain sense a beneficiary under a discretionary trust has an "interest": the nature of it may, sufficiently for the purpose, be spelt out by saying that he has a right to be considered as a potential recipient of benefit by the trustees and a right to have his interest protected by a court of equity. Certainly that is so, and when it is said that he has a right to have the trustees exercise their discretion "fairly" or "reasonably" or "properly" that indicates clearly enough that some objective consideration (not stated explicitly in declaring the discretionary trust, but latent in it) must be applied by the trustees and that the right is more than a mere spes.[40] But that does not mean that he has an interest which is capable of being taxed by reference to its extent in the trust fund's income: it may be a right, with some degree of concreteness or solidity, one which attracts the protection of a court of equity, yet it may still lack the necessary quality of definable extent which must exist before it can be taxed. . .. **12–022**
>
> The Master of the Rolls and Salmon L.J. in the Court of Appeal were persuaded by an argument which was suggested [by the Revenue] to meet this difficulty. The beneficiary's right, it was claimed, is analogous to that of a competitor in a beauty competition; she has a right to be considered for the prize: if she is excluded, she can be awarded damages which a jury can assess. The analogy was inevitably left at some distance because it could hardly be suggested that a charge for estate duty could be assessed by any similar procedure: and it is clear enough that it fails at the critical point, namely, of establishing that a person with a chance of success has an interest in more than the broadest popular sense, *in the fund*. **12–023**

As we will consider further below,[41] the mere fact that B's right under a particular type of trust is not regarded as an "interest" or even as "property", as that term is used by a specific statute, does not mean that such a trust must necessarily be regarded as consistent only with the obligational view rather than the proprietary view. This point is made by Nolan, who notes that:[42] **12–024**

> where a tax is levied by reference to the benefits of holding "property", or by reference to receipts from "property", then the notion of "property" is generally, and entirely understandably, taken to involve positive claims of access to some benefit of definable extent, unless the meaning of the word is deliberately extended.

So, the decision in *Gartside v IRC* does not mean that the right of B under a discretionary trust lies outside the definition of property which we have adopted, which looks not to the positive rights of B to a specific benefit, but rather to the rights of B to exclude others from access to the trust property. Indeed, under a discretionary trust as under any trust, B has a right which is capable of binding C, a third party who acquires the trust property through an unauthorised disposition by T;[43] and B is also protected should T go into insolvency. As Nolan notes,[44] therefore, the decision in *Gartside v IRC* does not, by itself, make it impossible to regard a beneficiary of a discretionary trust as having rights that are "proprietary" in the "general, negative, exclusionary sense". Nonetheless, consideration of the discretionary trust is important, as it shows that, even if though a possible object of the exercise of a discretion by the trustees cannot point to any asset which they will necessarily own, that party can still **12–025**

---

39 [1968] A.C. 553 at 617–618.

40 [i.e. more than a mere hope.]

41 See para.12–080.

42 R. Nolan, "Equitable Property" (2006) 122 L.Q.R. 232, 256 (footnotes omitted).

43 See paras 3–189 to 3–192 and note e.g. *Lewis v Tamplin* [2018] EWHC 777 (Ch) at [39] (HHJ Matthews): "If the trustee of a discretionary trust in breach of trust gave away a trust asset to a third party, no-one can doubt that even a discretionary object of the trust in whose favour an appointment could still be made would have standing to sue the third party for the return of the asset to the trust fund."

44 R. Nolan, "Equitable Property" (2006) 122 L.Q.R. 232, 257 (footnote omitted). See too *Lewis v Tamplin* [2018] EWHC 77 (Ch) at [39].

enforce the key duties of trustees, and the limits on the powers of the trustees, discussed in Chapters 3 and 11.[45]

ii. Looking Beyond Beneficiaries

12–026 In considering the diversity of trusts, it is also important to note that some effects fundamental to the nature of the trust can exist even if there is no individual who can claim equitable ownership of the trust assets. We saw in Chapter 3 that the duty of due administration is separate to, and arises independently of, any "equitable proprietary interest".[46] Parties without any "equitable proprietary interest" can have a right to due administration: for example, in Chapter 11 we saw that discretionary objects, who have no "equitable proprietary interest", can still enforce the trustee's duty of due administration.[47] Further, the duties of charitable trustees, and the limits on their powers, can be enforced and recognised in claims brought by the Attorney General, Charity Commission, or any person interested in the trust: this includes a claim to recover misapplied trust property from a third party.[48] It is for this reason that an analysis of the trust which prefers the proprietary view, and thus emphasises the importance of equitable ownership to a trust, might seek to distinguish charitable trusts, for example by seeing them as part of public law rather than private law,[49] or by pointing to their historical origins in the ecclesiastical rather than Chancery courts.[50] Similarly, as we noted in Chapter 8,[51] a preference for the proprietary view provides one means of explaining the general rule against private purpose trusts,[52] although an acceptance of the obligational view would not, in itself, require the courts to recognise all private purpose trusts as valid.[53]

12–027 In relation to charitable and other express trusts it is important to observe that a *trustee* also has a right to due administration that is enforceable against her co-trustee(s), and against former and replacement trustees.[54] For example, if T has breached a duty as trustee and is later replaced as a trustee by T2, then T2 may have the power, and indeed duty, to bring a claim against T.[55] Moreover, if a trustee misapplies the trust property, for example by distributing it in an unauthorised way, that trustee then has a duty to bring proceedings to recover the property or otherwise obtain relief on behalf of the beneficiaries.[56]

12–028 It would, therefore, be a mistake to think that the enforcement of the duties of trustees, and the recognition of limits on the powers of trustees, can occur only if there is a beneficiary who can be identified as an equitable owner of the trust property. It is also significant that, even in a simple case where T holds on trust for a single beneficiary, B, T also has powers in relation to the trust assets which can

---

45 See paras 3–143 to 3–192, 11–001ff.
46 See paras 3–145, 3–161 to 3–162.
47 See paras 11–020 to 11–022.
48 See paras 3–161 to 3–164.
49 See e.g. P. Matthews, "The Comparative Importance of the Rule in *Saunders v Vautier*" (2006) 122 L.Q.R. 266, 275: "the charitable trust is unusual, being for the benefit of society as a whole, rather than for that of private individuals. It is an instrument of public law rather than private law."
50 See e.g. P. Matthews, "From Obligation to Property and Back Again? The Future of Non Charitable Purpose Trusts" in D. Hayton (ed) *Extending the Boundaries of Trusts and Other Ring-Fenced Funds* (Kluwer Law International, 2002), 231.
51 See para.8–061.
52 See e.g. P. Matthews ibid fn.50 and "The New Trust: Obligations Without Rights?" in A.J. Oakley (ed.), *Trends in Contemporary Trust Law* (Oxford University Press, 1997).
53 Note e.g. the limits on valid non-charitable purpose trusts imposed even in legislation permitting such trusts: see e.g. Bermuda Trusts (Special Provisions) Act 1989 s.12A(2) (set out at para.8–056).
54 See para.11–015.
55 See paras 11–015ff.
56 See para.15–085.

take priority over the claims of B. We have seen that,[57] in relation to expenses incurred with authority under the trust (such as a debt owed to a third party who repaired trust property under a contract with the trustee) T has a "right of indemnity" and so can make use of the trust property to ensure that T does not have to bear the authorised trust expense from T's own pocket. As a result, it is impossible to say that B has an absolute entitlement to the trust property.[58] This "right of indemnity" can be seen to involve both a power of exoneration, which, in our example, permits T to use the trust assets directly to pay the debt to the third party, and a power of recoupment, available where T has already paid the debt using T's own funds and then "allows the trustee to treat trust property as her own, free of her duties as trustee, to the extent required to make good her loss . . .".[59] As noted by Kiefel CJ and Keane and Edelman JJ in *Carter Holt Harvey Woodproducts v Commonwealth of Australia*:[60]

> The trustee's rights take priority over those of the beneficiaries to the extent of the trustee's powers of indemnity. Where the "trust assets" need to be sold to reimburse or exonerate the trustee, the beneficiaries' rights have lower priority than the trustee's rights. A court may authorise the sale of assets held by the trustee so as to satisfy the power of indemnity, as a step in the process of the trustee exonerating itself from authorised liabilities, in the same manner as any other equitable charge.[61]

The reference in the quotation above to the trustee's power of indemnity as functioning in a similar way to an equitable charge might suggest that, in a simple case where T holds on trust for B, the power of indemnity is consistent with B's equitable ownership, as that ownership is simply subject to a competing property right which secures T's power of indemnity. Two points can be made in response. First, even on such an analysis, the power of indemnity, which arises as a matter of default whenever a trust is set up, constitutes a significant difference in the position of a beneficiary and that of a party who simply has unencumbered ownership of property. Second, as argued expressly by Hudson and Mitchell,[62] it may in any case be more accurate to see the protection of the trustee not as a charge over B's property but rather simply as a limit on the scope of the core duty of the trustee not to make use of the trust property for her own benefit. This analysis is suggested in the judgment of Bell, Gageler and Nettle JJ in the *Carter Holt* case:[63] **12-029**

> A court of equity will assist the trustee to realise trust assets to satisfy the trustee's right of indemnity, in priority to the beneficiaries' interests,[64] and thus it is said that the trustee has an equitable charge or lien over the trust assets.[65] It is not, however, a charge or lien comparable to a synallagmatic security interest over property of another. It arises endogenously as an incident of the office of trustee in respect of the trust assets.[66]

---

57 See paras 1-096 to 1-100 and 10-128 to 10-136.

58 See e.g. *Chief Commissioner of Stamp Duties (NSW) v Buckle* (1988) 192 CLR 226 at [47]-[48]; *CPT Custodian Pty Ltd v Commissioner of State Revenue (Vic)* (2005) 224 C.L.R. 98 at [51]; *Carter Holt Harvey Woodproducts v Commonwealth of Australia* [2019] HCA 20; (2019) 368 A.L.R. 390 at [80].

59 J. Hudson & C. Mitchell, "Trustee Recoupment: A Power Analysis" (2021) 35 Tru. L.I. 3, 7 [extracted at paras 10-131ff].

60 [2019] HCA 20; (2019) 368 A.L.R. 390 at [32].

61 *Chief Commisioner of Stamp Duties (NSW) v Buckle* (1998) 192 C.L.R. 226 at 247 [50]. See *Hewett v Court* (1983) 149 C.L.R. 639 at 663.

62 J. Hudson & C.Mitchell, "Trustee Recoupment: A Power Analysis" (2021) 35 Tru. L.I. 3, 7, 16-17.

63 [2019] HCA 20; (2019) 368 A.L.R. 390 at [83].

64 See e.g. *Grissell v Money* (1869) 38 LJ Ch 312 per Lord Romilly M.R.; cf *Darke v Williamson* (1858) 25 Beav 622 at 626-627 per Romilly M.R.

65 *Chief Commisioner of Stamp Duties (NSW) v Buckle* (1998) 192 CLR 226 at 247 [50] per Brennan CJ, Toohey, Gaudron, McHugh and Gummow JJ. See also *Bruton Holdings Pty Ltd (in liq) v Federal Commissioner of Taxation* (2009) 239 CLR 346 at 358-359 [43] per French CJ, Gummow, Hayne, Heydon and Bell JJ.

66 *Worrall v Harford* (1802) 8 Ves Jun 4 at 8 per Lord Eldon L.C. quoted in *Buckle* (1998) 192 CLR 226 at 245 [47]. See and compare *Hewett v Court* (1983) 149 CLR 639 at 663-664 per Deane J.

iii. Looking Beyond Trusts

12–030 We have so far encountered a number of situations, within the law of trusts, where the ability to enforce the duties of trustees, and the limits on their powers, can be held by a party, such as an object of a discretionary power, who cannot be seen in any realistic sense as having equitable ownership of the trust property. This is consistent with the fact that some of the key aspects of the operation of a trust, including both the shielding of assets in insolvency, and liability of third parties, are also features of other forms of arrangements in which a party holds assets subject to a duty of due administration, but there is no trust.

12–031 For example, we have seen in Chapter 3[67] that a personal representative in the course of administering a deceased person's estate is vested with particular assets (comprising the estate) but, like a trustee, is under a duty of due administration in relation to those assets, and so has limits on the lawful exercise of their powers in relation to the assets.[68] *Commissioner of Stamp Duties (Queensland) v Livingston*[69] shows that, while the estate is being administered (so that, for example, any debts owed by the deceased are met), an estate beneficiary (i.e a party who is due to receive a distribution from the estate, either as a legatee named in a will or as someone entitled on an intestacy) does not yet have any equitable proprietary right—she cannot point to any specific asset she will receive, as it may be that all the assets of the estate will be required to pay debts owed by the deceased. Nonetheless, as noted by Charles Mitchell:[70]

> . . . personal representatives must keep accurate records and produce these for inspection by estate beneficiaries.[71] A statutory provision also entitles estate beneficiaries to apply for an order that the personal representatives should supply them with information relating to the administration of the estate.[72]

12–032 The position of the estate beneficiary thus provides further evidence that duties which match key trustee duties (such as the duty to keep and provide accounts) can be owed to a party without that party having an equitable property interest. Moreover, the three aspects of a trust noted above[73] which distinguish the right of a trust beneficiary from a mere personal right (protection in the trustee's insolvency; the possibility of a claim against a third party receiving the trust assets; and the possibility of a claim in relation to new assets acquired using the trust assets) are all present when considering a deceased estate in the process of administration. Given such protection is available to an estate beneficiary, who cannot realistically be seen as an equitable owner of any specific assets, it would be dangerous to assume that the presence of such protection in the case of the trust requires us to regard the trust beneficiary as having such proprietary rights.[74]

12–033 In his analysis in the *Livingston* case, Viscount Radcliffe made a further point which is important when considering trusts more generally. It was argued that, as the personal representatives held the estate assets subject to duties, they could not be the beneficial owners of the property and, as

---

67 See paras 3–149 to 3–152.
68 See para.3–155.
69 [1965] A.C. 694 (PC).
70 See C. Mitchell, "*Commissioner of Stamp Duties (Queensland) v Livingston* (1964): Rights of Estate Beneficiaries and Trust Beneficiaries Compared" in B. Sloan (ed.) *Landmark Cases in Succession Law* (Hart Publishing, 2019), 265, 274.
71 Executors: *Freeman v Fairlie* (1812) 3 Mer. 29 at 43; *Ottley v Gilby* (1845) 8 Beav. 602; *Wroe v Seed* (1863) 4 Giff. 425 at 428–29; *Re Bosworth* (1889) 58 L.J. Ch. 432. Administrators: Administration of Estates Act 1925 s.21.
72 Administration of Estates Act 1925 s.25(b).
73 See para.12–003.
74 See C. Mitchell, "*Commissioner of Stamp Duties (Queensland) v Livingston* (1964): Rights of Estate Beneficiaries and Trust Beneficiaries Compared" in B. Sloan (ed.) *Landmark Cases in Succession Law* (Hart Publishing, 2019).

someone had to have such beneficial ownership, it could be seen as vested in the estate beneficiaries. Viscount Radcliffe rejected this argument as follows:[75]

> Where, it is asked, is the beneficial interest in those assets [i.e. the assets of the deceased husband] during the period of administration? It is not, ex hypothesi, in the executor: where else can it be but in the residuary legatee? This dilemma is founded on a fallacy, for it assumes mistakenly that for all purposes and at every moment of time the law requires the separate existence of two different kinds of estate or interest in property, the legal and the equitable. There is no need to make this assumption. When the whole right of property is in a person, as it is in an executor, there is no need to distinguish between the legal and equitable interest in that property, any more than there is for the property of a full beneficial owner. What matters is that the court will control the executor in the use of his rights over assets that come to him in that capacity; but it will do it by the enforcement of remedies which do not involve the admission or recognition of equitable rights of property in those assets. Equity in fact calls into existence and protects equitable rights and interests in property only where their recognition has been found to be required in order to give effect to its doctrines.

The application of such reasoning to trusts can be seen in, for example, *Westdeutsche Landesbank* **12–034**
Girozentrale v Islington LBC,[76] where the House of Lords rejected the view that a party who simply owns property has both a legal title and a distinct equitable title to that property. In Lord Browne-Wilkinson's words:[77]

> A person solely entitled to the full beneficial ownership of money or property, both at law and in equity, does not enjoy an equitable interest in that property. The legal title carries with it all rights. Unless and until there is a separation of legal and equitable estates, there is no separate equitable title.

It has therefore been accepted in more recent contributions to the debate,[78] and not only by those **12–035**
favouring the obligational view,[79] that the proprietary view, if it is to be justified, cannot be based on the argument that, as T is not permitted to use the property for her own benefit, B *must* have the beneficial interest in the trust property.

C. The Obligational View

i. Setting Out the Obligational View

The obligational view states that, in seeking to understand the nature of the trust, it is necessary to **12–036**
focus on the particular nature of T's duties to B, rather than on any direct link between B and the trust property. As the following extract demonstrates, the obligational view of the trust has a distinguished pedigree. This is worth noting as, whilst the proprietary view has been the prevailing one in modern times, Austin Scott, when advocating that view in 1917,[80] was disagreeing with a large number of past commentators.

---

75 [1965] A.C. 694 at 712.
76 [1996] A.C. 669 at 705–706.
77 [1996] A.C. 669 at 705–706.
78 See, e.g. L. Smith, "Unravelling Proprietary Restitution" (2004) 40 Can. Bus. L.J. 317; B. McFarlane & R. Stevens, "The Nature of Equitable Property" (2010) 4 J. Eq. 1.
79 See, e.g. J. Penner, "The (True) Nature of a Beneficiary's Equitable Proprietary Interest under a Trust" (2014) 27 Can. J.L. & Juris 473, 486–489.
80 A.W. Scott, "The Nature of the Rights of the 'Cestui Que Trust'" (1917) 17 Col. L. Rev. 269.

James Edelman, "Two Fundamental Questions for the Law of Trusts"

(2013) 129 L.Q.R. 66, 72–74

12–037 On one view. . .the interest of the beneficiary under a trust. . .is an interest or encumbrance upon the rights held by the trustee. Although this approach to the interest of a beneficiary may be inconsistent with modern nomenclature which equates common law and equity by common labels of "ownership" or "property right", it is a distinction with a distinguished lineage. Five examples can be given spanning two centuries.

12–038 First, in 1791, in Sanders' classic essay, which became *Sanders on Uses and Trusts*,[81] he explained that at common law the beneficiary under a trust had "neither *jus in re* nor *jus in rem*. The *jus in re* meant an estate, the *jus in rem* a demand."[82] Sanders then proceeded to enumerate the differences between the rights of the beneficiary and the rights of the legal owner.[83]

12–039 Secondly, in 1882, the definition of a trust in Dr Whitley Stokes' carefully drafted Indian Trusts Act 1882 s. 3, described the trustee's duties and the beneficiary's interest as "annexed" to the trustee's ownership of the trust property:

> "A 'trust' is an obligation annexed to the ownership of property, and arising out of confidence reposed in and accepted by the owner, or declared and accepted by him, for the benefit of another, or of another and the owner."

12–040 Thirdly, in 1899 the influential article by Walter Hart followed the same approach.[84] In this article, the many and varied definitions of a trust were considered. Hart explained that Sir Arthur Underhill's definition of a trust was "undoubtedly the best definition yet given".[85] That definition was:

> "an equitable obligation, either expressly undertaken or constructively imposed by the Court, whereby the obligor (who is called a trustee) is bound to deal with property over which he has control (which is called the trust property), for the benefit of persons (who are called the beneficiaries or *cestuis que trust*) of whom he may or may not himself be one."

The only doctrinal objection raised by Hart was that the enforceability of trusts only in courts of equity was merely a matter of history.[86] The objection was not entirely accurate. Historically there were instances where common law courts expressly took notice of a trust.[87]

12–041 Fourthly, from 1935, the *United States Restatement of the Law of Trusts § 2*, focussed on the nature of the express trust as concerned with the duties of the trustee in relation to the rights held by the trustee: "subjecting the person by whom the property is held to equitable duties to deal with the property for the benefit of another person."[88]

12–042 Fifthly, in the first edition of the leading Australian text on trusts in 1958,[89] Jacobs focussed upon the trustee's duties in relation to the trust rights he or she holds, describing the trust as existing when the:

> "holder of a legal or equitable interest in certain property is bound by an equitable obligation to hold his interest in that property not for his own exclusive benefit but for the benefit. . .of another person or persons. . .."

---

81 F.W. Sanders, *An Essay on Uses and Trusts*, 2nd edn (1799). The final edition was the 5th by G W Sanders and J Warner in 1844.

82 Sanders, *An Essay on the Nature and Laws of Uses and Trusts* (1791), p.107.

83 Sanders, *An Essay on the Nature and Laws of Uses and Trusts* (1791), pp.108–111.

84 W. Hart, "What is a Trust?" (1899) 15 L.Q.R. 294.

85 W. Hart, "What is a Trust?" (1899) 15 L.Q.R. 294 at 298.

86 W. Hart, "What is a Trust?" (1899) 15 L.Q.R. 294 at 298.

87 *Winch v Keeley* (1787) 1 Term Rep 619, 623; *Jonathan Scott v Robert Surman Salem Oewn* (1742) Willes 400, 402; *Boddington v Castelli* (1853) 1 El & Bl 879; discussion in *Duckworth v Water Corporation* [2012] WASC 30 at [66]–[70].

88 *American Law Institute, Restatement of the Law of Trusts* (1935). The reporter was Austin Scott. The definition was reproduced in the Second Restatement in 1957, and the Third Restatement in 2003, although "equitable duties" is replaced by "duties".

89 K. Jacobs, *The Law of Trusts in New South Wales* (1958) p. 7.

However, years later, as a Justice of the High Court of Australia, Jacobs J. saw "no difficulty" in describing a trust as involving a beneficiary as "the beneficial owner of the estate of which the vendor is the legal owner".[90]

Each of these definitions focussed attention on the beneficiary's power or right as one which relates to the rights of the trustee or, conversely, the particular liability or obligation of the trustee in relation to the trust rights which are held. Perhaps the best, and clearest, description of this conception of the trust which emphasises that the beneficiary's rights or powers are not directly in relation to the trust assets was given by F W Maitland, in his lectures at Cambridge, first published in 1910:[91] **12–043**

> "Equity did not say that the cestui que trust was the owner of the land, it said that the trustee was the owner of the land, but added that he was bound to hold the land for the benefit of the cestui que trust. There was no conflict here. Had there been a conflict here the. . .Judicature Act. . .would have abolished the whole law of trusts. Common law says that A is the owner, equity says that B is the owner, but equity is to prevail, therefore B is the owner and A has no right or duty of any sort or kind in or about the land. Of course the Judicature Act has not acted in this way; it has left the law of trusts just where it stood, because it found no conflict, no variance even, between the rules of the common law and the rules of equity."

This approach to understanding a beneficiary's interest as requiring as a necessary condition a particular encumbrance upon the rights that the trustee holds, rather than being an interest in the trust assets themselves, has gained significant academic support in recent years.[92] One commentator, Professor McFarlane, has suggested that the rights of the beneficiary should be described as "persistent rights"[93] to differentiate them very clearly from common law property rights and to elucidate that the rights of the beneficiary are not merely personal rights. As McFarlane has explained, the special nature of a beneficiary's rights is that they are not merely personal rights, but nor are they rights to the assets itself. The nature of the beneficiary's powers and rights, he argues, is that they are in relation to the trustee's rights, whatever the trustee's rights might be. This is why the beneficiary's rights under a trust are of the same nature whether the trust asset is a right to an intangible (a debt, shares) or a right to a tangible thing (land, chattels). It is also why, as Hart observed, the best descriptions of a beneficiary's rights have focussed on those rights being "annexed" to the trust property, or upon the nature of the obligation of the trustee to deal with the *trustee's* rights to the trust property.[94] **12–044**

The danger in using the label "proprietary" to describe a beneficiary's rights under a trust may be manifest unless lawyers recognise that the word "property" is like the word "love". It is often used in a number of different senses. It is essential not to forget that when we speak of "proprietary right" or "ownership" in equity we are using those terms in a very different sense from the sense in which they are used at common law. **12–045**

Some of the earlier obligational accounts of the trust seem to have regarded B's rights as essentially only personal rights against T.[95] The difficulty with such views, of course, lies in explaining any of the three key features of B's rights set out above:[96] in particular, the ability of B to make a claim against C, a third party acquiring the trust property in an unauthorised disposition by T. More recent proponents of the obligational view have therefore differentiated the rights of B from simply personal rights by focussing on the requirement that, for a trust to exist, T's duty to B must relate to the trust property: that is, to the specific rights held by T on trust for B. This emphasis has formed the basis of what has **12–046**

---

90 *Chang v Registrar of Titles* (1976) 137 CLR 177, 190.
91 F Maitland, *Equity: also The Forms of Action at Common Law* (1910) pp.12–18.
92 A Burrows, *The Law of Restitution* (3rd edn, 2010); R Chambers, "Constructive Trusts in Canada" (1999) Alberta Law Rev 173; L Smith, "Unravelling Proprietary Restitution" [2004] Canadian Business Law Journal 317; B McFarlane & R Stevens, "The Nature of Equitable Property" (2010) 4 J Eq 1.
93 B McFarlane, *The Structure of Property Law* (2008) at p. 364.
94 W Hart, "What is a Trust?" (1899) 15 LQR 294 at 302.
95 See, e.g. F.W. Maitland, *Lectures on Equity* (1929), Chs 9–11; H. Stone, "The Nature of the Rights of the 'Cestui Que Trust'" (1917) 17 Col. L. Rev. 467, esp. 477–480.
96 See para.12–003.

been called the "new obligational" view,[97] according to which the rights of B are best seen *neither* as proprietary rights in the trust property nor as personal rights against T.

Ben McFarlane & Robert Stevens, "The Nature of Equitable Property"

(2010) 4 J. Eq. 1, 3–6

THE NEW ANALYSIS

A. Equitable property rights and rights against a thing

12–047 The chief characteristic of a property right in relation to a thing is that it allows B to exclude others from making use of that thing. It has been argued that equitable property rights possess this characteristic.[98] The most obvious problem with that argument is that B may have an equitable property right in relation to an intangible asset. For example, A can hold a personal right against Z, such as a bank account, on trust for B. In such a case, there is no independent physical thing against which B has a right. After all, there is no thing against which A has a right: A merely has a right to receive payment from Z. If I have title to land or a car I can exclude others from making use of it, it is not meaningful to speak of excluding another from making use of a debt owed to me.

12–048 One possible reason for the view that an equitable property involves the creation of a right to a thing is that the common law permits several people to hold rights in relation to a single thing at the same time. In relation to land, for example, a lessee, his landlord, and a neighbour with an easement over the property all have rights in relation to the land that are *prima facie* exigible against all others. In relation to goods, relativity of title means that many persons may have a right in relation to the thing exigible against all others save such person or persons with a better title to the thing. However, the right to an intangible asset, such as a bank account, is incapable of division in this way. The one and only right is the contractual right against the bank, and this is vested in the person who has contracted with the bank by opening the account. The possibility of an equitable property right in relation to a bank account therefore demonstrates that equitable property rights cannot be understood as depending on the divisibility of an initial common law property right.

12–049 Indeed, even where an equitable property right relates to a physical thing, it does not give its holder a right to that thing. For example, let us say A has title to a car and declares that he holds his right to the car on trust for B. If X then steals that car, or carelessly damages it, B has no direct claim against X. X is not liable to B for conversion[99] or for negligently causing damage.[100] This is not simply a matter of B's equitable right being invisible to the common law court: B has no claim, either at law or in equity, against X. B therefore does not have a right against the car: he does not have a right to exclude *all* non-beneficiaries from the enjoyment of the trust assets.[101]

12–050 As A has title to the car, X's interference with that thing means that A can bring a claim against X. As A holds his title on trust for B, A is under a duty to use that right, and its products, for B's benefit. So, if A refuses to bring a claim against X, B can apply to court to force A to do so. B can use an expedited procedure to combine such an application with A's claim against X.[102] However, that procedural concession

---

97 The term used (in an article rejecting that view) by J. Penner, "The (True) Nature of a Beneficiary's Equitable Proprietary Interest under a Trust" (2014) 27 Can. J.L. & Juris 473.

98 See for example R Nolan, 'Equitable Property' (2006) 122 LQR 232 at 233.

99 See, e.g. *MCC Proceeds v Shearson Lehmann* [1998] 4 All ER 675; A Tettenborn, 'Trust Property and Conversion: An Equitable Confusion' [1996] CLJ 36. If B happens to have possession of the car at the time of X's intervention, he will be able to bring a claim in conversion against X: see *Healey v Healey* [1915] 1 KB 938. That claim, however, is based on the property right B acquires as a result of his possession (see, e.g. *Armory v Delamirie* (1722) 5 Strar 505), not on his position as beneficiary.

100 See, e.g. *Leigh and Sillivan Ltd v Aliakmon Shipping Co Ltd (The Aliakmon)* [1986] AC 785 at 812 *per* Lord Brandon.

101 See too *The Lord Compton's Case* (1587) 3 Leo 197: where feoffees to uses are disseised, and then release to the disseisor, the cestui que use has no claim against the disseisor, even if the disseissor has notice of the use.

102 That expedited procedure is commonly referred to as the *Vandepitte* procedure (see e.g. *Barbados Trust Company Ltd v Bank of Zambia* [2007] EWCA Civ 148 at [30] and [35] *per* Waller LJ) and is named for the case: *Vandepitte v Preferred Accident Insurance Corporation of New York* [1933] AC 70.

does not hide the key fact that two separate claims must be made: B has no direct claim against X as X has infringed no right of B.[103] It has been suggested that B can be seen as having an "indirect" right *in rem*:[104] that is, B has a right prima facie binding on anyone interfering with the car, but that right is indirect as it must be asserted through A. That suggestion must be rejected, as any "indirect" claim depends not on X's interference with the car itself, but rather on X's interference with A's right. For example, if A consents to X's interference with the car then X's interference, by itself, gives B no direct or indirect claim against X.[105]

B. Equitable property rights and rights against a person

Attempts have been made to argue that an equitable property right, such as a right under a trust, is no more than a personal right.[106] These attempts generally start from the insight that an equitable property right cannot plausibly be seen as a right against a thing.[107] The acceptance of the traditional, exhaustive dichotomy between rights against a thing and rights against a person then leads to the conclusion that an equitable property right must be in the latter category. However, such attempts fail to account for the key conceptual and practical difference between an equitable property right and a personal right. **12–051**

This difference can be seen by returning to the position where A has title to a car and declares that he holds his right to the car on trust for B. If A then makes a gift of the car to C, B will be able to bring a claim directly against C. Attempts have been made to argue that this is consistent with B's right under the trust being no more than a personal right against A. These attempts depend on showing that B's claim against C is based on a *new* direct right that B acquires against C because of C's unconscientious conduct in accepting the gift from A.[108] **12–052**

However, B can bring a claim directly against C even if C, when acquiring his right from A, had no actual knowledge or constructive notice of the trust. It therefore seems very difficult to argue that B's ability to bring a direct claim against C rests on B's having acquired a new right against C. Rather, it is B's *pre-existing* right under the trust that binds C. The ability of an equitable property right to bind a third party such as C also explains a key feature of such rights: their protection if A becomes bankrupt. On that event, A's rights pass to his trustee in bankruptcy. Like C in our example, that trustee in bankruptcy will be bound by any pre-existing equitable property right of B. **12–053**

C. Equitable property rights and rights against a right

The key to understanding equitable property rights lies in explaining why such a right is capable of binding a third party, such as C in the example above, who acquires a right from A; yet is not capable of binding a third party, such as X in the prior example, who steals or carelessly damages a thing to which B's right relates. The crucial difference between the position of C and of X is that the former, unlike the latter, has acquired a right that *derives from the right which A holds on trust for B*. If A gives his car to C, or C acquires the car in his capacity as A's trustee in bankruptcy, C acquires A's right to the car. As that right was held by A on trust for B, B's right is prima facie binding on C. It is only prima facie binding, as C may have a defence to B's right: for example, C may be able to show that he is a bona fide purchaser i.e. that he acquired A's right for value and had no actual knowledge or constructive notice of B's right. However, in our example, C cannot rely on that defence as he has not acquired A's right for value. In contrast, where X steals or carelessly damages A's car, X does not acquire a right that depends on A's ownership of the car. If X takes possession of the car he will acquire a right against the car, but that right does not derive from A: it is **12–054**

103 See *Barbados Trust Company Ltd v Bank of Zambia* [2007] EWCA Civ 148 *per* Waller LJ.
104 See J Penner, '*The Structure of Property Law (Book Review)*' [2009] RLR 250 at 254.
105 It will be possible for B to assert a right directly against X if it can be shown that X has dishonestly assisted in a breach of trust by A. The right that B has that others do not dishonestly assist A's breach of trust is, observably, not the same right that B has against A and is analogous to the right that a promisee has against third parties to a contract, see further B McFarlane, 'Equity, Obligations and Third Parties' [2008] Sing J LS 308.
106 See, e.g. F Maitland *Lectures on Equity* (1929) chs. 9–11; H Stone, 'The Nature of the Rights of the Cestui Que Trust' (1917) 17 Col L Rev 467.
107 For example Stone, *ibid* at 470; L Smith, 'Unravelling Proprietary Restitution' [2004] Canadian Business Law Journal 317.
108 See e.g. F Maitland, *Lectures on Equity* (1929), ch.9 at pp.112–121; Stone, *ibid* at 474ff. Smith, *ibid* suggests that, originally at least, B's new right against C was based on C's unjust enrichment at B's expense.

original, coming from X's own conduct in taking possession. As a result, B cannot assert his right under the trust against X.[109]

12-055 This analysis explains why it is vital to talk of A holding a *right* on trust for B (eg A's ownership of a car) rather than of A holding a *thing* on trust for B (eg the car itself).[110] It also explains why an equitable property right can exist in relation to a personal right.[111] If A has a personal right against Z, such as a bank account, B can have a right against A's right against Z. So, if C acquires A's personal right, for example because A makes a statutory assignment of the right to C, or because C is A's trustee in bankruptcy, B's right against A's right will be prima facie binding on C.

12-056 The analysis in the extract above can be related to the meaning of "property" adopted in this chapter, which follows that adopted by Richard Nolan for the purpose of his analysis in the extract set out above.[112] On that definition, the proprietary view regards B as having a right to exclude others from the trust assets; if B has no such general right of exclusion, B's right cannot be regarded as truly proprietary. This explains why McFarlane and Stevens consider the case where the trust property consists of a physical thing and a stranger, X, then interferes with that thing: if B has a right to exclude others, it might be expected that, in such a case, it would be possible for B to bring a claim directly against X. As noted by McFarlane and Stevens, the orthodox position in such a case, however, is that B has no such direct claim,[113] but must rather rely on, or compel, T to sue X, with any damages acquired by T then being held on trust for B.

12-057 The indirectness of B's protection against X is particularly important if T permits X to interfere physically with the trust property: in such a case, it seems that B's only claim is a personal claim against T. Yet one would think that if B's right were truly proprietary, B would necessarily have a claim against a party who has physically interfered, without B's authority, in the trust property. This question is not of purely academic interest: indeed, it was central to a Court of Appeal decision, *Shell UK Ltd v Total UK Ltd*,[114] made after the publication of McFarlane and Stevens' article. As we will see later in this chapter,[115] however, that decision does not provide any decisive support either for or against the new obligational view of the trust; indeed, its reasoning has been widely criticised, by commentators who adopt a proprietary view, as well as by those who subscribe to the obligational view.

12-058 The model proposed by McFarlane and Stevens is consistent with the differences which have been explained already,[116] between the rights of B under a trust and the rights of O, an outright owner of property. In particular, it explains why it is possible for B to have an "equitable property right" in relation to a purely personal right of T, such as a bank account. It is, therefore, consistent with the fact that a very broad range of rights (including even a non-assignable right held by T against X) are capable of forming the subject-matter of a trust.[117] It also explains why B has no claim against C where C acquired trust property in an unauthorised disposition from T as an innocent donee and later

---

[109] The distinction between the positions of C, a party acquiring a right that depends on A's right, and of X, a party who does not, also explains the effect on B of a forfeiture or escheat of an estate held by A on trust for B. Where A's estate is forfeited, A's right is acquired by the superior landlord who is *prima facie* bound by B's right against A's estate: see Stone 'The Nature of the Rights of the Cestui Que Trust' (1917) 17 Col L Rev 467 at 481. When A's estate is subject to an escheat, A's right is instead lost and B cannot assert his right against the superior lord, who can prevent B from enjoying the land without relying on any right acquired from A: see Maitland, *Lectures on Equity* (1929), lecture 9 at p.120.

[110] See W Swadling in A Burrows (ed), *English Private Law* (2nd edn, 2007) at 4.140–4.153.

[111] See, e.g. R Chambers, *An Introduction to Property Law in Australia* (2nd edn, 2008) at [13–90].

[112] See paras 12–011 to 12–013.

[113] In addition to the cases cited in the extract above (see fn.99–101), see, e.g. Restatement (Third) of Trusts §§ 107–108 (2003) (for the position in the US).

[114] [2011] Q.B. 186.

[115] See paras 12–092 to 12–110.

[116] See para.12–006.

[117] See paras 4–029 to 4–033.

disposed of the trust property herself, so that she no longer has either that property or its traceable proceeds.[118] Again, in such a case, C can be seen to have interfered with the trust property, and has perhaps been enriched as a result, yet B has no claim. On the obligational view of the trust, this can be explained: first, any enrichment of C as a result of acquiring the trust property was at the expense of T, who had ownership of that property, not of B, who had no true proprietary right in that property; second, there was no point in time when C can be said to have been under a duty to B in relation to the trust property, as no such duty can be imposed on C when C is unaware of the initial trust in B's favour and thus innocent.

The "right against a right" model is also consistent with a particular feature of equity that we encountered in Chapters 2 and 3. Rules and principles relating to trusts can be seen as depending on equity's role as a supplemental to the common law. Whilst the common law may establish the allocation of property rights or personal rights by, for example, deciding if T is an owner of a car, or if T has a contractual right against X, equity can then come in and impose a duty on T in relation to such rights, such as a duty to use that right for the benefit of B. **12-059**

As argued by McFarlane and Stevens later in their article,[119] the obligational model provides a relatively simple means of explaining the incidence of constructive and resulting trusts. On the proprietary view, such trusts may be somewhat difficult to explain:[120] as no-one has exercised a power to give B a proprietary right, why should the courts intervene to recognise a right that will interfere with the defendant's ownership of the property? On the obligational view, however, the key feature of the trust is that T holds a right subject to a duty to B to use that right for the benefit of B, and not to use it for T's own benefit (unless and to the extent that T is also a beneficiary of the trust). This means that, if the *content* of T's duty matches that description, a trust exists, irrespective of the grounds on which that duty arose.[121] So in a case such as *Attorney General for Hong Kong v Reid*,[122] for example, the crucial question is simply as to whether the agent who receives a bribe is under an immediate duty to the principal to give the bribe *itself* to the principal, or is instead under a duty to pay the *value* of the bribe to the principal. In the former case, on the obligational view, a trust necessarily arises: there is then no further question of policy as to whether the principal's right should count as proprietary. **12-060**

The challenge for any obligational view of the trust, of course, is to explain the three key features of the trust identified at the start of this chapter,[123] as it is those features which most commonly lead judges and commentators to describe B's rights as proprietary. The model proposed by McFarlane and Stevens builds on an insight of Robert Chambers:[124] the subject matter of a trust, strictly speaking, is always a right or rights held by T.[125] So, even though we would naturally speak of a trust of land, for example, in such a case it is in fact a specific estate in land (e.g. a legal freehold) that is held by T on trust for B. On the obligational model of the trust, it is the nature of T's duty to B, as a duty relating **12-061**

---

118 If C had acquired such knowledge, a claim in knowing receipt could be made against her: see paras 14–017ff.

119 B. McFarlane & R. Stevens, "The Nature of Equitable Property" (2010) 4 J. Eq. 1, 15–22.

120 As noted at para.4–019.

121 See too B. McFarlane, "The Centrality of Constructive and Resulting Trusts" in C. Mitchell (ed.), *Constructive and Resulting Trusts* (Hart Publishing, 2010). For a different view, see W Swadling, "Unjust Enrichment: Value, Rights, and Trusts" (2021) 137 L.Q.R. 56.

122 [1994] 1 A.C. 324; approved in *FHR European Ventures LLP v Cedar Capital Partners LLC* [2014] UKSC 45; [2015] A.C. 250.

123 See para.12–003.

124 First apparent in R. Chambers, *An Introduction to Property Law in Australia* (Law Book Co, 2001), p.115; see now R. Chambers, *An Introduction to Property Law in Australia*, 4th edn (Thomson Reuters, 2018) 13.90.

125 It is notable that in *Carter Holt Harvey Woodproducts v Commonwealth of Australia* [2019] HCA 20; (2019) 368 A.L.R. 390, Kiefel CJ and Edelman and Nettle JJ are careful in their joint judgment to refer to the *rights* held on trust and note at [24] that the expression "trust assets" is "simply shorthand for . . . the rights held on trust by the trustee".

to a specific right or rights of T, that justifies B's protection in insolvency; it also justifies B's ability to make a claim against C where T makes an unauthorised disposition of trust property to C.

12-062 Of course, if one's definition of property is such that *any* right protected in insolvency or capable of binding certain third parties counts as proprietary, then B's right under a trust is necessarily a property right.[126] Yet such a right nonetheless varies in significant ways from the right of O, an absolute owner of physical property, and the new obligational view of the trust attempts to explain those differences.

D. Possible Objections to The Obligational View

12-063 There has of course been criticism of both the general obligational view of the trust and of the new obligational view. It is impossible to cover all the points made in this debate,[127] but we will focus here on some of the most prominent.

i. The *Saunders v Vautier* Power

12-064 The *Saunders v Vautier* principle[128] allows all of the beneficiaries of a trust, if they have full capacity and act together, to call for the trust property to be transferred to them by the trustees: if that power is exercised by the beneficiaries, they then have the trust property itself, and the trust comes to an end.[129] As in *Saunders v Vautier* itself, the exercise of this power can trump an outstanding duty of T, such as a duty not to pay out capital to a beneficiary with a current entitlement.

Saunders v Vautier

Master of the Rolls (1841) 4 Beav. 115

12-065 A testator bequeathed his stock on trust to accumulate the dividends until V should attain the age of twenty-five, and then to transfer the principal, together with the accumulated dividends, to V. V, having attained twenty-one, claimed to have the fund transferred to him. It was contended for him that he had "a vested interest, and that as the accumulation and postponement of payment was for his benefit alone, he might waive it and call for an immediate transfer of the fund."

12-066 LORD LANGDALE M.R.: I think that principle has been repeatedly acted upon; and where a legacy is directed to accumulate for a certain period, or where the payment is postponed the legatee, if he has an absolute indefeasible interest in the legacy, is not bound to wait until the expiration of that period, but may require payment the moment he is competent to give a valid discharge.

12-067 On a question raised, with reference to a previous order for maintenance, as to whether there was a vested interest in V before he attained twenty-five, the petition stood over, with liberty to apply to the Lord Chancellor. Held, by the Lord Chancellor, the fund was intended wholly for the benefit of V, although the enjoyment of it was postponed: it vested immediately, and he could now claim the transfer.

12-068 This power of the beneficiaries cannot be denied by the settlor, even if an express declaration is made when setting up the trust.[130] Moreover, if all the beneficiaries of a discretionary trust are of full capacity

---

126 See para.12-016.

127 For further grounds of disagreement with the obligational view, see, e.g. S. Gardner, "'Persistent Rights' Appraised" in N. Hopkins (ed.) *Modern Studies in Property Law: Vol.7* (Hart Publishing, 2013); P. Jaffey, "Explaining the Trust" (2015) 131 L.Q.R. 377; E. Zaccaria, "The Nature of the Beneficiary's Right Under a Trust" (2019) 133 L.Q.R. 460.

128 (1841) 4 Beav. 115.

129 As noted at para.12-069, the *Saunders v Vautier* power is not recognised in all legal systems that have a concept of a trust, and so the argument based on that power, whilst applicable to the analysis of the trust in English law, would not be determinative of the nature of the trust in, for example, jurisdictions of the US. See further P. Matthews, "The Comparative Importance of the Rule in *Saunders v Vautier*" (2006) 122 L.Q.R. 266.

130 *Stokes v Cheek* (1860) 28 Beav. 620.

and are entitled absolutely to the property between them, then they too may call for a transfer, provided that they act together.[131] Indeed, the rule in *Saunders v Vautier* applies even where there are nothing more than powers of appointment with a gift over in default of appointment.[132] In practice, however, it is relatively easily for a well-advised settlor to avoid the operation of the principle, as it does not apply where a beneficiary has only a contingent interest: i.e. where his entitlement under the trust does not arise until the happening of a specified event, such as the beneficiary attaining 25 years of age.[133] Nor does it apply where there is a fluctuating body of beneficiaries from time to time within a class,[134] even where the likelihood of another beneficiary being born before the fund is exhausted is remote.[135] Nor does it apply where other persons have an interest in the accumulations of income which the beneficiaries would like to stop.[136] Where trusts arise out of contractual relationships it is possible for the parties who are beneficiaries to contract out of their *Saunders v Vautier* powers. So, for example, unit-holders in a unit trust cannot terminate the trust and claim the trust property while the trust is operating as a going concern and before it is wound up as agreed pursuant to the trust deed.

It would be difficult to argue that the *Saunders v Vautier* power is an inherent part of the very concept of a trust as many other jurisdictions recognise trusts but do not recognise the power;[137] nonetheless it could be seen as an important part of the English law of trusts. Certainly, in English law, it is a right held by the beneficiaries in many, but not all, trusts. As it allows direct access to the trust property itself, it might be thought to be consistent only with a proprietary view of the trust, in the particular sense identified in the following extract. In that article, Paul Matthews draws a link between the power and the further rule of English law that prohibits restraints on the inalienability of trust interests.[138] **12–069**

Paul Matthews, "The Comparative Importance of the Rule in *Saunders v Vautier*"

(2006) 122 L.Q.R. 266, 273–281

. . . Why does this rule matter? First, it illustrates and exemplifies the idea of beneficial (or "equitable") ownership or property. But we must be careful what we mean by this. It is true that the rights of trust beneficiaries are good against many—if not in practice most—third parties. They fail only when the asset concerned[139] reaches the hands of a bona fide purchaser for value without notice. And a property right need not be absolute. Indeed, in most civil law systems, good faith purchase by a third party defeats the **12–070**

---

131 *Re Nelson* [1928] Ch. 920n.; *Re Smith* [1928] Ch. 915; *Sir Moses Montefiore Jewish Home v Howell & Co (No.7) Pty Ltd* [1984] 2 N.S.W.L.R. 406 at 410.

132 *Schmidt v Rosewood Trust* [2003] UKPC 26; [2003] 2 A.C. 709 at [41].

133 *Re Couturier* [1907] 1 Ch. 470 at 473, where Joyce J points out the distinction between giving a person an interest *contingent* on her reaching a specified age, and giving her a *vested* interest and postponing the enjoyment of it to a specified age. See too *Gosling v Gosling* (1859) John 265; *Re Lord Nunburnholme* [1912] 1 Ch. 489; *Thorpe v HMRC* [2010] S.T.C. 964. If a contingent interest is given, but the specified event does not occur, then either the trust deed will specify that someone else then becomes entitled to the trust property, as in, e.g. *Re Bellville's ST* [1964] Ch. 163, or it will go to the settlor or her estate on a resulting trust.

134 *Re Levy* [1960] Ch. 346 at 363; *Re Westphal* [1972] N.Z.L.R. 792 at 794–795.

135 *Thorpe v HMRC* [2009] S.T.C. 2107 at [14]–[15].

136 *Berry v Geen* [1938] A.C. 575.

137 For example, many American jurisdictions follow *Claflin v Claflin* 149 Mass. 19; 20 N.E. 454 (1889) in holding that, if a material purpose of the settlor remains to be carried out, the beneficiaries cannot call for a transfer of the trust property. For discussion see e.g. J. Langbein, "Why the Rule in *Saunders v Vautier* is Wrong" and P. Matthews, "Why the Rule in *Saunders v Vautier* is Wrong: A Commentary" in P Turner (ed) *Equity and Administration* (Cambridge University Press, 2016), 189 and 203.

138 For which see *Brandon v Robinson* (1811) 18 Ves. 429; *Green v Spicer* (1830) Russ. & My. 395; *Re Dugdale* (1888) 38 Ch.D. 176 at 182.

139 We are not here concerned with the debate over how the position changes when the asset is itself a personal right, e.g. an institutional or governmental bond.

original owner's proprietary claim to a stolen asset,[140] although in some cases it may give rise to an option for the original owner to repurchase it from the third party.[141] At all events, persistence of rights in a thing against third parties is the hallmark of the property idea,[142] and equity lawyers have therefore found it convenient to borrow from the common law the language and vocabulary of ownership.[143]

12-071 However, it is not this aspect of "property" that the rule in *Saunders v Vautier* illustrates.[144] Instead, it is the idea of exclusive decision-making. If I give something to you, then the "property" idea should mean that it is yours to deal with as you please. "Property" means—indeed, etymologically, has to mean—that you decide. I should not be able, consistently with the idea of property, to make something your "property", and then tell you how to deal with it.[145] So equity used the same idea, and for example, generally forbade the attempt to impose a restraint on the alienation of an equitable interest.[146] *Saunders v Vautier* is in one sense merely an application of the same principle: if there is only one beneficiary of a particular trust, that beneficiary must be entitled to take the property subject to the trust and decide what he wishes to do with it.[147] The same is true if two or more persons are interested, and they are agreed on what should happen.[148] In English law the settlor cannot oust this principle even by express declaration.[149] Related to this is the principle that a settlor or testator cannot create a trust to destroy property, or to waste it, as by blocking up a house for 20 years,[150] or by throwing money into the sea.[151] Whatever the subject-matter of the trust, it no longer belongs to the settlor or (obviously) the testator, and the decision whether to enjoy it or destroy it is no longer one for him. Instead it is ultimately a decision for those who benefit from the trust.[152]

12-072 It is, however, possible to recognise a collective power in all the beneficiaries of a trust to acquire the trust property in the future without admitting that each specific beneficiary has a current, individual, proprietary right. Certainly, if we are regarding the right to exclude others as the key indicator of a property right, the potential to acquire the trust property in the future, after a transfer by T, does not by itself make B's right proprietary. As noted, for example, by the authors of a leading Australian work[153] "a power to become the owner of trust assets in the future is different from being the owner, legal or equitable, of the trust assets at present." This can be seen, for example, in *re Brockbank*,[154] where

[140] *Code Civil*, art.2279; *Codice Civile*, art.1153.

[141] *Code Civil*, art.2280; *Código Civil*, art.464.

[142] See, e.g. Birks, in Bright and Dewar (eds), *Land Law: Themes and Perspectives* (1998), p.473; Smith in Birks and Pretto (eds), *Breach of Trust* (2002), pp.112–114.

[143] See generally Matthews, "From Obligation to Property and Back Again? The Future of Non Charitable Purpose Trusts" in Hayton (ed.), *Extending the Boundaries of Trusts and Other Ring-Fenced Funds* (2002). Whether there is a numerus clausus principle at work here is another matter, and beyond the scope of this paper. But see, e.g. Merrill and Smith (2000) 110 Yale L.J. 1; Hansmann and Kraakman (2002) 31 J. Leg. Stud. 383.

[144] Cf. Underhill and Hayton, *Trusts and Trustees*, 16th edn (2003), p.52. The rights of trust beneficiaries only became exigible against third parties later on in the development of the trust idea, but there is no a priori reason why imposing obligations on third parties should have altered the nature of the beneficiaries' relationship with the trustee. More likely, the right of the beneficiaries to collapse the trust was developed independently of the third- party idea, and may even have been present from the beginning.

[145] See, e.g. *Ware v Cann* (1830) 10 B. & C. 433; *Hood v Oglander* (1865) 34 Beav. 513; *Re Rosher* (1884) 26 Ch.D. 801; *Corbett v Corbett* (1889) 14 P.D. 7; *Harbin v Masterman* [1894] 2 Ch. 184, affd [1895] A.C. 186; *Re Nelson* [1928] Ch. 920n; *Re Brown* [1954] Ch. 39. Cf. the similar idea in civil law systems: e.g. the French *Code Civil*, art.544.

[146] *Brandon v Robinson* (1811) 18 Ves. 429; *Re Dugdale* (1888) 38 Ch.D 176 at p.182.

[147] See, e.g. *Younghusband v Gisborne* (1844) 1 Coll. 400; *Stokes v Cheek* (1860) 28 Beav. 620; *Weatherall v Thornburgh* (1878) 8 Ch.D 261 at 270; *Re Johnston* [1894] 3 Ch. 204; *Re Robbins* [1907] 2 Ch. 8, CA; *Re Brunning* [1909] 1 Ch. 276; *Re Lipinski's WT* [1976] Ch. 235.

[148] *Barton v Briscoe* (1822) Jac. 603; *Re Bowes* [1896] 1 Ch. 507.

[149] *Stokes v Cheek* (1860) 28 Beav. 620.

[150] *Brown v Burdett* (1882) 21 Ch.D. 667.

[151] *McCaig v University of Glasgow* 1907 S.C. 231.

[152] The civilian idea of property includes the power to destroy it (abuses): see, e.g. Mazeaud and Mazeaud, *Leçons de Droit Civil, Biens* (5th edn, 1994), Vol.II, paras 1332–1333; cf. Mattei, *La Proprietà* (2001), pp.259–262.

[153] *Meagher, Gummow and Lehane's Equity: Doctrines and Remedies*, edited by J.D. Heydon et al, 5th edn (LexisNexis, 2015), 4.105.

[154] [1948] Ch. 206.

the beneficiaries of a trust, acting together, attempted to compel the trustees to appoint their own nominee as a new trustee of that trust. It was acknowledged that the beneficiaries could exercise the *Saunders v Vautier* power, receive the trust property themselves and thus terminate the trust, but that did not mean that they had a power, not given to them under the terms of the trust, to keep the trust on foot and compel the trustees to act in a particular way.[155] Further, the *Saunders v Vautier* power is subject, like other rights of B, to the trustees' powers of indemnity, so that the trustees can first use the trust assets to meet any outstanding authorised expenses before needing to make any requested transfer of the trust assets to B.[156]

It is also possible to make sense of the *Saunders v Vautier* power even if adopting an obligational view of the trust.[157] This can be seen by considering the argument successfully made in *Saunders* itself—the terms of the trust required the trustee to accumulate the dividends and preserve the principal until V should reach the age of 25, but as V was the sole beneficiary, that duty was owed to V alone and, as V was an adult and had capacity, V could waive that duty. We are then in effect left with a bare trust, and in such a case, where the trustees have a duty to use the trust assets for the benefit of V, and V is an adult and has the capacity to judge what is to V's own benefit, the fulfilment of that duty requires the trustees to comply with an instruction of V to terminate the trust by means of a transfer of the trust property to V. Indeed, in such a bare trust, even if the beneficiary does not wish to receive the trust property, it is equally open to the trustees to end their role as trustees by paying the trust funds into court.[158] **12–073**

ii. A Trust Shall Not Fail for Want of a Trustee

As discussed in Chapter 4,[159] trusteeship can be regarded as an office, and the position of T is thus different from that of a contracting party such as, for example a debtor who simply owes a creditor £100. For example, if T is not properly performing her duties as trustee, a court can remove and replace her; a court cannot do the same to the debtor. The notion of an office can also be seen to lie behind the maxim, discussed in Chapter 4,[160] that "a trust shall not fail for want of a trustee". That maxim might suggest that the relationship between T and B, and the obligations imposed on T, are not central to a trust; rather, it is the existence of B's proprietary right that motivates the courts' protection of B. **12–074**

The notion of trusteeship as an office is, as identified in Chapter 4, an important part of the operation of a trust. It is not, however, inconsistent with an obligational view of the trust.[161] On that view, the obligation owed by T is a *special* one, which differs in its nature and effects from a purely contractual duty such as a duty to pay a debt: the notion of trusteeship as an office can help to explain more precisely the special nature of T's duty. The key point, made in the following extract, is that the trust involves a form of *depersonalised* duty. **12–075**

---

155 Although note that under the Trusts of Land and Appointment of Trustees Act 1996 ss.19 and 20, it is now possible for beneficiaries of full capacity acting collectively to force trustees to retire in favour of new trustees whom they have nominated.

156 *X v A* [2000] 1 All E.R. 490; *CPT Custodian Property Co v State Trading Commissioner* [2005] HCA 53 at [49]–[51].

157 See too T. Cutts, "The Nature of 'Equitable Property': A Functional Analysis" (2012) 6 J. Eq. 44, 45 using the *Saunders v Vautier* power as the basis of an obligational account of the trust, under which "the settlor confers upon the beneficiary an unconditional power to impose on the trustee a duty to transfer to the former the rights to the trust res."

158 See *IRC v Hamilton-Russell Executors* [1943] 1 All E.R. 474 (CA).

159 See paras 4–054 to 4–060.

160 See para.4–025.

161 The discussion here in some ways demonstrates the point made that no single aspect of a trust's operation is likely to be decisive when assessing the obligational and proprietary views.

Ben McFarlane "The Trust and its Civilian Analogues"

in L. Smith (ed.), *The Worlds of the Trust* (Cambridge University Press, 2013), pp.522–523

12–076 [Some civilian commentators] have objected to the notion that a right can be separated from its holder: on this view, a right against a right cannot be distinguished from a right against a person. The concept of a persistent right, as developed by equity, precisely allows this separation. This can be seen not only in. . .the ability of the beneficiary to assert his right against particular strangers to the initial trust relationship. . .but also in the phenomenon. . .of the trust as office. This latter phenomenon allows, for example, for the replacement of a trustee, and so for a trust to continue despite the death or removal of an initial trustee. This depersonalisation of the trust obligation is permitted by the trust's focus on the duties of a trustee *in his capacity as* holder of a particular right. After all, the defining feature of a trustee is that he both holds a right and has a duty not to use that right for his own benefit. The personality, or creditworthiness, of the trustee is not critical to the performance of that core duty: its negative nature thus permits its extension to strangers to the trust, provided that such a stranger also holds the right initially held on trust, or a product of that right. This may finally account for the fact that the right of a beneficiary occupies an awkward position between property and obligation. The trust requires a relationship between beneficiary and trustee—unlike the ancient use, the trust does not permit a beneficiary to have a direct, unmediated relationship with an asset. Yet the *particular identity* of the trustee is not critical to the relationship, as the relationship is defined by the holding of a right subject to a negative duty. On the view that a beneficiary of a trust has a right against a right (the "persistent rights" theory), the trustee is necessary; but only because the object of a trust must be a right, and all rights must be held by someone.

12–077 The notion of trusteeship as an office may also be apparent in the power of a court to supervise the administration of a trust. The obligational view also gains some support from the approach of the Privy Council in *Schmidt v Rosewood Trust Ltd*,[162] when dealing with requests, made by an object of a power held by trustees, for disclosure by the trustees of information relating to the trust. It was stated that, even in a case where a court orders disclosure of trust documents to a beneficiary of a fixed trust, that decision is based not on recognising any proprietary right of B to such documents, but is rather made as an exercise of the court's general jurisdiction "to supervise (and where appropriate intervene in) the administration of trusts".[163] On this view, at least some of the protection given to B under a trust can be seen as based not on any proprietary entitlement of B, but rather on the particular means of enforcement and protection given to the duty owed by T to B; a duty which, owing to its content, is a special type of duty.

iii. Lord Sumption's Analysis in *Akers v Samba Financial Group*

12–078 *Akers v Samba Financial Group*,[164] concerned the possible application of s.127 of the Insolvency Act 1986 to a case where it was assumed that T had, in breach of trust, transferred shares held on trust for B to C, a third party against whom B would not be able to bring a claim to the shares. We saw above[165] that the Supreme Court's willingness to see B's right as "property" for the purposes of the very broad definition of that term under the Insolvency Act 1986 is not inconsistent with an obligational view of the trust. Nonetheless, the following statement of Lord Sumption, in his analysis of B's rights, is on its face inconsistent with such a view:[166]

---

162 [2003] 2 A.C. 709. See paras 10–063 to 10–078.
163 [2003] 2 A.C. 709 at [66] (extracted at para.10–075).
164 [2017] A.C. 424.
165 See para.12–016.
166 [2017] A.C. 424 at [82].

> As a beneficiary of a trust, [B] had two main legal rights. First, it had a right to have the trust administered according to its terms. This was a personal right against the trustee . . . Secondly, [B] had a true proprietary right. The proprietary character of an equitable interest in property has sometimes been doubted, but in English law (which is in this respect the same as Cayman Islands law), the position must be regarded as settled. An equitable interest possesses the essential hallmark of any right in rem, namely that it is good against third parties into whose hands the property or its traceable proceeds may have come, subject to the rules of equity for the protection of bona fide purchasers for value without notice: see *Westdeutsche Landesbank Girozentrale v Islington London Borough Council*.[167]

Care must however be taken in understanding Lord Sumption's analysis. For example, later in his judgment, he stated that:[168] **12-079**

> . . . equitable interests arise from equity's recognition that in some circumstances the conscience of the holder of the legal interest may be affected. When the asset is transferred to a third party, the question becomes whether the conscience of the transferee is affected. On the facts pleaded in the present case, the equitable interest of [B] was defeated not by the act of the transferor [T] but by absence of anything affecting the conscience of the transferee [C]. The rules of equity which protect transferees acquiring in good faith and without notice are among the most fundamental conditions on which equitable interests can exist without injustice.

It is clear therefore that Lord Sumption is using the term *"in rem"* in a specific, somewhat limited way.[169] He is not suggesting that an equitable interest, like a legal property right, is prima facie binding on *all* third parties. Rather, the focus is on a particular set of third parties—those who acquire the trust property or its traceable proceeds—and in those cases the third party will be bound only if their conscience is affected, presumably by their acquiring knowledge of B's interest and the facts meaning the transfer was unauthorised whilst still holding the trust property or its traceable proceeds. This is consistent with the analysis of Lord Browne-Wilkinson in the *Westdeutsche* case, cited by Lord Sumption: there again, the language of equitable property is used, but emphasis is placed on the need for a party's conscience to be affected before they can be subject to a claim by the beneficiary. **12-080**

McFarlane and Stevens argue that the restriction on the class of third parties identified by Lord Sumption to those who receive the trust property or its traceable proceeds is consistent with their analysis of the beneficiary having a right in relation to the trustee's rights rather than an abstract right to property, and with the broader idea that equity operates in a secondary fashion to control primary rights:[170] **12-081**

> It is certainly the case, for example, that if T holds a right on trust for B, and then transfers that right to C, it may be possible for B to assert a right against C. In that case the relevant 'property' that has 'come into the hands of' C is T's *right*: the right initially held on trust for B. Our point is that such a third party effect can be recognized without allowing B's right to be prima facie binding on *any* third party whose action may affect the trust property.[171] It may be the case that a third party has the potential to come under a duty to B *if* that third party acquires a particular right, as the third party's assertion of that right may then be restrained. As a result, B can be seen as having more than a merely personal right against T. This does not mean,

---

167 [1996] A.C. 669, 705 (Lord Browne-Wilkinson).

168 [2017] A.C. 424 at [89].

169 See further see B. McFarlane, "The Persistence of Equity: Lessons from the Trust" (Inaugural Lecture, Oxford 2022): recording available at: *https://www.youtube.com/watch?v=TNUQ96ik2tQ*.

170 B. McFarlane and R. Stevens, "What's Special About Equity? Rights About Rights" in D. Klimchuk et al (eds) *Philosophical Foundations of the Law of Equity* (Oxford University Press, 2021), 191, 197–198.

171 See J. Penner, "Duty and Liability in Respect of Funds" in J. Lowry and L. Mistelis (eds) *Commercial Law: Perspectives and Practice* (Butterworths 2006) 207–225, distinguishing between successor and trespassory liability.

> however, that all third parties are under a general, prima facie duty to B as soon as the trust is established. Indeed, rather than imposing a primary, general duty of non-interference, an equitable property right may be seen instead as imposing a second-order liability on third parties: one that serves only to regulate the enforcement of a particular *right* by such a third party. The liability of T's successor in title, identified by Lord Sumption, does not show that B's right has the same *in rem* quality as a legal property right: a third party, C, does not owe a primary duty of non-interference to B. Rather, equity again operates in a specific second-order fashion: it regulates C's acquisition and enforcement of a right, by recognizing that C may come under a duty to B in relation to the right acquired from T. The (limited) third party effect of an equitable property right can thus be recognized without undermining the point that it is T, rather than B, who has a primary entitlement to the subject matter of the trust.[172]

12–082 Indeed, as McFarlane and Stevens go on to argue,[173] the actual result in *Akers* demonstrates a crucial difference between the nature of B's rights and the rights of O, a party with unencumbered ownership of property. The Supreme Court found that, whilst B's interest could be regarded as "property", there had been no *disposition* of B's property on the assumed facts, as, when making the transfer of the shares to C, T had simply transferred T's right to the shares.[174] There was then a separate question of whether C was bound by any claim of B. Even if, under the applicable rules, C was able to take the shares free from any claim of B, this did not mean there had been a disposition of B's property, with C acquiring any equitable rights *from* B: rather, C had simply acquired T's right to the shares. That finding was consistent with the earlier analysis of Lloyd LJ in *Independent Trustee Services Ltd v GP Noble Trustees Ltd*:[175]

> a transferee of the legal title to property under a disposition made in breach of trust, or a successor in title to such a person, does not have the beneficial title to the property, which remains held on the original trusts, unless either the transferee, or a successor in title, was a bona fide purchaser for value without notice. The trustee acting in breach of trust can transfer the legal title, but cannot vest the beneficial interest in the property in a bona fide purchaser for value without notice, since he does not own that title and is not acting in a way which enables him, under the trust, to overreach the beneficiaries' equitable interest. Despite that inability, the availability of the bona fide purchaser defence means that a transaction in favour of a bona fide purchaser for value without notice is as effective as it would be if he could vest the beneficial title in the purchaser. Therefore the purchaser can deal with the asset free from any prior claim of the beneficiaries.

iv. The Nature of B's Claims Against a Recipient of Trust Property

12–083 A crucial feature of the rights of B, a beneficiary of a trust, is that there are particular claims, not available to a party with a purely personal right, which B may bring against a third party, C, who receives

---

[172] See eg P Matthews, 'The Compatibility of the Trust with the Civil Law Notion of Property' in L Smith (ed) *The Worlds of the Trust* (CUP 2013) 313–339.

[173] B. McFarlane and R. Stevens, "What's Special About Equity? Rights About Rights" in D. Klimchuk et al (eds) *Philosophical Foundations of the Law of Equity* (Oxford University Press, 2021), 191, 200–201. See too S. Agnew and B. McFarlane, "The Nature of Trusts and the Conflict of Laws" (2021) 137 L.Q.R. 405, who argue, drawing on *Akers* as well as decisions such as *Webb v Webb* [1994] Q.B. 696, that the approach taken to trusts in international cases such as *Akers* depends on the courts seeing B's rights as depending on obligations owed to B by T or by third parties, rather than as standard property rights.

[174] Compare the discussion at 6–083 of the term "disposition of a subsisting beneficial interest" in s.53(1)(c) of the Law of Property Act 1925. Note that in *Akers v Samba*, Lord Neuberger, whilst agreeing with the other judgments, expressed some doubts at [61]–[77] as to how best to interpret "disposition" in the specific context of s.127 of the Insolvency Act 1986. Certainly, as noted by Briggs LJ (as he then was) writing extra-judicially, the interpretation in *Akers* means that the rules applying to a company's legal property rights are quite different to those applying to its equitable interests: M. Briggs, "*Akers v Samba*: Equity's Darling Reigns Supreme", Chancery Bar Association Annual Lecture (2017).

[175] *Independent Trustee Services Ltd v GP Noble Trustees Ltd* [2012] EWCA Civ 195; [2013] Ch. 91 at [106], cited in *Akers* by Lord Mance [2017] UKSC 6; [2017] A.C. 424 at [52]. See too para.10–031A.

the trust property or its traceable proceeds. There is said to be both a personal claim, based on C's knowing receipt of trust property (we will examine this claim in detail in Chapter 14) and a proprietary claim whereby B directly asserts that C is under a duty to B in relation to specific assets now held by C (we will examine this claim in detail in Chapter 15).

The question to consider here is whether the existence of such claims is necessarily inconsistent with an obligational view of the trust. Certainly, the ability to bind third parties is often said to be a distinguishing feature of a property right and we have already seen, for example, that Lord Sumption in *Akers v Samba* regarded B's ability to bring such claims against recipients of trust property as decisive in allowing B to be seen as having a right *in rem*. Nonetheless, the particular operation of these third party claims distinguishes them from legal property rights: first, they are effective not against *all* third parties, but only against recipients of the trust property or its traceable proceeds; second, they depend on the conscience of the third party being affected by knowledge of the initial trust. It has therefore been argued, as in the following extract (where the trustee is referred to as A) that the availability of these claims is consistent with an obligational, or relational, view of the trust. 12-084

Sinéad Agnew and Ben McFarlane, "The Nature of Trusts and the Conflict of Laws"

(2021) 137 L.Q.R. 405, 415–417 [footnotes omitted]

It might be thought that this relational analysis is inconsistent with the protection given to B against third parties, which is of course greater than the protection available where a party holds only a personal right against A. The first key point for present purposes is that Maitland was correct to argue against the (still) commonly held view that B's right under a trust is distinguished from full ownership only by its vulnerability to the defence of bona fide purchaser for value without notice. This can be seen by considering two cases. The first is where A, without authority under the trust, transfers the trust property to C, who provides no value in return. C is unaware of any trust and, before gaining such awareness, C disposes of the property without retaining any traceable proceeds. Here, C is *not* a bona fide purchaser for value without notice; yet it is clear in English law that B has no claim against C. C is free to deal with the asset unless and until C's conscience is affected by sufficient knowledge of B's interest to subject C to a duty towards B. It is only when C has that knowledge that C can reason as to what he or she *ought* to do, i.e. not deal with the asset other than for B's benefit: before then, there is no basis for equity to treat C as owing such a duty to B. Ultimately, therefore, B will recover from C only such assets as remain in C's hands when that duty arises (which may be as late as the date on which B notifies C of B's intention to bring proceedings). B's claim thus depends on showing that C's conscience was affected, through knowledge of B's position, at a point when C still held the trust property or its traceable proceeds. The second case is where X, a stranger, carelessly destroys or damages the trust property. The orthodox position is that B has no claim against X; but instead can, if necessary, compel A to enforce for B's benefit, any claim A has against X. 12-085

Taken together, these two cases help to explain the prominence of conscience when considering B's protection against third parties. B must provide a reason, grounded in moral standards and related to C's own position, why equity should recognise that C now has a duty to B. In some cases, that reason may be unconnected to C's acquisition of a particular asset: this is the case, for example, where B's claim is based on C's dishonest assistance in A's breach of fiduciary duty to B. The significance of B's initially having an equitable interest in a particular asset, rather than a merely personal right against A, is that it provides a different reason for why C's conscience can be affected. That reason depends on both C's acquisition of an asset, and C's conscience being affected by knowledge of A's pre-existing duty to B in respect of that asset. 12-086

On this obligational analysis, B's pre-existing equitable interest is crucial in allowing B to make a claim against C; but that interest, coupled with C's dealing with the trust property does not, *in itself*, lead to a claim against C. Rather, just as B's initial interest depends on T's being under a particular type of duty to B, so does B's claim against C, whether made in knowing receipt or by means of an 12-087 "equitable proprietary claim". Where O has a legal property right, in contrast, the rest of the world immediately owes a prima facie duty of non-interference to O, and it is such a duty which is breached when a third party deals with the property without O's consent or other lawful authority.

12–088 In *Byers v Saudi National Bank*,[176] the next stage of the dispute also litigated in *Akers v Samba Financial Group*, the Court of Appeal considered whether B could bring a knowing receipt claim against C, if it was the case that, under Saudi Arabian law, C would be regarded as having acquired the shares from T free of any claim of B. As confirmed by the Supreme Court in *Akers v Samba*, Saudi Arabian law did not govern the question of whether B could establish an initial trust of the shares when held by T. However, once a transfer of the shares to C took place, there are strong reasons for allowing Saudi Arabian law to govern the effects of that transfer. The Court of Appeal upheld the finding of Fancourt J at first instance that, as Saudi Arabian law did govern the effect of the transfer of the shares and would regard C as acquiring the shares free from any interest of B, it was not possible for B to make a knowing receipt claim against C. This analysis is consistent with the broader point (also relevant in the context of land registration rules) that no knowing receipt claim can be made where the rules governing the transfer to C provide that C will be protected from any pre-existing equitable interest of B.[177]

12–089 In supporting this conclusion, much of the analysis both at first instance and by the Court of Appeal makes reference to the "proprietary" nature of a knowing receipt claim. For example, Fancourt J, adopting the language used by Millett J in *Macmillan Inc v Bishopsgate Investment Trust Plc (No.3)*,[178] held that a knowing receipt claim depends on B's showing a "continuing proprietary base" and this was impossible if, under the law governing the transfer of the shares to C, C acquired those shares free from any pre-existing interest of B. Similarly, the Court of Appeal, regarding a knowing receipt claim as giving effect to a "custodial duty" of B, emphasised that C could not be under such a duty if C had acquired "full and unencumbered title" to the shares and further cited with approval a statement of Nugee J in *Courtwood Holdings SA v Woodley Properties Ltd* that:[179]

> the foundation of the claim in knowing receipt . . . is that a person has got their hands on property which belongs to someone else . . . what gives the equity to the claimants is . . . the fact that the transaction which is impugned is not one which transfers a good title to the recipient.

12–090 Such an analysis is, on its face, consistent only with a proprietary view of B's rights under a trust. Nonetheless, in *Byers v Saudi National Bank*, the Court of Appeal did also emphasize the importance of C's knowledge, so C's acquisition of the trust property or its traceable proceeds is clearly not *sufficient* for a knowing receipt claim. Indeed, where C is liable in knowing receipt, the judgment draws a link between the position of T and of C, approving the statement of Lord Sumption and Lord Briggs, with whom Lord Carnwath agreed, in *DD Growth Premium 2X Fund v RMF Market Neutral Strategies (Master) Ltd* that:[180]

> The liability of a constructive trustee [in knowing receipt] is essentially a custodial liability comparable to that of an express trustee, which is imposed on him because he has sufficient knowledge to affect his conscience.

---

176 [2022] EWCA Civ 43.
177 See paras 14–024 to 14–027.
178 [1995] 1 W.L.R. 978.
179 [2018] EWHC 2163 (Ch) at [201] quoting [59] of his own preliminary judgment in the case.
180 [2017] UKPC 36 at [58].

It seems then that, notwithstanding the proprietary language employed in cases such as *Byers v Saudi National Bank*, it is possible to regard B's claims against third party recipients of trust property or its traceable proceeds as depending, like B's claims against the initial trustee, on the existence of a particular duty owed by the third party to B, which relates to specific assets either held or formerly held by C, and which depends for its existence on C's conscience having been affected. Given, however, that such claims (in contrast, for example, to a dishonest assistance claim[181]) depend on C's acquisition of particular rights, there may be good reasons for the courts to find that if rules governing C's acquisition of the rights aim to protect C from a pre-existing right of B, then C should also be protected from a knowing receipt, or equitable proprietary claim, by B.[182] **12–091**

v. The Court of Appeal's Analysis in *Shell (UK) Ltd v Total (UK) Ltd*

As evidenced by the statement of Lord Sumption set out above,[183] it is generally accepted (both by proponents of proprietary views and supporters of obligational views) that the third party effect of B's rights under a trust are focussed on *recipients* of the trust property or its traceable proceeds, rather than strangers who instead simply interfere with the trust property. The following decision casts some doubt, however, on that key limit to the effect of B's rights under a trust. **12–092**

Shell (UK) Ltd v Total (UK) Ltd

Court of Appeal [2010] EWCA Civ 180; [2011] Q.B. 86

In December 2005, a number of very large explosions and fires occurred at the Buncefield Oil Storage Terminal in Hertfordshire, England. The explosions and fires were due to the carelessness of the defendant. No-one was killed or seriously injured, but a large amount of property was destroyed or damaged. The claimant, Shell UK Ltd, was one of a group of companies who used the oil storage terminal, and its pipelines, to store and distribute oil. As a result of damage to the terminal and pipelines, Shell was unable to distribute oil to its customers for a period and so suffered a large financial loss. It sued the defendant to recover that consequential loss. Shell, however, was not the registered owner of the terminal: instead, the terminal was registered to two trustee companies, who held their rights on trust for a number of companies, including Shell (and also the defendant). The defendant, Total UK Ltd, admitted that it was liable in negligence to the trust company but, relying chiefly on the decision of the House of Lords in *The Aliakmon*[184] argued that it was not liable in the tort of negligence to the beneficiaries of the trust, and therefore could not be made to pay for consequential loss suffered only by a beneficiary, and not by the trustee. **12–093**

WALLER LJ (giving the judgment of the court, to which LONGMORE and RICHARDS LJJ also contributed): Pursuant to two "Participants Agreements" Shell was entitled to the use of the relevant facilities, of which it was a part beneficial owner in common, for the purpose of receipt and delivery of the fuel. But its claims have failed before David Steel J largely because Shell was unable to overcome the rule that there can be no recovery for negligent infliction of mere economic loss. The House of Lords considered this aspect of the law over 20 years ago and reiterated English law's traditional refusal to allow recovery in such circumstances, unless such loss was the foreseeable consequence of physical injury to the claimant or the claimant's property. . .In *Leigh & Sillavan Ltd v Aliakmon Shipping Co Ltd, The Aliakmon* Lord Brandon of Oakbrook, setting out the exclusionary rule said:[185] **12–094**

---

181 See paras 14–101ff.

182 See further S. Agnew and B. McFarlane, "The Nature of Trusts and the Conflict of Laws" (2021) 137 L.Q.R. 405, 420–424. Note though that, as observed at para.14–027, there is room for further discussion on this point as the particular policy motivating the rule offering protection to C may vary with circumstances and so may not always be inconsistent with allowing a knowing receipt or equitable proprietary claim.

183 See para.12–078.

184 *Leigh & Sillivan Ltd v Aliakmon Shipping Co Ltd (The Aliakmon)* [1986] A.C. 785.

185 [1986] A.C. 785 at 809.

> "... in order to enable a person to claim in negligence for loss caused to him by reason of loss of or damage to property, he must have had either the legal ownership of or a possessory title to the property concerned at the time when the loss or damage occurred, and it is not enough for him to have only had contractual rights in relation to such property which have been adversely affected by the loss of or damage to it."

12-095 Shell's response to Total's defence is that (i) even if it had no possessory title to the damaged tanks and pipelines it had a (shared) equitable ownership of them and that is enough to give it title to claim for its economic loss. To the extent that it needs to join the legal owners of the pipelines, it has done so because the trustee companies are parties to the action; (ii) it anyway did have a good (shared) possessory title to the pipelines at the time of the damage; (iii) the rule requiring a legal or possessory title before recovering for economic loss has always been subject to exceptions (see the *Hedley Byrne* case)[186] and justice requires a further exception to be made to fit the facts of this case; (iv) the rule should anyway be abandoned, although Shell recognised that that is not an option open to this court; (v) whatever the law of negligence may be, Shell has alternative claims in nuisance and under the rule of *Rylands v Fletcher*,[187] which cover the same ground; beneficial ownership of land has always been sufficient to sustain a claim in nuisance, of which the rule in *Rylands v Fletcher* is an aspect.

12-096 For Shell, Mr Laurence Rabinowitz QC accepted that Lord Brandon in *The Aliakmon* had confined the right to sue for negligent loss of or damage to property to a person who had "the legal ownership of or a possessory title to" the relevant property but he submitted that his Lordship was not intending to rule out the owner in equity at any rate if that equitable owner had (as Shell had) joined the legal owner to the proceedings...

12-097 It is fair to say that Lord Brandon's speech in *The Aliakmon* does not resolve the question which divides the parties in this case. . .[But] [w]hat, after all, would be the point of requiring the beneficial owner to join the legal owner in the action if the beneficial owner could then recover only his physical loss, but not his associated economic loss.

12-098 In the absence of any directly applicable authority, it is necessary to look in a little more detail at the exclusionary rule and the rationale for it. The rule is:[188]

> "... no duty is owed by a defendant who negligently damages property belonging to a third party, to a claimant who suffers loss because of a dependence upon that property or its owner."

12-099 So on the facts of this case Total, who has admittedly damaged the pipelines owned by [the trustee companies], submits that it owes no duty to Shell who has a contractual right to have its fuel loaded into, carried and discharged from the pipelines. If Shell was a complete stranger to the transaction that would be understandable but Shell is not a complete stranger. It is the (co-) beneficial owner of the pipelines and the contract to use the pipeline is only an incident of its beneficial ownership (albeit a necessary incident, since it is a co-owner of the pipelines with others who also wish to use it). On the face of things, it is legalistic to deny Shell a right to recovery by reference to the exclusionary rule. It is, after all, Shell who is (along with BP, Total and Chevron) the "real" owner, the "legal" owner being little more than a bare trustee of the pipelines.

12-100 It can be seen that the judges [in cases establishing the "exclusionary rule" in relation to carelessly caused economic loss] were not particularly enamoured of the law that they were laying down but felt it necessary because otherwise many other actions from persons with a mere contractual interest would be well founded and that would mean the law would find itself redressing more than "the proximate and direct consequences of wrongful acts". This argument has come to be known as the "floodgates argument" which was, indeed, also relied on by Lord Brandon in *The Aliakmon* when refusing to carve out a specific exception to the exclusionary rule in favour of c&f (or cif) purchasers of goods at sea. But the floodgates argument does not apply with nearly as much force to the suggestion that the beneficial owner of land (or chattels) should be entitled to sue since it is his position as "owner" not as contractor which has been damnified.

12-101 The editors of *Clerk and Lindsell* summarise the position by saying:[189]

---

186 *Hedley Byrne & Co Ltd v Heller & Partners Ltd* [1964] AC 465.

187 (1868) LR 3 HL 330.

188 See *Clerk and Lindsell on Torts* (19th edn, 2006) p 470 (para 8–115).

189 *Clerk and Lindsell on Torts* (19th edn, 2006) p 472 (para 8–116).

"To allow all claims for such economic loss would lead to unacceptable indeterminacy because of the ripple effects caused by contracts and expectations. Proximity requires some special relationship between the defendant and the person suffering relational economic loss, one which goes beyond mere contractual or non-contractual dependence on the damaged property."

Beneficial ownership of the damaged property goes well beyond contractual or non-contractual dependence on the damaged property and does indeed constitute a special relationship of the kind required by the learned editors. It is, in fact, a closer relationship in many ways than that of a bare trustee having no more than the legal title. **12–102**

We would be prepared to hold that a duty of care is owed to a beneficial owner of property (just as much as to a legal owner of property) by a defendant, such as Total, who can reasonably foresee that his negligent actions will damage that property. If, therefore, such property is, in breach of duty, damaged by the defendant, that defendant will be liable not merely for the physical loss of that property but also for the foreseeable consequences of that loss, such as the extra expenditure to which the beneficial owner is put or the loss of profit which he incurs. Provided that the beneficial owner can join the legal owner in the proceedings, it does not matter that the beneficial owner is not himself in possession of the property. **12–103**

We must confess to being somewhat influenced by what Lord Goff of Chieveley called "the impulse to do practical justice".[190] It should not be legally relevant that the co-owners of the relevant pipelines, for reasons that seemed good to them, decided to vest the legal title to the pipelines in their service companies and enjoy the beneficial ownership rather than the formal legal title. Differing views about the wisdom of the exclusionary rule are widely held but however much one may think that, in general, there should be no duty to mere contracting parties who suffer economic loss as a result of damage to a third party's property, it would be a triumph of form over substance to deny a remedy to the beneficial owner of that property when the legal owner is a bare trustee for that beneficial owner. **12–104**

Permission to appeal to the Supreme Court was granted to Total, but the case was settled. As noted by the Court of Appeal,[191] Shell relied on a number of different grounds in claiming compensation for the consequential loss it had suffered as a result of the damage to the oil plant, and it may well have been that a decision in favour of Shell could have been reached on other grounds.[192] The Court of Appeal's reasoning is significant to the present discussion, however, given that we have identified the extent of B's protection against X, a stranger interfering with the trust property, as a potentially critical test of the proprietary status of B's rights under a trust. **12–105**

Unfortunately, however, the reasoning of the Court of Appeal is far from clear and has been subject to much criticism.[193] It is odd, for example, to suggest that to draw a distinction between the position of B and that of O, an absolute owner, is "legalistic":[194] as we noted above,[195] there are a number of significant differences between the rights of such parties. Of course, the finding in favour of B might seem to support the proprietary view but James Penner, one proponent of that view, has stated that:[196] **12–106**

---

190 See *White v Jones* [1995] 1 All ER 691 at 702–703, [1995] 2 AC 207 at 259–260.

191 [2010] EWCA Civ 180; [2011] Q.B. 86.

192 For example, it may be that, as in, e.g. *Healy v Healy* [1915] 1 K.B. 938, Shell was a beneficiary which also had, in fact, possession of the trust property and gained a common law proprietary right — enforceable, for example, through claims in conversion or negligence, by virtue of that possession.

193 See, e.g. A. Rushworth & A. Scott, "Total Chaos?" [2010] L.M.C.L.Q. 536; P. Turner, "Consequential Economic Loss and the Trust Beneficiary" [2010] C.L.J. 445; J. Edelman, "Two Fundamental Questions for the Law of Trusts" (2013) 129 L.Q.R. 66, 67–72; W. Swadling, "In Defence of Formalism" and B. McFarlane, 'Form and Substance in Equity' in J. Goudkmap and A. Robertson (eds) *Form and Substance in the Law of Obligations* (Hart Publishing, 2019) 95 and 197.

194 [2011] Q.B. 86 [132] (extracted at para.12–099).

195 See para.12–006.

196 J. Penner, "The (True) Nature of a Beneficiary's Equitable Proprietary Interest under a Trust" (2014) 27 Can. J.L. & Juris 473, 485 fn.36.

> McFarlane, Stevens and I could agree that *Shell UK v Total UK* is wrongly decided. There is no reason why a beneficiary without possession of the trust assets. . .should have a claim for consequential economic loss against a third party in virtue of his damaging those assets.

12–107 In fact, the result in the case notwithstanding, it can be argued that the reasoning of the Court of Appeal is founded on a rejection of the proprietary view of the trust. This is because the court views B's claim as falling within an exception to the "exclusionary rule" which prevents the recovery of carelessly caused pure economic loss. That analysis assumes, of course, that the rule prima facie applies. This in turn assumes that the defendant, X, did *not* interfere with any property right of B. After all, if such interference had occurred, B's loss would not be pure economic loss: no exclusionary rule applies to the recovery of economic loss flowing from damage to the claimant's property.

12–108 The mistake in the court's reasoning, it is submitted, lies in its misinterpretation of the exception to the exclusionary rule as formulated by *Clerk and Lindsell*.[197] That exception is based on "proximity" which is stated to require "some special relationship between the defendant and the person suffering relational economic loss". It therefore requires a special relationship between the claimant and the defendant. The court, however, states that the case falls within the exception as B's "[b]eneficial ownership of the damaged property goes well beyond contractual or non-contractual dependence on damaged property and does indeed constitute a special relationship of the kind required".[198] There is an obvious flaw in this reasoning. The existence of a trust means there is a special relationship between the claimant and the *trustee*. But the exception identified by *Clerk and Lindsell* instead requires a special relationship between the claimant and the *defendant*. No such relationship exists between B and X simply as a result of X, a stranger, damaging trust property.

12–109 It can also be noted that the court laid down a requirement that T must be joined by B if an action is to be brought by B against X. That requirement does preserve a difference between the position of B and of O, as an outright owner of property can clearly sue a party interfering with that property without needing to join any other party. On one view,[199] the joinder requirement is not merely procedural, but reflects the substantive point that the right being enforced against X is in truth T's right as owner of the property, which T enforces on B's behalf because T holds that right subject to a duty to B. The joinder requirement, however, is of no real comfort to X, not least because T can be compelled by B to join the action.[200] Moreover, the court in *Shell UK v Total UK* assumed that B could then recover consequential losses suffered by B, and not by T. That is the crucial practical point for a party in X's position: is X liable not only for consequential loss caused to T, who has the right to the trust property, but also to B, a beneficiary of the trust? There are, it is submitted, sound practical reasons for saying that X should not be so liable. There is no limit, after all, on the possible number of beneficiaries of a trust, or the possible losses that each could suffer from X's damage to the trust property. This is precisely why economic loss suffered by parties who have a contract with an owner of property, but no right to that property themselves, is not generally recoverable from a defendant who carelessly causes such loss. If an owner of property cannot impose the risk of such extended liability on third parties by merely entering a contract, why should it be possible for her to do so by setting up a trust?

---

[197] [2011] Q.B. 86 at [135] (extracted at para.12–101).

[198] [2011] Q.B. 186 at [136] (extracted at para.12–102).

[199] For discussion of the nature of the joinder requirement, see, e.g. *Roberts v Gill & Co* [2010] UKSC 22; [2011] 1 A.C. 240 at [55]–[72]: see too para.3–210.

[200] Indeed, B can bring one action combining both B's claim against T and then T's claim against X: this procedural concession to B derives from *Vandepitte v Preferred Accident Insurance Corp of New York* [1933] A.C. 70.

In considering any academic debate as to different conceptions of the law, it is important to ask why the debate matters: what turns on it in practice? The facts of *Shell UK v Total UK*, and the reasoning adopted by the Court of Appeal, provide a convincing example that it is important to be aware of the differences between the proprietary and obligational views. Not because the outcome will necessarily be dictated by which of those views is expressly or impliedly preferred by the court, but rather because, if the debate is simply overlooked, there is a great risk of confusion. **12–110**

vi. B's Protection Against T's Creditors

A crucial feature of the rights of B, a beneficiary of a trust, is that those rights are protected in the insolvency of T. This is a feature shared with legal property rights. So, for example, if O has ownership of a car, but that car happens to be in the possession of A, then both before and during any insolvency of A, the car will not be available to meet claims of A's creditors. Similarly, both before and during any insolvency of T, rights held on trust by T will not be available to T's creditors. In this way, the trust can be seen as having a practically important asset-partitioning effect. **12–111**

A proprietary approach to understanding B's rights provides a simple means of explaining this protection from T's creditors—if, for example, the trust assets are seen as in effect belonging to B rather than to T, then it is obvious that T's creditors should not have access to their value. However, it is not necessary to link this asset-partitioning effect to B's having a proprietary entitlement. The effect applies to other situations in which a party holds assets subject to rules imposing particular duties, and particular limits on their powers in relation to the assets, even if, in those cases, there is no other party who can be identified as having a proprietary entitlement in the assets.[201] So, for example, assets held on charitable trust are not available to the general creditors of the trustees, and assets held by a personal representative administering an estate are similarly not available to the general creditors of the personal representatives. **12–112**

It may also be possible to explain B's protection whilst adopting an obligational view of the trust. The key point again would be that at least some of the duties of T are of a special kind, as they relate precisely to particular rights held by T. Such duties are then recognised as having a different effect to duties, such as the simple duty to pay a party a sum of money, which do not relate to any specific rights held by the party subject to the duty. For example, insolvency legislation applying to natural persons now makes clear that any rights held by the insolvent party on trust do not form part of that party's estate for insolvency purposes and so are not, for example, acquired by a trustee in bankruptcy for distribution to creditors. However, this provision can be seen to reflect that, if trust assets were thus vested in the party administering the insolvent estate, that party, as a recipient of trust assets who is not a bona fide purchaser for value without notice, and has no other defence, would be liable to a claim by B, who could, for example, inform the party administering the estate of the trust and demand that they give up the trust assets. The protection of B in T's insolvency can thus be seen to flow from the general point that B may have a claim against third party recipients of the trust property. Indeed, such an analysis was adopted in the following extract. **12–113**

Carter Holt Harvey Woodproducts v Commonwealth of Australia

[2019] HCA 20; (2019) 368 A.L.R. 390 at [25]–[27]

KIEFEL CJ, KEANE AND EDELMAN JJ: Although a trustee is personally liable to creditors, it has been established for centuries in bankruptcy law that rights held by a bankrupt on trust do not generally form **12–114**

[201] See para.12–032.

part of the bankrupt's estate that is available for general distribution amongst creditors.[202] In this respect, the common law courts took notice of a trust.[203] Despite Australian bankruptcy legislation having adopted a broad definition of "property",[204] it also expressly adopted this principle by excluding from the property divisible among creditors all property held by the bankrupt on trust for another person.[205]

12–115 The Corporations Act contains a similarly broad definition of "property" to the bankruptcy legislation but it does not contain an equivalent express exclusion of property held by a company on trust for another person. However, the same "elementary, and fundamental" principle that generally precludes distribution of trust property from distribution among creditors has been consistently applied in Australia to trustee companies. It has been said that, as a general proposition, it would be "extraordinary, in the context of insolvency law, if "property of the company" included property of which it was a trustee and in which it had no beneficial interest. Hence, as the Court of Appeal correctly observed, the exclusion of property held on trust from the property of a trustee, while express in bankruptcy, applies "by undisputed analogy in the case of corporations."

12–116 The reason that rights held on trust by an insolvent company or bankrupt individual are generally excluded from division amongst the creditors of the company or of the bankrupt individual is that a liquidator's power over the rights of an insolvent company and the statutory assignment of rights in bankruptcy have always been concerned only with those rights that enure in law "for the benefit of" the *"personal estate"* of the bankrupt or insolvent person, even if in some cases that legal benefit might not be a "practical benefit". By contrast, other than as permitted by rules of law or terms of the trust, the trustee owes a "personal obligation to deal with the trust property for the benefit of the beneficiaries, and this obligation must be annexed to the trust property". The trustee does not generally have any entitlement to deal with the rights held on trust for the trustee's own benefit. Courts of law took notice of the trust because "it would be absurd" for rights to have vested in bankruptcy "for no other purpose but in order that there may be a bill in equity brought against [the trustee in bankruptcy]". Hence rights held on trust were, and are, generally excluded from inclusion in the statutory concepts of the "property" of the bankrupt or the "property" of the insolvent company.

12–117 However, the general principle that excludes those rights held on trust from division among creditors does not apply to the extent to which a trustee is permitted to benefit personally by "deriv[ing] any benefit" from the rights held on trust. One means by which a trustee can benefit personally from the trust rights is the trustee's power to use those trust rights to indemnify itself from liabilities. The existence of that "right of indemnity" means that, to the extent of the power, the trust rights are "no longer property held solely in the interests of the beneficiaries of the trust".

12–118 The reference above to the trustee's rights of indemnity is a useful reminder that, even in the simple case where T holds on a fixed trust for B1 and B2, there are some circumstances in which specific creditors of T may have a form of access to the trust assets. In carrying out the trusts or powers, T is personally liable to the extent of her whole fortune or patrimony for debts, contracts, torts or taxes arising in respect of her acts or omissions as trustee. This is the case even if T is exercising her powers in an authorised way, for example by entering into a contract with a third party for the repair of trust property. The position is usefully summarised in the following extract.

Investec Trust (Guernsey) Ltd v Glenalla Properties Ltd

Privy Council [2018] UKPC 7 at [57]

12–119 LORD HODGE (with whom LORD SUMPTION and LORD CARNWATH agreed): . . .it is necessary to start by setting out some well-established principles of English trust law which are relevant to the present issue:

[202] *Scott v Surman* (1742) Willes 400 at 402; *Winch v Keeley* (1787) 1 Term Rep. 619, 623; *Boddington v Castelli* (1853) 1 Wl. & Bl. 879, 885.

[203] *Winch v Keeley* (1787) 1 Term Rep. 619, 623. See also *Gladstone v Hadwen* (1813) 1 M. & S. 517, 526; *Britten v Perrott* (1834) 2 C. & M. 597, 602.

[204] Bankruptcy Act 1924 (Cth), s 4; Bankruptcy Act 1966 (Cth), s 5(1).

[205] Bankruptcy Act 1924 (Cth), s 91(a); Bankruptcy Act 1966 (Cth), s 116(2)(a).

(i) A trust is not a legal person. Its assets are vested in trustees, who are the only entities capable of assuming legal rights and liabilities in relation to the trust. In particular, they are not agents for the beneficiaries, since their duty is to act independently.

(ii) English law does not look further than the legal person (natural or corporate) having the relevant rights and liabilities . . .

(iii) The legal personality of a trustee is unitary. Although a trustee has duties specific to his status as such, when it comes to the consequences English law does not distinguish between his personal and his fiduciary capacity. It follows that the trustee assumes those liabilities personally and without limit, thus engaging not only the trust assets but his personal estate. As Lord Penzance put it in *Muir v City of Glasgow Bank*,[206] where debts are incurred by a trustee for the benefit of the beneficiaries, the trustee:

'could not avoid liability on these debts by merely shewing that they rose out of matters in which he acted in the capacity of trustee or executor only, even though he should be able to shew, I addition, that the creditors of the concern knew all along the capacity in which he acted.'

(iv) This liability may be limited by contract, but the mere fact of contracting expressly as trustee is not enough to limit it. It merely makes explicit the knowledge of the trustee's capacity which Lord Penzance regarded as insufficient . . . There must be words negativing the personal liability which is an ordinary incident of trusteeship.

(v) A trustee is entitled to procure debts properly incurred as trustee to be paid out of the trust estate, or, if he pays it in the first instance from his own pocket, to be indemnified out of the trust estate.[207] To secure his right of indemnity, the trustee has an equitable lien on the trust assets.[208] Because an equitable lien does not depend on possession, it normally survives after he has ceased to be a trustee.[209]

(vi) A creditor has no direct access to the trust assets to enforce his debt. His action is against the trustee, who is the only person whose liability is engaged and the only one capable of being sued. A judgment against the trustee, even for a liability incurred for the benefit of the trust, cannot be enforced directly against trust assets, which the trustee does not beneficially own. The creditor's recourse against the trust assets is only by way of subrogation to the trustee's right of indemnity.[210]

(vii) Because the creditor's recourse to the assets is derived from the trustee's right of indemnity, it is vulnerable. It is exercisable only to the extent that that right exists. It may be defeated if there are insufficient trust assts to satisfy his debt, or if the trustee's right of indemnity is defeated, for example because the debt was unreasonably or improperly incurred and the indemnity does not extend to such debts, or because the trust deed excludes it on account of the trustee's wilful default or gross negligence. More generally, a breach of trust by the trustee, even in relation to a matter unconnected with the incurring of the relevant liability, will, to the extent that it creates a liability to account on the part of the trustee, stand in the way of the enforcement of the indemnity. As has frequently been observed, this can be hard on the creditor, who will usually have no knowledge of the state of account between the trustee and the beneficiaries. But the creditor can in principle protect his position, for example by taking a fixed charge over the trust assets, or, as in the present case, by stipulating for a personal guarantee from the principal beneficiary.

Whilst noting the important limits on the protection of a trust creditor, Lord Hodge makes clear that in some circumstances, such a third party does have indirect access to the trust assets. As this occurs through subrogation to the trustee's powers of indemnity, the trust creditor will be able to take advantage of the fact that, as noted above,[211] the trustee can exercise those powers in priority to the **12–120**

[206] *Muir v City of Glasgow Bank* (1879) 4 App. Cas. 337, 368.
[207] *In re Blundell* (1888) 40 Ch D 370, 376.
[208] *Lewin on Trusts* (19th edn, 2017) [21–043].
[209] *In re Johnson* (1880) 15 Ch D 548, 552.
[210] *In re Johnson* (1880) 15 Ch D 548.
[211] See para.12–028.

claims of beneficiaries of the trust. This further demonstrates that, even where B has an interest under a fixed trust, any "equitable ownership" of B is limited by T's powers to make use of the trust property in ways necessary or reasonable to give effect to the terms of the trust.

3. The Significance of the Debate

i. Practical Aspects

12–121 The debate between the proprietary and obligational views of the trust is a debate as to how best to explain a set of core, accepted features of the trust. It is not primarily a debate as to how the trust *should* operate. Nonetheless, there are some important practical questions as to the law of trusts which may be answered differently according to whether a court, expressly or impliedly, adopts a proprietary or obligational view.

12–122 In Chapter 8, for example, we saw that a proprietary view of the trust can support English law's refusal to admit private purpose trusts: if all trusts necessarily involve specified individuals (the beneficiaries) with at least a potential collective right to the trust property under the principle in *Saunders v Vautier*,[212] that refusal could be easily explained. Indeed, the specific debate as to whether English law should move from a beneficiary principle to an enforcer principle has been influenced by participants' views on the wider debate as to the nature of a trust.[213] This does not mean, however, that English law's current attachment to the beneficiary principle is necessarily inconsistent with the obligational view. On that view, there is a separate question as to whether T's core trust duties must be owed to, and enforced by, someone who benefits from their performance.[214] There may be good reasons for recognising such a limit (to do, for example, with incentives for enforcement and to ensure that the choice to waive enforcement is given to those who would lose out from such waiver) even if one takes an obligational view of the trust.

12–123 In *Serious Fraud Office v Litigation Capital*,[215] Foxton J. considered different views of the nature of the trust when addressing a question which "might be thought to be a foundational issue of the law of trusts, which does not appear to have been directly considered in any authority."[216] That question was at the effect of conflicting trusts over the same rights, as may occur, for example, where T holds on trust for B1, and then declares a trust in favour of B2. Foxton J identified two competing approaches to that question. The first, described by the judge as the "priority model", and advocated by the litigants referred to in the judgment as "The Settlement Parties", recognises that T has come under inconsistent duties, and then applies priority rules to resolve any conflict between those duties. The second, described by the judge as the "disability model" instead holds that if "T declares or becomes subject to a valid trust over property in favour of B1, it thereby disables itself from declaring or constituting a valid trust over the same property to the same extent in favour of B2, and any such purported declaration of trust in favour of B2 is of no effect." Foxton J then linked each of these two models to "competing conceptual models of the law of trusts advanced in academic commentary". The "priority model" was

---

212 (1841) 4 Beav. 115.

213 See, e.g. and compare D. Hayton, "Developing the Obligation Characteristic of the Trust" (2001) 117 L.Q.R. 96 (favouring the enforcer principle and the obligational view); P. Matthews, "From Obligation to Property, and Back Again? The Future of the Non-Charitable Purpose Trust" in D. Hayton (ed.) *Extending the Boundaries of Trusts and Similar Ring-fenced Funds* (Kluwer Law International, 2002) (preferring the beneficiary principle and, to some extent, the proprietary view).

214 See e.g. K. Low, "Non-Charitable Purpose Trusts: The Missing Right to Forego Enforcement" in R. Nolan et al (eds), *Trusts and Modern Wealth Management* (CUP, 2018).

215 [2021] EWHC 1272.

216 [2021] EWHC 1272 at [272].

linked to an obligational view, whereas the "disability model" was linked to a proprietary view, as seen in the following extract.

Serious Fraud Office v Litigation Capital

[2021] EWHC 1272 (Comm)

FOXTON J. The Settlement Parties rely on the "rights against rights" model of trusts which is strongly supported by a number of academic commentators. That model argues that, for all the talk of equitable estates and equitable interests in property, trust rights and obligations are essentially bilateral obligations between the beneficiary and the trustee, which attach to the trustee's rights in relation to the legal estate (or, I suppose, in the case of a sub-trust, which attach to the sub-trustee's rights attaching to the trustee's rights in relation to the legal estate). In the course of their argument, the Settlement Parties placed particular reliance on the analysis of Professor Lionel Smith, appearing among other places in "Trust and Patrimony".[217] Professor Smith challenges the suggestion that the creation of a trust involves the split of property in trust assets between the legal and equitable estates (however prevalent that language in case law). At [16] he observes: 12–124

"Equitable title suggests a direct relationship between a beneficiary and the trust property. This does not exist. All equitable proprietary rights require at least two people, in addition to the object of the right. I mean that the beneficiary's right itself cannot be understood as a direct relationship between the beneficiary and the trust property. The trustee has rights in the object; that is, rights in the trust property. The trust beneficiary's rights are rights in the rights the trustee holds in the object."

[Foxton J. also then referred to similar analyses in J. Edelman, "Two Fundamental Questions for the Law of Trusts" (2013) L.Q.R. 129 (parts of which are extracted at paras 12–037 to 12–045) and S. Agnew and B. McFarlane, "The Paradox of the Equitable Proprietary Claim" in B. McFarlane and S. Agnew (eds) *Modern Studies in Property Law (Vol.10)* (Hart Publishing, 2019).] 12–125

On the basis of this conceptual framework, the Settlement Parties submit that once it is recognised that trust rights and obligations involve correlative rights and obligations between the relevant beneficiary and the trustee in relation to the trustee's rights in the legal estate, there is no reason why a trustee might not place itself under conflicting trust obligations in relation to its rights in the same legal estate (just as a person can assume conflicting contractual obligations). 12–126

There is also academic support for the disability model and the *nemo dat* comparison. Professor James Penner in "The (True) Nature of a Beneficiary's Equitable Proprietary Interest Under a Trust",[218] squarely addressing the "right against a right" proponents, and in support of his defence of "the orthodox" conceptual understanding of the trust under which the trust beneficiaries are regarded as the "beneficial owners" of the property held on trust for them, posited the following example: 12–127

"Take the case where A enters into successive contracts for the sale of Blackacre, first to Y and then to Z. Hasn't A created two trusts over the same asset, with Y's merely having priority over Z's? If that is the right analysis it would suggest that A is a residual claimant, for he retains an interest in the trust asset that is sufficient to declare a trust in Z's favour, even though the entire beneficial interest has been created in Y's favour by the first trust. I dispute that this is the correct analysis of the fact situation. Cases such as *re Hay's Settlement Trusts* tell us so. Those cases concern the validity of an exercise of a power to dispose of trust assets by transferring them to a new settlement; a bad exercise is considered null and void, there is no whiff of 'a priorities analysis'.

A fortiori, a trustee declaring a trust of the asset he holds in favour of some third party, when he has no power to do so under the terms of the trust, does nothing at all. Such a declaration would be no more effective to displace B's interest under a trust than would my contract to sell you London Bridge displace the interest of whoever has title to sue. I have no power to sell London Bridge because I don't own it, and the trustee has no power to declare a trust of assets in which, in the eyes of equity, he has no beneficial interest."

---

217 (2008) *Revue Générale de Droit* 38(2) 379 (also printed at (2008–09 28 E.T. & P.J. 332).

218 (2014) 27 *Canadian Journal of Law and Jurisprudence* 473.

12–128 Foxton J also then referred to "passages in some trust text books which support, at least in certain contexts, the disability thesis".[219] In the end, Foxton J found that, on the facts of the case, even if the "priority model" applied, it would not give the Settlement Parties the assistance they required, and so it was not necessary to resolve the "fundamental" question. He nonetheless stated that, whilst the "priority model" derived some support from the rules relating to successive equitable assignments, and "offers a more intuitively appealing answer to certain hypotheticals explored in argument", the "disability model better coheres with the nature of a trustee's obligations, and in particular the 'duty of single-minded loyalty'.[220] It also has the support of the textbook passages I have referred to, and provides a better fit with the 'equitable property' approach to trusts, which, although subject to significant academic challenge, remains a substantial presence in the decided cases."[221]

12–129 It would be foolish of course to think that any single decision, much less a first instance one, can give a definitive answer to the nature of a beneficiary's rights under a trust, a question which has been fiercely debated across the common law world for over a century. Nonetheless, the analysis of Foxton J. in *Serious Fraud Office v Litigation Capital* is significant as it shows a judicial willingness to recognise the potential practical significance of the academic debate. As Hohfeld put it:[222]

> the true analysis of trusts and other equitable interests is a matter that should appeal to even the most extreme pragmatists of the law.

ii. Broader Conceptual Aspects: Common Law and Equity

12–130 In Chapter 1, we discussed the debate as to fusion between common law and equity, and whether there are distinctive functions which are pursued by equitable rules and principles. In concluding this chapter, it is worth briefly noting that the proper understanding of the rights of a beneficiary of a trust is clearly linked to the resolution of that debate. We saw,[223] for example, that Maitland's analysis of the relationship between common law and equity was intertwined with his obligational understanding of the trust: he argued that the trust does not involve a separation between legal and equitable ownership, as it would mean "civil war and utter anarchy"[224] if common law and equity gave different answers to a question as fundamental as "who is the owner of this property?" Similarly, the "right against a right" view of the trust, whilst different from Maitland's view, can be seen as consistent with a view of equity as supplementing the common law by controlling, in B's favour, A's exercise of legal entitlements.[225]

12–131 Conversely, a proprietary view of the trust may in some ways lend itself to a more fused understanding of the relationship between common law and equity. On that view, equity could be seen as simply adding to the list of property rights recognised at common law, by recognising further property rights, such as those of a beneficiary of a trust. On this view, there need not be anything distinctive about the form of such equitable property rights, as compared to legal property rights. It is perhaps significant

---

[219] The passages referred to were para.1–054 of the 14th edition of this work, and also J. McGhee and S. Elliott (eds), *Snell's Equity*, 34th edn (Sweet & Maxwell, 2019) at para.10–005.

[220] *Lehtimaki v Cooper* [2020] UKSC 53; [2020] 3 W.L.R. 461 at [43]–[45].

[221] [2021] EWHC 1272 (Comm) at [292].

[222] W. Hoheld, "Some Fundamental Legal Conceptions as Applied in Judicial Reasoning" (1913) 23 Yale L.J. 16, 18.

[223] See para.1–064.

[224] Maitland, *Lectures in Equity*, Lecture II: p.11 of A. Chaytor and W. Whittaker (eds) *Equity: also The Forms of Action at Common Law* (Cambridge University Press, 1909).

[225] See e.g. B. McFarlane and R. Stevens, "What's Special About Equity? Rights About Rights" in D. Klimchuk et al (eds), *Philosophical Foundations of the Law of Equity* (Oxford University Press, 2021) 191, 200–201.

though that, as we saw when considering the analysis of Burrows,[226] even pro-fusion commentators have generally accepted the continued utility of distinguishing between legal property rights on the one hand, and the rights of a beneficiary on the other.

Questions

1. In what ways do the rights of a beneficiary of a trust differ from purely personal rights?
2. How do the courts distinguish between those aspects of a trustee's duties under a trust which may bind a third party and those which may not?
3. What does it mean to see a beneficiary of a trust as having a right against the rights of the trustee?
4. Did the Court of Appeal in *Shell UK Ltd v Total UK Ltd* reach the correct result? If so, did it adopt the best reasoning in support of that result?
5. Does it matter whether one adopts a proprietary view or an obligational view of the trust?

[226] A. Burrows, "We Do This At Common Law But That in Equity" (2002) 22 O.J.L.S. 1, 4. See paras 1–158ff.

PART IV

BREACH OF TRUST

13

PERSONAL LIABILITY OF TRUSTEES FOR BREACH OF TRUST

1. Introduction

A breach of trust is any failure by a trustee to perform a duty or comply with a rule governing the exercise of trustee powers. Various duties and rules were discussed in Chapter 11, where it was noted that failure to perform some of these duties or comply with some of these rules can render trustees personally liable to pay compensation. Two situations where trustee can incur such liability are examined in Section 2 of this chapter: first, where trustees transfer ownership of trust property to a recipient in a transaction that is not permitted by the trust terms, so that the trustees fail to obtain a discharge from their ongoing duty to preserve the trust property; and, second, where trustees fail to act with reasonable skill and care with the result that the value of the trust fund is depleted. In Chapter 18, we also discuss the compensatory liability of fiduciaries, including trustees, who fail to comply with the "no conflicts rule".[1] A key point emerging from all this discussion is that the principles of assessment governing the compensatory liability of trustees vary according to the breach of trust which has occurred. In Section 3 of this chapter, we examine some defences which trustees can raise against proceedings for breach of trust, and in Section 4 we discuss the liability of trustees between themselves when one pays more than their fair share of a common liability for loss. 13–001

2. Compensation Claims Against Trustees

Equity recognises two types of compensation claim against trustees, which will be termed "substitutive performance claims" and "reparation claims", using language that was first propounded by Steven Elliott, some of whose work is excerpted below.[2] Substitutive performance claims are discussed in part A.[3] These are claims for money payment as a substitute for performance of the trustees' continuing duty to preserve trust property and produce it on demand, save in cases where they can 13–002

1 See paras 18–007 to 18–025. See also paras 17–011 to 17–053, discussing when a constructive trust is imposed on unauthorised profits by fiduciaries.

2 See paras 13–004 to 13–008. The fullest version of Elliott's work is contained in his Oxford DPhil thesis: S.B. Elliott, *Compensation Claims against Trustees* (University of Oxford, 2002), parts of which were published in S.B. Elliott and J. Edelman, "Money Remedies against Trustees" (2004) 18 Tru. L.I. 116. Various other scholars have adopted Elliott's analysis in their own work, including C. Rickett, "Understanding Remedies for Breach of Trust" (2008) 11 Otago L.R. 603; L. Smith, "The Measurement of Compensation Claims against Trustees and Fiduciaries" in E. Bant and M. Harding (eds), *Exploring Private Law* (Cambridge University Press, 2010); D. Sheehan, "Equitable Remedies for Breach of Trust" in R. Halson and D. Campbell (eds), *Research Handbook on Remedies in Private Law* (Edward Elgar, 2019).

3 See paras 13–009 to 13–089.

show that the property was disbursed in an authorised transaction. Claims of this sort are apposite when trust property has been disbursed in an unauthorised transaction, and the amount claimed is the value of the "missing" property.

13–003 Reparation claims are discussed in Part B.[4] These are claims for a money payment to make good loss caused to the trust fund by a breach of trust. Claims of this sort can be brought, e.g. where trustees have carelessly mismanaged trust property or have taken a profit-making opportunity for themselves which they should have taken on behalf of the beneficiaries. Both types of claim were traditionally mediated through proceedings for an account, discussed below in Part C,[5] although it has been possible since the nineteenth century to dispense with the accounting process in cases where a single breach of trust caused a discrete loss.[6] However, these two types of claim are different, essentially because reparation claims rest on the assertion that the trustees have committed a wrong, while substitutive performance claims do not. Finally in Part D we discuss awards of pre-judgment interest on compensatory awards against trustees.

S. Elliott and C. Mitchell, "Remedies for Dishonest Assistance"

(2004) 67 M.L.R. 14, 23–25

Money Claims against Trustees

13–004 . . . Equity allows two types of claim against errant trustees that may be described as compensatory. Both types of claim have traditionally been mediated through the trustee's account, but they are claims of fundamentally different types. One is a claim that the trustee perform his primary obligations to apply the trust property in accordance with the trust deed, by a payment of monetary compensation where he cannot perform *in specie*.[7] This is a type of performance claim. The other is a claim that the trustee make good loss suffered by the beneficial interests by reason of his breach of trust. This is a type of reparation claim, because the compensation he must pay is calculated to repair the loss. . .

Compensation and Loss

13–005 Claims for performance and claims for reparation may both yield compensatory relief, but the relief is compensatory in different senses of the word. Both concepts of compensation carry the idea of an equivalent,[8] but the object of the equivalence is different in each case. A failure to discriminate between these two senses has become a prime source of confusion in this branch of equity.

13–006 In its dominant sense compensation consists in a money equivalent to the injury or loss that a person has suffered. This may be called reparative compensation because it is calculated to repair the loss. The measure of reparative compensation is the difference between the claimant's present position and the position he would have occupied if he had not sustained the wrong.[9] This hypothetical comparison is drawn pursuant to a causal inquiry linking the defendant's misconduct with deterioration in the claimant's position. Reparative compensation matches injury caused by the defendant's misconduct. In its second sense compensation consists in a money equivalent to property of which a person has been deprived or denied. This may be called substitutive compensation because it is calculated to provide a substitute for the property. Substitutive compensation is a familiar object of relief in expropriation cases: compensation

---

4 See paras 13–090 to 13–110.

5 See paras 13–111 to 13–122.

6 *Barnett v Creggy* [2016] EWCA Civ 1004; [2017] Ch. 273 at [22].

7 Where the primary obligation is performed by payment of substitutive compensation, it is performed transformatively rather than in terms. We are grateful to Dr Rafal Zakrzewski for this insight.

8 J.A. Simpson and E.S.C. Weiner (gen eds), *Oxford English Dictionary* (Oxford: O.U.P., 2nd ed., 1989) s.v. "Compensation", sense 2a; J. Burke (ed.), *Jowitt's Dictionary of English Law* (London: Sweet & Maxwell, 2nd ed., 1977) s.v. "Compensation".

9 *Livingston v Rawlands Coal Co* (1880) 5 App. Cas. 25 at 39. The measure is formulated differently in claims for breach of contract, where it is the difference between the claimant's present position and the position she would have occupied, had the agreement been performed.

is given in lieu of the property being taken.[10] Causal connection between the claimant's injury and the defendant's act is not to the point where compensation is used in the substitutive sense because the compensation is an equivalent to the property and not to whatever injury there may be.

These two concepts of compensation imply correspondingly different concepts of loss. Reparative compensation responds to loss in the figurative sense of injury or damage. Loss in this sense is subjective in that it is concerned with injury or damage to a particular claimant. It is harm to the claimant's interests such that his position is worse than it would have been if he had not suffered the wrong or if his contract had been performed. This idea includes foregone gains as well as consequential losses. Loss of this sort may be called reparable loss. **13-007**

Substitutive compensation, by contrast, meets the loss of property to the claimant, whether by deprivation or denial. Substitutive compensation is measured by the property's objective value or by the objective value of some deterioration or diminution. How the property is to be valued is always a question for decision. Whether the claimant's overall financial position or personal well-being is diminished or improved by the deprivation of the property is not material to that valuation. Consequential loss is likewise conceptually inapposite to compensation of the substitutive variety. **13-008**

A. Substitutive Performance Claims

i. Basic Principles

A trustee owes "a duty to preserve the assets of the trust except in so far as the terms of the trust permit the trustee to do otherwise".[11] At any given moment, the trustee must therefore be able to prove to the beneficiaries (or some other person with enforcement rights) that she continues to be the owner of the original trust property. Depending on the trust terms, however, she may be able to obtain a discharge from this duty in various ways, by showing e.g. that she has used trust property to acquire substitute property in an authorised transaction, that she has distributed trust property to an authorised beneficiary (or in the case of a charitable trust spent it on an authorised purpose), or that she has used trust property to pay an expense incurred while carrying out the due administration of the trust. To prove she is entitled to such a discharge, the trustee must produce a set of accounts which record her dealings with the trust property and also records of all relevant transactions, such as documents of sale, bank account records showing fund transfers, etc. **13-009**

A trustee will be unable to prove that she is still the owner of trust property, and unable to show that she has been discharged from her duty to preserve the property, where she no longer own the property because she has transferred ownership to another person in an unauthorised transaction, e.g. because she has distributed it to someone who is not a beneficiary, or have used it to pay an unauthorised expense. In such cases, there is no need for the beneficiaries to plead or prove that the trustee has done anything wrong in order to obtain her remedy.[12] The trustee's duty to preserve the property continues unless she obtains a discharge and the beneficiaries are therefore entitled an order that she performs this duty, either by producing the very property which she should still be able to produce because she should still be the owner of it, or by substitutively performing this duty by the payment of a money sum. **13-010**

[10] The distinction between these two types of compensation is drawn in the famous U.S. Supreme Court case *Monoghela Navigation Co. v United States*, 148 U.S. 312 (1893) 326.

[11] *AIB Group (UK) Plc v Mark Redler & Co Solicitors* [2014] UKSC 58; [2015] A.C. 1503 at [51]. See too *Low v Bouverie* [1891] 3 Ch. 82 at 99.

[12] *Bacon v Clarke* (1837) 2 My. & Cr. 294; Re Stevens [1898] 1 Ch. 162; *Ahmed Angullia bin Hadjee Mohamed Salleh Angullia v Estate and Trust Agencies (1927) Ltd* [1938] A.C. 624 at 637. See also W. Ashburner, *Principles of Equity* (Butterworth, 1902), p.710.

13-011 Claims of this kind are not claims that the beneficiaries should be paid compensation for harm suffered as a result of the trustee's failure to perform her obligation to produce the relevant property *in specie* and the amount payable in such a case is measured by the objective value of the property which the trustee should be able to produce: it "looks not so much to the loss suffered as to what is required to restore the trust fund".[13] The amount is calculated by requiring the trustee to produce accounts which omit no relevant incomings and record only authorised outgoings, by inspecting these to determine what property makes up the trust fund, and then, if the trustee cannot produce this property *in specie*, by ordering them to pay over a money substitute—either directly to the beneficiaries, or more usually, into the trust fund so that the trust can remain on foot. Thus, as Kekewich J held in *Head v Gould*:[14]

> As against a trustee who, on the accounts being taken, is shewn to have improperly applied part of the trust estate, the right of a cestui que trust is to have those accounts set straight—that is, to compel the trustee to pay such a sum as will make them balance.

13-012 In cases of this kind, there is no need to prove that the trustee's actions or omissions have caused a loss,[15] nor do the concepts of remoteness[16] and contributory negligence[17] have any bearing on their claim. Nor is any deduction made for tax which would have been payable by the trustees on the relevant property but for their default,[18] and the beneficiaries' tax liabilities are irrelevant because they arise only when a distribution of trust property is made and not when the trustee pays the value of the relevant asset back into the trust fund.

13-013 The amount due from the trustee may be the value of misapplied (or wrongfully retained) trust income,[19] or of a misapplied capital sum,[20] plus interest.[21] Where some other property than money has been misapplied, the trustee may be liable to pay the market value of the property at the date of misapplication plus interest,[22] or, if this is a higher sum, the market value of the property at the date of judgment.[23]

---

13 *New Cap Reinsurance Corp Ltd v General Cologne Re Australia Ltd* (2004) 7 I.T.E.L.R. 295 at [55], per Young CJ in Eq. See too *Re Anglo-French Co-operative Soc* (1882) 21 Ch.D. 492 at [506]; *Re Windsor Steam Coal Co (1901) Ltd* [1929] 1 Ch. 151 at 166–167; *Knight v Haynes Duffell, Kentish & Co (a firm)* [2003] EWCA Civ 223 at [36]–[39]; *Re Lehman Brothers International (Europe) (in admin.) (No.2)* [2009] EWHC 2141 (Ch) at [53], per Blackburne J: a beneficiary's remedy for breach of trust is "principally directed to securing performance of the trust, rather than to the recovery of compensation or damages". See also *Crossman v Sheahan* [2016] NSWCA 200 at [313], per Ward JA: trust terms exempting a trustee from liability for "loss" did not affect a trustee's liability in a case of unauthorised disbursement because the trustee's "liability to account . . . i.e. the obligation to make good the trust . . . is not dependent on any 'loss' being established beyond the fact of the unauthorised disbursement."

14 [1898] 2 Ch. 250 at 266. See too *Wiglesworth v Wiglesworth* (1852) 16 Beav. 269 at [272]; *Chaplin v Young* (1864) 33 Beav. 330 at 343.

15 *Cocker v Quayle* (1830) 1 Russ. & M. 353; *Salway v Salway* (1831) 2 Russ. & M. 215; *White v Baugh* (1835) 3 C. & F. 44 at [66]; *Youyang Pty Ltd v Minter Ellison Morris Fletcher* (2003) 212 C.L.R. 484 at [63], [69].

16 *Clough v Bond* (1838) 3 My. & Cr. 490; *Magnus v Queensland National Bank* (1888) 37 Ch.D. 466; *Re Dawson* [1966] 2 N.S.W.R. 211 at 214; *Re Duckwari Plc (No.2)* [1999] Ch. 268 at 272; *McCann v Switzerland Insurance Australia Ltd* (2000) 203 C.L.R. 579 at [621]–[622].

17 *Alexander v Perpetual Trustees (WA) Ltd* (2004) 216 C.L.R. 109 at [44] and esp. [104]: contributory negligence is inapt because "the basic principle that a fiduciary's liability to a beneficiary for breach of trust is one of restoration."

18 *Bartlett v Barclays Bank Trust Co Ltd (No.2)* [1980] Ch. 515 at 543; *Re Bell's Indenture* [1980] 1 W.L.R. 1217; *John v James* [1986] S.T.C. 352 at 361.

19 *Sharma v Farlam Ltd* [2009] EWHC 1622 (Ch) at [401] ff.

20 *Docker v Somes* (1834) 2 My. & K. 655; *Burdick v Garrick* (1870) 5 Ch. App. 233; *Re Davis* [1902] 2 Ch. 314; *Gordon v Gonda* [1955] 1 W.L.R. 885; *Kemp v Sims* [2008] EWHC 2579 (Ch); [2009] Pens. L.R. 83.

21 As to which, see paras 13-123 to 13-131.

22 *Shepherd v Mouls* (1845) 4 Hare 500 at 504.

23 *Re Massingberd's Settlement* (1890) 63 L.T. 296; *Re Bell's Indenture* [1980] 1 W.L.R. 1217.

When deciding whether a trustee's payments are justified and should therefore be allowed to stand on the taking of the account, the court will generally disallow unauthorised disbursements, with the result that unauthorised purchases are treated as having been made with the trustee's own money.[24] However, there are exceptional cases where unauthorised disbursements are allowed, and the trustee is exonerated from performance of her duty to hold the relevant property for the beneficiaries. One such case is where the beneficiaries elect to adopt the trustee's actions and ask the court to treat these as though they had been authorised all along. Beneficiaries would wish to do this where the trustee has bought an unauthorised investment which has increased in value,[25] or where the trustee has wrongfully sold trust property whose current market value is lower than the value of the sale proceeds plus interest.[26] **13–014**

In the following extract the foregoing principles are reviewed by an Australian judge, Street J, whose statement of the law has been endorsed by the English courts.[27] **13–015**

Re Dawson

New South Wales Supreme Court [1966] 2 N.S.W.R. 211

STREET J.: The obligation of a defaulting trustee is essentially one of effecting a restitution to the estate. The obligation is of a personal character and its extent is not to be limited by common law principles governing remoteness of damage. In *Caffrey v Darby*,[28] trustees were charged with neglect in failing to recover possession of part of the trust assets. The assets were lost and it was argued by the trustees that the loss was not attributable to their neglect. The Master of the Rolls, in stating his reasons, asked "will they be relieved from that by the circumstance that the loss has ultimately happened by something that is not a direct and immediate consequence of their negligence?" His answer to this question was that, even supposing that "they could not look to the possibility" of the actual event which occasioned the loss, "yet, if they have already been guilty of negligence they must be responsible for any loss in any way to that property; for whatever may be the immediate cause the property would not have been in a situation to sustain that loss if it had not been for their negligence. If they had taken possession of the property it would not have been in his possession. If the loss had happened by fire, lightning, or any other accident, that would not be an excuse for them, if guilty of previous negligence. That was their fault." *Caffrey v Darby* is consistent with the proposition that if a breach has been committed then the trustee is liable to place the trust estate in the same position as it would have been in if no breach had been committed. Considerations of causation, foreseeability and remoteness do not readily enter into the matter. To the same effect is the case of *Clough v Bond*.[29] It was argued before Lord Cottenham L.C. that "the principle of the court is to charge persons in the situation of trustees as parties to the breach of trust, wherever they have acted irregularly, and the irregularity, however well intended, has in the result enabled their co-trustees to commit a breach of trust, or has been, however remotely, the origin of the loss." . . . The principles embodied in this approach do not appear to involve any inquiry as to whether the loss was caused by or flowed from the breach. Rather the inquiry in each instance would appear to be whether the loss would have happened if there had been no breach. **13–016**

. . . The cases to which I have referred demonstrate that the obligation to make restitution, which courts of equity have from very early times imposed on defaulting trustees and other fiduciaries, is of a more absolute nature than the common-law obligation to pay damages for tort or breach of contract. . . . Moreover **13–017**

---

24 *Jackson v Dickinson* [1903] 1 Ch. 947, esp. at 951–952 (where the consequences of this rule are fully explored).

25 *Re Patten* (1883) 52 L.J. Ch. 787; *Re Jenkins* [1903] 2 Ch. 362; *Wright v Morgan* [1926] A.C. 788 (PC) 799. If the beneficiaries choose to adopt the investment, they cannot *also* demand that the trustees pay in the difference between the current value of the investment and the (higher) current value of an authorised asset that was sold to make the purchase: *Thornton v Stokill* (1855) 1 Jur. 751, which should be preferred on this point to *Re Lake* [1903] 1 K.B. 439.

26 *Harrison v Harrison* (1740) 2 Atk. 121; *Bostock v Blakeney* (1794) 2 Bro. C.C. 653 at 656; *Pocock v Reddington* (1801) 5 Ves. Jun. 794 at 800.

27 e.g. *Bartlett v Barclays Bank Trust Co Ltd (No.2)* [1980] Ch. 515 at 543, per Brightman LJ.

28 (1801) 6 Ves. 488.

29 (1838) 3 My. & Cr. 490.

the distinction between common law damages and relief against a defaulting trustee is strikingly demonstrated by reference to the actual form of relief granted in equity in respect of breaches of trust. The form of relief is couched in terms appropriate to require the defaulting trustee to restore to the estate the assets of which he deprived it. Increases in market values between the date of breach and the date of recoupment are for the trustee's account: the effect of such increases would, at common law, be excluded from the computation of damages but in equity a defaulting trustee must make good the loss by restoring to the estate the assets of which he deprived it notwithstanding that market values may have increased in the meantime. The obligation to restore to the estate the assets of which he deprived it necessarily connotes that, where a monetary compensation is to be paid in lieu of restoring assets, that compensation is to be assessed by reference to the value of the assets at the date of restoration and not at the date of deprivation. In this sense the obligation is a continuing one and ordinarily, if the assets are for some reason not restored in specie, it will fall for quantification at the date when recoupment is to be effected, and not before.

ii. Disapplication of the Basic Rules Where the Trust Has Been Exhausted and the Fund Has Become Absolutely Vested in Possession and/or Where Money Has Been Paid out of a Bare Trust Arising as an Incident of a Wider Commercial Transaction

13–018 In *Target Holdings Ltd v Redferns*,[30] excerpted below, the claimant company agreed to lend money to a borrower to purchase property. Repayment of the loan was to be secured by a charge on the property. The money was placed with the defendant solicitors on trust for payment to the borrower's order, once a duly executed charge over the property and supporting documents of title were delivered. The solicitors paid the money over to the borrower's order without first obtaining the charge or other documents, although these were later delivered. The borrower defaulted on the loan and it then transpired that the property had been fraudulently overvalued, so that the claimant was left substantially out of pocket after it had exercised its power of sale. The Court of Appeal held that the solicitors had committed a breach of trust by releasing the money before receiving the documents, and that at this moment there had been "an immediate loss placing the trustee under an immediate duty to restore the moneys to the trust fund".[31] The court concluded that the solicitors were liable for the full amount of the money, but to prevent double recovery they required the claimant to give credit for the amount realised by the sale of the property.

13–019 The House of Lords agreed that there had been a breach of trust, but disagreed that the clock should be stopped at the date of breach for the purpose of quantifying the solicitors' liability. Their Lordships held that the relevant date was the date of judgment, i.e. after the transaction had been completed, and that the solicitors would therefore be liable only if the claimant could prove that its loss would not have occurred but for the early payment of the money without taking any security. Hence the case was sent back to the High Court for determination of this point.

13–020 In his leading speech Lord Browne-Wilkinson recognised that the principles stated in the previous section comprise the basic rules governing liability to reconstitute the funds of a "traditional" trust depleted by an unauthorised disposal of the trust funds. However, the application of these rules would have led to a result he wished to avoid, namely that the solicitors would then have had to pay for the claimant's entire loss, including loss caused by the fact that the property had been fraudulently overvalued. Lord Browne-Wilkinson therefore held that they would be liable for the difference between the amount of the purchase money which they had released in breach of trust and the amount realised by sale of the property only if it could be shown that the claimant would not have sustained this loss if the defendants had not made their unauthorised payment.

---

30 [1996] 1 A.C. 421.

31 [1994] 1 W.L.R. 1089 at 1103, per Peter Gibson LJ.

Target Holdings Ltd v Redferns (a firm)

House of Lords [1996] 1 A.C. 421

The claimant mortgagee alleged that it had been the victim of a mortgage fraud as part of which the insolvent second defendant had overvalued the mortgaged property at £2 million. The first defendant, a firm of solicitors, had acted not just for the claimant but also for the mortgagor, Crowngate Ltd, and also for two other companies, Kohli Ltd and Panther Ltd. The owner of the property, Mirage Ltd, had agreed to sell to Crowngate for £775,000, but Crowngate had arranged matters so that Mirage would sell to Panther for £775,000, which would then sell the property on to Kohli for £1,250,000, which would then sell to Crowngate for £2 million. The claimant knew nothing of these arrangements, the point of which was to create a false impression of the property's value. **13–021**

The claimant paid £1,525,000 to the defendant solicitors to be held on a bare trust to pay the money to Crowngate's order only when the property was transferred to Crowngate and charges over it were executed in the claimant's favour. In breach of trust the money was paid over a month before the charges were executed. Crowngate became insolvent and the claimant sold the property for only £500,000. The claimant sued the defendant solicitors for breach of their duty of care as the claimant's solicitor in failing to alert the claimant to the suspicious circumstances, and also for breach of trust in paying the money away without authority. The claimant sought summary judgment for breach of trust; Warner J. granted leave to defend, conditional upon payment into court of £1 million. The Court of Appeal granted summary judgment. **13–022**

LORD BROWNE-WILKINSON (with whom LORD KEITH, LORD ACKNER, LORD JAUNCEY and LORD LLOYD agreed): Peter Gibson L.J., with whom Hirst L.J. agreed, held that the basic liability of a trustee in breach of trust is not to pay damages but to restore to the trust fund that which has been lost to it or to pay compensation to the beneficiary for what he has lost. He held that, in assessing the compensation payable to the beneficiary, causation is not irrelevant but common law rules of causation, as such, do not apply: the beneficiary is to be put back in the position he would have been in but for the breach of trust. He held that in cases where the breach of trust does not involve paying away trust money to a stranger (e.g. making an unauthorised investment), the answer to the question whether any loss has been thereby caused and the quantification of such loss will depend upon events subsequent to the commission of the breach of trust. But he held that in cases such as the present where the trustee has paid away trust moneys to a stranger, there is an immediate loss to the trust fund and the causal connection between the breach and the loss is obvious: the trustee comes under an immediate duty to restore the moneys to the trust fund. He held that the remedies of equity are sufficiently flexible to require Target (as it has always accepted) to give credit for the moneys received on the subsequent realisation of its security. But otherwise Redferns' liability was to pay to Target the whole of the moneys wrongly paid away. . . **13–023**

Before considering the technical issues of law which arise, it is appropriate to look at the case more generally. Target alleges, and it is probably the case, that it was defrauded by third parties (Mr Kohli and Mr Musafir and possibly their associates) to advance money on the security of the property. If there had been no breach by Redferns of their instructions and the transaction had gone through, Target would have suffered a loss . . . [which] would have been wholly caused by the fraud of the third parties. The breach of trust committed by Redferns left Target in exactly the same position as it would have been if there had been no such breach: Target advanced the same amount of money, obtained the same security and received the same amount on the realisation of that security. In any ordinary use of words, the breach of trust by Redferns cannot be said to have caused the actual loss ultimately suffered by Target unless it can be shown that, but for the breach of trust, the transaction would not have gone through, e.g. if Panther could not have obtained a conveyance from Mirage otherwise than by paying the purchase money to Mirage out of the moneys paid out, in breach of trust, by Redferns to Panther on 29 June. If that fact can be demonstrated, it can be said that Redferns' breach of trust was a cause of Target's loss: if the transaction had not gone through, Target would not have advanced the money at all and therefore Target would not have suffered any loss. But the Court of Appeal decided,[32] and it is common ground before your Lordships, that there is a triable issue as to whether, had it not been for the breach of trust, the transaction would have gone through. Therefore the decision of the Court of Appeal in this case can only be maintained on the basis that, even if there is no causal link between the breach of trust and the actual loss eventually suffered **13–024**

[32] See [1994] 1 W.L.R. 1089 at 1100 and 1104, per Ralph Gibson and Peter Gibson L.JJ.

by Target (i.e. the sum advanced less the sum recovered) the trustee in breach is liable to bear (at least in part) the loss suffered by Target. . . .

13-025 At common law there are two principles fundamental to the award of damages. First, that the defendant's wrongful act must cause the damage complained of. Second, that the plaintiff is to be put "in the same position as he would have been in if he had not sustained the wrong for which he is now getting his compensation or reparation".[33] Although, as will appear, in many ways equity approaches liability for making good a breach of trust from a different starting point, in my judgment those two principles are applicable as much in equity as at common law. Under both systems liability is fault based: the defendant is only liable for the consequences of the legal wrong he has done to the plaintiff and to make good the damage caused by such wrong. He is not responsible for damage not caused by his wrong or to pay by way of compensation more than the loss suffered from such wrong. The detailed rules of equity as to causation and the quantification of loss differ, at least ostensibly, from those applicable at common law. But the principles underlying both systems are the same. On the assumptions that had to be made in the present case until the factual issues are resolved (i.e. that the transaction would have gone through even if there had been no breach of trust), the result reached by the Court of Appeal does not accord with those principles. Redferns as trustees have been held liable to compensate Target for a loss caused otherwise than by the breach of trust. I approach the consideration of the relevant rules of equity with a strong predisposition against such a conclusion.

13-026 The considerations urged before your Lordships, although presented as a single argument leading to the conclusion that the views of the majority in the Court of Appeal are correct, on analysis comprise two separate lines of reasoning, viz.:

(A) an argument developed by Mr Patten Q.C. (but not reflected in the reasons of the Court of Appeal) that Target is now (i.e. at the date of judgment) entitled to have the "trust fund" restored by an order that Redferns reconstitute the trust fund by paying back into client account the moneys paid away in breach of trust. Once the trust fund is so reconstituted, Redferns as bare trustee for Target will have no answer to a claim by Target for the payment over of the moneys in the reconstituted "trust fund". Therefore, Mr Patten says, it is proper now to order payment direct to Target of the whole sum improperly paid away, less the sum which Target has received on the sale of property; and

(B) the argument accepted by the majority of the Court of Appeal that, because immediately after the moneys were paid away by Redferns in breach of trust there was an immediate right to have the "trust fund" reconstituted, there was then an immediate loss to the trust fund for which loss Redferns are now liable to compensate Target direct.

13-027 The critical distinction between the two arguments is that argument (A) depends upon Target being entitled now to an order for restitution to the trust fund whereas argument (B) quantifies the compensation payable to Target as beneficiary by reference to a right to restitution to the trust fund at an earlier date and is not dependent upon Target having any right to have the client account reconstituted now.

13-028 Before dealing with these two lines of argument, it is desirable to say something about the approach to the principles under discussion. The argument both before the Court of Appeal and your Lordships concentrated on the equitable rules establishing the extent and quantification of the compensation payable by a trustee who is in breach of trust. In my judgment this approach is liable to lead to the wrong conclusions in the present case because it ignores an earlier and crucial question, viz. is the trustee who has committed a breach under any liability at all to the beneficiary complaining of the breach? There can be cases where, although there is an undoubted breach of trust, the trustee is under no liability at all to a beneficiary. For example, if a trustee commits a breach of trust with the acquiescence of one beneficiary, that beneficiary has no right to complain and an action for breach of trust brought by him would fail completely. Again there may be cases where the breach gives rise to no right to compensation. Say, as often occurs, a trustee commits a judicious breach of trust by investing in an unauthorised investment which proves to be very profitable to the trust. A carping beneficiary could insist that the unauthorised investment be sold and the proceeds invested in authorised investments: but the trustee would be under no liability to pay compensation either to the trust fund or to the beneficiary because the breach has caused no loss to the trust fund. Therefore, in each case the first question is to ask what are the rights of the beneficiary: only if

---

33 See *Livingstone v Rawyards Coal Co.* (1880) 5 App. Cas. 25 at 39, per Lord Blackburn.

some relevant right has been infringed so as to give rise to a loss is it necessary to consider the extent of the trustee's liability to compensate for such loss.

The basic right of a beneficiary is to have the trust duly administered in accordance with the provisions of the trust instrument, if any, and the general law. Thus, in relation to a traditional trust where the fund is held in trust for a number of beneficiaries having different, usually successive, equitable interests (e.g. A for life with remainder to B), the right of each beneficiary is to have the whole fund vested in the trustees so as to be available to satisfy his equitable interest when, and if, it falls into possession. Accordingly, in the case of a breach of such a trust involving the wrongful paying away of trust assets, the liability of the trustee is to restore to the trust fund, often called "the trust estate", what ought to have been there. 13-029

The equitable rules of compensation for breach of trust have been largely developed in relation to such traditional trusts, where the only way in which all the beneficiaries' rights can be protected is to restore to the trust fund what ought to be there. In such a case the basic rule is that a trustee in breach of trust must restore or pay to the trust estate either the assets which have been lost to the estate by reason of the breach or compensation for such loss. Courts of Equity did not award damages but, acting in personam, ordered the defaulting trustee to restore the trust estate.[34] If specific restitution of the trust property is not possible, then the liability of the trustee is to pay sufficient compensation to the trust estate to put it back to what it would have been had the breach not been committed.[35] Even if the immediate cause of the loss is the dishonesty or failure of a third party, the trustee is liable to make good that loss to the trust estate if, but for the breach, such loss would not have occurred.[36] Thus the common law rules of remoteness of damage and causation do not apply. However, there does have to be some causal connection between the breach of trust and the loss to the trust estate for which compensation is recoverable, viz. the fact that the loss would not have occurred but for the breach.[37] 13-030

Hitherto I have been considering the rights of beneficiaries under traditional trusts where the trusts are still subsisting and therefore the right of each beneficiary, and his only right, is to have the trust fund reconstituted as it should be. But what if at the time of the action claiming compensation for breach of trust those trusts have come to an end? Take as an example again the trust for A for life with remainder to B. During A's lifetime B's only right is to have the trust duly administered and, in the event of a breach, to have the trust fund restored. After A's death, B becomes absolutely entitled. He of course has the right to have the trust assets retained by the trustees until they have fully accounted for them to him. But if the trustees commit a breach of trust, there is no reason for compensating the breach of trust by way of an order for restitution and compensation to the trust fund as opposed to the beneficiary himself. The beneficiary's right is no longer simply to have the trust duly administered: he is, in equity, the sole owner of the trust estate. Nor, for the same reason, is restitution to the trust fund necessary to protect other beneficiaries. Therefore, although I do not wholly rule out the possibility that even in those circumstances an order to reconstitute the fund may be appropriate, in the ordinary case where a beneficiary becomes absolutely entitled to the trust fund the court orders, not restitution to the trust estate, but the payment of compensation directly to the beneficiary. The measure of such compensation is the same, i.e. the difference between what the beneficiary has in fact received and the amount he would have received but for the breach of trust. . . . 13-031

Argument (A)

As I have said, the critical step in this argument is that Target is now entitled to an order for reconstitution of the trust fund by the repayment into client account of the moneys wrongly paid away, so that Target can now demand immediate repayment of the whole of such moneys without regard to the real loss it has suffered by reason of the breach. 13-032

Even if the equitable rules developed in relation to traditional trusts were directly applicable to such a case as this, as I have sought to show, a beneficiary becoming absolutely entitled to a trust fund has no automatic right to have the fund reconstituted in all circumstances. Thus, even applying the strict rules so developed in relation to traditional trusts, it seems to me very doubtful whether Target is now entitled to have the trust fund reconstituted. But in my judgment it is in any event wrong to lift wholesale the detailed 13-033

34 See *Nocton v Lord Ashburton* [1914] A.C. 932 at 952, per Viscount Haldane L.C.

35 See *Caffrey v Darby* (1801) 6 Ves. 488 and *Clough v Bond* (1838) 3 My. & Cr. 490.

36 See Underhill and Hayton, *Law of Trusts and Trustees* 14th edn (1987), pp. 734–736, *Re Dawson (decd)* [1966] 2 N.S.W.R. 211 and *Bartlett v Barclays Bank Trust Co. Ltd (No.2)* [1980] 2 Ch. 515.

37 See also *Re Miller's Deed Trusts* (1978) 75 L.S. Gaz. 454 and *Nestlé v National Westminster Bank Plc* [1993] 1 W.L.R. 1260.

rules developed in the context of traditional trusts and then seek to apply them to trusts of quite a different kind. In the modern world the trust has become a valuable device in commercial and financial dealings. The fundamental principles of equity apply as much to such trusts as they do to the traditional trusts in relation to which those principles were originally formulated. But in my judgment it is important, if the trust is not to be rendered commercially useless, to distinguish between the basic principles of trust law and those specialist rules developed in relation to traditional trusts which are applicable only to such trusts and the rationale of which has no application to trusts of quite a different kind.

13–034 This case is concerned with a trust which has at all times been a bare trust. Bare trusts arise in a number of different contexts: e.g. by the ultimate vesting of the property under a traditional trust, nominee shareholdings, and, as in the present case, as but one incident of a wider commercial transaction involving agency. In the case of moneys paid to a solicitor by a client as part of a conveyancing transaction, the purpose of that transaction is to achieve the commercial objective of the client, be it the acquisition of property or the lending of money on security. The depositing of money with the solicitor is but one aspect of the arrangements between the parties, such arrangements being for the most part contractual. Thus, the circumstances under which the solicitor can part with money from client account are regulated by the instructions given by the client: they are not part of the trusts on which the property is held. I do not intend to cast any doubt on the fact that moneys held by solicitors on client account are trust moneys or that the basic equitable principles apply to any breach of such trust by solicitors. But the basic equitable principle applicable to breach of trust is that the beneficiary is entitled to be compensated for any loss he would not have suffered but for the breach. I have no doubt that, until the underlying commercial transaction has been completed, the solicitor can be required to restore to client account moneys wrongly paid away. But to import into such trust an obligation to restore the trust fund once the transaction has been completed would be entirely artificial. The obligation to reconstitute the trust fund applicable in the case of traditional trusts reflects the fact that no one beneficiary is entitled to the trust property and the need to compensate all beneficiaries for the breach. That rationale has no application to a case such as the present. To impose such an obligation in order to enable the beneficiary solely entitled (i.e. the client) to recover from the solicitor more than the client has in fact lost flies in the face of common sense and is in direct conflict with the basic principles of equitable compensation. In my judgment, once a conveyancing transaction has been completed the client has no right to have the solicitor's client account reconstituted as a "trust fund".

Argument (B)

13–035 . . . The key point in the reasoning of the Court of Appeal is that where moneys are paid away to a stranger in breach of trust, an immediate loss is suffered by the trust estate: as a result, subsequent events reducing that loss are irrelevant. They drew a distinction between the case in which the breach of trust consisted of some failure in the administration of the trust and the case where a trustee has actually paid away trust moneys to a stranger. There is no doubt that in the former case, one waits to see what loss is in fact suffered by reason of the breach, i.e. the restitution or compensation payable is assessed at the date of trial, not of breach. However, the Court of Appeal considered that where the breach consisted of paying away the trust moneys to a stranger it made no sense to wait: it seemed to Peter Gibson L.J. obvious that in such a case "there is an immediate loss, placing the trustee under an immediate duty to restore the moneys to the trust fund".[38] The majority of the Court of Appeal therefore considered that subsequent events which diminished the loss in fact suffered were irrelevant, save for imposing on the compensated beneficiary an obligation to give credit for any benefit he subsequently received. In effect, in the view of the Court of Appeal one "stops the clock" at the date the moneys are paid away: events which occur between the date of breach and the date of trial are irrelevant in assessing the loss suffered by reason of the breach.

13–036 A trustee who wrongly pays away trust money, like a trustee who makes an unauthorised investment, commits a breach of trust and comes under an immediate duty to remedy such breach. If immediate proceedings are brought, the court will make an immediate order requiring restoration to the trust fund of the assets wrongly distributed or, in the case of an unauthorised investment, will order the sale of the unauthorised investment and the payment of compensation for any loss suffered. But the fact that there is an accrued cause of action as soon as the breach is committed does not in my judgment mean that the quantum of the compensation payable is ultimately fixed as at the date when the breach occurred. The quantum is fixed at the date of judgment, at which date, according to the circumstances then pertaining,

[38] [1994] 1 W.L.R. 1089 at 1103.

the compensation is assessed at the figure then necessary to put the trust estate or the beneficiary back into the position it would have been in had there been no breach. I can see no justification for "stopping the clock" immediately in some cases but not in others: to do so may, as in this case, lead to compensating the trust estate or the beneficiary for a loss which, on the facts known at trial, it has never suffered.

Moreover, in my judgment the distinction is not consistent with the decision in *Re Dawson (decd)*.[39] In that case a testator had established separate executors for his New Zealand and his Australian estates. In 1939 the New Zealand estate was under the administration of attorneys for, among others, PSD. PSD arranged that New Zealand £4,700 should be withdrawn from the New Zealand estate and paid away to a stranger, X, who in turn was supposed to lend the moneys to an Australian company in which PSD was interested. X absconded with the money. In that case, therefore, the trust money had been paid away to a stranger. Street J. had to decide whether the liability of PSD to compensate the estate was to be satisfied by paying sufficient Australian pounds to buy New Zealand £4,700 at the rate of exchange at the date of breach (when there was parity between the two currencies) or at the date of judgment (when the Australian pound had depreciated against the New Zealand pound). He held that the rate of exchange was to be taken as at the date of judgment. Although, contrary to the present case, this decision favoured the beneficiaries at the expense of the defaulting trustee, the principle is of general application whether operating to the benefit or the detriment of the beneficiaries. The equitable compensation for breach of trust has to be assessed as at the date of judgment and not at an earlier date. **13–037**

In *Canson Enterprises Ltd v Boughton & Co.*[40] the plaintiffs had bought some property in a transaction in which they were advised by the defendant, a solicitor. To the knowledge of the solicitor, but not of the plaintiffs, there was an improper profit being made by the vendors. If the plaintiffs had known that fact, they would not have completed the purchase. The defendant solicitor was in breach of his fiduciary duties to the plaintiffs. After completion the plaintiffs built a warehouse on the property, which due to the negligence of engineers and builders, was defective. The question was whether the defendant solicitor was liable to compensate the plaintiffs for the defective building, the plaintiffs contending that "but for" the defendant's breach of fiduciary duty they would not have bought the property and therefore would not have built the warehouse. Although the Supreme Court of Canada were unanimous in dismissing the claim, they reached their conclusions by two differing routes. The majority considered that damages for breach of fiduciary duty fell to be measured by analogy with common law rules of remoteness, whereas the minority considered that the equitable principles of compensation applied. Your Lordships are not required to choose between those two views. But the judgment of McLachlin J. (expressing the minority view) contains an illuminating exposition of the rules applicable to equitable compensation for breach of trust. Although the whole judgment deserves study, I extract the following statements: **13–038**

> "While foreseeability of loss does not enter into the calculation of compensation for breach of fiduciary duty, liability is not unlimited. Just as restitution in specie is limited to the property under the trustee's control, so equitable compensation must be limited to loss flowing from the trustee's acts in relation to the interest he undertook to protect. Thus, Davidson states 'It is imperative to ascertain the loss *resulting from breach of the relevant equitable duty*.'"[41] . . .
>
> "A related question which must be addressed is the time of assessment of the loss. In this area tort and contract law are of little help. . . . The basis of compensation at equity, by contrast, is the restoration of the actual value of the thing lost through the breach. The foreseeable value of the items is not in issue. As a result, the losses are to be assessed as at the time of trial, *using the full benefit of hindsight*."[42] . . .
>
> "In summary, compensation is an equitable monetary remedy which is available when the equitable remedies of restitution and account are not appropriate. By analogy with restitution, it attempts to restore to the plaintiff what has been lost as a result of the breach, i.e. the plaintiff's lost opportunity. The plaintiff's actual loss as a consequence of the breach is to be assessed with the full benefit of hindsight. Foreseeability is not a concern in assessing compensation, but it is essential that the losses made good are only those which, *on a common sense view of causation*, were caused by the breach."[43]

---

39 [1966] 2 N.S.W.R. 211.
40 [1991] 3 S.C.R. 534.
41 I. Davidson, "The Equitable Remedy of Compensation" (1982) 3 Melb. U.L.R. 349, 354 (McLachlin J.'s emphasis).
42 McLachlin J.'s emphasis.
43 Lord Browne-Wilkinson's emphasis.

13–039 In my view this is good law. Equitable compensation for breach of trust is designed to achieve exactly what the word compensation suggests: to make good a loss in fact suffered by the beneficiaries and which, using hindsight and common sense, can be seen to have been caused by the breach. . . .

13–040 Mr Patten for Target relied on *Nant-y-glo and Blaina Ironworks Co. v Grave*[44] as showing that a trustee can be held liable to recoup to the trust fund the value of shares at the highest value between the date of breach and the date of judgment. In my view that case has no relevance. The claim there was not for breach of trust but for account of profits made by a fiduciary (a company director) from shares which he had improperly received in breach of his duty. The amount recoverable in an action claiming an account of profits is dependent upon the profit made by the fiduciary, not the loss suffered by the beneficiary.

13–041 Mr Patten also relied on *Jaffray v Marshall*,[45] where the principles applicable in an action for an account of profits were, to my mind wrongly, applied to a claim for compensation for breach of trust. In my judgment that case was wrongly decided not only because the wrong principle was applied but also because the judge awarded compensation by assessing the quantum on an assumption (viz. that the house in question would have been sold at a particular date) when he found as a fact that such sale would not have taken place even if there had been no breach of trust.

13–042 For these reasons I reach the conclusion that, on the facts which must currently be assumed, Target has not demonstrated that it is entitled to any compensation for breach of trust. Assuming that moneys would have been forthcoming from some other source to complete the purchase from Mirage if the moneys had not been wrongly provided by Redferns in breach of trust, Target obtained exactly what it would have obtained had no breach occurred, i.e. a valid security for the sum advanced. Therefore, on the assumption made, Target has suffered no compensatable loss. Redferns are entitled to leave to defend the breach of trust claim.

13–043 However, I find it very difficult to make that assumption of fact. There must be a high probability that, at trial, it will emerge that the use of Target's money to pay for the purchase from Mirage and the other intermediate transactions was a vital feature of the transaction. The circumstances of the present case are clouded by suspicion, which suspicion is not dissipated by Mr Bundy's untruthful letter dated 30 June informing Target that the purchase of the property and the charges to Target had been completed. If the moneys made available by Redferns' breach of trust were essential to enable the transaction to go through, but for Redferns' breach of trust Target would not have advanced any money. In that case the loss suffered by Target by reason of the breach of trust will be the total sum advanced to Crowngate less the proceeds of the security. It is not surprising that Mr Sumption Q.C. was rather muted in his submission that Redferns should have had unconditional leave to defend and that the order for payment into court of £1m. should be set aside. In my judgment such an order was fully justified.

13–044 I would therefore allow the appeal, set aside the order of the Court of Appeal and restore the order of Warner J.

13–045 McLaughlin J's judgment in *Canson Enterprises Ltd v Boughton*[46] was a weak starting-point for Lord Browne-Wilkinson's analysis, since the case concerned a compensatory claim for breach of fiduciary duty rather than a compensatory claim following an unauthorised disposal of trust funds, and McLachlin J's own analysis suffers from a failure to distinguish between the different rules by which such claims are respectively governed.[47] In extra-judicial writing that is excerpted below, Lord Millett makes two further criticisms of Lord Browne-Wilkinson's speech. First, he questions the relevance of the distinction drawn by Lord Browne-Wilkinson between ongoing "traditional" trusts, terminated "traditional" trusts with a single absolutely entitled beneficiary, and "bare" trusts in a commercial transaction.[48] Second, he argues that Lord Browne-Wilkinson's approach was unsatisfactory because

[44] (1878) 12 Ch.D. 738.
[45] [1993] 1 W.L.R. 1285.
[46] [1991] 3 S.C.R. 534.
[47] See paras 18–011 to 18–012.
[48] See too J. Edelman, "Money Awards of the Cost of Performance" (2010) 4 J. Eq. 122: "[Lord Browne-Wilkinson's] assertion that the commercial trust would be rendered 'commercially useless' was unsupported by any reference to any empirical study."

claims for substitutive compensation are not claims for loss founded on the breach of a primary duty that triggers a secondary duty to pay compensation, so that it is incoherent to introduce a requirement into such claims that there must be a causal link between the breach of a primary duty committed by the trustee and a loss by the beneficiaries.

P.J. Millett, "Equity's Place in the Law of Commerce"

(1998) 114 L.Q.R. 214, 224–227

Lord Browne-Wilkinson distinguished between traditional family trusts on the one hand and the bare trust which has become a valuable device in commercial and financial dealings. He accepted that the fundamental principles of equity apply as much to such trusts as they do to the traditional trust in relation to which those principles were originally formulated. But he suggested that it was important, if the trust concept was not to be rendered commercially useless, to distinguish between the basic principles of trust law and those specialist rules developed in relation to traditional trusts which are applicable only to such trusts and the rationale of which has no application to trusts of a quite different kind. 13–046

It is difficult to know what to make of this. It is impossible to dissent from the proposition that equity is flexible and that circumstances alter cases. It is also true that, as Lord Browne-Wilkinson pointed out, the circumstances in which the solicitor [in *Target Holdings*] was entitled to part with his client's money were regulated by the client's instructions and were not part of the trusts on which the money was held. This is plainly correct. The only trust was a bare trust for the client; its instructions were superimposed on that trust. It was a form of *Quistclose* trust. But nothing turns on this, except that it made the instructions revocable. Application of trust money in such circumstances otherwise than in accordance with the unrevoked instructions of the beneficial owner is still a breach of trust. Likewise trustee investment powers are not part of the trusts on which trust money is held, but an unauthorised investment of trust money is still a breach of trust. . . 13–047

Lord Browne-Wilkinson's speech is, with respect, disappointing in a second respect. He begins his analysis by referring to the basic right of a beneficiary to have the trust duly administered in accordance with the provisions of the trust instrument, if any, and the general law, and of the trustee's liability to pay compensation for any loss to the trust estate which may be occasioned by his breach of trust. From there he proceeds to speak exclusively in terms of causation, introducing the "but for" test while at the same time rejecting other tests of causation and remoteness of damage which have been adopted by the common law. This fails to explain why the trustee's liability is strict, or why equity should not adopt the common law rules of causation and remoteness in toto. 13–048

It is misleading to speak of breach of trust as if it were the equitable counterpart of breach of contract at common law; or to speak of equitable compensation for breach of fiduciary duty as if it were common law damages masquerading under a fancy name. Forty years ago, the Chancery Judges bore down heavily on such solecisms. Woe betide a Chancery Junior who spoke of "damages for breach of trust" or "damages for breach of fiduciary duty". The judges knew that misuse of language often conceals a confusion of thought. Nowadays these misleading expressions are in common use. It is time that the usage was stamped out. 13–049

Lord Diplock has said that a contracting party is under a primary obligation to perform his contract and a secondary obligation to pay damages if he does not.[49] It is tempting, but wrong, to assume that a trustee is likewise under a primary obligation to perform the trust and a secondary obligation to pay equitable compensation if he does not. The primary obligation of a trustee is to account for his stewardship. The primary remedy of the beneficiary—any beneficiary no matter how limited his interest—is to have the account taken, to surcharge and falsify the account, and to require the trustee to restore to the trust estate any deficiency which may appear when the account is taken. The liability is strict. The account must be taken down to the date on which it is rendered. That is why there is no question of "stopping the clock". 13–050

If the beneficiary is dissatisfied with the way in which the trustee has carried out his trust—if, for example, he considers that the trustee has negligently failed to obtain all that he should have done for the benefit of the trust estate, then he may surcharge the account. He does this by requiring the account to be taken on the footing of wilful default. In this context "wilful default" bears a special and unusual meaning; 13–051

---

49 *Moschi v Lep Air Services Ltd* [1973] A.C. 331.

it means merely lack of ordinary prudence or due diligence.[50] The trustee is made to account, not only for what he has in fact received, but also for what he might with due diligence have received. Since the trustee is, in effect, charged with negligence, and the amount by which the account is surcharged is measured by the loss occasioned by his want of skill and care, the analogy with common law damages for negligence is almost exact.[51] Although he is a fiduciary, his duty of care is not a fiduciary duty.[52] In this context it must be right to adopt the common law rules of causation and remoteness of damage to their fullest extent. The trustee's liability is enforced in the course of taking the trust account rather than by an action for damages, but the obligation of skill and care is identical to the common law duty of care.

13–052 *Target Holdings Ltd v Redferns* was concerned with the other side of the account. Where the beneficiary complains that the trustee has misapplied trust money, he falsifies the account, that is to say, he asks for the disbursement to be disallowed. If, for example, the trustee lays out trust money in an unauthorised investment which falls in value, the beneficiary will falsify the account by asking the court to disallow both the disbursement and the corresponding asset on the other side of the account. The unauthorised investment will then be treated as having been bought with the trustee's own money and on his own behalf. He will be required to account to the trust estate for the full amount of the disbursement – not for the amount of the loss. That is what is meant by saying that the trustee is liable to restore the trust property; and why common law rules of causation and remoteness of damage are out of place.

13–053 If the unauthorised investment has appreciated in value, then the beneficiary will be content with it. He is not obliged to falsify the account which the trustee renders; he can always accept it. (It goes without saying that the trustee cannot simply "borrow" the trust money to make a profitable investment for his own account and then rely on the fact that the investment was unauthorised to avoid bringing the transaction into the account. He must account for what he has done with the trust money, not merely for what he has properly done with it.) Where the beneficiary accepts the unauthorised investment, he is often said to affirm or adopt the transaction. That is not wholly accurate. The beneficiary has a right to elect, but it is merely a right to decide whether to complain or not.

13–054 Where the beneficiary accepts the unauthorised investment, the account must be taken as if the investment were fully authorised in every respect. The investment is shown as a trust asset and the cost of acquisition as an authorised disbursement. But the converse is equally true. Where the beneficiary elects to falsify the account, the unauthorised investment is not shown as an asset, the disbursement is disallowed, and the trustee is accountable in every respect as if he had not disbursed the money. He is liable to restore the money to the trust estate; as notionally restored it remains subject to all the trusts powers and provisions of the trust as if it had never been disbursed; and the account is taken accordingly.

13–055 All this is elementary, but it provides the solution to the problem in *Target Holdings Ltd v Redferns*. The solicitor held the plaintiff's money in trust for the plaintiff but with its authority to lay it out in exchange for an executed mortgage and the documents of title. He paid it away without obtaining these documents. This was an unauthorised application of trust money which entitled the plaintiff to falsify the account. The disbursement must be disallowed and the solicitor treated as accountable as if the money were still in his client account and available to be laid out in the manner directed. It was later so laid out. The plaintiff could not object to the acquisition of the mortgage or the disbursement by which it was obtained; it was an authorised application of what must be treated as trust money notionally restored to the trust estate on the taking of the account. To put the point another way; the trustee's obligation to restore the trust property is not an obligation to restore it in the very form in which he disbursed it, but an obligation to restore it in any form authorised by the trust.

13–056 Lord Millett's analysis leaves intact Lord Browne-Wilkinson's finding that although a trustee who disposes of trust property in an unauthorised transaction comes under an immediate liability to restore the property, the quantum of the trustee's liability is not determined at the date of breach. However, this does not mean that the court can look at events occurring after the breach to see whether the

---

50 See e.g. *Re Chapman* [1896] 2 Ch. 763.

51 See *Henderson v Merrett Syndicates Ltd* [1995] 2 A.C. 145 at 205 per Lord Browne-Wilkinson.

52 See *Permanent Building Society v Wheeler* (1994) 14 A.C.S.R. 109 at 157–158 per Ipp J. approved in *Bristol & West B. S. v. Mothew* [1997] 2 WLR 436 at 448–449.

beneficiaries would ultimately have suffered the same loss anyway.[53] Rather, its significance lies in the fact that the court can look to see whether the trustee has rectified matters in an authorised fashion since the date of breach.[54] Also, if the trustee has not done this, the value of her obligation to hand over the property will vary according to its current market value, or, where the property is money, according to the amount of interest accrued on the money between the date of breach and the date of judgment.

Lord Millett's analysis was considered by the High Court of Australia in *Youyang Pty Ltd v Minter Ellison Morris Fletcher*,[55] the facts of which were materially identical to those of *Target Holdings*, with the important difference that the defaulting trustee in *Youyang* never "cured" the breach of trust it had committed. Citing Lord Millett's article, the court distinguished *Target Holdings* on this ground and ordered the trustee to pay the whole amount of its unauthorised disbursements as compensation,[56] although some of the trust money would have been lost even if the trustee had complied with its instructions. **13–057**

The result and reasoning in *Youyang* encouraged the claimant lender in *AIB Group (UK) Plc v Mark Redler & Co Solicitors*[57] to make the same argument. Again, the facts of *AIB* were materially identical to those of *Target Holdings*, with the difference that the defendants had not put things right by the time that proceedings were issued. The claimant sought to distinguish *Target Holdings* on the ground that the breach of trust had not been "cured" by the defendants; it also argued that the cases were distinct because in *AIB* the transaction in respect of which the lender had advanced its money had never relevantly been "completed". For the reasons set out in the following excerpt, however, the Supreme Court rejected both of these arguments. **13–058**

AIB Group (UK) Plc v Mark Redler & Co Solicitors

Supreme Court [2015] A.C. 1503

The defendant solicitors acted for the claimant bank in connection with a remortgage advance of £3.3 million on the security of the borrowers' home, which was then worth £4.25 million. The claimant instructed the solicitors that an existing mortgage over the property securing two loans totalling £1.5 million by Barclays Bank should be discharged and that a first charge over the property in the claimant bank's favour should be acquired before the funds were paid over. The solicitors negligently paid only one of the Barclays loans, worth £1.2 million, out of the advance, and paid the rest of the advance to the borrowers. Barclays' mortgage therefore remained as a first charge on the property to secure repayment of the £300,000 it was still owed, and the claimant's charge had to be registered as a second charge. The borrowers defaulted and became insolvent, the property was sold for £1.2 million after a collapse in the property market, and the claimant received only £900,000 after Barclays had been paid. **13–059**

The claimant sued the solicitors for £2.4 million, arguing that they had committed a breach of trust when they disbursed the £3.3 million without obtaining a first charge on the property in accordance with their instructions; that they were therefore liable to reconstitute the trust fund in full, subject to a credit for the £900,000 which had been recovered. The solicitors replied that if there had been a breach of trust (which they denied), their liability should be limited to the loss in value of the claimant's security caused by the solicitors' partial failure to pay off Barclays, quantified as the sum paid to Barclays from the sale proceeds (£300,000). **13–060**

---

[53] *Cocker v Quayle* (1830) 1 Russ. & M. 535.

[54] M. Conaglen, "Explaining *Target Holdings v Redferns*" (2010) J.Eq. 288, noting that the question whether the trustee has cured her breach in an authorised way is a different question from whether the beneficiaries have adopted her unauthorised actions, a point misunderstood in J. Edelman, "Money Awards of the Cost of Performance" (2010) 4 J.Eq. 122, 128.

[55] (2003) 212 C.L.R. 484, noted S. Elliott and J. Edelman "*Target Holdings* Considered in Australia" (2003) 119 L.Q.R. 545.

[56] (2003) 212 C.L.R. 484 at [45]–[48].

[57] [2014] UKSC 58; [2015] A.C. 1503.

13-061 The trial judge held that the solicitors had committed a breach of trust, but that they had partially satisfied the conditions on which the money could legitimately have been released, and payment to the borrowers had therefore been a breach of trust only to the extent that the solicitors had received a security that was worth £300,000 less than it should have been. The claimant's proper remedy was therefore restoration of that amount. The Court of Appeal upheld this result but on different reasoning. The court held that payment of the entire £3.3 million had been a breach of trust. Following *Target*, however, the measure of compensation payable by the solicitors should be calculated by asking what loss had been caused by the breach of trust. This should be done by asking the counterfactual question, what would have happened if there had been no breach of trust? The answer was that Barclays would have been paid off in full, the claimant would have acquired a first charge, and would have recovered the whole of the proceeds when the property was sold. Hence the only recoverable loss which the claimant had suffered was £300,000. This result and reasoning were upheld by the Supreme Court.

13-062 LORD TOULSON (with whom LORD NEUBERGER, LADY HALE, LORD WILSON agreed; LORD REED gave a concurring judgment): . . . The determination of this appeal involves two essential questions. The more important question in the appeal is whether Lord Browne-Wilkinson's statement in *Target Holdings* of the fundamental principles which guided him in that case should be affirmed, qualified or (as the bank would put it) reinterpreted. Depending on the answer to that question, the second is whether the Court of Appeal properly applied the correct principles to the facts of the case.

13-063 Two main criticisms have been made of Lord Browne-Wilkinson's approach. They have been made by a number of scholars, most recently by Professor Charles Mitchell in a lecture on "Stewardship of Property and Liability to Account" delivered to the Chancery Bar Association on 17 January 2014,[58] in which he described the Court of Appeal's reasoning in this case as incoherent. He expressed the hope that "if the case reaches the Supreme Court their Lordships will recognise that Lord Browne-Wilkinson took a false step in *Target* when he introduced an inapt causation requirement into the law governing . . . substitutive performance claims." He added that if it is thought too harsh to fix the solicitors in this case with liability to restore the full amount of the loan (subject only to a deduction for the amount received by the sale of the property), the best way to achieve this is "not to bend the rules governing substitutive performance claims out of shape", but to use the Trustee Act 1925, section 61, to relieve them from some or all of their liability.

13-064 The primary criticism is that Lord Browne-Wilkinson failed to recognise the proper distinctions between different obligations owed by a trustee and the remedies available in respect of them. The range of duties owed by a trustee include:

(1) a custodial stewardship duty, that is, a duty to preserve the assets of the trust except insofar as the terms of the trust permit the trustee to do otherwise;
(2) a management stewardship duty, that is, a duty to manage the trust property with proper care;
(3) a duty of undivided loyalty, which prohibits the trustee from taking any advantage from his position without the fully informed consent of the beneficiary or beneficiaries.

13-065 Historically the remedies took the form of orders made after a process of accounting. The basis of the accounting would reflect the nature of the obligation. The operation of the process involved the court having a power, where appropriate, to "falsify" and to "surcharge".

13-066 According to legal scholars whose scholarship I have no reason to doubt, in the case of a breach of the custodial stewardship duty, through the process of an account of administration in common form, the court would disallow (or falsify) the unauthorised disposal and either require the trust fund to be reconstituted in specie or order the trustee to make good the loss in monetary terms. The term "substitutive compensation" has come to be used by some to refer to a claim for the value of a trust asset dissipated without authority. (See the erudite judgment in *Agricultural Land Management Ltd v Jackson (No.2)*[59] of Edelman J., who attributes authorship of the term to Dr Steven Elliott.)

13-067 In a case of breach of a trustee's management stewardship duty, through the process of an action on the basis of wilful default, a court could similarly falsify or surcharge so as to require the trustee to make good the loss resulting from the breach. The phrase "wilful default" is misleading because, as Brightman

[58] [Editors' note: this lecture has been published as C. Mitchell, "Stewardship of Property and Liability to Account" [2014] Conv. 215.]

[59] [2014] WASC 102.

L.J. explained in *Bartlett v Barclays Bank Trust Co. Ltd (Nos 1 and 2)*,[60] conscious wrongdoing is not required. In this type of case the order for payment by the trustee of the amount of loss is referred to by some as "reparative compensation", to differentiate it from "substitutive compensation", although in a practical sense both are reparative compensation.

In a case of breach of the duty of undivided loyalty, there are possible alternative remedies. If the trustee has benefited from it, the court will order him to account for it on the application of the beneficiary. In *Bristol and West Building Society v Mothew*[61] Millett L.J. described such relief as "primarily restitutionary or restorative rather than compensatory". Alternatively, the beneficiary may seek compensation in respect of his loss. 13-068

The history of the account of profits is more complex than this summary might suggest, and the whole concept of equitable compensation has developed and become far more prominent in the law since *Nocton v Lord Ashburton*. However, what I have said is sufficient to identify the main criticism advanced against Lord Browne-Wilkinson's approach in *Target Holdings*. It is said that he treated equitable compensation in too broad-brush a fashion, muddling claims for restitutive compensation with claims for reparative compensation. 13-069

The relevant principle, it is suggested, in a case of unauthorised dissipation of trust funds is that "the amount of the award is measured by the objective value of the property lost, determined at the date when the account is taken and with the benefit of hindsight", per Millett N.P.J. in *Libertarian Investments Ltd v Hall*.[62] In determining the value of what has been lost, the court must take into account any offsetting benefits received, but it is not relevant to consider what the trustee ought to have done. The court is concerned only with the net value of the lost asset. 13-070

. . . According to the bank's argument, [the solicitors are] . . . responsible for loss which it would have suffered on the judge's findings if they had done what they were instructed to do. This involves effectively treating the unauthorised application of trust funds as creating an immediate debt between the trustee and the beneficiary, rather than conduct meriting equitable compensation for any loss thereby caused. I recognise that there are statements in the authorities which use that language to describe the trustee's liability. For example, in *Ex parte Adamson*,[63] James and Baggallay L.JJ. said that the Court of Chancery never entertained a suit for damages occasioned by fraudulent conduct or for breach of trust, and that the suit was always for "an equitable debt, or liability in the nature of a debt". This was long before the expression "equitable compensation" entered the vocabulary. Equitable monetary compensation for what in that case was straightforward fraud was clothed by the court in the literary costume of equitable debt, the debt being for the amount of the loss caused by the fraud. Whatever label is used, the question of substance is what gives rise to or is the measure of the "equitable debt or liability in the nature of a debt", or entitlement to monetary compensation, and what kind of "but for" test is involved. It is one thing to speak of an "equitable debt or liability in the nature of a debt" in a case where a breach of trust has caused a loss; it is another thing for equity to impose or recognise an equitable debt in circumstances where the financial position of the beneficiaries, actual or potential, would have been the same if the trustee had properly performed its duties. 13-071

. . . There are arguments to be made both ways, as the continuing debate among scholars has shown, but absent fraud, which might give rise to other public policy considerations that are not present in this case, it would not in my opinion be right to impose or maintain a rule that gives redress to a beneficiary for loss which would have been suffered if the trustee had properly performed its duties. 13-072

The same view was expressed by Professor Andrew Burrows,[64] where he applauded *Target Holdings* for impliedly rejecting older cases that may have supported the view that the accounting remedy can operate differently from the remedy of equitable compensation. Despite the powerful arguments advanced by Lord Millett and others, I consider that it would be a backward step for this court to depart from Lord Browne-Wilkinson's fundamental analysis in *Target Holdings* or to "re-interpret" the decision in the manner for which the bank contends. 13-073

---

60 [1980] Ch. 515 at 546.
61 [1998] Ch. 1.
62 [2014] 1 HKC 368 at [168].
63 (1878) 8 Ch.D. 807 at 807 and 819.
64 In Burrows and Peel (eds), *Commercial Remedies*, 2003, pp.46–47.

13-074 All agree that the basic right of a beneficiary is to have the trust duly administered in accordance with the provisions of the trust instrument, if any, and the general law. Where there has been a breach of that duty, the basic purpose of any remedy will be either to put the beneficiary in the same position as if the breach had not occurred or to vest in the beneficiary any profit which the trustee may have made by reason of the breach (and which ought therefore properly to be held on behalf of the beneficiary). Placing the beneficiary in the same position as he would have been in but for the breach may involve restoring the value of something lost by the breach or making good financial damage caused by the breach. But a monetary award which reflected neither loss caused nor profit gained by the wrongdoer would be penal.

13-075 The purpose of a restitutionary order is to replace a loss to the trust fund which the trustee has brought about. To say that there has been a loss to the trust fund in the present case of £2.5m by reason of the solicitors' conduct, when most of that sum would have been lost if the solicitors had applied the trust fund in the way that the bank had instructed them to do, is to adopt an artificial and unrealistic view of the facts.

13-076 I would reiterate Lord Browne-Wilkinson's statement, echoing McLachlin J.'s judgment in *Canson*, about the object of an equitable monetary remedy for breach of trust, whether it be sub-classified as substitutive or reparative. As the beneficiary is entitled to have the trust properly administered, so he is entitled to have made good any loss suffered by reason of a breach of the duty.

13-077 A traditional trust will typically govern the ownership-management of property for a group of potential beneficiaries over a lengthy number of years. If the trustee makes an unauthorised disposal of the trust property, the obvious remedy is to require him to restore the assets or their monetary value. It is likely to be the only way to put the beneficiaries in the same position as if the breach had not occurred. It is a real loss which is being made good. By contrast, in *Target Holdings* the finance company was seeking to be put in a better position on the facts (as agreed or assumed for the purposes of the summary judgment claim) than if the solicitors had done as they ought to have done.

13-078 Other considerations reinforce my view that the House of Lords did not take a wrong step in *Target Holdings*.

13-079 Most critics accept that on the assumed facts of *Target Holdings* the solicitors should have escaped liability. But if causation of loss was not required for them to be liable, some other way had to be found for exonerating them from liability (unless the court was to use section 61 of the 1925 Act as a deus ex machina). The solution suggested by the bank is that the solicitors in *Target Holdings* should be treated as if the moneys which had been wrongly paid out had remained in or been restored to the solicitors' client account and had then been properly applied after the solicitors had obtained the necessary paperwork. There is something wrong with a state of the law which makes it necessary to create fairy tales.

13-080 As to the criticism of the passage in *Target Holdings* where Lord Browne-Wilkinson said that it would be "wrong to lift wholesale the detailed rules developed in the context of traditional trusts" and apply them to a bare trust which was "but one incident of a wider commercial transaction involving agency", it is a fact that a commercial trust differs from a typical traditional trust in that it arises out of a contract rather than the transfer of property by way of gift. The contract defines the parameters of the trust. Trusts are now commonly part of the machinery used in many commercial transactions, for example across the spectrum of wholesale financial markets, where they serve a useful bridging role between the parties involved. Commercial trusts may differ widely in their purpose and content, but they have in common that the trustee's duties are likely to be closely defined and may be of limited duration. Lord Browne-Wilkinson did not suggest that the principles of equity differ according to the nature of the trust, but rather that the scope and purpose of the trust may vary, and this may have a bearing on the appropriate relief in the event of a breach. Specifically, Lord Browne-Wilkinson stated that he did not cast doubt on the fact that monies held by solicitors on client account are trust monies, or that basic equitable principles apply to any breach of such trust by solicitors. What he did was to identify the basic equitable principles. In their application, the terms of the contract may be highly relevant to the question of fact whether there has been a loss applying a "but for" test, that is, by reference to what the solicitors were instructed to do. If the answer is negative, the solicitors should not be required to pay restitutive monetary compensation when there has in fact been no loss resulting from their breach. That is not because special rules apply to solicitors, but because proper performance of the trustee's obligations to the beneficiary would have produced the same end result.

13-081 I agree with the view of Professor David Hayton, in his chapter "Unique Rules for the Unique Institution, the Trust" in Degeling & Edelman (eds), *Equity in Commercial Law* (2005), pp.279–308, that in circumstances such as those in *Target Holdings* the extent of equitable compensation should be the same as

> if damages for breach of contract were sought at common law. That is not because there should be a departure in such a case from the basic equitable principles applicable to a breach of trust, whether by a solicitor or anyone else. (If there were a conflict between the rules of equity and the rules of the common law, the rules of equity would prevail by reason of section 49(1) of the Senior Courts Act 1981, derived from the provisions of the Judicature Act 1875.) Rather, the fact that the trust was part of the machinery for the performance of a contract is relevant as a fact in looking at what loss the bank suffered by reason of the breach of trust, because it would be artificial and unreal to look at the trust in isolation from the obligations for which it was brought into being. I do not believe that this requires any departure from proper principles.
>
> There remains the question whether the Court of Appeal properly applied the reasoning in *Target Holdings* to the facts of the present case. It was argued on behalf of the bank that this case falls within Lord Browne-Wilkinson's statement that "[u]ntil the underlying commercial transaction has been completed, the solicitor can be required to restore to the client account monies wrongly paid away." **13–082**
>
> This argument constricts too narrowly Lord Browne-Wilkinson's essential reasoning. Monetary compensation, whether classified as restitutive or reparative, is intended to make good a loss. The basic equitable principle applicable to breach of trust, as Lord Browne-Wilkinson stated, is that the beneficiary is entitled to be compensated for any loss he would not have suffered but for the breach. In this case, proper performance of the obligations of which the trust formed part would have resulted in the solicitors paying to Barclays the full amount required to redeem the Barclays mortgage, and, as Patten L.J. said, the bank would have had security for an extra £300,000 or thereabouts of its loan. **13–083**
>
> When Lord Browne-Wilkinson spoke of completion he was talking about a commercial transaction. The solicitors did not "complete" the transaction in compliance with the requirements of the CML Handbook. But as a commercial matter the transaction was executed or "completed" when the loan monies were released to the borrowers. At that moment the relationship between the borrowers and the bank became one of contractual borrower and lender, and that was a fait accompli. The Court of Appeal was right in the present case to understand and apply the reasoning in *Target Holdings* as it did. **13–084**

Lord Toulson's reasoning in *AIB*, like Lord Browne-Wilkinson's reasoning in *Target Holdings*, attaches special significance to the fact that the case concerned a trust of short duration created as an incident of a commercial arrangement between the parties. It is hard to make out the scope of this idea, to discern when the *Target Holdings / AIB* rule applies and when it does not. Nor can the answer to this question be inferred from the content of their Lordships' rule, since they did not clearly explain this either. Nor can it be said that the law has been made clearer by two more recent decisions of the Court of Appeal where these issues have arisen. **13–085**

iii. Further Developments

The first of these is *Main v Giambrone & Law (a firm)*.[65] This concerned a scheme to build apartments in Italy that were sold "off-plan" to purchasers in the UK and Ireland. Only a few apartments were built and most of the disappointed buyers rescinded their purchase contracts. They were unable to recover their deposits from the sellers, however, and so they sued the solicitors' firm which had made the legal arrangements. After signing preliminary contracts, the buyers had transferred their deposits to the solicitors who had held them on trust, with authority to release them only on the issue of a guarantee issued by a certain type of bank. Guarantees had then been given by a different, less secure, type of bank but the solicitors had released the deposits anyway. The solicitors argued that following *AIB* they would be liable to reconstitute the trust funds only if their failure to comply with the trust terms had caused the purchasers to lose their deposits and on the facts it had made no difference what kind of **13–086**

65 [2017] EWCA Civ 1193; [2018] P.N.L.R. 2, discussed in P. Davies (2018) 134 L.Q.R. 165 and S. Williams "Equitable Compensation, Trustees, and Disobedience in the Court of Appeal" [2021] Conv. 13.

bank had issued the guarantees because on the events which had occurred no liability would have arisen under the guarantees issued by any bank.

13-087 This argument was rejected by the Court of Appeal which distinguished *Target* and *AIB* and said that *Giambrone* did not fall within the scope of the rules they laid down. So the case was governed by the traditional rules and causation was irrelevant. Jackson LJ said that the key difference between the three cases was that the solicitors in *Target* and *AIB* had owed what he called "a duty to take active steps" whereas the solicitors in *Giambrone* had not.[66] However, the judge did not clearly explain why the factual dissimilarities between the tasks performed by the firms should have justified making a different kind of award in *Giambrone*.

13-088 *Target* and *AIB* were also considered in *Auden McKenzie (Pharma Division) Ltd v Patel*,[67] where the defendant director had caused the claimant company to make unauthorised payments against bogus invoices submitted by other companies controlled by the director as part of a scheme to evade tax. David Richards LJ could "see no reason why there should be a difference"[68] between the case and *Holland v HMRC*,[69] where members of the Court of Appeal and Supreme Court had reaffirmed a line of older cases in which the traditional rules governing trustee liability to reconstitute misapplied trust funds had been applied to directors who had caused their companies to make unauthorised dividend payments. In *Patel*, the court refused summary judgment because it was at least arguable that the defendant director could rely on a "want of causation" defence by analogy with *AIB*. However, David Richards LJ doubted whether this argument would succeed on a full trial. One reason was that it was unclear that the rule laid down in *AIB* rather than the rule laid down in *Holland* should apply in *Patel*.[70] Another was that *Target* and *AIB* allow a defendant to disprove causation by leading evidence either that the claimant has "obtained the full benefit for which it bargained" between the date of breach and the date of judgment or that "if the trustee had fully performed its obligations, the loss would have been less than the amount of the unauthorised payment made by the trustee".[71] However, the defendant's argument in *Patel* was different because it depended on positing a counterfactual situation in which no breach of duty had occurred. So it was not an argument of the kind contemplated by the courts in *Target* and *AIB*.

13-089 Obviously, decisions of the senior appellate court are binding on lower courts. However, *Target* and *AIB* are not so well reasoned, and their departures from previous authority are not so clearly justified, that it is easy to identify the content and scope of the rules they lay down. The courts in *Giambrone* and *Patel* appear to have found this difficult and they displayed little enthusiasm for following *Target* and *AIB*. Instead, they took a narrow view of the circumstances in which departures from the traditional rules are permitted, distinguishing *Target* and *AIB* on grounds that seem strained, and they also took a narrow view of the types of argument that these decisions permit defendants to make. This has made it harder to state the law as it now stands and harder to predict what the English courts will do next.

---

66 [2017] EWCA Civ 1193; [2018] P.N.L.R. 2 at [60]–[61].
67 [2019] EWCA Civ 2291; [2020] W.T.L.R. 1133.
68 Ibid at [58].
69 [2009] EWCA Civ 625; [2010] Bus. L.R. 259; [2010] UKSC 51; [2011] Bus. L.R. 111..
70 [2019] EWCA Civ 2291; [2020] W.T.L.R. 1133 at [5]–[59].
71 Ibid at [49].

B. Reparation Claims

13–090 Reparation claims are claims that trustees should make good loss caused by their breaches of duty,[72] including the loss of a chance to avoid a detriment or make a gain,[73] using a "but-for" causation test in all cases, whether the breach was innocent, negligent or fraudulent.[74] Canadian authorities also indicate that such claims are subject to the principle of novus actus interveniens,[75] and that where the beneficiaries have become aware that their trustees are not to be trusted, losses flowing from clearly unreasonable behaviour by the beneficiaries thereafter will be judged to have been caused by this behaviour and not by the breach.[76]

13–091 A reparation claim might be brought, for example, where a trustee fails to exhibit an appropriate degree of care in negligently making an authorised investment which subsequently declines in value,[77] or again, where she has failed to do something, e.g. to collect the rents payable on the trust property,[78] or to diversify investments,[79] or to sell particular assets,[80] or to monitor the activities of a 99% owned company, as in *Bartlett v Barclays Bank Trust Co Ltd (No.2)*,[81] which is excerpted below.[82] In cases of this sort, it must be shown that the loss could not have occurred, but for the trustee's failure to do what no reasonable trustee (viz., a properly informed trustee exhibiting the due standard of care) could have failed to do. Proving this can be difficult,[83] but it seems that a claim would lie where trustees positively decide to take specific action, e.g. to sell particular shares as soon as practicable, and then fail to implement their decision without any conscious reason. Another way of analysing this situation, however, would be to draw an analogy with the case where a trust instrument requires a particular original investment to be sold as soon as practicable. If the trustees fail to perform this duty, then a substitutive performance claim will lie against them for the amount that would have been realised if they had sold investment within a reasonable time.[84]

13–092 In the *Bartlett* case, Brightman LJ thought that where trustees are ordered to pay money to make good the harm caused to the beneficiaries by the trustees' negligence, the award is "not readily

---

72 *Partington v Reynolds* (1858) 4 Drew 253 at 255–256; *Dowse v Gorton* [1891] A.C. 190 at 202; *Re Stevens* [1898] 1 Ch. 162 at 170; *Elder's Trustee and Executor Co Ltd v Higgins* (1963) 113 C.L.R. 426 at 453; *Fales v Canada Permanent Trust Co* [1977] 2 S.C.R. 302 at 320.

73 *Sanders v Parry* [1967] 1 W.L.R. 753 at 767; *Nestlé v National Westminster Bank Plc* [1993] 1 W.L.R. 1260 at 1269; *Colour Control Centre Pty Ltd v Ty*, N.S.W. Sup. Ct. (Eq. Div.) 24 July 1995; *Bank of New Zealand v New Zealand Guardian Trust Co Ltd* [1999] 1 N.Z.L.R. 664 at 685–686.

74 *Target Holdings Ltd v Redferns* [1996] A.C. 421 at 436; *Collins v Brebner* [2000] Lloyds Rep. P.N. 587; *Hulbert v Avens* [2003] EWHC 76 (Ch) at [56]; *Gwembe Valley Development Co Ltd v Koshy (No.3)* [2003] EWCA Civ 1048; [2004] 1 B.C.L.C. 131 at [147]. But cf. *Bairstow v Queen's Moat Houses Plc* [2001] EWCA Civ 712; [2001] 2 B.C.L.C. 531 at [53]–[54]. On the question whether reparation claims are subject to a remoteness cap, see S.B. Elliott, "Remoteness Criteria in Equity" (2002) 65 M.L.R. 588; and also *Olszanecki v Hillocks* [2002] EWHC 1997 (Ch); [2004] W.T.L.R. 975.

75 *Hodgkinson v Simms* [1994] 3 S.C.R. 377 at 443; *Waxman v Waxman* (2004) 7 I.T.E.L.R. 162 at [663].

76 *Canson Enterprises Ltd v Boughton & Co* [1991] 3 S.C.R. 534 at 554, endorsed in *Corporaçion del Cobre de Chile v Sogemin Metals Ltd* [1997] 1 W.L.R. 1396 at 1403–1404. See too *Lipkin Gorman v Karpnale Ltd* [1992] 4 All E.R. 331 at 361.

77 In these circumstances no question can arise of the beneficiaries choosing whether to adopt or reject the transaction: the investment forms part of the trust estate, but the trustee may be personally liable to pay compensation for the loss caused by her negligence: *Re Salmon* (1888) 42 Ch.D. 351 at 369, 371.

78 *M'Donnel v White* (1865) 9 HLC 570 at 584.

79 *Nestlé v National Westminster Bank* [1993] 1 W.L.R. 1265 at 1281; *Re Mulligan* [1998] 1 N.Z.L.R. 181.

80 *Wight v Olswang (No.2)* [2000] W.T.L.R. 783, reversed [2001] W.T.L.R. 291; *Re Ambrazevicius Estate* (2002) 164 Man. R. (2d) 5.

81 [1980] Ch. 515. See also *Zhang Hong Li v DBS Bank (Hong Kong) Ltd* (2019) 22 H.K.C.F.A.R. 392 at [125]–[127].

82 At paras 13–097 to 13–110.

83 Consider *Nestlé v National Westminster Bank* [1993] 1 W.L.R. 1265 and *Daniel v Tee* [2016] EWHC 1538 (Ch); [2016] 4 W.L.R. 115.

84 *Fry v Fry* (1859) 27 Beav. 144; *Fales v Canada Permanent Trust Co* (1976) 70 D.L.R. (3d) 257 at 274.

distinguishable from damages except with the aid of a powerful legal microscope".[85] This comment was later echoed by Millett LJ in *Bristol & West BS v Mothew*, who held that:[86]

> Equitable compensation for breach of the duty of skill and care [owed by a fiduciary] resembles common law damages in that it is awarded by way of compensation to the plaintiff for his loss. There is no reason in principle why the common law rules of causation, remoteness of damage and measure of damages should not be applied by analogy in such a case.

13–093 These dicta were followed by Newey J in *Brudenell-Bruce v Moore*,[87] where he held that a trustee who carelessly allows trust property to fall into disrepair is not liable for the costs of reinstatement where these would be much greater than the resulting enhancement of the property's value. In so holding, the judge drew an analogy with *Ruxley Electronics Ltd v Forsyth*,[88] a case concerning compensatory liability for breach of contract.

13–094 It is a controversial question whether trustees and other fiduciaries who harm their principals by their negligent acts or omissions should be treated in the same way as contract-breakers or tortfeasors at common law, or whether the fact that they are fiduciaries justifies treating them more stringently. When considering this question, it is important to distinguish clearly between substitutive performance claims and reparation claims, and to bear in mind that either type of claim might lie on some sets of facts, e.g. where trustees make an unauthorised negligent investment. As Millett LJ stresses in the passage quoted above, analogies with tort claims are simply inapt if a substitutive performance claim is brought, but we may legitimately ask whether a reparation claim should be governed by rules of causation, remoteness and contributory negligence which are identical with, or more claimant-friendly than, the rules which apply to tort claims for compensatory damages.

13–095 The authorities are divided on this point. Some stress that a fiduciary and her principal are not "independent and equal actors, concerned primarily with their own self-interest" but parties in a special relationship under which one "pledges itself to act in the best interest of the other", so that "when breach occurs, the balance favours the person wronged".[89] Others deny that there is a valid reason to treat a trustee or other fiduciary differently from anyone else who injures another person by her negligence, and that "regardless of the doctrinal underpinning, plaintiffs should not be able to recover higher damage awards merely because their claim is characterised as a breach of fiduciary duty, as opposed to breach of contract or tort".[90]

---

85 [1980] Ch. 515 at 545.

86 [1998] Ch. 1 at 18, adopting *Permanent BS v Wheeler* (1994) 11 W.A.R. 187 at 237. See too *Bank of New Zealand v New Zealand Guardian Trust Co Ltd* [1999] 1 N.Z.L.R. 664 at 687; *Hilton v Barker Booth & Eastwood (a firm)* [2005] UKHL 6; [2005] 1 W.L.R. 567 at [29]; *Langlands v SG Hambros Trust Co (Jersey) Ltd* [2007] EWHC 627 (Ch) at [25].

87 [2014] EWHC 3679 (Ch) at [144]–[155].

88 [1996] A.C. 344.

89 *Canson Enterprises Ltd v Boughton & Co* [1991] 3 S.C.R. 534 at 543, per McLachlin J, quoted with approval in *Youyang Pty Ltd v Minter Ellison Morris Fletcher* (2003) 212 C.L.R. 484 at [40]. See too *Norberg v Wynrib* [1992] 2 S.C.R. 226 at [272], quoted with approval in *Pilmer v Duke Group Ltd (In Liquidation)* (2001) 207 C.L.R. 165 at [71]; *Maguire v Makaronis* (1997) 188 C.L.R. 449 at 473. The argument that equity should exert prophylactic pressure on fiduciaries by stringent treatment of their breaches of skill and care as well as their breaches of fiduciary duty has been made by Joshua Getzler in three articles: "Equitable Compensation and the Regulation of Fiduciary Relationships" in P. Birks and F.D. Rose (eds), *Restitution and Equity: Resulting Trusts and Equitable Compensation* (Mansfield Press, 2000); "Duty of Care" in P. Birks and A. Pretto (eds), *Breach of Trust* (Hart Publishing, 2002); "Am I My Beneficiary's Keeper? Fusion and Loss-Based Fiduciary Remedies" in *Equity in Commercial Law* (Law Book Company, 2005).

90 *Martin v Goldfarb* (1998) 41 O.R. (3d) 161 at 173, per Finlayson JA. See too *Day v Mead* [1987] 2 N.Z.L.R. 443 at 451; *Canson Enterprises Ltd v Boughton & Co.* [1991] 3 S.C.R. 534 at 585–589, per La Forest J; *Waxman v Waxman* (2004) 7 I.T.E.L.R. 162 at 660–662; J. Edelman and S. B. Elliott, "Money Remedies against Trustees" (2004) 18 Tru L.I. 116, 119–122.

This debate is often conducted in all-or-nothing terms, but in our view the best way forward is for the courts to acknowledge that it can be appropriate to treat different kinds of trustee in different ways.[91] For example, there is an important difference between traditional family trusts and modern commercial trusts for absolutely entitled beneficiaries where the parties are on a more equal footing and the management role of the trustee is extensive and complex. In the latter case at least, the justification is much weaker for imposing a more stringent liability for negligent conduct than the trustee would incur at common law. **13–096**

Bartlett v Barclays Bank Trust Co Ltd

Chancery Division [1980] Ch. 515

The claimant sued the trustees for failing to exercise proper supervision over the management of the family company, "BTL", which they controlled through possession of a 99.8 per cent shareholding. Subsequently BTL became a wholly-owned subsidiary of another company, "BTH", which the trustees also controlled through a 99.8 per cent shareholding. The trustees' failure to supervise BTL and then BTH led to the company losing over £1/2 million in a disastrous property speculation. **13–097**

BRIGHTMAN J.: The situation may be summed up as follows. BTH made a large loss as a result of the involvement of itself and BTL in the Old Bailey project. This loss reduced the value of the BTH shares and thereby caused a loss to the trust fund of the 1920 settlement. The bank, had it acted in time, could by reason of its shareholding have stopped the board of BTL embarking on the Old Bailey project; and, had it acted in time, could have stopped the board of BTL and later the board of BTH (it is unnecessary to differentiate) from continuing with the project; and could, had it acted in time, have required BTH to sell its interest in Far to Stock Conversion on the no-loss or small-loss terms which (as I find) were available for the asking. This would not have necessitated the draconian course of threatening to remove, or actually removing, the board in favour of compliant directors. The members of the board were reasonable persons, and would (as I find) have followed any reasonable policy desired by the bank had the bank's wishes been indicated to the board. The loss to the trust fund could have been avoided (as I find) without difficulty or disruption had the bank been prepared to lead, in a broad sense, rather than to follow. **13–098**

What, then, was the duty of the bank and did the bank fail in its duty? It does not follow that because a trustee could have prevented a loss it is therefore liable for the loss. The questions which I must ask myself are: (i) what was the duty of the bank as the holder of 99.8 per cent of the shares in BTL and BTH? (2) Was the bank in breach of duty in any and if so what respect? (3) If so, did that breach of duty cause the loss which was suffered by the trust estate? (4) If so, to what extent is the bank liable to make good that loss? In approaching these questions, I bear in mind that the attack on the bank is based, not on wrongful acts, but on wrongful omissions, that is to say, non-feasance not misfeasance. **13–099**

The cases establish that it is the duty of a trustee to conduct the business of the trust with the same care as an ordinary prudent man of business would extend towards his own affairs.[92] In applying this principle, Lindley L.J. added in *Re Whiteley*:[93] **13–100**

> ". . . care must be taken not to lose sight of the fact that the business of the trustee, and the business which the ordinary prudent man is supposed to be conducting for himself, is the business of investing money for the benefit of persons who are to enjoy it at some future time, and not for the sole benefit of the person entitled to the present income. The duty of a trustee is not to take such care only as a prudent man would take if he had only himself to consider; the duty rather is to take such care as an ordinary prudent man would take if he were minded to make an investment for the benefit of other people for whom he felt morally bound to provide. The is the kind of business the ordinary prudent man is supposed to be engaged in; and unless this is borne in mind the standard of a trustee's duty

---

91 See further C.E.F. Rickett, "Compensating for Loss in Equity: Choosing the Right Horse for Each Course" in P. Birks and F.D. Rose (eds), *Restitution and Equity* (Informa, 2000), Vol.1; D.J. Hayton "Unique Rules for the Unique Institution, the Trust" in *Equity in Commercial Law* (Law Book Company, 2005).

92 See *Re Speight* (1883) 22 Ch.D. 727 at 739, per Jessel M.R., and 762, per Bowen L.J.; affirmed on appeal (1883) 9 App. Cas. 1., and see Lord Blackburn at 19.

93 (1886) 33 Ch.D. 347 at 355.

will be fixed too low; lower than it has ever yet been fixed, and lower certainly than the House of Lords or this Court endeavoured to fix it in [*Re Speight*]."

13–101 . . . If the trust had existed without the incorporation of BTL, so that the bank held the freehold and leasehold properties and other assets of BTL directly on the trusts of the settlement, it would in my opinion have been a clear breach of trust for the bank to have hazarded trust money in the Old Bailey development project in partnership with Stock Conversion. The Old Bailey project was a gamble, because it involved buying into the site at prices in excess of the investment values of the properties, with no certainty or probability, with no more than a chance, that planning permission could be obtained for a financially viable redevelopment, that the numerous proprietors would agree to sell out or join in the scheme, that finance would be available on acceptable terms, and that the development would be completed, or at least become a marketable asset, before the time came to start winding up the trust. However one looks at it, the project was a hazardous speculation on which no trustee could properly have ventured without explicit authority in the trust instrument. I therefore hold that the entire expenditure in the Old Bailey project would have been incurred in breach of trust, had the money been spent by the bank itself. The fact that it was a risk acceptable to the board of a wealthy company like Stock Conversion has little relevance.

13–102 I turn to the question, what was the duty of the bank as the holder of shares in BTL and BTH? I will first answer this question without regard to the position of the bank as a specialist trustee, to which I will advert later. The bank, as trustee, was bound to act in relation to the shares and to the controlling position which they conferred, in the same manner as a prudent man of business. The prudent man of business will act in such manner as is necessary to safeguard his investment. He will do this in two ways. If facts come to his knowledge which tell him that the company's affairs are not being conducted as they should be, or which put him on enquiry, he will take appropriate action. Appropriate action will no doubt consist in the first instance of enquiry of and consultation with the directors, and in the last but most unlikely resort, the convening of a general meeting to replace one or more directors. What the prudent man of business will not do is to content himself with the receipt of such information on the affairs of the company as a shareholder ordinarily receives at annual general meetings. Since he has the power to do so, he will go further and see that he has sufficient information to enable him to make a responsible decision from time to time either to let matters proceed as they are proceeding, or to intervene if he is dissatisfied. This topic was considered by Cross J. in *Re Lucking's Will Trusts*.[94] In that case nearly 70 per cent of the shares in the company were held by two trustees, L and B, as part of the estate of the deceased; about 29 per cent belonged to L in his own right, and 1 per cent belonged to L's wife. The directors in 1954 were Mr and Mrs L and D, who was the manager of the business. In 1956 B was appointed trustee to act jointly with L. The company was engaged in the manufacture and sale of shoe accessories. It had a small factory employing about 20 people, and one or two travellers. It also had an agency in France. D wrongfully drew some £15,000 from the company's bank account in excess of his remuneration, and later became bankrupt. The money was lost. Cross J. said this:[95]

> "The conduct of the defendant trustees is, I think, to be judged by the standard applied in *Re Speight*, namely, that a trustee is only bound to conduct the business of the trust in such a way as an ordinary prudent man would conduct a business of his own. Now, what steps, if any, does a reasonably prudent man who finds himself a majority shareholder in a private company take with regard to the management of the company's affairs? He does not, I think, content himself with such information as to the management of the company's affairs as he is entitled to as shareholder, but ensures that he is represented on the board. He may be prepared to run the business himself as managing director or, at least, to become a non-executive director while having the business managed by someone else. Alternatively, he may find someone who will act as his nominee on the board and report to him from time to time as to the company's affairs. In the same way, as it seems to me, trustees holding a controlling interest ought to ensure so far as they can that they have such information as to the progress of the company's affairs as directors would have. If they sit back and allow the company to be run by the minority shareholder and receive no more information than shareholders are entitled to, they do so at their risk if things go wrong."

---

94 [1968] 1 W.L.R. 866.
95 [1968] 1 W.L.R. 866 at 874–875.

I do not understand Cross J. to have been saying that in every case where trustees have a controlling interest in a company it is their duty to ensure that one of their number is a director or that they have a nominee on the board who will report from time to time on the affairs of the company. He was merely outlining convenient methods by which a prudent man of business (as also a trustee) with a controlling interest in a private company, can place himself in a position to make an informed decision whether any action is appropriate to be taken for the protection of his asset. Other methods may be equally satisfactory and convenient, depending on the circumstances of the individual case. Alternatives which spring to mind are the receipt of the copies of the agenda and minutes of board meetings if regularly held, the receipt of monthly management accounts in the case of a trading concern, or quarterly reports. Every case will depend on its own facts. The possibilities are endless. It would be useless, indeed misleading, to seek to lay down a general rule. The purpose to be achieved is not that of monitoring every move of the directors, but of making it reasonably probable, so far as circumstances permit, that the trustee or (as in *Re Lucking's Will Trusts*) one of them will receive an adequate flow of information in time to enable the trustees to make use of their controlling interest should this be necessary for the protection of their trust asset, namely the shareholding. The obtaining of information is not an end in itself, but merely a means of enabling the trustees to safeguard the interest of their beneficiaries. 13–103

. . . So far, I have applied the test of the ordinary prudent man of business. Although I am not aware that the point has previously been considered, except briefly in *Re Waterman's Will Trusts*,[96] I am of opinion that a higher duty of care is plainly due from someone like a trust corporation which carries on a specialised business of trust management. A trust corporation holds itself out in its advertising literature as being above ordinary mortals. With a specialist staff of trained trust officers and managers, with ready access to financial information and professional advice, dealing with and solving trust problems day after day, the trust corporation holds itself out, and rightly, as capable of providing an expertise which it would be unrealistic to expect and unjust to demand from the ordinary prudent man or woman who accepts, probably unpaid and sometimes reluctantly from a sense of family duty, the burdens of a trusteeship. Just as, under the law of contract, a professional person possessed of a particular skill is liable for breach of contract if he neglects to use the skill and experience which he professes, so I think that a professional corporate trustee is liable for breach of trust if loss is caused to the trust fund because it neglects to exercise the special care and skill which it professes to have. The advertising literature of the bank was not in evidence (other than the scale of fees) but counsel for the bank did not dispute that trust corporations, including the bank, hold themselves out as possessing a superior ability for the conduct of trust business, and in any event I would take judicial notice of that fact. Having expressed my view of the higher duty required from a trust corporation, I should add that the bank's counsel did not dispute the proposition. 13–104

In my judgment the bank wrongfully and in breach of trust neglected to ensure that it received an adequate flow of information concerning the intentions and activities of the boards of BTL and BTH. It was not proper for the bank to confine itself to the receipt of the annual balance sheet and profit and loss account, detailed annual financial statements and the chairman's report and statement, and to attendance at the annual general meetings and the luncheons that followed, which were the limits of the bank's regular sources of information. Had the bank been in receipt of more frequent information it would have been able to step in and stop, and ought to have stopped, Mr Roberts and the board embarking on the Old Bailey project. That project was imprudent and hazardous and wholly unsuitable for a trust whether undertaken by the bank direct or through the medium of its wholly owned company. Even without the regular flow of information which the bank ought to have had, it knew enough to put it on enquiry. There were enough obvious points at which the bank should have intervened and asked questions. Assuming, as I do, that the questions would have been answered truthfully, the bank would have discovered the gamble on which Mr Roberts and his board were about to embark in relation to the Old Bailey site, and it could have, and should have, stopped the initial move towards disaster, and later on arrested further progress towards disaster. . . . 13–105

I hold that the bank failed in its duty whether it is judged by the standard of the prudent man of business or of the skilled trust corporation. The bank's breach of duty caused the loss which was suffered by the trust estate. If the bank had intervened as it could and should have, that loss would not have been incurred. By "loss", I mean the depreciation which took place in the market value of the BTL and BTH shares, by comparison with the value which the shares would have commanded if the loss on the Old Bailey project 13–106

96 [1968] 1 W.L.R. 866.

had not been incurred, and reduction of dividends through loss of income. The bank is liable for the loss so suffered by the trust estate, except to the extent that I shall heareafter indicate. . . .

13–107 The bank also relies on clause 18 of the settlement. Clause 18 entitled the bank to:

> "act in relation to [BTL] or any other company and the shares securities and properties thereof in such way as it shall think best calculated to benefit the trust premises and as if it was the absolute owner of such shares securities and property."

In my judgment this a clause which confers on the bank power to engage in a transaction which might otherwise be outside the scope of its authority; it is not an indemnity protecting the bank against liability for a transaction which is a breach of trust because it is one that a prudent man of business would have eschewed. . . .

13–108 Section 61 of the Trustee Act 1925 is pleaded. There is no doubt that the bank acted honestly. I do not think it acted reasonably. Nor do I think it would be fair to excuse the bank at the expense of the beneficiaries.

13–109 There remains this defence, which I take from paragraph 26 of the amended pleading:

> "In about 1963 the Old Company purchased a site at Woodbridge Road, Guildford, pursuant to the policy pleaded in paragraph 19 hereof, for the sum of £79,000, and re-sold the same for £350,000 to MEPC Ltd in 1973. The net profit resulting from such sale was £271,000. If, which is denied, the Defendant is liable for breach of trust, whether as alleged in the amended Statement of Claim or otherwise, the Defendant claims credit for such sum of £271,000 or other sum found to be gained in taking any accounts or inquiries."

13–110 The general rule as stated in all the textbooks, with some reservations, is that where a trustee is liable in respect of distinct breaches of trust, one of which has resulted in a loss and the other in a gain, he is not entitled to set off the gain against the loss, unless they arise in the same transaction. . . . The relevant cases are, however, not altogether easy to reconcile. All are centenarians and none is quite like the present. The Guildford development stemmed from exactly the same policy and (to a lesser degree because it proceeded less far) exemplified the same folly as the Old Bailey project. Part of the profit was in fact used to finance the Old Bailey disaster. By sheer luck the gamble paid off handsomely, on capital account. I think it would be unjust to deprive the bank of this element of salvage in the course of assessing the cost of the shipwreck. My order will therefore reflect the bank's right to an appropriate set-off. . . .

C. Accountability

13–111 At the core of an express trust is the trustees' duty to account to the beneficiaries for what they have done with the trust property. Beneficiaries are entitled to ask their trustees for such an account as a matter of right, but they can also obtain a court order directing the trustees to account for the trust property in the course of proceedings to enforce their rights to (specific or substitutive) performance of the trustees' primary duties or to recover reparative compensation for losses flowing from the trustees' breaches of duty. In this context, the taking of the account is the first step in a two-step process that starts with the identification of deficits in the trust fund (usually undertaken by a Chancery Master or district judge) and is followed by the issuing of judgment for the balance found to be due. Sitting as a judge in the Hong Kong Final Court of Appeal, Lord Millett NPJ explained this process in *Libertarian Investments Ltd v Hall*,[97] in a passage that is excerpted below.

13–112 Before the Judicature Acts, beneficiaries could only make hostile claims against their trustees by bringing an administration suit. This was a suit for the judicial execution of the trust, asking the court to assume responsibility for the trust's performance. Beneficiaries can still bring full execution proceedings, but they can now also bring narrower proceedings for discrete relief by asking the court for

[97] (2013) 16 H.K.C.F.A.R. 681; noted L. Ho and R. Lee (2014) 130 L.Q.R. 542. See too *Ultraframe (UK) Ltd v Fielding* [2005] EWHC 1638 (Ch); [2007] W.T.L.R. 835 at [1513].

an order that the trustees should present an account of their dealings for judicial scrutiny, adding the common form plea for administration of the trust estate "if and so far as necessary".[98]

Two types of accounting order can be made in cases where the beneficiaries seek to fix the trustees with a compensatory liability.[99] An order for an account in common form is the most common, as the name suggests. Such accounts must generally "be able to show from period to period (the frequency of accounts is not fixed) how the trust assets have been dealt with, including what distributions and disposals have taken place" and a beneficiary reading them "must be in a position to assess whether the trust assets conform with the trust instrument [and] that the class of assets held is appropriate for the trust."[100] Typically, therefore, the trustees are directed to submit records which identify the original trust property, what the trustees have subsequently received, what investments they have made, what they have distributed to the beneficiaries, what they have disbursed for costs and expenses, and what remains. These accounts can be challenged by the beneficiaries, but the fact that a court has ordered trustees to present accounts in this form need not imply that the trustees have done anything wrong, and the beneficiaries need not allege any wrongdoing before such an order will be made: they simply need to establish that the trustee is an accounting party.[101] **13–113**

In contrast, an order for an account on the basis of wilful default is always grounded on the trustees' misconduct, at least one incident of which must be pleaded and proved by the beneficiaries.[102] The term "wilful default" is a misleading one in this context since it extends to all breaches of duty, including those committed carelessly as well as those committed fraudulently.[103] Accounts on the footing of wilful default require the trustees to account not only for what they have received but also for what they would have received if they had not committed a breach of duty.[104] Beneficiaries alleging that their trustees have negligently failed to collect assets which they should have collected must therefore bring proceedings for an account on the footing of wilful default. Proceedings for a common account are not an appropriate or sufficient way of advancing such a claim because "in substance [this would be tantamount to making] a claim for damages without making any allegation of a breach of duty".[105] **13–114**

In all cases where there is a dispute between trustees and beneficiaries as to whether the trustees have acted properly, "the beneficiary carries the burden of proving surcharges and the [trustee] carries the burden of proving [her] discharge"; hence the trustee must be able to document each item, and presumptions may be made against her if she has not kept proper records or has destroyed them.[106] **13–115**

---

98 *Iliffe v Trafford* [2002] W.T.L.R. 507 at [8].

99 As discussed by Austin J in *Glazier Holdings Pty Ltd v Australian Men's Health Pty Ltd (No.2)* [2001] NSWSC 6. See too S. Elliott, "Accounting in Equity" in H.G. Hanbury, "Forms of Account against Executors and Trustees" (1936) 108 L.Q.R. 365; J. McGhee (ed.), *Snell's Equity*, 34th edn (Sweet & Maxwell, 2019) paras 20.12–20.27; *The Business and Property Courts of England & Wales Chancery Guide 2022* at [29.4] and [29.11], *https://www.judiciary.uk/announcements/the-chancery-guide-2022/*.

100 *Henchley v Thompson* [2017] EWHC 225 (Ch); [2017] W.T.L.R. 1289 at [62].

101 *Partington v Reynolds* (1858) 4 Drew 253 at 255–256: "it is sufficient that the defendant holds the office". See too *Dowse v Gordon* [1891] A.C. 190 at 204; *Attorney General v Cocke* [1988] Ch. 414 at 420.

102 *Knott v Cottee* (1852) 16 Beav. 77 at 79; *Re Stevens* [1898] 1 Ch. 162 at 170; *Re Duckwari Plc* [1999] Ch. 253 at 265; *White v Thompson* [2011] NSWCA 161 at [46].

103 *Walker v Symonds* (1818) 3 Swan. 1 at 69; *Re Chapman* [1896] 2 Ch. 763 at 776 and 779–780. See too J.H. Stannard "Wilful Default" [1979] Conv. 345, esp. at 348.

104 *Gordon v Gonda* [1955] 2 All E.R. 762 at 768; *Re Tebbs* [1976] 2 All E.R. 858; *Armitage v Nurse* [1998] Ch. 241 at 252; *Garcia v Delfino* [2003] NSWSC 1001 at [31]–[33].

105 *Sinclair v Glatt* [2015] EWHC 1673 (Admin); [2015] Lloyd's Rep. F.C. 481 at [36]. It is possible, however, for an account taken in common form to be surcharged with an amount received by the trustees which they are not authorised to take themselves but which they have not entered into the accounts as trust income, as would be the case e.g. if the trustees receive dividends paid on shares held on trust.

106 *Exsus Travel Ltd v Turner* [2014] EWCA Civ 1331 at [22]. See too *Campbell v Gillespie* [1899] 1 Ch. 225 at 229; *Campbell v Hogg* [1930] 3 D.L.R. 673; *Sinclair v Sinclair* [2009] EWHC 926 (Ch) at [39]–[41].

If the trustee can show that he paid trust funds away in an authorised transaction which entailed no breach of duty he will be discharged from his duty to hold the relevant funds for the beneficiaries.[107] However, where the court decides, following its scrutiny of the accounts, that the trustees owe the beneficiaries a personal liability, different forms of order can be made against them, according to the nature of the trust. Where the trust is absolute and there is no need to reconstitute the fund, the court can simply order them to transfer property or pay money to the beneficiaries.[108] Where the trust is still on foot, the trustees will be ordered to reconstitute the fund in a proper state, or where they have been replaced by new trustees, to transfer assets or pay money to the new trustees, to be held by them under the terms of the trust.[109]

13–116 The different types of claim which can be brought against trustees are mediated through proceedings for an account in different ways. In the case of a substitutive performance claim where the trustees have made an unauthorised distribution, the court will not permit the trustees to enter the distribution into the accounts as an outgoing.[110] Instead, they will be treated as though they have spent their own money and kept the trust assets intact. The accounts will be "falsified" to delete the unauthorised outgoing, and the trustees will be ordered to produce the relevant trust property *in specie* or pay a money substitute out of their own pockets.[111] Reparation claims are brought into the conceptual scheme of the accounts in a different way. The loss claimed by the beneficiaries is translated into an accounting item by "surcharging" the trustees with the amount of the loss as if the trustees had already received this amount for the beneficiaries. They must then pay an equivalent amount into the trust fund out of their pockets in order to balance the accounts.[112]

Libertarian Investments Ltd v Hall

Hong Kong Court of Final Appeal (2013) 16 H.K.C.F.A.R. 681 at [167]–[172]

13–117 LORD MILLETT N.P.J.: . . . It is often said that the primary remedy for breach of trust or fiduciary duty is an order for an account, but this is an abbreviated and potentially misleading statement of the true position. In the first place an account is not a remedy for wrong. Trustees and most fiduciaries are accounting parties, and their beneficiaries or principals do not have to prove that there has been a breach of trust or fiduciary duty in order to obtain an order for account. Once the trust or fiduciary relationship is established or conceded the beneficiary or principal is entitled to an account as of right. Although like all equitable remedies an order for an account is discretionary, in making the order the court is not granting a remedy for wrong but enforcing performance of an obligation.

13–118 In the second place an order for an account does not in itself provide the plaintiff with a remedy; it is merely the first step in a process which enables him to identify and quantify any deficit in the trust fund and seek the appropriate means by which it may be made good. Once the plaintiff has been provided with an account he can falsify and surcharge it. If the account discloses an unauthorised disbursement the plaintiff may falsify it, that is to say ask for the disbursement to be disallowed. This will produce a deficit which the

---

107 *Pitt v Holt* [2011] EWCA Civ 197; [2012] Ch. 132 at [99]: "The interest of a beneficiary in the trust property continues until it is brought to an end by an act of the trustees done in accordance with the terms of the trust (or the general law)." See too *Nightingale v Lawson* (1784) 1 Cox 23; *Worral v Harford* (1802) 8 Ves. Jun. 4 at 8; *Soar v Ashwell* [1893] 2 Q.B. 390 at 394; *McGill v Huang* [2021] EWHC 938 (Ch) at [51].

108 *Target Holdings Ltd v Redferns* [1996] A.C. 421 at 435; *Roxborough v Rothmans of Pall Mall Australia Ltd* (2001) 208 C.L.R. 516 at [67].

109 *Partridge v Equity Trustees Executors and Agency Co Ltd* (1947) 75 C.L.R. 149; *Hillsdown Plc v Pensions Ombudsman* [1997] 1 All E.R. 862 at 897; *Chellaram v Chellaram (No.2)* [2002] EWHC 632 (Ch); [2002] 3 All E.R. 17 at [159]; *Patel v Brent LBC (No.2)* [2003] EWHC 3081 (Ch);[2004] W.T.L.R. 577 esp. at [32].

110 *Re Smith* [1896] 1 Ch. 71 at 77; *Re Biss* [1903] 2 Ch. 40.

111 *Knott v Cottee* (1852) 16 Beav. 77 at 79–80; *Re Bennion* (1889) 60 L.T. 859; *Re Salmon* (1889) 42 Ch. D. 351 at 357. Where trustees have received trust income but have failed to record this, the accounts can be "surcharged" by the amount and the trustees can be ordered to produce the very moneys they received or to pay an equivalent sum.

112 *Meehan v Glazier Holdings Pty Ltd* (2002) 54 N.S.W.L.R. 146 at 149–150; *Re Ambrazevicius Estate* (2002) 164 Man. R. (2d) 5.

defendant must make good, either in specie or in money. Where the defendant is ordered to make good the deficit by the payment of money, the award is sometimes described as the payment of equitable compensation; but it is not compensation for loss but restitutionary or restorative. The amount of the award is measured by the objective value of the property lost determined at the date when the account is taken and with the full benefit of hindsight.

But the plaintiff is not bound to ask for the disbursement to be disallowed. He is entitled to ask for an inquiry to discover what the defendant did with the trust money which he misappropriated and whether he dissipated it or invested it, and if he invested it whether he did so at a profit or a loss. If he dissipated it or invested it at a loss, the plaintiff will naturally have the disbursement disallowed and disclaim any interest in the property in which it was invested by treating it as bought with the defendant's own money. If, however, the defendant invested the money at a profit, the plaintiff is not bound to ask for the disbursement to be disallowed. He can treat it as an authorised disbursement, treat the property in which it has been invested as acquired with trust money, and follow or trace the property and demand that it or its traceable proceeds be restored to the trust in specie. **13–119**

If on the other hand the account is shown to be defective because it does not include property which the defendant in breach of his duty failed to obtain for the benefit of the trust, the plaintiff can surcharge the account by asking for it to be taken on the basis of "wilful default", that is to say on the basis that the property should be treated as if the defendant had performed his duty and obtained it for the benefit of the trust. Since ex hypothesi the property has not been acquired, the defendant will be ordered to make good the deficiency by the payment of money, and in this case the payment of "equitable compensation" is akin to the payment of damages as compensation for loss. **13–120**

In an appropriate case the defendant will be charged, not merely with the value of the property at the date when it ought to have been acquired or at the date when the account is taken, but at its highest intermediate value. This is on the footing either that the defendant was a trustee with power to sell the property or that he was a fiduciary who ought to have kept his principal informed and sought his instructions. **13–121**

At every stage the plaintiff can elect whether or not to seek a further account or inquiry. The amount of any unauthorised disbursement is often established by evidence at the trial, so that the plaintiff does not need an account but can ask for an award of the appropriate amount of compensation. Or he may be content with a monetary award rather than attempt to follow or trace the money, in which case he will not ask for an inquiry as to what has become of the trust property. In short, he may elect not to call for an account or further inquiry if it is unnecessary or unlikely to be fruitful, though the court will always have the last word. **13–122**

D. Interest

Beneficiaries can ask for statutory awards of pre-judgment interest on claims against trustees which count as claims for the recovery of a debt or damages for the purposes of the Senior Courts Act 1981 s.35A.[113] However it is far more common for beneficiaries to ask the courts to exercise their equitable jurisdiction to award interest. Usually, the courts make an award of simple interest,[114] but they may award compound interest if they think this is warranted. This has been done e.g. where a trustee has disobeyed a direction to accumulate or distribute income and has retained trust income in their own hands,[115] and where a trustee has used trust funds in their own business, compound interest then being awarded not as a punishment but as fairly representing the profits which the trustee is presumed to have made.[116] Australian judges have held that the court may also award compound **13–123**

---

113 As noted in *Glenn v Watson* [2018] EWHC 2016 (Ch) at [540](5); *Re Axminster Carpets Group Retirement Benefits Plan* [2021] EWHC 1652 (Ch); [2022] Pens. L.R. 1 at [326]–[327]. Interest awarded under s.35A can only be simple interest, but the rate is at the court's discretion.

114 *Lloyds Banking Group Pensions Trustees Ltd v Lloyds Bank Plc* [2018] EWHC 2839 (Ch); [2019] Pens. L.R. 5 at [462]: "It is still the normal practice of the court to award simple rather than compound interest."

115 *Raphael v Boehm* (1805) 11 Ves. Jun. 92; *Re Emmet's Estate* (1881) 17 Ch.D. 142.

116 *Burdick v Garrick* (1870) L.R. 5 Ch. App. 233 at 241; *Wallersteiner v Moir (No.2)* [1975] Q.B. 373 at 397; *Westdeutsche Landesbank Girozentrale v Islington LBC* [1996] A.C. 669 at 701–702; *Harris v Digital Pulse Pty Ltd* (2003) 56 N.S.W.L.R. 298 at [303]–[304]; *Grimaldi v Chameleon Mining NL (No.2)* (2012) 200 F.C.R. 296 at [548]–[552] and [753].

interest in cases of fraud or gross misconduct, even when the trustee has derived no personal benefit from the breach of trust,[117] but English judges have refused to make such awards on the grounds that they would be "penal",[118] a stance that is hard to reconcile with their willingness to award compound interest in fraud cases outside the trust context.[119]

13–124 The court also has a discretion to set the rate of interest payable by a trustee. Judicial practices in this regard were surveyed, and a new approach taken, by Nugee J in *Watson v Kea Investments Ltd*, whose analysis and findings were endorsed on appeal.[120] *Watson* concerned claims against several defendants, none of whom was an express trustee, but one of whom was liable as a constructive trustee for knowing receipt of funds paid in breach of fiduciary duty. The extent of this defendant's liability to pay interest was decided on the basis that the rules governing interest awards against knowing recipients are the same as those governing interest awards against express trustees who have lost trust property in unauthorised transactions.[121]

13–125 Nugee J and the Court of Appeal found that the rates of interest awarded in such cases have changed with time, not because the courts' objectives in making such awards have changed but because market interest rates have changed and so have the investment practices which trustees are expected to follow. When making an interest award in a case where a trust fund has been depleted in an unauthorised transaction, but the defendant trustee has derived no personal benefit from this and has acted honestly, the courts have awarded interest as a proxy for the beneficiaries' loss suffered because the "missing" property was not invested for their benefit. The interest rate set in cases of this kind is commonly called the "standard" or "trustee rate". Matters are different where a trustee has improperly used trust funds for their own purposes, as here the courts' goal has been to award interest as a proxy for the gain which the trustee has made or can reasonably be deemed to have made. The rate of interest set in such cases is called the "higher" or "commercial rate".

13–126 Applying these principles in nineteenth century cases, the courts generally concluded that interest should be awarded at 4% simple in a standard case,[122] the rationale having been that 4% was the average return on government debt, the main authorised trust investment at that time.[123] However, in the changing economic circumstances of the twentieth century, it came to be felt that 4% was no longer an accurate proxy for the beneficiaries' loss, and other rates were used, still pegged to lending rates, such as the rate allowed from time to time on the court's short-term investment account.[124]

---

117 *Southern Cross Commodities Pty Ltd (In Liq) v Ewing* (1987) 11 A.C.L.R. 818 at 843; *Duke Group Ltd (In liq) v Pilmer* (1999) 73 S.A.S.R. 64 at [237]; *Themis Holdings Pty Ltd v Canehire Pty Ltd* (2014) 17 I.T.E.L.R. 75 at [243].

118 *AG v Alford* (1855) 4 De G.M. & G. 843 (where Lord Cranworth LC reduced the award made by Stuart V-C in *AG v Alford* (1854) 2 Sm. & Giff. 488); *Burdick v Garrick* (1870) L.R. 5 Ch. App. 233 at 241 and 243; *Vyse v Foster* (1872) L.R. 8 Ch. App. 309 at 333; *Belmont Finance Corp Ltd v Williams Furniture Ltd* [1980] 1 All E.R. 393 at 419; *Wallersteiner v Moir (No.2)* [1975] Q.B. 373 at 388. See also S. Elliott, "Rethinking Interest on Withheld and Misapplied Trust Money" [2001] Conv. 313, 317–318.

119 As to this, see e.g. *President of India v La Pintada Compania Navigacion SA* [1985] A.C. 104 at 116; *Westdeutsche Landesbank Girozentrale v Islington LBC* [1996] A.C. 669 at 696 and 701.

120 [2018] EWHC 2483 (Ch); affd [2019] EWCA Civ 1759; [2019] 4 W.L.R. 145. Nugee J's findings on liability were given in an earlier judgment: [2018] EWHC 2016 (Ch), but his earlier judgment also contains some observations about interest awards at [545]–[553].

121 See too *Belmont Finance Corp Ltd v Williams Furniture Ltd* [1980] 1 All E.R. 393 at 419; *El Ajou v Dollar Land Holdings Plc (No.2)* [1995] 2 All E.R. 213 at 224; *CMOC Sales and Marketing Ltd v Persons Unknown* [2018] EWHC 2230 (Comm); [2019] Lloyd's Rep. F.C. 62 at [165].

122 *AG v Alford* (1855) 4 De G.M. & G. 843 at 853; *Fletcher v Green* (1864) 33 Beav. 426 at 430; *Re Emmet's Estate* (1881) 17 Ch.D. 142 at 150–151.

123 *Re Lambert* [1897] 2 Ch. 169 at 180.

124 *Bartlett v Barclays Bank Trust Co Ltd* [1980] Ch. 515 at 546–547. At that time the court's short-term investment account rate stood at 15%. Under the Court Funds Rules 2011 this account is now called the special account.

Following *Watson*, findings to this effect must be treated with caution. There McCombe LJ agreed with Nugee J that in most standard cases it is now likely to be more appropriate to peg the rate of interest not to market lending rates but to a standardised marker of trust investment returns. This is because it is now:[125] **13–127**

> unrealistic to assume that the trust fund, duly replaced, would have been placed (in breach of trust, one might add) on deposit with no regard to capital accretion; it would not have been so placed. That is simply not the real world of trustee investment and it is also unlike the world in the 19th century when trustees' investment powers were substantially more restricted.

For these reasons, the judges concluded that in standard cases a preferable approach will now usually be to set a rate that reflects the total return that would have been achieved by investment of the "missing" funds, taking both capital growth and income into account. Hence the Court of Appeal upheld the award made by Nugee J, fixed at the rate of 6.5% per annum compounded annually. When setting this rate, the judge consciously took:[126] **13–128**

> a broad brush approach based on what a person with the general characteristics of the claimant might have received by way of investment on trustee investments, not a rate that reflects what the individual claimant would itself have done [with the relevant funds].

In arriving at the 6.5% compound rate, the judge relied on information published by STEP and Asset Risk Consultants on the performance of "medium risk" trust investments during the relevant period,[127] which McCombe LJ agreed was evidence that "illustrated precisely what a deprived fund of this type would have done with the misappropriated money."[128]

Turning to the "higher" or "commercial" rates that were historically awarded, 5% was generally set during the nineteenth century and much of the twentieth.[129] The basis for this was that trustees who used trust funds in their businesses could be expected to have earned at least 5%,[130] and where there was reason to think that a trustee had earned more, an account of profits could be awarded as an alternative to a 5% interest award (although this had the disadvantage that it might require a costly enquiry into the trustee's business affairs[131]). Then in *Wallersteiner v Moir (No.2)*,[132] decided at a time of high inflation, the 5% rate was thought to be too low because it failed to reflect the market lending rate. Instead, the court held that the defendant company director (to whom the rules affecting trustees were held to apply) should be charged with compound interest at the commercial rate of 1% above the minimum lending rate (or official bank rate) with yearly rests. It remains to be seen what effect *Watson* has on the courts' thinking about the setting of higher rates against trustees who have **13–129**

125 [2019] EWCA Civ 1759; [2019] 4 W.L.R. 145 at [73]. For Nugee J's approach at first instance see [2018] EWHC 2483 (Ch) at [46]–[49].
126 [2018] EWHC 2016 (Ch) at [549], followed in *Van Zuylen v Whiston-Dew* [2021] EWHC 2219 (Ch) at [318].
127 [2018] EWHC 2483 (Ch) at [14]–[17] and [51]–[55].
128 [2019] 4 W.L.R. 145 at [74]. Cf. *Lewin on Trusts*, 20th edn (2020) para 41.060, n.225: "If the trust fund would in fact have diminished in value during the period if properly invested, such that the breach caused no loss, there would be appear to be good grounds in principle for declining to award interest."
129 *AG v Alford* (1855) 4 De G.M. & G. 843 at 852; *Re Jones* (1883) 49 L.T. 91; *Re Waterman's WT* [1952] W.N. 538; *Gordon v Gonda* [1955] 1 W.L.R. 885.
130 *Re Roberts* (1880) 14 Ch.D. 49 at 52.
131 See Lord Brougham's comments in *Docker v Somes* (1834) 2 My. & K. 655 at 664–665; and also S. Elliott "Rethinking Interest on Withheld and Misapplied Trust Money" [2001] Conv. 313, 319–320.
132 [1975] Q.B. 373 at 388, 399 and 406. See too *Belmont Finance Corp v Williams Furniture Ltd (No.2)* [1980] 1 All E.R. 393 at 418; *O'Sullivan v Management Agency and Music Ltd* [1985] Q.B. 428; *Re Duckwari (No.2)* [1999] Ch. 268 at 273.

improperly used trust funds for their own purposes, but it may be that in this context, too, they might consider awarding a rate that takes account of capital accretion as well as income yield, depending on the nature of the trustee's activities.

13–130 The foregoing discussion concerns awards of interest where trust funds have been misapplied in an unauthorised transaction. In *Davies v Ford*,[133] the judge held that cases where no misapplication of trust property has occurred, and where an award of reparative compensation has been made for breach of duty, are more closely akin to cases where awards of common law damages have been made and that for this reason the rules governing interest awards on such claims are the same as those governing statutory awards of pre-judgment interest on common law damages, as described in *Carrasco v Johnson*.[134] There, Hamblen LJ said inter alia that interest is awarded to compensate claimants for being kept out of money which ought to have been paid to them rather than as compensation for damage done or to deprive defendants of profit they may have made from the use of the money, and that the court will consider the position of persons with the claimants' general attributes, but will not attend to their particular attributes or any special position in which they may have been.

13–131 In *Watson* McCombe LJ said that interest awards against trustees should not be calculated by reference to *Carrasco* because the principles stated there were not designed to respond to the unique character of the trustee-beneficiary relationship.[135] However, this difference of opinion can be resolved by saying that different approaches should be taken to the setting of interest rates in different types of case—that it may be appropriate to treat interest awards in cases where trustees are ordered to reconstitute depleted trust funds differently from interest awards made in cases are ordered to pay reparative compensation, and that even in reparation cases, reference to *Carrasco* may be more apt in some cases (e.g. where the claim is for negligence) than in others (e.g. where the claim is for breach of fiduciary duty[136]).

3. Defences

A. Power of the Court to Relieve Trustees from Personal Liability

Trustee Act 1925 s.61

13–132 If it appears to the court that a trustee, whether appointed by the court or otherwise, is or may be personally liable for any breach of trust, whether the transaction alleged to be a breach of trust occurred before or after the commencement of this Act, but has acted honestly and reasonably, and ought fairly to be excused for the breach of trust and for omitting to obtain the directions of the court in the matter in which he committed such a breach, then the court may relieve him either wholly or partly from personal liability for the same.

13–133 The main purpose of this statutory rule[137] has always been to shield honest trustees from liability.[138] However, all three of the conditions identified in the section must be satisfied before relief can be

[133] [2021] EWHC 2550 (Ch) at [211]–[212].
[134] [2018] EWCA Civ 87.
[135] [2019] 4 W.L.R. 145 at [68]–[70].
[136] Cf. *Tuke v Hood* [2021] EWHC 74 (Comm) at [34]–[35] where the judge followed *Watson* when making an award of 4.5% compound interest on an award of equitable compensation for breach of fiduciary duty by a defendant who was not a trustee.
[137] The section was originally enacted as the Judicial Trustees Act 1896 s.3.
[138] For historical surveys, see Lord Maugham, "Excusable Breaches of Trust" (1898) 14 L.Q.R. 159; L. Sheridan, "Excusable Breaches of Trust" (1955) 19 Conv. (N.S.) 420; C. Stebbings, *The Private Trustee in Victorian England* (Cambridge University Press, 2002), Ch.6; J. Lowry and R. Edwards, "Excuses" in P. Birks and A. Pretto (eds), *Breach of Trust* (2002).

granted,[139] i.e. the trustee must not only have acted honestly but must also have acted reasonably, and it must also be "fair" to excuse her although the result will be to deny compensation to the beneficiaries. The burden lies on the trustee to prove that all three of these conditions hold.[140] The reference in the section to cases where a trustee "is *or may be* personally liable" should not be understood to mean that a trustee can use the section to obtain immunity in respect of contemplated future actions: these words mean only that relief can be granted in respect of past actions whether or not it has been established in court that these amount to a breach of trust.[141]

The section is broad enough to enable the court to excuse trustees who mismanage trust property[142] and also trustees who make unauthorised distributions to the wrong persons[143] and who make unauthorised acquisitions of property.[144] However, the section empowers the court to relieve trustees from "personal liability" only, and so it does not protect them from proprietary claims by beneficiaries, i.e. claims that property owned by trustees is held subject to the beneficiaries' equitable interests.[145] Appellate courts are generally reluctant to interfere with a lower court's exercise of discretion,[146] but *Santander UK Plc v R.A. Legal Solicitors*,[147] excerpted below, shows that they will do so if the lower court's order rested on an error of law. **13–134**

In the *Santander* case, Briggs LJ rejected Andrew Smith J's finding at first instance that an analogy could be drawn between s.61 and the equivalent relieving provision in the companies legislation under which directors can be said to have acted "reasonably" although they have breached their duty of care to the company.[148] Briggs LJ also held that if a defendant trustee's negligence has increased the risk of loss caused by a fraud perpetrated by a third party then it should not be excused on the basis that the fraud would have been carried through even if the trustee had acted with reasonable care. These findings closed down a possible route to rescuing solicitors from liability to pay the orthodox measure of substitutive compensation in conveyancing cases exemplified by *AIB Group (UK) Plc v Mark Redler & Co Solicitors*,[149] discussed above.[150] **13–135**

A different point arose in two conjoined cases, *P & P Property Ltd v Owen White & Catlin LLP* and *Dreamvar (UK) Ltd v Mishcon de Reya (a firm)*.[151] Both concerned transactions where the seller was a fraudster impersonating the real owner and had no legal title to the property he was purporting to sell. The purchase money was paid by the intending buyers to their solicitors who paid it over to the fraudster's solicitors although the transactions had not been completed because the buyers had not received good title. The fraudster's solicitors then paid it over to the fraudster, who absconded, **13–136**

---

139 *Marsden v Regan* [1954] 1 W.L.R. 423 at 434–435. See too *Mitchell v Halliwell* [2005] EWHC 937 (Ch) at [49] (no relief for honest trustee who unreasonably failed to ensure that beneficiaries took independent advice); *Re Clapham (deceased)* [2005] EWHC 3387 (Ch); [2006] W.T.L.R. 203 at [98] (no relief for honest trustee who carelessly paid trust assets to wrong people).

140 *Re Turner* [1897] 1 Ch. 536; *Ikbal v Sterling Law* [2013] EWHC 3291 (Ch); [2014] P.N.L.R. 9 at [226]; *Santander UK v RA Legal Solicitors* [2014] EWCA Civ 183; [2014] P.N.L.R. 20 at [20]; *Agouman v Leigh Day (a firm)* [2016] EWHC 1324 (QB); [2016] P.N.L.R. 32 at [135].

141 *Re Rosenthal* [1972] 1 W.L.R. 1273.

142 *Re Smith* (1902) 86 L.T. 401.

143 *Re Allsop* [1914] 1 Ch. 1; *Re Wightwick* [1950] 1 Ch. 260; *Re Evans* [1999] 2 All E.R. 777.

144 *Perrins v Bellamy* [1898] 2 Ch. 521, affd [1899] 1 Ch. 797.

145 Contrast the similarly but not identically worded Companies Act 2006 s.1157 which extends to cases where a company director receives an unauthorised disposal of company funds and the company seeks a declaration of ownership: *Dickinson v NAL Realisations (Staffordshire) Ltd* [2019] EWCA Civ 2146; [2020] 1 W.L.R. 1122 at [37]–[44].

146 *Marsden v Regan* [1954] 1 W.L.R. 423.

147 [2014] P.N.L.R. 20; excerpted at paras 13–138 to 13–158.

148 *Santander UK Plc v RA Legal Solicitors* [2013] EWHC 1380 (QB); [2013] P.N.L.R. 24 at [65]–[70].

149 [2014] UKSC 58; [2015] A.C. 1503.

150 See paras 13–018 to 13–085.

151 [2018] EWCA Civ 1082; [2019] Ch. 273.

and the buyers sued both sets of solicitors alleging among other things that the buyers' solicitors had committed a breach of trust because they had been instructed not to transfer the money prior to completion. The buyers' solicitors asked for s.61 relief, which was refused by Patten and Floyd LJJ essentially because the buyers' solicitors were insured and could therefore afford to bear the loss. However, there is much to commend the dissenting judgment of Gloster LJ, who observed that there was no evidence to suggest the fraudster's solicitors did not also carry insurance, and that as between the two firms it was the fraudster's solicitors rather than the buyers' solicitors who should have borne primary responsibility for checking his identity.[152]

13–137 The courts are reluctant to grant relief to a paid trustee but may do so in special circumstances.[153] The taking of legal advice will be a significant consideration if such advice is followed but a breach of trust occurs because the advice was erroneous. Relevant considerations will include the standing of the legal adviser and the value of the property affected by the advice,[154] whether the adviser was given full and accurate information by the trustee,[155] and whether the trustee is herself a solicitor (in which case she cannot shelter unthinkingly behind counsel and still has a duty to consider the matter for herself).[156] If the adviser was negligent then the trustee should sue her to recover the loss for the trust and it seems hardly likely that the court would excuse the trustee if she failed to sue.[157] One must distinguish between trustees obtaining advice on behalf of the trust beneficiaries and trustees obtaining advice for their own personal protection and benefit. In the former case any cause of action arising from negligent advice will be a trust asset so that, if not barred by the limitation period, the beneficiaries could sue for themselves on joining the trustees as co-defendants with the adviser if the trustees refused to sue; in the latter case the beneficiaries generally have no rights against the adviser, being able only to sue the trustees for any breach of trust.[158]

Santander UK Plc v RA Legal Solicitors

Court of Appeal [2014] P.N.L.R. 20

13–138 The claimant bank agreed to lend £150,000 to a borrower for the purpose of buying property. The defendant firm of solicitors undertook the conveyancing for the bank and the borrower, and the claimant transferred the money to the defendant to be held on trust and released to the vendor only when the documents of title had been obtained and a charge in favour of the bank created. The defendants dealt with a second firm of solicitors who fraudulently presented themselves as acting for the vendor. However, the vendor had never agreed to sell the property. On the day before completion, the defendant released the bank's money in the belief that they were completing the sale. However, completion never took place, and the bank never obtained a charge over the property. The money was not recovered from the fraudsters and so the bank sued the defendant solicitors for breach of trust on the basis that it had acted without authority when it had released the funds without completion having taking place.

13–139 Andrew Smith J. held that the defendants had acted in breach of trust, but had done so in the genuine belief that completion was taking place. He excused the defendants from liability under the Trustee Act

---

[152] See also R. Kennedy (2018) 34 P.N. 205, 208: the upshot of the majority's decision is that "property conveyancing solicitors will be invariably left bearing responsibility for property developers' opportunistic and risky endeavours".

[153] *National Trustees Co of Australasia v General Finance Co* [1905] A.C. 373; *Re Windsor Steam Coal Co* [1929] 1 Ch. 151; *Hawkesley v May* [1956] 1 Q.B. 304; *Re Pauling's Settlement Trusts (No.1)* [1964] Ch. 303 (partial relief); *Re Rosenthal* [1972] 1 W.L.R. 1273.

[154] *National Trustees Co of Australasia v General Finance Co* [1905] A.C. 373; *Re Allsop* [1914] 1 Ch. 1 at 13; *Marsden v Regan* [1954] 1 All E.R. 475 at 482; *Wong v Burt* (2004) 7 I.T.E.L.R. 263 at [49]–[58]; *Re Equilift Ltd* [2010] B.P.I.R. 116 at [15].

[155] *Cherney v Neuman* [2011] EWHC 2156 (Ch) at [311].

[156] *Cherney v Neuman* [2011] EWHC 2156 (Ch) at [319].

[157] *National Trustees Co of Australasia v General Finance Co* [1905] A.C. 373.

[158] *Wills v Cooke* (1979) 76 L.S.G. 706; *Parker-Tweedale v Dunbar Bank Plc* [1990] 2 All E.R. 577 at 583. But for exceptions to this rule, see *Hayim v Citibank NA* [1987] A.C 730 at 747–748; *Bradstock Trustee Services Ltd v Nabarro Nathanson* [1995] 1 W.L.R. 1405; *HR v JAPT* [1997] P.L.R. 99.

1925 s.61, reasoning that the bank's loss had been caused by a third party's fraud for which the defendants could not fairly be treated as responsible. The bank successfully appealed from his findings in connection with s.61.

BRIGGS L.J. (with whom ETHERTON C. and PROUDMAN J. agreed): . . . Section 61 of the Trustee Act 1925 has become the principal mechanism by which the law tempers the rigour of a trustee's otherwise strict (i.e. not fault based) liability where a fraudulent intervention in a conveyancing transaction of which the purchaser's solicitor is entirely unaware causes an unauthorised disposal of the lender's advance in breach of trust. It is precisely because of the strictness of the solicitor's trust liability that lenders which are the victims of such fraud prefer to base their claims for recovery upon breach of trust rather than breach of contract or negligence, because both of those causes of action generally require the lender to prove that the solicitor has been guilty of a breach of a duty of care. The formulation now in s.61 dates back at least to the nineteenth century (see s.3 of the Judicial Trustees Act 1896) and applies to all kinds of trustees, lay and professional, in the following terms: 13–140

> "If it appears to the court that a trustee. . . is or may be personally liable for a breach of trust. . ., but has acted honestly and reasonably and ought fairly to be excused for the breach of trust. . ., then the court may relieve him either wholly or partly from personal liability for the same."

Invocation of s.61 involves at least two main stages. First, the trustee must show (the onus being on him) that he has acted both honestly and reasonably. In the context of mortgage fraud, institutional lenders have tended to focus upon the second of those requirements, and to dispute it in individual cases by citing a litany of examples, large and small, of aspects of the handling of the transaction where the solicitor trustee departed from standard or best practice. The present case is no exception, and Abbey's criticisms included matters happening well before and well after the transfer and loss of its advance, with apparent disregard of the question whether those alleged departures from best practice had anything at all to do with its loss. 13–141

In the context of mortgage fraud, this court has interpreted s.61 as requiring the trustee to prove that he acted reasonably only in relation to those aspects of his conduct which are connected with the beneficiary lender's loss. This is best expressed by Sir Andrew Morritt C. in the *Davisons* case:[159] 13–142

> "The section only requires Mr Wilkes (the trustee) to have acted reasonably. That does not, in my view, predicate that he has necessarily complied with best practice in all respects. The relevant action must at least be connected with the loss for which relief is sought and the requisite standard is that of reasonableness not of perfection."

There was considerable debate on this appeal as to precisely what type of "connection" this judicial interpretation of s.61 requires. Mr Pooles submitted that the relevant conduct had to be causative of the loss. Mr Grant submitted that this imposed too narrow a range of relevant conduct, and that the concept of connection should be liberally applied on a case by case basis, rather than by reference to a rigid formula. 13–143

There are, I think, competing policy issues which affect this question. On the one hand, the court should be slow to gloss the general words of a statute, all the more so where it confers a broad discretion. On the other hand, mortgage fraud of this kind occurs in a business context in which those advising the lender and the solicitors, and their respective insurers, need to have reasonable clarity as to the application of s.61, so as to avoid every case having to be taken all the way to trial, with a full investigation of all potentially relevant circumstances, so as to obtain a particular trial judge's discretionary decision. 13–144

It is in my view clear that a strict causation test casts the net too narrowly for the purpose of identifying relevant conduct. In most mortgage fraud cases, the effective, primary or predominant cause of the loss is the third party's fraud rather than the conduct of the solicitor trustee. 13–145

Furthermore, it is also too restrictive to apply a "but for" test which disregards conduct, however unreasonable, on the basis that even if the solicitor had acted reasonably in that respect, the fraud, and therefore the loss, would still have occurred. The current best practice for conveyancing solicitors has evolved over many years, in the light of developing experience, for the purpose (among others) of providing reasonable, albeit not cast-iron, protection from fraud, both to lenders and purchasers. In my judgment it would not be appropriate to exclude as irrelevant conduct which consisted of a departure from best or reasonable 13–146

159 *Davisons Solicitors v Nationwide Building Society* [2012] EWCA Civ 1626; [2013] P.N.L.R. 12 at [48].

practice which increased the risk of loss caused by fraud, even if the court concludes that the fraudster would nonetheless have achieved his goal if the solicitor had acted reasonably.

13–147 In this respect the *Markandan* case provides a useful example.[160] There, the fraudster was an imposter who pretended to be operating a branch office of a well-known firm of solicitors. The purchaser's solicitors failed to check whether that branch office existed: see per Rimer L.J. at [60]. Plainly, that omission increased the risk that the fraudster would succeed in his plan.

13–148 On the other hand, it would in my view extend the net too wide if it accommodated every aspect and detail of the solicitor trustee's conduct which occurred, or played any part in, the process which began with the transfer of the loan money by the lender to the solicitor trustee and ended with its theft by the fraudster. As would appear, the criticisms of RA Legal's conduct in the present case appear to have been pleaded on that broad assumption.

13–149 Between those extremes, it seems to me that some element of causative connection will usually have to be shown, and that conduct (even if unreasonable) which is completely irrelevant or immaterial to the loss will usually fall outside the court's purview under s.61. This is, again, well illustrated by a careful comparison between the *Markandan* and *Davisons* cases. In the former, the Court of Appeal refused relief under s.61 because of two aspects of the solicitor trustee's conduct. The first, which I have already described, plainly increased the risk of the already-planned fraud succeeding. The second was a failure by the trustee solicitor to have regard to an earlier breach of undertaking by the fraudster when parting with the money for a second time. Again, the relevance or materiality of that conduct to the loss is clear. By contrast, although departures from best practice were identified both by the trial judge and by the Court of Appeal in the *Davisons* case, they had no causative significance at all. At [50], the Chancellor concluded that even if Davisons had in all respects acted in accordance with best practice, the impostor would have complied with the requisitions, supplied written undertakings, and still disappeared with the balance of the purchase money. He concluded:

> "the lapse from best practice, if any, did not cause the loss to Nationwide."

It may be said that this part of the Chancellor's analysis was concerned with the second question, namely whether the solicitor trustee ought fairly to be excused. Nonetheless the presence in the first case and absence in the second case of some causative element between the conduct complained of and the lender's loss cannot sensibly be ignored.

13–150 I would, finally, caution against an over-mechanistic application of the requirement to show the necessary connection between the conduct complained of and the lender's loss. There may be highly unreasonable conduct which lies at the fringe of materiality in terms of causation, and only slightly unreasonable conduct which goes to the heart of a causation analysis. It would be wrong in my view to allow this purely mechanistic application of a causation-based test for the identification of relevant conduct to exclude the former from any consideration under s.61.

13–151 An important issue in the present case relates to the standard to be applied to conduct connected with the loss. I have referred to the former Chancellor's summary in the Davisons case, at [48], as that of reasonableness not of perfection. It is well-established that the standard is likely to be higher for a paid than for an unpaid trustee: see *Lewin on Trusts* (18th edn.) at paras 39–145.

13–152 In the present case the judge sought to derive assistance from the jurisprudence about the similarly-worded provisions of s.727(1) of the Companies Act 1985 (now s.1157(1) of the Companies Act 2006), which provides that:

> "If in any proceedings for negligence, default, breach of duty or breach of trust against an officer of a company or a person employed by a company as auditor (whether he is or is not an officer of the company) it appears to the court hearing the case that that officer or person is or may be liable in respect of the negligence, default, breach of duty or breach of trust, but that he has acted honestly and reasonably, and that having regard to all the circumstances of the case (including those connected with his appointment) he ought fairly to be excused for the negligence, default, breach of duty or breach of trust, that court may relieve him, either wholly or partly, from his liability on such terms as it thinks fit."

160 *Lloyds TSB plc v Markandan & Uddin (a firm)* [2012] P.N.L.R. 20.

He referred to *Barings plc v Coopers & Lybrand*,[161] and also to *Maelor-Jones v Heywood-Smith*,[162] as suggesting that something approaching "pervasive and compelling" negligence must be shown before a trustee is cut off from relief under s.61.

The difficulty with equating s.61 with s.727(1), at least for the purpose of interpreting s.61, is that s.727(1) appears to contemplate that a company officer or auditor may have acted honestly and reasonably, even though negligent, whereas s.61 contemplates no such thing in relation to trustees. It would in my judgment be wrong, by any process akin to reverse engineering, to interpret s.61 by reference to the historically more recent and undoubtedly more difficult provisions now to be found in s.727 of the Companies Act 1985. Generally, negligence requires a finding of unreasonable conduct, in the sense that the defendant must be found to have failed to apply reasonable care and skill to the task in hand. In the *Re D'Jan of London* case, Hoffman L.J. said of s.727 that:[163] 13–153

> "It may seem odd that a person found to have been guilty of negligence, which involves failing to take reasonable care, can ever satisfy a court that he acted reasonably. Nevertheless, the section clearly contemplates that he may do so."

No such oddity appears in s.61, and in my view the judge was wrong to equate the two relieving provisions. I consider that the test of reasonableness rather than perfection identified in the *Davisons* case is amply sufficient for comparable cases under s.61, and calls for no further elaboration.

The second main stage of the s.61 analysis, usually described as discretionary, consists of deciding whether the trustee ought fairly to be excused for the breach of trust. This requires that regard be had to the effect of the grant of relief not only upon the trustee, but also upon the beneficiaries.[164] Furthermore, s.61 makes it clear that even if the trustee ought fairly to be excused, the court still retains the discretionary power to grant relief from liability, in whole or in part, or to refuse it. In the context of relief sought by solicitor trustees from liability for breach of trust in connection with mortgage fraud, much may depend at this discretionary stage upon the consequences for the beneficiary. An institutional lender may well be insured (or effectively self-insured) for the consequences of third party fraud. But an innocent purchaser may have contributed his life's savings to the purchase and have no recourse at all other than against his insured solicitor, where for example the fraudster is a pure interloper, rather than a dishonest solicitor in respect of whose fraud the losers may have recourse against the Solicitors' Compensation Fund. 13–154

Relief under s.61 is often described as an exercise of mercy by the court. In my judgment the requirement to balance fairness to the trustee with a proper appreciation of the consequences of the exercise of the discretion for the beneficiaries means that this old-fashioned description of the nature of the s.61 jurisdiction should be abandoned. In this context mercy lies not in the free gift of the court. It comes at a price. 13–155

[His Lordship reviewed the facts of the case and continued:] In the wholly exceptional circumstance that the fraudster was a solicitor, rather than a mere imposter, I am prepared to assume that the fraud would probably have been successfully achieved even if RA Legal had acted reasonably . . . [However, a] conclusion that, but for those aspects where RA Legal's conduct fell seriously and unreasonably short of best practice, the fraud would probably have succeeded by no means leads to the result that those parts of RA Legal's conduct are unconnected with the loss. They all represent departures from a sophisticated regime, worked out over many years, whereby risks of loss to lenders and lay clients are minimised, even if not wholly eradicated. Where solicitors fail, in serious respects, to play their part in that structure, and at the same time are swindled into transferring and then releasing trust money to a fraudster without authority, they cannot expect to persuade the court that it is fair to excuse them from liability, upon the basis that they have demonstrated that they have in all respects connected with that loss, acted reasonably. 13–156

. . . In the present case I have come to the clear conclusion that the particular failures which I have described, beginning with the inadequate making of Requisitions on Title, transferring the completion money without the adoption of the Completion Code by Sovereign, and then failing to deal with the absence of a prior mortgage discharge on the pretended completion, were indeed unreasonable, and sufficiently connected with Abbey's loss. In any event, those failings of RA Legal formed part of a larger 13–157

---

161 [2003] P.N.L.R. 34.

162 (1989) 54 S.A.S.R. 285.

163 *Re D'Jan of London Ltd* [1993] B.C.C. 646.

164 See *Marsden v Regan* [1954] 1 W.L.R. 423 at 434, per Evershed M.R. and *Bartlett v Barclays Trust Co. (No.1)* [1980] Ch. 515 at 538, per Brightman J.

picture of the shoddy performance of a conveyancing transaction from start to finish, which leaves me in no doubt that it would not be fair to excuse the firm from liability, in whole or in part.

13–158 The discretion is of course conferred upon the judge, and falls to be exercised by this court only if the judge has made an error of law, failed to take (and take only) the appropriate matters into account, or otherwise reached an irrational decision. I consider that the judge erred in law in adopting an over-lenient view about the requirement to show reasonable conduct, attributable to an incorrect attempt to construe s.61 by reference to the similar, but by no means identical, provisions in the Companies Act. His conclusion that the failure to obtain from Sovereign its commitment to the Completion Code in advance of the transfer of the completion money was inconsequential was, in my view, an error about a matter of legal analysis. The result is that his exercise of discretion cannot stand. Since RA Legal have not shown that they acted reasonably in all respects connected with Abbey's loss, the discretion does not, strictly, arise at all. But even if it had done, and fell to be undertaken afresh by this court, I would have not have regarded it as fair to grant RA Legal any relief from liability for breach of trust, for the reasons given in the previous paragraph. I would therefore allow the appeal.

B. Exemption Clauses

13–159 The jurisdiction of the court as to pure matters of law cannot be ousted by provisions in a trust deed giving the trustees power to determine all questions arising in the execution of the trusts under the deed.[165] However, the decision of trustees or of a third party can be binding and conclusive on matters of fact, assuming that the specified factual circumstances are conceptually certain,[166] while the decision of someone with expert knowledge in the relevant factual area can conclusively determine an incidental question of construction.[167]

13–160 It is also impermissible for a settlor to oust the jurisdiction of the court by including a clause in the trust deed which prevents the beneficiaries from applying to the court for the ascertainment and protection of their rights or for directions about the construction and exercise of the trustees' powers.[168] Such a clause would effectively render the beneficiaries' rights unenforceable so that it could not be said that a trust existed at all.

13–161 These points aside, a settlor can include a clause in the trust deed exempting the trustees from liability for a breach of trust provided that the trustees' conduct was not dishonest. This rule is established by *Armitage v Nurse*,[169] which concerned an exemption clause in a trust deed which stated that "No trustee shall be liable for any loss or damage which may happen to [the claimant beneficiary's] fund or any part thereof or the income thereof at any time or from any cause whatsoever unless such loss or damage shall be caused by his own actual fraud." The question was whether this clause was effective to absolve the trustees from liability for several pleaded breaches of trust committed when control of land held for the claimant was transferred to a family company run by her mother (who

---

165 *Re Wynn* [1952] Ch. 271.

166 *Re Coxen* [1948] Ch. 747; *Re Jones* [1953] Ch. 125; *Re Wright's Will Trusts* [1981] Law.S. Gaz 841.

167 *The Glazier* (1996) 1 Ll. Rep. 370; *Re Tuck's Settlement Trusts* [1978] Ch. 49; *Dundee General Hospitals Board v Walker* [1952] 1 All E.R. 896.

168 *Adams v Adams* (1882) 1 Ch. 369; *Permanent Trustee Co v Dougall* (1934) 34 S.R. (N.S.W.) 83 at 86–87; *AN v Barclays Private Bank & Trust (Cayman) Ltd* [2007] W.T.L.R. 565 at 597. But cf. *In the Matter of an Application for Information about a Trust* [2013] CA (Bda) 8 Civ, where the Supreme Court of Bermuda held that an information control clause in a trust instrument enabling the trust protector to veto the disclosure of trust information to beneficiaries was not invalid on its face, given: (1) that it did not purport to exclude the court's supervisory jurisdiction over the trust generally; and (2) that other mechanisms were in place to ensure due administration of the trust, viz the trustees were required to have the accounts independently audited; the protector was empowered to obtain financial information from the trustees; and the protector was required to have regard to the interests of the beneficiaries when exercising her supervisory powers.

169 [1998] Ch. 241. See too *Wight v Olswang (No.1)* (1999) 1 I.T.E.L.R. 783; *Wight v Olswang (No.2)* (2000) 2 I.T.E.L.R. 689; *Walker v Stones* [2001] Q.B. 902 at 935, 941; *Bonham v Blake Lapthorn Linell (a firm)* [2006] EWHC 2513 (Ch); [2007] W.T.L.R. 189 at [177].

was also a beneficiary) and her grandmother; the company then farmed the land for the company's benefit. It was alleged that all of this was contrary to the trust terms (which provided that no trust property should "in any circumstances whatsoever be paid or applied beneficially (save for full consideration) or be applied for the benefit whether directly or indirectly of [the claimant's] mother or grandmother"); that the trustees had pursued "a deliberate course of conduct . . . to disregard the [claimant's] interests and subordinate them to the interests of her mother or other members of the family who were not objects of the trust, or at the very least a conscious indifference to [the claimant's] interests"; and that as a result of the company's mismanagement of the land it had fallen in value, and that this had occurred as a consequence of the trustees' failure to take reasonable steps to supervise the company.[170] However it was not alleged that the trustees had been motivated by any dishonest purpose.

The Court of Appeal held that even if the alleged breaches of duty had been committed, the trustees would owe no personal liability because the clause was a valid one and the breaches of duty pleaded by the claimant all fell within its scope. Millett LJ accepted that settlors cannot validly relieve trustees of certain "core" duties, a feature of his judgment discussed elsewhere in this book,[171] but that was not a problem for the defendants because this principle was not infringed by the clause in question. Millett LJ also held that the term "fraud" used in the clause simply meant dishonesty which connoted "at the minimum an intention on the part of the trustee to pursue a particular course of action, either knowing that it is contrary to the interests of the beneficiaries or being recklessly indifferent whether it is contrary to their interests or not".[172] **13–162**

It has since been held that the question whether a trustee has acted "fraudulently" or "dishonestly" for the purposes of similarly worded exemption clauses should be tested against objective standards of conduct and it is irrelevant whether the trustee knows that their conduct would be thought dishonest by other people, i.e. there is no need to show that they have been "self-consciously dishonest".[173] This finding aligns with the still more recent decision of the House of Lords in *Ivey v Genting Casinos (UK) Ltd*,[174] that "objective" rather than "self-conscious" dishonesty is the general test for dishonesty in a criminal context. However, while he accepted that this is now the meaning of "dishonesty" and "fraud" when these terms appear in trustee exemption clauses, the judge in *Sofer v Swissindependent Trustees SA*[175] also followed Lewison J's earlier finding in *Fattal v Walbrook Trustees (Jersey) Ltd* that a professional trustee is not dishonest for the purpose of such a clause where they commit a deliberate breach of trust in the belief that this is for the benefit of the beneficiaries—unless their belief is "so unreasonable that, by any objective standard, no reasonable professional trustee could have thought that what [she] did or agreed to do was for the benefit of the beneficiaries."[176] **13–163**

As English law now stands, therefore, it is permissible for a clause to exempt a trustee from liability for loss arising from negligence of whatever kind, in contrast to Scots law, which follows other civil law systems in distinguishing "gross" and "ordinary" negligence, and which does not permit exemption **13–164**

---

170 [1998] Ch. 241 at 249–250.
171 See paras 11–145 to 11–148.
172 *Armitage* [1998] Ch. 241 at [251].
173 *Barnes v Tomlinson* [2006] EWHC 3115 (Ch); [2007] W.T.L.R. 377 at [78].
174 [2017] UKSC 67; [2018] A.C. 391. "Objective dishonesty" is also now the test for civil liability as a dishonest assistant in a breach of trust: *Group Seven Ltd v Notable Services LLP* [2019] EWCA Civ 614; [2020] Ch. 129 at [52]–[58]; *Byers v Saudi National Bank* [2022] EWCA Civ 43; [2022] 4 W.L.R. 22 at [13]. Discussion at paras 14–112 to 14–148.
175 [2019] EWHC 2071 (Ch) at [56]–[62] (not challenged on appeal: [2020] EWCA Civ 699; [2020] W.T.L.R. 1075 at [22]).
176 [2019] EWHC 2071 (Ch) at [63]–[64], following *Fattal v Walbrook Trustees (Jersey) Ltd* [2010] EWHC 2767 (Ch) at [79]–[81].

clauses that protect trustees from liability for gross negligence.[177] Similarly, the Trusts (Guernsey) Law 2007 s.39(7) provides that:[178]

> the terms of a trust may not (a) relieve a trustee of liability for a breach of trust arising from his own fraud, wilful misconduct or gross negligence, or (b) grant him any indemnity against the trust property in respect of any such liability.

13–165 In its 2006 Report on exemption clauses, the Law Commission considered whether a similar measure should be introduced into English law, but rejected this because English law does not clearly distinguish between gross and ordinary negligence.[179]

13–166 In its 2003 Consultation Paper on exemption clauses, the Law Commission proposed drawing a distinction between lay and professional trustees, suggesting that lay trustees should generally still be able to rely on trustee exemption clauses,[180] but that professional trustees should be unable to rely on an exemption clause where their conduct has been so unreasonable, irresponsible or incompetent that in fairness to the beneficiaries their conduct should not be excused.[181] However, in its 2006 Report on the subject, the Law Commission changed tack, concluding that reform would be undesirable because it could lead to increased costs, delays in trust administration, a greater tendency towards defensive trusteeship, and a general loss of flexibility in the operation of trusts.[182] Instead it suggested that a rule of practice should be recognised and enforced by regulatory and professional bodies along the following lines:[183]

> Any paid trustee who causes a settlor to include a clause in a trust instrument which has the effect of excluding or limiting liability for negligence must before the creation of the trust take such steps as are reasonable to ensure that the settlor is aware of the meaning and effect of the clause.

C. Limitation

13–167 Claims for breach of trust are subject to the limitation rules contained in the Limitation Act 1980 s.21. This section establishes a distinction between proceedings against express trustees who are guilty of fraud and/or have retained trust property (or its product) or converted it to their use, and proceedings against express trustees who have committed an "innocent" or "negligent" breach of trust and who have not retained trust property (or its product) or converted it to their use. In the former case no statutory limitation period applies with the result that claims may be unaffected by any limitation rule, although in some cases the trustees may plead laches—an equitable doctrine that is discussed elsewhere.[184] In the latter case a six-year limitation period applies. The following discussion is only concerned with claims for breach of trust against express trustees. Claims against constructive and resulting trustees raise additional issues that are not discussed here.

---

177 *Seton v Dawson* (1841) 4 D 310 at 316–317; *Knox v Mackinnon* (1888) 13 App. Cas. 753 at 765; *Clarke v Clarke's Trustees*, 1925 S.C. 693; *Lutea Trustees Ltd v Orbis Trustees* [1998] S.L.T. 471.

178 Considered by the Privy Council in *Spread Trustee Co Ltd v Hutcheson* [2011] UKPC 13; [2012] 2 A.C. 194.

179 Law Commission, *Trustee Exemption Clauses* (2006), Law Com. No.301, Cm.6874.

180 Law Commission, *Trustee Exemption Clauses* (TSO, 2003), LCCP No.171, para.4.39.

181 Law Commission, *Trustee Exemption Clauses*, para.4.78.

182 Law Commission, *Trustee Exemption Clauses*, para.5.99.

183 Law Commission, *Trustee Exemption Clauses*, para.6.65.

184 See paras 22–035 to 22–063.

Limitation Act 1980 s.21

(1) No period of limitation prescribed by this Act shall apply to an action by a beneficiary under a trust, being an action: 13–168
   (a) in respect of any fraud or fraudulent breach of trust to which the trustee was a party or privy; or
   (b) to recover from the trustee trust property or the proceeds thereof in the possession of the trustee, or previously received by the trustee and converted to his use.

(2) Where a trustee who is also a beneficiary under the trust receives or retains trust property or its proceeds as his share on a distribution of trust property under the trust, his liability in any action brought by virtue of subsection (1)(b) above to recover that property or its proceeds after the expiration of the period of limitation prescribed by this Act for bringing an action to recover trust property shall be limited to the excess over his proper share.
This subsection only applies if the trustee acted honestly and reasonably in making the distribution.

(3) Subject to the preceding provisions of this section an action by a beneficiary to recover trust property or in respect of any breach of trust, not being an action for which a period of limitation is prescribed by any other provision of this Act,[185] shall not be brought after the expiration of six years from the date on which the right of action accrued. For the purposes of this subsection the right of action shall not be treated as having accrued to any beneficiary entitled to a future interest in the trust property until the interest fell into possession.

(4) No beneficiary as against whom there would be a good defence under this Act shall derive any greater or other benefit from a judgment or order obtained by any other beneficiary than he could have obtained if he had brought the action and this Act had been pleaded in defence.

i. Section 21(1) Cases Where No Statutory Limitation Period Applies

Section 21(1)(a) provides that no statutory limitation period shall apply to proceedings against a trustee who has acted fraudulently or been "party or privy" to a fraud committed by another.[186] When deciding whether a trustee was "a party or privy to fraud or fraudulent breach of trust", what matters is the quality of the trustee's own conduct and not that of other people. Lindley LJ made this point in *Thorne v Heard*, when he said that:[187] 13–169

> It is only by a misuse of language that a person who in fact knows absolutely nothing of the fraudulent conduct of another, and who in no way benefits by it or ratifies it, can be said to be party or privy to it. One person may be, and often is, liable in law for frauds which he has not committed; but to say that he is party or privy to them is quite another matter, and is only true when he has personally in some way participated in them.

Accordingly, an "innocent" trustee who acts in good faith is not "a party or privy to fraud" for the purposes of s.21(1)(a) merely by dint of the fact that a fraud has been perpetrated by their co-trustee,[188] or by their solicitor or other agent,[189] or by their partner.[190] 13–170

---

185 Where personal representatives have become trustees upon completing administration of an estate the relationship between s.21(3) and s.22 is unclear. It would seem that the breadth of s.22 (formerly s.20 of the 1939 Act) makes the 12-year period applicable: *Re Diplock* [1948] Ch. 465 at 511–513; *Ministry of Health v Simpson* [1951] A.C. 251 at 276–277.

186 See *North American Land Co v Watkins* [1904] 1 Ch. 242; [1904] 2 Ch. 233; *Vane v Vane* (1872) L.R. 8 Ch. 383; *Armitage v Nurse* [1998] Ch. 241 at 260.

187 [1894] 1 Ch. 599 at 606. See also 608 where Kay LJ spoke of the need for "moral complicity". Their findings were upheld on appeal: [1895] A.C. 495 at 503 and 504–505.

188 *Re Tufnell* (1902) 18 T.L.R. 705.

189 *Thorne v Heard* [1895] A.C. 495; *Re Fountaine* [1909] 2 Ch. 382.

190 *Dixon Coles & Gill (a firm) v Baines* [2021] EWCA Civ 1097; [2022] Ch. 195.

13–171 Section 21(1)(b) provides that no statutory limitation period shall apply to proceedings to recover trust property or its proceeds in her possession, or who has previously received trust property and converted it to her use. The rule that trustees in possession of trust property are liable without limit of time (in the absence of laches) is often said to be justified by the reason given by Lord Redesdale in *Hovenden v Lord Annesley*,[191] that the trustees can only be possessed of the trust estate for, and on behalf of, the beneficiaries, and so time can never run against the beneficiaries in favour of the trustees. However, doubts are expressed about this rationale by Christian Daly and Charles Mitchell in the following extract.

C. Daly and C. Mitchell, "*Paragon Finance plc v D.B. Thakerar & Co. (a firm)* (1999)"

in C. Mitchell and P. Mitchell (eds), *Landmark Cases in Equity* (Hart Publishing, 2012), pp.655–656

13–172 [The rule that delay did not bar claims by a beneficiary against an express trustee, now found in the Limitation Act 1980 s.21(1)] . . . is usually attributed to the judgment of Lord Redesdale in *Hovenden v Lord Annesley*,[192] where he offered the following explanation:[193]

> "[I]f a trustee is in possession, and does not execute his trust, the possession of the trustee, is the possession of the cestui que trust; and if the only circumstance is, that he does not perform his trust, his possession operates nothing as a bar, because his possession is according to his title."

Lord Redesdale's statement of the principle, and, more importantly, his explanation for it . . . has been (almost) universally and uncritically followed.[194] His explanation certainly has a superficial attractiveness in relation to claims to recover trust property from an express trustee. However, its explanatory force does not extend much further, because it is premised on the idea that the trustee is in possession of the trust property. This premise necessarily circumscribes the scope of operation of the principle, which does not obviously extend to a claim based on misapplication of trust property or a claim based on the trustee's negligence. In both of these cases the gravamen of the beneficiary's complaint is that the trustee is not in possession of property that ought to be in his possession.

13–173 A different explanation of the *Hovenden* principle might run as follows. There are two types of claim that a beneficiary may make against an express trustee: performance claims and reparation claims . . . The objective of a performance claim is to enforce the performance of the trust according to its terms: to compel performance by the trustee of his primary obligation to apply the trust property in accordance with the trust deed, either in specie or substitutively (by paying a money substitute for the relevant property). By contrast, the objective of a reparation claim is to make good a loss occasioned by the trustee's breach of a primary obligation, such as his duty of care. Performance claims involve the assertion and vindication of pre-existing rights. They do not involve an allegation of breach of trust, or the enforcement of new rights arising from such a breach. Accordingly, it is inappropriate to apply the statutes of limitation by analogy to such claims because it is impossible to identify any breach of duty in respect of which time can run, and it is equally impossible to identify the moment from which it should start to run.[195]

---

191 (1806) 2 Sch. & Lef. 607 at 633–634; cited in, e.g. *Williams v Central Bank of Nigeria* [2014] UKSC 10; [2014] A.C. 1189 at [13]–[14]. See also A. Televantos "Trusts, Limitation Periods, and Unauthorised Gains" [2020] Conv. 330 at pp.334–5.

192 In fact the principle is much—at least 150 years—older: J. Brunyate, *Limitation of Actions in Equity* (Stevens & Sons, 1932) 50.

193 (1806) 2 Sch. & Lef. 607 at 633.

194 See *Chalmer v Bradley* (1819) 1 J. & W. 51 at 67–68; *Christ's Hospital v Grainger* (1849) 1 M & G 460 at 465; JGN Darby and FA Bosanquet, *A Practical Treatise on the Statutes of Limitations in England and Ireland* (William Maxwell & Son, 1867) 182–83; W. Ashburner, *Principles of Equity* (Butterworth & Co., 1902) 710–711; J.M. Lightwood, *The Time Limit on Actions* (Butterworth & Co., 1909) 68–69; contrast W. Swadling, "Limitation" in P. Birks and A. Pretto (eds), *Breach of Trust* (Hart, 2002) 326–27. For a particularly striking application of the principle, see *Lister v Pickford* (1865) 34 Beav. 576.

195 Compare *Christ's Hospital v Grainger* (1849) 1 M & G 460 at 466; *Re Nisbet and Potts' Contract* [1906] 1 Ch. 386 at 401–02. A similar kind of argument appealed to Moore-Bick L.J. in *P. & O. Nedlloyd B.V. v Arab Metals Co. (The UB Tiger) (No.2)* [2007] 1 W.L.R. 2288 at [47].

This account is confronted by at least four obstacles. First, both Lord Redesdale and Lord Eldon were of the view that the principle stated in *Hovenden*, and the explanation for that principle, was not limited to claims by beneficiaries against express trustees, but also applied to claims by landlords against their tenants.[196] This suggests that the principle was not attracted by the particular duties of an express trustee or the particular nature of a performance claim. Rather, the principle appears to be part of the law of adverse possession, in which case its explanatory force in the context of trusts is particularly limited. It merely operates to disable a person who enters into possession of land in the capacity of an express trustee from asserting a claim to the land adversely to his beneficiary. Its explanatory force extends no further. **13–174**

Secondly, although the matter is not free from doubt, it appears that the *Hovenden* principle applied to reparation claims.[197] Claims of this type involve the assertion of a new right to compensation for losses occasioned by reason of a breach of duty. The application of the principle to claims of this type is difficult to reconcile with the account being considered. **13–175**

Thirdly, the operation of Lord Redesdale's principle cannot be justified by appealing to the fact that the claims to which it was applied were performance claims. Since equity was applying the statutes of limitation by analogy, there is no reason why it should have set its face against barring performance claims because the statutes themselves were applicable to such claims.[198] In fact, equity did apply the statute by analogy to performance claims, including bills for an account by a principal against a fiduciary.[199] **13–176**

Fourthly, claims by beneficiaries against express trustees were subject to the equitable doctrine of laches or acquiescence,[200] and some accounts of this doctrine emphasise the violation of the claimant's rights or the breach of the defendant's duty.[201] If these accounts are correct then the applicability of laches and acquiescence to performance claims against trustees is inconsistent with the notion that such claims do not involve any allegation of a breach of duty. **13–177**

Neither Lord Redesdale's explanation of the *Hovenden* rule nor the only other plausible account of that rule is satisfactory. Hence we are forced to conclude that the rule is inexplicable. **13–178**

In *Re Axminster Carpets Group Retirement Benefits Plan*,[202] members of a pension scheme were underpaid benefits and they sued the trustees for the difference between the amounts they had been paid and the amounts they should have been paid. The trustees argued that these were not claims to "recover" trust property for the purposes of s.21(1)(b) because they were not proprietary claims against the trustees. The beneficiaries accepted that they had not made proprietary claims but said this did not matter because the s.21(1)(b) wording should be construed more broadly. The essence of their claims was that they were entitled to the arrears under the trust terms and since these would be paid by the trustee out of the trust fund if they succeeded they were relevantly claims to "recover" trust property. **13–179**

Morgan J accepted the beneficiaries' argument,[203] among other reasons because the construction advocated by the trustees was inconsistent with the policy of the statute, as stated in *Re Timmis*, where Kekewich J had held that the statutory precursor to s.21 had not been "intended to protect [a trustee] where, if he pleaded the statute, he would come off with something he ought not to have, i.e., **13–180**

---

196 *Hovenden v Lord Annesley* (1806) 2 Sch. & Lef. 607 at 633; *Cholmondeley v Clinton* (1821) 4 Bligh 1 at 40.

197 *Smith v Pococke* (1854) 2 Drew 197; *Bright v Legerton* (1860) 29 Beav. 60; (1861) 2 De G. F. & J. 606; *Brittlebank v Goodwin* (1868) L.R. 5 Eq. 545; *Stone v Stone* (1869) L.R. 5 Ch. 74. See also Ashburner at pp. 710–11.

198 Thus actions to recover debts were subject to a statutory limitation period: 21 James 1 c. 16, ss. 1 and 3.

199 *Lockey v Lockey* (1719) Prec. Ch. 518; *Knox v Gye* (1872) L.R. 5 H.L. 656. [Remainder of footnote omitted.]

200 *Bright v Legerton* (1860) 29 Beav. 60; (1861) 2 De G. F. & J. 606; *Re Cross* (1882) 20 Ch. D. 109; *Rochefoucauld v Boustead* [1897] 1 Ch. 196; *Re Taylor* (1900) 81 L.T. 812.

201 *Mills v Drewitt* (1855) 20 Beav. 632 at 638; Lightwood *The Time Limit on Actions* (Butterworth & Co, 1909), pp.252–255.

202 [2021] EWHC 1652 (Ch); [2022] Pens. L.R. 1, where Morgan J revisited and reaffirmed his own earlier decisions in *Lloyds Banking Group Pension Trustees Ltd v Lloyds Bank Plc (Nos 1 and 2)* [2018] EWHC 2839 (Ch); [2019] Pens. L.R. 5 and [2020] EWHC 3135 (Ch); [2021] Pens. L.R. 10.

203 [2021] EWHC 1652 (Ch); [2022] Pens. L.R. 1 at [110]–[156].

the money of the trust."[204] On the construction for which the trustee had argued in *Axminster Carpets*, a trustee who innocently underpaid beneficiaries over a long period would be free to raise a limitation defence against claims for payment of arrears dating from a time more than six years previously and could then "decide to use them in some other way or even possibly retain them for himself"—and this was incompatible with the policy of the statute as stated in *Re Timmis*.[205]

ii. Section 21(3) Cases Where the Statutory Limitation Period Does Apply

13–181 Section 21(3) stipulates a six-year limitation period for actions "to recover trust property or in respect of any breach of trust", time running from the date when the breach of trust occurred (and not, e.g. from the date when the beneficiary suffered a loss).[206] The first class of action referred to in subs.(3) can only include actions against third parties, since actions against trustees in possession of trust property are covered by s.21(1)(b), and the second class of action referred to in subs.(3) cannot include actions against fraudulent trustees, since these are covered by s.21(1)(a). Since the sub-section is expressed to apply only to actions by a beneficiary, it does not apply to bar an action by the Attorney General to enforce a charitable trust.[207]

13–182 Section 21(3) takes in cases, e.g. where a trustee has obtained only an indirect benefit from their breach of trust,[208] where she has disobeyed a direction in the trust deed to realise trust assets,[209] where she has disobeyed an instruction in the trust deed to accumulate income,[210] and where she has misused a power of advancement.[211]

13–183 The last sentence of s.21(3) protects reversionary interests by enacting that time shall not run against a beneficiary until their interest has fallen into possession.[212] Even before that date a remainderman can sue for breach of trust. In such a case if the prior beneficiary is themselves barred the trustees must nevertheless replace the fund at the suit of the remainderman, but during the continuance of the prior beneficiary's interest they will be entitled to the income of the property: for a judgment recovered by one beneficiary is not to improve the position of one who is already barred.[213]

D. Consent

13–184 There are different types of "consent" and the rules shielding trustees from liability may work differently depending on the type of "consent" which has been given.[214] Broadly speaking, however, a trustee can escape liability whenever a beneficiary[215] has assented to or concurred in a breach of

---

204 [1902] 1 Ch. 176 at 186, endorsed in *Burnden Holdings (UK) Ltd v Fielding* [2018] UKSC 14; [2018] A.C. 857 at [17], where Lord Briggs also stressed that the "starting point in the construction of section 21(1)(b) is to pay due regard to its purpose".

205 [2021] EWHC 1652 (Ch); [2022] Pens. L.R. 1 at [140].

206 *Vant v Campain* (1893) 9 T.L.R. 254; *Re Somerset* [1894] 1 Ch. 231; *Thorne v Heard* [1895] A.C. 495.

207 *Attorney General v Cocke* [1988] Ch. 414.

208 *Re Gurney* [1893] 1 Ch. 590.

209 *Re Swain* [1891] 3 Ch. 233.

210 *How v Earl Winterton* [1896] 2 Ch. 626.

211 *Re Pauling's Settlement Trusts (No.1)* [1962] 1 W.L.R. 86 at 115, approved [1964] Ch. 303 at 353.

212 Consent by a life-tenant to an advance in favour of a remainderman does not amount to a release of the life interest so as to convert the remainderman's interest into an interest in possession: *Re Pauling's Settlement Trusts (No.1)* [1964] Ch. 303.

213 *Re Somerset* [1894] 1 Ch. 231; s.19(3) of the Limitation Act 1939 and s.21(4) of the 1980 Act; *Mara v Browne* [1895] 2 Ch. 69 reversed on another point [1896] 1 Ch. 199.

214 J. Payne, "Consent" in P. Birks and A. Pretto (eds), *Breach of Trust* (2002), p.301.

215 In charitable trusts only the Attorney General can consent or acquiesce in a breach of trust: *Re Freeston's Charity* [1978] 1 All E.R. 481 at 490, though the Court of Appeal found it unnecessary to say anything on this point: [1979] 1 All E.R. 51 at 63.

trust,[216] or confirmed it after the event,[217] or acquiesced in it,[218] provided that the beneficiary was of full age and capacity when they gave their consent,[219] had full knowledge of the facts, and was not unduly influenced.[220] Many of the cases, such as the concurrence and confirmation cases, can be explained as an application of estoppel doctrine, but others, such as the acquiescence cases, do not lend themselves so readily to this analysis.[221]

The general position was summarised by Wilberforce J in *Re Pauling's Settlement Trusts (No.1)*:[222] **13–185**

> The court has to consider all the circumstances in which the concurrence of the cestui que trust was given with a view to seeing whether it is fair and equitable that, having given his concurrence, he should afterwards turn round and sue the trustees: that, subject to this, it is not necessary that he should know that what he is concurring in is a breach of trust, provided that he fully understands what he is concurring in, and that it is not necessary that he should himself have directly benefited by the breach of trust.

Wilberforce J's approach was approved by the Court of Appeal in *Holder v Holder*,[223] which is excerpted in Chapter 22.[224] So if a beneficiary consents to an act which the trustees know to be unauthorised although they refrain from telling her this, she may still sue them. The trustees must put the beneficiaries fully in the picture and must not withhold crucial information.[225] As Cotton LJ said in *Re Garnett*:[226] **13–186**

> the trustee ought not to be allowed . . . to shield herself from accounting for trust money in her hands simply by putting forward a document which has been signed and sealed without any knowledge of the real facts without any communication of their rights, though the release in its terms would bar the parties from insisting upon them.

If, however, the trustees themselves do not appreciate that what they propose is a breach of trust and the beneficiary fully understands and agrees with the proposal then she cannot sue them if things turn out badly. *Fletcher v Collis*,[227] excerpted below, establishes that these principles apply whether the beneficiary's consent or acquiescence[228] is before or after the breach of trust, and they prevent them from suing for breach of trust, whether or not she benefited from consenting to such breach. **13–187**

---

216 *Walker v Symonds* (1818) 3 Swan. 1; *Wilkinson v Parry* (1828) 4 Russ. 272; *Evans v Benyon* (1887) 37 Ch.D. 329; Re Pauling's S.T. [1964] Ch. 303.

217 *French v Hobson* (1803) 9 Ves 103; *Cresswell v Dewell* (1863) 4 Gif.f 460.

218 *Stafford v Stafford* (1857) 1 De G. & J. 193; *Re Jarvis* [1958] 1 W.L.R. 815; *Re Pauling's ST* [1964] Ch. 303.

219 *Lord Montford v Lord Cadogan* (1816) 19 Ves. Jun. 635; *Overton v Banister* (1844) 3 Hare 503 at 506.

220 *Earl Chesterfield v Janssen* (1751) 2 Ves. Sen. 125; *Bowles v Stewart* (1803) 1 Sch. & Lef. 209; *Stevens v Robertson* (1868) 18 L.T. 427.

221 Further see *Spellson v George* (1992) 26 N.S.W.L.R. 666 and *Byrnes v Kendle* (2011) 243 C.L.R. 253, critiqued in T. Economou, "The Defence of Acquiescence to a Breach of Trust" (2013) 15 *Flinders Law Journal* 115. See also L. Ho, "The Importance of Being Earnest: The Doctrines of Laches and Acquiescence" in P. Davies et al (eds) *Defences in Equity* (2018). Acquiescence is discussed further at paras 22–064 to 22–135.

222 [1962] 1 W.L.R. 86 at 108.

223 *Holder v Holder* [1968] Ch. 353 at 369. See too *Brudenell-Bruce v Moore* [2014] EWHC 3679 (Ch) at [195]–[197].

224 See paras 22–088 to 22–119.

225 *Phipps v Boardman* [1964] 2 All E.R. 187 at 204–205; *Mitchell v Halliwell* [2005] EWHC 937 (Ch) esp. at [41]–[52].

226 (1885) 31 Ch.D. 1 at 16.

227 [1905] 2 Ch. 24.

228 Mere delay (subject to Limitation Act 1980) is not enough; there must be conduct and circumstances making it inequitable to assert a claim, e.g. having knowledge of entitlement to sue but doing nothing, so that the trustee does things that would otherwise not have been done: *De Busche v Alt* (1877) 8 Ch.D. 286 at 314; *Nelson v Rye* [1996] 1 W.L.R. 1378; *Pullan v Wilson* [2014] EWHC 126 (Ch); [2014] W.T.L.R. 669.

13–188 As we said at the start of this chapter, the term "breach of trust" takes in non-compliance with various rules and the effects of beneficiary consent to non-compliance can vary according to the rule which has not been followed. Most notably, cases where beneficiaries consent to an unauthorised act by a trustee differ from other cases insofar as beneficiary consent to unauthorised acts can have the effect of retrospectively authorising the trustee's actions.[229] This has the result not only that the trustee incurs no personal compensatory liability (a result which also follows from consent to other types of breach), but also that the situation is treated as though no breach has ever taken place, with consequences for third parties with whom the trustees have dealt and also for the content of the beneficiaries' rights and the trustees' powers and duties going forward. As James Penner has observed, the "substance" of a trust subsists for as long as there are trustee obligations, and their character determines the nature of the trust whether or not the trustee incurs any liability for breaching them; furthermore, "dealings with trust property in compliance with the terms of the trust are the justification in law for those transactions being valid for the parties involved."[230]

Fletcher v Collis

Court of Appeal [1905] 2 Ch. 24

13–189 Securities were settled on trust for the husband for life, remainder to the wife for life, remainder to children. At the request of the wife and with the (written) consent of the husband, the trustee in 1885 sold off the whole of the trust fund and handed the proceeds to the wife, who spent them. In June 1891 the husband was adjudicated bankrupt. In August 1891 the present action was commenced by the remaindermen against the trustee to make him replace the loss, but proceedings were stayed on an undertaking by the trustee, on the security of (inter alia) certain policies on his life, to make good the trust fund. By means of payments by the trustee and of the policies which fell in on his death in 1902, the whole of the trust fund was replaced, together with interest from August 1891.

13–190 The personal representative of the deceased trustee then took out a summons for a declaration that she was entitled, during the life of the husband, to the income of the trust fund replaced by the deceased trustee. It was argued for her that a beneficiary who concurs in a breach of trust cannot afterwards complain of it against his trustee. The capital had in fact been replaced by the trustee at the instance of the remaindermen, but since the husband himself had by virtue of his concurrence no claim against the trustee, the income of the capital so replaced should (during the life of the husband) go to her as personal representative of the trustee who replaced it.

13–191 For the husband's trustee in bankruptcy, who resisted the claim of the personal representative, it was contended that the authorities showed that mere concurrence by a beneficiary does not preclude him from complaining against his trustee: it must be shown that the beneficiary also derived a personal benefit from the breach of trust, which was not the case here.

13–192 ROMER L.J. (with whom VAUGHAN WILLIAMS and STIRLING L.JJ. agreed): There was one proposition of law urged by the counsel on behalf of the respondents before us to which I accede. It is this: If a beneficiary claiming under a trust does not instigate or request a breach of trust, is not the active moving party towards it, but merely consents to it, and he obtains no personal benefit from it, then his interest in the trust estate would not be impoundable in order to indemnify the trustee liable to make good loss occasioned by the breach. I think this is what was meant and referred to by Chitty J. in his judgment in *Sawyer v Sawyer*,[231] where he says:

> "It strikes me as a novelty in law, and a proposition not founded on principle, to say that the person who merely consents is bound to do more than what he says he consents to do. It does not mean that he makes himself personally liable, nor does he render any property liable to make it good."

---

229 *Pettigrew v Edwards* [2017] EWHC 8 (Ch); [2017] W.T.L.R. 675 at [46]. Further see Y.K. Liew and C. Mitchell, "Beneficiaries' Consent to Trustees' Unauthorised Acts" in P. Davies et al (eds), *Defences in Equity* (2018).

230 J. Penner, "Exemptions" in P. Birks and A. Pretto (eds), *Breach of Trust* (2002), p.252.

231 (1885) 28 Ch.D. 595 at 598.

But that proposition of law must be taken to be subject to the following right of the trustee as between himself and the beneficiaries. In the case I have before referred to in respect to the general proposition, the beneficiary who knowingly consented to the breach could not, if of full contracting age and capacity, and in the absence of special circumstances, afterwards be heard to say that the conduct of the trustee in committing the breach of trust was, as against him the particular beneficiary, improper, so as to make the trustee liable to the beneficiary for any damage suffered in respect of that beneficiary's interest in the trust estate by reason of the loss occasioned by the breach, and of course if satisfactorily proved the consent of the beneficiary to the breach need not be in writing.

I will illustrate what I have said by a concrete case, not only to make my meaning perfectly plain, but also because the illustration will have a bearing upon the case now before us. Take a simple case of a trust under a settlement, say, of £3,000, for a tenant for life, and after the death of the tenant for life for certain remaindermen. Suppose the trustee commits a breach of trust and sells out £1,000, and pays it over to some third person, so that the cestui que trust does not benefit by it himself, and suppose that the tenant for life, being of full age and sui juris, knows of that act of the trustee and consents to it. What would be the position of the trustee in reference to that breach of trust if he were made liable at the instance of the remaindermen for the loss accruing to the trust estate by the breach of trust, assuming the £1,000 to have been lost? The remaindermen would have the right of saying, so far as their interest in remainder is concerned, the capital must be made good by the trustee; but the tenant for life who consented could not himself have brought an action against the trustee to make him liable for the loss of income suffered by the tenant for life by reason of the breach of trust as to the £1,000. On the other hand, the trustee would not have had a right, as against the cestui que trust, the tenant for life, to have impounded the tenant for life's interest on the remaining £2,000 of the trust fund in order to indemnify himself. Now suppose the remaindermen having brought an action to make good the breach of trust against the trustee, and the tenant for life is a co-plaintiff, a defence is put in by the trustee raising his right as against the tenant for life seeking relief in respect of the loss of income, but admitting the right of the remaindermen: what would the court in such a case do if the question between the tenant for life and the trustee had to be tried out, and the tenant for life was found to have consented knowingly to the breach of trust? To my mind the right thing for the court to do would have been clear. It might order the £1,000 to be paid into court by the trustee; but, pending the life of the tenant for life, it might also order the income to be paid to the trustee, because the income of the £1,000 would have been out of the pocket of the trustee just as much as the corpus from which it proceeded, and not to have given that relief to the trustee would have been to ignore his right, and to have acceded to the claim of the tenant for life in the action by him that I have indicated. Now suppose that the tenant for life is not a plaintiff, but co-defendant with the trustee, so that the question cannot be tried out at the trial as between the tenant for life and the trustee: what might the court do, if so advised, in that case? It might order the £1,000 to be paid into court by the trustee, and it might reserve the question of the right as between the tenant for life and the trustee to the income to be determined at some later period. It will be found that that illustration is pertinent to the case that is now before us. In such a case when the question as to income arose the trustee would be able to say: "The remaindermen are clearly not entitled to the income on the trust fund I have replaced, if the tenant for life is not entitled to it as against me. I replaced it; it is my money, and I am entitled to it"; and, therefore, when the question came to be tried out ultimately as between the tenant for life and the trustee, if that income was still under the control of the court, the court would again have the right to say to the trustee who replaced the corpus: "The income is yours in the absence of the right of the beneficiary, the tenant for life, to claim as against you to make you liable for that income." 13–193

Now that right of a trustee which I have been dealing with, the right to resist the claim by the beneficiary to make good as against him the income, has clearly not been affected either by section 6 of the Trustee Act of 1888, or by section 45 of the Trustee Act of 1893. As I pointed out in *Bolton v Curre*,[232] those sections were intended to and did extend the powers of the court for the benefit of the trustee. They clearly extended the powers of court so far as concerns the case of a married woman restrained from anticipation; but they also extended them in another respect by giving power to the court to impound any part of the interest in the trust property of any beneficiary who consented to a breach of trust, provided that consent was in writing. But clearly there was nothing in those sections which was intended to, and nothing in my opinion which operated so as to, deprive the trustee of the right I previously indicated, namely, the right of saying 13–194

[232] [1895] 1 Ch. 544 at 549.

as against a beneficiary who has consented to a breach of trust that the beneficiary cannot make him, the trustee, personally liable to recoup, to the beneficiary who consented, the loss accruing to that beneficiary by the breach of trust committed with his consent. The beneficiary, if he consented to the breach of trust, could not be heard to make that a ground of complaint or a ground of action as against the trustee. . . .

13–195 Is not this matter that we have to deal with on this appeal in substance one where a beneficiary who has consented to a breach of trust is now for his own benefit calling upon the trustee to make good the loss accruing to the beneficiary by reason of the breach? I think it is . . . .

13–196 Held, therefore, by the Court of Appeal that the personal representative of the deceased trustee was entitled, during the life of the husband tenant for life, to the income of the fund replaced by the trustee.

4. Liability of Trustees Between Themselves

A. Joint and Several Liability of Co-trustees

13–197 Trustees are liable only for their own breaches of trust and they are not vicariously liable for breaches by co-trustees. However, a trustee is not allowed to leave trust affairs in the hands of a co-trustee to be dealt with as she sees fit,[233] or to leave trust property in her sole control,[234] or to stand by with knowledge that she is committing a breach of trust,[235] or to do nothing to obtain redress on becoming aware that she has committed a breach of trust,[236] or to retire from being a trustee with the object of facilitating a breach of trust which the remaining, or new, trustees commit.[237] If a trustee does any of these things and a loss ensues then the trustee may incur a personal compensatory liability.

13–198 Trustees who cause the same loss by their respective breaches of trust are jointly and severally liable, meaning that two or more of them jointly, or one individually, can be ordered to discharge the whole of their common liability.[238] However, a trustee who pays more than a fair share of this common liability may be able to recover a contribution from the others, the amount of which will vary with circumstances. Contribution claims between trustees formerly lay in equity but now lie under the Civil Liability (Contribution) Act 1978 between trustees who are liable "in respect of the same damage".[239] Note, however, that no contribution claim will lie against a co-trustee who is not so liable, e.g. because she has been excused from liability under the Trustee Act 1925 s.61;[240] nor will a claim lie against a co-trustee who is liable only in respect of damage other than the damage for which the claimant trustee was liable to pay compensation.[241]

13–199 When apportioning liability between trustees for the purposes of a claim under the 1978 Act the courts are likely to draw on principles developed in the Chancery jurisdiction prior to the statute's enactment.[242] So it is likely that the courts will start with the presumption that co-trustees should

---

233 *Wynne v Tempest* (1897) 13 T.L.R. 360; *Re Lucking's Will Trusts* [1968] 1 W.L.R. 866. This assumes that there has been no proper delegation, e.g. under the Trustee Act 2000 ss.11, 12.

234 *Lewis v Nobbs* (1878) 8 Ch.D. 591. This assumes that the co-trustee is not an authorised nominee or custodian under the Trustee Act 2000 s.19.

235 *Booth v Booth* (1838) 1 Beav. 125; *Gough v Smith* [1872] W.N. 18.

236 *Wilkins v Hogg* (1861) 8 Jur. 25 at 26.

237 *Head v Gould* [1898] 2 Ch. 250; *Kingdom v Castleman* (1877) 36 L.T. 141.

238 *Charitable Corp v Sutton* (1742) 2 Atk. 400 at 406; *Walker v Symonds* (1818) 3 Swan 1 at 75; *Ashurst v Mason* (1875) L.R. 20 Eq. 225 at 233; *Re Duckwari Plc* [1999] Ch. 253 at 262.

239 Civil Liability (Contribution) Act 1978 ss.1 and 6. Reimbursement, which is the same thing as a 100% contribution, is expressly allowed for by s.2(2) of the 1978 Act.

240 Cf. *Purrunsing v A'Court & Co* [2016] EWHC 789 (Ch); [2016] 4 W.L.R. 81 at [62].

241 Cf. *Alexander v Perpetual Trustee (WA) Ltd* (2004) 216 C.L.R. 109.

242 Although they have departed from them in one respect. The "clean hands" rule formerly debarred a fraudulent trustee from recovering a contribution from another fraudulent trustee: *Attorney General v Wilson* (1840) Cr. & Ph. 1 at 28. But the 1978 Act was enacted with the express purpose of allowing claimants to rely on their own wrongdoing when seeking

share equal responsibility for loss,[243] and will then look to see whether there is any reason for departing from this rule. A trustee who has wrongfully misapplied trust funds to her own exclusive use,[244] or who has exclusively benefited as a beneficiary from the breach of trust,[245] must reimburse the others in full. So too must a trustee who has acted fraudulently if the others have acted in good faith.[246] The court may also take the relative causative potency and moral blameworthiness of the trustees' actions into account, although if these are of equal weight the court may make an equal apportionment and thus reach the same result as would follow from application of the default rule.[247]

The courts' initial tendency in the case law pre-dating the 1978 Act was to reject any argument that a trustee who played an active part in the management of trust affairs should be liable for a greater share of trust losses than a passive trustee who did nothing and so failed to prevent the losses from occurring.[248] However, once it had become common practice in the nineteenth century for solicitors and other professionals to be appointed as trustees of family settlements, the courts' tough line on this issue was moderated and lay trustees were permitted to shift the burden of paying for trust losses on to professional trustees, upon whose expertise the lay trustees had reasonably relied.[249] **13-200**

Contribution claims also lie between defaulting trustees and third parties who have incurred liability for knowing receipt of misdirected trust property or for dishonest assistance in a breach of trust.[250] The same general principles of apportionment apply to these claims as to claims between co-trustees. Hence unequal apportionments are made when one party has acted in good faith and another in bad faith, and when one party has made a gain and another has not. For example, in *Dubai Aluminium Co Ltd v Salaam*,[251] the House of Lords agreed with Rix J's finding at first instance that two fraudsters who had received all the money extracted from the claimant company by a wrongdoing fiduciary should reimburse the other defendants who had compensated the company for its loss, because "it cannot be just and equitable to require one party to contribute in a way which would leave another party in possession of his spoils."[252] **13-201**

Similar findings were made by the High Court of Australia in *Burke v LFOT Pty Ltd*,[253] and by the Court of Appeal in *Niru Battery Manufacturing Co v Milestone Trading Ltd (No.2)*, where Clarke LJ held that the principle applies both where the recipient still has the money at the time of the contribution proceedings, and where she has paid it away other than in good faith.[254] In *Charter Plc v City Index* **13-202**

---

contribution from other wrongdoers, and this led Ferris J to hold that "the *ex turpi causa* defence is not available" against a claim under the statute: *K v P* [1993] Ch. 140 at 148–149.

243 *Lingard v Bromley* (1812) 1 V. & B. 114: *Jesse v Bennett* (1856) 6 De G.M. & G. 609; *Robinson v Harkin* [1896] 2 Ch. 415 at 426; *Gilchrist v Dean* [1960] V.R. 266 at 270–271.

244 *Lincoln v Wright* (1841) 4 Beav. 427; *Thompson v Finch* (1856) 22 Beav. 316 at 327; *Bahin v Hughes* (1886) 31 Ch.D. 390 at 395; *Wynne v Tempest* [1897] 1 Ch. 110; *Goodwin v Duggan* (1996) 41 N.S.W.L.R. 158 at 166.

245 *Chillingworth v Chambers* [1896] 1 Ch. 685.

246 *Baynard v Woolley* (1855) 20 Beav. 583 at 585–586; *Elwes v Barnard* (1865) 13 L.T. 426; *Bellemore v Watson* (1885) 1 T.L.R. 241 at 242; *Re Smith* [1896] 1 Ch. 71.

247 *Purrunsing v A'Court & Co* [2016] EWHC 789 (Ch); [2016] 4 W.L.R. 81 at [62]–[67].

248 *Lingard v Bromley* (1812) 1 V. & B.114 at 117; *Wilson v Moore* (1833) 1 My. & K. 126 at 147; *Bahin v Hughes* (1886) 31 Ch.D. 390 at 396; *Bacon v Camphausen* (1888) 55 L.T. 851 at 852.

249 *Lockhart v Reilly* (1856) 25 L.J. Ch. 697, affirmed (1857) 27 L.J. Ch. 54: *Thompson v Finch* (1856) 22 Beav. 316; *Wilson v Thomson* (1875) L.R. 20 Eq. 459: *Re Partington* (1887) 57 L.T. 654; *Re Turner* [1897] 1 Ch. 536; *Re Linsley* [1904] 2 Ch. 785; and cf. *Linsley v Kirstiuk* (1986) 28 D.L.R. (4th) 495. For an interesting historical account of the C19 courts' reluctant acceptance of the principle that a lay trustee might rely on a professional trustee, see C. Stebbings, *The Private Trustee in Victorian England* (Cambridge University Press, 2002), Ch.4.

250 For general discussion of third party liability for breach of trust, see Ch.14.

251 [2002] UKHL 48; [2003] 2 A.C. 366 at [50]–[54] and [162]–[164], followed in *Pulvers (a firm) v Chan* [2007] EWHC 2406 (Ch); [2008] P.N.L.R. 9 at [401] and *Cherney v Neuman* [2011] EWHC 2156 (Ch) at [324]–[325].

252 [1999] 1 Lloyd's Rep. 415 at 475, following Ferris J's observations to the same effect in *K v P* [1993] Ch. 140 at 149.

253 (2002) 209 C.L.R. 282.

254 [2004] EWCA Civ 487; [2004] 2 All E.R. (Comm.) 289 at [50].

Ltd,[255] Morritt C was led by this dictum to conclude that there was no prospect of the claimant recovering a contribution and therefore struck out the claim. On appeal, Carnwath LJ disagreed because he thought that a party who receives money for her own benefit and then pays it away should be in a "similar position" to a party who never receives anything.[256] However, this is only true if the party has acted in good faith. If she has not (and in *City Index* the claimant had not), it would be inequitable to let her recover a portion of her bad faith expenditure from the defendant.

Questions

1. "It is misleading to speak of breach of trust as if it were the equitable counterpart of breach of contract at common law. . . . It is tempting, but wrong, to assume that a trustee is . . . under a primary obligation to perform the trust and a secondary obligation to pay equitable compensation if he does not. . . . The primary remedy of the beneficiary . . . is to have the account taken, to surcharge and falsify the account, and to require the trustee to restore to the trust estate any deficiency which may appear when the account is taken." (Lord Millett, writing in the *Law Quarterly Review* in 1998.) **Discuss.**
2. What should the measure of liability be in the following alternative circumstances where, in breach of trust, Samantha Smith and Roger Robinson, trustees of a family trust:
   (a) transfer the £2 million portfolio of investments and cash to a discretionary portfolio manager and either: (i) two months later before any of the investments have been replaced there is a stock-market collapse, so that the portfolio is worth only £1.5 million; or (ii) four years later, after the original investments have all been replaced, there is a stock-market collapse, so that the portfolio is worth only £1.5 million, having been worth £2.5 million earlier;
   (b) transfer investments worth £200,000 to their children Amanda Smith and Jack Robinson in consideration of their marriage and either: (i) two months later before any of the investments have been sold there is a stock-market collapse, so that the investments are worth only £150,000; or (ii) four years later, after the investments have been sold and used to purchase a £250,000 house (now worth £300,000) there is a stock-market collapse, so that if the investments had been retained they would have depreciated from £250,000 to £150,000.
3. Mega Trustee Corporation Ltd instructs you to draft provisions for its standard forms of trust instrument. In particular, it would like provisions which: (a) exclude as much trustee liability for breach of trust as possible; (b) deny the beneficiaries access to as much trust information as possible; and (c) make clear that the trustee has no duty to supervise the activities of any company in which it owns shares (even a majority shareholding) or to seek representation on the board of directors.

   Advise the company how far (if at all) it is possible in English law to achieve these objectives.

[255] [2006] EWHC 2508 (Ch); [2007] 1 W.L.R. 26 at [33]–[53].
[256] [2007] EWCA Civ 1382; [2008] Ch. 313 at [59].

14

PERSONAL LIABILITY OF THIRD PARTIES INVOLVED IN A BREACH OF TRUST

1. Introduction

Third parties involved in a breach of trust may commit an equitable wrong and incur a personal liability to the beneficiaries for that reason. Three possibilities are discussed in this chapter. First, a person who is neither a trustee, nor authorised by the trustees, but who takes it on herself to deal with trust property that comes into her hands as though she were a trustee, may incur liability as a trustee *de son tort*. **14–001**

Second, a person who acts unconscionably by receiving trust property for her own benefit with knowledge that it was transferred in breach of trust, or by receiving such property innocently but later acquiring such knowledge while she is still the owner, may incur liability for knowing receipt. It is a controversial question whether such a person may also incur strict liability in unjust enrichment (which is not itself a wrong-based liability). Third, a person who assists in a breach of trust with a dishonest state of mind may incur liability for dishonest assistance. **14–002**

A. Personal Liability to Account as a Constructive Trustee

Trustees *de son tort*, knowing recipients, and dishonest assistants are all said to owe a personal liability to account to the beneficiaries as constructive trustees. Some courts and commentators have said that this phrase has no particular significance when used in this context and is merely an empty formula for relief. That is incorrect, for the reasons given by Charles Mitchell and Stephen Watterson in the following extract. **14–003**

C. Mitchell and S. Watterson, "Remedies for Knowing Receipt"

in C. Mitchell (ed.), *Constructive and Resulting Trusts* (Hart Publishing, 2010), pp.128–130

Over the past twenty years it has become fashionable to say that nothing is added to our understanding of liability for knowing receipt by the language of constructive trusteeship, and indeed that this language obscures the true nature of the liability. This was a recurring theme in the work of Peter Birks,[1] which **14–004**

1 Although Birks' understanding of the relationship between knowing receipt and unjust enrichment changed he never shifted from his view that the language of constructive trusteeship was a "mystifying label" that should be discarded: e.g. P. Birks *An Introduction to the Law of Restitution* (Clarendon Press, 1985) 80–82; P. Birks "Persistent Problems in

seems to have exercised a strong influence on the thinking of some members of the senior judiciary. For example, Lord Nicholls has written extra-judicially that:[2]

> "The traditional approach to [knowing recipients and dishonest assistants] involves interposing a deemed ('constructive') trusteeship between the wrongful conduct (dishonest participation) and the remedy (liability in equity). This intermediate step seems otiose and, indeed, confusing."

Similarly, in *Paragon Finance plc v D B Thakerar & Co. (a firm)*, Millett L.J. observed of liability for both dishonest assistance and knowing receipt that:[3]

> "Equity has always given relief against fraud by making any person sufficiently implicated in the fraud accountable in equity. . . Such a person is not in fact a trustee at all, even though he may be liable to account as if he were. He never assumes the position of a trustee, and if he receives the trust property at all it is adversely to the plaintiff by an unlawful transaction which is impugned by the plaintiff. In such a case the expressions 'constructive trust' and 'constructive trustee' are misleading for there is no trust and usually no possibility of a proprietary remedy; 'they are nothing more than a formula for equitable relief'."

14–005 To the extent that these comments concern liability for dishonest assistance, their Lordships are right to say that a dishonest assistant need not receive property, with the result that his liability cannot depend on his owing duties as trustee in his own right. But even so their Lordships do not tell the whole story, because this form of liability can entail fixing the defendant with a duplicative liability which mirrors that of the trustee whose breach has been assisted. Hence it can meaningfully be said that he is "constructively liable as a trustee" in the sense that he is deemed to be liable to pay over the same sums as the trustee .. . . Leaving that point to one side, and focusing our attention on liability for knowing receipt, their Lordships also miss something fundamental when they dismiss the language of constructive trusteeship when it is applied to knowing recipients.[4]

14–006 In our view, when the courts say that a knowing recipient is personally liable to account as a constructive trustee, this language accurately conveys the distinctive nature of liability for knowing receipt, which many modern accounts of the subject misunderstand or ignore.[5] Many of these accounts are motivated by a proper desire to rationalise equitable principles, but they are misguided to the extent that they attempt to characterise liability for knowing receipt in terms of common law models of liability. This project can only be accomplished at the cost of ignoring what the courts actually do—and explicitly tell us that they do—in knowing receipt cases. Liability for knowing receipt cannot be collapsed into a liability for unjust enrichment, nor a liability for primary equitable wrongdoing which mirrors the common law tort of conversion, nor a liability for secondary equitable wrongdoing which mirrors the common law economic torts. Liability for knowing receipt is a distinctive, primary, custodial liability, which closely resembles the liability of express trustees to account for the trust property with which they are charged.

14–007 In short, when the courts say that a knowing recipient is "personally liable to account as a constructive trustee", they mean exactly what they say: because of the circumstances in which knowing recipients

---

Misdirected Money: A Quintet" [1993] L.M.C.L.Q. 218, 236; P. Birks *Unjust Enrichment* 2nd edn (O.U.P., 2005) 293–5. Like views are expressed in C. Rickett "The Classification of Trusts" (1999) 18 N.Z.U.L.R. 305, 321–4; A. Burrows *The Law of Restitution* 2nd edn (Sweet & Maxwell, 2005) 196–7; M. Cope *Equitable Obligations: Duties, Defences and Remedies* (Lawbook Co., 2007) 224 – although Cope also states at 224, n 39, that 'the personal liability [of a knowing recipient] is the same as the personal liability of an express trustee', a statement with which we broadly agree.

2 Lord Nicholls "Knowing Receipt: The Need for a New Landmark" in W.R. Cornish et al (eds) *Restitution: Past, Present, and Future* (Hart, 1998) 231, 243.

3 [1999] 1 All E.R. 400 at 409, quoting *Selangor United Rubber Estates Ltd v Cradock (No.3)* [1968] 1 W.L.R. 1555, 1582. The view that Millett L.J. meant to speak of knowing receipt as well as dishonest assistance in this passage is expressed by Rimer J. in *DEG-Deutsche Investitions-und Entwicklungsgesellschaft mbH v Koshy (No.2)* [2002] 1 B.C.L.C. 478 [288] and in *Sinclair Investment Holdings S.A. v Versailles Trade Finance Ltd (in admin recship)* (2007) 10 I.T.E.L.R. 58 [122]; also by Lawrence Collins J. in *Nabb Brothers Ltd v Lloyds Bank International (Guernsey) Ltd* [2005] EWHC 405 (Ch) [70] and *Pakistan v Zardari* [2006] EWHC 2411 (Comm) [88].

4 They also appear to be motivated by the wish to merge dishonest assistance and knowing receipt into a single equitable wrong of "dishonest participation in a breach of trust", something that we believe would be a false step.

5 But see S. Gardner *An Introduction to the Law of Trusts* 2nd edn (O.U.P., 2003) 281–2; S. Worthington *Equity* 2nd edn (O.U.P., 2006) 179–189, esp. 180 and 188; Cope (n.1), 342–3.

acquire title to the misapplied property, Equity fixes them with custodial duties which are the same as some of the duties which are voluntarily assumed by express trustees. In cases where a knowing recipient breaches these duties, the accounting mechanisms through which he can be forced to make things right are the same as those through which trust beneficiaries can take action against express trustees.

Proceeding on the basis that the courts do mean something when they say that third parties involved in a breach of trust are personally liable to account as constructive trustees, we next meet the problem that the courts do not always mean the same thing, as the phrase has a different significance according to whether it is used to describe the liability of a trustee *de son tort*, a knowing recipient or a dishonest assistant. **14–008**

In the case of a trustee *de son tort*, the courts mean that when the defendant acquires trust property and deals with it as though she were an express trustee, she is personally liable to account for what she does with it in the same way as an express trustee of the property is liable to account for her stewardship of the property to the beneficiaries.[6] **14–009**

Similarly, when a knowing recipient acquires trust property she is liable to account for what she does with it to the beneficiaries as though she were an express trustee of the property for them.[7] Consistently with this, the remedies awarded against trustees *de son tort* and knowing recipients who fail to deal with the trust property in accordance with the beneficiaries' rights are essentially the same as those which are awarded against express trustees who fail to act in accordance with the terms of the trust: claims are made through the same proceedings for an account, and liability is quantified by reference to the same principles as those which have been described in the discussion of express trustee liability in Chapter 13. **14–010**

In the case of dishonest assistants, however, the expression means something different. Liability for dishonest assistance can be incurred by defendants who handle misdirected trust property which might be impressed with a constructive trust for the beneficiaries (e.g. someone who dishonestly receives misdirected trust funds and pays them over to a third party). However liability can also be incurred by defendants whose assistance does not entail receiving misapplied property[8]—and indeed, can be incurred by defendants who assist in a breach of fiduciary duty that does not itself involve any misapplication of property.[9] It follows that when the courts say that a dishonest assistant is personally liable to account to the beneficiaries as a constructive trustee, they cannot mean that the assistant is a trustee of property for which she must account to the beneficiaries: "there is no real trust and usually no chance of a proprietary remedy" against her.[10] **14–011**

Arguably, what they mean instead is that the dishonest assistant can be treated, by a legal fiction, as though she were the trustee or fiduciary whose breach of duty she had assisted, so as to fix her with the same personal liabilities as are owed by that trustee or fiduciary: her liability derives from and duplicates the liability of that primary wrongdoer.[11] In other words, dishonest assistants can incur **14–012**

6 e.g. *Rackham v Siddall* (1850) 1 Mac. & G. 607 at 621; *Jasmine Trustees Ltd v Wells & Hind (a firm)* [2007] EWHC 38 (Ch); [2008] Ch. 194 at [42]; *Williams v Central Bank of Nigeria* [2014] UKSC 10; [2014] A.C. 1189 at [9].

7 e.g. *Jesse v Bennett* (1856) 6 De G.M. & G. 609 at 612; *John v Dodwell & Co Ltd* [1918] A.C. 563 at 569; *Williams v Central Bank of Nigeria* [2014] UKSC 10; [2014] A.C. 1189 at [31]; *DD Growth Premium 2X Fund v RMF Market Neutral Strategies (Master) Ltd* [2017] UKPC 36; [2018] Bus. L.R. 1595 at [58]; *Watson v Kea Investments Ltd* [2019] EWCA Civ 1759; [2019] 4 W.L.R. 145 at [40]; *Byers v Saudi National Bank* [2022] EWCA Civ 43; [2022] 4 W.L.R. 22 at [47]–[54].

8 *Royal Brunei Airlines Sdn Bhd v Tan* [1995] 2 A.C. 378 at 382; *Houghton v Fayers* [2000] Lloyd's Rep. Bank. 145 at 149.

9 *Novoship (UK) Ltd v Mikhaylyuk* [2014] EWCA Civ 908; [2015] Q.B. 499.

10 *Coulthard v Disco Mix Club Ltd* [2000] 1 W.L.R. 707 at 731.

11 *US Surgical Corp v Hospital Products International Pty Ltd* (1982) 2 N.S.W.L.R. 766 at 817 (not considered on appeal); *Royal Brunei Airlines Sdn Bhd v Tan* [1995] 2 A.C. 378 at 385; *Australian Securities Commission v AS Nominees Ltd* (1995) 62 F.C.R. 504 at 523; *Equiticorp Industries Ltd v R. (No.47)* [1998] 2 N.Z.L.R. 481 at 658; *Grupo Torras SA v Al-Sabah (No.5)* [2001] Lloyd's Rep. Bank. 36 at 61–62.

a civil secondary liability, analogous to the criminal secondary liability of those who procure, aid or abet a crime.[12] If this conceptualisation of liability for dishonest assistance is correct, then it suggests that the remedies awarded against defendants may simply duplicate the remedies awarded against the trustees or fiduciaries whose breaches of duty they have assisted. However, dishonest assistants can also incur a direct primary liability in their own right, to disgorge profits which they have made for themselves through their equitable wrongdoing, whether or not the trustees have shared in these profits, and whether or not they correspond to a loss to the trust estate.[13]

2. Trusteeship De Son Tort

14–013 In *Mara v Browne*, AL Smith LJ held that:[14]

> If one, not being a trustee and not having authority from a trustee, takes upon himself to intermeddle with trust matters or to do acts characteristic of the office of trustee he may thereby make himself what is called in law a trustee of his own wrong, i.e. a trustee *de son tort*, or as it is also termed, a constructive trustee.

14–014 A trustee *de son tort* does not purport to act for themselves, but for the beneficiaries,[15] as their trustee.[16] They may act in good faith and be actuated by selfless motives. For these reasons, in *Dubai Aluminium Co Ltd v Salaam,* Lord Millett preferred the term "de facto trustee" to the term "trustee *de son tort*".[17] Nevertheless, intermeddling with the beneficiaries' rights in this way is a civil wrong and despite the connotations of morally blameworthy behaviour that are sometimes associated with the term "tort",[18] the traditional language of "trusteeship *de son tort*" therefore says something important about the nature of liability under this head that is not captured by the language of "de facto trusteeship".

14–015 There is no need to show that an intermeddler has acted dishonestly in order to fix them with liability as a trustee *de son tort*. She may have been an honest and well intentioned busybody,[19] and/or have mistakenly believed herself to be an express trustee, although she was not, e.g. because she was invalidly appointed.[20] However, to show that a defendant has relevantly "intermeddled" with the trust affairs, she must have taken an active role in the administration of the trust estate that exceeds a de minimis threshold—it does not suffice that she has signed a few cheques or attended trustee meetings without participating in any decision making.[21]

---

12 *Ultraframe (UK) Ltd v Fielding* [2005] EWHC 1638 (Ch); [2007] W.T.L.R. 835 at [1506], per Lewison J: "liability as a dishonest assistant, as the law has developed, is a secondary liability akin to the criminal liability of one who aids and abets the commission of a criminal offence."

13 *Novoship (UK) Ltd v Mikhaylyuk* [2014] EWCA Civ 908; [2015] Q.B. 499.

14 [1896] 1 Ch. 199 at 209. See too *Carl Zeiss Stiftung v Herbert Smith (No.2)* [1969] 2 Ch. 276 at 289.

15 *Nolan v Nolan* [2004] VSCA 109 at [29]; *Haastrup v Okorie* [2016] EWHC 12 (Ch); [2016] W.T.L.R. 803 at [62]; *Green Light Solutions Corp v Baker* [2021] BCCA 287 at [41].

16 *Twigg v Twigg* [2022] NSWCA 68 at [57]: "before one can be liable as a trustee *de son tort* for a breach of trust, one must first have assumed the trust by purporting to act as if one were the trustee."

17 [2002] UKHL 48; [2003] 2 A.C. 366 at [138],

18 Cf. *High Commissioner for Pakistan in the UK v Prince Muffakham Jahat* [2019] EWHC 2551 (Ch); [2020] Ch. 421 at [251]: describing the defendant as a trustee *de son tort* was a "misnomer" because he could not be criticised for having accepted the duties of an express trustee when he was unaware that his appointment as such was invalid.

19 *Kennedy v Lyell* (1889) 14 App. Cas. 437 at 459; *Mara v Browne* [1896] 1 Ch. 199 at 209; *Dubai Aluminium Co Ltd v Salaam* [2002] UKHL 48; [2003] 2 A.C. 366 at [138].

20 As in e.g. *Re BB's Representation* (2011) 15 I.T.E.L.R. 51. See too *Williams v Central Bank of Nigeria* [2014] UKSC 10; [2014] A.C. 1189 at [54]

21 *Holder v Holder* [1968] Ch. 353 at 391, 396–397, 404; *Clay v Clay* (1999) 20 W.A.R. 427 at [16].

As Lord Millett said in *Dubai Aluminium Co Ltd v Salaam*, a trustee *de son tort* is treated "in every respect as if [she] had been duly appointed", with the result that she is "fully subject to fiduciary obligations".[22] Hence the court will treat her as having assumed a duty to account for her management of the trust property.[23] Her conduct is equated to a declaration of herself as a trustee,[24] and she is expected to familiarise herself with the extent of her duties on taking office, and thereafter she may be liable for a breach of these duties, as though she were an express trustee.[25] In this way her position may be contrasted with that of a knowing recipient, who owes a duty to account for and return the trust property she receives, but who does not owe the full range of duties associated with many forms of express trusteeship. However, a trustee *de son tort* does not have the full range of powers that she would have if she were an express trustee, and she cannot validly exercise dispositive discretions conferred on properly appointed express trustees by the trust instrument.[26] **14–016**

3. Knowing Receipt

In *El Ajou v Dollar Land Holdings Plc*,[27] Hoffmann LJ stated that for the purposes of a claim for knowing receipt the claimant must show: **14–017**

> first, a disposal of his assets in breach of fiduciary duty; secondly, the beneficial receipt by the defendant of assets which are traceable as representing the assets of the plaintiff; and thirdly, knowledge on the part of the defendant that the assets he received are traceable to a breach of fiduciary duty.

A. Disposal of Assets in Breach of Fiduciary Duty

As discussed in Chapter 2,[28] the term "fiduciary duty" is commonly used by the courts in two different senses. Sometimes they use it to describe a duty to avoid conflicts of interest owed by a person in whom another person reposes trust and confidence; and sometimes they use it to describe a trustee-like "stewardship" duty of due administration, to comply with instructions when dealing with property for another person's benefit.[29] In *El Ajou*, when Hoffmann LJ spoke of a disposal of the claimant's assets in breach of "fiduciary duty", he had the second sense in mind: the issue is not whether the person from whom the defendant received the property breached a duty to avoid a conflict of interest; rather, it is whether this person owed a duty of due administration and if so whether she acted within the scope of her authority to deal with the property. **14–018**

---

22 [2002] UKHL 48; [2003] 2 A.C. 366 at [138]–[139], following *Taylor v Davies* [1920] A.C. 636 at 651. See too *Selangor United Rubber Estates Ltd v Cradock (No.3)* [1968] 1 W.L.R. 1555 at 1579; *Paragon Finance Plc v DB Thakerar & Co* [1999] 1 All E.R. 400 at 408–409; *Williams v Central Bank of Nigeria* [2014] UKSC 10; [2014] A.C. 1189 at [9].

23 *Henchley v Thompson* [2017] EWHC 225 (Ch); [2017] W.T.L.R. 1289 at [15]–[17] and [71].

24 *Life Association of Scotland v Siddal* (1861) 3 De G. F. & J. 58 at 72.

25 *Pearce v Pearce* (1856) 22 Beav. 248 at 252.

26 *Jasmine Trustees Ltd v Wells & Hind (a firm)* [2007] EWHC 38 (Ch); [2008] Ch. 194 at [52]–[57].

27 [1994] 2 All E.R. 685 at 700.

28 See paras 2–078 to 2–090.

29 "Stewardship" is not a legal term of art and is used here in a loose sense to describe the control and management of property for another person's benefit. For judicial use of the word in this sense, see e.g. *Bairstow v Queens Moat Houses Plc* [2001] EWCA Civ 712; [2001] 2 B.C.L.C. 531 at [53]; *AIB Group (UK) Plc v Mark Redler & Co Solicitors* [2014] UKSC 58; [2015] A.C. 1503 at [39]; *Burnden Holdings (UK) Ltd v Fielding* [2018] UKSC 14; [2018] A.C. 857 at [11]. Judicial use of the term "duty of due administration" can be found in e.g. *Chief Commissioner of Stamp Duties (NSW) v Buckle* (1998) 192 C.L.R. 226 at 242; *Whaley v Whaley* [2011] EWCA Civ 617; [2011] 2 F.C.R. 323 at [112]. For further discussion see 11–024 to 11–029.

14–019 Liability for knowing receipt depends on receipt of assets in breach of a duty of due administration. As discussed in Chapter 3,[30] express trustees owe a duty of due administration, but so also do constructive and resulting trustees and liability for knowing receipt can therefore be incurred by defendants who receive property transferred in breaches of this duty by trustees of the latter sort.[31] Liability for knowing receipt can also be incurred by defendants who receive property transferred in breaches of the same duty of due administration owed by other people who are not trustees at all, including agents,[32] partners,[33] executors and administrators of deceased persons' estates,[34] and company directors.[35] This is why many claims for knowing receipt are concerned not with misapplied trust assets but with misapplied corporate assets.[36] Also, knowing recipients themselves owe a duty of due administration, and so liability for knowing receipt can be incurred by a defendant who receives improperly distributed funds from someone who is a knowing recipient.[37] However, if the person from whom a defendant received the relevant property owed no duty of due administration to the claimant, and was free to deal with the property as they chose, then no question can arise of the defendant incurring liability for knowing receipt.[38]

B. Beneficial Receipt of the Claimant's Property or its Traceable Proceeds

14–020 Receipt of property is the "gist of the action" for knowing receipt.[39] It does not suffice for liability that the defendant has been benefited in the abstract sense that their overall wealth has been increased, e.g. because their debt to a third party has been discharged: they must have received property.[40] This includes rights to real property and chattels and also choses in action (e.g. the benefit of a contract with a third party or a debt).[41] However the courts have shown little enthusiasm for arguments that in this context "property" includes more inchoate forms of right, e.g. the right to confidential information

---

30 See paras 3–143 to 3–156.

31 *Hotel Portfolio II UK Ltd (In Liquidation) v Ruhan* [2022] EWHC 383 (Comm) at [276]–[277].

32 *Pearse v Green* (1819) 1 Jac. & W. 135 Ct of KB 140–141; 37 E.R. 327 at 329; *Attorney General v Cocke* [1988] Ch. 414 at 420; *Maloney v Filtons Ltd* [2012] EWHC 1395 (Ch) at [97].

33 *London Financial Association v Kelk* (1884) 26 Ch. D. 107 at 151; *Platt v Butcher* unreported 11 November 2005, County Court (Bristol).

34 *Piety v Stace* (1799) 4 Ves. Jr. 620 at 622; *Freeman v Fairlie* (1817) 3 Mer. 29 at 43–44; *Wroe v Seed* (1863) 4 Giff. 425 at 428–429; Administration of Estates Act 1925 s.21.

35 *Re Exchange Banking Co (Flitcroft's Case)* (1882) 21 Ch. D. 519 at 525 and 535–536; *Re Lands Allotment Co* [1894] 1 Ch. 616 CA at 638; *Selangor United Rubber Estates Ltd v Cradock (No.3)* [1968] 1 W.L.R. 1555 at [1575]; *Revenue and Customs Commissioners v Holland* [2010] UKSC 51; [2011] Bus. L.R. 111 at [56]; *Sinclair Investments (UK) Ltd v Versailles Trade Finance Ltd (In Administration)* [2011] EWCA Civ 347; [2011] Bus. L.R. 1126 at [34].

36 *Russell v Wakefield Waterworks Co* (1875) L.R. 20 Eq. 474 at 479; *Belmont Finance Corp Ltd v Williams Furniture Ltd (No.2)* [1980] 1 All E.R. 393; *Agip (Africa) Ltd v Jackson* [1991] Ch. 547; *CMS Dolphin Ltd v Simonet* [2001] 2 B.C.L.C. 704; *Relfo Ltd (In Liquidation) v Varsani* [2014] EWCA Civ 360; [2015] 1 B.C.L.C. 14.

37 *Bracken Partners Ltd v Gutteridge* [2003] EWCA Civ 1875; [2004] 1 B.C.L.C. 377; *Evans v European Bank Ltd* (2004) 7 I.T.E.L.R. 19.

38 *Tuthill v Equine FX Ltd* [2013] EWHC 1207 (Comm) at [32]; *Gabriel v Little* [2013] EWCA Civ 1513; (2013) 16 I.T.E.L.R. 567 at [46]; *Dhir v Flutter Entertainment Plc* [2021] EWHC 1510 (QB) at [137]–[180].

39 *Novoship (UK) Ltd v Mikhaylyuk* [2014] EWCA Civ 908; [2015] Q.B. 499 at [89].

40 *Satnam Investments Ltd v Dunlop Heywood & Co Ltd* [1999] 1 B.C.L.C. 385 at 404; *Trustor AB v Smallbone (No.2)* [2001] 1 W.L.R. 1177 at [18]–[19]; *Quince v Varga* (2008) 11 I.T.E.L.R. 939 at [52]; *Westpac Banking Corp v Bell Group Ltd (In Liquidation) (No.3)* (2012) 270 Fed. L.R. 1 at [2137]ff; *Labrouche v Frey* [2016] EWHC 268 (Ch) at [267]–[279]; *Vancouver Coastal Health Authority v Moscipan* [2019] BCCA 17 at [64]–[82]. In this respect liability in knowing receipt differs from liability in unjust enrichment, discussed at paras 14–094 to 14–100.

41 Further see J. Glister, "Trust Property and Knowing Receipt" (2020) 34 Tru. L.I. 3.

and the right to develop and exploit business opportunities. Authorities on this point were reviewed in *Davies v Ford* where the judge concluded that:[42]

> in order to be trust property for the purpose of knowing receipt, there has to be either: (i) a pre-existing asset belonging to [the claimant] (which can include the benefit of a contract [already] entered into by it); or (ii) an asset (including the benefit of a contract) [already] acquired by the [trustee or] fiduciary ... in breach of duty which has subsequently been transferred or assigned to the knowing recipient.

Where a trustee transfers legal title to trust property to a defendant in an unauthorised transaction,[43] and the defendant still has the legal title at the time of the beneficiaries' claim, they will usually seek an order that it be reconveyed,[44] i.e. a proprietary rather than a personal remedy. There is no rule forbidding them to sue for a personal remedy in knowing receipt in such cases if they wish. Most often, however, claims in knowing receipt are brought where the defendant no longer has legal title to the property, e.g. because she transferred it to a third party, as a proprietary remedy is then no longer an option.[45] **14–021**

In *El Ajou*, Hoffmann L.J. stipulated that claims in knowing receipt lie not only in cases where defendants receive trust "assets"—meaning rights to land or chattels or choses in action—but also where they receive "assets which are traceable as representing the assets of the plaintiff". To bring themselves within the scope of this rule, a claimant must satisfy any relevant rules of tracing and following,[46] as in e.g. *Relfo Ltd (In Liq) v Varsani*,[47] where the Court of Appeal accepted that money credited to a bank account held by the defendant in Singapore represented the traceable proceeds of money debited from the claimant's bank account in England. **14–022**

A defendant must have received title to the relevant property beneficially for herself: she will not be liable if she receives property ministerially, i.e. as agent for a principal to whom they owe an immediate duty to account for the property, and who is himself immediately liable to the beneficiaries from the date of his receipt.[48] **14–023**

Does a claim in knowing receipt lie where a transfer has occurred prior to the defendant's receipt which extinguishes the claimant's equitable proprietary interest in the relevant trust property or its traceable proceeds? Suppose, for example, that the property is registered land, title to which is **14–024**

---

42 [2021] EWHC 2550 (Ch) at [245]. See also *Cook v Deeks* [1916] 1 A.C. 554, followed in *Akita Holdings Ltd v Attorney General of the Turks and Caicos Islands* [2017] UKPC 7; [2017] A.C. 590 at [15].

43 Trustees can validly transfer legal title to the trust property to a third party although the transfer is unauthorised, but if they do so under a contract with the recipient, the question whether there is a claim in knowing receipt then turns on whether the contract was binding so that the recipient was legally entitled to receive it: M. Conaglen and R. Nolan, "Contracts and Knowing Receipt: Principles and Application" (2013) 129 L.Q.R. 359. Similar rules affect recipients of corporate property from directors acting beyond their powers: *Rolled Steel Products (Holdings) Ltd v British Steel Corp* [1986] Ch. 246 at 303; *Criterion Properties Ltd v Stratford UK Properties LLC* [2002] EWCA Civ 1883; [2003] 1 W.L.R. 2108 at [4]; *Grimaldi v Chameleon Mining NL (No.2)* (2012) 200 F.C.R. 296 at [254]; *Great Investments Ltd v Warner* (2016) 243 F.C.R. 516 at [56]–[57]; *Tuke v Hood* [2020] EWHC 2843 (Comm) at [176]–[181].

44 *Ultraframe (UK) Ltd v Fielding* [2005] EWHC 1638 (Ch); [2007] W.T.L.R. 835 at [1486].

45 *Ultraframe (UK) Ltd v Fielding* [2005] EWHC 1638 (Ch); [2007] W.T.L.R. 835 at [1577].

46 See Chapter 15 for general discussion.

47 [2014] EWCA Civ 360; [2015] 1 B.C.L.C. 14. See too *Agip (Africa) Ltd v Jackson* [1990] Ch. 265 at 289–292; *El Ajou v Dollar Land Holdings Plc* [1994] 2 All E.R. 685 at 700; *Boscawen v Bajwa* [1996] 1 W.L.R. 328 at 334; *Foskett v McKeown* [2001] 1 A.C. 102 at 128; *Trustor AB v Smallbone (No.2)* [2001] 1 W.L.R. 1177 at 1184.

48 *Barnes v Addy* (1874) 9 Ch. App. 244 at 254–255; *Agip (Africa) Ltd v Jackson* [1990] Ch. 265 at 291–292; *Twinsectra Ltd v Yardley* [2002] UKHL 12; [2002] 2 A.C. 164 at 194; *Evans v European Bank Ltd* (2004) 7 I.T.E.L.R. 19 at [164]–[176]; *Sixteenth Ocean GmbH & Co KG v Société Générale* [2018] EWHC 1731 (Comm); [2018] 2 Lloyd's Rep. 465 at [109]. In these circumstances, the defendant may still be liable for dishonest assistance, depending on her state of mind, as in, e.g. *British North American Elevator Co v Bank British North American* [1919] A.C. 658; *Papamichael v National Westminster Bank Plc (No.2)* [2003] EWHC 164 (Comm); [2003] 1 Lloyd's Rep. 341.

transferred in exchange for valuable consideration so that the beneficiaries' interest is extinguished by the Land Registration Act 2002 s.29;[49] or suppose that title to the property is transferred to a party in a civil jurisdiction which does not recognise equitable proprietary rights under trusts and that a knowing receipt claim is subsequently made under English law. In *Courtwood Holdings SA v Woodley Properties Ltd*, Nugee J held that a claim in knowing receipt will not lie in circumstances of this sort, stating that:[50]

> what gives the equity to the claimants is not the knowledge of the defendants by itself, or antecedent breaches of duty, but the fact that the transaction which is impugned is not one which transfers a good title to the recipient. It is in those circumstances that the recipient, unless a bona fide purchaser for value without notice, is liable, if he still has the property, to give it back, and can be made liable to account as constructive trustee, whether he still has the property or not, if he received it in circumstances that make his receipt unconscionable.

14–025 In *Byers v Samba Financial Group*,[51] Fancourt J drew the same conclusion in a judgment that was upheld on appeal: according to the Court of Appeal in *Byers v National Saudi Bank*:[52]

> [Fancourt J] was right to conclude that a knowing recipient "must have held trust property, not property to which from the moment of receipt he had good title" and that "a claim in knowing receipt ... will fail if, at the moment of receipt, the beneficiary's equitable proprietary interest is destroyed or overridden so that the recipient holds the property as beneficial owner of it". That conclusion is, as the Judge said, borne out by "a consistent line of case law" in which it has either been decided that "a claim in knowing receipt cannot succeed unless the claimant has a continuing proprietary interest following the impugned transfer" or that has been assumed to be correct.

14–026 The Court of Appeal's reasoning in *Byers* turned on the fact that liability in knowing receipt is historically sourced in decisions of the Chancery courts where the duties of an express trustee were imposed on third party recipients of misapplied trust funds in which the beneficiaries continued to have an equitable proprietary interest. Thus Newey LJ observed that:[53]

> The cases in which the Courts have accepted that knowing recipients have "custodial" obligations, including in particular an obligation to restore the property, also tend to suggest that, to succeed in a knowing receipt claim, a claimant must have had a proprietary interest in the property when it was in the hands of the defendant. It makes sense to think of a knowing recipient owing such duties in circumstances where the property is subject to an interest having priority to the recipient's. It is much more difficult to see why a recipient should be bound to "restore" property or otherwise to have "custodial" responsibilities in respect of it if he has an unimpeachable title to it.

14–027 The point has already been made at the start of this chapter that this is why knowing recipients are said to be liable "as constructive trustees",[54] and as we discuss below, this has consequences for the remedies which are awarded against knowing recipients.[55] While Newey LJ's dicta are consistent with

---

49 A situation considered in M. Conaglen and A. Goymour, "Knowing Receipt and Registered Land" in C. Mitchell (ed.), *Constructive and Resulting Trusts* (Hart Publishing, 2010). Cf. A. See, "Recovering Misdirected Trust Assets in the Face of Torrens Indefeasibility" (2019) 13 J. Eq. 1; R. Havelock, "Reconciling Equitable Claims with Torrens Title" (2019) 41 Sydney L.R. 455.

50 [2018] EWHC 2163 (Ch) at [201] quoting [59] of his own preliminary judgment in the case.

51 [2021] EWHC 60 (Ch). See too *Courtwood Holdings SA v Woodley Properties Ltd* [2018] EWHC 2163 (Ch).

52 [2022] EWCA Civ 43; [2022] 4 W.L.R. 22 at [78].

53 [2022] EWCA Civ 43; [2022] 4 W.L.R. 22 at [75].

54 See paras 14–003 to 14–010.

55 See paras 14–081 to 14–093.

the historical development of knowing receipt liability, however, it does not follow from the history that it is now impossible for the courts to develop the law by imposing liability on a defendant who receives property that is not subject to a subsisting equitable interest at the time of receipt. Whether or not that would be desirable is a policy question the answer to which may vary with circumstances, but Newey LJ did not discuss this in his judgment. Following *Byers*, a claimant who seeks redress in a case of this kind is debarred from claiming in knowing receipt and must rely on a claim where there is no need to show that the property received by the defendant was subject to an equitable interest.[56] Dishonest assistance is one possibility, but the fault element for liability under this head is harder to prove.[57] Alternatively a claim might be made in unjust enrichment, where liability is strict and it suffices to show only that the defendant has received a benefit which need not be title to property, but which is subject to other requirements that claimants may not always find it easy to satisfy.[58] In some situations, claimants may therefore be left without a remedy, an outcome which may be justifiable in principle, but which the Court of Appeal did not attempt to justify in *Byers*.

C. Requirement of Knowledge

Until 2000, the starting point when asking whether a defendant had the requisite degree of knowledge for liability as a knowing recipient was *Baden, Delvaux v Société Générale pour Favoriser le Développement du Commerce et de l'Industrie en France SA*.[59] This case concerned liability for assisting in a breach of trust, but Peter Gibson J adopted a five-fold classification of knowledge in the case that was later used in knowing receipt cases as well. He distinguished: (i) actual knowledge; (ii) wilfully shutting one's eyes to the obvious; (iii) wilfully and recklessly failing to make such inquiries as an honest and reasonable man would make; (iv) knowledge of circumstances which would indicate the facts to an honest and reasonable man; and (v) knowledge of circumstances which would put an honest and reasonable man on inquiry.[60] **14–028**

There was no clear alignment between actual knowledge, *Baden, Delvaux* categories (i)–(iii), and dishonesty, on the one hand, and between constructive knowledge, *Baden, Delvaux* categories (iv)–(v), and negligence, on the other. Hence it is difficult to translate decisions expressed in the language of the *Baden, Delvaux* classification into the language of dishonesty and negligence. Nevertheless, the weight of authority indicated that dishonesty of the sort typically displayed by defendants falling into categories (i)–(iii) was sufficient, but not necessary, for liability,[61] and these cases were probably inconsistent with others which held that carelessness of the kind typically exhibited by defendants falling into categories (iv)–(v) was not enough.[62] **14–029**

---

56 See also *ED & F Man Capital Markets v Come Harvest Holdings Ltd* [2022] EWHC 229 (Comm) (no liability for knowing receipt where D received absolute ownership of property, knowing that the transfer had been procured by fraud, with the result that C was entitled to rescind and thereby cause a trust of the property to arise in C's favour). *Grimaldi v Chameleon Mining NL (No.2)* (2012) 287 A.L.R. 22 at [254] is to the same effect.

57 See paras 14–112 to 14–152.

58 See para.14–100.

59 [1993] 1 W.L.R. 509 (the case was decided in 1983).

60 *Baden, Delvaux* [1993] 1 W.L.R. 509 at 575–587.

61 *Selangor United Rubber Estates Ltd v Cradock (No.3)* [1968] 1 W.L.R. 1555; *Belmont Finance Corp v Williams Furniture Ltd (No.2)* [1980] 1 All E.R. 399 at 405; *International Sales and Agencies Ltd v Marcus* [1982] 3 All E.R. 551 at 558; *Baden, Delvaux v Société Générale pour Favoriser le Développement du Commerce et de l'Industrie en France SA* [1993] 1 W.L.R. 509 at 582; *Houghton v Fayers* [2000] 1 B.C.L.C. 511.

62 *Re Montagu's Settlement Trusts* [1987] Ch. 264; *Lipkin Gorman v Karpnale Ltd* [1987] 1 W.L.R. 987 at 1005; *Barclays Bank Plc v Quincecare Ltd* [1992] 4 All E.R. 363 at 375; *Eagle Trust Plc v SBC Securities Ltd* [1992] 4 All E.R. 488 at 509; *Cowan de Groot Properties Ltd v Eagle Trust Plc* [1991] B.C.L.C. 1045 at 1110; *Polly Peck International Plc v Nadir (No.2)* [1992] 4 All E.R. 769 at 777; *Jonathan v Tilley* (1988) 12 Tru. L.I. 36.

14–030 In 1995, in *Royal Brunei Airlines Sdn Bhd v Tan*,[63] the Privy Council held that liability for assisting in a breach of trust should no longer be decided with reference to the *Baden, Delvaux* classification, which had become over-theorised and obscure.[64] In 2000, in *Bank of Credit and Commerce International (Overseas) Ltd v Akindele*,[65] the Court of Appeal then said the same thing with respect to knowing receipt. Nourse LJ held that dishonesty will suffice, but is not required, to make a defendant liable where she has received and dealt with misapplied trust property for her own benefit,[66] and that as a general rule a defendant will be liable whenever her "state of knowledge [is] . . . such as to make it unconscionable for [her] to retain the benefit of the receipt."[67]

Bank of Credit and Commerce International (Overseas) Ltd v Akindele

Court of Appeal [2001] Ch. 437

14–031 The defendant, Chief Akindele, entered a contract with two companies, ICIC (Overseas) Ltd and BCCI (Overseas) Ltd, for the purchase of shares in their holding company, BCCI Holdings (Luxembourg) SA. The contract provided that the defendant would pay US$10 million to BCCI (Overseas) Ltd in exchange for 250,000 shares in the holding company, and on terms that after two years BCCI (Overseas) Ltd would arrange for their sale at a price that would give the defendant a 15 per cent annual return on his investment. The defendant paid the money, and by a further agreement, the shares were later sold and the defendant was paid US$16.679 million. Following the insolvent liquidation of ICIC (Overseas) Ltd and BCCI (Overseas) Ltd, it emerged that these arrangements had been procured as part of a fraudulent scheme by officers of the BCCI group, acting in breach of their fiduciary duty to their employers, the point of which had been to give the false impression that certain dummy loans had been performing normally. The liquidators of the two companies claimed that the defendant was liable to account to them for US$6.679m as a constructive trustee on the basis that he had knowingly assisted the breaches of fiduciary duty or had received the US$16.679 million with knowledge of these breaches. At first instance Carnwath J. dismissed the action on the ground that dishonesty by the defendant was the essential foundation of the claimants' case whether under the head of knowing assistance or of knowing receipt and that this had not been established by the claimants. The liquidators appealed.

14–032 NOURSE L.J. (with whom WARD L.J. and SEDLEY L.J. agreed) stated the facts and then continued:

The Claimants' Case in this Court

14–033 The judge[68] identified the two main issues arising on the pleadings as being, first, was the defendant liable for dishonestly assisting or participating in breaches of trust by Mr Naqvi, Mr Hafeez and Mr Kazmi (knowing assistance) and, secondly, was the defendant liable for receiving the divestiture payment with knowledge of the breaches of trust (knowing receipt). In this court the claimants' case has been maintained under both heads. In regard to knowing assistance, while accepting the judge's findings of primary fact, Mr Sheldon submitted that he was wrong not to infer from them that the defendant had acted dishonestly. I cannot accept that submission. Having seen and heard the defendant give evidence and found him to be a credible witness on most points, and after a conscientious consideration of the evidence as a whole, the judge was entitled to find that he had acted honestly. It cannot be said either that there was no evidence to support that finding or that it was against the weight of the evidence as a whole. The defendant not having acted dishonestly, the case in knowing assistance is bound to fail. If the claim is to succeed at all, it can only be in knowing receipt.

63 [1995] 2 A.C. 378.
64 See paras 14–112 to 14–146.
65 [2001] Ch. 437.
66 *Bank of Credit and Commerce International (Overseas) Ltd v Akindele* [2001] Ch. 437 at 440.
67 *Bank of Credit and Commerce International (Overseas) Ltd v Akindele* [2001] Ch. 437 at 455.
68 [1999] B.C.C. 669 at 675–676.

Knowing Receipt

The essential requirements of knowing receipt were stated by Hoffmann L.J. in *El Ajou v Dollar Land Holdings Plc*:[69] 14–034

> "For this purpose the plaintiff must show, first, a disposal of his assets in breach of fiduciary duty; secondly, the beneficial receipt by the defendant of assets which are traceable as representing the assets of the plaintiff; and thirdly, knowledge on the part of the defendant that the assets he received are traceable to a breach of fiduciary duty."

In the present case the first two requirements were satisfied in relation to the defendant's receipt of the US$16.679m paid to him pursuant to the divestiture agreement. But the satisfaction of the third requirement, knowledge on the part of the defendant that the sum received by him was traceable to a breach or breaches of fiduciary duty by Mr Naqvi, Mr Hafeez and Mr Kazmi, is problematical. 14–035

So far as the law is concerned, the comprehensive arguments of Mr Sheldon and Mr Moss have demonstrated that there are two questions which, though closely related, are distinct: first, what, in this context, is meant by knowledge; second, is it necessary for the recipient to act dishonestly? Because the answer to it is the simpler, the convenient course is to deal with the second of those questions first. 14–036

Knowing Receipt—Dishonesty

As appears from the penultimate sentence of his judgment, Carnwath J. proceeded on an assumption that dishonesty in one form or another was the essential foundation of the claimants' case, whether in knowing assistance or knowing receipt. That was no doubt caused by the acceptance before him (though not at any higher level) by Mr Sheldon, recorded at p.677f, that the thrust of the recent authorities at first instance was that the recipient's state of knowledge must fall into one of the first three categories listed by Peter Gibson J. in *Baden, Delvaux v Société Générale pour Favoriser le Développement du Commerce et de l'Industrie en France SA*,[70] on which basis, said Mr Justice Carnwath, it was doubtful whether the test differed materially in practice from that for knowing assistance. However, the assumption on which the judge proceeded, derived as I believe from an omission to distinguish between the questions of knowledge and dishonesty, was incorrect in law. While a knowing recipient will often be found to have acted dishonestly, it has never been a prerequisite of the liability that he should. 14–037

An authoritative decision on this question, the complexity of whose subject transactions has sometimes caused it to be overlooked in this particular context, is *Belmont Finance Corporation v Williams Furniture Ltd (No.2)*,[71] where the plaintiff ("Belmont") was the wholly-owned subsidiary of the second defendant ("City"), which in turn was the wholly-owned subsidiary of the first defendant ("Williams"). The chairman of all three companies and the sole effective force in the management of their affairs was Mr John James. Reduced to its essentials, what had happened there was that the shareholders of a fourth company ("Maximum") had agreed to sell its shares to Belmont for £500,000 and to buy the share capital of Belmont from City for £489,000, a transaction which, as carried out, constituted a contravention of section 54 of the Companies Act 1948 (prohibition of provision of financial assistance by a company for the purchase of its own shares) and was thus a misapplication of Belmont's funds. 14–038

Belmont having subsequently become insolvent, its receiver obtained an independent valuation of the shares in Maximum as at the date of the transaction which suggested that, instead of being worth £500,000, they were only worth some £60,000. The receiver brought an action in Belmont's name principally against Williams, City and the shareholders of Maximum, claiming that they were liable to Belmont, first, for damages for conspiracy and, secondly, as constructive trustees on the grounds of both knowing assistance and knowing receipt. At the trial, Foster J. found that Mr James genuinely believed that to buy the capital of Maximum for £500,000 was a good commercial proposition for Belmont. He held that there had been no contravention of section 54 and dismissed the action. 14–039

---

69 [1994] 2 All E.R. 685 at 700.
70 [1993] 1 W.L.R. 509 at 575–576.
71 [1980] 1 All E.R. 393.

14–040 On Belmont's successful appeal to this court Buckley L.J. is recorded[72] as having pointed out that Mr James had genuinely believed that the transaction was a good commercial proposition for Belmont without having any good grounds for that belief. He continued:

> "After careful consideration I do not feel that we should be justified in disturbing the judge's finding that Mr James genuinely believed that the agreement was a good commercial proposition for Belmont. It was a belief which, on his view of the commercial aspects of the case, Mr James could have sincerely held."

14–041 Having observed that Mr James, as a director of both Williams and City knew perfectly well what the objects of the transaction were, that other officers of City had the same knowledge and that their knowledge must be "imputed" to the respective companies,[73] and having referred[74] to the judgment of Lord Selborne L.C. in *Barnes v Addy*,[75] Buckley L.J. dealt with the claim in constructive trust:[76]

> "In the present case, the payment of the £500,000 by Belmont to [the shareholders of Maximum], being an unlawful contravention of section 54, was a misapplication of Belmont's money and was in breach of the duties of the directors of Belmont. £489,000 of the £500,000 so misapplied found their way into the hands of City with City's knowledge of the whole circumstances of the transaction. It must follow, in my opinion, that City is accountable to Belmont as a constructive trustee of the £489,000 under the first of Lord Selborne L.C.'s two heads. There remains the question whether City is chargeable as a constructive trustee under Lord Selborne's second head on the ground that Belmont's directors were guilty of dishonesty in buying the shares of Maximum and that City with knowledge of the facts assisted them in that dishonest design. As I understand Lord Selborne L.C.'s second head, a stranger to a trust notwithstanding that he may not have received any of the trust fund which has been misapplied will be treated as accountable as a constructive trustee if he has knowingly participated in a dishonest design on the part of the trustee to misapply the fund; he must himself have been in some way a party to the dishonesty of the trustees. It follows from what I have already held that the directors of Belmont were guilty of misfeasance but not that they acted dishonestly."

14–042 Goff L.J. also held that City was liable in knowing receipt.[77] Waller L.J. did not add anything of his own on the question of constructive trust. Accordingly, though the claim in knowing assistance failed because the directors of Belmont did not act dishonestly, the claim in knowing receipt succeeded. I will return to that decision when dealing with the question of knowledge.

14–043 *Belmont Finance Corporation v Williams Furniture Ltd (No.2)* is clear authority for the proposition that dishonesty is not a necessary ingredient of liability in knowing receipt. There have been other, more recent, judicial pronouncements to the same effect. Thus in *Polly Peck International Plc v Nadir (No.2)*,[78] Scott L.J. said that liability in a knowing receipt case did not require that the misapplication of the trust funds should be fraudulent. While in theory it is possible for a misapplication not to be fraudulent and the recipient to be dishonest, in practice such a combination must be rare. Similarly, in *Agip (Africa) Ltd v Jackson*,[79] Millett J. said that in knowing receipt it was immaterial whether the breach of trust was fraudulent or not. The point was made most clearly by Vinelott J. in *Eagle Trust Plc v SBC Securities Ltd*:[80]

> "What the decision in *Belmont (No. 2)* shows is that in a 'knowing receipt' case it is only necessary to show that the defendant knew that the moneys paid to him were trust moneys and of circumstances which made the payment a misapplication of them. Unlike a 'knowing assistance' case it is not necessary, and never has been necessary, to show that the defendant was in any sense a participator in a fraud."

---

72 At 403.
73 At 404.
74 At 405.
75 (1874) L.R. 9 Ch. App. 244 at 251.
76 At 405.
77 At 410–412.
78 [1992] 4 All E.R. 769 at 777.
79 [1990] Ch. 265 at 292.
80 [1993] 1 W.L.R. 484 at 497.

Knowing Receipt—The Authorities on Knowledge

With the proliferation in the last 20 years or so of cases in which the misapplied assets of companies have come into the hands of third parties, there has been a sustained judicial and extra-judicial debate as to the knowledge on the part of the recipient which is required in order to found liability in knowing receipt. Expressed in its simplest terms, the question is whether the recipient must have actual knowledge (or the equivalent) that the assets received are traceable to a breach of trust or whether constructive knowledge is enough. The instinctive approach of most equity judges, especially in this court, has been to assume that constructive knowledge is enough. But there is now a series of decisions of eminent first instance judges who, after considering the question in greater depth, have come to the contrary conclusion, at all events when commercial transactions are in point. In the Commonwealth, on the other hand, the preponderance of authority has been in favour of the view that constructive knowledge is enough. **14–044**

In *Karak Rubber Co Ltd v Burden*,[81] Brightman J. referred to a person: **14–045**

"who is a constructive trustee because (though not nominated as a trustee) he has received trust property with actual or constructive notice that it is trust property transferred in breach of trust . . .".

In *Belmont (No.2)*,[82] Buckley L.J. referred to the principle, established by the decision of this court in *Re Lands Allotment Co*,[83] that the directors of a company are treated as if they were actual trustees of the assets of the company which are in their hands or under their control. He continued: **14–046**

"So, if the directors of a company in breach of their fiduciary duties misapply the funds of their company so that they come into the hands of some stranger to the trust who receives them with knowledge (actual or constructive) of the breach, he cannot conscientiously retain those funds against the company unless he has some better equity. He becomes a constructive trustee for the company of the misapplied funds."

Goff L.J. said that what Belmont had to show, among other things, was that City received all or part of the £500,000 "knowing or in circumstances in which it ought to know, that it was a breach of trust".[84] He answered that question, saying:[85] **14–047**

"In my judgment the answer to that question must plainly be Yes for they are fixed with all the knowledge that Mr James had. Now, he had actual knowledge of all the facts which made the agreement illegal and his belief that the agreement was a good commercial proposition for Belmont can be no more a defence to City's liability as constructive trustees than in conspiracy. Apart from this, clearly, in my judgment, Mr James knew or ought to have known all the facts that I have rehearsed, showing that there was in any event a misfeasance apart from illegality."

Similarly, in *Rolled Steel Products (Holdings) Ltd v British Steel Corporation*,[86] Browne-Wilkinson L.J. said: **14–048**

"A third party who has notice—actual or constructive—that a transaction, although intra vires the company, was entered into in excess or abuse of the powers of the company cannot enforce such transaction against the company and will be accountable as constructive trustee for any money or property of the company received by [him]."

In *Agip (Africa) Ltd v Jackson*,[87] Millett J., in reference to a person who receives for his own benefit trust property transferred to him in breach of trust, said: **14–049**

"He is liable as a constructive trustee if he received it with notice, actual or constructive, that it was trust property and that the transfer to him was a breach of trust. . .".

---

[81] [1972] 1 W.L.R. 602 at 632.
[82] At 405.
[83] [1894] 1 Ch. 616.
[84] At 410.
[85] At 412.
[86] [1986] Ch. 246 at 306.
[87] At 291.

14–050 In *Houghton v Fayers*,[88] I myself said that it was enough for the claimant company to establish that the second defendant "knew or ought to have known that the money had been paid to him in breach of [the first defendant's] fiduciary duty to [the claimant]".

14–051 Collectively, those observations might be thought to provide strong support for the view that constructive knowledge is enough. But it must at once be said that in each of the three cases in this court (including, despite some apparent uncertainty in the judgment of Goff L.J.,[89] *Belmont (No.2)*) actual knowledge was found and, further, that the decisions in *Karak* and *Agip* were based on knowing assistance, not knowing receipt. Thus in none of the five cases was it necessary for the question to be examined in any depth and there appears to be no case in which such an examination has been conducted in this court. The groundwork has been done in other cases at first instance. I will refer to those of them in which the question has been considered in depth.

14–052 The seminal judgment, characteristically penetrative in its treatment of authority and, in the best sense, argumentative, is that of Megarry V.C. in *Re Montagu's Settlement Trusts*.[90] It was he who first plumbed the distinction between notice and knowledge. It was he who, building on a passage in the judgment of this court in *Re Diplock*,[91] first emphasised the fundamental difference between the questions which arise in respect of the doctrine of purchaser without notice on the one hand and the doctrine of constructive trusts on the other. Reading from his earlier judgment in the same case, he said:[92]

> "The former is concerned with the question whether a person takes property subject to or free from some equity. The latter is concerned with whether or not a person is to have imposed upon him the personal burdens and obligations of trusteeship. I do not see why one of the touchstones for determining the burdens on property should be the same as that for deciding whether to impose a personal obligation on a [person]. The cold calculus of constructive and imputed notice does not seem to me to be an appropriate instrument for deciding whether a [person's] conscience is sufficiently affected for it to be right to bind him by the obligations of a constructive trustee."

14–053 He added that there is more to being made a trustee than merely taking property subject to an equity.

14–054 The practical importance of that distinction had been explained by the Vice-Chancellor in his earlier judgment. The question in that case was whether the widow and executrix of the will of the 10th Duke of Manchester was liable to account to the 11th Duke in respect of certain settled chattels or the proceeds of sale thereof. Having found that the 10th Duke had had no knowledge that the chattels received by him were still subject to any trust and that he believed that they had been lawfully and properly released to him by the trustees, Megarry V.C. continued:[93]

> "If liability as a constructive trustee depended on his knowledge, then he was not liable as a constructive trustee, and his estate is not liable for any chattels that have been disposed of, as distinct from any traceable proceeds of them. Even if he was not a constructive trustee and was a mere volunteer, his estate is liable to yield up any chattels that remain, or the traceable proceeds of any that have gone. . . . But unless he was a constructive trustee, there appears to be no liability if the chattels have gone and there are no traceable proceeds."

14–055 Megarry V.C. summarised his conclusions in eight subparagraphs.[94] I read the first three:

> "(1) The equitable doctrine of tracing and the imposition of a constructive trust by reason of the knowing receipt of trust property are governed by different rules and must be kept distinct. Tracing is primarily a means of determining the rights of property, whereas the imposition of a constructive trust creates personal obligations that go beyond mere property rights. (2) In considering whether a constructive trust has arisen in a case of the knowing receipt of trust property, the basic question is whether the conscience of the recipient is sufficiently affected to justify the imposition of such a trust.

---

88 [2000] 1 B.C.L.C. 511 at 516.
89 At 412.
90 [1987] Ch. 264.
91 [1948] Ch. 465 at 478–479.
92 At 278.
93 At 272.
94 At 285.

(3) Whether a constructive trust arises in such a case primarily depends on the knowledge of the recipient, and not on notice to him; and for clarity it is desirable to use the word 'knowledge' and avoid the word 'notice' in such cases."

The effect of the Vice-Chancellor's decision, broadly stated, was that, in order to establish liability in knowing receipt, the recipient must have actual knowledge (or the equivalent) that the assets received are traceable to a breach of trust and that constructive knowledge is not enough. **14-056**

In *Eagle Trust Plc v SBC Securities Ltd*,[95] Vinelott J. did not think it would be right to found a decision that the statement of claim in that case disclosed no cause of action solely on the authority of *Re Montagu's Settlement Trusts*. However, on the ground that he (unlike Megarry V.C.) was dealing with a commercial transaction, he arrived at the same conclusion and held that in such a transaction constructive knowledge is not enough. He cited[96] a well known passage in the judgment of Lindley L.J. in *Manchester Trust v Furness*,[97] the latter part of which reads thus: **14-057**

"In dealing with estates in land title is everything, and it can be leisurely investigated; in commercial transactions possession is everything, and there is no time to investigate title; and if we were to extend the doctrine of constructive notice to commercial transactions we should be doing infinite mischief and paralyzing the trade of the country."

The decision of Vinelott J. was followed by Knox J. in *Cowan de Groot Properties Ltd v Eagle Trust Plc*[98] (another case of a commercial transaction) and the decisions of both of them by Arden J. at the trial of the action in *Eagle Trust Plc v SBC Securities Ltd*.[99] **14-058**

We were also referred to three decisions in New Zealand and one in Canada. In each of *Westpac Banking Corp v Savin*,[100] *Equiticorp Industries Group Ltd v Hawkins*,[101] and *Lankshear v ANZ Banking Group (New Zealand) Ltd*,[102] the preferred view was that constructive knowledge was enough, although in the last-named case the point went by concession. All of them were cases of commercial transactions. In *Westpac Banking Corp v Savin*, a decision of the Court of Appeal, Richardson J., having expressed a provisional preference for the view that constructive knowledge was enough, said:[103] **14-059**

"Clearly Courts would not readily import a duty to enquire in the case of commercial transactions where they must be conscious of the seriously inhibiting effects of a wide application of the doctrine. Nevertheless there must be cases where there is no justification on the known facts for allowing a commercial man who has received funds paid to him in breach of trust to plead the shelter of the exigencies of commercial life."

In *Citadel General Assurance Co.v Lloyds Bank Canada*,[104] another case of a commercial transaction, the Supreme Court of Canada held, as a matter of decision, that constructive knowledge was enough. **14-060**

The *Baden* Case

It will have been observed that up to this stage I have made no more than a passing reference to the five-fold categorisation of knowledge accepted by Peter Gibson J. in the *Baden* case:[105] (i) actual knowledge; (ii) wilfully shutting one's eyes to the obvious; (iii) wilfully and recklessly failing to make such enquiries as an honest and reasonable man would make; (iv) knowledge of circumstances which would indicate the facts to an honest and reasonable man; (v) knowledge of circumstances which will put an honest and reasonable man on inquiry. Reference to the categorisation has been made in most of the knowing receipt cases to which I have referred from *Re Montagu's Settlement Trusts* onwards. In many of them it has **14-061**

95 At 503.
96 At 504.
97 [1895] 2 Q.B. 539 at 545.
98 [1992] 4 All E.R. 700.
99 See [1996] 1 B.C.L.C. 121.
100 [1985] 2 N.Z.L.R. 41.
101 [1991] 3 N.Z.L.R. 700.
102 [1993] 1 N.Z.L.R. 481.
103 At 53.
104 (1997) 152 D.L.R. (4th) 411.
105 [1993] 1 W.L.R. 509, 575–576.

been influential in the decision. In general, the first three categories have been taken to constitute actual knowledge (or its equivalent) and the last two constructive knowledge.

14–062 Two important points must be made about the *Baden* categorisation. First, it appears to have been propounded by counsel for the plaintiffs, accepted by counsel for the defendant and then put to the judge on an agreed basis. Secondly, though both counsel accepted that all five categories of knowledge were relevant and neither sought to submit that there was any distinction for that purpose between knowing receipt and knowing assistance (a view with which the judge expressed his agreement[106]), the claim in constructive trust was based squarely on knowing assistance and not on knowing receipt.[107] In the circumstances, whatever may have been agreed between counsel, it is natural to assume that the categorisation was not formulated with knowing receipt primarily in mind. This, I think, may be confirmed by the references to "an honest and reasonable man" in categories (iv) and (v). Moreover, in *Agip* Millett J. warned against over refinement or a too ready assumption that categories (iv) and (v) are necessarily cases of constructive knowledge only.[108]

Knowing Receipt—The Recipient's State of Knowledge

14–063 In *Royal Brunei Airlines Sdn Bhd v Tan*,[109] which is now the leading authority on knowing assistance, Lord Nicholls of Birkenhead, in delivering the judgment of the Privy Council, said that "knowingly" was better avoided as a defining ingredient of the liability, and that in that context the *Baden* categorisation was best forgotten.[110] Although my own view is that the categorisation is often helpful in identifying different states of knowledge which may or may not result in a finding of dishonesty for the purposes of knowing assistance, I have grave doubts about its utility in cases of knowing receipt. Quite apart from its origins in a context of knowing assistance and the reservations of Millett and Knox JJ., any categorisation is of little value unless the purpose it is to serve is adequately defined, whether it be fivefold, as in *Baden*, or twofold, as in the classical division between actual and constructive knowledge, a division which has itself become blurred in recent authorities.

14–064 What then, in the context of knowing receipt, is the purpose to be served by a categorisation of knowledge? It can only be to enable the court to determine whether, in the words of Buckley L.J. in *Belmont (No.2)*, the recipient can "conscientiously retain [the] funds against the company" or, in the words of Megarry V.C. in *Re Montagu's Settlement Trusts*, "[the recipient's] conscience is sufficiently affected for it to be right to bind him by the obligations of a constructive trustee". But if that is the purpose, there is no need for categorisation. All that is necessary is that the recipient's state of knowledge should be such as to make it unconscionable for him to retain the benefit of the receipt.

14–065 For these reasons I have come to the view that, just as there is now a single test of dishonesty for knowing assistance, so ought there to be a single test of knowledge for knowing receipt. The recipient's state of knowledge must be such as to make it unconscionable for him to retain the benefit of the receipt. A test in that form, though it cannot, any more than any other, avoid difficulties of application, ought to avoid those of definition and allocation to which the previous categorisations have led. Moreover, it should better enable the courts to give common-sense decisions in the commercial context in which claims in knowing receipt are now frequently made, paying equal regard to the wisdom of Lindley L.J. on the one hand and of Richardson J. on the other.

Knowing Receipt—A Footnote

14–066 We were referred in argument to "Knowing Receipt: The Need for a New Landmark", an essay by Lord Nicholls;[111] a work of insight and scholarship taking forward the writings of academic authors, in particular those of Professors Birks, Burrows and Gareth Jones. It is impossible to do justice to such a work within the compass of a judgment such as this. Most pertinent for present purposes is the

---

106 At 582.
107 See 572.
108 [1990] Ch. 265 at 293, reservations which were shared by Knox J. in *Cowan de Groot* [1992] 4 All E.R. 700 at 761.
109 [1995] 2 A.C. 378.
110 At 392.
111 In Cornish, Nolan, O'Sullivan and Virgo (eds) *Restitution Past, Present and Future* (1998).

suggestion made by Lord Nicholls,[112] in reference to the decision of the House of Lords in *Lipkin Gorman v Karpnale Ltd*:[113]

> "In this respect equity should now follow the law. Restitutionary liability, applicable regardless of fault but subject to a defence of change of position, would be a better-tailored response to the underlying mischief of misapplied property than personal liability which is exclusively fault-based. Personal liability would flow from having received the property of another, from having been unjustly enriched at the expense of another. It would be triggered by the mere fact of receipt, thus recognising the endurance of property rights. But fairness would be ensured by the need to identify a gain, and by making change of position available as a default in suitable cases when, for instance, the recipient had changed his position in reliance on the receipt."

Lord Nicholls goes on to examine the *Re Diplock*[114] principle, suggesting that it could be reshaped by being extended to all trusts but in a form modified to take proper account of the decision in *Lipkin Gorman v Karpnale Ltd*.[115] 14–067

No argument before us was based on the suggestions made in Lord Nicholls' essay. Indeed, at this level of decision, it would have been a fruitless exercise. We must continue to do our best with the accepted formulation of the liability in knowing receipt, seeking to simplify and improve it where we may. While in general it may be possible to sympathise with a tendency to subsume a further part of our law of restitution under the principles of unjust enrichment, I beg leave to doubt whether strict liability coupled with a change of position defence would be preferable to fault-based liability in many commercial transactions, for example where, as here, the receipt is of a company's funds which have been misapplied by its directors. Without having heard argument it is unwise to be dogmatic, but in such a case it would appear to be commercially unworkable and contrary to the spirit of the rule in *Royal British Bank v Turquand*[116] that, simply on proof of an internal misapplication of the company's funds, the burden should shift to the recipient to defend the receipt either by a change of position or perhaps in some other way. Moreover, if the circumstances of the receipt are such as to make it unconscionable for the recipient to retain the benefit of it, there is an obvious difficulty in saying that it is equitable for a change of position to afford him a defence. 14–068

Knowing Receipt—The Facts of the Present Case

I return to the facts of the present case, in order to determine whether the defendant is liable in knowing receipt to repay (together with interest) US$6.679m of the sum received by him pursuant to the divestiture agreement, being the excess over the US$10m he paid to ICIC Overseas pursuant to the 1985 agreement. (By a decision whose forensic good sense dispensed with an analysis of its juristic foundation the claimants abandoned a claim for the full US$16.679m.) The answer to that question depends on whether the judge's findings, though made in the course of an inquiry as to the defendant's honesty, are equally supportive of a conclusion that his state of knowledge was not such as to make it unconscionable for him to retain the benefit of the receipt. 14–069

I start with the defendant's state of knowledge at the date of the 1985 agreement. As to that, the judge found that there was no evidence that anyone outside BCCI had reason to doubt the integrity of its management at that time. More specifically, it is clear that the judge was of the view that the defendant had no knowledge of the underlying frauds within the BCCI group either in general or in relation to the 1985 agreement. He found that the defendant saw it simply as an arm's-length business transaction. Moreover, he was not prepared to draw the conclusion that the high rate of interest and the artificial nature of the agreement were sufficient to put an honest person in the defendant's position on notice that some fraud or breach of trust was being perpetrated. He said that the defendant would have had no reason to question the form of the transaction. 14–070

Those findings, expressed in language equally appropriate to an inquiry as to constructive notice, appear to me to be consistent only with the view that the defendant's state of knowledge at the date of the 1985 agreement was not such as to make it unconscionable for him to enter into it. However, that 14–071

[112] At p.238.
[113] [1991] 2 A.C. 548.
[114] [1948] Ch. 465.
[115] At p.241.
[116] (1856) 6 E. & B. 327.

point, though of great importance, is not in itself decisive. We have also to consider the defendant's state of knowledge at the date of the divestiture agreement, by which time, as the judge said, he did have suspicions as to the conduct of BCCI's affairs.

14-072 In order to understand the judge's reference, it is necessary to go back to what he said[117]:

"Towards the end of 1988 the defendant decided to end his relationship with BCCI, and in particular to terminate the share agreement. A number of factors led to this decision. In late 1987 there had been rumours in the Nigerian press of irregularities involving BCCI. He had received warnings from senior business figures in Nigeria. One was Dr Onaolapo Soleye, a former Nigerian Minister of Finance, who has provided a witness statement. He says that he informed the defendant of 'unorthodox and irregular banking practices around the world', and warned him of the effect a scandal relating to BCCI could have on his business image and that of BCCI Nigeria. The defendant also became aware later in 1988 that various BCCI officials had been arrested by US Customs in Tampa in connection with money laundering offences. He considered selling his shares in BCCI Nigeria, but was dissuaded from doing so by Dr Soleye and others, because of the tribal imbalance it would create within the bank. At this time the defendant was seeking to realise £20m of his own money, and to raise a further £40m, to finance a property investment venture in the UK. The major banks involved including NM Rothschild in London and BNP, objected to him raising part of the finance from BCCI."

14-073 So in late 1987, more than two years after the 1985 agreement was entered into, there were press rumours of irregularities involving BCCI and warnings to the defendant from senior business figures in Nigeria of unorthodox and irregular banking practices around the world. Later in 1988 the defendant became aware that various BCCI officials had been arrested in connection with money laundering offences. He also knew that the major banks involved in financing his property investment venture in the United Kingdom objected to his raising part of the finance from BCCI.

14-074 There having been no evidence that the defendant was aware of the internal arrangements within BCCI which led to the payment to him of the US$16.679m pursuant to the divestiture agreement, did the additional knowledge which he acquired between July 1985 and December 1988 make it unconscionable for him to retain the benefit of the receipt? In my judgment it did not. The additional knowledge went to the general reputation of the BCCI group from late 1987 onwards. It was not a sufficient reason for questioning the propriety of a particular transaction entered into more than two years earlier, at a time when no one outside BCCI had reason to doubt the integrity of its management and in a form which the defendant had no reason to question. The judge said that the defendant was entitled to take steps to protect his own interest, and that there was nothing dishonest in his seeking to enforce the 1985 agreement. Nor was there anything unconscionable in his seeking to do so. Equally, had I thought that that was still the appropriate test, I would have held that the defendant did not have actual or constructive knowledge that his receipt of the US$6.79m was traceable to a breach or breaches of fiduciary duty by Messrs Naqvi, Hafeez and Kazmi.

Conclusion

14-075 For these reasons, though by a different route in relation to knowing receipt, I have come to the conclusion that Mr Justice Carnwath's decision to dismiss the action was correct. I would affirm it and dismiss the claimants' appeal.

14-076 Four points should be made here about *Akindele*. First, it may be doubted whether unconscionability is a sufficiently certain concept to bring clarity and predictability to the law in this area.[118] Indeed, it was rejected by Lord Nicholls in *Royal Brunei* as the test for assistance liability for precisely this reason. However, it is doubtful that any other test would achieve that either and there is much to be said for abandoning the over-subtle distinctions of *Baden, Delvaux*. In practice, the courts do not find it hard to apply the "unconscionability" test, and although a sceptic might say that this is because it makes

117 At p.675.

118 Consider the different readings of *Akindele* in *Papamichael v National Westminster Bank Plc (No.2)* [2003] EWHC 164 (Comm); [2003] 1 Lloyd's Rep. 341 at [246]–[247] and *Criterion Properties Plc v Stratford UK Properties LLC* [2002] EWCA Civ 1883; [2003] 1 W.L.R. 2108 at [20]–[39], not reviewed on appeal [2004] UKHL 28; [2004] 1 W.L.R. 1846.

liability turn on judicial discretion, the courts themselves regard this as a desirable feature because the facts of cases are various and the test enables them "to set a standard that is appropriate to the exigencies of the transaction in question".[119] *Akindele* has been reaffirmed by the Court of Appeal on several occasions[120] and judicial use of the term "unconscionable receipt" is increasing.[121]

Second, in *Agip (Africa) Ltd* v *Jackson*,[122] Millett J held that: **14–077**

> the person who receives for his own benefit trust property transferred to him in breach of trust ... is liable as a constructive trustee if he received it with notice, actual or constructive, that it was trust property and that the transfer to him was a breach of trust; or if he received it without such notice but subsequently discovered the facts. In either case he is liable to account for the property, in the first case as from the time he received the property, and in the second as from the time he acquired notice.

To establish a claim in knowing receipt it is therefore sufficient, but not necessary, for a claimant to show that the defendant had knowledge at the time of receipt, since the acquisition of knowledge at a later date can also suffice, though only if the defendant still owned the relevant property when he acquired this knowledge.[123] **14–078**

Third, liability will be incurred by a defendant who knows that as a matter of law a breach of trust or fiduciary duty was committed when property was transferred to her, but liability may also be incurred by a defendant who only knows the facts which make this transfer a breach of trust. So it suffices, for example, that a defendant knows that money she receives was "fraudulently obtained by deceit and illegal hacking" and in such a case it is immaterial whether she also knows "the actual identity of the victim, i.e. the true underlying beneficiary of the trust monies".[124] There is, however, a difference between knowing that property has been misappropriated and knowing that a legal claim has been made with respect to disputed property—and knowledge of the latter kind is not "sufficient to amount to notice of a trust or notice of misapplication of the moneys."[125] Hence solicitors who act for a party defending a proprietary claim can rely on a bona purchase defence against a claim for knowing receipt in respect of money they have received as fees.[126] **14–079**

Fourth, the court in *Akindele* seems to have thought that it could not recognise a strict liability claim in unjust enrichment against recipients of misdirected trust funds without departing from many cases requiring proof of fault for liability in knowing receipt. However, no such departure would be needed if the courts were to recognise that a claim in unjust enrichment against a recipient of misdirected trust funds can lie concurrently with a compensatory claim for knowing receipt. This is discussed further in Part E. **14–080**

---

119 *Moody v Estate of Jones (Deceased)* [2021] EWHC 3443 (Ch) at [302].

120 *Criterion Properties Plc v Stratford UK Properties LLC* [2002] EWCA Civ 1883; [2003] 1 W.L.R. 2108 at [20]–[39], not reviewed on appeal [2004] UKHL 28; [2004] 1 W.L.R. 1846; *City Index Ltd v Gawler* [2007] EWCA Civ 1382; [2008] Ch. 313; *Uzinterimpex JSC v Standard Bank Plc* [2008] EWCA Civ 819; [2008] Bus. L.R. 1762. See too *Arthur v Attorney General of the Turks and Caicos Islands* [2012] UKPC 30 at [33].

121 *Brent LBC v Davies* [2018] EWHC 3129 (Ch); *Group Seven Ltd v Notable Services LLP* [2019] EWCA Civ 614; [2020] Ch. 129; *Libyan Investment Authority v Credit Suisse International* [2021] EWHC 2684 (Comm) at [117].

122 [1990] Ch. 265 at 291; reversed on other grounds [1991] Ch. 547.

123 Further cases endorsing this statement of the law are *Pakistan v Zardari* [2006] EWHC 2411 (Comm) at [89]; *Relfo Ltd (In Liq) v Varsani* [2012] EWHC 2168 (Ch) at [80]; *Ali v Dinc* [2020] EWHC 3055 (Ch); [2021] 2 P. & C.R. 19 at [221]; *Byers v Saudi National Bank* [2022] EWCA Civ 43; [2022] 4 W.L.R. 22 at [19]–[20]. And cf. *Heperu Pty Ltd v Belle* (2009) 76 N.S.W.L.R. 230 at [92] and [154]; *Great Investments Ltd v Warner* (2016) 243 F.C.R. 516 at [55], [60] and [65]; *Smith v Leveraged Equities Ltd* [2020] WASCA 122 at [58].

124 *CMOC Sales and Marketing Ltd v Persons Unknown* [2018] EWHC 2230 (Comm); [2019] Lloyd's Rep. F.C. 62 at [134].

125 *Carl Zeiss Stiftung v Herbert Smith & Co (No.2)* [1969] 2 Ch. 276 at 290.

126 Ibid. See too *Sinclair Investments (UK) Ltd v Versailles Trade Finance Ltd (In Admin)* [2011] EWCA Civ 347; [2012] Ch. 453 at [108]; *Re Smith* [2021] EWHC 1272 (Comm) at [468]; *AA v BB* [2021] EWHC 1833 (Ch) at [22]–[35].

D. Remedies

14-081 In the following excerpt, Charles Mitchell and Stephen Watterson argue that a knowing recipient's core duty as constructive trustee of the property she receives is to restore the property immediately.[127] If she breaches this duty by dealing with the property for herself, or by applying it in any other way that is inconsistent with the beneficiaries' rights, then the mechanisms by which they can hold her liable to account are essentially the same as those by which they can hold an express trustee liable to account for unauthorised expenditure.[128] By analogy with the express trustee cases, the knowing recipient can be ordered to restore the property *in specie* if it is still in her hands. By the same analogy, if she has disposed of the property then she must show that this disposal was authorised, or the account will be falsified, and an order for substitutive performance will be made, requiring her to pay the current monetary value of the property, or where the property was money, the capital sum plus interest. A further possibility is that she has used the property to make a profit, in which case the court may exercise its discretion to order an account of profits and order that she pay over the amount of her profit.[129]

14-082 This analysis of the law was approved by the Privy Council in *Arthur v Attorney General of the Turks and Caicos Islands*[130] and by the Federal Court of Australia in *Grimaldi v Chameleon Mining NL (No.2)*.[131] It is also consistent with Lloyd LJ's statement in *Independent Trustee Services Ltd v GP Noble Trustees Ltd* that once a recipient of misdirected trust funds becomes aware of their improper provenance she comes "under a duty not to part with the remaining funds (and the traceable proceeds in her hands of any which had already gone) otherwise than by restoring them to or for the benefit of the beneficiaries."[132] As discussed above, the analysis also formed an important part of the Court of Appeal's reasoning in *Byers v National Saudi Bank*.[133]

C. Mitchell and S. Watterson, "Remedies for Knowing Receipt"

in C. Mitchell (ed.), *Constructive and Resulting Trusts* (Hart Publishing, 2010), pp.131–138

14-083 . . . The duties of a knowing recipient are rarely stated, but one cannot fully understand the nature of his liability to account as a constructive trustee without identifying these duties and the mechanisms by which they are enforced.

1. The Core Restorative Duty

(a) The nature of the duty

14-084 A knowing recipient's core duty, and generally his only duty of practical significance, is to restore the misapplied trust property.[134] His duty is to restore the property immediately, rather than to restore it on

---

127 For the view that this is usually the only duty of any practical significance owed by knowing recipients, see also D. Reynolds, "What Are the Duties of Constructive Trustees?" (2018) 41 U.N.S.W.L.J. 1297.

128 Discussed in Chapter 13.

129 *Cook v Deeks* [1916] 1 A.C. 554 at 565, endorsed in *Novoship (UK) Ltd v Mikhaylyuk* [2014] EWCA Civ 908; [2015] Q.B. 499 at [82]–[83]; *Akita Holdings Ltd v Attorney General of the Turks and Caicos Islands* [2017] UKPC 7; [2017] A.C. 590 at [16]; *Davies v Ford* [2021] EWHC 2550 (Ch) at [236] (though at [275] the judge declined to order an account of profits as he considered this inappropriate on the facts).

130 [2012] UKPC 30 at [37].

131 (2012) 200 F.C.R. 296 at [559].

132 [2013] Ch. 91 at [81].

133 [2022] EWCA Civ 43; [2022] 4 W.L.R. 22; discussed at paras 14–024 to 14–027.

134 Cf. *Re Holmes* [2004] EWHC 2020 (Admin); [2005] 1 W.L.R. 1857 at [22]; *Darkingjung Pty Ltd v Darkingjung Local Aboriginal Land Council* [2006] NSWSC 1217 at [47].

demand.[135] In this respect his position can be contrasted with that of an express bare trustee, who holds the trust property to the order of the beneficiary while the trust subsists, and whose continuing retention of this property is authorised, and therefore legitimate, until the beneficiary gives contrary instructions. In contrast, a knowing recipient's continuing retention of misapplied trust property is unauthorised and illegitimate, and so he owes an immediate restorative duty which does not depend on any demand for restoration having been made.

Although an action to enforce the knowing recipient's restorative duty can be brought by the beneficiaries,[136] it does not follow that performance of the duty necessarily entails transfer or payment to them. On the contrary, the duty is essentially to restore the misapplied property to the trustees, so that that the trust can be reconstituted and duly administered. However, much depends on the basis on which the property was held. If it was held on a bare trust, then, whilst the knowing recipient's duty is essentially a duty to restore the property to the trustees (assuming that the trust is still on foot), he could discharge his duty by restoring it directly to the absolutely entitled beneficiary instead.[137] But if the trust is a more elaborate continuing trust, where there is no single absolutely entitled beneficiary, then he cannot perform his duty in this way, and must instead restore the property to the trustees so that the trust can be reconstituted, and the trust fund administered for all of the beneficiaries. **14-085**

When can a knowing recipient claim to have performed his duty to restore the trust property? Obviously, if he hands over the property *in specie* then he will have done what he was meant to do . . . By analogy with the express trustee cases, he may also perform his duty by paying a money substitute for the property . . . But what if he hands over different property in lieu of the property which he received? This question arose in *Morlea Professional Services Pty Ltd v Richard Walter Pty Ltd*,[138] where a corporate trustee, which had misapplied trust money by making sham loans to another company, accepted from the other company the transfer of a debt equal in value to the sham loans, with 15% interest. According to the Full Court of the Federal Court of Australia, this "did not effect actual (in the sense of precisely equivalent) restoration to the trusts"; rather its effect "was to bring a new asset into the trusts by way of substitution for what was misappropriated", namely "a debt equivalent in sum to the moneys misappropriated, [which] asset was treated by the trustees as being subject to the trusts and was dealt with accordingly".[139] In the court's view, trustees who act in this way are bound by their actions vis-à-vis the knowing recipient, but the beneficiaries are not. They might disavow the trustees' actions and refuse to accept the new property as a substitute for the misapplied property. If they take this course then the knowing recipient will be unable to say that he has performed his duty, and will remain liable for the current market value of the property which he received.[140] **14-086**

Can the knowing recipient discharge his duty by returning the property to the wrongdoing trustee from whom he received it? In principle, the duty can generally be discharged in this way, consistently with the fact that, at least until he is replaced by another trustee, the wrongdoing trustee has a duty to recover the misapplied trust property . . . More difficult, though, are cases where the knowing recipient knows that the wrongdoing trustee will misapply the property again if it is returned to him, and will not use it to reconstitute the trust fund as he should. It may be that in this case, the knowing recipient's restorative duty would not be discharged if he retransferred the property to the trustee. This is suggested **14-087**

---

135 Notwithstanding Colman J.'s dictum to the contrary in *Allied Carpets Group Plc v Nethercott* [2001] B.C.C. 81 at 89–90.

136 The trustees can also bring an action for knowing receipt in a representative capacity, as discussed in *Morlea Professional Services Pty Ltd v Richard Walter Pty Ltd* (1999) 34 A.C.S.R. 371. In rare cases, a knowing recipient may also bring an action in knowing receipt against a knowing recipient from her, pursuant to her duty to get in the property so that the trust fund can be reconstituted: *Bracken Partners Ltd v Gutteridge* [2004] 1 B.C.L.C. 373 (CA); *Evans v European Bank Ltd* (2004) 7 I.T.E.L.R. 19.

137 Cf *Soar v Ashwell* [1893] 2 Q.B. 390 at 395, where Kay L.J. refers to a defendant who has "concurred with the trustee in committing a breach of trust, and has taken possession of the trust property, knowing that it was trust property, and has not duly discharged himself of it by handing it over to the proper trustees or to the persons absolutely entitled to it". And cf *Target Holdings Ltd v Redferns* [1996] A.C. 421 at 435 (express trustees).

138 (1999) 34 A.C.S.R. 371. Cf *Lander v Weston* (1853) 3 Drew. 389 at 394 (Kindersley V-C): express trustees who wrongfully sell trust stock cannot obtain a discharge by replacing some other stock in the fund unless the beneficiaries adopt their transactions – 'they are not discharged by substituting something different'.

139 Ibid at [75].

140 Ibid at [76].

by *Blyth v Fladgate*,[141] where solicitors acting for a set of trustees were held not to have been discharged from their liability to account for trust property which they had paid over at the direction of the trustees for the purposes of an investment which they actually or constructively knew to be improper. Another way of approaching this question, however, might be to say that, whether or not the knowing recipient's restorative duty is discharged, he may in any event incur an independent liability for dishonestly assisting the wrongdoing trustee's further breach of trust.

14-088 . . . [Might the court] ever excuse the knowing recipient from performance, or relieve him from liability for non-performance, in the same way that it sometimes relieves express trustees under the Trustee Act 1925 s 61? Consider a case where the property is lost or destroyed or stolen before the knowing recipient can return it. If the loss would not have occurred but for a delay by the knowing recipient in performing his duty of immediate restoration, then it can usually be said that he was at fault and should not be excused.[142] However this may not always be the case. Suppose, for example, that he cannot immediately restore the trust property, because he cannot identify or ascertain the whereabouts of the parties to whom restoration should be made – a rare situation, but one which arose in *Evans v European Bank Ltd*.[143] Or again, suppose that the parties to whom restoration should be made mistakenly deny that restoration is required and refuse to take the property back – another rare situation, but analogous to that which arose in *National Bank of New Zealand v Waitaki International Processing (NI) Ltd*.[144] In either case, if the knowing recipient takes reasonable steps to preserve the property pending performance of his duty, and yet it is unexpectedly lost or destroyed in the interim, then it would seem unfair to force him to pay a money substitute in lieu of delivering the property once all the relevant facts are known.

(b) Remedial implications

14-089 What remedy do the beneficiaries have if a knowing recipient fails to perform his primary restorative duty? By analogy with the express trustee cases, he can clearly be ordered to restore the property *in specie* if it is still in his hands. By the same analogy, if he disposed of the property then he must show that this disposal was authorised, or else the account will be falsified, and an order for substitutive performance made, requiring him to pay the current monetary value of the property, or where the property is money, the capital sum plus interest . . . [The] beneficiaries would not have to allege a breach of duty against an express trustee before they could obtain an order of either kind, and for exactly the same reasons they do not have to allege a breach of duty against the knowing recipient either. In other words, once they have established that he knowingly received the trust property and was therefore placed under a primary restorative duty, the beneficiaries need not show that he breached this duty by failing to return the property, as they are entitled without more to an order for specific or substitutive performance of his primary duty.

14-090 Authority for this is *Green v Weatherill*,[145] where a daughter received money from her father, to be held on trust for him, and transferred part of the money to her sister, who knew that this transfer constituted a breach of trust. The sister was ordered to pay the relevant sum into court, although there was no allegation in the pleadings that she had committed any breach of her duty as a constructive trustee of the money. Maughan J. explained this as follows:[146]

> "In the present action [the defendant] is sued as a constructive trustee of the sum so paid to her with full knowledge of the action and of the nature of the claim was being made as to the sum deposited by her sister with Martin's Bank. In my opinion those facts having been established; she must be taken to be a trustee. It is not alleged in the action that she has committed any breach of trust, and counsel for

---

141 [1891] 1 Ch. 337. See too *Morgan v Stephens* (1861) 3 Giff. 226 at 236–237. Neither case concerned liability for knowing receipt, since the defendants did not initially receive the relevant property in breach of duty, but the result would have been the same if they had: *Bank of China v Kwong Wa Po* [2005] HKCFI 422 at [90], where a recipient of moneys stolen from the claimant bank by ex-employees was not discharged when it repaid the moneys, not to the claimant, but to one of these ex-employees and/or the company which was the vehicle for their frauds.

142 An express trustee would no doubt be in the same position, if it was the case that he had come under a duty immediately to transfer a particular asset to a beneficiary. Bailees of chattels are similarly placed once they have come under a duty to deliver the goods: they are then strictly liable for the goods' loss or destruction.

143 (2004) 7 I.T.E.L.R. 19.

144 [1999] 2 N.Z.L.R. 211.

145 [1929] 2 Ch. 213.

146 Ibid. at 222–3.

the plaintiff would be entitled on the pleadings as they stand to ask for an account of the sum received by her with notice of the plaintiff's claim. It is not disputed that the sum paid to the defendant . . . is the sum of 135l, and an account against her is therefore unnecessary. This, therefore, is a case where the Court has ascertained to its satisfaction that the sum of 135l is in the hands of the defendant . . . as a constructive trustee, and I can see no reason why the Court should not order payment by the said defendant of that amount into Court."

Because the main liability of a knowing recipient is to perform his primary duty of restoration in just the same way as an express trustee, it is a distinctive form of liability which cannot be collapsed into other forms of liability which arise in the law of wrongs or the law of unjust enrichment. Several points can be made in this connection. First, because the knowing recipient is liable to perform or render substitutive performance of his restorative duty, and this liability does not depend on an allegation of a breach of duty, it is easy to see why the knowing receipt cases look like plausible candidates for re-characterisation as claims in unjust enrichment. Claims of this sort also generate a "restitutionary" liability which entails performance of a primary duty to pay the value of benefits received by the defendant, rather than performance of a secondary duty to pay money triggered by breach of a primary duty . . . However, a liability to make restitution of an unjust enrichment is a crucially different liability from a liability to effect restoration of misapplied trust property, and it is important that this distinction should not be obscured by the latent ambiguity in the term "restitution". . . 14–091

Secondly, the fact that the beneficiaries can get a remedy against the knowing recipient without asserting that he has breached his duty as constructive trustee has some implications for the defences that he can raise. If claims for knowing receipt were wrong-based, in the sense that they depended on the knowing recipient's breach of duty, then this might suggest that he was entitled to the defence of contributory negligence.[147] One response might be that contributory negligence is not available as a defence to every wrong; that the courts have been prepared to deny the defence to particular types of wrongdoer on policy grounds; and that this defence may be unavailable against claims for breach of fiduciary duty, because admitting the defence might undermine the fiduciary's core duty of undivided loyalty.[148] However, this response assumes a particular answer to a different question, namely whether knowing recipients owe fiduciary duties. . . And there is a different and better reason why contributory negligence cannot be pleaded against claims for actual or substitutive performance of their restorative duty.[149] Because the beneficiaries need not allege a breach of this duty in order to obtain an order for performance, there is no room for argument that they have been a partial cause of their own loss, because it makes no difference whether they have been caused a loss, whether by the knowing recipient's fault or their own. Where the beneficiaries were aware of the transfer to the knowing recipient, however, the knowing recipient might instead be able to escape liability by arguing that the beneficiaries acquiesced in the trustee's breach of duty, with the result that no claim lies against him at all because the case is effectively one of authorised transfer. 14–092

Thirdly, the measure of a knowing recipient's liability may be very different from the measure of other liabilities which he might owe on a different footing. Suppose, for example, that a defendant receives and then disposes of property that subsequently increases in value. If he owed a liability in unjust enrichment, then assuming that a change of position defence were disallowed, the measure of his liability would most probably be the value of the property at the time of receipt, and would certainly be no more than the value of the property when he disposed of it . . . However, if he were chargeable with the property as a knowing recipient, then he would be liable as constructive trustee to pay its current monetary value. An example is an American case, *Re Rothko*,[150] where executors of the renowned painter, Mark Rothko, improperly 14–093

---

[147] P. Jaffey 'The Nature of Knowing Receipt' (2001) 15 Tru. L.I. 151, 157–8.

[148] See *Pilmer v Duke Group Ltd* (2001) 207 C.L.R. 165 at [86] and [171]–[172], quoting His Honour Justice W.M.C. Gummow "Compensation for Breach of Fiduciary Duty" in T.G. Youdan (ed.) *Equity, Fiduciaries and Trusts* (Toronto, Carswell, 1989) 57, 86, and His Honour Justice K.R. Handley "Reduction of Damages Awards" in P.D. Finn (ed.) *Essays on Damages* (Sydney, Lawbook Co, 1992) 113, 127.

[149] This is not to rule out the possibility that a defence of contributory negligence might be raised against a knowing recipient where a reparation claim is made against him, for example where he has lost trust property through his negligence. Cf *Permanent Building Society (in liq) v Wheeler* (1994) 12 A.C.L.C. 674, where Ipp J. correctly noted the difference between a trustee's duty to account, and his duty of care, which can bring issues of causation and relative fault into play.

[150] 43 N.Y. 2d 305; 372 N.E. 2d 291 (1977).

transferred a large number of his paintings to third parties, who subsequently disposed of them. The value of Rothko's works then appreciated hugely, and in proceedings by the beneficiaries of his estate, the New York Court of Appeals held that the third parties were liable for the current market value of the paintings.

E. Concurrent Liability in Unjust Enrichment for Misdirected Trust Funds?

14–094 Some legal scholars have argued that recipients of misdirected trust property should owe a strict liability in unjust enrichment for the value of the property received.[151] This argument has been endorsed extra-judicially by some eminent judges,[152] but in *BCCI (Overseas) Ltd v Akindele,*[153] Nourse LJ thought that a decision of the House of Lords would be needed to recognise a strict liability claim in English law. He believed that recognising such a claim would be inconsistent with all the knowing receipt cases since *Barnes v Addy,*[154] which require proof of fault. However, these cases only make fault a prerequisite for compensatory, wrong-based liability in knowing receipt to account for misdirected trust funds as a constructive trustee, and they do not establish that fault is also a prerequisite for restitutionary liability in unjust enrichment to repay the value of the benefit received. Once it is recognised that these are different types of liability, Nourse LJ's objection falls away—and in *DD Growth Premium 2X Fund (In Liq) v RMF Market Neutral Strategies (Master) Ltd,* a decision of the Privy Council, Lord Sumption and Lord Briggs did recognise this, stating (with Lord Carnwath's agreement) that liability in unjust enrichment is "conceptually ... very different" from liability for knowing receipt, because:[155]

liability in restitution depends on the defendant having been unjustly enriched by the receipt. The liability of a constructive trustee is essentially a custodial liability comparable to that of an express trustee, which is imposed on him because he has sufficient knowledge to affect his conscience.

14–095 It follows that the question is not, as Nourse LJ supposed,[156] whether wrong-based liability for knowing receipt should be abolished and replaced with a different type of liability, i.e. liability in unjust enrichment, but whether the law should recognise that *both* types of claim can potentially lie against recipients of misdirected trust funds. If that were done, then in cases where no fault can be proved against recipients, or where they have been enriched but have not received property impressed with a claimant's subsisting equitable interest,[157] they still might be liable in unjust enrichment to make restitution. Meanwhile in cases where they had unconscionable knowledge, they might be concurrently liable, meaning that claimants have a choice of claims (being prevented from bringing both cumulatively if that would result in their recovering twice for the same loss).

---

151 e.g. P. Birks, "Receipt" in P. Birks and A. Pretto (eds) *Breach of Trust* (Hart Publishing, 2002), p.213; R. Chambers and J. Penner, "Ignorance" in S. Degeling and J. Edelman (eds), *Restitution in Commercial Law* (Law Book Co, 2008) (identifying "want of authority" rather than "ignorance" as the reason for restitution). Contra, L.D. Smith, "Unjust Enrichment, Property, and the Structure of Trusts" (2000) 116 L.Q.R. 412.

152 Lord Nicholls, "Knowing Receipt: The Need for a New Landmark", in W.R. Cornish et al. (eds) *Restitution: Past, Present and Future* (Hart Publishing, 1998); Lord Walker, "Dishonesty and Unconscionable Conduct in Commercial Life—Some Reflections on Accessory Liability and Knowing Receipt" (2005) 27 Sydney L.R. 187, 202; Lord Millett, "Proprietary Restitution" in S. Degeling and J. Edelman (eds) *Equity in Commercial Law* (Law Book Co, 2005), p.311.

153 [2001] Ch. 437 at 456.

154 (1874) L.R. 9 Ch. App. 244.

155 [2017] UKPC 36; [2018] Bus. L.R. 1595 at [58].

156 And as the Court of Appeal also seems to have thought in *Byers v Saudi National Bank* [2022] EWCA Civ 43; [2022] 4 W.L.R. 22 at [16]–[17].

157 As to this, see paras 14–024 to 14–027.

Three strands of authority could be drawn upon by a claimant bringing a claim in unjust enrichment. First, it was held by the House of Lords in *Ministry of Health v Simpson*[158] that the recipients of funds improperly distributed in the administration of a deceased person's estate are strictly liable to repay the persons properly entitled to the estate, and it could be argued that there is no compelling reason why this situation should be treated differently from the situation where a defendant receives misdirected trust assets. **14–096**

Second, it was held by Lord Nicholls in *Criterion Properties Ltd v Stratford UK Properties LLC* that if the directors of a company (A) act for an improper purpose when causing A to transfer assets to B, then:[159] **14–097**

> irrespective of whether B still has the assets in question, A will have a personal claim against B for unjust enrichment, subject always to a defence of change of position. B's personal accountability will not be dependent upon proof of fault or 'unconscionable' conduct on his part. B's accountability, in this regard, will be "strict".

This dictum was followed by Sales J in *Relfo Ltd (In Liq) v Varsani*[160] to support his finding that the claimant not only had a claim in knowing receipt against the defendant recipient of the traceable proceeds of the claimant's misdirected assets, but also had a claim in unjust enrichment. This was upheld by the Court of Appeal.[161] **14–098**

Third, it has been held that where trust assets are misappropriated by a trustee and used to pay off a security charged on property belonging to an innocent third party, the beneficiaries are entitled to be subrogated to the extinguished rights which were formerly possessed by the charge-holder, and to be treated, by a legal fiction, as though these rights were not extinguished, but were instead assigned to the beneficiaries in order that they might enforce them against the innocent third party.[162] The English courts have held that subrogation is a remedy awarded to reverse unjust enrichment,[163] and if beneficiaries are entitled to acquire proprietary rights against good faith third parties via subrogation on the ground of unjust enrichment, then a fortiori they should also be entitled to a direct personal claim in unjust enrichment against good faith third parties who have been enriched at the beneficiaries' expense.[164] **14–099**

Claims in unjust enrichment are governed by rules which a claimant might sometimes find it difficult to satisfy. In particular, the Supreme Court held in *Investment Trust Companies (In Liq) v Revenue and* **14–100**

---

158 [1951] A.C. 251.

159 [2004] UKHL 28; [2004] 1 W.L.R. 1846 at [3]–[4]. Lord Nicholls' reference in this passage to the "defence of change of position" is to a defence that can be raised against claims in unjust enrichment by defendants who have incurred expenditure in good faith as a consequence of receiving a benefit, so that it would be unfair to make them worse off than they were prior to receipt by ordering them to make restitution: *Lipkin Gorman v Karpnale Ltd* [1991] 2 A.C. 548. Change of position is not a defence to claims in knowing receipt, first, because it is only a defence to claims in unjust enrichment, and, second, because the unconscionability of the defendant's behaviour in a knowing receipt case would anyway debar them from relying on the defence, which is only available to those who have acted in good faith.

160 [2012] EWHC 2168 (Ch) at [86].

161 [2014] EWCA Civ 360; [2015] 1 B.C.L.C. 14. See also *Atkinson v Varma* [2021] EWHC 2027 (Ch).

162 *McCullough v Marsden* (1919) 45 D.L.R. 645 at 646–647; *Primlake Ltd (In Liq) v Matthews Associates* [2006] EWHC 1227 (Ch); [2007] 1 B.C.L.C. 666 at [340].

163 *Banque Financière de la Cité v Parc (Battersea) Ltd* [1999] A.C. 221 at 228 and 234, followed in *Niru Battery Manufacturing Co v Milestone Trading Ltd (No.2)* [2004] EWCA Civ 487; [2004] 2 All E.R. (Comm.) 289 at [27]–[28]; *Filby v Mortgage Express (No.2) Ltd* [2004] EWCA Civ 759 at [62].

164 The majority of the court made heavy weather of this point in *Menelaou v Bank of Cyprus UK Ltd* [2015] UKSC 66; [2016] A.C. 176 at [55], [80]–[82] and [141]. They held that the claimant bank was entitled to a lien over the defendant's property but were unsure whether it was also entitled to a personal claim against her. Since a lien necessarily secures the performance of an obligation, these doubts were misplaced.

Customs Commissioners[165] that as a general rule claims can be brought only where a benefit has been "directly transferred" from a claimant to a defendant. Where a series of transfers involving third parties occurs, this rule is not generally satisfied, even if it can be said that there is a causal connection between a claimant's loss and a defendant's gain. Many cases involving misdirected trust funds are like this and to succeed a claimant would therefore have to bring herself within one of the exceptions to the general rule that were also identified in the *Investment Trust Companies* case, e.g. by showing that a fraud was committed, that a set of "co-ordinated transactions" occurred or that the claimant had a continuing "equitable interest" in property or its traceable proceeds as it passed through the ownership of intermediaries before ending up with the defendant. In some, even many, cases, claimants will be able to do this, as illustrated by *Relfo Ltd (In Liquidation) v Varsani*,[166] but this may not always be so.

4. Dishonest Assistance

14–101 To make a defendant personally liable for dishonest assistance in a breach of trust or other fiduciary duty it is necessary to establish:[167]

(1) a breach of trust or fiduciary duty;

(2) assistance by the defendant in the breach;

(3) a causal link between the breach and a loss to the beneficiaries, or between the breach and a gain to the defendant, depending on the remedy which is sought; and

(4) a dishonest state of mind on the part of the assistant.

14–102 Liability for dishonest assistance can "arise even though no trust property has reached the hands of the accessory".[168] Where a defendant has in fact received trust property, there is nothing to stop the beneficiaries from suing in dishonest assistance if they wish,[169] but in practice, they usually prefer to make a proprietary claim, or to make a claim in knowing receipt, for which the mental element is easier to prove.[170] However, they may be unable to pursue the first option if the property has been dissipated, and the second if the defendant has received the property ministerially and not beneficially.[171]

A. The Primary Breach

14–103 Claims for dishonest assistance lie against defendants who assist in misapplications of property by trustees, and other stewards of property, e.g. company directors.[172] Claims also lie against defendants

[165] [2017] UKSC 29; [2018] A.C. 275.

[166] [2014] EWCA Civ 360; [2015] 1 B.C.L.C. 14.

[167] This formula combines the statements in *Group Seven Ltd v Notable Services LLP* [2019] EWCA Civ 614; [2020] Ch. 129 at [29] and [110](1). See too *FM Capital Partners Ltd v Marino* [2018] EWHC 1768 (Comm) at [82] (not considered on appeal: [2020] EWCA Civ 245; [2021] Q.B. 1).

[168] *Royal Brunei Airline Sdn Bhd v Tan* [1995] 2 A.C. 378 at 382. See too *Houghton v Fayers* [2000] Lloyd's Rep. Bank. 145 at 149; *Byers v Saudi National Bank* [2022] EWCA Civ 43; [2022] 4 W.L.R. 22 at [13].

[169] *Baden, Delvaux v Société Générale pour Favoriser le Développement du Commerce et de l'Industrie en France SA* [1993] 1 W.L.R. 509n at 572–573; *Primlake Ltd (in liquidation) v Matthews Associates* [2006] EWHC 1227 (Ch); [2007] 1 B.C.L.C. 666 at [334].

[170] As in e.g. *Starglade Properties Ltd v Nash* [2010] EWHC 148 (Ch); [2010] W.T.L.R. 1267 (not considered on appeal: [2010] EWCA Civ 1314).

[171] *Twinsectra Ltd v Yardley* [2002] UKHL 12; [2002] 2 A.C. 164 at [106].

[172] *Selangor United Rubber Estates Ltd v Cradock (No.3)* [1968] 1 W.L.R. 1555; *Belmont Finance Corp Ltd v Williams Furniture Ltd (No.2)* [1980] 1 All E.R. 393; *Group Seven Ltd v Notable Services LLP* [2019] EWCA Civ 614; [2020] Ch. 129.

who assist not in a breach of a duty of due administration, but in a breach of fiduciary duty, meaning a duty to avoid conflicts of interest. The Court of Appeal's finding to the latter effect in *Novoship (UK) Ltd v Mikhaylyuk*[173] is consistent with the courts' general desire to preserve the integrity of fiduciary relations.

There was originally no requirement that a defendant should have assisted in a breach of duty which was itself dishonest.[174] Then, in an unreserved judgment not discussing the earlier cases, Lord Selborne LC held that assistants in a breach of trust could not be liable unless "they assist with knowledge in a dishonest and fraudulent design on the part of the trustees".[175] In his speech for the Privy Council in *Royal Brunei Airlines Sdn Bhd v Tan*, Lord Nicholls declined to apply this rule, holding that the claimant did not need to show that the breach of trust assisted by the defendant had been a dishonest breach.[176] This finding was affirmed by the House of Lords in *Twinsectra Ltd v Yardley*.[177] **14–104**

B. Assistance

The word "assistance" suggests that a defendant has played a subsidiary part in a design orchestrated by the trustee or fiduciary whose breach of duty the defendant has facilitated and that is indeed the fact-pattern of many cases. However, there are also cases where accessory liability has been incurred by defendants who have instigated the primary breach of duty. An example is *Royal Brunei Airlines Sdn Bhd v Tan*,[178] where the defendant caused the company of which he was the majority shareholder and director to misdirect funds that it held on trust for the claimant. Liability has also been incurred in cases where the defendant has bribed a fiduciary to breach her duty to act exclusively in the interests of her principal.[179] **14–105**

A failure to act is capable of amounting to "assistance", albeit that a claimant will usually find assistance easier to prove where the defendant has taken some positive step.[180] Whether the claim relates to an action or an omission, a defendant cannot have "assisted" a breach of duty if her conduct has made no difference whatsoever to the accomplishment of the primary wrongdoer's design, or indeed has made this more difficult.[181] This brings us to the rules of causation. **14–106**

C. Causation

Generally speaking, the law of civil wrongs, like the criminal law, is "moulded on the philosophy of autonomy",[182] with the result that it does not generally regard loss flowing from the actions of a primary wrongdoer as having been caused by the actions of a participant who has induced or assisted in the **14–107**

---

173 [2014] EWCA Civ 908; [2015] Q.B. 499 (where previous case law is discussed). See too *Barrowfen Properties Ltd v Patel* [2021] EWHC 2055 (Ch) at [562].

174 *Fyler v Fyler* (1841) 3 Beav. 550; *Att-Gen v Corp of Leicester* (1844) 7 Beav. 176.

175 *Barnes v Addy* (1874) L.R. 9 Ch. App. 244 at 252, confirmed in *Belmont Finance Corp v Williams* [1979] Ch. 250 at 257.

176 [1995] 2 A.C. 378 at 385.

177 [2002] UKHL 12; [2002] 2 A.C. 164 at 171 and 195. See too *Williams v Central Bank of Nigeria* [2014] UKSC 10; [2014] A.C. 1189 at [35] and [178]; *FM Capital Partners Ltd v Marino* [2018] EWHC 1768 (Comm) at [82](3) (not considered on appeal: [2020] EWCA Civ 245; [2021] Q.B. 1).

178 [1995] 2 A.C. 378.

179 e.g. *Fyffes Group Ltd v Templeman* [2000] 2 Lloyd's 643; *Novoship (UK) Ltd v Mikhaylyuk* [2014] EWCA Civ 908; [2015] 2 W.L.R. 526.

180 As noted in *Fitzalan-Howard v Hibbert* [2009] EWHC 2855 (QB); [2010] P.N.L.R. 11 at [47]–[48]. See too *Barrowfen Properties Ltd v Patel* [2021] EWHC 2055 (Ch) at [564] (no liability incurred by a solicitor who failed to give advice to a client).

181 *Baden, Delvaux v Société Générale pour Favoriser le Développement du Commerce et de l'Industrie en France SA* [1993] 1 W.L.R. 509n at 574.

182 G. Williams, "Complicity, Purpose and the Draft Code" [1990] Crim. L.R. 4, 6.

commission of the wrong.[183] However, liability for dishonest assistance is an exception to this general rule: a defendant is liable for loss flowing from the primary wrong even if there is no direct causal link between her actions and the loss. Thus, in *Grupo Torras SA v Al-Sabah (No.5)* Mance LJ held that:[184]

> The starting point . . . is that the requirement of dishonest assistance relates not to any loss or damage which may be suffered, but to the breach of trust or fiduciary duty. The relevant enquiry is . . . what loss or damage resulted from the breach of trust or fiduciary duty which has been dishonestly assisted.

14–108 This was affirmed on appeal,[185] and then reaffirmed by a differently constituted Court of Appeal, in *Casio Computer Co Ltd v Sayo (No.3)*, where Tuckey LJ stated that:[186]

> *Grupo Torras* . . . establishes that in a claim for dishonest assistance it is not necessary to show a precise causal link between the assistance and the loss . . . [and that loss] caused by the breach of fiduciary duty is recoverable from the accessory.

14–109 Where a defendant's actions have made no difference at all to the implementation of a breach of trust or fiduciary duty, "there is no causative effect and therefore no assistance . . . [so that] the requirements of conscience [do not] require any remedy."[187] Hence a claimant must at least show that the defendant's actions made the fiduciary's breach of duty easier than it would otherwise have been. But the causation requirement for dishonest assistance is no stronger than this. There is no need for the claimant to show that the dishonest assistant's action or omission "inevitably [had] the consequence that a loss [was suffered]",[188] nor is it an answer to a claim that she "only participated in a part of a chain of events all of which led to [the breach], or to assert that the [breach] would probably have occurred without his assistance".[189] Thus a defendant can be liable for actions or omissions which precede the breach,[190] although she cannot be liable if her actions or omissions only occurred after the breach was fully implemented.[191]

14–110 However, where the breach has entailed the misapplication of funds, the courts are likely to hold that it was not fully implemented until the funds were hidden away where the beneficiaries could not find them, with the consequence that those who assist in money-laundering activities after trust funds have been removed from a trust account can be fixed with liability for dishonest assistance.[192] For the same reason, a defendant may also be liable if they have fraudulently mispresented the whereabouts of misapplied funds and have by that means discouraged the claimant from making prompt efforts to recover the funds.[193]

---

183 H.L.A. Hart and A.M. Honoré, *Causation in the Law*, 2nd edn (Oxford University Press, 1985), p.385.

184 [1999] C.L.C. 1469 at 1667.

185 [2001] Lloyd's Rep Bank 36 at 61.

186 [2001] EWCA Civ 661; [2001] I.L.Pr. 43 at [16].

187 *Brown v Bennett* [1999] 1 B.C.L.C. 649 at 659, per Morritt LJ.

188 *Baden, Delvaux v Société Générale pour Favoriser le Développement du Commerce et de l'Industrie en France SA* [1993] 1 W.L.R. 509n at 575.

189 *Balfron Trustees Ltd v Peterson* [2001] I.R.L.R. 758 at 761. Nor is this an answer to claims to recover the amount of a dishonest assistant's gain: *Ancient Order of Foresters in Victoria Friendly Society Ltd v Lifeplan Australia Friendly Society Ltd* (2018) 265 C.L.R. 1 at [9].

190 R.P. Austin, "Constructive Trusts" in P.D. Finn (ed.), *Essays in Equity* (Law Book Co, 1985), pp.196, 236–237, discussing *Adams v Bank of New South Wales* [1984] 1 N.S.W.L.R. 285. See too *Aequitas Ltd v Sparad No.100 Ltd* (2001) 19 A.C.L.C. 1006; *Law Society of England and Wales v Isaac & Isaac International Holdings Ltd* [2010] EWHC 1670 (Ch) at [75].

191 *Brown v Bennett* [1998] 2 B.C.L.C. 97 at 105.

192 *Heinl v Jyske Bank (Gibraltar) Ltd* [1999] Lloyd's Rep. Bank. 511 at 523, approving *Agip (Africa) Ltd v Jackson* [1990] Ch. 265 at 293. See too *Independent Trustee Services Ltd v GP Noble Trustees Ltd* [2010] EWHC 1653 (Ch) at [242]–[244].

193 *Latchworth Ltd v Dryer* [2016] EWHC 3424 (Ch) at [162]–[177].

If some of a claimant's losses were caused by a defendant's actions but others were not, a defendant's compensatory liability might be limited to losses where there was a causal link.[194] Much can turn, however, on how a defendant's "actions" are conceived. For example, in *Ancient Order of Foresters in Victoria Friendly Society Ltd v Lifeplan Australia Friendly Society Ltd*, employees of the claimant company breached their fiduciary duties to the claimant when they supplied the defendant company with confidential information and developed a business plan that the defendant successfully followed to win clients from the claimant. The claimant brought an action for "knowing assistance" (as it is termed in Australia), seeking an account of the defendant's profits and an order that these should be disgorged to the claimant. The defendant sought to limit the amount of its liability by arguing that this should be confined to the profits which were the direct result of each of the particular acts which constituted its equitable wrong. A majority of the High Court of Australia rejected this, stating that:[195] **14–111**

> By focusing on each act of knowing assistance and its direct consequences, rather than the overall effect of [the defendant's] wrongful conduct, the submission ignores the obvious reality that [the defendant's] particular interactions with [the defaulting employees] resulted ... in the wholesale acquisition by [the defendant] of the [claimant's] business connections ... . Another way of putting this point is to say that [the defendant] could not limit its liability to disgorge profits by claiming that only limited profits were caused by particular acts of knowing assistance when the consequences of those acts were inseparable from the consequences of [the employees'] general scheme of breach of fiduciary duty.

D. The Defendant's State of Mind

After some confused back and forth in the cases, it is now clearly established that the leading authority on this topic is *Royal Brunei Airlines Sdn Bhd v Tan*,[196] where the advice of the Privy Council was given by Lord Nicholls. He held, in essence, that a defendant must have had an objectively dishonest state of mind, which he understood to be a lower degree of fault than the "self-conscious dishonesty" described by the House of Lords in an earlier criminal case, *R. v Ghosh*.[197] However, Lord Nicholls' discussion must additionally be read in the light of the House of Lords' subsequent decision in *Ivey v Genting Casinos (UK) Ltd*,[198] that "objective" rather than "self-conscious" dishonesty is the general test for dishonesty in a criminal context, and in the light of the Court of Appeal's decision in *Group Seven Ltd v Notable Services LLP*,[199] where the court reaffirmed the rule established by *Royal Brunei* that "objective dishonesty" is the test for civil liability as a dishonest assistant, this test being consistent with the general test for dishonesty in the criminal context following *Ivey*. **14–112**

The cases bearing on the fault element for assistance liability had got into a sorry state prior to *Royal Brunei*. In the *Baden, Delvaux* case,[200] Peter Gibson J had held that a defendant might be liable for assisting in a breach of trust even if her behaviour fell short of dishonesty,[201] and he had accepted that any of the five types of knowledge he identified there would serve to render a defendant liable as an assistant in a breach of trust.[202] Subsequently a consensus had emerged that, contrary to Peter **14–113**

---

194 *Goldtrail Travel Ltd (In Liquidation) v Aydin* [2016] EWCA Civ 371; [2016] 1 B.C.L.C. 635.
195 (2018) 265 C.L.R. 1 at [5]–[6].
196 [1995] 2 A.C. 378.
197 [1982] Q.B. 1053.
198 [2017] UKSC 67; [2018] A.C. 391.
199 [2019] EWCA Civ 614; [2020] Ch. 129 at [52]–[58]. See too *Byers v Saudi National Bank* [2022] EWCA Civ 43; [2022] 4 W.L.R. 22 at [13].
200 [1993] 1 W.L.R. 509 (the case was decided in 1983).
201 *Baden, Delvaux* [1993] 1 W.L.R. 509 at 577. For Peter Gibson J's five-fold classification, see para.14–028.
202 *Baden, Delvaux* [1993] 1 W.L.R. 509 at 575–587.

Gibson J's view, a defendant must have been dishonest to incur liability,[203] but a line of cases predating *Baden, Delvaux*, and holding that a defendant can be liable if she has honestly but negligently failed to investigate the circumstances of an impugned transaction, had never been overruled.[204] The body of law founded on the *Baden, Delvaux* classification also suffered from the more general problem that it had become over-theorised: as Lord Nicholls put it in *Royal Brunei*, the courts had been led into "tortuous convolutions" in their efforts to investigate the "sort" of knowledge possessed by defendants, "when the truth is that 'knowingly' is inapt as a criterion when applied to the gradually darkening spectrum where the differences are of degree and not kind."[205]

14–114 In *Royal Brunei*, Lord Nicholls therefore decided to start afresh. He held that knowledge is best avoided as a defining ingredient of liability, and that the *Baden, Delvaux* scale is best forgotten in this context.[206] He rejected the idea that unconscionability should be the touchstone for liability,[207] and held that defendant must be shown to have acted dishonestly. He emphasised that the test for dishonesty in this context is not purely subjective, in the sense that individuals are not "free to set their own standards of honesty in particular circumstances",[208] and must be judged by the standards of right-thinking members of society. So, as the courts put it in later cases, there is no "Robin Hood" defence to an action for dishonest assistance.[209]

Royal Brunei Airlines Sdn Bhd v Tan

Privy Council [1995] 2 A.C. 378

14–115 LORD NICHOLLS (giving the advice of the Board): The proper role of equity in commercial transactions is a topical question. Increasingly plaintiffs have recourse to equity for an effective remedy when the person in default, typically a company, is insolvent. Plaintiffs seek to obtain relief from others who were involved in the transaction, such as directors of the company, or its bankers, or its legal or other advisers. They seek to fasten fiduciary obligations directly onto the company's officers or agents or advisers, or to have them held personally liable for assisting the company in breaches of trust or fiduciary obligations.

14–116 This is such a case. An insolvent travel agent company owed money to an airline. The airline seeks a remedy against the travel agent's principal director and shareholder. Its claim is based on the much-quoted dictum of Lord Selborne L.C., sitting in the Court of Appeal in Chancery, in *Barnes v Addy*:[210]

> "[The responsibility of a trustee] may no doubt be extended in equity to others who are not properly trustees, if they are found . . . actually participating in any fraudulent conduct of the trustee to the injury of the cestui que trust. But . . . strangers are not to be made constructive trustees merely because they act as the agents of trustees in transactions within their legal powers, transactions, perhaps of which a court of equity may disapprove, unless those agents receive and become chargeable with some part of the trust property, or unless they assist with knowledge in a dishonest and fraudulent design on the part of the trustees."

14–117 In the conventional shorthand, the first of these two circumstances in which third parties (non-trustees) may become liable to account in equity is "knowing receipt", as distinct from the second, where liability arises from "knowing assistance". Stated even more shortly, the first limb of Lord Selborne L.C.'s

---

[203] e.g. *Agip (Africa) Ltd v Jackson* [1990] 1 Ch. 265 at 292–293, on appeal: [1991] Ch. 547 at 569; *Lipkin Gorman v Karpnale Ltd* [1989] 1 W.L.R. 1340 at 1354–1355.

[204] *Selangor United Rubber Estates Ltd v Cradock (No.3)* [1968] 1 W.L.R. 1555; *Karak Rubber Co Ltd v Burden (No.2)* [1972] 1 W.L.R. 602; *Rowlandson v National Westminister Bank Ltd* [1978] 1 W.L.R. 798.

[205] [1995] 2 A.C. 378 at 391.

[206] *Royal Brunei* [1995] 2 A.C. 378 at 392.

[207] *Royal Brunei* [1995] 2 A.C. 378 at 392 (original emphasis).

[208] *Royal Brunei* [1995] 2 A.C. 378 at 389.

[209] *Grupo Torras SA v Al-Sabah (No.5)* [2001] Lloyd's Rep. Bank. 36 at 60; *Walker v Stones* [2001] Q.B. 902 at 939; *Twinsectra Ltd v Yardley* [2002] UKHL 12; [2002] 2 A.C. 164 at 172. Cf. *Consul Developments Pty Ltd v DPC Estates Pty Ltd* (1975) 132 C.L.R. 373 at 398.

[210] (1874) L.R. 9 Ch. App. 244 at 251–252.

formulation is concerned with the liability of a person as a recipient of trust property or its traceable proceeds. The second limb is concerned with what, for want of a better compendious description, can be called the liability of an accessory to a trustee's breach of trust. Liability as an accessory is not dependent upon receipt of trust property. It arises even though no trust property has reached the hands of the accessory. It is a form of secondary liability in the sense that it only arises where there has been a breach of trust. In the present case the plaintiff airline relies on the accessory limb. The particular point in issue arises from the expression "a dishonest and fraudulent design on the part of the trustees . . .".

In short, the issue on this appeal is whether the breach of trust which is a prerequisite to accessory liability must itself be a dishonest and fraudulent breach of trust by the trustee. 14–118

The Honest Trustee and the Dishonest Third Party

It must be noted at once that there is a difficulty with the approach adopted on this point in the *Belmont* case.[211] Take the simple example of an honest trustee and a dishonest third party. Take a case where a dishonest solicitor persuades a trustee to apply trust property in a way the trustee honestly believes is permissible but which the solicitor knows full well is a clear breach of trust. The solicitor deliberately conceals this from the trustee. In consequence, the beneficiaries suffer a substantial loss. It cannot be right that in such a case the accessory liability principle would be inapplicable because of the innocence of the trustee. In ordinary parlance, the beneficiaries have been defrauded by the solicitor. If there is to be an accessory liability principle at all, whereby in appropriate circumstances beneficiaries may have direct recourse against a third party, the principle must surely be applicable in such a case, just as much as in a case where both the trustee and the third party have been dishonest. Indeed, if anything, the case for liability of the dishonest third party seems stronger where the trustee is innocent, because in such a case the third party alone was dishonest and that was the cause of the subsequent misapplication of the trust property. 14–119

The position would be the same if, instead of procuring the breach, the third party dishonestly assisted in the breach. Change the facts slightly. A trustee is proposing to make a payment out of the trust fund to a particular person. He honestly believes he is authorised to do so by the terms of the trust deed. He asks a solicitor to carry through the transaction. The solicitor well knows that the proposed payment would be a plain breach of trust. He also well knows that the trustee mistakenly believes otherwise. Dishonestly he leaves the trustee under his misapprehension and prepares the necessary documentation. Again, if the accessory principle is not to be artificially constricted, it ought to be applicable in such a case. 14–120

These examples suggest that what matters is the state of mind of the third party sought to be made liable, not the state of mind of the trustee. The trustee will be liable in any event for the breach of trust, even if he acted innocently, unless excused by an exemption clause in the trust instrument or relieved by the court. But his state of mind is essentially irrelevant to the question whether the third party should be made liable to the beneficiaries for the breach of trust. If the liability of the third party is fault-based, what matters is the nature of his fault, not that of the trustee. In this regard dishonesty on the part of the third party would seem to be a sufficient basis for his liability, irrespective of the state of mind of the trustee who is in breach of trust. It is difficult to see why, if the third party dishonestly assisted in a breach, there should be a further prerequisite to his liability, namely that the trustee also must have been acting dishonestly. The alternative view would mean that a dishonest third party is liable if the trustee is dishonest, but if the trustee did not act dishonestly that of itself would excuse a dishonest third party from liability. That would make no sense. 14–121

Earlier Authority

The view that the accessory liability principle cannot be restricted to fraudulent breaches of trust is not to be approached with suspicion as a latter-day novelty. Before the accessory principle donned its *Barnes v Addy* strait-jacket, judges seem not to have regarded the principle as confined in this way. In *Fyler v Fyler*,[212] Lord Langdale M.R. expressed the view that, if trustees invested in an unauthorised investment, solicitors who knowingly procured that to be done for their own benefit "ought to be considered as partakers in the breach of trust" even though the trustees intended in good faith that the investment would be beneficial to 14–122

[211] [1979] Ch. 250.
[212] (1841) 3 Beav. 550 at 568.

the life tenant and not prejudicial to the beneficiaries with interests in capital. The same judge, in *Attorney-General v Corporation of Leicester*,[213] stated:

> "it cannot be disputed that, if the agent of a trustee, whether a corporate body or not, knowing that a breach of trust is being committed, interferes and assists in that breach of trust, he is personally answerable, although he may be employed as the agent of the person who directs him to commit that breach of trust."

14–123 In *Eaves v Hickson*[214] trustees, acting in good faith, paid over the fund to William Knibb's adult children on the strength of a forged marriage certificate produced to them by William Knibb. Sir John Romilly M.R. held that William Knibb was liable to replace the fund, to the extent that it was not recovered from his children, and to do so in priority to the liability of the trustees. Far from this being a case of fraud by the trustees, Sir John Romilly M.R.[215] described it as a very hard case on the trustees, who were deceived by a forgery which would have deceived anyone who was not looking out for forgery or fraud.

14–124 This point did not arise in *Barnes v Addy*. There the new sole trustee was engaged in a dishonest and fraudulent design. He intended to misapply the trust fund as soon as it reached his hands. The two solicitors were held not liable because there was no evidence that either of them had any knowledge or suspicion of this.

14–125 What has gone wrong? Their Lordships venture to think that the reason is that, ever since the *Selangor* case[216] highlighted the potential uses of equitable remedies in connection with misapplied company funds, there has been a tendency to cite and interpret and apply Lord Selborne L.C.'s formulation in *Barnes v Addy* as though it were a statute. This has particularly been so with the accessory limb of Lord Selborne L.C.'s apothegm. This approach has been inimical to analysis of the underlying concept. Working within this constraint, the courts have found themselves wrestling with the interpretation of the individual ingredients, especially "knowingly" but also "dishonest and fraudulent design on the part of the trustees", without examining the underlying reason why a third party who has received no trust property is being made liable at all. . . .

14–126 To resolve this issue it is necessary to take an overall look at the accessory liability principle. A conclusion cannot be reached on the nature of the breach of trust which may trigger accessory liability without at the same time considering the other ingredients including, in particular, the state of mind of the third party. It is not necessary, however, to look even more widely and consider the essential ingredients of recipient liability. The issue on this appeal concerns only the accessory liability principle. Different considerations apply to the two heads of liability. Recipient liability is restitution-based; accessory liability is not. . . .

Fault-Based Liability

14–127 Given, then, that in some circumstances a third party may be liable directly to a beneficiary, but given also that the liability is not so strict that there would be liability even when the third party was wholly unaware of the existence of the trust, the next step is to seek to identify the touchstone of liability. By common accord dishonesty fulfils this role. Whether, in addition, negligence will suffice is an issue on which there has been a well-known difference of judicial opinion. The *Selangor* decision in 1968 was the first modern decision on this point. Ungoed-Thomas J. held that the touchstone was whether the third party had knowledge of circumstances which would indicate to "an honest, reasonable man" that the breach in question was being committed or would put him on inquiry.[217] Brightman J. reached the same conclusion in *Karak Rubber Co. Ltd v Burden (No.2)*.[218] So did Peter Gibson J. in 1983 in *Baden v Société Générale pour Favoriser le Développement du Commerce et de l'Industrie en France SA*.[219] In that case the judge accepted a five-point scale of knowledge which had been formulated by counsel.

---

213 (1844) 7 Beav. 176 at 179.
214 (1861) 30 Beav. 136.
215 At 141.
216 [1968] 1 W.L.R. 1555.
217 [1968] 1 W.L.R. 1555 at 1590.
218 [1972] 1 W.L.R. 602.
219 [1993] 1 W.L.R. 509.

Meanwhile doubts had been expressed about this test by Buckley and Goff L.JJ. in the *Belmont* case.[220] Similar doubts were expressed in Australia by Jacobs P. in *DPC Estates Pty Ltd v Grey and Consul Development Pty Ltd*.[221] When that decision reached the High Court of Australia, the doubts were echoed by Barwick C.J., Gibbs and Stephen JJ.[222] **14–128**

Since then the tide in England has flowed strongly in favour of the test being one of dishonesty: see, for instance, Sir Robert Megarry V.C. in *Re Montagu's Settlement Trusts*[223] and Millett J. in *Agip (Africa) Ltd v Jackson*.[224] In *Eagle Trust Plc v SBC Securities Ltd*,[225] Vinelott J. stated that it could be taken as settled law that want of probity was a prerequisite to liability. This received the imprimatur of the Court of Appeal in *Polly Peck International Plc v Nadir (No.2)*.[226] . . . **14–129**

Dishonesty

Before considering this issue further it will be helpful to define the terms being used by looking more closely at what dishonesty means in this context. Whatever may be the position in some criminal or other contexts (see, for instance, *R. v Ghosh*[227]), in the context of the accessory liability principle acting dishonestly, or with a lack of probity, which is synonymous, means simply not acting as an honest person would in the circumstances. This is an objective standard. At first sight this may seem surprising. Honesty has a connotation of subjectivity as distinct from the objectivity of negligence. Honesty, indeed, does have a strong subjective element in that it is a description of a type of conduct assessed in the light of what a person actually knew at the time, as distinct a from what a reasonable person would have known or appreciated. Further, honesty and its counterpart dishonesty are mostly concerned with advertent conduct, not inadvertent conduct. Carelessness is not dishonesty. Thus for the most part dishonesty is to be equated with conscious impropriety. However, these subjective characteristics of honesty do not mean that individuals are free to set their own standards of honesty in particular circumstances. The standard of what constitutes honest conduct is not subjective. Honesty is not an optional scale, with higher or lower values according to the moral standards of each individual. If a person knowingly appropriates another's property, he will not escape a finding of dishonesty simply because he sees nothing wrong in such behaviour. **14–130**

In most situations there is little difficulty in identifying how an honest person would behave. Honest people do not intentionally deceive others to their detriment. Honest people do not knowingly take others' property. Unless there is a very good and compelling reason, an honest person does not participate in a transaction if he knows it involves a misapplication of trust assets to the detriment of the beneficiaries. Nor does an honest person in such a case deliberately close his eyes and ears, or deliberately not ask questions, lest he learn something he would rather not know, and then proceed regardless. However, in the situations now under consideration the position is not always so straightforward. This can best be illustrated by considering one particular area: the taking of risks. **14–131**

Taking Risks

All investment involves risk. Imprudence is not dishonesty, although imprudence may be carried recklessly to lengths which call into question the honesty of the person making the decision. This is especially so if the transaction serves another purpose in which that person has an interest of his own. **14–132**

This type of risk is to be sharply distinguished from the case where a trustee, with or without the benefit of advice, is aware that a particular investment or application of trust property is outside his powers, but nevertheless he decides to proceed in the belief or hope that this will be beneficial to the beneficiaries or, at least, not prejudicial to them. He takes a risk that a clearly unauthorised transaction will not cause loss. A risk of this nature is for the account of those who take it. If the risk materialises and causes loss, those who knowingly took the risk will be accountable accordingly. This is the type of risk being addressed by **14–133**

220 [1979] Ch. 250 at 267 at 275.
221 [1974] 1 N.S.W.L.R. 443 at 459.
222 See *Consul Development Pty Ltd v DP Estates Pty Ltd* (1975) 132 C.L.R. 373 at 376, 398, 412.
223 [1987] Ch. 264 at 285.
224 [1990] Ch. 265 at 293.
225 [1993] 1 W.L.R. 484 at 495.
226 [1992] 4 All E.R. 769 at 777, per Scott L.J.
227 [1982] Q.B. 1053.

Peter Gibson J. in the *Baden* case,[228] when he accepted that fraud includes taking "a risk to the prejudice of another's rights, which risk is known to be one which there is no right to take."

14–134 This situation, in turn, is to be distinguished from the case where there is genuine doubt about whether a transaction is authorised or not. This may be because the trust instrument is worded obscurely, or because there are competing claims, as in *Carl Zeiss Stiftung v Herbert Smith & Co (No.2)*,[229] or for other reasons. The difficulty here is that frequently the situation is neither clearly white nor clearly black. The dividing edge between what is within the trustee's powers and what is not is often not clear-cut. Instead there is a gradually darkening spectrum which can be described with labels such as clearly authorised, probably authorised, possibly authorised, wholly unclear, probably unauthorised and, finally, clearly unauthorised.

14–135 The difficulty here is that the differences are of degree rather than of kind. So far as the trustee himself is concerned the legal analysis is straightforward. Honesty or lack of honesty is not the test for his liability. He is obliged to comply with the terms of the trust. His liability is strict. If he departs from the trust terms he is liable unless excused by a provision in the trust instrument or relieved by the court. The analysis of the position of the accessory, such as the solicitor who carries through the transaction for him, does not lead to such a simple, clear-cut answer in every case. He is required to act honestly; but what is required of an honest person in these circumstances? An honest person knows there is doubt. What does honesty require him to do?

14–136 The only answer to these questions lies in keeping in mind that honesty is an objective standard. The individual is expected to attain the standard which would be observed by an honest person placed in those circumstances. It is impossible to be more specific. Knox J. captured the flavour of this, in a case with a commercial setting, when he referred to a person who is "guilty of commercially unacceptable conduct in the particular context involved".[230] Acting in reckless disregard of others' rights or possible rights can be a tell-tale sign of dishonesty. An honest person would have regard to the circumstances known to him, including the nature and importance of the proposed transaction, the nature and importance of his role, the ordinary course of business, the degree of doubt, the practicability of the trustee or the third party proceeding otherwise and the seriousness of the adverse consequences to the beneficiaries. The circumstances will dictate which one or more of the possible courses should be taken by an honest person. He might, for instance, flatly decline to become involved. He might ask further questions. He might seek advice, or insist on further advice being obtained. He might advise the trustee of the risks but then proceed with his role in the transaction. He might do many things. Ultimately, in most cases, an honest person should have little difficulty in knowing whether a proposed transaction, or his participation in it, would offend the normally accepted standards of honest conduct.

14–137 Likewise, when called upon to decide whether a person was acting honestly, a court will look at all the circumstances known to the third party at the time. The court will also have regard to personal attributes of the third party, such as his experience and intelligence, and the reason why he acted as he did.

14–138 Before leaving cases where there is real doubt, one further point should be noted. To inquire, in such cases, whether a person dishonestly assisted in what is later held to be a breach of trust is to ask a meaningful question, which is capable of being given a meaningful answer. This is not always so if the question is posed in terms of "knowingly" assisted. Framing the question in the latter form all too often leads one into tortuous convolutions about the "sort" of knowledge required, when the truth is that "knowingly" is inapt as a criterion when applied to the gradually darkening spectrum where the differences are of degree and not kind.

Negligence

14–139 It is against this background that the question of negligence is to be addressed. This question, it should be remembered, is directed at whether an honest third party who receives no trust property should be liable if he procures or assists in a breach of trust of which he would have become aware had he exercised reasonable diligence. Should he be liable to the beneficiaries for the loss they suffer from the breach of trust?

---

228 [1993] 1 W.L.R. 509 at 574.

229 [1969] 2 Ch. 276.

230 *Cowan de Groot Properties Ltd v Eagle Trust Plc* [1992] 4 All E.R. 700 at 761.

The majority of persons falling into this category will be the hosts of people who act for trustees in various ways: as advisers, consultants, bankers and agents of many kinds. This category also includes officers and employees of companies in respect of the application of company funds. All these people will be accountable to the trustees for their conduct. For the most part they will owe to the trustees a duty to exercise reasonable skill and care. When that is so, the rights flowing from that duty form part of the trust property. As such they can be enforced by the beneficiaries in a suitable case if the trustees are unable or unwilling to do so. That being so, it is difficult to identify a compelling reason why, in addition to the duty of skill and care vis-à-vis the trustees which the third parties have accepted, or which the law has imposed upon them, third parties should also owe a duty of care directly to the beneficiaries. They have undertaken work for the trustees. They must carry out that work properly. If they fail to do so, they will be liable to make good the loss suffered by the trustees in consequence. This will include, where appropriate, the loss suffered by the trustees, being exposed to claims for breach of trust. 14–140

Outside this category of persons who owe duties of skill and care to the trustees, there are others who will deal with trustees. If they have not accepted, and the law has not imposed upon them, any such duties in favour of the trustees, it is difficult to discern a good reason why they should nevertheless owe such duties to the beneficiaries. 14–141

There remains to be considered the position where third parties are acting for, or dealing with, dishonest trustees. In such cases the trustees would have no claims against the third party. The trustees would suffer no loss by reason of the third party's failure to discover what was going on. The question is whether in this type of situation the third party owes a duty of care to the beneficiaries to, in effect, check that a trustee is not misbehaving. The third party must act honestly. The question is whether that is enough. 14–142

In agreement with the preponderant view, their Lordships consider that dishonesty is an essential ingredient here. There may be cases where, in the light of the particular facts, a third party will owe a duty of care to the beneficiaries. As a general proposition, however, beneficiaries cannot reasonably expect that all the world dealing with their trustees should owe them a duty to take care lest the trustees are behaving dishonestly. . . . 14–143

The Accessory Liability Principle

Drawing the threads together, their Lordships' overall conclusion is that dishonesty is a necessary ingredient of accessory liability. It is also a sufficient ingredient. A liability in equity to make good resulting loss attaches to a person who dishonestly procures or assists in a breach of trust or fiduciary obligation. It is not necessary that, in addition, the trustee or fiduciary was acting dishonestly, although this will usually be so where the third party who is assisting him is acting dishonestly. "Knowingly" is better avoided as a defining ingredient of the principle and in the context of this principle the *Baden* scale of knowledge is best forgotten. 14–144

Conclusion

From this statement of the principle it follows that this appeal succeeds. The money paid to BLT on the sale of tickets for the airline was held by BLT upon trust for the airline. This trust, on its face, conferred no power on BLT to use the money in the conduct of its business. The trust gave no authority to BLT to relieve its cash flow problems by utilising for this purpose the rolling 30-day credit afforded by the airline. Thus BLT committed a breach of trust by using the money instead of simply deducting its commission and holding the money intact until it paid the airline. The defendant accepted that he knowingly assisted in that breach of trust. In other words, he caused or permitted his company to apply the money in a way he knew was not authorised by the trust of which the company was trustee. Set out in these bald terms, the defendant's conduct was dishonest. By the same token, and for good measure, BLT also acted dishonestly. The defendant was the company, and his state of mind is to be imputed to the company. 14–145

The Court of Appeal held that it was not established that BLT was guilty of fraud or dishonesty in relation to the amounts it held for the airline. Their Lordships understand that by this the Court of Appeal meant that it was not established that the defendant intended to defraud the airline. The defendant hoped, maybe expected, to be able to pay the airline, but the money was lost in the ordinary course of a poorly-run business with heavy overhead expenses. These facts are beside the point. The defendant had no right to employ the money in the business at all. That was the breach of trust. The company's inability to pay the airline was the consequence of that breach of trust. 14–146

14–147 It is plain that Lord Nicholls did not mean to lay down a test of self-conscious dishonesty analogous to the test that was previously laid down in criminal law by Lord Lane CJ in *R. v Ghosh.*[231] In *Twinsectra Ltd v Yardley*, however, the House of Lords oddly construed his words to mean that self-conscious dishonesty was needed. Lord Hutton said that "dishonesty requires knowledge by the defendant that what he was doing would be regarded as dishonest by honest people",[232] and Lord Hoffmann found that there must be "a dishonest state of mind, that is to say, consciousness that one is transgressing ordinary standards of honest behaviour."[233] The point was then revisited by the Privy Council, in *Barlow Clowes International Ltd v Eurotrust International Ltd*,[234] where Lord Hoffmann said that there had been "an element of ambiguity" in Lord Hutton's remarks in *Twinsectra* and asserted that neither he nor Lord Hutton had said that a defendant must have considered what normally acceptable standards of honest conduct might be: they had merely said that a defendant must have known about the aspects of the relevant transaction which made his participation transgress those standards.[235]

14–148 This was itself a strained reading of the judgments in *Twinsectra*, but in later cases, the courts took Lord Hoffmann at his word and followed *Eurotrust* rather than *Twinsectra*,[236] although *Eurotrust* was decided by the Privy Council and *Twinsectra* by the House of Lords. This difficult line of authority was then overtaken by the House of Lords' finding in *Ivey*, that "objective" rather than "self-conscious dishonesty" is the general test for dishonesty in the criminal context, and *Ivey* was then relied on by the Court of Appeal in the *Group Seven* case to support its finding that "objective dishonesty" is also the test for liability in dishonest assistance.[237] The law was thereby returned to its earlier state immediately following *Royal Brunei*.[238]

14–149 Although he held that knowledge is not the defining ingredient of liability in *Royal Brunei*, Lord Nicholls acknowledged that the honesty of a defendant's conduct can only be assessed in the light of what she knew at the time when she acted. It follows that a "fairly extensive investigation of the state of mind and knowledge of the relevant person who is alleged to have been dishonest" is usually necessary, making this an issue that is generally unsuitable for determination in proceedings for summary judgment.[239] Note, also, that special rules govern the pleading of claims founded on allegations of dishonesty.[240]

14–150 Lord Nicholls stated in *Royal Brunei*, and the Court of Appeal confirmed in *Group Seven*, that knowledge in this context is not limited to actual knowledge, but includes "blind-eye knowledge". This concept had previously been explained in *The Star Sea*,[241] where Lord Scott had said that blind-eye

---

231 [1982] Q.B. 1053.
232 [2002] UKHL 12; [2002] 2 A.C. 164 at [36].
233 [2002] UKHL 12; [2002] 2 A.C. 164 at [20].
234 [2005] UKPC 37; [2006] 1 W.L.R. 1476.
235 [2005] UKPC 37; [2006] 1 W.L.R. 1476 at [15]–[16].
236 e.g. *Abou-Rahmah v Abacha* [2006] EWCA Civ 1492; [2007] Bus. L.R. 220 at [43]; *Central Bank of Ecuador v Conticorp SA* [2015] UKPC 11; [2016] 1 B.C.L.C. 26 at [9].
237 [2019] EWCA Civ 614; [2020] Ch. 129 at [52]–[58].
238 See also *Royal Bank of Scotland International Ltd v JP SPC 4* [2022] 3 W.L.R. 261; [2022] UKPC 18 at [85]–[88], confirming that *Royal Brunei* is the governing authority (and holding that it would undermine the court's finding that accessory liability is not incurred by defendants who have merely been negligent if banks were held to owe a tortious duty of care to third parties to prevent breaches of fiduciary duty owed to such parties by the banks' customers).
239 *Umbrella Care Ltd (In Liq) v Nisa* [2022] EWHC 86 (Ch) at [184], noting *FM Capital Partners Ltd v Marino* [2018] EWHC 1768 (Comm) at [83].
240 For which see *Three Rivers DC v Bank of England (No.3)* [2001] UKHL 16; [2003] 2 A.C. 1 at [184]–[186]; *Sofer v SwissIndependent Trustees SA* [2020] EWCA Civ 699; [2020] W.T.L.R. 1075 at [23].
241 [2001] UKHL 1; [2003] 1 A.C. 469 at [112] and [116], discussed in *Group Seven Ltd v Notable Services LLP* [2019] EWCA Civ 614; [2020] Ch. 129 at [59]–[61], itself considered in *Natwest Markets Plc v Bilta (UK) Ltd (in liq)* [2021] EWCA Civ 680 at [130]–[133]. See also *Assets Co Ltd v Mere Roihi* [1905] A.C. 176 at 201: 'If it can be shown that his suspicions were aroused and that he abstained from making inquiries for fear of learning the truth . . . fraud may be ascribed to him.' See too

knowledge "requires an amalgam of suspicion that certain facts may exist and a decision to refrain from taking any step to confirm their existence", but that this must be a "targeted and firmly grounded suspicion of specific facts" and that blind-eye knowledge is not "constituted by a decision not to enquire into an untargeted or speculative suspicion". As noted in *Group Seven*,[242] *The Star Sea* also establishes that "the existence of the suspicion is to be judged subjectively by reference to the beliefs of the relevant person, and that the decision to avoid obtaining confirmation must be deliberate."

The facts which a defendant must have known before she can be said to have acted dishonestly will vary from case to case, but at the very least they must have known that the person assisted "is not entitled to do what he is doing".[243] The defendant need not have understood the legal characterisation of the primary wrongdoer's actions, so that "a person may dishonestly assist in the commission of a breach of trust without any idea of what a trust means".[244] Nor need she have known all the details of the primary wrongdoer's whole design, according to Lewison J in *Ultraframe (UK) Ltd v Fielding*,[245] although by analogy with criminal accessory liability, she must have known in broad terms what the design was, and her liability does not extend to unforeseen and uncontemplated actions by the primary wrongdoer which lay outside the scope of the joint enterprise in which he participated. This was endorsed by Vos LJ in *Goldtrail Travel Ltd (In Liq) v Aydin*,[246] although he also held that there is no liability where a defendant "lacked vital pieces of information known only to the primary fraudster". **14–151**

Is a defendant relevantly dishonest if she thinks that she is participating in some wrongful transaction other than the breach of trust or breach of fiduciary duty in which she is actually participating? The courts have given a positive answer, reasoning that defendants cannot be allowed to make the disreputable argument that they did not think they were helping to steal from the claimant because they thought they were helping to steal from someone else. As Fox LJ held in *Agip (Africa) Ltd v Jackson*, "persons who [need] to demonstrate that they [have] acted honestly [cannot] shelter behind transactions or objects which [are] themselves disreputable."[247] **14–152**

E. Remedies

Different remedies can be awarded against dishonest assistants in different situations. Arguably, some are made on the basis that the dishonest assistant owes a civil secondary liability which derives from and duplicates the liability of the trustee, so that once the amount of the trustee's liability is determined, the dishonest assistant is jointly and severally liable with the trustee for the same **14–153**

Westpac New Zealand Ltd v Map & Associates Ltd [2011] 3 N.Z.L.R. 751 at [24]–[27]; *Vestergaard Frandsen A/S v Bestnet Europe Ltd* [2013] UKSC 31; [2013] 1 W.L.R. 1556 at [26]; *Sandman v McKay* [2019] 1 N.Z.L.R. 519 at [77]–[78]; *Magner v Royal Bank of Scotland International Ltd* [2020] UKPC 5; (2020) 22 I.T.E.L.R. 863 at [10].

242 [2019] EWCA Civ 614; [2020] Ch. 129 at [59].

243 *Ultraframe (UK) Ltd v Fielding* [2005] EWHC 1638 (Ch); [2007] W.T.L.R. 835 at [1504]. See too *FM Capital Partners Ltd v Marino* [2018] EWHC 1768 (Comm) at [83](2); *CMOC Sales and Marketing Ltd v Persons Unknown* [2018] EWHC 2230 (Comm) at [117]–[127].

244 *Twinsectra Ltd v Yardley* [2002] UKHL 12; [2002] 2 A.C. 164 at [19]. See too *Barlow Clowes International Ltd (In Liq) v Eurotrust International Ltd* [2005] UKPC 37; [2006] 1 W.L.R. 1476 at [28]; *Abou-Rahmah v Abacha* [2005] EWHC 2662 (QB); [2006] 1 All E.R. (Comm.) 247 at [43], affirmed [2006] EWCA Civ 1492; [2007] Bus L.R. 220 at [23].

245 [2005] EWHC 1638 (Ch); [2007] W.T.L.R. 835 at [1506].

246 [2016] EWCA Civ 371; [2016] 1 B.C.L.C. 635 at [46] and [48]. See too *UBS AG (London Branch) v Kommunale Wasserwerke Leipzig GmbH* [2017] EWCA Civ 1567; [2017] 2 Lloyd's Rep. 621 at [361].

247 [1991] Ch. 547 at 569, affirming [1990] Ch. 265 at 295. See too *Barlow Clowes International Ltd (In Liq) v Eurotrust International Ltd* [2005] UKPC 37;[2006] 1 W.L.R. 1476 at [28], rejecting the contrary view in *Brink's Ltd v Abu-Saleh* [1996] C.L.C. 133 that was also taken in *Grupo Torras SA v Al-Sabah (No.5)* [1999] C.L.C. 1469 at 1665–1666, affirmed [2001] Lloyd's Rep. Bank. 36 at 59; *Abou-Rahmah v Abacha* [2006] EWCA Civ 1492; [2007] Bus L.R. 220 at [39]; *Livewire Telecom Ltd Technology Ltd v Revenue and Customs Commissioners* [2009] EWHC 15 (Ch); [2009] S.T.C. 643 at [103].

amount.[248] If the wrongdoing trustee is liable to pay money as a form of substitutive performance of her obligation to account for trust property,[249] the dishonest assistant is jointly and severally liable for this amount as well.[250] Again, the dishonest assistant can also be ordered to pay the same measure of compensation as the trustee would have had to pay if the beneficiaries had sued her for reparation.[251] Again, there are a series of Canadian cases,[252] and several English decisions,[253] which hold that where the trustee has incurred a liability to disgorge unauthorised profits,[254] the dishonest assistant will be jointly and severally liable for the same amount—although in *Ultraframe (UK) Ltd v Fielding*,[255] Lewison J declined to make a finding to this effect because he thought it would amount to a punitive measure, and the High Court of Australia has also held that a primary wrongdoer and an assistant are not jointly liable for one another's profits, although they may be severally liable to disgorge their own profits.[256]

14–154 English law also holds that a dishonest assistant must disgorge profits she has made for herself out of her wrongdoing. The Court of Appeal's statement to this effect in *Novoship (UK) Ltd v Mikhaylyuk*[257] is reproduced below. Note, however, that the court refused to order an account of profits on the facts of the case as it considered that the defendants' profits were not relevantly caused by their wrongdoing. Note, too, that the availability of this remedy requires us to think that for some purposes, at least, dishonest assistance can be a form of wrongdoing for which a primary liability is incurred by the defendant.

Novoship (UK) Ltd v Mikhaylyuk

Court of Appeal [2015] 1 Q.B. 499

14–155 The claimant corporate group alleged that a director, Mikhaylyuk, committed breaches of fiduciary duty when he took bribes to arrange charters of the group's vessels to Henriot Finance Ltd, a company controlled by Nikitin, who made US$150m profits from the charters. Christopher Clarke J. found that Nikitin

[248] S.B. Elliott and C. Mitchell, "Remedies for Dishonest Assistance" (2004) 67 M.L.R. 16. Contra P. Ridge, "Justifying the Remedies for Dishonest Assistance" (2008) 124 L.Q.R. 445. Further discussion: M.S. Clapton, "Gain-Based Remedies for Knowing Assistance: Ensuring Assistants Do Not Profit From Their Wrongs" (2008) 45 Alberta L.R. 989; C. Mitchell and S. Watterson, "Remedies for Knowing Receipt" in C. Mitchell (ed.) *Constructive and Resulting Trusts* (2010), pp.150–154.

[249] See paras 13–009 to 13–017.

[250] See, e.g. *Macdonald v Hauer* (1976) 72 D.L.R. (3d) 110 at 129; *Re Bell's Indenture* [1980] 1 W.L.R. 1217 at 1231–1233; *Commercial Union Life Assurance Co of Canada v John Ingle Insurance Group Inc* (2002) 22 C.C.L.I. 221, affirmed (2002) 217 D.L.R. (4th) 178; *NCR Australia Pty Ltd v Credit Connection Pty Ltd (In Liquidation)* [2004] NSWSC 1 at [150].

[251] See paras 13–090 to 13–096. Awards of this sort were made against dishonest assistants in, e.g. *Colour Control Centre Pty Ltd v Ty* N.S.W.S.C. (Eq. Div.) 24 July 1995; *Equiticorp Industries Group Ltd v R. (No.47)* [1998] 2 N.Z.L.R. 481 at 658; *Fyffes Group Ltd v Templeman* [2000] 2 Lloyd's Rep. 643.

[252] Running from *Canada Safeway Ltd v Thompson* [1951] 3 D.L.R. 295, through *Glenko Enterprises Ltd v Keller* [2001] 1 W.W.R. 229 at 257–258, to *Extreme Venture Partners Fund I LP v Varma* [2021] ONCA 853, where it was said that the courts have a discretion to choose whether to make a dishonest assistant jointly and severally liable with a defaulting fiduciary for the fiduciary's unauthorised profits.

[253] *Ostrich Farming Corp Ltd v Wallstreet LLC* Ch. D., Lawtel Report 8 October 1998; *Comax Secure Business Services Ltd v Wilson* Q.B.D. 21 June 2001; *CMS Dolphin Ltd v Simonet* [2001] 2 B.C.L.C. 704, followed in *Quarter Master UK Ltd v Pyke* [2005] 1 B.C.L.C. 245.

[254] See paras 18–056 to 18–100.

[255] [2005] EWHC 1638 (Ch); [2007] W.T.L.R. 835 at [1589]–[1601]. See also *Novoship (UK) Ltd v Mikahlyuk* [2012] EWHC 3586 at [99] (not considered on appeal: [2015] 1 Q.B. 499); *Airbus Operations Ltd v Withey* [2014] EWHC 1126 (QB) at [504]; *Tuke v Hood* [2020] EWHC 2843 (Comm) at [162]–[172]; *Hotel Portfolio II UK Ltd (In Liq) v Ruhan* [2022] EWHC 383 (Comm) at [265].

[256] *Michael Wilson & Partners Ltd v Nicholls* (2011) 244 C.L.R. 427 at [106].

[257] [2014] EWCA Civ 908; [2015] 1 Q.B. 499. See too *Consul Development Pty Ltd v DPC Estates Pty Ltd* (1972) 132 C.L.R. 373 at 397, followed in *US Surgical Corp v Hospital Products International Pty Ltd* (1982) 2 N.S.W.L.R. 766 at [817]; *Crown Dilmun v Sutton* [2004] 1 B.C.L.C. 468 at [204]; *Ultraframe (UK) Ltd v Fielding* [2005] EWHC 1638 (Ch); [2007] W.T.L.R. 835 at [1595]; *Airbus Operations Ltd v Withey* [2014] EWHC 1126 (QB) at [506].

and Henriot had dishonestly assisted Mikhaylyuk's breaches of fiduciary duty and ordered them to disgorge their profits on the charters. They appealed from this order. The Court of Appeal held that an account of profits is available against a defendant who has dishonestly assisted a breach of fiduciary duty that did not involve a misapplication of property. However, this remedy should only be awarded where there is a causal link between the dishonest assistance and the profit for which the defendant must account. The benefit derived by Nikitin and Henriot from their dishonest assistance was merely the use of the vessels at the market rate and although they had made a profit on the deal as a result of an unexpected change in the market there had been no sufficiently direct causal link between their wrongdoing and their profits. Hence the judge had erred in ordering them to account for these profits.

LONGMORE, MOORE-BICK AND LEWISON L.JJ.: . . . The question arising on this part of the appeal is whether Mr Nikitin is liable to account for the profits that he (or his companies) made from the Henriot charters. The judge held that he was so liable, because he had dishonestly assisted in a breach of fiduciary duty by Mr Mikhaylyuk either in (a) negotiating the terms of the fixtures with him or (b) concluding charters resulting from those negotiations, in either case at a time when Mr Mikhaylyuk had not disclosed to his principals that he had been bribed by Mr Ruperti and that part of the bribe had been diverted to Mr Nikitin. **14–156**

This raises the following potential issues: (i) is the remedy of an account of profits available against a dishonest assistant as opposed to a fiduciary; (ii) if so, is there a requirement for some causal connection between the dishonest assistance and the profit for which the assistant is asked to account; (iii) if so, what is the nature of that causal connection; (iv) if there is a requirement for a causal connection was it satisfied on the facts of this case; (v) if it is, would it be right, on the facts of this case, to order an account of profits? **14–157**

Remedies against third parties

[The claimant] claims an account of Mr Nikitin's profits from the Henriot charters. This is a personal claim only: Mr Brindle accepted that there is no proprietary claim. Mr Berry in turn accepted that a fiduciary would be compelled to account for an unauthorised profit made and falling within the scope of his fiduciary duty. However, he submitted that (a) an account of profits could never be ordered against a third party who had not voluntarily assumed fiduciary obligations to the claimant; alternatively (b) that an account of profits could not be ordered against a third party whose liability arose only because of his dishonest assistance in a breach of fiduciary duty; alternatively (c) an account of profits could not be ordered against a third party unless there had been some misapplication of trust property. These arguments were not deployed below, and so the judge did not deal with them. **14–158**

Where a person is not himself a fiduciary, he may become mixed up in a breach by another of a fiduciary duty. He may be liable in one of two ways: (i) as a knowing recipient of trust property or its traceable proceeds or (ii) as a dishonest accessory to the fiduciary's breach of duty. **14–159**

The former is now known by the shorthand "knowing receipt" and the second by the shorthand "dishonest assistance". Although for the purpose of legal analysis it is convenient to distinguish between the two types of secondary liability, a person may be liable under both heads, depending on the facts of a particular case. Mr Berry correctly points out that neither a knowing recipient nor a dishonest assistant has ever promised either expressly or inferentially to subordinate his own interests to those of the beneficiary. Neither is a fiduciary. In some areas of the law this does lead to a different legal treatment of a dishonest assistant on the one hand, and a fiduciary on the other. This is now settled at the highest level in the case of limitation of actions. Whereas a trustee is not entitled to raise a defence of limitation against a beneficiary alleging a fraudulent breach of trust or seeking to recover trust property, a knowing recipient or a dishonest assistant is entitled to rely on the Limitation Act 1980. This is the result of the decision of the Supreme Court in *Williams v Central Bank of Nigeria*.[258] Mr Berry drew attention in particular to the observations of Lord Neuberger of Abbotsbury P.S.C.:[259] **14–160**

> "So far as raising a limitation defence is concerned, this conclusion places dishonest assisters and knowing recipients (i) in the same position as those who are liable in common law for improper or dishonest conduct, and (ii) in a better position than defaulting trustees. The first result seems appropriate: as Millett L.J. said in the *Paragon* case,[260] 'There is no case for distinguishing between an action

[258] [2014] A.C. 1189.
[259] At [118].
[260] [1999] 1 All E.R. 400 at 414.

for fraud at common law and its counterpart in equity'. As for the second result, it is plainly justifiable, as defaulting trustees have pre-existing fiduciary duties to claimants which dishonest assisters and knowing recipients do not."

14–161 Building on this distinction Mr Berry pointed out that in the case of a common law action based on fraud the response of the courts is to require the fraudster to compensate the victim for loss that he has suffered. The common law does not strip the fraudster of his gain.[261] As Longmore L.J. put it in *Devenish Nutrition Ltd v Sanofi-Aventis SA*:[262]

"Neither the law of restitution nor the law of damages is in the business of transferring monetary gains from one undeserving recipient to another undeserving recipient even if the former has acted illegally while the latter has not."

14–162 However, we note that Longmore L.J. excluded "fiduciary claims" from his reluctance to encourage a restitutionary system of damages.[263] Moreover in the *Williams* case itself Lord Sumption J.S.C. made it clear that equity's intervention in the case of a knowing recipient or dishonest assistant was "purely remedial";[264] and he was careful to distinguish between the question of limitation and the question of remedy. Nor did he rule out the possibility that a knowing recipient might be liable to account for profits.[265] At the heart of the issue, therefore, is the question whether a dishonest assistant should be treated differently from a true fiduciary; and, if so, to what extent.

14–163 There is now a body of modern case law at first instance which recognises that the court has the power to order an account of profits against a dishonest assistant, even where no corresponding loss has been suffered by the beneficiary. They include: *Fyffes Group Ltd v Templeman*;[266] *Ultraframe (UK) Ltd v Fielding*;[267] *Tajik Aluminium Plant v Ermatov (No. 3)*;[268] *OJSC Oil Co Yugraneft v Abramovich*;[269] *Fiona Trust & Holding Corpn v Privalov*;[270] and *Otkritie International Investment Management Ltd v Urumov*.[271] The proposition for which these cases stand is unequivocally supported by *Underhill & Hayton, Law of Trusts and Trustees*.[272] Ranged against this body of case law are the obiter doubts expressed by Rimer J. in *Sinclair Investment Holdings SA v Versailles Trade Finance Ltd*.[273]

14–164 Mr Berry correctly submitted that none of these cases are binding on this court; and further submitted that, apart from the *Sinclair* case, they are wrong. . .

14–165 [Their Lordships rejected this submission and agreed with the statement in *Snell's Equity*[274] that] both a liability to make good loss and a liability to account for profits "follow from the premise that the defendant is held liable to account as if he were truly a trustee to the claimant".

14–166 In our judgment this position is supported both by policy and authority. The policy was articulated by Gibbs J. in *Consul Development Pty Ltd v DPC Estates Pty Ltd*.[275] He said:

"If the maintenance of a very high standard of conduct on the part of fiduciaries is the purpose of the rule it would seem equally necessary to deter other persons from knowingly assisting those in a fiduciary position to violate their duty. If, on the other hand, the rule is to be explained simply because it would be contrary to equitable principles to allow a person to retain a benefit that he had gained from a breach of his fiduciary duty, it would appear equally inequitable that one who knowingly took part in the breach should retain a benefit that resulted therefrom. I therefore conclude, on principle, that

261 *Halifax Building Society v Thomas* [1996] Ch. 217 at 227 per Peter Gibson L.J. and 229 per Glidewell L.J.
262 [2009] Ch. 390 at [147].
263 At [149].
264 [2014] A.C. 1189 at [10].
265 See the *Williams* case, at [31].
266 [2000] 2 Lloyd's Rep. 643 (Toulson J.).
267 [2006] F.S.R. 293 at [1589]–[1594] (Lewison J.).
268 [2006] EWHC 7 (Ch) at [23] (Blackburne J.).
269 [2008] EWHC 2613 (Comm) at [377] and [392] (Christopher Clarke J.).
270 [2010] EWHC 3199 (Comm) at [66] (Andrew Smith J.).
271 [2014] EWHC 191 (Comm) at [79] (Eder J.).
272 18th ed (2010), para.98.3.
273 [2007] 2 All E.R. (Comm.) 993 at [129]–[134].
274 32nd ed (2010), para.30–079.
275 (1975) 132 C.L.R. 373 at 397.

a person who knowingly participates in a breach of fiduciary duty is liable to account to the person to whom the duty was owed for any benefit he has received as a result of such participation."

If the phrase "knowingly took part in" is replaced by "dishonestly assisted in" we cannot see that it undermines the policy as formulated. It is true that in Australia the concept of "knowing participation" does not correspond precisely to our concepts of knowing receipt and dishonest assistance. However, so far as accounting for profits are concerned, even in Australian law a knowing participant is not generally required to account for profits that he did not make.[276] **14–167**

[Their Lordships quoted passages from *Docker v Somes*,[277] *Rolfe v Gregory*[278] and *Barnes v Addy*,[279] which supported their conclusion, then continued:] . . . *Royal Brunei Airlines Sdn Bhd v Tan*[280] altered the conditions that must be satisfied before liability arises, but did not, in our judgment, alter the nature of the liability. The nature of the liability, as it seems to us, is that the knowing recipient or dishonest assistant has, in principle, the responsibility of an express trustee. That responsibility would include, in an appropriate case, a liability to account for profits. We can see the principle at work in *Cook v Deeks*,[281] a decision of the Privy Council. Messrs Deeks and Hinds were the directors of the Toronto Construction Company. They negotiated a lucrative construction contract with the Canadian Pacific Railway. During the course of the negotiations, they decided to enter into the contract personally, on their own behalves. However, they incorporated a new company, the Dominion Construction Company to carry out the work. It was that company that made the profit under the contract. The Privy Council held that Messrs Deeks and Hinds were guilty of a breach of duty in the course they took to secure the contract, and must be regarded as holding it for the benefit of the Toronto Construction Company. The Board added:[282] **14–168**

"Their Lordships have throughout referred to the claim as one against the defendants GS Deeks, GM Deeks, and TR Hinds. But it was not, and it could not be, disputed that the Dominion Construction Company acquired the rights of these defendants with full knowledge of all the facts, and the account must be directed in form as an account in favour of the Toronto Company against all the other defendants."

The reference to "all the other defendants" is a reference both to the directors and to the Dominion Construction Company. Thus the Dominion Construction Company was ordered to account for the profit that it had made. The Dominion Construction Company was not a fiduciary. This, then, is a case in which an account of profits was ordered against a non-fiduciary who became mixed up in a breach of fiduciary duty. . . **14–169**

[Counsel has also argued that] that the misapplication of trust property is a necessary condition for the availability of an account of profits. This is put in two ways. First, since the Henriot charters were time charters they were no more than contracts for services with no disposition of trust property. We would be surprised if equity were to take a radically different view according to whether a charter were a time charter or a demise charter (or if the dishonest assistant took a licence of land rather than a lease), so we approach this way of putting the point with some scepticism. The second way in which the point is put is that although Mr Mikhaylyuk was a fiduciary, he had no power of disposition over his principal's property (unlike a trustee in whom trust property is vested, or a company director, who has power to dispose of the company's property). *Lewin on Trusts*[283] says that in such a case it is an open question whether a misapplication of trust property is a necessary precondition to an order for an account of profits. **14–170**

[Their Lordships considered *Satnam Investments Ltd v Dunlop Heywood & Co Ltd*[284], *Brown v Bennett*[285] and *Goose v Wilson Sandford & Co*[286] before turning to Peter Smith J.'s decision in *JD Wetherspoon plc v Van* **14–171**

---

276 *Grimaldi v Chameleon Mining NL (No.2)* (2012) 287 A.L.R. 22 at [536].
277 (1834) 2 My. & K. 655 at 665.
278 (1865) 4 De G.J. & S. 576 at 578 and 579.
279 (1874) L.R. 9 Ch. App. 244 at 251–252.
280 [1995] 2 A.C. 378.
281 [1916] 1 A.C. 554.
282 At 565.
283 18th ed. (2008 and 2012 supplement), para.40–16.
284 [1999] 3 All E.R. 652.
285 [1999] 1 B.C.L.C. 649.
286 [2001] Lloyd's Rep P.N. 189.

de Berg & Co Ltd[287] that] . . . misuse of trust property was not a prerequisite to a liability to account for profits for dishonest assistance in a breach of fiduciary duty. He reasoned thus:

> "In my view in a case for accessory liability there is no requirement for there to be trust property. Such a requirement wrongly associates accessory liability with trust concepts. That has led to difficulties which were addressed by Lord Millett in *Paragon Finance*. Accessory liability does not involve a trust. It involves providing dishonest assistance to somebody else who is in a fiduciary capacity [and] has committed a breach of his fiduciary duties. The consequences of those breaches (as this case shows) might have different consequences. One might be that the fiduciary has received a bribe. Another is that the fiduciary has made a profit in breach of his fiduciary duty. Another possibility is that assets are available . . . which it can be shown were acquired in breach of the fiduciary duty. Third party recipients are also potential candidates. Finally the breach of fiduciary duty might only sound in damages. In all of those cases I can see no logic or grave difficulty where the fiduciary is involved who has committed a breach of his fiduciary duty that an accessory who acts dishonestly in relation to those breaches should not be liable. It must not be forgotten that in most cases the breach can only occur as a result of the activities of the [assister]."

14–172 In the *Fiona Trust* case[288] Andrew Smith J. said that he agreed with Peter Smith J. and adopted his reasons. So do we. But in addition as we have said it would be a triumph of form over substance if a dishonest assistant escaped liability by entering into a time charter but not if he entered into a demise charter, or took a licence of land rather than a lease . . . Because dishonesty can take many different forms (as well as having many different consequences) we do not agree that it makes all the difference that the dishonesty consists of receiving as opposed to paying a bribe. As we have said, the only question is whether liability as a dishonest assistant in a breach of fiduciary duty has been established. If it has, then an account of profits is one possible remedy.

14–173 We therefore conclude that the remedy of an account of profits is available against one who dishonestly assists a fiduciary to breach his fiduciary obligations, even if that breach does not involve a misapplication of trust property.

Causation

14–174 In the decision in the *Ultraframe* case[289] Lewison J. said that a dishonest assistant is liable to account "for any profit that he makes from his dishonest assistance or from the underlying breach of trust". However, he was not considering the precise nature of the test of causation which was not in issue. We have already referred to the observations of Gibbs J. in holding that questions of policy support the availability of the remedy of an account of profits against a dishonest assistant. Gibbs J. concluded in the *Consul* case that a dishonest assistant is "liable to account to the person to whom the duty was owed for any benefit he has received as a result of such participation."[290]

14–175 This also suggests that a causation test is appropriate. We note also that Gibbs J. referred to a benefit received as a result of the participation (rather than a benefit received as a result of the breach of fiduciary duty). *Snell* suggests that the test should be that of "a sufficiently direct causal connection between the defendant's assistance and the alleged profit accruing to him".[291]

14–176 A fiduciary's liability to account for a secret profit does not depend on any notion of causation. It is sufficient that the profit falls within the scope of his duty of loyalty to the beneficiary. Arden L.J. made this point in the *Murad* case:[292]

> "If there is a fiduciary duty of loyalty and if the conduct complained of falls within the scope of that fiduciary duty as indicated by Lord Wilberforce in *New Zealand Netherlands Society 'Oranje' Inc v Kuys*[293] then I see no justification for any further requirement that the profit shall have been obtained

[287] [2009] EWHC 639 (Ch) at [518].
[288] *Fiona Trust & Holding Corp. v Privalov* [2010] EWHC 3199 (Comm) at [61].
[289] [2007] W.T.L.R. 835 at [1594].
[290] 132 C.L.R. 373 at 397 (emphasis added).
[291] At para.30–081.
[292] [2005] W.T.L.R. 1573 at [57], by reference to the judgment of Morritt L.J. in *United Pan-Europe Communications NV v Deutsche Bank AG* [2000] 2 B.C.L.C. 461 at [47].
[293] [1973] 1 W.L.R. 1126.

by the fiduciary 'by virtue of his position'. Such a condition suggests an element of causation which neither principle nor the authorities require. Likewise it is not in doubt that the object of the equitable remedies of an account or the imposition of a constructive trust is to ensure that the defaulting fiduciary does not retain the profit; it is not to compensate the beneficiary for any loss. Accordingly comparison with the remedy in damages is unhelpful."

Jonathan Parker L.J. made the same point in the *Murad* case.[294] Mr Brindle argued that our conclusion on the question of causation should not run contrary to the decision of this court in the *Murad* case, and in particular what Arden and Jonathan Parker L.JJ. said about the decision of Toulson J. in *Fyffes Group Ltd v Templeman*.[295] Although he did not say that we were bound by the decision in the Murad case (which concerned a fiduciary rather than a dishonest assistant) he did say that we should give full effect to it. **14–177**

It is, therefore, necessary to go back to the *Fyffes* case, and then to see what this court said about it in the *Murad* case. In the *Fyffes* case the claimant employed Mr Templeman as its chartering manager. He negotiated a service agreement with Seatrade under which Seatrade was to provide shipping services to Fyffes. However, unknown to Fyffes Seatrade had agreed to bribe Mr Templeman by paying him a percentage of the freight earned. That was dishonest assistance by Seatrade in Mr Templeman's breach of fiduciary duty to Fyffes. The question was whether Fyffes could require Seatrade to account for the profit that it had made in providing the shipping services under the service agreement. Toulson J. said that there were "cogent grounds, in principle and in practical justice, for following the approach of Gibbs J." in the *Consul* case. He therefore held that "the briber of an agent *may* be required to account to the principal for benefits obtained from the corruption of the agent."[296] But he decided on the facts that he should not order an account. First, he said that Seatrade would have entered into a service agreement with Fyffes, even if Mr Templeman had not been dishonest. Second, he said that the ordinary profit that Seatrade made under the service agreement was not "caused by the bribery of Mr Templeman". Third, he did not see the equity of ordering Seatrade to account to Fyffes for the whole of its profit, because that would amount to the unjust enrichment of Fyffes. As we read this decision the first two reasons for refusing to order an account related to the question of causation; and the third to the overall equity of the result. **14–178**

In the *Murad* case Arden L.J. said:[297] **14–179**

"Reliance has been placed . . . on the *Fyffes* case where Toulson J. declined to make an order for an account of profits in favour of the principal of a bribed agent as against the briber because the transaction with the defrauded principal was one into which the defrauded principal would have entered in any event. Toulson J. held that those profits were attributable to the provision of services under the agreement, not the payment of the bribe. On the face of it, this holding is precluded by the *Regal* case.[298] However, while it is not entirely clear, it may be that this should be treated as a case where the wrongdoer was held to be entitled to an allowance for his services despite his fraudulent conduct."

The *Regal* case to which Arden L.J. referred was a case about true fiduciaries. The principle that it established was described by Lord Russell of Killowen thus:[299] **14–180**

"The rule of equity which insists on those, who *by use of a fiduciary position* make a profit, being liable to account for that profit, in no way depends on fraud, or absence of bona fides; or on such questions or considerations as whether the profit would or should otherwise have gone to the plaintiff, or whether the profiteer was under a duty to obtain the source of the profit for the plaintiff, or whether he took a risk or acted as he did for the benefit of the plaintiff, or whether the plaintiff has in fact been damaged or benefited by his action. The liability arises from the mere fact of a profit having, *in the stated circumstances*, been made."

---

294 At [112].
295 [2000] 2 Lloyd's Rep. 643.
296 Our emphasis.
297 [2005] W.T.L.R. 1573 at [69].
298 *Regal (Hastings) Ltd v Gulliver* [1967] 2 A.C. 134.
299 At 144–145 (emphasis added).

14–181 Toulson J. was not, however, dealing with the case of a fiduciary; but with a dishonest assistant. So the *Regal* case does not in terms preclude his decision. In the decision in the *Murad* case Jonathan Parker L.J. said:[300]

> "Like Arden L.J . . . I have difficulty in reconciling Toulson J.'s reasoning in the above passage with the authorities to which I have referred, and I note that it appears from the report of the case that none of those authorities was cited to Toulson J. apart from *Target v Redferns* (a case concerning equitable compensation for breach of trust). Had the judge been addressing a claim for equitable compensation for breach of trust, his reasoning would in my judgment have been entirely in accordance with authority . . . but in the context of the 'no conflict' rule, the authorities, as I read them, preclude such an approach."

14–182 It is fair to say that, although these passages do not in terms disapprove or overrule the *Fyffes* case, they proceed on the assumption that precisely the same principles as regards causation apply in the case of a dishonest assistant as apply in the case of a true (but defaulting) fiduciary. But whether that assumption is correct was not before the court and neither Arden L.J. nor Jonathan Parker L.J. explicitly considered the question. Moreover in the decision in the *Satnam* case[301] this court held that the principle in the *Regal* case and *Phipps v Boardman*[302] did not apply to one who was alleged to be no more than a knowing recipient of trust property. As Nourse L.J. put it: "In the absence of a fiduciary duty the principle of those cases cannot apply." The *Satnam* case was not referred to in the *Murad* case. We do not consider that the decision in *Murad* will bear the weight that Mr Brindle seeks to place on it. . .

14–183 It is important to appreciate the special position in which a fiduciary finds himself. The essence of the relationship between a fiduciary and beneficiary is that the latter has placed his trust in the former. The core duty of the fiduciary is single minded loyalty to his beneficiary. Thus the breach of duty does not consist in the making of a profit by the fiduciary, but in the keeping of it for himself. That is not a breach of a personal obligation; it is an abuse of the trust and confidence placed in him by his principal who put him in a position to make the profit because he trusted him not to serve his own interests. Equity's response to the breach of this trust is not to give redress for the breach in the form of equitable compensation but to enforce the duty.[303] It is this attitude of equity which explains why a true trustee cannot raise a limitation defence against his beneficiary.[304]

14–184 We agree with Mr Berry that in the case of one who is not a fiduciary this approach is inappropriate, for the dishonest assistant has no pre-existing duty whose scope can be determined and enforced. It seems to us therefore that the scope of the wrongdoer's liability must be determined by reference to some other principle. In the case of a claim against a fiduciary for equitable compensation (as opposed to an account of profits) in respect of a breach of duty a court of equity will apply a "but for" test of causation, thus precluding recovery for loss that would have occurred even if the breach of duty had not taken place, although the common law rules of causation and remoteness do not apply in such a case . . .

14–185 In our case Mr Nikitin was not a fiduciary either as regards NOUK or the shipowning companies. He is not sued for a breach of fiduciary duty. He is sued because he has committed an equitable wrong. Where a claim based on equitable wrongdoing is made against one who is not a fiduciary, we consider that, as in the case of a fiduciary sued for breach of an equitable (but non-fiduciary) obligation, there is no reason why the common law rules of causation, remoteness and measure of damages should not be applied by analogy. We recognise that these rules do not apply to the case of a fiduciary sued for breach of a fiduciary duty; but that is because the two cases are different. Arden L.J. made this clear in the decision in the *Murad* case.[305] We note also that in the *Satnam* case some three pages of the court's judgment[306] were devoted to considering the question of causation.

14–186 The common law does not usually apply a simple "but for" test of causation. The common law distinguishes between a breach which is the effective cause of a loss and one which is merely the occasion for the

300 [2005] W.T.L.R. 1573 at [120].
301 [1999] 3 All E.R. 652 at 671.
302 [1967] 2 A.C. 46.
303 See Millett, "Bribes and Secret Commissions Again" [2012] C.L.J. 583.
304 See the *Williams* case [2014] A.C. 1189 at [13].
305 [2005] W.T.L.R. 1573 at [74].
306 [1999] 3 All E.R. 652 at 665–668.

loss. How to distinguish between the two is a question of the application of common sense.[307] Common sense, as we have seen, also plays its part in determining the extent of equitable compensation.

The question of causation has a bearing on the fashioning of the account. Even in the case of a fiduciary the cases stress the importance of identifying as precisely as possible the extent of the benefit or profit attributable to the breach of fiduciary duty. 14–187

The judge dealt with the question of causation at a number of points in his judgment.[308] [First] he posed the question whether as regards causation the dishonest assistant was in the same position as a fiduciary.[309] He referred to the well-established proposition that, in the case of a fiduciary, it is no defence to say that the profit would have been earned anyway even if there had been no breach of fiduciary duty; and said, "It seems to me that the same should apply to the assister in respect of whom the need for deterrence is similar."[310] 14–188

However, in the following paragraph, he said:[311] 14–189

> "In the present case, a sufficiently direct casual connection between the assistance and the profit is to be found given that the profit from the deployment of the vessels the subject of the Henriot Finance charters could not have been earned unless those charters had been entered into, and is, thus, a profit which results from Henriot Finance entering into those charters—which, itself, constitutes the dishonest assistance given to Mr Mikhaylyuk's breach of fiduciary duty."

Thus he said that the same test should apply to the dishonest assistant as applies to a fiduciary;[312] and [later] he said first that there was a "sufficiently direct causal connection"[313] but then in the same paragraph he appears to us to apply a simple "but for" test of causation. But he then went on to say:[314] 14–190

> "It is no defence to say that the charters were at commercial rates and not disadvantageous to the owners; or that, if there had been no breach of fiduciary duty, they would have been made anyway and at the same rates or that Henriot Finance would have made the same profit anyway by the charter of other vessels."

We agree with Mr Berry that that paragraph appears to disavow even a "but for" test of causation. 14–191

For the reasons we have given we do not agree with the judge that the same considerations that apply to a fiduciary apply to a dishonest assistant who has no fiduciary duties. We agree with the judge that if Mr Nikitin (or his companies) had not entered into the Henriot charters, the profits would not have been made. In other words, "but for" entry into the charters the profits would not have been made. But in our judgment the simple "but for" test is not the appropriate test. In our judgment what Mr Nikitin acquired as a result of his dishonest assistance (and also as a result of Mr Mikhaylyuk's breach of fiduciary duty) was the use of the vessels at the market rate. That was merely the occasion for him to make a profit. The real or effective cause of the profits was the unexpected change in the market. As the judge recognised,[315] Mr Nikitin made the profits "because he judged the market well". 14–192

We would therefore hold that there was an insufficient direct causal connection between entry into the Henriot charters and the resulting profits. We must stress, however, that had Mr Nikitin been a true fiduciary, and had entry into the Henriot charters been a breach of fiduciary duty, then the causation test we have adopted would not have applied. 14–193

[Their Lordships also held that it would be disproportionate to order an account of profits in relation to the particular form and extent of wrongdoing committed by the defendants.] 14–194

---

307 *Galoo Ltd v Bright Graham Murray* [1994] 1 W.L.R. 1360.
308 [2012] EWHC 3586 (Comm).
309 At [513].
310 At [518].
311 At [519].
312 At [518].
313 At [519].
314 At [520].
315 At [525].

Questions

1. What do the courts mean when they say that trustees *de son tort*, knowing recipients and dishonest assistants variously owe a "personal liability to account" to the beneficiaries, and how does this affect the measure of compensation that each may have to pay following a breach of trust?
2. In *Barnes v Addy* (1874) L.R. 9 Ch. App. 244 at 252, Lord Selborne LC thought that "if persons dealing honestly as agents are at liberty to rely on the legal power of the trustees, [and] are not to have the character of trustees constructively thrust upon them, then the transactions of mankind can safely be carried through; and I apprehend those who create trusts do expressly intend, in the absence of fraud and dishonesty, to exonerate such agents of all classes from the responsibilities which are expressly incumbent by reason of the fiduciary relation upon the trustees." In light of these comments should fault be a prerequisite for third party liability for breach of trust; and if so, what degree of fault?
3. A stockbroker is directed by trustees to sell an authorised investment and to apply the proceeds to the purchase of an unauthorised investment. She knowingly does so because she bona fide believes this to be in the beneficiaries' best financial interests. Most surprisingly the unauthorised investment halves in value within a year. Can the beneficiaries sue the stockbroker if the trustees are now insolvent?
4. An accountant agrees to falsify her client's records, and certify them as accurate, in what she believes to be a conspiracy to evade the payment of VAT. In fact, her client has misappropriated trust funds and the beneficiaries now wish to know whether they can sue the accountant. Would it make any difference if the client would have stolen the money anyway?

15

PROPRIETARY CLAIMS FOLLOWING A BREACH OF TRUST

1. Introduction

A. Overview

According to Lord Browne-Wilkinson in *Westdeutsche Landesbank Girozentrale v Islington LBC*:[1] **15–001**

> Once a trust is established, as from the date of its establishment the beneficiary has, in equity, a proprietary interest in the trust property, which proprietary interest will be enforceable in equity against any subsequent holder of the property (whether the original property or substituted property into which it can be traced) other than a purchaser for value of the legal interest without notice.

This statement was affirmed in *Akers v Samba Financial Group*,[2] where Lord Sumption held that a beneficiary has "two main legal rights": "a right to have the trust administered according to its terms" and a "true proprietary right", regarding which he observed that: **15–002**

> The proprietary character of an equitable interest in property has sometimes been doubted, but in English law ... the position must be regarded as settled. An equitable interest possesses the essential hallmark of any right *in rem*, namely that it is good against third parties into whose hands the property or its traceable proceeds may have come, subject to the rules of equity for the protection of bona fide purchasers for value without notice.

In Chapter 12 we discuss what it might mean to say that a beneficiary has an "equitable proprietary interest" in trust property and we consider different ways in which the beneficiary's right might be conceived. The focus of discussion in this chapter is on the different "proprietary claims" which can be made against trustees and third parties, meaning claims which rest on the assertion that beneficiaries have an "equitable proprietary interest" in property owned by the defendant. If successful, claims of this kind will lead to a declaration that the property is held subject to the beneficiaries' interest and where necessary to an order that the owner convey title to the existing or new trustees so that the property can be duly administered in accordance with the terms of the trust. Where those terms confer on a beneficiary an entitlement to the beneficial enjoyment of trust property, the form of relief can be different, requiring the third party to convey title to the beneficiary directly.[3] It is important to **15–003**

1 [1996] A.C. 669 at 705.
2 [2017] UKSC 6; [2017] A.C. 424 at [82].
3 As in *Foskett v McKeown* [2001] 1 A.C. 102 excerpted at paras 15–095 to 15–127.

appreciate that in such cases this is because the order for relief "short circuits"[4] the step of return to the trustee, and the beneficiary's exercise of power to call for the trust property. So while there are references in this chapter and in the cases to the beneficiary being able to claim property against a third party, the substance of her claim is to require the third party to return the subject property to the trustee (or possibly a replacement trustee) to be duly administered in accordance with the trust terms.[5]

15-004 The proprietary claims considered in this chapter should be distinguished from personal claims against trustees for breach of trust or third parties for knowing receipt in cases where trust property has been misapplied, which lead to a different remedy, namely an order that the defendant pay a money sum to the trustees as a way of reconstituting the trust fund.[6]

15-005 The distinction between such proprietary and personal claims has been brought out in many cases, one example being *Byers v Saudi National Bank* where Newey LJ said that:[7]

> [A knowing receipt] claim is most obviously likely to be useful where the defendant no longer has the property. If the defendant yet retains the property, the claimant may be able to recover it by asserting proprietary rights rather than by making a personal claim for knowing receipt. In *Re Montagu's Settlement Trusts*, Sir Robert Megarry V-C distinguished between "the equitable doctrine of tracing" and "liability as a constructive trustee", pointing out that "if the recipient of trust property still has the property or its traceable proceeds in his possession, he is liable to restore it unless he is a purchaser without notice".[8] In *Arthur v Attorney General of the Turks & Caicos Islands*, Sir Terence Etherton, giving the judgment of the Privy Council, said:[9]
>
> > "When considering relief for the consequences of knowing receipt it is necessary to distinguish between proprietary and personal remedies. The beneficiaries or innocent trustees will pursue a proprietary claim by following the trust property wrongly transferred or tracing its inherent value into something substituted for it.[10] The claim for personal liability is for the recipient to account as a constructive trustee and will usually only be necessary where following or tracing is not possible because, for example, the property has been acquired by a bona fide purchaser for value without notice or has been dissipated and is otherwise no longer identifiable."

15-006 There is usually no need for beneficiaries to bring a proprietary claim against their trustees to establish that they have an equitable interest in trust property owned by the trustees, because in normal circumstances the trustees would not dispute this. However, disagreements can arise when the trustees (or the trustees' trustee in bankruptcy) claim to have a beneficial interest in property which the beneficiaries contend should be treated as forming part of the trust fund, the parties' dispute then turning on whether the trust terms permit the trustees to treat the relevant property as belonging to them absolutely. For example, the trustees may purport to recoup themselves for costs which the beneficiaries say were not incurred in the course of authorised trust business[11] or the trustees may say that they are beneficially entitled to property purchased with trust money or to income generated by trust property which the beneficiaries say should be treated as trust property.[12] Meanwhile, disputes

---

4 J. Hudson, "Equitable Ownership and Restitution of Misapplied Trust Property" (2017) 11 J. Eq. 245, 267.

5 As explained in *Akers* [2017] UKSC 6; [2017] A.C. 424 at [46], [82].

6 Further see paras 13-009 to 13-089 and 14-081 to 14-093.

7 [2022] EWCA Civ 43; [2022] 4 W.L.R. 22 at [23].

8 [1987] 1 Ch. 264 at 276.

9 [2012] UKPC 30 at [34].

10 *Foskett v McKeown* [2001] 1 A.C. 102 at 127–129 (Lord Millett).

11 As required by e.g. *Re Beddoe* [1893] 1 Ch. 547; *Re Grimthorpe* [1958] Ch. 615 at 623; *Chief Commissioner of Stamp Duties (NSW) v Buckle* (1998) 192 C.L.R. 226 at [47]; *Carter Holt Harvey Woodproducts Australia Pty Ltd v Commonwealth* (2019) 268 C.L.R. 524 at [40].

12 *Aberdeen Town Council v Aberdeen University* (1877) 2 App. Cas. 544; *Re EVTR Ltd* (1987) 3 B.C.C. 389 at 393; *Tang Ying Ip v Tang Ying Loi* (2017) 20 H.K.C.F.A.R. 53.

can arise between beneficiaries and third parties to whom trustees have transferred ownership of trust property in unauthorised transactions and who are neither beneficiaries entitled to a distribution nor bona fide purchasers of the property without notice of the trust, the beneficiaries asserting in such cases that the third parties took the property bound by their equitable interest.[13]

Where the trust property survives in its original form and is held either by a trustee or a third party, the beneficiaries may be able to claim a "subsisting" equitable interest in the property, i.e. they may say that they have never stopped having an interest in the property because nothing has happened to extinguish their right. Where the trust property is exchanged for other property, the beneficiaries may be able to claim a new equitable interest in the substitute property or alternatively to claim to an equitable lien over the substitute property to secure performance of the defendant's personal obligation to pay the value of "missing" funds. **15–007**

These claims differ in that the first and second are claims to an interest under a trust, while the third is a claim to a security interest in property held by the defendant, but beneficiaries with either type of interest can defeat the defendant's creditors in the event of their insolvency. **15–008**

Furthermore, if a claimant has an equitable interest under a trust in property that appreciates in value, the claimant will take the increase; and if a claimant has an equitable lien over a defendant's property to secure the payment of a particular sum, and the property depreciates in value, the claimant can nevertheless recover the whole amount of the obligation secured by the lien by obtaining an order for sale of the property, and if necessary they can also recover any amount outstanding by bringing a personal action. As Keene LJ said in *Serious Fraud Office v Lexi Holdings Plc (in admin)*,[14] an equitable lien is "a cumulative remedy in aid of an equitable *in personam* claim, not an alternative remedy". **15–009**

If a trustee has legal title to trust property which she takes for herself and retains in its original form, it is usually a simple matter for the beneficiaries to identify the property that forms the subject-matter of their proprietary claim. But more complicated situations can arise. If a trustee transfers legal title to trust property to a third party, the beneficiaries must "follow" the title from the trustee to the third party as a preliminary to asserting an equitable proprietary claim against the third party, i.e. they must prove that title to property now held by the third party was previously held for the beneficiaries by the trustee. And if either a trustee or a third party recipient exchanges title to trust property for title to different property, the beneficiaries must "trace" from the old to the new title, i.e. they must demonstrate that the new title was exchanged for the old, before they can assert an equitable proprietary claim to the substitute property. As we will see, the tracing rules vary according to whether a "clean" or "mixed substitution" has taken place, the former occurring where the new asset is acquired solely with misapplied trust property, the latter occurring where the new asset is acquired with a mixture of misapplied trust property and the defendant's own property.[15] **15–010**

B. Following, Tracing and Claiming

In *Foskett v McKeown* Lord Millett explained the relationship between following, tracing and claiming in these terms:[16] **15–011**

> [Following and tracing] are both exercises in locating assets which are or may be taken to represent an asset belonging to the plaintiffs and to which they assert ownership . . . Following is the process of following the

13 *Venables v Hornby (Inspector of Taxes)* [2002] EWCA Civ 1277; [2003] I.C.R. 186 at [27].
14 [2008] EWCA Crim 1443; [2009] Q.B. 376 at [40].
15 *Foskett v McKeown* [2001] 1 A.C. 102 at 130.
16 *Foskett v McKeown* [2001] 1 A.C. 102 at 127–128.

> same asset as it moves from hand to hand. Tracing is the process of identifying a new asset as the substitute for the old. Where one asset is exchanged for another, a claimant can elect whether to follow the original asset into the hands of the new owner or to trace its value into the new asset in the hands of the same owner. . . . Tracing is also distinct from claiming. It identifies the traceable proceeds of the claimant's property. It enables the claimant to substitute the traceable proceeds for the original asset as the subject matter of his claim. But it does not affect or establish his claim. That will depend on a number of factors including the nature of his interest in the original asset . . . [and] his claim may also be exposed to potential defences as a result of intervening transactions.

15-012 On Lord Millett's view, therefore, "the rules of following and tracing . . . [are] evidential in nature" and are distinct from "rules which determine substantive rights": "the former are concerned with identifying property in other hands or in another form; the latter with the rights that a claimant can assert against the property in its present form".[17] Where trust property has been wrongfully converted into a different form by the trustee, either by exchanging the trust property for another asset, or by mixing the trust property with other property, or by a combination of the two, and the substitute asset or mixture remains in the trustee's hands, there is no need for the beneficiaries to "follow" their property or its traceable product into the hands of anyone else, before they can assert a proprietary claim to the new asset or mixture. However, it will be necessary for the beneficiaries to invoke the tracing rules to establish that the new asset or mixture is the traceable product of trust property before they can make a proprietary claim; and "following" will be necessary in cases where ownership of trust property or its traceable proceeds has been transferred to a third party.

15-013 In the passage quoted above, Lord Millett speaks of a claimant "tracing the value" of one asset into a substitute asset,[18] terminology which he derived from Lionel Smith's book on the law of tracing.[19] This language signifies that the purpose of the tracing exercise is to identify the value inhering in one property right as representing the value inhering in another property right. As Tatiana Cutts has argued, however, this idea does not stand up to scrutiny.[20] If a defendant exchanges legal title to a painting worth £20,000 for legal title to a car worth £40,000, the rules of tracing hold that title to the car is the traceable substitute of title to the painting. From the point of view of a claimant who was the equitable beneficial owner of the painting, the fact that the car is worth more than the painting gives her a practical reason for wishing to assert an equitable proprietary interest in the car. But if we understand "value" simply to mean "market value", i.e. the measure of what a right is worth, it is meaningless to say that the £20,000 value of the painting "has become" or "is now represented by" the £40,000 value of the car. On this understanding of "value", it has no abstract existence that makes it possible to say that it has moved from one right to another in the same way that one can say that the ownership of rights has moved from one person to another.

15-014 It may be that Smith, and through his approval and adoption of Smith's terminology and analysis, Lord Millett, use the term "value" in a different sense, to connote the potential for exchange inherent in an assignable right. For example, they may mean that if a trustee holds title to a painting on trust and exchanges this for title to a car, the trustee exploits the exchange potential inherent in one right to acquire another. The continuity provided by the tracing process is then sourced in the fact that it is a single actor—the trustee—who uses one right to acquire another. However, as Cutts

---

17 *Glencore International AG v Metro Trading International Ltd* [2001] 1 Lloyd's Rep. 284 at [180], per Moore-Bick J. See too *Boscawen v Bajwa* [1996] 1 W.L.R. 328 at 334; *Waxman v Waxman* (2004) 7 I.T.E.L.R. 162 at [582].

18 See also *Relfo Ltd (in liq) v Varsani* [2014] EWCA Civ 360; [2015] 1 B.C.L.C. 14 at [45]; *Brazil v Durant International Corp* [2015] UKPC 35; [2016] A.C. 297 at [32].

19 L.D. Smith, *The Law of Tracing* (Oxford University Press, 1997), p.119.

20 T. Cutts, "Tracing, Value and Transactions" (2016) 79 M.L.R. 381.

has also shown,[21] this idea does not work for bank transfers, through which claimants are allowed to trace.[22] Suppose that a trustee holds a bank account on trust and that she arranges a fund transfer of £10,000 to a recipient's bank account by asking her bank to debit the trust account and request a second bank to credit the recipient's account with an equivalent sum (the banks' reciprocal rights and obligations being mediated through the bank settlement system). Here, there is no "exchange" by a single actor and hence no continuity.[23] In the extra-judicial words of an Australian judge, Edelman J:[24]

> [In such cases] there is no substitution of one right for another, through which transfer of value can be traced. Rather, there is simply a matched creation and destruction of value. . . . [Where there is] a series of transactions between a variety of bank accounts . . . at each stage, there is no exchange or substitution of one right for another. Rather, each recipient has an increase in the value of the debt owed to him by a particular bank with a corresponding (more or less) decrease in the value of the debt owed to the payer by her particular bank. What links the matched destruction and creation of value is a transaction. And it is only where there are a series of such transactions that are sufficiently linked that the law of tracing is engaged.

For these reasons we agree that talk of "tracing value" is misguided and distracting, and that it **15–015** is preferable to speak of "tracing" solely in terms of rules that enable claimants to show that one property right is the traceable substitute of another for the purposes of making claims including proprietary claims to the substitute property. As the Jersey Court of Appeal said in *Brazil v Durant International Corp*:[25]

> The starting point is to recognise the true nature of the exercise with which the court is engaged when it is asked to trace a plaintiff's property . . . [The] court is being asked to identify an asset which represents the plaintiff's property, in other words an asset which is not in reality the plaintiff's original property but one which the law is prepared to treat as a 'substitute' for that original. That being the true nature of the process, . . . the court is liable to be making an evaluative judgment . . . [and] is accordingly making a policy choice as to whether the law is prepared to recognise one asset as representing, or as a substitute for, another on the particular facts of the case in hand.

As implicitly suggested by this passage, however, a further problem arises with the idea that tracing **15–016** and following are "rights-neutral" evidential processes that are separate from the claiming process.[26] This problem was well described by Look Chan Ho when he wrote that it is:[27]

---

21 T. Cutts, "Tracing, Value and Transactions" (2016) 79 M.L.R. 381, developed in T. Cutts "Dummy Asset Tracing" (2019) 135 L.Q.R. 140.

22 See e.g. *Agip (Africa) Ltd v Jackson* [1990] Ch. 265; *El Ajou v Dollar Land Holdings* [1994] 2 All E.R. 685; *Foskett v McKeown* [2001] 1 A.C. 102; *Relfo Ltd (in liq) v Varsani* [2014] EWCA Civ 360; [2015] 1 B.C.L.C. 14; *Brazil v Durant International Corp* [2015] UKPC 35; [2016] A.C. 297.

23 Smith tries to explain tracing through bank transfers using the idea of "tracing in transit": L.D. Smith, *The Law of Tracing* (1997), p.144. The idea is that if X has a dog which she gives to Y on the understanding that Y will then give a cat to Z, we can say that X has effectively substituted the dog for the cat herself, with the result that the cat is the traceable product of the dog which can be followed into Z's hands. But bank transfers do not entail the transfer of any identifiable asset from one person to another.

24 Hon J. Edelman, "Understanding Tracing Rules" [2016] *QUT Law Review* 1.

25 [2013] J.L.R. 273 at [48]–[49].

26 For which see also P. Millett, "Proprietary Restitution" in S. Degeling and J. Edelman (eds) *Equity in Commercial Law* (2005), p.325.

27 Look Chan Ho, "Book Review" (2007) 21 Tru. L.I. 110, 112. Similar points are made in C. Rotherham, "The Metaphysics of Tracing: Substituted Title and Property Rhetoric" (1996) 34 O.H.L.J. 321; Sir P. Sales, "The Future of Tracing: Practical and Conceptual Issues" [2017] R.L.R. 183; D. Whayman, "Obligation and Property in Tracing Claims" [2018] Conv. 157; P. Ridge, "Tracing and Associated Claims in Australian Law" (2020) 14 J. Eq. 32.

paradoxical to say that tracing rules "dictate that the owner of an asset may assert ownership of its traceable proceeds", and yet they do not "establish" the owner's claim to those proceeds. If tracing does indeed carry or transmit property rights from one asset to another, it is manifestly not about tracing value; it evidently performs more than just an evidential function because it also specifies entitlement; it is hardly neutral as to rights because it does tell us something about the legal or equitable rights to the assets traced; and it does affect or establish a claimant's claim.

15–017 The same argument has been made by Aruna Nair[28] and Magda Raczynska.[29] They both reject the idea that the rules of tracing are "rights-neutral" rules of evidence and contend that they are rules which decide when one property right can be treated in law as the substitute of another for a specific purpose, viz to enable a claimant to say that she had (and perhaps still has) a proprietary interest in the substitute right. Assuming the correctness of this, one must then ask when claimants should be entitled to invoke these rules in their favour. Nair's answer is when another party with the power to acquire a new right in exchange for the claimant's right uses this power in an unauthorised way. Raczynska agrees that claimants can use the tracing rules in such cases of unauthorised exchange, but further argues that they can be used in cases of authorised exchange where this is consistent with an agreement between the parties. So far as cases of unauthorised exchange are concerned, however, both scholars contend that the key to understanding these is to see that they entail unauthorised exercises of power to destroy a claimant's interest in assets, and for Nair at least it is also a key point that these cases entail a breach of duty epitomised by the breach committed by trustees who exceed the scope of their authority when dealing with the trust funds.[30]

2. Following and Tracing

A. Following

15–018 Following legal title to misdirected trust property into the hands of a third party recipient often presents no great evidential difficulty, but problems can arise when the recipient mixes the property with other property in such a way that it loses its discrete identity.[31] Different rules are used to resolve these problems, according to whether the property has been incorporated into a fungible mixture, i.e. a mixture composed of mutually interchangeable units, each of which can readily be separated from the others without causing damage.[32]

---

28 A. Nair, *Claims to Traceable Proceeds: Law, Equity and the Control of Assets* (Oxford University Press, 2018).

29 M. Raczynska, *The Law of Tracing in Commercial Transactions* (Oxford University Press, 2018).

30 A. Nair, *Claims to Traceable Proceeds: Law, Equity and the Control of Assets* (Oxford University Press, 2018), paras 6.04 and 7.04–7.22.

31 See generally P. Birks, "Mixtures of Goods" in N. Palmer and E. McKendrick (eds), *Interests in Goods*, 2nd edn (Informa, 1993); P. Matthews, "The Limits of Common Law Tracing" in P. Birks (ed.), *Laundering and Tracing* (Oxford University Press, 1995), pp.42–46; Smith, *The Law of Tracing* (1997), Ch.2; R.J.W. Hickey, "Dazed and Confused: Accidental Mixtures of Goods and the Theory of Acquisition of Title" (2003) 66 M.L.R. 368; A. Waghorn, "Sorting Out Mixtures of Property at Common Law" (2021) 84 M.L.R. 61.

32 *Rysaffe Trustee Co (CI) Ltd v IRC* [2002] S.T.C. 872 at [32]; *Glencore International AG v Alpina Insurance Co Ltd (Further Quantum Issues)* [2004] EWHC 66 (Comm); [2004] 1 All E.R. (Comm.) 858 at [16]. See too J. Austin, *Lectures on Jurisprudence*, 4th edn (J. Murray, 1879), p.807; R. Goode, "Are Intangible Assets Fungible?" in P. Birks and A. Pretto (eds), *Themes in Comparative Law* (Oxford University Press, 2002).

i. Fungible Mixtures

Suppose that trust assets are mixed with other assets in such a way that no one can tell who has contributed what to the mixture, but it remains possible to divide the mixture into identical parts: suppose, for example, that trust crude oil is mixed with other crude oil,[33] or trust shares with other shares.[34] Where the whole mixture is still intact, the beneficiaries' contribution must still be somewhere in the mixture although it has lost its discrete identity, and so the rule in this case is that the beneficiaries can identify any proportionate part of the mixture as their property.[35] **15–019**

However, if part of the mixture is consumed or transferred to a third party, the evidential problem becomes more acute. In this case no one can know if the beneficiaries' contribution subsists in the remainder. Two rules are used to resolve this problem. In the absence of wrongdoing, the remainder is apportioned rateably between contributors to the mixture: e.g. if 10,000 barrels of trust oil are mixed with 50,000 barrels of oil belonging to others, and 30,000 barrels are consumed, one-sixth of the 30,000 barrels remaining (i.e. 5,000 barrels) are deemed to be trust oil.[36] However, where wrongdoing occurs, as in the case e.g. where a trustee mixes trust assets and other assets, and then loses some of the mixed assets in an unauthorised transaction, a different rule applies, namely that evidential uncertainty created by wrongdoing is resolved against the wrongdoer.[37] This does not mean that the wrongdoer is debarred from following her own contribution into the mixture, but it does mean that losses from the mixture are deemed to have come out of her portion first.[38] So if e.g. a trustee mixes 100 tons of trust gravel with 100 tons of her own gravel, and 80 tons of gravel are then stolen out of the mixture, the trustee can identify 20 tons of the remaining gravel as her own, but she must allow the beneficiaries to identify the remainder as theirs. **15–020**

ii. Non-Fungible Mixtures

The process of following legal title to property inevitably comes to an end if the property is destroyed. It also comes to an end because the property is deemed to have been destroyed, in three situations: **15–021**

- where the asset is physically attached to another, "dominant", asset so that it would cause serious damage, or be disproportionately expensive, to separate the two: here the asset is said to "accede" to the dominant asset:[39]

---

33 *Indian Oil Corp v Greenstone Shipping SA* [1988] Q.B. 345; *Glencore International AG v Metro Trading International Ltd* [2001] 1 Lloyd's Rep. 284.

34 *Brady v Stapleton* (1952) 88 C.L.R. 322.

35 *Lupton v White* (1808) 15 Ves. Jun. 432 at 441; *Indian Oil Corp v Greenstone Shipping SA* [1988] Q.B. 345 at 369–371; *Foskett v McKeown* [2001] 1 A.C. 102 at 143; *Glencore International AG v Metro Trading International Ltd* [2001] 1 Lloyd's Rep. 284 at [185].

36 *Spence v Union Marine Insurance Co* (1868) L.R. 3 C.P. 427.

37 This is a general rule of the law of evidence: *Armory v Delamirie* (1722) 1 Str. 505; *Infabrics Ltd v Jaytex Ltd* [1985] F.S.R. 75. In this situation the mixing is not wrongful per se since trustees owe no duty to segregate trust assets: see para.10.029; but the trustees cannot rely on an unauthorised depletion to resolve the evidential problem.

38 *Harris v Truman* (1881) 7 Q.B.D. 340 at 358, affirmed (1882) 9 Q.B.D. 264; *Indian Oil Corp v Greenstone Shipping SA* [1988] Q.B. 345 at 370–371; *Foskett v McKeown* [2001] 1 A.C. 102 at 132; *Glencore International AG v Metro Trading International Ltd (No.2)* [2001] 1 Lloyd's Rep. 284 at [159] and [182].

39 *Hendy Lennox (Industrial Engines) Ltd v Grahame Puttick Ltd* [1984] 1 W.L.R. 485; *McKeown v Cavalier Yachts Pty Ltd* (1988) 13 N.S.W.L.R. 303 at 311. Which of two assets accedes to the other depends on which is the "dominant" entity, a point which is decided rather impressionistically by reference to overall physical significance rather than monetary value. The doctrine of "accession" derives from the Roman doctrine of *accessio*.

- where the asset is physically attached to land in such a way that it would cause serious damage, or be disproportionately expensive, to separate the two: here the asset is said to become a "fixture" on the land:[40] and
- where the asset is combined with other items to create a wholly new product, under the doctrine of "specification".[41]

15-022 At least in the case of specification, however, these rules are modified where the mixing is performed by a wrongdoer. Here, despite the creation of the new thing, the owner of the assets which are wrongfully used to create the new asset can follow her assets into the new asset. So, in *Jones v De Marchant*,[42] a man wrongfully took 18 beaver skins belonging to his wife and used them, together with four skins of his own, to have a fur coat made up which he gave to his mistress. The wife was allowed to recover the coat, a result which can only be explained on the basis that she was permitted to follow her property into the new asset.

B. Tracing

15-023 The rules on tracing resemble the rules on following, to the extent that they also provide that gains and losses to a mixture must be shared rateably between innocent contributors to the mixture. They also provide that evidential uncertainty created by wrongdoing must be resolved against the wrongdoer.

i. Where a Trustee Mixes Trust Money with Her Own Money

15-024 Suppose that a trustee mixes £10,000 of her own money with £10,000 of trust money in such a way that the funds lose their separate identities. Suppose further that she takes £10,000 out of the mixture and dissipates it. It is impossible to say whose money has been lost and whose money remains. Where the mixing has taken place in a bank account the courts could conceivably have solved this evidential problem by using the "first in, first out" rule in *Clayton's* case,[43] which is discussed below.[44] In *Re Hallett's Estate*,[45] however, the Court of Appeal held that the "first in, first out" rule does not apply in this situation, and instead the court resolved the evidential uncertainty by deeming the trustee to have done the right thing by keeping the beneficiaries' money intact and spending his own money. In Jessel MR's words:[46]

---

40 *Hobson v Gorringe* [1897] 1 Ch. 182; *Reynolds v Ashby & Son* [1904] A.C. 466; *Melluish (Inspector of Taxes) v BMI (No.3) Ltd* [1996] A.C. 454; *Elitestone Ltd v Morris* [1997] 1 W.L.R. 687; *Chelsea Yacht & Boat Co Ltd v Pope* [2000] 1 W.L.R. 1941; *Savoye v Spicers Ltd* [2014] EWHC 4195 (TCC); [2015] Bus. L.R. 242 at [26]–[35]. See too H.N. Bennett, "Attachment of Chattels to Land" in Palmer and McKendrick (eds), *Interests in Goods*, 2nd edn (1993).

41 *International Banking Corp v Ferguson, Shaw & Sons*, 1910 S.C. 182; *Borden (UK) Ltd v Scottish Timber Products Ltd* [1981] Ch. 25. The doctrine derives from the Roman doctrine of *specificatio*.

42 (1916) 28 D.L.R. 561, endorsed in *Foskett v McKeown* [2001] 1 A.C. 102 at 132–133. See too *Spence v Union Marine Insurance Co Ltd* (1868) L.R. 3 C.P. 427 at [437]–[438]; *Sandeman & Sons v Tyzack and Branfoot Steamship Co Ltd* [1923] A.C. 680 at 694–695. An attempt to extend the principle to mixtures of ideas leading to the creation of a patentable product failed in *IDA Ltd v University of Southampton* [2006] EWCA Civ 145; [2006] R.P.C. 21 at [40]–[42].

43 (1816) 1 Mer. 529.

44 See para.15-032.

45 (1880) 13 Ch. D. 696.

46 (1880) 13 Ch. D. 696 at [727]. See too *Halley v Law Society* [2002] EWHC 139 (Ch) at [160].

> where a man does an act which may be rightfully performed . . . he is not allowed to say against the person entitled to the property or the right that he has done it wrongfully.

Suppose, again, that a trustee mixes £10,000 of her own money with £10,000 of trust money in such a way that the funds lose their separate identities. But now suppose that she takes £10,000 out of the mixture and uses it to buy a painting, and that she dissipates the remaining £10,000. In this situation, too, Equity resolves the evidential uncertainty against the trustee by deeming her to have used the beneficiaries' money to buy the painting. This is the rule in *Re Oatway*, where Joyce J said that the trustee:[47] **15–025**

> cannot maintain that the investment which remains represents his money alone and what has been spent and can no longer be traced or recovered was money belonging to the trust.

Joyce J also held that if the mixing takes place in a bank account, the "first in, first out" rule does not apply in this situation either.[48]

A third situation might arise, which requires us to ask whether beneficiaries can "cherry-pick" between the rule in *Re Hallett's Estate* and the rule in *Re Oatway*? Suppose that a trustee mixes £10,000 of her own money with £10,000 of trust money in such a way that the funds lose their separate identities, that she takes £10,000 out of the mixture and uses it to buy a painting that triples in value, but that £10,000 is left. Is the governing authority *Re Hallett's Estate*, deeming the trustee to have kept the beneficiaries' £10,000 intact, or is it *Re Oatway*, deeming the painting to have been bought with trust money? **15–026**

This question was considered in *Shalson v Russo*,[49] where Rimer J said this:[50] **15–027**

> Normally, it is presumed that if a trustee uses money from a fund in which he has mixed trust money with his own, he uses his own money first: *Re Hallett's Estate*. But [counsel] submits that this is not an inflexible rule and that if the trustee can be shown to have made an early application of the mixed fund into an investment, the beneficiary is entitled to claim that for himself. He says, and I agree, that this is supported by *Re Oatway*. The justice of this is that, if the beneficiary is not entitled to do this, the wrongdoing trustee may be left with all the cherries and the victim with nothing.

The same question then arose in *Turner v Jacob*, where *Shalson* was not cited to the judge, Patten J. He interpreted *Re Oatway* to stand for the rather different proposition that[51] **15–028**

> where the trustee maintains in the account an amount equal to the remaining trust fund, the beneficiary's right to trace is limited to that fund. It is not open to the beneficiary to assert a lien against an investment made using monies out of the mixed account unless the sum expended is of such a size that it must have included trust monies or the balance remaining in the account after the investment is then expended so as to become untraceable.

---

47 [1903] 2 Ch. 356 at 360. See too *Grey v Haig* (1855) 20 Beav. 214 at 226.

48 [1903] 2 Ch. 356at 360–361: "The order of priority in which the various withdrawals and investments may have been respectively made is wholly immaterial." But note that the rule in *Re Oatway* does not apply where the trustee's money and the beneficiary's money are deposited in different accounts held by the trustee at the same bank: *FHR European Ventures Ltd v Mankarious (No.2)* [2016] EWHC 359 (Ch) at [32]–[33].

49 [2005] Ch. 281.

50 [2005] Ch. 281 at [144].

51 [2006] EWHC 1317 (Ch); [2008] W.T.L.R. 307 at [102].

15-029 The cases are therefore inconsistent. We believe Patten J's statement of the decision in *Re Oatway* to be closer than Rimer J's statement to what the case actually decided. However we prefer Rimer J's view of the merits. If the principle that underlies the law in this area is that presumptions should be made against trustees who wrongfully create evidential uncertainty by taking money out of a mixed fund and using at least some of it in an unauthorised way, we believe that this principle should extend to giving beneficiaries the right to choose whichever presumption produces the best result for them.

15-030 Because the rules in *Re Hallett's Estate* and *Re Oatway* are designed to resolve evidential uncertainty they do not apply in a situation where there is no uncertainty. Suppose that a trustee mixes £50,000 of her own money and £50,000 of trust money and places the mixture in an empty bank account. Suppose that she withdraws £80,000, dissipates it, and then adds another £30,000 of her own money, so that there is now £50,000 in the account. Here, the beneficiaries cannot invoke the rule in *Re Hallett's Estate* to identify more than £20,000 in the account as their property because it is not evidentially uncertain that at least £30,000 of the remaining funds came from the trustee's own resources. This rule was established in *James Roscoe (Bolton) Ltd v Winder*.[52] It is known as "the lowest intermediate balance rule" and it has been stated thus:[53]

> absent any payment in of money with the intention of making good earlier depredations, tracing cannot occur through a mixed account for any larger sum than is the lowest balance in the account between the time the beneficiary's money goes in, and the time the remedy is sought.

ii. Where a Trustee Mixes Trust Funds Together

15-031 If trust funds are mixed together and the beneficiaries are equally innocent victims of the trustee's failure to keep track of whose money has gone where, the beneficiaries will generally have equally strong claims to a rateable share of gains, and equally weak claims to avoid taking a rateable share of losses, to the mixed fund. Hence, gains and losses are generally shared between the beneficiaries pro rata: this is the rule in *Re Diplock*.[54]

15-032 Until recently, there was thought to be an exception to this rule, deriving from *Clayton's* case.[55] This case concerned a dispute centring on the appropriation of payments as between a bank and its customer,[56] but it later came to be understood as an authority for the rule that if a trustee places money belonging to two different sets of beneficiaries into the same unbroken running account,[57] any withdrawals that she makes from the account are deemed to be made in the same order as the

---

52 [1915] 1 Ch. 62, endorsed in *Re Goldcorp Exchange Ltd* [1995] 1 A.C. 74 at 107–108, also in *Bishopsgate Investment Management Ltd v Homan* [1995] Ch. 211 at 219, 220. See too *Re Graphicshppe Ltd* (2005) 78 O.R. (3d) 401; *Boughner v Greyhawk Equity Partners Ltd* [2013] ONCA 26.

53 *Re French Caledonia Travel Service Pty Ltd* (2003) 59 N.S.W.L.R. 361 at [175], per Campbell J. For application of the principle where goods are successively withdrawn and deposited in a mixed bulk, see *Glencore International AG v Metro Trading International Ltd (No.2)* [2001] 1 Lloyd's Rep. 284 at [201]–[202], revisited in *Glencore International AG v Alpina Insurance Co Ltd (No.2)* [2004] 1 All E.R. (Comm.) 858 at [14]–[20]. For a case falling within the scope of Campbell J's proviso, see *Westdeutsche Landesbank Girozentrale v Islington LBC* [1994] 4 All E.R. 890 at 939 (not considered on appeal).

54 [1948] Ch. 465 at 533, 534 and 539. See also *Edinburgh Corp v Lord Advocate* (1879) 4 App. Cas. 823.

55 (1816) 1 Mer. 529. For the history of the case see Smith, *The Law of Tracing* (1997), pp.183–194; *Re French Caledonia Travel Service Pty Ltd* (2003) 59 N.S.W.L.R. 361 at [20]–[172].

56 This aspect of the rule established by the case has a continued practical significance for the relationship between banks and their customers, as discussed in P. Hood, "*Clayton's* Case and Connected Matters" [2013] J.R. 501.

57 E.g. a bank account or a solicitor's trust account. The rule does not apply where there are distinct and separate debts: *The Mecca* [1897] A.C. 286; *Re Sherry* (1884) 25 Ch. D. 692 at 702. Nor does the rule apply to entries on the same day: it is the end-of-day balance which counts: *The Mecca* at 291.

payments in, on a "first in, first out" basis.[58] Thus, for example, if she puts £10,000 from Trust A into her bank account, then puts in £10,000 from Trust B, and then withdraws £10,000 and loses it (or uses it to buy an asset which triples in value), the loss (or gain) will be attributed solely to the beneficiaries of Trust A.

As between the beneficiaries of Trust A and Trust B this is an arbitrary and unfair result, and for this reason the "first in, first out" rule has been discarded in many Commonwealth jurisdictions, in favour of the *Re Diplock* pro rata approach.[59] In *Barlow Clowes International Ltd v Vaughan*,[60] the Court of Appeal reaffirmed the general application of *Clayton's* case in English law, except where its application would be impracticable or would result in injustice between the parties. But more recent English cases suggest that the rule will now be applied only very rarely, if at all, for the courts are now swift to find that the rule is an impracticable or unjust method of resolving disputes between the victims of shared misfortune, particularly in cases of large-scale fraud.[61] **15–033**

Barlow Clowes concerned the liquidation of an investment company whose fraudulent managers had stolen most of the company's assets, leaving thousands of investors out of pocket. The question arose as to how the surviving assets should be distributed between the investors. The court held that the rule in *Clayton's* case should not be used to resolve this question because the investors had all intended that their money should be pooled in a single fund for investment purposes, so that it would conform with their original intentions if they all shared rateably in what remained in the pool. However, Woolf and Leggatt LJJ[62] also indicated that a "rolling charge" solution might be fairer than rateable sharing so that claimants should share losses and gains to the fund in proportion to their interest in the fund immediately prior to each withdrawal. **15–034**

This would work as follows.[63] Suppose that a trustee pays £2,000 from Trust A and then £4,000 from Trust B into an empty current bank account. She then withdraws £3,000 and loses it. She then pays in £3,000 from Trust C before withdrawing another £3,000 to buy shares whose value increases tenfold. She then withdraws the remaining £3,000 and loses it. Applying the "rolling charge" rule, the first loss must be borne by A and B in the ratio 1:2, and C need not bear this loss at all. Immediately after the first withdrawal the remaining £3,000 would be attributed to A and B in the ratio 1:2, and after the next deposit, the £6,000 in the account would be attributable to A, B, and C in the ratio 1:2:3. Hence, the shares should be attributed to them in the same proportion, leaving A with shares worth £5,000, B with shares worth £10,000 and C with shares worth £15,000. In contrast, the pro rata rule would attribute all gains and losses in proportion to the total contributions made by each Trust, giving **15–035**

58 *Pennell v Deffell* (1853) 4 De G.M. & G. 372; *Hancock v Smith* (1889) 41 Ch. D. 456 at [461]; *Re Stenning* [1895] 2 Ch. 433; *Re Diplock* [1948] Ch. 465 at 553–554.

59 *Re Ontario Securities Commission* (1985) 30 D.L.R. (4th) 1, affirmed (1998) 52 D.L.R. (4th) 767; *Re Registered Securities Commission* [1991] 1 N.Z.L.R. 545; *Keefe v Law Society of New South Wales* (1998) 44 N.S.W.L.R. 451; *ASIC v Enterprise Solutions 2000 Pty Ltd* [2001] Q.S.C. 82; *Re Esteem Settlement*, 2002 J.L.R. 53; *Re French Caledonia Travel Service Pty Ltd* (2003) 59 N.S.W.L.R. 361; *Re International Investment Unit Trust* [2005] 1 N.Z.L.R. 270.

60 [1992] 4 All E.R. 22.

61 *El Ajou v Dollar Land Holdings Plc (No.2)* [1995] 2 All E.R. 213 at 222; *Russell-Cooke Trust Co v Prentis (No.1)* [2002] EWHC 2227 (Ch); [2003] 2 All E.R. 478 at 495; *Commerzbank Aktiengesellschaft v IMB Morgan Plc* [2004] EWHC 2771 (Ch); [2005] 1 Lloyd's Rep. 298 at [43]–[49]; *Re Ahmed & Co* (2006) 8 I.T.E.L.R. 779 at [131]–[138]; *Charity Commission for England and Wales v Framjee* [2014] EWHC 2507 (Ch); [2015] 1 W.L.R. 16 at [49]. In *El Ajou (No.2)*, at 223–224, Robert Walker J held that where A and B's money is mixed in an account and *Clayton's* case deems A's money (and not B's) to have been paid to D, B can still trace into the money received by D and claim against her if A makes no claim and is unlikely to do so. This finding was followed in *Campden Hill Ltd v Chakrani* [2005] EWHC 911 (Ch) at [76]–[77].

62 *Barlow Clowes* at 35, 44.

63 Further see C. Chamorro-Courtland, "Demystifying the Lowest Intermediate Balance Rule: The Legal Principles Governing the Distribution of Funds to Beneficiaries of a Commingled Trust Account for Which a Shortfall Exists" (2014) 30 Banking and Finance L.R. 39; C. Chamorro-Courtland, "The Shortfall Conundrum: A New Framework for Allocating Losses in a Mixed Fund in Australia" (2019) 43 Melbourne University L.R. 133.

a ratio of 2:4:3, leaving A with shares worth £6,667, B with shares worth £13,333, and C with shares worth £10,000. The "first in, first out" rule, meanwhile, would produce the result that all of A's money is lost, £1,000 of B's money is lost, all of the shares belong to B, and all of C's money is lost.

15–036 In *Shalson v Russo*,[64] Rimer J suggested that the rolling charge rule should always be used to resolve cases of this kind, because the pro rata rule ignores evidence of what has actually happened to the claimants' money: thus, in the example, we know that no part of Trust C's £3,000 can have gone into the trustee's first withdrawal, suggesting that Trust C should not have to share this loss with Trust A and Trust B. Rimer J's position can be supported by reference to *Roscoe v Winder*,[65] but in a case involving thousands of investors and millions of deposits and withdrawals, the expense and practical difficulties of assembling the raw data needed to apply the rolling charge rule may be prohibitive, leaving the courts with a choice between the rough justice of the pro rata rule, and the even rougher justice of "first in, first out". In *Charity Commission for England and Wales v Framjee*,[66] a case where similar evidential problems arose, Henderson J applied the pro rata rule.

iii. Where Recipients of Trust Money Mix It with Their Own Money

15–037 Where a trustee misdirects trust property to a bona fide purchaser for value without notice of the beneficiaries' equitable interest, they may be able to follow the property into her hands and trace through any mixtures and substitutions that she later carries out into new property. However it will be pointless for them to undertake this exercise as she will have a defence to any proprietary claim that they might bring.

15–038 Where a trustee misdirects trust property to a recipient who is not a bona fide purchaser, the beneficiaries may well wish to follow the property into the recipient's hands and then trace through her subsequent mixtures and substitutions into new property against which they can claim. The tracing rules that apply in this case will vary according to whether the recipient has acted in good faith.

15–039 If she is a bona fide volunteer, the rules governing the situation will be the same as those which govern the case where money belonging to the innocent beneficiaries of separate trust funds is mixed together by the trustee.[67] Gains and losses will be shared rateably, possibly subject to the rule in *Clayton's* case[68] if the court sees fit to apply it.[69]

15–040 If the recipient takes the property with knowledge of the breach of trust, then whether or not she gives value in exchange for the property, she cannot innocently mix it with her own property and then use part of the mixture for her own purposes. She will owe the beneficiaries a duty as constructive trustee to account to them for the trust property.[70] If they mix it with their own property and then use part of the mixture for their own purposes they will therefore be in the same position as an express trustee who does this,[71] and the case will be governed by the same rules as would apply to the express trustee: evidential uncertainties will be resolved against the trustee.[72]

---

64 [2003] EWHC 1637 (Ch); [2005] Ch. 281 at [150].

65 [1915] 1 Ch. 62.

66 [2014] EWHC 2507 (Ch); [2015] 1 W.L.R. 16.

67 *Re Diplock* [1948] Ch. 465 at 524 and 539.

68 *Re Diplock* [1948] Ch. 465 at 554.

69 See paras 15–032 to 15–036. If the recipient pays the trust money into an interest-bearing account designated as a trust account as soon as she learns of the trust claim, this will be regarded as effectively unmixing the fund so that the trust claim will then relate only to the money in the designated account: *Re Diplock* [1948] Ch. 465 at 551–552, dealing with the claim against the National Institute for the Deaf, reversed on an amended statement of the facts: ibid., at 559.

70 See paras 14–003 to 14–007 and 14–010.

71 *Boscawen v Bajwa* [1996] 1 W.L.R. 328 at 336–338; *Banton v CIBC Trust Corp* (2001) 197 D.L.R. (4th) 212.

72 See paras 15–024 to 15–030.

iv. Payment of Debts

Like the process of following property rights from hand to hand, the process of tracing through mixtures and substitutions must come to an end when the trust property or its traceable proceeds are dissipated or destroyed. So, if a trustee (or third party recipient) uses trust funds to pay for a holiday, or to buy a house which burns down, there is no traceable residue (assuming that the house is uninsured), i.e. there is no property left to which the beneficiaries might assert a proprietary claim. As the Court of Appeal stated in *Re Diplock:*[73] **15–041**

> The equitable remedies [available to beneficiaries making proprietary claims] presuppose the continued existence of the [trust] money either as a separate fund or as part of a mixed fund or as latent in property acquired by means of such a fund. If such continued existence is not established equity is . . . helpless.

The rule that the tracing process comes to an end when property is dissipated generally applies where a defendant uses trust money to pay off a debt, e.g. when she pays the money into an overdrawn bank account.[74] However, there are two exceptions. First, if a debt paid off with misdirected trust funds was secured by a charge over the defendant's property, the beneficiaries can ask the court to treat them as though the creditor's charge has not been extinguished, but has instead been assigned by the creditor to the beneficiaries, so that they can enforce the charge against the trustee's property to secure restoration of the trust fund. This remedy is known as subrogation, which literally means "substitution": the beneficiaries are treated, by a legal fiction, as though they have been substituted for the creditor. An example is provided by *Menelaou v Bank of Cyprus Plc*,[75] which is discussed below. In *Banque Financière de la Cité v Parc (Battersea) Ltd*,[76] Lord Hoffmann stressed the fictional nature of the subrogation remedy, and held that it lies in the court's discretion to tailor the remedy to fit the circumstances of a case, by varying the extent to which a claimant is entitled to be treated as though he has acquired the creditor's rights, to avoid unfairly prejudicing the position of third parties. **15–042**

Second, if the trustee borrows £10,000 from a creditor, and uses this money to purchase an asset, and then uses money misappropriated from the trust fund to pay her debt, it seems that the beneficiaries can sometimes "trace backwards" through the payment of the debt into the asset which was purchased with the borrowed money, and identify the asset as the traceable product of the trust money. This analysis, proposed by Lionel Smith,[77] has been approved by the courts, subject to limitations that remain to be worked out. **15–043**

The leading case is *Federal Republic of Brazil v Durant International Corp.*[78] The mayor of Sao Paulo took bribes in connection with a road building contract and allegedly arranged for the traceable proceeds of this money to be paid to the defendant companies which were controlled by the mayor and his son. The municipality sued the companies for knowing receipt and they sought to reduce their liability from US$10.5 million down to US$7.7 million on the grounds that nearly $3 million was paid to them by an intermediate company *before* rather than *after* that company received an equivalent sum from the briber. The companies argued that there was no sound doctrinal basis for "backwards **15–044**

---

73 [1948] Ch. 465 at 521.

74 *Rea v Russell* [2012] NZCA 536 at [42]–[45].

75 [2015] UKSC 66; [2016] A.C. 176, discussed at para.15–132. See also *McCullough v Marsden* (1919) 45 D.L.R. 645; *Boscawen v Bajwa* [1996] 1 W.L.R. 328; *Scotlife Homes Ltd (No.2) v Melinek* [1999] NSWSC 898.

76 [1999] 1 A.C. 221 at 236. See also *Halifax Mortgage Services Ltd v Muirhead* (1997) 76 P. & C.R. 418; *Cheltenham & Gloucester Plc v Appleyard* [2004] EWCA 291 at [49]; *Filby v Mortgage Express (No.2) Ltd* [2004] EWCA Civ 759 at [63].

77 L.D. Smith, "Tracing into the Payment of a Debt" [1995] CLJ 290, esp. pp.292–295,

78 [2015] UKPC 35; [2016] A.C. 297.

tracing" with a view to "joining up" transactions that had taken place in reverse chronological order. The Royal Court of Jersey and the Jersey Court of Appeal both rejected this argument, and the defendants' appeal to the Privy Council was dismissed.

Federal Republic of Brazil v Durant International Corp

[2016] A.C. 297 at [17]–[42]

15–045 LORD TOULSON stated the facts and continued: The appellants' twin arguments have a common and simple logical parentage. The doctrine of tracing involves rules by which to determine whether one form of property interest is properly to be regarded as substituted for another. It is therefore necessary to begin with the original property interest and study what has become of it. If it has ceased to exist, it cannot metamorphose into a later property interest. Ex nihilo nihil fit: nothing comes from nothing. If the money in a bank account has dwindled from £1,000 to £1, only the remaining £1 is capable of being substituted by something else; the £999 has ceased to exist. This explains "the lowest intermediate balance" principle. Similarly, a property interest cannot turn into (or provide a substitute for) something which the holder already has; the later acquisition cannot be the source of the earlier. This explains the "no backward tracing" principle. The two are in a sense opposite sides of the same coin.

15–046 Conceptually the appellants' argument is coherent and it is supported by a good deal of authority.

15–047 In *James Roscoe (Bolton) Ltd v Winder*[79] a company sold its business under an agreement containing a promise by the purchaser to collect on behalf of the vendor the amount of the book debts owed to it at the date of the agreement. From the sums collected, the purchaser paid £455 into his general bank account, but he failed to account for the money to the vendor and made drawings from the account which reduced it at one stage to £25. He later made payments into the account from an unrelated source, and died with a balance in his account of £358, to which the vendor claimed to be beneficially entitled. Sargant J held that the maximum which the vendor was entitled to trace was £25, representing the lowest sum to which the balance on the account had fallen between the payment of the £455 into the account and the purchaser's death, on the ground that at that date of the lowest balance the purchaser must have denuded the account of all the trust moneys except to the extent of £25.

15–048 In *Re Goldcorp Exchange Ltd*[80] a company mixed bullion belonging to some of its customers with other bullion. It then reduced its stock to less than the amount which belonged to those customers. It later bought more bullion, but there was no evidence to link the later purchases with the earlier depletion of the stock. On the company being placed in receivership, the customers claimed an equitable lien over the stock of bullion held by the company at the time of the receivers' appointment. The judge found that the amount of bullion held by the receivers on behalf of those customers was an amount equal to the lowest balance of bullion held by the company at any time, applying *James Roscoe (Bolton) Ltd v Winder*. The Board upheld his decision. Lord Mustill[81] cited the judgment of the Court of Appeal in *Re Diplock* where it was said:[82]

> "The equitable remedies presuppose the continued existence of the money either as a separate fund or as part of a mixed fund or as latent in property acquired by means of such a fund. . . . It is, therefore, a necessary matter for consideration in each case where it is sought to trace money in equity, whether it has such a continued existence, actual or notional, as will enable equity to grant specific relief."

Lord Mustill observed that the law relating to equitable tracing was still in a state of development, but that it would be inequitable to impose an equitable lien in favour of the customers in that case, since there was no evidence that their bullion continued to exist as a fund latent in property held by the company.

15–049 In *Bishopsgate Investment Management Ltd (In Liquidation) v Homan*[83] large amounts of funds held by Bishopsgate on trust under various pension schemes were improperly paid into a bank account of Maxwell Communication Corporation plc ("Maxwell CC"). The account was either overdrawn at the time of the payments or subsequently became overdrawn. Maxwell CC was hopelessly insolvent and was subsequently

79 [1915] 1 Ch. 62.
80 [1995] 1 A.C. 74.
81 Ibid at 109.
82 [1948] Ch. 465 at 521.
83 [1995] Ch. 211.

placed in Chapter XI protection under the US Bankruptcy Code. The administrators wished to make an interim distribution to Maxwell CC's creditors, but Bishopsgate's liquidators claimed to be entitled to an equitable charge over the whole of the moneys in the account, which happened to be in credit at the time of the administrators' appointment.

At first instance Vinelott J held that Bishopsgate could not trace through an overdrawn bank account, whether it was overdrawn at the time when the relevant moneys were paid into it or became overdrawn by subsequent drawings, subject to a reservation if it were shown that there was a connection between a particular misappropriation and the acquisition by Maxwell CC of a particular asset. He considered that there could be backward tracing if, for example, an asset was acquired by Maxwell CC with moneys borrowed from an overdrawn account and there was an inference that when the borrowing occurred it was the intention that it should be repaid by misappropriation of Bishopsgate's moneys. His conclusion was that "proof that [money was] paid into an overdrawn account ... may not always be sufficient to bar a claim to an equitable charge". 15-050

Bishopsgate's liquidators appealed, and Maxwell CC's administrators served a respondent's notice by way of cross-appeal, asking the Court of Appeal to overrule the judge's reservations. Dillon LJ considered it to be at least arguable that if the connection postulated by the judge were proved, there ought to be an equitable charge in favour of Bishopsgate over the particular asset, and he held that both the appeal and the cross-appeal should be dismissed. By contrast, Leggatt LJ held that there could be no tracing remedy against an asset acquired before misappropriation of money took place, since the money could not be traced into something which had been acquired before the money was received and therefore without its aid; but he accepted that if an asset were used as security for an overdraft, which was then discharged by means of misappropriated money, the beneficiary might obtain priority by subrogation. He therefore considered that the judge came to the right conclusion, although he did not accept that it was possible to trace through an overdrawn account, or to trace misappropriated money into an asset bought before the money was received by the purchaser. The third member of the court, Henry LJ, stated laconically that he agreed with both judgments. 15-051

The Court of Appeal was again divided in *Foskett v McKeown*.[84] The claim was by purchasers who advanced money on trust under a property development scheme which was never carried out. The issue was whether they could trace their money into the proceeds of a life insurance policy. The matter came before the court on an application for summary judgment, before the facts had been fully investigated. In his judgment Sir Richard Scott V-C said:[85] 15-052

> "I regard it as likely, that [the purchasers] will establish that it was [the deceased's] intention throughout to use [the] purchasers' money to pay the 1988 premium. If that is the case, it does not seem to me at all obvious that the circumstance that the payment into the account of the purchasers' money was made very shortly after the payment of the premium, rather than before or at the same time as the payment, should be regarded as fatal to the purchasers' equitable tracing claim. The availability of equitable remedies ought, in my view, to depend upon the substance of the transaction in question and not upon the strict order in which associated events happen. Moreover, there is at least some authority which the purchasers could pray in aid: see *Agricultural Credit Corpn of Saskatchewan v Pettyjohn*[86] and [Professor Lionel Smith] 'Tracing into the Payment of a Debt'[87]."

The majority of the court took a different view. Hobhouse LJ and Morritt LJ both held that the doctrine of tracing does not extend to following value into a previously acquired asset. Morritt LJ said[88] that the claimants "must be able to identify the money of the purchasers at every stage of the process: *Re Diplock*[89]". 15-053

The point in question did not require to be decided and so these observations were obiter. It was not discussed when the case reached the House of Lords, but there is a relevant passage in the speech of Lord Millett:[90] 15-054

84 [1998] Ch. 265.
85 Ibid at 283–284.
86 (1991) 79 D.L.R. (4th) 22.
87 [1995] C.L.J. 290, pp.292–295.
88 [1998] Ch. 265 at 296.
89 [1948] Ch. 465 at 521.
90 [2001] 1 A.C. 102 at 127–128.

> "We speak of money at the bank, and of money passing into and out of a bank account. But of course the account holder has no money at the bank. Money paid into a bank account belongs legally and beneficially to the bank and not to the account holder. The bank gives value for it, and it is accordingly not usually possible to make the money itself the subject of an adverse claim. Instead a claimant normally sues the account holder rather than the bank and lays claim to the proceeds of the money in his hands. These consist of the debt or part of the debt due to him from the bank. We speak of tracing money into and out of the account, but there is no money in the account. There is merely a single debt of an amount equal to the final balance standing to the credit of the account holder. No money passes from paying bank to receiving bank or through the clearing system (where the money flows may be in the opposite direction). There is simply a series of debits and credits which are causally and transactionally linked. We also speak of tracing one asset into another, but this too is inaccurate. The original asset still exists in the hands of the new owner, or it may have become untraceable. The claimant claims the new asset because it was acquired in whole or in part with the original asset. What he traces, therefore, is not the physical asset itself but the value inherent in it."

15–055 When Lord Millett speaks of "money paid into a bank account" (which then "belongs legally and beneficially to the bank"), generally what happens, in law, is the extinction of one credit/debit and creation of another credit/debit through the banking system, although a bank may sometimes receive payment of money in specie. So if a customer "pays" a cheque into his account, his bank will present the cheque to the bank on which it is drawn ("the paying bank"), and – provided that the drawer has a credit balance with the paying bank, or a borrowing facility sufficient to cover the amount of the cheque – the paying bank will credit the presenting bank with the amount of the cheque through the banking system, and will debit its customer's account. The presenting bank may already have credited its own customer's account, in anticipation of the cheque being cleared, in which case a legal purist would say that the statement of account is for the moment inaccurate, and it will be corrected by a corresponding debit entry if the cheque is dishonoured (or should turn out to be a forgery).

15–056 The appellants' argument has academic support, most fully developed in Professor Matthew Conaglen's article "Difficulties with Tracing Backwards",[91] written in riposte to the argument of Professor Smith (to which Sir Richard Scott V-C referred in *Foskett v McKeown*).

15–057 Professor Conaglen begins with the proposition that "Tracing is the process of identifying a new asset as the substitute for the old".[92] He observes that the acquisition of an asset and the extinguishment of a debt are different things. A debt is an asset in the hands of the creditor, and so can provide a basis for traditional tracing in relation to the creditor's assets. But a debt has no asset value in the hands of the debtor; it is a liability which ceases to exist when it is paid.

15–058 Having said that, Professor Conaglen accepts that there is nothing conceptually impossible about the courts tracing trust funds through the payment of a debt into assets that the trustee had acquired, before that payment was made, by incurring the debt. But he argues that the support in the case law for such an approach is weak and that there is stronger authority against it.

15–059 Professor Conaglen recognises that it is ultimately a matter of legal policy whether the law ought to allow backward tracing. He concludes:[93]

> "When the already precarious position of unsecured creditors is weighed against the concomitantly far better protected position of trust beneficiaries, it is suggested that the law ought not to recognise the possibility of tracing backwards. The unsecured creditors should not have their position worsened further by effectively making them insurers for the beneficiaries against trustee defalcations. Trust beneficiaries whose money has been wrongly applied in satisfaction of a debt can stand in the position of the satisfied creditor (by subrogation), but it is a step too far, in policy terms, to allow them to stand in the position of the debtor and act as owners of property that the trustee acquired before the debt was paid.
>
> "Alternatively, if backward tracing is to be allowed, then the policy concerns that have been highlighted above suggest that the extent to which payment of the debt is considered attributable to acquisition of the asset should perhaps be limited in some way, such as by reference to whether

[91] (2011) 127 L.Q.R. 432.
[92] Per Lord Millett in *Foskett v McKeown* [2001] 1 A.C. 102 at 127.
[93] At p.455.

> the trustee intended at the time the asset was acquired to (mis)use trust funds to pay for it. . . . That would be consistent with equity's traditional concern for substance – meaning intention – over form. However, the evidential difficulties inherent in a test that is focused on the defalcating trustee's intentions provide yet further reasoning for concluding that the balance is appropriately struck by refusing to recognise backward tracing."

The respondents found their arguments on the passage already quoted from in Lord Millett's speech in *Foskett v McKeown*. They emphasise that it is inaccurate to speak of tracing one asset into another. Rather, the court is concerned with tracing the value inherent in a trust asset. Whether it can properly be traced into another asset depends on whether there is a sufficient transactional link. In considering that question the court should concentrate on the substance of the transaction and not the form. In general terms those propositions carry force, but they do not resolve the disputed issues. **15–060**

More particularly the respondents submit, as Professor Smith argues, that money used to pay a debt can in principle be traced into whatever was acquired in return for the debt. That is a very broad proposition and it would take the doctrine of tracing far beyond its limits in the case law to date. As a statement of general application, the Board would reject it. The courts should be very cautious before expanding equitable proprietary remedies in a way which may have an adverse effect on other innocent parties. If a trustee on the verge of bankruptcy uses trust funds to pay off an unsecured creditor to whom he is personally indebted, in the absence of special circumstances it is hard to see why the beneficiaries' claim should take precedence over those of the general body of unsecured creditors. **15–061**

However there may be cases where there is a close causal and transactional link between the incurring of a debt and the use of trust funds to discharge it. *Agricultural Credit Corpn of Saskatchewan v Pettyjohn*[94] provides a good example. In 1981 and 1984 Mr and Mrs Pettyjohn applied to the credit corporation for loans to purchase cattle. They were informed that their applications were approved and that they could proceed to make the purchases. The Pettyjohns went ahead and bought cattle using a credit line with their bank as their immediate source of funding. About the same time, or shortly afterwards, the loan agreements with the credit corporation were executed, under which the credit corporation was given security over the cattle, and the moneys advanced by the credit corporation were used to pay back the bank. Sometime later the Pettyjohns sold the cattle (without the credit corporation's agreement), bought replacement cattle and used the proceeds of sale to repay the loan for the purchase of the replacement cattle. They then became insolvent. **15–062**

The credit corporation claimed to have a purchase money security interest in the replacement cattle under the Personal Property Security Act. The claim gave rise to two issues: whether the lender had a right to security over cattle which were purchased after the loan application had been approved but before the loan moneys had been advanced: and, if so, whether the lender was entitled to trace the value of its original security into the replacement cattle. **15–063**

The Saskatchewan Court of Appeal decided the case in favour of the credit corporation. Its decision on the second point turned on the construction of the provisions of the Act, but its decision on the first point is of general interest. Under the Act it was necessary for the credit corporation to establish that it gave value to the debtor for the purpose of enabling the debtor to acquire rights in personal property (as it undoubtedly did) and, more importantly, that the value was applied to acquire the rights. On that issue the court said:[95] **15–064**

> "The . . . requirement, that the value have been used to acquire such rights, presents greater difficulties. How can it be said that the moneys advanced were used to acquire rights when the purchase had already taken place and the rights already acquired? It is, however, commercially unreasonable to divide the transactions so minutely. The Pettyjohns used the value given to them to pay off interim financing, but the interim financing had not been obtained as a separate transaction, but always with the view that it would be repaid through the moneys advanced by ACCS. The Pettyjohns used the value given as part of a larger, commercially reasonable transaction to acquire rights in the 1981 and 1984 cattle. The fact that the use of the value given was, due to the nature of the transaction, after the acquisition of rights does not alter the conclusion that the value given was used to acquire those rights."

---

94 (1991) 79 D.L.R. (4th) 22.

95 Ibid at 38.

15-065 On those facts the court was right in the view of the Board not to divide minutely the connected steps by which, on any sensible commercial view, the purchase of the cattle was financed by the credit corporation, but to look at the transaction overall. The interposition of the bank was purely to provide bridging finance to cover the gap in time between the purchase and the credit corporation's funds coming through as previously arranged.

15-066 The development of increasingly sophisticated and elaborate methods of money laundering, often involving a web of credits and debits between intermediaries, makes it particularly important that a court should not allow a camouflage of interconnected transactions to obscure its vision of their true overall purpose and effect. If the court is satisfied that the various steps are part of a coordinated scheme, it should not matter that, either as a deliberate part of the choreography or possibly because of the incidents of the banking system, a debit appears in the bank account of an intermediary before a reciprocal credit entry. The Board agrees with Sir Richard Scott V-C's observation in *Foskett v McKeown* that the availability of equitable remedies ought to depend on the substance of the transaction in question and not upon the strict order in which associated events occur.

15-067 Similarly, in a case such as *Agricultural Credit Corpn of Saskatchewan v Pettyjohn*, the Board does not consider that it should matter whether the account used for the purpose of providing bridging finance was in credit or in overdraft at the time. An account may be used as a conduit for the transfer of funds, whether the account holder is operating the account in credit or within an overdraft facility.

15-068 The Board therefore rejects the argument that there can never be backward tracing, or that the court can never trace the value of an asset whose proceeds are paid into an overdrawn account. But the claimant has to establish a coordination between the depletion of the trust fund and the acquisition of the asset which is the subject of the tracing claim, looking at the whole transaction, such as to warrant the court attributing the value of the interest acquired to the misuse of the trust fund. This is likely to depend on inference from the proved facts, particularly since in many cases the testimony of the trustee, if available, will be of little value.

15-069 The Board does not doubt the correctness of the decisions in *James Roscoe (Bolton) Ltd v Winder* and *Re Goldcorp Exchange Ltd*, but in neither case was there evidence of an overall transaction embracing the coordinated outward and inward movement of assets.

15-070 In the present case the Royal Court and the Court of Appeal were justified in concluding that the necessary connection between the bribes itemised in schedule 3 and the receipts itemised in schedule 5 was proved, having regard in particular to the admission in the pleadings as to the link between the sums received by the appellants and the Chanani account. The Board will therefore humbly advise Her Majesty that the appeal should be dismissed.

v. The Swollen Assets Theory

15-071 *Space Investments Ltd v Canadian Imperial Bank of Commerce Trust Co*[96] concerned a bank trustee that was empowered by the trust instrument to lend trust money to itself. The bank lawfully exercised this power, and then went into liquidation. The beneficiaries could not trace their money into any particular surviving asset and so the Privy Council held that their claims ranked as unsecured debts. In obiter dicta, however, Lord Templeman contrasted the facts of the case with the situation where a bank trustee unlawfully takes trust money and the beneficiaries cannot trace their money into any particular surviving asset. Here, in his Lordship's view, "equity allows the beneficiaries to trace the trust money to all the assets of the bank and to recover the trust money by the exercise of an equitable charge over all the assets of the bank."[97]

15-072 To support this statement he cited Jessel MR's comment in *Re Hallett's Estate*,[98] that "if a man mixes trust funds with his own, the whole will be treated as trust property". However, this was to misread Jessel MR's judgment, which was concerned with the case where a trustee mixes £X of trust

---

96 [1986] 3 All E.R. 75.

97 Ibid at 76–77, overlooking *Re Hallett & Co* [1894] 2 Q.B. 237 at 245.

98 (1880) 13 Ch. D. 696 at 719.

money with £Y of his own money in a particular account and then dissipates part of the mixture. Jessel MR said nothing to support Lord Templeman's assertion that in such a case the whole of the trustee's assets constitutes one colossal fund which should be regarded as having been mixed with the trust money, so that if the money in the account is dissipated the beneficiaries can simply switch their attention to some other asset in the trustee's hands. Moreover, Lord Templeman's analysis is inconsistent with the *Roscoe v Winder* principle discussed earlier,[99] that presumptions are made against wrongdoing trustees only where there is evidential uncertainty. In a case where it is certain that a trustee has dissipated trust money out of a particular bank account, this principle prevents the beneficiaries from arguing that some other asset in the trustee's hands should be deemed to represent the traceable proceeds of their property. Essentially for this reason, Lord Templeman's dicta were repudiated by the Court of Appeal in *Serious Fraud Office v Lexi Holdings Plc (in administration)*.[100]

Sinclair Investments (UK) Ltd v Versailles Trade Finance Ltd (in admin rec'ship)[101] concerned a fraud whereby money belonging to a company (TPL) was misdirected into a complex set of transactions referred to as "cross-firing arrangements", the point of which was to create the false impression that a second company (VTFL) had a larger turnover than was actually the case. The question arose whether the complexity and obscurity of these cross-firing arrangements made it impossible to trace through them into surviving assets because the money had effectively disappeared into a "black hole" or "maelstrom". Lord Neuberger MR held that:[102] **15–073**

> [tracing does not come to an end] simply because the defaulting fiduciary, while still holding much of the money, has acted particularly dishonestly or cunningly by creating a maelstrom. Where he has mixed the funds held on trust with his own funds, the onus should be on the fiduciary to establish that part, and what part, of the mixed fund is his property.

Hence he upheld Lewison J's finding at first instance, that: **15–074**

> once it is shown that money held on trust for TPL was paid into a "maelstrom" account, [VTFL bears] the burden of showing that money in that account is not that of TPL.[103]

This was consistent with Jessel MR's dictum in *Re Hallett's* but care should be taken not to misread Lord Neuberger MR as adopting Lord Templeman's discredited "swollen assets" theory. **15–075**

3. Claiming

In this section we consider the different types of proprietary claim that can be made against trust property or its traceable proceeds, assuming that all necessary following and tracing processes have been successfully completed. We then examine the possible reasons why the law gives the beneficiaries **15–076**

---

99 See para.15–030; and see also para.15–047.

100 [2008] EWCA Crim 1443; [2009] Q.B. 376 at [49]–[50]. Lord Templeman's dicta were restrictively distinguished in *Re Goldcorp Exchange Ltd* [1995] 1 A.C. 74 and *Bishopsgate Investment Management Ltd v Homan* [1995] Ch. 211; see also *Ultraframe (UK) Ltd v Fielding* [2005] EWHC 1638 (Ch); [2007] W.T.L.R. 835 at [1470]–[1475]; *Moriarty v Various Customers of BA Peters Plc* [2008] EWCA Civ 1604; [2009] B.P.I.R. 248; *Re Lehman Bros (International) Europe (in admin)* [2009] EWHC 3228 (Ch) at [190]ff; *Rheem Australia Pty Ltd v McInnes (No.1)* [2020] NSWSC 1313 at [139]–[183].

101 [2011] EWCA Civ 347; [2012] Ch. 453.

102 [2011] EWCA Civ 347; [2012] Ch. 453 at [138].

103 [2011] EWCA Civ 347; [2012] Ch. 453 at [141].

proprietary rights in different situations. Finally, we discuss the main defence[104] which can be raised against an equitable proprietary claim following an unauthorised transfer of trust property to a third party,[105] that she was a bona fide purchaser for value without notice of the beneficiaries' equitable interest in the property.

A. Different Types of Proprietary Claim

i. Where a Trustee Misappropriates Trust Property for Herself

15-077 If a trustee purports to be the beneficial owner of trust assets and retains them in their original form, the beneficiaries can require her to reconstitute the trust estate, where necessary by conveying legal title to the assets to new trustees who have been appointed in the meantime.[106] If a trustee misappropriates trust property and uses it exclusively to acquire different property for her own benefit (a "clean substitution"), the beneficiaries can elect either to claim the new property *in specie*, or to take an equitable lien over the new property to secure their personal claim against the trustee to reconstitute the trust fund.[107] If a trustee misappropriates trust property and mixes it with her own property before acquiring new property in exchange for the mixture (a "mixed substitution"), the beneficiaries can elect either to claim a proportion of the new property, or to enforce an equitable lien over the property to secure their personal claim against the trustee.[108] In all of these cases the beneficiaries' claim is a claim that the trustee should specifically or substitutively perform her duty to deliver up trust property in which they have a subsisting equitable interest.[109]

15-078 Where beneficiaries elect to treat new property acquired by a trustee with trust money in an unauthorised transaction they could conceivably claim that the new property is held on constructive trust for them, because the trustee is in breach of the "no profit rule" that governs all fiduciaries.[110] In some cases, however, this might create difficulties because the beneficiaries might be unable to satisfy the causation rules which govern such claims, and a simpler route to the same end, which would not create the same difficulties because causation would be irrelevant, would be for the beneficiaries to adopt the purchase and treat the trustee's actions as having been authorised all along so that the new asset forms part of the original trust fund.[111]

---

104 In certain contexts (such as the acquisition by the third party of registered title to land) there are other defences that may be available (see, e.g. Land Registration Act 2002 s.29, which in fact replaces the bona fide purchaser defence in relation to dealings with land covered by the Land Registration Act 2002).

105 Where the trustee transfers trust property to the third party in an *authorised* exercise of her powers, the third party will be protected from any proprietary claim by the beneficiaries through operation of overreaching.

106 Cf. *Thorpe v Revenue and Customs Commissioners* [2009] EWHC 611 (Ch); [2009] Pens. L.R. 139 at [19].

107 *Re Hallett's Estate* (1880) 13 Ch. D. 696 at 709; *Foskett v McKeown* [1998] Ch. 265 at 277; [2001] 1 A.C. 102 at 130.

108 *Scott v Scott* (1962) 109 C.L.R. 649; *Re Tilley's Will Trusts* [1967] Ch. 1178 (where the point was conceded); *British Columbia Teachers' Credit Union v Betterley* (1975) 61 D.L.R. (3d) 755; *Foskett v McKeown* [1998] Ch. 265 at 277; [2001] 1 A.C. 102 at 130–131; *Tang Ying Ip v Tang Ying Loi* (2017) 20 H.K.C.F.A.R. 53 at [25]. And note *Rheem Australia Pty Ltd v McInnes (No.2)* [2020] NSWSC 1665 at [15]: "if the plaintiff elects to take a charge, the amount secured by the charge should include interest on the traceable amount used in the purchase of the asset in question. Otherwise the proprietary relief given by the court would be incomplete. It would not reflect the full economic value, at the date of the trial, of the monies belonging to the plaintiff which the defendant used in the purchase."

109 See Chapter 13.

110 *Re EVTR Ltd* (1987) 3 B.C.C. 389 at 393 per Dillon LJ: "It is a long established principle of equity that, if a person who is a trustee receives money or property because of, or in respect of, trust property, he will hold what he receives as a constructive trustee on the trusts of the original trust property." For this proposition the judge cited *Keech v Sandford* (1726) Sel. Cas. Temp. King 61; see also *Aberdeen Town Council v Aberdeen University* (1877) 2 App. Cas. 544.

111 As explained by Lord Millett NPJ in *Tang Ying Ip v Tang Ying Loi* (2017) 20 H.K.C.F.A.R. 53, a trustee infringes two different rules simultaneously if she takes trust property for herself in an unauthorised transaction and the beneficiaries can choose

If a trustee misappropriates money from two different trust sources and uses it to buy a new asset, then, according to Scott VC in *Foskett v McKeown*:[112] 15–079

> neither set of beneficiaries can claim a first charge over the asset to recover its money. The equities as between the two sets of beneficiaries will be equal. Neither will be entitled to priority as against the other. It follows that they must share proportionately in the asset, bearing pro rata any shortfall and enjoying pro rata any increase in value.

If trust property generates income, the income is held on trust as well: so, for example, if a house is held on trust, the rent will also be held on trust.[113] If a trustee uses trust funds to buy a house in the trustee's name, with the help of a mortgage loan that the trustee personally covenants to repay, the courts do not treat the trustee as having personally contributed the mortgage money when calculating the quantum of the beneficiaries' claim. So, for example, if the trustee uses £25,000 of trust money to buy a house with the help of a £75,000 purchase loan secured by a mortgage on the property, and the house increases in value, the whole house will be held on trust, subject to a counter-claim for any mortgage payments actually made by the trustee: but for the £25,000 of trust funds the trustee would not have been able to provide the necessary security for the mortgage loan and so the fruits of the transaction should go to the beneficiaries.[114] 15–080

An equitable lien is "essentially a positive right to obtain . . . an order for sale of the subject property or for actual payment from the subject fund", and it 15–081

> may, in general, be enforced in the same way as any other equitable charge, namely, by sale in pursuance of court order or, where the lien is over a fund, by an order for payment thereout.[115]

Since a beneficial interest in property will "rise or fall in value with the property"[116] it will be to the beneficiaries' advantage to elect for an equitable lien in cases where the property has decreased in value, and pursue a personal claim against the defendant for the difference. 15–082

An equitable lien can also be a potent remedy in a case where the beneficiaries can trace into a number of different assets and funds. Suppose that a trustee has several bank accounts and mixes £100,000 of trust money with her own money in her No.1 account, then transfers money from the No.1 account to her No.2 and No.3 accounts, and then buys a painting with money from the No.1 account, a car with money from the No.2 account, and a flat with money from the No.3 account. In this case: 15–083

> as against the wrongdoer and [her] successors in title, the beneficiary is entitled to locate his contribution in any part of the mixture [i.e. in any of the three accounts, the painting, the car, and the flat] and to subordinate their claims to share in the mixture till his own contribution has been satisfied.[117]

---

which rule they wish to invoke when making their claim. One rule requires the trustee to obey the terms of the trust and holds that she cannot validly treat property as her own if the trust terms require her to hold it for the beneficiaries; the other rule requires the trustee to subordinate his personal interests to those of the beneficiaries. Non-compliance with the latter rule can lead to the imposition of a constructive trust on the trustee's unauthorised profits, as discussed at paras 17–011 to 17–053.

112 [1998] Ch. 265 at 278. See too Lord Millett's comments on appeal: [2001] 1 A.C. 102 at 132.

113 *Banton v CIBC Corp* (1999) 182 D.L.R. (4th) 486 at 504–505; *Greenwood v Lee* [2003] O.P.L.R. 1.

114 *Paul Davies Pty Ltd v Davies* [1983] N.S.W.L.R. 440; *Re Marriage of Wagstaff* (1990) 99 F.L.R. 390.

115 *Hewett v Court* (1983) 149 C.L.R. 638 at 664, per Deane J.

116 *Australian Postal Corp v Lutak* (1991) 21 N.S.W.L.R. 584 at 590, per Bryson J.

117 *Foskett v McKeown* [2001] 1 A.C. 102 at 132, per Lord Millett. See too *El Ajou v Dollar Land Holdings Plc* [1993] 3 All E.R. 713 at 735–736; on appeal: [1994] 2 All E.R. 685 at 701; *Re Goldcorp Exchange Ltd* [1994] 2 All E.R. 806 at 831.

15–084 If the trustee reinstates the trust by returning the trust property then the beneficiaries will have no claim against her. However, if a trustee uses trust money to buy assets which increase in value it is not enough for her to repay the value of the trust money originally taken: she must account to the beneficiaries for the increase in value as well.[118]

ii. Where Trust Property is Misdirected to a Third Party

15–085 Where a third party receives title to trust property or its traceable proceeds as a result of an unauthorised exercise of power by the trustee,[119] the beneficiary (including a discretionary object[120]) or a trustee[121] has a proprietary claim against the recipient, unless the recipient is a bona fide purchaser for value without notice of the beneficiaries' interest,[122] or other defences apply (e.g. laches or acquiescence). Even if the recipient has acted in good faith, she must "yield up any [trust property that remains], or the traceable proceeds of any that [has been exchanged for a new asset]".[123] This proprietary liability is dependent on the recipient having received, and still having, the trust property or its traceable proceeds,[124] and if the claimant cannot prove this no proprietary claim can be made. The claim is not dependent on proof of knowledge[125] or fault, albeit that the process of litigation will mean the recipient has knowledge of the claim at least through the commencement of proceedings. It is said that the recipient holds the property on constructive trust for the beneficiaries.[126] However, the proprietary claim must be distinguished from the personal claim in knowing receipt to make the recipient personally accountable for the property as a constructive trustee, in cases where she has received the property with a sufficient degree of knowledge to make her receipt unconscionable or has acquired such a degree of knowledge whilst still holding the property or its traceable proceeds.[127] This point is brought out in the following extract.[128]

Independent Trustee Services Ltd v GP Noble Trustees Ltd

Court of Appeal [2013] Ch. 91 at [77]–[80]

15–086 LLOYD L.J.: . . . in the case of an innocent volunteer recipient of money which is the product of a breach of trust, the legal title is in the recipient but the equitable title remains in the beneficiaries of the relevant trust throughout. Conventionally, in a situation where the legal title to an asset is held by A but the beneficial ownership is in B, A is regarded as holding the asset on trust for B. To say that, however, is only the

---

[118] *Scott v Scott* (1962) 109 C.L.R. 649; *Re Hughes* [1970] I.R. 237.

[119] The rules that determine whether an exercise of power is authorised or not are discussed in paras 11–024 to 11–029.

[120] *Lewis v Tamplin* [2018] EWHC 777 (Ch); [2018] W.T.L.R. 215 at [39]; *Serious Fraud Office v Litigation Capital Ltd* [2021] EWHC 1272 (Comm) at [203]–[205].

[121] See e.g. *Fouche v Superannuation Fund Board* (1952) 88 C.L.R. 609, 640 (the Court); *Young v Murphy* [1996] 1 V.R. 27 at 281–83 (Brooking J); *Morlea Professional Services Ltd v Richard Walter Pty Ltd (in liq)* (1999) 96 F.C.R. 217 at [51] (the Court); *Re Cemcon* [2009] FCA 696 at [20] (Gordon J); *Krnjulac v Lincu* [2015] NSWCA 367; *Presbyterian Church of Victoria Trusts Corp v Anstee* [2017] VSC 102 at [14]–[20] (Sifris J), see further: paras 11–013 to 11–023.

[122] *Foskett v McKeown* [2001] 1 A.C. 102 at 127 and 130. For discussion of the bona fide purchase defence, see paras 15–164 to 15–168.

[123] *Re Montagu's Settlement Trusts* [1987] Ch. 264 at 272, per Megarry VC.

[124] Although B may seek to make the recipient personally liable under a different claim, such as knowing receipt.

[125] As recognised in *Re Montagu's Settlement Trusts* [1987] 1 Ch. 264 at 271–272; *Krnjulac v Lincu* [2015] NSWCA 367 at [2]–[6], [24] Bathurst CJ expressly observed that B had not pleaded or proved X's knowledge, precluding any claim based on knowing receipt, yet the proprietary claim was successful.

[126] *Independent Trustee Services Ltd v GP Noble Trustees Ltd* [2012] EWCA Civ 195; [2013] Ch. 91 at [80].

[127] As to which see paras 14–017 to 14–093.

[128] See also *Agip (Africa) Ltd v Jackson* [1990] 1 Ch. 265 at 290; *Allan v Rea Brothers Trustees Ltd* [2002] EWCA Civ 85; [2002] Pens. L.R. 169 at [55]; *Waxman v Waxman* (2004) 7 I.T.E.L.R. 162 at [583]; *Nabb Brothers Ltd v Lloyds Bank International (Guernsey) Ltd* [2005] I.L.Pr. 37 at [72].

beginning of the analysis because it does not tell you what duties A owes to B in respect of the asset. The fact that A is not liable to account to B for the asset if A has parted with it (without receiving traceable proceeds) at a time when he had no knowledge of B's interest shows that this is not a case of a trustee who is subject to strict liability.

This situation is inherently unstable in two respects. For so long as A has no notice of B's interest, B's interest is fragile because A may dispose of the property in a way which leaves no traceable product. On the other hand A's immunity from claims in respect of his dealings with the assets is also at risk because it can be brought to an end (for the future) if notice is given to him of B's interest. **15-087**

In *Westdeutsche Landesbank Girozentrale v Islington LBC*[129] Lord Browne-Wilkinson said that innocent receipt by A of property in which B has a beneficial interest, A being unaware of that interest, "does not by itself make [A] a trustee despite the severance of the legal and equitable titles". He said this on the premise,[130] that if A held on trust despite his ignorance and therefore innocence, he would be personally liable, regardless of fault, for any subsequent payment of the money to any third party even though at the time of the payment he was still innocent of B's interest. He recognised[131] that whether A is regarded as a trustee may be no more than a semantic question, so long as it is accepted that A's accountability does not extend to property which left A's hands before he had notice of B's interest. . . **15-088**

Despite what Lord Browne-Wilkinson said, it seems to me that it is appropriate to speak of A holding on trust for B in this situation, provided that one is not misled into thinking that to call the relationship one of trustee and beneficiary tells you, of itself, what the duties and liabilities of the trustee are. Since the trust arises from the asset having been extracted, in breach of trust, from a fund held on express trusts, it seems correct to characterise the trust as a constructive trust, rather than a resulting trust. . . **15-089**

[Since] an innocent volunteer recipient of trust assets transferred in breach of trust, before he has notice of the trust interest, . . . cannot be made accountable for relevant assets disposed of at a time when he had no notice of the adverse interest, even though the beneficial interest of the beneficiaries continued to exist, the volunteer is (for the time being) able to mix the trust assets with his own, with impunity, and to dispose of them freely, despite the beneficiaries' continuing beneficial interest. So in that situation the volunteer, even if regarded as holding the property on trust, is not constrained by any imposed duty as regards his free powers of dealing with the assets, until he has notice of the inconsistent interest of the beneficiaries. Of course, if he gives a relevant asset away, the beneficiaries may be able to follow it into the hands of the later recipient, and if he disposes of it for value, then he may receive another asset which would represent the trust property in his hands, and the beneficiaries may then be able to assert a claim to that asset by way of tracing. Once he has notice of the beneficiaries' adverse interest, he is no longer free to deal with the assets as he pleases. At that stage there is no conceptual difficulty or oddity in calling him a (constructive) trustee, at least as from that time. . . **15-090**

If the recipient of misdirected trust property mixes it with her own property, the claimant can claim the traceable proceeds of their property,[132] the identity of the residue being determined by rules that vary according to whether or not the recipient has acted in good faith, as discussed above.[133] As previously noted,[134] these rules permit the claimant to trace into assets bought by an innocent recipient even though she can prove that she could have bought the asset with her own money, and that she would have done so, had she known that the money which she actually used to buy the asset belonged to the beneficiaries. In the event that the asset increases in value, then it follows from the foregoing discussion that the claimant can capture the whole of the increase via a claim to the asset. **15-091**

This outcome may not offend us in a case where the defendant is a wrongdoing trustee, or a donee from a wrongdoing trustee, as in *Foskett v McKeown*,[135] which is reproduced below. But where the **15-092**

---

129 [1996] A.C. 669 at 707.
130 Stated at 703.
131 At 707.
132 *Re Diplock* [1948] Ch. 465 at 524, 539.
133 See paras 15-038 to 15-040.
134 See para.15-040.
135 [2001] 1 A.C. 102; excerpted at paras 15-095 to 15-127.

defendant has acted in good faith, it is "an affront to our notions of justice" that she should be liable in this way, as Lord Millett has observed in extra-judicial writing.[136] Suppose that an innocent recipient uses £5 of misapplied trust funds to buy a lottery ticket which pays out £5 million and that she would have used her own £5 for the purpose, had she known of the trust money's tainted source. In our view, the most to which the beneficiaries should be entitled in this case is an equitable lien over the winnings to secure repayment of the £5.[137]

15-093 The facts of *Foskett v McKeown*[138] were similar but differed in an important respect. A trustee stole trust funds that he used to pay some of the premiums on a life insurance policy. The policy contained an investment element and part of the premiums were used to build up an investment fund inside the policy while another part bought the right to the payment of a death benefit to nominated beneficiaries on the death of the policyholder. The policy also contained a clause which provided that in the event that annual premiums were not paid the policy would not immediately lapse, and instead money would be taken out of the investment fund to keep up the policyholder's right to the payment of the death benefit (until the fund was exhausted).

15-094 The trustee died and the trust beneficiaries claimed a proportionate share of the £1 million death benefit on the ground that this represented the traceable proceeds of trust property. The trustee's children and mother who were the nominated beneficiaries under the policy argued that the trust beneficiaries should be restricted to a lien for the amount of the stolen money. The nominated beneficiaries said that if they had been given a choice whether the right to the death benefit should be paid for with the stolen money, or with money taken out of the investment fund, they would have chosen the latter course. Hence it would be unfair to make them surrender more than the value of the premiums paid with trust money. This argument appealed to a minority of the House of Lords,[139] but it was rejected by the majority, Lord Millett stating that on the facts as they happened, the trustee had made the opposite choice, and that for the purposes of the case the nominated beneficiaries were in no better a moral position than that which had been occupied by the trustee from whom their rights to the death benefit had derived.[140]

Foskett v McKeown

House of Lords [2001] 1 A.C. 102

15-095 The claimants paid money to Murphy on trust for themselves, intending that the money should be used to buy land for investment purposes in Portugal. Murphy had previously bought a life insurance policy on his own life, on trust for his children (who would receive 90 per cent of the policy proceeds in the event of his death) and his mother (who would receive 10 per cent). Murphy paid the first two annual premiums with his own money; the source of the money which he used to pay the third premium was disputed; and in breach of trust he used the claimants' money to pay the fourth and fifth premiums. Murphy then committed suicide and the insurer paid £1 million to the surviving trustees of the policy settlement. The claimants sued the trustees, arguing that they had an equitable proprietary interest in at least 40 per cent of the insurance proceeds because at least 40 per cent of the premiums had been paid with stolen trust money. A majority of the House of Lords allowed the claim, and refused to restrict the claimants to a lien over the proceeds for the amount of money paid towards the premiums.

---

[136] "Proprietary Restitution" in S. Degeling and J. Edelman (eds), *Equity in Commercial Law* (Law Book Co, 2005).

[137] An outcome which is supported by *Re Tilley's Will Trusts* [1967] Ch. 1179, as discussed in D.J. Hayton, "Equity's Identification Rules" in Birks (ed.) *Laundering and Tracing* (1995), pp.10–12.

[138] [2001] 1 A.C. 102.

[139] [2001] 1 A.C. 102 at 112–13 per Lord Steyn.

[140] [2001] 1 A.C. 102 at 130: "The trustee cannot be permitted to keep any profit resulting from his misappropriation for himself, and his donees cannot obtain a better title than their donor."

LORD MILLETT (with whom LORD BROWNE-WILKINSON and LORD HOFFMANN agreed, and with whom LORD STEYN and LORD HOPE disagreed on the question of remedy): My Lords, this is a textbook example of tracing through mixed substitutions. At the beginning of the story the purchasers were beneficially entitled under an express trust to a sum standing in the name of Mr Murphy in a bank account. From there the money moved into and out of various bank accounts where in breach of trust it was inextricably mixed by Mr Murphy with his own money. After each transaction was completed the purchasers' money formed an indistinguishable part of the balance standing to Mr Murphy's credit in his bank account. The amount of that balance represented a debt due from the bank to Mr Murphy, that is to say a chose in action. At the penultimate stage the purchasers' money was represented by an indistinguishable part of a different chose in action, viz. the debt prospectively and contingently due from an insurance company to its policyholders, being the trustees of a settlement made by Mr Murphy for the benefit of his children. At the present and final stage it forms an indistinguishable part of the balance standing to the credit of the respondent trustees in their bank account. 15–096

Tracing and Following

The process of ascertaining what happened to the purchasers' money involves both tracing and following. These are both exercises in locating assets which are or may be taken to represent an asset belonging to the purchasers and to which they assert ownership. The processes of following and tracing are, however, distinct. Following is the process of following the same asset as it moves from hand to hand. Tracing is the process of identifying a new asset as the substitute for the old. Where one asset is exchanged for another, a claimant can elect whether to follow the original asset into the hands of the new owner or to trace its value into the new asset in the hands of the same owner. In practice his choice is often dictated by the circumstances. In the present case the purchasers do not seek to follow the money any further once it reached the bank or insurance company, since its identity was lost in the hands of the recipient (which in any case obtained an unassailable title as a bona fide purchaser for value without notice of the purchasers' beneficial interest). Instead the purchasers have chosen at each stage to trace the money into its proceeds, viz. the debt presently due from the bank to the account holder or the debt prospectively and contingently due from the insurance company to the policy holders. 15–097

Having completed this exercise, the purchasers claim a continuing beneficial interest in the insurance money. Since this represents the product of Mr Murphy's own money as well as theirs, which Mr Murphy mingled indistinguishably in a single chose in action, they claim a beneficial interest in a proportionate part of the money only. The transmission of a claimant's property rights from one asset to its traceable proceeds is part of our law of property, not of the law of unjust enrichment. There is no "unjust factor" to justify restitution (unless "want of title" be one, which makes the point). The claimant succeeds if at all by virtue of his own title, not to reverse unjust enrichment. Property rights are determined by fixed rules and settled principles. They are not discretionary. They do not depend upon ideas of what is "fair, just and reasonable". Such concepts, which in reality mask decisions of legal policy, have no place in the law of property. 15–098

A beneficiary of a trust is entitled to a continuing beneficial interest not merely in the trust property but in its traceable proceeds also, and his interest binds everyone who takes the property or its traceable proceeds except a bona fide purchaser for value without notice. In the present case the purchasers' beneficial interest plainly bound Mr Murphy, a trustee who wrongfully mixed the trust money with his own and whose every dealing with the money (including the payment of the premiums) was in breach of trust. It similarly binds his successors, the trustees of the children's settlement, who claim no beneficial interest of their own, and Mr Murphy's children, who are volunteers. They gave no value for what they received and derive their interest from Mr Murphy by way of gift. 15–099

Tracing

We speak of money at the bank, and of money passing into and out of a bank account. But of course the account holder has no money at the bank. Money paid into a bank account belongs legally and beneficially to the bank and not to the account holder. The bank gives value for it, and it is accordingly not usually possible to make the money itself the subject of an adverse claim. Instead a claimant normally sues the account holder rather than the bank and lays claim to the proceeds of the money in his hands. These consist of the debt or part of the debt due to him from the bank. We speak of tracing money into and out of the account, but there is no money in the account. There is merely a single debt of an amount equal to the final balance standing to the credit of the account holder. No money passes from paying bank to receiving bank or through the clearing system (where the money flows may be in the opposite direction). There is simply a 15–100 series of debits and credits which are causally and transactionally linked. We also speak of tracing one asset into another, but this too is inaccurate. The original asset still exists in the hands of the new owner, or it may have become untraceable. The claimant claims the new asset because it was acquired in whole or in part with the original asset. What he traces, therefore, is not the physical asset itself but the value inherent in it.

15–101 Tracing is thus neither a claim nor a remedy. It is merely the process by which a claimant demonstrates what has happened to his property, identifies its proceeds and the persons who have handled or received them, and justifies his claim that the proceeds can properly be regarded as representing his property. Tracing is also distinct from claiming. It identifies the traceable proceeds of the claimant's property. It enables the claimant to substitute the traceable proceeds for the original asset as the subject matter of his claim. But it does not affect or establish his claim. That will depend on a number of factors including the nature of his interest in the original asset. He will normally be able to maintain the same claim to the substituted asset as he could have maintained to the original asset. If he held only a security interest in the original asset, he cannot claim more than a security interest in its proceeds. But his claim may also be exposed to potential defences as a result of intervening transactions. Even if the purchasers could demonstrate what the bank had done with their money, for example, and could thus identify its traceable proceeds in the hands of the bank, any claim by them to assert ownership of those proceeds would be defeated by the bona fide purchaser defence. The successful completion of a tracing exercise may be preliminary to a personal claim[141] or a proprietary one, to the enforcement of a legal right,[142] or an equitable one.

15–102 Given its nature, there is nothing inherently legal or equitable about the tracing exercise. There is thus no sense in maintaining different rules for tracing at law and in equity. One set of tracing rules is enough. The existence of two has never formed part of the law in the United States.[143] There is certainly no logical justification for allowing any distinction between them to produce capricious results in cases of mixed substitutions by insisting on the existence of a fiduciary relationship as a precondition for applying equity's tracing rules. The existence of such a relationship may be relevant to the nature of the claim which the plaintiff can maintain, whether personal or proprietary, but that is a different matter. I agree with the passages which my noble and learned friend Lord Steyn has cited from Professor Birks' essay "The Necessity of a Unitary Law of Tracing",[144] and with Dr Lionel Smith's exposition in his comprehensive monograph *The Law of Tracing*.[145]

15–103 This is not, however, the occasion to explore these matters further, for the present is a straightforward case of a trustee who wrongfully misappropriated trust money, mixed it with his own, and used it to pay for an asset for the benefit of his children. Even on the traditional approach, the equitable tracing rules are available to the purchasers. There are only two complicating factors. The first is that the wrongdoer used their money to pay premiums on an equity linked policy of life assurance on his own life. The nature of the policy should make no difference in principle, though it may complicate the accounting. The second is that he had previously settled the policy for the benefit of his children. This should also make no difference. The claimant's rights cannot depend on whether the wrongdoer gave the policy to his children during his lifetime or left the proceeds to them by his will; or if during his lifetime whether he did so before or after he had recourse to the claimant's money to pay the premiums. The order of events does not affect the fact that the children are not contributors but volunteers who have received the gift of an asset paid for in part with misappropriated trust moneys.

The Cause of Action

15–104 As I have already pointed out, the purchasers seek to vindicate their property rights, not to reverse unjust enrichment. The correct classification of the purchasers' cause of action may appear to be academic, but it has important consequences. The two causes of action have different requirements and may attract different defences.

15–105 A plaintiff who brings an action in unjust enrichment must show that the defendant has been enriched at the plaintiff's expense, for he cannot have been unjustly enriched if he has not been enriched at all. But the plaintiff is not concerned to show that the defendant is in receipt of property belonging beneficially to

---

141 As in *El Ajou v Dollar Land Holdings Plc* [1993] 3 All E.R. 717.
142 As in *Trustees of the Property of FC Jones & Sons (a firm) v Jones* [1997] Ch. 159.
143 See Scott, *The Law of Trusts* (4th edn, 1989), 605–609.
144 In R. Cranston (ed.), *Making Commercial Law: Essays in Honour of Roy Goode* (1997).
145 L.D. Smith, *The Law of Tracing* (1997). See particularly pp.120–130, 277–279 and 342–347.

the plaintiff or its traceable proceeds. The fact that the beneficial ownership of the property has passed to the defendant provides no defence; indeed, it is usually the very fact which founds the claim. Conversely, a plaintiff who brings an action like the present must show that the defendant is in receipt of property which belongs beneficially to him or its traceable proceeds, but he need not show that the defendant has been enriched by its receipt. He may, for example, have paid full value for the property, but he is still required to disgorge it if he received it with notice of the plaintiff's interest.

Furthermore, a claim in unjust enrichment is subject to a change of position defence, which usually operates by reducing or extinguishing the element of enrichment. An action like the present is subject to the bona fide purchaser for value defence, which operates to clear the defendant's title. 15–106

The Tracing Rules

The insurance policy in the present case is a very sophisticated financial instrument. Tracing into the rights conferred by such an instrument raises a number of important issues. It is therefore desirable to set out the basic principles before turning to deal with the particular problems to which policies of life assurance give rise. 15–107

The simplest case is where a trustee wrongfully misappropriates trust property and uses it exclusively to acquire other property for his own benefit. In such a case the beneficiary is entitled at his option either to assert his beneficial ownership of the proceeds or to bring a personal claim against the trustee for breach of trust and enforce an equitable lien or charge on the proceeds to secure restoration of the trust fund. He will normally exercise the option in the way most advantageous to himself. If the traceable proceeds have increased in value and are worth more than the original asset, he will assert his beneficial ownership and obtain the profit for himself. There is nothing unfair in this. The trustee cannot be permitted to keep any profit resulting from his misappropriation for himself, and his donees cannot obtain a better title than their donor. If the traceable proceeds are worth less than the original asset, it does not usually matter how the beneficiary exercises his option. He will take the whole of the proceeds on either basis. This is why it is not possible to identify the basis on which the claim succeeded in some of the cases. 15–108

Both remedies are proprietary and depend on successfully tracing the trust property into its proceeds. A beneficiary's claim against a trustee for breach of trust is a personal claim. It does not entitle him to priority over the trustee's general creditors unless he can trace the trust property into its product and establish a proprietary interest in the proceeds. If the beneficiary is unable to trace the trust property into its proceeds, he still has a personal claim against the trustee, but his claim will be unsecured. The beneficiary's proprietary claims to the trust property or its traceable proceeds can be maintained against the wrongdoer and anyone who derives title from him except a bona fide purchaser for value without notice of the breach of trust. The same rules apply even where there have been numerous successive transactions, so long as the tracing exercise is successful and no bona fide purchaser for value without notice has intervened. 15–109

A more complicated case is where there is a mixed substitution. This occurs where the trust money represents only part of the cost of acquiring the new asset. As James Barr Ames pointed out in "Following Misappropriated Property into its Product",[146] consistency requires that, if a trustee buys property partly with his own money and partly with trust money, the beneficiary should have the option of taking a proportionate part of the new property or a lien upon it, as may be most for his advantage. In principle it should not matter (and it has never previously been suggested that it does) whether the trustee mixes the trust money with his own and buys the new asset with the mixed fund or makes separate payments of the purchase price (whether simultaneously or sequentially) out of the different funds. In every case the value formerly inherent in the trust property has become located within the value inherent in the new asset. 15–110

The rule, and its rationale, were stated by Samuel Williston in "The Right to Follow Trust Property when Confused with Other Property":[147] 15–111

> "If the trust fund is traceable as having furnished in part the money with which a certain investment was made, and the proportion it formed of the whole money so invested is known or ascertainable, the cestui que trust should be allowed to regard the acts of the trustee as done for his benefit, in the same way that he would be allowed to if all the money so invested had been his; that is, he should be entitled in equity to an undivided share of the property which the trust money contributed to

[146] (1906) 19 Harvard L.R. 511.
[147] (1888) 2 Harvard L.R. 28, 29.

purchase—such a proportion of the whole as the trust money bore to the whole money invested. The reason in one case as in the other is that the trustee cannot be allowed to make a profit from the use of the trust money, and if the property which he wrongfully purchased were held subject only to a lien for the amount invested, any appreciation in value would go to the trustee."

15–112 If this correctly states the underlying basis of the rule (as I believe it does), then it is impossible to distinguish between the case where mixing precedes the investment and the case where it arises on and in consequence of the investment. It is also impossible to distinguish between the case where the investment is retained by the trustee and the case where it is given away to a gratuitous donee. The donee cannot obtain a better title than his donor, and a donor who is a trustee cannot be allowed to profit from his trust.

15–113 In *Re Hallett's Estate*,[148] Jessel M.R. acknowledged that where an asset was acquired exclusively with trust money, the beneficiary could either assert equitable ownership of the asset or enforce a lien or charge over it to recover the trust money. But he appeared to suggest that in the case of a mixed substitution the beneficiary is confined to a lien. Any authority that this dictum might otherwise have is weakened by the fact that Jessel M.R. gave no reason for the existence of any such rule, and none is readily apparent. The dictum was plainly obiter, for the fund was deficient and the plaintiff was only claiming a lien. It has usually been cited only to be explained away.[149] It was rejected by the High Court of Australia in *Scott v Scott*.[150] It has not been adopted in the United States.[151] In *Primeau v Granfield* Learned Hand J. expressed himself in forthright terms: "On principle there can be no excuse for such a rule."[152]

15–114 In my view the time has come to state unequivocally that English law has no such rule. It conflicts with the rule that a trustee must not benefit from his trust. I agree with Burrows that the beneficiary's right to elect to have a proportionate share of a mixed substitution necessarily follows once one accepts, as English law does, (i) that a claimant can trace in equity into a mixed fund and (ii) that he can trace unmixed money into its proceeds and assert ownership of the proceeds.

15–115 Accordingly, I would state the basic rule as follows. Where a trustee wrongfully uses trust money to provide part of the cost of acquiring an asset, the beneficiary is entitled at his option either to claim a proportionate share of the asset or to enforce a lien upon it to secure his personal claim against the trustee for the amount of the misapplied money. It does not matter whether the trustee mixed the trust money with his own in a single fund before using it to acquire the asset, or made separate payments (whether simultaneously or sequentially) out of the differently owned funds to acquire a single asset.

15–116 Two observations are necessary at this point. First, there is a mixed substitution (with the results already described) whenever the claimant's property has contributed in part only towards the acquisition of the new asset. It is not necessary for the claimant to show in addition that his property has contributed to any increase in the value of the new asset. This is because, as I have already pointed out, this branch of the law is concerned with vindicating rights of property and not with reversing unjust enrichment. Secondly, the beneficiary's right to claim a lien is available only against a wrongdoer and those deriving title under him otherwise than for value. It is not available against competing contributors who are innocent of any wrongdoing. The tracing rules are not the result of any presumption or principle peculiar to equity. They correspond to the common law rules for following into physical mixtures (though the consequences may not be identical). Common to both is the principle that the interests of the wrongdoer who was responsible for the mixing and those who derive title under him otherwise than for value are subordinated to those of innocent contributors. As against the wrongdoer and his successors, the beneficiary is entitled to locate his contribution in any part of the mixture and to subordinate their claims to share in the mixture until his own contribution has been satisfied. This has the effect of giving the beneficiary a lien for his contribution if the mixture is deficient.

15–117 Innocent contributors, however, must be treated equally inter se. Where the beneficiary's claim is in competition with the claims of other innocent contributors, there is no basis upon which any of the claims can be subordinated to any of the others. Where the fund is deficient, the beneficiary is not entitled to enforce a lien for his contributions; all must share rateably in the fund.

148 (1880) 13 Ch.D. 696 at 709.
149 See e.g. *Re Tilley's Will Trusts* [1967] Ch. 1179 at 1186, per Ungoed-Thomas J.; A. Burrows, *The Law of Restitution* (1993), p.368.
150 (1963) 109 C.L.R. 649 at 661–662, cited by Morritt L.J. below: [1998] Ch. 265 at 300–301.
151 See the American Law Institute, *Restatement of the Law, Trusts 2d* (1959) at p.202(h).
152 (1911) 184 F. 480 at 482.

The primary rule in regard to a mixed fund, therefore, is that gains and losses are borne by the contributors rateably. The beneficiary's right to elect instead to enforce a lien to obtain repayment is an exception to the primary rule, exercisable where the fund is deficient and the claim is made against the wrongdoer and those claiming through him. It is not necessary to consider whether there are any circumstances in which the beneficiary is confined to a lien in cases where the fund is more than sufficient to repay the contributions of all parties. It is sufficient to say that he is not so confined in a case like the present. It is not enough that those defending the claim are innocent of any wrongdoing if they are not themselves contributors but, like the trustees and Mr Murphy's children in the present case, are volunteers who derive title under the wrongdoer otherwise than for value. On ordinary principles such persons are in no better position than the wrongdoer, and are liable to suffer the same subordination of their interests to those of the claimant as the wrongdoer would have been. They certainly cannot do better than the claimant by confining him to a lien and keeping any profit for themselves. 15–118

Similar principles apply to following into physical mixtures.[153] There are relatively few cases which deal with the position of the innocent recipient from the wrongdoer, but *Jones v De Marchant*[154] may be cited as an example. A husband wrongfully took 18 beaver skins belonging to his wife and used them, together with four skins of his own, to have a fur coat made up which he then gave to his mistress. Unsurprisingly the wife was held entitled to recover the coat. The mistress knew nothing of the true ownership of the skins, but her innocence was held to be immaterial. She was a gratuitous donee and could stand in no better position than the husband. The coat was a new asset manufactured from the skins and not merely the product of intermingling them. The problem could not be solved by a sale of the coat in order to reduce the disputed property to a divisible fund, since (as we shall see) the realisation of an asset does not affect its ownership. It would hardly have been appropriate to require the two ladies to share the coat between them. Accordingly it was an all or nothing case in which the ownership of the coat must be assigned to one or other of the parties. The determinative factor was that the mixing was the act of the wrongdoer through whom the mistress acquired the coat otherwise than for value. 15–119

The rule in equity is to the same effect, as Page Wood V.C. observed in *Frith v Cartland*:[155] 15–120

> ". . . if a man mixes trust funds with his own, the whole will be treated as the trust property, except so far as he may be able to distinguish what is his own."

This does not, in my opinion, exclude a pro rata division where this is appropriate, as in the case of money and other fungibles like grain, oil or wine. But it is to be observed that a pro rata division is the best that the wrongdoer and his donees can hope for. If a pro rata division is excluded, the beneficiary takes the whole; there is no question of confining him to a lien. *Jones v De Marchant* is a useful illustration of the principles shared by the common law and equity alike that an innocent recipient who receives misappropriated property by way of gift obtains no better title than his donor, and that if a proportionate sharing is inappropriate the wrongdoer and those who derive title under him take nothing. 15–121

Insurance Policies

In the case of an ordinary whole-life policy the insurance company undertakes to pay a stated sum on the death of the assured in return for fixed annual premiums payable throughout his life. Such a policy is an entire contract, not a contract for a year with a right of renewal. It is not a series of single premium policies for one year term assurance. It is not like an indemnity policy where each premium buys cover for a year after which the policyholder must renew or the cover expires. The fact that the policy will lapse if the premiums are not paid makes no difference. The amounts of the annual premiums and of the sum assured are fixed in advance at the outset and assume the payment of annual premiums throughout the term of the policy. The relationship between them is based on the life expectancy of the assured and the rates of interest available on long term government securities at the inception of the policy. 15–122

In the present case the benefits specified in the policy are expressed to be payable "in consideration of the payment of the first Premium already made and of the further Premiums payable". The premiums are stated to be "£10220.00 payable at annual intervals from 06 Nov 1986 throughout the lifetime of the 15–123

---

153 See *Lupton v White* (1808) 15 Ves. Jun. 432; and *Sandeman & Sons v Tyzack and Branfoot Steamship Co Ltd* [1913] A.C. 680 at 695, where Lord Moulton said: "If the mixing has arisen from the fault of 'B', 'A' can claim the goods."

154 (1916) 28 D.L.R. 561.

155 (1865) 2 H. & M. 417 at 420.

life assured". It is beyond argument that the death benefit of £1m paid on Mr Murphy's death was paid in consideration for all the premiums which had been paid before that date, including those paid with the purchasers' money, and not just some of them. Part of that sum, therefore, represented the traceable proceeds of the purchasers' money.

15–124 It is, however, of critical importance in the present case to appreciate that the purchasers do not trace the premiums directly into the insurance money. They trace them first into the policy and thence into the proceeds of the policy. It is essential not to elide the two steps. In this context, of course, the word "policy" does not mean the contract of insurance. You do not trace the payment of a premium into the insurance contract any more than you trace a payment into a bank account into the banking contract. The word "policy" is here used to describe the bundle of rights to which the policyholder is entitled in return for the premiums. These rights, which may be very complex, together constitute a chose in action, viz. the right to payment of a debt payable on a future event and contingent upon the continued payment of further premiums until the happening of the event. That chose in action represents the traceable proceeds of the premiums; its current value fluctuates from time to time. When the policy matures, the insurance money represents the traceable proceeds of the policy and hence indirectly of the premiums.

15–125 It follows that, if a claimant can show that premiums were paid with his money, he can claim a proportionate share of the policy. His interest arises by reason of and immediately upon the payment of the premiums, and the extent of his share is ascertainable at once. He does not have to wait until the policy matures in order to claim his property. His share in the policy and its proceeds may increase or decrease as further premiums are paid; but it is not affected by the realisation of the policy. His share remains the same whether the policy is sold or surrendered or held until maturity; these are merely different methods of realising the policy. They may affect the amount of the proceeds received on realisation but they cannot affect the extent of his share in the proceeds. In principle the purchasers are entitled to the insurance money which was paid on Mr Murphy's death in the same shares and proportions as they were entitled in the policy immediately before his death.

15–126 Since the manner in which an asset is realised does not affect its ownership, and since it cannot matter whether the claimant discovers what has happened before or after it is realised, the question of ownership can be answered by ascertaining the shares in which it is owned immediately before it is realised. Where A misappropriates B's money and uses it to buy a winning ticket in the lottery, B is entitled to the winnings. Since A is a wrongdoer, it is irrelevant that he could have used his own money if in fact he used B's. This may seem to give B an undeserved windfall, but the result is not unjust. Had B discovered the fraud before the draw, he could have decided whether to keep the ticket or demand his money back. He alone has the right to decide whether to gamble with his own money. If A keeps him in ignorance until after the draw, he suffers the consequence. He cannot deprive B of his right to choose what to do with his own money; but he can give him an informed choice.

15–127 The application of these principles ought not to depend on the nature of the chose in action. They should apply to a policy of life assurance as they apply to a bank account or a lottery ticket . . . .

iii. Where a Trustee Makes an Unauthorised Investment

15–128 When an express trust is declared, "the trust fund" is generally defined in the trust deed in terms such as "property transferred to the trustees to hold on the terms of this trust and all the property from time to time representing the same". However, such a clause spells out what is usually involved in the settlor creating a trust in any case. This is because trustees will have the power as owners of the initial trust property to assign ownership to third parties and will be permitted to use these powers for the purposes of sale and investment. For this to work, the trustees must additionally be able to assign title to trust assets clear of any proprietary claim and they can do this because the doctrine of overreaching provides that when the trustees assign ownership of trust property in an authorised fashion, the recipient takes clear title, and in cases where the trust property is exchanged for other property, the trust will attach instead to the substitute property.[156]

[156] R.C. Nolan, "Property in a Fund" (2004) 120 L.Q.R. 108, 111–117; R.C. Nolan, "Understanding the Limits of Equitable Property" (2006) 1 J. of Eq. 18, 24–28.

Now consider the case where trustees act in an unauthorised way when they sell trust assets or use trust money to buy new assets. In *Wright v Morgan*, Viscount Dunedin held that where:[157] **15–129**

> a trustee has made an improper investment, the law is well settled. The *cestuis que trustent* as a whole have a right, if they choose, to adopt the investment and to hold it as trust property. But if there is not unanimity then it is not trust property, but the trustee who has made it must keep the investment himself. He is debtor to the trust for the money which has been applied in its purchase.

These rules would be worked out in proceedings for an account either by affirming the purchase in a case where the beneficiaries all consent to that outcome, or else, in a case where they do not, by falsifying the account to delete the unauthorised expenditure from the record and requiring the trustees to reconstitute the trust fund by paying over the amount of the outgoing from their own pockets.[158] **15–130**

iv. Where Trust Funds are Used to Pay Off a Charge on Property

Suppose that a trustee misappropriates trust money and uses it to pay off a debt secured by a mortgage on her house. Or suppose that a trustee uses trust money to buy property for a third party in an unauthorised transaction thereby extinguishing the unpaid vendor's lien over the property. In such cases the courts can allow the beneficiaries, by means of a legal fiction, to trace their money into the extinguished charge, and to be treated as though this has been "kept alive" and transferred to them as security for the repayment of their money. **15–131**

An example is provided by *Menelaou* v *Bank of Cyprus UK Ltd*.[159] The defendant's parents owed a debt to a bank secured by charges on the parents' house. The bank released the charges to enable the parents to sell the house, use part of the proceeds to repay part of their debt and use the rest to buy a new house for the defendant. This was done after a third-party charge securing the rest of the parents' debt had apparently been executed on the defendant's house. The parents then got into financial difficulties and it transpired that the third-party charge on the defendant's house was invalid because she had not agreed to it and her signature on the charging document had been forged. She sought rectification of the land charges register by removal of the entries relating to the bank's invalid charge on her house. The bank counterclaimed, arguing among other things that it was entitled to an equitable lien over the defendant's house via subrogation. The bank said that after the parents' house had been sold the sale proceeds had been paid into the client account operated by the solicitors acting for both the parents and the bank and had been held by the solicitors on trust for them both. The solicitors had been instructed to pay the money to the vendor of the daughter's house only once a valid third-party charge over the defendant's house was put in place. Hence they had committed a breach of trust when they had paid the money to the vendor although no valid charge had been obtained. The court agreed with this analysis and awarded the remedy, the majority holding that the defendant had been unjustly enriched at the bank's expense. **15–132**

---

157 [1926] A.C. 788 at 798, citing *Parker v McKenna* (1874) L.R. 10 Ch. 96. See too *Re Patten* (1883) 52 L.J. (Ch.) 787; *Power v Banks* [1901] 2 Ch. 487 at 496; *Re Jenkins and HE Randall and Co's Contract* [1903] 2 Ch. 362.

158 *Re Biss, (Deceased)* [1903] 2 Ch. 40. For discussion of the accounting process, see paras 13–111 to 13–122.

159 [2015] UKSC 66; [2016] A.C. 176.

B. Justifying Proprietary Claims

15–133 It is easier to describe the types of proprietary claim which the beneficiaries can bring following a breach of trust than to explain why the beneficiaries are entitled to bring such claims. One justification that has strong judicial support, having been given in many cases as well as academic commentaries, depends on the beneficiary's "equitable proprietary interest", which is also sometimes described as the beneficiary's "equitable" or "beneficial" "title" or "ownership".[160] On this view, the express trust confers on the beneficiary the equitable analogue or parallel to title to at law; just as an owner of property might have remedies available to vindicate ownership, so too might a beneficiary have equitable remedies available to vindicate equitable ownership. This view is evident in Lord Millett's judgement in *Foskett v Mckeown*, excerpted above,[161] and many other cases that essentially treat the beneficiary as the "true"[162] or "real"[163] "owner" of the subject property and can assert that ownership against the third-party recipient.

15–134 Despite the prevalence and strength of support for this justification, it has some problems. First, B is not the "real" or "true" owner of the trust property: the trustee is. For the reasons discussed in Chapter 12,[164] it is contested whether B should be understood as having a distinct proprietary right or title, equitable or otherwise, and this makes reliance on the "proprietary" character of B's interest less convincing.

15–135 Second, is that proprietary claims can be brought by parties who are not "equitable owners" of trust property, such as discretionary objects or the Attorney General, Charity Commission or an "interested party" in relation to a charitable trust, as discussed in Chapter 3.[165] In the event of a trustee's unauthorised transfer, they all have a claim against a third-party recipient of the original or traceable substitute to require them to transfer that property to the trustee (or [possibly a replacement trustee). As discussed in Chapter 3, the availability of a proprietary claim for recovery of misapplied property to parties without "equitable ownership" is a pattern replicated across other relationships of due administration, such as the deceased estate where the estate beneficiaries and estate creditors also have such a proprietary claim, despite not having "equitable ownership".

15–136 Third, is that this justification entails a circular argument. We saw in Chapter 12[166] that while "property" can have different meanings across different contexts, the necessary feature permitting a beneficiary's right to be characterised as "proprietary" is that it involves a "right to exclude" or, more precisely, that it imposes a prima facie duty of non-interference on third parties. In other words, the necessary feature permitting the proprietary description is the proprietary claim against a third party. It is thus logically impossible for the proprietary nature of B's entitlement(s) under a trust to justify her proprietary claim against a third party. To justify B's proprietary claim on B's "equitable ownership" or "proprietary interest" is circuitous logic[167] because the premise for the argument—the proprietary characterisation of B's interest, assumes the conclusion—the availability of the proprietary claim.[168]

---

160 In addition to the cases cited below see also *Re Diplock* [1948] Ch. 465 at 522; *Boscawen v Bajwa* [1996] 1 W.L.R. 328 at 334; R. Grantham and C. Rickett, "Property Rights as a Legally Significant Event" (2003) C.L.J. 717, 728–34; G. Virgo, *The Principles of the Law of Restitution*, 3rd edn (Oxford University Press, 2015), pp.11–18 and 559–565.

161 See paras 15–095 to 15–127.

162 *Agip (Africa) Ltd v Jackson* [1991] Ch. 547 at 566; *Grimaldi v Chameleon Mining NL (No.2)* (2012) 200 F.C.R. 296 at [251].

163 *Shropshire Union Railways and Canal Co v R* (1875) L.R. 7 H.L. 496 at 506.

164 See paras 12–008 to 12–035.

165 See paras 3–163 to 3–185.

166 See paras 12–015 to 12–025.

167 As discussed in: *Colbeam Palmer Ltd v Stock Affiliates Pty Ltd* (1968) 122 C.L.R. 25 at 34; *Yanner v Eaton* (1999) 201 C.L.R. 351 at [19].

168 See further J. Hudson, "Equitable Ownership and Restitution of Misapplied Trust Property" (2017) 11 J. Eq. 245.

Another justification is needed for the proprietary claim, especially when regard is had to the effect on the trustee's creditors as well as the third party recipient who is required to transfer *her title* to the trustee (or possibly a replacement trustee). These disruptions to the *ex ante* legal rules require careful justification, and while it is beyond the scope of this chapter to do this, we will outline some possible approaches. We will start by considering proprietary claims to trust property that subsists in its original form in the hands of the trustee or a third party recipient. We will then examine proprietary claims to the traceable proceeds of trust property. **15–137**

i. Rights in the Trust Property

When a trust is set up, the settlor either declares herself to be trustee of property which she owns, or transfers title to property to others to hold on trust. In either case, the reason why the beneficiaries then acquire an equitable beneficial interest in the trust property is that the settlor intended this to happen and exercised her power as owner of the property to bring the trust into existence. It follows that the new rights created for the beneficiaries when the trust is set up are sourced in consent: the settlor consents to the creation of these new rights which she gifts to the beneficiaries. **15–138**

The trustees' consent is also required for the arrangement to work: a trust will not fail for want of a trustee, but no one is legally compelled to become trustee of an express trust against their wishes.[169] Once the trustees' consent is given, however, they are not allowed to change their minds, and if necessary equity will enforce their agreement to hold the trust property for the beneficiaries by ordering them to perform their duties *in specie*. Suppose, for example, that a trustee improperly takes physical possession of a painting, legal title to which she holds on trust for the beneficiaries. In this case, nothing happens to interrupt the beneficiaries' continuing equitable rights to the painting, and they can enforce these rights (and oblige the trustee to perform her continuing duties) by obtaining a declaration of their equitable beneficial interest and an order for conveyance of the legal title to new trustees if necessary. **15–139**

Suppose, alternatively, that a trustee holds legal title to a painting on trust for the beneficiaries and that in breach of trust she transfers title (along with physical possession) to a third party recipient who is not a bona fide purchaser for value without notice. In this case, again, the beneficiaries can obtain a declaration of their equitable beneficial interest and an order for reconveyance against the recipient. These rights are sourced in the settlor's intention to create an express trust relationship, and in the case of a trust by transfer by the trustee's acceptance of her role. Equity responds to the parties' choices by affording a beneficiary or trustee an entitlement to relief against third party when there is a failure of due administration. The proprietary claim exists as an alternative to asserting a personal claim against the trustee, discussed in Chapter 13.[170] While the trustee's personal accountability for her due administration is central to the express trust, its enforcement will necessarily be dependent upon the trustee's solvency. A claim against a third a party recipient provides a means of repairing a breach of trust and securing its ongoing due administration irrespective of the trustee's solvency, providing the beneficiary is able, via the processes of following and claiming able to locate property to claim. **15–140**

Recall also from Chapter 11,[171] that the proprietary claim is available to a trustee to bring against a co-trustee, former trustee or third-party recipient. Even where the trustee is personally responsible for the unauthorised transfer, she will be able to choose to pursue a claim against a third party recipient, **15–141**

---

169 See paras 4–023 to 4–028.
170 See paras 13–009 to 13–017.
171 See paras 11–015 to 11–019.

the successful pursuit of which will discharge her personal obligation to reinstate the trust estate. The proprietary claim, again, is facilitating and supporting the trustee's due administration even to the point of absolving her own personal liability.

15–142 Proprietary claims are responding to a particular vulnerability of the express trust relationship, which inheres in equity's meta law or secondary operation. As discussed in Chapters 3 and 11,[172] the rules that control a trustee, such as those requiring a trustee's adherence with the terms and a proper purpose, define a sphere of permission in which the trustee may lawfully hold and use their legal entitlements the subject of trust, and conversely one in which action is unauthorised. What they do not do is change the *ex ante* legal rules that generate the trustee's legal entitlements, and in particular, they do not limit the scope of the trustee's power as titleholder. The express trust relationship does not disable the trustee from exercising their power as titleholder in a way that is contrary to the trust terms. As discussed in Chapter 1, there are good reasons for equity's secondary or meta law operation, which preserves the continuity and stability of the underlying legal rules that generate the legal entitlements held on trust, such as property law and contract law. Nonetheless, the express trust relationship is vulnerable to an unauthorised, yet effective exercise of power, that undermines the express trust relationship and contribution it makes to the legal system overall. One of equity's responses is the recognition of the proprietary claims in this chapter. We can observe that equity responds in a similar way for other relationships of due administration, such as for the deceased estate, and as discussed in Chapter 3, there are proprietary claims available against third parties in response to unauthorised transfers.[173]

ii. Rights in Traceable Substitutes

15–143 Now consider the case where a trustee uses trust property to acquire substitute property in an unauthorised transaction. If she acquires the new property from a bona fide purchaser for value without notice of the beneficiaries' equitable interest in the trust property then they will lose their equitable rights in the trust property because the bona fide purchaser will have a defence to any proprietary claim that they may bring.[174] However, the cases hold that the beneficiaries have an equitable interest in the substitute property.

15–144 In *Foskett v McKeown*,[175] the majority of the House of Lords said that this is because the beneficiaries have a subsisting equitable interest in the substitute property. The majority of the House of Lords in *Foskett* explained the beneficiaries' right in the traceable proceeds of trust property as a right which arose in order to "vindicate their property rights" in the original trust property.[176] Lord Browne-Wilkinson held that:[177]

> The only trusts at issue are the express trusts of the purchasers' trust deed. Under those express trusts the purchasers were entitled to equitable proprietary interests in the original moneys [which they paid over to the trustee]. Like any other equitable proprietary interest, those equitable proprietary interests under the purchasers' trust deed which originally existed in the moneys paid to [the trustee] now exist in any other property which, in law, now represents the original trust assets. . . . If, as a result of tracing, it can be said

[172] See paras 3–157 to 3–158 and 11–024 to 11–077.
[173] See paras 3–186 to 3–192.
[174] See paras 15–164 to 15–168.
[175] [2001] 1 A.C. 102.
[176] [2001] 1 A.C. 102 at 129, per Lord Millett. See too Lord Browne-Wilkinson's comments at 110 and Lord Hoffmann's comments at 115.
[177] [2001] 1 A.C. 102 at 110. Cf. *Taylor v Plumer* (1815) 3 M. & S. 562 at 575. See also Grantham and C. Rickett, "Property Rights: A Legally Significant Event" [2003] C.L.J. 417.

that certain of the policy moneys are what now represent part of the assets subject to the trusts of the purchasers trust deed, then as a matter of English property law the purchasers have an absolute interest in such moneys.

Similarly, Lord Millett held that the beneficiaries have "a continuing beneficial interest not merely in the trust property but in its traceable proceeds also",[178] and in reply to criticism that this reasoning entails the adoption of a fiction, he has written extra-judicially that "'the fiction of persistence' is not a fiction [because the] beneficiaries' interests in the new investment are exactly the same as their interest in the old."[179] **15–145**

One problem with this justification is its reliance upon the beneficiary's "equitable proprietary interest" or "ownership" as a source of justification, the problems with which have been discussed above.[180] Just as "equitable ownership" cannot explain the proprietary claim to the original property, it cannot explain the proprietary claim to traceable substitutes either. **15–146**

It has also been argued[181] that another problem with this justification is that the beneficiaries' right to the substitute property cannot be the same right as the right which they previously had to the trust property. The reason is that a property right is a right to specific property which cannot be detached from the property to which it relates and reattached to some new property. For example, an ownership right in land relates to the land, and so it cannot be the same right as the right to the sale proceeds of the land, even if one right is exchanged for the other. **15–147**

There is problem however, with this criticism of *Foskett,* which is that is makes the same error of relying on the beneficiary's interest as being "property" such that the parameters and limitations of property apply. For the reasons discussed in Chapter 12 it is controversial whether B has a property right at all, and as discussed in this chapter, to the extent we accept B as having an interest that can be described as being "proprietary" in character this flows from, and cannot explain, the availability of the proprietary claim against the original or traceable substitute. **15–148**

Another possible justification for the claim against the traceable substitute is that it gives effect to the intentions of the settlor, and in the case of a trust by transfer, the trustee.[182] To explain this further and identify the reason why the beneficiaries have rights to substitute property acquired through unauthorised transactions, we should start by recalling what happens when a trustee sells trust property using her power of sale to enter an authorised transaction with a buyer, or uses trust money to buy an authorised investment using her powers of investment to enter an authorised transaction with a seller.[183] In such cases, the beneficiaries' interest in the trust property is overreached, and they acquire a new interest in the substitute property, by a process which the beneficiaries cannot afterwards call into question.[184] The source of the beneficiaries' new rights in the substitute property is ultimately the settlor's intention that they should have rights in the original trust property and any new property **15–149**

---

178 *Foskett* at 127.

179 Lord Millett, "Proprietary Restitution" in Degeling and Edelman (eds), *Equity in Commercial Law* (2005), pp.315–316, adding that "wrongfully substituted assets are [not] held on a constructive trust . . . [but] continue to be held on the same trusts throughout. If the claimant was the beneficiary under an express trust, the substituted assets are held on the same express trusts."

180 See paras 15–133 to 15–136.

181 P. Birks, "Tracing, Property, and Unjust Enrichment" (2002) 54 C.L.P. 231, 244–245; R. Chambers, "Tracing and Unjust Enrichment" in J.W. Neyers et al. (eds), *Understanding Unjust Enrichment* (Hart Publishing, 2004), pp.273–274. See too A. Burrows, "Proprietary Restitution: Unmasking Unjust Enrichment" (2001) 117 L.Q.R. 412.

182 See Chambers, "Tracing and Unjust Enrichment" in Neyers et al. (eds), *Understanding Unjust Enrichment* (2004), pp.263, 267.

183 See generally paras 10–031 to 10–056 and 10–082.

184 *Independent Trustee Services Ltd v GP Noble Trustees Ltd* [2012] EWCA Civ 195; [2013] Ch. 91 at [76]–[77], [101]–[106]; *Akers v Samba Financial Group* [2017] UKSC 6; [2017] A.C. 424 at [52].

acquired in exchange for the original property, along with the trustee's intention that the beneficiaries should acquire rights in substitute property when she acquires these through an authorised exercise of her powers, to be held by her on the same terms as those on which she held the original trust property.

15–150 The same analysis can also be used to explain the case where trustees purport to acquire new property for the beneficiaries, but do so in breach of the trust terms. As noted above,[185] the beneficiaries can retrospectively adopt the unauthorised transaction, which looks like an ad hoc variation of the trust, retrospectively giving the beneficiaries rights whose source, again, is the settlor's intention, agreed to by the trustee, to create such rights in their favour.

15–151 What of the case where a trustee misappropriates trust property and uses it to acquire new property for herself? Here one can also say that when the trustee first takes office she agrees with the settlor that she will hold whatever traceable proceeds of trust funds come into her hands for the beneficiaries, and that the beneficiaries' equitable proprietary right to these therefore responds to the trustee's intention that the beneficiaries should have them. Obviously it is tempting to say of this situation that the trustee does not actually intend the beneficiaries to acquire an interest in the new property, as she actually intends to take them for herself. However, it is not the trustee's current intention, but her original intention at the time of taking office, which is the source of the beneficiaries' proprietary right. Equity will not allow the trustee to go back on her word, and will, in effect, specifically enforce her promise to act for the beneficiaries.

15–152 Finally, we come to the case where the traceable proceeds of misdirected trust assets are in the hands of third party recipients. Here, the recipients have not previously agreed to hold the new assets for the beneficiaries, and the beneficiaries' right to them could therefore be explained either on the basis that the recipient commits a wrong (analogous to conversion at common law) when she interferes with the beneficiaries' rights in the original trust property, or else that she is unjustly enriched at the beneficiaries' expense when trust assets are used to acquire new assets for the benefit of the recipient.[186]

15–153 In *Foskett*, Lord Millett denied that beneficiaries can claim the traceable proceeds of trust property in the hands of third parties on the ground of unjust enrichment.[187] However, his Lordship's reasons for saying this do not stand up to scrutiny. They depend on the premise that the law of property and the law of unjust enrichment cannot both be in issue in a single claim. This entails a categorical error, since property and unjust enrichment are not categories that can be opposed: the first is a type of right, the second is a source of rights.[188] Moreover, his Lordship purports to analyse claims to traceable proceeds in the hands of third parties in the same way that he analyses claims to traceable proceeds in the hands of trustees. Yet for the reasons we have explained, the two types of claim are different, since the trustees have previously agreed to hold the proceeds for the beneficiaries while the third parties have not.

15–154 Alternatively, a justification for the claim to traceable substitutes held by a third party can be sourced in equity's commitment to the parties' choices to create an express trust, the inherent vulnerability of which entails the concomitant commitment to securing the trustee's due administration and responding to unauthorised exercises of power. This idea has been introduced above[189] as a justification for the claim to the original trust property. It applies mutatis mutandis to the claim to the traceable

185 See para.15–078.
186 P. Birks, "Property and Unjust Enrichment: Categorical Truths" [1997] N.Z.L.R. 623, 661.
187 [2001] 1 A.C. 102 at 127.
188 P. Birks, *Unjust Enrichment*, 2nd edn (Oxford University Press, 2005), pp.32–38.
189 See paras 15–138 to 15–142.

substitute on the basis that the extension of the claim to the substitute(s) increases the likelihood of a successful claim being made, reinstatement of the trust fund and its ongoing due administration. A similar argument has been made by Jordan English and Mohammud Jaamae Hafeez-Baig,[190] who argue that rights arising through tracing are a means of securing next-best compliance with the primary obligation of the trustee to hold the initial right on trust. If the proprietary claim was not extended to traceable substitutes, then in effect, some trusts would have no protection in the form of the proprietary claim against third parties owing to the nature of the legal entitlements held on trust.

Take the common example of an express trust of a bank account: rarely will it be that the trustee transfers their chose in action against the bank to a third party such that it could be followed by a beneficiary. The usual pattern is that the trustee exercises one of their powers as the account holder to make an interbank transfer to a third party, and which necessarily means that any proprietary claim will be to the traceable substitute of the original trust property, the trustee's chose in action against the bank. If the proprietary claim were not possible against traceable substitutes, then trusts of bank accounts would be protected to a far lesser extent than trusts of other legal entitlements. On this view, the extension of the proprietary claim to traceable substitutes is not the necessary outcome of the proprietary character of B's interest. It rather reflects a policy choice made to secure the due administration of an express trust. **15–155**

In support of this justification, we can also observe that proprietary claims in relation to other relationships of due administration are also extended in the same way to traceable substitutes, as is discussed by Charles Mitchell in the following excerpt. **15–156**

C. Mitchell, "*Commissioner of Stamp Duties (Queensland) v Livingston* (1964): Rights of Estate Beneficiaries and Trust Beneficiaries Compared"

in B. Sloan (ed.) *Landmark Cases in Succession Law* (Hart Publishing, 2019) pp.278–282

. . . In *Livingston*, Viscount Radcliffe denied that the question whether a residuary legatee has a beneficial interest in an unadministered estate can be answered by "referring to those cases in Equity Courts in which a creditor or a pecuniary or residuary legatee has been allowed to follow and recover assets which have been improperly abstracted from an estate".[191] He did not identify any relevant cases, but the proposition that legatees can do this is supported by *Hill v Simpson*,[192] where an executor owed a debt to his bankers and used stock which formed part of the estate to pay off the debt. The bankers knew that the executor was acting in that capacity, and although he was also the residuary legatee, the specific legatees were able to recover the stock from the bank. There are also many cases which say that estate creditors can reclaim misapplied assets from third party recipients . . . **15–157**

The question therefore arises whether there is any other way to explain the rights which estate beneficiaries and creditors have to make claims in specie against third party recipients of misdirected estate assets. Viscount Radcliffe evidently thought that although they can do this, they cannot do it with a view to taking the recovered property for themselves but can only do it on behalf of everyone with an interest in the proper administration of the estate. A possible difficulty with this is that one would have thought that it was therefore a job for the personal representatives – and, indeed, that they would owe a duty – to pursue third parties and recover the assets. *Brooksbank v Smith*[193] shows us that they can: the executors there brought a proprietary claim against the recipient of funds paid out of the estate under a mistake of fact, and they **15–158**

---

[190] M.J. Hafeez-Baig and J. English, *The Law of Tracing* (Federation Press, 2021), paras [2.44]-[2.51], referring to: McFarlane and Stevens, "What's Special About Equity" in D. Klimchuk, I. Samet, and H.E. Smith, *Philosophical Foundations of the Law of Equity* (Oxford University Press, 2020), book 191, 204 and Agnew and McFarlane, "The Paradox of the Eq Prop Claim" (2019) *Modern Studies in Property Law*, Vol.10, 303, 307.

[191] *Livingston* at 713–714.

[192] (1802) 7 Ves Jun 152.

[193] (1836) 2 Y & C Ex 58.

would have succeeded but for the fact that their claim was out of time. However, it does not follow from the fact that personal representatives can and must sue third parties to reverse wrongful transfers that the legatees and next of kin cannot also do this, and circumstances can be imagined where it is desirable to let them: for example, where the personal representative has become insolvent or unreasonably refuses to act, or where she colluded with the third party and cannot now be relied upon to bring proceedings.

15–159 In fact, there are cases where legatees and next of kin have been allowed to do this for precisely these reasons. . . . It is important to understand, however, that in cases of this kind the estate beneficiaries do not sue in their own right: instead, they bring 'derivative proceedings' which entail 'stepping into the shoes' of the personal representative and bringing the claim that she would have brought if she had initiated the proceedings herself. ...

15–160 Looking across to trusts law, we find an identical set of rules which say that trust beneficiaries can bring derivative proceedings on behalf of all those interested in the trust fund ...

15–161 It follows that in cases where trustees have improperly transferred trust property to third parties it should sometimes be possible for the beneficiaries to bring derivative proceedings against the recipients with a view to obtaining an order that the misapplied property must be restored to the trust fund. Such proceedings would be materially identical to derivative proceedings brought by estate beneficiaries to recover misapplied estate assets, suggesting that we do not need to explain the right of trust beneficiaries to bring such actions by pointing to their beneficial ownership of the trust property. ... we can argue instead that they have the right to do this as an incident of their rights to enforce compliance with the trust terms.

15–162 Having said this, however, we also know at least some trust beneficiaries have a right to recover misapplied trust assets and their traceable proceeds not by bringing derivative proceedings on behalf of everyone interested in the trust fund, but by bringing an action on their own behalf, and that their right to do this follows from the fact that they had an equitable 'beneficial interest' in the original assets. ...

[After referring to the justification given in *Foskett* discussed above,[194] Mitchell goes on to state:] It should be recalled, however, that *Foskett* was a claim by the beneficiaries of a fixed trust to recover the traceable proceeds of trust property, and the question arises whether the beneficiaries of a discretionary trust are given the same rights for the same reason.

15–163 The problem with this, of course, is that the beneficiary of a discretionary trust only has the hope of a distribution following the exercise of a discretionary distributive power in her favour, and until then she has no specific right to any part of the fund or even to a share in the whole fund. Several cases have held for this reason that individual discretionary trust beneficiaries (unlike fixed trust beneficiaries) have no proprietary 'interest' in the trust assets for the purposes of tax legislation where this language has been used.[195] Since these cases turned on points of statutory construction, however, it can be said that they establish no general principle; and it can be argued that even if individual beneficiaries of discretionary trusts lack a beneficial interest in the trust property, all the beneficiaries collectively are nevertheless its owners in equity. In turn, this might form the basis of an argument that, at least collectively, their position is sufficiently analogous to that of a fixed trust beneficiary for the *Foskett* reasoning to apply to them as well. This seems rather strained, however, and in this context at least it seems more plausible to say that the position of a discretionary trust beneficiary more closely resembles that of an estate beneficiary during administration – suggesting that she should only have the right to bring derivative proceedings. ...

C. The Bona Fide Purchase Defence

15–164 The law generally holds that no one can pass a better title to property to another person than the title she possesses. Exceptionally, however, a bona fide purchaser for value of legal title to property can take free of any prior equitable interest in the property, provided that she had no notice of this equitable interest. This rule was largely settled during the Chancellorship of Lord Nottingham, in the late seventeenth century.[196]

---

194 See paras 15–133 to 15–136.

195 *Gartside* at 617. ...

196 See, generally, "Introduction" in D.E.C. Yale (ed), *Lord Nottingham's Chancery Cases* (Vol.II) (Selden Society, 1961), Vol.79. On the origins and development of the rule see also D. Fox, "Purchase for Value Without Notice" in P.S. Davies et al (eds), *Defences in Equity* (2018).

The burden of proof lies on the defendant to establish the provision of value, good faith, and lack of notice.[197] The question whether she acted in good faith is separate from the question whether she had notice,[198] but there are no clear examples of these two questions operating independently. Defendants must show not only that they had no actual notice but also that they had no constructive notice of the beneficiaries' interest.[199] **15–165**

The doctrine of constructive notice was explained by Lord Browne-Wilkinson as follows:[200] **15–166**

> if the party asserting that he takes free of the earlier rights of another knows of certain facts which put him on inquiry as to the possible existence of the rights of that other and he fails to make such inquiry or take such other steps as are reasonable to verify whether such earlier right does or does not exist, he will have constructive notice of the earlier right and take subject to it.

In *Crédit Agricole Corp and Investment Bank v Papadimitriou* Lord Clarke added that:[201] **15–167**

> [a] bank's knowledge of facts indicating the mere possibility of a third party having a proprietary right in funds received by the bank would not be enough to put the bank on inquiry but, on the other hand, it is not necessary for the bank to conclude that it probably had such a right. The test is somewhere in between. It may be formulated in this way. The bank must make inquiries if there is a serious possibility of a third party having such a right or, put in another way, if the facts known to the bank would give a reasonable banker in the position of the particular banker serious cause to question the propriety of the transaction.

Defendants must also show that they have given value,[202] but no enquiry is normally made into the adequacy of the consideration provided.[203] For the purposes of the defence the relevant value must have passed under a valid contract between the defendant and the party from whom she received the relevant property. Mere factual exchanges do not suffice. So, in *Banque Belge pour l'Etranger v Hambrouck*[204] the Court of Appeal held that the defence was not available to a woman who had received misappropriated money in exchange for cohabiting with her lover as this constituted an immoral consideration that was not recognised by law. The same point arose in *Independent Trustee Services Ltd v GP Noble Trustees Ltd*,[205] where misappropriated trust money was paid under a consent order that was later set aside. The order therefore fell to be treated as though it had never had any legal effect and so it could not be said that discharging the order counted as consideration given in exchange for the trust money. **15–168**

---

197 *Pilcher v Rawlins* (1873) L.R. 7 Ch. App. 259 at 268–269. *Attorney General v Biphosphated Guano Co* (1879) 11 Ch. D. 327; *Re Nisbet and Potts' Contract* [1906] 1 Ch. 386 at 404, 409 and 410; *GL Baker v Medway Supplies Ltd* [1958] 1 W.L.R. 1217 at 1220; *Barclays Bank Plc v Boulter* [1998] 1 W.L.R. 1 at 8; *Credit Agricole Corp and Investment Bank v Papadimitriou* [2015] UKPC 13; [2015] 1 W.L.R. 4265 at [21].

198 *Midland Bank Ltd v Green* [1981] A.C. 513 at 528.

199 *Pilcher v Rawlins* (1872) L.R. 7 Ch. App. 259; *Cave v Cave* (1880) 15 Ch. D. 639; *Northern Counties of England Fire Insurance Co v Whipp* (1884) 26 Ch. D. 482 at 495–496; *Earl of Sheffield v London Joint Stock Bank Ltd* (1888) 13 App. Cas. 333; *Thomson v Clydesdale Bank Ltd* [1893] A.C. 282; *Carl Zeiss Stiftung v Herbert Smith & Co (No.2)* [1969] 2 Ch. 276; *Kingsnorth Finance Co Ltd v Tizard* [1986] 1 W.L.R. 783. Note that the doctrine of notice now has only a very limited role to play in registered conveyancing.

200 *Barclays Bank Plc v O'Brien* [1994] 1 A.C. 180 at 195–196.

201 [2015] UKPC 13; [2015] 1 W.L.R. 4265 at [20], also reviewing Lord Neuberger MR's discussion of the same topic in *Sinclair Investments (UK) Ltd v Versailles Trade Finance Ltd (in admin)* [2011] EWCA Civ 347; [2012] Ch. 453 at [97]–[112]. Further see *Serious Fraud Office v Litigation Capital Ltd* [2021] EWHC 1272 (Comm) at [145]–[147].

202 The rule does not protect volunteers: *Mansell v Mansell* (1732) 2 P. Wms 678; *Re Strachan* (1876) 4 Ch. D. 123; *Banque Belge pour l'Etranger v Hambrouck* [1921] 1 K.B. 321; *Wu Koon Tai v Wu Yau Loi* [1997] A.C. 179 at 184 and 189–190.

203 *Basset v Nosworthy* (1673) Rep. temp. Finch 102; *Midland Bank Ltd v Green* [1981] A.C. 513.

204 [1921] 1 K.B. 321 at 326 and 329.

205 [2012] EWCA Civ 195; [2013] Ch. 91.

Questions

1. Is the following approach sensible for a claimant beneficiary where her trustees have misdirected trust funds?
   (a) Go for a proprietary claim to trust assets or their traceable proceeds, if possible.
   (b) Go for personal liability: (i) of the trustees for breach of trust; (ii) of any third party who has dishonestly assisted in a breach of trust and is therefore personally liable to the same extent as the trustee or fiduciary whose breach she has assisted; (iii) of any third party who has beneficially received the trust property but has disposed of it after her conscience was affected that she had improperly received the property; or (iv) of any third party who has beneficially received the trust property and who has disposed of it, on the basis that her knowledge or ignorance of its improper provenance is irrelevant because she is strictly liable to repay the value received in unjust enrichment unless she can establish a change of position defence.
2. Theo is the sole trustee of a trust for Baz. Theo enters a contract to buy a vintage car under which he pays the car dealer £40,000 and promises to pay him the £20,000 balance of the purchase price in one year's time. A year later, Theo decides not to make this payment out of his personal resources and instead transfers £20,000 to the car dealer's bank account from the Baz Trust Account, which he maintains at Caring Bank Plc. The car has now doubled in value. At the same time Theo transfers another £5,000 out of the trust account into his personal account with the bank, bringing the balance in that account from £5,000 up to £10,000. He then takes £5,000 out of his current account and uses it to buy shares which have now doubled in value. Finally he transfers another £5,000 out of the trust account into his girlfriend Gigi's personal account. Innocently believing the money to be a legitimate birthday gift, Gigi spends it all. Theo makes all three transfers from the trust account with the help of the bank manager Roxy, whom he tells untruthfully that the purpose of the transfers is to evade tax. Roxy is happy to assist him as she believes that paying tax is morally wrong because the Government spends some of it on nuclear weapons. **Advise Baz.**

PART V

TRUSTS IMPOSED BY LAW

16

RESULTING TRUSTS

1. Introduction

A. Trusts Imposed by Law

It is possible to categorise trusts according to the reason for which a particular trust arises.[1] An express trust arises where a party (the settlor) has successfully exercised her power to set up a trust, either by declaring that she holds property on trust, or by transferring property to trustees to hold on trust. All other trusts are imposed by law. If we put statutory trusts to one side, there are only two types of trust imposed by law: resulting trusts and constructive trusts.[2] We examine resulting trusts in this chapter, and we will examine constructive trusts in Chapter 17. **16–001**

When examining trusts imposed by law, we have to confront the question of justification. Once it is accepted that a holder of property has, in general, a power to set up a trust of that property,[3] the existence of an express trust can be justified simply by pointing to the settlor's successful exercise of that power.[4] In contrast, if the law imposes a trust, we need to ask two questions: first, why is it that the defendant has come under a duty to the claimant; and secondly, even if the imposition of that duty can be justified, why has a trust been imposed? As we saw in Chapter 4, the existence of a trust has significant consequences, not only for the beneficiary and the trustee, but also for third parties, such as creditors of the trustee. **16–002**

For example, in *Chase Manhattan Bank NA v Israel-British Bank (London) Ltd*,[5] the claimant bank had been instructed to pay (just over) $2 million to the defendant. By mistake, it made that payment twice. Goulding J found that the second payment was held by the defendant on trust for the claimant. The trust was clearly not an express trust, as neither party had attempted to exercise any power to set up a trust. The existence of the trust had important consequences for the creditors of the defendant, which was insolvent. It meant that those creditors had no access to the second payment: as that right was subject to a trust, the claimant's right to it was protected in the defendant's insolvency. **16–003**

1 See para.4–014. For a useful discussion of different possible approaches to classifying trusts, see N. McBride, "On the Classification of Trusts" in P. Birks and F. Rose (eds), *Restitution and Equity, Volume 1: Resulting Trusts and Equitable Compensation* (Informa, 2000).

2 See para.4–014 to 4-019.

3 As we noted at para.4–029, "property" here refers to any right held by a party, as it is possible for a settlor (S) to set up a trust of even a purely personal right against another (as occurs where the trust property is a bank account, i.e. S's personal right against S's bank).

4 At a deeper level, the justification for the existence of the power itself can be linked, for example, to the promotion of S's autonomy: see e.g. S. Agnew and S. Douglas, "Self-Declarations of Trust" (2019) 135 L.Q.R. 67; H. Dagan and I. Samet, "Express Trust: The Dark Horse of the Liberal Property Regime" in S. Degeling et al (eds), *Philosophical Foundations of the Law of Express Trusts* (Oxford University Press forthcoming).

5 [1981] Ch. 105.

16-004 When considering such a case, we have to ask the two questions set out above: why did the defendant come under a duty to the claimant; and why was a trust imposed? As to the first, it may be said that, as a recipient of a mistaken payment, the defendant would be unjustly enriched at the claimant's expense if it were not under a duty to make restitution of the value of the payment to the claimant.[6] As to the second, the question is why the defendant, rather than simply owing a personal obligation to make restitution to the claimant, held the second payment on trust for the claimant. Different explanations have been suggested for the trust[7]; it has also been argued that there is no need for a trust, and that the court should simply have found that the claimant had nothing more than a personal right to repayment of the value of the mistaken payment, with the result that it had no special protection in the defendant's insolvency.[8] This shows that when considering trusts imposed by law, we must be alert to the question of justification.[9]

16-005 When considering the justification of resulting and constructive trusts, we also need to be alert to the fact that some trusts commonly referred to as "resulting" or "constructive" may, on closer inspection, turn out to have been misclassified. That will be the case if a trust can be shown to have arisen as a result of an actual or presumed exercise by a party of a power to set up a trust.[10] The terms resulting and constructive should be applied only to trusts that arise by operation of law, i.e. for some reason other than a settlor's successful exercise of her power to set up a trust. Whilst it is important to be aware of this argument, it is clear, nonetheless, that many trusts currently classified as resulting or as constructive *cannot* be explained as express trusts: the trust recognised in the *Chase Manhattan* case, for example, is clearly not an express trust.

16-006 It is also important to note that, even if a trust is indeed imposed by law, this does not mean that the parties' intentions can have *no* role to play in its justification.[11] The distinction between express trusts and those imposed by law depends on the fact that in the former case, a party has successfully exercised her power to set up a trust. This does not preclude a party's intention to set up a trust as being *one* of the factors that may lead to the imposition of a resulting or constructive trust.[12]

---

6 See, e.g. *Barclays Bank Ltd v WJ Simms Son & Cooke (Southern) Ltd* [1980] Q.B. 677 at 695; *Kleinwort Benson Ltd v Lincoln CC* [1999] 2 A.C. 349.

7 See, e.g. *Westdeutsche Landesbank Girozentrale v Islington LBC* [1996] A.C. 669 at 715 per Lord Browne-Wilkinson: "Although the mere receipt of the moneys, in ignorance of the mistake, gives rise to no trust, the retention of the moneys after the recipient bank learned of the mistake may well have given rise to a constructive trust". This view focuses on the defendant's knowledge of the claimant's mistake: see too B. McFarlane, "Trusts and Knowledge: Lessons from Australia" in J. Glister and P. Ridge (eds), *Fault Lines in Equity* (Hart Publishing, 2012). For a different explanation, regarding the trust as a resulting trust, and arising independently of any knowledge by the defendant of the claimant's mistake, see, e.g. R. Chambers, *Resulting Trusts* (Oxford University Press, 1997), pp.125–135.

8 This argument has been made, e.g. in W. Swadling, "A New Role for Resulting Trusts" (1996) 16 L.S. 110 and W. Swadling, "Unjust Enrichment: Value, Rights, and Trusts" (2021) 137 L.Q.R. 56.

9 See, e.g. *Westdeutsche Landesbank Girozentrale v Islington LBC* [1996] A.C. 669 at [684] where Lord Goff, in rejecting the claim of a resulting trust of money paid by the claimant to the defendant under an ultra vires contract, asked "why should the plaintiff bank be given the additional benefits which flow from a proprietary claim, for example the benefit of achieving priority in the event of the defendant's insolvency? After all, it has entered into a commercial transaction, and so taken the risk of the defendant's insolvency, just like the defendant's other creditors who have contracted with it, not to mention other creditors to whom the defendant may be liable to pay damages in tort." For further consideration of this question, see A. Burrows, "Proprietary Restitution: Unmasking Unjust Enrichment" (2001) 117 L.Q.R. 412.

10 See, e.g. W. Swadling, "Explaining Resulting Trusts" (2008) 124 L.Q.R. 72, making that argument in relation to so-called presumed resulting trusts; and W. Swadling, "The Nature of the Trust in *Rochefoucauld v Boustead*" in C. Mitchell (ed.), *Constructive and Resulting Trusts* (Hart Publishing, 2010), making that argument in relation to the type of trust (often said to be constructive) in *Rochefoucauld*.

11 As noted by P. Birks, *An Introduction to the Law of Restitution*, rev edn (Clarendon Press, 1989), p.65, there is "a fine but important distinction between intent conceived as creative of rights, as in an express trust or contract, and intent conceived as a fact which, along with others, calls for the creation of rights by operation of law."

12 See, e.g. paras 16–170 to 16–176 and 17–231 to 17–232. This important point is emphasised by R. Chambers, "Constructive Trusts in Canada" (1999) 37 *Alberta Law Review* 173 (reproduced in (2001) 15 Tru. L.I. 214 and (2002) 16 Tru. L.I. 2).

A final point is that resulting and constructive trusts play an important role in the operation of express trusts, and in protecting beneficiaries of such express trusts.[13] For example, a key feature of a beneficiary's right under a trust is that it is capable of binding a third party who acquires the trust property, if the trustees had no authority under the terms of the trust to make the transfer to the third party. In such a case, it is clear that the third party is not, in general, subject to all the terms of the original trust.[14] As a result, although the point is controversial, it can be argued that the third party is bound not by the original express trust, but rather by a new trust, imposed by law. Indeed, in *Independent Trustee Services Ltd v GP Noble Trustees Ltd*, Lloyd LJ described the trust binding the third party as constructive, stating that "[s]ince the trust arises from the asset having been extracted, in breach of trust, from a fund held on express trusts, it seems correct to characterise the trust as a constructive trust, rather than a resulting trust."[15] **16–007**

B. The Structure of this Chapter

There is a well-established group of trusts known as resulting trusts. In *Westdeutsche Landesbank Girozentrale v Islington LBC*, Lord Browne-Wilkinson defined them by reference to the circumstances in which they arise. **16–008**

Westdeutsche Landesbank Girozentrale v Islington LBC

House of Lords [1996] A.C. 669 at 705–706

LORD BROWNE-WILKINSON: Under existing law a resulting trust arises in two sets of circumstances: **16–009**

(A) Where A makes a voluntary payment to B or pays (wholly or in part) for the purchase of property which is vested either in B alone or in the joint names of A and B, there is a presumption that A did not intend to make a gift to B: the money or property is held on trust for A (if he is the sole provider of the money) or in the case of a joint purchase by A and B in shares proportionate to their contributions. It is important to stress that this is only a presumption, which presumption is easily rebutted either by the counter-presumption of advancement or by direct evidence of A's intention to make an outright transfer.[16]

(B) Where A transfers property to B on express trusts, but the trusts declared do not exhaust the whole beneficial interest.[17]

In this chapter, resulting trusts arising in the first set of circumstances identified by Lord Browne-Wilkinson will be called "Type (A)" resulting trusts, and those arising in the second set of circumstances will be called "Type (B)" resulting trusts. In this chapter, we will also consider another type of trust which is often thought of as a form of resulting trust: the *Quistclose* trust. Whilst it is clear that a trust may arise in each of those three cases, important questions remain. First, why does a trust arise in those three sets of circumstances? Is the reason for which the trust arises the same in each case? Second, can the principle or principles underlying those cases operate more broadly, and so allow for the recognition of a trust in other circumstances? Note that, following Lord Browne-Wilkinson's **16–010**

---

13 See B. McFarlane, "The Centrality of Constructive and Resulting Trusts" in C. Mitchell (ed.), *Constructive and Resulting Trusts* (Hart Publishing, 2010), pp.195–199.

14 As explained by, e.g. R. Nolan, "Equitable Property" (2006) 122 L.Q.R. 232. See further paras 12–010 to 12–015.

15 [2013] Ch. 91 at [80]. See further paras 15–085 to 15–090.

16 *Vandervell v IRC* [1967] 2 A.C. 291 at 312ff.; *Re Vandervell's Trusts (No.2)* [1974] Ch. 269 at 288ff.

17 ibid. and *Barclays Bank Ltd v Quistclose Investments Ltd* [1970] A.C. 567.

example, we will refer to A as the party in whose favour the resulting trust may arise, and B as the party who may be holding rights on the resulting trust.[18]

16–011 In Sections 2 to 4 of this chapter, we will set out the nature and operation of these three types of trust; in Section 5 we will consider if there are any further types of resulting trust; and then in Sections 6 and 7 we will consider the possible justifications for resulting trusts.

C. Terminology

16–012 Why are trusts arising in the two sets of circumstances set out by Lord Browne-Wilkinson in *Westdeutsche* called "resulting trusts"? First, in each case, and in relation to *Quistclose* trusts, the party who ends up as the beneficiary of the resulting trust (A in Lord Browne-Wilkinson's examples) starts off with some property. In the Type (A) case, the beneficiary was, initially, the unencumbered holder of either the eventual trust property, or of money used to purchase that eventual trust property. In the Type (B) case, the beneficiary of the eventual trust was, initially, the unencumbered holder of the eventual trust property. The word "resulting" derives from the Latin *resalire*, meaning "to jump back".

16–013 It should be stressed that this notion of giving "back" is a very loose one,[19] as of course the beneficiary of the resulting trust ends up with an equitable interest, whereas she is likely to have started out with a full legal interest. For example, in a case where A makes a voluntary payment to B, which is then held by B on resulting trust for A, the final position is that A has only an equitable interest in the payment whereas, at the start of the story, A had a full legal interest. It is therefore clear that the right A acquires under a resulting trust is a new right that A never previously held. This can be seen from the fact that the resulting trust depends on B's being under a duty to A in relation to the right held by B, whereas B was previously under no such duty to A. As Lord Browne-Wilkinson pointed out in *Westdeutsche* this means, that in *both* Type (A) and Type (B) cases, the resulting trust confers a *new* equitable interest on A.[20]

16–014 The second reason for the use of the term "resulting trust" is to distinguish such trusts from other types of trust. First, the use of the term assumes that such trusts are not express trusts, and therefore assumes that the trusts do not arise simply as a result of a party having successfully exercised her power to set up a trust. Certainly, even though "jumping back" may be involved, the trust arising where a settlor S successfully sets up a trust by transferring property to a trustee T to hold on trust for S is not conventionally referred to as a "resulting trust". However, as we have said already,[21] this does not mean that the intentions of the parties necessarily have no role to play in resulting trusts. Indeed, in *Westdeutsche* itself, having described the two types of resulting trust, Lord Browne-Wilkinson went on to say that:[22]

> Both types of resulting trust are traditionally regarded as examples of trusts giving effect to the common intention of the parties. A resulting trust is not imposed by law against the intentions of the trustee (as is a constructive trust) but gives effect to his presumed intention.

---

[18] Note this means that, whilst B was used in previous chapters to denote the beneficiary of a trust, in this chapter and the next, B refers instead to the party holding on trust.

[19] The difficulties inherent in the view that the beneficiary of a resulting trust "retains" an equitable interest are discussed at para.16–013. For an in-depth discussion of the notion of "retention" in this context, see J. Mee, "'Automatic Resulting Trusts': Retention, Restitution, or Reposing Trust?" in Mitchell (ed.), *Constructive and Resulting Trusts* (2010).

[20] See too para.16–188.

[21] See para.16–006.

[22] [1996] A.C. 669 at 708.

That analysis is somewhat controversial, and it will be examined in more detail below.[23] But it does at least make it clear that, even if resulting trusts are imposed by law, we will have to consider the role played by the intentions of the parties. 16–015

On the approach taken here to questions of terminology, the field of non-express trusts is therefore divided into resulting trusts and constructive trusts, and in line with Lord Browne-Wilkinson's analysis, resulting trusts are sub-divided into two categories according to the circumstances which give rise to them. As mentioned already, *Quistclose* trusts are sometimes also considered a third category of resulting trusts, for reasons discussed further below. Constructive trusts, in contrast, are imposed in a wider range of situations, and more explanations have been advanced for their imposition: e.g. to perfect the defendant's intention to transfer beneficial ownership to the claimant; to compensate the claimant for the loss that she detrimentally incur in reliance on the defendant's assurances; to strip the defendant of the profits of her wrongdoing; or to reverse the defendant's unjust enrichment at the claimant's expense. These explanations are all reviewed in the next chapter.[24] 16–016

2. Type (A) Resulting Trusts

A. Overview

Lord Millett has written extra-judicially that:[25] 16–017

> Resulting trusts arise in three situations: voluntary payment or transfer; purchase in the name of another; and incomplete disposal of the beneficial interest. The first two have been described as "apparent gifts"; the last as "failing trusts".

The "apparent gift" cases constitute the first type of resulting trust identified by Lord Browne-Wilkinson in *Westdeutsche* and will be referred to here as "Type (A) resulting trusts". These trusts are also often referred to as "presumed resulting trusts". 16–018

In *Vandervell v IRC*,[26] Lord Upjohn attempted a brief statement of the relevant principles: 16–019

> Where A transfers, or directs a trustee for him to transfer, the legal estate in property to B otherwise than for valuable consideration it is a question of the intention of A in making the transfer whether B was to take beneficially or on trust and, if the latter, on what trusts. If, as a matter of construction of the document transferring the legal estate, it is possible to discern A's intentions, that is an end of the matter and no extraneous evidence is admissible to correct and qualify his intentions so ascertained . . . But if, as in this case (a common form share transfer), the document is silent, then there is said to arise a resulting trust in favour of A. But this is only a presumption and is easily rebutted. All the relevant facts and circumstances can be considered in order to ascertain A's intentions with a view to rebutting this presumption.

In a later instalment of the Vandervell saga, *Re Vandervell's Trusts (No.2)*,[27] Megarry J glossed this statement by noting that "Lord Upjohn is obviously assuming that A is not the husband or father of B, and does not stand *in loco parentis* to him, so that no question of presumption of advancement arises." In cases where that presumption of advancement applies, as we discuss below,[28] the 16–020

---

[23] See paras 16–170ff to 16–189ff.
[24] See Chapter 17.
[25] Lord Millett, "Pension Schemes and the Law of Trusts" (2000) 14 Tru L.I. 66, 73.
[26] [1967] 2 A.C. 291 at 312.
[27] [1974] Ch. 269 at 289.
[28] See para.16–035.

presumption is not that a trust was intended, but that A intended a simple gift,[29] and so intended B to hold the transferred right absolutely, free of any trust. Megarry J also referred to Type (A) resulting trusts as "presumed resulting trusts", noting that "the matter is one of intention, with the rebuttable intention of a resulting trust applying if the intention is not made manifest."[30]

16-021 An example of a Type (A) resulting trust is provided by the Supreme Court's decision in *Prest v Petrodel Resources Ltd*.[31] In a wife's claim for ancillary relief, it was found that certain property held by companies controlled by her husband were held by those companies on resulting trust for him. This meant that although there was no justification for "piercing the corporate veil" and regarding the company's property as being held by the husband, his beneficial interest in particular properties held by the company on resulting trust for him meant that the court, in exercising its jurisdiction to order ancillary relief, could make an order that the company should convey those properties to the wife.

16-022 For example, in relation to three flats acquired by a company (PRL) for a nominal consideration of £1, Lord Sumption stated that:

> [s]ince no explanation has been forthcoming for the gratuitous transfer of [such] properties to PRL, there is nothing to rebut the ordinary presumption of equity that PRL was not intended to acquire a beneficial interest in them. The only question is who did hold the beneficial interest.[32]

16-023 As one of the flats had been transferred directly to the company by the husband, "[t]here is therefore an ordinary resulting trust back to the husband".[33] A second flat had been transferred to the company by the husband's brother, but had been paid for by the husband, and

> there is no evidence to rebut the ordinary inference that the husband was the beneficial owner of the property at the time of the transfer to PRL, and that the company held it on a resulting trust for him.[34]

16-024 Each of those two examples from *Prest* represents one of the sub-groups of the Type (A) resulting trust: particular factual situations in which such a trust *may* arise. The first is where A makes a gratuitous transfer of property to B: it extends to cases in which A makes a gratuitous transfer of that right into the joint names of A and B. The second is where B acquires property, but all or part of the money for its acquisition is provided by A; it similarly extends to cases in which the right is jointly acquired by A and B. In such cases, if a resulting trust arises as a result of A's provision of part only of the purchase price, the extent of A's beneficial interest will be proportionate to A's contribution.

B. Presumptions

i. Presumption of Resulting Trust: General Position

16-025 If A makes a gratuitous transfer of property to B, or if A provides all or part of the purchase price of a property acquired by B, a Type (A) resulting trust *may* arise. It must be remembered, though, that in such cases the presumption of a resulting trust may be displaced. Indeed, as Lord Browne-Wilkinson noted in *Westdeutsche*, the presumption may be "easily rebutted" by direct evidence of A's intention

29 See, e.g. *Antoni v Antoni* [2007] UKPC 10 at [20] (Lord Scott).
30 [1974] Ch. 269 at [289].
31 [2013] UKSC 34; [2013] 2 A.C. 415.
32 [2013] 2 A.C. 415 at [49].
33 [2013] UKSC 34; [2013] 2 A.C. 415 at [49].
34 [2013] 2 A.C. 415 at [49].

to make an outright transfer to B.[35] This reflects a more general point about the nature of presumptions, colourfully made by an American judge: "presumptions may be looked on as the bats of the law, flitting in the twilight, but disappearing in the sunshine of actual facts."[36]

One such actual fact dispelling a presumption of resulting trust occurs where A simply makes a gift to B, i.e. transfers a right to B with a donative intent. The finding of a gift is not, however, the only means by which the presumption can be rebutted.[37] In *Westdeutsche* itself, for example, the claimant bank, when making payments to the defendant local authority in the mistaken belief that it had a contractual duty to do so, clearly did not intend to make gift. Nonetheless, as Lord Browne-Wilkinson explained, **16–026**

> any presumption of resulting trust is rebutted since it is demonstrated that the bank paid, and the local authority received, the upfront payment with the intention that the moneys so paid should become the absolute property of the local authority . . . the presumption of resulting trust is rebutted by evidence of any intention inconsistent with such a trust, not only by evidence of an intention to make a gift.[38]

ii. Presumption of Resulting Trust: Voluntary Conveyances of Land

Law of Property Act 1925 s.60

(1) A conveyance of freehold land to any person without words of limitation, or any equivalent expression, shall pass to the grantee the fee simple or other the whole interest which the grantor had power to convey in such land, unless a contrary intention appears in the conveyance . . . **16–027**

(3) In a voluntary conveyance a resulting trust for the grantor shall not be implied merely by reason that the property is not expressed to be conveyed for the use or benefit of the grantee.

Considering this section in *Lohia v Lohia*, HHJ Nicholas Strauss QC, at first instance, stated that:[39] **16–028**

> on a plain reading of s 60, the presumption [of resulting trust] has been abolished [in relation to a voluntary conveyance of land]. It seems to me that s 60(1) establishes a general rule that a conveyance should be construed according to the words it uses, so that it is possible to tell from it who holds the legal and beneficial estate in the land. Consistently with this, s 60(3) provides in effect that a voluntary conveyance means what it says; it is not necessary to use additional words to make it effective. It is likely that by 1925 the suspicion with which gifts of land were formerly viewed, which was at least one of the underlying reasons for the presumption, would no longer have been regarded as material, and the purpose of s 60(3) was accordingly to do away with the presumption of a resulting trust in the cases of voluntary conveyance and to make it necessary for the person seeking to establish a resulting trust to prove it.

It was also found on the facts of *Lohia* that A had in any case intended to make a gift to B, so that, even if a presumption of resulting trust had arisen, it would have been rebutted. On appeal, the Court of Appeal agreed with that finding of fact, and so did not take on what Sir Christopher Slade referred to there as "the knotty question [of] whether the presumption of resulting trust on the voluntary **16–029**

---

35 [1996] A.C. 669 at 708.

36 *Mackowick v Kansas City St J & CB Rwy* 196 Mo. 550 at 571; 94 S.W. 256 at 262 (1906), per Lamm J.

37 See too *Prest v Petrodel Resources Ltd* [2013] UKSC 34; [2013] 2 A.C. 415 at [50], where Lord Sumption noted that the presumption of resulting trust would have been rebutted if there had been evidence that money had been provided to PRL by the husband by way of loan or capital subscription.

38 [1996] AC 669 at 708, citing with approval the analysis of this point by W. Swadling, "A New Role for Resulting Trusts" (1996) 16 L.S. 110 at 133.

39 (2000) 3 I.T.E.L.R. 117 at 129.

conveyance of land survives the enactment of s.60(3)".[40] Mummery LJ similarly said that a court would be "bold" to decide that question "without having heard very extensive argument."[41] Whilst the analysis of HHJ Nicholas Strauss QC drew on powerful academic support,[42] it would be unwise to regard his judgment in *Lohia* as having finally determined the effect of s.60(3). First, in *Prest v Petrodel Resources Ltd*,[43] Lord Sumption, when considering the effect of the conveyances of land set out above,[44] simply did not refer to s.60(3) and instead seemed to make use of the standard presumptions.[45] Second, in *National Crime Agency v Dong*,[46] Chief Master Marsh thought it unlikely that s.60(3) could have been intended to have removed the presumption in such cases, noting that, if there had been such an intention: "it might have been expected that the Act would have said so in terms and it would be even more surprising for the presumption to have been abolished only in relation to land with a saving provision for chattels."[47] In that case, then, as in *Ali v Dinc*,[48] a first instance judge, whilst considering the differing views, "proceeded on the basis that the presumption remains in being despite what has been described as the literal effect of the words in s 60(3)."[49]

16–030 As John Mee has convincingly argued, it is impossible to have a full understanding of the purpose of s.60(3) without first undertaking a detailed historical examination of the position before 1926, and of the "complex relationship between resulting uses and resulting trusts."[50]

16–031 Perhaps the most important practical point is that when A conveys a legal estate in land to B and receives nothing directly in return, a court will simply focus on the available evidence in order to determine if, as was found to be the case in *Lohia*, A intended to make an outright transfer to B (for example by way of gift) or if, as was found to be the case in *Prest*, A intended that the estate would be held on trust for A. Given Lord Browne-Wilkinson's statement that the presumption of resulting trust can be "easily rebutted",[51] it may, therefore, be said that the position in relation to a voluntary conveyance of land is not so different from the case where A buys land that is put into B's name, or where A makes a voluntary conveyance of other property to B.

16–032 As noted in *Ali v Dinc*, the controversy over the technical effect of s.60(3) is "generally avoided since outcomes rarely turn on the issue".[52] In that case, as in *National Crime Agency v Dong*, there was sufficient evidence to allow the court to find that A's intention was that B would hold the legal estate in the land on trust for A.[53] Previously, establishing whether or not the presumption of resulting trust applied could be crucial in the application of the rule forbidding reliance on evidence of an achieved

---

40 [2001] EWCA Civ 1691 at [34].
41 [2001] EWCA Civ 1691 at [24].
42 See, e.g. Chambers, *Resulting Trusts* (1997), pp.18–19.
43 [2013] UKSC 34; [2013] 2 A.C. 415: see, e.g. at [52] per Lord Sumption.
44 See para.16–023.
45 As noted in *Ali v Dinc* [2020] EWHC 3055 (Ch) at [273]. An appeal against the judgment, made only on a procedural point, was dismissed: [2022] EWCA Civ 34.
46 [2017] EWHC 3116 (Ch).
47 [2017] EWHC 3116 (Ch) at [35].
48 [2020] EWHC 3055 (Ch) at [272]–[278].
49 [2017] EWHC 3116 (Ch) at [34].
50 J. Mee, "Resulting Trusts and Voluntary Conveyances of Land" [2012] Conv. 307, 308. See too J. Mee, "Resulting Trusts and Voluntary Conveyances of Land: 1674–1925" (2011) 32 J.L.H. 215. Mee's position is that, prior to 1926, the doctrine of resulting trusts itself (rather than merely the presumption of a resulting trust) did not apply in relation to land, as only a doctrine of resulting uses was applied. As s.60(3) then abolishes the doctrine of resulting uses in the context of land, there is no longer any resulting use or trust doctrine that can avail A, and so A must instead turn to other doctrines, such as that in *Rochefoucauld v Boustead* [1897] 1 Ch. 196 (see paras 17–077 to 17–093) to claim that B holds land on trust for A. It would seem, for example, that the *Rochefoucauld* doctrine is applicable to the facts of *Hodgson v Marks* [1971] Ch. 892.
51 [1996] A.C. 669 at 708.
52 [2020] EWHC 3055 (Ch) at [273].
53 [2020] EWHC 3055 (Ch) at [275].

improper purpose.[54] As will be seen below, however, that rule is no longer applied by the courts, with a different approach taken to determining the effect of illegal or improper purposes.[55]

It may be argued that, whether or not it is justifiable as a matter of statutory interpretation, the view of s.60(3) adopted at first instance in *Lohia*, with its special treatment of voluntary conveyances of land, can be justified as a matter of policy.[56] For example, special formality rules apply to conveyances of land and not to transfers of personal property, increasing the likelihood that a transferor has thought carefully about whether she really wants another person to have the benefit of her legal estate in land and so reducing the need for a rule that she should be presumed not to have intended this. **16–033**

Alternatively, the *Lohia* interpretation of s.60(3) could be seen as useful if it were to become part of a wider judicial move to reject the presumption of resulting trust, whether or not land is involved. In *Lohia*, for example, HHJ Nicholas Strauss QC noted that, by 1925, there was no longer any reason for equity to think it unlikely that A would have intended an outright gratuitous transfer of land to B. It can similarly be argued that there is no longer any reason to presume, in *any* context, that the fact of A's gratuitous transfer of property to B means that A intended to create a trust.[57] Certainly, the apparent weakness of the presumption, coupled with its apparent dispensability in relation to voluntary conveyances of land, prompts the thought that in all Type (A) cases a resulting trust should arise only if A can provide evidence of an intention, known to B, that B was to hold on trust for A.[58] **16–034**

iii. Presumption of Advancement

In *Westdeutsche*, Lord Browne-Wilkinson stated that in a Type (A) resulting trust the presumption of resulting trust can be rebutted "either by the counter-presumption of advancement or by direct evidence of A's intention to make an outright transfer."[59] The presumption of advancement is said to arise in specific factual circumstances where courts have assumed that the more likely default position is that A, rather than intending that B, the gratuitous transferee, is to hold on trust for A, instead intends to make a gift to B.[60] The specific circumstances in which this presumption of advancement applies have, traditionally, been very confined. They consist of cases where A is the father of B, or stands in loco parentis to B,[61] or is the husband of B, or the fiancé of B.[62] The presumption of advancement does not arise where A is merely cohabiting with B,[63] nor where A is the wife of B.[64] The English **16–035**

---

54 For that rule, see Lord Browne-Wilkinson in *Tinsley v Milligan* [1994] 1 A.C. 340 at 370 and 375–376.

55 See *Patel v Mirza* [2016] UKSC 42; [2017] A.C. 467.

56 R. Chambers (2001) 15 Tru. L.I. 26, 29.

57 J. Mee, "Resulting Trusts and Voluntary Conveyances of Land" [2012] Conv. 307, 325: "The presumption of resulting trust in this context is an anachronism which should not be tolerated in the modern law."

58 See para.16–053. for further discussion of this point.

59 [1996] A.C. 669 at 708.

60 See, e.g. *Antoni v Antoni* [2007] UKPC 10 at [20] (Lord Scott).

61 *Hepworth v Hepworth* (1870) L.R. 11 Eq. 10; *Shephard v Cartwright* [1955] A.C. 431; *Re Cameron The Times*, 2 April 1999; *Lavelle v Lavelle* [2004] EWCA Civ 223; [2004] 2 F.C.R. 418 at [14]. For a presumption of advancement to arise on the basis that a transferor is in loco parentis to a transferee, it must be shown that he assumed the duty of a father to make provision for a child: *Bennett v Bennett* (1876) 10 Ch.D. 414 at 477, followed in *Sansom v Gardner* [2009] EWHC 3369 (QB) (where this was not established on the facts).

62 *Tinker v Tinker* [1970] P. 136; *Silver v Silver* [1958] 1 W.L.R. 259; *Moate v Moate* [1948] 2 All E.R. 486 (intended husband: marriage afterwards solemnised); Law Reform (Miscellaneous Provisions) Act 1970 s.2(1); *Mossop v Mossop* [1988] 2 All E.R. 202.

63 *Chapman v Jaume* [2012] EWCA Civ 476; [2012] 2 F.L.R. 830 at [24]; *Stack v Dowden* [2007] UKHL 17; [2007] 2 A.C. 432 at [112]; *Calverley v Green* (1984) 56 A.L.R. 483.

64 *Re Curtis* (1885) 52 L.T. 244; *Mercier v Mercier* [1903] 2 Ch. 98; *Abrahams v Trustee of Property of Abrahams* [2000] W.T.L.R. 593.

cases are divided on the question whether the presumption arises as between a mother and her children,[65] but authorities from elsewhere in the Commonwealth say that it does.[66]

16-036 These distinctions derive from cases which date back several hundred years, and some have ceased to reflect contemporary socio-economic reality and ideas of gender equality. Specifically, there is no longer a good reason to think that fathers but not mothers have a duty to support their children[67] or the financial wherewithal to advance their children in life, nor to think that husbands but not wives have the duty and means to benefit their spouses.

16-037 The outdated nature of the presumption of advancement has not escaped the attention of Parliament, which has enacted legislation to abolish it,[68] although this has not been brought into force and the passing of time, and the swing of the political pendulum, makes it appear ever less likely that this will happen.

Equality Act 2010 s.199

16-038

(1) The presumption of advancement (by which, for example, a husband is presumed to be making a gift to his wife if he transfers property to her, or purchases property in her name) is abolished.
(2) The abolition by subsection (1) of the presumption of advancement does not have effect in relation to—
  (a) anything done before the commencement of this section, or
  (b) anything done pursuant to any obligation incurred before the commencement of this section.

16-039 Even if this section is not brought into force, it would be no surprise if the courts were to redress the present inequality of treatment by doing away with presumptions of advancement between spouses altogether, since the strength of the presumption between husband and wife is now said to be very weak.[69] Moreover, the gender bias inherent in the rules affecting spouses probably contravenes art.5 of the Seventh Protocol to the European Convention of Human Rights, which asserts the equality of spousal rights and responsibilities.[70] Similarly, Lord Neuberger in *Laskar v Laskar* considered the possibility that the presumption of advancement might apply as between a mother and a daughter, but noted that: "it was said as long ago as 1970 to be a relatively weak presumption which can be rebutted on comparatively slight evidence."[71] Any such presumption would be "even weaker where, as

---

65 Yes, at least where she is a widowed mother: *Garrett v Wilkinson* (1848) 2 De G. & Sm. 244 at 246; *Sayre v Hughes* (1886) L.R. 5 Eq. 376; *Re Grimes* [1937] I.R. 470. No: *Re De Visme* (1863) 2 De G.J. & S. 17; *Bennet v Bennet* (1879) 10 Ch.D. 474; *Sekhon v Alissa* [1989] 2 F.L.R. 94.

66 *Re Brownlie* [1990] 3 N.Z.L.R. 243; *Brown v Brown* (1993) 31 N.S.W.L.R. 582 at 591; *Re Dreger Estate* (1994) 97 Manitoba R. (2d) 39; *Nelson v Nelson* (1995) 184 C.L.R. 538; *Pecore v Pecore* [2007] 1 S.C.R. 795 at [32]–[33].

67 The duty to support was regularly relied on in older cases as the rationale for the presumption of advancement, so that, for example, the presumption would not apply if the child were "fully advanced in the father's lifetime" so that the duty to support had already been fully discharged: see *Grey v Grey* (1677) 2 Swans 594 at 600–601; 36 E.R. 742 at 744 per Lord Nottingham. The absence of such a duty on a mother to a child was given in *Bennet v Bennet* (1879) 10 Ch. D. 474 as a reason not to apply the presumption of advancement in such cases. For consideration of this, and other possible rationales for the presumption of advancement, see J. Glister, "The Presumption of Advancement" in Mitchell (ed.), *Constructive and Resulting Trusts* (2010).

68 For discussion of the Equality Act 2010 s.199, see e.g. W. Swadling, "Legislating in Vain" in A. Burrows et al (eds), *Judge and Jurist: Essays in Memory of Lord Rodger of Earlsferry* (Oxford University Press, 2013).

69 *Pettitt v Pettitt* [1970] A.C. 777 at 793; *McGrath v Wallis* [1995] 2 F.L.R. 114 at 155; *Ali v Khan* (2002) 5 I.T.E.L.R. 232 at [30]. In *Bhura v Bhura* [2015] 1 F.L.R. 153, the presumption of advancement between spouses was said to be "on its death-bed" given the passing of s.199 of the Equality Act 2010.

70 Written Answer, *Hansard*, HL Vol.588, col.197 (21 April 1998). Note however that the UK has not yet ratified the Seventh Protocol.

71 [2008] 1 W.L.R. 2695 (CA) at [20], citing Lord Upjohn in *Pettitt v Pettitt* [1970] A.C. 777 at 814.

here, the child was over 18 years of age and managed her own affairs at the time of the transaction."[72] So, even if the presumption were said to apply, it would have been rebutted on the facts of the case, where property was jointly purchased by mother and daughter as "an investment for rental income and capital appreciation",[73] and so a resulting trust arose to reflect the contribution to the purchase price made by the mother.

The legislative solution offered by s.199 is more radical, as it abolishes *all* presumptions of advancement, including that between a father (and possibly a mother) and a child. It should be remembered, however, that, in such circumstances, the particular relationship between A and B will clearly be an important factor to be taken into account by a court in determining whether or not a gratuitous transfer by A was intended to take effect as a trust for A. For example, it has been said that although the question whether the presumption arises between mother and child is uncertain, this is "of little practical importance, since very slight intention is sufficient to establish advancement, there being very little additional motive required beyond the mother/child relationship to induce a mother to make a gift to her child."[74] **16–040**

iv. Presumption of Resulting Trust: Family Homes

Until recently, it was clear that a Type (A) resulting trust might arise in a case where A and B buy a shared family home together but do not make an express written declaration of trust as to their shares.[75] Whether the home was conveyed into the joint names of A and B, or into the names of only one of them, in the absence of clear evidence as to their intentions, and in the absence of any operative presumption of advancement,[76] it would be presumed that a trust was intended under which each party's share would be proportionate to their contributions to the purchase price.[77] So, for example, in the case of a house costing £100,000, if A paid £40,000 and B paid £60,000, A would be entitled to 40% and B to 60%; and the position was the same if A did not pay £40,000 but obtained a £40,000 discount on the market price, as a sitting tenant of the house.[78] **16–041**

However, the relevance of resulting trusts to such cases has diminished as a result of the recognition of the common intention constructive trust of the family home, a concept discussed in Chapter 17.[79] Rather than being used to support a claim under a resulting trust, A's contribution to the purchase price can instead be used as evidence supporting an inference of a common intention to share beneficial ownership of the home; the extent of A's share is then determined by that common intention, and **16–042**

---

72 Note too that in *Pecore v Pecore* [2007] 1 S.C.R. 795 and *Madsen Estate v Saylor* [2007] 1 S.C.R. 838, the Supreme Court of Canada has held that the presumption of advancement should no longer apply to transfers by parents to their adult children. See, e.g. *Pecore* at [36] per Rothstein J: "[I]t is common nowadays for ageing parents to transfer their assets into joint account with their adult children in order to have that child assist them in managing their financial affairs. There should therefore be a rebuttable presumption that the adult child is holding the property in trust for the ageing parent to facilitate the free and efficient management of that parent's affairs."

73 [2008] EWCA Civ 347; [2008] 1 W.L.R. 2695 at [17].

74 *Crown Prosecution Service v Malik* [2003] EWHC 660 (Admin) at [27], per Richards J.

75 An express written declaration of trust signed by the parties is conclusive in the absence of fraud or mistake (*Goodman v Gallant* [1986] Fam. 106) or undue influence (*Humphreys v Humphreys* [2004] EWHC 2201 (Ch); [2005] 1 F.C.R. 712).

76 See paras 16–035 to 16–040.

77 *Pettitt v Pettitt* [1970] A.C. 777 at 814. It has been unclear whether acquisition costs, e.g. legal fees and stamp duty, count as part of the purchase price. *Huntingford v Hobbs* [1993] 1 F.L.R. 736 suggests that they do, but in *Curley v Parkes* [2004] EWCA Civ 1515 at [22], Peter Gibson LJ held otherwise. At [23] he also held that removal costs do not form part of the purchase price either.

78 *Abbey National BS v Cann* (1989) 59 P. & C.R 381; *Springette v Defoe* [1992] 2 F.L.R. 388; *Mckenzie v Mckenzie* [2003] EWHC 601 (Ch) at [81]; *R. (on the application of Kelly) v Hammersmith & Fulham LBC* [2004] EWHC 435 (Admin). See too *Laskar v Laskar* [2008] EWCA Civ 347; [2008] 1 W.L.R. 2695 at [22]–[26].

79 See paras 17–121ff.

in ascertaining the parties' common intention as to A's share, a court can look beyond the relative size of the contributions to the purchase price, and take account of other factors, looking at the parties' whole course of dealing in relation to the property.[80] In *Midland Bank Plc v Cooke*,[81] for example, A's financial contribution amounted to less than 7% of the purchase price, but it allowed for the inference of a common intention, and the court then found that the parties, a married couple, had intended to hold equal beneficial shares of the property.

16–043 The approach taken in cases such as *Midland Bank v Cooke* illustrates the weakness of the presumption of resulting trust: the courts' preference is to ascertain the parties' intentions as to their beneficial shares (even if this involves a process of inference, divination, or even, when considering the extent of a party's share, imputation[82]) rather than to apply the stark mathematics of the resulting trust. Indeed, in *Jones v Kernott*, the Supreme Court confirmed that the effect of the House of Lords' decision in *Stack v Dowden* was to prevent the presumption of resulting trust from operating in cases where a home is bought "in joint names for joint occupation by a married or unmarried couple, where both are responsible for any mortgage".[83] This leaves open the possibility that a Type (A) resulting trust may still be relevant in other domestic cases, for example where the shared home is bought in the name of B alone, or where it is bought by parents and children,[84] or siblings, rather than a couple.

16–044 In *Stack v Dowden*,[85] however, the majority of the court seemed to have in mind a wider prohibition on resulting trusts, with Lady Hale stating, for example, that the courts should generally avoid using resulting trust reasoning as a means of establishing equitable interests in shared homes,[86] because it is too focused on one type of contribution to the parties' relationship, viz. financial contributions, to the exclusion of other types, e.g. home-making, child-care, etc. with the result that it delivers outcomes that are unfair and discriminatory against women who support their partners by staying at home while their partners go out to work. Indeed, speaking for the Privy Council in *Abbott v Abbott*, a case in which legal title to the home was in the name of B alone, Baroness Hale reiterated this point, stating that: "It is now clear that the constructive trust is generally the more appropriate tool of analysis in most matrimonial cases."[87]

16–045 The more limited wording used in *Jones v Kernott* to formulate the bar on resulting trusts may perhaps be seen as a concession to Lord Neuberger's speech in *Stack v Dowden*, where he took a very different approach, albeit one that led, on the facts of the case, to the same outcome. He considered that resulting trusts should not be completely abandoned in the domestic context (not least because defining the scope of such a context is a very difficult exercise),[88] as he believed that they might still have a role to play.[89] In *Laskar v Laskar*,[90] a case in which he subsequently sat as a judge of the Court of Appeal, Lord Neuberger specifically rejected the argument that the only way to establish an equitable interest in a family home is by way of a constructive trust. A mother and daughter had bought a house together as an investment, without intending to live in it. The court used a traditional resulting trust analysis under which the parties' shares were allocated in proportion to their contributions to the

---

80 See *Stack v Dowden* [2012] 1 A.C. 776 at [36] and [61].
81 [1995] 2 F.L.R. 915.
82 See *Stack v Dowden* [2012] 1 A.C. 776 at [69].
83 [2012] 1 A.C. 776 at [25].
84 As in, e.g. *City of London Building Society v Flegg* [1988] A.C. 54.
85 [2007] UKHL 17; [2007] 2 A.C. 432.
86 *Stack* at [60], with the agreement of Lord Hoffmann at [1], Lord Hope at [3], and Lord Walker at [31]. See too *Fowler v Barron* [2008] EWCA Civ 377; [2008] 2 F.L.R. 831 at [30] and [52].
87 [2007] UKPC 53; [2008] 1 F.L.R. 1451 at [4].
88 See too N. Hopkins, "The Relevance of Context in Property Law: A Case for Judicial Restraint?" (2011) L.S. 175.
89 [2007] UKHL 17; [2007] 2 A.C. 432 at [110]ff.
90 [2008] EWCA Civ 347; [2008] 1 W.L.R. 2695.

purchase price, and Lord Neuberger said that "it would not be right to apply the reasoning in *Stack v Dowden* to such a case as this, where the parties primarily purchased the property as an investment for rental income and capital appreciation, even where their relationship is a familial one."[91] It seems, therefore, that there are still some family home cases in which resulting trust reasoning should be used to determine the parties' equitable interests.

It follows that at least in a *Laskar*-type "investment" case, the resulting trust may still be used to govern the allocation of equitable interests in a home.[92] It is however possible to exaggerate the differences between the underlying basis of a Type (A) resulting trust on the one hand and the common intention constructive trust on the other. In *Westdeutsche*, after all, Lord Browne-Wilkinson described the former as "traditionally regarded as examples of trusts giving effect to the common intention of the parties."[93] At a general level, it may be said that in each case the court wishes to uncover the intention of the parties, and in some cases a purely mathematical approach to the quantification of beneficial interests would clearly be at odds with such intentions. This view, put forward in the previous edition of this book, finds support in the Privy Council's analysis in *Marr v Collie*.[94] **16–046**

Marr v Collie

Privy Council [2018] A.C. 631 at [53]–[56], [60]

Terry Marr and Bryant Collie were in a personal relationship with each other between 1991 and 2008. When the relationship ended, there was a dispute as to property acquired during the relationship in their joint names. This included land bought for investment purposes, land intended to be their joint home, a truck and a boat. In general, Marr claimed full beneficial ownership of the property, on the basis that he made virtually all payments associated with their purchase. Collie resisted this claim, pointing out, for example, that he had undertaken extensive work on one of the properties, which had been intended to be their joint home. The first instance judge found that, in relation to all property other than the intended joint home, the presumption of resulting trust applied in favour of Marr, and Collie had not been able to rebut this by showing that Marr had intended gifts when financing the purchases. The Court of Appeal of the Bahamas allowed Collie's appeal in part, finding that, at the time of their purchase, the parties had a common intention to share beneficial ownership of the investment properties. The Privy Council rejected Marr's appeal, but remitted the case to the Bahamas as the courts below had not properly examined the parties' common intentions. The members of the panel included both Lord Neuberger and Lady Hale and the single judgment was delivered by Lord Kerr, who analysed *Stack v Dowden*, *Jones v Kernott* and *Laskar v Laskar*, before coming to the following conclusion. **16–047**

LORD KERR: A clash of presumptions? **16–048**

If what Lady Hale described as a "starting point" (that joint legal ownership should signify joint beneficial ownership) is to be regarded as a presumption, is it in conflict with the presumption of a resulting trust where the parties have contributed unequally to the purchase of property in their joint names? A simplistic answer to that question might be that, if the property is purchased in joint names by parties in a domestic relationship the presumption of joint beneficial ownership applies but if bought in a wholly non-domestic situation it does not. In the latter case, it might be said that the resulting trust presumption obtains.

The Board considers that, save perhaps where there is no evidence from which the parties' intentions can be identified, the answer is not to be provided by the triumph of one presumption over another. In this, as in so many areas of law, context counts for, if not everything, a lot. Context here is set by the parties' common intention – or by the lack of it. If it is the unambiguous mutual wish of the parties, contributing in unequal shares to the purchase of property, that the joint beneficial ownership should reflect their joint **16–049**

---

91 *Laskar* [2008] EWCA Civ 347; [2008] 1 W.L.R. 2695 at [17].

92 See, e.g. *R v Muzafar and Qurban* (unreported 10 June 2014, Leeds County Court): purchase by father of a property put in the names of two of his sons and used as a home for his daughter.

93 [1996] A.C. 669 at 708.

94 [2018] A.C. 631.

legal ownership, then effect should be given to that wish. If, on the other hand, that is not their wish, or if they have not formed any intention as to beneficial ownership but had, for instance, accepted advice that the property be acquired in joint names, without considering or being aware of the possible consequences of that, the resulting trust solution may provide the answer.

16–050 Of course, the initial intention (or lack of it) at the time of purchase may change. This was the reason that the majority in *Stack v Dowden* emphasised that examination of the course of conduct of the parties over the years in which they dealt with the property is relevant. And it is why an intense examination is warranted of why the properties acquired in this case in 2008 were purchased in joint names. By that time, many of the contributions which, according to Mr Marr, he expected Mr Collie to have made, had not materialised. Why did he continue to agree that the properties should be acquired in joint names?

16–051 **The centrality of the question of intention**

In this case, each party was relying on common intention, although they could not agree on what it was. Given the intention of the parties is central to the resolution of the issues in this appeal, has it been addressed sufficiently by the trial judge and/or the Court of Appeal?. . .

16–052 . . .The Board is conscious of the undesirability of prolonging what have already been protracted proceedings. It has concluded, however, that there is no feasible alternative to this course. No proper examination of the actual intentions of the parties has taken place . . . the Board considers that such an examination is unavoidable if a proper determination is to be made of the respective beneficial interests of the parties in respect of the investment properties, the truck and the boat.

16–053 It would be a mistake, in our view, to regard the law in this area as involving a clash between the resulting trust and a trust based instead on the parties' common intention. The point, emphasised by the reasoning and result in *Marr v Collie*, is that establishing the parties' common intention is key, however the trust is labelled.[95] This helps to avoid any arbitrary distinction between "domestic" and "non-domestic" cases: whilst the context is of course crucial when ascertaining the parties' intentions, the underlying principles to be applied are the same. Indeed, it seems that, in Lord Kerr's analysis, the idea of a resulting trust is used not to invoke a different set of rules for ascertaining the parties' rights, but rather as a label for a particular type of outcome that may result after having searched for the parties' common intention. On this view, the "resulting trust" label is reserved for cases either where the court's best judgment of that common intention is that the parties intended their rights under a trust of the property to correspond to the extent of their financial contributions to its acquisition, or where that solution is adopted where the parties had no common intention as to the extent of their beneficial shares.[96] As Lord Kerr notes, one situation in which this "resulting trust solution may provide the answer" is where the parties have "not formed any intention as to beneficial ownership".[97] However, given the procedural resources available to inquire into such factual questions, and the willingness of the courts to infer such intentions, such cases must be quite rare. Moreover, as John Mee has pointed out,[98] the mere fact that the extent of the parties' beneficial interests is determined by their financial contributions does not make the trust a resulting one:[99] it is

---

95 See, e.g. *Gallarotti v Sebastianelli* [2012] EWCA Civ 865; [2012] 2 F.L.R. 1231 where, as in *Stack v Dowden* [2007] 2 A.C. 432, the application of a common intention constructive trust led to the parties' beneficial interests almost exactly matching the extent of their contributions to the purchase price and mortgage.

96 Note that, as argued by L. Maniscalco, "Common Intention and Constructive Trusts: Unorthodoxy in Trusts of Land" [2020] Conv 124, 133, it should be emphasized that, in a common intention constructive trust, the parties' intention is not the only factor in establishing the trust. However, where the intention is inferred at least in part from the parties' conduct, then that conduct will often provide evidence of the detrimental reliance required for a constructive trust: see para.17–186.

97 [2017] UKPC 17; [2018] A.C. 631 at [54].

98 See J. Mee, "The Past, Present, and Future of Resulting Trusts" (2017) 70 C.L.P. 189, 217.

99 For example, under a resulting trust, the extent of A's beneficial interest would depend on A's contribution to the purchase price only, and would not include mortgage contributions, as these instead go to paying off the debt used to acquire the property.

still a common intention constructive trust, with a particular rule used to determine the extent of the beneficial interests arising.

A useful overview, confirming the judicial trend to place very little weight on the presumptions and instead seek the parties' intentions directly, is provided by Lord Briggs in *Gany Holdings (PTC) SA v Khan*,[100] a Privy Council decision on an appeal from the British Virgin Islands:[101] **16–054**

> It is convenient to begin with a re-statement of the basic principles by which equity (which in this respect is shared by England and Wales and the British Virgin Islands) provides for the identification of beneficial interests arising from a gratuitous transfer of property. First, if either the transferor or the transferee makes a written (or oral) declaration as to those beneficial interests, or they do so together in an agreed form, that will generally be decisive, regardless of the subjective intentions of either of them: see for example *Whitlock v Moree*.[102] Secondly, and in default of any such declaration, the court looks for evidence from which a common intention as to beneficial ownership may be inferred. This may include evidence of statements made by either party before, at the time of or even after the relevant transfer, the parties' conduct, and the factual context in which the transfer takes place. Sometimes, a choice between possible conclusions as to beneficial interest may properly be arrived at by a process of elimination, whereby the most unlikely conclusions are first removed, leaving the least unlikely as the correct one. Finally, recourse may be had to time-honoured presumptions, such as the presumption of advancement or the presumed resulting trust, where there really is no evidence from which an inference as to common intention may properly be drawn. But these are, in modern times, a last resort, now that historic restrictions on the admissibility of evidence have been removed, and the forensic tools for the ascertainment and weighing of evidence are more readily available to the court.

v. The Presumptions and Improper Purposes

The analysis so far has suggested that very little practical purpose is served by either the presumption of resulting trust or the presumption of advancement: in any case where a Type (A) resulting trust might arise, a court simply needs to establish whether or not A could objectively have been understood to have intended B to hold the right acquired on trust for A. The presumptions will therefore be useful only in the rare case where there is no relevant evidence as to the parties' intentions. Previously, the presumptions were, however, very important in cases where the evidence on which A would have to rely to establish such an intention involved reference to an achieved improper purpose. **16–055**

This prominence of presumptions was a result of the approach approved by the House of Lords in *Tinsley v Milligan*[103] for dealing with such cases of illegal or other improper purposes. On that approach, A is allowed to establish an equitable interest (or a legal property right) if A can do so without having to rely on the improper purpose. This test makes the presumptions crucial, as Lord Browne-Wilkinson explained in *Tinsley*:[104] **16–056**

> The presumption of a resulting trust is, in my view, crucial in considering the authorities. On that presumption (and on the contrary presumption of advancement) hinges the answer to the crucial question "does a plaintiff claiming under a resulting trust have to rely on the underlying illegality?" Where the presumption of resulting trust applies, the plaintiff does not have to rely on the illegality. If he proves that the property is vested in the defendant alone but that the plaintiff provided part of the purchase money, or voluntarily transferred the property to the defendant, the plaintiff establishes his claim under a resulting trust unless either the contrary presumption of advancement displaces the presumption of resulting trust or the defendant leads evidence to rebut the presumption of resulting trust. Therefore, in cases where the presumption of

---

100 (2018) 21 I.T.E.L.R. 310 (PC).
101 (2018) 21 I.T.E.L.R. 310 at [17].
102 [2017] UKPC 44.
103 [1994] 1 A.C. 340.
104 [1994] 1 A.C. 340 at 371.

> advancement does not apply, a plaintiff can establish his equitable interest in the property without relying in any way on the underlying illegal transaction.

16–057 The presumptions, no matter how weak and easily rebutted, could thus determine the outcome of a case. In *Tinsley* itself, for example, A had paid for property but the property was put in B's name as part of a plan (which A, in the end, confessed to) to allow A fraudulently to claim benefits from the state. A and B were in a cohabiting relationship, but A was not B's husband, and so no presumption of advancement applied: A could thus establish a resulting trust, relying merely on the fact of her payment of the purchase price, and without having to invoke the illegal purpose. If, however, the presumption of advancement had instead applied, A would be required to show why in fact no gift had been intended to B, but would have been prevented from relying on that illegal purpose to do so. Whatever one's general view of the "reliance approach" to illegality,[105] its combination with the presumptions led to potentially arbitrary results.[106] One way to resolve this problem, consistently with the analysis put forward here, would simply be to abandon the presumptions, establishing the parties' intentions directly instead. Another way to resolve is to reform the "reliance approach": this was recommended by the Law Commission,[107] and undertaken judicially by the Supreme Court in *Patel v Mirza*. The majority there rejected the "reliance approach", finding it was not the best way to deal with the specific problem raised by illegal or improper purposes: the risk of harming the integrity of the legal system, in a way contrary to the public interest, by allowing a claim tainted by illegality. As Lord Toulson explained:[108]

> One cannot judge whether allowing a claim which is in some way tainted by illegality would be contrary to the public interest, because it would be harmful to the integrity of the legal system, without (a) considering the underlying purpose of the prohibition which has been transgressed, (b) considering conversely any other relevant public policies which may be rendered ineffective or less effective by denial of the claim, and (c) keeping in mind the possibility of overkill unless the law is applied with a due sense of proportionality.

16–058 *Patel v Mirza* itself did not involve any claim to a trust, but Lord Touslon and Lord Neuberger did consider how the new, more flexible approach would apply in a case such as *Tinsley*. A key concern is that of proportionality: if, for example, the consequence of denying A's claim would be that A has no equitable interest in a property wholly paid for by A, and in which A and B intended A should have an equitable interest, so that B is left with a windfall, that it is a significant factor to weigh in the balance. Lord Toulson stated that:[109]

> even if [A] had not owned up and come to terms with [the state agency she had planned to defraud], it would have been disproportionate to have prevented her from enforcing her equitable interest in the property and conversely to have left [B] unjustly enriched.

---

105 For further support for that approach, see eg Lord Sumption's dissent in *Patel v Mirza* [2016]; KSC 42 [2017] A.C. 467.

106 See, e.g. *Tribe v Tribe* [1996] Ch. 107 (CA): A made a transfer to B, one of his children, and so the presumption of advancement applied. A was allowed to establish a resulting trust by bringing evidence to rebut the presumption, but only because the planned improper purpose of putting the assets into B's name to hide them from A's possible creditors, was not in the end "wholly or partly carried into effect" ([1996] Ch. 107 at 134). The resolution of that case under the *Patel v Mirza* approach is discussed in the latter case by Lord Neuberger: [2016] UKSC 42; [2017] A.C. 467 at [151] and [171]. For a general consideration of how the *Patel* rules apply to trusts, see eg R Nwabueze, "Illegality and Trusts: Trusts-Creating Primary Transactions and Unlawful Ulterior Purposes" [2019] Conv. 29.

107 Law Com No.320 (2010).

108 [2016] UKSC 42; [2017] A.C. 467 at [101].

109 [2016] UKSC 42; [2017] A.C. 467 at [112]. See too Lord Neuberger at [181].

3. Type (B) Resulting Trusts

A. Overview

These "failing trusts"[110] cases constitute the second type of resulting trust identified by Lord Browne-Wilkinson in *Westdeutsche*, and said by him to arise: "Where A transfers property to B on express trusts, but the trusts declared do not exhaust the whole beneficial interest."[111] These trusts have also often been referred to as "automatic resulting trusts",[112] although, as we will see,[113] Lord Browne-Wilkinson's speech in *Westdeutsche* warns of the dangers of the term "automatic", and so they will be referred to here as "Type (B) resulting trusts". **16–059**

A simple example occurs in a case such as *Re Shaw*,[114] where George Bernard Shaw, in his will, directed trustees to hold funds on trust for the purpose of undertaking research into the possibility of a 40-letter alphabet. As this purpose was found not to be charitable, his attempt to set up a purpose trust failed. It was clear, however, that the trustees were not intended to be free to use the funds for their own benefit. As a result, the funds were held on resulting trust for Shaw's estate. **16–060**

An important example, albeit arising on more complicated facts, is *Vandervell v IRC*,[115] the facts of which were explained in Chapter 6.[116] Shares were held on trust for Vandervell, and he directed that they be transferred to the Royal College of Surgeons, subject to an option to purchase the shares for a fixed sum. That option to purchase was granted to the Vandervell trustee company. It seemed clear that the trustee company was not intended to have the benefit of the option, but rather that it was intended to hold it on trust. It was not clear however who were the beneficiaries of the trust of the option. A majority of the House of Lords held that the option was held on resulting trust for Vandervell. In Lord Upjohn's view, it was simply a matter of "what is the proper inference to draw from the facts", with the most plausible interpretation being that, as no trusts had been declared of the option, the company should hold them on trust for Vandervell, subject to any trust that he might later declare.[117] **16–061**

Such Type (B) resulting trusts therefore arise where property is transferred by an intending settlor to trustees[118] on express trusts which fail, whether for failure of marriage consideration, uncertainty, lapse, disclaimer, perpetuity, illegality,[119] non-compliance with requisite statutory formalities, or for any other reason.[120] They also arise if settlors fail to dispose exhaustively of the whole beneficial **16–062**

---

110 See Lord Millett, "Pension Schemes and the Law of Trusts" (2000) 14 Tru L.I. 66, 73.

111 [1996] A.C. 669 at 706.

112 See, e.g. *Re Vandervell's Trusts (No.2)* [1974] Ch. 269 at 274 per Megarry J: such trusts arise "where the transfer to B [from A] is made on trusts which leave some or all of the beneficial interest undisposed of. Here B automatically holds on a resulting trust for A to the extent that the beneficial interest has not been carried to him or others."

113 See para.16–067.

114 [1957] 1 W.L.R. 729. See para.16–063.

115 [1967] 2 A.C. 291.

116 See paras 6–067 to 6–068.

117 [1967] 2 A.C. 291 at 315–317.

118 If a settlor declares herself trustee of a trust which fails, she will become absolute beneficial owner of the property once more. A resulting trust is not needed to accomplish this, and in fact would be impossible, as a person cannot be a trustee solely for her own benefit: *Westdeutsche Landesbank Girozentrale v Islington LBC* [1996] A.C. 669 at 703, per Lord Browne-Wilkinson.

119 See para.16–057 for the approach now taken to illegality. Where there is a claim that an intended trust should fail on account of illegality, a court, when considering if such a failure would be a proportionate means of furthering the policy behind the rule rendering the trust illegal, will presumably take into account the consequences of the resulting trust that would arise in the event of illegality.

120 *Hodgson v Marks* [1971] Ch. 892 at 933, per Russell LJ; *Re Ames's Settlement* [1946] Ch. 217 though see now ss.16 and 24 of the Matrimonial Causes Act 1973. If the settlor were a testator then the property would result to his estate: if the property were specifically devised or bequeathed it would fall into residue; if the property were comprised in the residuary gift then

interest under their express trusts:[121] this would occur, for example, if a settlor transfers property to trustees to hold on trust for a life tenant, and does not specify any remainder interest. Where express trusts of funds subscribed by many settlors do not exhaust the funds there is a resulting trust in favour of the settlors rateably in proportion to the amounts subscribed by them.[122] Note, however, that in the case of charitable trusts that fail, the funds are often applied cy-près.[123]

B. Finding a Type (B) Resulting Trust

i. General Principles

16–063 Where an intending settlor A has transferred property to B on trust, the crucial question is whether the trust is complete and therefore succeeds in "disposing of" or "exhausting" the entire beneficial interest. This question can also be understood in terms of a gap in the duties owed by B: if A's expressed, objectively understood intention is that B is not to be free to use the property for B's own benefit, then for whose benefit must B hold the property? A gap can arise if it is not clear for whose benefit B must, in some circumstances at least,[124] hold the property. In some cases, as in *Re Shaw*, an operation of a legal rule invalidates the planned trust and creates the potential space filled by the resulting trust. In other cases, the operation of a legal rule prevents such a gap occurring: there is no resulting trust, for example, if the doctrine of acceleration applies to prevent there being a temporary failure to exhaust the beneficial interest under a trust.[125] Thus, if A by will leaves property to B to hold on trust C for life and after C's death to D absolutely, and C disclaims her interest, D's interest is accelerated so as to take effect immediately, thereby ousting any possible resulting trust of the income until C's death. For the doctrine to apply the remainderman must have a vested interest and there must be no contrary intention manifested in the trust document.[126]

16–064 Likewise, there is no resulting trust where the rule in *Hancock v Watson*[127] applies. This rule states that:

> if you find an absolute gift to a legatee in the first instance, and trusts are engrafted or imposed on that absolute interest which fail, either from lapse or invalidity or any other reason, then the absolute gift takes effect so far as the trusts have failed to the exclusion of the residuary legatee or next-of-kin as the case may be.[128]

The rule is equally applicable to inter vivos settlements.[129]

---

it would pass to the next-of-kin under the intestacy rules set out in the Administration of Estates Act 1925 as amended. On the impact of illegality, see paras 16–055ff.

121 *Re West* [1900] 1 Ch. 84; *Re Gillingham Bus Disaster Fund* [1958] Ch. 300.

122 See too *Re British Red Cross Balkan Fund* [1914] 2 Ch. 419 (where in the absence of the Attorney General a resulting trust was erroneously admitted); *Re Welsh Hospital Fund* [1921] 1 Ch. 655 at 662; *Re Hobourn Aero Components Ltd's Air Raid Disaster Fund* [1946] Ch. 194; *Air Jamaica Ltd v Charlton* [1999] 1 W.L.R. 1399 (for which, see paras 16–108 to 16–116).

123 See para.9–010.

124 As in the example noted at para.16–062, where A transfers property to B to hold on trust for C for life, and A does not specify what B's duty is to be on C's death.

125 *Re Flower's Settlement Trusts* [1957] 1 W.L.R. 401.

126 *Re Scott* [1975] 2 All E.R. 1033.

127 [1902] A.C. 14. See too *Lassence v Tierney* (1849) 1 Mac. & G. 551.

128 *Hancock* [1902] A.C. 14 at 22, per Lord Davey.

129 *Attorney General v Lloyd's Bank* [1935] A.C. 382; *Re Burton's Settlement Trusts* [1955] Ch. 348; *Watson v Holland* [1985] 1 All E.R. 290.

In many cases, the question of whether the trust is complete depends on a careful and fact-specific analysis of A's intentions. As we saw in Chapter 8,[130] for example, there may be a fine line between a case such as *Re Abbott*,[131] (where it was found that there was room for a resulting trust, as A had intended funds held on trust to be used for the benefit of the beneficiaries only whilst at least one of them survived) and a case such as *Re Osoba*,[132] in which there was no room for a resulting trust as A was regarded as having set up a trust for the benefit of three beneficiaries absolutely as joint tenants, so that the whole beneficial interest was disposed of by the terms of the initial transfer. **16–065**

It is possible of course that, when transferring property to B, A intends B's duties to be limited, so that B is in some circumstances free to use the property for B's own benefit. In such a case, there is again no gap for a resulting trust to fill. Thus, in *Re Foord*,[133] where a testator left his estate to his sister "absolutely . . . on trust" to pay his widow an annuity and the estate exceeded the annuity the sister was held beneficially entitled to the balance. **16–066**

There is an important question as to whether a Type (B) resulting trust can arise in a case where A has clearly indicated that she does *not* wish or intend such a trust to arise. In *Westdeutsche*, Lord Browne-Wilkinson disapproved of the term "automatic" as a description of such trusts, as he thought that: **16–067**

> If [A] has expressly, or by necessary implication, abandoned any beneficial interest in the trust property, there is in my view no resulting trust: the undisposed-of equitable interest vests in the Crown as bona vacantia: see *Re West Sussex Constabulary's Widows, Children and Benevolent (1930) Fund Trusts*.[134]

This "bona vacantia" solution means that B still holds on trust, but on trust for the Crown rather than A, with the Crown stepping in to fill the gap in B's duties. We will consider the conceptual significance of this possibility below,[135] but it is first useful to note some specific contexts in which bona vacantia has been discussed, and to consider the *West Sussex* case relied on by Lord Browne-Wilkinson. **16–068**

ii. Dissolution of Unincorporated Associations

In Chapter 8, we considered how unincorporated associations can hold property.[136] When an unincorporated association is dissolved it is necessary to ascertain how its property falls to be distributed: one of the possibilities is that there is a resulting trust to the persons who provided such property to the association.[137] **16–069**

The fate of property on the dissolution of an unincorporated association will depend on how it was held before that point. As we saw in Chapter 8, in such case, the property is usually regarded as being owned by the current members of the association, but subject to an express or implied contract between them.[138] So, if the rules of the association by which the members are contractually bound **16–070**

---

130 See paras 8–012 to 8–014.
131 [1900] 2 Ch. 326.
132 [1979] 2 All E.R. 393.
133 [1922] 2 Ch. 519. See too *Cook v Hutchinson* (1836) 1 Keen 42. But contrast the resulting trust in *Re West* [1900] 1 Ch. 84.
134 [1996] A.C. 669 at 708.
135 See paras 16–189 to 16–194.
136 See paras 8–035ff.
137 As was the case, for example, in *Re St Andrew's (Cheam) Lawn Tennis Club Trust* [2012] EWHC 1040 (Ch); [2012] 1 W.L.R. 3487. Although note there that, seemingly in order to reach a practically workable solution, Arnold J identified a specific party as having provided the property even though other, smaller contributions were made to its acquisition. For discussion see, e.g. T. Boncey & F. Ng (2014) 20 *Trusts & Trustees* 287.
138 See paras 8–042 to 8–051.

inter se provide for a particular method of distribution when the association is dissolved, this method will be used,[139] subject to any rights of third parties to share in the surplus assets.

16-071 Even if a donor when making a gift to the association intended to do so on trust for carrying out the purposes of the association, in order to prevent that gift being invalid as an attempt to establish a non-charitable purpose trust, the gift will generally be treated as an accretion to the general funds of the association. So, on dissolution, such gifts will be dealt with in just the same way as the funds which the members themselves have subscribed to the association's funds.[140]

16-072 The present position is set out in *Re Bucks Constabulary Fund Friendly Society (No.2)*,[141] reproduced below. This decision should be preferred to *Re West Sussex Constabulary's Benevolent Fund*,[142] parts of which are also reproduced here, because it pays proper attention to the primacy of the members' contracts in determining beneficial entitlements to the assets of the association, as stipulated in *Re Recher's Will Trusts*.[143] Finally, however, we also reproduce part of Lewison J's judgment in *Hanchett-Stamford v Attorney General*,[144] where he considers the situation where an association becomes moribund because all the members but one have died, and refuses to follow Walton J's dictum in *Re Bucks (No.2)*, that in such a case the assets should be treated as bona vacantia and pass to the Crown.

Re West Sussex Constabulary's Widows, Childrenand Benevolent (1930) Fund Trusts

Chancery Division [1971] Ch. 1

16-073 In 1930 members of the West Sussex Constabulary established a fund to provide for their widows and orphans. In 1968 the West Sussex Constabulary was amalgamated with other forces, and the question arose how the assets of the fund should be dealt with. These came from (1) contributions of past and present members; (2) entertainments, raffles, sweepstakes; (3) collecting boxes; (4) donations and legacies. Goff J. held that (4) were held on resulting trusts for the donors while (1), (2), and (3) were bona vacantia. These holdings are now of doubtful value in view of *Re Bucks (No.2)*, but the following dicta are still good law.

16-074 GOFF J.: I must now turn to the moneys raised from outside sources. Counsel for the Treasury Solicitor made an overriding general submission that there cannot be a resulting trust of any of the outside moneys because in the circumstances it is impossible to identify the trust property; no doubt something could be achieved by complicated accounting, but this, he submitted, would not be identification but notional reconstruction. I cannot accept that argument. In my judgment, in a case like the present, equity will cut the Gordian knot by simply dividing the ultimate surplus in proportion to the sources from which it has arisen . . . . There may be cases of tolerable simplicity where the court will be more refined, but in general, where a fund has been raised from mixed sources, interest has been earned over the years and income—and possibly capital—expenditure has been made indiscriminately out of the fund as an entirety, and then the venture comes to an end prematurely or otherwise, the court will not find itself baffled but will cut the Gordian knot as I have said.

16-075 Then counsel divided the outside moneys into three categories, first, the proceeds of entertainments, raffles and sweepstakes; secondly, the proceeds of collecting-boxes; and, thirdly, donations, including legacies if any, and he took particular objections to each.

16-076 I agree that there cannot be any resulting trust with respect to the first category. I am not certain whether Harman J. in *Re Gillingham Bus Disaster Fund*[145] meant to decide otherwise. In stating the facts

---

139 Otherwise, distribution will be on the basis of equality.
140 *Re Recher's Will Trusts* [1972] Ch. 526; *Re Lipinski's Will Trusts* [1976] Ch. 235. See para.8-053.
141 [1979] 1 All E.R. 623.
142 [1971] Ch. 1.
143 [1972] Ch. 526 at 538–539. See paras 8-043 to 8-051.
144 [2008] EWHC 330 (Ch); [2009] Ch. 173.
145 [1958] Ch. 300.

he referred to "street collections and so forth".[146] In the further argument[147] there is mention of whist drives and concerts but the judge himself did not speak of anything other than gifts. If, however, he did, I must respectfully decline to follow his judgment in that regard, for whatever may be the true position with regard to collecting-boxes, it appears to me to be impossible to apply the doctrine of resulting trust to the proceeds of entertainments and sweepstakes and such-like money-raising operations for two reasons: first, the relationship is one of contract and not of trust, the purchaser of a ticket may have the motive of aiding the cause or he may not; he may purchase a ticket merely because he wishes to attend the particular entertainment or to try for the prize, but whichever it be, he pays his money as the price of what is offered and what he receives; secondly, there is in such cases no direct contribution to the fund at all; it is only the profit, if any, which is ultimately received and there may even be none.

In any event, the first category cannot be any more susceptible to the doctrine than the second to which I now turn. Here one starts with the well-known dictum of P.O. Lawrence J. in *Re Welsh Hospital (Netley) Fund* where he said:[148] **16–077**

> "So far as regards the contributors to entertainments, street collections etc., I have no hesitation in holding that they must be taken to have parted with their money out-and-out. It is inconceivable that any person paying for a concert ticket or placing a coin in a collecting-box presented to him in the street should have intended that any part of the money so contributed should be returned to him when the immediate object for which the concert was given or the collection made had come to an end. To draw such an inference would be absurd on the face of it."

This was adopted by Upjohn J., in *Re Hillier's Trusts*[149] where the point was actually decided.

. . . In *Re Ulverston and District New Hospital Building Trusts*[150] Jenkins L.J. threw out a suggestion that there might be a distinction in the case of a person who could prove that he put a specified sum in a collecting-box, and, in the *Gillingham* case[151] Harman J. after noting this, decided that there was a resulting trust with respect to the proceeds of collections. **16–078**

. . . [For] for my part I cannot reconcile the decision of Upjohn J. in *Re Hillier's Trusts* with that of Harman J. in the *Gillingham* case. As I see it, therefore, I have to choose between them. On the one hand it may be said that Harman J. had the advantage, which Upjohn J. had not, of considering the suggestion made by Jenkins L.J. On the other hand that suggestion with all respect, seems to me somewhat fanciful and unreal. I agree that all who put their money into collecting-boxes should be taken to have the same intention, but why should they not all be regarded as intending to part with their money out and out absolutely in all circumstances? I observe that P.O. Lawrence J. in *Re Welsh Hospital*[152] used very strong words. He said any other view was inconceivable and absurd on the face of it. That commends itself to my humble judgment, and I therefore prefer and follow the judgment of Upjohn J. in *Re Hillier's Trusts*. **16–079**

Re Bucks Constabulary Fund Friendly Society (No.2)

Chancery Division [1979] 1 W.L.R. 936

The Bucks Constabulary Fund Friendly Society was established to provide for the relief of widows and orphans of deceased members of the Bucks Constabulary. It was an unincorporated association registered under the Friendly Societies Act 1896 but it had no rules providing for the distribution of its assets in the event of it being wound up. When it was wound up the question arose whether the surplus assets were bona vacantia passing to the Crown or whether they should be distributed among the members equally per capita or on some other basis. **16–080**

---

146 Ibid. at 304.
147 Ibid. at 309.
148 [1921] 1 Ch. 655 at 660.
149 [1954] 1 W.L.R. 9.
150 [1956] Ch. 622 at 633.
151 [1958] Ch. 300.
152 [1921] Ch. 655 at 661.

16–081 WALTON J.: There are basically two claimants to the fund, the Solicitor for the Affairs of Her Majesty's Treasury, who claims the assets as ownerless property, bona vacantia, and the members of the friendly society at the date of its dissolution on 14th October 1969.

16–082 Before considering the relevant legislation . . . and the decided cases, it is I think desirable to view the question of the property of unincorporated associations in the round. If a number of persons associate together, for whatever purpose, if that purpose is one which involves the acquisition of cash or property of any magnitude, then, for practical purposes, some one or more persons have to act in the capacity of treasurers or holders of the property. In any sophisticated association there will accordingly be one or more trustees in whom the property which is acquired by the association will be vested. These trustees will of course not hold such property on their own behalf. Usually there will be a committee of some description which will run the affairs of the association; though of course in a small association the committee may well comprise all the members; and the normal course of events will be that the trustee, if there is a formal trustee, will declare that he holds the property of the association in his hands on trust to deal with it as directed by the committee. If the trust deed is a shade more sophisticated it may add that the trustee holds the assets on trust for the members in accordance with the rules of the association. Now in all such cases it appears to me quite clear that, unless under the rules governing the association the property thereof has been wholly devoted to charity, or unless and to the extent to which the other trusts have validly been declared of such property, the persons, and the only persons, interested therein are the members. Save by way of a valid declaration or trust in their favour, there is no scope for any other person acquiring any rights in the property of the association, although of course it may well be that third parties may obtain contractual or proprietary rights, such as a mortgage, over those assets as the result of a valid contract with the trustees or members of the committee as representing the association.

16–083 I can see no reason for thinking that this analysis is any different whether the purpose for which the members of the association associate are a social club, a sporting club, to establish a widows' and orphans' fund, to obtain a separate Parliament for Cornwall, or to further the advance of alchemy. It matters not. All the assets of the association are held in trust for its members (of course subject to the contractual claims of anybody having a valid contract with the association) save and expect to the extent to which valid trusts have otherwise been declared of its property. I would adopt the analysis made by Brightman J. in *Re Recher's Will Trusts*.[153] . . .

16–084 All this doubtless seems quite elementary, but it appears to me to have been lost sight of to some extent in some of the decisions which I shall hereafter have to consider in detail in relation to the destination on dissolution of the funds of unincorporated associations.

16–085 Now in the present case I am dealing with a society which was registered under the Friendly Societies Act 1896. This does not have any effect at all on the unincorporated nature of the society, or (as I have in substance already indicated) on the way in which its property is held. But the latter point is in fact made very explicit by the provisions of s.49(1) of the 1896 Act which reads as follows:

> "All property belonging to a registered society, whether acquired before or after the society is registered, shall vest in the trustees for the time being of the society, for the use and benefit of the society and the members thereof, and of all persons claiming through the members according to the rules of the society."

16–086 There can be doubt, therefore, that in the present case the whole of the property of the society is vested in the trustees for the use and benefit of the society and the members thereof and of all persons claiming through the members according to the rules of the society. I do not think I need go through the rules in detail. They are precisely what one would expect in the case of an association whose main purpose in life was to enable members to make provision for widows and orphans. Members paid a contribution in exchange for which in the event of their deaths their widows and children would receive various benefits. There is a minimal benefit for which provision is made in the case of a member suffering very severe illness indeed, but, as counsel for the Treasury Solicitor was able to demonstrate from an analysis of the accounts, virtually the entire expenditure of the association was, as indeed one would expect, on the provision of widows' and orphans' benefits. But, of course, there is no trust whatsoever declared in their favour. I am not called on, I think, to decide whether they are, within the meaning of s.49(1), persons claiming through the members according to the rules of the society, or whether they are simply the beneficiaries of stipulations

[153] [1972] Ch. 526 at 538–539.

by the members for the benefit of third parties. All parties are agreed that accrued rights of such persons must be given full effect. There is indeed no rule which says what is to happen to surplus assets of the society on a dissolution. But in view of s.49(1) there is no need. The assets must continue to be held, the society having been dissolved, and the widows and orphans being out of the way, simply for the use and benefit of the members of the society, albeit they will all now be former members.

This indeed appears so obvious that in a work of great authority on all matters connected with friendly societies, *Baden Fuller*, the learned author says this:[154] 16-087

> "If the rules provide for the termination of the society they usually also provide for the distribution of the funds in that event, but if on the termination of a society no provision has been made by the rules for the distribution of its funds, such funds are divisible among the existing members at the time of the termination or dissolution in proportion to the amount contributed by each member for entrance fees and subscriptions, but irrespective of fines or payments made to members in accordance with the rules."

In my judgment this accurately represents the law, at any rate so far as the beneficiaries of the trust on dissolution are concerned, although not necessarily so far as the quantum of their respective interests is concerned; a matter which still remains to be argued. The effective point is that the claims of the Treasury Solicitor to the funds as bona vacantia are unsustainable in the present case. I say "in the present case" because there are undoubtedly cases where the assets of an unincorporated association do become bona vacantia. To quote *Baden Fuller* again:[155] 16-088

> "A society may sometimes become defunct or moribund by its members either all dying or becoming so reduced in numbers that it is impossible either to continue the society or to dissolve it by instrument; in such cases the surplus funds, after all existing claims (if any) under the rules have been satisfied or provided for, are not divisible among the surviving members . . . or the last survivor . . . or the representative of the last survivor . . . nor is there any resulting trust in favour of the personal representatives of the members of the society . . . not even in favour of honorary members in respect of donations by them . . . but a society which, though moribund, had at a testator's death one member and three annuitant beneficiaries, was held to be existing so as to prevent the lapse of a legacy bequeathed to it by the testator . . . . In these circumstances two cases seem to occur: if the purposes of the society are charitable, the surplus will be applicable cy-près . . . but if the society is not a charity, the surplus belongs to the Crown as bona vacantia."

Before I turn to a consideration of the authorities, it is I think pertinent to observe that all unincorporated societies rest in contract to this extent, that there is an implied contract between all of the members inter se governed by the rules of the society. In default of any rule to the contrary, and it will seldom if ever be that there is such a rule, when a member ceases to be a member of the association he ipso facto ceases to have any interest in its funds. Once again, so far as friendly societies are concerned, this is made very clear by s.49(1), that it is the members, the present members, who, alone, have any right in the assets. As membership always ceases on death, past members or the estates of deceased members therefore have no interest in the assets. Further, unless expressly so provided by the rules, unincorporated societies are not really tontine societies, intended to provide benefits for the longest liver of the members. Therefore, although it is difficult to say in any given case precisely when a society becomes moribund, it is quite clear that if a society is reduced to a single member neither he, still less his personal representatives on his behalf, can say he is or was the society and therefore entitled solely to its fund. It may be that it will be sufficient for the society's continued existence if there are two members, but if there is only one the society as such must cease to exist. There is no association, since one can hardly associate with oneself or enjoy one's own society. And so indeed the assets have become ownerless. 16-089

[The judge referred to various cases and went on:] Finally . . . there comes a case which gives me great concern, *Re West Sussex Constabulary's Widows, Children and Benevolent (1930) Fund Trusts*.[156] The case is indeed easily distinguishable from the present case in that what was there under consideration was a simple unincorporated association and not a friendly society, so that the provisions of s.49(1) of the 1896 16-090

---

[154] *The Law of Friendly Societies* (4th edn, 1926), p.186.
[155] ibid., pp.186–187.
[156] [1971] Ch. 1.

Act do not apply. Otherwise the facts in that case present remarkable parallels to the facts in the present case. Goff J. decided that the surplus funds had become bona vacantia . . . .

16-091 It will be observed that the first reason given by the judge for his decision is that he could not accept the principle of the members' clubs as applicable. This is a very interesting reason, because it is flatly contrary to the successful argument of Mr Ingle Joyce who appeared for the Attorney-General in the case Goff J. purported to follow, *Cunnack v Edwards*. His argument was as follows:[157]

> "This society was nothing more than a club, in which the members had no transmissible interest: *Re St James' Club*.[158] Whatever the members, or even the surviving member, might have done while alive, when they died their interest in the assets of the club died with them";

and in the Court of Appeal[159] he used the arguments he had used below. If all that Goff J. meant was that the purposes of the fund before him were totally different from those of a members' club then of course one must agree, but if he meant to imply that there was some totally different principle of law applicable one must ask why that should be. His second reason is that in all the cases where the surviving members had taken, the organisation existed for the benefit of the members for the time being exclusively. This may be so, so far as actual decisions go, but what is the principle? Why are the members not in control, complete control, save as to any existing contractual rights, of the assets belonging to their organisation? One could understand the position being different if valid trusts had been declared of the assets in favour of third parties, for example charities, but that this was emphatically not the case was demonstrated by the fact that Goff J. recognised that the members could have altered the rules prior to dissolution and put the assets into their own pockets. If there was no obstacle to their doing this, it shows in my judgment quite clearly that the money was theirs all the time. Finally he purports to follow *Cunnack v Edwards* and it will be seen from the analysis which I have already made of that case that it was extremely special in its facts, resting on a curious provision of the 1829 Act which is no longer applicable. As I have already indicated, in the light of s.49(1) of the 1896 Act the case before Goff J.[160] is readily distinguishable, but I regret that, quite apart from that, I am wholly unable to square it with the relevant principles of law applicable.

16-092 The conclusion therefore is that, as on dissolution there were members of the society here in question in existence, its assets are held on trust for such members to the total exclusion of any claim on behalf of the Crown. The remaining question under this head which falls now to be argued is, of course, whether they are simply held per capita, or, as suggested in some of the cases, in proportion to the contributions made by each . . . .

16-093 I think that there is no doubt that, as a result of modern cases springing basically from the decision of O'Connor M.R. in *Tierney v Tough*,[161] judicial opinion has been hardening and is now firmly set along the lines that the interests and rights of persons who are members of any type of unincorporated association are governed exclusively by contract, that is to say the rights between themselves and their rights to any surplus assets. I say that to make it perfectly clear that I have not overlooked the fact that the assets of the society are usually vested in trustees on trust for the members. But that is quite a separate and distinct trust bearing no relation to the claims of the members inter se on the surplus funds so held on trust for their benefit.

16-094 That being the case, prima facie there can be no doubt at all but that the distribution is on the basis of equality, because, as between a number of people contractually interested in a fund, there is no other method of distribution if no other method is provided by the terms of the contract, and it is not for one moment suggested here that there is any other method of distribution provided by the contract. We are, of course, dealing here with a friendly society, but that really makes no difference to the principle. The Friendly Societies Acts do not incorporate the friendly society in any way and the only effect that it has is, as I pointed out in my previous judgment in this case, that there is a section which makes it crystal clear in the Friendly Societies Act 1896 that the assets are indeed held on trust for the members.

16-095 . . .An ingenious argument has been put up by counsel for the third and fifth defendants, who are ad idem on this particular point, which runs very simply as follows: the members of the society are entitled

157 [1895] 1 Ch. 489 at 494.
158 (1852) 2 De G. M. & G. 383 at 387.
159 [1896] 2 Ch. 679.
160 [1971 Ch. 1.
161 [1914] I.R. 142.

in equity to the surplus funds which are distributable among them, therefore they are to be distributed among them according to equitable principles and those principles should, like all equitable principles, be moulded to fit the circumstances of the case, and in one case it would therefore be equitable to distribute in equal shares, in another case it might be equitable to distribute in proportion to the subscriptions that they have paid, and I suppose that in another case it might be equitable to distribute according to the length of their respective feet, following a very well known equitable precedent. Well, I completely deny the basic premise. The members are not entitled in equity to the fund: they are entitled at law. It is a matter, so far as the members are concerned, of pure contract, and, being a matter of pure contract, it is, in my judgment, as far as distribution is concerned, completely divorced from all questions of equitable doctrines. It is a matter of simple entitlement, and that entitlement, in my judgment, at this time of day must be, and can only be, in equal shares.

Hanchett-Stamford v Attorney General

Chancery Division [2009] Ch. 173

In 1914 the Performing and Captive Animals Defence League was founded as an unincorporated association. Its purposes included bringing about a ban on performing animals. In 1949, following the decision in *National Anti-Vivisection Society v IRC*,[162] the Inland Revenue decided that the league did not have charitable status since its principal object was to change the law. Mr and Mrs Hanchett-Stamford joined the league as life members in the mid-1960s, and after her husband's death in 2006, Mrs Hanchett-Stamford was left as the sole surviving member. She decided to wind up the league and to transfer its assets to an active animal charity. Hence she sought a declaration that the work and objects of the league were charitable under the Charities Act 2006 s.2(2)(k) and an order appointing herself and her solicitor as trustees of the fund. Lewison J. refused the relief sought, holding that the league's purposes were not exclusively charitable because one of its objects was seeking a change in the law to ban performing animals. However he also held that on her husband's death the league had ceased to exist and its rules had ceased to bind Mrs Hanchett-Stamford, who was therefore entitled to its assets absolutely as its sole surviving member 16–096

LEWISON J. (after reviewing *Re Bucks (No.2)* continued): . . . There is, I think, no difficulty in accepting Walton J.'s ultimate conclusion. Nor is there any difficulty in accepting that the member's rights are contractual rather than equitable. Nor is there any difficulty in accepting that on a member's death he ceases to have any interest in the assets of the unincorporated association. Accretion on death is inherent in the beneficial interest in any asset being held by joint tenants in equity; and is no doubt reinforced by contractual restrictions such as the rules of an association. It, therefore, follows that the estate of a deceased member can have no claim to the assets. In *Neville Estates Ltd v Madden*[163] Cross J. applied the same principle to cessation of membership through resignation. This must be a facet of the contractual relations between members. Walton J. also said that if there is only one member of an unincorporated association, it must cease to exist. That, too, must I think be right both for the reasons that Walton J. gave; and also because if the members' rights are based in contract, a contract must cease to bind once there is no other party who can enforce it. 16–097

However, what I find more difficult to accept is that a member who has a beneficial interest in an asset, albeit subject to contractual restrictions, can have that beneficial interest divested from him on the death of another member. It leads to the conclusion that if there are two members of an association which has assets of, say £2m, they can by agreement divide those assets between them and pocket £1m each, but if one of them dies before they have divided the assets, the whole pot goes to the Crown as bona vacantia. Since Walton J. was not dealing with a case in which there was only one surviving member, his observations were obiter. Nor did he explain his reasoning on this question beyond the extract from his judgment that I have quoted. 16–098

I must, I think, look a little more carefully at the authorities that are said to have this effect. In *Cunnack v Edwards*[164] a society was established to raise a fund, by the subscriptions, fines and forfeitures of its members, to provide annuities for the widows of its deceased members. There was also a category of 16–099

[162] [1948] A.C. 31.
[163] [1962] Ch. 832.
[164] [1895] 1 Ch. 489 and (on appeal) [1896] 2 Ch. 679.

honorary members. In 1848 Mr Edwards became an ordinary member and remained a member until his death in 1878, when he died a widower. He was the last surviving ordinary member. It appeared that all the other members had predeceased him, except Sir Vyvyan, an honorary member, and it was believed the only honorary member of the society. On joining the society he had signed a declaration that his object in joining the society was not that any widow of his should claim any benefit from it (to which he relinquished his right), but merely for the encouragement of the society. Sir Vyvyan died in 1879. The last annuitant had also died. Thus at the date when the matter came before the court there were no surviving members of the society and all the widows' pensions had been paid. The question was: what was to happen to the surplus funds. The two original claimants were the personal representatives of Mr Edwards and the Crown. The personal representatives of Sir Vyvyan made no claim. The Crown argued that the surplus was either held on charitable trusts and ought to be applied cy-près; or that the surplus was bona vacantia. Chitty J. held that the fund was not a charitable fund, and stood over the question of bona vacantia, giving leave to add as a party a representative of deceased members of the society generally. The argument for the Crown was:[165]

> "This society was nothing more than a club, in which the members had no transmissible interest . . . Whatever the members, or even the surviving member, might have done while alive, when they died their interest in the assets of the club died with them. The earlier deceased members have had all the benefit they bargained for when they joined—their widows have received their annuities. When Edwards was alive he and Sir R. Vyvyan might have dissolved the society in the statutory way and voted themselves the funds; but they did not do so. As a fact, Sir R. Vyvyan was the surviving member, and his representatives disclaim all beneficial interest; still he had just as much right to this fund as Edwards."

16–100 Thus the argument for the Crown turned on the fact that at the date of the proceedings there were no surviving members, but it did not exclude the possibility that if there had been a surviving member that surviving member could have claimed the assets. Chitty J. dealt with the claim of the personal representatives of Mr Edwards as follows:[166]

> "The claim of the representative of the last surviving member may be disposed of in a few words. The society was not a tontine society, and there is no ground for saying that the fund belonged in equity to the last survivor. There is nothing in the rules, or in any principle of equity, applicable to the case on which this claim can be rested. It was said that the last surviving member might have held a meeting under section 26 of the statute of George IV, and voted the funds to himself. To this proposition, extravagant as it is, it is sufficient answer to say that the last survivor never attempted to do anything of the kind."

16–101 In the result Chitty J. held that the surplus was held on a resulting trust for its contributors. The case then went to the Court of Appeal. On appeal Mr Edwards's personal representatives abandoned his claim and the contest was between the deceased members generally on the one hand, and the Crown on the other. Counsel for the Crown repeated the same arguments that he had advanced before Chitty J., which included the passage I have emphasised. The Court of Appeal held that when each subscriber paid money to the society his entire beneficial interest in the money was exhausted. Lord Halsbury said:[167]

> "There never was and there never could be any interest remaining in the contributor other than the right that his wife, if she survived him, should become entitled to a widow's portion thus provided. This was the final and exhaustive destination of all the sums contributed to the common fund. Under these circumstances, I am at a loss to see what room there is for the contention that there is any resulting trust."

16–102 A.L. Smith L.J. said:[168]

> "As the member paid his money to the society, so he divested himself of all interest in this money for ever, with this one reservation, that if the member left a widow she was to be provided for during her widowhood. Except as to this he abandoned and gave up the money for ever."

165 [1895] 1 Ch. 489 at 494–495. (Emphasis added by Lewison J.).
166 At 496.
167 [1896] 2 Ch. 679 at 681.
168 At 683.

Accordingly, the case turned on the circumstances in which the money was paid to the society. Thus the entirety of the bargain was that the money was to be used to pay widows' pensions, and not to return any part of the money to the contributor. On the facts, there were no surviving members of the association when the case came to court, so that the question before me did not arise; and the successful argument for the Crown admitted of the possibility that a single surviving member could during his lifetime claim the assets of the friendly society. In addition, as Walton J. pointed out in *Re Bucks Constabulary (No.2)*, the case concerned a friendly society and the legislation then in force required the rules to state all the uses applicable to the assets of the society, and they stated none in favour of members. I do not consider that this case is authority for the proposition that the sole surviving member of an unincorporated association, while still alive, cannot lay claim to its assets. Moreover although it was no doubt true, as Chitty J. held and as Walton J. emphasised, that the society was not a tontine society in the sense that it was not its intention to provide benefits for the ultimate survivor, any case in which property is held on a joint tenancy in equity produces a tontine effect, even if that is not its purpose. 16–103

[He reviewed *Tierney v Tough*[169] and *Abbatt v Treasury Solicitor*,[170] then continued:] The thread that runs through all these cases is that the property of an unincorporated association is the property of its members, but that they are contractually precluded from severing their share except in accordance with the rules of the association; and that, on its dissolution, those who are members at the time are entitled to the assets free from any such contractual restrictions. It is true that this is not a joint tenancy according to the classical model; but since any collective ownership of property must be a species of joint tenancy or tenancy in common, this kind of collective ownership must, in my judgment, be a subspecies of joint tenancy, albeit taking effect subject to any contractual restrictions applicable as between members. In some cases (such as *Cunnack v Edwards*) those contractual restrictions may be such as to exclude any possibility of a future claim. In others they may not. The cases are united in saying that on a dissolution the members of a dissolved association have a beneficial interest in its assets, and Lord Denning M.R. goes as far as to say that it is a "beneficial equitable joint tenancy". I cannot see why the legal principle should be any different if the reason for the dissolution is the permanent cessation of the association's activities or the fall in its membership to below two. The same principle ought also to hold if the contractual restrictions are abrogated or varied by agreement of the members. I do not find in the authorities considered by Walton J. anything that binds me to hold that where there is one identifiable and living member of an unincorporated association that has ceased to exist, the assets formerly held by or for that association pass to the Crown as bona vacantia. In addition, article 1 of the First Protocol of the European Convention for the Protection of Human Rights and Fundamental Freedoms guarantees the peaceful enjoyment of possessions. It says: "No one shall be deprived of his possessions except in the public interest and subject to the conditions provided for by law . . .". 16–104

On the face of it for one of two members of an unincorporated association to be deprived of his share in the assets of the association by reason of the death of the other of them, and without any compensation, appears to be a breach of this article. It is also difficult to see what public interest is served by the appropriation by the state of that member's share in the association's assets. This, in my judgment, provides another reason why the conclusion that a sole surviving member of an unincorporated association, while still alive, cannot claim its assets is unacceptable. 16–105

I therefore respectfully decline to follow Walton J.'s obiter dictum that a sole surviving member of an unincorporated association cannot claim the assets of the association, and that they vest in the Crown as bona vacantia. I might add that the Attorney General suggested in argument, without arguing in favour of one outcome, that there were three possible outcomes: first, that the last surviving member is entitled to the assets; secondly, that the assets are held jointly between the last surviving member and the estate of the member whose death caused the dissolution; thirdly, that the assets were ownerless or bona vacantia. For the reasons I have given, I conclude the first outcome is correct and I reject the second and third. 16–106

---

[169] [1914] 1 I.R. 142.
[170] [1969] 1 W.L.R. 561.

iii. Pension Scheme Surpluses

16–107 A number of important cases in this area concern surpluses within a pension scheme. In *Davis v Richard & Wallington Ltd*,[171] for example, the funds of the scheme were held on trust but the trust deed was silent as to the destination of any surplus, and there was no way to amend the deed to deal with the surplus.[172] Scott J held that the surplus derived primarily from over-funding arising from the contributions of the employer (which was obliged to make up any deficiencies if the employees' contributions proved inadequate), and that the portion of the surplus which derived from the employer's contributions should be held on resulting trust for the employer. However, as regards the surplus derived from the employees' contributions he held that this should pass to the Crown as bona vacantia because the circumstances of the case pointed "firmly and clearly to the conclusion that a resulting trust in favour of the employees should be excluded". This was because there were significant practical difficulties in working out how the shares of different employees should be calculated, and no steps had been envisaged to meet those difficulties.[173] Nor should a resulting trust be imposed if this would lead to employees receiving more than the legislature intended when stipulating the statutory limits under exempt approved schemes. However, neither of those reasons against a resulting trust for employees applied in *Air Jamaica Ltd v Charlton*.[174]

Air Jamaica Ltd v Charlton

Privy Council [1999] 1 W.L.R. 1399

16–108 Air Jamaica Ltd was privatised and its employee pensions plan was discontinued, leaving a surplus of $400 million. The pensions plan was established by a trust deed, one clause of which (clause 13.3) provided that "any balance of the Fund shall be applied to provide additional benefits for Members and after their death for their widows or their designated beneficiaries in such equitable and non-discriminatory manner as the Trustees may determine". The surplus would have been distributed in line with this clause if it had been valid, but the Privy Council advised that it was void for perpetuity. Clause 4 of the trust deed stated: "No moneys which at any time have been contributed by the Company under the terms hereof shall in any circumstances be repayable to the Company". The company purported to amend the trust deed, by removing clause 4 and replacing clause 13.3 with a clause providing that the surplus would be held on trust for the company. The Privy Council advised that clause 4 invalidated these amendments, but that it did not prevent a resulting trust from arising in favour of the company, and of the contributing members, in respect of the surplus funds.

16–109 LORD MILLETT (speaking for the court, which also consisted of LORD STEYN, LORD HOPE, SIR CHRISTOPHER SLADE and SIR ANDREW LEGGATT): Prima facie the surplus is held on a resulting trust for those who provided it. This sometimes creates a problem of some perplexity. In the present case, however, it does not. Contributions were payable by the members with matching contributions by the company. In the absence of any evidence that this is not what happened in practice, the surplus must be treated as provided as to one half by the company and as to one half by the members.

16–110 The Attorney General contended that neither the company nor the members can take any part in the surplus, which has reverted to the Crown as bona vacantia. He argued that cl.4 of the trust deed precludes any claim by the company, while the members cannot claim any part of the surplus because they have received all that they are entitled to. There is authority for both propositions. Their Lordships consider that they can be supported neither in principle nor as a matter of construction.

16–111 In *Re ABC Television Ltd Pension Scheme*[175] Foster J. held that a clause similar to cl.4 of the present trust deed "negatives the possibility of implying a resulting trust". This is wrong in principle. Like a constructive

---

[171] [1990] 1 W.L.R. 1511.

[172] See now Pensions Act 1995 ss.68, 69.

[173] [1990] 1 W.L.R. 1511 at 1543. Note the analogy to *North v Wilkinson* [2018] EWCA Civ 161: see para.7–042.

[174] [1999] 1 W.L.R. 1399.

[175] May 22, 1973, unreported.

trust, a resulting trust arises by operation of law, though unlike a constructive trust it gives effect to intention. But it arises whether or not the transferor intended to retain a beneficial interest—he almost always does not—since it responds to the absence of any intention on his part to pass a beneficial interest to the recipient. It may arise even where the transferor positively wished to part with the beneficial interest, as in *Vandervell v IRC*.[176] In that case the retention of a beneficial interest by the transferor destroyed the effectiveness of a tax avoidance scheme which the transferor was seeking to implement. The House of Lords affirmed the principle that a resulting trust is not defeated by evidence that the transferor intended to part with the beneficial interest if he has not in fact succeeded in doing so. As Plowman J. had said in the same case at first instance:[177]

> "As I see it, a man does not cease to own property simply by saying 'I don't want it'. If he tries to give it away the question must always be, has he succeeded in doing so or not?"

Lord Upjohn expressly approved this.[178]

Consequently their Lordships think that clauses of this kind in a pension scheme should generally be construed as forbidding the repayment of contributions under the terms of the scheme, and not as a pre-emptive but misguided attempt to rebut a resulting trust which would arise dehors the scheme. The purpose of such clauses is to preclude any amendment that would allow repayment to the company. Their Lordships thus construe cl.4 of the trust deed as invalidating the 1994 amendments, but not as preventing the company from retaining a beneficial interest by way of a resulting trust in so much of the surplus as is attributable to its contributions. **16–112**

The members' contributions stand on a similar footing. In *Davis v Richards & Wallington Industries Ltd*[179] Scott J. held that the fact that a party has received all that he bargained for is not necessarily a decisive argument against a resulting trust, but that in the circumstances of the case before him a resulting trust in favour of the employees was excluded. The circumstances that impressed him were twofold. He considered that it was impossible to arrive at a workable scheme for apportioning the employees' surplus among the different classes of employees and he declined[180] to "impute to them an intention that would lead to an unworkable result". He also considered that he was precluded by statute from "imputing to the employees an intention" that they should receive by means of a resulting trust sums in excess of the maximum permitted by the relevant tax legislation. **16–113**

These formulations also adopt the approach to intention that their Lordships have already considered to be erroneous. Their Lordships would observe that, even in the ordinary case of an actuarial surplus, it is not obvious that, when employees are promised certain benefits under a scheme to which they have contributed more than was necessary to fund them, they should not expect to obtain a return of their excess contributions. In the present case, however, the surplus does not arise from over-funding but from the failure of some of the trusts. It is impossible to say that the members "have received all that they bargained for". One of the benefits they bargained for was that the trustees should be obliged to pay them additional benefits in the event of the scheme's discontinuance. It was the invalidity of this trust that gave rise to the surplus. Their Lordships consider that it would be more accurate to say that the members claim such part of the surplus as is attributable to their contributions because they have not received all that they bargained for. **16–114**

Pension schemes in Jamaica, as in England, need the approval of the Inland Revenue if they are to secure the fiscal advantages that are made available. The tax legislation in both countries places a limit on the amount which can be paid to the individual employee. Allowing the employees to enjoy any part of the surplus by way of resulting trust would probably exceed those limits. This fact is not, however, in their Lordships' view a proper ground on which to reject the operation of a resulting trust in favour of the employees. The Inland Revenue had an opportunity to examine the pension plan and to withhold approval on the ground that some of its provisions were void for perpetuity. They failed to do so. There is no call to distort principle in order to meet their requirements. The resulting trust arises by operation of the general law, dehors the pension scheme and the scope of the relevant tax legislation. **16–115**

---

176 [1967] 1 All E.R. 1.
177 [1966] Ch. 261 at 275.
178 [1967] 1 All E.R. 1 at 9.
179 [1991] 2 All E.R. 563.
180 At 1544.

16–116 Scott J. was impressed by the difficulty of arriving at a workable scheme for apportioning the surplus funds among the members and the executors of deceased members. This was because he thought it necessary to value the benefits that each member had received in order to ascertain his share in the surplus. On the separate settlement with mutual insurance analysis which their Lordships have adopted in the present case, however, no such process is required. The members' share of the surplus should be divided pro rata among the members and the estates of deceased members in proportion to the contributions made by each member without regard to the benefits each has received and irrespective of the dates on which the contributions were made.

4. Quistclose Trusts

A. Introduction

16–117 In *Barclays Bank Ltd v Quistclose Investments Ltd*,[181] Quistclose lent money to Rolls Razor, another company in the same corporate group, so that Rolls Razor could pay a dividend to its shareholders. Rolls Razor became insolvent before the dividend was paid.[182] The House of Lords held that the money was held by Rolls Razor on trust for Quistclose, so that it was not available to Rolls Razor's other creditors. Lord Wilberforce, with whom the rest of the panel agreed, reached that result by finding that the money had been initially held by Rolls Razor on a trust to pay the dividends and that, when it went into insolvency, that purpose failed and a second trust arose in favour of Quistclose.[183]

16–118 Lord Wilberforce's analysis thus depended on a primary trust having arisen; on its failure, it could then be said that a Type B resulting trust arose in favour of Quistclose. There are, however, some difficulties with that explanation. First, as noted in Chapter 8,[184] the recognition of the primary trust would involve a departure from the beneficiary principle, which would be surprising given the lack of discussion of that principle in Lord Wilberforce's speech. Second, the trust in favour of the lender would then arise only on the insolvency of the borrower, and a key principle of insolvency law is that proprietary interests should not arise for the first time on insolvency, given their effect on other creditors.[185] Third, why should the secondary trust arise at all, given that the insolvency does not by itself necessarily prevent payment of the money to the shareholders?[186]

16–119 In *Twinsectra Ltd v Yardley*,[187] Lord Millett, building on his own extra-judicial analysis of the so-called *Quistclose* trust,[188] as well as other academic criticism of Lord Wilberforce's reasoning,[189] put

---

181 [1970] A.C. 567. See too *Re ETVR* [1987] B.C.L.C. 646.

182 For an entertaining account of the factual background, see R. Stevens, "Rolls Razor Ltd" in W. Swadling (ed.), *The Quistclose Trust* (Hart Publishing, 2004).

183 [1970] A.C. 567 at 582: "the intention to create a secondary trust for the benefit of the lender, to arise if the primary trust, to pay the dividend could not be carried out, is clear and I can find no reason why the law should not give effect to it."

184 See para.8–032.

185 See R. Stevens, "Insolvency" in *The Quistclose Trust* (2004).

186 A point made by Lord Millett in *Twinsectra v Yardley* [2002] UKHL 12; [2002] 2 A.C. 164 at [98], extracted at para.16–138. Of course, an insolvent company cannot choose to pay debts that are due to some of its creditors and refuse to pay debts due to others, but, as Lord Millett notes, ibid, on the hypothesis that a primary trust exists, the money was not in any case beneficially owned by the company.

187 [2002] UKHL 12; [2002] 2 A.C. 164.

188 P.J. Millett QC, "The *Quistclose* Trust: Who Can Enforce It?" (1985) 101 L.Q.R. 269.

189 See, e.g. R. Chambers, *Resulting Trusts* (Oxford University Press, 1997), pp.68–89.

forward a different interpretation of the case, which was generally[190] accepted by the other members of the panel, and has been applied in subsequent cases.[191]

i. The *Twinsectra* Analysis

Twinsectra Ltd v Yardley

House of Lords [2002] 2 A.C. 164

Yardley needed a loan to complete a purchase of land. Twinsectra, the claimant, offered to lend him £1 million, but only if the loan was secured by a solicitor's personal undertaking (a very unusual requirement). Yardley's solicitor, Leach, refused to give the undertaking. Sims, another solicitor known to Yardley, but who was not acting for him in the purchase of the land, did agree to give the undertaking. By this point, Yardley had found another source of finance for the purchase of the land. He and Sims nonetheless decided to take up the offer of the £1 million loan from Twinsectra. As between them, the plan was that Sims would give the money to Yardley, to discharge a debt owed to Yardley, and Sims would then be primarily liable for repaying Twinsectra. Twinsectra was not told of this plan, nor was it told that the money was no longer to be used for buying the land. It paid the money to Sims on the basis that it would be used for acquiring property, and Sims promised (1) to keep the money until it was applied in buying land on behalf of Yardley, and (2) that the money would be used *solely* for that purpose. In breach of those conditions, Sims, on receiving the money from Twinsectra, released it to Leach, who received it on behalf of Yardley, and credited it to a client account. The money was then paid out in accordance with the instructions of Yardley or one of his co-directors. Some of the money was spent on the acquisition of property, but other sums (totalling £357,720.11) were not. Neither Yardley nor Sims repaid Twinsectra. Twinsectra therefore wished to sue Leach. It claimed that the money it advanced to Sims had been impressed with a *Quistclose* trust, that Sims had breached this trust, and that Leach had dishonestly assisted in the breach by advancing sums to Yardley that were not used in the acquisition of property. The House of Lords held unanimously that the loan money had indeed been impressed with a *Quistclose* trust, and the parts of Lord Millett's speech dealing with this issue are reproduced here. Their Lordships also held by a majority (Lord Millett dissenting) that Leach was not liable in dishonest assistance, as he had not acted with the requisite degree of dishonesty. This was a controversial finding, and the definition of dishonesty in this context was later revisited by the Privy Council in *Barlow Clowes International Ltd v Eurotrust International Ltd*.[192] **16–120**

LORD MILLETT: Was there a Quistclose trust?

Money advanced by way of loan normally becomes the property of the borrower. He is free to apply the money as he chooses, and save to the extent to which he may have taken security for repayment the lender takes the risk of the borrower's insolvency. But it is well established that a loan to a borrower for a specific purpose where the borrower is not free to apply the money for any other purpose gives rise to fiduciary obligations on the part of the borrower which a court of equity will enforce. In the earlier cases the purpose was to enable the borrower to pay his creditors or some of them, but the principle is not limited to such cases. **16–121**

Such arrangements are commonly described as creating "a *Quistclose* trust", after the well known decision of the House in *Barclays Bank Ltd v Quistclose Investments Ltd*[193] in which Lord Wilberforce confirmed the validity of such arrangements and explained their legal consequences. When the money is advanced, the lender acquires a right, enforceable in equity, to see that it is applied for the stated purpose, or more accurately to prevent its application for any other purpose. This prevents the borrower from obtaining any beneficial interest in the money, at least while the designated purpose is still capable of being carried out. Once the purpose has been carried out, the lender has his normal remedy in debt. If for any reason the purpose cannot be carried out, the question arises whether the money falls within the general fund **16–122**

190 Although note that on Lord Hoffmann's analysis at [11], the trust is express rather than resulting: see further para.16–144.

191 See, e.g. *Templeton Insurance Ltd v Penningtons Solicitors* [2006] EWHC 685 (Ch); [2007] W.T.L.R. 1103. In *Cooper v PRG Powerhouse Ltd* [2008] EWHC 498 (Ch); [2008] 2 All E.R. (Comm) 964, Evans-Lombe J also purported to follow *Twinsectra*, notwithstanding references throughout his judgment to "the purpose trust".

192 [2006] 1 W.L.R. 1476: [see paras 14-147 to 14-152].

193 [1970] A.C. 567.

of the borrower's assets, in which case it passes to his trustee in bankruptcy in the event of his insolvency and the lender is merely a loan creditor; or whether it is held on a resulting trust for the lender. This depends on the intention of the parties collected from the terms of the arrangement and the circumstances of the case.

16–123 In the present case Twinsectra contends that paragraphs 1 and 2 of the undertaking which Mr Sims signed on 24 December created a *Quistclose* trust. Mr Leach denies this and advances a number of objections to the existence of a trust. He says that Twinsectra lacked the necessary intention to create a trust, and relies on evidence that Twinsectra looked exclusively to Mr Sims' personal undertaking to repay the loan as its security for repayment. He says that commercial life would be impossible if trusts were lightly inferred from slight material, and that it is not enough to agree that a loan is to be made for a particular purpose. There must be something more, for example, a requirement that the money be paid into a segregated account, before it is appropriate to infer that a trust has been created. In the present case the money was paid into Mr Sims' client account, but that is sufficiently explained by the fact that it was not Mr Sims' money but his client's; it provides no basis for an inference that the money was held in trust for anyone other than Mr Yardley. Then it is said that a trust requires certainty of objects and this was lacking, for the stated purpose "to be applied in the purchase of property" is too uncertain to be enforced. Finally it is said that no trust in favour of Twinsectra could arise prior to the failure of the stated purpose, and this did not occur until the money was misapplied by Mr Yardley's companies.

Intention

16–124 The first two objections are soon disposed of. A settlor must, of course, possess the necessary intention to create a trust, but his subjective intentions are irrelevant. If he enters into arrangements which have the effect of creating a trust, it is not necessary that he should appreciate that they do so; it is sufficient that he intends to enter into them. Whether paragraphs 1 and 2 of the undertaking created a *Quistclose* trust turns on the true construction of those paragraphs.

16–125 The fact that Twinsectra relied for its security exclusively on Mr Sims's personal liability to repay goes to Twinsectra's subjective intention and is not relevant to the construction of the undertaking, but it is in any case not inconsistent with the trust alleged. Arrangements of this kind are not intended to provide security for repayment of the loan, but to prevent the money from being applied otherwise than in accordance with the lender's wishes. If the money is properly applied the loan is unsecured. This was true of all the decided cases, including the *Quistclose* case itself.

The Effect of the Undertaking

16–126 A *Quistclose* trust does not necessarily arise merely because money is paid for a particular purpose. A lender will often inquire into the purpose for which a loan is sought in order to decide whether he would be justified in making it. He may be said to lend the money for the purpose in question, but this is not enough to create a trust; once lent the money is at the free disposal of the borrower. Similarly payments in advance for goods or services are paid for a particular purpose, but such payments do not ordinarily create a trust. The money is intended to be at the free disposal of the supplier and may be used as part of his cashflow. Commercial life would be impossible if this were not the case.

16–127 The question in every case is whether the parties intended the money to be at the free disposal of the recipient.[194] His freedom to dispose of the money is necessarily excluded by an arrangement that the money shall be used exclusively for the stated purpose, for as Lord Wilberforce observed in the *Quistclose* case:[195]

> "A necessary consequence from this, by a process simply of interpretation, must be that if, for any reason, [the purpose could not be carried out,] the money was to be returned to [the lender]: the word 'only' or 'exclusively' can have no other meaning or effect." . . .

16–128 In the present case paragraphs 1 and 2 of the undertaking are crystal clear. Mr Sims undertook that the money would be used solely for the acquisition of property and for no other purpose; and was to be retained by his firm until so applied. It would not be held by Mr Sims simply to Mr Yardley's order; and it

---

194 *Re Goldcorp Exchange Ltd* [1995] 1 A.C. 74 at 100, per Lord Mustill.
195 [1970] A.C. 567 at 580.

would not be at Mr Yardley's free disposition. Any payment by Mr Sims of the money, whether to Mr Yardley or anyone else, otherwise than for the acquisition of property would constitute a breach of trust.

Mr Leach insisted that such a payment would, no doubt, constitute a breach of contract, but there was no reason to invoke equitable principles merely because Mr Sims was a solicitor. But Mr Sims's status as a solicitor has nothing to do with it. Equity's intervention is more principled than this. It is unconscionable for a man to obtain money on terms as to its application and then disregard the terms on which he received it. Such conduct goes beyond a mere breach of contract . . . .The duty is not contractual but fiduciary. It may exist despite the absence of any contract at all between the parties, as in *Rose v Rose*;[196] and it binds third parties as in the *Quistclose* case itself. The duty is fiduciary in character because a person who makes money available on terms that it is to be used for a particular purpose only and not for any other purpose thereby places his trust and confidence in the recipient to ensure that it is properly applied. This is a classic situation in which a fiduciary relationship arises, and since it arises in respect of a specific fund it gives rise to a trust. 16–129

. . .In "The *Quistclose* Trust: Who Can Enforce It?",[197] I argued that the beneficial interest remained throughout in the lender. This analysis has received considerable though not universal academic support.[198] It was adopted by the New Zealand Court of Appeal in *General Communications Ltd v Development Finance Corp of New Zealand Ltd*[199] and referred to with apparent approval by Gummow J. in *In re Australian Elizabethan Theatre Trust*.[200] Gummow J. saw nothing special in the *Quistclose* trust, regarding it as essentially a security device to protect the lender against other creditors of the borrower pending the application of the money for the stated purpose. 16–130

On this analysis, the *Quistclose* trust is a simple commercial arrangement akin (as Professor Bridge observes) to a retention of title clause (though with a different object) which enables the borrower to have recourse to the lender's money for a particular purpose without entrenching on the lender's property rights more than necessary to enable the purpose to be achieved. The money remains the property of the lender unless and until it is applied in accordance with his directions, and insofar as it is not so applied it must be returned to him. I am disposed, perhaps pre-disposed, to think that this is the only analysis which is consistent both with orthodox trust law and with commercial reality. Before reaching a concluded view that it should be adopted, however, I must consider the alternatives 16–131

It is plain that the beneficial interest is not vested unconditionally in the borrower so as to leave the money at his free disposal. That would defeat the whole purpose of the arrangements, which is to prevent the money from passing to the borrower's trustee in bankruptcy in the event of his insolvency. It would also be inconsistent with all the decided cases where the contest was between the lender and the borrower's trustee in bankruptcy, as well as with the *Quistclose* case itself . . .[201] 16–132

. . . The most serious objection to [the view that the beneficial interest is in third parties who will benefit from the performance of the purpose] is exemplified by the facts of the present case. In several of the cases the primary trust was for an abstract purpose with no one but the lender to enforce performance or restrain misapplication of the money . . .[202] The present case is another example. It is simply not possible to hold money on trust to acquire unspecified property from an unspecified vendor at an unspecified time. There is no reason to make an arbitrary distinction between money paid for an abstract purpose and money paid for a purpose which can be said to benefit an ascertained class of beneficiaries, and the cases rightly draw no such distinction. Any analysis of the Quistclose trust must be able to accommodate gifts and loans for an abstract purpose. 16–133

. . . The difficulty with [the view that the beneficial interest is in suspense until the stated purpose is carried out or fails] (apart from its unorthodoxy) is that it fails to have regard to the role which the resulting trust plays in equity's scheme of things, or to explain why the money is not simply held on a resulting trust for the lender. 16–134

---

196 (1986) 7 N.S.W.L.R. 679.

197 (1985) 101 L.Q.R. 269.

198 See for example Priestley L.J. "The *Romalpa* Clause and the *Quistclose* Trust" in *Equity and Commercial Relationships*, edited by P. D. Finn (1987), pp.217, 237; and M. Bridge "The *Quistclose* Trust in a World of Secured Transactions" (1992) 12 O.J.L.S. 333, 352; and others.

199 [1990] 3 N.Z.L.R. 406.

200 (1991) 102 A.L.R. 681.

201 See in particular *Toovey v Milne* (1819) 2 B. & Ald. 683; *In re Rogers, Ex p. Holland & Hannen* (1891) 8 Morr. 243.

202 [The cases cited by Lord Millett at this point include *In re EVTR* [1987] B.C.L.C. 646, where money was advanced "for the sole purpose of buying new equipment".]

16–135 . . . Lord Browne-Wilkinson [in *Westdeutsche Landesbank Girpcentrale v Islington Borough Council*[203]] explained that a resulting trust arises in two sets of circumstances. He described the second as follows: "Where A transfers property to B on express trusts, but the trusts declared do not exhaust the whole beneficial interest." The *Quistclose* case was among the cases he cited as examples . . .

16–136 Thus all the alternative solutions have their difficulties. But there are two problems which they fail to solve, but which are easily solved if the beneficial interest remains throughout in the lender. One arises from the fact, well established by the authorities, that the primary trust is enforceable by the lender. But on what basis can he enforce it? He cannot do so as the beneficiary under the secondary trust, for if the primary purpose is fulfilled there is no secondary trust: the precondition of his claim is destructive of his standing to make it. He cannot do so as settlor, for a settlor who retains no beneficial interest cannot enforce the trust which he has created.

16–137 Dr Chambers[204] insists that the lender has merely a right to prevent the misapplication of the money, and attributes this to his contractual right to specific performance of a condition of the contract of loan. As I have already pointed out, this provides no solution where the arrangement is non-contractual. But Lord Wilberforce clearly based the borrower's obligation on an equitable or fiduciary basis and not a contractual one. He was concerned to justify the co-existence of equity's exclusive jurisdiction with the common law action for debt. Basing equity's intervention on its auxiliary jurisdiction to restrain a breach of contract would not have enabled the lender to succeed against the bank, which was a third party to the contract. There is only one explanation of the lender's fiduciary right to enforce the primary trust which can be reconciled with basic principle: he can do so because he is the beneficiary.

16–138 The other problem is concerned with the basis on which the primary trust is said to have failed in several of the cases, particularly *Toovey v Milne*[205] and the *Quistclose* case itself. Given that the money did not belong to the borrower in either case, the borrower's insolvency should not have prevented the money from being paid in the manner contemplated. A man cannot pay some only of his creditors once he has been adjudicated bankrupt, but a third party can. A company cannot pay a dividend once it has gone into liquidation, but there is nothing to stop a third party from paying the disappointed shareholders. The reason why the purpose failed in each case must be because the lender's object in making the money available was to save the borrower from bankruptcy in the one case and collapse in the other. But this in itself is not enough. A trust does not fail merely because the settlor's purpose in creating it has been frustrated: the trust must become illegal or impossible to perform. The settlor's motives must not be confused with the purpose of the trust; the frustration of the former does not by itself cause the failure of the latter. But if the borrower is treated as holding the money on a resulting trust for the lender but with power (or in some cases a duty) to carry out the lender's revocable mandate, and the lender's object in giving the mandate is frustrated, he is entitled to revoke the mandate and demand the return of money which never ceased to be his beneficially . . . .

16–139 As Sherlock Holmes reminded Dr Watson, when you have eliminated the impossible, whatever remains, however improbable, must be the truth. I would reject all the alternative analyses, which I find unconvincing for the reasons I have endeavoured to explain, and hold the *Quistclose* trust to be an entirely orthodox example of the kind of default trust known as a resulting trust. The lender pays the money to the borrower by way of loan, but he does not part with the entire beneficial interest in the money, and in so far as he does not it is held on a resulting trust for the lender from the outset . . .

16–140 After this over-long exposition, it is possible to dispose of the remaining objections to the creation of a *Quistclose* trust very shortly. A trust must have certainty of objects. But the only trust is the resulting trust for the lender. The borrower is authorised (or directed) to apply the money for a stated purpose, but this is a mere power and does not constitute a purpose trust. Provided the power is stated with sufficient clarity for the court to be able to determine whether it is still capable of being carried out or whether the money has been misapplied, it is sufficiently certain to be enforced. If it is uncertain, however, then the borrower has no authority to make any use of the money at all and must return it to the lender under the resulting trust . . .

16–141 Like all resulting trusts, the trust in favour of the lender arises when the lender parts with the money on terms which do not exhaust the beneficial interest. It is not a contingent reversionary or future interest. It does not suddenly come into being like an 18th century use only when the stated purpose fails. It is a

---

[203] [1996] A.C. 669, 706].
[204] [*Resulting Trusts* (Clarendon, 1997)].
[205] (1819) 2 B. & Ald. 683.

default trust which fills the gap when some part of the beneficial interest is undisposed of and prevents it from being "in suspense".

Conclusion

In my opinion the Court of Appeal were correct to find that the terms of paragraphs 1 and 2 of the undertaking created a *Quistclose* trust. The money was never at Mr Yardley's free disposal. It was never held to his order by Mr Sims. The money belonged throughout to Twinsectra, subject only to Mr Yardley's right to apply it for the acquisition of property. Twinsectra parted with the money to Mr Sims, relying on him to ensure that the money was properly applied or returned to it. Mr Sims act in paying the money over to Mr Leach was a breach of trust, but it did not in itself render the money incapable of being applied for the stated purpose. In so far as Mr Leach applied the money in the acquisition of property, the purpose was achieved. **16–142**

ii. The Impact of the *Twinsectra* Analysis

On Lord Millett's view in a case where A lends money to B, stipulating that the money be used only for a specific purpose, the *Quistclose* trust responds to the objective intention of A that B should be under a duty to A to use the money only for the specified purpose, and not otherwise for B's benefit: "[t]he question in every case is whether the parties intended the money to be at the free disposal of the recipient."[206] The trust thus arises in A's favour as soon as the transfer to B occurs, but A's interest is defeasible by the exercise of a power vested in B to apply the money to the specified purpose.[207] If and when the money is so applied, the trust ends and B simply owes A a personal duty to repay the loan on the terms agreed between the parties. **16–143**

Lord Millett referred to an article he had written which set out his view that, from the moment of the transfer to B, a trust arose in favour of A.[208] The analysis there suggests that the *Quistclose* trust is an express trust, arising as a result of A's exercise of a power to set up a trust. His speech in *Twinsectra*, however, suggests that he was persuaded by Robert Chambers' general work on resulting trusts (whilst disagreeing with Chambers' specific view of the *Quistclose* trust) to modify this opinion[209] so that in cases where the transferor does not declare an express trust for herself, a resulting trust can arise in her favour.[210] However, it would be easy to exaggerate the significance of Lord Millett's shift from an express trust to a resulting trust analysis.[211] Lord Millett's central point is that the "question in every case is whether the parties intended the money to be at the free disposal of the recipient"[212] and so the governing factor in finding a trust is "the intention of the parties collected from the terms of the arrangement and the circumstances of the case".[213] **16–144**

---

206 [2002] 2 A.C. 164, [74] (extracted at para 16-127).

207 The nature of this power is discussed in L. Smith, "Understanding the Power" in W. Swadling (ed.), *The Quistclose Trust* (Hart Publishing, 2004).

208 (1985) 101 L.Q.R. 269.

209 Although not his analysis of the *Quistclose* case, which his Lordship thought vulnerable to the criticisms made in L. Ho and P. St.J. Smart "Reinterpreting the *Quistclose* Trust: A Critique of Chambers' Analysis" (2001) 21 O.J.L.S. 267. Chambers responds to these criticisms, and restates his position on *Quistclose*, in "Restrictions on the Use of Money" in Swadling (ed.), *The Quistclose Trust* (2004). See too J. Glister, "The Nature of *Quistclose* Trusts: Classification and Reconciliation" [2004] C.L.J. 632.

210 As noted in J. Penner, "Lord Millett's Analysis" in Swadling (ed.), *The Quistclose Trust* (2004), pp.50–56. See also Lord Millett's own comments in the foreword at p.ix. Whether the recipient is an express trustee or a resulting trustee with knowledge of X's equitable interest, Y must account to X for the money from the moment of receipt, and must pay X any profit she obtains by misapplication of the money: *Abraaj Investment Management Ltd v Bregawn Jersey Ltd* [2010] EWHC 630 (Comm) at [28]–[32].

211 As noted by eg E. Hudson, "A Normative Approach to the *Quistclose* Trust" (2017) 80 M.L.R. 775, 781, there are "doctrinal tensions in Lord Millett's reasoning" as to whether the trust is best seen as express or resulting.

212 [2002] UKHL 12; [2002] 2 A.C. 164 at [74] (extracted at para.16–127).

213 [2002] UKHL 12; [2002] 2 A.C. 164 at [69] (extracted at para.16–122). Note too J. Penner, "Lord Millett's Analysis" in Swadling (ed.) *The Quistclose Trust* (2004), pp.53–54 noting that, in this context, the distinction between A's having a

16–145 The centrality of A's objectively understood intention to the *Quistclose* trust can also be seen in later cases. The link to express trusts is also evident in further judicial formulations which emphasise that it is not enough for B simply to be under a contractual duty to A; rather the court must be satisfied that the intention of A and B was that the right transferred should be held for A's benefit, not for that of B.[214] This entails that B "understands that his use of the property is specifically restricted: he is not entitled to use the property as his own despite his legal ownership of it."[215]

Bellis v Challinor

[2015] EWCA Civ 59 at [56]–[65]

16–146 BRIGGS LJ: *Quistclose*-type trusts are a species of resulting trust which arise where property (usually money) is transferred on terms which do not leave it at the free disposal of the transferee. That restriction upon its use is usually created by an arrangement that the money should be used exclusively for a stated purpose or purposes.[216]

16–147 There must be an intention to create a trust on the part of the transferor. This is an objective question. It means that the transferor must have intended to enter into arrangements which, viewed objectively, have the effect in law of creating a trust.[217]

16–148 In this respect, *Quistclose*-type trusts are no different from any other trusts. In particular, they are not presumed to exist unless a contrary intention be proved, as in the case of the traditional type of resulting trust where a person makes a gratuitous transfer of property to an apparent stranger.

16–149 A person creates a trust by his words or conduct, not by his innermost thoughts. His subjective intentions are, as Lord Millett said, irrelevant. In the *Twinsectra* case, the *Quistclose* trust was established despite the transferor having no subjective intention to create a trust. But the objectivity principle works both ways. A person who does subjectively intend to create a trust may fail to do so if his words and conduct, viewed objectively, fall short of what is required. As with the interpretation of contracts, this process of interpretation is often called the ascertainment of objective intention. In the contractual context, the court is looking for the objective common intention, whereas in the trust context the search is for the objective intention of the alleged settlor . . .

16–150 . . . where it is not demonstrated that money apparently advanced by way of loan is not to be at the free disposal of the transferee, the ordinary consequence is that the money becomes the property of the transferee, who is free to apply it as he chooses, leaving the lender at risk of his insolvency.[218] This is the true default position, in which the transfer of the legal title carries with it the beneficial interest. Although Lord Millett speaks of the *Quistclose*-type trust as one under which the transferor "does not part with the beneficial interest in the money",[219] he was not, I am sure, intending thereby to depart from the following well-known dictum of Lord Browne-Wilkinson:

> "A person solely entitled to the full beneficial ownership of money or property, both at law and in equity, does not enjoy an equitable interest in that property. The legal title carries with it all rights. Unless and until there is a separation of the legal and equitable estate, there is no separate equitable title. Therefore to talk about [A] 'retaining' its equitable title is meaningless. The only question is whether the circumstances under which the money was paid were such, as in equity, to impose a trust on [B]. If so, an equitable interest arose for the first time under that trust."

---

positive intention that B hold on trust for A and A's instead having only an absence of intention to benefit B is so fine that it "is almost scholastic in its unreality".

214 See e.g. *Bieber v Teathers Ltd* [2012] EWCA Civ 1466 at [15]; *Ali v Dinc* [2020] EWHC 3055 (Ch) at [241]–[243]. An appeal against the judgment in *Ali v Dinc*, made only on a procedural point, was dismissed: [2022] EWCA Civ 34.

215 *Ali v Dinc* [2020] EWHC 3055 (Ch) at [245].

216 See *Twinsectra* [2002] 2 A.C. 164 at [71].

217 See *Twinsectra* [2002] 2 A.C. 164 at [71].

218 See *Twinsectra* [2002] 2 A.C. 164 at [68].

219 See *Twinsectra* [2002] 2 A.C. 164 at [100].

In *Bellis v Challinor*, the Court of Appeal reversed the first instance finding of a *Quistclose* trust: it was held that there was nothing to displace the general starting point that, when paying money into B's solicitor's client account at the request of B, A had simply been making a payment to B: there was no evidence of any objective intention that the solicitors, or B, should be under a duty to A not to use that money for anything other than a specific purpose. Similarly, in *First City Monument Bank Plc v Zumax Nigeria Ltd*,[220] the Court of Appeal overturned a first instance finding of a *Quistclose* trust on the basis that there was insufficient evidence of any objective intention of A that money paid to a bank, B, should be held by the bank on trust for A subject only to a power of the bank to apply the money to the credit of C. It was true that the purpose of the payment was that B should then credit C's account, but that could be met by B's being under a personal duty to A to do so, and it did not mean that B had to be under a duty in relation to the specific payments received. This was confirmed by the fact that (in contrast to the position in *Quistclose* or *Twinsectra*) the payments had not been made into a separate account, and also by the usual banking practice in which "the basic banker–customer relationship is that of debtor and creditor". As noted in Chapter 5 when discussing express trusts, the crucial question is not simply whether B is under a duty to A, but rather whether that duty is a duty to A not to use a specific right held by B for B's own benefit (albeit, in the case of a *Quistclose* trust, with a permission to use the right for a particular purpose). Certainly, it is clear that the mere fact that a payment is made by A to B with the intention that B use the payment for a specific purpose does not suffice for a trust:[221] "[c]ommercial life would be impossible if this were not the case."[222] **16–151**

A further example of a court failing to find a claimed *Quistclose* trust is *Prickly Bay Waterside Ltd v British American Insurance Co*.[223] The Privy Council held that the parties' arrangements had not been intended to impose a duty on B not to use money received from A for B's own benefit, and the lack of any intention that B should keep the money apart from B's general funds supported that overall finding. The Privy Council's advice, given by Lady Arden, contains the same tension apparent in Lord Millett's analysis in *Twinsectra*, and in that of Briggs LJ in *Bellis v Challinor*, as it does not make clear whether a *Quistclose* trust is best seen as an express or as a resulting trust. We will return to this question when considering the justification for such trusts. **16–152**

Prickly Bay Waterside Ltd v British American Insurance Co Ltd

[2022] UKPC 8 at [25] and [31]–[32]

LADY ARDEN: Lord Millett made it clear in [*Twinsectra*] . . . that the *Quistclose* trust was a default trust. This means two things. Firstly, the resulting trust which characterises the *Quistclose* trust arises as a matter of law and becomes unconditional on failure of the specified purpose. Secondly, the resulting trust does not override any arrangement on which the parties may have agreed for the destination of the funds previously earmarked for the purpose but takes subject to it . . . **16–153**

The third summarised principle[224] states that there must be a "mutual intention" of the payer and recipient that the funds transferred "should not be part of the general assets of the recipient" but should be used *exclusively* to effect particular identified payments. It is clear that Lord Millett did not consider that the intention had to be "mutual" in the sense of being shared or reciprocated. It would be **16–154**

---

220 [2019] EWCA Civ 294.
221 See [2019] EWCA Civ 294 at [33] and *Twinsectra* [2002] UKHL 12; [2002] 2 A.C. 164 at [100].
222 *Twinsectra* [2002] UKHL 12; [2002] 2 A.C. 164 at [73]. See too *First City Monument Bank Plc v Zumax Nigeria Ltd* [2019] EWCA Civ 294 at [33] and [36].
223 [2022] UKPC 8.
224 [This is a reference to the summary of principles governing the *Quistclose* trust set out in *Bieber v Teathers* [2012] EWHC 190 (Ch) at [18].]

enough if one party imposed it on the other who acquiesced in it (see his citation[225] from the judgment of North J in *Gilbert v Gonard*[226]). Moreover, the minimum necessary to constitute a *Quistclose* trust is not an intention that the funds transferred should not form part of the general assets of the recipient but is expressed more flexibly as an intention that the payer should retain some beneficial interest in the funds.[227] It is also possible that the trust does not require that property should be "exclusively" used for the purposes of the *Quistclose* trust. The payer or other transferor may have given other directions, or the parties may have agreed to other terms, since, as emphasised above, the *Quistclose* trust is only a default trust. As explained in para [25] above, that means that a resulting trust arises by operation of law only if and to the extent that the parties have not agreed what should happen to the trust property if the trust fails.

16–155 In the opinion of the Board, it follows from Lord Millett's injunction that subtle distinctions should not be drawn between different species of trust for the payment of creditors that the term *Quistclose* trust may commonly be used whenever a person provides assets to another for the purpose of paying debts under arrangements which create a trust.[228] A *Quistclose* trust can take many forms. It may be express as to what is to happen on failure of the specified purpose, or express only as to that purpose, or it may simply be a resulting trust arising by operation of law: such is the flexibility of equity. That flexibility makes an important and beneficial contribution to the legal system of the jurisdiction in question because it enables equity to respond to the need for different sorts of transactions, and also because in that way it contributes to the development of society and to the growth of its economy. However, to be a trust which enables the provider of the asset to enforce the return of those assets in specie in the event of exhaustion or failure to execute the purpose, and thus to obtain priority over other creditors of the recipient if insolvent, there must be a sufficient indication that the provider did not intend to dispose of the entire beneficial interest in the trust funds. Normally, that indication will be a mutual intention that there should be a trust, but it can also be an acceptance that the provider of the assets retains a partial beneficial interest by virtue of the resulting trust.

16–156 It should finally be noted that, as shown by Lady Arden's reference to cases where "a person provides assets to another", a *Quistclose* trust can arise in relation to rights other than money, and in cases where the specific purpose for which B is allowed to use the rights is something other than the payment of debts. In *Ali v Dinc*,[229] for example, Sarah Worthington QC (sitting as a Deputy High Court Judge) found that such a trust arose where A transferred legal estates in land ["the Properties"] to B, without receiving anything in return, for the specific purpose of allowing B to use those rights to raise money by granting charges over them in favour of third parties. It seems that the factor distinguishing the case from *Bellis v Challinor* and *Prickly Bay Waterside* was that it was "clear on the evidence that [A] did not intend that the Properties were to be at the free disposal of [B], *and* [B] also understood that to be the case."[230]

5. Further Examples of Resulting Trusts?

16–157 In *Westdeutsche Landesbank Girozentrale v Islington LBC*,[231] A (the bank) argued that a payment it had made to B (the local authority) under a void contract was, as soon as it was received by B, held on trust for A. Its reason for doing so was that, if a trust existed, B would be liable to pay compound interest, rather than only simple interest, on the payment. One of the arguments made by A was that, as the contract was void, its equitable title to the money had not passed to B. It was in rejecting that

225 *Twinsectra* [2002] 2 A.C. 164 at [76].
226 (1884) 54 LJ Ch 439, 440.
227 *Twinsectra* [2002] 2 A.C. 164 at [100].
228 *Twinsectra* [2002] 2 A.C. 164 at [68] and [69].
229 [2020] EWHC 3055 (Ch).
230 [2020] EWHC 3055 (Ch) at [200] (emphasis in original).
231 [1996] A.C. 669.

argument that Lord Browne-Wilkinson made the important observation, noted above,[232] that it is "fallacious" as "[a] person solely entitled to the full beneficial ownership of money or property, both at law and in equity, does not enjoy an equitable interest in that property."[233]

The bank also argued that a resulting trust could arise, even though the facts did not fall into either of the two types of resulting trust identified by Lord Browne-Wilkinson. One suggested basis for such a resulting trust was that it was needed to respond to an unjust enrichment of B at A's expense. As we will see below,[234] Peter Birks[235] and Robert Chambers[236] made the argument that unjust enrichment provides the best explanation for both Type (A) and Type (B) resulting trusts, and can also justify the recognition of resulting trusts in further situations. In *Westdeutsche*, however, the House of Lords rejected this argument for extending the types of resulting trust. **16–158**

Westdeutsche Landesbank Girozentrale v Islington LBC

House of Lords [1996] A.C. 669

The appellant bank sued the respondent council to recover £1,145,525 paid under an interest rate swap agreement that was void because beyond the powers of the council. The Court of Appeal upheld the judge's decision that the bank was entitled to recover the money on the ground that the council had been unjustly enriched at the bank's expense, with compound interest. The council appealed against the award of compound interest, arguing that the court could only have had jurisdiction to make such an interest award if the money had been held on trust for the bank, and arguing too that no trust had arisen in the bank's favour. The House of Lords unanimously held that although the bank had a personal claim to recover the money in a common law action for money had and received, it had no proprietary equitable claim; by a 3:2 majority, it followed that only simple interest was payable (Lords Goff and Woolf dissenting on the basis that compound interest should be awarded by way of an equitable remedy in aid of the common law, so that the bank could have restitution of the user value of its money[237]). **16–159**

LORD BROWNE-WILKINSON (with whom LORD SLYNN and LORD LLOYD agreed, but with whom LORD GOFF and LORD WOOLF disagreed): Before considering the legal merits of the submission, it is important to appreciate the practical consequences which ensue if the bank's arguments are correct. Those who suggest that a resulting trust should arise in these circumstances accept that the creation of an equitable proprietary interest under the trust can have unfortunate, and adverse, effects if the original recipient of the moneys becomes insolvent: the moneys, if traceable in the hands of the recipient, are trust moneys and not available for the creditors of the recipient. However, the creation of an equitable proprietary interest in moneys received under a void contract is capable of having adverse effects quite apart from insolvency. The proprietary interest under the unknown trust will, quite apart from insolvency, be enforceable against any recipient of the property other than the purchaser for value of a legal interest without notice. **16–160**

. . . My Lords, wise judges have often warned against the wholesale importation into commercial law of equitable principles inconsistent with the certainty and speed which are essential requirements for the orderly conduct of business affairs.[238] If the bank's arguments are correct, a businessman who has entered into transactions relating to or dependent upon property rights could find that assets which apparently belong to one person in fact belong to another; that there are "off balance sheet" liabilities of which he **16–161**

232 See paras 4–046 and 16–160.
233 [1996] A.C. 669 at 705–706.
234 See paras 16–182ff.
235 See, e.g. "Restitution and Resulting Trusts" in S. Goldstein (ed.), *Equity and Contemporary Legal Developments* (1992).
236 See, e.g. *Resulting Trusts* (Clarendon Press, 1997).
237 In *Sempra Metals Ltd v IRC* [2008] A.C. 561, the House of Lords later held that claims in unjust enrichment do lie to recover the user value of money as compound interest, thus vindicating the views of Lord Goff and Lord Woolf; however in *Prudential Assurance Co Ltd v HMRC* [2018] UKSC 39, [2019] A.C. 929, the Supreme Court reversed that position, denying the existence of a claim in unjust enrichment to recover compound interest.
238 *Barnes v Addy* (1874) L.R. 9 Ch. App. 244 at 251, 255, and *Scandinavian Trading Tanker Co AB v Flota Petrolera Ecuatoriana* [1983] 2 A.C. 694 at 703–704.

cannot be aware; that these property rights and liabilities arise from circumstances unknown not only to himself but also to anyone else who has been involved in the transactions. A new area of unmanageable risk will be introduced into commercial dealings. If the due application of equitable principles forced a conclusion leading to these results, your Lordships would be presented with a formidable task in reconciling legal principle with commercial common sense. But in my judgment no such conflict occurs. The resulting trust for which the bank contends is inconsistent not only with the law as it stands but with any principled development of it.

16–162 . . . This is not a case where the bank had any equitable interest which predated receipt by the local authority of the upfront payment. Therefore, in order to show that the local authority became a trustee, the bank must demonstrate circumstances which raised a trust for the first time either at the date on which the local authority received the money or at the date on which payment into the mixed account was made. Counsel for the bank specifically disavowed any claim based on a constructive trust. This was plainly right because the local authority had no relevant knowledge sufficient to raise a constructive trust at any time before the moneys, upon the bank account going into overdraft, became untraceable. Once there ceased to be an identifiable trust fund, the local authority could not become a trustee: *Re Goldcorp Exchange Ltd*.[239] Therefore, as the argument for the bank recognised, the only possible trust which could be established was a resulting trust arising from the circumstances in which the local authority received the upfront payment.

16–163 [His Lordship explained the circumstances under which resulting trusts arise, as set out at para.16–009, and continued:] Applying these conventional principles of resulting trust to the present case, the bank's claim must fail. There was no transfer of money to the local authority on express trusts: therefore a resulting trust of type (B) above could not arise. As to type (A) above, any presumption of resulting trust is rebutted since it is demonstrated that the bank paid, and the local authority received, the upfront payment with the intention that the moneys so paid should become the absolute property of the local authority. It is true that the parties were under a misapprehension that the payment was made in pursuance of a valid contract. But that does not alter the actual intentions of the parties at the date the payment was made or the moneys were mixed in the bank account. As the article by William Swadling demonstrates,[240] the presumption of resulting trust is rebutted by evidence of any intention inconsistent with such a trust, not only by evidence of an intention to make a gift.

16–164 Professor Birks,[241] while accepting that the principles I have stated represent "a very conservative form" of definition of a resulting trust, argues from restitutionary principles that the definition should be extended so as to cover a perceived gap in the law of "subtractive unjust enrichment"[242] so as to give a plaintiff a proprietary remedy when he has transferred value under a mistake or under a contract the consideration for which wholly fails. He suggests that a resulting trust should arise wherever the money is paid under a mistake (because such mistake vitiates the actual intention) or when money is paid on a condition which is not subsequently satisfied.

16–165 As one would expect, the argument is tightly reasoned but I am not persuaded. The search for a perceived need to strengthen the remedies of a plaintiff claiming in restitution involves, to my mind, a distortion of trust principles. First, the argument elides rights in property (which is the only proper subject matter of a trust) into rights in "the value transferred".[243] A trust can only arise where there is defined trust property: it is therefore not consistent with trust principles to say that a person is a trustee of property which cannot be defined. Second, Professor Birks' approach appears to assume (e.g. in the case of a transfer of value made under a contract the consideration for which subsequently fails) that the recipient will be deemed to have been a trustee from the date of his original receipt of money, i.e. the trust arises at a time when the "trustee" does not, and cannot, know that there is going to be a total failure of consideration. This result is incompatible with the basic premise on which all trust law is built, viz. that the conscience of the trustee is affected. Unless and until the trustee is aware of the factors which give rise to the supposed trust, there is nothing which can affect his conscience. Thus neither in the case of a subsequent failure of consideration nor in the case of a payment under a contract subsequently found to be void for mistake or

239 [1995] 1 A.C. 74.
240 "A New Role for Resulting Trusts?" (1996) 16 L.S. 110, 133.
241 "Restitution and Resulting Trusts" in S. Goldstein (ed.), *Equity and Contemporary Legal Developments* (1992), p.360.
242 ibid. at p.368.
243 ibid. at p.361.

failure of condition will there be circumstances, at the date of receipt, which can impinge on the conscience of the recipient, thereby making him a trustee. Thirdly, Professor Birks has to impose on his wider view an arbitrary and admittedly unprincipled modification so as to ensure that a resulting trust does not arise when there has only been a failure to perform a contract, as opposed to total failure of consideration.[244] Such arbitrary exclusion is designed to preserve the rights of creditors in the insolvency of the recipient. The fact that it is necessary to exclude artificially one type of case which would logically fall within the wider concept casts doubt on the validity of the concept.

If adopted, Professor Birks' wider concepts would give rise to all the practical consequences and injustices to which I have referred. I do not think it right to make an unprincipled alteration to the law of property (i.e. the law of trusts) so as to produce in the law of unjust enrichment the injustices to third parties which I have mentioned and the consequential commercial uncertainty which any extension of proprietary interests in personal property is bound to produce. **16–166**

. . . The argument for a resulting trust was said to be supported by the case of a thief who steals a bag of coins. At law those coins remain traceable only so long as they are kept separate: as soon as they are mixed with other coins or paid into a mixed bank account they cease to be traceable at law. Can it really be the case, it is asked, that in such circumstances the thief cannot be required to disgorge the property which, in equity, represents the stolen coins? Moneys can only be traced in equity if there has been at some stage a breach of fiduciary duty, i.e. if either before the theft there was an equitable proprietary interest (e.g. the coins were stolen trust moneys) or such interest arises under a resulting trust at the time of the theft or the mixing of the moneys. Therefore, it is said, a resulting trust must arise either at the time of the theft or when the moneys are subsequently mixed. Unless this is the law, there will be no right to recover the assets representing the stolen moneys once the moneys have become mixed. **16–167**

I agree that the stolen moneys are traceable in equity. But the proprietary interest which equity is enforcing in such circumstances arises under a constructive, not a resulting, trust. Although it is difficult to find clear authority for the proposition, when property is obtained by fraud equity imposes a constructive trust on the fraudulent recipient: the property is recoverable and traceable in equity. Thus, an infant who has obtained property by fraud is bound in equity to restore it.[245] **16–168**

Consistently with Lord Browne-Wilkinson's classification we will examine the trust said to arise in relation to theft or fraud in Chapter 17, when considering constructive trusts.[246] **16–169**

6. Justifying Type (A) Resulting Trusts

A. A Response to A's Intention to Create a Trust

Our view is that the best way for the current law to understand and justify such trusts is that they are based on A's intention (as objectively interpreted) that B should hold the property acquired on trust for A. In *Vandervell v IRC*, for example, Lord Upjohn identified the crucial question as being whether A intended B to "take beneficially or on trust".[247] **16–170**

This intention should be tested for in just the same way as an express trust, and as discussed in Chapter 7.[248] So, for example, it is not necessary that the term "trust" should be used, nor should B be expressly told to keep the property acquired separately from other property. The question is simply **16–171**

---

244 ibid. at pp. 356–359 and 362.

245 *Stocks v Wilson* [1913] 2 K.B. 235 at 244; *R. Leslie Ltd v Sheill* [1914] 3 K.B. 607. Moneys stolen from a bank account can be traced in equity: *Bankers Trust Co v Shapira* [1980] 1 W.L.R. 1274 at 1282. See also *McCormick v Grogan* (1869) L.R. 4 H.L. 82 at 97.

246 See paras 17–210 to 17–232.

247 [1967] 2 A.C. 291 at 312. See too Briggs LJ, writing extra-judicially: "Resulting Trusts after *Prest*" (2014) 181 *ACTAPS Newsletter* 4, 6: "I suggest that the only underlying principle of law is that a resulting trust will be inferred or implied (where not imposed in express terms) where to do so would give effect to the common intention or understanding of the parties."

248 See paras 7–007 to 7–033.

whether A objectively intended B, when acquiring the property, to be under a duty to A not to use that property for B's own benefit. As demonstrated by *Quistclose* trusts, such a duty can exist even if B also has a power to use the property for a specific purpose, such as the payment of a particular debt, which may benefit B. In our view, the presumption of resulting trust, and the presumption of advancement, are of use only to the extent that they help a court answer this key question as to the nature of A's objective intention.

16–172 The link drawn above between resulting trusts and the common intention constructive trust assists with this analysis: in each case, the focus is on the intentions of the parties. The difference with the resulting trust is that the claimant (A) begins with a particular right: either the claimed trust property itself, which A transferred to B; or money, or another right, which is used for B to acquire the claimed trust property. In such a case, to protect A's ability to benefit from the initial right, a resulting trust can arise simply because of A's objectively expressed intention that B should be under a duty to A not to use the claimed trust property for B's own benefit (other than to the extent that B is also a beneficiary of the trust, or for a specific permitted purpose). A common intention constructive trust, in contrast, can arise where the claimant (A) does not begin with a particular right but because, for example, A and B agree that B is to be under such a duty to A in relation to particular property held or to be acquired by B (or in the joint names of A and B); this is one reason why the common intention constructive trust has the further requirement of some detrimental reliance by A on the agreement.

16–173 On this analysis, the difference between, on the one hand, a Type A resulting trust and, on the other hand, an express trust, is slight. It may simply be that, in contrast to a case where A aims to set up a trust for C by transferring property to B to hold on trust for C, the former type of trust does not require a specific act of declaration by A, as settlor of the trust. The justification again may be that A's claim under the resulting trust, unlike C's under an express trust, need not depend on a successful exercise by A of A's power to set up a trust, as the resulting trust instead aims to protect A's ability to benefit from A's initial right. This different basis for the resulting trust would be consistent with the exemption of such trusts from general formality requirements applying to the creation of equitable interests.[249]

16–174 Academic support for the view that Type (A) resulting trusts are based on A's intention to create a trust is provided by John Mee, who has noted that:[250]

> Although in most cases the courts do not spell out the nature of the presumption of resulting trust, this seems quite natural. The label 'presumption of resulting trust' is fairly self-explanatory . . . since it is a 'presumption that it was a trust and not a gift.'

16–175 It is also useful to look at cases where a presumption of advancement has been rebutted, as in such cases A must prove directly the fact presumed in other cases. In *Sidmouth v Sidmouth*, for example, in considering whether the presumption of advancement was rebutted as between a father and a son, Lord Langdale MR asked if there was "anything to manifest an intention to make the son a trustee for the father".[251]

16–176 It should be noted that our view does not attempt to explain how Type (A) resulting trusts operated in the past. As John Mee has shown, the law of resulting trusts developed from that of resulting uses, and a focus on the presumed intention of A when making a gratuitous transfer of an estate in land to B.[252] At that point in time, A's motivation for making such a transfer was very likely to have been a

---

[249] See Law of Property Act 1925 s.53(2).
[250] J. Mee, "Presumed Resulting Trusts, Intention and Declaration" [2014] C.L.J. 86, 100.
[251] (1840) 2 Beav. 447 at 454, quoting *Fowkes v Pascoe* (1875) L.R. 10 Ch. App. 343 at 352.
[252] See e.g. J. Mee, "Presumed Resulting Trusts, Intention and Declaration" [2014] C.L.J. 86, 94–97.

wish that B hold the estate to A's use, so that A could, at a later point, specify for whose benefit the land should be used, thus gaining a power to control the use of the land even after A's death. It seems in such cases that the focus of the doctrine was on A's subjective intention, which need not have been manifested or apparent to B, and that this approach was carried into the law on resulting trusts.[253] It is difficult, however, to argue for such a view in the modern law,[254] both because, as a matter of fact, there is no need for A to set up a trust in A's own benefit in order to have freedom to dispose of her property on death and, as a matter of principle, by the need to prevent the position of B, and of third parties, being determined by an unexpressed subjective intention of A.[255] If, however, it can be inferred from an examination of the facts, that A objectively intended B to hold the right transferred subject to a basic duty to use the right for A's benefit, then, a trust in A's favour can be justified. Indeed, as Mee has argued, this now seems to be the basis on which the courts approach the form of resulting trust arising from A's contribution to the purchase price of a right held by B (or by A and B jointly),[256] and explains the close link between such a trust and the common intention constructive trust.[257]

B. Alternative Views

i. Type A Resulting Trusts as Presumed Declarations of Trust

We suggested above that, in the modern law, a Type (A) resulting trust is best seen as giving effect to an objective, expressed intention of A that B should hold the right, either acquired from A or acquired wholly or partly with A's money, on trust for A. William Swadling has argued that A's intention alone cannot suffice to generate a trust, because her intention must be *expressed* through the specific means of a declaration of trust.[258] On this view, in a presumed resulting trust, the fact presumed is A's successful exercise of a power to set up a trust by means of a declaration of trust.[259] In our view, Swadling is correct to be concerned about the possibility of a trust arising simply on the basis of an unexpressed, subjective intention of A. However, this concern can be met without requiring evidence, or a presumption, of a declaration of trust as such; instead evidence of an objective, expressed intention is required. It does not seem unreasonable to look to the objective intention of A (without also declaring a distinct declaration of trust) in attempting to answer the vital question of whether B takes the transferred property absolutely, or instead holds it on trust for A.[260] **16–177**

Moreover, there is only limited support in the case law for the idea that, in a presumed resulting trust, the court is presuming that A did in fact declare a trust in A's favour.[261] For example, Swadling **16–178**

[253] J. Mee, "Presumed Resulting Trusts, Intention and Declaration" [2014] C.L.J. 86, 107; J. Mee, "The Past, Present, and Future of Resulting Trusts" (2017) 70 C.L.P. 189, 199–200.
[254] See J. Mee, "The Past, Present, and Future of Resulting Trusts" (2017) 70 C.L.P. 189, 199–200: "It is common for commentators to recognize that the presumption of resulting trust is outdated but to fail to see that the doctrine itself – turning on a mere intention to create a trust – was also decisively influenced by the same historical circumstances."
[255] This is one of the concerns as to the result in *Re Vinogradoff [1935]* W.N. 68: see para.16–184.
[256] See J. Mee, "The Past, Present, and Future of Resulting Trusts" (2017) 70 C.L.P. 189, 212–214.
[257] See paras 16–046 to 16–054.
[258] W. Swadling, "Explaining Resulting Trusts" (2008) 124 L.Q.R. 72, 80.
[259] As Swadling notes, however, the question remains whether, in the modern world, we should continue to presume such a declaration of trust simply because, for example, A has made a gratuitous transfer to B. The presumption of a declaration of trust was arguably justifiable in the past in some contexts at least, given conveyancing practices, but those practices have long since changed: see eg W. Swadling, "Explaining Resulting Trusts" (2008) 124 L.Q.R. 72, 84.
[260] For further defence of the "intention to create a trust" argument from Swadling's objection, see Mee, "Presumed Resulting Trusts, Intention and Declaration" [2014] C.L.J. 86, 106–109.
[261] As noted by J. Mee, "Presumed Resulting Trusts, Intention and Declaration" [2014] C.L.J. 86, 90–94.

relies on the analysis of Lord Nottingham in *Cook v Fountain*,[262] but as Mike Macnair has shown in a thorough historical analysis of that decision, Lord Nottingham's analysis was quite unusual and may well have been skewed by a political desire to favour one of the parties. In any case, it is clear that the trust recognised in the case itself was not a resulting one, did not arise on a gratuitous conveyance, and was found as a result of circumstantial evidence rather than through the operation of a presumption.

16–179 It is true that, in *Westdeutsche*, Lord Browne-Wilkinson expressly adopted an important point made by Swadling: the presumption of a resulting trust may be rebutted not only by evidence of intention to make a gift to B, but "by evidence of any intention inconsistent with such a trust".[263] This is, however, consistent with our view of such Type A resulting trusts, as responses to A's intention to create a trust.

16–180 In any case, it may be that the line between our preferred view and that of Swadling is only a very fine one, turning as it does on what is meant by a "declaration" of trust, and how it differs from evidence of an objectively expressed intention. If the former term is understood broadly, then the difference, if any, between the two views is minimal.

16–181 It may nonetheless be that the link drawn, on Swadling's view, between Type (A) resulting trusts and express trusts is a weakness. If such resulting trusts are simply presumed express trusts, and so are not truly imposed by law, the structure of the formality provisions governing trusts of land may be difficult to justify.[264] Whilst s.53(1)(b) of the 1925 Act prevents A from proving an oral declaration of a trust of land, resulting trusts are expressly excluded from the scope of the formality rule by s.53(2) of the 1925 Act.[265] This is simple to explain if such trusts arise by operation of law, rather than by means of an exercise of a power to set up a trust,[266] but it is harder to justify if at least some resulting trusts rest on a presumption that an express trust has been declared.

ii. Resulting Trusts as Reponses to B's Unjust Enrichment at A's Expense

16–182 A third view of the reasons why Type (A) resulting trusts arise was developed by Robert Chambers,[267] building on the work of Peter Birks,[268] and has been given some support, both judicially and extra-judicially, by Lord Millett.[269] On this view, Type (A) and Type (B) resulting trusts, as well as *Quistclose* trusts, are imposed in order to reverse the unjust enrichment of the transferee at the transferor's expense.[270] Claims in unjust enrichment arise under English law when a defendant is enriched at the

---

262 (1733) 3 Swans. 585. See M. Macnair, "*Coke v Fountaine* (1676)" in C. Mitchell & P. Mitchell (eds) *Landmark Cases in Equity* (Hart Publishing, 2012).

263 [1996] A.C. 669 at 708.

264 This point is made by R. Chambers, "Is There a Presumption of Resulting Trust?" in Mitchell (ed.), *Constructive and Resulting Trusts* (2010), p.267, p.280. But cf. Mee, "Presumed Resulting Trusts, Intention and Declaration" [2014] C.L.J. 86, 105–06, who sees less force in this objection.

265 See, e.g. *Hodgson v Marks* [1971] Ch. 892 (CA).

266 See J. Mee, "Presumed Resulting Trusts, Intention and Declaration" [2014] C.L.J. 86, 104–105.

267 See, e.g. Chambers, *Resulting Trusts* (1997), R. Chambers, "Resulting Trusts in Canada" (2000) 38 Alberta L.R. 378, reprinted (2002) 16 Tru. L.I. 104 and 138; R. Chambers, "Resulting Trusts" in A. Burrows and Lord Rodger (eds), *Mapping the Law: Essays in Memory of Peter Birks* (Oxford University Press, 2006); R. Chambers "Is There a Presumption of Resulting Trust?" in Mitchell (ed.), *Constructive and Resulting Trusts* (2010), p.267.

268 P. Birks, "Restitution and Resulting Trusts" in S. Goldstein (ed.), *Equity and Contemporary Legal Developments* (Hebrew University of Jerusalem, 1992), p.361.

269 See his judgments in *Air Jamaica v Charlton* [1999] 1 W.L.R. 1399 and in *Twinsectra v Yardley* [2002] 2 A.C. 164. Note too Lord Millett, "Restitution and Constructive Trusts" (1998) 114 L.Q.R. 399, 416; Lord Millett, "The Law of Restitution: Taking Stock" (1999) 14 *Amicus Curiae* 1, 7–8.

270 P. Birks, "Restitution and Resulting Trusts" in Goldstein (ed.), *Equity and Contemporary Legal Developments* (1992), p.361; Chambers, *Resulting Trusts* (1997); R. Chambers, "Resulting Trusts in Canada" (2000) 38 Alberta L.R. 378, reprinted (2002) 16 Tru. L.I. 104 and 138; R. Chambers, "Resulting Trusts" in A. Burrows and Lord Rodger (eds), *Mapping the Law: Essays in Memory of Peter Birks* (2006).

expense of a claimant in circumstances which make her enrichment unjust,[271] the question whether her enrichment is relevantly unjust being governed by "the binding authority of previous decisions", so that the courts do *not* have "a discretionary power to order repayment whenever it seems in the circumstance of the particular case just and equitable to do so".[272]

On this view, resulting trusts are imposed not in response to A's actual or presumed intention to create a trust, or in response to a presumed declaration of trust by A, but rather in response to the fact that A (actually or presumably) did not intend to make a gift to B.[273] Intention can thus be said to play a negative, rather than a positive role. **16–183**

In contrast to the two views discussed so far, this view identifies a common underlying basis for each of Type (A) and Type (B) resulting trusts. It would also allow for such trusts to arise in further situations, in which it can also be said that B has been unjustly enriched by her receipt of property acquired at A's expense. As the question of unjust enrichment may focus on the intention of A alone, and does not require that A actually or presumably had a positive intention to create a trust, it may also seem to provide a readier explanation of cases in which it may seem unlikely that A intended B to hold on trust. One such case is *Re Vinogradoff*:[274] A transferred shares into the joint name of herself and her four-year-old niece; a resulting trust arose although it may seem unlikely that A wished to make her niece a trustee. As John Mee has noted, however,[275] three points can be made in response: first, it may simply be that the result in *Re Vinogradoff*, which has been criticised, is wrong;[276] second, A's plan in making the transfer was most likely to have been that she would have the benefit of the income from the shares during her lifetime, and B would then become solely entitled to the shares on A's death, so that, consistently with A's intentions, the right outcome should have been a resulting trust for A's lifetime only[277] (and not an absolute resulting trust as was found in the case); and third, if A's plan was merely that B should be a passive nominee, there is in fact nothing unlikely about A having intended that B would, during A's life at least, hold on a bare trust for A. **16–184**

The principal difficulty with the unjust enrichment analysis is that, as we have seen,[278] it was expressly rejected by the House of Lords in *Westdeutsche Landesbank Girozentrale v Islington LBC*.[279] A particular concern there was that the analysis would unduly extend the scope of resulting trusts, so that " new areas of unmanageable risk will be introduced into commercial dealings"[280] as parties might arrange their transactions on the basis that rights held by B are at B's free disposal, only later to discover that B holds those rights on resulting trust for A, in order to reverse an unjust enrichment of B at A's expense. Lord Browne-Wilkinson's analysis in that case also ascribes a more positive role to the intention of A, which is consistent with the view that a Type (A) resulting trust depends on A's having an actual or presumed intention to create a trust. His Lordship also stated that "a resulting **16–185**

---

271 *Banque Financière de la Cité v Parc (Battersea) Ltd* [1999] 1 A.C. 221 at 227 and 234; *Sempra Metals Ltd v IRC* [2007] UKHL 34; [2008] 1 A.C. 561 at [23].

272 *Kleinwort Benson Ltd v Birmingham CC* [1996] 4 All E.R. 733 at 737. See too *Sempra Metals Ltd v IRC* [2007] UKHL 34; [2008] 1 A.C. 561 at [46]; *Test Claimants in the FII Group Litigation v Revenue and Customs Commissioners* [2012] UKSC 19; [2012] 2 A.C. 337 at [162]. For an excellent introductory account of the circumstances which render a defendant's enrichment unjust, see A. Burrows *The Law of Restitution*, 3rd edn (Oxford University Press, 2010), Chs 3–13.

273 Chambers, *Resulting Trusts* (1997), pp.19–27; P. Birks, *Unjust Enrichment* (Oxford University Press, 2003), pp.136–137.

274 [1935] W.N. 68; discussed at para.16–090. See too *Lench v Lench* (1805) 10 Ves. Jun. 511; *Childers v Childers* (1857) 1 De G. & J. 482.

275 J. Mee, "Presumed Resulting Trusts, Intention and Declaration" [2014] C.L.J. 86, 99.

276 See, e.g. J. Penner *The Law of Trusts*, 11th edn (Oxford University Press, 2019), 5.10, referring to *Re Vinogradoff* as "an atrocity of a decision".

277 As was found in *Fowkes v Pascoe* (1875) L.R. 10 Ch. App. 343.

278 See paras 16–164 to 16–166.

279 [1996] A.C. 669.

280 [1996] A.C. 669 at 708.

trust arises in order to give effect to the intention of the parties".[281] It is less clear why B's intention should be relevant, but the point perhaps is that B's conscience can be said to be bound only if it was possible for B to have understood A's intention as being an intention to create a trust.[282] In either case, the focus of unjust enrichment analysis is misplaced, as it looks only to the question of A's absence of an intention to benefit B.

16–186 From the perspective of principle, rather than of authority, the main objection to the unjust enrichment theory is that it proves too much.[283] Pushed to its logical limits, it suggests that a resulting trust should arise whenever A transfers property to B, and A's intention to benefit B is vitiated by mistake or undue influence, or is conditional on the happening of a future event which subsequently fails to materialise. That view was rejected in *Westdeutsche*: even though A's intention to make the transfer to B was vitiated by the mistaken belief that there was a valid contract between the parties, no resulting trust arose, as it was clear that A had never intended B to hold on trust for A. Indeed, in principle, it seems very doubtful that claimants in all these various situations of unjust enrichment should be given equitable proprietary rights and thus priority over the defendant's unsecured creditors, rather than a personal restitutionary remedy.[284]

16–187 Certainly, the basic question of justification may be more difficult to answer on an unjust enrichment analysis than under either of the previous two analyses, as we have to explain not only why B is under a duty to A, but also why this duty takes the form of a trust. Even if it is accepted that A should have more than a merely personal right against B, it could still be argued that there is no need for an immediate trust.[285] For example, a case in which A transfers property to B following an innocent misrepresentation by B can be seen as another example of unjust enrichment. In such cases, the standard response is that A acquires an equitable power to rescind the transaction: unless and until that power is exercised, A thus has a "mere equity".[286] It might then seem strange to argue that an immediate trust should arise in the case where A makes a mistaken, gratuitous transfer to B.[287] Indeed, it may be that, whatever the outcome of the wider debate as to the circumstances in which unjust enrichment may give rise to a form of equitable property right,[288] Type (A) resulting trusts can be more easily explained on the classically accepted basis of A's intention to create a trust.[289]

---

281 "Constructive Trusts and Unjust Enrichment" (1996) 10 Tru L.I. 98, 99, echoed in *Tinsley v Milligan* [1994] 1 A.C. 340 at 371; *Westdeutsche Landesbank Girozentrale v Islington LBC* [1996] A.C. 669 at 708.

282 See para.16–165.

283 For further difficulties with the unjust enrichment analysis, see e.g. J. Mee, "The Past, Present, and Future of Resulting Trusts" (2017) 70 C.L.P. 189, 207–213.

284 Lord Millett, "Restitution and Constructive Trusts" (1998) 114 L.Q.R. 399, 416; Lord Millett, "The Law of Restitution: Taking Stock" (1999) 14 *Amicus Curiae* 1, 7–8. See e.g. W. Swadling, "Explaining Resulting Trusts" (2008) 124 L.Q.R. 72, 101.

285 As noted by J. Mee, "'Automatic' Resulting Trusts: Retention, Restitution or Reposing Trust?" in Mitchell (ed.), *Constructive and Resulting Trusts* (2010), p.227, the law has a number of different possible to cases where there is some form of flaw in A's intention to exercise a power to transfer a right to B, and a trust is just one possible response.

286 See paras 20–060 to 20–062.

287 See further B. Häcker, "Proprietary Restitution After Impaired Consent Transfers: A Generalised Power Model" [2009] C.L.J. 324.

288 For useful but contrasting contributions to that wider debate, see, e.g. A. Burrows, "Proprietary Restitution: Unmasking Unjust Enrichment" (2001) 117 L.Q.R. 412; J. Penner, "Value, Property and Unjust Enrichment: Trusts of Traceable Proceeds" in R. Chambers et al. (eds), *Philosophical Foundations of the Law of Unjust Enrichment* (Oxford University Press, 2009).

289 See J. Mee, "Presumed Resulting Trusts, Intention and Declaration" [2014] C.L.J. 86, 102–103, pointing out that, where judges viewed the characterisation of A's transfer of property to B as either being a gift, or a trust for A, then "a conclusion that [A] did not intend a gift (or, to use the language of retention, did not intend to pass the beneficial interest to [B]) is equivalent to the a conclusion that [A] did intend to create a trust."

7. Justifying Type (B) Resulting Trusts

William Swadling has argued that the Type (B) resulting trust simply "defies legal analysis" and that no convincing justification can be provided for it.[290] On this view, when A transfers a right to B on an intended trust that fails, there should be no trust in A's favour, but B will be liable to be ordered to pay to A the value of the right received from A.[291] Certainly, one justification previously made[292] for the this type of resulting trust has now been generally rejected. It is the view of Megarry J in *Re Vandervell's Trusts (No.2)*[293] that the trust arises automatically as a result of A's simply retaining an equitable interest. As was noted above,[294] that view depends on the misconception that A, when simply owning property outright, has both a distinct legal and equitable interest in that property: this idea was decisively rejected by Lord Browne-Wilkinson in *Westdeutsche Landesbank Girozentrale v Islington LBC*.[295] However, we need to examine two other suggestions as to the principle underlying the trust. 16–188

A. A Response to A's Intention to Create a Trust

In *Westdeutsche Landesbank Girozentrale v Islington LBC*,[296] Lord Browne-Wilkinson stated that each of Type (A) and Type (B) resulting trusts:[297] 16–189

> are traditionally regarded as examples of trusts giving effect to the common intention of the parties. A resulting trust is not imposed by law against the intentions of the trustee (as is a constructive trust) but gives effect to his presumed intention.

We have already considered this explanation of Type (A) resulting trusts.[298] There would seem to be an immediate difficulty, however, in extending it to Type (B) resulting trusts. On one view at least, such trusts may arise even in a case where A does not intend to have any beneficial interest: that is why such trusts have often been described as "automatic". Megarry J used that term in *Re Vandervell's Trusts (No.2)*,[299] when attempting to understand how, in *Vandervell v IRC*,[300] a resulting trust arose in favour of Mr Vandervell even when, for reasons of tax planning, he would presumably have been very keen to avoid such a result. 16–190

There may be three ways to respond to this criticism of Lord Browne-Wilkinson's view. First, as was noted by Lord Upjohn in *Vandervell* itself,[301] the finding of a resulting trust in a case of a failed express 16–191

---

290 W. Swadling, "Explaining Resulting Trusts" (2008) 124 L.Q.R. 72, 102.

291 Note that if B were ordered to return the specific right itself to A, then a constructive trust might arise on the principle discussed in Chapter 17, Section 4.

292 As noted by J. Mee, "The Past, Present, and Future of Resulting Trusts" (2017) 70 C.L.P. 189, 194–197, the idea of retention was more plausible in relation to resulting uses (the forerunners of resulting trusts) of estates in land, as it was thought then that A, an unencumbered holder of such an estate, held to A's own use, and this "use" was retained on a gratuitous transfer to B.

293 [1974] Ch. 269 at 294. See too *Vandervell v IRC* [1967] 2 A.C. 291 at 313, per Lord Upjohn "if the beneficial interest was in A and he fails to give it away effectively to another or others or on charitable trusts it must remain in him" and at 329 per Lord Wilberforce "the equitable, or beneficial interest, cannot remain in the air: the consequence in law must be that it remains in the settlor."

294 See para.16–150.

295 [1996] A.C. 669 at 706. See too W. Swadling, "Explaining Resulting Trusts" (2008) 124 L.Q.R. 72, 99–100.

296 [1996] A.C. 669 at 705–706.

297 [1996] A.C. 669 at 708.

298 See paras 16–170 to 16–176.

299 [1974] Ch. 269 at 294.

300 [1967] 2 A.C. 291.

301 [1967] 2 A.C. 291 at 315–317.

trust gives A the possibility of making a further attempt to dispose of a beneficial interest and, as Mee has argued:

> It seems plausible to suggest that such a rule would reflect the legal response which settlors *as an abstract class* would be likely to prefer in the scenario under discussion (even if some settlors might, in individual sets of circumstances, prefer a rule that the trustee would take beneficially).[302]

16–192 Indeed, Lord Upjohn's view of the facts of *Vandervell* was that the proper inference to be drawn was that A intended that B should hold the option of trust for A, subject to any trust that A might later declare.[303] The fact that tax consequences arose from A's failure to declare such trusts does not in itself render that view of the facts implausible.

16–193 The second response, developed by Lord Browne-Wilkinson in *Westdeutsche*,[304] is to argue that, if A does indeed, on the facts, make clear that he does not wish there to be any resulting trust, then B will hold on trust for the Crown rather than for A. Whilst his Lordship relied on the decision in *Re West Sussex Constabulary's Widows, Children and Benevolent (1930) Fund Trusts*[305] to support that view, we have seen that this case is controversial, and was rejected by Lord Millett in *Air Jamaica v Charlton*, where he regarded the decision in *Vandervell v IRC* as showing that "a resulting trust is not defeated by evidence that [A] intended to part with the beneficial interest if he has not in fact succeeded in doing so."[306] Nonetheless, in *Vandervell v IRC*, it was recognised that it is certainly open to A to intend that B (even if B is a trustee company) should take beneficially, and by so doing to dispose effectively of the beneficial interest, so to that extent A can ensure that no resulting trust arises. Indeed, Lord Millett himself, writing extra-judicially, has supported the view that if no resulting trust arises on the failure of an express trust, the trustees simply hold the property for their own benefit and thus free from any trust.[307]

16–194 The third response is to accept the importance of intention, but to modify Lord Browne-Wilkinson's view by drawing a distinction between Type (A) and Type (B) resulting trusts. In the former case, it can be argued that the trust arises as a response to A's objectively apparent intention that B hold on trust for A. In the latter case, the relevant intention of A may simply be that B should hold as trustee; there is no need to show that A intended B, in the circumstances which have occurred, to hold *for A*. After all, Type (B) resulting trusts arise in the case of failed trusts and A's actual intention was that the failed trust should succeed. The resulting trust can be seen as a practical, next best solution, which at least allows A another chance to create a trust:[308] as Maitland put it, from A's perspective, "I have made [B] a trustee for somebody, and a trustee he must be—if for no one else then for me or my representatives."[309]

---

302 J. Mee, "'Automatic' Resulting Trusts: Retention, Restitution or Reposing Trust?" in Mitchell (ed.), *Constructive and Resulting Trusts* (2010).

303 [1967] 2 A.C. 291 at 315–317.

304 [1996] A.C. 669 at 708.

305 [1971] Ch. 1.

306 [1999] 1 W.L.R. 1399 at 1412.

307 "Pension Schemes and the Law of Trusts" (2000) 14 Tru. L.I. 66, 74; a similar analysis can be applied to *Burgess v Wheate* (1759) 1 Wm. Bl. 123.

308 See J. Mee, "'Automatic' Resulting Trusts: Retention, Restitution or Reposing Trust?" in Mitchell (ed.), *Constructive and Resulting Trusts* (2010), pp.208–209: "the key feature in the relevant situation is the fact that the settlor has transferred property to another person, reposing trust in that person to hold the property according to the settlor's instructions".

309 F.W. Maitland, *Equity – A Course of Lectures*, 2nd edn (Cambridge University Press, 1936), p.77.

B. A Response to B's Unjust Enrichment at A's Expense

As we saw above,[310] it has been argued, notably by Chambers, that each of a Type (A) and Type (B) resulting trust can be seen as imposed to reverse B's unjust enrichment at A's expense. This analysis may seem particularly compelling when applied to the latter type of resulting trust: if A has transferred a right to B on the basis that B should hold it on a particular trust, and that planned trust has failed, it would seem clear that B would be unjustly enriched at A's expense were B to hold the right free from any trust. **16–195**

Support for this analysis can be derived from Lord Millett's formulation in *Air Jamaica v Charlton*:[311] **16–196**

> Like a constructive trust, a resulting trust arises by operation of law, though unlike a constructive trust it gives effect to intention. But it arises whether or not the transferor intended to retain a beneficial interest—he almost always does not—since it responds to the absence of any intention on his part to pass a beneficial interest to the recipient. It may arise even where the transferor positively wished to part with the beneficial interest, as in *Vandervell v IRC*.[312]

Many of the points made about this explanation of Type (A) trusts[313] are also relevant here, most notably the key one that, in *Westdeutsche*, the House of Lords rejected the view that resulting trusts are a response to B's unjust enrichment at A's expense. As a matter of principle, Swadling has also argued that "if our only desire is to strip out [B's] enrichment, a response in the nature of a personal claim for the value received serves that purpose perfectly well", so that a trust is not necessary.[314] If, however, the aim is to protect A's initial entitlement, and to give effect to A's objective intention that B should not be free to use the trust property for B's own benefit, then a resulting trust can be defended as an appropriate solution. **16–197**

8. Justifying *Quistclose* Trusts

As noted at para.16–144, and as reflected by Lord Millett's changing views on the matter, there is a clear tension between an express trust and a resulting trust characterisation of *Quistclose* trusts.[315] Addressing this tension is critical in suggesting a justification for such trusts but recent decisions have continued to equivocate between the two views.[316] **16–198**

The first point to make is that, on the definition of *Quistclose* trusts given in *Prickly Bay Waterside*, which can apply where A "provides assets to another for the purpose of paying debts under arrangements which create a trust",[317] such a trust can be set up by a settlor exercising their power to do so, and so can be a simple express trust.[318] The mere fact that the settlor becomes the beneficiary of the **16–199**

---

310 See paras 16–182 to 16–187.

311 [1999] 1 W.L.R. 1399 at 1412.

312 [1967] 2 A.C. 291.

313 See paras 16–184 to 16–187.

314 W. Swadling, "Explaining Resulting Trusts" (2008) 124 L.Q.R. 72, 101.

315 See too e.g. E. Hudson, "A Normative Approach to the *Quistclose* Trust" (2017) 80 M.L.R. 775.

316 See the extracts at paras 16–146 to 16–155 from *Bellis v Challinor* [2015] EWCA Civ 59 and *Prickly Bay Waterside Ltd v British American Insurance Co Ltd* [2022] UKPC 8.

317 *Prickly Bay Waterside Ltd v British American Insurance Co Ltd* [2022] UKPC 8 at [32], extracted at para.16–155.

318 In such cases, the justification for the trust depends on the justifications for allowing parties the power to set up such legal relationships: for discussion in the specific context of the *Quistclose* trust, see E. Hudson, "A Normative Approach to the *Quistclose* Trust" (2017) 80 M.L.R. 775, 789–791.

trust does not mean that any special justification is required for the existence of the trust.[319] In our view, however, such a trust can also arise even if the settlor has not exercised that power to set up a trust. This is consistent with Lady Arden's observation in the *Prickly Bay* case that a *Quistclose* trust may be "express as to what is to happen on failure of the specified purpose, or express only as to that purpose, or it may simply be a resulting trust arising by operation of law."[320]

16-200 Where a *Quistclose* trust arises without A having exercised her power to set up the trust, then it is most likely to share a justification with the Type (A) resulting trust arising in the case of a gratuitous conveyance: it arises because A has transferred a right to B, and the objective intention of A is that B should be under a duty to A not to use that right for B's own benefit. The need for an objective assessment of A's intention is seen in formulations which require there to be a "mutual understanding that [the property] should not be at the free disposal of [B], but should be used exclusively for a specific purpose".[321] The transfer to B need not be gratuitous, and B also has a power to make some specific use of the property (e.g. to pay particular debts) which may benefit B. Nonetheless, the broader point, seen also when we considered the relationship of resulting trusts and common intention constructive trusts, is that the existence of the trust depends on the court's finding in the parties' dealings sufficient evidence that A's intention, as reasonably apparent to B, was that B should be under a general duty to A not to use the right acquired by B for B's own benefit, albeit with a power to use the right for a specific agreed purpose. This explains why the factors considered by the court in deciding if a *Quistclose* trust has arisen are very similar to those applying when asking if A had the certainty of intention required to establish an express trust.[322] This view can explain why, as demonstrated by the analysis in a case such as *Bellis v Challinor*, there is no need for a *Quistclose* trust to depend on a declaration of trust by A:[323] as in the case of a Type (A) resulting trust, such a declaration is not required, given the context in which A transferred property to B. This explains why, as was held in *Ali v Dinc*,[324] a *Quistclose* trust can arise and be proved in relation to land even if there is no signed writing complying with s.53(1)(b) of the Law of Property Act 1925.

16-201 It is also possible for a *Quistclose* trust to share a justification with the Type (B) resulting trust. This could occur, consistently with Lord Millett's description of the trust as a "default trust", if A's objective intention was that B hold property on a non-charitable purpose trust, with the object of that trust being the performance of a particular purpose. As seen in our analysis of anomalous testamentary purpose trusts in Chapter 8,[325] the immediate failure of the intended purpose trust does not alter the fact that A objectively intended B to be subject to a duty not to hold the property for B's own benefit. This aspect of A's intention can be given effect to and whilst it is not possible for B to be under a duty, as trustee, to fulfil the private purpose, it is consistent with A's intention for B to have the freedom to

---

319 Although, as noted by e.g. E. Hudson, "A Normative Approach to the *Quistclose* Trust" (2017) 80 M.L.R. 775, 806–811, where a *Quistclose* trust is set up expressly to function, in effect, as a means for A to acquire security for B's performance of a duty, there is a question as to whether registration of A's interest should be required in order to alert other creditors of B.

320 Ibid.

321 *Ali v Dinc* [2020] EWHC 3055 (Ch) at [232] (Sarah Worthington QC (Hon), sitting as a Deputy High Court Judge). See too *Prickly Bay Waterside Ltd v British American Insurance Company* [2022] UKPC 8 at [31], extracted at para.16–154, where Lady Arden notes that the need for mutual intentions is met if A has such an intention and B acquiesces in it.

322 See the extracts at paras 16–146 to 16–155 from *Bellis v Challinor* [2015] EWCA Civ 59 and *Prickly Bay Waterside Ltd v British American Insurance Co Ltd* [2022] UKPC 8. See too E. Hudson, "A Normative Approach to the *Quistclose* Trust" (2017) 80 M.L.R. 775, 811 where (albeit on the view, slightly different from ours, that *Quistclose* trusts "are generally express), it is argued that "judges should pay proper regard to party intention when determining whether a trust has arisen".

323 M. Bryan, "The Inferred Trust: An Unhappy Marriage of Contract and Trust?" (2016) 69 C.L.P. 377, criticises the reasoning in *Bellis* on the basis that it was not stated that a declaration of trust by A was required but that aspect of *Belllis* is consistent with our view of the justification of that type of *Quistclose* trust.

324 [2020] EWHC 3055 (Ch) [232].

325 See para.8–009.

use the property for that purpose.[326] This is consistent with the justification we suggested above for the Type (B) resulting trust.

Questions

1. "The similarities between the two types of resulting trust identified by Lord Browne-Wilkinson in the *Westdeutsche* case are more important than their differences." **Discuss.**
2. Do the presumptions of resulting trust and of advancement have any role to play in a modern legal system?
3. "A resulting trust is a default mechanism to locate the beneficial ownership of property and not a proprietary remedy for unjust enrichment." **Discuss.**
4. When, if ever, is it helpful to think of a *Quistclose* trust as a resulting trust?
5. The members of the Ravers Anonymous Club, an unincorporated association whose purposes are not charitable, have dissolved the association one week after having received £10,000 from Sir Lancelot Hellfire for the purposes of the Club, and one month after having received £1,000 from various raffles and sweepstakes, along with £150 from collections taken at a public meeting held to publicise the Club. In accordance with the Club rules the members received ten days' written notice of the meeting called to dissolve the association. What should happen to the above sums?

326 See too the analysis at para.8–014 of *re Abbott* [1900] 2 Ch. 326.

17

CONSTRUCTIVE TRUSTS

1. Introduction

A. Trusts Imposed by Law

As explained in Chapter 1, we can categorise trusts according to the reason for which a particular trust arises.[1] An express trust arises when a party (the settlor) successfully exercises her power to set up a trust, either by declaring that she holds property on trust, or by transferring property to trustees to hold on trust. All other trusts are imposed by law. If we put statutory trusts to one side, there are only two types of trust imposed by law: resulting trusts and constructive trusts.[2] We examined resulting trusts in Chapter 16; we examine constructive trusts in this chapter. 17–001

When examining trusts imposed by law, we must confront the question of justification.[3] First, why has B been placed under a duty to A;[4] and second, even if the imposition of that duty can be justified, why has a trust been imposed? The existence of a trust has significant consequences, not only for the beneficiary and the trustee, but also for third parties, such as creditors of the trustee. 17–002

The practical importance of constructive trusts can be illustrated by *Attorney General for Hong Kong v Reid*.[5] The Privy Council advised that when F, a fiduciary, received a bribe to act in a way that was contrary to the interests of the principal, P, F did not merely incur a personal obligation to pay the value of the money to P, but also held the money on constructive trust for P. The significance of this in the factual circumstances of *Reid* was threefold. First, it meant that P could trace from the bribe money into assets, such as land, acquired by F with that money. Second, P had an equitable interest in such assets, which protected P in F's insolvency, and also gave P the benefit of any increase in the value of the assets. Third, P could assert a claim to such assets in the hands of third parties,[6] as those third parties, it seems,[7] were not bona fide purchasers for value of a legal estate without notice. 17–003

---

1 For a useful discussion of different possible approaches to classifying trusts, see N. McBride, "On the Classification of Trusts" in P. Birks and F. Rose (eds), *Restitution and Equity, Volume 1: Resulting Trusts and Equitable Compensation* (Informa, 2000).

2 See paras 4–014 to 4–019.

3 See para.4–019.

4 Consistently with Chapter 16, and the labels used by Lord Browne-Wilkinson in *Westdeutsche Landesbank Girozentrale v Islington LBC* [1996] A.C. 669, in a number of sections of this Chapter (not Sections 2 and 3) we will use "B" to refer to the party alleged to hold on constructive trust, and "A" as the beneficiary of the constructive trust. Note this means that, whilst B was used in some earlier chapters to denote the beneficiary of a trust, in this Chapter, B refers instead to the party holding on trust.

5 [1994] 1 A.C. 324; approved in *FHR European Ventures LLP v Cedar Capital Partners LLC* [2014] UKSC 45; [2015] A.C. 250.

6 Respectively the wife and the solicitor of the agent.

7 [1994] 1 A.C. 324 at 330.

17-004 The question of justification is, therefore, an urgent one. In a case such as *Reid*, we cannot justify the advantages gained by P by pointing to any party's successful exercise of a power to set up a trust. The third party paying the bribe or secret commission did not intend that it should be held on trust for P, nor did F when he received the bribe. Yet F's other creditors (and also third parties bound by P's interest) deserve a convincing explanation as to why P was given the important advantages of an equitable beneficial interest under the constructive trust.[8]

B. The Nature of Constructive Trusts

17-005 Under English law, constructive trusts arise as a result of rules which state that they arise in certain circumstances. These rules do not give the courts a discretion to impose constructive trusts—or to refuse to do so—according to their assessment of the equities of a case: the courts' role is purely declaratory. In contrast, some other Commonwealth jurisdictions, e.g. Canada[9] and Australia,[10] distinguish "substantive" or "institutional" constructive trusts from "remedial" constructive trusts, and recognise that the courts have the power to impose the latter type of constructive trust as well as the former. Different judges and scholars attach different meanings to the terms "institutional" and "remedial constructive trust",[11] but most use them to distinguish constructive trusts which arise through the operation of legal rules from constructive trusts which arise following the exercise of a judicial discretion,[12] either retrospectively or prospectively from the date of the court order.[13] It is controversial whether the courts should have a discretion to impose burdens on a holder of property in this way,[14] but whatever the rights and wrongs of this question, it is clear that English law does not expressly recognise "remedial" constructive trusts of this kind.[15] As Lord Sumption put it in *Bailey v Angove's Pty*

---

8 This point is particularly well-made by R. Goode, "Proprietary Liability for Secret Profit: A Reply" (2011) 127 L.Q.R. 493.

9 *Sorochan v Sorochan* [1986] 2 S.C.R. 38; *Lac Minerals Ltd v International Corona Resources Ltd* [1989] 2 S.C.R. 574; *Soulos v Korkontzilas* [1997] 2 S.C.R. 217; *Kerr v Baranow* [2011] 1 S.C.R. 269; *Sun Indalex Finance, LLC v United Steelworkers* [2013] 1 S.C.R. 271 at [228].

10 *Muschinski v Dodds* (1985) 160 C.L.R. 583; *Bathurst CC v PWC Properties Pty Ltd* (1998) 195 C.L.R. 566; *Giumelli v Giumelli* (1999) 196 C.L.R. 101; *John Alexander's Clubs Pty Ltd v White City Tennis Club Ltd* (2010) 241 C.L.R. 1 at [128]–[129]; *Grimaldi v Chameleon Mining NL (No.2)* (2012) 200 F.C.R. 296 at [504]–[511].

11 For an excellent survey of different usages of the term, see M. Bryan, "Constructive Trusts: Understanding Remedialism" in J. Glister and P. Ridge (eds), *Fault Lines in Equity* (Hart Publishing, 2012). See too C. Webb, "The Myth of the Remedial Constructive Trust" (2016) 69 C.L.P. 353. Some judges have used the term "remedial constructive trust" to refer to the personal liability of strangers who dishonestly participate in a breach of trust: e.g. *Clarke v Marlborough Fine Art (London) Ltd* [2002] 1 W.L.R. 1731 at [66]; *Kilcarne Holdings Ltd v Targetfollow (Birmingham) Ltd* [2004] EWHC 2547 (Ch); [2005] 2 P. & C.R. 8 at [261]. This usage seems to have been prompted by *Paragon Finance Plc v DB Thakerar & Co (a firm)* [1999] 1 All E.R. 400 at 408–409, where Millett LJ distinguished constructive trusts of property from the personal liability of dishonest participants in a breach of trust. However it is best avoided, lest this personal liability become confused with the "discretionary proprietary remedy" to which Millett LJ also refers at 415.

12 Cf. *Grimaldi v Chameleon Mining NL (No.2)* (2012) 200 F.C.R. 296 at [504] per Finn J: "We emphasise the remedial use of the constructive trust so as to exclude from consideration those classes of case where, on the proof of particular facts in a given context (e.g. the death of one party to an agreement for mutual wills: *Birmingham v Renfrew* (1937) 57 C.L.R. 666; or the entitlement under contract to an expectancy after the consideration for it is executed: cf. *Tailby v Official Receiver* (1888) 13 App. Cas. 523) the circumstances are 'construed' as giving rise to a constructive trust."

13 See, e.g. *Fortex Group Ltd v Macintosh* [1998] 3 N.Z.L.R. 171 at 172–173, endorsed in *Regal Casting Ltd v Lightbody* [2009] 2 N.Z.L.R. 433 at [162]–[163].

14 D. Wright, *The Remedial Constructive Trust* (1998), reviewed by P. Birks (1999) 115 L.Q.R. 681; P. Birks, "Rights, Wrongs, and Remedies" (2000) 20 O.J.L.S. 1; T. Etherton, "Constructive Trusts: A New Model for Equity and Unjust Enrichment" [2008] C.L.J. 265.

15 As noted by Y.K. Liew, "Reanalysing Institutional and Remedial Constructive Trusts" [2016] C.L.J. 528, the ability of a proprietary estoppel claim to give rise to a trust provides an example where English law, on one view, comes at least very close to recognising a type of remedial constructive trust. Whilst the court does have some discretion when giving effect to a proprietary estoppel claim it is, however, a structured discretion, as noted by Robert Walker LJ in *Jennings v Rice* [2002] EWCA Civ 159 at [43]: "It cannot be doubted that in this as in every other area of the law, the court must take a principled

Ltd:[16] "English law is generally averse to the discretionary adjustment of property rights, and has not recognised the remedial constructive trust favoured in some other jurisdictions, notably in the United States and Canada." Lord Sumption there adopted the distinction made by Lord Browne-Wilkinson in *Westdeutsche Landesbank Girozentrale v Islington LBC*:[17]

> Under an institutional constructive trust, the trust arises by operation of law as from the date of the circumstances which give rise to it: the function of the court is merely to declare that such trust has arisen in the past. The consequences that flow from such trust having arisen (including the possibly unfair consequences to the third parties who in the interim have received trust property) are also determined by rules of law, not under a discretion. A remedial constructive trust . . . is different. It is a judicial remedy giving rise to an enforceable equitable obligation: the extent to which it operates retrospectively to the prejudice of third parties lies in the discretion of the court.

C. *The Diversity of Constructive Trusts*

Constructive trusts have been imposed in a wide variety of circumstances. This makes it very difficult, if not impossible, to find any general underlying justification that explains each and every constructive trust.[18] To proceed, then, we need to break down the circumstances in which constructive trusts have been imposed into discrete categories, and to consider the possible justifications for each such type of constructive trust. At the end of the chapter we will see if any general themes emerge. **17–006**

We have already discussed several situations in which constructive trusts are imposed, namely: (a) cases concerning incomplete transfers and the rule in *Re Rose*;[19] (b) cases concerning secret and half-secret trusts;[20] (c) cases concerning mutual wills;[21] and (d) cases concerning a failure to comply with formality rules in relation to trusts of land.[22] In this chapter we shall look at some further situations, in the following sections: (2) proceeds of a breach of fiduciary duty; (3) proceeds of breach of confidence; (4) specifically enforceable contracts of sale; (5) assignments for value of future property; (6) receipt of property subject to an undertaking; (7) shared homes; (8) the *Pallant v Morgan* equity; (9) unlawful killing; and (10) four situations which all, in a general sense, involve the protection of pre-existing rights. **17–007**

In analysing these cases, we can bear in mind a useful distinction, made by Ying Khai Liew, between what he has called "qualified interest" and "absolute interest" cases. **17–008**

---

approach, and cannot exercise a completely unfettered discretion according to the individual judge's notion of what is fair in any particular case."

16 [2016] UKSC 47; [2016] 1 W.L.R. 3179 at [27]. See too *Crossco No.4 Unltd v Jolan Ltd* [2011] EWCA Civ 1619; [2012] 2 All E.R. 754 at [84] (Etherton LJ). See also *Re Goldcorp Exchange Ltd* [1995] 1 A.C. 74 at 104; *Sinclair Investments (UK) Ltd v Versailles Trade Finance Ltd* [2011] EWCA Civ 347; [2012] Ch. 453 at [37]; *FHR European Ventures LLP v Cedar Capital Partners LLC* [2014] UKSC 45; [2015] A.C. 250 at [47]. In *Thorner v Major* [2009] UKHL 18; [2009] 1 W.L.R. 776 at [20]–[21], Lord Scott would have preferred to base his finding for the claimant on the grounds of a remedial constructive trust, but none of the other members of the court took that view. Writing extra-judicially, the Chancellor, Sir Terence Etherton, has expressed support for the imposition of remedial constructive trusts in cases about shared homes: T. Etherton, "Constructive Trusts: A New Model for Equity and Unjust Enrichment" (2008) C.L.J. 265.

17 [1996] A.C. 669 at 714–715.

18 As was saw at para.1–112, Lord Briggs, "Equity in Business" (2019) 135 L.Q.R. 567, 583, it cannot usefully be said that all constructive trusts respond to cases where it would be unconscionable for B to deny A a beneficial interest in the property, as the idea of unconscionability, when used in such a way, is too general to be of any practical assistance.

19 See paras 5–023ff.

20 See paras 6–129ff.

21 See paras 6–172ff.

22 See paras 6–033ff.

Ying Khai Liew, *Rationalising Constructive Trusts* (Hart Publishing, 2017), p.15

17–009 There are two distinct and mutually exclusive situations in which constructive trusts arise. The first is where the property in question is at the outset owned *absolutely* by B, the person against whom the trust obligation arises. Here, one of the causative events to which the constructive trust responds is an act of B in relation to *his own* property. The second relates to property which B does not previously own. Here, one of the material events is an act of B in relation to property he has yet to acquire, and the result is that, when B later obtains title to the property in question, a constructive trust arises with the effect that he only ever takes a *qualified* interest in that property. These cases can respectively be referred to as AI and QI situations.

17–010 We can apply this distinction, for example, to the distinction between secret trusts and mutual wills, as discussed in Chapter 6. In the former case, a constructive trust is imposed because of B's prior agreement to hold rights acquired under A's will on trust for C: this is a "qualified interest" case as B only ever acquires the rights subject to the agreement. The mutual wills doctrine, in contrast, can apply to rights that B did not acquire under A's will, but held anyway, even before making an agreement with A as to how those rights would be disposed of on B's death. Mutual wills can therefore cover "absolute interest" cases. Liew's general argument is that equity, historically, was more reluctant to impose constructive trusts in these "absolute interest" cases, and this is reflected in the usually stricter requirements that apply before a constructive trust arises in such cases.[23] So, for example, the doctrine of mutual wills, unlike that of secret trusts, requires the agreement between A and B to be contractually enforceable.[24]

2. Proceeds of a Breach of Fiduciary Duty

A. Nature of the Trust

17–011 It was noted above that, in *Attorney General for Hong Kong v Reid*,[25] a constructive trust was imposed on a bribe acquired by F in breach of his fiduciary duty to P. We also saw in Chapter 2 that, in *Keech v Sandford*,[26] a trust was also imposed when T held a lease on trust for an infant B, and, having unsuccessfully sought to renew the lease on behalf of B, then took the renewal for himself. Lord King LC decreed that T held the renewed lease on trust for the infant. In each case, the fiduciary/trustee can be seen to have breached the "no conflicts" rule by putting himself in a position where his own interest might conflict with that of the principal/beneficiary. It can equally be said that, in those cases, there was also a breach of the "no profit" rule, as the fiduciary/trustee made an unauthorised profit by use of their fiduciary position; although, as noted in Chapter 2, we agree with Conaglen[27] that this rule is best seen not as a distinct one, but rather as an extension of the "no conflicts" rule.[28]

17–012 Constructive trusts have also been awarded in other cases where a fiduciary has misappropriated a profit-making opportunity which came to them in their fiduciary capacity. We saw in Chapter 2[29]

---

23 Y.K. Liew, *Rationalising Constructive Trusts* (Hart Publishing, 2017), 15–16, 349–351.

24 See para.6–173.

25 [1994] 1 A.C. 324; approved in *FHR European Ventures LLP v Cedar Capital Partners LLC* [2014] UKSC 45; [2015] A.C. 250.

26 (1726) Sel. Cas. T. King 61. For discussion of the case, see e.g. J. Getzler, "Rumford Market and the Genesis of Fiduciary Obligations" in A. Burrows and A. Rodger (eds), *Mapping the Law: Essays in Memory of Peter Birks* (Oxford University Press, 2006).

27 See Conaglen, *Fiduciary Loyalty: Protecting the Due Performance of Non-Fiduciary Duties* (Hart Publishing, 2010) pp.33–40.

28 See para.2–092.

29 See para.2–109.

that, at first instance in *Boardman v Phipps*,[30] Wilberforce J made a declaration that shares acquired in breach of fiduciary duty were held on constructive trust, and this order was affirmed by the appellate courts.[31] Similar declarations of trust have been made in many other "opportunity cases",[32] and indeed it has been said that "any property acquired, or profit made" by a fiduciary through a breach of fiduciary duty is held on constructive trust for her principal.[33] Moreover, in the words of Mason J:[34]

> Neither principle nor authority provide any support for the proposition that relief by way of constructive trust is available only in the case where a profit or benefit obtained by the fiduciary was one which it was an incident of his duty to obtain for the person to whom he owed the fiduciary duty. Once it is established that the fiduciary is liable to account for a profit or benefit which he has obtained there can be no objection to his being held to account as a constructive trustee of that profit or benefit. It can make no difference that it was not his duty to obtain the profit or benefit for the person to whom the duty was owed. What is important is that the advantage has accrued to him in breach of his fiduciary duty or by his misuse of his fiduciary position. The consequence is that he must account for it and in equity the appropriate remedy is by means of a constructive trust.

Where P claims that a constructive trust can be recognised in relation to proceeds of F's breach of fiduciary duty, it is of course necessary for P to identify those proceeds. As will be discussed in Chapter 18, taking an account of profits is a means of doing this. Such an account need not result in a constructive trust, however, as it could instead determine the value of P's personal claim against F: as a result, "equitable accounting can encompass both proprietary and non-proprietary claims."[35] **17–013**

B. Scope of the Trust

Notwithstanding the authorities set out above, English courts were formerly divided over the question of whether a constructive trust arises in cases where a fiduciary has received a secret commission or bribe from a third party. One line of cases, the best known of which is *Lister & Co v Stubbs*,[36] held that the fiduciary merely owed a personal liability to account for and pay over the amount of the bribe to her principal, while another, stemming from the Privy Council's decision in *Attorney General for Hong Kong v Reid*,[37] held that the money was additionally held by the fiduciary on a constructive trust. In *FHR European Ventures LLP v Cedar Capital Partners LLC*, this controversy was definitively resolved when a seven-member Supreme Court held that a constructive trust would be imposed on money paid to **17–014**

30 [1964] 1 W.L.R. 993.
31 See [1965] Ch. 992 (CA) and [1967] 2 A.C. 46 (HL).
32 e.g. *Carter v Palmer* (1842) 8 Cl. & Fin. 657; *Bowes v City of Toronto* (1858) 11 Moo. P.C. 463; *Bagnall v Carlton* (1877) 6 Ch. D. 371; *Cook v Deeks* [1916] 1 A.C. 554; *Furs Ltd v Tomkies* (1936) 54 C.L.R. 583 at 592; *Industrial Development Consultants Ltd v Cooley* [1972] 1 W.L.R. 443; *Bhullar v Bhullar* [2003] EWCA Civ 424; [2003] 2 B.C.L.C. 241.
33 *Keith Henry & Company Pty Ltd v Stuart Walker & Co Pty Ltd* (1958) 100 C.L.R. 342 at 350, per Dixon CJ, McTiernan and Fullagar JJ. See too *Chan v Zacharia* (1983) 154 C.L.R. 178 at 199. English dicta to like effect are set out in Lord Neuberger's judgment in *FHR European Ventures LLP v Cedar Capital Partners LLC* [2014] UKSC 45; [2015] A.C. 250 at [19]–[20].
34 *Hospital Products Ltd v US Surgical Corp* (1984) 156 C.L.R. 41 at 107–108, followed in *Grimaldi v Chameleon Mining NL (No.2)* (2012) 200 F.C.R. 296 at [575].
35 *FHR European Ventures LLP v Cedar Capital Partners LLC* [2014] UKSC 45; [2015] A.C. 250 at [36] (Lord Neuberger).
36 (1890) 45 Ch.D. 1. See too *Metropolitan Bank v Heiron* (1880) 5 Ex.D. 319; *Powell v Thomas & Evan Jones & Co* [1905] 1 K.B. 11; *Attorney General's Ref. (No.1 of 1985)* [1986] Q.B. 491 at 504–505; *Sinclair Investments (UK) Ltd v Versailles Trade Finance Ltd* [2011] EWCA Civ 347; [2012] Ch. 453.
37 [1994] 1 A.C. 324, followed in *Fyffes Group Ltd v Templeman* [2000] 2 Lloyd's Rep. 643; *Daraydan Holdings Ltd v Solland International Ltd* [2004] EWHC 622 (Ch); [2005] Ch. 119.

a fiduciary as a bribe or secret commission. This brought English law into line with the law of various Commonwealth jurisdictions which have the same rule.[38]

FHR European Ventures LLP v Cedar Capital Partners LLC

Supreme Court [2015] A.C. 250

17–015 The facts are given in the judgment of the court, which was delivered by LORD NEUBERGER. The other members of the court were LORD MANCE, LORD SUMPTION, LORD CARNWATH, LORD TOULSON, LORD HODGE and LORD COLLINS.

17–016 On 22 December 2004, FHR European Ventures LLP purchased the issued share capital of Monte Carlo Grand Hotel SAM (which owned a long leasehold interest in the Monte Carlo Grand Hotel) from Monte Carlo Grand Hotel Ltd ("the vendor") for €211.5m. The purchase was a joint venture between the claimants in these proceedings, for whom FHR was the vehicle. Cedar Capital Partners LLC provided consultancy services to the hotel industry, and it had acted as the claimants' agent in negotiating the purchase. It is common ground that Cedar accordingly owed fiduciary duties to the claimants in that connection. Cedar had also entered into an agreement with the vendor ("the exclusive brokerage agreement") dated 24 September 2004, which provided for the payment to Cedar of a €10m fee following a successful conclusion of the sale and purchase of the issued share capital of Monte Carlo Grand Hotel SAM. The vendor paid Cedar €10m on or about 7 January 2005.

17–017 On 23 November 2009 the claimants began these proceedings for recovery of the sum of €10m from Cedar (and others). The trial took place before Simon J., and the main issue was whether, as it contended, Cedar had made proper disclosure to the claimants of the exclusive brokerage agreement. Simon J. gave a judgment[39] in which he found against Cedar on that issue. There was then a further hearing to determine what order should be made in the light of that judgment, following which Simon J. gave a further judgment.[40] In that judgment he concluded that he should (i) make a declaration of liability for breach of fiduciary duty on the part of Cedar for having failed to obtain the claimants' fully informed consent in respect of the €10m, and (ii) order Cedar to pay such sum to the claimants, but (iii) refuse to grant the claimants a proprietary remedy in respect of the moneys.

17–018 The claimants appealed to the Court of Appeal against conclusion (iii), and it allowed the appeal[41] for reasons given in a judgment given by Lewison L.J., with supporting judgments from Pill L.J. and Sir Terence Etherton C. Accordingly, the Court of Appeal made an order which included a declaration that Cedar received the €10m fee on constructive trust for the claimants absolutely. Cedar now appeals to the Supreme Court on that issue. There is and was no challenge by Cedar to the judge's conclusions (i) and (ii), so the only point on this appeal is whether, as the Court of Appeal held, the claimants are entitled to the proprietary remedy in respect of the €10m received by Cedar from the vendor . . .

17–019 . . . the centrally relevant point for present purposes is that, at least in some cases where an agent acquires a benefit which came to his notice as a result of his fiduciary position, or pursuant to an opportunity which results from his fiduciary position, the equitable rule ("the rule") is that he is to be treated as having acquired the benefit on behalf of his principal, so that it is beneficially owned by the principal. In such cases, the principal has a proprietary remedy in addition to his personal remedy against the agent, and the principal can elect between the two remedies.

17–020 Where the facts of a particular case are within the ambit of the rule, it is strictly applied. The strict application of the rule can be traced back to the well-known decision in *Keech v Sandford*,[42] where a trustee held a lease of a market on trust for an infant, and, having failed to negotiate a new lease on behalf of the infant because the landlord was dissatisfied with the proposed security for the rent, the trustee negotiated a new lease for himself. Lord King L.C. concluded, at p 62, that, "though I do not say there is a fraud in this case" and though it "may seem hard", the infant was entitled to an assignment of the new lease and an account

---

[38] Australia: *Grimaldi v Chameleon Mining NL (No.2)* (2012) 200 F.C.R. 296; Canada: *Insurance Corp of British Columbia v Lo* (2006) 278 D.L.R. (4th) 148; Singapore: *Sumitomo Bank Ltd v Thahir* [1993] 1 S.L.R. 735; New Zealand: *Attorney General for Hong Kong v Reid* [1994] 1 A.C. 324.

[39] [2011] EWHC 2308 (Ch); [2012] 2 B.C.L.C. 39.

[40] [2011] EWHC 2999 (Ch).

[41] [2014] Ch. 1.

[42] (1726) Sel. Cas. Ch. 61.

of the profits made in the meantime—a conclusion which could only be justified on the basis that the new lease had been beneficially acquired for the infant beneficiary.

Since then, the rule has been applied in a great many cases. The question on this appeal is not so much concerned with the application of the rule, as with its limits or boundaries. Specifically, what is in dispute is the extent to which the rule applies where the benefit is a bribe or secret commission obtained by an agent in breach of his fiduciary duty to his principal. **17–021**

On the one hand, Mr Collings Q.C. contends for the appellant, Cedar, that the rule should not apply to a bribe or secret commission paid to an agent, because it is not a benefit which can properly be said to be the property of the principal. This has the support of Professor Sir Roy Goode, who has suggested that no proprietary interest arises where an agent obtains a benefit in breach of his duty unless the benefit either (i) flows from an asset which was (a) beneficially owned by the principal, or (b) intended for the principal, or (ii) was derived from an activity of the agent which, if he chose to undertake it, he was under an equitable duty to undertake for the principal. Sir Roy suggested that "to treat [a principal] as having a restitutionary proprietary right to money or property not derived from any asset of [the principal] results in an involuntary grant by [the agent] to [the principal] from [the agent's] pre-existing estate".[43] Professor Sarah Worthington has advanced a slightly different test. She suggests (summarising at the risk of oversimplifying) that proprietary claims arise where benefits are (i) derived from the principal's property, or (ii) derived from opportunities in the scope of the agent's endeavours on behalf of the principal, but not (iii) benefits derived from opportunities outside the scope of those endeavours.[44] **17–022**

On the other hand, it is suggested by Mr Pymont Q.C. on behalf of the respondent claimants in this appeal, that the rule does apply to bribes or secret commissions received by an agent, because, in any case where an agent receives a benefit, which is, or results from, a breach of the fiduciary duty owed to his principal, the agent holds the benefit on trust for the principal. This view has been supported by Lord Millett writing extra-judicially. In "Bribes and Secret Commissions",[45] he suggested that, on grounds of practicality, policy and principle, a principal should be beneficially entitled to a bribe or secret commission received by his agent.[46] He bases his conclusion on the proposition that equity will not permit the agent to rely on his own breach of fiduciary duty to justify retaining the benefit on the ground that it was a bribe or secret commission, and will assume that he acted in accordance with his duty, so that the benefit must be the principal's. This approach is also supported by Lionel Smith,[47] whose view, in short, is that the basic rule should be that an agent who obtains a benefit in breach of his fiduciary duty to his principal holds that benefit on trust for his principal. **17–023**

The decision as to which view is correct must be based on legal principle, decided cases, policy considerations, and practicalities . . . **17–024**

[Lord Neuberger then considered a large number of relevant authorities and found that they are] . . . all consistent with the notion that the rule should apply to bribes or secret commissions paid to an agent, so that the agent holds them on trust for his principal, rather than simply having an equitable duty to account to his principal. It is true that in many of those cases there was apparently no argument as to whether the benefit obtained by the fiduciary was actually held on trust for the principal. However, in some of the cases there was a dispute on the nature of the relief; in any event, the fact that it was assumed time and again by eminent barristers and judges must carry great weight. **17–025**

However, there is one decision of the House of Lords which appears to go the other way, and several decisions of the Court of Appeal which do go the other way, in that they hold that, while a principal has a claim for equitable compensation in respect of a bribe or secret commission received by his agent, he has no proprietary interest in it. [Lord Neuberger then considered the House of Lords decision is *Tyrrell v Bank of London*[48] *and* Court of Appeal decisions, particularly those in *Metropolitan Bank v Heiron*[49] and *Lister & Co v Stubbs*.[50]] **17–026**

---

43 "Proprietary Restitutionary Claims" in W.R. Cornish et al (eds), *Restitution: Past, Present and Future* (1998) p. 69 and see more recently (2011) 127 L.Q.R. 493.

44 "Fiduciary Duties and Proprietary Remedies: Addressing the Failure of Equitable Formulae" [2013] C.L.J. 720.

45 [1993] R.L.R. 7.

46 And see more recently [2012] C.L.J. 583.

47 "Constructive Trusts and the No-Profit Rule" [2013] C.L.J. 260.

48 (1862) 10 H.L. Cas. 26.

49 (1880) 5 Ex. D. 319.

50 (1890) 45 Ch. D. 1.

17–027 More recently, in 1993, in *Attorney General for Hong Kong v Reid*,[51] the Privy Council concluded that bribes received by a corrupt government legal officer were held on trust for his principal, and so they could be traced into properties which he had acquired in New Zealand. In his judgment on behalf of the Board, Lord Templeman disapproved the reasoning in *Heiron*, and the reasoning and outcome in *Lister*, and he thought his conclusion inconsistent with only one of the opinions, that of Lord Chelmsford, in *Tyrrell*. In *Daraydan Holdings Ltd v Solland International Ltd*,[52] Lawrence Collins J. indicated that he would follow *Reid* rather than *Lister*, as did Toulson J. in *Fyffes Group Ltd v Templeman*.[53] But in *Sinclair Investments (UK) Ltd v Versailles Trade Finance Ltd*,[54] in a judgment given by Lord Neuberger of Abbotsbury MR, the Court of Appeal decided that it should follow *Heiron* and *Lister*, and indeed *Tyrrell*, for a number of reasons,[55] although it accepted that this court might follow the approach in *Reid*. In this case, Simon J. considered that he was bound by *Sinclair*, whereas the Court of Appeal concluded that they could and should distinguish it . . .

17–028 The respondents' formulation of the rule, namely that it applies to all benefits received by an agent in breach of his fiduciary duty to his principal, is explained on the basis that an agent ought to account in specie to his principal for any benefit he has obtained from his agency in breach of his fiduciary duty, as the benefit should be treated as the property of the principal, as supported by many judicial dicta including those [quoted] above and can be seen to be reflected in Jonathan Parker L.J.'s observations above. More subtly, it is justified on the basis that equity does not permit an agent to rely on his own wrong to justify retaining the benefit: in effect, he must accept that, as he received the benefit as a result of his agency, he acquired it for his principal . . .

17–029 The appellant's formulation of the rule, namely that it has a more limited reach, and does not apply to bribes and secret commissions, has various different formulations and justifications. Thus, it is said that, given that it is a proprietary principle, the rule should not apply to benefits which were not derived from assets which are or should be the property of the principal, a view supported by the reasoning of Lord Westbury L.C. in *Tyrrell*.[56] It has also been suggested that the rule should not apply to benefits which could not have been intended for the principal and were, rightly or wrongly, the property of the agent, which seems to have been the basis of Cotton L.J.'s judgment in *Heiron*[57] and *Lister*.[58] In *Sinclair*[59] it was suggested that the effect of the authorities was that the rule should not apply to a benefit which the agent had obtained by taking advantage of an opportunity which arose as a result of the agency, unless the opportunity "was properly that of the [principal]" . . .

17–030 Each of [these] formulations . . . have their supporters and detractors. In the end, it is not possible to identify any plainly right or plainly wrong answer to the issue of the extent of the rule, as a matter of pure legal authority. There can clearly be different views as to what requirements have to be satisfied before a proprietary interest is created. More broadly, it is fair to say that the concept of equitable proprietary rights is in some respects somewhat paradoxical. Equity, unlike the common law, classically acts in personam;[60] yet equity is far more ready to accord proprietary claims than common law. Further, two general rules which law students learn early on are that common law legal rights prevail over equitable rights, and that where there are competing equitable rights the first in time prevails; yet, given that equity is far more ready to recognise proprietary rights than common law, the effect of having an equitable right is often to give priority over common law claims—sometimes even those which may have preceded the equitable right. Given that equity developed at least in part to mitigate the rigours of the common law, this is perhaps scarcely surprising. However, it underlines the point that it would be unrealistic to expect complete consistency from the cases over the past 300 years. It is therefore appropriate to turn to the arguments based on principle and practicality, and then to address the issue, in the light of those arguments as well as the judicial decisions discussed above.

51 [1994] 1 A.C. 324.
52 [2005] Ch. 119 at [75] ff.
53 [2000] 2 Lloyd's Rep. 643 at 668–672.
54 [2012] Ch. 453.
55 Set out ibid at [77]ff.
56 (1862) 10 H.L. Cas. 26.
57 (1880) 5 Ex. D. 319 at 325.
58 (1890) 45 Ch. D. 1 at 12.
59 [2012] Ch. 453 at [88].
60 See e.g. *Maitland on Equity* 2nd ed (1936), p. 322.

The position adopted by the respondents, namely that the rule applies to all unauthorised benefits which an agent receives, is consistent with the fundamental principles of the law of agency. The agent owes a duty of undivided loyalty to the principal, unless the latter has given his informed consent to some less demanding standard of duty. The principal is thus entitled to the entire benefit of the agent's acts in the course of his agency. This principle is wholly unaffected by the fact that the agent may have exceeded his authority. The principal is entitled to the benefit of the agent's unauthorised acts in the course of his agency, in just the same way as, at law, an employer is vicariously liable to bear the burden of an employee's unauthorised breaches of duty in the course of his employment. The agent's duty is accordingly to deliver up to his principal the benefit which he has obtained, and not simply to pay compensation for having obtained it in excess of his authority. The only way that legal effect can be given to an obligation to deliver up specific property to the principal is by treating the principal as specifically entitled to it. **17–031**

On the other hand, there is some force in the notion advanced by the appellant that the rule should not apply to a bribe or secret commission paid to an agent, as such a benefit is different in quality from a secret profit he makes on a transaction on which he is acting for his principal, or a profit he makes from an otherwise proper transaction which he enters into as a result of some knowledge or opportunity he has as a result of his agency. Both types of secret profit can be said to be benefits which the agent should have obtained for the principal, whereas the same cannot be said about a bribe or secret commission which the agent receives from a third party. **17–032**

The respondents' formulation of the rule has the merit of simplicity: any benefit acquired by an agent as a result of his agency and in breach of his fiduciary duty is held on trust for the principal. On the other hand, the appellant's position is more likely to result in uncertainty. Thus, there is more than one way in which one can identify the possible exceptions to the normal rule, which results in a bribe or commission being excluded from the rule . . . Clarity and simplicity are highly desirable qualities in the law. Subtle distinctions are sometimes inevitable, but in the present case, as mentioned above, there is no plainly right answer, and, accordingly, in the absence of any other good reason, it would seem right to opt for the simple answer . . . **17–033**

The notion that the rule should not apply to a bribe or secret commission received by an agent because it could not have been received by, or on behalf of, the principal seems unattractive. The whole reason that the agent should not have accepted the bribe or commission is that it puts him in conflict with his duty to his principal. Further, in terms of elementary economics, there must be a strong possibility that the bribe has disadvantaged the principal. Take the facts of this case: if the vendor was prepared to sell for €211·5m, on the basis that it was paying a secret commission of €10m, it must be quite likely that, in the absence of such commission, the vendor would have been prepared to sell for less than €211·5m, possibly €201·5m. While Simon J. was not prepared to make such an assumption without further evidence, it accords with common sense that it should often, even normally, be correct; indeed, in some cases, it has been assumed by judges that the price payable for the transaction in which the agent was acting was influenced pro rata to account for the bribe.[61] . . . **17–034**

The notion that an agent should not hold a bribe or commission on trust because he could not have acquired it on behalf of his principal is somewhat inconsistent with the long-standing decision in *Keech*, the decision in *Phipps* approved by the House of Lords, and the Privy Council decision in *Bowes*. In each of those three cases, a person acquired property as a result of his fiduciary or quasi-fiduciary position, in circumstances in which the principal could not have acquired it: yet the court held that the property concerned was held on trust for the beneficiary. In *Keech*, the beneficiary could not acquire the new lease because the landlord was not prepared to let to him, and because he was an infant; in *Boardman*, the trust could not acquire the shares because they were not authorised investments; in *Bowes*, the city corporation would scarcely have been interested in buying the loan notes which it had just issued to raise money. **17–035**

The respondents are also able to point to a paradox if the appellant is right and a principal has no proprietary right to his agent's bribe or secret commission. If the principal has a proprietary right, then he is better off, and the agent is worse off, than if the principal merely has a claim for equitable compensation. It would be curious, as Mr Collings frankly conceded, if a principal whose agent wrongly receives a bribe or secret commission is worse off than a principal whose agent obtains a benefit in far less opprobrious circumstances, eg the benefit obtained by the trustees' agents in *Boardman*. Yet that is the effect if the rule does not apply to bribes or secret commissions. **17–036**

---

61 See e.g. *Fawcett v Whitehouse* (1829) 1 Russ. & M. 132 at 136.

17–037 Wider policy considerations also support the respondents' case that bribes and secret commissions received by an agent should be treated as the property of his principal, rather than merely giving rise to a claim for equitable compensation. As Lord Templeman said giving the decision of the Privy Council in *Attorney General for Hong Kong v Reid*,[62] "bribery is an evil practice which threatens the foundations of any civilised society". Secret commissions are also objectionable as they inevitably tend to undermine trust in the commercial world. That has always been true, but concern about bribery and corruption generally has never been greater than it is now: see for instance, internationally, the OECD Convention on Combating Bribery of Foreign Public Officials in International Business Transactions 1999 and the United Nations Convention against Corruption 2003, and, nationally, the Bribery Acts 2010 and 2012. Accordingly, one would expect the law to be particularly stringent in relation to a claim against an agent who has received a bribe or secret commission.

17–038 On the other hand, a point frequently emphasised by those who seek to justify restricting the ambit of the rule is that the wide application for which the respondents contend will tend to prejudice the agent's unsecured creditors, as it will serve to reduce the estate of the agent if he becomes insolvent. This was seen as a good reason in *Sinclair*[63] for not following *Reid*. While the point has considerable force in some contexts, it appears to us to have limited force in the context of a bribe or secret commission. In the first place, the proceeds of a bribe or secret commission consists of property which should not be in the agent's estate at all, as Lawrence Collins J. pointed out in *Daraydan*[64] (although it is fair to add that insolvent estates not infrequently include assets which would not be there if the insolvent had honoured his obligations). Secondly, as discussed above, at any rate in many cases, the bribe or commission will very often have reduced the benefit from the relevant transaction which the principal will have obtained, and therefore can fairly be said to be his property.

17–039 None the less, the appellant's argument based on potential prejudice to the agent's unsecured creditors has some force, but it is, as we see it, balanced by the fact that it appears to be just that a principal whose agent has obtained a bribe or secret commission should be able to trace the proceeds of the bribe or commission into other assets and to follow them into the hands of knowing recipients (as in *Reid*). Yet, as Mr Collings rightly accepts, tracing or following in equity would not be possible, at least as the law is currently understood, unless the person seeking to trace or follow can claim a proprietary interest. Common law tracing is, of course, possible without a proprietary interest, but it is much more limited than equitable tracing. Lindley L.J. in *Lister*[65] appears to have found it offensive that a principal should be entitled to trace a bribe, but he did not explain why, and we prefer the reaction of Lord Templeman in *Reid*, namely that a principal ought to have the right to trace and to follow a bribe or secret commission.

17–040 Finally, on this aspect, it appears that other common law jurisdictions have adopted the view that the rule applies to all benefits which are obtained by a fiduciary in breach of his duties. In the High Court of Australia, Deane J. said in *Chan v Zacharia* that any benefit obtained:[66]

> "in circumstances where a conflict . . . existed . . . or . . . by reason of his fiduciary position or of opportunity or knowledge resulting from it . . . is held by the fiduciary as constructive trustee."

17–041 More recently, the Full Federal Court of Australia has decided not to follow *Sinclair*: see *Grimaldi*, where the decision in *Reid* was preferred.[67] Although the Australian courts recognise the remedial constructive trust, that was only one of the reasons for not following *Sinclair*. As Finn J. who gave the judgment of the court said[68] (after describing *Heiron* and *Lister* as imposing "an anomalous limitation . . . on the reach of *Keech v Sandford*"[69]), "Australian law" in this connection "matches that of New Zealand . . ., Singapore, United States jurisdictions . . . and Canada". As overseas countries secede from the jurisdiction of the Privy Council, it is inevitable that inconsistencies in the common law will develop between different jurisdictions.

62 [1994] 1 A.C. 324 at 330.
63 [2012] Ch. 453 at [83].
64 [2005] Ch. 119 at [78].
65 (1890) 45 Ch.D. 1 at 15.
66 (1984) 154 C.L.R. 178 at 199.
67 (2012) 287 A.L.R. 22 at [569]–[584].
68 Ibid. at [582].
69 Ibid. at [569].

However, it seems to us highly desirable for all those jurisdictions to learn from each other, and at least to lean in favour of harmonising the development of the common law round the world.

Conclusions

The considerations of practicality and principle discussed above appear to support the respondents' case, namely that a bribe or secret commission accepted by an agent is held on trust for his principal. The position is perhaps rather less clear when one examines the decided cases, whose effect we have summarised above. However, to put it at its lowest, the authorities do not preclude us adopting the respondents' case in that they do not represent a clear and consistent line of authority to the contrary effect. Indeed, we consider that, taken as a whole, the authorities favour the respondents' case **17–042**

. . .we consider that, the many decisions and the practical and policy considerations which favour the wider application of the rule and are discussed above justify our disapproving *Tyrrell*. In our judgment, therefore, the decision in *Tyrrell* should not stand in the way of the conclusion that the law took a wrong turn in *Heiron* and *Lister*, and that those decisions, and any subsequent decisions (*Powell & Thomas*, *Attorney General's Reference (No. 1 of 1985)* and *Sinclair*), at least in so far as they relied on or followed *Heiron* and *Lister*, should be treated as overruled. **17–043**

In this case, the Court of Appeal rightly regarded themselves as bound by *Sinclair*, but they managed to distinguish it. Accordingly, the appeal is dismissed. **17–044**

In *FHR*, the Supreme Court thus clearly held that a constructive trust is imposed on bribe money and secret commissions paid to a fiduciary to act against her principal's interests. To the extent that previous decisions held otherwise, they were overruled. But what did their Lordships make of the respondents' argument that *all* benefits received by a fiduciary in breach of her fiduciary duty are held on constructive trust? This rule would align the circumstances in which a constructive trust is imposed with the circumstances in which a fiduciary owes a personal liability to account for and pay over the value of gains made in breach of fiduciary duty. However, it was not necessary for the court to adopt this rule to decide the appeal and it is not clear from Lord Neuberger's judgment that they did in fact ground their decision on it. **17–045**

As Matthew Conaglen has noted, this leaves us with some unanswered questions:[70] **17–046**

For example, will benefits obtained indirectly from a breach of fiduciary duty, as in *Sinclair v Versailles*, be caught by the principle in *FHR*? In *Sinclair*, the fiduciary profited by selling shares which he did not hold, or deal with, in a fiduciary capacity, but where the fiduciary's misapplication of other funds (in a Ponzi scheme) allowed him to inflate the value of his shareholding. If the fiduciary must account for such profit, as the Court of Appeal indicated in *Sinclair*, *FHR* suggests that the principal will have a proprietary right to that profit (assuming it, or its traceable product, can be located). . .

Relatedly, if the fiduciary takes a loan from his principal in a way that involves a breach of fiduciary duty, will the principal have a proprietary claim in respect of any profits which the fiduciary generates from employment of the loan monies? Traditionally, a breach of fiduciary duty renders a transaction voidable, rather than void, which means that the principal can rescind the loan transaction, but has no proprietary interest (beyond the mere equity to rescind) in the loan monies (even assuming they can be identified or traced) until the transaction is rescinded.[71] It is unclear to what degree the decision in *FHR* might alter this position. Presumably, the results will be similar if the right to rescind is recognised as binding on unsecured creditors in the event of the fiduciary's insolvency.[72] **17–047**

---

70 M. Conaglen, "Proprietary Remedies for Breach of Fiduciary Duty" (2014) 73 C.L.J. 490, 492.
71 e.g. *Daly v Sydney Stock Exchange Ltd* (1986) 160 C.L.R. 371 at 387–88.
72 Although that issue is itself difficult: P. Watts, "Constructive Trusts and Insolvency" (2009) 3 J.Eq. 250.

C. Justifying the Trust

17–048 In *Attorney General for Hong Kong v Reid*, Lord Templeman justified the imposition of a constructive trust in the following way:[73]

> As soon as the bribe was received it should have been paid or transferred instanter to the person who suffered from the breach of duty. Equity considers as done that which ought to have been done. As soon as the bribe was received, whether in cash or in kind, the false fiduciary held the bribe on a constructive trust for the person injured.

17–049 There are, however, important difficulties with this reasoning, which provides a further example of the dangers of applying equitable maxims too loosely.[74] The unexamined premise in Lord Templeman's analysis is whether F really is under a duty to transfer the *bribe itself* to P, rather than just a duty (or liability) to pay its value to P. It may be though that Lord Templeman had in mind a different analysis, focussing not on F's breach of duty, but rather on a disability of F as against P.

17–050 As we saw in Chapter 2,[75] equity's treatment of fiduciaries originally took effect through rules imposing disabilities rather than duties, applying the idea that, as against P, F was simply unable to enter into certain types of transaction. Lionel Smith[76] has relied on similar reasoning to justify the constructive trust imposed in cases such as *Reid* and *FHR*. He emphasises the following statement of Lord Russell in *Regal (Hastings) Ltd v Gulliver*:[77]

> The rule of equity which insists on those, who by use of a fiduciary position make a profit, being liable to account for that profit, is no way depends on fraud, or absence of bona fides; or upon such questions or considerations as whether the profit would or should otherwise have gone to the plaintiff, or whether the profiteer was under a duty to obtain the source of the profit for the plaintiff, or whether he took a risk or acted as he did for the benefit of the plaintiff, or whether the plaintiff has in fact been damaged or benefitted by his action . . . The liability arises from the mere fact of a profit, having, in the stated circumstances, been made.

17–051 The argument is that P's claim thus does not depend on any breach of duty by F as such, but is rather, in Smith's words:[78]

> . . . a direct implication of the fact that a fiduciary acts, within a sphere of activity, for and on behalf of the principal. The implication is that whatever may be extracted from that sphere of activity is attributed, as between the fiduciary and the beneficiary, as a matter of primary right, to the beneficiary including that which was extracted without authority, should the beneficiary so choose. It is not necessary to say that opportunities or information 'belong' to the beneficiary in a legal sense; the rule is activated when opportunities or information are used to acquire rights, if they can be said to have been acquired from acting in the fiduciary role. Nor is it necessary to see the result as a remedy for wrongful conduct: profits are attributed to the beneficiary as an implication of the nature of the fiduciary relationship, not as a remedy for a wrong . . . The rule is not only about profits; rather it attributes to the beneficiary rights acquired from the fiduciary role.

---

[73] [1994] 1 A.C. 324 at 331.
[74] See paras 1–102 to 1–106.
[75] [1994] 1 A.C. 324 at 331.
[76] L. Smith, "Constructive Trusts and the No-Profit Rule" [2013] C.L.J. 260. See too D.J. Hayton, "Proprietary Liability for Secret Profits" (2011) 127 L.Q.R. 487; Lord Millett, "Bribes and Secret Commissions Again" (2012) 71 C.L.J. 583, 585 and 591–592.
[77] [1942] 2 A.C. 134 at 144–145.
[78] L. Smith, "Constructive Trusts and the No-Profit Rule" [2013] C.L.J. 260, 261–262.

There are some hints of this analysis in Lord Neuberger's judgment in *FHR*. For example, he states that:[79] **17–052**

> The principal is thus entitled to the entire benefit of the agent's acts in the course of his agency. This principle is wholly unaffected by the fact that the agent may have exceeded his authority. The principal is entitled to the benefit of the agent's unauthorised acts in the course of his agency, in just the same way as, at law, an employer is vicariously liable to bear the burden of an employee's unauthorised breaches of duty in the course of his employment.

Note that, on this model, the constructive trust arising in a case such as *Reid* or *FHR* is, in Liew's terms, a "qualified interest" trust,[80] as F never acquires the property free from the duty to P. This argument is predicated on the "disability" view of the rules governing fiduciary behaviour, and as noted in Chapter 2, that model is now coming under pressure from the "duty" model on which claims for equitable compensation are premised.[81] Laying that point to one side, however, and assuming the correctness of the "disability" model, the argument may still be problematic for the different reason that it is conclusory, i.e. it affirms what it seeks to prove.[82] One suggestion for a reason why F may be prevented, as against P, from denying that F has acquired the right on behalf of P is that this would conform to the policy of removing, as far as possible, incentives for F to act beyond F's authority: there may otherwise be situations where F would be tempted to accept a bribe, e.g. of a right to specific property such as land, as F would prefer to have that right than not, even if F is under a liability to pay its value to P.[83] It should not be overlooked, however, that thus furthering this policy of removing temptations from P necessarily comes at the expense of F's other creditors who would otherwise have access to the rights acquired by F. **17–053**

3. Proceeds of Breach of Confidence

A. The Nature of the Trust

As we saw in Chapter 3,[84] the equitable doctrine of breach of confidence, which now also extends to the protection of private information, **17–054**

> depends on the broad principle of equity that he who has received information in confidence shall not take unfair advantage of it. He must not make use of it to the prejudice of him who gave it without obtaining his consent.[85]

The equitable right of confidence can be protected by the grant of an injunction to prevent disclosure, but if it is too late and the confidence has been disclosed then B[86] may be entitled to an award of **17–055**

---

79 [2015] A.C. 250 at [33].

80 Y.K. Liew, *Rationalising Constructive Trusts* (Hart Publishing, 2017) 218. See para.17–009.

81 See paras 2–158 to 2–163.

82 J.E. Penner, "The Difficult Doctrinal Basis for the Fiduciary's Proprietary Liability to Account for Bribes" (2012) 18 T. & T. 1000.

83 See e.g. B. McFarlane and R. Stevens, "The Nature of Equitable Property" (2010) 4 J. Eq. 1, 18. Note this argument is not the same as simply saying that the trust is there for purposes of deterrence: as explored by Lionel Smith, there are some significant difficulties with a pure deterrence rationale for the trust: see L. Smith, "The Motive, Not the Deed", in J. Getzler (ed.), *Rationalizing Property, Equity and Trusts* (Oxford University Press, 2003), pp.60–61.

84 See paras 3–034ff.

85 *Seager v Copydex Ltd* [1967] 1 W.L.R. 923 at 931.

86 Note that here, consistently with the discussion of confidence in Chapter 3, B here refers to the party to whom the duty of confidence is owed.

monetary compensation against A,[87] or to a money award based on the value of A's profits[88]—although the trend of recent case law suggests where there is no fiduciary relationship between the parties, the court will usually restrict B to the compensatory award.[89] Where A acquires specific property by means of a breach of confidence, B may wish to argue that A is not only personally liable to pay the value of those profits to B, but in fact holds the property itself on trust for B.[90] If such a trust is imposed, it will clearly be constructive. It is far from clear, however, that such a trust can arise in English law.

B. The Scope of the Trust

17–056 There is Commonwealth authority suggesting that a constructive trust may sometimes be imposed on profits acquired through a breach of confidence or privacy. For example, in *LAC Minerals Ltd v International Corona Resources Ltd*,[91] the Supreme Court of Canada held that LAC was constructive trustee of land that it had bought for itself, because it had been told in confidence by a potential joint-venturer that the land could well contain gold deposits.

17–057 Dicta to the same effect can also be found in some English cases. In *Attorney General v Guardian Newspapers Ltd (No.2)*, Lord Goff considered obiter that if a confidant disclosed information in a book so that it lost its quality of confidentiality, and then sought to profit further from his wrongdoing by selling the film rights to the book "the copyright in the book, including the film rights, are held by him on constructive trust for the confider".[92] In *Ocular Sciences Ltd v Aspect Vision Care Ltd*,[93] Laddie J considered that the approach taken by the court in *LAC Minerals* "makes eminent sense" and, whilst refusing to find a constructive trust on the facts of the case, stated that "the imposition of a constructive trust is part of the equitable armoury of the court."[94] Similarly, in *United Pan-Europe Communications NV v Deutsche Bank AG*[95] the Court of Appeal stated that in principle a constructive trust could be awarded in response to a breach of confidence.

17–058 It seems, however, that there is no English case in which a constructive trust has actually been imposed in response to a breach of confidence, and it is important to note that, where the breach of confidence also involves a breach of fiduciary duty, any trust arising may more easily be seen as responding to the breach of fiduciary duty.

---

87 See, e.g. *Saltman Engineering Co Ltd v Campbell Engineering Co Ltd* (1948) 65 R.P.C. 203 at 219; *Seager v Copydex Ltd (No.1)* [1967] 1 W.L.R. 923 at 932; and *Seager v Copydex (No.2)* [1969] 1 W.L.R. 809; *Indata Equipment Supplies Ltd v ACL Ltd* [1998] F.S.R. 248 at 259–262, 263 and 264; *Campbell v Mirror Group Newspapers Ltd* [2002] E.M.L.R. 617 at [75], affirmed [2004] UKHL 22; [2004] 2 A.C. 457; *Douglas v Hello! Ltd (No.6)* [2005] EWCA Civ 595; [2006] Q.B. 125 at [120], [243]–[250] and [259]; *OBG Ltd v Allan* [2007] UKHL 21; [2008] 1 A.C. 1 at [276].

88 *Peter Pan Manufacturing Corp v Corsets Silhouette Ltd* [1964] 1 W.L.R. 96 at 106; *Attorney General v Observer Ltd* [1990] 1 A.C. 109 at 255–256, 262 and 288; *OBG Ltd v Allan* [2007] UKHL 21; [2008] 1 A.C. 1 at [276]; *Vestergaard Frandsen A/S v BestNet Europe Ltd* [2009] EWHC 1456 (Ch); [2010] F.S.R. 2 at [93].

89 *CF Partners (UK) LLP v Barclays Bank Plc* [2014] EWHC 3049 (Ch) at [1168]–[1181], considering *Experience Hendrix LLC v PPX Enterprises Inc* [2003] EWCA Civ 323; [2003] 1 All E.R. (Comm) 830; *Vercoe v Rutland Fund Management Ltd* [2010] EWHC 424; and *Walsh v Shanahan* [2013] EWCA Civ 411.

90 As noted at para.17–013 in relation to proceeds of a breach of fiduciary duty, the process of taking an account can be used to establish the extent of the proceeds acquired by A in breach of duty, and can then support either a personal claim against A or a claim that A holds those proceeds on constructive trust.

91 (1989) 61 D.L.R. (4th) 15. See too *Minera Aquiline Argentina SA v IMA Exploration Inc* (2007) 10 W.W.R. 648. Cf. *Australian Broadcasting Corporation v Lenah Game Meats Pty Ltd* (2001) 208 C.L.R. 199 at [311].

92 *Attorney General v Guardian Newspapers (No.2)* [1990] 1 A.C. 109 at 288.

93 [1997] R.P.C. 289 at 404.

94 [1997] R.P.C. 289 at 416.

95 [2000] 2 B.C.L.C. 461.

C. Justifying the Trust

Given the paucity of English authority supporting the imposition of a constructive trust in response to a breach of confidence, the question here is whether the recognition of such a trust *would* be justified. In a breach of confidence case which does not also feature a breach of fiduciary duty, B would face some significant obstacles in seeking to establish a constructive trust.[96] First, it would be necessary to show that a remedy responding to A's gain is required, as several recent cases have indicated that claimants do not have a right in every case simply to elect to receive an account of profits rather than a compensatory award.[97] It certainly seems that a remedy related to the gain of the defendant will not be awarded if the breach of confidence was not deliberate.[98] **17–059**

Second, even once that hurdle is cleared, the further question arises whether A should have only a personal duty to account for the profits, or whether A should also hold those profits on trust, an additional response to her wrongdoing that requires additional justification. One possibility would for B to make the form of argument we noted in relation to fiduciary duty cases, and argue that A was under a disability, as against B, to misuse the information, so that any right acquired by A by such misuse must be held on trust for B. There is no sign, however, of such a strict approach being adopted in all breach of confidence cases, and it would be particularly inappropriate in cases concerned with invasions of privacy given that, as noted in Chapter 3,[99] those cases seem unrelated to any disability of A. **17–060**

4. Specifically Enforceable Contracts of Sale

A. Nature of the Trust

If two parties enter a specifically enforceable contract to sell land or other property, then the vendor will hold the property on constructive trust for the purchaser until the contract is completed by conveyance of the property.[100] This form of constructive trust is very well-established: in *Lysaght v Edwards*, for example, Jessel MR found such a trust and said that the point had been settled "for more than two centuries".[101] **17–061**

There are, nonetheless, some uncertainties, in England and other common law jurisdictions,[102] as to the nature and operation of the purchaser's interest. Certainly, as noted by Lord Walker in *Jerome v Kelly (Inspector of Taxes)*,[103] "[it would] be wrong to treat an uncompleted contract for the sale of land as equivalent to an immediate, irrevocable declaration of trust." Lord Walker's approach has been elaborated by Peter Turner,[104] who argues that the vendor-purchaser constructive trust in fact consists of a number of distinct equitable rights, not all of which arise immediately, but that it is **17–062**

---

96 For further discussion see, e.g. M. Conaglen, "Thinking about Proprietary Remedies for Breach of Confidence" [2008] I.P.Q. 82; N. Witzleb, "Justifying Gain-Based Remedies for Invasions of Privacy" (2009) 29 O.J.L.S. 325.

97 See the cases cited at n.289.

98 See, e.g. *Seager v Copydex (No.1)* [1967] 1 W.L.R. 923 at 932 per Lord Denning MR; *Vercoe v Rutland Fund Management Ltd* [2010] EWHC 424 at [336].

99 See para.3–046.

100 *Holroyd v Marshall* (1862) 10 H.L.C. 191 at 209; *Dougan v Ley* (1946) 71 C.L.R. 152; *Oughtred v IRC* [1960] A.C. 206; *Neville v Wilson* [1997] Ch. 44.

101 (1876) 2 Ch. D. 499 at 506.

102 See, e.g. *Chang v Registrar of Titles* (1976) 137 C.L.R. 177 at 184 (Mason J). See too *Martin Commercial Fueling Inc v Virtanen* (1997) 154 D.L.R. (4th) 290, esp. at [8]–[10].

103 [2004] UKHL 25; [2004] 1 W.L.R. 1409 at [32].

104 P. Turner, "Understanding the Constructive Trust between Vendor and Purchaser" (2012) 128 L.Q.R. 582.

nonetheless reasonable to say that a "trust in some sense exists at every stage between the formation and discharge by performance of a specifically enforceable contract of sale." It is thus possible to agree with the view that a trust (in some sense) arises as soon as the contract for the sale of unique property is entered into, whilst also agreeing that the rights of the parties change over time, so that the purchaser acquires further rights only once the purchase price is paid.[105]

17–063 At the time of formation of the contract, for example, the vendor has the right to protect their own interest prior to completion.[106] She can keep the rents and profits until the date fixed for completion,[107] and retain possession of the property until the contract is completed by payment of the purchase price.[108] If the vendor parts with possession to the purchaser before actual completion, or even conveys the land, then the vendor may fall back on her equitable lien over the property to ensure that she is paid.[109] It is nonetheless possible to regard the purchaser as having an interest under a constructive trust from the time of formation of the contract because she is given potential protection against a third party receiving the property from the vendor and, as Turner argues:[110]

> A uniquely equitable feature of all trusts of property is that they keep the property available for the performance of an obligation. The property is kept alive through a general rule that, subject to defences, a person who acquires an interest in property takes subject to the interest anyone else may have acquired under a trust.

17–064 As explained by Lord Collins in *Scott v Southern Pacific Mortgages Ltd*,[111] "it does not follow that the purchaser has proprietary rights for all purposes."[112] So, whilst in such a case the purchaser's equitable interest can bind third parties, it does not mean that the purchaser has an interest which she can transfer to a sub-purchaser so as to bind the vendor,[113] nor does it mean that a party with a proprietary estoppel claim against the purchaser can acquire their own equitable interest before the point when the purchaser acquires legal title.[114]

17–065 If the vendor sells the property to a third party who has a defence to the purchaser's interest under the trust, the purchaser can trace into the sale proceeds received by the vendor, and assert a proprietary claim to these proceeds, subject to accounting to the vendor for the price agreed between the vendor and purchaser.[115] This will be useful if the vendor has generated a surplus through her dealings with the third party,[116] or if the vendor is insolvent and so a contractual claim for damages is not worthwhile.

---

105 *Miliangos v George Frank (Textiles) Ltd* [1976] A.C. 443 at 467. Note too *Baker v Craggs* [2016] EWHC 3250 (Ch); [2017] Ch. 295, where Newey J (in a point not considered by the Court of Appeal in that litigation) held that, after formation of the contract and pending its completion, the purchaser has an "estate contract" under the Law of Property Act 1925, whereas that estate contract disappears and is replaced by a full beneficial interest under a trust when the contract is completed by the vendor. Note of course that completion of the contract does not itself transfer the vendor's registered title to the purchaser as that occurs only on registration of the purchaser.

106 *Shaw v Foster* (1872) L.R. 5 H.L. 321 at 328; *Re Watford Corporation's Contract* [1943] Ch. 82 at 85.

107 *Cuddon v Tite* (1858) 1 Giff. 395.

108 *Gedge v Montrose* (1858) 26 Beav. 45; *Phillips v Silvester* (1872) L.R. 8 Ch. 173.

109 *Nives v Nives* (1880) 15 Ch. D. 649; *Re Birmingham* [1959] Ch. 523; *London & Cheshire Insurance Co Ltd v Laplagrene* [1971] Ch. 499.

110 Turner, "Understanding the Constructive Trust between Vendor and Purchaser" (2012) 128 L.Q.R. 582, 597.

111 [2014] UKSC 52; [2015] A.C. 385.

112 [2014] UKSC 52; [2015] A.C. 385 at [65].

113 *Ezair v Conn* [2020] EWCA Civ 687 at [49].

114 *Scott v Southern Pacific Mortgages Ltd* [2014] UKSC 52; [2015] A.C. 385.

115 *Bunny Industries Ltd v FSW Enterprises Pty Ltd* [1982] Qd. R. 712.

116 *Lake v Bayliss* [1974] 1 W.L.R. 1073.

B. Scope of the Trust

Whilst contracts for the sale of land constitute the core case of this form of constructive trust, it can also apply in other situations where a party is under a contractual duty to transfer unique property. For example, we saw in Chapter 6[117] that in *Neville v Wilson*,[118] adopting views expressed by Lord Radcliffe in the House of Lords in *Oughtred v IRC*,[119] the Court of Appeal found that a constructive trust arose on the making of a contract to transfer a beneficial interest in shares in a private company. Indeed, it seems that the same principle can apply even if the enforceable duty to make a transfer is non-contractual: in *Mountney v Treharne*,[120] for example, a court had made an order, in ancillary relief proceedings following a divorce, that the husband had to transfer his interest in the matrimonial home to his wife. It was held that, as a result of that order, a trust arose and so an immediate equitable interest arose in favour of the wife, which was critical given that the husband had subsequently been made bankrupt. **17–066**

It also seems that the underlying principle is not confined to constructive trusts, but can give rise to other forms of equitable interest. In *Walsh v Lonsdale*,[121] for example, it was held that where A is under a specifically enforceable contractual duty to grant a lease to B, B immediately acquires an equitable lease; in *Holroyd v Marshall*,[122] an immediate equitable security interest arose as a result of the borrower's contractual promise to transfer title to mill machinery to trustees, so that the title could be held as security for a debt owed by the transferor. However, a trust is appropriate where the duty is to make an outright transfer, rather than to grant a lease or to make a transfer by way of security. **17–067**

There is some debate as to the proper role, if any, of the availability of specific performance. For example, in *Tailby v Official Receiver*,[123] Lord Macnaghten stated, in the context of an agreement to give a security interest over receivables, that there was no requirement that the contract be capable of specific performance. Simon Gardner has also argued that, in the context of equitable leases, the supposed requirement of specific performance has no sound historical basis.[124] Peter Turner, in contrast, has supported the orthodox requirement, noting however that, at the time of the formation of the contract at least, it is the *potential* for specific performance, arising from the uniqueness of the property to be transferred, that is of importance.[125] **17–068**

C. Justifying the Trust

The vendor–purchaser constructive trust has been the subject of some fierce academic criticism. William Swadling, for example, has argued that it is a "fiction" which "cannot be justified", as the simple fact that a defendant may be ordered by a court to transfer property to the claimant is not, in itself, sufficient to justify giving the claimant all the advantages of a beneficial interest under a trust.[126] Certainly, Swadling is correct to doubt the usefulness of the formula often used to justify this form of constructive trust: that "equity looks upon as done that which ought to be done". The difficulty with **17–069**

---

117 paras 6–109ff.
118 [1997] Ch. 144.
119 [1960] A.C. 206 at 227. See too the views of Upjohn J at first instance in that case: [1958] Ch. 383 at 390.
120 [2003] Ch. 135.
121 (1882) 21 Ch. D. 9.
122 (1862) 10 H.L. Cas. 191.
123 (1888) 13 App. Cas. 523.
124 S. Gardner, "Equity, Estate Contracts and the Judicature Acts: *Walsh v Lonsdale* Revisited" (1987) 7 O.J.L.S. 60.
125 P. Turner, "Understanding the Constructive Trust between Vendor and Purchaser" (2012) 128 L.Q.R. 582, 589–592.
126 W. Swadling, "The Vendor-Purchaser Constructive Trust" in S. Degeling and J. Edelman (eds), *Equity in Commercial Law* (Sweet & Maxwell, 2005), pp.475–476, 487–488; Swadling, "The Fiction of the Constructive Trust" (2011) 64 C.L.P. 399, 408.

the formula, taken literally, is that where, for example, A is under a duty to grant B a lease, or to transfer a right to B, it seems odd that equity should pretend that this duty has already been performed. In any case, the outcome of the vendor-purchaser constructive trust, at least when it initially arises, is not that the purchaser is already regarded in equity as an owner: as previously noted,[127] the vendor retains certain valuable rights in relation to the property until the purchase price is paid.

17–070 The maxim may be of some assistance, however, if it is applied only "within the parameters of what are clearly understood boundaries"[128] and is not interpreted literally. It reflects an underlying principle that if A holds particular property and is under a duty to transfer that property to B, or to give B a right in relation to it, then B can acquire an immediate equitable interest in relation to the property.[129] As Peter Turner[130] and Lionel Smith[131] have noted, it is characteristic of equity to give B the benefit of protection against third parties where a duty of A relates to specific property held by A. In Turner's view, the vendor–purchaser constructive trust is justified as a means of protecting the purchaser's interest in due performance of the contract, responding in particular to the need to prevent the purchaser failing to obtain the property promised under the contract: "Equity's policy is that contracts to convey unique property need greater stability against third parties than contracts to convey non-unique property."[132]

17–071 The emphasis on uniqueness ties in with a requirement that the contract be, potentially at least, specifically enforceable. A different view, building on that requirement, is that whenever B has the power to acquire property held by A, B necessarily has an equitable interest in that property,[133] and so it is no surprise that a constructive trust arises when A is under a specifically enforceable duty to convey specific property to B.[134] A further view, which again builds on a conception of the nature of the trust, is that the fact of A's holding a specific right, and being under a duty to B in relation to that right, is itself sufficient to give B an equitable interest, as such interests, by definition, arise when B has a right in relation to another right.[135]

5. Assignments for Value of Future Property

A. Nature of the Trust

17–072 As Swinfen Eady LJ stated in *Re Lind*:[136]

> An assignment for value of future property actually binds the property itself directly it is acquired—automatically on the happening of the event, and without any future act on the part of the assignor—and does not merely rest in, and amount to, a right in contract, giving rise to an action. The assignor, having received the consideration, becomes in equity on the happening of the event, trustee for the assignee of the property devolving upon or acquired by him, and which she had previously sold and been paid for.

---

[127] See para.17–063.

[128] *HR Trustees Ltd v Wembley Plc (In Liquidation)* [2011] EWHC 2974 (Ch) at [59].

[129] W. Swadling, "Unjust Enrichment: Value, Rights, and Trusts" (2021) 137 L.Q.R. 56, 68–69 argues that, even if an equitable interest arises in such cases, it need not arise under a trust.

[130] P. Turner, "Understanding the Constructive Trust between Vendor and Purchaser" (2012) 128 L.Q.R. 582, 597–598.

[131] L. Smith, "Fusion and Tradition" in Degeling and Edelman (eds), *Equity in Commercial Law* (2005).

[132] Turner, "Understanding the Constructive Trust between Vendor and Purchaser" (2012) 128 L.Q.R. 582, 603.

[133] See the discussion at para.5–040 of the *re Rose* principle.

[134] See R. Chambers, "The Importance of Specific Performance" in Degeling and Edelman (eds), *Equity in Commercial Law* (2005).

[135] See, e.g. B. McFarlane and R. Stevens, "The Nature of Equitable Property" (2010) 4 J.Eq. 1, 16–17. As noted by W. Swadling, "Unjust Enrichment: Value, Rights, and Trusts" (2021) 137 L.Q.R. 56, 68–69, an equitable interest arising in such cases need not arise under a trust.

[136] [1915] 2 Ch. 345 at 360.

B. Scope of the Trust

The constructive trust arising in such a case is clearly related to that in *Pullan v Koe*,[137] which we examined in Chapter 5,[138] and to the underlying principle applied in cases of specifically enforceable contracts to transfer property. In *Pullan*, it was held that, as a result of a prior, binding promise to settle any property later acquired by the wife of the value of £100 or more, a sum of £285 later received by the wife was *immediately* held by her on a trust enforceable in favour of all those within the marriage consideration. The trust in such a case is constructive, rather than express, as it does not require any exercise of a power to set up a trust: such a power cannot be exercised in relation to property not yet held by the purported settlor; and, once the property is received, the trust arises immediately, without the need for any declaration of trust.[139] The point of the principle stated in *Re Lind* is that an ineffective attempt at an immediate assignment, if made for value, will be regarded in effect as a promise to make such an assignment when possible, and so will have the same effect as in *Pullan*.[140] **17–073**

It is important to note that this principle applies only where the attempted assignment was for value provided for or on behalf of the claimant. In the absence of such value, there is no reason to impose any duty on the party who attempted to make the assignment, who is simply regarded as having failed in an attempt to make a gift. This is, therefore, one of the contexts in which the maxim that "equity will not assist a volunteer" has some relevance. **17–074**

The principle is also limited to cases where the promise to assign, or the attempted assignment, related to specific, identifiable property. It therefore cannot apply in a case such as *Re Goldcorp Exchange Ltd*,[141] where the defendant has simply promised to transfer a particular quantity of unascertained goods to the claimant. The very reason that prevents property passing at common law in such a case,[142] the lack of identifiable property to which the vendor's duty may attach, also prevents a trust, as a trust must have identifiable subject matter.[143] **17–075**

C. Justifying the Trust

As the principle underlying this trust seems to be identical to that applying in the case of specifically enforceable contracts to transfer property, it stands or falls, as far as justification is concerned, with that principle.[144] The only significant difference is that, in the case of a failed assignment for value, it is also necessary to justify why the defendant, who is unlikely to have made an express contractual promise to assign in the future, should be under such a duty to make the assignment as soon as the property is received. It does not seem unreasonable, however, to imply a promise to make such an assignment, if the intention was that some specific, identifiable property should be transferred. **17–076**

---

137 [1913] 1 Ch. 9. See too *Re Gillott's Settlement* [1934] Ch. 97 at 157–159.

138 See paras 5–076ff.

139 See too *Barclays Bank Plc v Willowbank International Ltd* [1987] B.C.L.C. 717; *Associated Alloys Pty Ltd v ACN 001 452 106 Pty Ltd* (2000) 202 C.L.R. 588.

140 [1915] 2 Ch. 345 at 360. See too *Re Burton's Settlements* [1955] Ch. 82 at 103–104 and *Parker v Taswell* (1858) 2 De G. & J. 559.

141 [1995] 1 A.C. 74.

142 See Sale of Goods Act 1979 s.16.

143 See para.7–074.

144 For discussion of the effects of the principle on other creditors, see J. Getzler, "Assignment of Future Property and Preferences" in J. Glister and P. Ridge (eds), *Fault Lines in Equity* (Hart Publishing, 2012).

6. Receipt of Property Subject to an Undertaking

A. Nature of the Trust

17–077 In Chapter 6, when looking at the formal requirements applying in relation to trusts of land, we considered the Court of Appeal's decision in *Rochefoucauld v Boustead*.[145] It was held there that, even though no written evidence of a declaration of trust could be produced, the defendant had acquired title to land from the claimant's mortgagee on trust for the claimant. In *Bannister v Bannister*,[146] the Court of Appeal regarded the trust thus arising as a constructive trust, and found that such a trust also arose where A transferred her interest in two cottages to B, pursuant to an oral agreement that B would allow A to remain living rent-free in one of those cottages for the rest of her life. Giving the Court of Appeal's judgment, Scott LJ stated that:[147]

> It is, we think, clearly a mistake to suppose that the equitable principle on which a constructive trust is raised against a person who insists on the absolute character of a conveyance to himself for the purpose of defeating a beneficial interest, which, according to the true bargain, was to belong to another, is confined to cases where the conveyance itself was fraudulently obtained . . . Nor is it, in our opinion, necessary that the bargain on which the absolute conveyance is made should include any express stipulation that the grantee is in so many words to hold as trustee. It is enough that the bargain should have included a stipulation under which some sufficiently defined beneficial interest in the property was to be taken by another.

17–078 In each of *Rochefoucauld* and *Bannister*, it can be said that a trust arises where the defendant has acquired property following a promise made to another to hold that property, in some way, on trust for that other. The nature of this trust is a matter of some controversy. As we noted in Chapter 6, there are important practical reasons for wishing to know whether the trust is express or constructive.[148]

17–079 On one view, the trust is an express one. Certainly, in *Rochefoucauld* itself, the Court of Appeal classified the trust as express when establishing what limitation period should govern the beneficiary's claim.[149] As noted in Chapter 6,[150] however, this point may not be decisive, for to treat a trust as an express one "within the meaning" of a limitation statute does not mean that it necessarily arose as a result of a party's successful exercise of a power to set up a trust and was thus not imposed by law. In a case where the defendant did indeed agree to hold on trust, there may be good reasons for treating that defendant as an express trustee, and thus preventing her from taking advantage of a limitation period, even if the agreement (because for example of a failure to comply with formal requirements) cannot, in itself, establish a provable trust.[151]

---

145 [1897] 1 Ch. 196; discussed at paras 6–033 to 6–050.
146 [1948] 2 All E.R. 133.
147 [1948] 2 All E.R. 133 at 136.
148 See paras 6–048 to 6–049.
149 [1897] 1 Ch. 196 at 207–208. See too W. Swadling, "The Nature of the Trust in *Rochefoucauld v Boustead*" in C. Mitchell (ed.), *Constructive and Resulting Trusts* (Hart Publishing, 2010), pp.100–103.
150 See para.6–047.
151 On this point, note the analysis of Millett LJ in *Paragon Finance v Thakerar* [1999] 1 All E.R. 400, 408–409, distinguishing between different types of constructive trust when considering the relevant limitation rules. It is conceivable that a similar approach could be adopted when considering, for example, the application of conflicts of laws rules, so that a constructive trust arising in a case where the defendant had agreed to hold on trust would be treated in the same way as an express trust.

William Swadling has also argued in favour of the express trust view as a matter of principle.[152] Perhaps the strongest point is as to the effect of an oral declaration of a trust over land. As Swadling notes, the relevant formality rule in *Rochefoucauld*, the Statute of Frauds 1677 s.7, did not render such an oral declaration void, or even unenforceable; it was rather "a rule describing how, if it came to litigation, an allegation that a declaration of trust respecting land must be proved".[153] The same is true of the successor to s.7, the Law of Property Act 1925 s.53(1)(b), which specifies how a declaration of trust respecting any land or any interest therein must be manifested and proved. This means that an express trust of land can arise by oral declaration: the obstacle imposed by the statute is as to *proof* of that trust. In *Rochefoucauld*, the Court of Appeal was willing to allow proof of that express trust, as any attempt by the trustee to rely on the statutory formality rule would have been regarded as a "fraud",[154] and the trustee was thus disabled from pleading the statute.[155] On this view, the trust proved was necessarily express. 17-080

The alternative view is that the type of trust recognised in *Rochefoucauld* and in *Bannister* is a constructive trust. Certainly, *Bannister* is not the only case in which the constructive trust label has been applied by the courts to that type of trust.[156] This view of the trust also has substantial academic support.[157] Perhaps the strongest point in favour of this view is that it permits direct reliance on the statutory exception to the formality rules provided for constructive trusts by s.53(2) of the Law of Property Act 1925.[158] This means that a court does not have to deal with the difficult questions of when, precisely, it is fraudulent for a party to rely on the statutory formality rule[159] and why, precisely, it is constitutionally permissible for a court to read in a fraud-based exception which is not set out in the statute itself.[160] In addition, in a thorough analysis of the facts of *Rochefoucauld*, Ying Khai Liew has argued that, in that case "none of the parties could possibly have acted as settlor",[161] as there was no declaration by any party who had a power to declare a trust. First, the relevant land was not initially held by the beneficiary (the Comtesse) of the eventual trust, as title to it was held by mortgagees, who then sold the land to the eventual trustee (Boustead) using their power of sale as mortgagees. Second, there is no evidence that those mortgagees set up a trust in favour of the Comtesse 17-081

---

152 See, e.g. W. Swadling, "The Nature of the Trust in *Rochefoucauld v Boustead*" in Mitchell (ed.), *Constructive and Resulting Trusts* (2010).

153 W. Swadling, "The Nature of the Trust in *Rochefoucauld v Boustead*" in Mitchell (ed.), *Constructive and Resulting Trusts* (2010), p.104.

154 [1897] 1 Ch. 196 at 205–206.

155 See too A.B. Douglas, "Trusts, Formalities and the Doctrine in *Rochefoucauld v Boustead*" [2021] Conv. 128.

156 See too *Paragon Finance Plc v DB Thakerar & Co* [1999] 1 All E.R. 400 at 409 per Millett LJ; *Gissing v Gissing* [1971] A.C. 886 at 905, per Lord Diplock; *de Bruyne v de Bruyne* [2010] EWCA Civ 519 at [51], per Patten LJ; *Archibald v Alexander* [2020] EWHC 1621 at [33]–[35].

157 See, e.g. W. Ames, "Constructive Trusts Based on the Breach of an Express Oral Trust of Land" (1906–7) 29 Harvard L.R. 549; T. Youdan, "Formalities for Trusts of Land and the Doctrine in *Rochefoucauld v Boustead*" [1984] C.L.J. 306; B. McFarlane, "Constructive Trusts Arising on Receipt of Property *Sub Conditione*" (2004) 120 L.Q.R. 667; N. Hopkins, "Conscience, Discretion and the Creation of Property Rights" (2006) 26 L.S. 475; S. Gardner, "Reliance-Based Constructive Trusts" in Mitchell (ed.), *Constructive and Resulting Trusts* (2010); Y.K. Liew "*Rochefoucauld v Boustead* (1897)" in C. Mitchell and P. Mitchell (eds), *Landmark Cases in Equity* (Hart Publishing, 2012).

158 Section 8 of the Statute of Frauds 1677 played the same role, providing an exception for a trust arising by "the implication or construction of law".

159 Swadling himself admits that "there is no authoritative statement" of what amounts to fraud for the purposes of the doctrine: A. Burrows (ed.), *English Private Law*, 3rd edn (Oxford University Press, 2013), 4.208.

160 Those problems are discussed by N. Hopkins, *The Informal Acquisition of Rights in Land* (Sweet & Maxwell, 2000), pp.31–32 and P. Critchley, "Instruments of Fraud, Testamentary Dispositions, and the Doctrine of Secret Trusts" (1999) 115 L.Q.R. 631, pp.653–654.

161 Y.K. Liew, "*Rochefoucauld v Boustead* (1897)" in Mitchell and Mitchell (eds), *Landmark Cases in Equity* (2012), p.426. Although for a different analysis of when a party can act as settlor, see D. Wilde, "Valid Trust Declarations over Property Not Owned by the Settlor or Over Unascertainable Property" (2020) 26 *Trusts and Trustees* 168.

when transferring the land to Boustead, or that they would have had any interest in doing so. Third, Boustead himself could not have declared a trust as he had immediately remortgaged the land to the mortgagees who sold it to him. Liew argues that, as the court in *Rochefoucauld* focussed instead on the agreement between the Comtesse and Boustead, which occurred before any receipt of land by the latter, that agreement was part of the grounds justifying the imposition of a constructive trust.[162]

17–082 There is always a hurdle to be cleared if arguing that a trust is imposed by law, rather than as a result of a party's successful exercise of a power to set up a trust. It must be shown that there is a good reason for the law not only to impose a duty on the defendant, but also to do so by means of a trust, which gives the claimant an equitable proprietary right. We will consider below if such a justification can be found for the trust arising in cases such as *Rochefoucald* and *Bannister*, if indeed it is constructive.[163]

B. Scope of the Trust

i. General Position

17–083 On either of the express trust or constructive trust analyses of the trust in *Rochefoucald* and *Bannister*, there is an important question to be answered as to the precise requirements of the trust. On the former view, the question is as to the definition of fraud: when will the principle that a "statute cannot be used as an instrument of fraud" allow oral proof of the declaration of trust? On the latter view, the question is as to the precise ground on which a trust is imposed by law.

17–084 A requirement for this type of trust, it seems, is that there has been a promise by the recipient of the property to hold it on trust, so that any "fraud" involves reneging on that promise. The recipient must have "undertaken a new obligation, not otherwise existing" to the beneficiary;[164] no trust arises, for example, if the purchaser only acquires land subject to any rights that might already exist in relation to it.[165] As noted by Lord Diplock in *Gissing v Gissing*,[166] however, it would be surprising if an oral promise alone sufficed, where the trust property is land; something else[167] is required to permit an express trust to be proved or a constructive trust to arise without writing.

17–085 One suggestion is that the additional factor is provided by the prospect of detriment being suffered, usually by the claimant, as a result of action undertaken in reliance on the defendant's promise.[168] In *Bannister*, for example, it can be said that, as the vendor's decision to sell the cottages to the purchaser was influenced by the purchaser's promise to allow the vendor continued rights in one of those cottages, the vendor would be left to suffer a detriment if the purchaser were free to renege on the promise.

---

[162] Liew, "*Rochefoucauld v Boustead* (1897)" in Mitchell and Mitchell (eds), *Landmark Cases in Equity* (2012), p.432.

[163] See paras 17–091 to 17–093.

[164] *Lloyd v Dugdale* [2002] 2 P. & C.R. 13 at [52] per Sir Christopher Slade.

[165] See *Ashburn Anstalt v Arnold* [1989] Ch. 1 at 26, per Fox LJ: "We do not think it desirable that constructive trusts of land should be imposed in reliance on inferences from slender materials." In *Chaudhary v Yavuz* [2013] Ch. 249, the fact that the recipient acquired property sold subject to incumbrances "discoverable by inspection of the property before the contract" did not give rise to a trust, as it did not mean that the purchaser had made a promise to give effect to any such right.

[166] [1971] A.C. 886 at 905.

[167] See P. Critchley, "Instruments of Fraud, Testamentary Dispositions, and the Doctrine of Secret Trusts" (1999) 115 L.Q.R. 631, 646–653.

[168] See, e.g. S. Gardner, "Reliance-Based Constructive Trusts" in Mitchell (ed.), *Constructive and Resulting Trusts* (2010).

An alternative view is that the "something else" is provided by the prospect of the recipient acquiring an unfair advantage as a result of the promise;[169] if the promise relates to the very property acquired by the recipient, and if the promise also gave the recipient an advantage in relation to the acquisition of that property, the promise is then enforced. On this view, the key point in *Bannister* is that it would have been unconscionable for the purchaser to be free to use his legal rights in the land as he wished, given that those rights were acquired, in part, because of a promise to use those rights in a particular way. **17–086**

It is important to note that, whatever view is taken as to the basis of the type of trust in *Rochefoucauld* and *Bannister*, and even if they are seen as express trusts, there are clearly strong links between this type of trust and those we have seen in other areas of the law. For example, when considering secret trusts in Chapter 6,[170] we saw that there is a debate as to whether the trusts are properly seen as express or constructive, and also as to the precise grounds on which they arise, and whether the focus should be the risk of unjust detriment to the testator, or the risk of unjust gain to the secret trustee. On most views of the nature of secret trusts, it therefore seems possible to regard them as falling within the same principle as the trusts arising in *Rochefoucauld* and *Bannister*. **17–087**

If one adopts a constructive trust view of the *Rochefoucauld* and *Bannister* type of trust, however, it may be possible to find further cases which fall within the same underlying principle. For example, in *Neale v Willis*,[171] a husband received £50 from his mother-in-law, to enable him to buy a house: the money was provided subject to his express promise that the house would be conveyed into the joint names of himself and his wife. He had the house conveyed into his sole name, but the Court of Appeal, relying on *Bannister*, held that the husband's promise to his mother-in-law should be enforced "by holding that the husband holds the property on constructive trust for himself and his wife."[172] In that case, the mother-in-law was never in a position to create an express trust of the land, and the husband did not agree to hold on trust at a time when he held the land itself, making an express trust analysis more difficult.[173] Similarly, in the next section, we will consider the *Pallant v Morgan*[174] constructive trust, which arises as a result of an agreement made between the parties prior to the acquisition of any property: on one view, it might fall under the same general principle as the *Rochefoucauld* and *Bannister* trusts. **17–088**

ii. Fictional Trusts

In *Binions v Evans*,[175] Lord Denning MR relied on *Bannister* to find a constructive trust where the purchasers of land had promised, when acquiring that land, to allow a widow currently in occupation of a cottage on the land to continue living in the cottage for life, or for as long as she wished. The effect of the trust was thus to allow the widow to continue enjoying the right in the property which she had had before the sale of the land: in Lord Denning's view, that was a licence. Similarly, in *Ashburn Anstalt v Arnold*,[176] the Court of Appeal considered if a constructive trust arose to protect a **17–089**

---

169 See, e.g. B. McFarlane, "Constructive Trusts Arising on Receipt of Property *Sub Conditione*" (2004) 120 L.Q.R. 667. See too *de Bruyne v de Bruyne* [2010] EWCA Civ 519 at [51], per Patten LJ.

170 See paras 6–129ff.

171 (1968) 19 P. & C.R. 836 (CA).

172 (1968) 19 P. & C.R. 836 at 839.

173 It could be argued that the mother-in-law created a trust of the money advanced, but the extent of the wife's interest under the trust arising in *Neale v Willis* was determined by the content of the husband's promise, not by tracing from the money into a proportionate share of the house.

174 [1953] Ch. 43.

175 [1972] Ch. 359 (CA).

176 [1989] Ch. 1 (CA).

licensee in a case where land was sold by the licensor subject to that licence: no such trust arose as, on the facts, the purchaser had made no promise to undertake a new duty to the licensee.[177]

17–090 The difficulty in these cases is that it has been clearly determined by the House of Lords that a licence to occupy land, even if protected by a contract, gives the licensor only a personal right against the licensee.[178] It seems very strange, therefore, that a trust, presumably giving the beneficiary an equitable interest in land, should arise where the purchaser has simply promised to allow an existing licence to continue.[179] On the express trust view of *Rochefoucauld* and *Bannister*, the cases provide no assistance when the purchaser, rather than agreeing to hold on trust, makes some other promise. On the constructive trust view of those cases, it is possible in a case such as *Binions v Evans* to draw on the principle underlying *Rochefoucauld* and *Bannister*, but the operation of that principle should *not* lead to the imposition of a trust.[180] The point is that, on the constructive trust view, there may be a general principle about the need to enforce promises subject to which rights have been acquired, with that principle leading to a trust only if the promisor said that she would hold on trust (or transfer property outright), and leading instead to a different right (such as a licence) where the promisor instead said that she would give the claimant such a right. On either view, however, it seems reasonably clear that, despite its continued usage,[181] the language of trusts is misleading if the right that the recipient has promised to confer does not amount to a beneficial interest under a trust.

C. Justifying the Trust

17–091 As we have said, trusts are always easier to justify if they can be seen as express. However, the express trust view of the type of trust in *Rochefoucauld* and *Bannister* does require one to accept that the concept that "a statute cannot be used as an instrument of fraud" is sufficiently precise to be sensibly applied, and can be justifiably applied, even if it is not expressly contained in the statute imposing a formality rule.[182] The constructive trust view avoids the second of those problems, and can also avoid the first if the grounds on which the law imposes a trust are identified and defined. It should be noted too that, on Liew's terminology, such a trust is a "qualified interest" constructive trust, as the claim is that the defendant never held the rights free from the trust.

17–092 It seems clear that a promise made by the recipient of property to hold it on trust forms a central part of those grounds, and also that a promise alone cannot justify a trust, especially as the promise may not give rise to any contractual right in the claimant. As noted above,[183] the two principal views are, first, that the promise can be enforced to prevent a party suffering a detriment as a result of action undertaken on the basis of the promise and, second, that the promise can be enforced to prevent the recipient from enjoying property free from an obligation undertaken in relation to that property, where the promise to undertake it gave the recipient an advantage in relation to the acquisition of the property. On each of these views, the need to enforce the promise explains why a trust can arise in favour of a third party, if that was the content of the promise made by the party receiving the trust

---

177 See too *Lloyd v Dugdale* [2001] EWCA Civ 1754; [2002] 2 P. & C.R. 13 at [52] per Sir Christopher Slade and *Chaudhary v Yavuz* [2011] EWCA Civ 1314; [2013] Ch. 249.

178 See *King v David Allan* [1916] 2 A.C. 54, *National Provincial Bank v Ainsworth* [1965] A.C. 1175.

179 As pointed out by, e.g. W. Swadling in A. Burrows (ed.), *English Private Law* (Oxford University Press, 2013), 4.126; S. Bright, "The Third Party's Conscience and Land Law" [2000] Conv. 398, 402.

180 See, e.g. B. McFarlane, "Constructive Trusts Arising on Receipt of Property *Sub Conditione*" (2004) 120 L.Q.R. 667, 678–682.

181 See, e.g. *Chaudhary v Yavuz* [2013] Ch. 249.

182 See the discussion at para.6–170.

183 See paras 17–085 to 17–086.

property. In contrast, if the only relevant principle is the need to prevent the recipient benefitting by using the property for their own benefit, then, as discussed in Chapter 6,[184] this can be met by simply recognising a resulting trust in favour of the party who transferred the property, rather than a trust in favour of the third party.[185]

A difficulty with enforcing the promise on the basis of detriment to the transferor is that the trust does not always arise in favour of that transferor: this is the case, for example, in *Neale v Willis*[186] and in secret trust cases where the risk of detriment is to the party (the mother-in-law, or the testator) initially providing the property, and not to the party benefitting from the intended trust. A difficulty with the second view is that the principle does not fall easily into any recognised legal category:[187] it is, for example, based on a promise, but the promise need not be made to the claimant, and so it is clearly not based on the existence of a contract between the claimant and the recipient; and, whilst the prospect of an unjust benefit is emphasised, the response is to enforce the promise, and is not limited to removing that benefit from the recipient. It has also been pointed out that, at an abstract level, the second view overlaps with a possible justification for express trusts arising where S transfers property to T to hold on trust for B. This may, however, give some support to the second view: given the historical development of such express trusts, we should not be surprised to see equity continuing to intervene in a case where the defendant's receipt of property is coloured by a prior promise to hold that property for the benefit of another.[188] **17–093**

7. Trusts Arising through the Pallant v Morgan Equity

A. Nature of the Trust

In *Pallant v Morgan*,[189] land was sold at auction. Pallant's agent was authorised to bid up to £2,000 for lot 16; Morgan's agent could go up to £3,000. Not wanting to bid against each other and push the prices up, the agents agreed, in the auction room, that, if Morgan acquired both lots 15 and 16, he would sell on to Pallant part of lot 15 and part of lot 16. Pallant's agent therefore pulled out of the bidding for lot 16, which Morgan succeeded in buying for less than £2,000. Morgan also acquired lot 15. The parties then failed to agree on the details of how to divide the land, and so Morgan kept it all for himself. Harman J held that, whilst the agents had authority to bind their principals to an agreement, the auction room agreement was too uncertain to be specifically enforceable. Nevertheless, he held that Morgan should hold plot 16 on trust for himself and Pallant jointly because his bid had been made on the basis of an agreement for division and it would be "tantamount to sanctioning **17–094**

184 See para.6–048.
185 See the analysis of HHJ Matthews in *Solomon v McCarthy* [2020] 1 WLUK 130 at [43]. For discussion, see e.g. O. Foy (2020), "Receipt of Property Subject to an Undertaking in the Domestic Context", Oxford Property Law Blog: *https://www.law.ox.ac.uk/research-and-subject-groups/property-law/blog/2020/08/receipt-property-subject-undertaking-domestic.*
186 (1968) 19 P. & C.R. 836 (CA).
187 A point made by W. Swadling, "The Nature of the Trust in *Rochefoucauld v Boustead*" in Mitchell (ed.), *Constructive and Resulting Trusts* (2010), pp.106–107.
188 See B. McFarlane, "The Centrality of Constructive and Resulting Trusts" in Mitchell (ed.), *Constructive and Resulting Trusts* (2010), pp.199–201. See too *de Bruyne v de Bruyne* [2010] EWCA Civ 519 at [51] per Patten LJ, referring to a principle giving rise to a constructive trust where the defendant's unconscionable conduct is "in the form of a denial or refusal to carry out the agreement to hold the property for the benefit of the third party which was the only basis upon which the property was transferred."
189 [1953] Ch. 43.

fraud" to allow him to retain all of plot 16 for himself.[190] Pallant however had no rights in relation to plot 15.

17–095 The "*Pallant v Morgan* equity", like a specifically enforceable contract for sale,[191] can give rise to a trust. The principle was later summarised by Megarry J:[192]

> If A and B agree that A will acquire some specific property for the joint benefit of A and B on terms yet to be agreed and B in reliance on A's agreement is thereby induced to refrain from attempting to acquire the property equity ought not to permit A when he acquires the property to insist on retaining the whole benefit for himself to the exclusion of B.

17–096 It seems clear that a trust arising as a result of the *Pallant v Morgan* equity is properly seen as a constructive rather than an express trust. The agreement between the parties pre-dates the defendant's acquisition of the property, and the trust arises even if the defendant, having acquired the property, does not attempt to exercise her power to create a trust. The trust also differs from the form of constructive trust arising as a result of a specifically enforceable contract: as made clear in *Pallant* itself, there is no requirement that the parties' agreement be sufficiently certain to be contractually enforceable. The trust can also be based on an oral agreement in relation to land and it is clear that, as a result of the formality rule imposed by s.2 of the Law of Property (Miscellaneous Provisions) Act 1989, such an oral agreement is not contractually binding.

B. Scope of the Trust

17–097 The *Palllant v Morgan* equity was given a wide interpretation in *Banner Homes Group Plc v Luff Developments Ltd*,[193] where Chadwick LJ held that, whilst it is often triggered in cases where the claimant has suffered detriment, a constructive trust can also be imposed where the claimant has suffered no detriment, but the defendant has gained an advantage as a result of the parties' arrangement.

> *Banner Homes Group Plc v Luff Developments Ltd*
>
> Court of Appeal [2000] Ch. 372
>
> 17–098 CHADWICK L.J.: It is important . . . to identify the features which will give rise to a *Pallant v Morgan* equity and to define its scope; while keeping in mind that it is undesirable to attempt anything in the nature of an exhaustive classification . . .
>
> 17–099 (1) A *Pallant v Morgan* equity may arise where the arrangement or understanding on which it is based precedes the acquisition of the relevant property by one party to that arrangement. It is the pre-acquisition arrangement which colours the subsequent acquisition by the defendant and leads to his being treated as a trustee if he seeks to act inconsistently with it. Where the arrangement or understanding is reached in relation to property already owned by one of the parties, he may (if the arrangement is of sufficient certainty to be enforced specifically) thereby constitute himself trustee on the basis that 'equity looks on that as done which ought to be done;' or an equity may arise under the principles developed in the proprietary estoppel cases. As I have sought to point out, the concepts of constructive trust and proprietary estoppel have much in common in this area.. . .

---

190 [1953] Ch. 43 at 48.

191 See paras 15–011—15–024.

192 *Holiday Inns of America Inc v Broadhead* Ch. D. 19 December 1969 (where Megarry J considered interlocutory relief; for later proceedings see (1974) 232 E.G. 951, 1087); the words reproduced in the text are quoted in *Banner Homes Group Plc v Luff Developments Ltd* [2000] Ch. 372 at 391.

193 [2000] Ch. 372 at 396–399, followed in *Cox v Jones* [2004] EWHC 1486 (Ch); [2004] 2 F.L.R. 1010 at [46]. In both cases, the claimant suffered detriment on the facts.

(2) It is unnecessary that the arrangement or understanding should be contractually enforceable. Indeed, if there is an agreement which is enforceable as a contract, there is unlikely to be any need to invoke the *Pallant v Morgan* equity; equity can act through the remedy of specific performance and will recognise the existence of a corresponding trust. On its facts *Chattock v Muller*,[194] is, perhaps, best regarded as a specific performance case. In particular, it is no bar to a *Pallant v Morgan* equity that the pre-acquisition arrangement is too uncertain to be enforced as a contract—see *Pallant v Morgan* itself, and *Time Products Ltd. v. Combined English Stores Group Ltd*,[195] —nor that it is plainly not intended to have contractual effect—see *Island Holdings Ltd v Birchington Engineering Co Ltd*.[196] 17–100

(3) It is necessary that the pre-acquisition arrangement or understanding should contemplate that one party ("the acquiring party") will take steps to acquire the relevant property; and that, if he does so, the other party ("the non-acquiring party") will obtain some interest in that property. Further, it is necessary that (whatever private reservations the acquiring party may have) he has not informed the non-acquiring party before the acquisition (or, perhaps more accurately, before it is too late for the parties to be restored to a position of no advantage/no detriment) that he no longer intends to honour the arrangement or understanding. 17–101

(4) It is necessary that, in reliance on the arrangement or understanding, the non-acquiring party should do (or omit to do) something which confers an advantage on the acquiring party in relation to the acquisition of the property; or is detrimental to the ability of the non-acquiring party to acquire the property on equal terms. It is the existence of the advantage to the one, or detriment to the other, gained or suffered as a consequence of the arrangement or understanding, which leads to the conclusion that it would be inequitable or unconscionable to allow the acquiring party to retain the property for himself, in a manner inconsistent with the arrangement or understanding which enabled him to acquire it. *Pallant v Morgan* itself provides an illustration of this principle. There was nothing inequitable in allowing the defendant to retain for himself the lot (lot 15) in respect to which the plaintiff's agent had no instructions to bid. In many cases the advantage/detriment will be found in the agreement of the non-acquiring party to keep out of the market. That will usually be both to the advantage of the acquiring party—in that he can bid without competition from the non-acquiring party—and to the detriment of the non-acquiring party—in that he loses the opportunity to acquire the property for himself. But there may be advantage to the one without corresponding detriment to the other. Again, *Pallant v Morgan* provides an illustration. The plaintiff's agreement (through his agent) to keep out of the bidding gave an advantage to the defendant—in that he was able to obtain the property for a lower price than would otherwise have been possible; but the failure of the plaintiff's agent to bid did not, in fact, cause detriment to the plaintiff—because, on the facts, the agent's instructions would not have permitted him to outbid the defendant. Nevertheless, the equity was invoked. 17–102

(5) That leads, I think, to the further conclusions: (i) that although, in many cases, the advantage/detriment will be found in the agreement of the non-acquiring party to keep out of the market, that is not a necessary feature; and (ii) that although there will usually be advantage to the one and correlative disadvantage to the other, the existence of both advantage and detriment is not essential—either will do. What is essential is that the circumstances make it inequitable for the acquiring party to retain the property for himself in a manner inconsistent with the arrangement or understanding on which the non-acquiring party has acted. Those circumstances may arise where the non-acquiring party was never "in the market" for the whole of the property to be acquired; but (on the faith of an arrangement or understanding that he shall have a part of that property) provides support in relation to the acquisition of the whole which is of advantage to the acquiring party. They may arise where the assistance provided to the acquiring party (in pursuance of the arrangement or understanding) involves no detriment to the non-acquiring party; or where the non-acquiring party acts to his detriment (in pursuance of the arrangement or understanding) without the acquiring party obtaining any advantage therefrom 17–103

The *Pallant v Morgan* equity does not seek to give effect to the parties' bargain, still less to make for them some bargain which they have not themselves made, as the cases to which I have referred make clear. The equity is invoked where the defendant has acquired property in circumstances where it would be inequitable to allow him to treat it as his own; and where, because it would be inequitable to allow him to 17–104

194 (1878) 8 Ch. D. 177.

195 2 December 1974 (unrep).

196 7 July 1981 (unrep).

> treat the property as his own, it is necessary to impose on him the obligations of a trustee in relation to it. It is invoked because there is no bargain which is capable of being enforced; if there were an enforceable bargain there would have been no need for equity to intervene in the way that it has done in the cases to which I have referred . . .

17–105 As I have sought to show, the *Pallant v Morgan* equity is invoked where it would be inequitable to allow the defendant to treat the property acquired in furtherance of the arrangement or understanding as his own. It may be just as inequitable to allow the defendant to treat the property as his own when it has been acquired by the use of some advantage which he has obtained under the arrangement or understanding as it is to allow him to treat the property as his own when the plaintiff has suffered some detriment under the arrangement or understanding. That, as it seems to me, is this case.

17–106 Writing extra-judicially, Lord Briggs has described Chadwick LJ's analysis in *Banner Homes* as:

> a heroic attempt to make what turned out to be bricks without straw, based on only a tiny handful of cases. Upon later analysis they could not be explained in terms of how the equity actually worked.

17–107 Certainly, is important to note that later cases have been quite cautious in finding that a *Pallant v Morgan* equity has arisen. In particular, whilst the equity does not depend on there being a legally binding agreement between the parties, no claim will arise if the parties have a common intention not to be bound unless and until formal contracts have been exchanged.[197] In *Generator Developments Ltd v Lidl UK GmbH*,[198] Lewison LJ qualified the second of the five elements identified in *Banner Homes* by stating that: "[a]t least in the context of arms' length 'subject to contract' negotiations", an equity should not arise if the parties have "mutual knowledge that an 'agreement' is not legally binding." This built on the view of Arden LJ in *Herbert v Doyle*[199] that:

> if the parties intend to make a formal agreement setting out the terms on which one or more of the parties is to acquire an interest in property, or, if further terms for that acquisition remain to be agreed between them so that the interest in property is not clearly identified, or if the parties did not expect their agreement to be immediately binding, neither party can rely on constructive trust as a means of enforcing their original agreement.

17–108 Further, in *Cobbe v Yeoman's Row Management Ltd*,[200] one of the reasons given for denying a *Pallant v Morgan* constructive trust was the fact that the claimed agreement was made when the defendant already owned the property in question. In *Farrar v Miller*,[201] Kitchin LJ went against this trend of limiting the equity, and suggested that it may apply even if the parties' agreement is made after the acquisition of the property: this would allow it to give rise to, in Liew's terms, an "absolute interest" constructive trust.[202] On this view, however, it is difficult to distinguish the equity from other principles, such as proprietary estoppel and the common intention constructive trust, which, unlike the *Pallant v Morgan* equity, both require some prospect of detriment arising from reliance on the

---

197 See *London & Regional Investments Ltd v TBI Plc* [2002] EWCA Civ 355 at [47]–[50], per Mummery LJ.
198 [2018] EWCA Civ 396; [2018] 2 P. & C.R. 7 at [67].
199 [2010] EWCA Civ 1095 at [57]. Note that Arden LJ stated there that the same limit applies to a proprietary estoppel claim. However, there are certainly examples of such claims arising where the parties know that an agreement is not legally binding: see e.g. *Sutcliffe v Lloyd* [2007] EWCA Civ 153 at [38], where Wilson LJ explains that as the effect of a successful proprietary estoppel claim is not to make the agreement binding, it is hard to see why the claim can arise only where the parties mistakenly believe that it is.
200 [2008] UKHL 55; [2008] 1 W.L.R. 1752 at [33].
201 [2018] EWCA Civ 396; [2018] 2 P. & C.R. 7 at [42].
202 See para.17–009.

agreement.[203] Moreover, Kitchin LJ's analysis was based on a direct appeal to the broad concept of unconscionability[204] which, as Lord Briggs has noted extra-judicially, is of limited use in ascertaining the specific requirements of particular equitable doctrines. Indeed Lord Briggs wrote that the use of unconscionability "in *Farrar v Miller* in connection with the boundaries of the *Pallant v Morgan* equity led potentially to an uncontrolled invasion of equity into commerce."[205]

C. Justifying the Trust

A number of different explanations have been proposed for the *Pallant v Morgan* equity, and thus for constructive trusts arising on that basis. Indeed, as noted by Henderson LJ in *Kahrmann v Harrison-Morgan*:[206] "the correct legal basis of the doctrine is controversial . . . The whole subject is ripe for review by the Supreme Court".[207] The explanations share a desire to link such trusts to other types of constructive trust. For example, one academic suggestion[208] is that a *Pallant v Morgan* constructive trust is just one example of a trust arising in response to the prospect of a party's suffering a detriment as a result of an undertaking by the defendant to hold on trust: on this view, the same principle also underlies trusts arising in response to proprietary estoppel and mutual wills, secret trusts, and the *Rochefoucauld v Boustead* trust. The difficulty with this view, as applied to *Pallant v Morgan*, is that detriment does not in fact seem to be a requirement of the *Pallant v Morgan* equity (as Chadwick LJ pointed out in *Banner Homes*). Such a view also groups together both "absolute interest" constructive trusts, which bind the defendant even where she previously held the property free from any trust, and "qualified interest" constructive trusts which operate as soon as the defendant acquires the relevant property. It may be, as Liew suggests,[209] that detriment is required for a proprietary estoppel claim as it can relate to property initially held absolutely by the defendant, whereas it is not required for *Pallant v Morgan*, as that equity can only bind property acquired by the defendant on a particular basis. **17–109**

A second academic suggestion,[210] building on this point, sees a trust based on *Pallant v Morgan* instead as just one example of a trust arising to prevent the defendant holding property free from a promised right of the claimant, where the defendant's promise gave the defendant an advantage in relation to the acquisition of the property. On that view, the same principle also underlies secret trusts[211] and the *Rochefoucauld v Boustead* trust.[212] **17–110**

Two further views, each of which has attracted some judicial support, also seek to align trusts arising on the basis of *Pallant v Morgan* with other types of constructive trust. The view adopted by **17–111**

---

203 Note too that in *Ali v Dinc* [2020] EWHC 3055 (Ch), Sarah Worthington QC (sitting as a Deputy High Court Judge) held at [231] that "the *Pallant v Morgan* claim cannot be made out where the land subject to the 'joint venture' is already owned by one of the parties".

204 [2018] EWCA Civ 172 at [42].

205 Lord Briggs, "Equity in Business" (2019) 135 L.Q.R. 567, 583.

206 [2019] EWCA Civ 2094 at [127].

207 [2019] EWCA Civ 2094 at [127]. See too Lord Briggs, "Equity in Business" (2019) 135 L.Q.R. 567, 576 suggesting that, before the nature of the *Pallant v Morgan* equity can be determined, "Perhaps another airing in the Supreme Court is due".

208 See S. Gardner, "Reliance-Based Constructive Trusts" in Mitchell (ed.), *Constructive and Resulting Trusts* (2010).

209 Y.K. Liew, *Rationalising Constructive Trusts* (Hart Publishing, 2017), 15.

210 See B. McFarlane, "Constructive Trusts Arising on a Receipt of Property *Sub Conditione*" (2004) 120 L.Q.R. 667. See too *de Bruyne v de Bruyne* [2010] EWCA Civ 519 at [51] per Patten LJ, referring to a principle giving rise to a constructive trust where the defendant's unconscionable conduct is "in the form of a denial or refusal to carry out the agreement to hold the property for the benefit of the third party which was the only basis upon which the property was transferred."

211 See paras 6–129ff.

212 See paras 6–033 to 6–050.

Chadwick LJ in *Banner Homes* was that such a trust is an example of the common intention constructive trust.[213] In *Crossco No 4 Unltd v Jolan Ltd,*[214] a majority of the Court of Appeal felt bound to adopt that view. In the same case, Etherton LJ proposed instead that a trust arising on the basis of *Pallant v Morgan* is an example of a trust arising in response to a breach of fiduciary duty.[215]

Crossco No 4 Unltd v Jolan Ltd

Court of Appeal [2012] 2 All E.R. 754

17–112 ETHERTON L.J.: . . . It is not necessary to resort to the common intention constructive trust to provide an explanation for the cases in which the *Pallant v Morgan* equity was, or is said to have been, applied. They can all be explained, and, in my judgment, ought to be explained in wholly conventional terms by the existence and breach of fiduciary duty. In *Chattock v Muller*[216] Sir Richard Malins V.-C. held that the defendant had attended the auction as the plaintiff's agent. Similarly, in *Pallant v Morgan* Harman J. held that the defendant's agent bid for lot 16 on behalf of both parties. *Holiday Inns,*[217] *Time Products*[218] and *Island Holdings* [219] were joint venture cases, in which it is to be inferred that the particular nature of the relationship between the joint venturers was such as to give rise to fiduciary duties. In the absence of agency or partnership, it would require particular and special features for such fiduciary duties to arise between commercial co-venturers. It is clear, however, that in special circumstances they can arise . . . In my judgment, the result in *Banner Homes* can only properly be explained on that basis . . . .

17–113 It is not possible to do full justice in the context of this judgment to the alternative explanations put forward by McFarlane[220] and Gardner[221] for the *Pallant v Morgan* equity and *Banner Homes*. Their merit is that they are put forward as principled explanations for a range of constructive trusts, including, for example, (in addition to the *Pallant v Morgan* equity and *Banner Homes*) secret trusts, trusts arising under the doctrine of *Rochefoucauld v Boustead* and, in Gardner's case, those associated with mutual wills and proprietary estoppel. Neither [counsel] argued in favour of them. It is sufficient for the purpose of this judgment to say that: (1) they provide explanations of a range of constructive trusts at a high level of abstraction; but (2) the cases in which the *Pallant v Morgan* equity has been applied can be explained in a wholly conventional way as examples of breach of an existing fiduciary duty, and (3) it is a sound policy that they should be so explained and confined. It is sound policy because, by contrast with the common intention constructive trust, such a policy recognises the need for certainty in commercial transactions, and it reflects the usual practice and desirability for business transactions to be effected by binding written contracts, often after the receipt of legal advice.

17–114 If the cases in which the *Pallant v Morgan* equity has been applied are interpreted as I suggest, then they can be seen as cases in which the court is, pursuant to the constructive trust, depriving the defendant of the advantage obtained in breach of trust. The irrelevance of lack of complete agreement, whether documented or not, is then easily explained, as is the latitude with which the court devises the best way to deprive the defendant of the unconscionable advantage . . .

17–115 ARDEN L.J.: . . .*Banner Homes* is invoked, in practice, in circumstances where parties have been in commercial negotiations over the acquisition of some property but the negotiations have for some reason failed so that there is no legally enforceable agreement. The advantage of the re-interpretation of the case law proposed by Etherton L.J. would be that it would restrict the number of situations in which *Banner Homes* can be used. That would be consistent with developments in the law of proprietary estoppel. The House of Lords made it clear that where parties have been dealing on the basis that their negotiations are "subject to contract", proprietary estoppel will not ordinarily be available: see *Cobbe*. The result is not unconscionable because the disappointed party will always have known that that was the position .. . . For

---

213 For which, see paras 17–121ff.

214 [2011] EWCA Civ 1619; [2012] 2 All E.R. 754.

215 See paras 17–011ff.

216 (1878) 8 Ch. D. 177.

217 *Holiday Inns v Broadhead* (1974) 232 E.G. 951.

218 *Time Products v Ltd v Combined English Stores Group Ltd* 2 Dec 1974 (unrep).

219 *Island Holdings v Birchington Engineering Co Ltd* 7 July 1981 (unrep).

220 B. McFarlane, "Constructive Trusts Arising on a Receipt of Property *Sub Conditione*" (2004) 120 L.Q.R. 667.

221 S. Gardner, "Reliance-Based Constructive Trusts" in C. Mitchell (ed.), *Constructive and Resulting Trusts* (2010).

the law in general to provide scope for claims in respect of unsuccessful negotiations that do not result in legally enforceable contracts would, in my judgment, be likely to inhibit the efficient pursuit of commercial negotiations, which is a necessary part of proper entrepreneurial activity.

MCFARLANE L.J.: In order to arrive at his conclusion, Etherton L.J. has considered the development of the law in subsequent decisions, which include determinations by the UK Supreme Court and the House of Lords. The approach in those subsequent cases leads my lord to the conclusion that, by implication, the *Banner Homes* decision must now be seen to be based upon fiduciary duty. My lady, Arden L.J., sees advantage in the interpretation put forward by my lord. I for my part also understand the path that Etherton L.J. has threaded through the decisions and particularly see the attraction of his conclusion at that the line of cases from *Gissing* to *Jones v Kernott* relating to domestic arrangements are driven by different policy considerations and may have features which are distinct from those arising from strictly commercial circumstances. **17–116**

Whilst Etherton L.J. may well be correct to interpret the oblique consequences of subsequent decisions as developing a construction of *Banner Homes* which is based on fiduciary duty, that approach was not expressly described by Chadwick L.J. in the case itself, and has not been, or at least was not, the interpretation afforded to the decision at the time. Absent an express declaration from the Supreme Court, and despite being attracted to the analysis of Etherton L.J., I consider that the solid jurisprudential ground must remain as Arden L.J. has described and I therefore agree with her that it is not open to this court to reinterpret the ratio of *Banner Homes* a decade after its genesis. **17–117**

It is somewhat surprising that the majority in *Crossco* subscribed to the view that Chadwick LJ's analysis of the *Pallant v Morgan* equity continued to have binding effect, notwithstanding the developments in the common intention constructive trust, which will examine below,[222] in *Stack v Dowden* and *Jones v Kernott*. Certainly, as we will see,[223] there are real difficulties in providing a convincing justification of that type of trust, and so, if we wish to justify the *Pallant v Morgan* equity, it will be better to look elsewhere. **17–118**

Etherton LJ's suggestion that the *Pallant v Morgan* equity responds to a breach of fiduciary duty is an interesting one, and certainly accords with a desire to limit the applicability of the equity, at least in relation to pre-contractual negotiations.[224] It is well-recognised that, in a simple case of an agent and a principal, the agent has a duty to act exclusively in the principal's interest,[225] but it may be hard to find such a fiduciary duty in a joint venture case, where business rivals agree to co-operate, but in a specific and limited way.[226] It can be argued that, in a case such as *Pallant v Morgan* or *Banner Homes*, the relevant duty of the defendant is simply a duty to honour the terms of a promise,[227] and that it would be confusing to regard such a duty as fiduciary. **17–119**

There is of course a wider issue as to the extent to which equitable concepts should operate in the commercial context.[228] As shown by the promise-based strand of proprietary estoppel,[229] however, **17–120**

---

222 See paras 17–129ff.

223 See paras 17–196 to 17–204.

224 For academic support, see e.g. J. Grower, "Explaining the '*Pallant v Morgan*' Equity" [2016] Conv. 434.

225 See para.2–066. For the possible relevance of agency to the equity, see e.g. M. Yip, "The *Pallant v Morgan* Equity Reconsidered" (2013) 33 L.S. 549.

226 See paras 2–175 to 2–180. See too Lord Briggs, "Equity in Business" (2019) 135 L.Q.R. 567, 575, querying "by what yardstick do we decide which joint ventures do, and which do not, impose fiduciary duties upon the participants? And what fiduciary duties?".

227 In *Vercoe v Rutland Fund Management Ltd* [2010] EWHC 424 at [358], for example, Sales J stated that in a case such as *Pallant v Morgan*, "where property has been acquired by one person as a result of an explicit agreement with another that, in return for him not seeking to acquire the property himself, it will be held after acquisition for the benefit of both of them . . . a constructive trust may be imposed to give effect to the agreement." Although note M. Lower, "The *Pallant v Morgan* Equity" [2012] Conv. 379, 385–386 pointing out that, if it were seen as arising in response to a breach of fiduciary duty, the equity need not always give rise to a trust as in "exceptional cases" other relief might be appropriate.

228 See eg paras 7–086 to 7–088.

229 See paras 3–013ff.

the absence of a binding contract does not necessarily prevent a claim arising on the basis of a promise made by the defendant. Indeed, it may be that a promise-based analysis of *Pallant v Morgan* is consistent with the view of Etherton LJ, in as far as the defendant's promise is crucial in establishing that, in relation to the acquisition of particular property, and to an extent determined by the content of the defendant's promise,[230] the defendant must act for the benefit of the claimant.[231]

8. Shared Homes: The Common Intention Trust

A. Nature of the Trust

17–121 Since the decision of the House of Lords in *Gissing v Gissing*,[232] a particular type of constructive trust has been used by the courts to resolve disputes relating to the rights of parties in relation to a home where they have lived together in a marital or quasi-marital relationship. In cases where the parties are married, or in a civil partnership, and their relationship ends in divorce or dissolution, and there is no contest with a third party who has acquired rights in the home, such as a mortgage lender,[233] there is no need to ascertain the parties' pre-existing beneficial interests, as the court has a statutory discretion to vary those rights and in doing so can take account of a wide range of factors related to the parties' relationship. In cases where the parties determined their beneficial interests by means of a written declaration of trust, either before or after acquiring the property, that declaration will generally be decisive,[234] and the rights of the parties will arise under an express trust, which can be proved by the written declaration.

17–122 Nonetheless, the "common intention constructive trust" is of great practical importance: first, because no statutory discretion exists for couples who are neither married nor in a civil partnership; second, because where third parties are involved, it will be necessary to establish what beneficial interests the spouses or civil partners had at the point when the third party acquired its rights over the relevant property. Third, in practice, it seems that parties often fail to set out their rights by means of a written declaration of trust, notwithstanding judicial encouragement to do so.[235]

17–123 Where A has directly contributed to the costs of acquisition of a property, by providing some or all of a deposit, or some or all of the mortgage payments, one might have thought that her beneficial interest would be determined by means of a resulting trust. As we noted in Chapter 16,[236] however, the common intention constructive trust has displaced the resulting trust in many domestic cases,[237]

---

[230] cf. J. Edelman, "When Do Fiduciary Duties Arise?" (2010) 126 L.Q.R. 302, who argues that the incidence and content of fiduciary duties is determined by the parties' consent.

[231] Compare the general argument used by Lionel Smith to justify constructive trusts arising in cases of breach of fiduciary duty: see L. Smith, "Constructive Trusts and the No-Profit Rule" [2013] C.L.J. 260.

[232] [1971] A.C. 886.

[233] See, e.g. *Lloyds Bank v Rosset* [1991] 1 A.C. 107.

[234] See, e.g. *Goodman v Gallant* [1986] Fam. 106; *Pankhania v Chandegra* [2012] EWCA Civ 1438; [2013] 3 F.C.R. 16. Whilst decisive as to the parties' initial interests in the property, it is of course possible that those interests might change as a result of the parties' subsequent conduct if, for example, there is a later contrary agreement, or a proprietary estoppel arises: see *Stack v Dowden* [2007] UKHL 17; [2007] 2 A.C. 432 at [49] per Lady Hale.

[235] See e.g. *Carlton v Goodman* [2002] EWCA Civ 545; [2002] 2 F.L.R. 259 at [44] per Ward LJ. In *Stack v Dowden* [2007] UKHL 17; [2007] 2 A.C. 432 at [52] Lady Hale noted that, in a case where the legal title is conveyed to a couple, the Land Registry Form TR1 "provides a box for the transferees to declare whether they are to hold the property on trust for themselves as joint tenants, or on trust for themselves as tenants in common in equal shares, or on some other trusts which are inserted on the form. If this is invariably complied with, the problem confronting us here will eventually disappear. Unfortunately, however, the transfer will be valid whether or not this part of the form is completed." See further E. Cooke, "In the Wake of *Stack v Dowden*: The Tale of TR1" [2011] Fam. Law 1152.

[236] See paras 16–046ff.

[237] See, e.g. *Midland Bank Plc v Cooke* [1995] 2 F.L.R. 915, discussed at para.16–043.

and certainly where a home is bought "in joint names for joint occupation by a married or unmarried couple, where both are responsible for any mortgage".[238] The common intention constructive trust differs from the traditional resulting trust in some important respects: unlike a resulting trust, it can arise even if A has not provided any part of the purchase price, and the size of A's share depends on the parties' intentions, rather than on the percentage contribution made to the costs of acquisition. These features of the common intention constructive trust are fundamental to its existence: its recognition in *Gissing v Gissing*,[239] and its later development, can be seen in part as a response to the limited utility of the traditional resulting trust, which cannot recognise contributions made by the claimant other than the provision of money towards acquisition of the home.[240] Indeed, as noted in Chapter 16,[241] it can be argued that the logic of focussing on the parties' common intentions can now also be applied to many, if not all, cases of resulting trusts.

Given the role of intention in the common intention constructive trust, it has been suggested that the trust is in fact best seen as an express trust. The same argument can be made as in relation to the *Rochefoucauld v Boustead* trust: it is express as it depends on an oral declaration, proof of which is permitted, even in the absence of writing, in order to ensure that the statutory formality requirement imposed by s.53(1)(b) of the Law of Property Act 1925 is not used by the defendant as an instrument of fraud.[242] However, this argument is harder to sustain in relation to common intention constructive trusts, as such trusts have arisen even in cases where the parties have not discussed their beneficial interests, and it would be impossible on the facts to find any declaration of trust, even an oral one.[243] **17–124**

The speeches of Lord Diplock in *Gissing v Gissing*[244] and Lord Bridge in *Lloyds Bank Plc v Rosset*[245] **17–125** confirm that the common intention constructive trust has two key requirements: first, an agreement, arrangement or understanding that A is to have a beneficial share of the property; and second, action by A in reliance on that agreement, arrangement or understanding. We will see, however, that the way in which those requirements are applied suggests that the courts may have some doubts as to their suitability.

There is, in particular, a question of the circumstances in which a court may *infer* or even *impute* a **17–126** common intention to the parties. The distinction between imputing and inferring a common intention is an important one. As Lord Neuberger noted in *Stack v Dowden*:[246]

> An imputed intention is one which is attributed to the parties, even though no such actual intention can be deduced from their actions and statements, and even though they had no such intention. Imputing involves concluding what the parties would have intended, whereas inference involves concluding what they did intend.

---

238 *Jones v Kernott* [2011] UKSC 53; [2012] 1 A.C. 776 at [25], per Lord Walker and Lady Hale.

239 [1971] A.C. 886.

240 As noted by Lady Hale in *Stack v Dowden* [2007] UKHL 17; [2007] 2 A.C. 432 at [59]–[60].

241 See paras 16–170 to 16–176.

242 See, e.g. *Allen v Snyder* [1977] 2 N.S.W.L.R. 685 at 693 per Glass JA: "The trust is enforced, because it is unconscionable of the legal owner to rely on the statute to defeat the beneficial interest. It could justifiably be called an express trust, as it was in *Rochefoucauld v Boustead*."

243 See, e.g. *Midland Bank Plc v Cooke* [1995] 2 F.L.R. 915: when asked in cross-examination if he and his wife had ever discussed their rights in the home, Mr Cooke replied: "No. We were just happy, I suppose, you know." As noted by Lord Hodson in *Pettitt v Pettitt* [1970] A.C. 777 at 810: "The concept of a normal married couple spending the long winter evenings hammering out agreements about their possessions appears grotesque."

244 [1971] A.C. 886 at 904–905.

245 [1991] 1 A.C. 107.

246 [2007] UKHL 17; [2007] 2 A.C. 432 at [126].

17–127 As we will see, in that case, Lord Neuberger disagreed with the other members of the panel by finding that imputation has no role to play in the common intention constructive trust; nonetheless, his statement as to the difference between inference and imputation is helpful and has been widely accepted as a definition of the two concepts.[247]

17–128 The common intention constructive trust may be relevant both when legal title to the property is in the sole name of B, and also when legal title is in the joint names of A and B. In the first class of case, in the absence of any trust, A will have no beneficial interest in the property, and so A's purpose in establishing a common intention constructive trust is to show that she does in fact have some share of the beneficial ownership of the property. In the second class of case, in the absence of any express, resulting, or common intention constructive trust, A and B will hold their joint legal title on trust for each other as joint tenants in equity. This default trust is imposed by statute in cases of co-ownership of land.[248] If that equitable joint tenancy is severed, each party will then have a 50% share of the beneficial ownership of the property. In such a case, then, the purpose of A in establishing a common intention constructive trust is not to show that she has some beneficial interest: it is rather to show that she has an interest greater than the 50% share she would receive by severing the beneficial joint tenancy which arises in the absence of such a trust.

17–129 Whereas the key decisions in the development of the common intention constructive trust were cases where the land was registered in A's sole name,[249] it happens that the two most recent decisions of England's top court have dealt with registration in the joint names of A and B. This raises the question of whether separate principles govern each class of case: an issue considered by Lord Walker and Lady Hale in the later of those two recent decisions, *Jones v Kernott*.[250] As can be seen from the extract below, their joint judgment also considers the first of those two decisions, *Stack v Dowden*[251] and includes a discussion of the circumstances in which a common intention may be inferred or imputed.[252]

Jones v Kernott

Supreme Court [2012] 1 A.C. 776

17–130 Mr Kernott and Ms Jones bought a house in their joint names. Their relationship ended after ten years and Kernott moved out. Jones continued to live in the original home, assuming sole responsibility for payment of the mortgage and other outgoings, including repairs and improvements. In 1995, the parties cashed in a jointly owned life insurance policy and divided the proceeds equally. Kernott used his share to pay for the deposit on a house. In 2006, Kernott first sought to realise the financial value of his share of the original home. Jones claimed a declaration that, although legal title to the home was held by the parties jointly, she was the sole beneficial owner. In 2008, Kernott purported to sever the parties' beneficial joint tenancy. The majority of the Court of Appeal (Wall and Rimer L.JJ., with Jacob L.J. dissenting) found that there was no basis on which the parties' shares could be varied from the 50–50 split each would have received had the beneficial joint tenancy been severed immediately after their separation. The Supreme Court unanimously allowed Jones's appeal and re-instated the order of the first instance judge, which had also been confirmed in the High Court, that the parties held the joint legal title on a common intention constructive trust, under which Jones had a 90% share of the beneficial interest in the home.

17–131 In a joint judgment with which Lord Collins agreed, Lord Walker and Baroness Hale found clear evidence that the parties' intentions as to ownership of the property had changed over time. They inferred

---

247 See, e.g. *Jones v Kernott* [2012] 1 A.C. 776 at [26], [73] and [79].
248 Law of Property Act 1925, s 34.
249 See, e.g. *Gissing v Gissing* [1971] 1 A.C. 886; *Lloyds Bank Plc v Rosset* [1991] 1 A.C. 107.
250 [2011] UKSC 53; [2012] 1 A.C. 776.
251 [2007] UKHL 17; [2007] 2 A.C. 432.
252 [2011] UKSC 53; [2012] 1 A.C. 776.

that when, in 1995, the life insurance policy was cashed in and Kernott bought a new home, he did so on the basis that he would not be expected to contribute further to the mortgage on the original family home, so that "the logical inference is that they intended that his interest in [the family home] should crystallise then" with Jones taking the benefit of any increase in the value of the home from that point. On that view, the parties had an actual intention, established by inference from the evidence, not only that the parties' beneficial entitlements should differ from their legal rights as joint tenants, but also as to the size of each party's beneficial interest.

Lord Wilson and Lord Kerr reached the same result, but, in each case, their reasoning differed from that of the majority. Each found that there was insufficient evidence to infer that the parties had actually formed an intention as to the size of their beneficial interests, but that an intention to hold in proportions of (roughly) 90% and 10% could instead be *imputed* to the parties to meet the demands of fairness. Lord Kerr would have preferred, if possible, to avoid the language of imputation, and to have reached that outcome simply as a matter of fairness, without any reference to the parties' intentions. 17–132

LORD WALKER AND BARONESS HALE: This appeal gives the Supreme Court the opportunity to revisit the decision of the House of Lords in *Stack v Dowden*.[253] That case, like this, was concerned with the determination of the beneficial interests in a house acquired in joint names by an unmarried couple who intended it to be their family home.. . . 17–133

Mr Stack and Ms Dowden lived together for 19 years, from 1983 to 2002. They did not marry but they had four children born between 1986 and 1991. Ms Dowden was a well-qualified electrical engineer, and throughout the time when they lived together she worked full-time (except for periods of maternity leave) for the London Electricity Board and its successor. Mr Stack was a self-employed builder and decorator until 1987, after which he was employed by Hammersmith and Fulham London Borough Council. 17–134

They started living together in 1983 in a house acquired in Ms Dowden's sole name at the price of £30,000. The deposit of £8,000 was paid out of a building society account in Ms Dowden's sole name; there was a conflict of evidence as to whether Mr Stack had made any contributions to the account. The balance of £22,000 was raised on a mortgage for which Ms Dowden alone was responsible. She made the mortgage payments and paid other household outgoings. Mr Stack kept his finances separate (he had most of his post, including his bank statements, sent to his father's address). They carried out extensive repairs and improvements to the house. The judge found that Mr Stack was responsible for most of this work but could not put a figure on its contribution to the sale value of the house. 17–135

They moved house in 1993. Ms Dowden received over £66,000 from the sale of their first home. Their new home was bought for £190,000. Nearly £129,000 came from Ms Dowden's building society account and the balance from a bank loan secured on the house and on two endowment policies, one in joint names and one in Ms Dowden's sole name. The house was transferred into their joint names with no express declaration of trust, but a standard-form provision that the survivor could give a good receipt. 17–136

Mr Stack paid the mortgage interest and the premiums on the joint policy, to a total amount of nearly £34,000. The principal of the mortgage loan was repaid by a series of lump sum payments, to which Mr Stack contributed £27,000 and Ms Dowden over £38,000. The utility bills were in Ms Dowden's name and she paid all or most of them. There were some improvements to the property, but not on a large scale. The parties continued to maintain separate bank accounts and each made a number of separate investments. 17–137

In short, there was a substantial disparity between their respective financial contributions to the purchase. The trial judge held that the proceeds of sale should be divided in equal shares. Although Ms Dowden had been the bigger earner, "they have both put their all into doing the best for themselves and their family as they could". The Court of Appeal allowed Ms Dowden's appeal and divided the proceeds 65% to 35% as she had asked. The House of Lords (Lord Hoffmann, Lord Hope of Craighead, Lord Walker of Gestingthorpe, Baroness Hale of Richmond and Lord Neuberger of Abbotsbury) unanimously upheld that order, although Lord Neuberger did so for different reasons from the majority. 17–138

The curious feature of the decided cases up until then had been that, once an intention to share ownership had been established, the courts had tended to adopt a more flexible and "holistic" approach to the quantification of the parties' shares in cases of sole legal ownership than they had in cases of joint legal ownership. In the former, they had adopted a concept of the "common intention" constructive trust which depends upon the shared intentions of the parties. In the latter, they had tended to analyse the matter in 17–139

253 [2007] UKHL 17; [2007] 2 A.C. 432.

terms of a resulting trust, which depends upon the law's presumption as to the intention of the party who makes a financial contribution to the purchase. This point was made by Lady Hale in *Stack v Dowden*:[254] see also Peter Gibson L.J. in *Drake v Whipp*.[255]

17–140 The leading opinion in the House of Lords was that of Lady Hale. Lord Hoffmann, Lord Hope and Lord Walker all agreed with it, though Lord Hope and Lord Walker added some observations of their own . . .

17–141 The conclusions in Lady Hale's opinion were directed to the case of a house transferred into the joint names of a married or unmarried couple, where both are responsible for any mortgage, and where there is no express declaration of their beneficial interests. In such cases, she held that there is a presumption that the beneficial interests coincide with the legal estate. Specifically, "in the domestic consumer context, a conveyance into joint names indicates both legal and beneficial joint tenancy, unless and until the contrary is proved".[256]

17–142 Secondly, the mere fact that the parties had contributed to the acquisition of the home in unequal shares would not normally be sufficient to rebut the presumption of joint tenancy arising from the conveyance:

> "It cannot be the case that all the hundreds of thousands, if not millions, of transfers into joint names . . . are vulnerable to challenge in the courts simply because it is likely that the owners contributed unequally to their purchase".[257]

17–143 Thirdly, the task of seeking to show that the parties intended their beneficial interests to be different from their legal interests was not to be "lightly embarked upon. In family disputes, strong feelings are aroused when couples split up. These often lead the parties, honestly but mistakenly, to reinterpret the past in self-exculpatory or vengeful terms. They also lead people to spend far more on the legal battle than is warranted by the sums actually at stake. A full examination of the facts is likely to involve disproportionate costs. In joint names cases it is also unlikely to lead to a different result, unless the facts are very unusual".[258]

17–144 Fourthly, however, if the task is embarked upon, it is to ascertain the parties' common intentions as to what their shares in the property would be, in the light of their whole course of conduct in relation to it.[259] It is the way in which this point was made which seems to have caused the most difficulty in the lower courts. The difficulty is well illustrated in Lord Wilson J.S.C.'s judgment . . . which read the judgment in a way which we would not read it. It matters not which reading is correct. It does matter that any confusion is resolved.

17–145 It was also accepted that the parties' common intentions might change over time, producing what Lord Hoffmann referred to in the course of argument as an "'ambulatory' constructive trust".[260] An example[261] was where one party had financed or constructed an extension or major improvement to the property, so that what they had now was different from what they had first acquired. But of course there are other examples. The principal question in this case is whether this is one.

17–146 At its simplest the principle in *Stack v Dowden* is that a "common intention" trust, for the cohabitants' home to belong to them jointly in equity as well as on the proprietorship register, is the default option in joint names cases. The trust can be classified as a constructive trust, but it is not at odds with the parties' legal ownership. Beneficial ownership mirrors legal ownership. What it is at odds with is the presumption of a resulting trust.

A single regime?

17–147 . . . At a high level of generality, there is of course a single regime: the law of trusts (this is the second of Mustill L.J.'s propositions in *Grant v Edwards*[262]). To the extent that we recognise that a "common intention" trust is of central importance to "joint names" as well as "single names" cases, we are going some way to meet that hope. Nevertheless it is important to point out that the starting point for analysis

---

254 At [64]–[65].
255 [1996] 1 F.L.R. 826 at 827, cited in *Stack* at [29].
256 Lady Hale at [58]; Lord Walker at [33].
257 Lady Hale at [68].
258 Lady Hale at [68]; Lord Walker at [33].
259 Lady Hale at [60].
260 Lady Hale at [62].
261 *Stack* at [70].
262 [1986] Ch 638, 651.

is different in the two situations. That is so even though it may be necessary to enquire into the varied circumstances and reasons why a house or flat has been acquired in a single name or in joint names (they range, for instance, from *Lowson v Coombes*,[263] where the property was in the woman's sole name because the man was apprehensive of claims by his separated wife, to *Adekunle v Ritchie*,[264] where an enfranchised freehold was in joint names because the elderly tenant could not obtain a mortgage on her own).

The starting point is different because the claimant whose name is not on the proprietorship register has the burden of establishing some sort of implied trust, normally what is now termed a "common intention" constructive trust. The claimant whose name is on the register starts (in the absence of an express declaration of trust in different terms, and subject to what is said below about resulting trusts) with the presumption (or assumption) of a beneficial joint tenancy . . . 17–148

The presumption of a beneficial joint tenancy is not based on a mantra as to "equity following the law" (though many non-lawyers would find it hard to understand the notion that equity might do anything else). There are two much more substantial reasons (which overlap) why a challenge to the presumption of beneficial joint tenancy is not to be lightly embarked on. The first is implicit in the nature of the enterprise. If a couple in an intimate relationship (whether married or unmarried) decide to buy a house or flat in which to live together, almost always with the help of a mortgage for which they are jointly and severally liable, that is on the face of things a strong indication of emotional and economic commitment to a joint enterprise. That is so even if the parties, for whatever reason, fail to make that clear by any overt declaration or agreement . . . 17–149

The notion that in a trusting personal relationship the parties do not hold each other to account financially is underpinned by the practical difficulty, in many cases, of taking any such account, perhaps after 20 years or more of the ups and downs of living together as an unmarried couple. That is the second reason for caution before going to law in order to displace the presumption of beneficial joint tenancy.[265] Lady Hale pointed this out in *Stack v Dowden*[266] at para 68, as did Lord Walker at para 33: "In the ordinary domestic case where there are joint legal owners there will be a heavy burden in establishing to the court's satisfaction that an intention to keep a sort of balance-sheet of contributions actually existed, or should be inferred, or imputed to the parties. The presumption will be that equity follows the law. In such cases the court should not readily embark on the sort of detailed examination of the parties' relationship and finances that was attempted (with limited success) in this case." . . . 17–150

The time has come to make it clear, in line with *Stack v Dowden* (see also *Abbott v Abbott*),[267] that in the case of the purchase of a house or flat in joint names for joint occupation by a married or unmarried couple, where both are responsible for any mortgage, there is no presumption of a resulting trust arising from their having contributed to the deposit (or indeed the rest of the purchase) in unequal shares. The presumption is that the parties intended a joint tenancy both in law and in equity. But that presumption can of course be rebutted by evidence of a contrary intention, which may more readily be shown where the parties did not share their financial resources. 17–151

Inference or imputation?

In *Stack v Dowden* Lord Neuberger observed:[268] 17–152

> "While an intention may be inferred as well as express, it may not, at least in my opinion, be imputed. That appears to me to be consistent both with normal principles and with the majority view of this House in *Pettitt v Pettitt*, as accepted by all but Lord Reid in *Gissing v Gissing*[269] and reiterated by the Court of Appeal in *Grant v Edwards*.[270] The distinction between inference and imputation may appear a fine one (and in *Gissing v Gissing* Lord Pearson, who, on a fair reading I think rejected imputation, seems to have equated it with inference),[271] but it is important.

263 [1999] Ch. 373.
264 [2007] W.T.L.R. 1505.
265 Lady Hale in *Stack v Dowden* at [68], Lord Walker at [33].
266 At [68].
267 [2008] 1 F.L.R. 1551.
268 At [125]–[126].
269 [1971] A.C. 886 at 897, 898, 900, 901, and 904.
270 [1986] Ch. 638 at 651–653.
271 [1971] A.C. 886 at 902.

"An inferred intention is one which is objectively deduced to be the subjective actual intention of the parties, in the light of their actions and statements. An imputed intention is one which is attributed to the parties, even though no such actual intention can be deduced from their actions and statements, and even though they had no such intention. Imputation involves concluding what the parties would have intended, whereas inference involves concluding what they did intend."

Rimer L.J. made some similar observations in the Court of Appeal in this case.[272] . . .

17–153 The decision in *Stack v Dowden* produced a division of the net proceeds of sale of the house in shares roughly corresponding to the parties' financial contributions over the years. The majority reached that conclusion by inferring a common intention.[273] Only Lord Neuberger reached the same result by applying the classic resulting trust doctrine (which involved, it is to be noted, imputing an intention to the parties).

17–154 In deference to the comments of Lord Neuberger and Rimer L.J., we accept that the search is primarily to ascertain the parties' actual shared intentions, whether expressed or to be inferred from their conduct. However, there are at least two exceptions. The first, which is not this case, is where the classic resulting trust presumption applies. Indeed, this would be rare in a domestic context, but might perhaps arise where domestic partners were also business partners.[274] The second, which for reasons which will appear later is in our view also not this case but will arise much more frequently, is where it is clear that the beneficial interests are to be shared, but it is impossible to divine a common intention as to the proportions in which they are to be shared. In those two situations, the court is driven to impute an intention to the parties which they may never have had.

17–155 Lord Diplock, in *Gissing v Gissing*,[275] pointed out that, once the court was satisfied that it was the parties' common intention that the beneficial interest was to be shared in some proportion or other, the court might have to give effect to that common intention by determining what in all the circumstances was a fair share. And it is that thought which is picked up in the subsequent cases, culminating in the judgment of Chadwick L.J in *Oxley v Hiscock*[276] in particular the passage which was given qualified approval in *Stack v Dowden*: "the answer is that each is entitled to that share which the court considers fair having regard to the whole course of dealing between them in relation to the property."[277]

17–156 Chadwick L.J. was not there saying that fairness was the criterion for determining whether or not the property should be shared, but he was saying that the court might have to impute an intention to the parties as to the proportions in which the property would be shared. In deducing what the parties, as reasonable people, would have thought at the relevant time, regard would obviously be had to their whole course of dealing in relation to the property.

17–157 However, while the conceptual difference between inferring and imputing is clear, the difference in practice may not be so great. In this area, as in many others, the scope for inference is wide. The law recognizes that a legitimate inference may not correspond to an individual's subjective state of mind.. . .

17–158 In several parts of the British Commonwealth federal or provincial legislation has given the court a limited jurisdiction to vary or adjust proprietary rights in the home when an unmarried couple split up. Most require a minimum period of two years' cohabitation (or less if there are children) before the jurisdiction is exercisable. In England the Law Commission has made recommendations on similar lines, *Cohabitation: The Financial Consequences of Relationship Breakdown*,[278] but there are no plans to implement them in the near future.

17–159 In the meantime there will continue to be many difficult cases in which the court has to reach a conclusion on sparse and conflicting evidence. It is the court's duty to reach a decision on even the most difficult case . . . [the facts of the case were then examined.]

17–160 In this case, there is no need to impute an intention that the parties' beneficial interests would change, because the judge made a finding that the intentions of the parties did in fact change. At the outset, their intention was to provide a home for themselves and their progeny. But thereafter their intentions did change significantly. He did not go into detail, but the inferences are not difficult to draw. They separated

---

272 [2010] 1 W.L.R. 2401 at [76]–[77].
273 See Lady Hale's opinion at [92], following her detailed analysis of the facts starting at [86].
274 See *Stack v Dowden* at [32].
275 [1971] A.C. 886 at 909.
276 [2005] Fam 211 at [65], [66] and [69].
277 Ibid. at [69].
278 Law Com. No.307, 2007.

in October 1993. No doubt in many such cases, there is a period of uncertainty about where the parties will live and what they will do about the home which they used to share. This home was put on the market in late 1995 but failed to sell. Around that time a new plan was formed. The life insurance policy was cashed in and Mr Kernott was able to buy a new home for himself. He would not have been able to do this had he still had to contribute towards the mortgage, endowment policy and other outgoings on 39 Badger Hall Avenue [the original family home and thus the contested property]. The logical inference is that they intended that his interest in Badger Hall Avenue should crystallise then. Just as he would have the sole benefit of any capital gain in his own home, Ms Jones would have the sole benefit of any capital gain in Badger Hall Avenue. In so far as the judge did not in so many words infer that this was their intention, it is clearly the intention which reasonable people would have had had they thought about it at the time. But in our view it is an intention which he both could and should have inferred from their conduct.

A rough calculation on this basis produces a result so close to that which the judge produced that it would be wrong for an appellate court to interfere. If we take the value of the property as £60,000 in late 1993 (or £70,000 in late 1995) and the value in 2008 as £245,000, and share the £60,000 (or £70,000) equally between the parties, but leave the balance to Ms Jones, that gives him £30,000 (£35,000) and her £215,000 (£210,000), roughly 12% (15%) and 88% (86%) respectively. This calculation ignores the mortgage, which may be the correct approach, as in 2008 the mortgage debt was almost fully covered by the endowment policy which was always meant to discharge it. Introducing the mortgage liability in 1993 (or 1995) into the calculation would be to Mr Kernott's disadvantage, because at that stage the endowment policy would not have been sufficient to discharge the debt, so the equity would have been less. . . . 17–161

In summary, therefore, the following are the principles applicable in a case such as this, where a family home is bought in the joint names of a cohabiting couple who are both responsible for any mortgage, but without any express declaration of their beneficial interests. 17–162

(1) The starting point is that equity follows the law and they are joint tenants both in law and in equity.
(2) That presumption can be displaced by showing (a) that the parties had a different common intention at the time when they acquired the home, or (b) that they later formed the common intention that their respective shares would change.
(3) Their common intention is to be deduced objectively from their conduct: "the relevant intention of each party is the intention which was reasonably understood by the other party to be manifested by that party's words and conduct notwithstanding that he did not consciously formulate that intention in his own mind or even acted with some different intention which he did not communicate to the other party".[279] Examples of the sort of evidence which might be relevant to drawing such inferences are given in *Stack v Dowden*.[280]
(4) In those cases where it is clear either (a) that the parties did not intend joint tenancy at the outset, or (b) had changed their original intention, but it is not possible to ascertain by direct evidence or by inference what their actual intention was as to the shares in which they would own the property, "the answer is that each is entitled to that share which the court considers fair having regard to the whole course of dealing between them in relation to the property".[281] In our judgment, the whole course of dealing in relation to the property" should be given a broad meaning, enabling a similar range of factors to be taken into account as may be relevant to ascertaining the parties' actual intentions.
(5) Each case will turn on its own facts. Financial contributions are relevant but there are many other factors which may enable the court to decide what shares were either intended (as in case (3)) or fair (as in case (4)).

This case is not concerned with a family home which is put into the name of one party only. The starting point is different. The first issue is whether it was intended that the other party have any beneficial interest in the property at all. If he does, the second issue is what that interest is. There is no presumption of joint beneficial ownership. But their common intention has once again to be deduced objectively from their conduct. If the evidence shows a common intention to share beneficial ownership but does not show what shares were intended, the court will have to proceed as at (4) and (5) above. 17–163

---

279 Lord Diplock in *Gissing v Gissing* [1971] A.C. 886 at 906.
280 [2007] 2 A.C. 432 at [69]. [See the extract at para.17–172.]
281 *Oxley v Hiscock* [2005] Fam. 211 at [69].

B. Scope of the Trust

i. Common Intention that the Beneficial Entitlements Will Differ from the Position at Common Law

17–164 The common intention constructive trust requires a bilateral understanding between the parties that A's beneficial entitlement will differ from her rights at law. Where B is the sole legal owner, this requires a common intention that A should have *some* beneficial interest in the property. Where the claimant and defendant are joint legal owners, this requires a common intention that each should have a distinct (and therefore usually unequal)[282] beneficial interest in the property.

17–165 The parties' intentions are to be judged objectively in the usual way. In Lord Diplock's words:[283]

> the relevant intention of each party is the intention which was reasonably understood by the other party to be manifested by that party's words or conduct notwithstanding that he did not consciously formulate that intention in his own mind or even acted with some different intention which he did not communicate to the other party.

17–166 It does not suffice that each party happened separately to form the same intention, because an express common intention means one that is communicated between the parties: it is the external manifestation of intention by one party to the other that is crucial, regardless of uncommunicated private intentions.[284]

17–167 In *Lloyds Bank Plc v Rosset*,[285] Lord Bridge drew an important distinction between cases in which there is evidence capable of establishing an express agreement between the parties and cases where there is no such evidence, but where there is evidence of conduct from which the court can infer the existence of an agreement. For a court to hold that the parties formed an express common intention, evidence of discussions is required, "however imperfectly remembered and however imprecise their terms may have been".[286] For example, if the defendant gives the claimant an excuse (such as the age of the claimant, or the need to protect assets from the claimant's former spouse) as to why legal title to the property should be vested in the defendant's name alone, this may, depending on the wider factual context,[287] be interpreted as evidence from which the court can objectively determine that the parties commonly intended the beneficial ownership to be shared, if otherwise there would have been no need for such an excuse.[288] It should be noted, however, that there is a clear distinction between an intention to share the current use and possession of property and an intention that the claimant should have a share of ownership of the property, and vague statements made in a casual context will not, by themselves, establish an express agreement that the claimant should have a beneficial share.[289]

---

282 Strictly speaking, an intention that the parties should each have a 50% beneficial interest suffices, as in such a case the intention is that the parties will be tenants in common in equity, whereas they are necessarily joint tenants at law: see s.1(6) Law of Property Act 1925.

283 Lord Diplock in *Gissing v Gissing* [1971] A.C. 886 at 906. See too *Austin v Keele* (1987) 61 A.L.J.R. 605 at 610, per Lord Oliver.

284 *Springette v Defoe* (1992) 24 H.L.R. 552; *Mollo v Mollo* [2000] W.T.L.R. 227 at 242–243; *Lightfoot v Lightfoot-Brown* [2005] EWCA Civ 201; [2005] 2 P. & C.R. 22.

285 [1991] 1 A.C. 107.

286 *Lloyds Bank Plc v Rosset* [1991] 1 A.C. 107 at 132, per Lord Bridge.

287 Note the warning of Lewison LJ in *Curran v Collins* [2015] EWCA Civ 404 at [74]: an excuse does not "necessarily or even usually lead to an inference that the person to whom the excuse has been given can reasonably regard herself as having an immediate entitlement to an interest in the property in question."

288 See *Eves v Eves* [1975] 1 W.L.R. 1338; *Grant v Edwards* [1986] Ch. 638.

289 See, e.g. *Lissimore v Downing* [2003] 2 F.L.R. 308 and *James v Thomas* [2008] 1 F.L.R. 1598.

If there is no evidence of relevant express discussions between the parties, however reasonable it might have been for the parties to discuss the matter and reach an arrangement on beneficial ownership, then the common intention can only be established by inferences from the conduct of the parties. The judgment of Lord Walker and Lady Hale in *Jones v Kernott*, along with that of Lord Collins, makes it clear that it is *not* permissible for a court to impute a common intention that the parties' equitable rights are to differ from their legal entitlements.[290] At this stage of the inquiry, only an actual intention will suffice. In *Geary v Rankine*,[291] for example, Lewison LJ stated that: 17–168

> Whether the beneficial interests are to be shared at all is still a question of a party's actual shared intentions. An imputed intention only arises where the court is satisfied that the parties' actual common intention, express or inferred, was that the beneficial interest would be shared, but cannot make a finding about the proportions in which they were meant to be shared.

This is true in a case where the property is in the parties' joint names just as in a case where it is in the sole name of one of the parties: the *existence* of the common intention constructive trust must be based on an actual common intention, either expressed by the parties or inferred on the evidence. It is crucial to remember, therefore, that the initial common intention that the parties' equitable interests should differ from the position at law, *cannot* be imputed:[292] it must be found either as a result of express discussions or as a result of a process of inference.[293] 17–169

The question then is as to when a court will be willing to make an inference of such a common intention. In answering that question, it is useful to distinguish between those cases in which the legal title is in the joint names of A and B, and those in which it is in the sole name of B. 17–170

(1) Inferring a Common Intention Where the Legal Title is in the Joint Names of A and B

As was made clear by Lord Walker and Lady Hale in their statement of principle in *Jones v Kernott*, the "starting point is that equity follows the law and that [the parties] are joint tenants both in law and in equity."[294] In *Stack v Dowden*, Lord Walker and Lady Hale each suggested that there is a "considerable burden" on a claimant wishing to establish an inference that the parties had a common intention that they should have different beneficial interests, as such an inference could be supported only in "very unusual" cases.[295] At least where property is bought "in joint names for joint occupation by a married or unmarried couple, where both are responsible for the mortgage",[296] the fact that the parties made, overall, unequal financial contributions will not, by itself, justify a departure from the starting point of a beneficial joint tenancy. In the particular context of such cohabitation, it can easily be accepted that 17–171

---

290 In contrast, Lord Wilson's judgment at [78] emphasises the importance of imputation.

291 [2012] 2 F.L.R. 1409 at [19]. See too *Thompson v Hurst* [2015] 1 F.L.R. 238 at [22] per Etherton LJ: "In the case of a single legal owner, such as the present, where there is no express declaration of trust, the claimant has first to establish some sort of implied trust, normally what is now termed a common intention constructive trust . . . The claimant must show that it was intended that he or she was to have a beneficial interest at all. That can only be achieved by evidence of the parties' actual intentions, express or inferred, objectively ascertained."

292 See, e.g. *Barnes v Phillips* [2015] EWCA Civ 1056, where the first instance judge made that mistake and was corrected by the Court of Appeal, who were instead able, on the facts, to infer the existence of such a common intention.

293 See too *Capethorn v Harris* [2015] EWCA Civ 955 at [17] (Sales LJ).

294 [2011] UKSC 53; [2012] 1 A.C. 776 at [51].

295 [2007] UKHL 17; [2007] 2 A.C. 432 at [15] and [68].

296 See *Jones v Kernott* [2011] UKSC 53; [2012] 1 A.C. 776 at [25].

the parties' intentions are more likely to be informed by an ethos of equality and sharing rather than one of pure "balance-sheet" accounting.[297]

17–172 Whilst the starting point of a beneficial joint tenancy is hard to displace in such cases, the court can take account of a broad range of factors in determining if a contrary common intention can be inferred. In *Stack v Dowden*, Lady Hale stated that:[298]

> In law, 'context is everything' and the domestic context is very different from the commercial world. Each case will turn on its own facts. Many more factors than financial contributions may be relevant to divining the parties' true intentions. These include: any advice or discussions at the time of the transfer which cast light upon their intentions then; the reasons why the home was acquired in their joint names; the reasons why (if it be the case) the survivor was authorised to give a receipt for the capital moneys;[299] the purpose for which the home was acquired; the nature of the parties' relationship; whether they had children for whom they both had responsibility to provide a home; how the purchase was financed, both initially and subsequently; how the parties arranged their finances, whether separately or together or a bit of both; how they discharged the outgoings on the property and their other household expenses. When a couple are joint owners of the home and jointly liable for the mortgage, the inferences to be drawn from who pays for what may be very different from the inferences to be drawn when only one is owner of the home. The arithmetical calculation of how much was paid by each is also likely to be less important. It will be easier to draw the inference that they intended that each should contribute as much to the household as they reasonably could and that they would share the eventual benefit or burden equally. The parties' individual characters and personalities may also be a factor in deciding where their true intentions lay. In the cohabitation context, mercenary considerations may be more to the fore than they would be in marriage, but it should not be assumed that they always take pride of place over natural love and affection. At the end of the day, having taken all this into account, cases in which the joint legal owners are to be taken to have intended that their beneficial interests should be different from their legal interests will be very unusual.
>
> **17–173** This is not, of course, an exhaustive list. There may also be reason to conclude that, whatever the parties' intentions at the outset, these have now changed. An example might be where one party has financed (or constructed himself) an extension or substantial improvement to the property, so that what they have now is significantly different from what they had then.

17–174 Notwithstanding the court's emphasis on the "very unusual" circumstances required to support an inference of a common intention that the parties would have unequal beneficial shares, such an inference was made in both *Stack v Dowden* and *Jones v Kernott*. It also seems clear that the disparity in the parties' financial contributions to the costs of acquiring the property was crucial to that inference, and to the calculation of the individual beneficial shares arising under the common intention constructive trust. This demonstrates a point noted in Chapter 16:[300] whilst there is a clear conceptual difference between common intention constructive trust and resulting trust reasoning, it is possible to exaggerate the difference in the outcomes they produce.[301]

297 See *Stack v Dowden* [2007] UKHL 17; [2007] 2 A.C. 432 at [68]; *Jones v Kernott* [2011] UKSC 53; [2012] 1 A.C. 776 at [22].

298 [2007] UKHL 17; [2007] 2 A.C. 432 at [69].

299 [This point is mentioned as, prior to 1995, the form of transfer prescribed by the Land Registry in the case of a conveyance to two or more parties required the transferees to state if the survivor was able to give such a receipt. It was determined prior to *Stack v Dowden* that a positive answer to this question did not amount to an express declaration of a beneficial joint tenancy (see, e.g. *Huntingford v Hobbs* [1993] 1 F.L.R. 736), but it was stated in *Stack* that it was nonetheless a potentially relevant factor against a finding that the parties intended to hold as tenants in common in equity.]

300 See para.16–053.

301 In *Stack v Dowden* [2007] UKHL 17; [2007] 2 A.C. 432, for example, Lord Neuberger reached the same result as the other members of the panel, but by using resulting trust reasoning rather than finding a common intention constructive trust: see [122].

(2) Inferring a Common Intention Where the Legal Title is in the Sole Name of B

In *Lloyds Bank Plc v Rosset*, where legal title to the property was in the sole name of Mr Rosset, Lord Bridge stated that:[302] **17–175**

> direct contributions to the purchase price by the partner who is not the legal owner, whether initially or by payment of mortgage instalments, will readily justify the inference necessary to the creation of a constructive trust. But, as I read the authorities, it is at least extremely doubtful that anything less will do.

On this view, the wide list of factors identified by Lady Hale in *Stack v Dowden*,[303] set out in the previous extract, is not applicable in a case where A is not on the legal title and needs to resort to a common intention constructive trust in order to show that she has any beneficial interest in the property. **17–176**

The limit identified by Lord Bridge had the advantage of making it clear to the parties and their advisers what evidence was required in cases where there had been no express discussions as to beneficial ownership of the home.[304] As a matter of principle, however, it is very hard to justify such a limit on the evidence that can be used to support an inference of common intention. Whilst the making of a direct financial contribution may well provide support for such an inference, there is no reason to think that, in the absence of such a contribution by the claimant, the parties cannot possibly have intended that the parties' beneficial interests in the property should differ from their rights at law. **17–177**

In *Stack v Dowden*, Lord Walker stated that:[305] **17–178**

> Lord Bridge's extreme doubt 'whether anything less will do' was certainly consistent with many first-instance and Court of Appeal decisions, but I respectfully doubt whether it took full account of the views (conflicting though they were) expressed in *Gissing v Gissing*.[306] It has attracted some trenchant criticism from scholars as potentially productive of injustice.[307] . . . Whether or not Lord Bridge's observation was justified in 1990, in my opinion the law has moved on, and your Lordships should move it a little more in the same direction, while bearing in mind that the Law Commission may soon come forward with proposals which, if enacted by Parliament, may recast the law in this area.[308]

Lady Hale referred with approval to Lord Walker's view in her own speech in *Stack*, stating that:[309] **17–179**

> The law has indeed moved on in response to changing social and economic conditions. The search is to ascertain the parties' shared intentions, actual, inferred or imputed, with respect to the property in the light of their whole course of conduct in relation to it.

It might therefore seem that the *Rosset* limit on the evidence that may be used to infer a common intention that the parties' beneficial interests should differ from their entitlements at law has been rejected and that the wide list of factors identified by Lady Hale in *Stack*[310] is relevant to the inference of common intention in a case where the legal title is in the name of the defendant alone. **17–180**

---

302 [1991] 1 A.C. 107 at 133.
303 [2007] UKHL 17; [2007] 2 A.C. 432.
304 Although it can be argued that the advantages of certainty in this context are exaggerated: see L. Fox O'Mahony, "Property Outsiders and the Hidden Politics of Doctrinalism" (2015) 67 C.L.P. 409, 430–431.
305 [2007] UKHL 17; [2007] 2 A.C. 432 at [26].
306 [1971] A.C. 886, especially Lord Reid at 896–7 and Lord Diplock at 909.
307 See K. Gray and S.F. Gray, *Elements of Land Law* (4th edn, 2004) 10.132–10.137. [See now the 5th edn, 2008 at 7.3.62–7.3.66.]
308 [Those Law Commission proposals will be considered at para.17–204.]
309 [2007] UKHL 17; [2007] 2 A.C. 432 at [60].
310 [2007] UKHL 17; [2007] 2 A.C. 432.

17–181 In *Abbott v Abbott*, a sole name case, Lady Hale relied on *Stack*, noting that "the law has indeed moved on" since *Rosset*, and that "[t]he parties' whole course of conduct in relation to the property must be taken into account in determining their shared intentions as to ownership." Three factors, however, limit the weight of that decision. First, it was a Privy Council case and so does not have the binding weight in English law of a decision of the House of Lords or the Supreme Court; second, it was made after *Stack* and before the principles of that case were "revisited"[311] in *Jones v Kernott*; third, B had in any case conceded that A had some beneficial interest, and so the question on the facts was as to how to quantify that interest, not whether it could be established.

17–182 Indeed, there seems to be little evidence that the courts are reaching decisions inconsistent with the limits on inference imposed in *Rosset*.[312] There is, after all, a tension at the heart of *Stack* and *Jones*. On the one hand, there is a clear desire to tackle common intention constructive trusts generally, in sole name and joint name cases, and to show that the law has "moved on" since *Rosset*. On the other hand, there is the insistence that, in joint names cases at least, there is a heavy burden to displace in seeking to establish an inference that the parties' entitlements in equity differ from their rights at law, and the fact that the outcome in each case corresponded very closely to the extent of the parties' direct financial contributions to the costs of acquisition of the property. This contributes to the lack of clarity in the relevant principles which, as Sloan notes,[312a] makes it very difficult for lower courts confidently to develop the law.

ii. Detrimental Reliance

17–183 In a case where the required common intention is established by means of express discussions between the parties, it is clear that this expressed oral intention cannot, by itself, allow A to prove the existence of a trust.[313] In *Gissing v Gissing*, Lord Diplock's assumption was that the parties' common intention would be that A had to act in some specific way to facilitate the acquisition of the property, by:

> contributing to the purchase price or to the deposit or the mortgage instalments when it is purchased upon mortgage or to make some other material sacrifice by way of contribution to or economy in the general family expenditure.[314]

17–184 Since then, however, the courts have rejected the idea that the common intention must be that A would acquire an interest in the property in exchange for some quid pro quo. It will suffice if A has "acted to his or her detriment or significantly altered his or her position in reliance on the agreement".[315]

17–185 The action in reliance need not consist of making a direct financial contribution to the costs of acquisition of the property. In *Eves v Eves*,[316] for example, A's reliance was established by her having painted the house, broken up a patio with a sledgehammer, disposed of rubble, and built a new

311 [2011] UKSC 53; [2012] 1 A.C. 776.

312 See eg B. Sloan, "Keeping Up with the *Jones* Case: Establishing Constructive Trusts in 'Sole Legal Owner' Scenarios" (2015) L.S. 226.

312a ibid.

313 See Law of Property Act 1925 s 53(1)(b). See too *Gissing v Gissing* [1971] A.C. 886 at 805; *Grant v Edwards* [1986] Ch. 638 at 647 and 652. Note too L. Maniscalco, "Common Intention and Constructive Trusts: Unorthodoxy in Trusts of Land" [2020] Conv. 124, 133.

314 [1971] A.C. 886 at 905.

315 Lord Bridge in *Lloyds Bank Plc v Rosset* [1991] 1 A.C. 107 at 132.

316 [1975] 1 W.L.R. 1338. See too *Lalani v Crump Holdings Ltd* Ch. D. 18 June 2004, at [47]: the acts alleged to give rise to detriment need not be "dealings with the property by way of contributions or by way of improvements [and other] conduct, contributions or sacrifices may suffice".

garden shed. As a matter of principle, it would seem that the reliance requirement can be established by conduct with no direct relation to the property in question, such as giving up a job or accommodation elsewhere as a result of the common intention that A had or would acquire a beneficial interest in the shared home. That is certainly the case in relation to proprietary estoppel. That doctrine is distinct from the common intention constructive trust,[317] but, as it shares a requirement of detrimental reliance, decisions interpreting that requirement must also be of relevance to the common intention constructive trust.[318] The particular context in which the trust arises, however, may mean that the courts have to adopt a broad approach to the factual question of reliance,[319] lest it be too easy for a claim to be defeated by the allegation that A's conduct was motivated not by a belief as to her beneficial entitlement in the property, but rather by, for example, her love and affection for the defendant, or for any children.[320]

In a case where the required common intention is instead inferred from the parties' conduct in relation to the property, detrimental reliance is far less prominent. Indeed, the concept was mentioned in neither *Stack v Dowden*[321] nor *Jones v Kernott*.[322] This is easily explained by the fact that, in such cases, the very actions of A which support the inference of common intention, such as direct financial contributions to the costs of acquisition of the property, also provide evidence of reliance on that intention. Conversely, in a case where the conduct of the parties does not support such an inference, this is likely to be because that conduct can be explained as motivated not by any belief that A had or would acquire a beneficial interest different from his or her legal entitlement (if any), but rather by other factors.[323] **17–186**

iii. Quantifying the Interest under the Trust

The basic rule, applying in all cases, is that the size of A's beneficial interest under the common intention constructive trust will be determined solely by that common intention.[324] It may well be the case that, whilst there is an express or inferred common intention that A's beneficial interests should differ from her legal right (if any), it is not possible to find any express or inferred intention as to the *size* of that beneficial interest. In such a case, it is clear from *Stack v Dowden* and *Jones v Kernott* that the court may *impute* the missing intention. **17–187**

---

317 See paras 17–200 to 17–202.

318 See, e.g. *Grant v Edwards* [1986] 1 Ch. 638 at 657 per Browne-Wilkinson VC.

319 See, e.g. the approach adopted by Browne-Wilkinson VC in *Grant v Edwards* [1986] 1 Ch. 638 (looking at all acts done by the claimant as part of the couple's life together) which is broader than each of the approaches adopted in the same case by Nourse LJ (looking at conduct on which the claimant could not reasonably have been expected to embark but for having a beneficial interest) and Mustill LJ (preferring the quid pro quo approach which is now inconsistent with Lord Bridge's analysis in *Lloyds Bank Plc v Rosset* [1991] 1 A.C. 107 at 132). For discussion see, e.g. A. Lawson, "The Things We Do For Love: Detrimental Reliance in the Family Home" (1996) 16 L.S. 218.

320 The same concern is shown in proprietary estoppel cases, even where there is no romantic relationship between the claimant and the defendant: see, e.g. *Campbell v Griffin* [2001] EWCA Civ 990; [2001] W.T.L.R. 981 at [27] per Robert Walker LJ. Notwithstanding the view of Lord Denning MR in *Greasley v Cooke* [1980] 1 W.L.R. 1307, however, it may be going too far to say that a "presumption of reliance" operates, so that the defendant has to disprove reliance. Rather, as is usually the case, the claimant should prove each part of his claim: see, e.g. *Steria Ltd v Hutchison* [2006] EWCA Civ 1551; [2007] I.C.R. 445 at [129] per Neuberger LJ and *Sidhu v van Dyke* (2015) 251 C.L.R. 505. See further B. McFarlane, *The Law of Proprietary Estoppel*, 2nd edn (Oxford University Press, 2020), 3.98–3.283.

321 [2007] UKHL 17; [2007] 2 A.C. 432.

322 [2011] UKSC 53; [2012] 1 A.C. 776.

323 See, e.g. *James v Thomas* [2007] EWCA Civ 1212; [2008] 1 F.L.R. 1598 at [36] per Chadwick LJ.

324 See, e.g. *Clough v Killey* (1996) 72 P. & C.R. D22 per Peter Gibson LJ: "it is only common sense that where the parties form a common intention as to the specific shares they are to take, those shares prima facie are the shares to which the court will give effect."; *Oxley v Hiscock* [2004] EWCA Civ 546; [2005] Fam. 211 at [69] per Chadwick LJ.

17–188 In *Midland Bank Plc v Cooke*,[325] for example, A's direct financial contribution to the purchase price of the property, registered in the sole name of her husband, amounted to less than 7% of the costs of acquisition. Even under the limits imposed by *Rosset*,[326] this nonetheless allowed for the inference of a common intention that she should have a beneficial interest in the property. It was clear from the parties' evidence that they had not discussed, or even thought about, the size of any such share. Looking at the nature of their relationship, and their sharing of household expenses, the Court of Appeal found that the claimant had a 50% share in equity. Waite LJ stated starkly that:[327]

> positive evidence that the parties neither discussed nor intended any agreement as to the proportions of their beneficial interest does not preclude the court, on general equitable principles, from inferring one.

17–189 Despite the reference to "inferring", the decision must have involved an imputation: imposing on the parties an intention as to the size of A's share when no such intention actually existed.

17–190 In *Jones v Kernott*, Lord Walker and Lady Hale, with whom Lord Collins agreed, affirmed that imputation of intention as to the size of A's beneficial interest is permissible.[328] They nonetheless responded to Lord Neuberger's concern as expressed in *Stack* in two ways. First, they took a broad view of the process of inference, and thus argued that the line between inference and imputation is a fine one. Second, they affirmed that the process of imputation involves finding "the share which the court considers fair having regard to the whole course of dealing in relation to the property",[329] rather than the imposition of a result which the court deems fair on more general grounds, perhaps based on the parties' relationship and needs, but unconnected to their dealings in relation to the property itself. As Tomlinson LJ noted in *Graham-York v York*, even when imputation is permitted:[330]

> the court is not concerned with some form of redistributive justice. Thus it is irrelevant that it may be thought a 'fair' outcome for a woman who has endured years of abusive conduct by her partner to be allotted a substantial interest in his property on his death. The plight of [the claimant] attracts sympathy, but it does not enable the court to redistribute property interests in a manner which right-minded people might think amount to appropriate compensation. [A] is 'entitled' to the share which the court considers fair having regard to the whole course of dealing between them *in relation to the property*. It is these last words, which I have emphasised, which supply the confines of the enquiry as to fairness.

17–191 Two points in particular arise from *Jones v Kernott*. First, on what basis will a common intention as to the size of A's interest be inferred? Lord Walker and Lady Hale, with whom Lord Collins agreed, found that an agreement as to a 90:10 split could be inferred because the parties must have intended, when their insurance policy was cashed in and Mr Kernott bought a new home, that "his interest in [the property] should crystallise then."[331] This meant that Mr Kernott was denied any benefit from the significant appreciation in the value of the house after that point. In the absence of clear evidence, it may be doubted that Mr Kernott would have made such an agreement. Lord Kerr, along with Lord Wilson, and also Wall and Rimer LJJ in the Court of Appeal, found that no such inference could be made:

---

325 [1995] 2 F.L.R. 915.
326 Discussed at paras 17–175 to 17–182.
327 [1995] 2 F.L.R. 915 at 920.
328 [2011] UKSC 53; [2012] 1 A.C. 776 at [31] and [51] (extracted at paras 17–154 and 17–162).
329 [2011] UKSC 53; [2012] 1 A.C. 776 at [51] (extracted at para.17–162), quoting from the judgment of Chadwick LJ in *Oxley v Hiscock* [2005] Fam 211 at [69].
330 [2015] EWCA Civ 72 at [22].
331 [2011] UKSC 53; [2012] 1 A.C. 776 at [76].

> the bare facts of [Mr Kernott's] departure from the family home and acquisition of another property are a slender foundation on which to conclude that he had entirely abandoned whatever stake he had in the previously shared property.[332]

Second, what does it mean to impute a common intention? Why retain the language of intention at all, if the court is simply deciding what would be fair in light of the parties' whole course of dealing with the property? As Lord Kerr put it:[332A] **17–192**

> The reason that I question the aptness of the notion of imputing an intention is that, in the final analysis, the exercise is wholly unrelated to ascertainment of the parties' views. It involves the court deciding what is fair in light of the whole course of dealing with the property. That decision has nothing to do with what the parties intended, or what might be supposed to have been their intention had they addressed the question.

iv. Availability of the Trust in a Commercial Context

It is clear that the common intention constructive trust has been fashioned as a response to the specific and very difficult problem of affording sufficient protection to cohabitants, particularly on the termination of their relationship. As Etherton LJ put it in *Crossco No 4 Unltd v Jolan Ltd*:[333] **17–193**

> [The] line of cases on the common intention constructive trust can be seen clearly in retrospect as a specific jurisprudential response to the problem of a presumption of resulting trust and the absence of legislation for resolving disputes over property ownership where a married or unmarried couple have purchased property for their joint occupation as a family home. The jurisprudence in that distinctive area is driven by policy considerations and the special facts that normally apply in the dealings between those living in an intimate relationship . . . those rights and interests must be seen in the context of an enduring but often-changing relationship of inter-dependency, mutual co-operation, compromise and joint contributions.

Nonetheless, as a product of judicial rather than legislative development of the law, it is difficult arbitrarily to confine the scope of the constructive trust to "domestic" cases, however they may be identified. Indeed, we have seen already that the majority in *Crossco*, disagreeing with Etherton LJ on this point, considered themselves bound to follow the analysis of Chadwick LJ that the *Pallant v Morgan* equity, developed in the commercial context, is itself an example of a common intention constructive trust. Certainly, there are commercial cases in which the basic requirements of that type of trust are present: a common intention that beneficial interest should vary from the position at law, plus reliance on that agreement meaning the relying party would now suffer a detriment if the common intention were departed from. Moreover, whilst these cases could equally be seen as applications of proprietary estoppel, there are advantages to the claimant of pleading a common intention constructive trust.[334] **17–194**

In *Kahrmann v Harrison-Morgan*,[335] therefore, Henderson LJ cited with agreement, and applied, the observation in *Lewin on Trusts* that:[336] "An express agreement, relied on to the detriment of the party claiming a beneficial interest, may found an interest under a common intention constructive trust **17–195**

---

332 [2011] UKSC 53; [2012] 1 A.C. 776 at [76].
332a [2011] UKSC 53; [2012] 1 A.C. 776 at [74].
333 [2011] EWCA Civ 1619; [2011] EWCA Civ 1619 at [85].
334 See paras 17–201 to 17–202.
335 [2019] EWCA Civ 2094 at [99].
336 L. Tucker et al (eds) *Lewin on Trusts*, 19th edn (Sweet and Maxwell, 2014), para.9–064.

outside the scope of the domestic consumer context."[337] Nonetheless, as Henderson LJ observed, once outside the cohabitation context, a court will not have the same flexible approach to the "inference or imputation of a common intention retrospectively ascertained by examination of the whole course of conduct between co-habiting parties over many years, of the kind now routinely undertaken by the courts in a domestic context".[338] There is also a question of whether, in a commercial context, reliance on a non-contractual agreement should give rise to a common intention constructive trust (in which the claimant necessarily acquires the expected beneficial interest), rather than to a proprietary estoppel claim,[339] in which the extent of the claimant's actual and potential detriment can be used to limit the extent of the claimant's right.[340]

C. Justifying the Trust

i. Comparison with Related Doctrines

17–196 The common intention constructive trust has been described by the Canadian Supreme Court as "doctrinally unsound".[341] It suffers from the basic problem that it is premised on the parties' objectively established common intentions as to beneficial ownership when, in fact, such intentions rarely exist.[342] As a result, the cases consist of a "judicial quest for the fugitive or phantom common intention."[343] Indeed, the English courts' acceptance that it is permissible to *impute* such an intention, albeit only as to the size of the parties' beneficial shares, shows that the notion of the parties' intention is used as a fiction in an attempt to provide some justification for the imposition of a trust.

17–197 A further difficulty is caused by the pedigree of the common intention constructive trust. As John Mee has noted,[344] a number of distinct and competing principles have influenced its identification and development. On the one hand, Lord Diplock's discussion of the trust in *Gissing v Gissing*[345] proceeds from a discussion of presumed resulting trusts, and this influence can be seen from the fact that, where a common intention constructive trust is based on an inference as to the parties' intentions, the courts have traditionally focussed, particularly in cases where the legal title is in the sole name of the defendant, on the question of whether A has made any direct financial contribution to the costs of acquiring the property. Nonetheless, in contrast to the position under a resulting trust, the size of any interest arising under the common intention constructive trust is not determined solely by the extent of any such financial contributions, but is rather said to depend on the parties' actual or imputed intentions, even if that approach may lead in some cases to the same outcome as a resulting trust.

17–198 One attempt to justify the common intention constructive trust consists in seeing it as an application of the same principle underlying the promise-based strand of proprietary estoppel:[346] A's rights

---

337 For further examples of a common intention constructive trust arising outside the context of cohabitation, see e.g. *Kinane v Mackie-Conteh* [2005] EWCA Civ 45; *Matchmove Ltd v Dowding* [2016] EWCA Civ 1233; [2017] 1 W.L.R. 749. See too *re Lehman Brothers International (Europe) (In Administration)* [2010] EWHC 2914 (Ch) at [243]–[247] (Briggs J).

338 [2019] EWCA Civ 2094 at [99].

339 See Chapter 3, section 2.

340 Note that the forthcoming decision of the Supreme Court in *Guest v Guest* (o appeal from [2020] EWCA Civ 387) is likely to clarify the principles applied in determining the extent of a right arising through proprietary estoppel.

341 *Kerr v Baranow* [2011] 1 S.C.R. 269 at [25] per Cromwell J.

342 A point noted by, e.g. S. Gardner, "Rethinking Family Property" (1993) 109 L.Q.R. 263.

343 *Pettkus v Becker* (1980) 2 S.C.R. 834 at 843 per Dickson J.

344 See J. Mee, "*Pettitt v Pettitt* (1970) and *Gissing v Gissing* (1971)" in Mitchell and Mitchell (eds), *Landmark Cases in Equity* (2012) and, more generally, J. Mee, *The Property Rights of Cohabitees* (Hart Publishing, 1999).

345 [1971] A.C. 886 at 906-907.

346 See paras 3–013 to 3–033. Note that in Chapter 3, the party claiming the estoppel is referred to as B, and the defendant subject to the estoppel claim as A; the labels are reversed here, given that A is the party claiming the right under the

under the trust arise because it would be unconscionable for B to leave her to suffer a detriment as a result of her reasonable reliance on a seriously intended promise, made by B, that A had or would have an interest in B's land.[347] Certainly, some of the language employed by Lord Diplock in *Gissing v Gissing*[348] is very close to that used in proprietary estoppel, where *any* conduct of A is relevant if it is undertaken in reliance on a promise of a beneficial interest and gives rise to the prospect of detriment if the defendant were free to renege on the promise.

Given the nature of a proprietary estoppel claim,[349] however, this analogy with proprietary estoppel is far from straightforward and differing views have been expressed on it; even, as can be seen in the following extract, by the same judge. **17–199**

Stack v Dowden

House of Lords [2007] 2 A.C. 432 at [37]

LORD WALKER: I add a brief comment as to proprietary estoppel. In his judgment in *Oxley v Hiscock*,[350] Chadwick L.J. considered the conceptual basis of the developing law in this area, and briefly discussed proprietary estoppel, a suggestion first put forward by Sir Nicholas Browne-Wilkinson V.-C. in *Grant v Edwards*.[351] I have myself given some encouragement to this approach (see *Yaxley v Gotts*[352]), but I have to say that I am now rather less enthusiastic about the notion that proprietary estoppel and "common interest" constructive trusts can or should be completely assimilated. Proprietary estoppel typically consists of asserting an equitable claim against the conscience of the "true" owner. The claim is a "mere equity". It is to be satisfied by the minimum award necessary to do justice,[353] which may sometimes lead to no more than a monetary award. A "common intention" constructive trust, by contrast, is identifying the true beneficial owner or owners, and the size of their beneficial interests. **17–200**

Lord Walker's caution is well-placed. First, the breadth of the factors that a court may take into account in inferring a common intention that A's beneficial entitlement should differ from her legal rights (if any), at least where legal title is in the joint names of A and B, means that such an intention may be inferred in cases where it is unlikely that a court would find the express or implied promise required for proprietary estoppel claim. Second, as noted by Lord Walker, the effect of a successful proprietary estoppel claim differs from the finding of a common intention constructive trust. In the latter case, the parties' common intention, whether actual or imputed, determines the content of A's right in the property,[354] whereas in the former case, there is no guarantee that B's promise will be enforced,[355] since the court will carefully consider the nature of A's reliance and the extent of any detriment potentially arising from it.[356] **17–201**

---

common intention constructive trust.

347 For an excellent historical survey of the relationship between proprietary estoppel and common intention constructive trusts, see P. Matthews, "The Words Which Are Not There: A Partial History of the Constructive Trust" in Mitchell (ed.), *Constructive and Resulting Trusts* (2010), pp.24–60.

348 [1971] A.C. 886 at 905.

349 See paras 3–013 to 3–033.

350 [2005] Fam. 211 at [70]–[71].

351 [1986] Ch. 638 at 656.

352 [2000] Ch. 162 at 177.

353 *Crabb v Arun D.C.* [1976] Ch. 179 at 198.

354 See para.17–187.

355 See, e.g. *Jennings v Rice* [2002] EWCA Civ 159; [2003] 1 P. & C.R. 8; *Ottey v Grundy* [2003] W.T.L.R. 1253. Note too the analysis of Hoffmann LJ in *Walton v Walton* (CA, 15 April 1994).

356 See, e.g. *Powell v Benney* [2007] EWCA Civ 1283; *Henry v Henry* [2010] UKPC 3; [2010] 1 All E.R. 988. Note too *Southwell v Blackburn* [2014] EWCA Civ 1347: A and B had cohabited, and B's claim to a beneficial share of the property under a common intention constructive trust was rejected at first instance. B's proprietary estoppel claim, however, succeeded and, as confirmed by the Court of Appeal, A was ordered to pay a sum of money (£28,5000) to B.

17–202 Moreover, as noted by Lord Walker, a proprietary estoppel claim can be said to give rise to a "mere equity". The point seems to be that it does not impose an immediate duty on B to perform her promise: rather, a court looks back over the parties' conduct and asks if it would *now* be unconscionable for B to be wholly free to renege on her promise.[357] In contrast, at least in a case where the parties' common intention precedes, or arises at the same time as, the acquisition of the property in sole or joint names, the common intention constructive trust arises as soon as the property is acquired, even if it may be of an "ambulatory" nature, so that the extent of the parties' shares may change over time, as the common intention of the parties changes.[358] In fact, the better analogy in such a case may be with the constructive trust arising under *Rochefoucauld v Boustead*[359] or under the *Pallant v Morgan* equity.[360] Such cases are, to use Liew's terminology, "qualified interest" constructive trusts, whereas proprietary estoppel can operate to impose a trust even in an "absolute interest" case,[361] where B initially held the property free from any claim. Again, however, the difficulty is that each of those types of constructive trust, like the promise-based strand of proprietary estoppel, requires clear evidence of a specific promise by the defendant and does not permit the broad process of inference recognised in *Jones v Kernott*.

17–203 The difficulty of justifying the common intention constructive trust on doctrinal grounds may well result from the fact that the trust has been fashioned as a response to the specific and very difficult problem of affording sufficient protection to cohabitants, particularly on the termination of their relationship. From a policy perspective, however, there are still pressing difficulties in justifying the common intention constructive trust. For example, it may still be difficult, even after *Stack v Dowden* and *Jones v Kernott*, for a long-term cohabitant to show that he or she has a beneficial interest where the property is registered in the sole name of their partner, there is no evidence of an expressed agreement between the parties as to the claimant's having a beneficial share, and the claimant has made no direct financial contribution to the costs of acquiring the property. Yet many would argue that, in such a case, the nature of the claimant and defendant's relationship, and the broader contributions made by the former to the parties' lives together may mean that the claimant should not be left empty-handed if the relationship ends for reasons other than the death of the defendant.[362]

17–204 Of course, had the parties been married or in a civil partnership, much of the pressure would be taken off the law of constructive trusts, as the parties would then have been subject to a broad

---

357 See the analysis of Hoffmann LJ in *Walton v Walton* (CA, 15 April 1994). In a case concerning a third party, the court will instead have to establish the rights held by the claimant at the time when the third party acquired its rights, by asking if *at that time*, it would have been unconscionable for the defendant to be wholly free to renege on her promise. This is consistent with the fact that an "equity" arising by proprietary estoppel can have effect from the moment of the facts giving rise to it, and does not operate only prospectively from the time of a court order: see s.116(a) Land Registration Act 2002.

358 See *Stack v Dowden* [2007] UKHL 17; [2007] 2 A.C. 432 at [62] and [138], *Jones v Kernott* [2011] UKSC 53; [2012] 1 A.C. 776 at [15]. Note that Etherton C, writing extra-judicially, has suggested that the common intention constructive trust is in fact a form of remedial constructive trust: T. Etherton, "Constructive Trusts: A New Model for Equity and Unjust Enrichment" [2008] C.L.J. 265. On this view, contrary to Lord Walker's analysis in *Stack* at [37] (extracted at para.17–200), the trust would arise with prospective effect only.

359 See paras 6–033ff.

360 See para.17–009.

361 See para.17–009.

362 *Burns v Burns* [1984] Ch. 317 is often cited as an example of an unjust outcome: the parties' relationship ended after nearly 20 years, during which time the claimant had cared for the couple's children and had contributed to household expenses. The family home was registered in the sole name of the defendant, there had been no express discussions as to beneficial ownership, and the claimant had made no direct financial contribution to the purchase price or mortgage payments. No constructive trust arose and at 332 and 345, Fox and May LJJ, and whilst recognising the harshness of the claimant being left without a remedy, stated that any reform had to come from Parliament. For a nuanced examination of the decision, see J. Mee, "*Burns v Burns*: The Villain of the Piece?" in S. Gilmore et al., (eds), *Landmark Cases in Family Law* (Hart Publishing, 2011).

statutory jurisdiction allowing for the variation of their property rights, with consideration given to a broad range of factors, such as the nature of their relationship and their future needs.[363] Indeed, in an eminently sensible set of proposals, the Law Commission recommended that a similar (but not identical) statutory scheme should be put in place for cohabitants who are unmarried and not in a civil partnership, allowing for financial relief to be available to claimants.[364] One advantage of such a scheme is that the protection of a cohabitant would not then depend on whether or not a valuable right to *land* is held by one or both of the parties—financial relief could be available based on the holding of other assets, such as pensions. Such a scheme, if enacted, would not be a panacea, as of course there would still be cases (such as those involving third parties) where it is necessary for a court to establish the parties' individual beneficial entitlements in relevant land (if any) at a past point in time. Parliament's failure to implement such a scheme, however, raises a difficult dilemma: should the courts continue to develop the common intention constructive trust, stretching it so as to fill the gap left by an absence of statutory intervention? Or should the courts acknowledge that, in relation to a politically sensitive area of the law, they should not distort existing legal principles in order to achieve similar outcomes to those that Parliament has chosen not to impose through legislation?[365]

9. Unlawful Killing

A. The Nature of the Trust

There is a clear public policy in preventing one who has unlawfully killed another from enjoying the benefit of property that they would otherwise have gained as a result of that death: this has been recognised in legislation as the "forfeiture rule".[366] This rule applies, for example, where a murderer stands to gain under the will of her victim, or, where the victim left no will, under the usual intestacy rules. It also applies where one joint tenant kills another, and so would otherwise benefit from the operation of the doctrine of survivorship. **17-205**

There are different ways of giving effect to the rule.[367] The most direct is simply to find that the property has not in fact passed as it would have done had the death been lawful.[368] That was the approach adopted, for example, in the famous case of *Riggs v Palmer*, where the American court interpreted the relevant legislation in a creative way to find that no property passed to the unlawful killer. In such a case, no constructive trust is required. Another means, where property has already been acquired by the killer, is to impose a constructive trust of the property for the benefit of others.[369] **17-206**

---

363 Similarly, if the relationship had ended by the death of the defendant, and no adequate financial provision had been made for the claimant, some financial protection would be available to the claimant under the Inheritance (Provision for Family and Dependants) Act 1975.

364 Law Commission, *Cohabitation: The Financial Consequences of Relationship Breakdown* (TSO, 2007), Law Com. No.307, Cm.7182.

365 For discussion, see Mee "*Burns v Burns*: The Villain of the Piece?" in Gilmore et al., (eds), *Landmark Cases in Family Law* (2011). Indeed, protecting a claimant by means of a common intention constructive trust, and thus giving her a beneficial interest capable of binding third parties, would give her a more significant right than the right to financial relief proposed by the Law Commission.

366 Forfeiture Act 1982 s.1. See too Law Commission, *The Forfeiture Rule and the Law of Succession* (2005) Law Com. No.295, Cm.6625.

367 For a very useful survey, with consideration of the role of constructive trusts, see I. Williams, "How Does the Common Law Forfeiture Rule Work?" in B. Häcker and C. Mitchell (eds), *Current Issues in Succession Law* (Hart Publishing, 2016).

368 *Re Crippen* [1911] P. 108. See too *Re Sigsworth* [1935] Ch. 89.

369 *Schobelt v Barber* (1966) 60 D.L.R. (2nd) 519; *Re Pechar* [1969] N.Z.L.R. 574; *Rasmanis v Jurewitsch* [1970] N.S.W.L.R. 650; *Beresford v Royal Insurance Co Ltd* [1938] A.C. 586 at 600. See further G. Jones, "Stripping a Criminal of the Profits of

As noted by, for example, James Barr Ames,[370] this option requires less creativity in the interpretation of legislation and is consistent with equity's characteristic role of accepting (rather than contradicting) the location of legal entitlements, but then controlling, in favour of others, the exercise of those entitlements. Where the killer would otherwise have acquired rights under a will or an intestacy, the beneficiaries of such a constructive trust should be identified by asking what would have happened to the victim's property if the killer had died immediately before the victim.[371] Such a trust is clearly imposed by law, as it does not arise in response to any party choosing to set up a trust.

B. The Scope of the Trust

17-207 Murder[372] and manslaughter[373] including manslaughter by reason of diminished responsibility[374] invoke the forfeiture rule, as does incitement to murder,[375] but it does not apply to a killer who is found not guilty by reason of insanity.[376] The Forfeiture Act 1982 now enables the court to modify the effect of the forfeiture rule where the killer has not been convicted of murder, and the justice of the case requires it, if the killer brings proceedings within three months of conviction.[377]

17-208 Where property is held by two joint tenants, and one murders the other, it has been held that survivorship still operates to mean that the murderer is solely entitled at law, but that a constructive trust arises, under which a half share of the beneficial interest is held by the next of kin of the victim.[378] A different approach, reaching a very similar result, would be to apply the forfeiture rule to mean that that the killer and the next of kin each holds a half share of the property as tenants in common.[379] On one variant of the constructive trust approach, where property is held by three or more joint tenants, the policy of preventing the gain of the killer may be achieved by effecting a partial severance, so that the killer has a proportionate share as tenant in common with the remaining joint tenant(s), who hold the remaining share as joint tenants, with the doctrine of survivorship applying as between them to mean that nothing passes to the estate of the victim.[380] Where a remainderman murders the life tenant, it has been argued that the victim should be deemed to live her actuarial life-span (except for a death-bed mercy killing), so that for the period of this notional life-span the victim's interest should be held on constructive trust for her estate; thereafter, devolution should occur normally.[381]

Crime" (2000) 1 *Theoretical Inquiries in Law* 59.

370 J.B. Ames, "Can A Murdered Acquire Title By His Crime and Keep It?" in *Lectures on Legal History and Miscellaneous Legal Essays* (Harvard University Press, 1913), 310. See too H. Smith, "Equity As Meta-Law" (2021) 130 Yale L.J. 1050, 1124–1125 and J. Goldberg and B. Zipursky, "From *Riggs v Palmer* to *Shelley v Kraemer*: Judicial Power and the Law-Equity Distinctions" in D. Klimchuk et al (eds) *Philosophical Foundations of the Law of Equity* (Oxford University Press, 2020), 291, 298–299.

371 This is the position as from 1 February 2012 and is applied by Estates of Deceased Persons (Forfeiture Rule and Law of Succession) Act 2011. It means, for example, that if a daughter unlawfully kills her parents, who have left no will, her share under the intestacy rules should pass to the daughter's children, the deceased's grandchildren. The result in *Re Jones (Deceased)* [1998] 1 F.L.R. 246 would therefore be different if the same facts arose today.

372 See, e.g. *Beresford v Royal Insurance Co Ltd* [1938] A.C. 586 at 600.

373 *Davitt v Titcumb* [1990] Ch. 110.

374 *Re Giles* [1972] Ch. 544.

375 *Evans v Evans* [1989] 1 F.L.R. 351.

376 *Re Giles* [1972] Ch. 544; *Re Pitts* [1931] 1 Ch. 546; *Re Plaister* (1934) S.R. (N.S.W.) 547; *Permanent Trustee Co v Gillett* (2004) 6 I.T.E.L.R. 1063 at [36]ff.

377 See, e.g. *Re K* [1985] Ch. 85; *Dunbar v Plant* [1998] Ch. 412; *Dalton v Latham* [2003] EWHC 796 (Ch); [2003] W.T.L.R. 687.

378 *Schobelt v Barber* (1966) 60 D.L.R. (2nd) 519; *Re Pechar* [1969] N.Z.L.R. 574.

379 See, e.g. *Re K* [1985] Ch. 85 at 99.

380 *Rasmanis v Jurewitsch* [1970] N.S.W.L.R. 650.

381 T. Youdan "Acquisition of Property by Killing" (1973) 89 L.Q.R. 235 at 250–251.

C. Justifying the Trust

There is little controversy as to the underlying policy behind the forfeiture rule and so, where a constructive trust is required to give effect to it, such a trust can be justified simply by pointing to that policy. It might be observed that there are of course other means of confiscating property from criminals, and so, if the aim of the rule is simply to prevent the unlawful killer making a gain, it could be achieved by those means. The constructive trust, however, also ensures that the benefit of the property in question goes not to the state, but rather to an appropriate party, and so can also preserve the policy behind the underlying rules as to the destination of property on the death of the victim. **17–209**

10. The Protection of Pre-existing Rights: Four Examples

A. The Nature of the Trusts

In this section, we will examine four further types of constructive trust which have a common effect: each can operate to provide some protection to A's pre-existing right. By treating them together, we do not mean to assume that they are identical; rather, we simply wish to note that some common issues arise when considering them. **17–210**

One such issue is whether the trusts are best seen as constructive trusts or as resulting trusts.[382] The first of the four types of trust we will examine here can protect A's pre-existing right where A, by mistake, transfers that right to the defendant. In *Chase Manhattan Bank v Israel-British Bank (London) Ltd*,[383] for example, as we saw in Chapter 16,[384] Goulding J held that money paid in the mistaken belief that it was owed by the payor to the recipient was held on trust for the payor by the recipient.[385] We also saw that in *Westdeutsche Landesbank Girozentrale v Islington LBC*[386] Lord Browne-Wilkinson held that Goulding J had erred in assuming that the trust was based on a retention of an equitable property right by the payor and so would arise, in any case where such a mistake was made, as soon as the payor received the money. His Lordship stated that although: **17–211**

> the mere receipt of the moneys, in ignorance of the mistake, gives rise to no trust, the retention of the moneys after the recipient bank learned of the mistake may well have given rise to a constructive trust.[387]

---

382 As noted by Sarah Worthington QC (Hon) (sitting as a Deputy High Court Judge) in *Ali v Dinc* [2020] EWHC 3055 (Ch) at [229] there is general "no compelling consistency in terminology" when it comes to the use of the constructive or resulting label. On the facts of *Collings v Lee* [2001] 2 All E.R. 332, where A1 and A2 had transferred their legal title to land to B following a fraudulent misrepresentation from B, who was their agent, it was stated at [13] that whether the trust "should be characterised as implied, resulting or constructive is a matter of no importance."

383 [1981] Ch. 105.

384 See para.16–003.

385 *Chase Manhattan* remains good law in England, although its status has been diminished by Lord Browne-Wilkinson's gloss on the case in *Westdeutsche Landesbank Girozentrale v Islington LBC* [1996] A.C. 669, and by sceptical judicial reactions to this gloss in *Barclays Bank Plc v Box* [1998] Lloyd's Rep. Bank. 185 at 200–201; *Papamichael v National Westminster Bank Plc (No.2)* [2003] EWHC 164 (Comm); [2003] 1 Lloyd's Rep. 341 at [232]–[242]; *Shalson v Russo* [2003] EWHC 1637 (Ch); [2005] Ch. 281 at [108]–[127]; *Fitzalan-Howard v Hibbert* [2009] EWHC 2855 (QB); [2010] P.N.L.R. 11 at [49]; *Maqsood v Mahmood* [2012] EWCA Civ 251 at [35]–[38]; *Wuhan Guoyu Logistics Group Co Ltd v Emporiki Bank of Greece SA* [2013] EWCA Civ 1679; [2014] 1 All E.R. (Comm.) 870 at [19].

386 [1996] A.C. 669.

387 ibid., at 715, referring to *Metall und Rohstoff AG v Donaldson Lufkin & Jenrette Inc* [1990] 1 Q.B. 391 at 473–474. See too *Ali v Dinc* [2020] EWHC 3055 (Ch) at [222]–[223].

17–212 As Lord Browne-Wilkinson also noted, such a constructive trust may also protect A where A's transfer of the property right is procured by fraud of the recipient, B. He thought it "difficult to find clear authority for the proposition", but stated nevertheless that "when property is obtained by fraud equity imposes a constructive trust on the fraudulent recipient: the property is recoverable and traceable in equity."[388] As noted by Lewison LJ in *Nasrullah v Rashid*,[389] citing the analysis in *Snell's Equity*,[390] it is important, however, to distinguish between two different types of fraud. The first, "fraudulent taking" is the "outright taking of a person's property, wholly without his consent". Usually, of course, such fraud would prevent B, the fraudster, acquiring A's right; but, if, as in *Nasrullah*, A's right is a registered estate in land, and B succeeds in having the register changed so that B is now the registered proprietor, then B does acquire legal title to that registered estate, and a constructive trust will be imposed. The second case, "fraudulently induced transfer", occurs where B instead tricks A into exercising A's power to transfer A's property to B. Unlike in the fraudulent taking case, "the transaction is valid until [A] elects to rescind it." So, whilst B's right is immediately subject to A's equitable power to rescind the transaction,[391] and a trust will arise when A exercises that power, there is no immediate trust.[392]

17–213 The second type of trust can protect A's pre-existing right where A's property is stolen. Where the thief simply takes A's property, it might seem that there is no room for a trust, as the thief does not thereby acquire any right from A, and A can rely on A's original property right. However, where B, a thief takes possession of a physical thing owned by A, B does thereby acquire a possessory title to the thing, and it seems this can right can then be held by B on constructive trust for A. The advantage of a trust is said to be that it allows A to invoke equitable tracing rules if, for example, A wants to claim an interest in the proceeds of the theft. In *Westdeutsche*, for example, Lord Browne-Wilkinson stated that if stolen money is used to set up a bank account, the account will be held by the thief on trust for the victim of the theft.[393]

17–214 There is a question, in relation to each of these two types of trust, as to whether the trust is best seen as constructive or resulting. In *Westdeutsche*, Lord Browne-Wilkinson clearly said that each such trust is constructive, as it does not fall within either of the two traditional classes of resulting trust, and is inconsistent with their basis because "[a] resulting trust is not imposed by law against the intentions of the trustee (as is a constructive trust) but gives effect to his presumed intention."[394] Others have argued, however, that, the trusts, like those two traditional classes of resulting trust,

---

388 [1996] A.C. 669 at 716, referring to *Stocks v Wilson* [1913] 2 K.B. 235 at 244; *R. Leslie Ltd v Sheill* [1915] 3 K.B. 607; *Bankers Trust Co v Shapira* [1980] 1 W.L.R. 1274 at 1282; *McCormick v Grogan* (1869) L.R. 4 H.L. 82 at 97. Note that in *Shalson v Russo* [2005] Ch. 281 at [111], Rimer J doubted the strength of those authorities, as well as the proposition that property obtained by fraud is automatically held on trust for the person defrauded: see further para.17–224.

389 [2018] EWCA Civ 2685; [2019] 2 W.L.R. 1310 at [53].

390 J. McGhee and S. Elliott (eds), *Snell's Equity*, 33rd edn (Sweet & Maxwell, 2015), paras 26–012—26–013: see now 34th edn, 2019 at 26–012—26–013.

391 See para.20–060.

392 See *Nasrullah v Rashid* [2018] EWCA Civ 2685; [2019] 2 W.L.R. 1310 at [53]. Note that if A's right is transferred to B under a contract which was "not merely induced by fraudulent misrepresentation but [was] itself the instrument of fraud and no more than a vehicle for obtaining money by false pretences" then a trust can arise immediately: the apparent contract is seen as a "device" with no legal effect, making it unnecessary to require rescission by A: see *Global Currency Exchange Network Ltd v Osage 1 Ltd* [2019] EWHC 1375 (Comm); [2019] 1 W.L.R. 5865 at [40]–[47] and *Halley v Law Society* [2003] EWCA Civ 97 at [48].

393 [1996] A.C. 669 at 717–716. See too *Black & Black v S Freedman & Co* (1910) 12 C.L.R. 105. Note too *Banque Belge pour l'Etranger v Hambrouck* [1921] 1 K.B. 321; *Agip (Africa) Ltd v Jackson* [1991] Ch. 547.

394 [1996] A.C. 669 at 708.

are based on the need to prevent an unjust enrichment of the defendant, and so should be seen as resulting trusts.[395]

The question of terminology is not an important one. As far as the actual operation of A's rights under the trust are concerned, it makes no difference whether the trust is labelled as constructive or resulting. The key point, on either view, is that the trust is not an express one and so, for example, it falls outside the formality requirements imposed in cases where a party attempts to exercise a power to set up a trust.[396] The important question is rather as to the justification for the trusts: do they depend on the need to prevent unjust enrichment, or do they arise on some other basis? We will consider this question below.[397] **17–215**

The third type of trust arises where T holds a right on trust for A, and A is able to show that C, a third party who acquired the trust property as a result of an unauthorised disposition made by T, now holds on trust for A. We examined such "proprietary claims" in Chapter 15.[398] We noted there that, in *Independent Trustee Services Ltd v GP Noble Trustees Ltd*, Lloyd LJ described that claim of A as based on C's being subject to a trust and explained that:[399] **17–216**

> Since the trust arises from the asset having been extracted, in breach of trust, from a fund held on express trusts, it seems correct to characterise the trust as a constructive trust, rather than a resulting trust.

It is important to note that, on Lloyd LJ's analysis, if C receives the trust property as a gift from T, and without any knowledge of the trust, this constructive trust exists even before C has acquired such knowledge. On that view, which differs from that of Lord Browne-Wilkinson in *Westdeutsche*,[400] a trust can be said to exist even before C owes any duty to A not to use the trust property for C's own benefit. The difference between the views of Lloyd LJ and Lord Browne-Wilkinson is not large, however, as even on the latter's view, A has, in the period before C acquires knowledge of the initial trust, at least a *power* to impose a trust on C by informing C of the initial trust.[401] **17–217**

The fourth type of trust is also principally important in protecting the pre-existing equitable interest of a beneficiary of a trust. It can arise where T, holding on trust for A, uses the initial trust assets, without authority from A or under the terms of the trust, to acquire new assets. As we saw in Chapter 15,[402] it is possible for A, invoking tracing rules, to assert a proprietary claim, under a trust, in relation to those new assets. There is, again, a question as to the nature of such a trust. **17–218**

Where T held on an express trust for A, the analysis of the House of Lords in *Foskett v McKeown*[403] may support an express trust view, as in that case A's right in relation to the new assets was said to be based on A's subsisting equitable interest in the initial assets. In Chapter 15, however, we noted that there are some important problems with such a view: an inherent feature of any property right, whether legal or equitable, is that it must relate to a specific asset, and so it is very difficult to say that, because A's initial right is an equitable interest in the initial trust assets it *must* turn into a new equitable interest **17–219**

---

395 See, e.g. R. Chambers, *Resulting Trusts* (Oxford University Press, 1997), pp.125–132 (dealing with cases of mistake and fraud) and pp.116–118 (dealing with cases of theft). In the case of fraud, Millett J in *El Ajou v Dollar Land Holdings* [1993] 3 All E.R. 717 at 734 used the terminology of resulting trusts.

396 See, e.g. Law of Property Act 1925 s.53(2).

397 See paras 17–222ff.

398 See paras 15–085ff.

399 [2012] EWCA Civ 195; [2013] Ch. 91 at [80].

400 As acknowledged by Lloyd LJ in the *Independent Trustee Services* case: [2012] EWCA Civ 195; [2013] Ch. 91 at [80].

401 See e.g. S. Agnew and B. McFarlane, "The Paradox of the Equitable Proprietary Claim" in *Modern Studies in Property Law: vol 10* (2019).

402 See paras 15–077ff.

403 [2001] 1 A.C. 102: see paras 15–095 to 15–127.

in the *new* assets.[404] Again, the resulting trust analysis of the fourth type of trust depends on the view that it arises in response to the need to prevent the unjust enrichment of T, or C, at A's expense.[405]

B. The Scope of the Trusts

17–220 Constructive trusts have been recognised not only where property has been transferred by mistake, or in cases of fraudulent taking or theft, but also where the transfer was procured by the undue influence of B,[406] and where A's ability to make decisions as to the transfer of A's property has otherwise been comprised by their relationship with B.[407] Such "vitiation of intention" cases have even extended to cases where property has been transferred under a contract on the basis that A will receive counter-performance, and such counter-performance is not received; but, it was crucial in those cases that B knew, when it received the payment, that there was no prospect of its providing the contractual counter-performance;[408] and, in any case, the decision to find a constructive trust on such facts has been disapproved in the Supreme Court.[409]

17–221 It should also be emphasised that not all cases of vitiated intent give rise to an immediate trust. Where A's intention to make a contract is vitiated as a result of an innocent misrepresentation made by B, A instead acquires an equitable power to rescind the transaction. Whilst the exercise of that power may give rise to a trust, A before then has only a "mere equity". Similarly, where A's unilateral mistake suffices to allow a gift to be set aside, A is seen as having an equitable power to rescind the gift.[410]

C. Justifying the Trusts

17–222 A number of possible explanations have been suggested as to the basis on which each of the four types of trust considered here arises. The third type of trust is intimately connected with the ability of A's initial right under a trust to bind a third party, and thus with the proprietary status of such a right. Questions as to the justification of such a trust therefore depend on what underlying view one takes of the very nature of a beneficiary's rights under a trust: we considered those issues in Chapter 12.

i. Unjust Enrichment?

17–223 We have seen that, on one view, the first, second and fourth of the trusts considered in this section respond to the need to prevent B's being unjustly enriched at A's expense. This claim has been made as part of a broader argument about the role of unjust enrichment in the recognition of equitable property rights, and has been accompanied by the view that the trusts in question are best seen as

---

404 See paras 15–133 to 15-137.

405 See, e.g. R. Chambers, "Tracing and Unjust Enrichment" in J. W. Neyers et al. (eds), *Understanding Unjust Enrichment* (Hart Publishing, 2004); Birks, "Property and Unjust Enrichment: Categorical Truths" [1997] N.Z.L.R. 623, 661; A. Burrows, *The Law of Restitution*, 2nd edn (Oxford University Press, 2002), pp.64–66 and 208–209.

406 *Janz v McIntosh* (1999) 182 Sask. R. 197.

407 *Louth v Diprose* (1992) 175 C.L.R. 621; *McCulloch v Fern* [2001] NSWSC 406; *Smith v Smith* [2004] N.S.W.S.C. 663. On the Australian law governing unconscionable transactions and the law of unjust enrichment, see M. Bryan "Unjust Enrichment and Unconscionability in Australia: A False Dichotomy?" in Neyers et al., (eds), *Understanding Unjust Enrichment,* (2004).

408 *Neste Oy v Lloyd's Bank Plc* [1983] 2 Lloyds Rep. 658; *Re Farepak Food and Gifts Ltd* [2006] EWHC 3272 (Ch); [2007] 2 B.C.L.C. 1; subsequent proceedings [2009] EWHC 2580 (Ch); [2010] 1 B.C.L.C. 444.

409 *Bailey v Angove's Pty Ltd* [2016] UKSC 47 at [31] (Lord Sumption).

410 See para.20–025.

resulting trusts.[411] Nonetheless, even if the trusts are regarded as constructive in nature, it may still be possible to regard them as responses to unjust enrichment.

As we saw in Chapter 16,[412] there are some general difficulties with the unjust enrichment analysis, both as a matter of authority and of principle. The essential difficulty is in establishing when an unjust enrichment should give rise to a trust, rather than to a personal claim.[413] In *Westdeutsche*, for example, A's intention to make the transfer was vitiated by the mistaken belief that there was a valid contract between the parties, and so it seems clear that B was unjustly enriched at the expense of A, yet no trust arose. Lord Browne-Wilkinson insisted instead that a trust could arise if B's conscience is affected by knowledge of the circumstances making his enrichment unjust, at a time when he still holds the property received from A, or its traceable proceeds. Unjust enrichment is also present in cases where a contract is voidable as a result of an innocent misrepresentation, or where a gift can be rescinded for unilateral mistake, but in each of those cases, a trust can only arise if A elects to set aside the transaction.[414] In *Shalson v Russo*,[415] for example, Rimer J doubted that property received under a fraudulently induced contract is immediately held on trust by the recipient, before any rescission of the contract. **17–224**

It has been argued that an unjust enrichment analysis of these trusts is possible *if* one adopts Lord Browne-Wilkinson's requirement that no trust can arise unless and until B is aware of the facts alleged to affect her conscience.[416] On this view, the presence or absence of this knowledge of B determines if unjust enrichment gives rise to a trust or merely a personal claim.[417] So, where the claimed subject matter of the trust is held by a thief or fraudster herself, a constructive trust arises, as B was necessarily aware of the facts alleged to affect her conscience: A's prior entitlement and the fact that B's acquisition of the property occurred without A's authority. If, in contrast, the claim is based on A's unilateral mistake, or a non-fraudulent misrepresentation by B, then a trust can arise only if B later acquires knowledge of the mistake, or of the falsity of the representation, and still holds the property or its traceable proceeds at that point. **17–225**

Where the transfer occurs under a fraudulently induced contract, two analyses are possible.[418] On one view, there is no immediate trust,[419] as, unless and until the contract is rescinded, it provides a legal basis for B's holding of the property and so means that B is not unjustly enriched. On another view, there is an immediate trust, but A will lose her interest under that trust if A affirms the contract or otherwise loses the right to rescind it. It is certainly worth noting that the right held by A in such a case, even prior to rescission, behaves like a beneficial interest in as much as it is capable of binding **17–226**

---

[411] See, e.g. Chambers, *Resulting Trusts* (1997), Ch.5. For the view that a trust responding to unjust enrichment is necessarily resulting, see the suggestion of Millett J in *El Ajou v Dollar Land Holdings Plc* [1993] 3 All E.R. 717 at 734. Note too *Evans v European Bank Ltd* (2004) 7 I.T.E.L.R. 19 at [112], per Spigelman CJ; Millett, "Tracing the Proceeds of Fraud" (1991) 107 L.Q.R. 71, 81.

[412] See 16–182 to 16-187 and note eg *Shalson v Russo* [2005] Ch. 281 at [111] (Rimer J).

[413] See, e.g. *Scott v Bridge* [2020] EWHC 3116 (Ch) at [131]–[133]. For the argument that B should be subject to a duty to return the specific right acquired from A in cases where it is "necessary to restore [A] to his or her previous condition", because a personal claim against B for the value of that right would not adequately protect A, see J. Edelman, "Restitution of (Property) Rights" in E. Bant and M. Bryan (eds), *Principles of Proprietary Remedies* (Thomson Reuters, 2013).

[414] Prior to such rescission, the claimant has a "mere equity": see further para.20–060.

[415] [2003] EWHC 1637 (Ch); [2005] Ch. 281 at [111].

[416] *Westdeutsche Landesbank Girozentrale v Islington LBC* [1996] A.C. 669 at 705.

[417] See, e.g. *B. McFarlane,* "Trusts and Knowledge: Lessons from Australia" in J. Glister and P. Ridge (eds), *Fault Lines in Equity* (Hart Publishing, 2012). For an argument against this view, see e.g. W. Swadling, "Unjust Enrichment: Value, Rights, and Trusts" (2021) 137 L.Q.R. 56.

[418] For extended discussion, see B. Häcker, *Consequences of Impaired Consent Transfers* (Hart Publishing, 2009), pp.125–159; E. Bant, "Reconsidering the Role of Election in Rescission" (2012) 32 O.J.L.S. 467.

[419] See *Shalson v Russo* [2005] Ch. 281 at [111]. See too B. Häcker, "Proprietary Restitution After Impaired Consent Transfers: A Generalised Power Model" [2009] C.L.J. 324.

third parties, and, unlike a "mere equity", can bind a bona fide purchaser for value of a subsequent equitable interest.[420]

ii. Wrongs?

17–227 Another possible explanation for at least some of the four types of trust considered in this section looks to B's wrongful conduct. Certainly, in a case of fraud or theft, it can be said that B acquired particular rights only by breaching a duty owed to A. A wrongs-based analysis, however, is of no assistance in a case, such as *Chase Manhattan Bank v Israel-British Bank (London) Ltd*,[421] in which A simply makes a unilateral mistake when transferring rights to B. It should also be noted that there is clearly no general principle that a constructive trust arises in A's favour whenever B acquires property by committing a wrong against A. For example, damages based on B's gain rather than A's loss are only very rarely awarded in response to a tort or a breach of contract,[422] and it would be a step still further to say that B should also hold any profits gained through a wrong on trust for A.

iii. Enforcing a Subsisting Property Right?

17–228 We noted above[423] that, when considering the final type of the four trusts considered here, the House of Lords in *Foskett v McKeown*[424] regarded it as giving effect to a beneficiary's subsisting equitable property right. We also noted some important problems with such a view. Similarly, we have also seen that,[425] in *Westdeutsche Landesbank Girozentrale v Islington LBC*,[426] Lord Browne-Wilkinson held that Goulding J had erred in assuming that the trust arising in the case of a mistaken payment was based on a retention of an equitable property right by the payor. The point is that, whilst each of the four types of trust considered in this section has the *effect* of giving some protection to an initial right of A, that does not mean that each can be justified purely by referring to the existence of such a right.[427] The third type of constructive trust considered here, arising where C receives trust property through an unauthorised disposition by T, might seem to be a straightforward case of the assertion of a pre-existing equitable interest. Even in that case, however, we have noted[428] a disagreement between Lloyd LJ[429] and Lord Browne-Wilkinson[430] as to whether a further fact (C's knowledge of the initial trust) is required before a trust can arise.

---

420 See, e.g. *Car & Universal Finance v Caldwell* [1965] 1 Q.B. 525.
421 [1981] Ch. 105.
422 In *Attorney General v Blake* [2001] 1 A.C. 268, for example, the House of Lords, in awarding such damages, was at pains to emphasise the exceptional nature of the award: see, e.g. per Lord Nicholls at 284–285.
423 See paras 17–219ff.
424 [2001] 1 A.C. 102.
425 See para.17–228.
426 [1996] A.C. 669.
427 Although, as noted at para. 15–154, it may be possible to look to the specific reasons for a party's initial interest and then consider if those reasons continue to apply to justify the acquisition of a right in relation to different property.
428 See para.17–217.
429 In *Independent Trustee Services Ltd v GP Noble Trustees Ltd* [2013] Ch. 91 at [80].
430 In *Westdeutsche Landesbank Girozentrale v Islington LBC* [1996] A.C. 669 at 705.

11. Explaining Constructive Trusts: General Themes?

A. The Diversity of Constructive Trusts

This chapter has demonstrated the truth of the point made at its start: constructive trusts arise in a very diverse set of circumstances. This means that, in seeking to explain or justify why such trusts arise, it is best to break down the inquiry by looking at specific types of constructive trust. **17–229**

It is certainly hard to formulate a workable *positive* thesis as to why all constructive trusts arise. For example, it has often been said that unconscionability is at the heart of the constructive trust[431] or, similarly, that such trusts arise where "the defendant has acquired property in circumstances where it would be inequitable to allow him to treat it as his own."[432] The difficulty here is that broad concepts such as unconscionability or inequity, by themselves, can only state a conclusion: they cannot provide reasons for which that conclusion was reached.[433] As Lord Briggs has noted extra-judicially: "Unconscionable conduct may be a minimum condition, but never a sufficient condition, for the intervention of equity."[434] Broad concepts may also confuse the question of why B is under a duty to A with the crucial question of why that duty gives rise to a trust, rather than to a merely personal claim. More specifically, it has been suggested, principally in jurisdictions other than England, that constructive trusts are based on unjust enrichment. As noted in this chapter,[435] that concept may have a role to play in relation to some constructive trusts, but it clearly cannot explain those trusts where the content of A's rights depends not on the extent of the benefit acquired by B, but on the content of the promise made B, or on the extent of any detrimental reliance by A or another party. **17–230**

It is similarly difficult to support a *negative* thesis as to the basis of all constructive trusts. For example, it has sometimes been said that constructive trusts, in contrast to express or resulting trusts, are *not* concerned with the intention of the parties, but are instead imposed "against the intentions of the trustee".[436] Nevertheless it can be argued that in all of the cases discussed in Sections 4–8 of this chapter, as well as the constructive trust cases based on the principle in *Re Rose*,[437] mutual wills,[438] and secret trusts,[439] constructive trusts were imposed in order to give effect to an intention that the beneficiary of the constructive trust should acquire an interest in property, whether outright or under a trust.[440] **17–231**

---

431 See, e.g. the famous statement of Judge Cardozo in *Beatty v Guggenheim Exploration Co* (1919) 225 N.Y. 380 at 386: "a constructive trust is the formula through which the conscience of equity finds expression."

432 *Banner Homes Group Plc v Luff Developments Ltd* [2000] Ch. 372 at 400 per Chadwick LJ; also *Gissing v Gissing* [1971] A.C. 886 at 905 per Lord Diplock; *Paragon Finance Plc v DB Thakerar & Co* [1999] 1 All E.R. 400 at 408–409, per Millett LJ.

433 See, e.g. Smith, "Fusion and Tradition" in Degeling and Edelman (eds), *Equity in Commercial Law* (2005).

434 Lord Briggs, "Equity in Business" (2019) 135 L.Q.R. 567, 583.

435 See paras 17–223 to 17–226.

436 *Westdeutsche Landesbank Girozentrale v Islington LBC* [1996] A.C. 669 at 708, per Lord Browne-Wilkinson. See too *Rathwell v Rathwell* [1978] 2 S.C.R. 436 at 454, per Dickson J; *Air Jamaica Ltd v Charlton* [1999] 1 W.L.R. 1399 at 1512, per Lord Millett.

437 See paras 5–023ff.

438 See paras 6–172ff.

439 See paras 6–129ff.

440 In the terminology of G. Elias, *Explaining Constructive Trusts* (Clarendon Press, 1990), such constructive trusts are "perfectionary" as they give effect to a party's intention. See too R. Chambers, "Constructive Trusts in Canada" (1999) 37 Alberta L.R. 173, reprinted in (2001) 15 Tru L.I. 215 and (2002) 16 Tru. L.I. 2; *Bathurst CC v PWC Properties Pty Ltd* (1998) 195 C.L.R. 566 at [39]; *Paragon Finance Plc v DB Thakerar & Co* [1999] 1 All E.R. 400 at 408–409.

17–232 Of course, if a party has successfully exercised her power to set up a trust, and there are no formality requirements preventing proof of that trust, there is no need for a constructive trust. We have seen cases, however, in which an intention to create a trust was present, but it was not possible for the claimant to prove that an express trust was created.[441] In such cases, it seems, a constructive trust may still arise; but not *simply* as a result of the initial intention to create a trust. There must be some other factor which justifies the imposition of a constructive trust: as we have seen, it has been variously suggested that such a factor may be constituted by fraud,[442] detrimental reliance,[443] or the acquisition of an advantage by the defendant in relation to the receipt of property.[444]

B. A Common Thread?

17–233 It seems that asking why constructive trusts arise is rather like asking why a court awards damages. A damages award can be made on many different grounds: as a result of a contract; a non-contractual promise which is nonetheless binding; proprietary estoppel; a tort or a breach of contract; unjust enrichment; public policy, etc. The same is true of a constructive trusts. The common thread in such trusts is to do with the *content* of the claimant's right, not the basis on which it was acquired. If a constructive trust arises, the claimant has a beneficial interest in property, with all the advantages flowing from that.[445] So a general theme, relevant to all constructive trusts, is to ask why the claimant acquires such an interest, rather than a mere personal claim against the defendant.

17–234 One way of approaching this question is to look at the precise content of the defendant's duty, and to distinguish between cases where that duty does, or does not, relate to specific rights held by the defendant. For example, it is clear that, if the duty does not relate to specific rights, no constructive trust can arise. In *Re Goldcorp's Exchange Ltd*,[446] for example, the defendant had made a contractual promise to transfer ownership of gold bullion to the claimant. No legal title to property passed under the contract, however, because the promise did not relate to any specific or ascertained gold. For the same reason, no constructive trust of any bullion arose, even though the defendant had behaved badly in leading the claimant to believe that it would hold specific gold at the claimant's instructions. The problem for the claimant was that the defendant's contractual duty was simply to provide that quantity of gold, and so the duty did not relate to any *specific* rights held by the defendant. In contrast, in the type of constructive trust arising in a specifically enforceable contract to transfer property,[447] the defendant's duty clearly does relate to specific property.

17–235 Indeed, in the cases reviewed in this chapter where a constructive trust does arise, it is generally clear that the defendant's duty does relate to specific property held by the defendant. In many cases, this is because the defendant's duty is based on a promise, and that promise related to specific property that the defendant held at the time, or now holds. The more difficult cases, then, are where no such promise has been made. This is why cases involving unjust enrichment, or wrongful conduct (such as the receipt of a bribe) are more controversial. In those cases, however, it may be that Lord

---

441 See paras 17–077ff.

442 See, e.g. N. Hopkins, "Conscience, Discretion and the Creation of Property Rights" (2006) 26 L.S. 475; W. Swadling, "The Nature of the Trust in *Rochefoucauld v Boustead*" in Mitchell (ed.), *Constructive and Resulting Trusts* (2010) (although of course on Swadling's view the trust is an express one, with fraud operating so as to prevent the defendant relying on s.53(1)(b) of the Law of Property Act 1925 to object to the oral proof of the express trust).

443 See, e.g. S. Gardner, "Reliance-Based Constructive Trusts" in Mitchell (ed.), *Constructive and Resulting Trusts* (2010).

444 See, e.g. B. McFarlane, "Constructive Trusts Arising on Receipt of Property *Sub Conditione*" (2004) 120 L.Q.R. 667.

445 For which see para.12–003.

446 [1995] 1 A.C. 74. See para.17–075.

447 See paras 17–061 to 17–071.

Browne-Wilkinson's analysis in *Westdeutsche*,[448] albeit criticised in some quarters,[449] provides some assistance. The idea is that a trust involves the trustee's being under a duty not to use property for her own benefit (unless and to the extent permitted by the terms of the trust). For such a duty to arise, the defendant must be aware of the facts giving rise to the duty; if not, it would be unfair to say that the defendant somehow behaves wrongfully by using that property as her own. On that view, for example, the trust in the *Chase Manhattan* case was justified only from the point where the recipient bank discovered the mistake of the claimant,[450] but it is clear that a fiduciary who knowingly accepts a bribe holds it on trust from the moment when it is received.[451] The most difficult question,[452] which may be crucial for the future development of constructive trusts, is whether Lord Browne-Wilkinson's analysis is purely negative, so that no constructive trust can arise in the absence of such knowledge, or whether it can be used to support a positive formula, under which such a trust arises if: (i) the grounds on which the defendant's duty arises demand that the duty is one not to use specific property held by the defendant for the defendant's own benefit;[453] *and* (ii) the defendant is aware of the facts constituting the grounds on which that duty arises.[454]

Questions

1. Is the imposition of a constructive trust on the profits of a breach of fiduciary duty fair to the creditors of the fiduciary?
2. A specifically enforceable contract for the sale of land certainly gives the purchaser some equitable property rights, but it would be a mistake to say that those rights amount to a beneficial interest under a trust." **Do you agree?**
3. "The decisions in *Stack v Dowden* and *Jones v Kernott* have made the law less clear, without making it significantly more fair." **Do you agree?**
4. To what extent, if at all, do the trusts recognised in *Rochefoucauld v Boustead* and *Pallant v Morgan* have a common basis?
5. "The constructive trust plays an important role in protecting a party with a legal property right against the consequences of fraud." Do you agree?

---

448 [1996] A.C. 669 at [705].

449 See, e.g. W. Swadling, "Property and Conscience" (1998) 12 Tru. L.I. 228; *Meagher, Gummow & Lehane's Equity: Doctrines and Remedies*, 5th edn (LexisNexis, 2015), para.14–010.

450 See the analysis of Lord Browne-Wilkinson in *Westdeutsche Landesbank Girozentrale v Islington LBC* [1996] A.C. 669 at 714–715.

451 As was held by the Supreme Court in *FHR European Ventures LLP v Cedar Capital Partners LLC* [2015] A.C. 250.

452 For consideration of this question, see, e.g. B. McFarlane, "Trusts and Knowledge: Lessons from Australia" in J. Glister and P. Ridge (eds), *Fault Lines in Equity* (Hart Publishing, 2012).

453 There may of course be cases in which the grounds on which the duty arises are not inconsistent with the defendant using the property to her own benefit, to some extent: so the *Pallant v Morgan* equity can arise where the defendant's promise was that the parties would divide up the benefit of particular property (as in the case itself: [1953] Ch. 43), and a common intention constructive trust can arise where the common intention was that each party should have a share of the beneficial interest. A trust may still arise in such cases as the promise or common intention controls the extent to which the defendant can use the property for her own benefit.

454 For an example of a trust arising consistently with that positive formula, see *Ali v Dinc* [2020] EWHC 3055 (Ch) at [222]–[223]: where B had received rights from A under a void contract, and still had those rights when aware that the contract was void, a trust of those rights in favour of A could be recognised.

PART VI

EQUITABLE REMEDIES

18

EQUITABLE MONEY REMEDIES

1. Overview

This chapter concerns the courts' equitable jurisdiction to order defendants to pay money to claimants. Orders of this kind are "personal" remedies, in the sense that they place a defendant under a personal obligation to pay, which the defendant can satisfy by using any of the resources at her disposal. They can be supported by, but should be distinguished from, declarations that particular property owned by a defendant is impressed with an equitable lien to secure the performance of a defendant's obligation. In the event of a defendant's insolvency, a claimant who has won a personal money award is unlikely to recover the full amount, as her right is no stronger than that of any unsecured creditor. In contrast, a claimant with an equitable lien over property owned by a defendant can obtain an order for sale and insist on being paid first out of the sale proceeds. Further, if the value of the relevant property is less than the amount secured by the lien, she can take the whole of the sale proceeds and make a personal claim for the balance as well, since an equitable lien is "a cumulative remedy in aid of an equitable *in personam* claim, not an alternative remedy".[1] **18–001**

This chapter examines three types of equitable money remedy: equitable compensation, equitable damages in lieu of an injunction or specific performance, and an account of profits.[2] For reasons we will discuss, the law governing the circumstances in which such awards can be made, and the principles governing their assessment, have changed over the past hundred years and are still changing. Two points recur in the discussion: first, the courts now recognise a wide variety of different equitable claims which can lead to the award of money remedies and they acknowledge that it may be apt to apply different assessment principles in different classes of case; and, second, when selecting which rule to apply in a given case it may be helpful to analogise with other cases where similar awards have been made in equity and/or common law, but care must be taken when selecting an appropriate comparator from the range of possibilities. In a brief section at the end of the chapter we finally consider whether there also exists an equitable jurisdiction to award exemplary damages. **18–002**

---

1 *Serious Fraud Office v Lexi Holdings Plc (in administration)* [2008] EWCA Crim 1443; [2009] Q.B. 376 at [40].

2 These are not the only types of equitable money award that can be made. Some others are discussed in J. Hudson, "Equitable Compensation for Equitable Estoppels" and E. Bant, "Rescission, Restitution and Compensation", both in S. Degeling and J. Varuhas (eds), *Equitable Compensation and Disgorgement of Profit* (Hart Publishing, 2017).

2. Equitable Compensation

A. Introduction

18–003 To understand the law governing equitable compensation it is essential to grasp that such awards are not assessed by reference to a single set of rules. Consider claims that trustees should reconstitute trust funds depleted by unauthorised disposals of property, claims that trustees should make good loss caused by their negligence, claims that knowing recipients of misapplied trust property should reconstitute depleted trust funds, claims that dishonest assistants in a breach of trust should make good loss flowing from the trustees' unauthorised or negligent conduct, claims that fiduciaries should pay compensation for loss caused by breaches of fiduciary duty, and claims that recipients of confidential information should pay compensation for loss caused by breach of an equitable duty of confidence. The term "equitable compensation" is now often used to describe awards made in all these cases. However, it would be surprising if all such awards were calculated in the same way, given the differences that exist between all these claims, and in fact, it is now generally recognised that different rules may govern the quantification of awards in different types of case. Given that most of the claims developed in separate streams of authority, it might seem that this is hardly worth saying. During the 1990s, however, various Commonwealth courts held that awards of equitable compensation were governed by a single, one-size-fits-all, set of rules and it is only in more recent times that the courts have disavowed such statements as over-generalised and have held that a more nuanced approach is needed that aligns the rules governing quantification of remedy with the reasons why claims lie in different situations.

18–004 Historically, awards against trustees were made in line with trust accounting procedures that were not expressed in the language of "equitable compensation" but in the language of "falsifying" and "surcharging" trust accounts, as discussed in Chapter 13.[3] Historically, awards against knowing recipients and dishonest assistants were described in similar terms because liability for these wrongs was conceived as an extension of the liabilities owed by trustees, as noted in Chapter 14.[4] Meanwhile, the "no conflicts" rule to which fiduciaries are subject was not originally conceptualised as a rule that imposed a primary duty on a fiduciary to avoid conflicts of interest, breach of which triggered a secondary duty to pay compensation for loss, but as a rule which disabled the fiduciary from validly contracting with her principal.[5] On this view, no question arose of a fiduciary incurring compensatory liability for breach of duty, and it was only in the late 1900s that compensatory awards for breach of fiduciary duty began to be made on a large scale, forcing the courts to consider for the first time whether such awards should be subject to the same or different assessment rules as compensatory awards in other types of case. A similar point can be made about the rules governing the equitable duty of confidence which were first conceptualised as rules which disabled the recipients of confidential information from using it in certain ways, rather than as rules which might generate a compensatory liability.

18–005 It is only recently, therefore, that the courts have come to recognise that non-compliance with various equitable rules *can* lead to compensatory liability, and, further, that although it is sometimes appropriate to calculate the amount payable in the same way in different types of case, it is sometimes better to proceed differently. So, for example, it is now generally accepted that trustees typically owe different types of duty, breach of which can result in awards being made that are quantified in

---

3 See paras 13–111 to 13–122.

4 See paras 14–004 to 14–007 and 14–010.

5 For further discussion see paras 2–158 to 2–163.

accordance with several sets of principles. These include a duty to preserve the trust property except insofar as the trust terms permit the trustee to do otherwise and to use her powers as property owner only in ways that are authorised by the trust terms; a duty to act with reasonable care and skill; and a duty to avoid conflicts between the trustee's personal interests and the beneficiaries' interests and between the beneficiaries' interests and those of other people.[6]

The rules governing compensatory awards for breaches of the first two trustee duties are discussed in Chapter 13,[7] but in this section we discuss compensatory awards for the third, bearing in mind that breach of fiduciary duty is an equitable wrong which may be committed not only by trustees but also by other fiduciaries, as noted in Chapter 2;[8] we also discuss equitable compensation for breach of an equitable duty of confidence, the elements of which are discussed in Chapter 3.[9] **18–006**

B. Breach of Fiduciary Duty

i. Historical Development

The source of the rule entitling a principal to recover equitable compensation for breach of fiduciary duty is widely taken[10] to be *Nocton v Lord Ashburton*.[11] The claimant released a security over land belonging to a third party at the request of the defendant, who was the claimant's solicitor, and who had a second security over the land, the priority status of which was thereby advanced. The third party defaulted on his debt to the claimant, who successfully sued the defendant for the amount of his loss. Viscount Haldane LC held this result to follow from the fact that the defendant had breached his fiduciary duty, observing that:[12] **18–007**

> When, as in the case before us, a solicitor has had financial transactions with his client . . . a Court of Equity has always assumed jurisdiction to scrutinize his action . . . and in proper cases to order the solicitor to replace property improperly acquired from the client, or to make compensation if he had lost it by acting in breach of a duty which arose out of his confidential relationship to the man who had trusted him.

In this passage Viscount Haldane refers to earlier cases which established a number of connected rules: if a principal contracts with her fiduciary she may later be able to rescind the contract and if she has transferred legal title to property to the fiduciary under the contract then a trust may be retrospectively imposed on the property and the principal may then be entitled to an order that the legal title must be transferred back to her; if this is impossible because the fiduciary has resold the property to a bona fide purchaser, the principal can either claim the proceeds of the resale[13] or claim a money sum representing the current value of the property. The term "pecuniary rescission" has been used to describe awards of the latter type. These are compensatory, but their aim is not to compensate the **18–008**

---

6 *Bank of New Zealand v New Zealand Guardian Trust Co Ltd* [1999] 1 N.Z.L.R. 664 at 687; *Libertarian Investments Ltd v Hall* (2013) 16 H.K.C.F.A.R. 681 at [75]; *AIB Group (UK) Plc v Mark Re dler & Co Solicitors* [2014] UKSC 58;[2015] A.C. 1503 at [51]; *Zhang Hong Li v DBS Bank (Hong Kong) Ltd* (2019) 22 H.K.C.F.A.R. 392 at [115]–[120]; *Sim Poh Ping v Winsta Holding Pte Ltd* [2020] 1 S.L.R. 1199 at [86]–[126].

7 See paras 13–009 to 13–110.

8 See paras 2–164 to 2–194.

9 See paras 3–034 to 3–136.

10 e.g. *Breen v Williams* (1996) 186 C.L.R. 71 at 135–136; *Swindle v Harrison* [1997] 4 All E.R. 705 at 731–732; *Canson Enterprises Ltd v Boughton & Co* [1991] 3 S.C.R. 534 at 570; *Maguire v Makaronis* (1997) 188 C.L.R. 449 at 468–469.

11 [1914] A.C. 932.

12 [1914] A.C. 932 at 956–957.

13 *Ladywell Mining Co v Brookes* (1887) 35 Ch. D. 400 at 418.

principal for every loss caused by the fiduciary's breach of duty, but only to make the fiduciary pay the money value of the property that she would have had to return, had she not put this beyond her power by selling it to a bona fide purchaser. In other words, the fiduciary is ordered to pay the money as a form of substitutive performance of her duty to return the property *in specie*.[14]

18–009 *Nocton* was not a case in which property passed between the parties under a contract which the principal sought to rescind, and so the court's finding that the defendant was liable to compensate the claimant marked a new departure for the law, i.e. the court recognised a different type of remedy, assessed by reference to different principles. In the extra-judicial words of an Australian judge, Justice Gummow:[15]

> [The issues raised by "pecuniary rescission" cases] . . . do not arise where no property has passed between principal and fiduciary or vice versa and loss has been sustained by other means, for example, advice given in breach of duty. In such cases, and *Nocton v Lord Ashburton* may be considered one of them, greater assistance may be found in the common law principles regulating claims in tort or, perhaps, contract. In *Nocton v Lord Ashburton* the Court of Appeal had found deceit and awarded damages. While the House of Lords reversed that finding and Lord Haldane[16] said that the measure of damages in equity might not always be the same as in an action in deceit, he also said "in this case the question is of form only". Lord Dunedin said the equitable remedy would "practically come to much the same".[17]

18–010 The Commonwealth courts were slow to follow the lead established by *Nocton*, and it was not until the last decades of the twentieth century that they began to make awards of equitable compensation for breach of fiduciary duty on a regular basis. As a result, various questions about the assessment of such awards still await an answer. A significant barrier to the resolution of these issues has been the widespread misapprehension that "equitable compensation" is a remedy that operates in the same way in every case where a defendant has breached an equitable duty. This has led some courts to draw the wrong conclusion that equitable compensation awards for breach of fiduciary duty should be assessed in the same way as substitutive performance claims against trustees who have misapplied trust property.[18] It has also led them to form the mistaken belief that causation and remoteness are "common law concepts" that are irrelevant to compensatory awards for breach of fiduciary duty. This is discussed in the following excerpt.

C. Mitchell, "Equitable Compensation for Breach of Fiduciary Duty"

(2013) 66 C.L.P. 307, 19–20

18–011 [In] McLachlin J.'s minority concurring judgment in *Canson Enterprises Ltd v Boughton*[19] . . . she said that by analogy with "restitution" awards (by which she meant orders that a defaulting trustee should reconstitute the trust fund), the award of equitable compensation for breach of fiduciary duty also seeks "to restore to the plaintiff what has been lost as a result of the breach". However, she added that "the losses made good

---

14 *Re Leeds and Hanley Theatres of Varieties Ltd* [1902] Ch. 809; *McKenzie v McDonald* [1927] V.L.R. 134; *Coleman v Myers* [1977] 2 N.Z.L.R. 225 at 359–362 and 379; *Bristol & West Building Soc v Mothew* [1998] Ch. 1 at 17; *Mahoney v Purnell* [1996] 3 All E.R. 61 at 86–91.

15 The Hon Mr Justice Gummow, "Compensation for Breach of Fiduciary Duty" in T.G. Youdan (ed.), *Equity, Fiduciaries and Trusts* (Carswell, 1989), p.74. See also V. Vann, *Equitable Compensation in Australia: Principles and Problems* (Saarbrücken, 2009), pp.71–75.

16 [1914] A.C. 932 at 958.

17 Ibid. at 965.

18 For which see paras 13–009 to 13–089.

19 [1991] 3 S.C.R. 534 at 555.

are only those which, on a common sense view of causation, were caused by the breach". Steven Elliott and James Edelman comment that this reasoning runs:[20]

> "reparative and substitutive thinking together. In effect McLachlin J. wished to distinguish equitable compensation from common law damages on the basis that it is substitutive rather than reparative, but she was unable to make the analogy with restitution of trust property work because she could not convincingly describe the object of the substitution. Her Ladyship inevitably ended with a reparative model confusingly clothed in substitutive language."

The same criticism can be made of many Australian cases in which the courts have purported to analyse reparation claims for breach of fiduciary duty as though they were substitutive compensation claims to reconstitute a trust fund.[21] Typically they cite Street J.'s dicta in *Re Dawson*[22] about the reconstitution of trust funds, along with McLachlin J.'s judgment in *Canson* and Lord Browne-Wilkinson's speech in *Target Holdings Ltd v Redferns*,[23] as authority for the following propositions: because claims for equitable compensation for breach of fiduciary duty resemble claims to reconstitute a trust fund, the relevant question "is not whether the loss was caused by or flowed from the breach" and so "principles governing remoteness of damages" are irrelevant;[24] hence, also, "there is no translation into this field of discourse of the doctrine of novus actus interveniens";[25] but on the other hand, the court must still decide whether the fiduciary's breach of duty and the principal's loss were connected, using a "common sense" approach to causation with the full benefit of hindsight. These propositions are inconsistent because they are not founded on a single idea of the fiduciary's liability. They are also incoherent: it makes no sense to say, as Ipp J. has felt constrained to say, that:[26] **18–012**

> "I am required by the rules of equity, in assessing compensation, to leave aside questions of causation (save that compensation will only be awarded for losses caused by the breach of fiduciary duties)."

The Australian courts have tried to paper over the cracks in their theory by appealing to a grand but vague idea that equity does things differently from the common law, and that "common law concepts" of causation and remoteness are irrelevant to claims for equitable compensation.[27] Lionel Smith has observed that this reasoning will not do, either, not because it asserts that equity and the common law can do things differently, but because it ignores the differences between distinct types of equitable claim.[28] . . . The courts of every Commonwealth jurisdiction would do much better to recognize that the rules governing claims to reconstitute trust funds do not apply to claims for equitable compensation for breach of fiduciary duty. **18–013**

For these reasons, we share Justice Gummow's view, quoted above, that when asking what causation and remoteness rules govern equitable compensation claims for breach of fiduciary duty, analogies can more usefully be drawn with damages claims in tort than with claims against **18–014**

---

20 S.B. Elliott and J. Edelman, "Money Remedies against Trustees" (2004) 18 Tru. L.I. 116, pp.122–3. See too L. Smith, "The Measurement of Compensation Claims against Trustees and Fiduciaries" in E. Bant and M. Harding (eds), *Exploring Private Law* (2010), pp. 372–73.

21 e.g. *Hill v Rose* [1990] V.R. 129; *Gemstone Corp of Australia Ltd v Grasso* (1994) 13 A.C.S.R. 695 at 714; *O'Halloran v RT Thomas & Family Pty Ltd* (1998) 45 N.S.W.L.R. 262 at 272–73; *Aequitas v Sparad No.100 Ltd* (2001) 19 A.C.L.C. 1006 at [442]; *WA Fork Truck Distributors Pty Ltd v Jones* [2003] WASC 102 at [104]–[105]; *GM & AM Pearce & Co Pty Ltd v Australian Tallow Producers* [2005] VSCA 113 at [65]; *V-Flow Pty Ltd v Holyoake Industries (Vic) Pty Ltd* [2013] FCAFC 16 at [56]. For critical comment, see V. Vann, *Equitable Compensation in Australia: Principles and Problems* (2009), Ch.3, esp. pp.106–07.

22 [1966] 2 N.S.W.R. 211.

23 *Target Holdings Ltd v Redferns* [1996] 1 A.C. 421.

24 *Hill* at 144.

25 *Maguire v Makaronis* (1997) 188 C.L.R. 449 at 470.

26 *Biala Pty Ltd v Mallina Holdings Ltd* (1993) 13 W.A.R. 11 at 77–78.

27 *Canson* at 556; *Hill* at 144; *O'Halloran* at 273; *Harrison v Schipp* [2001] NSWCA 13 at [123]; *Re Purcom No 34 Pty Ltd (in liq) (No.2)* [2010] FCA 624 at [23]; *Secure Parking (WA) Pty Ltd v Wilson* [2012] WASCA 230 at [76]; *Michael Wilson & Partners Ltd* [2012] NSWCA 383 at [171].

28 Smith at p. 369. His criticism is aimed at McLachlin J.'s judgment in *Canson*, but it applies with equal force to the other cases cited in the previous footnote.

trustees following an unauthorised transfer of trust property, which are claims of a fundamentally different kind.[29]

ii. Causation

18–015 A principal seeking equitable compensation for breach of fiduciary duty must show that she suffered damage that was caused by the breach. As Mummery LJ held in *Swindle v Harrison*, "there is no equitable by-pass of the need to establish causation".[30] Harrison borrowed £180,000 from a loan company to buy a hotel. The loan was secured by a charge on her house. When the time came for completion, she was £75,000 short and so she took a bridging loan from her solicitor, Swindle, believing that she would be able to borrow this sum from a brewery later on. The bridging loan was secured by a charge on the hotel. Swindle failed to tell her that his firm was making a profit on this arrangement. Nor did he tell her that a loan from the brewery was unlikely to be forthcoming, as in fact turned out to be the case. Harrison's business failed and she defaulted on her debts. The loan company took her house, and Swindle sought possession of the hotel. She counter-claimed, arguing that Swindle's breach of duty had caused her to lose the value of the equity that she had formerly had in her house. The Court of Appeal accepted that he had breached his fiduciary duty, but held that even so the counterclaim failed. The judges gave different reasons for this, but each stressed that Harrison would have gone ahead with the purchase even if Swindle had committed no breach of duty, because she would have forfeited her deposit if she had not completed the hotel purchase, and she could not have borrowed the money elsewhere.

18–016 Does it suffice for a principal to show that her fiduciary's breach of duty was a material cause of her loss, or can the fiduciary escape liability if she can show that the principal would have entered the impugned transaction anyway? In *Brickenden v London Loan & Savings Co*,[31] the Privy Council took the former view. The claimant finance company lent money to a couple named Biggs. The defendant solicitor acted for the claimant in the transaction. He failed to disclose that Biggs owed him debts, which Biggs was able to repay with the loan money received from the claimant. The Biggses defaulted and the court ordered the defendant to compensate the claimant for the full amount of the loan. Lord Thankerton held that:[32]

> When a party, holding a fiduciary relationship, commits a breach of his duty by non-disclosure of material facts, which his constituent is entitled to know in connection with the transaction, he cannot be heard to maintain that disclosure would not have altered the decision to proceed with the transaction, because the constituent's action would be solely determined by some other factor, such as the valuation by another party of the property proposed to be mortgaged. Once the court has determined that the non-disclosed facts were material, speculation as to what course the constituent, on disclosure, would have taken is not relevant.

18–017 As we discuss below, a similar rule prevents fiduciaries from avoiding liability for gains by arguing that they would have made these even if they had performed their fiduciary duty.[33] But as Justice Heydon has extra-judicially observed, "it is one thing to strip a fiduciary of profit without much

---

29 As emphasised in *Sim Poh Ping v Winsta Holding Pte Ltd* [2020] 1 S.L.R. 1199 at [99]–[103].
30 [1997] 4 All E.R. 705 at 733.
31 [1934] 3 D.L.R. 465.
32 [1934] 3 D.L.R. 465 at 469.
33 See para.18–078.

inquiry . . . [and] another to hold him accountable for all loss without inquiry into relative causes."[34] Later courts have interpreted Lord Thankerton's words narrowly, to mean that they may not speculate as to the course a principal would otherwise have taken, but that a fiduciary can escape liability if she can prove that principal would not have acted any differently. This was the result of *Swindle*, and of other cases, including *Sim Poh Ping v Winsta Holding Pte Ltd*, where the Singapore Court of Appeal held that the rule governing causation in this context is that:[35]

> the principal bears the legal burden of establishing its claim, but the legal burden of proof of showing that the loss would have been sustained by the principal even if the fiduciary had not breached his or her fiduciary duty falls on the fiduciary.

Where a principal would not have entered an impugned transaction, but for the breach of fiduciary duty, a further question arises, as to what the principal would have done instead. The evidence may show that the principal would have maintained the status quo ante (i.e. would not have entered *any* transaction), and in such cases the principal can recover all the losses caused by the fiduciary's breach of duty (subject to any applicable remoteness cap).[36] In *Hodgkinson v Simms*, La Forest J stated that this should be presumed in every case,[37] but Sirko Harder has rightly observed that this will not do as a default rule because it does not always follow from the fact that a principal would not have entered the impugned transaction that he would not have entered *any* transaction.[38] Where the evidence shows that the principal would have entered into an alternative transaction, this should be taken into account when assessing compensation. **18–018**

iii. Remoteness and Intervening Cause

Should compensatory claims for breach of fiduciary duty be contained by a remoteness rule, and if so, what rule should this be? In our view, it would be appropriate for the courts to apply a remoteness rule, but to use a "directness" rule rather than a "reasonable foreseeability" rule, drawing an analogy with the remoteness rule that contains tortious liability for the tort of deceit[39] rather than the "reasonable foreseeability of damage" rule that contains liability for the tort of negligence.[40] Adoption of either test would produce the same results in many cases, but this might depend on how the claimant's loss were characterised for the purposes of a test which required the loss to be reasonably foreseeable rather than direct. For example, in *Schmidt v AHRKalimpa Pty Ltd*,[41] the defendant was liable to compensate the claimants for the loss of a misappropriated business and on the facts, the type of loss sustained by the claimants might or might not have been reasonably foreseeable, depending on how broad a view it was appropriate for the court to take of "loss of business". **18–019**

If our preferred remoteness test were adopted, then the courts should hold that loss is not too remote to be recoverable regardless of whether it is the type of damage one would expect, provided **18–020**

---

34 J.D. Heydon, "Causal Relationships Between a Fiduciary's Default and the Principal's Loss' (1994) 110 L.Q.R. 328, 332.

35 [2020] 1 S.L.R. 1199 at [240]. There is a detailed review of relevant case law and principles at [128]–[248]. See too J. Glister, "Equitable Compensation" in J. Glister and P. Ridge (eds), *Fault Lines in Equity* (2012), pp.162–167.

36 See, e.g. *Morkot v Watson & Brown Solicitors* [2014] EWHC 3439 (QB); [2015] P.N.L.R. 9 at [64]ff.

37 [1994] 3 S.C.R. 377 at 440–441.

38 S. Harder, "Equitable Compensation for a Fiduciary's Non-Disclosure and Hypothetical Courses of Events" (2011) 5 J. Eq. 22. See too S.M. Waddams, "Fiduciary Duties and Equitable Compensation" (1996) 27 Can. Bus. L.J. 466, 468; and cf *Stevens v Premium Real Estate Ltd* [2009] 2 N.Z.L.R. 284.

39 *Smith New Court Securities Ltd v Citibank NA* [1997] A.C. 254.

40 *Overseas Tankship (UK) Ltd v Morts Dock & Engineering Co Ltd (The Wagon Mound) (No.1)* [1961] A.C. 388.

41 [2020] VSCA 193.

that it is caused by the fiduciary's breach of duty and is not due to the operation of independent causes with no connection to the breach.[42] This would be consistent with the result in *Canson Enterprises Ltd v Boughton & Co.*[43] The defendant solicitor acted for the claimant company in the purchase of land for development. He failed to disclose that there had been an intermediate sale that had realised a profit of CAD 115,000 for the intermediate purchaser. The claimant would not have gone ahead with the deal if it had been aware of this. Following acquisition of the land the claimant employed engineers and contractors to construct a building on the property, work which was done negligently. The claimant won damages from them but failed to enforce its judgment. So it sued the solicitor, arguing that the losses flowing from the builders' negligence had been caused by his breach of fiduciary duty. The Supreme Court of Canada denied recovery, in effect because the negligence had been an intervening act that was a more proximate cause of the claimant's loss than the solicitor's breach of duty.[44]

iv. Contributory Fault

18–021 In *Day v Mead*,[45] the claimant invested money in a company that went into receivership the following year. He did so on the advice of the defendant solicitor, who was a director of the company and had other conflicts of interest. The trial judge awarded compensation for breach of fiduciary duty, but reduced the sum payable on the basis that the claimant had acted imprudently in failing to obtain independent and competent financial advice before making such a large investment. This was upheld by the New Zealand Court of Appeal, where Cooke P said that:[46]

> Whether or not there are reported cases in which compensation for breach of a fiduciary obligation has been assessed on the footing that the plaintiff should accept some share of the responsibility, there appears to be no solid reason for denying jurisdiction to follow that obviously just course . . . Of course, before reducing an award on the ground that the claimant has been partly the author of his or her own loss, the court will have to give much weight to the well established principle that, largely for exemplary purposes, high standards are expected of fiduciaries. A strong case is needed to relieve the fiduciary of complete responsibility.

18–022 This has also been accepted in Canada, where the courts have held that recovery may be reduced where the principal has "failed to take some reasonable step that might have reduced or eliminated the loss"[47] and that "losses that are the result of the plaintiffs' unreasonable actions may be barred".[48]

18–023 In contrast, the Australian courts have held that the compensation payable by a defaulting fiduciary should never be reduced on the ground that the principal contributed to his loss in a blameworthy way. In *Pilmer v Duke Group Ltd (In Liquidation)*,[49] the majority considered that this idea suffered from "severe conceptual difficulties". These were essentially the same as those which had previously been identified by Justice Gummow in extra-judicial writing:[50]

---

42 *Re Polemis* [1921] 3 K.B. 560 at 577.

43 [1991] 3 S.C.R. 534. See too *Hodgkinson v Simms* [1994] 3 S.C.R. 377 at [93].

44 Cf. *Corr v IBC Vehicles Ltd* [2008] UKHL 13; [2008] 1 A.C. 884 at [15], per Lord Bingham: "It is not fair to hold a tortfeasor liable, however gross his breach of duty may be, for damage caused to the claimant not by the tortfeasor's breach of duty but by some independent, supervening cause . . . for which the tortfeasor is not responsible."

45 [1987] 2 N.Z.L.R. 443.

46 [1987] 2 N.Z.L.R. 443 at 450–51.

47 *Lemberg v Perris* (2010) 76 C.C.L.T. (3d) 276 at [88].

48 *Wardrope v Smith* [2013] ONSC 330 at [167]. In neither case did the court hold that a reduction for contributory negligence was appropriate on the facts.

49 (2001) 207 C.L.R. 165 at [85]–[86].

50 The Hon Mr Justice Gummow, "Compensation for Breach of Fiduciary Duty" in T. Youdan (ed.), *Equity, Fiduciaries and Trusts* (1989), p.86, cited with approval in *Pilmer* at [171]. See too the Hon Mr Justice Handley, "Reduction of Damages Awards"

> While negligence is concerned with the taking of reasonable care, a fiduciary traditionally has more expected of him. His duty is one of undivided and unremitting loyalty. The fiduciary acts in a 'representative' capacity in the exercise of his responsibility. One must fear that introduction of concepts of contributory negligence into that setting inevitably will work a subversion of fundamental principle.

The English courts have taken an intermediate position. The leading case is *Nationwide Building Society v Balmer Radmore (a firm)*.[51] The claimant building society suffered losses on around 400 residential mortgage loans when the borrowers defaulted and the properties were repossessed and sold at a loss. The defendant solicitors had breached their fiduciary duty to the claimant when they had failed to disclose features of the purchase transactions of which they were aware and knowledge of which would have affected the claimant's lending decisions: e.g. the fact that a property had been substantially overvalued by the surveyors, or that a very recent (or even simultaneous) sale of the property to the borrower's vendor had taken place at a price significantly lower than the price agreed between the vendor and the borrower. The question arose whether the defendant's liability should be reduced to reflect the claimant's contributory negligence, and Blackburne J held that it should not.[52] He distinguished *Day* on the basis that the defendant there had acted in good faith, whereas the defendant firm in the present case had acted with conscious disloyalty, and he held that in these circumstances the defence should not be allowed. **18–024**

Later English cases have assumed that *Balmer Radmore* disables fiduciaries from pleading a principal's contributory negligence in every case, regardless of the character of the fiduciary's breach,[53] but that is not what the case decided, and it must still be regarded as an open question whether English law allows contributory negligence to be pleaded by a defaulting fiduciary who has acted in good faith. **18–025**

C. Breach of Confidence

i. Historical Development

The law relating to the equitable duty of confidence originated in cases where a claimant sought either an injunction against disclosure of confidential information or an account of the profits made by a defendant through the use of such information. Equitable compensation was not thought to be an available remedy, and compensatory awards were made only in cases where a duty of confidence owed by a defendant was contractual (so that damages could be awarded for breach of contract) and/or where the claimant was entitled to an injunction (so that the court could award equitable damages in lieu of an injunction under what is now the Senior Courts Act 1981 s.50[54]). However, the law has moved on and it is now accepted that equitable compensation can be awarded for breach of an equitable duty of confidence, whether or not an injunction is available.[55] **18–026**

---

in P.D. Finn (ed.), *Essays on Damages* (Law Book Co, 1992), p.127; M. Conaglen *Fiduciary Loyalty* (Hart Publishing, 2010), pp.172–176.

51 [1999] P.N.L.R. 606.

52 [1999] P.N.L.R. 606 at 676–677.

53 *Day v Cook* [2001] EWCA Civ 592; [2002] 1 B.C.L.C. 1 at [47]; *Leeds & Holbeck Building Society v Arthur & Cole (a firm)* [2002] P.N.L.R. 4 at [3]; *De Beer v Kanaar & Co (No.2)* [2002] EWHC 688 (Ch) at [92].

54 For discussion of which see paras 18–033 to 18–050.

55 The law's development can be tracked through: *Proctor v Bayley* (1889) 42 Ch.D. 390; *Robb v Green* [1895] 2 Q.B. 315; *Nichrotherm Electrical Ltd v Percy* [1957] R.P.C. 207 at 213; *Seager v Copydex Ltd (No.2)* [1969] 1 W.L.R. 109; *Malone v Metropolitan Police Commissioner (No.2)* [1979] Ch. 344 at 360; *Concept Television Productions Pty Ltd v Australian Broadcasting Corp* (1988) 12 I.P.R. 129, 136; *Attorney General v Guardian Newspapers Ltd (No.2)* [1990] 1 A.C. 109 at 286;

18–027 The courts have recognised that when awarding remedies for breach of confidence, it can be useful to draw analogies with awards made in response to other types of claim, but that the circumstances in which claims for breach of confidence can lie are various and that different analogies are apposite in different types of case. The clearest judicial statement to this effect appears in Sales J's judgment in *Vercoe v Rutland Fund Management Ltd*,[56] which is reproduced below.[57] His comments there concerned the types of remedy which might be awarded for breach of confidence and he concluded on the facts that it would be appropriate to make a compensatory award but not to order an account of profits. However, the logic of his approach suggests that factual variations may also lead the courts to apply different rules when quantifying compensatory awards, and in *MVF 3 Apps v Bestnet Europe Ltd*,[58] Floyd LJ confirmed that this is indeed the general approach to be taken, i.e. depending on the facts the courts may accept that loss suffered by the claimant should be characterised in one way or another, and/or that they should apply causation and remoteness rules of one kind or another.

ii. Recoverable Loss

18–028 Some cases concern personal information which has no economic value to the claimant, but disclosure of which causes her distress or disappointment, and awards can be made for loss of this kind.[59] They are usually modest but may be larger where the claimant has been the victim of an egregious indignity.[60]

18–029 Other cases concern information that the claimant would have used to make a profit, e.g. by using technical know-how in a manufacturing process, or by licensing the use of such information to other people. In cases of the first kind an award might be made to compensate the claimant for loss of manufacturing profits;[61] in cases of the second kind an award might be made to compensate her for loss of the licence fee that she would have charged.[62] These types of loss were distinguished by Lord Wilberforce in a well-known patent case, *General Tire and Rubber Co v Firestone Tyre and Rubber Co (No.2)*,[63] and came to be known as "lost manufacturing profits" and "lost royalty profits". As Lord Wilberforce also said, however, there is a difference between cases where a patentee's business is to sell licenses, and cases where it is not and there is no evidence that she would have done this. In cases of the latter sort, it can still be said that the patentee has suffered a loss, but the amount cannot be assessed by reference to a standard rate and instead the court must postulate a hypothetical negotiation between the patentee and an infringer on a willing buyer/willing seller basis.

Kitchenology BV v Unicor Gmbh Plastmaschinen [1995] F.S.R. 765 at 777–778; *Indata Equipment Supplies Ltd v ACL Ltd* [1998] 1 B.C.L.C. 412; *Aquaculture Corp v New Zealand Green Mussel Co Ltd* [1990] 3 N.Z.L.R. 299 at 301; *Smith Kline & French Laboratories (Aust) Ltd v Secretary, Department of Community Services & Health* (1990) 22 F.C.R. 73 at 83; *Cadbury Schweppes Inc v FBI Foods Ltd* [1999] 1 S.C.R. 142 at [59]–[61]; *Vercoe v Rutland Fund Management Ltd* [2010] EWHC 424 (Ch); *Force India Formula One Team Ltd v 1 Malaysia Racing Team* [2012] EWHC 616 (Ch) at [392]; *MVF 3 Apps v Bestnet Europe Ltd* [2016] EWCA Civ 541; [2017] F.S.R. 5. at [85]–[89].

56 [2010] EWHC 424 (Ch) at [344], approved in *MVF 3 Apps v Bestnet Europe Ltd* [2016] EWCA Civ 541; [2017] F.S.R. 5 at [85]–[86].

57 See paras 18–102 to 18–115.

58 [2016] EWCA Civ 541; [2017] F.S.R. 5 at [86]–[89].

59 *Douglas v Hello! Ltd (No.6)* [2003] EWHC 2629 (Ch); [2004] E.M.L.R. 2 at [57], affirmed [2005] EWCA Civ 595; [2006] Q.B. 125.

60 *Mosley v News Group Newspapers Ltd* [2008] EWHC 1777 (QB); [2008] E.M.L.R. 20 at [216].

61 *Dowson & Mason v Potter* [1986] 1 W.L.R. 1419; *Universal Thermosensors Ltd v Hibben* [1992] 1 W.L.R. 840; *Flogas Britain Ltd v Calor Gas Ltd* [2013] EWHC 3060 (Ch).

62 *Gorne v Scales* [2006] EWCA Civ 311; *MVF 3 Apps v Bestnet Europe Ltd* [2016] EWCA Civ 541; [2017] F.S.R. 5.

63 [1975] 1 W.L.R. 819 at 824–5.

The latter rules were confirmed in *One Step (Support) Ltd v Morris-Garner*.[64] By the time this reached the House of Lords it was solely concerned with breaches of non-compete and non-solicit clauses in a contract for the sale of a business, an additional claim for breach of an equitable duty of confidence having fallen away. However, Lord Reed's leading judgment contains a general survey of the law governing "negotiating damages", as he termed them, which he held to be available not only in patent infringement cases,[65] but also in cases where claimants have "lost a valuable opportunity to exercise their right to control the use of information".[66] Lord Reed took such awards to be compensatory and seems to have thought that they compensate claimants for a loss of factual control over property and analogous rights.[67] It is likely that this category includes cases where a claimant has been deprived of the ability to decide for herself whether confidential information should be disclosed. **18–030**

iii. Causation and Remoteness

Claimants seeking equitable compensation for breach of confidence must show that the losses for which they seek compensation were caused by the defendant's breach. This was discussed in *MVF 3 Apps*, where the claimant employed an expert on insecticides who developed a formula for use in the manufacture of mosquito nets. He left the claimant's employment and set up competing companies which manufactured nets using the same formula; using this formula as a starting point, he then developed another formula which was used to make a new type of net. He and his companies were liable for breach of a non-compete clause in his employment contract and for breach of an equitable duty of confidence,[68] and when the claimant's remedies were assessed it was assumed that the same rules would govern the assessment of damages and equitable compensation. **18–031**

Rose J awarded compensation for lost sales caused by the defendant's sales of the first formula nets and for loss of a licence fee in respect of the defendant's other sales of first formula nets. She declined to award compensation for lost sales in respect of the defendant's sales of the later formula nets and instead awarded a "quasi-consultancy" fee in respect of the defendants' use of confidential information in manufacture of the later formula nets. The Court of Appeal upheld all these findings. Floyd LJ emphasised in connection with the judge's rejection of the claim for lost sales caused by the defendant's sales of later formula nets that "rules which award the injured party all the consequences of [a] wrongful act are exceptional, and need to be justified by some policy consideration" and he concluded that this was not a case "in which the measure of damages should extend to cover all the foreseeable consequences of the defendant's acts."[69] **18–032**

3. Equitable Damages in Addition to or in Lieu of Injunctions and Specific Performance

A. Jurisdiction

Section 2 of the Chancery Amendment Act 1858, known as Lord Cairns' Act, gave the Court of Chancery a discretionary power, in cases where it had jurisdiction to grant an injunction or to order **18–033**

---

64 [2018] UKSC 20; [2019] A.C. 649.
65 [2018] UKSC 20; [2019] A.C. 649at [26]–[30].
66 [2018] UKSC 20; [2019] A.C. 649 at [84], instancing *Vercoe v Rutland Fund Management Ltd* [2010] EWHC 424 (Ch). See too *Seager v Copydex Ltd (No.2)* [1969] 1 W.L.R. 809.
67 C. Mitchell and L. Rostill, "Making Sense of Mesne Profits: Remedies" [2020] C.L.J. 552, 553–560.
68 *Vestergaard Frandsen A/S v Bestnet Europe Ltd* [2009] EWHC 657 (Ch) at [642].
69 [2016] EWCA Civ 541; [2017] F.S.R. 5 at [90]–[91]. Rose J's decision is at [2014] EWHC 3159 (Ch).

specific performance, to award damages to the injured party "either in addition to or in substitution for" the other relief. The courts' jurisdiction to award such damages now derives from the Senior Courts Act 1981 s.50. The main purpose of the 1858 statute was to save plaintiffs who had unsuccessfully sought equitable relief from the Court of Chancery from having to start new proceedings at common law to obtain a damages award, by empowering the Court of Chancery to award damages on the same principles as those which a common law court would have applied.[70] However, the statute also empowered the Court of Chancery to do two things which the common law courts could not do—award damages for breach of purely equitable rights and award damages for future wrongs.[71] The same is true of s.50 of the 1981 Act.

18-034 In *Pell Frischmann Engineering Ltd v Bow Valley Iran Ltd*, Lord Walker observed that:[72]

> Although damages under Lord Cairns's Act are awarded in lieu of an injunction it is not necessary that an injunction should actually have been claimed in the proceedings, or that there should have been any prospect, on the facts, of it being granted.

18-035 In other words, the courts have a statutory jurisdiction to award damages in lieu even in cases where they would not have awarded a remedy of specific performance or injunction, provided that they had the *power* to do so.

18-036 In *Shelfer v City of London Electric Lighting Co*,[73] AL Smith LJ said that as a "working rule" four conditions should be met before equitable damages are awarded: the injury to the claimant's rights should be small, capable of being estimated in money, and adequately compensable by a small sum; and granting the injunction should be oppressive to the defendant.[74] These criteria were interpreted narrowly and applied rigidly in later cases.[75] In addition, a divergence of view opened up between courts who thought that public interest considerations might justify the withholding of an injunction and the making of an award of equitable damages in lieu[76] and courts who thought that such considerations would justify such an approach only in "marginal" cases where the damage to the defendant was "minimal".[77]

18-037 These matters were considered in *Lawrence v Fen Tigers Ltd*.[78] In 2006 the claimants bought a house in the country situated near a motor racing stadium and motocross track run by the defendants in accordance with planning permissions which placed limits on the frequency and times of stadium and track activities but which placed no conditions on the level of noise emitted by these activities. The claimants brought an action in nuisance. The trial judge held the permissions could not relevantly have changed the character of the area so as to affect his assessment of whether the noise amounted

---

70 *Ferguson v Wilson* (1866) L.R. 2 Ch. App. 77 at 88.

71 *Eastwood v Lever* (1863) 4 De G.J. & S. 114; *Leeds Industrial Co-operative Society Ltd v Slack* [1924] A.C. 851; *Hooper v Rogers* [1975] Ch. 43; *Jaggard v Sawyer* [1995] 1 W.L.R. 269. Discussion in J.A. Jolowicz, "Damages in Equity—A Study of Lord Cairns' Act" [1975] C.L.J. 224; P.M. McDermott, *Equitable Damages* (Butterworths, 1994), Ch.3.

72 [2009] UKPC 45; [2011] 1 W.L.R. 2370 at [48](5), citing *Jaggard v Sawyer* [1995] 1 W.L.R. 269 at 285 (but cf. at p.291); *Attorney General v Blake* [2001] 1 A.C. 268 at 282; *WWF World Wide Fund for Nature v World Wrestling Federation Entertainment Inc* [2007] EWCA Civ 286; [2008] 1 W.L.R. 445 at [54]. Earlier cases in point are *City of London Brewery Co v Tennant* (1873) L.R. 9 Ch. App. 212; *Lavery v Pursell* (1888) 39 Ch. D. 508 at 519; *Hooper v Rogers* [1975] Ch. 43.

73 [1895] 1 Ch. 287 at 322–323.

74 [1995] 1 W.L.R. 269 at 280–281.

75 M. Wilde, "Nuisance Law and Damages in Lieu of an Injunction: Challenging the Orthodoxy of the *Shelfer* Criteria" in S.G.A. Pitel et al (eds), *Tort Law: Challenging Orthodoxy* (Hart Publishing, 2013).

76 *Wheeler v JJ Saunders Ltd* [1996] Ch. 19; *Marcic v Thames Water Utilities Ltd* [2002] EWCA Civ 64; [2002] Q.B. 929 (overturned by the HL on other grounds).

77 *Watson v Croft Promo-Sport* [2009] EWCA Civ 15; [2009] 3 All E.R. 249 at [51].

78 [2014] UKSC 13; [2014] A.C. 822.

to a nuisance. On the facts it had and so the claimants were entitled to an injunction, although the defendants could ask for this order to be discharged and replaced with an award of damages in lieu. The Court of Appeal disagreed but the Supreme Court agreed with the trial judge on the question whether the noise was a nuisance and restored the judge's order for injunctive relief with the inclusion of orders allowing the defendants to apply for damages to be awarded in lieu of an injunction.

The Justices of the Supreme Court gave five separate judgments. So far as the court's jurisdiction to award damages in lieu was concerned, they all moved away from the rigid and formulaic application of *Shelfer* but they had rather different ideas of the starting point for deciding when an injunction should be awarded for nuisance and of the significance of the grant of planning permission for the activity constituting the nuisance. **18–038**

Lord Neuberger's starting point was that an injunction will be awarded to restrain the continuation of a nuisance, and the legal burden is on the defendant to show why an injunction should not be granted.[79] He said that a "much more flexible"[80] approach should be taken when deciding whether to award equitable damages in lieu. A court had jurisdiction to refuse an injunction for reasons beyond those permitted by *Shelfer,* such as the parties' conduct and impact on third parties, e.g. the potential loss of work for the defendant's employees.[81] He disavowed a "mechanical application of A.L. Smith L.J.'s four tests" in *Shelfer*, stating that "an approach which involves damages being awarded only in 'very exceptional circumstances'" is "simply wrong in principle".[82] In relation to the significance of planning permission, Lord Neuberger indicated that this can be a factor in favour of refusing the injunction.[83] **18–039**

Lord Sumption agreed with Lord Neuberger but his starting position was different:[84] **18–040**

> The ordinary principle is that the court does not grant an injunction in a case where there is an adequate legal remedy. In particular, it does not do so where damages would be an adequate remedy. Where an injunction is granted, it is usually because the injury to the claimant is "irreparable", in the sense that money cannot atone for it. However, this principle has never been consistently followed in cases of nuisance. The leading case is *Shelfer v City of London Electric Lighting Co* which created a strong presumption in favour of an injunction to be displaced only in the four narrowly defined categories identified by A.L. Smith L.J . . .

He also disavowed a slavish application of *Shelfer,* stating the test it proposed was:[85] **18–041**

> devised for a time in which England was much less crowded, when comparatively few people owned property, when conservation was only beginning to be a public issue, and when there was no general system of statutory development control. The whole jurisprudence in this area will need one day to be reviewed in this court. There is much to be said for the view that damages are ordinarily an adequate remedy for nuisance and that an injunction should not usually be granted in a case where it is likely that conflicting interests are engaged other than the parties' interests. In particular, it may well be that an injunction should as a matter of principle not be granted in a case where a use of land to which objection is taken requires and has received planning permission. However, at this stage, in the absence of argument on these points, I can do no more than identify them as calling for consideration in a case in which they arise.

---

79 *Lawrence* [2014] UKSC 13; [2014] A.C. 822 at [101], [121].
80 *Lawrence* [2014] UKSC 13; [2014] A.C. 822 at [119].
81 *Lawrence* [2014] UKSC 13; [2014] A.C. 822 at [120]–[121].
82 *Lawrence* [2014] UKSC 13; [2014] A.C. 822 at [119], and see [123].
83 *Lawrence* [2014] UKSC 13; [2014] A.C. 822 at [125]–[126].
84 *Lawrence* [2014] UKSC 13; [2014] A.C. 822 at [159].
85 *Lawrence* [2014] UKSC 13; [2014] A.C. 822 at [161].

18–042 Lord Mance agreed with Lord Neuberger[86] save to the extent that he agreed with Lord Carnwath that the grant of planning permission should not give rise to any presumption against an injunction.[87] Lord Mance also expressed reservations as to Lord Sumption's view that an injunction should not ordinarily be granted when in conflict with a grant of planning permission as giving undue prioritisation to the significance of planning permission and the public benefit.[88]

18–043 Lord Clarke agreed with Lord Neuberger but reserved on the question as to who bore the burden[89] and agreed with Lord Sumption's view as to the starting position that an injunction will only be awarded when damages are inadequate and the need to avoid a slavish application of *Shelfer*.[90] He also agreed with Lord Neuberger, Lord Sumption and Lord Carnwath that planning permission for the activity complained of may be relevant to the remedy granted.[91]

18–044 Lord Carnwath agreed with Lord Neuberger as to the need to "signal a move away from the strict criteria derived from *Shelfer*" and in particular where "an injunction would have serious consequences for third parties, such as employees of the defendant's business . . .".[92] However, Lord Carnwath added the caveat that planning permission should not in itself give rise to a presumption against an award of an injunction, albeit that this may be an important factor in the court's assessment.[93]

B. Quantification

i. Damages in Lieu of an Injunction

18–045 In *Lawrence*, the Supreme Court seems to have accepted the view expressed by the Court of Appeal in *Jaggard v Sawyer*[94] that at least in cases of trespass and breach of restrictive covenant, the best approach to quantifying the damages awarded in lieu of an injunction is to ask what price the parties would have agreed should be paid by the defendant in exchange for the claimant releasing her rights. Lord Carnwath denied that this was a viable approach in nuisance cases, because he considered the inchoate nature of the claimant's injury to make it harder for the courts to assess an appropriate price. Given the artificial nature of the assessment exercise even in trespass cases, however, that was a weak reason for taking a different approach in nuisance cases, and to make matters worse his Lordship did not explain what else the courts are meant to do.

18–046 Damages of this kind were formerly known as "*Wrotham Park*" damages, after *Wrotham Park Estate Co Ltd v Parkside Homes Ltd*,[95] where Brightman J awarded damages in lieu of an injunction for breach of a restrictive covenant in a sum equal to 5% of the defendant property developer's anticipated profit, which he calculated to be the price the parties would have agreed should be paid for relaxation of the covenant. Nowadays, they are known as "negotiating damages" the term preferred by Lord Reed in his leading judgment in *One Step (Support) Ltd v Morris-Garner*.[96] In that case Lord Reed undertook

---

[86] *Lawrence* [2014] UKSC 13; [2014] A.C. 822 at [162].
[87] *Lawrence* [2014] UKSC 13; [2014] A.C. 822 at [167].
[88] *Lawrence* [2014] UKSC 13; [2014] A.C. 822 at [168].
[89] *Lawrence* [2014] UKSC 13; [2014] A.C. 822 at [170].
[90] *Lawrence* [2014] UKSC 13; [2014] A.C. 822 at [171].
[91] *Lawrence* [2014] UKSC 13; [2014] A.C. 822 at [169].
[92] *Lawrence* [2014] UKSC 13; [2014] A.C. 822 at [239].
[93] *Lawrence* [2014] UKSC 13; [2014] A.C. 822 at [246].
[94] [1995] 1 W.L.R. 269.
[95] [1974] 1 W.L.R. 798.
[96] [2018] UKSC 20; [2019] A.C. 649.

a survey of the cases where such damages have been awarded, and observed in connection with equitable damages that:[97]

> it is necessary to treat with care Lord Wilberforce's remark in *Johnson v Agnew*[98] that he found in Lord Cairns' Act "no warrant for the court awarding damages differently from common law damages". As Millett LJ explained in *Jaggard v Sawyer*[99] all that *Johnson v Agnew* decided was that damages [for breach of an obligation to pay money under a contract for the purchase of land], whether at common law or under the Act, are not invariably to be measured by reference to "the value of the land ascertained at the date of the breach of contract". Lord Wilberforce's words should not be read out of context and taken to imply that damages awarded in substitution for an injunction must necessarily be measured in the same way as damages recoverable at common law. That is hardly to be expected, given that the damages are available on a different basis, in different circumstances, and in respect of different types of wrong (past, on the one hand, and future or continuing, on the other).

The obvious difficulty with quantifying equitable damages in lieu of an injunction is that they depend on the premise that the parties are willing to sell and buy a licence for the relaxation of the claimant's right, when the reality is often that the parties do not wish to do this. Nonetheless that is the approach the courts must take. In *One Step*, Lord Carnwath accepted that in trespass cases the hypothetical negotiation should be assumed to take place at the start of the defendant's infringement,[100] and Lord Reed was "inclined to agree", although he chose not to express a concluded view as it was not a live issue in the case.[101] "Both parties are to be assumed to act reasonably",[102] and the sum they would agree will partly depend on the options available to a reasonable person in the defendant's position—on whether there are other ways for her to achieve her ends, or whether the claimant holds a "trump card".[103] However, it is not permissible for a court to conclude in cases where the defendant could have lawfully achieved her ends without reaching an agreement with the claimant, that no price at all would have been agreed in the negotiations.[104] **18–047**

ii. Damages in Lieu of Specific Performance

According to Megarry J in *Wroth v Tyler*,[105] the purpose of an award of equitable damages in lieu of specific performance is to provide the claimant with a true substitute for the equitable remedy, and since this remedy can only be refused at trial, the date of trial, rather than the date of the defendant's breach of contract, may be the relevant one for the purpose of assessing the equitable damages. Various Commonwealth cases have adopted Megarry J's reasoning in *Wroth* to develop special principles of assessment for equitable damages in cases where common law damages could alternatively have been awarded. For instance, in *Semelhago v Paramadevan*,[106] the parties entered a contract for **18–048**

---

97 [2018] UKSC 20; [2019] A.C. 649 at [47].
98 [1980] A.C. 367 at 400.
99 [1995] 1 W.L.R. 269 at 290–291.
100 [2018] UKSC 20; [2019] A.C. 649 at [159]. Cf. *Lunn Poly Ltd v Liverpool & Lancashire Properties Ltd* [2006] EWCA Civ 430; [2006] 2 E.G.L.R. 29 at [17]–[37]; *Pell Frischmann Engineering Ltd v Bow Valley Iran Ltd* [2009] UKPC 45; [2011] 1 W.L.R. 2370 at [50]–[51].
101 Ibid at [56].
102 *Pell Frischmann* [2009] UKPC 45; [2011] 1 W.L.R. 2370 at [49]; *One Step* [2018] UKSC 20; [2019] A.C. 649 at [75].
103 Cf. *Sinclair v Gavaghan* [2007] EWHC 2256 (Ch) at [16]–[17]; *Stadium Capital Holdings (No.2) Ltd v St Marylebone Property Co Plc* [2011] EWHC 2856 (Ch); [2012] 1 P. & C.R. 7 at [69] and [78]–[84].
104 Cf. *Enfield LBC v Outdoor Plus Ltd* [2012] EWCA Civ 608; [2012] 2 E.G.L.R. 105.
105 [1974] Ch. 30.
106 [1996] 2 S.C.R. 415. See too *Souster v Epsom Plumbing Contractors Ltd* [1974] 2 N.Z.L.R. 515; *Metropolitan Trust Co of Canada v Pressure Concrete Services Ltd* (1975) 60 D.L.R. (3d) 431; *Kopec v Pyret* (1987) 36 D.L.R. (4th) 1; *Mills v Ruthol Pty Ltd*

the sale of a house for CAD 205,000 with a closing date at the end of October 1986. The purchaser had CAD 75,000 in cash, and he planned to mortgage his existing house to secure a loan for the remaining CAD 130,000. To this end he negotiated a six-month open mortgage, intending to sell his existing house over the next six months and repay the loan with the proceeds. However, the vendor reneged on the deal and transferred title to a third party in December 1986. The purchaser therefore issued a writ for specific performance or damages in lieu, and stayed in his existing house. This was worth CAD 190,000 in the autumn of 1986, but had risen in value to CAD 300,000 by the time of trial. By then the new house which he had planned to buy from the vendor had also risen in value, to CAD 325,000.

18–049 At trial the purchaser elected to take damages rather than specific performance, and in line with *Wroth* the trial judge assessed these at CAD 120,000, representing the difference between the purchase price and the value of the new house at the time of trial. The Ontario Court of Appeal reduced this to CAD 81,000, accepting the vendor's argument that certain items should be deducted, namely the interest which the purchaser had avoided paying on the CAD 130,000 loan which would have been needed to finance the purchase, the interest earned on the CAD 75,000 that he would have used for the down payment, and the legal fees which he would have incurred. The vendor appealed, arguing that a deduction should also be made to reflect the fact that the purchaser's existing house had risen in value, a gain which he would not have made if he had sold it as planned. The Supreme Court of Canada rejected this, Sopinka J stating that:[107]

> If the respondent had received a decree of specific performance, he would have had the property contracted for and retained the amount of the rise in value of his own property. Damages are to be substituted for the decree of specific performance. I see no basis for deductions that are not related to the value of the property which was the subject of the contract. To make such deductions would depart from the principle that damages are to be a true equivalent of specific performance.

18–050 This result seems to overcompensate by the claimant by overriding the normal rule that a claimant must mitigate her loss between the date of breach and the date of judgment. However, *Semelhago* is a logical extension of the *Wroth* principle that equitable damages under Lord Cairns' Act are a monetised substitute for specific performance. As Lionel Smith has observed,[108] the purpose of an order for specific performance is not to compensate the claimant for the loss of her expectation interest, but to vindicate her performance right by compelling the defendant to perform her promise. If equitable damages in lieu of specific performance are awarded with the same goal in mind, the duty to mitigate has no application for the same reasons that it has no application to a claim for specific performance: since neither remedy is designed to compensate the claimant for her expectation loss, complaints that the claimant has been "overcompensated" miss the point.

(2004) 61 N.S.W.L.R. 1. In *Semelhago* at [22] Sopinka J also held that contracts for the sale of land are not routinely specifically enforceable, and that claimants must produce evidence that the property is "unique to the extent that its substitute is not readily available". For critical comment on this aspect of the case, see R. Chambers, "The Importance of Specific Performance" in S. Degeling and J. Edelman (eds), *Equity in Commercial Law* (Sweet & Maxwell, 2005).

107 *Semelhago* at [19].

108 L.D. Smith, "Understanding Specific Performance" in N. Cohen and E. McKendrick (eds), *Comparative Remedies for Breach of Contract* (Hart Publishing, 2005). See too C. Webb, "Performance and Compensation: An Analysis of Contract Damages and Contractual Obligation" (2006) 26 O.J.L.S. 41, developing ideas in D. Friedmann, "The Performance Interest in Contract Damages" (1995) 111 L.Q.R. 628.

4. Accounts of Profits

A. Terminology

"A claim for equitable compensation for losses sustained by a claimant is in principle a quite different remedy from a claim for an account of profits".[109] The "amount recoverable in an action claiming an account of profits is dependent upon the profit made by the [defendant], not the loss suffered by the [claimant]",[110] and it is no bar to a claim for an account of profits that the claimant has suffered no loss.[111] Where the claimant's loss and the defendant's gain are the same, e.g. because the claimant has taken property for herself that she should have taken for her principal, it may not matter which remedy is awarded. However, it often happens that the claimant's loss and defendant's gain do not coincide, and the question whether an account of profits is a more or less advantageous remedy than equitable compensation then depends on the facts: in some cases it may be "a more advantageous remedy . . . because the actual profits obtained by the [defendant are] higher than [the loss] suffered by the [claimant]";[112] in other cases it may be less advantageous, e.g. because the "defendant may have run his business as loss-leader, or not competently, or it may be that for some other reason, as it turns out on the evidence, the defendant has made little or no profit."[113] **18–051**

We start with these points because in *Sinclair Investments (UK) Ltd v Versailles Trade Finance Ltd (in admin)*[114] and again in *FHR European Ventures LLP v Cedar Capital Partners LLC*,[115] Lord Neuberger described an order that a fiduciary pay the profits of a breach of fiduciary duty as an award of "equitable compensation" in a sum corresponding to the value of the fiduciary's gains. This language was rightly described as "confusing" and disavowed by Lord Stephens in *Crown Prosecution Service v Aquila Advisory Ltd*,[116] where he said that an order to pay the amount brought out by an account of profits is "restitutionary, reversing the value of a benefit received, and is not concerned to compensate for a loss." **18–052**

The reasoning which led Lord Neuberger to use compensatory language rested on the erroneous premise that all personal claims in equity are the same. In *Sinclair*, he noted that trustees are accountable to beneficiaries for trust property and owe them a personal compensatory liability to reconstitute the trust fund if they dissipate the property in an unauthorised transaction:[117] that fiduciaries owe a personal duty to account to principals for gains received in breach of their fiduciary duty:[118] and that knowing recipients of misapplied trust funds and dishonest assistants in a breach of trust are **18–053**

---

109 *Barnsley v Noble* [2014] EWHC 2657 (Ch) at [300].

110 *Target Holdings Ltd v Redferns* [1996] A.C. 421 at 440. See too *Celanese International Corp v BP Chemicals Ltd* [1999] R.P.C. 203 at [35]–[36]; *United Pan-Europe Communications NV v Deutsche Bank AG* [2000] 2 B.C.L.C. 461 at [47]; *Attorney General v Blake* [2001] 1 A.C. 268 at 280; *Murad v Al-Saraj* [2005] EWCA Civ 959; [2005] W.T.L.R. 1573 at [108]; *Chirnside v Fay* [2007] 1 N.Z.L.R. 433 at [17].

111 *Boardman v Phipps* [1967] 2 A.C. 46.

112 *CMS Dolphin Ltd v Simonet* [2001] 2 B.C.L.C. 704 at [97]. See too *Colbeam Palmer Ltd v Stock Affiliates Pty Ltd* (1968) 122 C.L.R. 25 at 32; *Tang Man Sit v Capacious Investments Ltd* [1996] 1 A.C. 514 at 520. And cf. *Attorney General v Guardian Newspapers Ltd (No.2)* [1990] 1 A.C. 109 at 262: an account of profits "may provide some compensation to the claimant for loss which he has suffered" as a result of wrongdoing, but "damages are the main remedy for such loss".

113 *Edwards Lifesciences LLC v Boston Scientific SCIMED Inc* [2018] EWHC 664 (Pat) at [31].

114 [2011] EWCA Civ 347; [2012] Ch. 453.

115 [2014] UKSC 58; [2015] A.C. 250 at [1].

116 [2021] UKSC 49; [2021] 1 W.L.R. 5666 at [48], noting Lord Reed's observations in *AIB Group (UK) Ltd Plc v Mark Redler & Co Solicitors* [2014] UKSC 58; [2015] A.C. 1503 at [120].

117 [2011] EWCA Civ 347; [2012] Ch. 453 at [40]–[41], citing *Target Holdings Ltd v Redferns* [1996] A.C. 421 at 434, and *Foskett v McKeown* [2001] 1 A.C. 102 at 130. See Ch.13.

118 [2011] EWCA Civ 347; [2012] Ch. 453 at [42], citing *Chan v Zacharia* (1984) 154 C.L.R. 178 at 199.

"accountable in equity" to compensate the beneficiaries.[119] These observations then led him to say that "the traditional way in which a non-proprietary claim is assessed in equity is through the medium of an equitable account, which in turn leads to equitable compensation"[120]—including claims against fiduciaries for an account of profits. However, it does not follow from the fact that accounting mechanisms are used to quantify the loss-based compensatory liabilities of trustees, knowing recipients and dishonest assistants that the function of accounting mechanisms used to identify gains made by defaulting fiduciaries must be to quantify a compensatory liability. There are different types of accounting order and they support different types of claim: accounts in common form and accounts on the footing of wilful default support loss-based claims, and accounts of profits support gain-based claims.

18–054 A second terminological problem concerns the expression "account of profits". As in the passages quoted at the start of this section, the courts often use this term to describe a two-part order that can be made where a claimant has established that a defendant has made an improper gain:[121] first, the court directs that an inquiry should be undertaken into the relevant transactions (usually by a Chancery Master or district judge) to ascertain what profit the defendant has made; and, second, the court orders the defendant to pay the amount of this profit to the claimant once it has been identified. Strictly speaking, however, an order for an "account of profits" is only the first of these, i.e. an order that the amount of the defendant's profit should be established by investigating what has happened. Different orders for consequential or declaratory relief can then follow: that the defendant pay the amount of the profit or that particular property acquired through the defendant's wrongdoing is held on a constructive trust. This is what Lord Neuberger meant when he said in *FHR* that the term "equitable accounting can encompass both proprietary and non-proprietary claims".[122]

18–055 In this section we discuss the first type of award only, looking at the personal liability of fiduciaries and the personal liability of recipients of confidential information to pay the amount of wrongful gains. Note that courts may additionally direct that the performance of such a payment obligation is secured by an equitable lien over property belonging to the defendant;[123] or they may make a declaration that gains are held on constructive trust, the circumstances in which such declarations are made being discussed in Chapter 17.[124]

B. Personal Liability for the Profits of a Breach of Fiduciary Duty

i. Jurisdiction

18–056 Since an account of profits is an equitable remedy, one might have expected the courts to hold in cases concerning breaches of fiduciary duty that the award of the remedy is discretionary, just as in every other case. According to the Court of Appeal in *Novoship (UK) Ltd v Nitikin*,[125] however, there is an "inflexible rule of equity that where a fiduciary has made an unauthorised profit within the scope of his duty he is bound to account for it to his principal", in contrast to cases "where a claim for an

---

119 [2011] EWCA Civ 347; [2012] Ch. 453 at [43], citing *Paragon Finance Plc v DB Thakerar & Co* [1999] 1 All E.R. 400 at 408–409 and *Dubai Aluminium Co Ltd v Salaam* [2002] UKHL 48; [2003] 2 A.C. 366 at [142]. See further Chapter 14.

120 [2011] EWCA Civ 347; [2012] Ch. 453 at [45].

121 The court will not order an account of profits if the principal has failed to explain in her pleadings what gain she alleges the fiduciary to have made: *City of London Group Plc v Lothbury Financial Services Ltd* [2012] EWHC 3148 (Ch) at [89]–[91].

122 [2014] UKSC 45; [2015] A.C. 250 at [36].

123 As in e.g. *Warman International Ltd v Dwyer* (1995) 182 C.L.R. 544 at 570.

124 See paras 17–014 to 17–047.

125 [2014] EWCA Civ 908; [2015] Q.B. 499 at [118]–[119].

account of profits is made against one who is not a fiduciary, and does not owe fiduciary duties . . . [and where] the court has a discretion to grant or withhold the remedy." It is hard to know what to make of these dicta, but it seems unlikely that the court can have meant that there is no discretion to withhold the remedy in a case e.g. where the fiduciary has made a profit in good faith and the principal has behaved badly and/or said that she will not claim and has not done so for a long time, so that the "clean hands" doctrine and/or doctrine of laches might otherwise be expected to apply.[126]

ii. What Counts as a "Profit"?

As Lord Reed observed in *AIB Group (UK) Plc v Mark Redler & Co Solicitors*,[127] in cases where a fiduciary has made a gain by a breach of fiduciary duty, the principal has "a personal claim to payment of the amount brought out by an account of profits". As the name suggests, the purpose of an account of profits is to identify the fiduciary's net profits, as opposed to her gross receipts,[128] and the burden of proving that expenses and overheads should be deducted lies on the fiduciary.[129] Broadly speaking, a fiduciary "should be accountable for the profits properly attributable to the breach of fiduciary duty, taking into account the expenses connected with those profits and a reasonable allowance for overheads (but not necessarily salary . . .)".[130] The "object of the exercise is to deprive . . . wrongdoers of the benefit of their wrong"[131] but to do no more than this, since the "fashioning of an account should not be allowed to operate as the unjust enrichment of the claimant."[132] Thus, to give a simple example, if a fiduciary buys shares in breach of her fiduciary duty, and the principal claims the current value of the shares, the price paid by the fiduciary must be deducted when her "profits" are calculated. **18–057**

Special difficulties arise in cases where a fiduciary takes property or profit-making opportunities which should go to her principal and uses them in her own business. In this situation the court may regard the entire capital value of the fiduciary's business as representing the profit flowing from her breach of duty, and order her to disgorge that amount.[133] Or the court may apportion the profits of the business between the principal and the fiduciary according to their contributions—e.g. property or opportunities derived from the principal, and time, skill and effort from the fiduciary.[134] These possibilities are discussed by Finn J, an Australian judge and well-known expert on fiduciary law, in the following extract. **18–058**

Grimaldi v Chameleon Mining NL (No.2)

Full Court of the Federal Court of Australia (2012) 200 F.C.R. 296 at [515]–[531]

FINN J: . . . In many contexts the identification of the breach and of the benefit or profit resulting from it will be straightforward and uncontroversial, as where a trustee improperly purchases a house with a mixed fund of his own and trust moneys. In such a case, where a proportionate interest in the property itself is not **18–059**

---

126 As in e.g. *Re Jarvis (deceased)* [1958] 1 W.L.R. 815. See too *Edmonds v Donovan* (2005) 12 V.R. 513 at [76]–[77]; *Murdoch v Mudgee Dolomite & Lime Pty Ltd (in liq)* [2022] NSWCA 12 at [195]–[217].

127 [2014] UKSC 58; [2014] 3 W.L.R. 1367 at [120].

128 *Regal Hastings Ltd v Gulliver* [1967] 2 A.C. 134 at 154, followed in *Patel v Brent LBC* [2003] EWHC 3081 (Ch); [2004] W.T.L.R. 577 at [29].

129 *Murdoch v Mudgee Dolomite & Lime Pty Ltd (in liq)* [2022] NSWCA 12 at [239].

130 *CMS Dolphin Ltd v Simonet* [2001] 2 B.C.L.C. 704 at [97].

131 *TCP Europe Ltd v Perry* [2012] EWHC 1940 (QB) at [120].

132 *Ultraframe (UK) Ltd v Fielding* [2005] EWHC 1638 (Ch); [2007] W.T.L.R. 835 at [1588]. See too *Roadchef (Employee Benefits Trustees) Ltd v Hill* [2014] EWHC 109 (Ch) at [186].

133 *Fanmailuk.com v Cooper* [2011] EWHC 902 (Ch).

134 *Docker v Somes* (1834) 2 My. & K. 655; *Wedderburn v Wedderburn* (1838) 4 My. & Cr. 41; *Page v Rattiffe* (1896) 75 L.T. 371; *Manley v Sartori* [1927] 1 Ch. 157; *Re Jarvis* [1958] 1 W.L.R. 815; *CMS Dolphin Ltd v Simonet* [2001] 2 B.C.L.C. 704.

sought, then, apart from his liability to account for the moneys misused, the fiduciary will be liable in the usual case for the same proportion of any profit from the purchase as the trust moneys bore to the total purchase price.[135] This will be because the sole source of profit will generally be the capital outlaid.[136] . . .

18-060 The courts have long recognised that benefits or the profits derived by a misbehaving fiduciary may be attributable to multiple sources only one of which was the breach of fiduciary duty or trust; personal skill, expertise and exertion, goodwill or the financial contributions of the fiduciary and of third parties may have played their part as well in generating profits. In such circumstances, the assessment of the actual profit or benefit derived may involve a difficult, complex and costly exercise of attribution. If such an exercise is to be undertaken—and at best it can only result in some reasonable approximation of the profit for which the fiduciary must account[137]—the remedy invoked will be by way of an account of profits. What requires emphasis is that the profits inquiry in cases involving, variously, the establishment of a competing business by utilising the resources of the fiduciary's former employer,[138] using "trust" moneys in the fiduciary's own business,[139] reviving a trust business for the fiduciary's own benefit,[140] or misappropriating an opportunity,[141] raise their own particular concerns. They are not resolved by the application of a common "general rule".[142]

18-061 . . . [Finn J turned to consider "that category of case where profits are sought to be recovered from trust moneys improperly introduced into a trade or business either at its inception or afterwards":] The leading authority is *Docker v Somes*[143] which established that, if trust moneys were improperly employed in a trustee's own trade or business, the beneficiaries were entitled to insist upon having a proportionate share of the profits instead of, as previously, interest only on the amount of the trust moneys so employed. Though of some length Lord Brougham's reasoning is revealing. He began with what was the then orthodoxy:[144]

> "Wherever a trustee, or one standing in the relation of a trustee, violates his duty, and deals with the trust estate for his own behoof, the rule is that he shall account to the cestui que trust for all the gain which he has made. Thus, if trust money is laid out in buying and selling land, and a profit made by the transaction, that shall go not to the trustee who has so applied the money, but to the cestui que trust whose money has been thus applied. In like manner (and cases of this kind are more numerous), where a trustee or executor has used the fund committed to his care in stock speculations, though the loss, if any, must fall upon himself, yet for every farthing of profit he may make he shall be accountable to the trust estate. So, if he lay out the trust money in a commercial adventure, as in buying or fitting out a vessel for a voyage, or put it in the trade of another person, from which he is to derive a certain stipulated profit, although I will not say that this has been decided, I hold it to be quite clear that he must account for the profits received by the adventure or from the concern. In all these cases it is easy to tell what the gains are; the fund is kept distinct from the trustee's other monies, and whatever he gets he must account for and pay over. It is so much fruit, so much increase on the estate or chattel of another, and must follow the ownership of the property and go to the proprietor . . ."

18-062 His Lordship went on to explain why the then orthodoxy was that profits could not be claimed where money had been mixed:[145]

> "The reason which has induced Judges to be satisfied with allowing interest only I take to have been this: they could not easily sever the profits attributable to the trust money from those belonging to the whole capital stock; and the process became still more difficult, where a great proportion of the gains proceeded from skill or labour employed upon the capital."

---

135 *Scott v Scott* (1963) 109 C.L.R. 649.

136 For examples in other fiduciary contexts where the calculation is simple, see *McKenzie v McDonald* [1927] V.L.R. 134 (profit made on a purchase and resale) and *Attorney- v Edmunds* (1868) L.R. 6 Eq. 381.

137 *My Kinda Town Ltd v Soll* [1982] F.S.R. 147 at 159.

138 *Timber Engineering Co Pty Ltd v Anderson* [1980] 2 N.S.W.L.R. 488.

139 *Willett v Blanford* (1841) 1 Hare 253.

140 *Re Jarvis* [1958] 1 W.L.R. 815.

141 *Green & Clara Pty Ltd v Bestobell Industries Pty Ltd (No.2)* [1984] W.A.R. 32.

142 cf. *Re Jarvis* at 820.

143 (1834) 2 My. & K. 655.

144 Ibid. at 664–5.

145 Ibid. at 665.

Confronted by counsel with an example which was designed to deter him permitting apportionment ("from taking the course which all principle points out"), Lord Brougham made the important comment:[146] 18–063

> "[Counsel] feigned the instance of an apothecary buying drugs with £100 of trust money, and earning £1000 a year by selling them to his patients; and so he might have taken the case of trust money laid out in purchasing a piece of steel or skein of silk, and these being worked up into goods of the finest fabric, Birmingham trinkets or Brussels lace, where the work exceeds by 10,000 times the material in value. But such instances, in truth, prove nothing; for they are cases not of profits upon stock, but of skilful labour very highly paid; and no reasonable person would ever dream of charging a trustee, whose skill thus bestowed had so enormously augmented the value of the capital, as if he had only obtained from it a profit."

Apportionment was permissible. The profits "which might be supposed to come from the money misapplied [could be severed] from the rest of the capital embarked".[147] Nonetheless an escape route was left:[148] 18–064

> "Should in any case a serious difficulty arise in tracing and apportioning the profits, this may be a reason for preferring a fixed rate of interest in that case."

A significant body of nineteenth century case law built on *Docker v Somes*.[149] Many of the cases involved the shares of deceased partners being improperly left in the new partnership.[150] 18–065

The subsequent case law did not attempt to trace the precise application of the moneys misused. It had been "mixed up with the consequences and liabilities" of the business.[151] That was sufficient. Nor was it the case, where the trustee/fiduciary started a business on his own account using a mixed fund, or used trust moneys in an existing business, that the profits should necessarily be apportioned according to the respective contributions of his own and trust moneys to the business' capital. 18–066

As was affirmed in *Vyse v Foster* . . . by James L.J.:[152] 18–067

> ". . . there was no rule for apportioning the profits according to the respective amounts of the capital, but that the division would be affected by considerations of the source of the profit, the nature of the business, and the other circumstances of the case. It is obvious that it must be so, for it would be easy to suggest a number of instances in which the profit of a business has no ascertainable reference to the capital – e.g. solicitors, factors, brokers . . . Indeed, in almost every case where the business consists of buying and selling, the difference between prosperity and ruin mainly depends on the skill, industry, and care of the dealers."

The need to apportion commonly requires the court to direct inquiries concerning the sources of profit in the particular business concerned and then to determine the profits which are attributable to those sources[153]; a like need to apportion can arise, we note in passing, where intellectual property is misused in another business.[154] 18–068

Contemporary Australian authority conforms to the above: where a portion of the profits made is "not the product or consequence of the plaintiff's property but the product of the fiduciary's skill, efforts, property and resources", it would be inequitable to order an account of the "entire profits".[155] However, it is for the fiduciary to establish that inequity.[156] 18–069

---

146 Ibid. at 667–8.
147 Ibid. at 666.
148 Ibid. at 673.
149 See, e.g. *Wedderburn v Wedderburn* (1838) 4 My. & Cr. 41; *MacDonald v Richardson* (1858) 1 Giff 81.
150 See *Lindley & Banks on Partnership* (19th edn, 2010) paras 26–40—26–41. See also *Lewin on Trusts* (18th edn, 2008), para.20–33.
151 *Flockton v Bunning* (1872) L.R. 8 Ch. App. 323n at 326n; see also *Primeau v Granfield* 184 F. 480 (1911) – a tracing/accounting case.
152 Ibid. at 331. See also *Willett v Blanford* (1842) 1 Hare 253.
153 See *Manley v Sartori* [1927] 1 Ch. 157; *Page v Rattiffe* (1896) 75 L.T. 371.
154 See, e.g. *Colbeam Ltd v Stock Affiliates Pty Ltd* (1968) 122 C.L.R. 25 at 42; see also Ricketson, *The Law of Intellectual Property: Copyright, Designs and Confidential Information* para.[2.75].
155 *Warman v Dwyer* (1995) 182 C.L.R. 544 at 561.
156 Ibid.

18-070 The courts have on occasion sought, understandably, to short-circuit the apportionment inquiries by resort to the device of awarding "just allowances" to the fiduciary. This can take the form of dividing between the fiduciary and the principal all the profits made in the proportions that the fiduciary's own and the trust's money bore to the total capital, but only after making an allowance to the fiduciary for his or her own skill and exertion.[157] The same just allowances device has been employed where the capital or business used when generating the profit represented, or was constituted by, the trust property misused;[158] or, for that matter, in exceptional circumstances where, without misusing trust property at all, but in consequence of a breach of fiduciary duty, the fiduciary has made profits by deploying his or her own knowledge, skill and experience.[159] In cases of the latter two varieties, the courts have shown quite some reticence in granting just allowances, as of course.

18-071 As was said in *Warman v Dwyer*:[160]

> "Whether it is appropriate to allow an errant fiduciary a proportion of profits or to make an allowance in respect of skill, expertise and other expenses is a matter of judgment which will depend on the facts of the given case. However, as a general rule, in conformity with the principle that a fiduciary must not profit from a breach of fiduciary duty, a court will not apportion profits in the absence of an antecedent arrangement for profit-sharing but will make allowance for skill, expertise and other expenses."

18-072 Allowances are not granted as of right and it is here that a court will exercise its powers to do what is "practically just". Considerations such as whether the fiduciary has acted honestly or dishonestly; how and for what has the fiduciary been remunerated; would the denial of an allowance leave the principal unjustly enriched; what risk has been borne by the principal; etc, come into play.[161]

18-073 Three points should be made about cases where a fiduciary has contributed time, skill and effort to the generating of profits. First, there is a difference between an order that these profits should be apportioned between the parties (as in e.g. *Docker v Somes*[162]) and an order that all of the profits should be allocated to the principal, subject to the making of an allowance to the fiduciary for the value of her work (as in e.g. *Boardman v Phipps*[163]). The court has a discretion to make one order or the other—or neither—depending on the facts.

18-074 This leads to the second point, which is that the courts have said that they can order an allowance on the basis that "it would be inequitable . . . for the [principal] to step in and take the profit without paying for the skill and labour which has produced it";[164] but in *Guinness Plc v Saunders*,[165] Lord Goff conversely held that the exercise of the courts' discretion to order an allowance should be restricted to cases where an award would not have the effect of encouraging fiduciaries to put themselves in a position of conflict. It can be assumed that the courts will be guided by the same considerations when deciding whether to apportion profits. It is not always easy to predict how the courts will balance one

---

157 See *Yates v Finn* (1880) 13 Ch. D. 839; *Lord Provost of Edinburgh v Lord Advocate* (1879) 4 App. Cas. 823 at 838–9.

158 See *Boardman v Phipps* [1967] 2 A.C. 46 at 104; *Timber Engineering Co Pty Ltd v Anderson* [1980] 2 N.S.W.L.R. 488 at [13]–[27]; *Paul A. Davies (Aust) Pty Ltd v Davies* [1983] 1 N.S.W.L.R. 440 at 448 and 451; *Re Jarvis* [1958] 1 W.L.R. 815 at 820.

159 cf. *O'Sullivan v Management Agency and Music Ltd* [1985] Q.B. 428.

160 (1995) 182 C.L.R. 544 at 562.

161 See generally *Harris v Digital Pulse Pty Ltd* (2003) 56 N.S.W.L.R. 298 at 311–336; and see Ford and Lee, *Principles of the Law of Trusts*, vol. 2, para.[17.2650].

162 (1834) 2 My. & K. 655.

163 [1967] 2 A.C. 46.

164 *Phipps v Boardman* [1964] 1 W.L.R. 993 at 1018, per Wilberforce J; affirmed [1967] 2 A.C. 46 at 104 and 112. See too *O'Sullivan v Management Agency and Music Ltd* [1985] Q.B. 42; *Badfinger Music v Evans* [2001] W.T.L.R. 1.

165 *Guinness Plc v Saunders* [1990] 2 A.C. 663 at 701, followed in, e.g. *Quarter Master UK Ltd (In Liquidation) v Pyke* [2004] EWHC 1815 (Ch); [2005] 1 B.C.L.C. 245 at [76]–[77] and *Cobbetts LLP v Hodge* [2009] EWHC 786 (Ch); [2010] 1 B.C.L.C. 30 at [118]; though cf. *Nottingham University v Fishel* [2000] I.C.R. 1462 at 1499–1500, and see too *Imageview Management Ltd v Jack* [2009] EWCA Civ 63; [2009] Bus. L.R. 1034 at [54]–[60].

consideration against the other,[166] although it is safe to assume that they will be less likely to favour a dishonest fiduciary than an honest one.[167]

18–075 Third, the burden of proof lies on the fiduciary to show that she has incurred a deductible expense.[168] The exercise of matching receipts against costs is essentially mathematical, but there is a margin of discretion insofar as a doubtful expense may be allowed to an honest fiduciary but disallowed to a dishonest one.[169] Further, as Lord Millett NPJ said in the Hong Kong Court of Final Appeal:[170]

> Where the absence of evidence is the consequence of the fiduciary's own breach of duty the court is not without resource, for it can have resort to three principles. First, it may be able to take the fiduciary at his own word and use his falsehoods to establish the facts as if they were true even though they are known to be untrue. Secondly the court is entitled to make every assumption against the party whose conduct has deprived it of necessary evidence. And thirdly the court is entitled to be robust and do rough and ready justice without having to justify the amount of its award with any degree of precision.

iii. Causation

18–076 In *Ultraframe (UK) Ltd v Fielding*, Lewison J said that profits claimed by a principal must "bear a reasonable relationship" to the breach of duty committed by the fiduciary,[171] and in *Murad v Al-Saraj* Arden LJ accepted that some rule is needed to distinguish between the gains which a fiduciary derives from her breach and the gains which she derives from other sources—for "no fiduciary is liable for all the profits [she] ever made from any source".[172] The question arises, though, what this should be? In *United Pan-Europe Communications NV v Deutsche Bank AG*,[173] Morritt LJ said that the court should ask whether the gains made by the fiduciary fall within the scope of her duty. He took this to be a different question from the question whether the fiduciary's receipt of a gain was caused by her breach of duty, which he believed to be an irrelevant issue. His comments to this effect have been endorsed by the Court of Appeal on several occasions.[174]

18–077 It may be that these dicta reflect an understanding of the rules governing gain-based liability for breach of fiduciary duty that considers the fiduciary to be disabled from taking gains for herself, and does not consider her to owe a positive duty to avoid conflicts of interest, breach of which triggers a gain-based liability.[175] However, Arden LJ appears to have thought in *Murad* that the same rules of

---

166 Compare the views taken by Elias CJ and by Tipping and Blanchard JJ in *Chirnside v Fay* [2007] 1 N.Z.L.R. 433.

167 Cf. *Phipps v Boardman* [1965] Ch. 992 at 1021.

168 *Warman v Dwyer* (1995) 182 C.L.R. 544 at 561–562, endorsed in *Chirnside v Fay* [2007] 1 N.Z.L.R. 433 at [131]; *Imageview Management Ltd v Jack* [2009] EWCA Civ 63; [2009] Bus. L.R. 1034 at [56]; *Gray v Global Energy Horizons Corp* [2020] EWCA Civ 1668; [2021] 1 W.L.R. 2264 at [239].

169 *Colburn v Simms* (1843) 2 Hare 543 at 560.

170 *Libertarian Investments Ltd v Hall* (2013) 16 H.K.C.F.A.R. 681 at [174].

171 [2005] EWHC 1638 (Ch); [2007] W.T.L.R. 835 at [1518]. Lewison LJ (as he had by then become) made the same point in *Keystone Healthcare Ltd v Parr* [2019] EWCA Civ 1246; [2019] 4 W.L.R. 99 at [18]: there "must . . . be a sufficient degree of connection between the breach of duty and the receipt of the secret profit."

172 [2005] EWCA Civ 959; [2005] W.T.L.R. 1573 at [62]. cf. *3464920 Canada Inc v Strother* (2005) 7 I.T.E.L.R. 748 at [47].

173 [2000] 2 B.C.L.C. 461 at [47].

174 *Murad v Al-Saraj* [2005] EWCA Civ 959; [2005] W.T.L.R. 1573 at [57]; *Novoship (UK) Ltd v Mikhaylyuk* [2014] EWCA Civ 908; [2015] Q.B. 499 at [96]; *Keystone Healthcare Ltd v Parr* [2019] EWCA Civ 1246; [2019] 4 W.L.R. 99 at [17]–[18]; *Gray v Global Energy Horizons Corp* [2020] EWCA Civ 1668; [2021] 1 W.L.R. 2264 at [128]. Cf. M. Conaglen "Identifying the Profits for which a Fiduciary Must Account" (2020) 79 C.L.J. 38, 60 and 62–67, equivocating between the view that a causative analysis can provide the requisite link and the view that scope of duty analysis is preferable because the "liability is focused more on the fact that making and retaining the profit is itself the breach of fiduciary duty, than on whether the breach caused a profit to be made."

175 See paras 2–158 to 2–163.

attribution would apply whichever way the fiduciary's liability is analysed,[176] and if one takes the latter view of the fiduciary's duty (as the courts clearly do in the equitable compensation cases considered above[177]), then it is unhelpful to collapse the question whether there was a duty at all (which requires one to consider what function or responsibility the fiduciary undertook) into the question whether this duty was breached with the result that the fiduciary made a gain that she should now be ordered to disgorge (which requires one to consider why she acquired particular gains). Hence we prefer the view that a principal must establish a causal link between the gain and the breach of duty before the fiduciary should have to pay the value of the gain (or hold it on constructive trust for the principal).[178]

18–078 This still leaves us with the question of what test should be used to decide whether a fiduciary's gain has been caused by a breach of duty. The answer is a simple one. The breach must have been one cause of the gain. It need not have been the only cause, nor need it have been the predominant cause, for "in this sort of case the court 'does not allow an examination into the relative importance of contributory causes'".[179] The court "lays the burden on the defaulting fiduciary to show that the profit is not one for which [she] should account",[180] and she cannot escape liability by proving that she would have made the gain even if she had not breached his duty because "the question whether or not the benefit would have been obtained but for the breach of trust has always been treated as irrelevant".[181] In Lord Radcliffe's words:[182]

> If a trustee has placed himself in a position in which his interest conflicts with his duty and has not discharged himself from responsibility to account for the profits that his interest has secured for him, it is neither here nor there to speculate whether, if he had done his duty, he would not have been left in possession of the same amount of profit.

18–079 In effect, therefore, the fiduciary must prove that her breach of duty had no causative effect at all, by showing that she acquired the gain solely as a result of activities legitimately undertaken in her own interest. In *Murad v Al-Saraj*, the defendant fiduciary failed to do this, with the result that liability was imposed.

Murad v Al-Saraj

Court of Appeal [2005] W.T.L.R. 1573

18–080 The claimants agreed to participate in a property development deal with the defendant who owed them a fiduciary duty. The claimants put up £1 million in cash in the belief that he would also contribute cash towards the purchase price, but in fact he never paid any cash to the vendor who instead released him from a legally unenforceable liability arising out of their prior personal dealings. Had the claimants been aware of this fact, they would have gone ahead with the deal but rather than agreeing to a half and half

---

176 [2005] EWCA Civ 959; [2005] W.T.L.R. 1573 at [49].

177 See paras 18–007 to 18–025.

178 Cf. *Maguire v Makaronis* (1997) 188 C.L.R. 449 at 468: there is "a need to specify criteria for a sufficient connection (or 'causation') between breach of duty and the profit derived." See too *Swain v Law Society* [1982] 1 W.L.R. 17 at 37; *Estate Realties Ltd v Wignall* [1992] 2 N.Z.L.R. 615 at 631; *Button v Phelps* [2006] EWHC 53 (Ch) at [66].

179 *Fexuto Pty Ltd v Bosnjak Holdings Pty Ltd (No.2)* (1998) 29 A.C.S.R. 290 at 297.

180 *Murad v Al-Saraj* [2005] EWCA Civ 959; [2005] W.T.L.R. 1573 at [77]. See too *Condliffe v Sheingold* [2007] EWCA Civ 1043 at [23]; *Ross River Ltd v Waveley Commercial Ltd* [2014] 1 B.C.L.C. 545 at [94]; *Global Energy Horizons Corp v Gray* [2015] EWHC 2232 (Ch) at [133], Asplin J adding at [134] that "the evidential burden is on [the fiduciary] to establish that there is no sufficient causal relationship with the breach of fiduciary duty."

181 *Brickenden v London Loan & Savings Co* [1934] 3 D.L.R. 465 at 469; *Industrial Development Consultants Ltd v Cooley* [1972] 1 W.L.R. 443 at 453; *Beach Petroleum NL v Kennedy* (1999) 48 N.S.W.L.R. 1 at [440]; *Gwembe Valley Development Co Ltd (in rec.) v Koshy (No.3)* [2004] 1 B.C.L.C. 131 at [145]–[146].

182 *Gray v New Augarita Porcupine Mines Ltd* [1952] 3 D.L.R. 1 at 15. See too *Manley v Santori* [1927] 1 Ch. 157.

capital profit split on resale of the hotel, they would have insisted on a higher profit share for themselves. After the hotel was sold, the facts came to light, and the claimants asserted that the defendant was liable to account for the whole of his share of the profits to them, as the proceeds of his breach of fiduciary duty, and that he held these profits on constructive trust for them. The defendant claimed to keep that portion of the profits which the claimants would have let him take even if he had made full disclosure. This was rejected by a majority of the court.

ARDEN L.J. (with whom JONATHAN PARKER L.J. agreed; CLARKE L.J. gave a dissenting judgment): . . . **18–081**
The judge gave a remedy of account because there was a fiduciary relationship. For wrongs in the context of such a relationship, an order for an account of profits is a conventional remedy. The Murads considered that that remedy would be more beneficial to them because, if they were awarded damages at common law, they would simply be entitled to recover the difference between the profit share to which they agreed and that which they would have negotiated if the true position had been disclosed to them. The reference to deceit is, however, a reminder that the judge's finding was that Mr Al-Saraj's failure to disclose the set off arrangement to the Murads was both deliberate and fraudulent, a point to which I shall have to return.

A distinguishing feature of this case is that, because the claim was brought both in tort and for breach **18–082**
of fiduciary duty, the judge carefully made all the findings which might be relevant if his conclusion on fiduciary duty was reversed on appeal. He accordingly made a finding as to what the Murads would have done if they had been given the information withheld from them. As I have explained, he held that the Murads would still have entered into a joint venture with Mr Al-Saraj but they would have agreed with him that he should have a reduced profit share. The appellants seize on that finding as relevant also to the question of liability to account as a fiduciary. The finding is highly compressed, and it is not clear, on the facts as found by the judge, exactly why the Murads would have agreed to give Mr Al-Saraj a profit share in the changed circumstances. I consider it most likely that what the judge had in mind was that the Murads would have agreed to give Mr Al-Saraj a profit share in return for a cash injection (other than by way of loan). In other words, what the judge found was that the Murads would have given him a profit share in return for an investment not as a reward for the service of introducing the Murads to the Park Hotel venture. If the position had been the latter, the more obvious course for Mr Al-Saraj would have been to attempt to convince the judge on the taking of the account that he ought to be allowed a profit share as an introductory fee.

. . . [Counsel for Al-Saraj argued that] the account ordered by the judge would . . . result in unjust **18–083**
enrichment of the Murads. It is (he submits) wrong in principle that the Murads should receive the benefit of any profits which, if there had been full disclosure, they would have been content for Mr Al-Saraj to have. They all along anticipated being co-venturers with him and so expected him to have a share of the profits from the acquisition of Parkside Hotel. Increases in profits not attributable to his wrongful conduct should be excluded from the profits for which he has to account . . . To test [this] argument . . . it is necessary to go back to first principle. It has long been the law that equitable remedies for the wrongful conduct of a fiduciary differ from those available at common law . . . Equity recognises that there are legal wrongs for which damages are not the appropriate remedy. In some situations therefore, as in this case, a court of equity instead awards an account of profits. As with an award of interest . . . the purpose of the account is to strip a defaulting fiduciary of his profit . . .

[The] liability of a fiduciary to account does not depend on whether the person to whom the fiduciary **18–084**
duty was owed could himself have made the profit . . . [This] is established by numerous authorities. It is sufficient for me to cite the well-known passage from the speech of Lord Russell of Killowen in the *Regal* case:[183]

> "The rule of equity which insists on those, who by use of a fiduciary position make a profit, being liable to account for that profit, in no way depends on fraud, or absence of bona fides; or upon such questions or considerations as whether the profit would or should otherwise have gone to the plaintiff, or whether the profiteer was under a duty to obtain the source of the profit for the plaintiff, or whether he took a risk or acted as he did for the benefit of the plaintiff, or whether the plaintiff has in fact been damaged or benefited by his action. The liability arises from the mere fact of a profit having, in the stated circumstances, been made."

---

[183] *Regal Hastings Ltd v Gulliver* [1967] 2 A.C. 134 at 144–5.

18–085 . . . The fact that the fiduciary can show that that party would not have made a loss is, on the authority of the *Regal* case, an irrelevant consideration so far as an account of profits is concerned. Likewise, it follows in my judgment from the *Regal* case that it is no defence for a fiduciary to say that he would have made the profit even if there had been no breach of fiduciary duty.

18–086 In the present case, the conduct of Mr Al-Saraj was held to be fraudulent. This was not the position of the directors in the *Regal* case. The principle, however, established by the *Regal* case applies even where the fiduciary acts in the mistaken belief that he is acting in accordance with his fiduciary duty. As Lord Russell made clear in the passage cited above, liability does not depend on fraud or lack of good faith. The existence of a fraudulent intent will, however, be relevant to the question of the allowances to be made on the taking of the account . . .

18–087 I accept that any rule that makes a wrongdoer liable for all the consequences of his wrongful conduct or for actions which did not cause the injured party any loss needs to be justified by some special policy. But . . . in the field of fiduciaries there are policy reasons which have for a long time been accepted by the courts.

18–088 For policy reasons, the courts decline to investigate hypothetical situations as to what would have happened if the fiduciary had performed his duty. In *Regal* case Lord Wright made the following point, to which I shall have to return below:[184]

> "Nor can the court adequately investigate the matter in most cases. The facts are generally difficult to ascertain or are solely in the knowledge of the person being charged. They are matters of surmise; they are hypothetical because the inquiry is as to what would have been the position if that party had not acted as he did, or what he might have done if there had not been the temptation to seek his own advantage, if, in short, interest had not conflicted with duty."

18–089 Again, for policy reasons, on the taking of an account, the court lays the burden on the defaulting fiduciary to show that the profit is not one for which he should account.[185] This shifting of the onus of proof is consistent with the deterrent nature of the fiduciary's liability. The liability of the fiduciary becomes the default rule.

18–090 . . . I have already set out Lord Wright's observations in the *Regal* case about the difficulties of investigating the conduct of a defaulting trustee. Under the rule of equity applied in that case . . . cases can be found where the fiduciary or trustee acted in all good faith believing that he was acting in the interests of his beneficiary but yet has been made to account for the profits obtained as a result of the breach of trust without limitation. Now, in a case like the *Regal* case, if the rule of equity under which the defendants were held liable to account for secret profits were not inflexible, the crucial issue of fact would be: what the company would have done if the opportunity to subscribe for shares in its subsidiary had been offered to it? In the passage just cited, as I have said, Lord Wright makes the point that it is very difficult to investigate that issue. However, while that may have been so in the past in the days of Lord Eldon and Lord King, that would not be the case today. The court has very extensive powers under the Civil Procedure Rules for instance to require information to be given as to a party's case. If the witness cannot attend the hearing, it may be possible for his evidence to be given by way of a witness statement or it may be possible for him to give evidence by video-link. The reasons for the rule of equity are many and complex . . . There have been calls for its re-examination . . . It may be that the time has come when the court should revisit the operation of the inflexible rule of equity in harsh circumstances, as where the trustee has acted in perfect good faith and without any deception or concealment, and in the belief that he was acting in the best interests of the beneficiary. I need only say this: it would not be in the least impossible for a court in a future case, to determine as a question of fact whether the beneficiary would not have wanted to exploit the profit himself, or would have wanted the trustee to have acted other than in the way that the trustee in fact did act. Moreover, it would not be impossible for a modern court to conclude as a matter of policy that, without losing the deterrent effect of the rule, the harshness of it should be tempered in some circumstances. In addition, in such cases, the courts can provide a significant measure of protection for the beneficiaries by imposing on the defaulting trustee the affirmative burden of showing that those circumstances prevailed.

---

184 Ibid. at 154.

185 See, for example, *Manley v Sartori* [1927] Ch 157.

Certainly the Canadian courts have modified the effect of equity's inflexible rule[186] though I express no view as to the circumstances in which there should be any relaxation of the rule in this jurisdiction. That sort of question must be left to another court.

In short, it may be appropriate for a higher court one day to revisit the rule on secret profits and to make it less inflexible in appropriate circumstances, where the unqualified operation of the rule operates particularly harshly and where the result is not compatible with the desire of modern courts to ensure that remedies are proportionate to the justice of the case where this does not conflict with some other overriding policy objective of the rule in question. **18–091**

However that is not this case. Mr Al-Saraj was found to have made a fraudulent misrepresentation to the Murads who had placed their trust in him. I do not consider that, even if we were free to revisit the *Regal* case, this would be an appropriate case in which to do so. The appropriate remedy is that he should disgorge all the profits, whether of a revenue or capital nature, that he made from inducing the Murads by his fraudulent representations from entering into the Parkside Hotel venture, subject to any allowances permitted by the court on the taking of the account. **18–092**

The imposition of liability to account for secret profits and the placing of the burden of proof on the defaulting trustee are not, however, quite the end of the matter. The kind of account ordered in this case is an account of profits, that is a procedure to ensure the restitution of profits which ought to have been made for the beneficiary and not a procedure for the forfeiture of profits to which the defaulting trustee was always entitled for his own account. That is [counsel for Al-Saraj's] case and I agree with him on this point. Even when the fiduciary is not fraudulent, the profit obtained from the breach of trust has to be defined. It may indeed be derivative, as where a trustee misappropriates trust property and then sells it and make a profit out of something else. But equity does not take the view that simply because a profit was made as part of the same transaction the fiduciary must account for it. I can give an example of that. In *Giddings v Giddings*,[187] a tenant for life renewed a lease belonging to the trust. The renewed lease, however, included land which had not been within the original lease. Sir John Copley M.R. dealt with the point briefly. He held that the remaindermen were only entitled to the benefit of the lease so far as it related to the land originally leased to the tenant for life. Another example is *Docker v Somes*,[188] where Lord Brougham expressed the view that in some circumstances a trustee who had applied considerable skill and labour to trust property which he had misapplied would be awarded a share of the product of his skill and labour: **18–093**

> "Mr. Solicitor General might have taken the case of trust money laid out in purchasing a piece of steel or skein of silk, and these being worked up into goods of the finest fabric, Birmingham trinkets or Brussels lace, where the work exceeds by 10,000 times the material in value. But such instances, in truth, prove nothing; for they are cases not of profits upon stock, but of skilful labour very highly paid; and no reasonable person would ever dream of charging a trustee, whose skill thus bestowed had so enormously augmented the value of the capital, as if he had only obtained from it a profit; although the refinements of the civil law would certainly bear us out, even in charging all gains accruing upon those goods as in the nature of accretions belonging to the true owners of the chattels."

In the present case, any recognisable contribution made by Mr. Al-Saraj was to the business of the joint venture. As the *Warman* case[189] shows, there can be particular difficulty applying the above principles where the trustee mixes trust property with his own business. The profit which belongs to the trust has to be disentangled from that which belongs to the defaulting trustee because it is a profit of his business. I have explained above how these difficulties were resolved in the Warman case by limiting the account to two years' profits. The problem in the *Warman* case has also faced courts within our own jurisdiction. In *Vyse v Foster*,[190] one of the partners in a business died but his capital remained in the business and was thus used by the surviving partners. One of the residuary legatees of the deceased partner sought an account of the share of the profits of the business to which she was entitled. The matter came before James and Mellish L.JJ. (Mellish L.J. did not deliver a separate judgment). This court was prepared in principle to **18–094**

---

[186] See *Peso Silver Mines Ltd v Cropper* (1966) 58 D.L.R. (2d) 1; see also the decision of the Privy Council on appeal from Australia in *Queensland Mines Ltd v Hudson* (1978) 52 A.J.L.R. 399.

[187] (1826) 3 Russ. 241.

[188] (1834) 2 My. & K. 655 at 688.

[189] *Warman v Dwyer* (1995) 182 C.L.R. 544.

[190] (1872) 9 Ch. App. 309.

ascertain the share of the profits of the business but when it came down to working out how this was to be done this court decided that the appropriate remedy would be to order repayment of the capital with interest. In his judgment, James L.J. held that the share of profits to which the plaintiff was entitled could not simply be ascertained by working out the proportion of the capital to which she was entitled:

"But it was pointed out by Vice-Chancellor Wigram, in the case of *Willett v Blanford*,[191] and his judgment was afterwards repeated and approved of by the Lords Justices, that there was no rule for apportioning the profits according to the respective amounts of the capital, but that the division would be affected by considerations of the source of the profit, the nature of the business, and the other circumstances of the case. It is obvious that it must be so, for it would be easy to suggest a number of instances in which the profit of a business has no ascertainable reference to the capital—e.g., solicitors, factors, brokers, or, as was the case before the Lords Justices, bankers. Indeed, in almost every case where the business consists of buying and selling, the difference between prosperity and ruin mainly depends on the skill, industry, and care of the dealers; no doubt also greatly on their credit and reputation, and the possession of ready money to take advantage of favourable opportunities and to enable them to bide their time in unfavourable states of the market, and also greatly on established goodwill and connection of the house."

18–095 In the end, as I have said, James L.J. held that it would be too difficult to work out the share of profits to which the legatee was entitled and instead this court awarded her interest on her share of the residue to compensate her for the fact that her capital had been employed in the partnership business.

18–096 Does this line of authority help Mr Al-Saraj in this case? I think not. The hypothetical share, which the Murads would have given him if he had disclosed the set off arrangement, is not relevant to this argument because it was never actually agreed or put up as his contribution. Mr Al-Saraj under this approach would have to say that the £500,000 which he actually put up by way of set off should be treated as his investment in the joint venture. But that was the very sum that he lied to the Murads about. It was not a cash sum as they had been led to believe and accordingly I do not consider that he can say that he is entitled to an order which treats the £500,000 as his contribution to the profits made by the venture . . .

18–097 Finally, we note the statements of principle by Kiefel CJ, Keane J and Edelman J in *Ancient Order of Foresters in Victoria Friendly Society Ltd v Lifeplan Australia Friendly Society Ltd*.[192] This was a claim to recover the profits made by defendants who had dishonestly assisted in a breach of fiduciary duty, but the Justices considered that the same rules govern dishonest claims of this kind as govern claims for the profits of a breach of fiduciary duty. They observed that:[193]

While it is true that equity will not require an errant fiduciary or a participant in a breach of fiduciary duty to account for an advantage which the breach of fiduciary duty has not caused or to which it has not sufficiently contributed,[194] where causation is sufficiently established the onus is upon the errant fiduciary or participant to show that he or she should not account for the full value of the advantage. That onus is not discharged by mere conjecture or supposition giving the benefit of the doubt to a proven wrongdoer. The requirement of proof conforms with the obligation of a party charged with a breach of fiduciary duty to show why the full value of an advantage obtained in a situation of conflict of duty should not be disgorged.[195]

[One way in which the wrongdoer might discharge that onus and reduce the extent of the liability to disgorge profits] . . . is by demonstrating that the benefit or advantage is beyond the scope of the liability for which the wrongdoer should account for profits. A wrongdoer might prove that some profit or benefit is beyond the scope of liability for which he or she should account if the profit or benefit has no reasonable connection with the wrongdoing.[196]

---

[191] (1842) 1 Hare 253.
[192] (2018) 265 C.L.R. 1.
[193] (2018) 265 C.L.R. 1 at [13] and [15].
[194] Citing *Warman International Ltd v Dwyer* (1995) 182 C.L.R. 544 at 557 and 561.
[195] Citing *Birtchnell v Equity Trustees, Executors and Agency Co Ltd* (1929) 42 C.L.R. 384 at 398.
[196] Citing two U.S. cases: *Frank Music Corp v Metro-Goldwyn-Mayer Inc* 886 F. 2d 1545 (1989) at 1553; *Polar Bear Productions Inc v Timex Corp* [2004] 384 F. 3d 700 at 714.

In contrast to English authorities suggesting that "scope of duty" is the only relevant issue for the court to consider when identifying the gains for which a fiduciary must account,[197] the view taken in this passage is that "scope of duty" analysis acts as a check on the imposition of "too much" liability after a causal link between breach and profit has been identified. In our view this is a preferable approach, but we would add that a remoteness rule might also be used for this purpose. **18–098**

iv. Remoteness

In his dissenting judgment in *Murad v Al-Saraj*,[198] Clarke LJ discussed an Australian case, *Warman v Dwyer*.[199] Warman was the distribution agent for an Italian company that manufactured gearboxes. In breach of fiduciary duty, Warman's employee, Dwyer, formed a joint venture with the Italian manufacturer in competition with his employer, and made substantial profits. The question arose whether Dwyer and his associated companies should account for all of these profits, and the court held not, ordering them instead to account only for the profits made in the first two years of business. The court made the following comments:[200] **18–099**

> In the case of a business it may well be inappropriate and inequitable to compel the errant fiduciary to account for the whole of the profit of his conduct of the business or his exploitation of the principal's goodwill over an indefinite period of time. In such a case, it may be appropriate to allow the fiduciary a proportion of the profits, depending upon the particular circumstances. That may well be the case when it appears that a significant proportion of an increase in profits has been generated by the skill, efforts, property and resources of the fiduciary, the capital which he has introduced and the risks he has undertaken, so long as they are not risks to which the principal's property has been exposed. Then it may be said that the relevant proportion of the increased profits is not the product or consequence of the plaintiff's property but the product of the fiduciary's skill, efforts, property and resources.

Clarke LJ interpreted *Warman* to mean that a "but-for" causation test can sometimes be used to determine the scope of a fiduciary's liability to account. His Lordship considered that proof of this lay in the attention paid by the court to the trial judge's finding that Warman's business relationship with the Italian manufacturer would only have continued for about another year even if Dwyer had not breached his duty. However, a different view of the case is possible, namely that the court effectively held that the profits made by Dwyer and his companies after the first two years were too remote a consequence of his breach of duty to justify ordering them to account for these later profits. On this view, the significance of the trial judge's finding about the counterfactual was that it gave the court one means of assessing the point in time at which the defendant's gains could fairly be attributed to his own efforts rather than his breach of duty.[201] **18–100**

---

197 See paras 2–195 to 2–203.

198 [2005] W.T.L.R. 1573 at [154].

199 (1995) 182 C.L.R. 544.

200 ibid., at 561.

201 For the view that *Warman* is explicable on the basis that a remoteness rule was applied, see also *Kao Lee & Yip v Koo Hoi Yan* [2003] 3 H.K.L.R.D. 296; P. Devonshire "Account of Profits for Breach of Fiduciary Duty" (2010) 32 Sydney L.R. 389, 397–402; L. Ho "Deemed Performance in Account of Profits" in P. Devonshire and R. Havelock (eds), *The Impact of Equity and Restitution in Commerce* (Hart, 2019), pp.194–195.

C. Personal Liability for the Profits of a Breach of Confidence

i. Jurisdiction

18–101 Claimants are not automatically entitled to an account of profits as a remedy for breach of confidence and a court might refuse to make such an award, for example, where the costs of taking the account would be disproportionately large.[202] As Rimer LJ said of breach of confidence cases in *Walsh v Shanahan*,[203] "the award of an account of profits is a discretionary matter", adding that "the objective in any case is to identify the appropriate remedy for the circumstances of the wrongdoing." He also endorsed Sales J's statement of the approach to be taken when deciding the appropriateness of remedies which appears immediately below.

Vercoe v Rutland Fund Management Ltd

Chancery Division [2010] EWHC 424 (Ch) at [333]–[345]

18–102 The claimants identified a profit-making opportunity which entailed the purchase of a pawnbroking company and the claimants becoming part of the management team and acquiring shares in the company thereafter. They approached the defendant venture capital company with a request for finance and the parties signed a confidentiality agreement. The defendant proposed, and the claimants accepted, an arrangement under which the defendant would fund the purchase of the company and the claimants would be assigned management roles following the purchase. However the defendant then purchased the company, cut the claimants out, developed the business itself and made substantial profits when the company was floated on the stock market. The claimants brought proceedings for breach of the confidentiality agreement and it was agreed that they were entitled to an award of what are now called "negotiating damages" (for discussion of which see paras 18–030 and 18–045 to 18–047). The claimants argued that they were entitled to elect for an account of profits but this part of their claim was rejected. The following excerpt concerns the principles which the judge held to govern the latter point.

18–103 SALES J: Mr Newey [counsel for the claimants] submitted that in relation to the claimants' claim based on breach of obligations of confidentiality they had a complete discretion to choose between claiming compensation assessed by reference to the loss of the notional transaction to buy release from their rights . . . and claiming an account of profits. He relied in particular upon *Peter Pan Manufacturing Corporation v Corsets Silhouette Ltd*[204] (in a case where the claimant had supplied the defendant with confidential information regarding the design of a brassiere and the defendant made unauthorised use of that information to manufacture and sell brassieres according to that design, the judge said that the claimant had the right to elect to claim either damages or an account of profits) and *Siddell v Vickers*[205] (a claimant in a breach of patent case has a right to elect to take damages or an account of profits:). In the alternative, if the court has power to control the choice between those forms of relief, he submitted that in this case an account of profits was appropriate and should be ordered.

18–104 I do not accept either of these submissions. As to Mr Newey's primary submission, I consider that it has long been recognised that in relation to a claim based on breach of confidence there are circumstances in which the claimant will not be allowed to choose a remedy in the form of an account of profits, and may be confined to an award of damages (which will often be assessed by reference to the value of a notional reasonable agreement to buy release from the claimant's rights, as in relation to the breach of contract claim in this case). Recent developments in the law and wider considerations of justice tend to reinforce this approach.

---

202 *Fortuity Pty Ltd v Barcza* (1995) 32 I.P.R. 517 at 532.
203 [2013] EWCA Civ 411 at [64].
204 [1964] 1 W.L.R. 96 at 106 per Pennycuick J.
205 [1892] R.P.C. 152 at 162 per Lindley LJ.

The first obstacle for Mr Newey is the decision of the Court of Appeal in *Seager v Copydex Ltd.*[206] In that case the claimant had come up with an idea for a design for a new type of carpet grip and had provided the defendant with confidential information about that design in the course of negotiations for the defendant to market his grip; the negotiations came to nothing, but a little later the defendant started to manufacture and sell its own new carpet grip, which the court found had been designed by the defendant by making unauthorised use of the claimant's confidential information without appreciating that it was breaching its obligations to him. The claimant claimed "an inquiry as to damages by reason of the defendants' breaches of confidence . . . or alternatively an account of profits"[207] and thus appears to have been claiming the right to elect between those two remedies. The Court of Appeal found there had been a breach of confidence by the defendant, but that the appropriate remedy was for damages to be awarded, not an account of profits: see in particular [Lord Denning MR's statement that]:[208] 18–105

> "[The recipient of confidential information] should not get a start over others by using the information which he received in confidence. At any rate, he should not get a start without paying for it. It may not be a case for injunction or even an account, but only for damages, depending on the worth of the confidential information to him in saving him time and trouble;"

he then analysed the frame of mind of the defendant and gave judgment for damages to be assessed.

Mr Newey submitted that the court in that case did not actually decide that the claimant should be confined to an award of damages. I do not agree. In my view it is clear from the way in which the claimant had pleaded his case for a remedy in the form of an award of damages or an account of profits, from the terms of what Lord Denning said[209] and from the order the court made that the court positively decided the claimant should be limited to that remedy, even though he had asked for what might well have been a far more valuable remedy of an account. The court did not give the claimant an opportunity to elect between these different remedies. . . . *Seager v Copydex* therefore shows that there are cases involving a claim for breach of confidence where the claimant will not be afforded a right of election to choose the remedy of an account of profits, but will be confined to an award of damages. 18–106

This conclusion is also supported by later case law. [*Attorney General v Blake*[210]] is of great importance in the development of the law in this area. In the leading speech in that case, Lord Nicholls confirmed that the court always had a discretion regarding the grant of the remedy of an account of profits,[211] explained that in relation to other discretionary remedies in relation to breach of contract, such as specific performance and injunctive relief, they might be refused if to grant them would be oppressive[212] and then used the analogy with such remedies as the foundation for his analysis that in certain exceptional cases the remedy of an account of profits will be available in respect of breach of contract.[213] As he said:[214] 18–107

> "Remedies are the law's response to a wrong (or, more precisely, to a cause of action). When, exceptionally, a just response to a breach of contract so requires, the court should be able to grant the discretionary remedy of requiring a defendant to account to the plaintiff for the benefits he has received from his breach of contract. In the same way as a plaintiff's interest in performance of a contract may render it just and equitable for the court to make an order for specific performance or grant an injunction, so the plaintiff's interest in performance may make it just and equitable that the defendant should retain no benefit from his breach of contract."

Lord Nicholls also identified certain remedial differences between equity and common law in relation to infringement of rights of property as being the product of mere accidents of history rather than any valid underlying principle[215] and rejected the sophistry involved in saying that the remedy of an account of 18–108

---

206 [1967] 1 W.L.R. 923.
207 Ibid at 924.
208 Ibid at 931–932.
209 Ibid at 932.
210 [2001] 1 A.C. 268.
211 Ibid at 279.
212 Ibid at 282.
213 Ibid at 284–5.
214 Ibid at 284–5.
215 Ibid at 280.

profits may be available for breach of confidence but not for breach of contract, where the equitable and contractual obligations are in substance the same.[216]

18-109 In my view, Lord Nicholls' speech in *Blake* has opened the way to a more principled examination of the circumstances in which an account of profits will be ordered by the courts and where it will not. His reasoning,[217] comparing remedies available in contract and for breach of confidence in relation to the same underlying facts, flows in both directions. It both opens up the possibility of an award of an account of profits in relation to breach of contract relating to confidential information and also opens up the possibility for a more principled debate about when an account of profits should be refused in relation to a breach of confidence, and a damages award (typically assessed by reference to a notional reasonable price to buy release from the claimant's rights . . .) made instead. Both in cases of breach of contract and in cases of breach of confidence, the question (at a high level of generality) is, what is the just response to the wrong in question?[218] In both cases, to adapt Lord Nicholls' formulation . . . the test is whether the claimant's interest in performance of the obligation in question (whether regarded as an equitable obligation or a contractual obligation) makes it just and equitable that the defendant should retain no benefit from his breach of that obligation. Again, I think that there is a broad parallel with the way in which the courts will, as in *Ruxley Electronics and Construction Ltd v Forsyth*,[219] control the amount of damages to be awarded in a contract case by reference to the strength of the claimant's interest in performance of a contractual obligation, judged on an objective basis and weighing that against countervailing legitimate interests of the defendant, to ensure that the remedy awarded is not oppressive and is properly proportionate to the wrong done to the claimant.

18-110 Although in a certain sense the courts' decisions about these matters might be described as discretionary, in truth I think the courts are now seeking to articulate underlying principles which will govern the choices to be made as to the remedy or remedies available in any given case. In some situations, where the rights of the claimant are of a particularly powerful kind and his interest in full performance is recognised as being particularly strong, there may well be a tendency to recognise that the claimant should be entitled to a choice of remedy (both as between damages and an account of profits, and also possibly as between different bases of calculation of damages, such as by reference to loss actually suffered or by reference to a notional reasonable agreement to buy release from his rights). There are indications in the authorities that this may more readily be found to be appropriate in cases involving infringement of property rights.[220] This may reflect the particular importance usually attached to property rights and the extent of protection they are to be afforded in law—although one might think that in relation to ordinary rights in relation to property of a kind which is regularly bought and sold in a market, damages assessed by reference to a notional buy-out fee may often represent an appropriate and fair remedy, and it is possible that the law may develop in that way. By contrast, it may be more appropriate to award an account of profits where the right in question is of a kind where it would never be reasonable to expect that it could be bought out for some reasonable fee, so that it is accordingly deserving of a particularly high level of protection (such as the promise to keep state secrets which was in issue in *Blake*, which was classified as an exceptional case meriting such an award, and rights to protection under established fiduciary relationships, where trust between the parties rather than a purely commercial relationship is regarded as central to the obligations in question).

18-111 Cases will frequently arise where a significant choice falls to be made between damages calculated by reference to a notional reasonable buy out fee and an account of profits. Then in my judgment, in the light of *Blake*, where one is not dealing with infringement of a right which is clearly proprietary in nature (such as intellectual property in the form of a patent, as in *Siddell v Vickers*) and there is nothing exceptional to indicate that the defendant should never have been entitled to adopt a commercial approach in deciding how to behave in relation to that right, the appropriate remedy is likely to be an award of damages assessed by reference to a reasonable buy out fee rather than an account of profits. The law will control the choice between these remedies, having regard to the need to strike a fair balance between the interests of

---

216 Ibid at 285.

217 Ibid at 285.

218 Ibid at 284.

219 [1996] A.C. 344.

220 See, for an historic example, *Siddell v Vickers* [1892] R.P.C. 152, and also *Blake* at 278–280 and *Devenish Nutrition Ltd v Sanofi-Aventis SA* [2009] Ch. 390 at [75] and [155], cf [144]).

the parties at the remedial stage, rather than leaving it to the discretion of the claimant. The significance of *Seager v Copydex* is that it shows that, even in relation to confidential information closely akin to a patent (such as a secret manufacturing design or process), the law will not necessarily afford protection to the claimant extending to an account of profits. Still more strongly will that be the case as one moves further away from confidential information in a form resembling classic intellectual property rights towards forms of obligation in respect of confidential information more akin to purely personal obligations in contract and tort.

This approach is, I think, supported by the judgments in the Court of Appeal in *Experience Hendrix LLC v PPX Enterprises Inc.*[221] In that case the defendant licensed masters of recordings of certain music in breach of its agreement with the claimant that they should should not be licensed, and thereby made a profit. The claimant's claim for an account of profits arising from the breach of the agreement was dismissed, even though the breach was deliberate, because the case was not exceptional (there was no special interest of the claimant in having its rights protected, unlike in *Blake*) but rather arose in a commercial context, and the defendant was not in the position of a fiduciary or any position analogous to that. The claimant was instead awarded a payment equivalent to the reasonable notional royalties which would have been paid by the defendant to buy release from its obligations so as to be able to license the masters as it did.[222] **18–112**

The approach which I adopt also, in my view, produces a coherent picture regarding the extent of protection afforded by the law, moving from lesser protection in relation to an ordinary commercial context to greater protection where there is a fiduciary relationship, rather than too readily equiparating the two. In a commercial context, as reflected in *Experience Hendrix*, a degree of self-seeking and ruthless behaviour is expected and accepted to a degree. In a fiduciary relationship, by contrast, self-seeking behaviour is required to be reined in on the grounds that special obligations of trust have been assumed by the fiduciary to the other party. It seems natural that the law governing the extent of the remedies available in these different contexts should reflect the strength of the interest which the law recognises in each case as deserving protection and the increased importance of deterring abusive behaviour in a fiduciary relationship. As observed by James Edelman,[223] it is not obvious why the remedies for breach of confidence should necessarily be the same as for breach of fiduciary duty, so as to allow an account of profits; nor is it obvious why they should be more than the remedy available for, say, the tort of deceit. **18–113**

The law relating to breach of confidence covers a very wide range of different factual situations, and it is unsurprising that the strength of the arguments in favour of any particular remedy or set of remedies in respect of a particular breach of confidence varies across that range. Sometimes the nature of the obligation of confidence may be closely similar to a fiduciary obligation (as in the special context of obligations imposed on officers of the Secret Intelligence Service in *Blake*), in which case it may be appropriate for remedies to be available similar to those in respect of a breach of fiduciary duty; sometimes the nature of the obligation may be closely similar to the obligations which protect forms of intellectual property (as in *Corsets Silhouette* and *Seager v Copydex*), in which case it may be appropriate for remedies to be fashioned equivalent to those available in that context; sometimes (as observed by Lord Nicholls in *Blake's* case) the obligation may spring from a contract, or arise in circumstances closely similar to a contractual relationship, in which case the appropriate remedy (in the absence of exceptional circumstances) is likely to be similar to those available for breach of contract; in yet other cases, e.g. where the law of confidence is used to address use of private information obtained by a stranger, a relevant analogy may be drawn from the law of tort. **18–114**

In the present case, I consider that an award of an account of the profits made by the defendants would not be an appropriate remedy in relation to the claimants' breach of confidence claim. For reasons given below, there was no fiduciary relationship between [the defendant] and the claimants. Nor did the claimants provide [the defendant] with information about a secret design or process analogous to other forms of intellectual property. The relationship between them was founded upon a contractual relationship, in which each side bargained at arm's length to define the obligations to be accepted by [the defendant] in respect of the business idea or opportunity which [the claimants] had identified. The negative covenant given by [the defendant] as to use of the confidential information was broadly equivalent to the restrictive covenant in [*Wrotham Park Estate Co Ltd v Parkside Homes Ltd*[224]], and a remedy fashioned by reference **18–115**

---

221 [2003] 1 All E.R. (Comm.) 830.

222 See in particular [37] and [43]-[45] (Mance LJ) and [55] (Peter Gibson LJ).

223 J. Edelman, *Gain-Based Damages: Contract, Tort, Equity and Intellectual Property* (Hart, 2002), p.214.

224 [1974] 1 W.L.R. 798.

to the same kind of notional reasonable transaction to buy release from the claimant's rights as was considered in that case seems eminently suitable in this case. There are the same sufficient means of determining the notional fair or reasonable price appropriate for this case as there were in that case.

ii. Quantification

18–116 Matters may be relatively simple in cases where the entirety of a defendant's profits can be attributed to her breach of confidence, although questions may still arise as to the costs which should be deducted from the defendant's receipts when calculating the net profit she has made, in which case the same points may arise as also arise when calculating the net profits of a breach of fiduciary duty.[225] *Peter Pan Manufacturing Corp v Corsets Silhouette Ltd*[226] was a case of this kind: the defendant's brassieres were made to a design that would not have existed but for its misuse of the claimant's confidential information and so it was appropriate to make the defendant disgorge the whole of its profits. As Pennycuick J said, however, "profits" are different from receipts, and to calculate the former one must ask: "What has the [relevant party] expended on manufacturing these goods? What is the price which he has received on their sale? And the difference is profit."[227]

18–117 Potentially much more complex are cases where a defendant has used the claimant's confidential information, but has also used her own information, knowhow and/or skill to generate profits which should therefore be proportionately allocated between the defendant's wrongdoing and her non-wrongful conduct. How this should be done is likely to vary with circumstances, but the problem has often arisen in intellectual property cases to which a court is likely to attend, at least in cases concerned with a breach of confidence that has occurred in a commercial setting.[228]

5. Exemplary Damages in Equity?

18–118 Can an award of exemplary damages be made in equity in cases of outrageous misconduct by a trustee or fiduciary or recipient of confidential information? In *Re Brogden*,[229] North J said that "the court will not punish a trustee pecuniarily for his breach of trust except so far as loss has resulted therefrom to the trust estate", and to date no English court has awarded exemplary damages against a defaulting trustee.[230] It was once thought that the English courts could not award exemplary damages in respect of any kind of equitable wrongdoing because there was no case pre-dating 1964 where this had been done, as required by the "cause of action" test for the award of exemplary damages laid down in *AB v South West Water Services Ltd*.[231] However, the disavowal of this test in *Kuddus v Chief*

---

225 See paras 18–057 to 18–075.

226 [1964] 1 W.L.R. 96. See too *Attorney General v Blake* [2001] 1 A.C. 268 at 288; and cf *Dart Industries Inc v Decor Corp Pty Ltd* (1993) 179 C.L.R. 101 (breach of patent).

227 [1964] 1 W.L.R. 96 at 108.

228 e.g. *Cartier v Carlisle* (1862) 31 Beav. 292; *United Horse Shoe & Nail Co Ltd v Stewart* (1888) 5 R.P.C. 260; *Potton Ltd v Yorkclose Ltd* [1990] F.S.R. 11; *Celanese International Corp v BP Chemicals Ltd* [1999] R.P.C. 203; *OOO Abbott v Design & Display Ltd* [2016] EWCA Civ 98.

229 (1886) 38 Ch.D. 546 at 557. See too *Attorney General v Alford* (1855) 4 De G.M. & G. 843; *Vyse v Foster* (1872) L.R. 3 Ch. App. 309 at 333, affirmed (1874) L.R. 7 H.L. 318.

230 But note that the Pensions Act 1995 s.10 empowers the Pensions Regulator to levy penalty fines for maladministration of occupational pension schemes, as discussed in *All Metal Services Ltd v Pensions Regulator* [2017] UKUT 323 (TCC); [2017] Pens. L.R. 21; *Vive-Kananda v Pensions Regulator* [2019] UKUT 138 (TCC); [2019] Pens. L.R. 18.

231 [1993] Q.B. 507. See too Law Commission, *Aggravated, Exemplary, and Restitutionary Damages* (1997), Law Com. No.247, HC Paper No.346 (Session 1997–98), paras [5.54]–[5.56], recommending legislation to give the courts a power to award exemplary damages in relation to breaches of equitable duty. This recommendation has not been acted upon by Parliament.

Constable of Leicestershire[232] means that the courts could now make such awards if they believed this to be appropriate.

Canadian and New Zealand courts have held that exemplary damages can be awarded in response to a breach of fiduciary duty.[233] In Australia, the leading case on this subject is *Harris v Digital Pulse Pty Ltd*,[234] where Heydon JA opposed the award of exemplary damages for equitable wrongs, but Mason P favoured their award in suitable cases. Supporters of the latter view argue that like cases should not be treated differently because they have historically fallen within the separate jurisdictions of the common law and Chancery courts, and that breaches of trust and fiduciary duty resemble torts for which exemplary damages can be awarded.[235] It might be countered, however, that to the extent that trustees and other fiduciaries voluntarily assume their duties, breaches of trust and fiduciary duty more closely resemble breaches of contract, for which exemplary damages are not available under English law.[236] **18–119**

In *Mosley v News Group Newspapers Ltd*,[237] Eady J held that awards of exemplary damages could not be made in breach of privacy cases, but this cannot be viewed as the last word on the topic under English law,[238] and courts in Hong Kong and New Zealand have held that awards of exemplary damages can be made in breach of confidence cases where outrageous conduct has occurred.[239] **18–120**

Many discussions of the issue whether exemplary damages should be awarded in equity start from the premise that they are—and should be—available at common law in some situations, so that the reluctance of courts to award them in equity requires explanation. It is arguable, however, that exemplary damages should never be awarded because they disrupt the internal rationality of private law by looking outside the relationship between claimants and defendants to policy goals of deterrence and punishment that are more appropriately dealt with in the public law sphere.[240] On this view, it is not the English courts' refusal to award exemplary damages in equity that appears anomalous but their willingness to do so at common law. **18–121**

Questions

1. Clement wishes to invest £10 million in buy-to-let property in London. He consults a friend, Dave, who is a property developer. Dave undertakes to find a suitable property for Clement and later says that he has found a suitable block of flats selling for £10 million, but that the building needs renovation which will cost a further £2 million. He proposes that they enter a joint venture under which Clement will put up £10 million and Dave will put up the remaining £2 million, and Dave will also oversee all the building works and manage the letting of the property. Dave also proposes that they should split the rental income 75% to Clement and 25% to Dave, and that

---

232 [2001] UKHL 29; [2002] 2 A.C. 122.

233 Canada: *Norberg v Wynrib* [1992] 2 S.C.R. 226; *KM v HM* [1992] 3 S.C.R. 6; *Whiten v Pilot Insurance Co* [2002] 1 S.C.R. 595; *Chudy v Merchant Law Group* (2008) 300 D.L.R. (4th) 56. New Zealand: *Cook v Evatt (No.2)* [1992] 1 N.Z.L.R. 676.

234 (2003) 56 N.S.W.L.R. 298.

235 e.g. A. Burrows, "Remedial Coherence and Punitive Damages in Equity" in S. Degeling and J. Edelman (eds), *Equity in Commercial Law* (Law Book Company, 2005).

236 *Johnson v Unisys Ltd* [2001] UKHL 13; [2003] 1 A.C. 518 at [15]; *Devenish Nutrition Ltd v Sanofi-Aventis SA* [2008] EWCA Civ 1086; [2009] Ch. 390 at [143].

237 [2008] EWHC 1777 (QB); [2008] E.M.L.R. 20.

238 *PJS v News Group Newspapers Ltd* [2016] UKSC 26; [2016] A.C. 1081 at [42] and [92]; *Salt Ship Design AS v Prysmian Powerlink SRL* [2021] EWHC 2633 (Comm) at [452].

239 Hong Kong: *China Light & Power Co Ltd v Ford* [1996] 1 H.K.L.R. 57, followed in *Allan v Ng & Co (a firm)* [2012] 2 H.K.L.R.D. 160. New Zealand: *Aquaculture Corp v New Zealand Green Mussel Co. Ltd* [1990] 3 N.Z.L.R 299 at 302.

240 A. Beever, "The Structure of Aggravated and Exemplary Damages" (2003) 23 O.J.L.S. 87.

any profit on an eventual resale of the property should be split in the same way. Clement agrees and the deal goes ahead: the building is bought and renovated, the flats are let, and 5 years later they sell the building for £20 million.

Clement then discovers that Dave never put any cash into the project: the building vendor owed Dave a debt of £2 million and agreed to sell him the building in exchange for £8 million in cash and a write-off of the debt. Had Clement been aware of this, he would have gone ahead with the deal but would have insisted on taking a 90% share of all the profits. Clement also discovers that Dave let half the flats in the building at reduced rates to his friends and members of his family. Clement calculates that if all the flats had been let at market rates, this would have generated a rental income of £5 million over the 5-year period prior to resale, but the rental income actually generated was only £3 million.

Advise Clement.

2. When awarding remedies for breach of fiduciary duty, the courts must weigh up "the need the need to deter fiduciaries from abusing their trust on the one hand, and the goal of achieving a remedy that is fair to all those affected, on the other": *3464920 Canada Inc v Strother* [2007] 2 S.C.R. 177 at [156] per McLachlin CJ.

   Have the courts struck the right balance between principals and fiduciaries when assessing loss-based and gain-based awards for breach of fiduciary duty?

3. The courts' approach to deciding which remedies (if any) to award for breach of confidence affords them great flexibility to do justice on a case-by-case basis but it makes their decision-making very unpredictable with the result that parties have an incentive to litigate rather than settling their disputes.

   Discuss.

19

SPECIFIC PERFORMANCE, INJUNCTIONS AND DECLARATIONS

1. Overview

This chapter examines specific performance, injunctions, and declarations. They are important in practice as they can be a more effective remedy to realise equitable or common law rights than the remedy afforded at law to realise common law rights or other entitlements, usually damages, and are sometimes the only remedy available. Across private and public law; and common law, statute and equity, these remedies instantiate equity's commitment to furthering law's ends either by: (i) providing a remedy in aid of a legal entitlement recognised by common law rules when the remedy afforded at law is inadequate; or, (ii) providing a remedy in aid of a legal entitlement recognised by equitable rules that prevent the unconscientious assertion of some *ex ante* legal entitlement afforded by law (or equity). **19-001**

Orders for specific performance or an injunction are enforced either by empowering a person other than the defendant to take the required action,[1] or, more generally, by committing the defendant to prison on account of her contempt[2] (i.e. disobedience to the order of the court) until she complies with the court order and purges her contempt. Orders for specific performance and injunction are thus of a very different nature and significance from the defendant's perspective than the remedy afforded at law, as they restrict her choices to either: performing her obligation, or, face contempt of court. Orders for specific performance and injunctions remove the option of paying a monetary sum in lieu of performance. It should not be surprising then, that historically, and today, these remedies are not available as of right in response to common law or equitable rights. As we will see in this chapter, there are well defined equitable rules that guide the exercise of judicial discretion to award an injunction or specific performance, in addition to the rules that condition the availability of these equitable remedies in response to common law rights on the inadequacy of the remedy at law. **19-002**

1 Senior Courts Act 1981 s.39.

2 Sequestration of assets until compliance is also available against both individuals and corporations and is the only way of proceeding against corporations for contempt, although their directors may, of course, be imprisoned. Fines may also be imposed.

A. Definition and Classification

19–003 A starting point for describing an injunction is an order of the court forbidding the initiation or the continuance of some act or state of affairs or commanding that an act be done. In one sense however, this description is overinclusive insofar as it takes in all remedies, save declarations:[3]

> All court orders forbid or command one person to whom they are directed to refrain from doing something or not to do something, but not all court orders are injunctions. Legal usage alone, and not logic, decides which court orders can, and which cannot, accurately be described as injunctions.

19–004 Cases and commentaries tend instead to distinguish between different categories of injunctions to identify which rules determine their availability. Some of these categorial distinctions and their implications will be discussed below.[4] Relevant to our initial definition of, and distinction between, injunctions and specific performance, is that between *prohibitory* and *mandatory* injunctions. This distinction is drawn substantively, that is by asking whether the order requires a defendant's action or inaction for compliance.[5] Where an order requires a defendant to take action to comply it is mandatory. Where an order requires a defendant to refrain from taking action it is prohibitory. This is opposed to asking how the order is framed. For example, a court order requiring the demolition of a house could be framed in the negative as an order not to leave it standing; the order would nonetheless be mandatory on the basis that it requires the defendant to take action to demolish the house and does not prohibit the defendant from taking inaction. In addition, whereas the execution of prohibitory injunctions generally needs no supervision (the defendant simply has to refrain from committing the prohibited act), the execution of a mandatory order may do so, e.g. in the case of an order to demolish a house in a particular manner.

19–005 Primary contractual obligations that require a party to take action are enforced by orders for specific performance rather than mandatory injunctions.[6] Whereas a secondary obligation, whether arising in contract, such as the duty to pay damages for breach, or in tort, such as a tortfeasor's duty to pay damages for nuisance or trespass, is usually enforced via a mandatory injunction. Another way of distinguishing between specific performance and mandatory injunctions is that specific performance is sometimes reserved for orders compelling one party to perform the entirety of their side of a contract, and a mandatory injunction is reserved for orders compelling performance of part of a party's contractual obligations, or performance on a temporary basis. What is the point of insisting on this difference? Does it matter whether a claimant obtains a mandatory injunction or a decree of specific performance? In terms of enforcement, it cannot matter for both remedies are enforced in the same way: in the case of an individual defendant, by imprisonment,[7] fine or sequestration of assets (or any combination of these) and in the case of a corporation (whose officers may, additionally, be punished in their individual capacities), by fine or sequestration of assets, or both.[8]

19–006 Nonetheless, it does matter which order a claimant must ask for because, as will be seen, the number of grounds on which a decree for specific performance may be refused is greater than the

---

3 J.D. Heydon, M.J. Leeming and P.G. Turner, *Meagher, Gummow & Lehane's Equity Doctrines & Remedies*, 5th edn (LexisNexis Butterworths, 2015), para.21–005. This passage appears in a paragraph that was approved by Millett J in *ISC Technologies Ltd v Radcliffe* (Ch.D., 7 December 1990, unreported).

4 See paras 19–118 to 19–124.

5 *Truckell v Stock* [1957] 1 W.L.R. 161.

6 See para.19–015.

7 Contempt of Court Act 1981 s.14(1), discussed in *Lomas v Parle* [2003] EWCA Civ 1804; [2004] 1 W.L.R. 1642 and *Re W (A Child) (Abduction: Committal)* [2011] EWCA Civ 1196; [2012] 1 W.L.R. 1036.

8 RSC Orders 45 and 52, as incorporated into the Civil Procedure Rules 1998.

number of grounds on which a final injunction may be refused. This appears to be for a justifiable reason: by contract, a party may either, by negative stipulation, put herself under prohibitions that she does not have under the general law; or, by positive stipulation, impose on herself obligations which she does not have under the general law (apart from the contract). In the former case, the party merely restricts her freedom to act, which can be enforced by a prohibitory injunction without imposing burdens on her over and above those which the general law imposes. But in the latter case, where a party has agreed to do something which the general law does not require her to do, the court will be astute to enquire into the justice of making the party perform her promise in kind. It will want to be certain that, for example, the counter-party seeking relief is ready, willing and able to perform her own contractual obligation(s), that there is "mutuality" between the parties, and so on.

Moreover, it is often said that, unlike the case with mandatory injunctions, no decree of specific performance will be made on an interim basis (i.e. pending trial). If true, it would matter very much whether a claimant's claim was for a mandatory injunction or a decree of specific performance, for in the first case she might obtain interim relief, but in the second she could not. The case of *Sky Petroleum Ltd v VIP Petroleum Ltd*,[9] however, tends to blur the distinction and, indeed, suggests that specific performance may lie on an interim basis. There, the claimant applied for an interim prohibitory injunction restraining the defendant from failing to supply it with petrol, which failure was allegedly in breach of contract. Goulding J treated the motion as one for an interim decree of specific performance, looking at the substance rather than the form, and granted it. **19–007**

Sky Petroleum Ltd v VIP Petroleum Ltd

Chancery Division, [1974] 1 W.L.R. 576 at 578–579

The claimants had contracted to purchase all their petrol, at fixed prices, from the defendants. During a petrol shortage the defendants purported to terminate the contract on the ground of breach of certain credit provisions therein by the claimants. Pending trial of that issue, the claimants sought an injunction to restrain the defendants from withholding supplies. **19–008**

GOULDING J.: . . . What I have to decide is whether any injunction should be granted to protect the plaintiffs in the meantime. There is trade evidence that the plaintiffs have no great prospect of finding any alternative source of supply for the filling stations which constitute their business. The defendants have indicated their willingness to continue to supply the plaintiffs, but only at prices which, according to the plaintiffs' evidence, would not be serious prices from a commercial point of view. There is, in my judgment, so far as I can make out on the evidence before me, a serious danger that unless the court interferes at this stage the plaintiffs will be forced out of business. In those circumstances, unless there is some specific reason which debars me from doing so, I should be disposed to grant an injunction to restore the former position under the contract until the rights and wrongs of the parties can be fully tried out. The most serious hurdle in the way of the plaintiffs is the well known doctrine that the court refuses specific performance of a contract to sell and purchase chattels not specific or ascertained. That is a well-established and salutary rule, and I am entirely unconvinced by Mr Christie, for the plaintiffs, when he tells me that an injunction in the form sought by him would not be specific enforcement at all. The matter is one of substance and not of form, and it is, in my judgment, quite plain that I am, for the time being, specifically enforcing the contract if I grant an injunction. However, the ratio behind the rule is, as I believe, that under the ordinary contract for the sale of non-specific goods, damages are a sufficient remedy. That, to my mind, is lacking in the circumstances of the present case. The evidence suggests, and indeed it is common knowledge that the petroleum market is in an unusual state in which a would-be buyer cannot go out into the market and contract with another seller, possibly at some sacrifice as to price. Here, the defendants appear for practical purposes to be the plaintiffs' sole means of keeping their business going, and I am **19–009**

9 [1974] 1 W.L.R. 576. See also *Capita Trust Co (Channel Islands) Ltd v Chatham Maritime J3 Developments Ltd* [2006] EWHC 2596 (Ch); [2007] L. & T.R. 2; *Ashworth v Royal National Theatre* [2014] EWHC 1176 (QB); [2014] 4 All E.R. 238. As to the distinction between primary and secondary obligations see paras 13–050 and 19–034.

> prepared so far to depart from the general rule as to try to preserve the position under the contract until a later date. I therefore propose to grant an injunction.

19-010 A declaration is a final decree or pronouncement of the court as to the existence of a party's legal entitlement(s), such as a right or power, and correlatively another party's duty(ies) or liability(ies).[10] Unlike specific performance or an injunction, a declaration is not enforceable by further proceedings, such as via execution or contempt of court. The finality of a declaration is achieved via res judicata or an issue estoppel; either of which mean that the parties to a declaration cannot contest the issue again in later proceedings.[11]

B. Equitable or Common Law Legal Entitlements

19-011 Injunctions and declarations can be awarded in response to a legal entitlement generated by equitable rules. This does not raise the jurisdictional question of whether or not the remedy available at law is adequate. In these instances, they also do not raise the broader questions as to the interconnections between common law and equity, which arise when injunctions, declarations and specific performance are awarded in response to common law rights.

19-012 It is a controversial issue whether equitable remedies in aid of common law rights should be treated separately from common law remedies. On one view,[12] it is misleading to distinguish equitable and common law remedies on the ground that the former are discretionary and the latter are not, given that both are granted and withheld in line with clearly established rules and principles. Some of these equitable remedies allow the courts a wide discretion when exercising their equitable jurisdiction, the same can also be said of certain common law principles (e.g. the rules limiting the award of compensatory damages, and the rules authorising the award of punitive damages). Moreover, it is untrue that the common law lacks the means to compel the performance of primary obligations, for this is the function of the award of an agreed sum in contract cases. It is also said to diminish our understanding of the law to consider equitable and common law remedies separately, because this obscures the full range of the courts' remedial armoury in private law, and disguises the similarities which exist between some equitable and common law remedies, e.g. an account of profits in equity and an award of restitutionary damages at common law. While there are differences between equitable and common law remedies (e.g. common law damages, in contrast to equitable damages awarded in lieu of an injunction, are not awarded in response to an anticipated wrong);[13]

> nothing would be lost, and some simplicity and rationality would be gained, if one took the small steps necessary to move to a fully-fused system of remedies where it would be unnecessary to use the labels common law and equitable.

19-013 On this view of the law, the discussion which follows in this chapter would serve a better purpose if it appeared alongside a discussion of common law remedies in books on contract, tort, unjust enrichment, and remedies.

---

10 See further Heydon, Leeming and Turner, *Meagher, Gummow and Lehane's Equity Doctrines and Remedies* 5th edn (2014), paras 19-010—19-070.

11 A declaration is final for the purposes of an appeal; *Becker v Marion City Corp* [1977] A.C. 271.

12 A. Burrows, *Fusing Common Law and Equity: Remedies, Restitution and Reform* (Hochelaga Lecture, 2002), pp.1–26; A.Burrows, "We Do This at Common Law But That in Equity" (2002) 22 O.J.L.S. 1; cf. S. Worthington, *Equity*, 2nd edn (Oxford University Press, 2006), Ch.2.

13 A. Burrows, *Remedies for Torts and Breach of Contract*, 3rd edn (Oxford University Press, 2004), pp.11–12.

There is another view,[14] however, namely that it is desirable to treat equitable remedies differently because they possess unique characteristics, most notably that they are subject to discretionary defences, unlike common law remedies which may be claimed as of right on proof of a legal wrong (with or without proof of consequent loss, depending on the cause of action). Equitable remedies also have a distinctive means of enforcement, the effect of which is to force a defendant, through the threat of punishment or otherwise, to comply with her legal obligations in kind.[15] So, for example, a defendant who is made the subject of injunctive relief or a decree of specific performance may not leave her "primary" contractual or tortious obligations unfulfilled, and may not choose instead to fulfil the "secondary" obligation to pay damages which arises on breach of a primary duty of performance, as she can at common law. Further, when a defendant is subject to a common law remedy, such as damages, the processes for enforcement does not threaten her personal liberty. When subject to an equitable order of an injunction or specific performance, however, the defendant must, on pain of contempt of court, act or refrain from acting in the manner specified in the court order. Indeed, even if she chooses to take the punishment rather than act as she should, the court may simply by-pass her and in an appropriate case empower someone else to do the act instead. On this view of the law, it makes sense to consider equitable remedies alongside one another, because this enables us to gain a better understanding of their common features. **19–014**

2. Specific Performance

A. Overview

Specific performance compels a defendant to perform a contractual obligation that is positive in the sense that performance requires action to be taken and breach occurs upon a failure to act. This is in distinction to the remedy of a prohibitory injunction, discussed below, that compels performance of contractual obligations that are negative in the sense that they prohibit action from being taken and are breached by the prohibited action being taken.[16] As we will see, prohibitory and mandatory injunctions are also awarded to compel performance of other non-contractual obligations. Specific performance is a remedy awarded exclusively in response to positive contractual obligations.[17] **19–015**

A distinction has sometimes been made between specific performance of "executory contracts", regarded as "specific performance, in the proper sense";[18] and specific performance of "executed contracts". In this context an "executory contract" is one that requires the further exercise of a power, such as a conveyance of title, to finally settle the parties' legal relations and give effect to their intentions. An example is a contract for the sale of property. This is in contrast to an "executed contract" where the parties intend for the contract itself to determine the parties' legal relationship, such as a contract for the supply of services for payment. The use of the labels "executory" and "executed" can make it seem as if the distinction is referring to relative stages of performance of a contract. While this is an important consideration, as we will see in relation to mutuality, the distinction being drawn by the labels of "executed" and "executory" is rather as to whether the parties' intended their legal relations **19–016**

---

14 Heydon, Leeming and Turner, *Meagher, Gummow and Lehane's Equity Doctrines and Remedies*, 5th edn (2014) Ch.2.
15 *"In specie"* in Latin, from which root the term "specific performance" derived.
16 As to this distinction, see further *JC Williamson Ltd v Lukey and Mulholland* (1931) 45 C.L.R. 282, 298–99 (Dixon J).
17 See paras 19–005 to 19–006.
18 *JC Williamson Ltd v Lukey and Mulholland* at 297–78 (Dixon J). See also *Wolverhampton and Walsall Railway Co v London and North Western Railway Co* (1873) L.R. 16 Eq. 433 at 439.

to be determined by the contract, or, to be determined according to some other exercise of power that one party has promised to effect, such as to convey title to land.

19–017 The relevance of this distinction today is that it can mean some of the rules pertaining to the availability of specific performance can apply differently, albeit the cases have largely accepted that specific performance is, prima facie, available regardless of whether a contract is "executory" or "executed". This can be seen from Lord Radcliffe's response in *Australian Hardwoods Pty Ltd v Commissioner for Railways*, excerpted below, to counsel's submission that the specific relief asked for in that case was not specific performance "proper", and that specific performance ought to be confined to "executory" agreements which were not intended in their nature to be the final instrument regulating the mutual relations of the parties.

Australian Hardwoods Pty Ltd v Commissioner for Railways

Privy Council, [1961] 1 W.L.R. 425 at 433–434

19–018 LORD RADCLIFFE (for the Board): Now it is true that on one occasion Lord Selborne L.C. did advert to such a distinction, stating that

> the common expression 'specific performance' as applied to suits known by that name, presupposes an executory as distinct from an executed agreement, something remaining to be done, such as the execution of a deed or a conveyance, in order to put the parties in the position relative to each other in which by the preliminary agreement they were intended to be placed.[19]

The same distinction has been adverted to in a case in the High Court of Australia — *J.C. Williamson Ltd. v Lukey*.

19–019 Their Lordships are of opinion, however, that this distinction between executory and executed agreements (to adopt Lord Selborne's nomenclature for this occasion) in connection with the jurisdiction to grant specific performance does not suggest any line of argument that can be of assistance to this appellant. The distinction certainly cannot be taken as warrant for the idea that the jurisdiction to give specific relief by ordering the performance of particular acts is confined to the enforcement of agreements that are executory in this sense; nor can it mean that when a court is invited to order specific performance of an agreement which is not executory, or some part of that agreement, it should not pay attention to considerations as to the conduct and position of the plaintiff which are similar to those it attends to in the "proper" cases. Lord Selborne, in the passage referred to, made only the broad distinction between the class of executory agreements, such as agreements for the sale of land and marriage articles, and the principles applicable to specific performance of them on the one hand, and on the other a very different class of agreement, which he described as "ordinary agreements for work and labour . . . hiring and service and things of that sort." Such a division leaves uncategorised a great many agreements of various kinds which are not inherently unsuitable for specific performance in the sense that contracts for work and labour, hiring and service are normally regarded as being by their very nature so unsuitable. As to this intermediate class it does not appear to their Lordships that there is any obvious reason why, even if their terms do not call for the execution of a further instrument regulating the rights of the parties, the equitable right to specific relief in respect of them should be tried by principles which are in any way different from those applicable to executory agreements "proper."

B. Effect(s) and Enforcement

19–020 When an order for specific performance is made, what happens to the parties' legal relations under the contract? In *Johnson v Agnew*,[20] Lord Wilberforce explained the effect of an order for specific performance as to place the matter:[21]

---

19 *Wolverhampton and Walsall Railway Co v London and North Western Railway Co* at 439.

20 [1980] A.C. 367.

21 *Johnson v Agnew* [1980] A.C. 367 at 398.

> in the hands of a court of equity, or one exercising equity jurisdiction, the subsequent control of the matter will be exercised according to equitable principles. The court would not make an order dissolving the decree of specific performance and terminating the contract (with recovery of damages) if to do so would be unjust, in the circumstances then existing, to the other party, in this case to the purchaser. This is why there was, in the Court of Appeal, rightly, a relevant and substantial argument, repeated in this House, that the non-completion of the contract was due to the default of the vendors: if this had been made good, the court could properly have refused them the relief sought. But the Court of Appeal came to the conclusion that this non-completion, and the ultimate impossibility of completion, was the fault of the purchaser. I agree with their conclusion and their reasons on this point and shall not repeat or add to them . . .

This enables the court to prevent a claimant who has won an order for specific performance from changing her mind and asserting a right to damages after the defendant has detrimentally relied on the original order. However, it also means that whenever an order for specific performance is made, the parties' original rights under the contract are subject to equitable principles that would not have affected the parties' original rights at common law.[22] However, and as pointed out by Charles Mitchell:[23] **19–021**

> This model of the law is complex, and it is also inconsistent with Lord Wilberforce's own statement that "if an order for specific performance is sought and is made, the contract remains in effect and is not merged in the judgment for specific performance"[24] – not to mention Clawson LJ's previous statement in *John Barker & Co Ltd v Littman* that the court has no "dispensing power" to dissolve an order for specific performance and order the forfeiture of a purchaser's deposit, because a vendor has the right to these things *ex debito justitiae*.[25] Hence there is much to be said for the different view that even after an order for specific performance has been made, both parties' common law rights under the contract subsist, including the right to terminate for breach and sue for damages, and that either party can exercise these rights without complying with equitable requirements such as the rule that a claimant must come into court with clean hands.

Enforcement of a decree of specific performance may take various forms, e.g. empowering a person other than the defendant to execute a conveyance which the latter has promised but refused to execute,[26] or, more generally, committing the defendant to prison on account of her contempt[27] (i.e. disobedience to the order of the court) until she complies with the court order and purges her contempt. **19–022**

Specific performance can thus be a strategic and powerful remedy for a plaintiff as it compels the defendant's actual performance of her contractual obligations, and thereby alleviates a plaintiff of the requirement to take (in)action as necessary to mitigate her loss, as well as protect her from losses that might otherwise be recoverable as being too remote or unforeseeable. Equally, the remedy has special significance for the defendant, removing the choice to perform in specie or to pay monetary compensation that is otherwise afforded to a contractual party at law, and replacing it with the choice between performance to comply with the court order or liability for contempt of court. Specific **19–023**

---

[22] M. Hetherington, "Keeping the Plaintiff out of His Contractual Remedies: The Heresies That Survive *Johnson v Agnew*" (1980) 96 L.Q.R. 403.

[23] C. Mitchell, "*Johnson v Agnew* (1979)" in C. Mitchell and P. Mitchell (eds) *Landmark Cases in the Law of Contract* (Hart Publishing, 2008), Pt E.

[24] *Johnson v Agnew* [1980] A.C. 367 at 393, citing *Austins of East Ham Ltd v Macey* [1941] Ch. 338 at 341, where Sir Wilfrid Greene MR stressed that after an order for specific performance has been made "the contract is still there".

[25] [1941] Ch. 405 at 412.

[26] Senior Courts Act 1981 s.39.

[27] Sequestration of assets until compliance is also available against both individuals and corporations and is the only way of proceeding against corporations for contempt, although their directors may, of course, be imprisoned. Fines may also be imposed.

performance means that the defendant's performance is sanctioned by the quasi-criminal regime for contempt of court, not just the regime for damages at law. It should not be surprising, then, that the availability of specific relief is guarded; a contractual party does not have an entitlement to specific performance, and indeed any consideration of a plaintiff's entitlement depends first on her satisfying a court that it has the jurisdiction to award specific performance in the first place. To this end, it can be helpful to distinguish between the jurisdictional question or factors pertaining to whether specific performance is even an option, and the discretionary factors that guide a court's determination of whether it should be awarded on the particular facts.

19–024 As we will see, there is a range of rules pertaining to the availability of specific performance, and cases and commentaries do not always expressly categorise any individual one as being a jurisdictional or discretionary factor. It is useful, however, to keep in mind whether a particular rule is one going to the jurisdiction or prima facie availability of specific performance, or rather pertains to the more general question of whether equitable relief should be awarded in the case. This is to have a better understanding of the rule and its application and as it interlinks with other potential issues, such as the availability of equitable damages in lieu of specific performance. These damages are only available when the specific performance was prima facie available, i.e. the jurisdictional factors have been made out, but owing to some discretionary reason was not granted on the facts; this has been discussed in Chapter 18.[28]

19–025 Finally, the special treatment of specific performance as an exceptional add on to the default or core remedy of damages is in contrast to some civil law jurisdictions which treat specific performance as the core remedy to which a contractual party is entitled.[29] This suggests a greater commitment by in these jurisdictions to claimants' performance interest in contracts, though historically it is only post-Judicature that the English emphasis on damages became dominant following the marginalisation of equitable doctrine in contract cases.[30]

C. Jurisdictional Factors

i. A valid contract for adequate consideration or part performance

19–026 One pre-requisite to the availability of specific performance is that there is a valid and binding contract in existence between the parties. Without a valid contract, there is no obligation to order the defendant to specifically perform. Specific performance will not be ordered in relation to a contract that is voided for fraud or mistake, for example.

19–027 As part of this requirement, the party seeking specific performance must have given adequate consideration.[31] The consideration provided by a deed, although sufficient for the courts to discover a binding contract at law, is inadequate for the courts to hold that this contract is specifically enforceable in equity.[32] Neither will past consideration,[33] nor a promise to perform a contractual duty already

---

28 See paras 18–048 to 18–050.

29 See generally: J. Oosterhuis, *Specific Performance in German, French and Dutch Law in the Nineteenth Century – Remedies in an Age of Fundamental Rights and Industrialization* (Martinus Nijhoff & Brill, 2011) and para.19–071.

30 W.R. Cornish, et al, *Law and Society in England: 1750–1950*, 2nd edn (Hart Publishing, 2019), pp.215–216.

31 *Jefferys v Jefferys* (1841) Cr. & Ph. 138.

32 *Re Pryce* [1917] 1 Ch. 234 at 241 (Eve J); *Cannon v Hartley* [1949] Ch. 213. In marriage settlement cases, however, children of a marriage may obtain specific performance, as they are treated in equity as having provided consideration: *Re Pryce; Re Kay's Settlement* [1939] Ch. 329.

33 *Robertson v St John* (1786) 2 Bro. C.C. 140.

in existence,[34] suffice. Beyond these limits, there is no positive test for adequacy of consideration and cases have taken different views as to whether nominal consideration, such as £1, will suffice.[35]

Exceptionally, this requirement will be met for some contracts that are otherwise invalid or unenforceable at law owing to a failure to comply with writing requirements under the Statute of Frauds 1677, or other legislation, such as the Law of Property Act 1925, via the doctrine of part performance. The doctrine of part performance is discussed in more detail elsewhere,[36] and it is another example of how equity operates to prevent subversion of the law via its exceptional application to prevent one party from relying on the legal entitlements afforded to them by law in a way that undermines law's ends. Part performance has been rationalised on the basis that "[c]ourts of Equity will not permit the statute to be made an instrument of fraud".[37] Part performance applies where one party, the claimant, C, has acted (or omitted to act) on the faith of there being a contract with another party, the defendant, D, who will not be permitted to rely on a statutory writing requirement to avoid enforcement of D's obligation thereunder. The gist of this doctrine was summarised by Fry in a passage of his text on *Specific Performance* that was approved in *Chaproniere v Lambert*:[38] **19–028**

> If a man have made a bargain with another, and allowed that other to act upon it, he may have created an equity against himself which he cannot resist by setting up the want of formality in the evidence of the contract out of which the equity in part arose.

The interaction of part performance and specific performance is that D is ordered to bring a valid contract into existence, i.e. by signing the relevant documentation, and which is then the basis for orders for specific performance. This interaction is discussed by Dixon J in the following excerpt. **19–029**

J C Williamson Ltd v Lukey and Mulholland

High Court of Australia, (1931) 45 C.L.R. 282 at 300

DIXON J.: In cases of specific performance, the party is said to be charged upon the equities arising out of the acts of part performance and not merely upon the contract. The acts of part performance must be such as to be consistent only with the existence of a contract between the parties, and to have been done in actual performance of that which in fact existed. But in such a case the equity which so arises is to have the entire contract carried into execution by both sides. Because the acts done upon the faith of the contract could not have taken place if it had not been made, and the contract is of a kind which it is considered equitable to enforce in specie, a party who has so acted in partial execution of the contract obtains an equity to its complete performance. **19–030**

ii. Inadequacy of damages

The requirement for inadequacy of damages is explained by Lord Hoffmann in *Co-operative Insurance Society Ltd v Argyll Stroes (Holdings) Ltd* and is set out in the excerpt from para.19–067. **19–031**

The requirement of inadequacy of damages is sometimes explained by reference to various categories or types of contracts, and this can provide a useful means of understanding the application of this rule to specific cases. It is important to keep in mind, however, that the overarching criterion is not how a contract is categorised; rather, it is whether in the circumstances, the remedy afforded at law will **19–032**

---

[34] *Stilk v Myrick* (1809) 2 Camp 317; 170 E.R. 1168.

[35] In *Mountford v Scott* [1975] Ch. 258 £1 was sufficient consideration, although fell short of valuable consideration in *Milroy v Lord* (1862) 4 De G.F. & J. 264 and *Peffer v Rigg* [1977] 1 W.L.R. 285.

[36] See, e.g. I.F.C. Spry, *Equitable Remedies*, 9th edn (Thomson Reuters, 2013), Ch.23.

[37] *Maddison v Alderson* (1883) 8 App Cas 467 at 474–476 (Lord Selborne LC).

[38] *Chaproniere v Lambert* [1917] 2 Ch. 356 at 361.

effect law's end(s), and if not, then inadequacy is made out. Usually, the aim of damages for breach of contract is to put the plaintiff in the position, as close as possible, to that they would be in but for the breach, or if the contract had been performed.[39] Usually, this is the expectation measure of damages, a sub-species of which includes damages for reliance loss,[40] the end or remedial aim of which is to put the plaintiff in the position she would have been in had there been no breach. Sometimes, for one reason or another, damages will not achieve this result, being inadequate to meet their stated aim, and it is for this reason that equity steps in to supply a remedy that will further law's ends in another way, relevantly to compel the defendant's performance of her contractual obligation.

19–033 An example where damages are inadequate is a contract for the sale of specific property, such as land.[41] Each piece of real estate is regarded as unique and, therefore, damages will be an inadequate remedy for a purchaser, in the sense that, damages will not enable her to buy a replacement in the market, as held in *Adderley v Dixon*.[42]

Paul Davies, "Being Specific About Specific Performance"

[2018] Conv. 324, 327–330

The uniqueness of property

19–034 It is generally thought that specific performance is most appropriate where the subject-matter of the contract is unique.[43] English law has traditionally accepted that each parcel of land is unique, since no parcel of land can be exactly the same as another; as a result, specific performance is available as a matter of course.[44] This was explained by Lord Diplock in *Sudbrook v Eggleton*:[45]

> "Since if [the purchasers] do not acquire the fee simple they will not have to pay that price, the damages for loss of such a bargain would be negligible and, as in most cases of breach of contract for the sale of land at a market price by refusal to convey it, would constitute a wholly inadequate and unjust remedy for the breach. That is why the normal remedy is by a decree for specific performance by the vendor of his primary obligation to convey, upon the purchaser's performing or being willing to perform his own primary obligations under the contract."

19–035 This approach to contracts for the sale of land has strong historical roots. By the 15th century, the jurisdiction to award specific performance was both well-known and well-established, and "most petitioners sought the enforcement of agreements to sell land".[46] Indeed, specific performance may have been especially important at a time when land was relatively difficult to obtain and there was no open market for real property.[47]

---

39 *Robinson v Harman* (1848) 1 Ex. 850, (Parke B); *Morris-Garner v One Step (Support) Ltd* [2018] UKSC 20; [2019] A.C. 649 at [35] (Lord Reed with whom the President, Lady Hale, and Lords Wilson and Carnwath agreed). See further H. Beale, *Chitty on Contracts*, 30th edn (Sweet & Maxwell, 2008), Ch.29.

40 *Omak Maritime Ltd v Mamola Challenger Shipping Co Ltd* [2010] EWHC 2026; [2010] W.L.R. 230 at [42]–[57].

41 "[D]amages have traditionally not been regarded as an adequate remedy on the basis that each piece of land is unique"; *Mungalsingh v Juman* [2015] UKPC 38 at [33] (Lord Neuberger).

42 (1824) 1 Sim. & St. 607 at 610–612. See too *Hall v Warren* (1804) 9 Ves. 605. In *Verrall v Great Yarmouth BC* [1981] 1 Q.B. 202, the Court of Appeal affirmed the grant of specific performance to enforce a contractual licence to occupy premises. As no other premises could be found, damages would have been an inadequate remedy (the promisee being unable to hire any premises with any damages awarded).

43 A. Kronman, "Specific Performance" (1978) 45 Univ. Chicago L.R. 351.

44 *Hall v Warren* (1804) 9 Ves. Jr. 605 at 608; 32 E.R. 738; *Adderley* [rest of footnote omitted].

45 *Sudbrook v Eggleton* [1983] 1 A.C. 444 at 478; [1982] 3 W.L.R. 315.

46 G. Jones and W. Goodhart, *Specific Performance* 2nd edn (Butterworths, 1996), p. 6.

47 P. Brenner, "Specific Performance of Contracts for the Sale of Land Purchased for Resale or Investment" (1978) 24 McGill L.J. 513, 516–517 [rest of footnote omitted].

However, the situation may no longer be so clear.[48] Land is bought and sold on the open market. And although each parcel of land is unique in the sense that the fixed location of each unit cannot be precisely the same as any other, increasingly for commercial purchasers, at least, one property may be just as good as another. This might be particularly significant where the intention is to sell the property for a profit, or to rent out the property: two similar properties may be susceptible to the same growth due to a rise in the market, or produce the same rental yield. If the only interest the purchaser has in the property is its financial value, then there may be a strong case for awarding damages rather than specific performance if the vendor breaches the contract to sell. **19–036**

In contract law generally, the burden should be on the innocent party to show that damages are not adequate and specific performance should be awarded.[49] But that burden seems to be reversed in contracts for the sale of land, since the assumption has consistently been that land is unique so damages will not be adequate because no satisfactory substitute can be acquired.[50] That approach has prevailed even in the commercial context. . . . **19–037**

Specific performance in favour of the vendor

That the desired property is "unique" may explain why the purchaser should be granted specific performance. But it does not explain why the vendor should also be granted specific relief. After all, the vendor is really interested in receiving money[51] in return for the property, and, potentially, anyone can provide money for the property: it does not have to be the purchaser's money. Indeed, it is generally thought that an obligation to pay money should not be specifically enforced, and these cases concerning the vendor represent an unusual anomaly.[52] **19–038**

Early authorities appeared to accept that since the vendor only wanted the purchaser's money, he should be limited to remedies at law and specific performance should not be awarded. . . . **19–039**

Nevertheless, that early preference for common law remedies over specific performance has been discarded and the current position in English law is that the vendor can "thrust the property down the purchaser's throat"[53] through an order for specific performance. It is not entirely clear what brought about the change in approach. . . . The real driver of the change was more likely to have been a new emphasis upon "mutuality"[54]: since specific performance is available to the purchaser, it should be available to the vendor.[55] Yet in more recent times, the requirement of "mutuality" in the law of specific performance has been persuasively criticised,[56] and it is a weak basis for such strong protection in favour of the vendor. The focus should be on whether the court's discretion to grant specific performance should properly be exercised. **19–040**

Clearly, the vendor may have good reasons for wanting specific performance. It may be difficult to re-sell the property if the property market has crashed, and the vendor may want the hassle of selling an unwanted property to be placed on the (breaching) purchaser rather than himself. But that is true in all sorts of contexts, and it is not clear that real property merits different treatment.[57] Indeed, given that the vendor will have already gone through the process of selling the property once, it is strongly arguable that the vendor is better-placed than the purchaser to sell the property after the failed initial transaction . . . **19–041**

---

48 M. Chen-Wishart, "Specific Performance and Change of Mind" in G. Virgo and S. Worthington (eds), *Commercial Remedies: Resolving Controversies* (CUP, 2017), p.122: "English law's reservation of a special position for land derives from socio-political circumstances that have little relevance today"; J. McGhee (ed), *Snell's Equity*, 33rd edn (Sweet & Maxwell, 2015), para.[17–008]: "However, it is unrealistic today to regard land as inevitably a unique item for which damages are an inadequate remedy".

49 *The Stena Nautica (No.2)* [1982] 2 Lloyd's Rep. 336 at 348.

50 This apparently extends to transient interests: *Verrall v Great Yarmouth BC* [1981] Q.B. 202; [1980] 3 W.L.R. 258.

51 The consideration provided by the purchaser is virtually always money; in the rare circumstances that the consideration provided is unique then specific performance is much easier to justify.

52 E. Peel, *Treitel: The Law of Contract*, 14th edn (Sweet & Maxwell, 2015), para.[21–001].

53 *Hope v Walter* [1900] 1 Ch. 257 at 258 (Lindley LJ) [rest of footnote omitted].

54 E. Hewitt and M. Overton (eds), *Dart's Treatise on the Law and Practice Relating to Vendors and Purchasers of Real Estate*, 8th ed (Stevens and Sons, 1929), p.878 [rest of footnote omitted].

55 See, e.g. *Lewis v Lord Lechmere* (1721) 10 Mod. 503; 88 E.R. 828 [rest of footnote omitted].

56 *Price v Strange* [1978] Ch. 337; [1977] 3 W.L.R. 943; A. Burrows, *Remedies for Torts and Breach of Contract*, 3rd edn (Oxford University Press, 2014), pp.491–493.

57 Cf *AIB Group (UK) Plc Ltd v Redler & Co Solicitors* [2014] UKSC 58, the result of which means the hassle of selling the unwanted property now clearly rests with the beneficiary rather than trustee.

19-042 Nevertheless, there may be good practical reasons for generally granting the vendor specific performance, based upon maintaining the integrity of the system concerning transactions for real property. Property transactions often form part of a longer chain: the vendor may need the money from the purchaser immediately in order to buy a different property, and so on. Absent a quick order of specific performance, it is likely that the vendor would be unable to complete on the other property, and the chain might collapse. In those circumstances, it is suggested that specific performance may still be the more appropriate remedy. The recognition that specific performance will generally be quickly granted may help to keep a number of chains alive, and the very threat of specific performance might discourage a purchaser from backing out, thereby preventing chains from collapsing.

19-043 Mutuality is discussed further below. Another reason given in favour of specific performance of a vendor is that:[58]

> A contract to mortgage property, real or personal, will, normally at least, be specifically enforceable, for a mere claim to damages or repayment is obviously less valuable than a security in the event of the debtor's insolvency.

19-044 Damages might also be inadequate for a contract to convey chattels that are special or unique, as an award of damages would be inadequate to put the plaintiff in the position as if the defendant had not breached her obligation to convey title, because a replacement cannot be readily obtainable on market. A related example is where the nature of the property to be conveyed by the defendant is such that it is very difficult or impossible to quantify the value, putting the plaintiff to an impossible standard of proof and such that damages might be unavailable altogether.[59]

19-045 The categories of contracts for which damages are less likely to be adequate, and some of the significant authorities on this and other issues concerning the award of specific performance, such as court supervision and mutuality, are discussed by Dixon J in the following excerpt from the High Court of Australia case of *Dougan v Ley*. In this case, the plaintiff sought specific performance of a contract for the transfer of a statutory registration and licence to operate a taxi-cab. The registration and licence were difficult to obtain, requiring the Commissioner's approval under the relevant statutory regime, and the market for their transfer was limited, and prices fluctuated. At first instance, the defendant was ordered to do all things necessary to enable plaintiff to present an application for approval from the Commissioner to affect the transfer of the registration and licence under the applicable statutory regime, and upon the application being accepted, the plaintiff was ordered to pay the balance of the purchase price. The appeal against this order was unanimously dismissed by the High Court of Australia.

Dougan v Ley

High Court of Australia, (1946) 71 C.L.R. 142 at 149–152

19-046 DIXON J.: [After summarising the terms of the contract and the applicable statutory regime the judge continued:] . . . It follows that the appellant is bound to take certain formal steps and the respondents, on their part, must satisfy the Commissioner of their fitness and that they will have the use, control and management of the vehicle. There is nothing in this, in respect of either side, calling for the continued supervision of the Court. The appeal is based primarily upon the contention that the contract is not one appropriate for the equitable remedy of specific performance.

19-047 The subject matter, it is said, is the sale of a chattel and, in general, a suit for the specific performance of an agreement to sell and deliver chattels will not be entertained. But, when the substance of the matter

[58] *Swiss Bank Corp v Lloyd's Bank Ltd* [1980] 2 All E.R. 419 at 425 (Buckley LJ).
[59] See e.g.: *Fells v Read* (1796) 3 Ves. Jun. 371; 30 E.R. 899 at 899–900, excerpted below in Question 1.

is considered, the agreement is not of this simple character. The legislation has resulted in a restriction upon the number of registered and licensed vehicles with which the calling of taxi-driving may be pursued. The contract is in fact for the transfer of a valuable privilege annexed to a chattel. Of the amount of the consideration, somewhat the greater part appears to represent the registration and licence and the lesser part the vehicle itself. . . . The subject of the sale is thus shown to be a special right attached to a chattel, transferable only with it, and numerically restricted.

Though in earlier times the absence of an adequate theory of simple contract had led to the interposition of chancery on wider grounds, by the seventeenth century, if not before, it had come to be "taken for a good cause of dismission" of a bill "in most causes, to say that he" the plaintiff "hath remedy at the common law".[60] So it became the received doctrine that the foundation of decrees for specific performance was "that damages at law would not give the party the compensation to which he was entitled; that is, would not put him in a situation as beneficial to him as if the agreement were specifically performed".[61] **19–048**

> The Court gives specific performance instead of damages, only when it can by that means do more perfect and complete justice.[62]

In the case of goods or securities obtainable upon the market, damages at law place the disappointed buyer or seller in as good a position as delivery of the articles or receipt of the price because it enables him to go upon the market. But damages at law for the refusal of a vendor of land to go on with the contract might not be a complete remedy to the purchaser, to whom the land might have a special value[63] and the vendor's failure to complete through defect of title left the purchaser without any adequate remedy at law.[64] But specific performance is also the right of a vendor of land against a defaulting purchaser. "It has been said, but has long since been overruled, that a seller may go to law, as he only wants the money, whereas the purchaser wants the estate; but a seller wants the exact sum agreed to be paid to him, and he wants to divest himself legally of the estate, which after the contract was no longer vested in him beneficially".[65] **19–049**

But apart from land, a contract for which has always been considered a proper subject of specific performance, the question raised for the Court of Chancery was to say in what circumstances equity considered the purchaser entitled to the specific thing contracted to be sold or the vendor to divest himself of it and receive the price, rather than in either case being bound to accept damages as the price of the loss of the contract. **19–050**

It was not difficult to say that a purchaser of "articles of unusual beauty rarity and distinction" was entitled to obtain them in specie.[66] Though a less obvious case, it was settled that "a certain number of railway shares of a particular description, which railway shares are limited in number" and are not to be obtained by going on the share market, are a subject in respect of which a contract of sale will be enforced specifically.[67] But though it is within the power of a court of equity to decree specific performance of a contract for the sale and purchase of shares, yet when shares are dealt in largely on the market and anyone can go and buy them, there is no reason why they should not be in the same position as government stock is, in a contract for its sale and purchase.[68] Where chattels are sold or otherwise disposed of by contract as part of the particular equipment of a business, there is ground for equity granting specific relief. There appears to be no direct case of specific performance.[69] **19–051**

In the present case I think that we should have no difficulty in concluding that, because of the limited number of vehicles registered and licensed as taxi-cabs, because of the extent to which the price represents the value of the licence, and because of the essentiality to the purchasers' calling of the chattel and **19–052**

---

60 (circa 1602) Cary 20; 21 E.R. 11.

61 *Harnett v Yeilding* (1805) 2 Sch. & Lef. 549 at 553; 9 R.R. 98 at 100, 101 (Lord Redesdale).

62 *Wilson v Northampton and Banbury Junction Railway Co* (1872) L.R. 14 Eq. 477 (Lord Selborne).

63 *Adderley v Dixon* (1824) 1 Sim. & St. at 610; 57 E.R. at 239–41.

64 *Flureau v Thornhill* [1746] EngR 175; (1776) 2 Black. W. 1078; *Bain v Fothergill* (1874) L.R. 7 H.L. 158 at 201, 207–10.

65 *Eastern Counties Railway Co v Hawkes* [1855] EngR 697; (1855) 5 H.L.C. 331 at 376 (Lord St. Leonards).

66 *Falcke v Gray* [1859] EngR 710; (1859) 4 Drew 651 at 658.

67 *Duncuft v Albrecht* (1841) 12 Sim. at 199; 59 E.R. at 1108.

68 *Stern v Schwabacher* (1907) 98 L.T. 127 at 128 (Parker J).

69 But compare *North v Great Northern Railway Co* [1860] EngR 382; (1860) 2 Giff. 64 at 68, 69; *Nutbrown v Thornton* (1804) 10 Ves. Jun. 160; 32 E.R. 805

> the licence annexed thereto, we should treat the contract as within the scope of the remedy of specific performance.
>
> 19-053 An answer was attempted on the part of the appellant to the effect that the respondents in fact succeeded in buying another taxi-cab. This, I think, is not material. It was not an election on their part to obtain a substitute at the expense, in damages, of the appellant. They were entitled to obtain an additional car, if they could, for their business without prejudicing their right to obtain in specie the taxi-cab registration and licence already contracted for.
>
> 19-054 An argument was advanced that there was a lack of mutuality because, as against the respondents as purchasers, the contract could not be enforced without a continued supervision or superintendence, which the Court would not undertake.[70] But it is evident from the nature of the statutory provision that the argument is misconceived. All the respondents must do is to submit the materials for satisfying the Commissioner. If they fail to satisfy him the decree has no further operation.
>
> 19-055 The conditional form of decree made in the present case accords with settled practice in Australia, where a contract to be specifically performed involves obtaining the consent, approval or other sanction of a public authority.

19-056 Other examples include a contract for the sale or issue of shares in private companies:[71] damages will normally be an inadequate remedy.[72]

19-057 A contract to leave personal or real property by will is not enforceable directly (which would interfere with freedom of testamentary power) but a legatee who receives it in breach will be ordered to yield it up[73] and, before death of the testator, the promisee can obtain a declaration of right and an injunction restraining any inconsistent disposition.[74]

19-058 A contract promising to pay money to a third party "will not generally be a contract for the breach of which damages will be an adequate remedy" and therefore such a contract will be specifically enforceable by the parties to it.[75] In *Beswick v Beswick*,[76] the contract was to pay an annuity to a third party. It was enforced because damages would have been an inadequate remedy in the sense that either: (i) damages awarded to the promisee would have been nominal; (ii) a multiplicity of suits might need to be brought if there were future breaches; or (iii) the worth of an annuity, depending on the longevity of the annuitant, might be too conjectural to quantify.[77]

19-059 Ultimately, however, it is important to bear in mind that the adequacy of damages, not the categorization of the contract or subject property, is what matters. Contracts that are usually not specifically enforceable such as for the sale of shares in which there is a ready market, i.e. those of a quoted public company, may exceptionally be specifically enforced if it can be shown on the specific facts that damages are inadequate. Conversely, in *South African Territories Ltd v Wallington*,[78] a contract to make a loan which is usually specifically enforced, was not specifically enforced because damages were an adequate remedy in the circumstances.

---

70 *Peto v Brightons Uckfield and Tunbridge Wells Railway Co* (1863) 1 H. & M. 468; 71 E.R. 205; *Pickering v Bishop of Ely* (1843) 2 Y. & C.C.C. 249 at 266–68; 63 E.R. 109 at 117.

71 In light of the restriction on the transferability of shares in private companies and of the criminal prohibition in s.755 of the Companies Act 2006, against a private company (other than a company limited by guarantee and not having a share capital) from offering its securities to the public directly or indirectly.

72 See, e.g. *Pena v Dale* [2004] 2 B.C.L.C. 508; *Gaetano Ltd v Obertor Ltd* [2009] EWHC 2653 at [48]; *ANZ Executors and Trustees Ltd v Humes Ltd* [1990] V.R. 615 (Brooking J), affirmed on appeal *Humes Ltd v PS (Enterprises) Nominees Pty Ltd* (1989) 7 A.C.L.C. 992.

73 *Synge v Synge* [1894] 1 Q.B. 466 (on the ground that the legatee is a volunteer and takes subject to the equity).

74 *Schaefer v Schumann* [1972] A.C. 572 (PC).

75 *Beswick v Beswick* [1968] A.C. 58; *Woodar Investment Development Ltd v Wimpey Construction UK Ltd* [1980] 1 W.L.R. 277 at 293; *Coulls v Bagot's Executor & Trustee Co Ltd* (1967) 119 C.L.R. 460 at 478.

76 [1968] A.C. 58.

77 But query: actuaries and judges in personal injury cases do it routinely.

78 [1898] A.C. 309.

iii. Contracts for personal services are not specifically performable

One instance where the category or type of contract will itself be determinative is in relation to contracts for personal services, which are not generally amenable to specific performance, either as a result of statute,[79] or equitable principle, the rationale for which is illustrated by Fry LJ's comment in *De Francesco v Barnum*: "[t]he courts are bound to be jealous lest they should turn contracts of service into contracts of slavery".[80] In *Chappell v Times Newspapers Ltd*, Geoffrey Lane LJ further explained that "if one party has no faith in the honesty or integrity or the loyalty of the other, to force him to serve or to employ that other is a plain recipe for disaster".[81] **19–060**

However there seems to be no hard and fast rule. In *Geys v Société Générale, London Branch*,[82] Lord Wilson noted that it is a "big question whether nowadays the more impersonal, less hierarchical, relationship of many employers with their employees requires review of the usual unavailability of specific performance." In *Giles (CH) & Co Ltd v Morris*,[83] Megarry J denied that there was a rule preventing enforcement: it was, rather, a question of looking at the particular obligations in question. In *Hill v CA Parsons & Co Ltd*,[84] the Court of Appeal by a majority enforced a contract for personal services in what were described as exceptional circumstances. In *Lumley v Wagner*,[85] a singer was prevented by injunction from breaching her promise to sing only at the plaintiff's theatre, thereby being forced to sing for the plaintiff. This and other cases were reviewed in the Court of Appeal by Mance LJ in *Lady Navigation Inc v Lauritzencool AB*[86] where he concluded that there is no general rule that injunctive relief will be withheld if the practical effect would be to compel performance of a contract for personal services. **19–061**

D. Discretionary Factors

The award of specific performance is discretionary, and like other equitable remedies, is subject to a range of rules that guide a court's exercise of discretion whether to award equitable relief. Those which are generally applicable to equitable remedies are discussed in Chapter 22, e.g. laches, acquiescence, and unclean hands. Discussed here are some of the discretionary factors that relate only to an award of specific performance. **19–062**

i. Mutuality

In *Price v Strange*[87] Buckley LJ explained the rationale for mutuality as that:[88] **19–063**

> . . . the court will not compel a defendant to perform his obligations specifically if it cannot at the same time ensure that any unperformed obligations of the plaintiff will be specifically performed, unless, perhaps, damages would be an adequate remedy to the defendant for any default on the plaintiff's part.

---

79 Trade Union and Labour Relations (Consolidation) Act 1992 s.236: "no court shall . . . by way of an order of specific performance . . . compel an employee to do any work or to attend at any place for the doing of any work."
80 (1890) 45 Ch. D. 430.
81 [1975] 1 W.L.R. 482 at 506.
82 [2012] UKSC 63; [2013] 1 A.C. 523 at [77].
83 *Giles (CH) & Co Ltd v Morris* [1972] 1 W.L.R. 307.
84 *Hill v CA Parsons & Co Ltd* [1972] Ch. 305.
85 *Lumley v Wagner* (1852) 1 De G.M. & G. 604.
86 *Lady Navigation Inc v Lauritzencool AB* [2005] EWCA Civ 579; [2005] 2 All E.R. (Comm.) 183.
87 *Price v Strange* [1978] Ch. 377.
88 *Price v Strange* at 367–368.

19–064 It used to be said that specific performance will not be granted to a promisee who could not herself be the subject of a decree,[89] i.e. all the obligations imposed by the contract upon the claimant promisee must themselves be specifically enforceable. This is the traditional statement of the requirement of mutuality. However, Fry LJ's statement of it, which required mutuality at the time of entering into the contract (rather than it sufficing at the date of the hearing) was rejected in *Price v Strange*.[90] There Goff LJ stated that "want of mutuality raises a question of the court's discretion to be exercised according to everything that has happened up to the decree", so that "the court will grant specific performance if it can be done without injustice or unfairness to the defendant".[91] This might involve some payment to the defendant as in *Price*.[92] Likewise, Buckley LJ emphasised that "considerations of mutuality go to discretion, not to jurisdiction"[93] and this means that some inability of the plaintiff to perform her obligation(s) in specie will not be fatal to her claim for specific performance where any injustice to the defendant can be avoided by the imposition of terms on the plaintiff or an award of damages to the defendant.[94]

ii. Need for constant supervision

19–065 *Ryan v Mutual Tontine Westminster Chambers Association*[95] holds that a breach of a contract which would need constant supervision by the court if it were to be performed *in specie* will only sound in damages. In *Posner v Scott-Lewis*,[96] however, Mervyn Davies J at a tenant's request, and on facts difficult to distinguish from *Ryan*, made an order against the landlord for the appointment of a resident porter whom the landlord had covenanted to employ for the purpose of carrying out certain duties at a block of flats: he found that there was a sufficient definition of what had to be done in order to comply with the order of the court.

19–066 *Cooperative Insurance Society Ltd v Argyll Stores (Holdings) Ltd*[97] provided the House of Lords with the opportunity to review and reconcile the authorities clustered around this principle. The owner of Safeway supermarkets was the anchor-tenant in a new shopping mall in Hillsborough. It covenanted to keep the demised premises open for retail trade during normal business hours, but then decided to close all of its loss-making stores of which the demised premises were one. The tenant was content to pay damages for breach but resisted an order for specific performance. The Court of Appeal, by a majority, granted a decree which the House of Lords discharged in accordance with the practice not to grant specific performance or mandatory injunctions[98] requiring persons to carry on a business.

---

89 *Flight v Bolland* (1828) 4 Russ. 298 (minor failing to obtain decree because, *qua minor,* suit could not be maintained against him).

90 [1978] 1 Ch. 337.

91 *Price v Strange* at 354. At 368–369 Buckley LJ stated: "The court will not compel a defendant to perform his obligations specifically if it cannot at the same time ensure that any unperformed obligations of the plaintiff will be specifically performed unless, perhaps, damages would be an adequate remedy to the defendant for any default on the plaintiff's part."

92 *Price v Strange* at 357.

93 *Price v Strange* at 369.

94 *Rainbow Estates Ltd v Tokenhold Ltd* [1999] Ch. 64.

95 [1893] 1 Ch. 116 (lessor's covenant to provide resident porter who would always be in attendance at block of flats). See also *Dowty Boulton Paul Ltd v Wolverhampton Corporation* [1971] 2 All E.R. 277 (mandatory injunction refused to enforce covenant to maintain aerodrome for period of over 60 years: same principle applied).

96 [1987] Ch. 25.

97 [1998] A.C. 1.

98 See paras 19–118ff.

Cooperative Insurance Society Ltd v Argyll Stores (Holdings) Ltd

House of Lords, [1998] A.C. 1 at 9, 11–19

LORD HOFFMANN (with whom LORD BROWNE-WILKINSON, LORD SLYNN, LORD HOPE and LORD CLYDE agreed): . . . In 1955 Lord Goddard C.J. said:[99] **19–067**

> No authority has been quoted to show that an injunction will be granted enjoining a person to carry on a business, nor can I think that one ever would be, certainly not where the business is a losing concern.

In this case his prediction has been falsified. The appellant defendants, Argyll Stores (Holdings) Ltd ("Argyll"), decided in May 1995 to close their Safeway supermarket in the Hillsborough Shopping Centre in Sheffield because it was losing money. This was a breach of a covenant in their lease, which contained in clause 4(19) a positive obligation to keep the premises open for retail trade during the usual hours of business. Argyll admitted the breach and, in an action by the landlord. Co-operative Insurance Society Ltd ("CIS") consented to an order for damages to be assessed. But the Court of Appeal,[100] reversing the trial judge, ordered that the covenant be specifically performed. It made a final injunction ordering Argyll to trade on the premises during the remainder of the term (which will expire on 3 August 2014) or until an earlier subletting or assignment. The Court of Appeal suspended its order for three months to allow time for Argyll to complete an assignment which by that time had been agreed. After a short agreed extension, the lease was assigned with the landlord's consent. In fact, therefore, the injunction never took effect. The appeal to your Lordships is substantially about costs. But the issue remains of great importance to landlords and tenants under other commercial leases **19–068**

The judge refused to order specific performance. He said that there was on the authorities a settled practice that orders which would require a defendant to run a business would not be made. . . . **19–069**

There is no dispute about the existence of the settled practice to which the judge referred. It sufficient for this purpose to refer to *Braddon Towers Ltd v International Stores Ltd* where Slade J said:[101] **19–070**

> Whether or not this may be properly described as a rule of law. I do not doubt that for many years practitioners have advised their clients that it is the settled and invariable practice of this court never to grant mandatory injunctions requiring persons to carry on business.

But the practice has never, so far as I know, been examined by this House and it is open to CIS to say that it rests upon inadequate grounds or that it has been too inflexibly applied.

Specific performance is traditionally regarded in English law as an exceptional remedy, as opposed to the common law damages to which a successful plaintiff is entitled as of right. There may have been some element of later rationalisation of an untidier history, but by the 19th century it was orthodox doctrine that the power to decree specific performance was part of the discretionary jurisdiction of the Court of Chancery to do justice in cases in which the remedies available at common law were inadequate. This is the basis of the general principle that specific performance will not be ordered when damages are an adequate remedy. By contrast, in countries with legal systems based on civil law, such as France, Germany and Scotland, the plaintiff is prima facie entitled to specific performance. The cases in which he is confined to a claim for damages are regarded as the exceptions. In practice, however, there is less difference between common law and civilian systems than these general statements might lead one to suppose. The principles upon which English judges exercise the discretion to grant specific performance are reasonably well settled and depend upon a number of considerations, mostly of a practical nature, which are of very general application. I have made no investigation of civilian systems, but a priori I would expect that judges take much the same matters into account in deciding whether specific performance would be inappropriate in a particular case. **19–071**

The practice of not ordering a defendant to carry on a business is not entirely dependent upon damages being an adequate remedy. In *Dowty Boulton Paul Ltd v Wolverhampton Corporation*[102] Sir John Pennycuick V.C. refused to order the corporation to maintain an airfield as a going concern because: "It is very well **19–072**

---

99 *Attorney General v Colchester Corp* [1955] 2 Q.B. 207 at 217.
100 [1996] Ch. 286.
101 [1987] 1 E.G.L.R. 209 at 213.
102 [1971] 1 W.L.R. 204.

established that the court will not order specific performance of an obligation to carry on a business."[103] He added: "It is unnecessary in the circumstances to discuss whether damages would be an adequate remedy to the company."[104] Thus the reasons which underlie the established practice may justify a refusal of specific performance even when damages are not an adequate remedy.

19–073 The most frequent reason given in the cases for declining to order someone to carry on a business is that it would require constant supervision by the court. In *JC Williamson Ltd v Lukey and Mulholland*[105] Dixon J said flatly: "Specific performance is inapplicable when the continued supervision of the court is necessary in order to ensure the fulfilment of the contract."

19–074 There has, I think, been some misunderstanding about what is meant by continued superintendence. It may at first sight suggest that the judge (or some other officer of the court) would literally have to supervise the execution of the order. In *CH Giles & Co Ltd v Morris,*[106] Megarry J said that "difficulties of constant superintendence" were a "narrow consideration" because:

> there is normally no question of the court having to send its officers to supervise the performance of the order . . . Performance . . . is normally secured by the realisation of the person enjoined that he is liable to be punished for contempt if evidence of his disobedience to the order is put before the court . . .

This is, of course, true but does not really meet the point. The judges who have said that the need for constant supervision was an objection to such orders were no doubt well aware that supervision would in practice take the form of rulings by the court, on applications made by the parties, as to whether there had been a breach of the order. It is the possibility of the court having to give an indefinite series of such rulings in order to ensure the execution of the order which has been regarded as undesirable.

19–075 Why should this be so? A principal reason is that, as Megarry J pointed out in the passage to which I have referred, the only means available to the court to enforce its order is the quasicriminal procedure of punishment for contempt. This is a powerful weapon: so powerful, in fact, as often to be unsuitable as an instrument for adjudicating upon the disputes which may arise over whether a business is being run in accordance with the terms of the court's order. The heavyhanded nature of the enforcement mechanism is a consideration which may go to the exercise of the court's discretion in other cases as well, but its use to compel the running of a business is perhaps the paradigm case of its disadvantages and it is in this context that I shall discuss them.

19–076 The prospect of committal or even a fine, with the damage to commercial reputation which will be caused by a finding of contempt of court, is likely to have at least two undesirable consequences. First, the defendant, who *ex hypothesi* did not think that it was in his economic interest to run the business at all, now has to make decisions under a sword of Damocles which may descend if the way the business is run does not conform to the terms of the order. This is, as one might say, no way to run a business. In this case the Court of Appeal made light of the point because it assumed that, once the defendant had been ordered to run the business, self-interest and compliance with the order would thereafter go hand in hand. But, as I shall explain, this is not necessarily true.

19–077 Secondly, the seriousness of a finding of contempt for the defendant means that any application to enforce the order is likely to be a heavy and expensive piece of litigation. The possibility of repeated applications over a period of time means that, in comparison with a once-and-for-all inquiry as to damages, the enforcement of the remedy is likely to be expensive in terms of cost to the parties and the resources of the judicial system.

19–078 This is a convenient point at which to distinguish between orders which require a defendant to carry on an activity, such as running a business over or more or less extended period of time, and orders which require him to achieve a result. The possibility of repeated applications for rulings on compliance with the order which arises in the former case does not exist to anything like the same extent in the latter. Even if the achievement of the result is a complicated matter which will take some time, the court, if called upon to rule, only has to examine the finished work and say whether it complies with the order. This point was

---

103 *Dowty Boulton Paul Ltd v Wolverhampton Corporation* at 211.
104 *Dowty Boulton Paul Ltd v Wolverhampton Corporation* at 212.
105 (1931) 45 C.L.R. 282 at 297–98.
106 [1972] 1 W.L.R. 307 at 318.

made in the context of relief against forfeiture in *Shiloh Spinners Ltd v Harding*.[107] If it is a condition of relief that the tenant should have complied with a repairing covenant, difficulty of supervision need not be an objection. As Lord Wilberforce said:[108]

> what the court has to do is to satisfy itself, ex post facto, that the covenanted work has been done, and it has ample machinery, through certificates, or by inquiry, to do precisely this.

This distinction between orders to carry on activities and orders to achieve results explains why the courts have in appropriate circumstances ordered specific performance of building contracts and repairing covenants.[109] It by no means follows, however, that even obligations to achieve a result will always be enforced by specific performance. There may be other objections, to some of which I now turn.

One such objection, which applies to orders to achieve a result and a fortiori to orders to carry on an activity, is imprecision in the terms of the order. If the terms of the court's order, reflecting the terms of the obligation, cannot be precisely drawn, the possibility of wasteful litigation over compliance is increased. So is the oppression caused by the defendant having to do things under threat of proceedings for contempt. The less precise the order, the fewer the signposts to the forensic minefield which he has to traverse. The fact that the terms of a contractual obligation are sufficiently definite to escape being void for uncertainty, or to found a claim for damages, or to permit compliance to be made a condition of relief against forfeiture, does not necessarily mean that they will be sufficiently precise to be capable of being specifically enforced. So in *Wolverhampton Corporation v Emmons*, Romer L.J. said that the first condition for specific enforcement of a building contract was that[110]: 19–079

> the particulars of the work are so far definitely ascertained that the court can sufficiently see what is the exact nature of the work of which it is asked to order the performance.

Similarly in *Morris v Redland Bricks Ltd*,[111] Lord Upjohn stated the following general principle for the grant of mandatory injunctions to carry out building works: 19–080

> the court must be careful to see that the defendant knows exactly in fact what he has to do and this means not as a matter of law but as a matter of fact, so that in carrying out an order he can give his contractors the proper instructions.

Precision is of course a question of degree and the courts have shown themselves willing to cope with a certain degree of imprecision in cases of orders requiring the achievement of a result in which the plaintiffs' merits appeared strong; like all the reasons which I have been discussing, it is, taken alone, merely a discretionary matter to be taken into account.[112] It is, however, a very important one.

I should at this point draw attention to what seems to me to have been a misreading of certain remarks of Lord Wilberforce in *Shiloh Spinners Ltd v Harding*.[113] He pointed out, as I have said, that to grant relief against forfeiture subject to compliance with a repairing covenant involves the court in no more than the possibility of a retrospective assessment of whether the covenanted work has been done. For this reason, he said: 19–081

> Where it is necessary, and, in my opinion, right, to move away from some 19th century authorities, is to reject as a reason against granting relief, the impossibility for the courts to supervise the doing of work.

This is plainly a remark about cases involving the achievement of a result such as doing repairs, and, within that class, about making compliance a condition of relief against forfeiture. But in *Tito v Waddell (No.2)*[114] Sir Robert Megarry V.C. took it to be a generalisation about specific performance and, in particular, a rejection of difficulty of supervision as an objection, even in cases of orders to carry on an activity. Sir Robert Megarry V.C. regarded it as an adoption of his own views (based, as I have said, on incomplete analysis of

---

107 [1973] A.C. 691.
108 *Shiloh Spinners Ltd v Harding* at 724.
109 *Wolverhampton Corporation v Emmons* [1901] 1 K.B. 515 (building contract) and *Jeune v Queens Cross Properties Ltd* [1974] Ch. 97 (repairing covenant).
110 *Wolverhampton Corporation v Emmons* at 525.
111 [1970] A.C. 652 at 666.
112 See Spry, *Equitable Remedies*, 4th edn (1990), p.112.
113 *Shiloh Spinners Ltd v Harding* at 724.
114 [1977] Ch. 106 at 322.

what was meant by difficulty of supervision) in *CH Giles & Co Ltd v Morris*.[115] In the present case[116] Leggatt L.J. took this claim at face value. In fact, Lord Wilberforce went on to say that impossibility of supervision "is a reality, no doubt, and explains why specific performance cannot be granted of agreements to this effect . . .". Lord Wilberforce was in my view drawing attention to the fact that the collection of reasons which the courts have in mind when they speak of difficulty of supervision apply with much greater force to orders for specific performance, giving rise to the possibility of committal for contempt, than they do to conditions for relief against forfeiture. While the paradigm case to which such objections apply is the order to carry on an activity, they can also apply to an order requiring the achievement of a result.

19–082 There is a further objection to an order requiring the defendant to carry on a business, which was emphasised by Millett L.J. in the Court of Appeal. This is that it may cause injustice by allowing the plaintiff to enrich himself at the defendant's expense. The loss which the defendant may suffer through having to comply with the order (for example, by running a business at a loss for an indefinite period) may be far greater than the plaintiff would suffer from the contract being broken. As Professor R.J. Sharpe explains[117]:

> In such circumstances, a specific decree in favour of the plaintiff will put him in a bargaining position vis-à-vis the defendant whereby the measure of what he will receive will be the value to the defendant of being released from performance. If the plaintiff bargains effectively, the amount he will set will exceed the value to him of performance and will approach the cost to the defendant to complete.

19–083 This was the reason given by Lord Westbury L.C. in *Isenberg v East India House Estate Co Ltd*[118] for refusing a mandatory injunction to compel the defendant to pull down part of a new building which interfered with the plaintiff's light and exercising instead the Court of Chancery's recently acquired jurisdiction under Lord Cairns's Act 1858 to order payment of damages:

> . . . I hold it . . . to be the duty of the court in such a case as the present not, by granting a mandatory injunction, to deliver over the defendants to the plaintiff bound hand and foot, in order to be made subject to any extortionate demand that he may by possibility make, but to substitute for such mandatory injunction an inquiry before itself, in order to ascertain the measure of damage that has been actually sustained.

19–084 It is true that the defendant has, by his own breach of contract, put himself in such an unfortunate position. But the purpose of the law of contract is not to punish wrongdoing but to satisfy the expectations of the party entitled to performance. A remedy which enables him to secure, in money terms, more than the performance due to him is unjust. From a wider perspective, it cannot be in the public interest for the courts to require someone to carry on business at a loss if there is any plausible alternative by which the other party can be given compensation. It is not only a waste of resources but yokes the parties together in a continuing hostile relationship. The order for specific performance prolongs the battle. If the defendant is ordered to run a business, its conduct becomes the subject of a flow of complaints, solicitors' letters and affidavits. This is wasteful for both parties and the legal system. An award of damages, on the other hand, brings the litigation to an end. The defendant pays damages, the forensic link between them is severed, they go their separate ways and the wounds of conflict can heal.

19–085 The cumulative effect of these various reasons, none of which would necessarily be sufficient on its own, seems to me to show that the settled practice is based upon sound sense. Of course the grant or refusal of specific performance remains a matter for the judge's discretion. There are no binding rules, but this does not mean that there cannot be settled principles, founded upon practical considerations of the kind which I have discussed, which do not have to be reexamined in every case, but which the courts will apply in all but exceptional circumstances. As Slade J. said, in the passage which I have quoted from *Braddon Towers Ltd v International Stores Ltd*,[119] lawyers have no doubt for many years advised their clients on this basis. In the present case. Leggatt L.J.[120] remarked that there was no evidence that such advice had been given. In my view, if the law or practice on a point is settled, it should be assumed that persons entering into legal

---

[115] [1972] 1 W.L.R. 307 at 318.
[116] [1996] Ch. 286 at 292–93.
[117] In "Specific Relief for Contract Breach", Ch.5 of *Studies in Contract Law* (1980), edited by Reiter and Swan p.129.
[118] (1863) 3 De G.J. & S. 263 at 273.
[119] [1987] 1 E.G.L.R. 209 at 213.
[120] [1996] Ch. 286 at 294.

transactions will have been advised accordingly. I am sure that Leggatt L.J. would not wish to encourage litigants to adduce evidence of the particular advice which they received. Indeed, I doubt whether such evidence would be admissible.

The Decision of the Court of Appeal

I must now examine the grounds upon which the majority of the Court of Appeal[121] thought it right to reverse the judge. . . . 19–086

The Court of Appeal thought that once Argyll had been ordered to comply with the covenant, it was, as Roch L.J. said,[122] "inconceivable that they would not operate the business efficiently." Leggatt L.J. said,[123] that the requirement 19–087

> was quite intelligible to the defendants, while they were carrying on business ther . . . . If the premises are to be run as a business, it cannot be in the defendants' interest to run it half-heartedly or inefficiently . . . .

This treats the way the tenant previously conducted business as measuring the extent of his obligation to do so. In my view this is a non sequitur: the obligation depends upon the language of the covenant and not upon what the tenant has previously chosen to do. No doubt it is true that it would not be in the interests of the tenant to run the business inefficiently. But running the business efficiently does not necessarily mean running it in the way it was run before. Argyll had decided that, from its point of view, the most efficient thing to do was to close the business altogether and concentrate its resources on achieving better returns elsewhere. If ordered to keep the business open, it might well decide that the next best strategy was to reduce its costs as far as was consistent with compliance with its obligations, in the expectation that a lower level of return would be more than compensated by higher returns from additional expenditure on more profitable shops. It is in my view wrong for the courts to speculate about whether Argyll might voluntarily carry on business in a way which would relieve the court from having to construe its order. The question of certainty must be decided on the assumption that the court might have to enforce the order according to its terms.

. . .

Finally, all three judges in the Court of Appeal took a very poor view of Argyll's conduct. Leggatt L.J. said that they had acted "with gross commercial cynicism"[124]; Roch L.J. began his judgment by saying that they had "behaved very badly" and Millett L.J. said that they had no merits.[125] The principles of equity have always had a strong ethical content and nothing which I say is intended to diminish the influence of moral values in their application. I can envisage cases of gross breach of personal faith, or attempts to use the threat of non-performance as blackmail, in which the needs of justice will override all the considerations which support the settled practice. But although any breach of covenant is regrettable, the exercise of the discretion as to whether or not to grant specific performance starts from the fact that the covenant has been broken. Both landlord and tenant in this case are large sophisticated commercial organisations and I have no doubt that both were perfectly aware that the remedy for breach of the covenant was likely to be limited to an award of damages. The interests of both were purely financial: there was no element of personal breach of faith, as in the Victorian cases of railway companies which refused to honour obligations to build stations for landowners whose property they had taken: compare *Greene v West Cheshire Railway Co.*[126] No doubt there was an effect on the businesses of other traders in the Centre, but Argyll had made no promises to them and it is not suggested that CIS warranted to other tenants that Argyll would remain. Their departure, with or without the consent of CIS, was a commercial risk which the tenants were able to deploy in negotiations for the next rent review. On the scale of broken promises, I can think of worse cases, but the language of the Court of Appeal left them with few adjectives to spare. . . . 19–088

---

121 [1996] Ch. 286.
122 *Cooperative Insurance Society Ltd v Argyll Stores (Holdings) Ltd* at 298.
123 *Cooperative Insurance Society Ltd v Argyll Stores (Holdings) Ltd* at 292.
124 [1996] Ch. 286 at 295.
125 [1996] Ch. 286 at 301.
126 (1871) L.R. 13 Eq. 44.

Conclusion

19-089 I think that no criticism can be made of the way in which Judge Maddocks exercised his discretion. All the reasons which he gave were proper matters for him to take into account. In my view the Court of Appeal should not have interfered and I would allow the appeal and restore the order which he made.

19-090 As Lord Hoffmann discusses in the excerpt above, the reluctance to award specific performance requiring court supervision is in part to ensure the efficient use of court resources and a concern about litigation expenses. In addition, is the rule of law concern that a defendant should only be subject to a court order that is accessible in the sense that the defendant can understand the (in)action to avoid being in contempt of court. In *Cooperative Insurance Society Ltd v Argyll Stores (Holdings) Ltd*, Lord Hoffmann explains that a contractual obligation that requires a party to achieve a defined and objectively ascertainable result, such as the transfer of legal title to identified property, is one that the party subject to it can fairly determine for herself what is it that she needs to do to ensure the complies with the contract, and would be capable of court supervision. This is in distinction to a contractual obligation to carry out an activity, such as to carry on a business, and the performance of which is not easily assessed according to clear cut objective criteria. This consideration also explains why a contract that fails to specifically identify the subject property to which a defendant's obligation relates will not be capable of specific performance, and thus will not be one that creates and equitable proprietary interest in favour of the purchaser.

19-091 This consideration regarding the certainty or specificity with which the parties have defined their contractual relationship must be distinguished from that forming part of the rules for contract formation and which asks whether the parties manifested an intention to create binding legal relations.[127]

19-092 The rules for contract formation ask whether the parties have manifested an intention to create a binding legal relationship and expresses the rationale that the parties should only be held to a contractual relationship if they manifested an intention to create one. Certainty of intention can be made out even if the parties choose to define the content of that relationship by reference to standards of conduct that are not easily assessed, such as the obligation to carry on a business, or perform some service, such as a singer's obligation to perform a musical. It might seem curious that a contract for the transfer of the goodwill of a business is certain enough to create a contract but too uncertain to enforce *in specie*.[128] We can make sense of this as an application of the rule of law imperative requiring definitional certainty or specificity not applying in the same way to contract formation, because contractual performance is enforced by damages for breach of contract. The monetary sum a defendant is ordered to pay in response to a breach of contract makes clear what it is the defendant must do, even if the parties defined their contractual relationship in vague terms or that require a qualitative assessment of performance.

19-093 At the stage of considering the award of specific performance, however, the court is no longer ordering a defendant to pay a fixed monetary sum to an identified person, the payment of which is enforced by various types of execution proceedings. For specific performance, the court is considering ordering the defendant to take some other (in)action that is enforced by the quasi-criminal proceedings of contempt of court. Different rule of law considerations apply to the court's discretion whether to order specific performance, which explain the application of this discretionary factor to specific performance, and as we will see, injunctions as well, particularly when the prima facie remedy at law is damages.

---

127 *Baird Textile Holdings Ltd v Marks & Spencer Plc* [2001] EWCA Civ 274; [2002] 1 All E.R. (Comm) 737 at [30], [59]. See further, H. Beale, *Chitty on Contracts*, para.4–206.

128 *Darbey v Whitaker* (1857) 4 Drew. 134 (unless premises or other business assets are contracted to be transferred with it). See too *Buxton v Lister* (1746) 3 Atk. 383 at 386 (Lord Hardwicke LC).

Finally, it is helpful to observe that the discretionary concern of court supervision is less obvious when specific relief is being ordered in response to legal relations recognised by equitable rules, such as an injunction compelling a trustee's performance of trust. This is because the rule of law concern around court supervision and certainty is in-built to the equitable rules determining the creation or recognition of a plaintiff's underlying entitlement to equitable relief, and so do not arise at the stage when relief is sought. The rules for trust creation, for example, ensure that a trustee is only subject to trustee obligations, the performance of which can be specifically compelled, if the parties have clearly defined the trust property and its terms.[129] The trustee needs to know for whom she holds what property and what it is that she is and is not allowed to do with it. Likewise, in relation to proprietary estoppel, which will not be enforced against a promisor where the terms of the promise are so unclear that they are not amendable to specific relief.[130] **19–094**

It is interesting that some cases have tended to regard proprietary estoppel as having a *lower* certainty requirement than that of contract (or promissory estoppel).[131] This comparison, however, is made in relation to the other certainty requirement, discussed above, and which is whether the parties have manifested an intention to be legally bound. The higher standard in contract is whether the parties intended to create a legally binding relationship. Proprietary estoppel, on the other hand, asks whether the promissor intended for the promisee to rely on her promise. The other certainty requirement is not asking whether the parties intended their actions to change or create a legal relationship and is rather concerned with whether they have manifested their intentions sufficiently clearly to permit the accessible expression of court orders compelling a defendant to act in accordance with those intentions under the threat of contempt of court. **19–095**

iii. Hardship

Specific performance may be refused if undue hardship will be caused to either of the contracting parties or a third party.[132] The decisions in individual cases tend to turn on the facts, but *Patel v Ali*[133] is reproduced here by way of illustration. There is Commonwealth authority requiring the hardship to have existed at the date of contract formation,[134] but in England it has been held that specific performance can also be refused on the ground of hardship arising after contract formation. **19–096**

The gist of this discretionary factor is hardship that would be suffered by a defendant or third party from the award of specific relief and which is distinct or over and above that which would be suffered if the plaintiff is left to her remedy at law, usually damages. In other words, to make out hardship, the defendant must point to the hardship caused by having to perform her contractual obligation(s) as distinct from paying damages for breach. **19–097**

The considerations relevant to this discretionary factor and its operation are discussed by Goulding J in *Patel v Ali*, where an award of specific performance of a contract for the sale of land was overturned on the basis of hardship and damages in lieu were awarded instead. **19–098**

---

129 See Chapter 7.

130 In relation to proprietary estoppel generally, see Chapter 4. In relation to the certainty requirement for proprietary and promissory estoppel, see J. Hudson, "Certainty in equitable estoppels: Questions of taxonomy, unification and coherence" (2016) 10 J. Eq. 137.

131 See, e.g. *Crown Melbourne Ltd v Cosmopolitan Hotel (Vic) Pty Ltd* [2016] HCA 26; (2016) 260 C.L.R. 1 at [133]–[159] (Keane J), [210]–[218] (Nettle J).

132 *Thomas v Dering* (1837) 1 Keen 729 at 747–48. For discussion of the limits to hardship in the context of large financial cost to the defendant, see *ANZ Executors and Trustees Ltd v Humes Ltd* [1990] VR 615 (Brooking J), affirmed on appeal *Humes Ltd v PS (Enterprises) Nominees Pty Ltd* (1989) 7 A.C.L.C. 992.

133 [1984] Ch. 238.

134 See, e.g. *Nicholas v Ingram* [1958] N.Z.L.R. 972.

Patel v Ali

Chancery Division [1984] Ch. 283 at 285–289

19–099 GOULDING J.: . . . The circumstances of the case are unusual and it has caused me some anxiety. . . .

19–100 The material facts are not in dispute and can be shortly stated. In the year 1979 the defendant was living in the property with her husband, Mr. Ali. They occupied it as their matrimonial home. Another couple, Mr. and Mrs. Nazir Ahmed, were also living in the house. Mr. Ahmed is the second defendant to the action. The property was freehold and was registered in the name of Mr. Ahmed and the defendant, who claim to be not only legally but beneficially entitled thereto. On 31 July 1979 the contract was entered into between both defendants as vendors and the plaintiffs, Mr. and Mrs. Patel, as purchasers. The price was £24,000, the contractual completion date 28 August 1979.

19–101 The performance of the contract has been subject — and this is a circumstance which, to my mind, is of the greatest importance in the case — to a quite extraordinary delay, for which neither side on this appeal has sought to blame the other. The causes of the delay have not been explored in detail in the evidence, but it appears that a great deal of it can be put down to two difficulties. In the first place, the trustee in bankruptcy of Mr. Ali has made claim to a beneficial interest in the property. . . . The second cause of delay, so it is said, was a succession of difficulties experienced by the plaintiffs in effecting service of proceedings on Mr. Ahmed, who has returned to Pakistan. . . .

19–102 Meanwhile, the circumstances of the defendant had changed disastrously. At the date of the contract she had one child who was still a baby; and, so far as she knew, she was in good health. She was about 23 years old. She spoke and still speaks, in the words of her solicitor's affidavit, "virtually no English at all." In the summer of 1980 she was found to have a bone cancer in her right thigh. On 24 July 1980, that is three days after the order of Fox J. in the bankruptcy proceedings, her right leg was amputated at the hip joint. She was then in an advanced state of pregnancy and gave birth to her second child on 31 August 1980. In the spring of 1981 her husband went to prison and remained there until mid-summer 1982. After his release she became pregnant again and her third child was born in August 1983.

The defendant has been fitted with an artificial leg. She is able to walk about the house and dress herself, but not to do shopping, and she needs help with household duties and with the children. She is greatly dependent on friends and relations to enable her to keep her home going and to look after her children, especially on her sister who, I was told, lives only a few doors away, and on a friendly neighbour, Mrs. Dhillon.

19–103 It is in these circumstances that the defendant asks the court to refuse specific performance of the contract and to leave the plaintiffs to their remedy in damages. Her advisers recognise that the court must be satisfied that the legal remedy will be effective, and there is evidence that sympathetic persons in the Muslim Community in which she lives are willing to put up money for that purpose.

19–104 That the hardship to the defendant of enforced removal from the property would be great is, on the evidence, beyond doubt. Any accommodation which the local authority could immediately provide for the defendant is likely to deprive her of the daily assistance on which she relies, or at least greatly to diminish it. The move would necessarily cause much more severe disturbance to the lives of the children, now aged five years, three years and four or five months, than a family removal does in ordinary cases, and might even make it impossible for the defendant to keep them with her, handicapped as she is by her physical disability.

19–105 The hardship which would be caused to the plaintiffs if specific performance were refused and adequate pecuniary compensation were available is not, so far as the evidence reveals, greater than what is necessarily involved in being disappointed of the purchase after so long a delay. Since the contractual date for completion in 1979 the plaintiffs have lived in accommodation rented from their local authority, Brent London Borough Council.

19–106 It is not in dispute that, like other equitable relief, the specific performance of contracts is a discretionary remedy; but, in the ordinary case of a sale of land or buildings, the court normally grants it as of course and withholds it only on proof of special facts. The textbooks and reported decisions have long recognised hardship as one ground on which, in a proper case, a purchaser or vendor may be refused specific performance and be left to his right to damages for breach of contract at law. The difficulty is to determine within what limits hardship to a defendant can properly be said to justify this exercise of judicial discretion. There is no doubt that, in the majority of cases, the hardship which moves the court to refuse specific performance is either a hardship existing at the date of the contract or a hardship due in some way to the plaintiff. In the present case, neither of those conditions being satisfied, the plaintiffs rely strongly on that principle or practice, which is stated in varying terms in all the well-known textbooks. It is sufficient for me to cite a passage from *Fry* on Specific Performance[135]:

> It is a well-established doctrine that the court will not enforce the specific performance of a contract, the result of which would be to impose great hardship on either of the parties to it; and this although the party seeking specific performance may be free from the least impropriety of conduct. The question of the hardship of a contract is generally to be judged of at the time at which it is entered into: if it be then fair and just and not productive of hardship, it will be immaterial that it may, by the force of subsequent circumstances or change of events, have become less beneficial to one party, except where these subsequent events have been in some way due to the party who seeks the performance of the contract. For whatever contingencies may attach to a contract, or be involved in the performance of either part, have been taken upon themselves by the parties to it. It has been determined that the reasonableness of a contract is to be judged of at the time it is entered into, and not by the light of subsequent events, and we have already seen that the same principle applies in considering the fairness of a contract.

However, the principle so stated cannot be erected into a fixed limitation of the court's equitable jurisdiction. It is recognised, both by Fry L.J. in his book and in the argument of Mr. Simpkiss for the plaintiffs in the present action, that the court has sometimes refused specific performance because of a change of circumstances supervening after the making of the contract and not in any way attributable to the plaintiff. . . . Thus, I am satisfied that the court's discretion is wide enough, in an otherwise proper case, to refuse specific performance on the ground of hardship subsequent to the contract and not caused by the plaintiff. **19–107**

Another limitation suggested by Mr. Simpkiss was that, in the reported cases, as he said, hardship successfully relied on has always related to the subject matter of the contract and has not been just a personal hardship of the defendant. Certainly, mere pecuniary difficulties, whether of purchaser or of vendor, afford no excuse from performance of a contract. In a wider sense than that, I do not think the suggested universal proposition can be sustained. . . . **19–108**

The important and true principle, in my view, is that only in extraordinary and persuasive circumstances can hardship supply an excuse for resisting performance of a contract for the sale of immovable property. A person of full capacity who sells or buys a house takes the risk of hardship to himself and his dependants, whether arising from existing facts or unexpectedly supervening in the interval before completion. This is where, to my mind, great importance attaches to the immense delay in the present case, not attributable to the defendant's conduct. Even after issue of the writ, she could not complete, if she had wanted to, without the concurrence of the absent Mr. Ahmed. Thus, in a sense, she can say she is being asked to do what she never bargained for, namely to complete the sale after more than four years, after all the unforeseeable changes that such a period entails. I think that in this way she can fairly assert that specific performance would inflict upon her "a hardship amounting to injustice".[136] Equitable relief may, in my view, be refused because of an unforeseen change of circumstances not amounting to legal frustration, just as it may on the ground of mistake insufficient to avoid a contract at law. **19–109**

In the end, I am satisfied that it is within the court's discretion to accede to the defendant's prayer if satisfied that it is just to do so. And, on the whole, looking at the position of both sides after the long unpredictable delay for which neither seeks to make the other responsible, I am of opinion that it is just to leave the plaintiffs to their remedy in damages if that can indeed be effective. **19–110**

In *Wroth v Tyler,* a different type of hardship precluded specific performance, on the basis that "the court would be reluctant to make an order which requires a husband to take legal proceedings against his wife, especially while they are still living together."[137] **19–111**

Another example of the type of another type of hardship that precludes specific performance is where, for one reason or another, it is impossible for the defendant to perform her contractual obligation and any court order compelling its performance. The concern here is that specific performance **19–112**

---

135 E. Fry, *A Treatise on the Specific Performance of Contracts*, 6th edn (Sweet & Maxwell, 1921), p.199.
136 *Tamplin v James* (1880) 15 Ch. D. 215 at 221 (James LJ).
137 *Wroth v Tyler* [1974] Ch. 30 at 51.

subjects the defendant to a court order she cannot comply with and thus compels a defendant to contempt of court. This is explained in *Matila Ltd v Lisheen Properties*:[138]

> If the court is satisfied that a defendant against whom an order is sought is simply not in a position to comply, then it would not be equitable to order him to comply nonetheless and thus put him at risk of committal, even if in fact an order for committal should not be made unless the court was satisfied that the defendant was able to comply but had chosen not to do so.

19–113 Hardship in the sense of impossibility is a "high hurdle"[139] and depends on the court's assessment of the facts, not whether the defendant subjectively believes that performance is impossible.[140]

19–114 If made out, hardship precludes the award of specific relief. The defendant is not exonerated completely, and equitable damages may be awarded in lieu. In *Patel v Ali*, for example, Goulding J explained that in order to refuse specific relief on the basis of hardship, the court must be satisfied that damages will be effective. To this end, counsel for the first defendant indicated to the court that members to the first defendant's community had been willing to put up the money to enable her to pay an order for damages.[141] In *Wroth v Tyler*,[142] for example, damages in lieu of specific performance were awarded, and being assessed as at the date of judgment, resulted in a higher award of damages than if contractual damages assessed at the expectation measure at the date of breach were awarded, as the price of the property to be transferred had risen since the date of breach.

iv. Breach of contract

19–115 It is a well-established principle that the court will not grant a decree if compliance with it would involve the defendant in breach of a prior contract[143] or trust.[144]

v. Laches and acquiescence

19–116 There being no statutory limit on the time after which a claim for specific performance may be brought,[145] equitable considerations govern and may deprive a claimant of the right to performance *in specie* where there is delay either sufficient to be evidence of the plaintiff's abandonment of the contract,[146] or coupled with circumstances which make it unjust to order specific performance.[147] This

---

138 *Matila Ltd v Lisheen Properties* [2010] EWHC 1832 (Ch) at [256] (Stephen Davies J).

139 *Matila v Lisheen Properties* [2010] EWHC 1832 (Ch) at [259].

140 *North Est Lincolnshire Borough Council v Millenium Park (Grimsby) Ltd* [2002] EWCA Civ 1718 (CA); H. Beale, *Chitty on Contracts*, para.27–041.

141 *Patel v Ali* at 286.

142 [1974] Ch. 30.

143 *Harvela Investments Ltd v Royal Trust Co of Canada Ltd* [1985] Ch. 103 at 122.

144 *Dunn v Flood* [1885] 28 Ch. D. 586 (CA) at 593 (Bowen LJ), 595–96 (Fry LJ). A trust beneficiary can seek equitable relief to prevent the trustee's unauthorised execution in performance of an obligation owed to a third party, as in *Palmer v Monk* [1962] N.S.W.R. 786 (Jacobs J).

145 Limitation Act 1980 s.36. Nor do the Limitation Acts apply by analogy: *Talmash v Mugleston* (1826) 4 L.J.O.S. Ch. 200.

146 *Parkin v Thorold* (1852) 16 Beav. 59 at 73. The claimant will still have their legal remedy.

147 Where the plaintiff took possession and waited 10 years before seeking a decree to have the legal title vested in him, mere delay with no injustice to the defendant was no bar: *Williams v Greatrex* [1957] 1 W.L.R. 31. See too *Ridgeway Motors (Isleworth) Ltd v Michael* Ch. D. 13 June 1996 (claim for specific performance after 17 years struck out for laches); *Yewbelle Ltd v London Green Developments Ltd* [2007] 1 E.G.L.R. 137 at [92], where Lewison J held that: "In cases where the contract in question concerns land to be exploited for commercial purposes, the period of delay that can lead to the refusal of specific performance may be comparatively short."

discretionary factor is one that is applicable to other equitable remedies and is discussed further in Chapter 22.

vi. Lack of clean hands

If the claimant is guilty of some impropriety connected to the contract[148] she may not be entitled to an equitable remedy. This discretionary factor is one that is applicable to other equitable remedies and is discussed further in Chapter 22. **19–117**

3. Injunctions

A. Types of Injunctions

As mentioned already, cases and commentaries tend to distinguish between different categories of injunctions. The reason is that the type of injunction tends to have implications for the rules that guide the court's exercise of discretion whether to grant one, and what terms, if any may apply. For this reason, this textbook's discussion will outline the types of injunctions and give an overview of the principles relevant to their award. To this end, injunctions have been distinguished according to different variables, and some of the main distinctions are set out in the following excerpt from *Snell's Equity*. **19–118**

Paul Davies, "Injunction" in John McGhee et al (eds), *Snell's Equity*, 34th edn (Sweet & Maxwell, 2021), paras 18–002–18–004

(a) Perpetual or interlocutory.

A perpetual (or final) injunction can only be granted after the court has been able to adjudicate upon the matter. A perpetual injunction is so called because it is granted at the final determination of the parties' rights and not because it will necessarily operate forever. For instance, a perpetual injunction may be granted so as to continue only during the currency of a lease. **19–119**

By contrast, an interlocutory (or interim) injunction is granted before the trial of an action; its object is to keep matters in status quo until the question at issue between the parties can be determined. Where the claimant seeks a final injunction, that fact may be sufficient to justify the grant of an interlocutory injunction until trial or sooner order. Interlocutory injunctions may also be granted as an aid to the proper determination of the case or as an aid to enforcement: in appropriate cases, such injunctions may be granted for the period between the trial of the action and completion of the enforcement process. **19–120**

(b) Prohibitory or mandatory.

A prohibitory (or restrictive) injunction is an order which requires a person not to do some wrongful act. A mandatory injunction is an order which requires a person (i) not to continue some wrongful omission; or (ii) to undo the consequences of a wrongful act. Prohibitory injunctions are far more common than mandatory. Indeed, owing to doubts as to the jurisdiction to grant mandatory injunctions, until late in the nineteenth century all injunctions were collected in prohibitive form. Thus a court which wished to secure the removal of buildings wrongfully erected formerly used to order the defendant not to allow them to remain on the land, a form of order which seems strange in a jurisdiction which traditionally looks to the substance rather than the form. Now, however, a mandatory injunction is made in a positive form, ordering some act to be done. **19–121**

---

[148] *Moody v Cox* [1917] 2 Ch. 71 at 87–88; *van Gestel v Cann, The Times*, 7 August 1987 (claim that plaintiff guilty of fraud unconnected with contract of no assistance to defendant).

(c) Common or special.

19–122 Before 1875, the Court of Chancery might grant an injunction restraining a person from proceeding in the common law courts or from executing a judgment obtained there. Such injunctions were known as common injunctions, and like all injunctions they were directed not to the court but to the parties to the proceedings, in accordance with the principle that equity acts in personam. An injunction granted to give effect to an equitable right, or to provide an additional remedy in aid of rights enforceable at common law, was known as a special injunction. With the fusion of the administration of law and equity, common injunctions were no longer required and were abolished. As all injunctions are now technically "special", the terms have dropped out of use.

19–123 In addition to the types outlined above is a *"quia timet"* injunction and which can be granted where there is a threatened breach of a claimant's right or other legal entitlement. This means that a court can order a defendant to take (in)action to prevent a breach or infringement of a plaintiff's right.

19–124 These categories are not mutually exclusive and can overlap. A final injunction might be mandatory or prohibitory, just as an interim injunction might be. Any of which might be awarded to restrain a threatened breach, i.e. a *quia timet* injunction, or might be awarded in response to an actual breach.

B. Jurisdiction

19–125 A general jurisdiction to award injunctions is contained in the Senior Courts Act 1981 s.37, which states:

> The High Court may by order (whether interlocutory or final) grant an injunction . . . in all cases in which it appears to the court to be just and convenient to do so.
>
> (1) Any such order may be made either unconditionally or on such terms and conditions as the court thinks fit.

19–126 This broad jurisdiction allows the court to order injunctions to realise a right or other legal entitlement, whether recognised by common law, statute or equity and which is justiciable by a court[149] and excluding that in relation to a criminal sanction.[150] Examples include orders restraining a trustee from dealing with trust funds contrary to the trust terms;[151] orders to restrain a defendant from taking action in breach of a statutory provision, such as one to prevent publication of evidence given in matrimonial proceedings, as in *Duchess of Argyll v Duke of Argyll*;[152] orders restraining an opera singer performing in breach of her contractual obligation to perform exclusively for the plaintiff;[153] orders restraining trespass[154] or nuisance;[155] or orders restraining a defendant passing off a product as being that of the plaintiff's.[156]

---

149 *Siskina (Owners of cargo lately laden on board) v Distos Compania Naviera SA* [1979] A.C. 210 at 254–57 (Lord Diplock); *Fourie v Le Roux* [2007] UKHL 1; [2007] 1 W.L.R. 320 at [30]–[35].

150 Jurisdiction to award an injunction is where the claimant has an entitlement to a civil remedy as distinct from being in lieu of a criminal sanction, see, e.g. *Di Marco v Morshead Mansions Ltd* [2014] EWCA Civ 96; [2014] 1 W.L.R. 1799 (a landlord's obligations under the Landlord and Tenant Act 1985 s.21 and s.22 could not be enforced by way of injunction).

151 *Howden v Yorkshire Miners Association* [1905] A.C. 256.

152 [1967] Ch. 302.

153 *Lumley v Wagner* (1852) 1 De. G.M. & G. 604.

154 *Patel v WH Smith (Eziot) Ltd* [1987] 1 W.L.R. 853.

155 *Soltau v De Held* (1851) 2 Sim. (N.S.) 133 at 151 (Kindersley VC).

156 The classic statement of principle is in the speech of Lord Parker in *AG Spalding & Bros v AW Gamage Ltd* (1915) 32 R.P.C. 273 at 283. See too the speeches of Lord Diplock and Lord Fraser in *Warnink (Erven) BV v J Townend & Sons Mull Ltd* [1979] A.C. 731 at 742 and 755, 756 respectively.

In addition to this general statutory jurisdiction, there are specific legislative provisions conferring jurisdiction to award specific types of injunctive orders in certain instances, such as freezing or "Mareva" injunctions[157] which prevent a defendant dissipating his assets to frustrate enforcement of a prospective judgment, and search orders or "Anton Pillar" orders, which allows the applicant to enter and search the defendant's premises and force the defendant to allow the applicant to inspect documents and withdraw those documents from the defendant's possession, with a view to preserving evidence for trial.[158] In addition, there are a range of legislative provisions providing for the award of injunctions; for example, as part of the remedial regime for actions taken by companies via their corporate officers,[159] judicial review of the actions of public officials,[160] or in relation to intellectual property.[161] The breadth and depth of rules and materials on injunctions necessitates a high-level consideration of the factors guiding the court's assessment of whether to grant an injunction, namely whether (a) there is a need for an injunction in the circumstances; and (b) damages are inadequate. **19–127**

i. The need for an injunction

A claimant must do more than show she has some right or other legal entitlement, and instead must establish that there is a present need for an injunction to prevent the defendant's continuing or imminent breach. An injunction may be refused if the breach has ceased prior to trial, or is of a temporary nature and the defendant has no intention to commit the same breach again.[162] However, a defendant cannot resist an injunction simply by disavowing any intention to breach in the future, especially when the defendant has already breached or infringed the claimant's rights.[163] The claimant will not be able to show a need for an injunction if she has other means available to her to prevent the breach, such as in *Elliman Sons & Co v Carrington & Son Ltd*[164] where the claimant could prevent a defendant's dealing with goods in breach of contract by not providing those goods to the defendant in the first place. **19–128**

The factors relevant to the discretion to award a *quia timet* injunction have been summarised by Marcus Smith J in the following excerpt from *Vastint Leeds BV v Persons Unknown*.[165] **19–129**

---

157 Senior Courts Act 1981 s.37(3); Civil Procedure Rules r.25.1(1)(f).
158 Civil Procedure Act 1997 s.7.
159 Companies Act 2006 s.178 (directors' statutory duties are enforceable in the same way as the corresponding common law rule or equitable principle, including by way of injunction), s.757 (Enforcement of prohibition: order restraining proposed contravention).
160 Senior Courts Act 1981 s.31(2) confers a power on the High Court to award a declaration or injunction where "it would be just and convenient" for the remedy to be awarded having regard to the nature of the matters in respect of which relief by one of the prerogative writs might be granted. The statutory replacement of the injunction and declaration was a response to the Law Commission's recommendation for the declaration and injunction to be made available through a new method for judicial review. The Commission otherwise recommended that the "essential characteristics of these remedies remain": Law Commission, *Remedies in Administrative Law* (1976) Law Com. No.73, para.[43], including the discretionary nature of the remedies.
161 See, e.g. Copyright, Designs and Patents Act 1988 s.96; Trade Marks Act 1994 s.14.
162 *Leader v Moody* (1875) L.R. 20 Eq. 145.
163 *Proctor v Bayley* (1889) 42 Ch. D. 390 at 399, 400.
164 *Elliman Sons & Co v Carrington & Son Ltd* [1901] 2 Ch. 275.
165 *Vastint Leeds BV v Persons Unknown* [2018] EWHC 2456 (Ch) at [31] (Marcus Smith J).

Vastint Leeds BV v Persons Unknown

Chancery Division, [2018] EWHC 2456 at [31]

19–130 MARCUS SMITH J.:

(1) A distinction is drawn between final mandatory and final prohibitory quia timet injunctions. Because the former oblige the defendant to do something, whilst the latter merely oblige the defendant not to interfere with the claimant's rights, it is harder to persuade a court to grant a mandatory than a prohibitory injunction. That said, the approach to the granting of a quia timet injunction, whether mandatory or prohibitory, is essentially the same.

(2) Quia timet injunctions are granted where the breach of a claimant's rights is threatened, but where (for some reason) the claimant's cause of action is not complete. This may be for a number of reasons. The threatened wrong may, as here, be entirely anticipatory. On the other hand, as in *Hooper v. Rogers*, the cause of action may be substantially complete. In *Hooper v. Rogers*, an act constituting nuisance or an unlawful interference with the claimant's land had been committed, but damage not yet sustained by the claimant but was only in prospect for the future.

(3) When considering whether to grant a quia timet injunction, the court follows a two-stage test:

(a) First, is there a strong probability that, unless restrained by injunction, the defendant will act in breach of the claimant's rights?

(b) Secondly, if the defendant did an act in contravention of the claimant's rights, would the harm resulting be so grave and irreparable that, notwithstanding the grant of an immediate interlocutory injunction (at the time of actual infringement of the claimant's rights) to restrain further occurrence of the acts complained of, a remedy of damages would be inadequate?

(4) There will be multiple factors relevant to an assessment of each of these two stages, and there is some overlap between what is material to each . . .

(5) Turning to the second stage, it is necessary to ask the counterfactual question: assuming no quia timet injunction, but an infringement of the claimant's rights, how effective will a more-or-less immediate interim injunction plus damages in due course be as a remedy for that infringement? Essentially, the question is how easily the harm of the infringement can be undone by an ex post rather than an ex ante intervention, but the following other factors are material:

(a) The gravity of the anticipated harm. It seems to me that if the some of the consequences of an infringement are potentially very serious and incapable of ex post remedy, albeit only one of many types of harm capable of occurring, the seriousness of these irremediable harms is a factor that must be borne in mind.

(b) The distinction between mandatory and prohibitory injunctions.

19–131 A court's jurisdiction is not confined to ordering a defendant's future performance, and can extend to ordering a defendant to take action as necessary to rectify or repair the consequences of a defendant's past breach, such as an order requiring a defendant to remove a skylight erected in breach of a plaintiff's access to light,[166] or an order requiring a defendant to remove a fence erected in breach of the plaintiffs' right of way.[167]

ii. Inadequacy of damages

19–132 Like the court's jurisdiction to award specific performance, the jurisdiction to award an injunction in aid of a common law entitlement depends on the claimant showing that the remedy afforded her at law, usually damages, is inadequate.[168] Adequacy is a question of whether the remedy afforded at law will be sufficient to achieve the law's ends when applied to the facts of the case. The remedy at law will be

166 *McManus v Cooke* (1887) 35 Ch. D. 681.
167 *Higson v Guenault* [2014] EWCA Civ 703.
168 *London and Blackwall Ry v Cross* (1886) 31 Ch. D. 354 at 369 (Lindley LJ).

adequate and an injunction not available, when a monetary sum will put the plaintiff in the position as if there were no breach.[169] Conversely, inadequacy of damages, and the prima facie availability of injunctive relief, will be made out when, for example: the defendant is poor (making it unlikely that she will pay any damages award),[170] or, assessment of the plaintiff's loss is difficult such that only nominal damages might be available,[171] or, where the plaintiff has a right to performance, and not simply to compensation for breach, and tends toward inadequacy of damages in cases concerning continuing nuisances[172] reflecting the strong protection afforded by the law to a landowner's right to the quiet enjoyment of her property.[173] Injunctions can be awarded to restrain other torts, too,[174] and breaches of a negative contractual obligation,[175] regarding which Sachs LJ observed in *Evans Marshall & Co Ltd v Bertola SA* that:[176]

> The courts have repeatedly recognised there can be claims under contracts in which, as here, it is unjust to confine a plaintiff to his damages for their breach. Great difficulty in estimating these damages is one factor that can be and has been taken into account. Another factor is the creation of certain areas of damage which cannot be taken into monetary account in a common law action for breach of contract. Loss of goodwill and trade reputation are examples. Generally, indeed, the grant of injunctions in contract cases stems from such factors.

An example of the court's assessment of the need for an injunction, adequacy of damages and the application of some discretionary factors is supplied by the following excerpt from *Wood v Sutcliffe*,[177] where the plaintiff sought an injunction to restrain the defendants from discharging pollutant materials or liquids into a stream, the water from which the plaintiffs had a right (acquired by long user) to use for the purposes of their wool mill. The defendants operated a dye works upstream and effluent ran from the defendants' works into the stream. In the period between the construction of the plaintiffs' mills and acquisition of the right of long user, and the construction of the defendants' dye works, some 16,000 dwellinghouses had been erected on, or near the banks of the stream. The plaintiffs' bill for an injunction was dismissed. **19–133**

169 *Wood v Sutcliffe* (1851) 2 Sim. (N.S.) 163; *Garden Cottage Foods Ltd v Milk Marketing Board* [1984] A.C. 130.

170 *Hodgson v Duce* (1856) 2 Jur. (N.S.) 1014.

171 *John Trenberth Ltd v National Westminster Bank Ltd* (1979) 39 P. & C.R. 104 at 107 (Walton J).

172 *Martin v Nutkin* (1725) 2 P.Wms. 266; *Shelfer v City of London Electric Lighting Co* [1895] 1 Ch. 287.

173 See, e.g. *Hodgson v Duce* (1856) 2 Jur. N.S. 1014; *Eardley v Granville* (1876) 3 Ch. D. 826; *Litchfield-Speer v Queen Anne's Gate Syndicate (No.2) Ltd* [1919] 1 Ch. 407; *Anchor Brewhouse Developments Ltd v Berkley House (Docklands Developments) Ltd* (1987) 38 B.L.R. 82; *Harrow LBC v Donohue* [1995] 1 E.G.L.R. 257 (distinguishing acts of mere trespass—where damages might be substituted for an injunction—and dispossession—where a claimant is entitled as a matter of right to the protection of an injunction).

174 As noted in J. Murphy, "Rethinking Injunctions in Tort Law" (2007) 27 O.J.L.S. 509, arguing that the law attaches just as much importance to, and so should be just as willing to award injunctions to protect, other interests besides proprietary interests, e.g. bodily integrity.

175 See, e.g. *Lumley v Wagner* (1852) 1 De. G.M. & G. 604; *Doherty v Allman* (1878) 3 App. Cas. 709 at 720; *Dyson Technology Ltd v Pellerey* [2016] EWCA Civ 87; [2016] I.C.R. 688. For the enforcement of positive contractual obligations, see Part 2 above on specific performance.

176 [1973] 1 W.L.R. 349 at 380. See too *Manning v AIG Europe UK Ltd* [2004] EWHC 1760 (Ch); [2005] 1 B.C.L.C. 1 (breach of subordinated debt agreement); *Sheffield United Football Club Ltd v West Ham United Football Club Plc* [2008] EWHC 2855 (Comm); [2009] 1 Lloyd's Rep. 167 (breach of arbitration clause).

177 *Wood v Sutcliffe* (1851) 2 Simons, New Series 163, 61 E.R. 303 at 303–305.

Wood v Sutcliffe

Court of Chancery, (1851) 2 Simons, New Series 163, 61 E.R. 303 at 303–305

19–134 KINDERSLEY V.C.: Now I conceive that if parties have established such a legal right as the Plaintiffs in this case have established, and another person comes and erects works on the same stream above their works, and by his manufacturing process so fouls the water of the stream as seriously and continuously to obstruct the effective carrying on of their manufacture; and if the granting of an injunction will restore or tend to restore those parties to the position in which they previously stood, and in which they have a right to stand, and if the injury complained of is of such a nature that damages will not be an adequate compensation, that is, such a compensation as will in effect, though not in specie, place them in the position in which they previously stood; and if, moreover (for there are several conditions), they use due diligence in vindicating their rights, they have, in general, a right to come to a Court of Equity and say, "Do not leave us to bring action after action for the purpose of recovering damages, but interfere with a strong hand, and prevent the continuance of the acts we complain of, in order that our legal right may be protected and preserved to us." I say in general, because whenever a Court of Equity is asked for an injunction in cases of such a nature as this, it must have regard not only to the dry strict rights of the Plaintiff and Defendant, but also to the surrounding circumstances, to the rights or interests of other persons which may be more or less involved: it must, I say, have regard to those circumstances before it exercises its jurisdiction (which is unquestionably a strong one), of granting an injunction. . . .

19–135 Having stated the conditions which are requisite to induce the Court to grant an injunction in such a case, I proceed to consider how far those conditions are satisfied in the present case. One of those conditions is that the injunction, by stopping the acts complained of, will restore or tend to restore the party complaining to the enjoyment of that right which he has established against the Defendant. I say "restore or tend to restore," because I conceive it is no answer to an application of this sort for the Defendant to say that other persons as well as he are polluting the stream, and that therefore the injunction will not restore the Plaintiff to the enjoyment of his legal right, inasmuch as it will not prevent those other persons from continuing to pollute the water; for the Plaintiff must sue each of the wrongdoers separately, unless indeed they are acting in partnership or in concert together; and the obtaining of an injunction against any one of the wrongdoers, though it may not actually restore, does tend to restore the Plaintiff to the enjoyment of his right, as it is a step towards obtaining an injunction against each of them.

19–136 Now, the Plaintiffs require water for three purposes: namely, washing wool, generating steam and condensing steam; for the first two of which purity is an essential quality. Not only the Defendants, but the Messrs. Ripley and other persons, have manufactories on the banks of the stream above the Plaintiffs' mills. The works of Messrs. Ripley, who are dyers, were established long before the Plaintiffs' mills were; but the works of the other persons were established at a comparatively recent period. Besides those various works, a very large and dense population has gradually grown up on or near to the banks of the stream. No doubt, however, there was a time, and probably not a very remote one, when the stream, or that portion of it which lies between Messrs. Ripley's works and the Plaintiffs' mills, flowed through open fields, pure and unpolluted, to the Plaintiffs' mills. But whenever human beings congregate in large numbers on the banks of a stream, the inevitable consequence is that a great quantity of sewerage is discharged into the stream, which necessarily has the effect of polluting it. Therefore, to some considerable extent, the pollution of this stream is inevitable. Not all the Courts of law and Equity in the kingdom can prevent it; for they cannot remove the mass of human beings who are congregated on the banks of the stream. . . . Therefore, if this injunction were granted, it would not have the effect of restoring or tending to restore the Plaintiffs to the position in which they originally stood; for the water would still flow to their mills in so polluted a state that they could not use it, as they originally did, for either washing wool or generating steam.

19–137 On the other hand, to grant the injunction would have the effect of seriously injuring, if not ruining, the Defendants. Weighing, then, the injury that may accrue to the one party or the other by granting or refusing the injunction, I think that, if my decision were to turn upon this point alone, I should be bound to refuse it.

19–138 Another condition which, as I have said, is necessary in order to induce a Court of Equity to interfere by injunction in a case similar to that now before me is that the mischief complained of is such that it cannot be properly and adequately compensated by pecuniary damages. Now let us see how the matter stands in this respect. Many years before the Defendants' works were commenced. Mr. Dixon, Messrs. Greenwood, and other individuals had works in what is, aptly enough, called the nest of factories immediately above the Plaintiffs' mills; and they also having polluted the stream, the Plaintiffs threatened to bring actions against them; where-upon they entered into deeds of arrangement with the Plaintiffs by which, in order to

> avoid litigation, they agreed to pay the Plaintiffs at the rate of £2 per annum per horse-power for the right of polluting the water. Now, if such an arrangement as that can be made, ought I to grant an injunction in order to compel the Defendants to enter into it, when the bringing of an action would be almost (I will not say quite) as efficacious? If the Plaintiffs desire to apply to the Defendants a certain pressure in order to bring them to terms, I think that I ought to leave Plaintiffs to that pressure which may be applied by means of an action or actions at law. If the Plaintiffs brought an action, and, the matter being represented to the jury, the jury were satisfied that the Defendants ought to come to terms, they might give the Plaintiffs £50 or £100 damages, instead of a farthing, a shilling, or forty shillings. On the ground, therefore, that the Plaintiffs themselves have shewn that the injury they complain of is one which, in some way, may be compensated by money, I think that I ought not to grant the injunction.
>
> But I do not rest my decision upon either of the grounds which I have mentioned. The principal ground upon which I conceive that I must refuse this injunction is that the Plaintiffs have not used due diligence in vindicating their rights. They stood by whilst the Defendants were constructing their works, and they suffered the Defendants to use their works after they were constructed, from the beginning of 1845 until the beginning of 1850, a period of very nearly five years, without giving them any hint that they were doing anything that they had not a lawful right to do; and, if there had been nothing else in this case, I should have been of opinion, on this ground alone, that the Plaintiffs were not entitled to the injunction. **19–139**
>
> I incline to think also that the injunction ought to be refused on the ground that the injury complained of is capable of being compensated by money; and, in my opinion, it ought also to be refused on the ground that the granting of it would inflict serious damage upon the Defendants, without doing any real practical good to the Plaintiffs. **19–140**

It is possible to observe some fluctuation(s) in the courts' conception of the requirement of inadequacy of damages: from a strict jurisdictional precondition expressing the default position in favour of the remedy available at law, to the different starting position that a claimant is entitled to an injunction subject to discretionary considerations "as to the remedy which the court will provide for the invasion of the plaintiff's rights", such as adequacy of damages.[178] **19–141**

The requirement of inadequacy of damages does not apply where an injunction is sought in aid of statutory rights, or some equitable entitlement,[179] such as when a trust beneficiary seeks an injunction to restrain a trustee's threatened or continuing breach of trust. **19–142**

C. Discretionary Bars to Relief

i. Supervision and certainty

Important considerations that tend against the award of an injunction is the extent to which court supervision is required and the degree of certainty with which the order(s) can be framed. These have discussed already in relation to specific performance, and apply mutatis mutandis to injunctions owing to their enforcement mechanism. This is particularly for mandatory injunctions which, like specific performance, compel the defendant to take action under the pain of contempt of court. Indeed, the excerpt from Lord Hoffmann's judgment in *Argyll*,[180] was expressed in relation to specific performance and mandatory injunctions indiscriminately. **19–143**

---

178 *Bristol City Council v Lovell* [1998] 1 W.L.R. 446 at 453 (Lord Hoffman). See also *Evans v Marshall & Co Ltd v Bertola SA* [1973] 1 W.L.R. 349 at 379. However, see the different preference for the remedy at law when adequate, as expressed by Lord Sumption in *Lawrence v Fen Tigers Ltd* [2014] UKSC 13; [2014] A.C. 822 at [168]. See also the dissenting judgment of Millett L.J. in the Court of Appeal in *Co-operative Insurance Society Ltd v Argyll Stores (Holdings) Ltd* [1996] Ch. 286 at 304, upheld in the House of Lords [1998] A.C. 1.

179 See, e.g. *Fox v Fox* (1870) L.R. 11 Eq. 142; *Buttle v Saunders* [1950] 2 All E.R. 193.

180 See paras 19–067ff.

ii. Laches and acquiescence

19–144 Laches and acquiescence are bars to an injunction, as illustrated by *Wood v Sutcliffe*,[181] excerpted above. Each of these discretionary bars are discussed further in Chapter 22.

iii. Lack of clean hands

19–145 Unclean hands is discussed further in Chapter 22 and is another discretionary bar that can bar an injunction where the claimant's misbehaviour is sufficiently closely connected with the relief sought to justify withholding the remedy. An example is *Royal Bank of Scotland Plc v Highland Financial Partners LP*,[182] where the Court of Appeal declined to grant an anti-suit injunction restraining the defendants from pursuing proceedings in Texas because the claimant had suppressed facts in the course of the substantive proceedings before the English court and had continued to argue, even after discovery of the true position, that it had not concealed those facts. On the other side of the line is *Grobelaar v News Group Newspapers Ltd*,[183] where the House of Lords granted an injunction restraining a newspaper from repeating an unproven allegation that a footballer had thrown football matches, although he was proven to have taken bribes, to have told his co-conspirator that he had thrown matches in exchange for the money, and to have lied about this in court.

iv. Hardship

19–146 Interim and mandatory injunctions (interim or perpetual), in particular, provide scope for an argument that an injunction ought to be refused as a matter of discretion on the ground of hardship to the defendant. In the former case, this is because, ex hypothesi, the claimant has not yet established her right to any relief because there has not yet been a trial.[184] In the latter, the reason is that compliance with a mandatory injunction will often involve the defendant in expenditure which may be out of all proportion to the benefit which the claimant will derive from the grant of an injunction.

19–147 As discussed elsewhere,[185] the Senior Courts Act 1981 s.50 gives the court a statutory jurisdiction to award damages in lieu of an injunction, in recognition of the fact that the award of injunctions can sometimes be oppressive to defendants (particularly mandatory ones requiring, for example, the demolition of buildings). By giving courts of equity the power to award damages in lieu, Parliament made it easier to justify declining to grant injunctions in such cases.

19–148 If issuing an injunction would be futile and subject a defendant to the certain outcome of contempt of court, no injunction will be issued. In Arden LJ's words, "the court must be astute to see that there is a real prospect that something will be gained".[186] An injunction will not be issued if it is impossible for the defendant to comply with the order (because, for example, in a case where a mandatory injunction was sought requiring her to tear down a building, she no longer owned the land and had no right to

---

181 *Wood v Sutcliffe* at 303–305.

182 [2013] EWCA Civ 328; [2013] 1 C.L.C. 596.

183 [2002] UKHL 40; [2002] 1 W.L.R. 3024.

184 The position is slightly different where the claimant has won proceedings, but the defendant appeals and the claimant seeks an interim injunction pending resolution of the appeal: *Novartis AG v Hospira UK Ltd* [2013] EWCA Civ 583; [2014] 1 W.L.R. 1264 at [41].

185 See para.18-035.

186 *Dadourian Group International Inc v Simms (Practice Note)* [2006] 1 W.L.R. 2499 at [35]. See also *Wookey v Wookey* [1991] Fam. 121.

tear down any building upon it). Another illustration is provided by the *Spycatcher* case,[187] where a final injunction was refused against a newspaper preventing it from publishing certain information. The information had been confidential, but it had already been published in a book that had become widely available in the UK by the time of the litigation.

Another context in which hardship can have a particular application is for contracts for personal service and employment contracts. An injunction will not be awarded that compels a defendant to work for a plaintiff on the threat of contempt of court as this is tantamount to slavery.[188] An injunction prohibiting a defendant from working for another person, will not be awarded if its effect is indirectly to compel the defendant to work for the plaintiff, where for example the defendant would not be able to find work elsewhere. A range of factors will be taken into account, so that an injunction restraining the defendant for a short period may be granted,[189] as opposed to a long period of restraint is so long that the defendant will be compelled to work for the plaintiff or act in contempt of court to find work.[190] **19–149**

D. Specific Applications

The jurisdictional and discretionary considerations outlined in Parts B and C above apply across the various types of injunctions outlined in Part A above. They can have particular meaning and emphasis depending on the type of injunction, and the nature of the imposition on the defendant relative to the contribution the remedy makes to ensuring law's ends are met, as is discussed in the excerpts below. **19–150**

i. Mandatory injunctions

Redland Bricks Ltd v Morris

House of Lords, [1970] A.C. 652 at 665–666

LORD UPJOHN: The grant of a mandatory injunction is, of course, entirely discretionary and unlike a negative injunction can never be "as of course." Every case must depend essentially upon its own particular circumstances. Any general principles for its application can only be laid down in the most general terms: **19–151**

1. A mandatory injunction can only be granted where the plaintiff shows a very strong probability upon the facts that grave damage will accrue to him in the future. As Lord Dunedin said in 1919 it is not sufficient to say "timeo."[191] It is a jurisdiction to be exercised sparingly and with caution but in the proper case unhesitatingly.
2. Damages will not be a sufficient or adequate remedy if such damage does happen. This is only the application of a general principle of equity; it has nothing to do with Lord Cairns' Act or *Shelfer's case*.[192]
3. Unlike the case where a negative injunction is granted to prevent the continuance or recurrence of a wrongful act the question of the cost to the defendant to do works to prevent or lessen the likelihood of a future apprehended wrong must be an element to be taken into account:
   (a) where the defendant has acted without regard to his neighbour's rights, or has tried to steal a march on him or has tried to evade the jurisdiction of the court or, to sum it up, has acted wantonly and quite unreasonably in relation to his neighbour he may be ordered to repair his wanton and unreasonable acts by doing positive work to restore the status quo

---

[187] *Attorney General v Observer Ltd* [1990] 1 A.C. 109.
[188] *De Francesco v Barnum* (1890) 45 Ch.D. 430 at 438.
[189] *Lumley v Wagner* (1852) 1 De. G.M.&G. 604.
[190] *Warren v Mendy* [1989] 1 W.L.R. 853.
[191] *Attorney General for the Dominion of Canada v Ritchie Contracting and Supply Co* [1919] A.C. 999 at 1005.
[192] [1895] 1 Ch. 287.

even if the expense to him is out of all proportion to the advantage thereby accruing to the plaintiff. As illustrative of this see *Woodhouse v. Newry Navigation Co.*[193]

(b) but where the defendant has acted reasonably, though in the event wrongly, the cost of remedying by positive action his earlier activities is most important for two reasons. First, because no legal wrong has yet occurred (for which he has not been recompensed at law and in equity) and, in spite of gloomy expert opinion, may never occur or possibly only upon a much smaller scale than anticipated. Secondly. because if ultimately heavy damage does occur the plaintiff is in no way prejudiced for he has his action at law and all his consequential remedies in equity.

So the amount to be expended under a mandatory order by the defendant must be balanced with these considerations in mind against the anticipated possible damage to the plaintiff and if, on such balance, it seems unreasonable to inflict such expenditure upon one who for this purpose is no more than a potential wrongdoer then the court must exercise its jurisdiction accordingly. Of course, the court does not have to order such works as upon the evidence before it will remedy the wrong but may think it proper to impose upon the defendant the obligation of doing certain works which may upon expert opinion merely lessen the likelihood of any further injury to the plaintiff's land. Sargant J. pointed this out in effect in the celebrated "Moving Mountain" case, *Kennard v. Cory Bros. & Co. Ltd.*[194]

4. If in the exercise of its discretion the court decides that it is a proper case to grant a mandatory injunction, then the court must be careful to see that the defendant knows exactly in fact what he has to do and this means not as a matter of law but as a matter of fact, so that in carrying out an order he can give his contractors the proper instructions.

ii. Interim injunctions

American Cyanamid Co v Ethicon Ltd

House of Lords, [1975] A.C. 396 at 405–409

19–152 LORD DIPLOCK: The grant of an interlocutory injunction is a remedy that is both temporary and discretionary. . . .

19–153 My Lords, when an application for an interlocutory injunction to restrain a defendant from doing acts alleged to be in violation of the plaintiff's legal right is made upon contested facts, the decision whether or not to grant an interlocutory injunction has to be taken at a time when ex hypothesi the existence of the right or the violation of it, or both, is uncertain and will remain uncertain until final judgment is given in the action. It was to mitigate the risk of injustice to the plaintiff during the period before that uncertainty could be resolved that the practice arose of granting him relief by way of interlocutory injunction; but since the middle of the 19th century this has been made subject to his undertaking to pay damages to the defendant for any loss sustained by reason of the injunction if it should be held at the trial that the plaintiff had not been entitled to restrain the defendant from doing what he was threatening to do. The object of the interlocutory injunction is to protect the plaintiff against injury by violation of his right for which he could not be adequately compensated in damages recoverable in the action if the uncertainty were resolved in his favour at the trial; but the plaintiff's need for such protection must be weighed against the corresponding need of the defendant to be protected against injury resulting from his having been prevented from exercising his own legal rights for which he could not be adequately compensated under the plaintiff's undertaking in damages if the uncertainty were resolved in the defendant's favour at the trial. The court must weigh one need against another and determine where "the balance of convenience" lies.

19–154 In those cases where the legal rights of the parties depend upon facts that are in dispute between them, the evidence available to the court at the hearing of the application for an interlocutory injunction is incomplete. It is given on affidavit and has not been tested by oral cross-examination. The purpose sought to be achieved by giving to the court discretion to grant such injunctions would be stultified if the discretion were

---

193 [1898] 1 I.R. 161.

194 [1922] 1 Ch. 265 at 274, affirmed on appeal [1922] 2 Ch. 1.

clogged by a technical rule forbidding its exercise if upon that incomplete untested evidence the court evaluated the chances of the plaintiff's ultimate success in the action at 50 per cent. or less, but permitting its exercise if the court evaluated his chances at more than 50 per cent.

The notion that it is incumbent upon the court to undertake what is in effect a preliminary trial of the action upon evidential material different from that upon which the actual trial will be conducted, is, I think, of comparatively recent origin, . . . judges generally treated as sufficient to justify their considering the balance of convenience upon applications for interlocutory injunctions, at any rate up to the time when I became a member of your Lordships' House. . . . 19–155

It is no part of the court's function at this stage of the litigation to try to resolve conflicts of evidence on affidavit as to facts on which the claims of either party may ultimately depend nor to decide difficult questions of law which call for detailed argument and mature considerations. These are matters to be dealt with at the trial. . . .So unless the material available to the court at the hearing of the application for an interlocutory injunction fails to disclose that the plaintiff has any real prospect of succeeding in his claim for a permanent injunction at the trial, the court should go on to consider whether the balance of convenience lies in favour of granting or refusing the interlocutory relief that is sought. 19–156

As to that, the governing principle is that the court should first consider whether, if the plaintiff were to succeed at the trial in establishing his right to a permanent injunction, he would be adequately compensated by an award of damages for the loss he would have sustained as a result of the defendant's continuing to do what was sought to be enjoined between the time of the application and the time of the trial. If damages in the measure recoverable at common law would be adequate remedy and the defendant would be in a financial position to pay them, no interlocutory injunction should normally be granted, however strong the plaintiff's claim appeared to be at that stage. If, on the other hand, damages would not provide an adequate remedy for the plaintiff in the event of his succeeding at the trial, the court should then consider whether, on the contrary hypothesis that the defendant were to succeed at the trial in establishing his right to do that which was sought to be enjoined, he would be adequately compensated under the plaintiff's undertaking as to damages for the loss he would have sustained by being prevented from doing so between the time of the application and the time of the trial. If damages in the measure recoverable under such an undertaking would be an adequate remedy and the plaintiff would be in a financial position to pay them, there would be no reason upon this ground to refuse an interlocutory injunction. 19–157

It is where there is doubt as to the adequacy of the respective remedies in damages available to either party or to both, that the question of balance of convenience arises. It would be unwise to attempt even to list all the various matters which may need to be taken into consideration in deciding where the balance lies, let alone to suggest the relative weight to be attached to them. These will vary from case to case. 19–158

Where other factors appear to be evenly balanced it is a counsel of prudence to take such measures as are calculated to preserve the status quo. If the defendant is enjoined temporarily from doing something that he has not done before, the only effect of the interlocutory injunction in the event of his succeeding at the trial is to postpone the date at which he is able to embark upon a course of action which he has not previously found it necessary to undertake; whereas to interrupt him in the conduct of an established enterprise would cause much greater inconvenience to him since he would have to start again to establish it in the event of his succeeding at the trial. 19–159

Save in the simplest cases, the decision to grant or to refuse an interlocutory injunction will cause to whichever party is unsuccessful on the application some disadvantages which his ultimate success at the trial may show he ought to have been spared and the disadvantages may be such that the recovery of damages to which he would then be entitled either in the action or under the plaintiff's undertaking would not be sufficient to compensate him fully for all of them. The extent to which the disadvantages to each party would be incapable of being compensated in damages in the event of his succeeding at the trial is always a significant factor in assessing where the balance of convenience lies, and if the extent of the uncompensatable disadvantage to each party would not differ widely, it may not be improper to take into account in tipping the balance the relative strength of each party's case as revealed by the affidavit evidence adduced on the hearing of the application. This, however, should be done only where it is apparent upon the facts disclosed by evidence as to which there is no credible dispute that the strength of one party's case is disproportionate to that of the other party. The court is not justified in embarking upon anything resembling a trial of the action upon conflicting affidavits in order to evaluate the strength of either party's case. 19–160

19–161 For a summary of these principles when applied to a *quia timet* injunction sought on an interim basis against an unknown person(s) and which would interfere with freedom of expression under the Human Rights Act 1998 s.12, see *Shell UK Oil Products Ltd v Persons Unknown.*[195]

E. The Parties

19–162 Sometimes, the legal rules being enforced by the injunction make it clear who is the proper applicant with a power to seek court relief in aid of a legal entitlement generated by the law in her favour. An injunction can be awarded in favour of a trust beneficiary, a co-trustee or replacement trustee to compel a trustee's due administration;[196] a party to the contract can seek injunctive relief to restrain a breach of contract; the person to whom the defendant assumed a duty of care can seek injunctive relief to restrain a breach; and a titleholder can seek injunctive relief to restrain another party's trespass or nuisance.[197] These and other rules identify to whom a legal entitlement accrues and with it a power of enforcement against either a private legal person (including a company) or a public official. What is more difficult is when a legal rule (be it one of common law, statute or equity) is of general application and which operates for the benefit of the public as a whole, rather than to generate a legal entitlement for specifically identified legal persons, be they private or public. Generally speaking, the Attorney General is the party who may seek an injunction to restrain a breach, and sometimes to compel performance of a duty or other requirement.[198] This is because the Attorney General has the duty of protecting public rights, and which they can do on their own motion, or at the relation of a private individual. Exceptionally, a private individual may have a sufficient interest to seek an injunction to enforce a legal rule of general application,[199] usually against a public official, and the question of when and why an individual should be allowed to do this raises difficult questions of standing in public law which are beyond the scope of this textbook. The aim for now is to point out that when an injunction is sought by the Attorney General in the public interest, this has implications for how the range of discretionary considerations, set out above, are applied, and as is discussed by Lord Wilberforce in the excerpt from *Associated Minerals Consolidated Ltd v Wyong Shire Council.*[200]

Associated Minerals Consolidated Ltd v Wyong Shire Council

Privy Council, [1975] A.C. 538 at 559–560

19–163 LORD WILBERFORCE: . . . The law on this subject, which was correctly applied by the judge contains two propositions. First, even in cases where relief is being sought by the Attorney-General in the public interest (and the respondent council, acting under section 587 of the Local Government Act 1919, is placed in a similar position), the granting of an injunction is discretionary.[201]

19–164 Secondly, however, it is necessary to take into account that the plaintiff is acting on behalf of the public and in the public interest. It is necessary therefore to base the granting or denial of equitable relief on broader grounds than would normally apply as between private citizens. As was said in *Attorney-General*

---

195 [2022] EWHC 1215 at [23].

196 See paras 3–143ff.

197 *Malone v Laskey* [1907] 2 K.B. 141; *Hunter v Canary Wharf* [1997] A.C. 655.

198 *Attorney General v Logan* [1891] 2 Q.B. 100; *Attorney General v Cockermouth Local Board* (1874) L.R. 18 Eq. 172 at 176; *Attorney General v PYA Quarries Ltd* [1957] 2 Q.B. 169.

199 *Lyon v Fishmongers' Co* (1876) 1 App. Cas. 662; *Vanderpant v Mayfair Hotel Co Ltd* [1930] 1 Ch. 138; *Boyce v Paddington BC* [1903] 1 Ch. 109 at 114 (reversed: [1903] 2 Ch. 556; restored: [1906] A.C. 1).

200 *Associated Minerals Consolidated Ltd v Wyong Shire Council* [1975] A.C. 538.

201 *Attorney General v Johnson* (1819) 2 Wils. Ch. 87; *Attorney General v Sheffield 560Gas Consumers Co* (1853) 3 De G.M. & G. 304; *Attorney-General and County Council of Down v Newry No. 1 Rural District Council* [1933] N.I. 50.

and County Council of Down v. Newry No. 1 Rural District Council,[202] the courts are somewhat slower to deny the Attorney-General, as the custodian of the public rights, relief on this ground (sc. delay) than in the case of an individual. The injury to a public interest by denial of relief, its extent and degree of irremediability, must be weighed against any loss which the defendant may have sustained by the plaintiff standing by while the defendant incurs expense or, if such is the case, misleading the defendant into supposing that its activities were or would be permitted. . . .

An injunction can be awarded against a group or representative of a group. An injunction, like other equitable remedies, usually operates in personam between the parties to the proceedings. However, an injunction can also be granted *contra mundum*, and operate against persons not party to the proceedings or even named in the orders. An example includes an injunction against all the legal persons in the world, for example, preventing the publication of certain facts[203] such as where this is necessary and proportionate to the protection of rights under the Human Rights Act 1998.[204] **19–165**

An injunction cannot be made against the Crown, and no finding of contempt of court can be made against the Crown.[205] However, a government department or a minister of the Crown can be subject to injunctive relief and contempt of court, even when acting in their official capacity, for the reasons outlined by Lord Templeman in the following excerpt from *M v Home Office*.[206] **19–166**

M v Home Office

House of Lords, [1994] 1 A.C. 377 at 395

LORD TEMPLEMAN: My Lords, Parliament makes the law, the executive carry the law into effect and the judiciary enforce the law. The expression "the Crown" has two meanings; namely the monarch and the executive. In the 17th century Parliament established its supremacy over the Crown as monarch, over the executive and over the judiciary. Parliamentary supremacy over the Crown as monarch stems from the fact that the monarch must accept the advice of a Prime Minister who is supported by a majority of Parliament. Parliamentary supremacy over the Crown as executive stems from the fact that Parliament maintains in office the Prime Minister who appoints the ministers in charge of the executive. Parliamentary supremacy over the judiciary is only exercisable by statute. The judiciary enforce the law against individuals, against institutions and against the executive. The judges cannot enforce the law against the Crown as monarch because the Crown as monarch can do no wrong but judges enforce the law against the Crown as executive and against the individuals who from time to time represent the Crown. A litigant complaining of a breach of the law by the executive can sue the Crown as executive bringing his action against the minister who is responsible for the department of state involved, in the present case the Secretary of State for Home Affairs. To enforce the law the courts have power to grant remedies including injunctions against a minister in his official capacity. If the minister has personally broken the law, the litigant can sue the minister, in this case Mr. Kenneth Baker, in his personal capacity. For the purpose of enforcing the law against all persons and institutions, including ministers in their official capacity and in their personal capacity, the courts are armed with coercive powers exercisable in proceedings for contempt of court. **19–167**

---

202 [1933] N.I. 50 at 71.

203 As in *Venables v News Group Newspapers Ltd* [2001] Fam. 430; [2001] 2 W.L.R. 1038.

204 *OPQ v BJM* [2011] EWHC 1059 (QB); [2011] E.M.L.R. 23 at [16]–[18] (Eady J).

205 *Crown Proceedings Act* 1947 s.21; *M v Home Office* [1994] 1 A.C. 377 at 395–396C, 424D–E, 425E–426B, 427.

206 See also *M v Home Office* [1994] 1 A.C. 377 at 412–23 (Lord Woolf, with whom Lord Keith, Lord Templeman, Lord Griffiths and Lord Browne-Wilkinson agreed); Sir William Wade Q.C. "Injunctive Relief against the Crown and Ministers" (1991) 107 L.Q.R. 4, 4–5.

4. Declarations

A. Jurisdiction and Scope—When Can a Declaration be Made?

19–168 Historically, declarations were developed and made by the Court of Chancery, and primarily as orders that were ancillary to the primary orders for relief, such as an injunction. A "naked"[207] declaration, one made without any other order for relief, was not possible until after legislative reforms broadened the jurisdiction to award declarations so that the Court of Chancery,[208] and, after the Judicature Acts,[209] the High Court, could grant a declaration independent of any other order for relief, in relation to equitable, common law or statutory entitlements and obligations.[210] The jurisdiction to grant declarations has been described in wide terms, including as being "almost unlimited; I might say only limited by its own discretion".[211]

19–169 Today this general statutory power to grant declarations is conferred by the Civil Procedure Rules Part 40.20:

> The court may make binding declarations whether or not any other remedy is claimed.

19–170 This wide-ranging statutory jurisdiction subsumes the equitable one. Nonetheless and given the equitable origins of declarations, it is useful to give a brief outline of the operation and availability of declarations. As we will see, the declaration is another example of how an equitable remedy contributes to the normative force of law, specifically, by making clear to the parties, and the public generally, the (non-)existence and content of a particular legal right or other entitlement(s) and/or obligation(s).

19–171 To further understand the nature of a declaration, it is useful to distinguish it from other types of judgments that can be given by a court.[212] A declaration is distinguishable from orders enforceable by execution, such as orders to pay damages. A declaration is not enforced by execution against a defendant's assets, for example. A declaration is distinguishable from orders that are constitutive or investitive in the sense of creating a new right in the successful party, such as orders for specific performance, or other forms of specific relief such as to transfer or deal with title to specific property in specified ways. A declaration declares or affirms the (non-) existence of a legal entitlement or obligation and does not of itself create any such entitlement. A declaration can also be distinguished from interlocutory or procedural orders, such as interim injunctions,[213] or Mareva orders, which for a set period of time, require one party to take some (in)action, usually to maintain the status quo in the period prior to a final determination, and does not finally determine the rights and other legal entitlements between the parties. As discussed already, a declaration finally determines the parties' legal entitlements the subject of the declaration.

---

207 *Clough v Ratcliffe* (1847) 1 De G. & Sm. 164 at 178 (Knight-Bruce VJ).

208 Chancery Act 1850 13 & 14 Vict. c.35; Chancery Procedure Act 1852 15 & 16 Vict. c.86.

209 Supreme Court of Judicature Act 1873 36 & 37 Vict. 66; Supreme Court of Judicature Act 1875 38 & 39 Vict. c.77.

210 O XXV, r.5 of the rules of the Supreme Court 1883. As to the history of the power to grant naked declarations see further *Guaranty Trust Co of New York v Hannay* [1915] K.B. 536 at 567–70 (Bankes LJ).

211 *Hanson v Radcliffe Urban DC* (1922) 2 Ch. 490 at 507. See also *Barnard v National Dock Labour Board* (1953) 2 Q.B. 18 at 41; *Ibeneweka v Egbuna* (1964) 1 W.L.R. 219 at 225.

212 See further P. Young, C. Croft and M. Smith, *On Equity* (Thomson Reuters, 2008), para.16.750.

213 See paras 19–120 and 19–152ff.

The utility or benefit of declarations has been acknowledged in cases and commentaries.[214] In the decision of *Bass v Permanent Trustee Co Ltd (Homefund Case)*,[215] Kirby J expressed the view that the statutory conferral of a wide jurisdiction to make a declaration was "one of the most important and beneficial advances in the administration of justice during [the twentieth] century". **19–172**

Utility is sometimes equated with the breadth of the scope of declarations. Declarations have been made in relation to a person's title to land;[216] the existence of a contract;[217] or particular contractual terms;[218] one party's breach of a contract;[219] the consequences of breach of contract;[220] one party's termination of a contract;[221] whether there has been a valid assignment of a contractual right or other chose in action;[222] and a person's membership of a club,[223] church[224] or trade union.[225] **19–173**

In addition to declarations as to the legal relations between legal persons are declarations as to the existence of legal relations between a legal person and the Crown,[226] such as to the validity of orders made by municipal authorities under legislation,[227] that a tribunal has no jurisdiction to determine a certain issue;[228] a declaration that the Chief Constable of North Wales had unlawfully induced the plaintiff's resignation as a police officer such that the plaintiff was entitled to the same rights and remedies as if he had been unlawfully dismissed, excluding reinstatement;[229] or, that Parliament has not been prorogued as the Order in Council purporting to prorogue Parliament was ineffective, having been made on the basis of the unlawful advice given by the Prime Minister.[230] Declarations are also useful because they may be available when no other remedy is, and can sometimes provide more cost and/or time efficient solution to a legal controversy. **19–174**

The utility or benefit of a declaration, like other equitable rules and remedies, can be explained in relation to the contribution it makes to the normative force of law. A declaration, literally, ensures the accessibility of the legal rules in question, by finally declaring the consequence(s) of application of those rules in creating, or not, a given legal relationship(s) between the parties. This will be of particular significance where the legal dispute arises due to the parties' disagreement as to the existence or application of one or more legal rules, as opposed to a party's reluctance to follow and abide by the law. When law operates as a guide for the parties' actions this obviates the need for orders that can be enforced via execution or contempt of court. A declaration is of particular use where the parties are willing to abide by a declaration and what they need is a determination of the existence and application of those rules so that they may adopt them as reasons for action. While not always expressed in **19–175**

---

214 See generally Hon. Justice R French, "Declarations: Homer Simpson's Remedy – Is There Anything They Cannot Do?" in K. Dharmananda and A. Papamatheos (eds), *Perspectives on Declaratory Relief* (Federation Press, 2009), p.28. The authors of the 4th edition of *Meagher Gummow and Lehane's Equity Doctrines and Remedies* (LexisNexis, 2002) express "no doubt" as to the utility and scope of the remedy: at para.19–075.

215 *Bass v Permanent Trustee Co Ltd (Homefund Case)* (1999) 198 C.L.R. 334 at [89].

216 *Bridges v Mees* [1957] Ch. 475.

217 *Jager v Tolme & Runge* [1916] 1 K.B. 939.

218 *West v Gwynne* [1911] 2 Ch. 1.

219 *Union of India v Compania Naviera Aeolus SA* [1962] 1 Q.B. 1.

220 *Rajbenbach v Mamon* [1955] 1 Q.B. 283.

221 *Schering Ltd v Stockholms Enkilda Bank* [1946] A.C. 219.

222 *Societe Martime et Commercial v Venus Shipping Co* (1904) 9 Com. Cas. 289.

223 *Young v Ladies Imperial Club Ltd* [1902] 2 K.B. 523.

224 *Stuart v Haughley Parochial Church* [1936] Ch. 32.

225 *Bonsor v Musicians' Union* [1956] A.C. 104.

226 Senior Court Act 1981 s.31(2) confers a power on the High Court to award a declaration or injunction; see paras 1–139 and 19–128.

227 *Brownsea Haven Properties Ltd v Poole Corp* [1958] Ch. 574.

228 *Govt of Gibraltar v Kenney* [1956] 2 Q.B. 410.

229 *Chief Constable of the North Wales Police v Evans* [1982] 1 W.L.R. 1155 at 1176.

230 *R. (on the application of Miller) v Prime Minister* [2019] UKSC 41 at [70] (the Court).

these rule of law terms, we can observe this is a theme underlying the principles guiding the exercise of the discretion to award a declaration, and which are briefly summarised next.

B. Discretion—Should a Declaration be Made?

19–176 A useful summary of the principles guiding the exercise of discretion to the award of declarations is contained in the excerpt from *Fujifilm Kyowa Kirin Biologics Co Ltd v AbbVie Biotechnology Ltd.*

Fujifilm Kyowa Kirin Biologics Co Ltd v AbbVie Biotechnology Ltd

Court of Appeal, [2017] EWCA Civ 1 at [58]–[61]

19–177 THE COURT: The modern approach to the grant of declarations can be taken from two cases: *Messier-Dowty Ltd v Sabena SA*[231] and *Financial Services Authority v Rourke*.[232] In *Messier-Dowty* the court held that the grant or refusal of declaratory relief in relation to commercial disputes should not be constrained by artificial limits wrongly related to jurisdiction. Instead, it should be kept in proper bounds by the exercise of the court's discretion. Negative declarations were an unusual remedy which can result in procedural complications resulting in unfairness to the defendant. But subject to appropriate circumspection, there should be no reluctance to grant negative declarations "when it is useful to do so".

19–178 In *Financial Services Authority v Rourke* Neuberger J (as he then was) proposed the following, with which we respectfully agree:

> It seems to me that, when considering whether to grant a declaration or not, the court should take into account justice to the claimant, justice to the defendant, whether the declaration would serve a useful purpose whether there are any other special reasons why or why not the court should grant the declaration.

19–179 Older cases suggested that there had to be "a claim of right" by the defendant before a declaration could be made against him. The modern rule is not interpreted so rigidly, although if no claim of right has been made (or is likely to be made) this may show why a declaration would not be useful. In *Nokia Corp v Interdigital Technology Corp*,[233] this court upheld the granting of declarations that patents did not cover that which was "essential" to do to comply with a particular telecommunications standard. If the patents were essential in this sense it would mean that Nokia's phones were infringing. One of the points taken by the patentees was that there had been no, or no sufficient claim of right so as to give rise to the declaratory jurisdiction. Jacob LJ (with whom Ward and Carnwath LJJ agreed) rejected this argument: Nokia had a manifest and real commercial interest in a decision of the kind sought: they were "technically infringing" if they were wrong.[234]

19–180 Accordingly, so far as the CPR are concerned, the power to make declarations appears to be unfettered. As between the parties in the section, it seems to me that the court can grant a declaration as to their rights, or as to the existence of facts, or as to a principle of law, where those rights, facts, or principles have been established to the court's satisfaction. The court should not, however, grant any declarations merely because the rights, facts or principles have been established and one party asks for a declaration. The court has to consider whether, in all the circumstances, it is appropriate to make such an order.

19–181 In *Patten v Burke*,[235] Millett LJ stated that, in effect, it was the court's duty "to do the fullest justice to the plaintiff to which he is entitled", and he went on to hold that there was no rule of law which prevented a declaration of fraudulent conduct.

19–182 In *Messier-Dowty v Sabena*[236] the issue was whether a negative injunction should be granted. Lord Woolf said this:

---

[231] [2001] 1 All E.R. 275 at [41]–[42] (Lord Woolf MR).
[232] [2002] CP Rep 14 (Neuberger J, as he then was).
[233] [2006] EWCA Civ 1618.
[234] *Nokia Corp v Interdigital Technology Corp* at [19].
[235] [1994] 1 W.L.R. 541.
[236] [2001] 1 All E.R. 275.

> The deployment of negative declarations should be scrutinised and their use rejected where it would serve no useful purpose. However, where a negative declaration would help to ensure that the aims of justice are achieved, the courts should not be reluctant to grant such declarations. They can and do assist in achieving justice. . . .
>
> So in my judgment the development of the use of declaratory relief in relation to commercial disputes should not be constrained by artificial limits wrongly related to jurisdiction. It should instead be kept within proper bounds by the exercise of the courts' discretion. **19–183**
>
> It seems to me that, when considering whether to grant a declaration or not, the court should take into account justice to the claimant, justice to the defendant, whether the declaration would serve a useful purpose and whether there are any other special reasons why or why not the court should grant the declaration. **19–184**

As is evident from the excerpt above, the court has a wide discretion whether to award a declaration, and the guiding principle is that the declaration will serve a useful purpose having regard to the dispute between the parties and justice to each. As Lord Radcliffe said in *Ibeneweka v Egbuna*:[237] **19–185**

> After all, it is doubtful if there is more of principle involved than the undoubted truth that the power to grant a declaration should be exercised with a proper sense of responsibility and a full realisation that judicial pronouncements ought not to be issued unless there are circumstances that call for their making. Beyond that there is no legal restriction on the award of a declaration.

Courts have articulated a range of specific concerns that give shape to this overriding principle and which have been summarised in different ways in cases and commentaries. One example is Lord Goff's outline in *Re F (Mental Patient: Sterilisation)*:[238] **19–186**

> There are of course some limits which have been established to the exercise of the discretion under the Rules. In *Russian Commercial and Industrial Bank v British Bank for Foreign Trade Ltd*,[239] Lord Dunedin said with reference to the ancient Scottish action of declarator: **19–187**
>
>> The rules that have been elucidated by a long course of decisions in the Scottish courts may be summarized thus: The question must be a real and not a theoretical question; the person raising it must have a real interest to raise it; he must be able to secure a proper contradictor, that is to say, someone presently existing who has a true interest to oppose the declaration sought.
>
> Subsequently, in *Vine v National Dock Labour Board*,[240] Viscount Kilmuir L.C. found this Scottish approach to be helpful; and indeed there is authority in the English cases that a declaration will not be granted where the question under consideration is not a real question, nor where the person seeking the declaration has no real interest in it, nor where the declaration is sought without proper argument, e.g. in default of defence or on admissions or by consent. **19–188**

In summary, a court will take into account the following considerations: **19–189**

(a) the declaration must be directed to the resolution of a legal controversy and concern the existence of some legal entitlement or other legal relationship, and which will be of consequence for the parties;[241]

---

237 *Ibeneweka v Egbuna* (1964) 1 W.L.R. at 225.

238 *Re F (Mental Patient: Sterilisation)* [1990] 2 A.C. 1 at 82.

239 [1921] 2 A.C. 438 at 448.

240 [1957] A.C. 488 and 500.

241 The power to make declarations is confined to making declarations on matters that are justiciable in the courts; *Malone v Laskey* [1907] 2 K.B. 141 at 354, see too at 353.

(b) a declaration cannot be sought in relation to circumstances that do not exist or might not happen, nor relate to the hypothetical question of law;[242]

(c) the party seeking declaratory relief must have a real or sufficient interest in the issue;[243] and

(d) the claim for a declaration must identify a party who is a proper contradictor.[244]

19–190 In relation to (a)–(b), the requirement for the declaration to concern a controversy between the parties and which concerns a legal right or other entitlement: "Such matters include but are not confined to legal (including equitable rights) and extend to the existence, scope and content of other legal entitlements, such as privileges, powers, liabilities and immunities, for example."[245] This is in distinction to "merely moral, social or political rights or liabilities".[246] Examples of matters outside the justiciability of a court and which are not amenable to declarations, include the effect of a financial agreement made between the governments of the United Kingdom and Italy;[247] in relation to the engagement between an Army or Navy Officer and the Crown;[248] or, as to the "decency" of a burial.[249]

19–191 A distinction is sometimes drawn between a "positive" declaration as to the existence of a legal entitlement, such as a right or power, as opposed to the more exceptional situation where a "negative" declaration is made as to the non-existence of a right or power, i.e. a freedom from a duty or liability.[250] Depending on how various legal entitlements are characterised,[251] the non-existence of a right or power can still be positive in so far as it means that another party has a privilege or immunity, and which makes the positive–negative distinction artificial, at least in some instances. As we can see from the excerpt below, the question of whether a negative declaration will be made will be determined by reference to the same discretionary considerations as set out above.

Messier-Dowty Ltd v Sabena SA

Court of Appeal, [2000] 1 W.L.R. 2040 at [39]–[42]

19–192 WOOLF L.J.: . . . there are the numerous cases where without objection negative declarations have been granted. There are also the judgments of Lord Denning M.R. in this court and Lord Wilberforce in the House of Lords in *Camilla Cotton Oil Co. v. Granadex S.A.*:[252]

> It has been said that a declaration as to non-liability ought very rarely to be made.[253] And *In re Clay*[254] is sometimes cited for the proposition that it cannot be made. But it is nothing of the kind. In modern times, I think that a declaration as to non-liability can be made whenever it will serve a useful purpose. I would not limit it in any way.[255]

---

242 *Aberdeen Development Co v Mackiel, Ramsay & Taylor* [1977] S.L.T. 177 at 181; *Lever Bros & Unilever Ltd v Manchester Ship Canal Co* (1945) 78 Lloyd's Rep. at 509–10 (Vaisey J).

243 *Russian Commercial and Industrial Bank v British Bank for Foreign Trade Ltd* [1921] 2 A.C. 438 at 448 (Lord Dunedin).

244 *Russian Commercial and Industrial Bank v British Bank for Foreign Trade Ltd* at 448 (Lord Dunedin).

245 *Russian Commercial and Industrial Bank v British Bank for Foreign Trade Ltd* at 448 (Lord Dunedin). *Nixon v Attorney-General* [1930] 1 Ch. 566 at 574 (Clauson J): a declaration could only be made "of legal right, between a subject and the Crown".

246 *Malone v Laskey* at 353.

247 *Republic of Italy v Hambros Bank Ltd* [1950] Ch. 314 at 329 (Vaisey J).

248 *Hanson v Radcliffe Urban DC* [1922] 2 Ch. 490, affirmed on appeal: (1933) 49 T.L.R. 300.

249 *Ganoun v Joshi* [2020] EWHC 2743 (Ch).

250 See, e.g. *Re Clay* [1919] 1 Ch. 66; *Midland Bank Plc v Laker Airways Ltd* [1986] Q.B. 689 at 700–701 (Lawton L.J., with whom Dillon and Neill L.JJ. agreed).

251 See paras 2–002 to 2–009.

252 [1975] 1 Lloyd's Rep. 470; [1976] 2 Lloyd's Rep. 10.

253 *Dyson v Attorney-General* [1911] 1 K.B. 410; *Guaranty Trust Co. of New York v Hannay & Co.* [1915] 2 K.B. 536.

254 [1919] 1 Ch. 66.

255 [1975] 1 Lloyd's Rep. 470 at 474–75 (Lord Denning M.R).

In the House of Lords Lord Wilberforce stated the position in his own words but the effect was very much the same. He said:[256]

> The declaration claimed is of a negative character and as Lord Sterndale himself had said: '. . . a declaration that a person is not liable in an existing or possible action is one that will hardly ever be made.'[257] 'Hardly ever' is not the same as 'never' but the words warn us that we must apply some careful scrutiny. So I inquire whether to grant such a negative declaration would be useful. The liability which the English court is asked to negative is any possible liability of the respondents on the basis of agency . . .

Lord Wilberforce and Lord Denning M.R. differed in the circumstances of that case as to whether the declaration would serve a useful purpose. However, if it would, that it would then be appropriate to grant a declaration was agreed. The approach is pragmatic. It is not a matter of jurisdiction. It is a matter of discretion. The deployment of negative declarations should be scrutinised and their use rejected where it would serve no useful purpose. However, where a negative declaration would help to ensure that the aims of justice are achieved the courts should not be reluctant to grant such declarations. They can and do assist in achieving justice. For example, where a patient is not in a position to consent to medical treatment declarations have an important role to play. Without the use of negative declarations, recent extensions in the use of declaratory relief, including the beneficial intervention of the courts in cases concerning mentally incapacitated people would not have been possible. As Sir Thomas Bingham M.R. said in *In re S. (Hospital Patient: Court's Jurisdiction)*:[258] **19–193**

> Any statutory rule, unless framed in terms so wide as to give the court an almost unlimited discretion, would be bound to impose an element of inflexibility which would in my view be wholly undesirable.

He considered that the different situation he was there considering was "pre-eminently an area in which the common law should respond to social needs." So in my judgment the development of the use of declaratory relief in relation to commercial disputes should not be constrained by artificial limits wrongly related to jurisdiction. It should instead be kept within proper bounds by the exercise of the courts' discretion. **19–194**

While negative declarations can perform a positive role, they are an unusual remedy in so far as they reverse the more usual roles of the parties. The natural defendant becomes the claimant and vice versa. This can result in procedural complications and possible injustice to an unwilling "defendant." This in itself justifies caution in extending the circumstances where negative declarations are granted, but, subject to the exercise of appropriate circumspection, there should be no reluctance to their being granted when it is useful to do so. **19–195**

In relation to (c)–(d), the party seeking the declaration must have a proper or tangible interest in obtaining a declaration, and this issue is sometimes referred to as "standing" or "locus standi"[259] and the declaration must identify a proper contradictor. These parties will sometimes be relatively easily identified when the legal entitlement exists as a bilateral or otherwise specifically delineated legal relationship between the legal person who has the power to seek relief in relation to a legal entitlement, including a declaration, as well as the person who is the proper contradictor. Contract law, generally, confers a power of enforcement on the parties to the contract; tort, generally, confers this power on the legal person whose right was infringed by another party's breach of duty owed to them; as we have discussed in Chapter 12, trusts law identifies the (co- or replacement) trustee and/or beneficiary as the person who has the power to enforce the duty of administration. Across these and other areas of law are rules providing for when other parties, exceptionally, will have a power to **19–196**

---

[256] [1976] 2 Lloyd's Rep. 10 at 14.
[257] *Guaranty Trust Co. of New York v Hannay & Co.* [1915] 2 K.B. 536 at 564 (Pickford L.J).
[258] *In re S. (Hospital Patient: Court's Jurisdiction)* [1996] Fam 1 at 19 (Thomas Bingham M.R.).
[259] T. Liau, "Privity: Rights, Standing, and the Road Not Taken" (2021) 41 O.J.L.S. 803.

enforce a right to accrues to another.[260] However, in some situations it can be difficult to identify who is the person who has a sufficient interest to seek,[261] or who is the proper contradictor to, a declaration as to how law applies to a government or other public body.[262] These are difficult questions beyond the scope of this text.[263]

19–197 In one way or another, all these considerations express the one broader concern: to only award a declaration where it would assist in the administration of justice by enhancing its guidance function. It should not be surprising, then, that they are interrelated. A declaration must relate to law and how it applies to real circumstances in existence between the parties, and thus not relate to hypothetical or non-existent circumstances. This is because a declaration will not enhance the normative force of law if the parties are not sufficiently interested in law as a reason for action. Equally, the identification of who those parties are, and their interests, will be difficult where a party is seeking a declaration that does not relate to the existence of a *legal* entitlement of one sort or another. The High Court of Australia in *Bateman's Bay Local Aboriginal Land Council v Aboriginal Community Benefit Fund Pty Ltd* has explained this interconnection as that "the requirement of a legal right determines the availability of injunctive relief and there is no separate requirement which determines the entitlement to approach a court of equity".[264] In other words, if the applicant's claim for a declaration does not relate to a *legal* entitlement, then she will not be able to rely on any legal rule to identify her as the particular legal person that has a real interest in the matter, such as being the person to whom a legal entitlement accrues, or exceptionally is given standing to sue on behalf of another. Equally, there will be no identified legal rule that identifies a proper contradictor.

Questions

1. In *Fells v Read*, Lord Loughborough LC granted specific performance of a defendant's obligation to deliver up possession of a silver tobacco-box enclosed in two large silver cases, all which were adorned with several engravings, and gave the following reasons as to inadequacy of damages at law:[265]

> I am sorry this cause has come into this Court: but the regret I feel is no other than that, one always feels, that litigation and expense should have been occasioned by the peevishness and obstinacy of the parties. The value I cannot measure. The Pusey horn, the Patera of the Duke of Somerset, were things of that sort of value, that a jury might not give two-pence beyond the weight. It was not to be cast to the estimation of people, who have not those feelings. In all cases, where the object of the suit is not liable to a compensation by damages, it would be strange, if the law of this country did not afford any remedy. It would be great injustice, if an individual cannot have his property without being liable to the estimate of people, who have not his feelings upon it.

Discuss.

---

260 Such as when a beneficiary can assert rights accruing to the trustee as titleholder via *Vandepitte* procedure, see para.12–109, or when a shareholder can bring derivative proceedings in the company's name: *Foss v Harbottle* (1843) 2 Hare 661 (Ch); Companies Act 2006 Pt 11.

261 Senior Courts Act 1981 s.31(3).

262 See generally *Worthington v Jeffries* (1875) L.R. 10 C.P. 379 at 382 (Brett J); *Boyce v Paddington Borough Council* [1903] 1 Ch. 109 at 114.

263 See generally W. Wade and C. Forsyth, *Administrative Law*, 11th edn (Oxford University Press, 2014), Pt VII.

264 *Bateman's Bay Local Aboriginal Land Council v Aboriginal Community Benefit Fund Pty Ltd* [1998] HCA 49; (1998) 194 C.L.R. 247 at [43] (Gaudron, Gummow and Kirby JJ).

265 *Fells v Read* (1796) 3 Ves. Jun. 371; 30 E.R. 899 at 899–900.

2. Should specific performance be confined to a secondary remedy available only after damages have been assessed as "inadequate"?
3. When are damages an "*inadequate* remedy"? Do you agree with the decisions on this point in *Sky Petroleum v VIP* and *Argyll Stores*?
4. Is the decision in *Argyll Stores* best explained as being based upon the objection of "constant supervision" or "severe hardship"?
5. Given that the general objective of tort damages is to restore the claimant to her *ex ante* position, why should it matter whether tortious harm is prevented by way of injunction or compensated by way of damages?
6. Cosmo and Jaffa enter into an agreement according to which Cosmo promises to build Jaffa "a house to the highest architectural standards of design and craftsmanship."
   (a) Can Jaffa seek specific performance of this obligation?
   (b) Would it make a difference if Cosmo had instead promised to build Jaffa "a house according to the specifications set out in the architectural drawings annexed to this Contract"?
   (c) Cosmo has also promised Jaffa that Cosmo will not allow the building works to cause any damage or nuisance to adjoining properties. Cosmo has commenced building works and has not taken the necessary precautions to prevent dust and other run-off from the building works flowing onto Jaffa's neighbour, Luna's, property. Can Luna or Jaffa obtain an injunction and against whom?
7. When and why might a court award a declaration? What purpose can "naked declarations" serve?

20

RESCISSION

1. What is Rescission?

Sometimes, for one reason or another, the exercise of a legal power, such as entry into a contract, transfer of title to property, or declaration of an express trust, will be reversed or avoided. This process of reversal is referred to as rescission. An example is when one party to a contract can rescind the contract, placing the parties in the position as if the contract had never been created. Rescission can also occur in other situations, which differ from the contractual example either because rescission is sought in relation to some other type of transaction or exercise of power, such as the settlement of a trust or the transfer of some property, or because the person seeking rescission of a contract, transfer of property or other exercise of power is not the person who exercised the relevant power. **20–001**

As will be discussed further in this chapter, rescission can occur via different legal mechanisms, taking effect either (1) by the actions of a party (C) in electing to rescind, or (2) by orders of a court made on the application of a party (C) seeking rescission. Either way, rescission "rewrites history",[1] avoiding the legal consequences of a prior exercise of power so that the parties are put into the position they would have occupied if there had been no exercise of power. Rescission of a contract, for example, means that the parties no longer have, and never had contractual relations. Rescission of a transfer of title to property means that the recipient no longer has, and never had, title. **20–002**

Sometimes, rescission of one exercise of power may mean that subsequent exercises of power can also be rescinded. An example is when one party has transferred title to property under a rescinded contract for sale. When the contract itself effects the transfer of title, rescission of the contract will also rescind the transfer of title, revesting it in the seller.[2] In other situations, rescission of a contract for sale of property will mean that rescission of the separate transfer of title is possible. Rescission might also mean that other forms of relief may be available to restore the parties to their previous position, such as restitution of the value of money paid or services rendered under a rescinded contract.[3] **20–003**

There are various reasons why an exercise of power might be rescinded, across common law and equity, some of which are outlined below and have already been discussed in earlier chapters. **20–004**

The law governing rescission is complex and controversial. In *Revenue and Customs Commissioners v IGE USA Investments Ltd*, Henderson LJ described rescission as "a notoriously difficult subject, on which the authorities are in such a state of disarray that, in my judgment, only the Supreme Court can **20–005**

---

1 N. McBride, "Rescission" in S. Worthington and G. Virgo (eds), *Commercial Remedies* (Hart Publishing, 2018), Ch.7, p.151.

2 *Load v Green* (1846) 15 M. & W. 216 at 221; 153 E.R. 828 at 830; *Car & Universal Finance Co Ltd v Caldwell* [1965] 1 Q.B. 525 at 532.

3 About which, see further C. Mitchell, P. Mitchell and S. Watterson, *Goff & Jones The Law of Unjust Enrichment*, 9th edn (Sweet & Maxwell, 2016).

reconcile them."[4] Dame Sarah Worthington has written "almost every aspect of the law of rescission is now contentious".[5] Some of these problems stem from the fact that the term "rescission" has not been used exclusively to describe the legal phenomena outlined above and has also been used to describe the termination of a contract following discharge by breach. The distinction between these is explained in the following excerpt.[6]

Johnson v Agnew

House of Lords, [1980] A.C. 367 at 392–393

20-006 LORD WILBERFORCE (with whom LORD SALMON, LORD FRASER, LORD KEITH and LORD SCARMAN agreed): . . . In this situation it is possible to state at least some uncontroversial propositions of law. . . . First, in a contract for the sale of land, after time has been made, or has become, of the essence of the contract, if the purchaser fails to complete, the vendor can either treat the purchaser as having repudiated the contract, accept the repudiation, and proceed to claim damages for breach of the contract, both parties being discharged from further performance of the contract; or he may seek from the court an order for specific performance with damages for any loss arising from delay in performance. (Similar remedies are of course available of purchasers against vendors.) This is simply the ordinary law of contract applied to contracts capable of specific performance.

20-007 Secondly, the vendor may proceed by action for the above remedies (viz., specific performance or damages) in the alternative. At the trial he will however have to elect which remedy to pursue.

20-008 Thirdly, if the vendor treats the purchaser as having repudiated the contract and accepts the repudiation, he cannot thereafter seek specific performance. This follows from the fact that, the purchaser having repudiated the contract and his repudiation having been accepted, both parties are discharged from further performance.

20-009 At this point it is important to dissipate a fertile source of confusion and to make clear that although the vendor is sometimes referred to in the above situation as "rescinding" the contract, this so-called "rescission" is quite different from rescission ab initio, such as may arise for example in cases of mistake, fraud or lack of consent. In those cases, the contract is treated in law as never having come into existence. (Cases of a contractual right to rescind may fall under this principle but are not relevant to the present discussion.) In the case of an accepted repudiatory breach the contract has come into existence but has been put an end to or discharged. Whatever contrary indications may be disinterred from old authorities, it is now quite clear, under the general law of contract, that acceptance of a repudiatory breach does not bring about "rescission ab initio".

20-010 When an exercise of power is susceptible to rescission "ab initio", it is sometimes referred to as "voidable".[7] Voidability describes the fact that the powerholder's actions *are effective* to produce the legal consequences she manifested an intention to produce, such as the creation of a contract or the transfer of title to property, but for one reason or another, these consequences can be retrospectively reversed or avoided from the beginning, i.e. "ab initio". However, unless and until rescission occurs, the exercise of power is effective, and the parties' legal relations are determined as such. Rescission is needed precisely when the impugned exercise of power was effective but for one reason or another should be reversed. In contrast is the situation where the powerholder's action is "void ab initio". Voidness describes the situation where the powerholder's actions were *never effective* to produce the legal consequences she manifested an intention to produce.

20-011 Rescission occurs in two different ways, which are discussed next.

---

4 [2021] EWCA Civ 534 at [91], referring to D. O'Sullivan, S. Elliott and R. Zakrzewski, *The Law of Rescission*, 2nd edn (Oxford University Press, 2014), paras 11.107–11.108, and J. O'Sullivan, "Rescission as a Self-Help Remedy: A Critical Analysis" (2000) 59 C.L.J. 509.

5 S. Worthington, "Proprietary Consequences of Rescission" [2002] 10 R.L.R. 28, 28.

6 See also *Photo Production Ltd v Securicor Transport Ltd* [1980] A.C. 827 at 844.

7 *Erlanger v New Sombrero Phosphate Co* (1878) 3 App. Cas. 1218 at 1278–79; *Pitt v Holt* [2013] 2 A.C. 108 at [93]–[94].

A. Rescission as a Legal Power Exercisable by the Rescinding Party

Rescission can occur as the result of C's action in disaffirming, i.e. rescinding, an exercise of power, such as the creation of a contract or transfer of title. As discussed below, there are different grounds that give rise to an election to affirm or rescind a prior exercise of power. Election is made via C's conduct in manifesting her choice either way.[8] **20–012**

Once made, C's election to affirm or rescind is final.[9] A prior exercise of power, once affirmed, cannot be rescinded, and once rescinded, cannot be affirmed.[10] **20–013**

An election to rescind is retrospective, avoiding the exercise of power ab initio. A contract that did exist no longer does, and any title to property transferred by way of the contract revests immediately upon rescission of the contract. This is explained in the following excerpt from *Abram Steamship Co Ltd (In Liquidation) v Westville Shipping Co Ltd (In Liquidation)*:[11] **20–014**

> Where one party to a contract expresses by word or act in an unequivocal manner that by reason of fraud or essential error of a material kind inducing him to enter into the contract he has resolved to rescind it, and refuses to be bound by it, the expression of his election, if justified by the facts, terminates the contract, puts the parties in status quo ante and restores things, as between them, to the position in which they stood before the contract was entered into. It may be that the facts impose upon the party desiring to rescind the duty of making restitutio in integrum. If so, he must discharge that duty before the rescission is, in effect, accomplished; but if the other party to the contract questions the right of the first to rescind, thus obliging the latter to bring an action at law to enforce the right he has secured for himself by his election, and the latter gets a verdict, it is an entire mistake to suppose that it is this verdict which by itself terminates the contract and restores the antecedent status. The verdict is merely the judicial determination of the fact that the expression by the plaintiff of his election to rescind was justified, was effective, and put an end to the contract. Questions as to whether the judgment relates back to a date earlier than its own are really irrelevant.

C's election to rescind has been understood as a legal power under what is sometimes called the "power-model" of rescission.[12] Conceived in this way, rescission is a form of self-help remedy, as it allows C to affect a reversal of an impugned exercise of power by her own action. Court relief is not needed to avoid the exercise of power, and is needed only when remedies are necessary to enforce the parties' legal relation(s) prior to the impugned exercise of power to which they are restored by C's exercise of her power to rescind. **20–015**

B. Rescission as a Court Order

Sometimes rescission only takes effect according to the terms of a court order. C does not have a legal power to rescind and rather has an equity to rescind which is an entitlement to apply for the court for order(s) for rescission, and any consequential relief.[13] **20–016**

An example is when a court makes orders setting aside the creation of a contract, and awards consequential relief to restore the parties to the position they were in prior to execution, such as ordering **20–017**

---

8 *Car & Universal Finance Co Ltd v Caldwell* [1965] 1 Q.B. 525 at 550–51, finding that exceptionally no communication need be made where to require would be "to allow a fraudulent contracting party to prevent the innocent party exercising his undoubted right".

9 *Peyman v Lanjani* [1985] Ch. 457.

10 *Clough v London and North Western Railway Co* (1871) L.R. 7 Ex. 26 at 34.

11 [1923] A.C. 773 at 781.

12 S. Worthington, "Proprietary Consequences of Rescission" [2002] 10 R.L.R. 28, 28; B. Häcker, *Consequences of Impaired Consent Transfers: A Structural Comparison of English and German Law* (Hart Publishing, 2013).

13 J. McGhee (ed) et al, *Snell's Equity*, 34th edn (Sweet & Maxwell, 2021), para.15–012.

the payment of money or transfer of property.[14] Further examples include when a court sets aside an exercise of a power to amend the terms of an express trust on the basis that the powerholder failed to take only relevant considerations into account,[15] or was mistaken,[16] for example. Depending on the circumstances, further orders for consequential relief may be made, for example, requiring a recipient to repay funds paid under terms that have since been rescinded.

2. Common Law vs Equitable Rescission

20–018 This chapter focuses on the equitable remedy of rescission, although it is necessary to explain some of the differences between common law and equitable rescission as this is a distinction that underpins some of the reasoning in the cases on the equitable remedy of rescission.

20–019 Common law rescission is a legal power vested in C, and is a consequence of C's act in disaffirming the exercise of power. Common law rescission may also mean C has a claim in unjust enrichment for a personal order for restitution of the value of money or another benefit transferred under the contract, or a declaration that particular property is held on trust as a remedy for unjust enrichment.[17] However, where the revesting of legal title required further acts (such as the registration of an ordinary share, or registration of title to land) then a party needed to seek a remedy of the court to order the defendant to take the action(s) necessary to affect rescission and put the parties in the position prior to the impugned exercise of power. Historically, courts of common law did not have the power to grant such relief, but equity did, and so rescission at common law was affected by orders made by the Court of Chancery, the effect of which was to produce a substantially similar outcome as would have followed from 's exercise of her power to rescind as recognised by common law rules.

20–020 The differences between common law rescission and equitable rescission are historically sourced in the different jurisdictional origins of the rules, but the substantive distinction that matters nowadays is between rescission at common law, which is a self-help remedy or legal power conferred on a person to set aside some prior exercise of power, and equitable rescission, which largely takes effect via a court's power to grant certain forms of relief as necessary to put the parties in the same position as if the power had not been exercised.[18]

20–021 Having said that, the extent to which *equitable* rescission takes effect as the result of a court order is a controversial issue that has been examined in detail by the authors of *The Law of Rescission*.[19] They argue that equitable rescission for fraud takes effect via C's actions, i.e. is a legal power, albeit that

---

14 As in *O'Sullivan v Management Agency and Music Ltd* [1985] 1 Q.B. 428, see 5th edn, paras 20–040ff.

15 *Smithson v Hamilton* [2007] EWHC 2900 at [79]–[80]; *Pitt v Holt* [2013] 2 A.C. 108 at [60], [70], [93], [99]–[101].

16 A possibility contemplated in *AMP (UK) Ltd v Barker* [2001] Pens. L.R. 77 at [80]–[82] and *Gallaher Ltd v Gallaher Pensions Ltd* [2005] EWHC 42 (Ch); [2005] Pens. L.R. 103 at [153], though Sir Andrew Park declined to follow these dicta in *Smithson v Hamilton* at [114], [119], [121]. See also N. Stallworthy, "Rationalising Mistake in the Law of Trusts: *Smithson v Hamilton*" (2009) 23 T.L.I. 51; *Pitt v Holt* [2013] 2 A.C. 108 at [114]; C. Mitchell, "Rescission of Voluntary Settlements and Dispositions of Trust Property on the Ground of Mistake" (2017) 2 *Private Client Business* 41.

17 See, e.g. *Vale SA v Steinmetz* [2021] EWCA Civ 1087 at [16]: "if a contract is voidable for fraud, the innocent party's right to rescind the contract gives rise to an equity . . . such that upon rescission a payment made by the rescinding party is impressed with a constructive trust (a 'rescission trust')".

18 Excepting the instances where equitable rescission also operates as a legal power conferred on C, similar to common law rescission, see paras 20–018 to 20–022. See further *Nadinic v Drinkwater* (2017) 94 N.S.W.L.R. 518 at [28]–[30].

19 O'Sullivan, Elliott and Zakrzewski, *The Law of Rescission*, paras 11–56–11–108. A sample includes: *Reese River Silver Mining Co Ltd v Smith* (1869) L.R. 4 H.L. 64; *Abram Steamship*; *Horsler v Zorro* [1975] 1 Ch. 302 at 310; *Brotherton v Aseguradora Colseguros SA* [2003] EWCA Civ 705; [2003] 2 All E.R. (Comm) 298 at [27], [45]–[48].

outside of the fraud cases, there are other cases where equitable rescission occurs via the award of court orders.[20]

In so far as equitable rescission takes effect by court orders, the substantive differences between common law rescission as a legal power and equitable rescission in the form of a court order helps to explain why common law and equitable rescission differ in relation to factors such as the grounds for rescission, the requirement of *restitutio in integrum* and totality, matters to which we now turn. **20–022**

3. Grounds for rescission

A. Grounds for Rescission at Law

Contract law recognises a power to rescind a contract on certain grounds including for fraud,[21] duress,[22] some defined instances in relation to contracts of insurance,[23] and some instances of bribery.[24] **20–023**

The rules determining when rescission of a contract at law is possible are examined elsewhere.[25] What is important for present purposes is that, in one way or another, these rules give C the choice to disaffirm their prior choice when that choice was flawed or vitiated in some way, such as if there is fraud or duress. **20–024**

B. Grounds for Rescission in Equity

Equity is prepared to rescind an exercise of power on the same grounds as common law, and more, including: **20–025**

(a) a fraudulent misrepresentation;[26]

(b) duress;[27]

(c) an innocent misrepresentation,[28] although the court now has a discretion to award damages in lieu of rescission if it would be equitable to do so;[29]

---

20 See, e.g. *Erlanger v The New Sombrero Phosphate Co* (1878) 3 App. Cas. 1218 at 1278; *Spence v Crawford* [1939] 3 All E.R. 271; *Cooper v Phibbs* (1867) L.R. 2 H.L. 149; *O'Sullivan v Management Agency and Music Ltd* at [45]; *Goldsworthy v Bricknell* [1987] Ch. 378 at 409–10; *Wilson v Hurstanger Ltd* [2007] EWCA Civ 299; [2007] 1 W.L.R. 2351 at [47]; *Hurstanger Ltd v Wilson* [2007] EWCA Civ 299; [2008] Bus L.R. 216 at [48]–[51]. See also *UBS AG (London Branch) v Kommunale Wasserwarker Leipzig GmbH* [2017] EWCA Civ 1567; [2017] 2 Lloyd's Rep. 621 at [157]: "[a] claim (at least of this kind) for rescission is a claim for an equitable remedy." See also A. Reilly, "Is the 'Mere Equity' to Rescind a Legal Power?" (2019) 39 O.J.L.S. 779, arguing that rescission in equity is best understood as a court ordered remedy rather than a legal power.

21 *Load v Green* (1846) 15 M. & W. 216 at 221; *Car & Universal Finance Co Ltd v Caldwell* [1965] 1 Q.B. 525 at 532; P. Turner, "Rescission of the Doctrine of Rescission for Fraud" [2016] C.L.J. 206, 207.

22 *Dimskal Shipping Co SA v International Transport Workers Federation (The Evia Luck) (No.2)* [1992] 2 A.C. 152; *Universe Tankships Inc of Monrovia v International Transport Workers Federation* [1983] 1 A.C. 366 at 383 (Lord Diplock), 400 (Lord Scarman).

23 *Manifest Shipping Co Ltd v Uni-Polaris Insurance Co Ltd (The Star Sea)* [2001] UKHL 1; [2003] 1 A.C. 469.

24 *Conway v Prince Eze* [2018] EWHC 29 at [148] explaining "Bribery is treated as a special form of fraud at common law". See also *Ross River Ltd v Cambridge City Football Club Ltd* [2007] EWHC 2115 at [203] (Briggs J).

25 See further Mitchell et al, *Goff & Jones The Law of Unjust Enrichment*; H. Beale, *Chitty on Contracts*, 34th edn (Sweet & Maxwell, 2021), Pt 3.

26 As in *Banwaitt v Dewji* [2014] EWCA Civ 67.

27 *Barton v Armstrong* [1976] A.C. 106 at 118.

28 *Redgrave v Hurd* (1881) 20 Ch. D. 1 at 12–13; *Alati v Kruger* (1955) 94 C.L.R. 216: *Shalson v Russo* [2003] EWHC 1637 (Ch); [2005] Ch. 281; *Nadinic v Drinkwater* [2017] NSWCA 114 at [23]–[26] (Leeming JA).

29 Misrepresentation Act 1967 s.2(2).

(d) unconscionable dealing or special disadvantage;[30]

(e) breach of a duty of disclosure in connection with an insurance contract;[31]

(f) in relation to a voluntary exercise of power, such as a transfer of property or settlement on trust, C's unilateral mistake where it is of sufficient gravity to make it unconscionable to deny relief;[32]

(g) breach of a fiduciary duty;[33]

(h) bribery or secret commission;[34]

(i) inadequacy of deliberation;[35] and

(j) a director's or agent's fraud on a power, or improper purpose.[36]

20-026 Another way of understanding the different grounds for equitable rescission is according to the type of power that is the object of rescission. Equitable rescission is available in relation to different powers: entry to a contract, or a party's exercise of power to vary the terms of contract; a transfer of title to property; declaration of trust; the issue of company shares; an agent or mortgagee's exercise of a power of sale, and a variation to the terms of a trust, just to name a few. A distinction is sometimes drawn between rescission of contracts and gifts, although there are other powers the exercise of which can be rescinded and which do not fit so easily into this twofold classification, such as powers by directors, agents, trustees and mortgages, for example.

20-027 The type of power being rescinded matters as it can determine the grounds for rescission. A common mistake[37] or unilateral mistake is not a ground for rescission of a contract. However, the making of a gift,[38] as well as other exercises of power, such as a trustee's exercise of power to vary the terms of a trust,[39] may be rescinded where there was a causative unilateral mistake of "sufficient gravity" to make it unconscionable to refuse relief.[40]

20-028 The type of power in relation to which rescission is sought also matters when it comes to assessing whether rescission is barred in the specific circumstances, and the orders for consequential relief, as discussed next.

---

30 *Cresswell v Potter* [1978] 1 W.L.R. 255; *Crédit Lyonnais Nederland NV v Burch* [1997] 1 All E.R. 144; *Portman Building Society v Dusangh* [2001] W.T.L.R 117.

31 *Pan Atlantic Insurance Co Ltd v Pine Top Insurance Co Ltd* [1995] 1 A.C. 501; *Manifest Shipping Co Ltd v Uni-Polaris Insurance Co Ltd* [2001] UKHL 1; [2003] 1 A.C. 469; but note the Consumer Insurance (Disclosure and Representations) Act 2012; Insurance Act 2015.

32 *Pitt v Holt* [2013] 2 A.C. 108 at [121]–[122].

33 *Maguire v Makaronis* (1997) 188 C.L.R. 449; *Johnson v EBS Pensioner Trustees Ltd* [2002] EWCA Civ 164; [2002] Lloyd's Rep. P.N. 309; *Wilson v Hurstanger Ltd* [2007] EWCA Civ 299 at [33]–[47]. See further Chapter 2, Pt 3.

34 *Wood v Commercial First Business Ltd* [2021] EWCA Civ 471; [2022] Ch. 123 at [46]–[50], [92]–[102]; *Prince Eze v Conway* [2019] EWCA Civ 88 at [149]–[157]; *Ross River Ltd v Waveley Commercial Ltd* [2013] EWCA Civ 910; [2014] 1 B.C.L.C. 545 at [203].

35 *Pitt v Holt* [2013] 2 A.C. 108 at [60], [70], [93], [99]–[100]; *Smithson v Hamilton* at [79]–[80].

36 As in *Howard Smith Ltd v Ampol Petroleum Ltd* [1974] A.C. 821; *Latec Investments Ltd v Hotel Terrigal Pty Ltd* (1965) 113 C.L.R. 265; *Criterion Properties Plc v Stratford UK Properties LLC* [2004] UKHL 28 at [4] (Lord Nicholls). Note that in other circumstances, fraud on a power results in a different claim for equitable proprietary relief and the reasons for this are discussed in Chapter 11, paras 11-066ff.

37 *Great Peace Shipping Ltd v Tsavliris Salvage (International) Ltd* [2002] EWCA Civ 1407; [2003] Q.B. 679.

38 *Pitt v Holt* [2013] 2 A.C. 108 at [99]–[123]; Mitchell, "Rescission of Voluntary Settlements and Dispositions of Trust Property on the Ground of Mistake". See further: Mitchell et al, *Goff & Jones The Law of Unjust Enrichment*, paras 9-134–9-142.

39 As considered in *AMP (UK) Ltd v Barker* [2001] Pens. L.R. 77 at [80]–[82]; *Gallaher Ltd v Gallaher Pensions Ltd* [2005] EWHC 42 at [153], although compare *Smithson v Hamilton* at [114], [119], [121] where Sir Andrew Park declined to follow these dicta.

40 *Pitt v Holt* [2013] 2 A.C. 108 at [121]–[122].

A final point of distinction between the different grounds for rescission is that sometimes the party with an equity for rescission, C, is the powerholder wanting to undo her previous exercise of power, whereas in other situations, C is not the powerholder and is wanting to undo another person's exercise of power, such as when a beneficiary seeks rescission of a trustee's exercise of power, or a company seeks rescission of a director's or other corporate agent's exercise of power to act for the company. **20–029**

4. Bars to Equitable Rescission

Once C has made out one or more grounds for orders for rescission, a court must determine whether rescission should be awarded in the circumstances. This will depend on whether rescission is barred by one or more of the factors which are outlined next. If a bar applies, this does not necessarily mean that C will be awarded no relief at all, since a money remedy might be available—either common law damages or an equitable money remedy of the kind discussed in Chapter 18. **20–030**

A. An Election to Affirm

C's equity for rescission will be lost if she affirms the contract or other consequences of the impugned exercise of power. Affirmation occurs through C's unequivocal conduct showing her choice to treat the contract as being on foot, such as when C sues for damages for breach of a contract or accepts a benefit thereunder.[41] C must have known of the facts giving rise to her equity for rescission,[42] although the precise requirement of knowledge is controversial and is an issue discussed in relation to the general equitable discretionary bar of acquiescence in Chapter 22. **20–031**

B. Restitutio in Integrum

Equitable rescission is barred if *restitutio in integrum* is not possible. C must be "able to put those against whom [rescission] is asked in the same situation in which they stood when the contract was entered into".[43] For example, if C seeks equitable rescission of a loan agreement with D under which C is the borrower, C will be required to repay the principal sum and interest, usually at market rates, to D. The authors of *Snell's Equity* explain that the:[44] **20–032**

> . . . concern of the bar is to protect the defendant from unjustified prejudice; that circumstances have changed such that it is no longer possible fully to restore the claimant will not preclude rescission.[45] In making their election, it is for the claimant to decide whether they are content to get back less than they gave. The bar is usually applied in cases where the party seeking rescission is unable to make satisfactory counter-restitution of what they have received, but it may also apply where the circumstances have changed in some other way such that the defendant would be unjustifiably prejudiced were the contract now set aside, particularly where the defendant has not been guilty of conscious wrongdoing.[46]

Restitutio in integrum is relevant to rescission at common law and equity. However, the requirement operates as a pre-condition to rescission at law and is assessed to a stricter degree. Common law **20–033**

---

41 *Insurance Corp of the Channel Islands Ltd v The Royal Hotel Ltd* [1998] Lloyd's Rep. I.R. 151 at 161, 174.
42 *Peyman v Lanjani* [1985] Ch. 457.
43 *The Western Bank of Scotland v Addie* (1867) L.R. 1 Sc. App. 145 at 164–65.
44 S. Elliott, "Rescission" in J. McGhee et al (eds), *Snell's Equity*, para.15–014.
45 *Spence v Crawford* [1939] 3 All E.R. 271 at 279.
46 *Erlanger v The New Sombrero Phosphate* (1878) 3 App. Cas. 1218 at 1278–79; *Spence v Crawford* at 281–82.

rescission is only possible if *precise restitutio in integrum* can be made. In *Blackburn v Smith*,[47] rescission was barred because the plaintiff had taken possession of the land pursuant to the impugned contract and it was not possible to return the use of the land for the period of possession. Rescission was refused. Likewise, in *Clarke v Dickson*, where it was found that a plaintiff could not rescind a purchase of company shares despite having been made in reliance on fraudulent misrepresentations about the company by the defendant directors. In principle, the defendants' fraudulent misrepresentation was a ground for rescission of the purchase of shares but did not arise on the facts as counter restitution was not possible, for the reasons exampled in the excerpt below.

Clarke v Dickson

Queens Bench, (1858) Ellis, Blackburn and Ellis 148, 120 E.R. 463 at 466

20-034 ERLE J.: I am of opinion that the nonsuit was right. The plaintiff claims to repudiate the contract under which shares were allotted to him; to give up the shares, and recover back the price. There are several grounds of objection, all falling under the same principle: the plaintiff cannot avoid the contract under which he took the shares, because he cannot restore them in the same state as when he took them. In 1853 the plaintiff accepted the shares; and from that time he was, in point of law, in possession of the mine, and worked it by his agent the purser. After three years working of the mine, and trying to make a profit, he cannot restore the shares as they were before this was done. But, further, he not only had the chance of profit, but dividends were declared, and received by him . . . rendering it impossible for him to rescind.

20-035 CROMPTON J: When once it is settled that a contract induced by fraud is not void, but voidable at the option of the party defrauded, it seems to me to follow that, when that party exercises his option to rescind the contract, he must be in a state to rescind; that is, he must be in such a situation as to be able to put the parties into their original state before the contract . . . what did he buy? Shares in a partnership with others. He cannot return those; he has become bound to those others. Still stronger, he has changed their nature: what he now has and offers to restore are shares in a quasi corporation now in process of being wound up. That is quite enough to decide this case. The plaintiff must rescind in toto or not at all; he cannot both keep the shares and recover the whole price. . . . The true doctrine is, that a party can never repudiate a contract after, by his own act, it has become out of his power to restore the parties to their original condition.

20-036 In contrast, *restitutio in integrum* operates as a discretionary bar to equitable rescission and as such it allows a court to take a more flexible approach. *Resitutio in integrum* can be affected via consequential orders for relief requiring one or both parties to take further action as necessary to restore them to the position prior to the exercise of power.

Erlanger v New Sombrero Phosphate Company

House of Lords, (1878) 3 App. Cas. 1218 at 1278

20-037 LORD BLACKBURN: . . . It is, I think, clear on principles of general justice, that as a condition to a rescission there must be a restitutio in integrum. The parties must be put in status quo. . . . It is a doctrine which has often been acted upon both at law and in equity. But there is a considerable difference in the mode in which it is applied in courts of law and equity, owing, as I think, to the difference of the machinery which the courts have at command. I speak of these courts as they were at the time this suit commenced, without inquiring whether the Judicature Acts make any, or if any, what difference. It would be obviously unjust that a person who has been in possession of property under the contract which he seeks to repudiate should be allowed to throw that back on the other party's hands without accounting for any benefit he may have derived from the use of the property, or if the property, though not destroyed, has been in the interval deteriorated, without making compensation for that deterioration. But as a court of law has no machinery at its command for taking an account of such matters, the defrauded party, if he sought his remedy at law, must in such cases keep the property and sue in an action for deceit, in which the jury, if properly directed, can

[47] (1848) 2 Ex. 783. See also *Hunt v Silk* (1804) 5 East 449.

do complete justice by giving as damages a full indemnity for all that the party has lost . . . But a court of equity could not give damages, and, unless it can rescind the contract, can give no relief. And, on the other hand, it can take account of profits, and make allowance for deterioration. And I think the practice has always been for a court of equity to give this relief whenever, by the exercise of its powers, it can do what is practically just, though it cannot restore the parties precisely to the state they were in before the contract.

Alati v Kruger

High Court of Australia (1955) 94 C.L.R. 216 at 223–224

DIXON C.J., WEBB, KITTO and TAYLOR J.J.: . . .[E]quity has always regarded as valid the disaffirmance of a contract induced by fraud even though precise restitutio in integrum is not possible, if the situation is such that, by the exercise of its powers, including the power to take accounts of profits and to direct inquiries as to allowances proper to be made for deterioration, it can do what is practically just between the parties, and by so doing restore them substantially to the status quo . . . The difference between the legal and the equitable rules on the subject simply was that equity, having means which the common law lacked to ascertain and provide for the adjustments necessary to be made between the parties in cases where a simple handing back of property or repayment of money would not put them in as good a position as before they entered into their transaction, was able to see the possibility of restitutio in integrum, and therefore to concede the right of a defrauded party to rescind, in a much wider variety of cases than those which the common law could recognize as admitting of rescission. Of course, a rescission which the common law courts would not accept as valid cannot of its own force revest the legal title to property which had passed, but if a court of equity would treat it as effectual the equitable title to such property revests upon the rescission. 20–038

An illustrative example of equity's more flexible approach to restitutio in integrum is *O'Sullivan v Management Agency and Music Ltd*. The claimant, "O'Sullivan", had been an aspiring music composer and performer and relied on the defendant, "Mills", an established and experienced music producer and performer, for his advice and assistance. O'Sullivan entered into a series of agreements with Mills and Mills's companies (also defendants) appointing Mills as O'Sullivan's managing agent and giving Mills ownership of the copyright in music composed by O'Sullivan. O'Sullivan went on to be hugely successful artist and Mills made large profits as a result of O'Sullivan's success and Mills's expertise and effort in managing, producing and publishing O'Sullivan's music. O'Sullivan later sought rescission of the management agreements between him and Mills and Mills's companies. At trial, the trial judge declared the agreements to be void and ordered the reconveyance of the copyrights and delivery up of the master tapes because the contracts, and Mills and his companies appealed. 20–039

O'Sullivan v Management Agency and Music Ltd

Court of Appeal, [1985] 1 Q.B. 428 at 448–449, 458–460

The trial judge's findings which were not challenged on appeal and repeated by DUNN L.J.: [Mills and his companies] took it upon themselves to look after [O'Sullivan] . . . They knew they were dealing with a young an inexperienced man who was content to put himself entirely in their hands and relied entirely on them to give [O'Sullivan] a fair deal. They were responsible for the contractual arrangements and they were just as much in a confidential relationship to O'Sullivan as was Mills himself. In those circumstances the judge was right to hold that the companies as well as Mills were fiduciaries. 20–040

On the footing therefore that the companies were in a fiduciary relationship with O'Sullivan, and consequently all the agreements were obtained by undue influence, the principal question on the appeal was what is the appropriate remedy against Mills and the companies? 20–041

[After reviewing the authorities as to the requirement of restitutio in integrum, DUNN L.J. went on to state:] This analysis of the cases shows that the principles of restitutio in integrum is not applied with its full rigour in equity in relation to transactions entered into by persons in breach of a fiduciary relationship, and that such transactions may be set aside even though it is impossible to place the parties precisely in 20–042

> the position in which they were before, provided that the court can achieve practical justice between the parties by obliging the wrongdoer to give up his profits and advantages, while at the same time compensating him for any work that he has actually performed pursuant to the transaction. . . .
>
> 20–043 In my judgment the judge was right to set the agreements aside and to order an account of the profits and payment of the sums found due on the taking of the account. But in taking the account the defendants are entitled to an allowance . . . for reasonable remuneration including a profit element for all work done in promoting and exploiting O'Sullivan and his compositions, whether such work was done pursuant to a contractual obligation or gratuitously. What constitutes "reasonable remuneration" will depend on evidence on the taking of the account . . .
>
> 20–044 The assignments of the copyrights were made pursuant to the agreements. It was said on behalf of the defendants that each separate assignment was made for good consideration, and consequently that the copyrights cannot be re-assigned. [Counsel for O'Sullivan] submitted that the individual assignments were made for no consideration and that the only consideration was contained in the agreements themselves. However that may be I accept that the validity of the individual assignments depends on the validity of the agreements themselves, and if the agreements are set aside I see no reason why the copyrights should not be re-assigned to O'Sullivan.
>
> 20–045 The same consideration applies to the delivery up of the master tapes. . . . and if the original copyrights are to be re-assigned, and O'Sullivan's consent to the use of the copyrights in the tapes is withdrawn by the setting aside of the agreements, then the defendants have no right to use the tapes and they must be returned to O'Sullivan.

20–046 The Court of Appeal found the management agreements, while initially valid, were voidable and ordered rescission of the agreements, and delivery up of the copyright and master tapes. The remedy of equitable rescission was possible even though the management agreements were complete, and the parties could not be restored to their initial positions given Mills (and his companies') receipt of substantial profits from third parties. In the circumstances, rescission depended on the court making orders as was practically just between the parties and required Mills to account for the profits reduced to give an allowance for Mills's skill and labour in promoting O'Sullivan and contributing to his success.[48]

20–047 Along similar lines, a more flexible approach to restitio in integrum, and equitable rescission generally, was taken by the Court of Appeal in *UBS AG (London Branch) v Kommunale Wasserwarker Leipzig GmbH*, again where rescission was sought on the ground of breach of fiduciary duty and bribery, and in which Lord Briggs and Hamblen L.J. explained:[49]

> A claim (at least of this kind) for rescission is a claim for an equitable remedy. Where a prima facie right to rescission is demonstrated, the court nonetheless retains what is traditionally called a discretion to refuse it where it would be unfair or disproportionate, or to afford some other more suitable remedy, such as equitable compensation or an account. Further, the claim is subject to the usual equitable defences including laches and lack of clean hands.

C. Intervention of Third-Party Rights

20–048 Equitable rescission is barred when it would defeat the legal or equitable rights acquired by a third party without notice of the facts giving rise to rescission, and if they have provided consideration.[50]

---

48 See also Fox L.J. at 465–69. In relation to an account of profits, see Chapter 18, Pt 4.

49 *UBS AG (London Branch) v Kommunale Wasserwarker Leipzig GmbH* [2017] EWCA Civ 1567; [2017] 2 Lloyd's Rep. 621 at [157], see also [223]–[229].

50 *Car & Universal Finance Co Ltd v Caldwell* [1965] 1 Q.B. 525; *Tennent v The City of Glasgow Bank and Liquidators* (1879) 4 App. Cas. 615 at 620–21; *Hunter BNZ Finance Ltd v CG Maloney Pty Ltd* (1988) 18 N.S.W.L.R. 420 at 433–34, 438; *Latec Investments Ltd v Hotel Terrigal Pty Ltd* (1965) 113 C.L.R. 265.

When rescission is sought in relation to a transaction involving multiple exercises of power, such as a contract for the transfer of title to property, third party rights may bar rescission of the transfer of title such as when the purchaser, D, has since sold title to a third party. Rescission may still, however be possible in relation to the contract between C and D and following which C may be entitled to trace into and claim the proceeds of sale if identifiable in D's hands[51] or seek orders for account.[52] **20-049**

D. No Partial Rescission

Partial rescission is not possible in relation to contracts. In *TSB Bank Plc v Camfield*,[53] the Court of Appeal held that if a claimant can set aside a transaction for misrepresentation (or undue influence) then it must be set aside entirely rather than partially. So, a claimant who has agreed to mortgage her house for £30,000 can escape liability for the entire sum, although she would have agreed to liability for £15,000 irrespective of the misrepresentation (or undue influence). Note, however, that she must return any benefit she has personally received under the contract before it can be set aside, such as repayment of the loan sum and interest.[54] **20-050**

Albeit a contract can be rescinded in part if it is severable.[55] **20-051**

A different approach is taken when equitable rescission is sought of a voluntary disposition on the ground of mistake. In *Kennedy v Kennedy*,[56] Etherton C ordered partial rescission of a trustee's exercise of a power of appointment on the ground of mistake, stating: **20-052**

> There is authority that there cannot be partial rescission of a contract; it must be set aside as a whole and not only as to part . . . That limitation makes sense in a contractual context and as preventing the court in effect imposing a different contract to the one the parties actually made. I see no reason, however, why that limitation should apply to a self-contained and severable part of a non-contractual voluntary transaction.

E. Other Equitable Discretionary Bars

As an equitable remedy, rescission is subject to the general equitable discretionary factors and bars to relief, such as laches and unclean hands and which are discussed in Chapter 22. In the context of rescission, the equitable discretionary factor of acquiescence will usually amount to an election to affirm, precluding rescission in the first place. **20-053**

---

51 See, e.g. *El Ajou v Dollar Land Holdings Plc* [1993] 3 All E.R. 717 at 735; *Twinsectra Ltd v Yardley* [1999] Lloyd's Rep. Bank 438 CA at 461–62; *Shalson v Russo* [2003] EWHC 1637 (Ch); [2005] Ch. 281 at 320–322.

52 *New Sombrero Phosphate Co v Erlanger* (1877) 5 Ch. D. 73 at 125; *Lagunas Nitrate Co v Lagunas Syndicate* [1899] 2 Ch. 392 at 434.

53 [1995] 1 W.L.R. 430.

54 *TSB Bank Plc v Camfield* at 432 at 437; *Dunbar Bank Plc v Nadeem* [1998] 3 All E.R. 876 at 883. Although a different approach is taken in Australia, *Vadasz v Pioneer Concrete SA* (1995) 184 C.L.R. 102 and New Zealand in *Scales Trading Co Ltd v Far Eastern Shipping Co Public Ltd* [1999] 3 N.Z.L.R. 26.

55 *Myddleton v Lord Kenyon* (1794) 2 Ves. 391 at 408; *Rawlins v Wickham* (1858) 3 De. G. & J. 304 at 321–322; *The Sheffield Nickel and SilverPlating Co Ltd v Unwin* (1877) 2 Q.B.D. 214 CA at 223.

56 *Kennedy v Kennedy* [2014] EWHC 4129 at [46]. See also *Mackay v Wesley* [2020] EWHC 3400 (Ch); [2020] W.T.L.R. 1359 at [26]–[44] where rescission was possible of a "self-contained and severable part of a [deed of trustee appointment and retirement]". See further Mitchell, "Rescission of Voluntary Settlements and Dispositions of Trust Property on the Ground of Mistake", [2017] P.C.B. 41, 47–48.

5. Proprietary Consequences of Rescission

20-054 An important effect of rescission is its proprietary consequences, and, again, a distinction is often drawn between the proprietary consequences of rescission at common law and equity. Sometimes, the effect of C's exercise of her power to rescind a contract at law is to avoid the contract and re-vest title to specific property transferred by the contract,[57] unless it has reached the hands of a bona fide purchaser.[58] C can then rely on that title to recapture the goods still in D's possession, or to bring other claims against D, such as conversion or trespass.

20-055 Common law rescission does not always have this effect for all contracts involving the transfer of title to property, and, whether rescission automatically revests title depends on the property transfer rules for the subject property. If these rules provide for the transfer of title upon the execution of the contract, then according to those rules, if the contract is rescinded, then so is the transfer of title.[59] When the rules for property transfer are different, so too are the proprietary implications of rescission at law. Rescission of a contract for the sale of shares, or title to land, for example, will not revest title as the transfer of title depends, according to the applicable rules, on registration. This means that when C rescinds, she will also need to seek consequential relief to give effect to the exercise of power to rescind, i.e. by obtaining a court order that the owner of the shares or land must take the necessary action to have the other party re-registered as the owner. These equitable orders are often referred to as "rescission" but are really giving legal effect to the consequences of C's exercise of her power to rescind at law.

20-056 For rescission in response to grounds recognised by equitable rules (whether in the form of a legal power conferred on a legal person or a court ordered remedy), consequential court orders may be required to restore the parties to the position they were in prior to the impugned exercise of power, such as orders requiring the return of title to specific property, or monetary orders. Unless such property has come into the hands of a bona fide purchaser, the court will declare it to have been held on trust and provide in its order for the reconveyance of legal title and delivery up of possession, as appropriate.[60]

20-057 The availability of such relief has led courts and commentators to find that equitable rescission of a contract under which legal title to property was transferred leads to the retrospective imposition of a trust on the property with the consequence that C can trace into substitute assets held by the defendant and assert an equitable proprietary claim to them.[61] Likewise, in relation to rescission of a voluntary transaction rescinded for mistake.[62]

20-058 In the following passage of Potter LJ's judgment in *Twinsectra Ltd v Yardley*, it is left unclear whether the trust imposed on the property is a constructive or resulting trust, a question that has not been

---

57 *Load v Green* (1846) 15 M. & W. 216 at 221; 153 E.R. 828 at 830; *Clough v London and North Western Railway* (1871) L.R. 7 Ex. 26, 32; *Car & Universal Finance Co Ltd v Caldwell* [1965] 1 Q.B. 525 at 532.

58 *White v Garden* (1851) 10 C.B. 919.

59 B. Häcker, "Proprietary Restitution After Impaired Consent Transfers: A Generalised Power Model" (2009) 68 C.L.J. 324, 329–331, 335–337.

60 As in, e.g. *Transvaal Lands Co v New Belgium (Transvaal) Land & Development Co* [1914] 2 Ch. 488 at 505 (company shares); *Clark v Malpas* (1862) 4 De G.F. & J. 401 (unregistered land); *Norwich Peterborough Building Soc v Steed* [1993] Ch. 116 at 132–33.

61 *Small v Attwood* (1832) You. 407 at 533–538; *Banque Belge pour l'Etranger v Hambrouck* [1921] 1 K.B. 321 at 332; *Daly v Sydney Stock Exchange Ltd* (1986) 160 C.L.R. 371 at 387–90; *El Ajou v Dollar Land Holdings Plc* [1993] 3 All E.R. 717 at 735; *Shalson v Russo* [2003] EWHC 1637 (Ch); [2005] Ch. 281 at [120]–[127]. See too S. Worthington "The Proprietary Consequences of Rescission" [2002] 10 R.L.R. 28, 37–38.

62 *Bainbridge v Bainbridge* [2016] EWHC 898 at [30], applying *Shalson v Russo* at [122]. See further Mitchell, "Rescission of Voluntary Settlements and Dispositions of Trust Property on the Ground of Mistake", [2017] P.C.B. 41, 48–49.

resolved by more recent English authorities,[63] although the Australian courts have decided that this trust is a ("remedial"[64]) constructive trust.[65]

Twinsectra Ltd v Yardley

Court of Appeal, [1999] Lloyd's Rep. Bank. 438 at [99]

POTTER L.J. (with whom SIR IAIN GLIDEWELL and SIR DAVID HIRST agreed) . . .[The] distinction of importance here is that between non-consensual transfers and transfers pursuant to contracts which are voidable for misrepresentation. In the latter case, the transferor may elect whether to avoid or affirm the transaction and, until he elects to avoid it, there is no constructive (resulting) trust; in the former case, the constructive trust arises upon the moment of transfer. The result, so far as third parties are concerned, is that, before rescission, the owner has no proprietary interest in the original property; all he has is the "mere equity" of his right to set aside the voidable contract. That equity binds volunteers and those taking with notice of the equity, but not purchasers for value without notice.[66] Despite dicta of Lord Mustill in *Re Goldcorp Exchange Ltd*[67] (a case in which the purchase monies sought to be traced were unidentifiable), which, if generally applied beyond the context of the facts in that case, would suggest that equitable title does not (or in appropriate circumstances may not) revest on rescission, the general position seems to me that summarised in *Underhill and Hayton*.[68] It is there stated that equity imposes a constructive trust on property where a transferor's legal and equitable title to his property has passed to the transferee according to basic principles of property law but in circumstances (e.g. involving fraud and misrepresentation) where the transferor has an equitable right (i.e. mere equity) to recover the property by having the transfer set aside, and the court declares that from the outset the transferee has held the property to transferor's order, though nowadays it seems better to regard a restitutionary resulting trust as arising. **20–059**

Regardless of how the trust is characterised, it arises as a consequence of rescission and, unless and until rescission occurs, the recipient, D, has an unencumbered title to the property. Prior to rescission, C does not have an equitable interest under a trust and has rather been understood as having a "power in rem" or "proprietary power" to rescind, and which is a "mere equity" for rescission.[69] C's equity for rescission is fragile, and will be deferred in priority to a bona fide purchaser for value without notice of the legal *or equitable interest* in property.[70] After rescission occurs, however, things change and C has an equitable interest under a trust over the property as discussed in the excerpt from *Twinsectra* above, and means that C has an interest that will take priority over equitable interests arising after the point in time from when rescission takes effect. **20–060**

---

63 *Papamichael v National Westminster Bank (No.2)* [2003] EWHC 164 (Comm); [2003] 1 Lloyd's Rep. 341; *London Allied Holdings Ltd v Lee* [2007] EWHC 2061 at [276]; *National Crime Agency v Robb* [2014] EWHC 4384 (Ch); [2015] Lloyd's Rep. F.C. 161 at [43]–[44].

64 See para.17–005.

65 *Robins v Incentive Dynamics Pty Ltd (In Liquidation)* (2003) 175 Fed. L.R. 286 at [74]; *Grimaldi v Chameleon Mining NL (No.2)* (2012) 200 F.C.R. 296 at [277].

66 See generally S. Worthington, *Proprietary Interests in Commercial Transactions* (Clarendon Press, 1996), pp.163–165, 167.

67 [1995] 1 A.C. 74 at 102–103.

68 15th edn, (Butterworth & Co, 1995), p.372(f).

69 See: Worthington, "Proprietary Consequences of Rescission"; Häcker, "Proprietary Restitution After Impaired Consent Transfers". Exceptionally, it seems that some impaired consent transfers do not give rise to rescission, and rather create an equitable proprietary interest in property or funds transferred by the claimant in her favour: *Global Currency Exchange Network Ltd v Osage 1 Ltd* [2019] 1 W.L.R. 5865 at [41] (followed in *Van Zuylen v Whiston-Dew* [2021] EWHC 2219 at [238]–[239]): holding that where a contract is not merely induced by fraudulent misrepresentation and is itself the instrument of fraud, being no more than a vehicle for obtaining money by false pretences, then the payers under the fraudulent contract would still own the funds in equity without the need to rescind, likening the position to theft with the result that the funds would be immediately traceable by investors, referring to *Westdeutsche Landesbank Girozentrale v Islington LBC* [1996] A.C. 669 at 705, 715, see para.17–213.

70 *Phillips v Phillips* (1861) 4 De G.F. & J. 208; *Latec Investments Ltd v Hotel Terrigal Pty Ltd* (1965) 113 C.L.R. 265.

20-061 Much turns then on the timing of how and when equitable rescission occurs and this brings us back to the controversial question of whether equitable rescission is affected by a court order, or C's actions in manifesting her intention to rescind, and to which courts orders later give effect.[71] As a power exercisable by C, rescission occurs on C's actions, and after which C has "a sufficient proprietary title to enable him to trace, follow and recover what, by virtue of such revesting, can be regarded as having always been in equity his own property".[72] The earlier C exercises that power, the less likely it is that rescission will be barred because third parties have acquired rights in relation to the property in the meantime.

20-062 As a court order, the timing for when a trust consequent upon rescission arises depends on the exercise of the court's discretion. Courts will take account of intervening factors, including third party interests, in determining whether to award rescission and if so, from what date rescission will take effect, such as from the date or order, or backdated to some earlier time.[73] It is important to remember that C's actions in manifesting her choice to affirm or rescind may still have some impact in relation to the availability and form of rescission as a court order. C's actions may mean that a third party has knowledge of C's equity for rescission and may not then be able to avail herself of the protection afforded to innocent recipients of legal or equitable title, making rescission in C's favour more likely. To this extent, the difference between rescission as a power or court ordered remedy may have less significance for the proprietary consequences of rescission.

Questions

1. In *Photo Production Ltd v Securicor Transport Ltd,*[74] Lord Wilberforce stated:

> A vast number of expressions are used to describe situations where a breach has been committed by one party of such a character as to entitle the other party to refuse further performance: discharge, rescission, termination, the contract is at an end, or dead, or displaced; clauses cannot survive, or simply go. I have come to think that some of these difficulties can be avoided; in particular the use of "rescission," even if distinguished from rescission ab initio, as an equivalent for discharge, though justifiable in some contexts may lead to confusion in others. To plead for complete uniformity may be to cry for the moon.

Discuss.

2. Cosmo agrees to sell her run-down vintage bike to Jaffa for £100 as a result of Jaffa's undue influence over Cosmo. The contract is completed, Jaffa pays the purchase price and Cosmo delivers the bike to Jaffa. Three years later, Cosmo sends Jaffa a letter stating the agreement with Jaffa was for an undervalue and that Cosmo wants her bike back and offers to repay the purchase price paid by Jaffa. In the period prior to receiving Cosmo's letter, Jaffa undertakes extensive restoration work on the bike and has since sold the bike to Luna for £10,000. Luna has no notice of the circumstances pertaining to Cosmo's claim. Does Cosmo have an equity for

---

71 See paras 20-011 to 20-022.

72 *Shalson v Russo* [2003] EWHC 1637 (Ch); [2005] Ch. 281 at [136]. It can also affect the personal liability of third parties, as discussed by Rimer J. in *Shalson v Russo* at [106]–[119], whose comments were approved in *Nasrullah v Rashid* [2018] EWCA Civ 2685; [2020] Ch. 37 at [53]–[55]. And see too *ED & F Man Capital Markets Ltd v Come Harvest Holdings Ltd* [2022] EWHC 229 at [620]ff, as to which see para.14-029, n.46.

73 This can be of particular importance in the context of rescission of exercises of amendment powers in pension trusts, see further *Breadner v Granville-Grossman* [2001] Ch. 523 at [533]; *Smithson v Hamilton* [2007] EWHC 2900 at [79].

74 [1980] A.C. 827 at 844.

rescission against Jaffa or Luna? Would your answer change if Luna bought the bike from Jaffa after Jaffa received Cosmo's letter?

3. Burt is a trustee of a discretionary family trust, and Leigh is one of the beneficiaries. Burt borrows funds from Alyssa to invest as trustee with a view to making higher investment returns for the trust fund. Under the agreement, Burt grants Alyssa an equitable security interest over the shares that Burt holds on trust. Burt's actions were authorised by the trust terms and he was acting in good faith. Burt did not, however, give adequate consideration to the investment, failing to survey the market, and simply approached the first lender he could find. Does Burt or Leigh have an equity for rescission of the loan agreement against Alyssa?

21

RECTIFICATION

1. What is Rectification?

Across multiple areas of law, the existence and/or content of legal relations is determined by the meaning of one or more parties' actions in manifesting their intentions for what they want their legal relations to be, such as contract, express trusts, and dealings with property. Sometimes, the parties will manifest their intention via execution of a deed or signing a document that contains written provisions purporting to manifest the parties' intentions. The document provides evidence of the parties' intentions and usually will be determinative exclusively thereof, on the basis that the parties either expressly or impliedly manifested their intentions to be exclusively determined by the written document.[1] For example, the existence and content of a contractual relationship will be determined by the written provisions of the parties' document. There are also various statutory regimes conditioning the validity or enforceability of certain transactions to the extent they are evidenced by writing.[2] In addition, some documents, such as deeds, give rise to various forms of estoppels, as a result of which the parties' legal relationships are determined according to the state of affairs represented by the document.[3] The centrality of the written provisions of a document to determining the existence and content of legal relationships means that parties will usually ensure the written provisions correctly record their intention about their legal relationships, and indeed, a key role played by lawyers and other advisers is ensuring that their clients' intentions are accurately recorded. 21–001

However, mistakes can sometimes be made in the preparation and execution of written documents with the result that they do not accurately record the parties' intentions. It may be that words are added, omitted or wrongly written as a result of carelessness, or that particular words were "purposely used but it was mistakenly considered that they bore a different meaning from their correct meaning as a matter of true construction."[4] Left uncorrected, such errors mean that the parties' legal relationship will be determined by reference to a document that does not manifest their intention, thereby frustrating the goals of various legal doctrines, such as those governing the construction of documents and the implication of terms, whose central purpose is to give effect to the parties' intentions. Equity's solution is rectification, a doctrine in accordance with which the court can order that 21–002

[1] *Tartsinis v Navona Management Co* [2015] EWHC 57 at [84]–[86]; *FSHC Group Holdings Ltd v GLAS Trust Corp Ltd* [2019] EWCA Civ 1361; [2020] Ch. 365 at [144].

[2] See, e.g. Law of Property Act 1925 s.53(1)(c) and s.136, about which see further Chapter 6.

[3] See, e.g. *Prime Sight Ltd v Lavarello* [2013] UKPC 22; [2014] A.C. 436.

[4] *Re Butlin's ST* [1976] Ch. 251 at 260–61; *Day v Day* [2013] EWCA Civ 280; [2014] Ch. 114 at [21]–[22].

the written provisions of a document should be altered, with retrospective effect,[5] so that it accurately expresses the parties' intentions.

21-003 Rectification is concerned with "the mistaken implementation of intention".[6] Rectification supports or facilitates law's ends by ensuring that the relevant documentation accurately expresses the parties' intentions. This in turn ensures that other legal rules affording primacy to the documentary evidence, such as the parol evidence rules in contract, some estoppels and legislative writing requirements, do not operate in a self-defeating or unjust way owing to one or more parties' mistake in creating a document. Cases and commentaries sometimes speak in terms of "rectification of a contract" or other legal relationship, such as an express trust, but this is imprecise because "[c]ourts of Equity do not rectify contracts; they may and do rectify instruments . . .".[7] The written document is not literally the parties' legal relationship, such as a contract or express trust and rectification does not change the legal relationship. It (only) changes the documentary evidence of the parties' legal relationship. Paul Davies has explained this point in the following way:[8]

> Where the terms of a written instrument do not accord with the true agreement between the parties, equity has the power to reform, or rectify, that instrument so as to make it accord with the true agreement.[9] What is rectified is not a mistake in the transaction itself, but a mistake in the way in which that transaction has been expressed in writing.[10]

21-004 Rectification has been understood in a similar way in the context of express trusts, as explained by Simon Douglas:[11]

> The purpose of rectification, as stated by Mummery L.J. in *Allnutt v Wilding*, is to bring the "trust document into line with the true intentions of the settlor as held by him at the date when he executed the document".[12] The principal requirements were stated by Barling J. in *Giles v The Royal National Institute for the Blind*:
>
> > "[T]here must be a flaw in the written document such that it does not give effect to the parties'/donor's agreement/intention, as opposed to the parties/donor merely being mistaken as to the consequences of what they have agreed/intended . . . [and the] specific intention of the parties/donor must be shown; it is not sufficient to show that the parties did not intend what was recorded; they also have to show what they did intend, with some degree of precision . . ."[13]
>
> What rectification appears to do is to enable the court to ignore this aspect of the settlor's intent, i.e. the intention that the final trust deed be the sole source of the terms of the trust. The justification for this is that the settlor, when executing this document, was mistaken as to its contents . . .

---

5 *Lake v Lake* [1989] S.T.C. 865.

6 *Day v Day* at [25]; *Britoil Plc v Hunt Overseas Oil Inc* [1994] C.L.C. 561 at 573–574.

7 *Mackenzie v Coulson* (1869) L.R. 8 Eq. 368 at 375. See also *Frederick E Rose (London) Ltd v William H Pim Jnr & Co Ltd* [1953] 2 Q.B. 450.

8 P. Davies, "Rectification" in J. McGhee et al (eds), *Snell's Equity*, 34th edn (Sweet & Maxwell, 2021), para.16–001.

9 See *M'Cormack v M'Cormack* (1877) 1 L.R. Ir. 119; *Frederick E Rose v William H Pim*. For a more detailed study of this area, see D. Hodge, *Rectification: The Modern Law and Practice Governing Claims for Rectification for Mistake* (Sweet & Maxwell, 2010).

10 See *Racal Group Services v Ashmore* [1995] S.T.C. 1151 at 1154; *Allnutt v Wilding* [2007] EWCA Civ 412; [2007] W.T.L.R. 941.

11 S. Douglas, "Misuse of Rectification in the Law of Trusts" (2018) 134 L.Q.R. 138, p.138. See also P. Matthews, C. Mitchell, J. Harris and S. Agnew, *Underhill and Hayton: Law of Trusts and Trustees*, 19th edn (LexisNexis, 2022), Art.17.

12 *Allnutt v Wilding* at [11].

13 *Giles v Royal National Institute for the Blind* [2014] S.T.C. 1631 at [25]. Barling J. was here summarising Peter Gibson L.J.'s judgment in *Racal Group v Ashmore*.

Franklins Pty Ltd v Metcash Trading Ltd

New South Wales Court of Appeal, (2009) N.S.W.L.R. 603 at [431]–[447]

CAMPBELL J.A. (with whom ALLSOP P. and GILES J.A. agreed): In considering whether to grant rectification of a written contract, equity does not use any of its own principles to decide what the terms of the contract are, or how they are construed — those matters are decided solely by the common law. Rather, equity focuses on what it is unconscientious for a party to assert about the contract. The rationale is that it is unconscientious for a party to a contract to seek to apply the contract inconsistently with what he or she knows to be the common intention of the parties at the time that the written contract was entered. In other words, when a plaintiff succeeds in a claim for rectification, the plaintiff is found to have been justified in effect saying to the defendant "you and I both knew, when we entered this contract, what our intention was concerning it, and you cannot in conscience now try to enforce the contract in accordance with its terms in a way that is inconsistent with our common intention." . . . **21–005**

The remedy that is granted is, as with all equity's remedies, one that will seek to undo, so far as is in practice possible, the departure, that the litigation has shown to exist, from equity's standards of conscientious behaviour. The way this is achieved, when a remedy of rectification is granted, is by rewriting the contract so that it . . . no longer departs from the common intention of the parties. The rewriting is done in a quite literal sense — the proper form of order identifies the precise words of the contract that are to be struck out, the precise words that are to be inserted, and where those words are to be inserted.[14] As well the order usually[15] involves calling in the original document and actually endorsing the order on the instrument that is to be rectified . . . In that way the executed contractual document is no longer able to be a potential source of error and confusion, by appearing to state legal relations that in truth are not as the document says. . . . **21–006**

The rewriting should not do anything more than rewrite the contract to the minimum extent that is necessary for it to no longer fail to express the common subjective intention the parties had when the contract was entered. Thus, to the extent that the words of the contract cover some situation concerning which the parties had no common subjective intention, the words of the contract continue to govern that situation. **21–007**

Crafting a remedy in rectification involves close attention to the words of the document. However, in the prior step of making a finding about a common intention, for the purpose of a rectification order, it is important that the court not confine itself to a narrow focus on particular words of the document. It is the document as a whole that is rectified, and the point of the exercise is that, once rectified, the document will not be contrary to the common intention of the parties to the document. Thus if a particular change to some words will result in some other words of the document operating in a different way, rectification will be justified only if that different operation of those other words is shown to be in accordance with the common intention of the parties. **21–008**

The way in which rectification operates has particular significance when rectification of a deed of trust, or other document, is sought for taxation motivations. Rectification allows for the provisions of a written document to be changed to express the parties' intentions at the time the document was created. Depending on those intentions, rectification may have taxation implications. However rectification will not allow the parties to correct their intentions to achieve a more tax efficient outcome than that which they had intended for at the time the document was created.[16] **21–009**

---

14 H.W. Seton, *Forms of Judgments and Orders in the High Court of Justice and Court of Appeal*, 7th edn (Stevens and Sons Ltd, 1912), Vol.2, pp.1638–643 ("Judgments and Orders").

15 But not always — for example, *Wilson v Registrar-General* (NSW) [2004] NSWSC 1220 at [13]–[14].

16 See further *Allnutt v Wilding* at [19]–[20]; Mitchell et. al., *Underhill*, paras [17.9]–[17.12]; S. Douglas, "Misuse of Rectification in the Law of Trusts" (2018) 134 L.Q.R. 138.

2. When is Rectification Possible?

A. Documents That Can Be Rectified

21–010 The jurisdiction to rectify is quite general[17] and can be exercised to correct documents recording one or more parties' intentions across a range of contexts, such as: contracts,[18] transfers of shares,[19] conveyancing documents for transfer of ownership,[20] leases,[21] express trusts,[22] appointments and other exercises of power by trustees and other donees[23] and notice of severance of a joint tenancy.[24]

B. Rectification for Common Mistake

21–011 Whether rectification is possible will depend on the party seeking rectification, C, providing convincing evidence that the document does not align with her, and in some instances, another party's intentions.[25] To do this, C must prove the relevant intentions, and that these are not expressed by the document. It is not enough for C to prove the negative: that the parties did not have the intentions which *are* expressed in the document. The standard of proof is the balance of probabilities, but strong evidence is required to displace "the inherent probability that [a] written instrument truly represents the parties' intentions because it is a document signed by the parties".[26]

21–012 Depending on the situation, the intention that C needs to prove may be that of C alone, as in cases concerning some voluntary settlements, where C's unilateral mistake may suffice for rectification, as discussed next. In other cases, however, such as those concerning contracts, C must prove that the mutual or common intention which she shared with one or more others is not accurately expressed by the document due to their common mistake as to the meaning of the document.

21–013 The approach to determining the availability of rectification for a common mistake is set out in the "seminal"[27] judgment of Leggatt LJ in *FSHC Group Holdings Ltd v GLAS Trust Corp Ltd*,[28] which affirmed the "subjective" approach to common mistake and departed from the "objective" approach preferred by Lord Hoffmann in obiter dicta in *Chartbrook Ltd v Persimmon Homes Ltd*.[29] These differing approaches are explained by Paul Davies in the following excerpt.

---

17 Excluding rectification of wills which is covered by statutory provisions, especially the Administration of Justice Act 1982 s.20, and see generally *Marley v Rawlings* [2014] UKSC 2; [2015] A.C. 129; B. Häcker, "What's in a Will? Examining the Modern Approach Towards the Interpretation and Rectification of Testamentary Instruments" in C. Mitchell and B. Häcker (eds), *Current Issues in Succession Law* (Hart Publishing, 2016), Ch.6. For further examples of rectification, see P. Davies, "Rectification" in J. McGhee and S. Elliott (eds), *Snell's Equity*, paras 16–004–16–005.

18 *FSHC Group Holdings Ltd v GLAS Trust.*

19 *Re International Contract Co* (1872) 7 Ch. App. 485.

20 *Beale v Kyte* [1907] 1 Ch. 564; *Wilson v Wilson* [1969] 1 W.L.R. 1470; *Re Colebrook's Conveyances* [1972] 1 W.L.R. 1397. In relation to the different process of rectification of the Land Register, see Land Registration Act 2002 s.65 and Sch.4; *Cherry Tree Investments Ltd v Landmain Ltd* 2012] EWCA Civ 736; [2013] Ch. 305.

21 *Thomas Bates and Son v Wyndham's (Lingerie) Ltd* [1981] 1 W.L.R. 505.

22 *Lawie v Lawie* [2012] EWHC 2940 (Ch); [2013] W.T.L.R. 85.

23 *Day v Day* [2013] EWCA Civ 280; [2014] Ch. 114; *AMP (UK) Plc v Barker* [2001] Pens. L.R. 77; *Merchant Navy Officers Pension Fund Trustees v Watkins* [2013] EWHC 4741.

24 *Lee v Lee* [2018] EWHC 149; *Thin v Thin* (1650) 1 Rep. Ch. 162.

25 *Joscelyne v Nissen* [1970] 2 Q.B. 86; *FSHC Group Holdings Ltd v GLAS Trust* at [46].

26 *Thomas Bates and Son v Wyndham's (Lingerie) Ltd* [1981] 1 W.L.R. 505 at 521.

27 *Ralph v Ralph* [2021] EWCA Civ 1106 at [14].

28 See paras 21–019 to 21–025. See also: *Britoil v Hunt* [1994] C.L.C. 561; *Simic v New South Wales Land and Housing Corp v New South Wales Land and Housing Corp* (2016) 260 C.L.R. 85.

29 *Chartbrook Ltd v Persimmon Homes Ltd* [2009] UKHL 38; [2009] 1 A.C. 1101.

Paul Davies, "Rectification Rectified" (2020) 79 C.L.J. 8, 8–9

In *Chartbrook Ltd. v Persimmon Homes Ltd*, Lord Hoffmann expressed the view that a contract could be rectified for common mistake even where one party was not actually mistaken: it was sufficient that a reasonable observer would conclude, objectively, that both parties had made a common mistake. The other members of the House of Lords agreed with Lord Hoffmann's speech, but his Lordship's views on rectification were, strictly, obiter. This left the law in a troublesome position: should judges follow Lord Hoffmann's lead, or continue to apply the orthodox test that required both parties actually (or "subjectively") to have made a mistake? The answer to this question has not been clear for over a decade. In *Daventry District Council v Daventry & District Housing Ltd*[30] the parties assumed, without further argument, that the objective approach to rectification favoured in *Chartbrook* should be applied, and the Supreme Court frustratingly refused permission to appeal. However, in *FSHC Group Holdings Ltd v Glas Trust Corporation Ltd* the Court of Appeal was able to examine common mistake rectification thoroughly. In an excellent judgment, Leggatt L.J. (with whom Rose LJ and Flaux L.J. joined) restored traditional orthodoxy and rejected the objective approach to establishing a common mistake where the parties had not concluded a binding contact before producing the written instrument. **21–014**

FSHC was a parent company which entered into a private equity financing transaction in 2012 that required it to provide security over a shareholder loan. In 2016, its lawyers spotted that the relevant security documentation had either never been provided or could not be located. They drafted Accession Deeds to provide that security, which FSHC entered into with the defendant bank. By mistake, the Accession Deeds were drafted such that much more onerous obligations were undertaken by FSHC than was required. **21–015**

FSHC successfully brought a claim to rectify the deeds by deleting the additional obligations that were not necessary. The trial judge found that the lawyers and relevant directors on both sides all subjectively intended the Accession Deeds only to provide the missing security and no more, and that this was also what a reasonable observer would understand the parties to have intended. The Court of Appeal agreed. **21–016**

The decision is therefore explicable on both a "subjective" or "objective" approach to common mistake rectification, and the result must be right. The case is significant since it "provide[d] the opportunity for an appellate court to clarify the correct test to apply in deciding whether the written terms of a contract may be rectified because of a common mistake".[31] **21–017**

Space does not permit a long excerpt from Leggatt LJ's judgment, which provides a detailed and illuminating examination of rectification,[32] as well as the question of when the Court of Appeal can depart from obiter comments of the Supreme Court. The key passages in relation to rectification for unilateral and common mistake, as well as the underlying rationale, are set out below. **21–018**

FSHC Group Holdings Ltd v GLAS Trust Corp Ltd

Court of Appeal, [2020] Ch. 365 at [76]–[77], [143]–[148]

LEGGATT L.J. (with whom ROSE and FLAUX L.J.J. agreed) . . . In any case, *Joscelyne v Nissen*[33] clearly held that it is essential for rectification of a written contract to show an agreement, not in the sense of a prior concluded contract but "in the more general sense of an outwardly expressed accord of minds", and this requirement has been affirmed by the Court of Appeal on many subsequent occasions, as we will see. **21–019**

We also consider that the requirement is sound in principle. As has often been observed, the power of the court to rectify a contractual document is not a power to make an agreement for the parties; it is a power to correct mistakes in recording what the parties have actually agreed. Moreover, the effect of rectification is not merely to prevent a party from enforcing the written terms of a contract: it is to alter those terms so as to establish legal rights and obligations which differ from those recorded in the original **21–020**

---

30 [2012] 1 W.L.R. 1333.
31 *FSHC Group Holdings Ltd v GLAS Trust* at [1].
32 For a useful summary see *Ralph* [2021] EWCA Civ 1106 at [14]–[20].
33 [1970] 2 Q.B. 86 at 93.

contractual document. Leaving aside for the time being cases of rectification for unilateral mistake, establishing new contractual rights and obligations in this way is only justified if they are founded on mutual agreement. Whether the test applied is subjective or objective, it is fundamental that contractual rights and obligations should be based on mutual assent which the parties have manifested to each other and not on uncommunicated intentions which happen, without the parties knowing it, to coincide. Thus, as noted in *Tartsinis v Navona Management Co*,[34] it would be capricious if a document which the parties have agreed as the formal record of their contract could be altered to make it conform to the private intention of a party just because, although unknown to that party at the time, it turns out that the other party had a similar intention. We agree with the answer implied to the following question posed by Campbell J.A. in the Australian case of *Ryledar Pty Ltd v Euphoric Pty Ltd*:[35]

> If two negotiating parties each had a particular intention about the agreement they would enter, and their intentions were identical, but that intention was disclosed by neither of them, and they later entered [into] a document that did not accord with that intention, what would be the injustice or unconscientiousness in either of them enforcing the document according to its terms? . . .

Principle

21-021 . . . The principle that a contractual document should be reformed so as to enforce what the parties have (objectively) agreed has no validity where the prior "agreement" is not a legally binding contract but a non-binding expression of intent. There is no principle which requires or justifies a court in holding the parties to the terms of an objective consensus reached during negotiations but never intended to be binding: it is in the very nature of such a consensus . . . that it should not have any legal effect and represents only a stage in negotiations from which either party is free to walk away. Still less does the principle that parties should keep their promises to each other justify giving such a consensus priority over the terms of a formal written contract by which (objectively) the parties did intend to be bound. To adopt this course is to impose on the parties a contract they never made in place of one which they did make. It is to do exactly what . . . courts should not do: it is to rectify the contract made by the parties and not simply a document which fails to give effect to the terms of a contract.

21-022 It is in the very nature of a formal written contract that it is objectively intended to have priority over any earlier informal non-binding record of the parties' intention, as objectively assessed. In so far as there is a difference between them, it is therefore the contractual document which must prevail. As Professor Paul Davies has aptly put it:

> The objective approach to rectification involves too much objectivity: objectively, a binding written contract with a particular meaning, ascertained through the process of interpretation, has been concluded.

. . .

21-023 The justification for rectifying a contractual document to conform to a "continuing common intention" is therefore not to be found in the principle that agreements (as objectively determined) must be kept. It lies elsewhere. It rests on the equitable doctrine that a party will not be allowed to enforce the terms of a written contract, objectively ascertained, when to do so is against conscience because it is inconsistent with what both parties in fact intended (and mutually understood each other to intend) those terms to be when the document was executed. This basis for rectification is entirely concerned with the parties' subjective states of mind. The underlying moral principle can be characterised . . . as being that persons who make a contract have to observe certain standards of good faith.

21-024 It is not, however, a new principle . . . Nor is it limited, as also there suggested, to cases of unilateral mistake. We have seen that the principle is of ancient origin and was, historically, the rationale for granting rectification in cases of common mistake. Moreover, it is just as contrary to good faith – if not more obviously so – for a party to take advantage of a mistake about the content or effect of a written contract in a case where both parties were mistaken in believing when the contract was executed that it faithfully recorded their common intention than it is to do so in a case where only one party made such a mistake (to the other's knowledge). Rectification for unilateral mistake can, as we noted earlier . . . be understood as

[34] [2015] EWHC 57 at [88].
[35] [2007] N.S.W.L.R. 603 at 315.

> an extension of the same basic equitable principle. It is fundamental to the doctrine, in either aspect, that an actual mistake was made by one or more real people in believing that the written contract gave effect to what either was or was understood by one party to be the parties' actual common intention. As it was put in the passage from *Story's Commentaries*,[36] quoted earlier, to allow the terms of the written contract to prevail where such a mistake was made:
>
> > would be to allow an act, originating in innocence, to operate ultimately as a fraud, by enabling the party, who receives the benefit of the mistake, to resist the claims of justice, under the shelter of a rule framed to promote it.
>
> . . .
>
> **Conclusion on the law**
>
> For all these reasons, we are unable to accept that the objective test of rectification for common mistake articulated in Lord Hoffmann's obiter remarks in the *Chartbrook* case correctly states the law. We consider that we are bound by authority, which also accords with sound legal principle and policy, to hold that, before a written contract may be rectified on the basis of a common mistake, it is necessary to show either (1) that the document fails to give effect to a prior concluded contract or (2) that, when they executed the document, the parties had a common intention in respect of a particular matter which, by mistake, the document did not accurately record. In the latter case it is necessary to show not only that each party to the contract had the same actual intention with regard to the relevant matter, but also that there was an "outward expression of accord" – meaning that, as a result of communication between them, the parties understood each other to share that intention. **21–025**

In addition to setting out the tests for common mistake[37] and unilateral mistake,[38] Leggatt LJ also clarified that the requirement of an outward expression of accord is necessary for common mistake in contracts and other transactions.[39] However, this requirement is not as onerous as is sometimes assumed. The communication necessary to establish an outwardly expressed accord or common intention which each party understands the other to share, need not involve declaring that agreement or intention in express terms, and could include understandings that are so obvious as to go without saying, or that were reached without being spelled out in so many words. Leggatt LJ accepted that there could be cases where, depending on the circumstances and the context, the fact that an intention or understanding is shared may be apparent from the fact that nothing is said.[40] **21–026**

The requirement for a common continuing intention in the context of other transactions is not the same as for contract. Other transactions do not depend for their validity on a mutually shared and communicated intention and thus rectification does not depend on a common intention being communicated between the parties. It is sufficient if the parties both had the same or convergent intentions, and that these differed from the written document.[41] So while a common intention and a mistake are both required, there is a difference in the extent to which that intention must be shared or communicated between them, as is discussed in the following excerpt from *FSHC*. **21–027**

---

36 J. Story, *Commentaries on Equity Jurisprudence*, 4th edn (1846), Vol.1, Ch.5, para.155.

37 See paras 21–011ff.

38 See para.21–031.

39 See paras 21–025 and 21–028. See further *Ralph v Ralph* at [18]; *Ryledar Pty Ltd v Europhic Pty Ltd* (2007) N.S.W.L.R. 603 at [281].

40 *FSHC Group Holdings Ltd v GLAS Trust* at [81]–[83].

41 *AMP v Barker* at [65]–[66]. See also P. Davies, "Rectification in Pension Schemes" in S. Agnew, P. Davies and C. Mitchell, *Pensions: Law, Policy and Practice* (Hart Publishing, 2020), pp.101–102.

FSHC Group Holdings Ltd v GLAS Trust Corp Ltd
Court of Appeal, [2020] Ch. 365 at [78]–[79]

LEGGATT L.J. (with whom ROSE and FLAUX L.J.J. agreed):

The pension cases

21–028 The nature of the requirement to show an outward expression of accord can be further brought out by contrasting a line of cases involving the rectification of amendments made to the rules of employee pension schemes where the trustees of the scheme have the power to alter the rules provided they obtain the consent of the employer. As analysed by Lawrence Collins J in *AMP (UK) plc v Barker*,[42] in this situation no agreement between the trustees and the employer is needed in order to effect a change in the rules: it is sufficient that the employer gives its consent to the proposed change. In such a case it is sufficient to justify rectification that the intentions of the trustees and the employer coincide in that they both independently have the same intention regarding the effect of the amendment. It is not necessary to show that the trustees and the employer had a common intention as a result of communication with each other because the validity of an amendment does not depend on the parties having mutually agreed it – only on one having approved what the other has done.

21–029 This analysis has been followed in later cases.[43] In *Re IBM Pension Plan* Warren J said:[44]

> There needs to be cogent evidence of the intentions of both the trustee and the employer where the power of amendment requires the consent of both. . . . In a case such as *Chartbrook* or *Daventry*, what is sought to be rectified is a contract; it makes sense that, in order to displace the contract actually made by rectifying it, there should be found a consensus, albeit not one giving rise to a legally binding agreement. In contrast, in a case such as the present, no sort of agreement is required for there to be a valid deed of amendments. What is needed is an exercise of the power of amendment by the trustee and the consent of the employer to the exercise of the power. If that is to be called a consensus, so be it, but it is a different animal from the agreement or consensus which is relevant in a contractual case . . .

C. Rectification for Unilateral Mistake

21–030 Rectification is sometimes possible for a unilateral mistake and means the relevant document will be corrected to reflect one party's intention.[45] Examples include rectification of a deed poll,[46] or some provisions in deeds of settlement,[47] ante-nuptial marriage settlement,[48] or conveyance of property.[49]

21–031 The existence of a unilateral mistake is assessed subjectively and according to whether the document fails to reflect the intention of the relevant party.[50] The document will then be rectified to accurately express that intention.

21–032 It will sometimes be easier to make out a unilateral mistake than a common mistake as it is only necessary to prove the subjective intention of one party and it is not necessary to prove another party's intention with a common accord between the parties' understanding of the document.[51] Given the differences between common mistake and unilateral mistake, it is important to be sure whether rectification is justified on a unilateral mistake alone, or whether a common mistake must be shown.

42 [2001] Pens L.R. 77.
43 *Gallaher v Gallaher Pensions* at [117]; *Re IBM Pension Plan* [2012] P.L.R. 469.
44 *IBM Pension* at [19].
45 *Wright v Goff* (1856) 22 Beav. 207 at 214; *Walker v Armstrong* [1856] 8 De G.M. & G. 531; *Re Butlin's ST* [1976] Ch. 251.
46 *Bonhote v Henderson* [1895] 2 Ch. 202.
47 *Maunsell v Maunsell* (1877) 1 L.R.Ir. 529 at 539–40; *Van der Linde v Van der Linde* [1947] Ch. 306.
48 *Lackersteen v Lackersteen* (1860) 30 L.J. Ch. 5; *Behrens v Heilbut* (1956) 222 L.T. Jo. 290.
49 As in *Day v Day* at [22] and [50].
50 *FSHC Group Holdings Ltd v GLAS Trust* at [105], [147].
51 *Day v Day* at [22].

Rectification for a unilateral mistake is possible in two situations: (i) when the other party(s) to the transaction knows that her counterparty is mistaken as to the meaning of the document such that the document does not express the intention of that party; or (ii) when the nature of the transaction is such that its validity depends only on one party's intention, sometimes referred to as a unilateral transaction, and in which case that party's unilateral mistake is sufficient, and it is not necessary to prove whether another party shared the same mistake or had knowledge of her counterparty's. Each are discussed in turn. **21–033**

i. Unilateral mistake known by the other party

Some transactions depend for their validity on two or more parties' intentions, and them having mutual or convergence intentions, a key of example of which is contract. That is why rectification is usually only possible to correct a document to reflect an intention shared by both parties. Rectification for a unilateral mistake would hold the non-mistaken party to an agreement to which she did not intend, and violate the:[52] **21–034**

> . . . ordinary rule that it is the objective intention of the parties which determines the construction of the contract and not the subjective intention of one of them. Also, it would generally be inequitable to compel the other party to execute a contract, which he had no intention of making, simply to accord with the mistaken interpretation of the other party.[53]

An exception is when the non-mistaken party knew, or was wilfully blind to the possibility, that her counterparty was mistaken as to the meaning of the document such that it does not express her counter-party's intention.[54] In this situation rectification is possible on the basis of a unilateral mistake, for reasons discussed by Leggatt LJ in the following excerpt from *FSHC*.[55] **21–035**

FSHC Group Holdings Ltd v GLAS Trust Corp Ltd

Court of Appeal, [2020] Ch. 365 at [103]–[105]

Unilateral mistake

It has come to be accepted that the jurisdiction to rectify a written contract is not limited to cases where there was a common mistake and that in certain circumstances rectification may be granted even though at the time of execution of the contract only one of the parties was mistaken about its terms or effect. The development of the modern doctrine stems from the approval in *A Roberts & Co Ltd v Leicestershire County Council*[56] of the following statement of principle in *Snell's Equity*:[57] **21–036**

> . . . a party is entitled to rectification of a contract upon proof that he believed a particular term to be included in the contract, and that the other party concluded the contract with the omission or a variation of that term in the knowledge that the first party believed the term to be included.

---

52 *Commission for New Towns v Cooper* [1995] Ch. 259 at 279.
53 *Olympia Sauna Shipping Co SA v Shinwa Kaiun Kaisha Ltd* [1985] 2 Lloyd's Rep. 364 at 371.
54 *Crossco No.4 Unltd v Jolan Ltd* [2011] EWHC 803 at [234]–[250] affd in [2011] EWCA Civ 1619 at [43]–[45]. See further: D. McLauchlan, "The 'Drastic' Remedy of Rectification for Unilateral Mistake" (2008) 124 L.Q.R. 608.
55 See also *Holaw (470) Ltd v Stockton Estates Ltd* (2001) 81 P. & C.R. 29 at [41] approved in *FSHC Group Holdings Ltd v GLAS Trust* at [106].
56 [1961] Ch. 555.
57 R. Megarry, *Snell's Equity*, 25th edn (Sweet & Maxwell, 1960), p.570.

> 21-037 The precise scope of this principle remains controversial. But there is no doubt that it covers at least a case, such as the facts found in *Thomas Bates & Son Ltd v Wyndham's (Lingerie) Ltd*,[58] where the parties had a common intention that each had communicated to the other but one party before executing the contract realised that the document did not give effect to that intention and changed their mind without telling the other party.
>
> 21-038 The recognition of this principle is consistent with the traditional rationale of rectification for common mistake and gives effect to the same underlying equity. In the case of common mistake it is inequitable for a party to the contract to seek to apply the contract inconsistently with what that party knew to be the common intention of the parties when the written contract was executed. The doctrine of unilateral mistake extends this principle to the situation where a party seeks to apply the contract inconsistently with what that party knew the other party believed to be the common intention of the parties when the written contract was executed. . . .

ii. Unilateral mistake in a unilateral transaction

21-039 A unilateral mistake of itself will be sufficient for rectification in some situations and mean that the party seeking rectification need only show that the document fails to express the party's true intention, without needing to know another party's knowledge or shared mistake.

21-040 It is important to identify precisely when rectification for a unilateral mistake is possible and to this end a distinction is usually[59] drawn between: (a) contracts and other transactions involving consideration or bargain, in which case only a common mistake, or a unilateral mistake known to the other party will suffice for rectification; and (b) a voluntary transaction, in which case a unilateral mistake, even if unknown to the other party, may suffice for rectification. This is why a unilateral mistake suffices for rectification in the context of a self-declaration of trust, some gifts or notice of severance of a joint tenancy, to name a few.

21-041 However, we think that a focus on a lack of a bargain or the voluntary nature of a transaction to ascertain the scope of rectification for a unilateral mistake is problematic. This is because there are some voluntary transactions that do not involve consideration or a bargain, but which do depend for their validity on two or more parties' manifestation of their intentions, and to an extent, the convergence of those intentions. This is explained by his Honour Judge Matthews in *Scott v Bridge*:[60]

> A gift is often considered to be an entirely unilateral transaction, perhaps because it is not a (simple) contract. Yet the reason it is not a contract is because it lacks consideration. The position in the civil law is different: the concept of consideration is absent, and the contract of gift is well-known. But in fact, at common law, a gift is a bilateral (or multilateral) transaction whereby property in a thing is immediately and gratuitously vested by its owner in another or others. However, in English common law, each party to a gift has to consent to it, even though in some cases the relevant consent may be supplied by way of a presumption, and if the presumption is rebutted there is no gift. As Ventris J once put it in an old case, "a man cannot have an estate put into him in spight of his teeth".[61] Thus, in *Cochrane v Moore*,[62] Lord Esher MR said:
>
> > "It is a transaction consisting of two contemporaneous acts, which at once complete the transaction, so that there is nothing more to be done by either party. The act done by the one is that he gives; the act done by the other is that he accepts. These contemporaneous acts being done, neither party has anything more to do."

---

58 [1981] 1 W.L.R. 505.
59 See, e.g. *Re Butlin's ST* at 260–62; *Day v Day* at [21], [47].
60 [2020] EWHC 3116 at [122]–[123].
61 *Thompson v Leach* (1689) 2 Vent 198 at 206.
62 (1890) 25 Q.B.D. 57 at 76.

> ... So far as concerns the position of the recipient, as I have said, it is necessary that the recipient should accept the property given. There is here a presumption that, when a gift of property is made, the donee is presumed to accept it unless, upon learning of the gift, the recipient repudiates it.

In these types of voluntary yet bilateral or interconnected unilateral transactions, rectification on the basis of a unilateral mistake may mean that another party is held to a transaction to which they did not consent or intend to be bound by, and thereby undermine the underlying legal rules aiming to give effect to the parties' intentions. **21–042**

This point was made by Lawrence Collins LJ in *AMP v Barker*, where rectification was ordered to correct documentation which had been created by a trustee in the exercise of an amendment power and to which the employer had given its consent.[63] Lawrence Collins LJ referred to the traditional distinction between rectification in the context of a contract or other bargain transaction and rectification in the context of a voluntary settlement. He went on to explain that while the facts did not involve a contract or bargain requiring agreement *inter se*, rectification was not available on the basis of a unilateral mistake. This is because the validity of the transaction depended on two parties' manifestation of intentions that, to an extent, needed to converge: the pension trustee had to manifest an intention to exercise a power to amend the terms of the pension scheme and the employer had to manifest an intention to consent to the trustee's specific amendment.[64] Lawrence Collins LJ explained:[65] **21–043**

> Consequently, the intentions of the Trustees and the Principal Employer must converge. But they do not have to agree *inter se*. The Resolution, however cannot be rectified to reflect the intentions of the Trustees when that is not also the intention of the Principal Employer, for otherwise the Resolution could take a form to which the Principal Employer had not consented, and the consent of the Principal Employer is an essential part of the machinery of amendment. ... There must, therefore, be cogent evidence of the intentions both of the Trustees and of NPI, but not necessarily of their agreement or accord. ...

Thus, rectification was only possible to correct documentation to give effect to the parties' common continuing intention,[66] and as mentioned above, it is not necessary to show the common intention was communicated between the parties as is the case for rectification of a contract. It is sufficient if they both had the same or convergent intentions, and which differs from the written document.[67] **21–044**

There are other cases that might on first blush suggest a wider scope for rectification for a unilateral mistake, but which, in one way or another affirm its limits. First there are cases where rectification corrects a document to implement a unilateral mistake known to the other party.[68] **21–045**

Second, are cases where rectification for a unilateral mistake is subject to equitable discretion taking account of the other party's different intention. An example is *Re Butlin's ST*,[69] where a settlor had mistakenly thought the trust deed contained provisions for trustees to make decisions by majority, when in fact it did not. Rectification was ordered, despite some of the trustees not having had any intention as to the ability to decide by majority, and one trustee opposing the claim for rectification. Brightman J held:[70] **21–046**

---

63 Another example is when joint settlors or trustees intend to settle property on trust, rectification will depend on them having the same intention that is not accurately recorded by the document they execute, see: *Kennedy v Kennedy* [2014] EWHC 4129.

64 *AMP v Barker* at [64]–[67].

65 *AMP v Barker* at [65]–[66].

66 *AMP v Barker* at [67].

67 See paras 21–028 and 21–043.

68 See, e.g. *Day v Day* at [15] and [19], [45].

69 *Re Butlin's ST* at 262.

70 *Re Butlin's ST* at 262.

> In the absence of an actual bargain between a settlor and trustees: (i) a settlor may seek rectification by proving that the settlement does not express his true intention, or the true intention of himself and any party with whom he has bargained, such as a spouse in the case of an antenuptial settlement; (ii) it is not essential for him to prove that the settlement fails to express the true intention of the trustees if they have not bargained; but (iii) the court may in its discretion decline to rectify a settlement against a protesting trustee who objects to rectification.

21–047 Brightman J qualified this finding on the basis that (i) there was one trustee who did share the same mistake as the settlor and accepted the trusteeship on this basis;[71] and (ii) the trustee opposing rectification had provided no evidence or reasons for opposition.[72] Brightman J also went on to suggest that:[73]

> It may be — it is not necessary to decide the point — that the court would never be willing to rectify a settlement in the face of the reasonable opposition of a trustee, whether original or subsequent, who had accepted office upon the faith of the settlement as executed and in ignorance of the mistake. To override reasonable opposition on the part of a blameless trustee to suit the wishes of a settlor who, or whose advisers, have ex hypothesi fallen into error might well be thought unjust.

21–048 This makes sense because the validity of the express trust by transfer depends not just on a settlor's unilateral action, but also on the trustee's action in accepting her title subject to the trust terms.[74] While a court may appoint a replacement trustee if the settlor's nominated trustee will not act as such,[75] no one can be forced to be an express trustee. If a trustee's acceptance (or non-disclaimer) turns out to be on an understanding of a written document not shared by the settlor seeking rectification, then this should be a bar to rectification. To rectify in accordance with the settlor's unilateral intention would be to force the trustee to accept her office on terms she did not accept and violate the "the important principle of liberty that rights or liabilities are not generally to be conferred or imposed upon a person independently of that person's actions."[76] Indeed, rectification for a settlor's unilateral mistake may be a ground for the trustee to seek rescission of her acceptance. The question of whether a document can be rectified to implement a unilateral intention should depend on whether the legal relationship(s) evidenced by the document depend on a unilateral intention or the intentions of two or more parties' common or convergent intention.

3. Bars to Rectification

21–049 Rectification is a "cautiously watched and jealously guarded"[77] remedy, the award of which depends on there being no other way in which the parties' intentions can be given effect, such as via interpretation,[78] or via a further agreement between the parties.

---

71 *Re Butlin's ST* at 259.
72 *Re Butlin's ST* at 263–63.
73 *Re Butlin's ST* at 263.
74 See para.10–006.
75 See para.10–006.
76 *Commissioner of Taxation v Carter* [2022] HCA 10 at [48] (Edelman J), in relation to why a beneficiary can retrospectively disclaim her entitlement under an express trust.
77 *Whiteside v Whiteside* [1950] Ch. 65 at 71; *Racal Group Services v Ashmore* at 1154; *Pitt v Holt* [2013] 2 A.C. 108 at [131].
78 See Part 4.

Rectification will not be granted where a bona fide purchaser for value without notice has acquired a proprietary interest under the document.[79] Laches or acquiescence will also bar the claim[80] equitable doctrines which are discussed further in Chapter 22. **21–050**

Rectification will not be ordered where performance is impossible, or when subsequent circumstances have intervened, such as the passing of a statute frustrates performance.[81] **21–051**

4. Rectification and Interpretation

Rectification is not the only way in which the parties' mistake in recording their intentions might be overcome. Interpretation may be another option. Interpretation refers to the process of deriving the meaning of the parties' actions and in this context, in their creation of a document. That meaning will predominately be derived from the text of the document and the parties' actions in executing it. This meaning is ascertained objectively and restricts the parties' ability to hold each other to some other subjectively held intention to the extent it differs from the objective meaning of their actions. However, a more flexible approach to interpretation can exceptionally allow for mistakes to be corrected via interpretation. This approach can be taken when the mistake is apparent but the corrected meaning is objectively clear to a reasonable person with the relevant background knowledge,[82] such as when written provisions do not make grammatical sense,[83] are ambiguous[84] or use a technical term with definition.[85] **21–052**

Interpretation goes to the meaning of the parties' actions and will not actually change the written provisions of the document, and which is the provenance of rectification. As Lord Neuberger explains in *Marley v Rawlings*:[86] **21–053**

> If it is a question of interpretation, then the document in question has, and has always had, the meaning and effect as determined by the court, and that is the end of the matter. On the other hand, if it is a question of rectification, then the document, as rectified, has a different meaning from that which it appears to have on its face, and the court would have jurisdiction to refuse rectification or to grant it on terms (eg if there had been delay, change of position, or third party reliance).

Implication of terms by law may also be employed to correct the parties' failure to include an obvious or necessary provision in their written document. Implication gives effect to the parties' presumed intentions, while rectification gives effect to their actual intentions.[87] **21–054**

---

79 *Smith v Jones* [1954] 1 W.L.R. 1089; *Thames Guaranty Ltd v Campbell* [1985] Q.B. 210 at 240.

80 *Beale v Kyte* [1907] 1 Ch. 564; *Milton Keynes BC v Viridor (Community Recycling MK) Ltd* [2017] EWHC 239 (TCC) at [100]–[111].

81 *Pyke v Peters* [1943] 1 K.B. 242.

82 *Investors Compensation Scheme Ltd v West Bromwich Building Society* [1998] 1 W.L.R. 896 at 912–913.

83 *Homburg Houtimport BV v Agrosin Private Ltd (The Starsin)* [2003] UKHL 12; [2004] 1 A.C. 715 at [23].

84 *L Schuler AG v Wickman Machine Tool Sales Ltd* [1974] A.C. 235.

85 *ProForce Recruit Ltd v Rugby Group Ltd* [2006] EWCA Civ 69.

86 *Marley v Rawlings* at [40].

87 *FSHC Group Holdings Ltd v GLAS Trust* at [85]–[87]; *Codelfa Construction Pty Ltd v State Rail Authority (NSW)* (1982) 149 C.L.R. 337 at 346; *Simic v New South Wales Land and Housing Corp v New South Wales Land and Housing Corp* (2016) 260 C.L.R. 85 at [18]–[20]. See further A. Burrows, "Construction and Rectification" in A. Burrows and E. Peel (eds), *Contract Terms* (Oxford University Press, 2007); R. Buxton "'Construction' and Rectification after *Chartbrook*" [2010] C.L.J. 253; P. Davies, "Rectification versus Interpretation: The Nature and Scope of the Equitable Jurisdiction" [2016] C.L.J. 62.

5. Rectification and Rescission

21–055 Rectification is forward looking in that it implements and gives effect to the parties' intentions by correcting a document to record them accurately. Rectification ensures the parties are held to their intentions, properly recorded. This is in distinction to rescission which is backward looking in that it allows for one or more parties' exercise of power to be reversed or rescinded, placing the parties in the position prior to the impugned exercise of power.

21–056 Rectification and rescission are sometimes considered together on the basis they are both a response to mistake. In *Day v Day*,[88] Lewison LJ expressed the view that in the context of voluntary dispositions, rectification and rescission should be governed by the same principles. However, Birke Häcker has argued that this idea is misleading because the kind of mistake that calls for rectification is different from the kind of mistake that is typically addressed through rescission.[89] Rectification deals with a mistake in the way one or more parties have recorded their intentions. In contrast, rescission reverses an exercise of power in response to a different kind of mistake, which can be termed a "motivational mistake": the settlor (or transferor) has a piece of incorrect data in her mind which leads her to enter a transaction that she does not "truly" intend to enter. She is not mistaken about the means by which she records her intention, but she would not have entered it if she had known the relevant facts at the time when she decided to do so.

21–057 Rectification and rescission should be seen as complementary remedies aimed at different objectives, and not as alternative remedies aimed at the same objective. Rectification holds parties to their intentions by correcting the written evidence of their intentions. Mistake has a more confined role in the context of rectification in explaining why a document fails to express the parties' intention and justifying the court's departure from the strong presumption that parties intend for a written document to exclusively manifest their intention. Rescission, on the other hand, responds to a vitiation of intention, such as mistake, or some other problem with the exercise of power by reversing the consequences of execution.

Questions

1. What is corrected via rectification, a document or a legal relationship?
2. Why is rectification only possible to correct a document to implement an intention common to two or more parties in some situations while in others, rectification can correct a document to implement one party's intention?
3. In *Pitt v Holt*[90] Lord Walker said:

   Rectification is a closely guarded remedy, strictly limited to some clearly-established disparity between the words of a legal document, and the intentions of the parties to it. It is not concerned with consequences.

   Discuss.
4. Molly and Bob have a series of email exchanges to negotiate the terms of a contract under which Molly will supply coffee beans to Bob for his café. Over emails they agree that Molly

---

88 *Day v Day* at [41].

89 B. Häcker, "Mistaken Gifts after *Pitt v Holt*" (2014) 67 C.L.P. 333, 346–370.

90 [1909] 1 Ch. 476 at 481.

will supply Bob with 10 bags of coffee per week in return for Bob's weekly payment of £100. They forward their email exchanges to their solicitors to draft a formal document which they both sign, and includes clause 2 which states: "Molly will supply Bob with 100 bags of coffee per week in return for Bob's weekly payment of £100 each week for 1 year from the date of this agreement."

There is a typographical error in clause 2 as an additional "0" has been added to the number of bags Molly must supply Bob, reading "100". Can Molly seek rectification?

Bob is unhappy with the length of the contract as he did not think he and Molly agreed to a 1-year period. He has gone back through his emails and his personal notes and cannot find any indication they had previously agreed a 1-year period. Can Bob seek rectification for the documentation to be corrected to being terminable by either party with 1 month's notice?

22

EQUITABLE DISCRETIONARY FACTORS AND BARS TO RELIEF

1. Introduction

A. Equitable Discretionary Factors and Bars to Relief

Once a claimant, C, has made out the elements of her claim for equitable relief, a court must consider: (i) the extent of C's equity for relief; (ii) whether any relief should be awarded against the defendant, D; and, (iii) the form of relief necessary to satisfy C's equity.[1] The scope of inquiry (i) may vary from one claim to another: sometimes the extent of C's equity is relatively fixed, while for other equitable claims a court must ascertain where on a spectrum the extent of C's equity sits. We saw in Chapter 3, for example, that the extent of C's equity for relief for a proprietary estoppel ranges from vindication of C's expectation to removal of her detriment. This is in contrast to the extent of C's equity for relief against a third-party recipient of misapplied trust property, which is fixed: that the recipient must return the subject property (or its value) to the (sometimes replacement) trustee.[2] While the scope of inquiry (i) varies across equitable doctrines, it is not a matter of equitable discretion. Inquiries (ii) and (iii), however, are, and the aim of this chapter is to explore what it means for these inquiries to be discretionary and the implications of this for our understanding of equity, and to give an overview of some of the equitable rules that inform the exercise of these discretions. 22-001

Equitable discretionary factors and bars to relief guide a court in making two distinct choices of whether to award relief at all in favour of C against D and if so, what type of relief (inquiries (ii) and (iii)). "Equitable discretionary bars to relief"[3] is the label given to the equitable rules that inform the court's discretionary choice whether to award relief at all in favour of C (inquiry (ii)). Examples include laches and acquiescence. "Equitable discretionary factors" is the label given to the set of rules that inform the court's discretionary choice as to the kind of remedy necessary to meet C's equity for relief (inquiry (iii)). We have considered some of these already in relation to the courts' assessment of the questions whether to award specific performance, injunctions, or equitable damages in lieu: examples are the need for court supervision, certainty and hardship. Equitable discretionary factors and bars to relief overlap and some rules can inform both inquiries (ii) and (iii). C's delay in bringing a claim against D, for example, may mean that prejudice is caused to D or third parties such that relief is not awarded at all, or that a different form of relief is appropriate. 22-002

---

1 *Boscawen v Bajwa* [1996] 1 W.L.R. 328 at 334–35 (Millett LJ).

2 As in *Foskett v McKeown* [2001] 1 A.C. 102. See further Chapter 15.

3 See further E. Bant and M. Bryan, "Defences, Bars and Discretionary Factors" in E. Bant and M. Bryan (eds), *Principles of Proprietary Remedies* (Thomson Reuters, 2013), pp.185–87.

22–003 Generally speaking, equitable discretionary factors operate as *defences*, providing reasons why relief should not be awarded against D, despite C having made out her claim, or, a reason why C should only be awarded some different form of relief; examples include laches, acquiescence, and unclean hands. Sometimes an equitable discretionary factor will be relevant to another aspect of the court's discretion, which is the form of relief necessary to satisfy C's equity, and the terms on which relief is granted[4] (inquiry (iii)); examples include third party interests and (again) unclean hands. The effect of one or more discretionary factors and/or bars to relief is that even though C has made out her prima facie entitlement to equitable relief, she may not be awarded the precise form of relief she might otherwise have been awarded: relief might be awarded on terms requiring the plaintiff to take some (in)action, or might not be awarded at all.

22–004 A defence can be contrasted with a denial,[5] and which is an argument that D can make to negate one, or more, of the elements of C's claim; for example, when a defaulting trustee shows that a beneficiary gave consent to the trustee's (in)action, making (in)action that would otherwise have been unauthorised, authorised, thereby negating one of the main elements to C's claim for relief in response to an unauthorised execution.[6] However, and as we will see below, some equitable discretionary factors, such as acquiescence, may in some instances operate as a denial, negating an element of C's claim from the outset.

22–005 One or more equitable discretionary factors might be raised by D as part of a range of other denials or defences, some of which have been considered in previous chapters, such as a plea of bona fide purchaser,[7] a defaulting fiduciary's defence of informed consent,[8] or a defaulting trustee's exculpation by the trust terms or statute,[9] or the discretionary factors relevant to the award of specific relief,[10] or an account of profits,[11] or operate as a result of other principles of common law, such as illegality[12] or statute, such as registration of title to land[13] or statutory periods of limitation.[14] Like other defences or denials, D bears the burden of pleading and proving any discretionary factor or bar to relief.

22–006 The discretionary nature of equitable relief has been understood to mean different things over time, two of which are explained by the authors of *Snell's Equity* in the following excerpt.

---

4 S. Smith, "Form and Substance in Equitable Remedies" in D. Robertson and M. Tilbury (eds), *Divergences in Private Law* (Hart Publishing, 2016); J. Campbell, "When and Why a Bribe Is Held on a Constructive Trust: The Method of Reasoning towards an Equitable Remedy" (2015) 39 A.C.R. 320, 325–330.

5 As to the distinction between defences and denials generally, see, e.g. J. Goudkamp, *Tort Law Defences* (Hart Publishing, 2013), pp.1–7; J. Goudkamp and C. Mitchell, "Denials and Defences in the Law of Unjust Enrichment" in C. Mitchell and W. Swadling (eds), *The Restatement Third, Restitution and Unjust Enrichment: Comparative and Critical Essays* (Hart Publishing, 2013), pp.137–139.

6 See para.13–188.

7 See paras 15–164ff.

8 In relation to the defence as it applies to a breach of fiduciary duty see paras 2–210ff and in relation to a breach of trust see paras 13–184ff.

9 In relation to statutory exemption see paras 13–132ff and in relation to exemption clauses see paras 13–159ff.

10 See paras 19–062ff.

11 See paras 18–070 to 18–075.

12 See paras 22–156 to 22–158.

13 See, eg,: Land Registration Act 2002 s.29, which in fact replaces the bona fide purchaser defence in relation to dealings with land covered by the Land Registration Act 2002.

14 See paras 13–167ff.

Steven Elliott, "Introduction to Equitable Remedies" in John McGhee et al (eds), *Snell's Equity*, 34th edn (Sweet & Maxwell, 2020), para.14-002

It is sometimes said that the remedies treated in this part of the book are discretionary. The extent of the freedom the court enjoys in deciding whether to grant these remedies, as compared with the freedom it enjoys in relation to other remedies, can be overstated. It consists principally in the need to make what are sometimes fine judgments in order to apply more or less settled principles to the factual circumstances of particular cases. In some cases the description of a remedy as being discretionary only means that its principles are still being worked out.[15] To illustrate, while the decision to rescind a contract is said to be discretionary, the principles according to which that discretion must be exercised have been settled over the years through the articulation of the bars. If rescission has become barred, the court will exercise its discretion to refuse rescission. But it is well established that if restitutio in integrum is possible, and if rescission is not otherwise barred, the claimant is entitled to have the contract rescinded as of right.[16] The same is true of the jurisdiction to compel the performance of a contract, which was said over a century ago to be discretionary but "confined within well-known rules".[17] Of the discretion the court enjoys in deciding whether to grant an injunction, it has been said that "the discretion is not one to be exercised according to the fancy of whoever is to exercise the jurisdiction of equity".[18] And again in relation to the jurisdiction to order that an account of profits be taken, one finds statements that "although an account of profits, like other equitable remedies, is said to be discretionary, it is granted or withheld according to settled principles".[19] **22-007**

The discretionary nature of equitable relief does not mean that judges are deciding cases according to rules that are not clear, or without reference to legal rules; despite having been criticised as allowing for the arbitrary exercise of judicial power.[20] This point has been made by Lord Eldon in *White v Damon*,[21] the award of equitable relief "is not an arbitrary, capricious, discretion. It must be regulated upon grounds, that will make it judicial." As we will see in this chapter, equitable discretion does not import a broad-ranging remedial inquiry and is a structured form of judicial discretion bound by defined equitable rules, which themselves are largely consistent with rules of law demands.[22] There are a range of established rules, some of which are outlined below, that guide and structure the court's exercise of discretion in balancing "justice and injustice in taking one course or the other, so far as relates to the remedy."[23] **22-008**

Discretion describes how C's claim for equitable relief asserts a "construct of values and standards against which the conduct of 'suitors'—not only defendants—is to be judged."[24] If C wishes to engage and rely on one or more equitable rules to hold D to a set of values and standards, then C herself must also submit to those same values and standards. Discretion means that the outcome of cases is determined by the court's consideration of variables relating to, and beyond, the plaintiff's claim for **22-009**

---

15 *Vercoe v Rutland Fund Management Ltd* [2010] EWHC 424 (Ch); [2010] Bus. L.R. D141 at [340].

16 *Lagunas Nitrate Co v Lagunas Syndicate* [1899] 2 Ch. 393 at 456; *Spence v Crawford* [1939] 3 All E.R. 271 at 280.

17 *Ryan v Mutual Tontine Westminster Chambers Association* [1893] 1 Ch. 116 at 126.

18 *Doherty v Allman* (1878) 3 App.Cas. 709 at 728–29.

19 *Warman International Ltd v Dwyer* (1995) 182 C.L.R. 544 at 559. cf. *Walsh v Shanahan* [2013] EWCA Civ 411 at [63], [66] and *Novoship (UK) Ltd v Nikitin* [2014] EWCA Civ 908; [2015] Q.B. 499 at [120].

20 See, e.g. P. Birks, "Equity in the Modern Law: An Exercise in Taxonomy" (1996) 26 U.W.D.L.R. 1, 16–17, 97–99; P. Birks, "Three Kinds of Objection to Discretionary Remedialism" (2000) 29 U.W.D.L.R. 1, 2, 15–17.

21 *White v Damon* (1802) 7 Ves. Jun. 30 at 35 (Lord Eldon).

22 See further M. Harding, "Equity and the Rule of Law" (2016) 132 L.Q.R. 278, 293–295.

23 *Lindsay Petroleum Co v Hurd* (1894) L.R. 5 P.C. 221 at 239–40.

24 *Kakavas v Crown Melbourne Ltd* (2013) 250 C.L.R. 392 at [15]–[18], referring to W. Gummow, *Change and Continuity: Statute, Equity, and Federalism* (Clarendon Press, 1999), pp.44–51; J. Pomeroy, *A Treatise on Equity Jurisprudence*, 5th edn (Bancroft-Whitney & Lawyers Cooperative, 1941), Vol.1, p.74.

relief, including the position of the plaintiff, the defendant and third parties. There are good reasons for the self-reflexive nature of equity, which are outlined further below.[25]

22-010 Another route to understanding the discretionary nature of the court's power to award equitable relief is by way of reference to the limited grounds on which an appellate court will intervene in a trial judge's decision. The circumstances of any given case may mean that there are two or more possible options for the award of equitable relief, "any one of which might reasonably be thought to be the best, and any one of which therefore a judge may make without being held to be wrong".[26] The first instance judge thus has a "generous ambit within which reasonable disagreement is possible"[27] in relation to her decision whether to award relief in favour of C against D, and the type of relief. An appellate court will defer to the trial judge's exercise of discretion and will not intervene with the exercise of discretion simply on the basis that a different decision might have been made. An appellant must show that the exercise of discretion was so plainly wrong that the decision made was not within the ambit of discretion at all. An appellant will thus have a higher bar if she is to convince an appellate court to overturn the award of equitable relief than what she might if appealing a trial judge's award of non-discretionary relief, such as an award of damages at law.

B. Scope of Application

22-011 Cases have sometimes taken a restrictive view as to the scope of application of equitable discretionary factors and bars to relief. Strong judicial statements have been made to the effect that discretion has no application to certain types of claims for equitable relief, such as a trust beneficiary's claims against an express trustee, or the proprietary claim against a third party. For example, in *Foskett v McKeown*,[28] Lord Millett stated that equitable discretion did not apply to a trust beneficiary's proprietary claim against an innocent third party as "[p]roperty rights are determined by fixed rules and settled principles. They are not discretionary." In the same case, Lord Browne-Wilkinson[29] stated, "[t]here is no discretion vested in the court", going on to say "[i]t is a fundamental error to think that, because certain property rights are equitable rather than legal, such rights are in some way discretionary. . . . It is a case of hard-nosed property rights." These statements have since been relied on in finding that relief in response to the beneficiary's proprietary claim is not subject to discretionary factors or bars to relief.[30] In addition are older cases to the effect that equitable discretionary factors and bars to relief would be harder to make out against a trust beneficiary and that only "gross laches", for example, would suffice.[31]

22-012 Other cases show, however, that a trust beneficiary's entitlement to relief against the trustee or against a third party is subject to equitable discretionary factors like any other claim for equitable relief. Laches and acquiescence did bar a beneficiary's claims for administration, accounts and

---

25 See para.22-034.

26 *G v G (Minors: Custody Appeal)* [1985] 1 W.L.R. 647 at 651. In relation to equitable discretionary factors in particular, see *Lucas Stuart Pty Ltd v Hemmes Hermitage Pty Ltd* [2010] NSWCA 283 at [7].

27 *Bellenden (formerly Satterthwaite) v Satterthwaite* [1948] 1 All E.R. 343 at 345.

28 *Foskett v McKeown* [2001] 1 A.C. 102 at 127.

29 *Foskett v McKeown* [2001] 1 A.C. 102 at 109.

30 See, e.g. *Ultraframe (UK) Ltd v Fielding* [2005] EWHC 1638 at [1522]; *Zarbafi v Zarbafi* [2014] EWCA Civ 1267; [2014] 1 W.L.R. 4122 at [70] (Briggs LJ) "there is much to be said for the judge's instinctive reaction that a defence of laches in relation to the assertion of a beneficial interest (rather than, for example, the pursuit of an equitable remedy, or a mere equity) would, if successful, produce a surprising and at first sight unfair outcome"; *Gadson v Gadson* [2003] WASC 48 at [86]; *K & S Corp Ltd v Sportingbet Australia* (2003) 86 S.D.S.R. 312 at [157]; W. Swadling, "The Nature of Knowing Receipt" in P. Davies and J. Penner (eds), *Equity, Trusts and Commerce* (Hart Publishing, 2017), p.309.

31 See, e.g. *Re Cross* (1882) 20 Ch. D. 109 at 121.

recovery of specific property against an express trustee in *Hourigan v Trustees, Executors & Agency Co Ltd*.[32] In *Orr v Ford*,[33] the High Court of Australia expressly stated that laches may bar a trust beneficiary's claim to specific property which is the subject of an express trust, albeit that laches was not made out on the facts in that case.

Orr v Ford

High Court of Australia, (1989) 167 C.L.R. 316 at 330 and 340

WILSON, TOOHEY AND GAUDRON JJ: . . . The substance of the respondent's case in relation to laches was that of prejudice in defending the appellant's claim by reason that evidence which might earlier have been available was lost to them. Prejudice is a consideration properly to be taken into account in relation to laches, although the respondents were not able to point to any authority where such a consideration had defeated the claim of a beneficiary to specific property the subject of an express trust. However, where entitlement depends on factual matters which are fairly open to dispute we see no reason why prejudice occasioned by the loss of evidence as a result of delay on the part of the claimant might not be raised in answer to such a claim. **22–013**

DEANE J: . . . Delay and acquiescence are invoked as part of the circumstances of the case which are said to found a defence of laches notwithstanding that Mr. Orr's claim is that of a beneficiary for the enforcement of an alleged express trust. . . . **22–014**

. . . Laches is an equitable defence and is not available in answer to a legal claim. It has been said that, even in the case of equitable claims, "laches . . . finds a Bluebeard's Chamber . . . in a claim [by a beneficiary] against an express trustee for recover of trust property"[34] and less colourfully, per Jessel M.R., *Browne v Radford*,[35] "who knew of now cases where acquiescence had been held to be a bar to an express trust". As Professor Hanbury recognized, however, that broad statement requires qualification. The qualification is that "the doctrine . . . that where there is an express trust lapse of time is to be entirely disregarded" does not apply to a case in which there has been "gross laches". . . . One searches in vain in the judgements in the above mentioned cases (and, for that matter, elsewhere) for nay satisfactory comprehensive description of the combinations of circumstances which will suffice to attract the label "gross" for the purposes of that qualification. That is not surprising since any attempt to specify exhaustively those combinations of circumstances would be likely to introduce an inappropriately arbitrary and technical element into an area of equity doctrine which has traditionally been kept free of arbitrary and technical constraints. On balance, the preferable approach is to treat the phrase "gross laches" as an intentionally imprecise one which involves not merely considerations of the period of the relevant delay but which invokes the traditional notions of equity and good conscience which are the general determinants of whether a plaintiff should be refused relief by reason of laches in the circumstances of a particular case. On that approach, the phrase refers to circumstances where inaction or standing by (with knowledge) by a plaintiff over a substantial period of time assumes an aggravated character in that it will, if the plaintiff is granted the relief which he seeks, give rise to serious and unfair prejudice to the defendant or a third party. So understood, the use of the phrase "gross laches" does little to aid in the identification of particular circumstances in which a defence of laches will preclude relief being granted to a beneficiary in an action for the enforcement of an express trust. The ultimate test effectively remains that enunciated by Lord Selborne L.C. (not, as is often said, Sir Barnes Peacock (see Errata)), speaking for the Privy Council, in *Lindsay Petroleum Co. v Hurd*,[36] namely, whether the plaintiff has, by his inaction and standing by, placed the defendant or a third party in a situation in which it would be inequitable and unreasonable "to place him if the remedy were afterwards to be asserted" . . . **22–015**

Ordinarily, it is difficult to envisage circumstances, falling short of waiver, release, election or estoppel, in which the laches of a beneficiary would produce a situation in which it was inequitable and unreasonable to grant relief in proceedings for the enforcement of an express trust in relation to trust property which **22–016**

---

[32] *Hourigan v Trustees, Executors & Agency Co Ltd* (1934) 51 C.L.R. 619 at 629 (Rich J), 651 (Dixon J).

[33] *Orr v Ford* (1989) 167 CLR 316 at 330 (Wilson, Toohey and Gaudron JJ), 340–41 (Deane J).

[34] H.G. Hanbury, *Modern Equity*, 6th edn (Steven and Sons Ltd,1952), p.349.

[35] (1874) W.N. 124.

[36] [1874] LR 5 PC 221.

remained in the possession of the trustee (or his personal representative). There are, however, at least two categories of case where that is not so. The first is where there is or has been dispute or mistake about the existence of the trust or the identity or extent of the trust property. The second category is where prejudice to third parties, such as other beneficiaries, is involved. . . .

22–017 In addition to the cases mentioned in *Orr v Ford*, there are further cases where laches and/or acquiescence were considered capable of barring a trust beneficiary's proprietary claim against a third party for recovery of trust property,[37] including *Patel v Shah*.

Patel v Shah

Court of Appeal, [2005] EWCA Civ 157 at [23]–[38]

22–018 MUMMERY L.J. (with whom Keene L.J. and Mr Kevin Garnett Q.C. agreed): As for an action to recover trust property from the trustees, the authorities, [Mr Hodge, counsel for the beneficiary] submitted, show that such a claim cannot be defeated by the defence of laches. He cited *Mills v Drewitt*,[38] which was relied on by Mr Brunyate in his work *Limitation of Actions in Equity*[39] as authority for the proposition that:

> D trustee who is in possession of property which he admits to be trust property cannot plead the laches of the cestui que trust in a suit to enforce the trust in respect of that property.

22–019 In other words, a beneficiary cannot be divested of his beneficial interest in the capital of the trust by the operation of the doctrine of laches.

22–020 Mr Hodge went on to submit that this was a matter within the exclusive jurisdiction (as distinct from the auxiliary jurisdiction) of courts of equity, and that a denial of equitable relief on the grounds of laches would in effect deprive the claimant of all relief. Equity, he said, was particularly reluctant to refuse a beneficiary relief on the grounds of delay or laches.[40]

22–021 Such an extreme step was not justified in the case of claims in respect of properties vested in the defendants in trust for the claimants. . . .

22–022 Mr Hodge referred in detail to a number of authorities. . . . *Knight v Bowyer*,[41] was cited for the proposition that the doctrine of laches and delay did not apply to an express trust, save possibly where there was a release or abandonment by the beneficiary and that was capable of being presumed from the facts of the case. The overriding duty of the trustee was to apply the trust property according to the trusts. He cited the case of *Bright v Legerton*,[42] to the same effect. *In re Cross*[43] was cited as an example of the application of laches and delay to a claim against a trustee, not for the recovery of trust property, but for breach of trust.

22–023 Mr Hodge also cited two Australian cases. In *Hourigan v Trustees Executors and Agency Co Ltd*,[44] it was stated that the defence of laches may be raised in answer to a claim by a beneficiary of an express trust where there had been acquiescence or "gross laches". *Orr v Ford* was also cited, particularly for the passage in the judgment of Deane J that ordinarily the laches of a beneficiary would not make it inequitable or unreasonable to grant relief in proceedings for the enforcement of an express trust in relation to property in the possession of the trustee.

22–024 I do not doubt that, in the general run of claims by a beneficiary against a trustee for the recovery of a beneficial interest in trust property, Mr Hodge's analysis is apposite. The key question is whether it applies

---

[37] *Pearce v Newlyn* (1818) 3 Madd. 186 at 189 (Sir John Leach), where laches was considered as potentially applying to defeat the beneficiary's proprietary claim but not raised on the facts; *Harper v Brown* (1884) 8 L.R. (NSW) Eq. 86 at 107 (Manning PJ), affirmed on appeal [1887] N.S.W.R. 116 at 121 (the Court); *Mallott v Wilson* [1903] 2 Ch. 494 at 504 (Byrne J); *Fernandes v Fernandes* [2015] EWHC 814 (Ch), laches was considered (but found inapplicable on the facts) in relation to an assertion of a beneficial interest; *Halford v Halford* [2022] WASCA 1 at [179].

[38] (1855) 20 Beav. 632 at 638.

[39] J. Brunyate, *Limitations of Actions in Equity* (Stevens and Sons, 1932), p.234.

[40] I.C.F. Spry, *Principles of Equitable Remedies: Specific Performance, Injunctions, Rectification and Equitable Damages*, 6th edn (Lawbook Company, 2001), pp.437–438.

[41] (1858) 2 De. G. & J. 421 at 443.

[42] (1860) 29 Beav. 606 at 615–616.

[43] (1882) 20 Ch D 109.

[44] (1934) 51 C.L.R. 619 at 650.

to the trusts affecting the properties in this case, bearing in mind that these trusts arose, and are sought to be enforced, in a commercial context, not in the donative context of orthodox inter vivos and testamentary trusts, in which a beneficiary is not expected by anyone to do anything other than to receive the gift. . . .

. . . There is . . . in my judgment a wider principle, which embraces the defences of laches and delay, and can be invoked in answer to claims which are made to equitable interests in property arising in circumstances affecting the sale and purchase of property. I refer to the principle formulated by Aldous LJ on the *Frawley v Neill*[45]. Aldous LJ (with whose judgment Ward and Swinton Thomas LJJ agreed) stated, having discussed instances of the doctrines of laches, acquiescence and estoppel, the following principle: 22–025

> In my view, the more modern approach should not require an inquiry as to whether the circumstances can be fitted within the confines of a preconceived formula derived from earlier cases. The inquiry should require a broad approach, directed to ascertaining whether it would in all the circumstances be unconscionable for a party to be permitted to assert his beneficial right. No doubt the circumstances which gave rise to a particular result in decided cases are relevant to the question whether or not it would be conscionable or unconscionable for the relief to be asserted, but each case has to be decided on its facts applying the broad approach.[46]

The effect of conduct by the claimants, which may properly be described as unconscionable, is to release a defendant trustee from the equitable trust obligation, which binds his conscience as the holder of the legal title for the benefit of others. In the case of an ordinary trust by way of gift to trustees for the benefit of the beneficiaries, where the beneficiary is not required or expected to do more than receive what has been given for his benefit, it will obviously be extremely rare for laches and delay on the part of the beneficiary to make it unconscionable for that beneficiary to assert his claim to the beneficial interest, or for the trustee to claim that he has been released from the equitable obligations that bind his conscience. . . . 22–026

In my judgment, the deputy judge was right to regard the conduct of the claimants as conduct on which he was entitled to dismiss the claim as unconscionable and barred by laches. 22–027

Equitable discretionary factors may also lead a court to vary the form of relief given in cases concerned with equitable proprietary claims (inquiry (iii)). For example, in *The Attorney-General v Kerr*,[47] orders for recovery of property misapplied by trustees of a charitable trust were made conditional on counter-restitution of the value of the improvements the third party had made to the property. Lord Langdale MR explained that:[48] 22–028

> The charity having equity, must on its part do equity, and the question is, what ought to be done with regard to the very great and valuable expenditure which has been made?

Lord Langdale MR went on to state that relief on terms requiring counter-restitution was "no more than just and reasonable".[49] Similarly, in *Palmer v Monk*,[50] where a trust beneficiary's claim for an injunction to prevent a trustee from transferring title to trust property under a contract for sale with a third party, relief was awarded on terms requiring the beneficiary to perform counter-restitution for the defendant's improvements to the property. Terms requiring counter-restitution will not be imposed where a third party's expenditure has gone to the defaulting trustee personally, rather than to the trust estate the subject of relief. In *Dudley v Champion*,[51] and *Devaynes v Robinson*,[52] relief was 22–029

---

45 [2000] C.P. Reports 20.
46 [2000] C.P. Reports 20.
47 *The Attorney-General v Kerr* (1840) 2 Beav. 420 at 429.
48 *The Attorney-General v Kerr* at 429.
49 *The Attorney-General v Kerr* at 429.
50 *Palmer v Monk* [1962] N.S.W.R. 786 at 790.
51 *Dudley v Champion* [1893] 1 Ch. 101 at 114–116 (Lindley LJ).
52 *Devaynes v Robinson* (1856) 24 Beav. 86 at 97 (Sir John Romilly MR).

conditional upon the trust beneficiary making counter-restitution to the third party only to the extent of the amount of the funds applied to the trust estate the subject of relief.

22-030 In addition, there are cases showing that a trust beneficiary's assertion of priority against a later third party claiming a later equitable interest in the subject property will be barred or deferred by her disentitling conduct, and which is a discretionary assessment of whether it would be fair to allow the trust beneficiary's claim to prevail over that of another in the circumstances, according to discretionary factors and bars to relief such as laches or acquiescence.[53] In *Fung v Tong*, C's prior equitable interest under a trust was deferred in priority to a later equitable mortgage on account of C's conduct.[54]

22-031 These cases show that equitable discretionary factors and bars to relief apply to a trust beneficiary's claim against an express trustee and/or third parties. The other cases[55] disavowing the role of discretion, such as *Foskett v McKeown*, could be understood as saying the assessment of the extent of a trust beneficiary's equity for relief against an innocent third party recipient (inquiry (i)) is not discretionary. These cases are not disavowing the role of discretion in relation to the availability and form of relief (inquiries (ii) and (iii)). Further, those other cases insisting on "gross laches" should be understood as an application of the principle that C's conduct in allowing T to retain trust property will not count against C. This reflects the trustee's status as an accounting party and that a trust beneficiary is not required or expected to monitor a trustee's performance and administration. In turn, a beneficiary's reliance on her entitlement to due administration cannot be barred simply by her conduct in allowing the trustee to have title to property and in not monitoring the trustee. These cases do not otherwise support the more general proposition that C's conduct can never count against her at all.

C. Implications for Understanding Equity

22-032 The discretionary nature of equitable relief has some important implications for our understanding of equity.

22-033 First, it means that C's so-called "right" or "entitlement" to equitable relief is never absolute. As mentioned in Chapter 1, it is the discretionary nature of an entitlement to equitable relief that is captured by the phrase "an equity for relief". The conditional nature of C's equity for relief is very different to a plaintiff's right to relief at common law. A plaintiff who makes out her claim for breach of contract, for example, has an entitlement to damages, even if nominal in the circumstances.

22-034 Second, it shows how equity, via its various equitable discretionary factors and bars to relief, looks inwards to prevent C's unconscientious assertion of the entitlements that equity generates, and thereby preserves the normative force of equitable rules. The underlying idea is that if C seeks to hold D to equity's standards to prevent D from abusing the law afforded to D, then C should be subject to the same standards to ensure C does not abuse the legal entitlements equity generates in C's favour against D. We have already seen how equity's rules that control how D uses the legal entitlement(s) generated by common law rules apply equally to D's legal entitlement generated by equitable rules, such as when a promissory estoppel is raised to prevent assertion of an entitlement to *equitable* relief, or when an express (sub-)trust is declared over an equitable chose in action. In addition, there are the equitable discretionary factors and bars to relief which ensure that equitable relief is not awarded

---

53 *Shropshire Union v R.* (1865) L.R. 7 H.L. 496 at 506–508 (Lord Cairns LC), 512 (Lord Hatherley), 514 (Lord O'Hagan); *Taylor v London & County Banking Co* [1901] 2 Ch. 231 at 261–262 (Stirling LJ); *Powell v London & Provincial Bank* [1893] 1 Ch. 610 at 617 (Wright J), affd on appeal [1893] 2 Ch. 555. See generally in relation to the assessment of priorities between competing equitable interests: *Rice v Rice* (1853) 2 Drew 73 at 78–79 (Sir Kindersley VC); *Lapin v Abigail* (1930) 44 C.L.R. 166 at 196–97 (Duffy and Starke JJ), 204–05 (Dixon J); *Moffett v Dillon* [1999] 2 V.R. 480 at [77] (Ormiston JA).

54 *Fung v Tong* [1918] A.C. 403 at 408–411 (the Board).

55 See para.22-011.

when it would be unconscionable to do so in the given circumstances. Equity's self-reflexive nature is echoed in cases such as *Kakavas v Crown Melbourne Ltd*,[56] explaining that equity is a "construct of values and standards against which the conduct of "suitor"—not only defendants—is to be judged."[57] Some of the equitable discretionary factors and bars to relief are set out in the rest of this Chapter 22.

2. Laches

A. Introduction

Laches (pronounced "lay-cheese") is an old Law French term that means "neglect" or "slackfulness". It applies as a discretionary bar to C's claim for equitable relief where C has delayed in prosecuting her claim to the disadvantage of D (or a third party) such that the balance of justice favours withholding relief to C. This discretionary bar is different to statutory periods of limitation, which can also bar C's claim after a period of time. We discuss the interconnections between laches and statutory limitation periods further below. **22-035**

The justification for laches is based on the maxim that equity "aids the vigilant, not the indolent".[58] In *Lindsay Petroleum Co v Hurd*, Lord Selborne LC writes that:[59] **22-036**

> the doctrine of laches in Courts of Equity is not an arbitrary or a technical doctrine. Where it would be practically unjust to give a remedy, either because the party has, by his conduct, done that which might fairly be regarded as equivalent to a waiver of it, or where by his conduct and neglect he has, though perhaps not waiving that remedy, yet put the other party in a situation in which it would not be reasonable to place him if the remedy were afterwards to be asserted, in either of these cases, lapse of time and delay are most material. But in every case, if an argument against relief, which otherwise would be just, is founded upon mere delay, that delay of course not amounting to a bar by any statute of limitations, the validity of that defence must be tried upon principles substantially equitable. Two circumstances, always important in such cases, are, the length of the delay and the nature of the acts done during the interval, which might affect either party and cause a balance of justice or injustice in taking the one course or the other, so far as relates to the remedy.

In that case, the delay in itself was not of a long duration and there was no prejudicial change of circumstances. The doctrine was therefore not enlivened:[60] **22-037**

> The situation of the parties having, therefore, in no substantial way been altered, either by the delay or by anything done during the interval, there is in these circumstances nothing to give special importance to the defence founded on time.

Laches does not operate as a technical rule, but as a discretionary doctrine. This was explained by Laddie J in *Nelson v Rye*:[61] **22-038**

> It can be misleading to approach the equitable defences of laches and acquiescence as if they consisted of a series of precisely defined hurdles over each of which a litigant must struggle before the defence is made

---

56 *Kakavas v Crown Melbourne Ltd* (2013) 250 C.L.R. 392.

57 *Kakavas v Crown Melbourne Ltd* at [16], quoting Gummow, *Change and Continuity: Statute, Equity, and Federalism*, pp.44–51.

58 See generally *Partridge v Partridge* [1894] 1 Ch. 351 at 359, 360; J. Brunyate, *Limitation of Actions in Equity* (Stevens & Sons, 1932), p.188; McGhee et al, *Snell's Equity*, 34th edn, Ch.5.

59 *Lindsay Petroleum Co v Hurd* at 239–240.

60 *Lindsay Petroleum Co v Hurd* at 239–240.

61 *Nelson v Rye* [1996] 1 W.L.R. 1378 at 1392.

> out. . . . So here, these defences are not technical or arbitrary. The courts have indicated over the years some of the factors which must be taken into consideration in deciding whether the defence runs. Those factors include the period of the delay, the extent to which the defendant's position has been prejudiced by the delay and the extent to which that prejudice was caused by the actions of the plaintiff. I accept that mere delay alone will almost never suffice, but the court has to look at all the circumstances, including in particular those factors set out above, and then decide whether the balance of justice or injustice is in favour of granting the remedy or withholding it. If substantial prejudice will be suffered by the defendant, it is not necessary for the defendant to prove that it was caused by the delay. On the other hand the plaintiff's knowledge that the delay will cause such prejudice is a factor to be taken into account.

B. Circumstances of Delay with Prejudice

22-039 The point from which time begins to run is when C has "sufficient knowledge of the facts constituting the title to relief".[62]

22-040 While laches is framed in general terms of "delay", "disadvantage", and "the balance of justice", it is important to understand that laches is not concerned with mere delay (although, the length of delay can be a relevant factor), nor with any form of prejudice or disadvantage. Laches is only concerned with delay during which there is a change in D's (or a third party's) circumstances such that, to allow C to maintain her claim against D would now cause prejudice or disadvantage to D (or possibly a third party) and it would therefore now be unconscionable for C to be granted equitable relief.

22-041 The types of disadvantage or prejudice can vary and may depend on the nature of C's claim and the relief sought by C. So, where C is seeking rescission of a sale of property, laches may bar C's claim where there are intervening interests of third parties and/or where the passage of time means that it is no longer possible to put the parties in the position they occupied prior to the sale. This is explained in *Bonney v Ridgard*,[63] where Sir Lloyd Keyon MR held that a fraudulent sale of property will not be rescinded if a great length of time has run against the parties seeking relief:[64]

> . . . the common case is that of mortgagor and mortgagee; when mortgagee has been in possession for twenty years, without any particular impediment to the mortgagor, or if such impediment has been removed for ten years, it shall be a bar to the redemption. So in this case, I think the length of time ought to bar, and if the authority did not say so, I would make the precedent, for this very case shews the good policy of the rule. Here the many persons, through whose hands this property has passed, have relied upon the undisturbed possession, and have laid out considerable sums of money in the improvement of it upon that idea. It would be too much at this length of time to give the plaintiffs the relief required when the accounts cannot be taken. If these plaintiffs had made their claims when they all came of age, it would have been very different; but upon the whole, weighing the convenience with the inconvenience, I think it right to say that the length of time is a bar in this case.

22-042 Laches may bar C's claim where the passage of time has resulted in a loss of evidence that would have "cast a different complexion on the matter", although the loss of evidence that is only suppositional and not likely to have made a difference to the outcome of the case will not constitute prejudice sufficient to bar C's claim. As is explained in the High Court of Australia case of *Orr v Ford* below, whether a loss of evidence amounts to prejudice will require an examination of the probative value of the evidence lost, and whether, in light of the other evidence available, the evidence lost would have shed a different light on facts material to the outcome of the case.

---

62 *Lindsay Petroleum Co v Hurd* at 241; *Twigg v Twigg* [2022] NSWCA 68 at [86]–[88].

63 *Orr v Ford* at 342.

64 *Bonney v Ridgard* (1784) 1 Cox 145; 29 E.R. 1101 at 149.

Orr v Ford

High Court of Australia, (1989) 167 C.L.R. 316 at 330 and 345–346.

[In 1968, Stone acquired a leasehold interest in land for $156,000.00. Orr contributed $30,000.00 to the purchase price, on the basis Stone would hold a one-half interest on trust for Orr (the appellant). Stone later suffered mental illness, and with the deterioration of his faculties, Stone came to regard the land as solely his own. Stone granted a sublease of the land to his manager, and by a will made in 1978, he purported to dispose of the entire leasehold interest to his manager and housekeeper. Probate of the will was granted in November 1985. Up to, and until December 1985, Orr had done nothing to assert his rights to the land. In December 1985, Orr commenced an action against Stone's executors (the respondents) claiming a half beneficial interest in the land under an express trust, and in the alternative a beneficial interest proportionate to his contribution to the purchase price under a resulting trust. By then, persons who might have been witnesses had died. The judge held that an express trust of the one-half interest had been created in favour of Orr, and, that his claim to a declaration of trust had not been defeated by laches and acquiescence, but that the trust was illegal and unenforceable by certain statutory provisions. On appeal to the High Court of Australia, it was held that those statutory provisions did not preclude or render illegal the existence of the trust, nor was laches established by reason of no loss of crucial or material evidence, and consequently no prejudice to the defendant, Stone.] 22–043

WILSON, TOOHEY AND GAUDRON J.J.: The question of prejudice resulting from unavailability of evidence necessarily involves some degree of speculation, but it is not a question of pure speculation. The issue is not whether evidence may have been lost but whether evidence which may have cast a different complexion on the matter has been lost. Thus in *Crago v. McIntyre* a defence of laches was successful because a different conclusion may have been reached "if all of the witnesses, including the doctors, who could have given first-hand accounts of the plaintiff's behaviour, and of other relevant circumstances, had been available to be called as witnesses". 22–044

In the present case the witnesses whose evidence was said to have been lost were the appellant's parents-in-law, Dr. Stone and Mrs. Nickerson. The loss of the evidence of the appellant's parents-in-law occurred prior to December 1977, the time at which the respondents assert that the appellant knew that his interest was impugned and whose delay thereafter is said to constitute laches. The loss of this evidence is therefore not a matter to be taken into account. 22–045

The evidence of Dr. Stone falls for consideration by reference to other factors. Assuming that after 1977 Dr. Stone was in a position to give evidence, testimony contrary to the creation of a trust pursuant to agreement would be contrary to two letters written by him in January 1968 corroborating the existence of the trust as claimed by the appellant. At this distance the probative value of any such hypothetical evidence must be adjudged so slight that its loss does not amount to prejudice. 22–046

Dr. Stone might also have been able to give evidence of subsequent matters amounting to an answer to the appellant's claim, as for example, release, abandonment or discharge of the trust or conduct inducing an assumption by Dr. Stone as to such matters and amounting to an estoppel. It was said that Mrs. Nickerson might also have been able to give such evidence. If the evidence were such as to make an inference as to any of these matters at all likely then the evidence of Dr. Stone and Mrs Nickerson might well have cast a difference complexion on the appellant's claimed entitlement to a half interest in "Cockatoo". But the evidence gives rise to no such likelihood. On the view least favourable to the appellant the most that can be said was that he was content to stand by and let matters take their course in the expectation that they could be resolved within the family after the death of Dr. Stone. This falls far short of release, abandonment, discharge or of conduct in inducing an assumption as to such matters by Dr. Stone. The question of the loss of evidence as to such matters is entirely suppositional and is thus not a matter which can properly be said to amount to prejudice of the character which might defeat the appellant's claim. 22–047

. . .

DEANE J. (IN DISSENT): Whether, at the end of the day, the defence of laches should prevail in the present case "is necessarily a matter of degree and must depend on the circumstances of the given case" (cf. Haas Timber & Trading Co. Pty. Ltd. v. Wade and see, e.g., C. M. Auto Sales Pty. Ltd. v. Budget Rent A Car System). As has been seen, those circumstances include: the nature of the claim as a claim to the fruits of what was (to the extent it exceeded a proportionate share) in substance an alleged gift made by Dr. Stone; the long period of standing by in the face of an unequivocal and undisputed assertion by Dr. Stone, who was by then an old man, that he remained sole owner of the leasehold selection; the deliberate and calculated character of the standing by until Dr. Stone was dead; and, the grave unfairness

> and injustice of the consequences if Mr. Orr is permitted to enforce his claim at this late stage. On balance, and notwithstanding any hardship to Mr. Orr, the circumstances of the case compel the conclusion that Mr. Orr's conduct in standing by for some eight years constituted "gross laches" which precludes the grant of the equitable relief which he seeks. That does not, however, mean that the order of the learned trial judge that the action should be dismissed should be allowed to stand. As has been said, it is conceded that the effect of the conclusion that the Act did not preclude or render unenforceable any trust of a share of "Cockatoo" is that Mr. Orr was beneficially entitled to a 30/156 share of "Cockatoo" and it has not been argued that laches precludes the grant of declaratory relief in relation to that beneficial interest. Subject to the appropriate allowance being made for the cost of the improvements that the learned trial judge found had been made by Dr. Stone, it should be declared that Mr. Orr is beneficially entitled to that share.

22-049 Laches may also be established where the delay has ameliorated a speculative risk of the transaction that is the subject of the claim, to the prejudice of C, in allowing D to "lie by and remain passive while [C] is incurring all the risk of loss, and only to claim to participate after the affairs have turned out to be prosperous".[65]

22-050 Laches may also be established in respect of delay causing prejudice to third parties, for example, where a third party has since acquired an interest in the property subject to the dispute.[66] Another example is *Re Cachar Co*,[67] where laches barred C's claim for rescission of an allotment of shares. Cairns LJ writes:[68]

> it would, in my opinion, be contrary to the first principles of justice to hold that Mr. Lawrence was at liberty to remain wholly passive, content to trust to what was stated in the prospectus, and, while he knew that an authority to register his name and hold him out as a shareholder had been given and probably acted on, keeping himself in a position to ratify all that had been done if the company turned out prosperous, but for the first time to inquire, and, if possible, repudiate, should a financial panic come, or the speculation turn out unsuccessful. Admitting that there existed no memorandum of association which Mr. Lawrence could have seen when he applied for shares, he was, in my opinion, entitled to a reasonable time after the registration of the memorandum to acquaint himself with, and, if so disposed, to object to its contents.

22-051 The prejudice in that case was to third party subscribers, who would otherwise be going on taking shares on the faith of the claimant being on the register and holding himself out as a shareholder, while they assumed the risk of applying their own paid-up capital.

22-052 In *Fisher v Brooker*,[69] Lord Neuberger suggested that "some sort of detrimental reliance is usually an essential ingredient of laches". Lord Neuberger's statement is best understood as a reiteration of the point that mere delay alone is insufficient to make out laches. Laches is not confined to where D can show detrimental reliance on her part or that of another on C's delay, and as discussed above, there are a range of facts showing disadvantage or prejudice sufficient to bar C's claim on the basis of laches, including where no action has been taken by D or third party in reliance on C's delay.

22-053 Laches is sometimes considered alongside estoppel, and the interconnection and distinction between the doctrines is explained in *Lester v Woodgate*.

---

65 *Clements v Hall* (1858) 2 De. Gex. & Jones 173; 44 E.R. 954 at 959.

66 As in *Hourigan v Trustees, Executors & Agency Co Ltd* (1934) 51 C.L.R. 619 at 651. Another example is when the possibility of a third party having an equitable proprietary interest in the same property the subject of C's claim for a proprietary estoppel, meant that equitable compensation secured by a lien, rather than a constructive trust, was awarded in *Sidhu v Van Dyke* (2014) 251 C.L.R. 505; *Giumelli v Giumelli* (1999) 196 C.L.R. 101, referring to *Soulos v Korkontzilas* [1997] 2 S.C.R. 217 at 236, 241, 243 (McLachlin J). See also T. Oakley, "The Precise Effect of the Imposition of a Constructive Trust" in Goldstein (ed.), *Equity and Contemporary Legal Developments* (1992), pp.427, 451–56.

67 *In Re Cachar Co* (1867) L.R. 2 Ch. App. 412.

68 *In Re Cachar Co* at 425.

69 *Fisher v Brooker* [2009] UKHL 41 at [64].

Lester v Woodgate

Court of Appeal, [2010] EWCA Civ 199 at [20]–[21]

PATTEN L.J.: Although the Recorder mentions laches and estoppel together in his judgment, they are separate defences with different and distinct consequences. Laches is a general equitable defence which bars the grant of equitable relief when the claimant has been guilty of undue delay in asserting his rights . . . 22–054

The word laches is also sometimes used to denote the type of passive conduct which can amount to acquiescence and so found an estoppel when it can be shown that the party standing by has induced the would-be defendant to believe that his rights will not be enforced and that other party has, as a consequence, acted in a way which would make the subsequent enforcement of those rights unconscionable. 22–055

C. Scope of Application

Laches cannot be raised against a claim at law and can only bar a claim to equitable relief. Thus in *Lester v Woodgate*, Patten L.J. wrote that:[70] 22–056

But where the conduct relied on consists of no more than undue delay, it operates only to bar the grant of equitable relief such as an injunction. It does not extinguish the claimants' legal right or bar its enforcement by, for example, the award of common law damages. For the same reason, mere delay or inactivity by a landowner in respect of the enforcement of his legal rights will not necessarily prevent a successor in title from obtaining even equitable relief for their infringement. The conduct of earlier owners of the property since the date of the trespass or nuisance will be one of a number of relevant factors for the court to consider in determining whether it is appropriate to grant equitable relief to the successor in title having regard to the circumstances relevant to both parties at the time when the court is called upon to make its decision. 22–056

Laches may bar claims for rescission,[71] rectification,[72] injunctions[73] and specific performance.[74] As discussed above,[75] laches (and other equitable discretionary factors and bars to relief) can apply to a trust beneficiary's claims against a trustee or third party. 22–058

However, the application of laches to these and other equitable claims is subject to any statutory period of imitation, that applies to C's claim. In *Re Pauling's Settlement Trusts*,[76] laches was excluded in its application to a trust beneficiary's claim against an express trustee for breach of trust on the basis that there was an express statutory provision providing a period of limitation for C's claim. 22–059

Whether laches is excluded by application of a statutory period of limitation will depend on the construction of various statutory provisions.[77] If a statutory period of limitation applies (including by analogy), then laches cannot operate to bar C's claim before expiry of the statutory period. If no limitation period applies directly or by analogy, then D can raise laches as a bar to C's claim. 22–060

Chadwick LJ in *In Re Loftus (deceased)*[78] found that for claims to which s.21(1)(b) of the Limitation Act 1980 applied to *exclude* any statutory period of limitation, laches and acquiescence may still apply to bar a beneficiary's claim. 22–061

---

70 *Lester v Woodgate* [2010] EWCA Civ 199; [2010] 2 P. & C.R. 21 at [21]–[22], citing *Nwakobi v Nzekwu* [1964] 1 W.L.R. 1019 at 1024.

71 *Lindsay Petroleum Co v Hurd*.

72 *Beale v Kyte* [1907] 1 Ch. 564 at 566–67.

73 *GW Railway v Oxford Railway* (1853) 3 De. G.M. & G. 341

74 *Mills v Haywood* (1877) 6 Ch. D. 196; *MEPC Ltd v Christian-Edwards* [1978] Ch. 281, affirmed on more general grounds: [1981] A.C. 205.

75 See paras 22–031 to 22–032.

76 *Re Pauling's Settlement Trusts* [1962] 1 W.L.R. 86 at 115, affirmed on appeal [1964] Ch. 303 at 353.

77 The application of statutory period of limitation to a beneficiary's claim against a trustee is discussed at paras 13-167ff.

78 *Re Loftus (deceased)* [2006] EWCA Civ 1124; [2007] 1 W.L.R. 591 at [33]–[41].

22-062 Further, s.36(2) of the Limitation Act has been held to preserve the equitable jurisdiction to refuse relief on grounds of laches:

> s.36 Equitable jurisdictions and remedies.
>
> . . .
>
> (2) Nothing in this Act shall affect any equitable jurisdiction to refuse relief on the ground of acquiescence or otherwise.

22-063 Chadwick LJ in *In Re Loftus (deceased)* writes that "acquiescence or otherwise" should be taken to encompass laches,[79] quoting with approval Mummery LJ in *Patel v Shah*:[80]

> No period of limitation is prescribed by the Limitation Act 1980 for an action by a beneficiary under a trust to recover from the trustee trust property or the proceeds of trust property in the possession of the trustee, or previously received by the trustee and converted to his own use (section 21(1)(b)). It was accepted that section 36 of the 1980 Act preserved equitable jurisdiction to refuse relief on the grounds of acquiescence or otherwise and that that would include laches.

3. Acquiescence

A. Introduction

22-064 Acquiescence is an equitable discretionary bar that denies relief to C when C has, via her inaction, accepted or acquiesced to D's conduct that is the subject of C's complaint. Cottenham LC in *Duke of Leeds v Earl of Amherst*, described acquiescence as follows:[81]

> If a party, having a right, stands by and sees another dealing with the property in a manner inconsistent with that right, and makes no objection while the act is in progress, he cannot afterwards complain. That is the proper sense of the word acquiescence.

22-065 Acquiescence has similarly been described in the High Court of Australia by Deane J in *Orr v Ford*:[82]

> acquiescence is used . . . to refer to conduct by a person, with knowledge of the acts of another person, which encourages that other person reasonably to believe that his acts are accepted (if past) or not opposed (if contemporaneous). . . . acquiescence is . . . calculated (i.e. deliberate and informed) inaction or standing by which encouraged another reasonably to believe that his assertion of rights and consequent actions were accepted or not opposed.

22-066 Acquiescence is a term used in different ways, and which has made it hard for courts to pin down an exact formulation for when C's claim for equitable relief against D will be barred on account of acquiescence. Some of the different meanings of acquiescence are set out by Deane J in *Orr v Ford*,[83] excerpted above, and later summarised by Heydon and Crennan JJ in *Byrnes v Kendle*,[84] after observing the "unclarity of the applicable laws", in the following excerpt.

---

79 *Re Loftus* at [33].
80 *Patel v Shah* [2005] EWCA Civ 157 at [22].
81 *Duke of Leeds v Earl of Amherst* (1846) 2 Phillips 117 at 123.
82 *Orr v Ford* at 338, 340.
83 *Orr v Ford* at 337–341.
84 *Byrnes v Kendle* (2011) 243 C.L.R. 253 at [132].

Byrnes v Kendle

High Court of Australia, (2011) 243 C.L.R. 253 at [132]–[140]

HEYDON and CRENNAN J.J.: Was there contemporaneous or subsequent conduct by the second appellant disentitling the appellants from relief? 22–067

In *Orr v Ford* Deane J. set out various meanings of "acquiescence". It is convenient to consider the circumstances of this case in the light of his analysis. 22–068

Deane J. said: 22–069

> "Strictly used, acquiescence indicates the contemporaneous and informed ("knowing") acceptance or standing by which is treated by equity as "assent" (i.e. consent) to what would otherwise be an infringement of rights . . ."

There was no evidence to support contemporaneous consent by the second appellant. 22–070

Deane J. then said that the word "acquiescence" is commonly used also to refer "to a representation by silence of a type which may found an estoppel by conduct". The respondent did not attempt to establish the ingredients of an estoppel by silence. 22–071

Deane J. further said that "acquiescence" is commonly used to refer to "acceptance of a past wrongful act in circumstances which give rise to an active waiver of rights or a release of liability". The conditions for "active waiver" were not established. Nor were the conditions for a "release of liability". Lord Westbury L.C. described those conditions thus in *Farrant v Blanchford*: 22–072

> "Where a breach of trust has been committed, from which a trustee alleges that he has been released, it is incumbent on him to shew that such release was given by the cestui que trust deliberately and advisedly, with full knowledge of all the circumstances, and of his own rights and claims against the trustee; for it is impossible to allow a trustee who has incurred personal liability to deal with his cestui que trust for his own discharge upon any other ground than the obligation of giving the fullest information, and of shewing that the cestui que trust was well acquainted with his own legal rights and claims, and gave the release freely and without pressure or undue influence of any description."

The evidence does not establish that the second appellant was acting deliberately and advisedly or with knowledge of her own rights and claims against the respondent. 22–073

Deane J. then said that "acquiescence" is commonly used to refer to "an election to abandon or not enforce rights". The evidence does not support election. 22–074

Deane J. then referred to two usages of the word "acquiescence" which he found unhelpful: 22–075

> "First, it is sometimes used as an indefinite overlapping component of a catchall phrase also incorporating 'laches' or 'gross laches' and/or 'delay'. . . . Secondly, acquiescence is used as a true alternative to 'laches' to divide the field between inaction in the face of 'the assertion of adverse rights' ('acquiescence') and inaction 'in prosecuting rights' ('laches')."

He then gave a third meaning: 22–076

> "Thirdly, and more commonly, acquiescence is used, in a context where laches is used to indicate either mere delay or delay with knowledge, to refer to conduct by a person, with knowledge of the acts of another person, which encourages that other person reasonably to believe that his acts are accepted (if past) or not opposed (if contemporaneous)."

There is no evidence of that encouragement, and the respondent did not give evidence that he had that belief. 22–077

22–078 Finally, Deane J. said that the expression "gross laches" referred to:

> "circumstances where inaction or standing by (with knowledge) by a plaintiff over a substantial period of time assumes an aggravated character in that it will, if the plaintiff is granted the relief which he seeks, give rise to serious and unfair prejudice to the defendant or a third party."

22–079 The grant of relief to the plaintiff appellants here will cause no prejudice to third parties and no prejudice (beyond the justice of the case) to the respondent.

22–080 In the same case, French CJ gave another description of acquiescence:[85]

> Acquiescence as a defence to a claim for equitable relief is used in at least two different senses:
>
> A person who is aware that an act is about to be done to his or her prejudice takes no step to object to it.
>
> A person being aware of a violation his or her rights which has occurred fails to take timely proceedings to obtain equitable relief. This is acquiescence after the event which founds the defence of laches.

22–081 In the same case, Gummow and Hayne JJ explained acquiescence as:[86]

> . . . requiring calculated (that is, deliberate and informed) inaction by [C] or standing by, which encouraged [D] reasonably to believe that [D's] omissions were accepted or not opposed by [C].

22–082 In *Byrnes v Kendle*, acquiescence was raised by a trustee in defence to a beneficiary's claim for an account and consequent orders requiring the trustee to pay a sum of money for the trustee's failure to render the trust property profitable, and to collect rent. The High Court of Australia unanimously overturned the decisions at trial and on appeal, that acquiescence barred the beneficiary's claim. The relevant facts were that the beneficiary did not press the trustee to insist upon payment of rent from the tenant of the trust property "[f]or the sake of matrimonial harmony".[87] The trustee could not have reasonably formed a belief that the beneficiary's inaction amounted to assent to the trustee's breach of his duties as such.

22–083 DA lack of a settled view as to the meaning of acquiescence has made it more difficult to be sure about the elements, and has also meant that it is hard to be sure about the distinction between acquiescence as a discretionary bar to relief and other rules that may operate to bar C's claim against D.

B. C's Inaction with Knowledge Inducing D's Belief

22–084 While there is some ambiguity as to the meaning of acquiescence, it is relatively clear that for acquiescence to operate as a discretionary bar to C's claim for equitable relief, at a minimum, D must show that: (i) C had knowledge of the relevant facts of D's conduct; (ii) C failed to assert her entitlement to equitable relief or complain of D's conduct; (iii) C's inaction with knowledge encouraged D to believe that D's conduct is accepted or not opposed by C; and, (iv) that D's belief is reasonably formed.

22–085 C must have knowledge for her inaction to amount to acquiescence. In the case of *In Re Pauling's Settlement Trusts*, an express trustee's reliance on acquiescence against a trust beneficiary's claim for an account failed on the basis the trust beneficiary did not have knowledge of the relevant facts.

---

85 *Byrnes v Kendle* at [27].

86 *Byrnes v Kendle* at [79].

87 *Byrnes v Kendle* at [24], [29], [75].

In Re Pauling's Settlement Trusts

Court of Appeal, [1964] Ch. 303 at 353

UPJOHN L.J.: As to acquiescence, we think that this must be looked at rather broadly. We were, of course, pressed with the leading case of *Allcard v. Skinner*, but in that case the plaintiff had had her rights fully explained to her by a brother, who was a barrister, and by her solicitor, and yet she took no steps until five or six years later. Even that gave rise to a difference of opinion in a very strong Court of Appeal. In this case it would be wrong, we feel, to place any disability upon the beneficiaries because it so happened that George was a member of the bar, and had been in well-known chambers. He had not been in Chancery chambers where it may be said that these things are better understood; but the real truth of the matter is that a party cannot be held to have acquiesced unless he knew, or ought to have known, what his rights were. On the facts of this case we cannot criticise any of the plaintiffs for failing to appreciate their rights until another junior counsel, whom they consulted on a far-fetched and futile scheme of George's for avoiding estate duty on his mother's death, advised that the advances might be improper That was in 1954, and thereupon the family, headed, of course, by George, took immediate steps to explore this matter. This is a most complicated action, and many matters had to be explored before an action for breach of trust could properly be mounted. The writ was issued in 1958, and we do not think it right to hold that the plaintiffs were debarred by acquiescence from bringing an action which otherwise, to the extent we have indicated, is justified. 22–086

While it is clear that acquiescence cannot be raised where C did not have knowledge, a more difficult issue for courts is the type of knowledge required, and in particular, whether acquiescence requires C to have knowledge of the facts and to have appreciated the legal significance of those facts.[88] This issue and the differing cases are summarised in the following excerpt from the decision of the Court of Appeal in *Holder v Holder*. This case concerned a claim by a plaintiff beneficiary for rescission to set aside a sale of trust property by executors holding as trustees under a testamentary trust to one of the executors, referred to as Victor in the excerpt below, in circumstances where Victor and the other executors thought Victor had renounced his role as executor, but in fact this had not occurred. 22–087

Holder v Holder

Court of Appeal, [1968] Ch. 353 at 393–395, 398–401, 403–406

[After finding that Victor was not disentitled from purchasing the trust property, HARMAN L.J. went onto to consider the alternative issue of whether the beneficiary's claim for rescission would have been barred by the beneficiary's consent or acquiescence.] There arises a further defence, namely, that of acquiescence, and this requires some further recital of the facts. 22–088

Completion of the sale was due for Michaelmas, 1961, but by that time the third defendant was not in a position to find the purchase money. The proving executors served a notice to complete in October, 1961, and, the validity of this notice being questioned, served a further notice in December. In February 1962 the plaintiff's solicitor pressed the defendants to forfeit the third defendant's deposit and this was a right given by the contract of sale and is an affirmation of it. Further, in May, 1962, the plaintiff issued a writ for a common decree of administration against the proving executors, seeking thus to press them to complete the contract and wind up the estate. The contract was in fact completed in June, 1962, and in the same month £2,000 on account was paid to and accepted by the plaintiff as his share and he thereupon took no further steps with his action. In order to complete, the third defendant borrowed £21,000 from the Agricultural Mortgage Corporation with interest at 7 1/2 per cent. He also borrowed £3,000 from his mother with interest at 6 1/2 per cent, and a like sum from his sister at a similar rate of interest. In November 1962 the third defendant demanded possession of Glebe Farm house from the plaintiff, who at that time changed his solicitors, and it was suggested by the new solicitors in February 1963 that the third defendant was disqualified from bidding at the auction. This was the first time any such suggestion had been made by anyone. The writ was not issued till a year later. 22–089

[88] *Twigg v Twigg* [2022] NSWCA 68 at [88]–[89].

22–090 I have found this question a difficult one. The plaintiff knew all the relevant facts but he did not realise nor was he advised till 1963 that the legal result might be that he could object to his brother's purchase because he continued to be a personal representative. There is no doubt strong authority for the proposition that a man is not bound by acquiescences until he knows his legal rights. In *Cockerell v Cholmeley*[89] Sir John Leach M.R. said this:

> It has been argued that the defendant, being aware of the facts of the case in the lifetime of Sir Henry Englefield has, by his silence, and by being a party to the application to Parliament, confirmed the title of the plaintiffs. In equity it is considered, as good sense requires it should be, that no man can be held by any act of his to confirm a title, unless he was fully aware at the time, not only of the fact upon which the effect of title depends, but of the consequence in point of law; and there is no proof that the defendant, at the time of the acts referred to, was aware of the law on the subject . . .

22–091 There, however, the judge was asked to set aside a legal right. In *Willmott v. Barber*[90] Fry J. said:

> A man is not to be deprived of his legal rights unless he has acted in such a way as would make it fraudulent for him to set up those rights. What, then, are the elements or requisites necessary to constitute fraud of that description? In the first place the plaintiff must have made a mistake as to his legal rights. Secondly, the plaintiff must have expended some money or must have done some act (not necessarily upon the defendant's land) on the faith of his mistaken belief. Thirdly, the defendant. the possessor of the legal right, must know of the existence of his own right which is inconsistent with the right claimed by the plaintiff. If he does not know of it he is in the same position as the plaintiff, and the doctrine of acquiescence is founded upon conduct with a knowledge of your legal rights.

22–092 On the other hand, in *Stafford v Stafford*[91] we find Knight Bruce L.J. saying; "Generally, when the facts are known from which a right arises, the right is presumed to be known . . ."

22–093 Like the judge, I should desire to follow the conclusion of Wilberforce J. who reviewed the authorities in *In re Pauling's Settlement Trusts*[92] and this passage was mentioned without dissent in the same case in the Court of Appeal:[93]

> "The result" (says the judge) "of these authorities appears to me to be that the court has to consider all the circumstances in which the concurrence of the cestui que trust was given with a view to seeing whether it is fair and equitable that having given his concurrence, he should afterwards turn round and sue the trustees: that, subject to this, it is not necessary that he should know that what he is concurring in is a breach of trust, provided that he fully understands what he is concurring in, and that it is not necessary that he should himself have directly benefited by the breach of trust."

22–094 There is therefore no hard and fast rule that ignorance of a legal right is a bar, but the whole of the circumstances must be looked at to see whether it is just that the complaining beneficiary should succeed against the trustee.[94]

22–095 On the whole I am of opinion that in the circumstances of this case it would not be right to allow the plaintiff to assert his right (assuming he has one) because with full knowledge of the facts he affirmed the sale. He has had £2,000 as a result. He has caused the third defendant to embark on liabilities which he cannot recoup. There can in fact be no restitutio in integrum, which is a necessary element in rescission.

22–096 The plaintiff is asserting an equitable and not a legal remedy. He has by his conduct disentitled himself to it. It is extremely doubtful whether the order if worked out would benefit anyone. I think we should not assent to it, on general equitable principles.

22–097 DANCKWERTS L.J. (after agreeing with HARMAN L.J. that there was no reason why the trustee could not bid at the auction of trust property went on to consider whether the plaintiff's claim for rescission

---

89 (1830) 1 Russ. & M. 418 at 425.

90 (1880) 15 Ch.D. 96 at 105.

91 (1857) 1 De G. & J. 193 at 202.

92 [1961] 3 All E.R. 713 at 730.

93 [1964] Ch. 303.

94 Endorsed in *Re Freeston's Charity* [1979] 1 All E.R. 51 at 62. The third proposition of Fry J. in *Wilmott v Barber* (1880) 15 Ch.D. 96 at 105 has also been rejected in *Taylor Fashions Ltd v Liverpool Victoria Trustees Co. Ltd* [1981] 1 All E.R. 897 at 915–918 and *Habib Bank Ltd v Habib Bank AG Zurich* [1981] 2 All E.R. 650 at 666, 668.

would be barred by acquiescence) . . . But the plaintiff's right of action may be barred by acquiescence or confirmation. The cases on this subject are rather confusing in regard to the knowledge that a beneficiary must have in order to prevent his knowledge barring him in a subsequent attempt to set the transaction aside, and how far the beneficiary must know the legal result of the facts of which he was aware.

The matter of the purchase of the farms was discussed fully and at length at the family meetings and I find it impossible to believe that [the plaintiff] did not know the facts. No one seems to have objected to Victor buying on the ground that he was an executor. [The plaintiff] treated him as not being an executor when he brought his action against the proving executors alone. He accepted the benefits of the sale when he received £2,000. None of the four solicitors involved in the discussions which took place questioned Victor's right to purchase. [The plaintiff] had his own solicitor at his elbow, and that solicitor should have advised him on the legal position. Instead he apparently said nothing, stood by with [the plaintiff], and allowed the sale to be completed by conveyance of the farms to Victor by the proving executors and the payment of the purchase price by Victor, who has altered his position by mortgaging the farms and carrying on the farming business on the farms. **22–098**

As to the cases, *Cockerell v Cholmeley*[95] and *Stafford v Stafford*[96] show different views on the point whether appreciation of the situation in law is necessary. **22–099**

. . . Like Harman L.J., I prefer the view expressed by Wilberforce J. in *In re Pauling's Settlement Trusts*[97] that all the circumstances must be considered and there is no hard and fast rule. **22–100**

In my opinion [the plaintiff] has acted in such a way in the present case in regard to Victor's purchase of the farms that he must be taken to have acquiesced in or to have confirmed the sale and cannot now claim to have the sale set aside. **22–101**

There is authority for the general rule that, in the absence of fraud, a transaction which has been completed will not be set aside . . . that the rule does not apply where there is a fiduciary position. But in that case there seems to have been fraud. **22–102**

Whether that be the case or not, on general equitable grounds I am of opinion that in the present case the transaction should not be set aside. The transaction is not void. It is one which is voidable and is liable to be set aside if a proper case is made out for that relief. **22–103**

As has been pointed out by Harman L.J., the plaintiff is claiming equitable relief against Victor, who is the legal owner of the farms and is in occupation of them. He has paid what was a good price at the time of the sale. Much hardship would be caused to Victor if the transaction was set aside now. He purchased the farms in good faith, believing that there was no bar to that course. The plaintiff stood by and benefited along with the other beneficiaries by the sale. He had legal advice to hand and made no attempt to stop the completion of the sale. Now, after completion, he is attacking the sale for purely selfish reasons. He cares nothing for the effect that setting aside will have upon the estate of the testator and the other beneficiaries under the will. The costs of the sale (some £875) will all be thrown away. **22–104**

The order made by the judge will cause some unfairness to Victor and is so complicated that it will be difficult and expensive to work out. In fact, it is not really possible in the circumstances to carry out restitution, which is a condition of the equitable relief which the plaintiff seeks. The plaintiff's position would have been expressed in former times by the words "he has no equity." **22–105**

For all these reasons, in my opinion the court should not grant the equitable relief of setting aside or rescission in the present case. **22–106**

SACHS L.J. (after considering the issue of whether executors were disabled from selling trust property to Victor, went on to consider whether the plaintiff's claim for rescission would be barred by acquiescence, and held that acquiescence would apply to bar the claim, agreeing with HARMAN and DANCKWERTS L.JJ.) . . . Next I turn to . . . whether the plaintiff acquiesced in Victor's purchase of the property . . . **22–107**

The plea of acquiescence in this particular case seems to me to have a close resemblance to one of estoppel: and it is to be noted that in *Halsbury's Laws of England*,[98] it is stated: **22–108**

> Acquiescence operates by way of estoppel. It is quiescence in such circumstances that assent may reasonably be inferred, and is an instance of estoppel by words or conduct.

---

95 (1830) 1 Russ. & M. 418 at 425.

96 (1857) 1 De G. & J. 193 at 202.

97 [1961] 3 All E.R. 713 at 730.

98 3rd edn (Butterworths, 1956), vol. 14, pp.638.

22–109 Whilst recognising that these two pleas are not necessarily coterminous it yet seems to me that in the present case if the facts are sufficient to create an estoppel then a fortiori, a plea of acquiescence must succeed.

22–110 . . . [the plaintiff's] conduct falls to be assessed on the basis of that knowledge unless he can successfully provide himself with an escape route upon asserting that he was not aware of the legal effect of matters within his knowledge. With that last point I will deal separately later.

22–111 Next there falls to be considered his conduct in relation to the sale to Victor. In the first place it is to be noted that he himself by his solicitor suggested that he and Victor should join in purchasing the property: a direct encouragement of the view that Victor could purchase property from the estate. Thereafter during the preparations for an auction the plaintiff did nothing which could in any way be construed as an objection to Victor bidding and indeed it is obvious that all concerned assumed that he would. At the auction itself the plaintiff by his solicitor raised an objection to the plaintiff being regarded as a licensee (as opposed to a tenant) of part of the property and perhaps also objected to Victor being regarded as anything but a licensee: but not a word was raised against Victor bidding at the auction where such bidding would almost certainly enure to the benefit of the estate.

22–112 Thus by his conduct he expressly and impliedly represented that Victor could properly do the very act to which he now objects — purchase the property.

22–113 Moreover after the auction the plaintiff pressed for the rigour of the contract to be enforced and for Victor's deposit to be forfeited: indeed he went so far as to issue a writ against the executors, the ostensible object of which was to compel them to enforce the contract in the above way. Then when the contract had been completed he duly received a cheque for £2,000 from the proceeds and must have disposed of most of those proceeds in a way which has rendered him eligible for legal aid.

22–114 It was in these circumstances that Victor made his bid at the auction, completed the sale having paid full value for the property, and involved himself in all the expenses such operations entail. Later — still in the absence of any indication from the plaintiff that he desired to upset the sale — he expended money on improving the property.

22–115 To my mind (subject to the escape route point) this is a case of the plaintiff being estopped from now saying that Victor should never have bid or completed. Incidentally it is also a case of approbation by subsequent conduct from which the plaintiff cannot now resile. A fortiori it is a case of acquiescence.

22–116 Next comes the point whether ignorance of the effect in law of facts which constitute an intermeddling can avail the plaintiff. This is a case where the plaintiff and the defendant were on a completely equal footing. Both were laymen whose occupation had been on the land, and each was at all material times armed with professional advice in the shape of a solicitor. . . .

22–117 Once one comes to the conclusion that the plaintiff and Victor were indeed upon an equal footing, each with professional advisers, there seems to me to be no reason why one should not apply the normal rule that the effect in law of a person's conduct should be assessed by having regard to his actions in a common-sense way. In all common sense the plaintiff did in fact assent to Victor bidding and did so with knowledge of the relevant facts. To provide him with an escape route of the type propounded by [counsel for the plaintiff] would seem to work injustice and to open the way in a great many cases to suggesting that a man with appropriate professional advisers should be allowed to say that he was personally ignorant of the law when he wished to reopen a concluded transaction. It would also open the way in a great many cases where the law might be doubtful for a man to come in at almost any stage after a transaction had been completed and say: "Well, the law is now shown to be different from what I thought at the time and I object to what has happened although I had full opportunity to object earlier." Accordingly I reject the "escape route" submissions . . .

22–118 It may well be that ignorance of the legal effect of facts may in certain circumstances afford an answer to a plea of acquiescence where conduct does not amount to an estoppel. But I know of no authority for such a proposition in relation to estoppel: indeed having regard to the judgments in *Holt v Markham*[99] (a case in which both parties were ignorant of the legal effect of certain regulations) I doubt if there is any warrant for it in estoppel in pais.

99 [1923] 1 K.B. 504.

> In so far as there may be cases of acquiescence to which the normal rules of estoppel do not apply I too agree that the judgment of Wilberforce J. in *Pauling's case*[100] provides the correct guide and that upon that basis too the plaintiff would fail. 22–119

In addition to C's knowledge, D must also show that C's inaction or standing by, such as C's failure to prosecute her claim or assert her complaint as to D's conduct, has encouraged a belief in D that C assents to, or has confirmed, D's conduct *and* that D's belief is reasonable.[101] This element was made out in *Holder v Holder* for reasons discussed in the excerpt above. In contrast, D failed to make out the last objective element in *Byrnes v Kendle*[102] for reasons set out above in the excerpt from this case. In short, C's failure to commence proceedings against the trustee, and failure to agitate her concerns for the "sake of matrimonial harmony" could not reasonably induce a belief in D that C assented or confirmed D's conduct in failing to render the trust property profitable and collect rent. 22–120

C. Distinguishing Acquiescence as a Discretionary Bar to Relief from the Acquiescence Based Strand of Estoppel

There are some significant overlaps between acquiescence as a discretionary bar to relief and some forms of estoppel, particularly when a promissory estoppel (see Chapter 2) or proprietary estoppel (see Chapter 3) is raised on the basis of one party's silence or inaction. The overlap between estoppel and acquiescence is a theme running through some of the case excerpts above, although the cases and commentaries have conceived of the nature of the overlap in different ways and this can make it hard to be certain whether acquiescence is an independent discretionary bar to relief, or is simply an application of estoppel to prevent one party asserting a legal entitlement in the specific instance where that legal entitlement is generated by equitable rules. This question matters for the sake of being clear about what rules apply and why and it also has implications for an appellate court's jurisdiction and the deference typically given to discretionary decisions made at first instance, as well as for our understanding of equity's self-reflexive nature and whether the assertion of legal entitlements will be controlled by different standards depending on whether those legal entitlements are generated by legal or equitable rules. 22–121

Acquiescence and estoppel are sometimes considered to be the same, or acquiescence is considered part of, and subsumed by, estoppel. For example, Lord Neuberger in *Fisher v Brooker*,[103] "was not convinced" that "acquiescence adds anything to estoppel and laches." In the excerpt above from *Holder v Holder*,[104] Sachs LJ notes that the authors of *Halsbury's Laws of England* regard acquiescence as being entirely subsumed by, and an instance of estoppel. 22–122

In the same excerpt from *Holder v Holder*, Sachs LJ, however, expressed a different view, noting that the "two pleas are not necessarily coterminous", yet, acknowledged they have significant overlap because "if the facts are sufficient to create an estoppel then a fortiori, a plea of acquiescence must succeed".[105] Sachs LJ also later contemplated "there may be cases of acquiescence to which the normal rules of estoppel do not apply".[106] 22–123

---

[100] [1961] 3 All E.R. 713 at 730.
[101] *Byrnes v Kendle* (2011) 243 C.L.R. 253 at [30] (French CJ), [79] (Gummow and Hayne JJ), [138] (Heydon and Crennan JJ).
[102] *Byrnes v Kendle*.
[103] *Fisher v Brooker* [2009] UKHL 41 at [62].
[104] *Holder v Holder*; see para.22–108.
[105] *Holder v Holder*; see para.22–109.
[106] *Holder v Holder*; see para.22–119.

22–124 Part of the difficulty in distinguishing between acquiescence and estoppel is that estoppel itself is not a uniform body of rules, and within which, there are various areas of uncertainty. Nonetheless, it is possible to make some distinctions between estoppels when they arise in response to one party's silence or inaction, and acquiescence as a discretionary bar to relief. One is that pointed out by Sachs LJ which is the nature and type of C's knowledge; in particular, that C's ignorance of the legal effect of facts would preclude acquiescence being raised against C, albeit an estoppel might still be raised against C. If we recall the discussion of estoppels in Chapters 2 and 3, it is possible to observe that there are some further distinctions between acquiescence as a discretionary bar to equitable relief and estoppels.

22–125 First, acquiescence as a discretionary bar to relief applies only to bar C's assertion of an equitable entitlement (which may itself be one founded on an equitable estoppel) and has a different scope of application to acquiescence-based promissory and proprietary estoppels which may operate in relation to legal or equitable entitlements.

22–126 Second, the reliance element of acquiescence as a discretionary bar to relief has a different content to the reliance element of acquiescence-based estoppels. For D to raise acquiescence as a discretionary bar to C's claim for equitable relief, D must show that D relied on C's (in)action coupled with C's knowledge in forming the (reasonably held) belief that C acquiesced or assented to D's action in enjoying D's legal entitlement in some way. To raise a promissory or proprietary estoppel against C, D would need to show that D relied on C's (in)action in forming the (reasonably held) belief that C would not enforce C's legal entitlement against D in some way.

22–127 *Third* relates to detriment. For D to raise acquiescence as a discretionary bar to relief, it is only necessary for D to show that D has reasonably formed a belief that C accepts or consents to D's conduct in reliance on C's inaction. D does not also need to show that they have taken some (in)action on the faith of that belief, such that they will suffer detriment if C is granted equitable relief. Whereas for D to raise an acquiescence-based promissory or proprietary estoppel against C, D must show that D has taken some (in)action on the faith of D's belief induced by C's (in)action, and such that D will suffer detriment if the estoppel is not upheld.[107]

D. Distinguishing Acquiescence as a Discretionary Bar to Relief from the Defence of Consent

22–128 The differences between estoppel, consent (discussed in Chapter 13) and acquiescence is discussed in the separate judgements delivered in *Byrnes v Kendle*.[108]

Byrnes v Kendle

High Court of Australia, (2011) 243 C.L.R. 253 at [25]–[27], [77]–[80]

22–129 [FRENCH C.J. explains that concurrence (also referred to as consent) and acquiescence] . . . are not congruent. Consent, of course, may be expressed in a number of ways some of which may overlap with conduct constituting acquiescence. As Handley JA said in *Spellson v George*[109]:

> Consent may take various forms. These include active encouragement or inducement, participation with or without direct financial benefit, and express consent. Consent may also be inferred from silence and lack of activity with knowledge. However consent means something more than a state of mind. The trustee must know of the consent prior to the breach.

---

107 In relation to the requirement of detriment for promissory estoppel, see Pt 2 in Chapter 2 and for proprietary estoppel, Pt 2 in Chapter 3.

108 *Byrnes v Kendle*, referring to *Spellson v George* (1992) 26 N.S.W.L.R. 666.

109 *Spellson* at 669–670.

Handley J.A. quoted a number of authorities for the proposition that consent to a breach of trust operates as an estoppel and observed[110]: 22–130

> If this defence does operate by way of estoppel it would require proof of inducement and reliance thereon by the trustee.

Young A.J.A., in the same case, distinguished between concurrence in a breach and acquiescence after breach. . . . Hope A.J.A., who agreed with Young A.J.A., said it was necessary, in determining whether a defence of consent to a breach of trust was made out, to consider all the circumstances with a view to determining whether it was fair and equitable to allow the plaintiff to sue the defendants for the breaches of trust. 22–131

GUMMOW and HAYNE J.J.: The term "consent", when used with respect to breach of trust, expresses the principle that "[t]here is no reason for a court of Equity to enforce an equitable obligation in favour of a party who consented to its breach against a party who acted with knowledge of that consent". The words are those of Handley J.A. in *Spellson v George*. His Honour added that while consent may take various forms, and while consent may operate as an estoppel, it means "something more than a state of mind", and that "[t]he trustee must know of the consent prior to the breach".[111] 22–132

The findings by the primary judge in the above passage fell short of providing sufficient basis for defences of consent and estoppel. 22–133

There remains the defence of acquiescence by Mrs Byrnes in the breach of trust. This, as explained by Deane J. in *Orr v Ford*,[112] is best understood as requiring calculated (that is, deliberate and informed) inaction by her or standing by, which encouraged Mr Kendle reasonably to believe that his omissions were accepted or not opposed by her. Counsel for the appellants correctly emphasised the absence of evidence by Mr Kendle that there was no need for him to take steps to recover arrears of rent or to evict Kym because Mrs Byrnes accepted the actions and did not oppose their continuation. 22–134

There was no pleading of a defence of laches. In any event, where presented in answer to a claim of breach of an express trust such as that manifested in the 1997 Deed, the defence would require aggravating circumstances such that the granting of the relief sought by the beneficiary would "give rise to serious and unfair prejudice to the defendant or a third party". No such case was presented by the defendant in this litigation. 22–135

4. Unclean Hands

A. Scope of Application

Another bar to relief is that of unclean hands, and which is also understood as a specific application of the equitable maxim that "He who comes to equity must come with clean hands".[113] Unclean hands, in principle, can bar any claim for equitable relief, whether in aid of legal entitlements generated by common law, such as an injunction to prevent a breach of contract,[114] specific performance of a contract;[115] or, equitable rules, such as rescission of a transaction entered into in breach of fiduciary duty;[116] relief to prevent disclosure of confidential and privileged documents;[117] or, relief in response to 22–136

---

110 *Spellson v George* at 670

111 *Spellson v George* at 669–670.

112 *Orr v Ford* at 337–338, 340.

113 McGhee et al, *Snell's Equity*, 34th edn, para.5–010, comparing this backward-looking maxim with the forward-looking maxim of "He who seeks equity must do equity".

114 Unclean hands precluded the award of an anti-suit injunction to prevent proceedings in breach of an exclusive jurisdiction clause in *Royal Bank of Scotland Plc v Highland Financial Partners LP* [2013] EWCA Civ 328.

115 For discussion see, *ANZ Executors and Trustees Ltd v Humes Ltd* [1990] V.R. 615 (Brooking J), affirmed on appeal *Humes Ltd v PS (Enterprises) Nominees Pty Ltd* (1989) 7 A.C.L.C. 992, although unclean hands was not made out on the facts.

116 As contemplated in *UBS AG (London Branch) v Kommunale Wasserwerke Leipzig GmbH* [2017] EWCA Civ 1567; [2017] 2 Lloyd's Rep. 621, but not made out on the facts.

117 *Simpkin v Berkeley Group Holdings Plc* [2017] EWHC 1472 (QB); [2017] 4 W.L.R. 116 at [48] (Garnham J).

a proprietary estoppel.[118] The gist of this discretionary bar to relief is that C has engaged in improper (in)action that has a connection to C's claim for equitable relief such that it would be unequitable to grant relief to C.[119] While descriptions of the unclean hands doctrine (or clean hands maxim) are broadly framed in relation to C's conduct, this does not import a broad ranging inquiry as to the moral turpitude of C, and cases have sought to define the limits to the scope of inquiry as being that: "[e]quity does not demand that its suitors shall have led blameless lives";[120] and equity does not "enforce manners, or require apology", unclean hands applies in[121] "exceptional cases" against those who:[122]

> put themselves beyond the pale by reason of serious immoral and deliberate misconduct such that the overall result of equitable intervention would not be an exercise but a denial of equity.

22–137 Further, a court will take account of the context so that a party's "brusque and impatient" way of dealing will not engage unclean hands when "well within the rough and tumble of a fraught commercial negotiation".[123] A useful summary of the scope and limits of unclean hands, and cases in which it has barred C's claim for equitable relief is summarised by Campbell J in *Black Uhlans Incorporated v New South Wales Crime Commission*.[124]

Black Uhlans Inc v New South Wales Crime Commission

Supreme Court of New South Wales, [2002] NSWSC 1060 at [158]–[161], [164]–[165], [178]–[179]

22–138 CAMPBELL J.: That someone who comes to equity must have clean hands is an equitable maxim. Such a maxim provides an explanation for the circumstances in which equity recognises rights, and confers remedies, across a broad range of equity's jurisdiction. The approach to the recognition of rights and conferring of remedies which the maxim articulates has resulted in various specific principles of law which are recognised as part of the substantive law of equity. The law of promissory estoppel provides one example. However, the maxim remains of ongoing importance, as a guide to how cases not governed by specific rules of substantive law ought be decided, or as a guide to how specific rules of substantive law ought be extrapolated.

22–139 The unclean hands maxim requires the Court to look at the conduct of the litigant who seeks the assistance of equity, rather than the conduct of the defendant. Further, it is conduct which the litigant who seeks the assistance of equity has engaged in in the past which is required to be looked at. In this way it differs from the maxim that he who seeks equity must do equity, which looks at the conduct which a litigant who seeks the assistance of equity undertakes to engage in in the future.

22–140 Some examples of the circumstances in which the maxim has been the basis on which a case has been decided illustrate the breadth of application of the maxim. Thus, specific performance of a contract will not be granted at the suit of a plaintiff who has made a relevant misrepresentation to the defendant.[125] Unclean hands can be a ground for refusing relief against forfeiture of a lease.[126] It can be a ground on which a court declines to enforce a trust.[127] It can be a basis upon which the beneficiary of a trust, who has led the trustee to commit a breach of trust, can be denied a remedy for that breach.[128] It can provide

---

118 *Murphy v Rayner* [2011] EWHC 1 (Ch) at [351].
119 *Dering v Earl of Winchelsea* (1787) 1 Cox 318 at 319 (Eyre LBC).
120 *Loughran v Loughran*, 292 U.S. 216 at 229 (1934) (Brandeis J).
121 Cf. *Partners (UK) LLP v Barclays Bank Plc* [2014] EWHC 3049 (Ch) at [1133] (Hildyard J).
122 Cf. *Partners (UK) LLP v Barclays Bank Plc* at [1133] (Hildyard J).
123 *Gamatronic (UK) Ltd v Hamilton* [2016] EWHC 2225 (QB) at [227] per Choudhury QC, sitting as a Deputy High Court judge.
124 [2002] NSWSC 1060.
125 *Cadman v Horner* (1810) 18 Ves Jun 10; 34 E.R. 221; *Wall v Stubbs* (1815) 1 Madd 80; 56 E.R. 31.
126 *Gill v Lewis* [1956] 2 Q.B. 1.
127 *Gascoigne v Gascoigne* [1918] 1 Q.B. 223; *In Re Emery's Investment Trusts* (1959) Ch. 410.
128 *Cory v Gertcken* (1816) 2 Madd 40; 56 E.R. 250.

a ground for refusing an injunction to enforce a negative contractual stipulation, if that contract has been procured by a misrepresentation of the plaintiff.[129] It can provide a basis for refusing an injunction to enforce a restrictive covenant, if a person entitled to the benefit of the covenant has represented it will not be enforced, and that representation is acted upon by the person bound by the covenant.[130] Where the plaintiff and the defendant are both bound by restrictive covenants arising under a common building scheme, and the plaintiff is in serious breach of the covenant, unclean hands provides a basis on which the plaintiff cannot obtain an injunction to require the defendant to observe the restrictive covenant.[131] It can provide a basis for refusing an injunction to prevent passing off, where the reputation which the plaintiff seeks to have protected has itself been built up by deceptive means.[132] It can provide a basis for refusing equitable relief to prevent a breach of copyright where the work contained false statements calculated to deceive the public.[133] Further, some cases have held that it can provide a basis for refusing equitable relief in circumstances where a plaintiff has engaged in, or advocated, immorality of some kind . . . .

However, the operation of the maxim is not triggered by any act of wrongful conduct by a defendant, regardless of its nature or connection to the subject matter of the suit. . . . **22–141**

A test for the circumstances in which the maxim operates was provided in *Dering v Earl of Winchelsea*.[134] **22–142**
That case arose from the appointment of a Mr Dering as a collector of customs duties. In connection with the appointment, bonds for his proper performance were given to the Crown by his elder brother (Sir Edward Dering) and two others. When Mr Dearing fell into arrears in making payments to the Crown, the Crown sued Sir Edward Dering on his bond, and recovered the full amount of the arrears. In this action, Sir Edward Dering sought contribution from the other two sureties. Those sureties resisted the action on the ground that Sir Edward Dering had unclean hands. This argument was dealt with by Lord Chief Baron Eyre as follows[135]:

> The misconduct imputed to Sir Edward is that he encourages his brother in gaming and other irregularities; that he knew his brother had no fortune of his own, and must necessarily be making use of the public money, and that Sir Edward was privy to his brother's breaking the orders of the Lords of the Treasury, to keep the money in a particular box, and in a particular manner, &c this may all be true, and such a representation of Sir Edward's conduct certainly places him in a bad point of view; and perhaps it is not a very decorous proceeding in Sir Edward to come into this Court under these circumstances: he might possibly have involved his brother in some measure, but yet it is not made out to the satisfaction of the Court, that these facts will constitute a defence. It is argued that the author of the loss shall not have the benefit of a contribution; but no cases have been cited to this point, nor any principle which applies to this case. It is not laying down any principle to say that his ill conduct disables him from having any relief in this court. If this can be founded on any principle, it must be, that a man must come into a Court of Equity with clean hands; but when this is said, it does not mean a general depravity; it must have an immediate and necessary relation to the equity sued for; it must be a depravity in a legal as well as in a moral sense. In a moral sense, the companion, and perhaps the conductor, of Mr Dering, may be said to be the author of the loss, but to legal purposes, Mr Dering himself is the author of it, and if the evil example of Sir Edward led him on, this is not what the Court can take cognisance of.

What is meant by the expression "an immediate and necessary relation to the equity sued for" is best explained by reference, first, to cases where an allegation of unclean hands was made, but did not result in the plaintiff failing to be granted relief. . . . **22–143**

Gascoigne v Gascoigne[136] was a case where a husband put a lease of land in his wife's name and built a house upon the land with his own money. He used his wife's name in the transaction, with her knowledge and connivance, for the purpose of misleading, defeating and delaying present or future creditors. After **22–144**

---

129 *Hewson v Sydney Stock Exchange Ltd* [1968] 2 N.S.W.R. 224.
130 *Greater Sydney Development* Association *Ltd v Rivett* (1929) 29 S.R. (NSW) 356 at 360–361.
131 *Goddard v Midland Railway Company* (1891) 8 T.L.R. 126.
132 *Kettles and Gas Appliances Ltd v Anthony Hordern and Sons Ltd* (1934) 35 S.R. (NSW) 108.
133 *Slingsby v Bradford Patent Truck and Trolley Co* [1905] W.N. 122; [1906] W.N. 51.
134 (1787) 1 Cox 318; 29 E.R. 1184.
135 *Dering v Earl of Winchelsea* at 319–320.
136 [1918] 1 KB 223.

the parties separated, the husband sought a declaration that the wife was trustee for him of the property. He succeeded at first instance, but on appeal he failed. The Divisional Court (Lawrence and Lush JJ) said[137]:

> . . . What the learned judge has done is this: he has permitted the plaintiff to rebut the presumption [of advancement] which the law raises by setting up his own illegality and fraud, and to obtain relief in equity because he has succeeded in proving it. The plaintiff cannot do this; and, whether the point was taken or not in the County Court this court cannot allow a judgment to stand which has given relief under such circumstances as that.

22–145 *Gascoigne* was a case where it was necessary for the plaintiff to prove his own bad conduct to rebut the presumption of advancement and thus to establish the trust he sued to enforce. . . . If a plaintiff needs to prove his own bad conduct to be able to prove the circumstances which he says entitles him to an equitable remedy, that bad conduct has an immediate and necessary relation to the equity sued for.

22–146 Care is thus needed when considering whether C's conduct is such that relief should be denied on the basis of unclean hands, as it is not any conduct of C, morally reprehensible or not, that disentitles C to relief. It is only when C has engaged in some misconduct or impropriety that has "an immediate and necessary relation to the equity sued for".[138] To raise this bar, D must show that C is seeking "to derive advantage from [C's] dishonest conduct in so direct a manner that it is considered unjust to grant [C] relief".[139]

22–147 In *UBS AG (London Branch) v Kommunale Wasserwerke Leipzig GmbH*, the Court of Appeal considered whether unclean hands would bar one party, KWL, from obtaining equitable rescission of a transaction between KWL and UBS on account of UBS's having knowledge that the transaction was affected by two of KWL's directors who were paid a bribe. The majority, Lord Briggs and Hamblen LJ, upheld the trial judge's decision that the bar of unclean hands did not apply. Gloster LJ dissented, finding that KWL's inequitable conduct in making of fraudulent misrepresentations was "so closely connected with the relief sought" that relief should not be granted.[140]

UBS AG (London Branch) v Kommunale Wasserwerke Leipzig GmbH

Court of Appeal, [2017] 2 Lloyd's Rep. 621 at [169]–[171]

22–148 LORD BRIGGS and HAMBLEN L.J.: We have however concluded that UBS's conscience was affected by the bribe. The discretion whether or not to grant equitable rescission is exercised by the court as a court of conscience[141]. . .

22–149 There remains the question whether KWL is barred from obtaining rescission by coming to equity without clean hands. In addressing this submission at trial, the judge directed himself as to the law by reference to the following passage in the judgment of Aikens L.J. in *Royal Bank of Scotland Plc v Highland Financial Partners LP*[142]:

22–150

> There is no dispute that there exists in English law a defence to a claim for equitable relief, such as an injunction, which is based on the concept encapsulated in the equitable maxim "he who comes into equity must come with clean hands". Mr Nicholls accepted that the doctrine applies to a claim for an anti-suit injunction where the claim is based on an allegation that the defendant has started proceedings in a foreign jurisdiction in breach of contract because the claimant and defendant had agreed to an exclusive jurisdiction clause in favour of the English courts. It is clear from the speech of Lord

---

137 *Gascoigne v Gascoigne* at 226.

138 *Royal Bank of Scotland Plc v Highland Financial Partners LP* [2013] EWCA Civ 328 at [159] (Aikens LJ), quoting *Dering v Earl of Winchelsea* at 319.

139 *Royal Bank of Scotland* [2013] EWCA Civ 328 at [159], quoting I.C.F. Spry, *Principles of Equitable Remedies: Specific Performance, Injunctions, Rectification and Equitable Damages*, 8th edn (Lawbook Company, 2010).

140 *UBS AG (London Branch) v Kommunale* at [376].

141 *Cheese v Thomas* [1994] 1 W.L.R. 129 at 137.

142 [2013] EWCA Civ 328 at [158]–[159].

> Bingham in *Donohue v Armco Inc* that this defence is distinct from that of there being "strong reason" not to grant an anti-suit injunction.
>
> It was common ground that the scope of the application of the "unclean hands" doctrine is limited. To paraphrase the words of Lord Chief Baron Eyre in *Dering v Earl of Winchelsea* the misconduct or impropriety of the claimant must have "an immediate and necessary relation to the equity sued for". That limitation has been expressed in different ways over the years in cases and textbooks. Recently in *Fiona Trust & Holding Corporation and others v Yuri Privalov and others* Andrew Smith J. noted that there are some authorities in which the court regarded attempts to mislead it as presenting good grounds for refusing equitable relief, not only where the purpose is to create a false case but also where it is to bolster the truth with fabricated evidence. But the cases noted by him were ones where the misconduct was by way of deception in the course of the very litigation directed to securing the equitable relief. *Spry: Principles of Equitable Remedies*, suggests that it must be shown that the claimant is seeking "to derive advantage from his dishonest conduct in so direct a manner that it is considered to be unjust to grant him relief". Ultimately in each case it is a matter of assessment by the judge, who has to examine all the relevant factors in the case before him to see if the misconduct of the claimant is sufficient to warrant a refusal of the relief sought. **22–151**
>
> Neither Lord Falconer nor Mr Lord criticised the judge's reliance upon this statement of principle, and we are content to adopt it. The key part of it, which dates back to the 18th century, is that the misconduct or impropriety of the claimant must have "an immediate and necessary relation to the equity sued for", and that it must be shown that the claimant is seeking "to derive advantage from his dishonest conduct in so direct a manner that it is considered unjust to grant him relief". As the last five lines of the quoted passage show, this is one of those multi-factorial assessments to be conducted by the trial judge, with which an appellate court will be slow to intervene, unless the judge's conclusion was clearly wrong, or based upon some evident failure of analysis. **22–152**

Lord Briggs and Hamblen LJ went on to apply these principles in finding that the fraudulent conduct of KWL's own managing partner, Mr Heininger, including in making fraudulent misrepresentations to UBS about the transaction, did not give rise to a bar of unclean hands against KWL's claim for equitable rescission.[143] In summary, Mr Heininger's conduct did not cause the transaction KWL sought to rescind; the conduct could not be imputed to KWL in order to "sully KWL's hands for the purpose of the grant or refusal of rescission in equity"; and, the party seeking to rely on the bar of unclean hands, UBS, in paying a bribe to Mr Heininger, played a part in inducing Mr Heininger's conduct in making the fraudulent misrepresentation. **22–153**

Gloster L.J. reached a different view, finding unclean hands did bar KWL's claim for rescission, largely differing in relation to the application of principle to the facts, finding that KWL was vicariously liable for Mr Heininger's conduct "with the result that KWL's hands are, through Mr Heininger, relevantly sullied . . .";[144] Mr Heininger's conduct was sufficiently connected because the transaction KWL sought rescission of would not have been concluded without the impugned conduct; and the fact that Mr Heininger's conduct was procured by UBS' bribe was irrelevant owing to the way the case had been pleaded. Gloster LJ summarised the argument in favour of unclean hands applying as a bar to KWL's claim as being:[145] **22–154**

> that, despite having deceived UBS into entering into the contract, the contract ought to be rescinded at KWL's election. In my view equity debars KWL from doing so.

---

143 *UBS AG (London Branch) v Kommunale* at [171]–[177].

144 *UBS AG (London Branch) v Kommunale* at [376].

145 *UBS AG (London Branch) v Kommunale* at [376].

22–155 In *Dering v Earl of Winchelsea*, Eyre LCC confines unclean hands to where C's conduct is depraved "in a legal as well as in a moral sense".[146] Later cases, however, suggest that unclean hands might be raised where C's conduct is not unlawful in the sense of transgression of some legal or equitable rule, but is of such a nature that C should be denied relief. Examples of conduct that is lawful but otherwise triggers application of unclean hands and precludes C of equitable relief, includes "trickery" in commercial dealings between parties as in *Quadrant Visual Communications Ltd v Hutchison Telephone (UK)*,[147] and in *Pitt v Holt*,[148] the Supreme Court indicated that "at the extreme end of artificiality" unclean hands might deny equitable relief to trusts used for "artificial tax avoidance". This question of whether unclean hands denies C relief on account of her morally depraved, yet otherwise lawful conduct, has important implications for the relationship between unclean hands and illegality, discussed next. This question also raises a rule of law concern to the extent that C is being denied relief according to some non-legal reason, such as a judge's assessment of the morality of C's conduct, as opposed to the lawfulness of that conduct.[149]

B. Unclean Hands and Illegality

22–156 Unclean hands shares some aspects with the doctrine of illegality, which has been discussed already in Chapter 16. Both may apply to bar C's claim for equitable relief against D and involve balancing a range of considerations, including the relative moral turpitude or the respective wrongdoing of D and C.[150] In *Ball v de Marzo*,[151] Morgan J noted that "it is not obvious why the public policy considerations relied on in *Patel v Mirza* should not equally apply to the equitable maxim", although did not consider the point further as it did not make a difference to the outcome, having determined that neither unclean hands nor illegality applied to bar the claim for equitable relief, nor was it fully argued.

22–157 The impact of *Patel v Mirza* on unclean hands and the relationship between illegality and unclean hands, has been the object of academic attention.[152] One issue is whether unclean hands underpins,[153] or is subsumed by,[154] the doctrine of illegality when applied to C's conduct that is illegal or unlawful in the sense of a transgression of some legal or equitable rule. In *Patel v Mirza*,[155] illegality is expressed as relating only to where C's conduct is unlawful in the sense of being a transgression of a legal rule and would not arise where C's conduct, while reprehensible for one reason or other, is not a breach or infringement of a legal rule. Less clear is whether, for illegality, C's conduct is assessed by reference to common law rules alone or also takes account of C's adherence with equitable standards. If not, then unclean hands has a distinct role in responding to situations where C's conduct falls short of one or more of equity's rules, but not common law ones. Further, and to the extent that unclean hands

---

146 *Dering v Earl of Winchelsea* at 319–320.

147 *Quadrant Visual Communications Ltd v Hutchison Telephone (UK)* [1993] C.C.L.C. 442 (CA) at 451.

148 *Pitt v Holt* [2013] UKSC 26; [2013] 2 A.C. 108 at [135].

149 N. McBride, "The Future of Clean Hands" in P. S. Davies et al (eds), *Defences in Equity* (Hart Publishing, 2018), pp.273–274.

150 Cf. *Partners (UK) LLP v Barclays Bank Plc* [2014] EWHC 3049 (Ch) at [1133].

151 *Ball v de Marzo* [2019] EWHC 1587 (Ch) at [52].

152 For academic views, see N. McBride, "The Future of Clean Hands" and P.S. Davies, "Illegality in Equity" in P. S. Davies et al (eds), *Defences in Equity* (Hart Publishing, 2018); P.S. Davies, "Ramifications of Patel v Mirza in the Law of Trusts" in S. Green and D. Bogg (eds), *Illegality After Patel v Mirza* (Hart Publishing, 2018); I. Samet, *Equity: Conscience Goes to Market* (Oxford University Press, 2018), Ch.4; T.L. Anenson, *Judging Equity: The Fusion of Unclean Hands in US Law* (Cambridge University Press, 2019).

153 See, e.g. *Tinsley v Milligan* [1994] 1 A.C. 340 (HL) at 357–358, 362 (Lord Goff).

154 *Tinsley v Milligan* [1992] Ch. 310 (CA) at 324 (Nicholls LJ), 341 (Lloyd LJ).

155 *Patel v Mirza* [2016] UKSC 42; [2017] A.C. 467 at [99], [101].

denies relief where C's conduct is morally depraved but otherwise lawful, unclean hands has a scope of application beyond illegality which is concerned only with cases where C's conduct is unlawful.

The interconnections between illegality and unclean hands bring us back to foundational questions about equity's role as meta or secondary rules that preserve the normative force of the primary legal system by preventing people from abusing the legal entitlements afforded to them by the primary legal system, or equity itself. If one accepts this bifurcated conception of the distinct roles, this might provide a basis on which to further distinguish between illegality and unclean hands. Illegality reconciles the tension(s) between different legal rules irrespective of their jurisdictional origins. Unclean hands has a different orientation as it preserves equity's guidance function by preventing C's abuse of the entitlement to relief generated by equitable rules in C's favour. **22–158**

Questions

Milly wants to take advantage of a government scheme that provides funding to disadvantaged university students to help with the cost of university fees. The scheme is means tested according to the value of all property to which Milly has legal title and precludes Milly as she owns a townhouse in London worth £1,500,000. Milly asks her trusted friend, Bobbie, to help her out by agreeing to accept a transfer of title to the townhouse to hold on express trust for Milly. Bobbie agrees, Milly transfers ownership of the townhouse to Bobbie who executes a deed of trust in Milly's favour. Milly applies to the government scheme and declares that she has legal title to property worth less than £1,000. Milly is successful and her university fees (£40,000) are paid for under the scheme. Milly continues living in her townhouse and completes university. Milly would like to ask Bobbie to reconvey ownership of the townhouse to her, although, they have had a falling out and Milly is too upset and hurt to approach Bobbie again. Time passes by and Millie and Bobbie never reconcile. Some 20 years later, after Bobbie's death, Milly sends a copy of the Deed of Trust executed by Milly and Bobbie and asks Bobbie's personal representative to reconvey ownership of the London townhouse to her. In answer to a claim by Milly for recovery of the trust property, can Bobbie's personal representative raise any of the following:

1. Unclean hands and/or illegality?
2. Acquiescence?
3. Laches?
4. "In my view, recognising that an order of a court concerning disclosure of information relating to a trust to a beneficiary or potential beneficiary is discretionary does not involve deserting the firm ground of sure principles for a trackless sea of uncertainty"; J. Campbell, "Access by Trust Beneficiaries to Trustees' Documents, Information and Reasons" (2009) 3 J. Eq. 97, 145. **Discuss.**

INDEX

LEGAL TAXONOMY
FROM SWEET & MAXWELL

This index has been prepared using Sweet and Maxwell's Legal Taxonomy. Main index entries conform to keywords provided by the Legal Taxonomy except where references to specific documents or non-standard terms (denoted by quotation marks) have been included. These keywords provide a means of identifying similar concepts in other Sweet & Maxwell publications and online services to which keywords from the Legal Taxonomy have been applied. Readers may find some minor differences between terms used in the text and those which appear in the index. Suggestions to *sweetandmaxwell.taxonomy@thomson.com*.

Also available:

English Legal System – The Fundamentals, 4th edn
Michael Bromby
ISBN: 9780414089723
Publication date: November 2022
Formats: Paperback/ProView eBook/WestlawUK

English Legal System – The Fundamentals presents a clear and detailed explanation of the area, with features that aid comprehension and understanding, providing an excellent grounding in the subject and a solid basis for the study of law.

The Fundamentals series introduces students to the principles of the law by way of clear text combined with visual aids, tools and diagrams to enable an easy understanding of the subject without sacrificing the detail that is required for proper comprehension. Each title assumes no level of prior knowledge, allowing the book to be used for those new to the subject and for distance learning.

Commercial Law – Textbook Series, 10th edn
Professor Rob Stokes
ISBN: 9780414103412
Publication date: October 2022
Formats: Paperback and ProView eBook

Commercial Law presents a clear and detailed account of commercial law, covering the fundamental principles and how the law works in practice. The work concentrates on those topics common to the majority of undergraduate law courses such as sale of goods, consumer credit and agency.
In addition, Commercial Law:

- Includes topical and relevant practical examples to help draw out key principles
- Uses introductions to parts to link the law into its wider context
- Contains references to further reading and web-based sources at the end of each chapter to enable further study of the subject

Commercial Law is an essential textbook for those studying law at degree or graduate diploma level. Its clarity and comprehensive coverage also make it an indispensable resource.